W9-CHD-049

The American Critical Tradition

M. Thomas Inge
General Editor

Theodore Dreiser: The Critical Reception
Edited by Jack Salzman
Long Island University

Thomas Wolfe: The Critical Reception
Edited by Pascal Reeves
University of Georgia

Ernest Hemingway: The Critical Reception
Edited by Robert O. Stephens
University of North Carolina

William Faulkner: The Critical Reception
Edited by M. Thomas Inge
Virginia Commonwealth University

Theodore Dreiser:
The Critical Reception

Theodore Dreiser

The Critical Reception

Edited with an Introduction by

Jack Salzman

David Lewis New York 1972

Library of Congress Card Number: 73–78882
Manufactured in the United States by
Haddon Craftsmen, Inc.
Design by Ronald Gordon
First Edition

To the Memory of my Grandfather,
Samuel Wehrman, and my Father-in-Law,
Philip Falkenstein

General Editor's Preface

When we speak of a writer's reputation in critical terms, we should recognize that he actually has two: the response of book reviewers and critics during his own lifetime to each of his works as it was published, and the retrospective evaluation of his achievement by literary historians and academic critics in the decades after his career is concluded. The primary concern of modern scholarship has been the latter, on the assumption that the passage of time is essential before a writer's achievement can be objectively viewed and assessed. The purpose of the volumes in the American Critical Tradition series, however, is to provide overviews of the critical reputations earned by major American authors in their own times. Such overviews are necessary before the full impact of a writer's influence can be properly evaluated and an understanding of how he related to his contemporary cultural milieu achieved.

The few efforts hitherto made in summarizing a writer's contemporary critical standing have usually been based on a reading of sample reviews or vague impressions retained by veterans of the era. Seldom have literary historians gone back to locate and read all or most of the comment elicited by a career in progress. In the present volumes, the editors have sought to unearth every known review of each book in the contemporary newspapers, journals, and periodicals, and to demonstrate the critical response chronologically through reprint, excerpt, or summary. Exhaustive checklists of reviews not included in the text are appended to each chapter, and the editor has provided an introduction summarizing the major trends observable in the criticism. The results not only elucidate the writer's career, but they reveal as well intellectual patterns in book reviewing and the reception of serious writing by the American reading public. Each volume is, therefore, a combined literary chronicle and reference work of a type previously unavailable.

M. Thomas Inge
General Editor

Contents

Acknowledgements

The editor wishes to thank the following newspapers, journals, and individuals for permission to reprint reviews: Albany *Knickerbocker Press* for "Free," "Hand of the Potter," "Tragic America," "Dreiser Says His Say on Russia." Ashville *Times* for "Gold in the Ore." Atlanta *Constitution* for " 'The Bulwark' Accentuates Dreiser's Loss to Letters." Atlantic Monthly Co., for "The Atlantic's Bookshelf," "Dreiser Reconsidered." Baltimore *News* for "Hey Rub-A-Dub-Dub." Baltimore *Evening Sun* for "Dreiser's Rare Genius is Shown in 'Twelve Men,' " "Mencken Becomes Reminiscent Over Dreiser's New York." Boston *Globe* for "Unchanging Dreiser." Chicago *News* for "Dreiser's 'The Stoic' Powerful," "Hey Rub-A-Dub-Dub," "Chains," "A Hoosier Holiday." Chicago *Sun* for "Dreiser's Final Novel of Cowperwood Series." Chicago *Tribune* for "Does Dreiser's Final Novel Reveal Spiritual Creed," "Mr. Dreiser Goes Travelling," "Hey Rub-A-Dub-Dub," "Dreiser True Realist in His Final Novel." Cleveland *Press* for "Book Review." Colorado *Sunday Gazette & Telegraph* for "Theodore Dresier," "Chains." Columbia *Dispatch* for "Dreiser Trilogy Completed." Commonweal Publishing Co., Inc. for "The Bulwark," "The Stoic," "An American Tragedy." Dallas *News* for "New York's Color," "After Long Silence Dreiser Writes Two-Volume 'American Tragedy,' " "Experimental Poetry of Theodore Dreiser," "Dawn," "Books-Old and New: Dreiser's Posthumous Novel." Dallas *Times Herald* for "Dreiser's Last Novel." Davenport *Times* for "Color of A Great City." Des Moines *Register* for "Strength and Compassion Set Dreiser's Posthumous Novel Apart." Detroit *News* for "Frank Exposition of Dreiser's Philosophy." Detroit *Free Press* for "Theodore Dreiser Surpasses Even Himself," "A Book About Himself." Detroit *News* for "Life's Ironies," "Tragedy of Empire and the New Russia." El Cajon *Valley News* for "Books in Review." James T. Farrell for "Dreiser's Last Book Ends the Cowperwood Saga." Granville Hicks for "The Bulwark." Houston *Post* for "Completing the Record of a Notable Career." Indianapolis *Star* for "Theodore Dreiser Revisits Indiana," "A Reader's Notes," "A Play by Theodore Dreiser," "The Stoic," "An American Tragedy." John Lydenberg for "The Anatomy of Exhaustion." H. L. Mencken by permission of Mercantile Trust Co. Minneapolis

Tribune for "Living This Life," "Dreiser Power Holds in his Final Novel." Muskeegan *Democrat* for "Book Worm." *The Nation* for "Dreiser and the Liberal Mind," "American Types," "According to Dreiser," "Plays of the Natural and Supernatural," "Two Americans Look at Russia," "Dreiser as Economist." New York *Post* for "Hoosier Holiday," "Free," "Hey Rub-A-Dub-Dub," "An American Tragedy," "A Pachyderm Needs Room to Run In," "A Book on Our Table," "Tragic America," "Dreiser's Last Testament." The New York Times Co. for "Theodore Dreiser Looking Backward," "As the Uncommercial Traveller," "Dreiser's Undisciplined Power," "As Usual, Mr. Dreiser Spares Us Nothing," "Soviet Russia at the Beginning of the Second Decade," "Theodore Dreiser in the Maze of Feminine Psychology," "Dreiser's Confession of His Early Years," "Mr. Dreiser Prescribes for Us," "Theodore Dreiser Mounts the Soapbox," "Books of the Times," "God, Mammon and Mr. Dreiser," "Ending Dreiser's 'Trilogy of Desire'." The New Yorker Magazine, Inc. for "America is Worth Saving." Newsweek, Inc. for "Dreiser the Great," "Unfinished Trilogy." Omaha *Sunday World Herald* for "Dreiser's Last Novel." Philadelphia Inquirer for "Three Books About Russia," "Book of the Day," "Dreiser's Despair Reaffirmed in 'The Stoic'." Pittsburgh *Press* for "Dreiser Looks at Russia," "Dreiser's Moods Are Published," "The Stoic." Portland *Oregonian* for "The Work of Ten Years." Providence *Journal* for "Twelve Men." Pueblo *Star Journal* for "Moods." Annette T. Rubinstein for "The Bulwark." San Francisco *Chronicle* for "A Book About Myself," "Bookman's Notebook," "Twelve Men," "Moods." The Saturday Review Company, Inc. for "Dreiser" by Sherwood Anderson, "Odds and Ends" by Gorham B. Munson, "Fifteen Women" by Rollo Walter Brown, "Dreiseriana" by Robert Herrick, "Dreiser vs. the U.S." by Eliot Jones, "The Red Peril" by Elmer Davis, "Dreiser to the Rescue," "Dreiser as Master Craftsman," "The Anatomy of Exhaustion." Scribner's Magazine for "As I Like It." Edwin Seaver for "A Book About Myself," and "The Bulwark." *The Sewanee Review* for "An American Tragedy." Robert E. Spiller for "The Bulwark." St. Louis *Globe Democrat* for "Word Pictures of Life of Working Class Thrill," "Moods." St. Louis *Dispatch* for "What Happens?" Syracuse *Post Standard* for "Moods." Terre Haute *Tribune* for "A Book About Myself." Time, Inc., "Valedictory," "The Last of Dreiser." Reprinted by permission of The Viking Press, Inc. for "Words, Words, Words." Washington *Star* for "Twelve Men," "A Hoosier Holiday," "New Books at Random," "Hand of the Potter," "Reviewing the New Books." Edmund Wilson for "Theodore Dreiser's Quaker and Graham Greene's Priest." Worcester *Telegram* for "Last Novel by Dreiser." *The Yale Review* for "Self Revelations," "Outstanding Books," "Russia Today."

Introduction

Theodore Dreiser's significance in the history of American letters is no longer a matter for dispute. We may continue to debate his merits as an artist, but his importance to American literature has been well established. Dreiser was the writer, as Sherwood Anderson appreciatively wrote in *Horses and Men,* who by himself cleared the wilderness of Puritan denial. His novels frequently were as huge and ungainly as he himself was (though, like the man, the novels achieved some of their fascination just because of their size and crudity). But none of Dreiser's defects as a craftsman can deny his singular importance: though there is much in the writings of Stephen Crane, Kate Chopin, and Frank Norris to have offended the souls of the genteel tradition, it is Dreiser and Dreiser alone who, in Sinclair Lewis' words, is to be credited with having "cleared the trail from Victorian and Howellsian timidity and gentility in American fiction to honesty and boldness and passion of life."

Dreiser's reputation is of a legendary nature and is tied to a particular incident. His great first novel, as Sinclair Lewis told the Nobel Prize audience in 1930, "came to housebound and airless America like a great free Western wind, and to our stuffy domesticity gave us the first fresh air since Mark Twain and Whitman." But this great novel—*Sister Carrie*—did not come to housebound and airless America without a struggle. For, as most history books of American literature tell us, the philistine publishers tried to suppress the novel, and when they failed, the critics refused to review the book upon its publication in November, 1900. It is the events surrounding Dreiser's now-legendary attempt to get *Sister Carrie* published which have defined his position in American literary history. *An American Tragedy* may be a greater artistic achievement than *Sister Carrie,* and to H. L. Mencken even *Jennie Gerhardt* was better than Dreiser's first novel (which suffered from what Mencken called a "broken back"), but none of this is of much matter: Dreiser essentially is *Sister Carrie.*

Thirty-one years after the fact, Dreiser wrote an account for *The Colophon* of "the trials and tribulations attendant upon the publication of [his] first novel—*Sister Carrie.*" The story he told was the same one he had related to Mencken several years earlier, and which by then had become fairly wide-spread in literary circles. After Harper & Bros. had rejected the novel, Dreiser took it to Doubleday, Page & Co. There, it was read by Frank Norris, who enthusiastically recommended the novel as the best work he yet had read in manuscript. According to Dreiser, a contract was signed, the book was printed, and then the trouble began. Mrs. Frank Doubleday—again according to Dreiser—read the manuscript, was horrified by its frankness, and had the book withdrawn from circulation. Then, the story went, Frank Norris persuaded Dreiser to insist that Doubleday carry out the contract. Doubleday's legal adviser, Thomas McKee, "advised the firm that it was legally obliged to go on with the publication, it having signed a contract to do so, but that this did not necessarily include selling; in short, the book, after publication, might be thrown into a cellar! I believe this advice was followed to the letter," Dreiser wrote, "because no copies were ever sold." Copies, perhaps a hundred in all, were sent to book reviewers, who responded with the same outrage as Mrs. Doubleday. Even when the novel was reissued in 1908, Dreiser contended, "the outraged protests far outnumbered the plaudits."

This is a fine story. But, much of Dreiser's account seems to be just that: a fine story. Doubleday, Page & Co. was not bound by any contract because no agreement was signed until August 20, 1900, and Dreiser, who was always obsessed with money, surely knew that there was no truth to the contention that no copies were ever sold. In fact, 456 copies of *Sister Carrie* were sold and Dreiser received $68.40 in royalties. But the inaccuracies in Dreiser's tale did not bother very many people. This was the kind of story of which legends are made, and as Alfred Kazin wrote in the introduction to *The Stature of Theodore Dreiser,* "the legend that *Sister Carrie* had been suppressed by the publisher's wife was now so dear to the hearts of the rising generation that Mrs. Doubleday became a classic character, the Carrie Nation of the American liberal epos, her ax forever lifted against 'the truth of American life'." Because of *Sister Carrie* and *l'affaire Doubleday* Dreiser quickly came to embody, to again quote Kazin, "the whole struggle of the new American literature."

The distortions in Dreiser's account of the publication of *Sister Carrie* do not mean, of course, that the story is without truth. Doubleday clearly did not want to publish the novel, and just as clearly Frank Norris did urge the firm to publish it. But after this, fact frequently gives way to fabrication. For example, Frank Norris, who was himself a young writer as well as a reader for the firm, could exert just so much influence and could say just so much before he would endanger his position with Doubleday, Page. There is no reason to believe that Norris ever insisted upon the publication of Dreiser's novel to the point where his job was jeopardized. Nor is there much evidence to support the contention that it was Mrs. Doubleday who wanted to prevent the book's publication. It makes a better story to see Mrs. Doubleday as the villain, but it is rumor alone which has made her the Carrie Nation of American literature. What we do know about the publication of *Sister Carrie* is that Doubleday, Page & Co. led Dreiser to believe that it would publish his novel and then tried to back out of its commitment. When Dreiser decided to contest the firm's decision, a formal "Memorandum of Agreement" was signed and *Sister Carrie* was published on November 8, 1900.

Although the book was neither suppressed nor withdrawn, as legend would have us believe, it is true that Doubleday did not make any attempt to advertise the novel. Yet, from a business point of view, this is quite understandable. The books most frequently bought during the first few years of the twentieth century were Maurice Thompson's *Alice of Old Vincennes,* Mary Johnston's *To Have and to Hold,* Winston Churchill's *The Crisis,* Alice Hegan Rice's *Mrs. Wiggs of the Cabbage Patch,* and Owen Wister's *The Virginian.* These books, together with John Fox, Jr.'s *The Little Shepherd of Kingdom Come,* and Kate Wiggins' *Rebecca of Sunnybrook Farm,* were the most popular books at the turn of the century, and it is little wonder that Frank Doubleday chose to advertise Ellen Glasgow's *The Voice of the Turtle* in *Publisher's Weekly* rather than *Sister Carrie.* What is to be wondered at, however, is why as late as September 30, 1935, a representative for Doubleday & Co. would tell Arthur Hobson Quinn that the "early criticisms [of *Sister Carrie*] were not good." This is an opinion expressed by the firm which published *Sister Carrie,* by its author, and, consequently, by almost every critic who has written about the novel's publication. From Mencken to Dorothy Dudley to Stephen Stepanchev to W. A. Swanberg, critics seem to agree with Burton Rascoe's claim in his *Theodore Dreiser* that the reviews of *Sister Carrie* "were overwhelmingly denunciatory"; Dreiser was "this and that and everything that was vile, untruthful, and godless." But such a view has little basis in fact; it belongs to the great legend that publisher and reviewers alike tried to keep *Sister Carrie* from coming before the American public.

The fact is that had Frank Doubleday so chosen, there were many favorable reviews from which he might have quoted for publicity purposes. For, at the very least, to use Kazin's terms, *Sister Carrie* did not so much have a bad press as it did a frightened press. Yet even such a claim detracts somewhat from the reception accorded *Sister Carrie.* There were, to be sure, several unfavorable notices: the reviewers for the Indianapolis *News,* Toledo *Blade,* and Minneapolis *Journal* agreed that the story was "too realistic, too somber to be altogether pleasing" (Toledo *Blade,* December 8, 1900); and A. Schade Van Westrum, writing in the March, 1901, issue of *Book Buyer,* foreshadowed the attacks to be made on Dreiser by the Humanists when he dismissed *Sister Carrie* because "Life seems to have no deeper and no higher meaning for [Dreiser] than the semi-accidental progress of Sister Carrie towards the rewards of her greater beauty, the rise of the drummer to partnership dinners at the Waldorf-Astoria, and stage-door intimacies; and the descent of the salon keeper to Bowery lodging houses, soup kitchens, and suicide. All this happens automatically, by physical processes only; if these bodies have souls and minds, the author knows and tells us nothing of them." Such, in essence, was the negative criticism leveled against *Sister Carrie* upon its publication. Even when most vituperative (i.e., Van Westrum's review), there is nothing in these early reviews to support the contention that "The protest against *Sister Carrie* was so vehement that the publishers voluntarily withdrew it . . . (Irene and Allen Cleaton, *Book and Battles* [Boston, 1937]).

Many reviewers were disturbed by certain aspects of the novel, but they were still impressed by its power. "It is a study, and a very strong one," wrote the reviewer for the Louisville *Courier-Journal* on February 23, 1901, "of the development of a soul that seeks the unattainable, whose goal flies before it." Similarly, the critic for the mid-Western weekly, *Interior,* noted that although the novel had weaknesses, "it is undeniably true that Mr. Dreiser has made a noteworthy addition to American literature" (February 21, 1901). Dreiser was favorably compared with Zola (Chicago *Tribune,* February 25, 1901), Balzac (New Haven *Journal Courier,* January 12, 1901), and Norris (Louisville *Times,* November 30, 1900), while William Marion Reedy, who, like many critics, felt that it was in Hurstwood's "gradual sinking or slinking into degradation" that Dreiser showed his real power, offered the opinion that the veritism of *Sister Carrie* "out-Howells Mr. Howells and out-Garlands Mr. Hamlin Garland" (*Reedy's Mirror,* January 3, 1901). And at least one critic, the reviewer for the Chicago *Times Herald,* was moved to exclaim: "Here, at last, is, in its field, a great American novel" (January 16, 1901).

As these reviews of the time clearly show, there is little basis for the generally held belief that the press accorded *Sister Carrie* in 1900 was overwhelmingly denunciatory. While some of the reviewers were frightened, even horrified, by the intensity and realism of Dreiser's story, many who read the novel were able to recognize an element of greatness in the book. The point to be noted here, then, is not that *Sister Carrie* received a bad press or even a frightened press but that it did not receive an adequate one. For, whatever the reasons may have been, such important periodicals as *North American Review, Atlantic Monthly, Critic, Arena, Ainslee's, Catholic World, Independent, Literary Digest,* and *Review of Reviews* failed to notice the publication of *Sister Carrie,* while *Outlook,*

Dial, Current Literature, and *The Nation* listed the novel as received for review but did not review it.

Not long after its publication, someone, perhaps Frank Norris, sent a copy of *Sister Carrie* to William Heinemann, the British publisher, and that proved to be a more fortuitous move than all the copies sent for review in the United States. In 1901 Heinemann had begun publishing "The Dollar Library: A Monthly Series of American Fiction." It was his belief that a school of talented writers were growing up in America to whom respect could not be denied and whom England could no longer afford to ignore. In The Dollar Library Series, Heinemann therefore wanted to publish the works not only of Stephen Crane and Harold Frederic, the two writers he regarded as being most responsible for the new development in American literature; he also intended to use The Dollar Library to introduce unknown writers, thereby affording "an opportunity to English readers of gaining an impression of the mercurial genius picturesquely expressing itself on the other side of the Atlantic. . . ."

Heinemann was very interested in *Sister Carrie,* and by May 6, 1901, he had practically concluded negotiations with Doubleday, Page & Co. to include Dreiser's novel in The Dollar Library. The only stipulation made by Heinemann was that the first 200 pages of the novel be condensed into eighty pages. The London publisher did not want Dreiser to expurgate the novel; he simply wanted *Sister Carrie* to conform in length to the other volumes in the Series. Dreiser had no objections to doing this, and with the assistance of his friend, Arthur Henry, he did as Heinemann had requested. Not long after, on July 31, 1901, *Sister Carrie,* now 357 pages long, was published in England.

The reviews which *Sister Carrie* received in Great Britain were not unlike those it received upon its publication in the United States. Some reviewers (the one for the Liverpool *Daily Post,* for example), found that "although its cleverness is undeniable, 'Sister Carrie' leaves a somewhat objectionable impression on the mind" (September 11, 1901). But, again, even many of the reviewers who found the story to be disagreeable did not deny the strength of Dreiser's novel. And, as was true of the American critics, many singled out Dreiser's portrayal of Hurstwood for special praise. The Eversham *Journal* found that Carrie herself was not too convincing, but "in drawing the portrait of Hurstwood Mr. Dreiser has been entirely successful. In few books has the gradual deterioration of a man's character been so cruelly exposed" (September 7, 1901). Similarly, the critic for *The Spectator* commented that "the really powerful study is the figure of Hurstwood, Carrie's second lover. The picture of the sapping of the man's whole nature by the inertia which attacks him in his weary search for work is most subtly and strongly drawn. The reader follows each weakening struggle to its inevitable defeat with something of the sickening sensation which a real spectator must have felt, indeed, the whole situation is almost too poignant in its hopelessness." In short, the reviewer concluded, *Sister Carrie* "is at once an engrossing and depressing book" (August 24, 1901).

This last review is of considerable importance simply because it did appear in *The Spectator.* No American journal of comparable importance —with the possible exception of *Book Buyer*—reviewed *Sister Carrie.* In Great Britain, however, The Dollar Library edition of Dreiser's novel was reviewed not only by *The Spectator* but by *The Athenaeum* as well (both of which were among England's most important literary organs of the time). In a lengthy and favorable review in the September 7, 1901, issue of *The Athenaeum,* Theodore Watts-Dunton wrote that *Sister Carrie* "is a creditable piece of work, faithful and rich in the interest which pertains to genuinely realistic fiction. It is further of interest by reason that it strikes a key-note and is typical both in the faults of its manner and in the wealth and diversity of its matter, of the great country which gave it birth. Readers there are who, having perused the three hundred and odd pages which go to the making of 'Sister Carrie' will find permanent place upon their shelves for the book beside M. Zola's 'Nana.' "

The reaction in the United States to the critical success of the Heinemann edition of *Sister Carrie* (and particularly to the review of Watts-Dunton) was as immediate as it was positive. Within weeks after the appearance of the reviews in *The Athenaeum* and *The Spectator,* Dreiser received a letter from George Brett of the Macmillan Company, who wrote to tell Dreiser that *Sister Carrie* had not escaped him on its first appearance, nor had he failed to note the favorable reviews in the English papers: "I must say," Brett wrote on September 21, 1901, "that I have been looking forward to the receipt of [your next manuscript] and trust still to have the pleasure of perusing it." But by this time Dreiser already had arranged with a small firm, J. F. Taylor Company, for the publication of the novel that was to become *Jennie Gerhardt,* as well as the possible republication of *Sister Carrie.* Still, words of congratulations continued to arrive. In December, 1901, Dreiser received a letter from Ripley Hitchcock, of D. Appleton & Company (and a friend of Stephen Crane), who wrote: "I am frankly disappointed that you have arranged for the new novel elsewhere, because your work has interested me greatly. . . . As a reader and a literary man the quality of the work which you have done in 'Sister Carrie' has made a very strong impression upon me and I feel very honestly in your debt for the opportunity of studying the work which you have been doing. . . ."

Despite such letters of encouragement—and a small advance from J. F.

Taylor—Dreiser was too depressed to be able to complete work on his new novel, now called *The Transgressor.* For a while, he did no work at all on the story; then, in 1904, he returned to the manuscript, wrote until Chapter 41, once again set the manuscript aside, and this time did not go back to it for another six years. In the meantime, he resumed his editorial work, which enabled him to save enough money to repay Taylor the money advanced on *The Transgressor* and to purchase the plates of *Sister Carrie.* Then, in 1906, he learned of a new firm, B.W. Dodge & Company, that was interested in republishing his novel. Dodge offered Dreiser a ten per cent royalty fee on the first three thousand copies sold and agreed to consult him in matters of publicity; Dreiser, for his part, was to give Dodge the plates to the novel. Dreiser agreed to the arrangement, and on May 18, 1907, *Sister Carrie* was reissued in the United States.

Unlike Doubleday, Page & Co., B.W. Dodge effectively advertised *Sister Carrie.* On the day of publication, Dodge printed an ad which read: "The Curtain Raised/on a generally unwritten/Phase of life/Sister Carrie/By Theodore Dreiser/Greatest novel of the times."/ Two weeks later, *Sister Carrie* was given a half-page spread in the June 1, 1907, issue of *Publisher's Weekly,* where it was called "the most realistic novel of our times" and included words of praise from Hamlin Garland and Thomas Bigelow Paine. Dodge also capitalized upon the favorable English reviews by quoting their comparisons of Dreiser with Balzac and Zola—and then went them one better by advertising that "The tone of Theodore Dreiser's story is better than anything written by the great French realists because our country is better."

Whether it was due to the advertising, a change in critical taste, the cordial reception of the English reviewers, or the underground reputation it had attained, the Dodge reissue of *Sister Carrie* attracted considerably more critical attention than did the first edition. *The Nation* and *Literary Digest,* it is true, did no more than mention *Sister Carrie* among the "Books Received." But *Forum, North American Review, Current Literature,* and the New York *Times* did review it for the first time, and the influential *Bookman* printed two reviews in the May, 1907, issue.

Of course, not all the reviews were favorable. There were still those critics who were indignant at what they considered to be the novel's immorality. ("A volume containing a terrible warning to men and one that women had better not read is *Sister Carrie,*" wrote the reviewer for Chicago *Advance* on June 27, 1907.) But even those reviewers who disliked the novel now approached it with an attitude very much like that of the critic for the Los Angeles *Times,* who wrote, " 'Sister Carrie' is a book which must be regarded seriously, whatever opinion of its value and propriety the reader may form." Here, after all, was a novel that supposedly had been sabotaged by publisher and reviewers alike in the United States but which had been warmly praised by the critics in Great Britain; its republication could now be seen, as the Baltimore *Sun* put it on June 26, 1907, as the "Triumphant Vindication of a Suppressed Novel." This, at least, was the starting point of many of the reviews which greeted the Dodge reissue. On June 6, 1907, William Reedy, whom F. O. Matthiessen was to call Dreiser's "first real champion," reprinted his original review of *Sister Carrie* with a new opening paragraph:

> A novel that a man will read through at one sitting is, in these days of novels *ad nauseam*, a rarity, and yet the writer found one the other day—a novel that, upon its original appearance in 1900, was suppressed, for its startling naturalism, by its publishers, Doubleday, Page & Co., though enthusiastically reviewed in many of the best journals of criticism here and in England, and now reissued by the new publishing firm of B.W. Dodge & Co., New York. The title is 'Sister Carrie.' The author is Theodore Dreiser.

Some reviewers, such as the one for the Chicago *Tribune*, devoted a good deal of attention to the novel's publishing history. And most of the reviewers found occasion to either mention or quote from the British reviews. Among the journals and newspapers which referred to the English reviews, in addition to *Reedy's Mirror*, one can list *Current Literature*, New York *Evening Sun*, Baltimore *Sun*, Mobile *Register*, *Independent*, Chicago *Evening Post*, Houston *Daily Post*, Philadelphia *Public Ledger*, and *Bookman*. (The Louisville *Times* reviewer apparently was so impressed with the English reviews that he began his review of June 19, 1907, by stating that "[*Sister Carrie*] was first printed in England, where the critics have treated it with flattering attention. . . .") The attitude of the American reviewers in general perhaps was best expressed by the critic for the New York *Evening Sun*, who quoted the last lines of Watts-Dunton's *Athaneaum* review and explained: "We quote this passage, not because we want to thrust the opinions of the author of 'The Coming of Love' down the throat of any virtuous New York publisher, but for fear anybody should accuse us of being 'coarse and vulgar' ourselves, seeing that we too admire this story" (June 1, 1907).

The review in *The Athenaeum* had made *Sister Carrie* respectable. Whatever Dreiser's weaknesses as a stylist, his novel no longer was to be faulted on moral grounds. What the Philistines had to recognize about Dreiser was that *Sister Carrie*, as Watts-Dunton so aptly had put it, "strikes a keynote and is typical, both in the faults of its manner and the wealth and diversity of its matter, of the great country which gave it birth." Whether the wealth of matter in a Dreiser novel does overcome the faults of its manner is, of course, still *the* question to be argued about Dreiser's work. In the early 1900s, however, what was of prime importance was that the dictum of Watts-Dunton and several of his colleagues made it possible for such an influential American critic as Frederic Taber Cooper to write in the May, 1907, *Bookman* that although "Mr. Dreiser is no stylist," his novel "gripped the present writer with a force unequalled by any other American novel that has appeared within five years of it. . . ."

A year after B. W. Dodge reissued *Sister Carrie,* the novel was published by Grosset & Dunlap, who had contracted with Dodge for an edition of 10,000 copies. By the end of the year, more than half of the copies had been sold. In the same year, 1908, William J. Locke came to the United States from England and told reporters that in Great Britain *Sister Carrie* was regarded as the finest American novel of the last twenty years and Dreiser as "the biggest American novelist who has sent us anything . . ." (New York *Times,* November 21, 1908). England's reading public apparently did not agree with Locke, for *Sister Carrie* did not sell well. But the critics continued to express high praise for the novel. Frank Harris included *Sister Carrie* in a list of his favorite books, saying that it was "a better story than any of Hawthorne's—the best story, on the whole, which has yet come to America, perhaps better than any realistic story which has yet been produced in America" (*Academy,* May 27, 1911), while Arnold Bennett thought the novel to be "eye-openingly good" (*North American Review,* January, 1912).

During this period, Dreiser devoted his energies largely to editorial work with the Butterick Publishing Co. and to his love for young Thelma Cudlipp—the girl he called Honeypot. But in October, 1910, because of his infatuation for Honeypot, Dreiser was fired from his position at Butterick and the next month Mrs. Cudlipp took her seventeen year old daughter to Europe. Dreiser, somewhat distraught and bewildered, returned to the manuscript of *Jennie Gerhardt.* A draft was quickly completed, and Dreiser sent the work to Harper & Bros., the same company that had refused *Sister Carrie* in 1900. This time they accepted Dreiser's novel for publication, some revisions were hurriedly made, and *Jennie Gerhardt* was brought out on October 19, 1911.

As was the case with the Dodge reissue of *Sister Carrie,* many of the reviewers of *Jennie Gerhardt* began their critiques with the comment about *l'affaire Doubleday.* Their account of the publication of *Sister Carrie* varied greatly—one critic wrote that "It is more than a decade since Theodore Dreiser's remarkable book, 'Sister Carrie,' appeared, and was immediately smothered under a 'conspiracy of silence' " (New Orleans *Times Democrat,* November 19, 1911) and another, apparently unaware of the fact that *Jennie* was Dreiser's first novel since *Sister Carrie,* began his review with the observation that *Jennie Gerhardt* "is the best book from the facile pen of Mr. Dreiser since he wrote his famous book 'Sister Carrie' " (Waterbury [Conn.] *Democrat,* November 25, 1911). But such differences were of little importance; the story of Dreiser's struggle with the Philistines was becoming an established part of our literary history. This is not to say, of course, that Dreiser had become a national folk hero. There were still many critics who were disturbed by his "lack of style and proportion, baldness and commonplaceness of diction" (New York *Daily Tribune,* October 21, 1911). And there were just as many reviewers who, despite Watts-Dunton, were offended by his world view—his immorality. Frederic Blount, writing in the New York *Telegraph,* was certain that Dreiser would write "the big story that is in him . . . but he ought to choose a bigger theme than the story of a kept woman" (November 5, 1911). Much the same sentiment was expressed by the reviewer for the Detroit *Free Press,* who wrote that *Jennie Gerhardt* "is not a book one enjoys, it is too bald and naked, yet there is nothing sensational in it. There is simply no need that it should have been written. It can do no good; it may do harm, for in spite of Jennie's immoral life, we can hardly condemn her as unmoral" (November 4, 1911). And Edwin Markham, who acknowledged that Dreiser had once again shown himself "master of a pen that etches with power the dark side of poverty with all its cares and despairs," felt compelled to tell his readers that a woman is never "justified in smirching her womanhood, in staining her virtue . . . even to save [her relatives] from starvation." "The wise are aware," he wrote in the New York *American* on October 25, 1911, "that there are some misfortunes that are worse than starvation."

But such exclamations of moral concern notwithstanding, this time there was no doubt that the favorable reviews far outweighed the unfavorable ones. As if anticipating the moral stance of a Blount and Markham, Dreiser's admirers were quick to note that "The book neither is moral nor immoral—it is art" (Kansas City *Journal,* October 22, 1911); or, as Mencken put it, "A moral tale? Not at all. It has no more moral than a string quartet or the first book of Euclid." It was also Mencken, who would prove to be Dreiser's staunchest and most articulate champion in the years to come, who made the most extravagant claim on *Jennie*'s behalf: "I am firmly convinced," he wrote in the November, 1911, *Smart Set,* "that 'Jennie Gerhardt' is the best American novel I have ever read, with the lonesome but Himalayan exception of 'Huckleberry Finn,' and so I may as well say it aloud and at once and have done with it." Other reviewers were somewhat less bold. Floyd Dell, for example, was content to simply call *Jennie Gerhardt* "a great book" (Chicago *Evening Post Literary Review,* November 3, 1911). Rowana Landon, writing in the Columbus [Ohio] *Dispatch,* asked, "What constitutes greatness in a novel?" and responded by saying, "If it be a vitally human motif, wrought into adequate literary form, then is 'Jennie Gerhardt' but entering into a deserved inheritance of fame destined to prove abiding" (May 11, 1912). Even a critic such as Calvin Winter, who had serious reservations about the novel, told the readers of *Bookman* that although *Jennie* was "not a great book," it was "a big book, undeniably, full of rugged sincerity, a fearless devotion to truth, and undisguised pity for the impotence of human nature under its double handicap of heredity and environment" (December, 1911).

Such extravagant praise obviously represents an extreme attitude toward Dreiser and *Jennie Gerhardt.* But, at the same time, these reviews make it quite clear that with only two novels to his credit, and those published eleven years apart, Dreiser was already a dominant figure in American letters. As the reviewer for the Brooklyn *Eagle* wrote on November 2, 1912, "The time has already arrived in the literary career of Theodore Dreiser when the publication of a new novel by him may be called an event." The event in 1912 was the publication in October of the first volume of Dreiser's Trilogy of Desire, *The Financier.*

On the whole, *The Financier* was extremely well received. There were, to be sure, occasional demurers. The reviewer for New York *Evening Mail,* for example, considered the novel to be less "solid" than Dreiser's two previous novels: "He has attempted to handle material which is not his to command," wrote the reviewer on November 9, 1912; and H.L. Mencken wrote what was for him a guarded review: *The Financier,* he stated in the New York *Times Book Review* on November 10, 1912, was "the prologue rather than the play." But Dreiser's other champion, William Marion Reedy, considered *The Financier* to be better than either *Sister Carrie* or *Jennie Gerhardt,* an opinion shared by the reviewers for the New York *Evening Sun* and Cleveland *Leader,* among others. What dominated almost all the reviews, favorable and unfavorable alike, was the length of the novel. In review after review, the same observation could be noted: " 'The Financier' reaches to 780 compact pages, printed from a clear and readable type upon paper of a weight and thinness that keep the book within easily portable compass, and it contains nearly three hundred thousand words, thereby extending to more than twice the length of the average long novel" (Boston *Evening Transcript,* November 6, 1912); " 'The Financier,' the latest production of Theodore Dreiser, is printed in small type and fills 780 narrow-margined pages" (*McClure's,* March, 1913); "A novel of almost 800 pages is a portentous publication" (New York *Evening Sun,* November 11, 1912). In ensuing years, the length of Dreiser's novels was to become a major issue of discontent with those critics who regarded Dreiser as a writer who was most notably lacking a sense of style and proportion, and the response to *The Financier* foreshadowed the battles that were to come. Some critics felt that Dreiser had not justified "the 780 substantial pages to which his book extends" (Providence [R.I.] *Journal,* November 17, 1912); as William Payne wrote in *Dial,* "There are nearly eight hundred pages in this book, and the story that they tell might have been more effectively set forth with half the words" (February 1, 1913). But others—Reedy, most notably—related the length of the novel to its dramatic power: "If you read novels," Reedy wrote in his *Mirror,* "let me recommend Theodore Dreiser's 'The Financier.' It's big—physically and intellectually. It is bigger than his powerful books, 'Sister Carrie' and 'Jennie Gerhardt.' Bigger as a man's sphere of action is bigger than woman's" (January 2, 1913). And, wrote Frederic Cooper in the December issue of The *Bookman,* whatever its crudities, and despite its unwarranted length, *The Financier* "must be recognized as a novel of the first magnitude." Most of the critics agreed. Indeed, the same assessment was made of Dreiser himself: whatever his crudities, his flaws as a writer, he obviously was a writer of the first magnitude. He was the American Balzac, Hardy, and Zola; with the lone exception of Howells, he was "the greatest of contemporary novelists" (Carl Robertson, Cleveland *Plain Dealer,* November 16, 1912), the one American novelist "who takes himself seriously and whose novels may be spoken of in the same breath with those of the great European realists" (Herbert Bashford, San Francisco *Bulletin,* November 16, 1912).

About a year before *The Financier* was published, Dreiser left the United States for a tour of Europe. For some time, he had been anxious to go abroad to research the activities of Charles Yerkes—the prototype for Frank Cowperwood—and through the intercession of Grant Richards, the English publisher, he finally was able to get together enough money to allow him to sail to Europe. Richards, who had business ties with the Century Company in New York, convinced the company's president to give Dreiser an advance on three articles he would write about Europe for *Century Magazine* upon his return; in addition, Century was given the option on a travel book Dreiser agreed to write about his impressions of Europe. Dreiser made the trip—leaving for Europe on November 22, 1911, and returning on April 23, 1912—and by June, 1913, he published the first of his European sketches, "Lilly Edwards: An Episode," in Mencken's *Smart Set.* This was followed in quick order by the three sketches for *Century Magazine,* as well as a completed draft of his impressions of Europe, which Dreiser sent to Douglas Z. Doty at Century. The editors at Century were troubled by the length of the manuscript, as well as Dreiser's frankness about his encounters with prostitutes. The manuscript was shown to Grant Richards, the "Barfleur" of the book, who was to write in *Author Hunting by an Old Literary Sportsman:* "Reticence on any matter and Theodore Dreiser were as far apart as the poles. As I read [the manuscript] I discovered that George Moore at his frankest was, compared with Dreiser, the essence of discretion. No confidence was sacred, no actual, or imagined, secret respected." The manuscript was heavily cut —especially, as Dreiser wrote Mencken on November 18, 1913, "a lot of woman stuff which [Century] objected to like hell"—and on November 25, 1913, *A Traveler at Forty* was published.

Dreiser's first book of non-fiction was received with respect rather than excitement. There was general agreement that *A Traveler at Forty* was not an ordinary travel book; what the reviewers were unable to agree upon was whether the unusual aspects of the book were deserving of praise. Dreiser had made himself the center of the work; it was clear to all that Dreiser was more fascinated by his own response to Europe than he was by Europe itself. Some reviewers inevitably found this offensive. The critic for *Town & Country,* for example, wrote that "The very tone of 'A Traveler at Forty' is irritating and unfortunate. Mr. Dreiser's style has been an intensification of the commonplace; now it has fused into smugness" (February 7, 1914). And, as more than one critic noted, this smugness was particularly evident in Dreiser's disdainful attitude toward the Church. But most critics found Dreiser's approach refreshingly different: "As in 'Sister Carrie,' in 'Jennie Gerhardt' and in 'The Financier' Mr. Dreiser was no ordinary novelist," wrote E.F. Edgett in the Boston *Evening Transcript,* "so in 'A Traveler at Forty' he is no ordinary tourist" (December 3, 1913). Not only was the book filled with Dreiser's own experiences and impressions; it also contained, in the words of the critic for the Boston *Globe,* "the philosophy of the novelist, to whom the study of human nature is the occupation and chief end of life" (December 13, 1913). This clearly was the real interest of the book for many reviewers: it helped them to better understand Dreiser the novelist. As Mencken wrote in the February, 1914, issue of *Smart Set,* although *A Traveler at Forty* was occasionally hackneyed, the empty impressions were outnumbered and outweighed by "the pregnant observations of an old hand at looking, the sharp remarks and annotations of the creator of Hurstwood, Cowperwood, and Père Gerhardt." And as a result, Dreiser's travel book "differs enormously from the customary travel books; it is not a mere description of places and people, but a revelation of their impingement upon an exceptional and almost eccentric personality. Whoever has got civilized pleasure out of the Dreiser novels will read it with joy. It is, in a sense, a free commentary upon those novels, a sort of epilogue mufti. It makes a bit clearer the Dreiser philosophy, the Dreiser view of life. . . ."

For all the merit the critics may have found in *A Traveler at Forty*— and the Philadelphia *Record* considered it to be "one of the great works of

American travel writing" (December 6, 1913)—the book was but an interlude between novels. It was to be a relatively short interlude, however, for Dreiser soon was ready with the second volume of his Cowperwood saga. Only, once again and quite unexpectedly, he encountered difficulty finding a publisher for his new novel. The completed manuscript naturally enough had been sent to Harper's, who advertised the forthcoming publication of *The Titan* and printed 8,500 sets of sheets (Dreiser's figure was 10,000 sets). Then, perhaps because, as Dreiser wrote Mencken on March 6, 1914, they found the realism "too hard and uncompromising and their policy cannot stand it," Harper's decided against publication. Proofs of the novel were sent to several publishers, but it was not until Dreiser sent them to the John Lane Company, a British firm which recently had opened an office in New York, that *The Titan* found a publisher. J. Jefferson Jones, director of Lane's New York branch, wired Dreiser that they would be "proud to publish [*The*] *Titan,*" Dreiser was delighted to find a publisher, and the novel was brought out on May 10, 1914.

Two months before *The Titan* was published, Mencken, who had read an unbound copy of the novel, wrote Dreiser (on March 23) that "it is the best thing you have ever done, with the possible exception of *Jennie Gerhardt,* and the superiority there is only in the greater emotional appeal." When he reviewed *The Titan* for *Smart Set* in August of that year, Mencken went even further: "But what of 'The Titan' as a work of art?" he wrote. "To me, at least, it comes closer to what I conceive to be Dreiser's ideal than any other story he has done." He was not alone in lavishing such praise on *The Titan.* The reviewer for the Baltimore *Evening Sun* called it an "epoch in American fiction" (May 23, 1914), while the critic for *Life* wrote that together with *The Financier, The Titan* offered "what is undoubtedly, in several important respects, the nearest approximation yet arrived at to that figment of our fictional dreams, the Great American Novel" (August 13, 1914).

Most of the reviewers, however, were somewhat more tempered in their praise. Ethel Colson, writing in the Chicago *Record-Herald,* commented that *The Titan* was vigorous and arresting, but it was "neither finished nor fine" (June 13, 1914). And Frederic T. Cooper, who had no quarrel with Dreiser's method or outlook on life, was bothered by his sense of proportion: "it is not enough to tell the reader the truth, the whole truth, and nothing but the truth," he wrote in the June, 1914, *Bookman;* "it is necessary also to hold his interest—and to do that, an author must be careful not to try the reader's patience too far nor too long." Other voices were considerably more strident in their objections to Dreiser's novel. The New York *Evening Sun*'s reviewer wrote that in *The Titan,* Dreiser "mauls and mutilates the English language with more brutal carelessness than any literate person we have ever known" (June 22, 1911); and in a review entitled "A Master of Immorality," a writer for the Providence *Journal* found *The Titan* to be "both profoundly immoral and profoundly inartistic" (June 14, 1914). Still, by 1914 there were few reviewers who seemed to disagree with the assessment of Dreiser offered by the New York *Tribune*'s reviewer: "While Robert Herrick is still pleading for greater freedom for the American novelist," he wrote on May 23, 1914, "Theodore Dreiser long ago took it, and by the mere weight of his ponderous talent imposed himself upon our literature. Others have done this, and continue to do it, but he is our arch-realist, unrestrained and unafraid."

That Dreiser was unrestrained *and* unafraid was eminently reinforced by the publication in 1915 of *The "Genius."* This, the most autobiographical of his novels, was also the longest and most sexually preoccupied work he had written. The response to it shows just how strong Dreiser's position had become by this time. Today, *The "Genius"* clearly seems to be one of Dreiser's weaker literary efforts, and one might well have thought that both the subject matter and length of the novel would have left Dreiser vulnerable to a sharp critical attack. And, indeed, there were a number of strongly dissenting reviews. (Dreiser himself was quick to note in letters to Arthur Ficke [October 17, 1915] and Harold Hersey [November 18, 1915] that his latest novel was receiving unfavorable notices: "They knock and knock and knock me but even so I do the best I can.") The ever-loyal Mencken and Floyd Dell, who had helped with the editing of the original manuscript, were hard pressed to find any kind words for the novel, and some less sympathetic critics found it easy to dismiss the book, in varying tones of indignation, as either depressing or unpleasant or depressing *and* unpleasant. But what now seems remarkable about the critical reception of *The "Genius"* is not the unfavorable notices which appeared in the New York *Times,* Providence *Journal,* Los Angeles *Graphic,* and St. Louis *Post Dispatch,* but that, Dreiser to the contrary, the majority of reviews were not unfavorable. The most unreadable of Dreiser's novels was in fact frequently greeted in the most laudatory terms. The review in *Little Review* began with the unequivocal statement that "Theodore Dreiser is the greatest novelist in America" (October, 1915). Albrecht Monteglas, writing in the Chicago *Examiner,* modified this view somewhat by stating, "In 'The Genius'[sic] Theodore Dreiser has proven that he is the greatest living American epic writer of life as it is" (December 11, 1915), a view which may have been inspired by John Cowper Powys' contention that *"The 'Genius'* is an epic work" (*Little Review,* November, 1915). Edgar Lee Masters did not see the novel in such grand terms (nor did Elia Peattie, who wrote in the December 4, 1915, Chicago *Tribune* that if *The "Genius"* is an epic, "it is the epic of a human Tom-Cat."), but he did consider *The "Genius"* to be a greater book than any previously written by the writer who "has revolutionized American fiction" (Chicago *Evening Post,* October 22, 1915). So, too, William Reedy, who mistakenly thought *The "Genius"* to be the final volume in the Trilogy of Desire: *The "Genius"*, he wrote in the *Mirror* on October 8, 1915, "is a work of art to which Dreiser has risen from mere works of devoted craft." Most impressive of all, though considerably less exuberant than others, was the balanced and thoughtful assessment of Randolph Bourne: "I trust [Bourne wrote in the November 20, 1915, issue of *The New Republic*] that the quotation marks in the title indicate Mr. Dreiser's realization that he has created only a second-rate personality, that he never, indeed, creates any but second-rate personalities. In the Genius he has made, however, a grandiose caricature of the masculine soul. And his real hero, anyway, is not his second-rate personality, but the desire of life. For this, much shall be forgiven him."

Due in large part no doubt to such reviews, sales of *The "Genius"* got off to a good start; more than 6,500 copies were sold in the first three months of publication. An additional 1,685 copies of the novel were sold in the first six months of 1916, and then came the event that was to make *The "Genius"* a cause célèbre: in July, with John S. Sumner leading the way, The New York Society for the Suppression of Vice banned *The "Genius"* on grounds of obscenity. The Society contended that there were more than ninety offensive pages in the novel, and in the words of Mr. Sumner, "It is wholly conceivable that the reading of such a book by a young woman would be very harmful." John Lane, who had published *The "Genius"* the previous October, recalled all copies of the novel from the bookstores and the fight was on. Mencken took charge: "On with the machine guns!", he wrote Dreiser. "Forward the Zepplins! I am planning a general offensive." Little happened: some meetings were held, petitions were signed, and two years after the novel had been suppressed, the case finally came to court. It was thrown out on a technicality, and the situation remained as it had been for the previous two years; Dreiser was unable to force Lane to publish the book or to sell their rights to it. As a result, only bootleg copies of *The "Genius"* were obtainable, and they were the only ones to be had until 1923, when the novel was reissued by Boni & Liveright.

Whatever the total effect of the suppression of *The "Genius"* may have been upon Dreiser, a decade would pass before another of his novels was published. His various publishers—especially Boni & Liveright—tried to get him to complete *The Bulwark* (which he had begun some time between 1910–1914), but Dreiser was unable to do so. Instead, he quickly followed *The "Genius"* with *Plays of the Natural and Supernatural*

(1916), *A Hoosier Holiday* (1916), *Free and Other Stories* (1918), *Hand of the Potter* (1919), *Twelve Men* (1919), and *Hey Rub-a-Dub-Dub* (1920). By this time, an exasperated Horace Liveright wrote Dreiser on June 28, 1920, that although he would be glad to read the manuscript of *Newspaper Days,* "frankly, what I want is *The Bulwark*. . . . Everybody is waiting for a Dreiser novel." But Dreiser still could not deliver *The Bulwark,* or any other novel. So Liveright took *Newspaper Days,* which was published in 1922 as *A Book About Myself* (and reissued as *Newspaper Days* in 1931), and the next year published *The Color of a Great City.*

None of these works in any way notably affected Dreiser's reputation. However, it was during this period following the publication of *The "Genius"* that Dreiser's writings and reputation were subjected to their first intensive evaluation. The catalyst for this assessment was the publication in the December 2, 1915, issue of *The Nation* of Stuart Sherman's article, "The Naturalism of Mr. Dreiser." In this piece, which remains among the severest rejections of Dreiser's art, Sherman harshly criticized all of Dreiser's novels, contending that in none of them was he able to find either "moral value" or "memorable beauty." Dreiser, he wrote, was a naturalist, not a realist; he had adopted a mode of writing which was a representation based upon a theory of animal behavior. And "since a theory of animal behavior can never be an adequate basis for a representation of the life of man in contemporary society, such a representation is an artistic blunder. When half the world attempts to assert such a theory, the other half rises in battle. And so [he concluded] one turns with relief from Mr. Dreiser's novels to the morning papers."

Two years later, Sherman retitled his essay "The Barbaric Naturalism of Theodore Dreiser" and included it in his volume *On Contemporary Literature.* This time, however, the attack did not go unanswered. In the same year, 1917, Mencken published *A Book of Prefaces,* which contained a long and generally laudatory estimate of Dreiser's work. Mencken began by writing that "Out of the desert of American fictioneering, so populous and yet so dreary, Dreiser stands up—a phenomenon unescapably visible, but disconcertingly hard to explain." Then, after trying to explain the phenomenon, Mencken directed his attention to those academics who, like William Lyon Phelps, continued to ignore Dreiser, or, like Sherman and H.W. Boynton, derided his efforts. Because Boynton was "a mere parrotor of conventional phrases," Sherman bore the brunt of Mencken's counter-attack: "As for the animal behaviour prattle of the learned headmaster," wrote Mencken, "it reveals, on the one hand, only the academic fondness for seizing upon high-sounding but empty phrases and using them to alarm the populace, and on the other hand, only the academic incapacity for observing facts correctly and reporting them honestly."

Mencken was joined in his defense of Dreiser by Randolph Bourne and Burton Rascoe. On June 14, 1917, *Dial* published Bourne's essay, "The Art of Theodore Dreiser," in which Bourne wrote that Sherman's antithesis between the realism that was based on a theory of human conduct and the naturalism that reduced life to a mere animal behavior was "silly" and "nonsensical." Dreiser had done a real service to the American imagination by going gravely about the business of portraying sex as it is found in the "personal relations of bungling, wistful, or masterful men and women." A good novelist, Bourne explained, "catches hold of the thread of human desire. Dreiser does this, and that is why his admirers forgive him so many faults." Rascoe, in the first book devoted solely to Dreiser, continued the counter-attack by suggesting that Sherman's essay be read as the sort of "critical yelping" that had pursued Dreiser throughout his career: Sherman, wrote Rascoe, "sets up a false premise in regard to Dreiser and argues from that false premise by a most astonishing misrepresentation of the facts."

Rascoe's *Theodore Dreiser* came out in 1925. That was, coincidentally, the same year in which Horace Liveright finally got to publish his Dreiser novel. *The Bulwark* still was not finished, and would not be for another twenty years, but *An American Tragedy* was, and it was this most successful of all Dreiser's works which Boni & Liveright issued in a two-volume edition on December 14, 1925. Almost immediately upon its publication, the novel was reviewed in the New York *Herald Tribune* (January 3, 1926), where, under the heading, "Mr. Dreiser in Tragic Realism," it was called "the worst written great novel in the world." Despite its faults, wrote the reviewer, "the work as a whole is massively impressive. I do not know where else in American fiction one can find the situation here presented dealt with so fearlessly, so intelligently, so exhaustively, so veraciously, and *therefore* with such unexceptionable moral effect." The reviewer was Stuart Sherman.

Sherman was hardly alone in his praise for *An American Tragedy.* To be sure, William Lyon Phelps, whom Mencken had chastized for ignoring Dreiser, now expressed his displeasure with the novel, as did Ernest Brennecke, Jr. in *Commonweal,* and Mencken, in a piece entitled, "Dreiser in 840 pages," advised his readers to "Hire your pastor to read the first volume for you. But don't miss the second!" (*American Mercury,* March, 1926). There were not very many more dissenting opinions. *An American Tragedy* was a stunning success. In addition to Sherman, the novel was lauded by such diverse figures as Sherwood Anderson ("Get and read 'An American Tragedy' for yourself if you have any feeling for American writing. That's all I can say"[*Saturday Review of Literature,* January 9, 1926].), Burton Rascoe, Clarence Darrow, Donald Davidson, Joseph Wood

Krutch ("Mr. Dreiser's new novel is the crowning achievement of the work he began a quarter of a century ago"[*Nation*, February 10, 1926].), Heywood Broun, R. N. Linscott, John Cowper Powys, and Carl Van Doren ("Only 'Moby Dick' among American novels moves with the same fateful tread, carrying all its documents on its back, and yet never seriously delaying"[*Century Magazine*, April, 1926].) Even before these reviews came out, *An American Tragedy* sold close to 14,000 copies, earning Dreiser $11,872.02 in royalties. By March, such was the fame of *An American Tragedy* that Dreiser was able to sell the film rights to the novel for $90,000 (of which $10,000 went to Liveright). *An American Tragedy* cost Dreiser Mencken's friendship—Dreiser would never forgive Mencken his unenthusiastic review—but it finally gave him the critical renown and financial independence for which he had so long waited.

Yet, just as the suppression of *The "Genius"* may account, at least in part, for Dreiser's failure to complete a novel in almost ten years, so too the extraordinary success of *An American Tragedy* may have had a detrimental artistic effect on Dreiser. Whatever the reason, Dreiser failed to complete another novel for twenty years. In 1926, a limited edition of *Moods, Cadenced and Declaimed* was issued. The following year, Dreiser published *Chains*, a collection of lesser novels and stories; and later that year, at the invitation of the Soviet government, he made his famous journey to Russia. This resulted in the publication the following year of *Dreiser Looks at Russia*, which in turn brought forth charges of plagiarism from Dorothy Thompson. In the same year (1928), Dreiser added twenty-six poems to the limited edition of *Moods, Cadenced and Declaimed*, and the expanded volume was published in a trade edition. *A Gallery of Women* was published in 1929, and in 1931 Dreiser published the second volume of his autobiography, *Dawn*, as well as his indictment of the capitalistic system, *Tragic America*. More poems were added to *Moods*, which then was reissued in 1935 as *Moods: Philosophical and Emotional (Cadenced and Declaimed)*. And in 1941 *American Is Worth Saving* was brought out by Modern Age; it was the last book written by Dreiser to be published before his death in December, 1945.

Unlike the period between the publication of *The "Genius"* and *An American Tragedy*, Dreiser's reputation underwent a considerable change in the twenty years following the publication of *An American Tragedy*. Literary tastes were changing, and Dreiser's position changed with them. As he moved further in time from *An American Tragedy*, he was no longer regarded as the greatest of American novelists. Nor was he a dynamic force in American letters. He was a man of the past, a writer to whom many of the younger authors now paid their tribute. His legendary past became his present; he became a public figure. But for all this, there were still two novels which had to be finished, and Dreiser spent the last years of his life working on the manuscripts of his Quaker novel, *The Bulwark,* and the final volume of the Trilogy of Desire, *The Stoic.* He approved the galleys of *The Bulwark* on December 22, 1945, just seven days before his death; *The Stoic* was left unfinished, and was published with an appendix prepared by Helen Dreiser from the notes left by her husband.

Neither novel was greeted with much enthusiasm. *The Bulwark* did receive words of praise from Robert Spiller and Edmund Wilson, and James T. Farrell wrote reviews extolling the two posthumously published novels. For the most part, however, *The Bulwark* and *The Stoic* were regarded with more curiosity than excitement. Both novels were seen as the work of a tired man who was speaking with a voice that belonged to a different generation. There was some interest in *The Bulwark*'s religious affirmation (especially since Dreiser had joined the Communist Party at the same time he was completing the story of Solon Barnes), and some critics were interested in comparing *The Stoic* with the earlier volumes in the Trilogy of Desire. But it was Dreiser, really, rather than his last two novels, with whom many critics decided to concern themselves. This obviously was an apt occasion for the reviewers to present an overview of Dreiser's career.

The results were, in effect, a summation of the critical response which had been accorded Dreiser throughout his life. Lionel Trilling, for example, in a now-famous essay in *The Nation* (April 20, 1946), that in some ways recalled Stuart Sherman's "The Naturalism of Mr. Dreiser," used the publication of *The Bulwark* to attack the liberal judgment which excused Dreiser's penchant for thinking stupidly and writing badly. But, more often than not, the critical response was as it long had been: whatever weaknesses there were in Dreiser's style, they *were* to be excused, for as Jack Conroy wrote in the Chicago *Sun,* Dreiser's principal contribution "has been a conceptual and thematic, not a stylistic, one" (December 3, 1947). Dreiser, that is, for all his weaknesses, was still the author of *Sister Carrie* and *An American Tragedy;* and, to quote from John Lydenberg's review of *The Stoic,* his "contribution to American literature is as great, for all his limitations, as that of any other novelist; he fought stubbornly and often alone a battle that had to be fought" (*Saturday Review of Literature,* December 6, 1947).

There was also a somewhat different view of Dreiser offered in these reviews of his last two novels, one which stressed that Dreiser's significance was not limited to his historical function as the "courageous opener of doors for later writers like Sherwood Anderson and Farrell." This view was best expressed by F. O. Matthiessen, whose sensitive study of Dreiser ironically was left unfinished at *his* death: "The emotional force of [Dreiser's] novels rises from his own involvement in his material," Matthiessen wrote in a front page review of *The Bulwark* for the New York *Times Book Review* (March 24, 1946). " 'Sister Carrie' exudes the glamour of a chromo, the glamour of the big cities as Carrie herself was drawn to them. The liability in what Santayana called the genteel tradition was due to its being the product of the mind apart from experience. Dreiser gave us the stuff of our common existence, not as it was hoped to be by any idealizing theorist, but as it actually was in its crudity."

No one has offered a better estimate of Dreiser's art. Of course, Dreiser's detractors remain unconvinced; to many, his writings are still to be regarded as nothing less than stylistic abominations. In the past few years, however, we have seen the publication of a number of impressive studies of Dreiser's novels as works of art. Whether they in any way will help resolve the debate that has always surrounded Dreiser seems unlikely. But it is time nevertheless for Dreiser to be explained. His position in American letters has been clearly defined. Now, we must elucidate the fascination, even the eloquence, of his extraordinary crudity.

A few words, not of Dreiserian proportion, are in order about the making of this volume. In the balcony of the Rare Book Room at the University of Pennsylvania, where the Dreiser Papers are kept, there are two grey steel filing cabinets which contain the reviews Dreiser had sent to him by various clipping services. The reviews in these two cabinets formed the core for this collection. Clipping agencies, unfortunately, are frequently careless in dating the reviews they send their clients, and although I have tried to verify the dates on the reviews in the clipping file, I am sure that the source and dates of some of the reviews are inaccurate. (There is a review in the *Gallery of Women* folder, for example, which is marked *Atlantic Monthly,* April, 1930; neither I nor the staff at *Atlantic Monthly* has been able to locate the review which is so dated.) In addition, though the clipping file at the University of Pennsylvania is immense, it is far from complete. I have managed to ferret out a number of reviews not in the clipping file; but, again, I am certain that there are still many more reviews to be located. (There must, for example, have been more reviews of *Tragic America* and *America Is Worth Saving* than I have found.) The general editor and I will appreciate and gratefully acknowledge any reviews brought to our attention.

This volume is intended to reflect the development of Theodore Dreiser's critical reputation in the United States. Therefore, with one exception, the reviews which are here reprinted or listed in the checklist are those which appeared in American newspapers and journals. The exception is the reviews accorded *Sister Carrie* upon its publication in Great Britain in 1901. These reviews had a dominating influence on Dreiser's entire career, and for that reason I have included reviews from the British press of the 1901 Heinemann edition of *Sister Carrie.* No reviews, on the other hand, have been included of Dreiser works which were printed in limited editions: for example, *Fine Furniture, Epitaph, The Aspirant,* and the 1926 collection of *Moods, Cadenced and Declaimed.*

The organization of this volume is chronological, beginning with *Sister Carrie* in 1900 and concluding with the publication of *The Stoic* in 1947. (*Hand of the Potter,* incidentally, has a 1918 publishing date on its title page; but, it actually was not published until September, 1919, and that is the date which I have used for this volume.) As for the reviews themselves, I have tried to avoid reprinting only reviews which appeared in major newspapers. My aim has been to include a representative sampling of opinion from across the nation. Hopefully, at least most of the reviews which have been reprinted will be found to be substantial unto themselves, as well as reflective of the critical opinion of the time.

To avoid a sense of repetitiveness, plot summaries often have been deleted; such deletions are always noted by the use of ellipsis. Three kinds of silent changes have been made: the deletion of publishing information (unless it is an integral part of the text); the deletion of section headings in newspaper reviews; and the correction of obvious typographical errors (e.g. Drieser for Dreiser). For the most part, brief notices have not been included, and the checklist does not list all of the appearances of a syndicated review. (But it does include, at the end of the list, those reviews in the clipping file at the University of Pennsylvania which do not contain sufficient publishing information to appear chronologically in the body of the checklist). Finally, it should be noted that Stuart Sherman's "The Naturalism of Mr. Dreiser" and Randolph Bourne's "The Art of Theodore Dreiser" are not included in this volume because they are not reviews of any particular book by Dreiser.

No volume of this sort can be put together without the help and assistance of many people. I have had more than my share. A much-needed grant from the Penrose Fund of the American Philosophical Society helped with the cost of xeroxing and several trips to the University of Pennsylvania. Mrs. Neda M. Westlake, curator of the Rare Book Collection at the University of Pennsylvania, to whom all Dreiser scholars are indebted, allowed me access to the fading and crumbling reviews in the clipping file; without her cooperation this volume would have been impossible. She and her staff—David Kelly Kegan, Patricia Bridges, and Eileen Garafano—helped in innumerable ways to lighten the burden of drudging through the clipping file, and I am extremely grateful to them. I am equally indebted to Joseph Duchac, Edward Casson, and Gina Guastella, of the Periodicals Division of Long Island University, who were extraordinarily patient and cooperative. My thanks, too, to Miss Lois M. Jones, Department Librarian at the Los Angeles Public Library, who helped locate several Dreiser reviews in the Library's collection. And to Richard Dowell, Richard Lehan, and Joseph Slade, my gratitude for their help at various stages of this project. My friends, M. Thomas Inge and Stanley Lewis, proved to be very much like Dilsey: they endured. My wife, Cecily, spent many days going through the Dreiser clipping file with me, and she, together with my daughters, Ellie and Linda, helped with the scissors and paste. Words of thanks would hardly be adequate or appropriate. Better to say: Done, at last.

Jack Salzman

Sister Carrie

By

Theodore Dreiser

NEW YORK

Doubleday, Page & Co.

1900

Sister Carrie

Louisville *Times*, November 20, 1900.

Out in the highways and hedges of life you find a phase of realism that has not found its way into many books. It is sometimes morbid and sometimes forbidding. At its best it is grim and shadowy. It reeks of life's sordid endeavor; of the lowly home and the hopelessly restricted existence. Its loves, its joys, its sorrows, are narrow. There is little sunshine. It is plain realism.

When a man puts this sort of thing in a book he cannot expect to hear the plaudits of an admiring host or know the lavish tribute that goes out to men who write successful fiction. But he is an artist nevertheless. Fiction must reflect life, and all life does not present itself in the drawing-room, in the palace car or in the luxurious home. Because Theodore Dreiser has chosen to tell of the other side, not the "other half" about which so much has been written, but the other side of the social scale, he may not have brilliant success, but he will have the credit that must be accorded a man who has written faithfully and impressively.

"Sister Carrie" is the name of his book. It is a homely name; there is no suggestion of the girl with the laughing eye and the glowing cheek, and there is no thought of rustling silk and dancing lace. Instead, there comes into the mind the picture of a plain woman, plain in the sense of being of the great common people. And you are not mistaken.

Only once before in our recent fiction has this life been exploited, and then it was done by the brilliant young realist, Frank Norris. What happened in San Francisco in the brutal dentist's home happens in Chicago with "Sister Carrie." Where "McTeague" ended in hopeless tragedy and thrilling detail, "Sister Carrie" closes with a superficial triumph. But even then there is the shadow of a man's mistaken life and the inevitable sorrow of bitter defeat.

"Sister Carrie" is the story of a poor girl who gets into the glamor and the excitement of a great city. She is caught up in its dizzy whirl. She is exposed to temptation and she falls. What she does, what she says, what she lives for, are all told with minute detail and vivid realism. There is not the remarkable detail that has made Norris a master in his way, but it is the fine attention to the little things that makes Dreiser a factor in that sort of fiction which must be read and which we must have. It is a remarkable book, strong, virile, written with the clear determination of a man who has a story to tell and who tells it.

Detroit *Free Press*, November 24, 1900.

The tangle of life sweeps "Sister Carrie" into its maze and she rises—in her own estimation—by her fall in the eyes of others. Coming to Chicago poor, pretty and unsophisticated, with a girl's natural love of gaiety and finery; finding "honest labor" at a wage that barely fed and lodged her, falling into the clutches of a man who knew how to appeal to her vanity, what marvel that she chose the path that seemed to lead to all she thought best and most necessary to her happiness? Mr. Theodore Dreiser has portrayed in detail the conditions and temptations that lead a girl from virtue to the cheap theater. "Sister Carrie" is neither a pleasant nor an edifying book, but it is written out of real life. The problem in the reader's mind is: Was it worth the doing?

Life, November 24, 1900.

"Sister Carrie", by Theodore Dreiser, is a Chicago story of over five hundred pages. It is an exposition in great detail of the dangers which beset a young woman who goes to the city and is obliged to earn her living. She ends her variegated career at the head of the Casino Opera Company in New York. Such girls, however, as imagine that they can follow in her footsteps will probably end their days on the Island or in the gutter. . . .

Edna Kenton. Chicago *Daily News*, November, 30, 1900.

Nowadays when a writer dares to offer a 600-page novel to the public he has the courage of his convictions. One begins reading Theodore Dreiser's "Sister Carrie" with a sensation of wrath at the author's deliberation, and ends with the feeling that he has been treated to some remarkable character dissection. Mr. Dreiser writes painstakingly, he is apt to shovel on "local color," but he does not err on the side of over-elaboration, and that is what makes his picture of Carrie, of Drouet and Hurstwood so really worthy of respect. In the beginning Carrie comes to Chicago from a little Wisconsin town. She is 18 and is going to live with her sister, who is married to a stolid husband, Hansen. The girl's search for work, her experience in the grinding shoe factory, is deftly told. On the train to Chicago she had met Drouet, who is a type of the jolly, prosperous, good liver, fond of women, but meaning them no harm according to his point of view as to morality. In simple good-nature he rescues Carrie, as, penniless and discouraged, she thinks of going back to Wisconsin. She needs new clothes and she is hungry, and Drouet buys them for her in the same spirit he would have tossed a quarter to a starving man with a careless "Poor beggar!" The rest follows so logically that Carrie's downfall does not surprise the reader. Hurstwood next comes on the scene. He is a middle-aged and prosperous manager of a fashionable drinking place in Chicago. His home life is not happy, but he is true to his family. Gradually he becomes an admirer of Carrie, and his brilliance enables him to undermine whatever affection she has for Drouet, who in reality, with all his kindness and good-nature, is a little beneath the girl, who possesses a sort of innate refinement from which she never varies throughout the story. How Hurstwood is tempted and steals $10,000 from his employers, how he lures Carrie away with him under a pretext that Drouet has sent for her, is skillfully told. In a moment of weakness Hurstwood has tossed aside his home, his assured position, his friends. The couple finally settle in New York and Hurstwood sends back the money to his former employers, Carrie knowing nothing of his financial transactions, good or bad. The rest of the novel is its strong portion. It relates Carrie's success on the stage until she has reached comparative wealth, and it pictures Hurstwood's downfall, after she deserts him. There is something painful in the remorseless way the writer shows step by step the sinking of the once prosperous manager into a listless seeker for work, a penniless vagrant, a tattered, hopeless Bowery tramp and beggar, living on the various charities of New York, and his final horrible end. There is nothing melodramatic about it—it is too logical and photographic to own one unreal note. The book is well worth reading simply for this account of Hurstwood.

Hartford [Conn.] *Courant*, December 6, 1900.

"Sister Carrie" is a novel dealing with the sunny side of life in a manner which it is not too much to say is like that of Balzac. The writer shows insight into human nature and power of analysis and description. If this is, as some indications seem to show, his first book, and, if he is young, which nothing indicates, he ought to do some great work in the future. There is nothing more impressive in the year's novel-writing than the description of Hurstworth's [sic] last days, and death in New York. The book is rather long—556 pages—but it is full of action. One or two people of a moderate amount of honor would have strengthened the character group by contrast. All the people in the world are not hateful.

Toledo *Blade*, December 8, 1900.

The search for happiness, that will-o'-the-wisp so many go about the wrong way to seek, is what makes the story in Theodore Dreiser's novel, Sister Carrie. The tale is one of Chicago and New York, among people who are neither rich nor of high social position. There are really only three characters in the romance, if so may be called, for it carries with it an air of truth, and the circumstances are so constantly recurring that the events are more like a drama of real life. . . .

The character drawing of these people [Carrie, Hurstwood, and Drouet] is skilfully done, and the novel is a faithful portraiture of the conditions it represents, showing how the tangle of human life is knotted thread by thread. It is a gloomy story, and, while it is well told, it is too realistic, to sombre to be altogether pleasing.

New York *Commercial Advertiser*, December 19, 1900.

It may as well be said at the very outset that the titular heroine of *Sister Carrie* is a very frequent and commonplace type, unredeemed by even a touch of the basic honesty and inner charm of Du Maurier's Trilby, and yet the imperfect sketch which Mr. Dreiser has rendered of her detracts but little from the value of his work, for the reason that she plays a subordinate part in the development of the story. She is interesting as an unconscious tool in the shaping of events and as exhibiting in her own career the occasional absurd disproportion of motives to results. The extraordinary power with which this novel is vested, and which should, but probably will not, give it wide recognition, has little to do with the delineation of foolish, worldly wise Carrie; the power of the novel resides in a concrete and detailed proof of a truth too little understood.

The facts of the life of George Hurstwood, for some time the lover of Carrie, constitute a series of pictures, vivid to intensity, hard to deny, and illustrative of the maxim of Turgot: "Civilization is at bottom an economic fact." Hurstwood, as we first see him, is a prosperous business man of a prevalent type. Perhaps he has too much girth, is a trifle flabby-fleshed; is used too much to social success, too little to hardening effort. Still he is the eminently well-groomed, pleasant-faced man, whose contemporaries we negligently admire every day of our lives, in the cafés, the brokers' offices and at dinner, because of their unassuming but well-marked success, their buoyancy and their *savoir faire.* Of these men the workers of hand and brain have always been envious. By what diverse law are these happier soldiers of fortune enabled to turn genial ways into gold, and by a facile twist of wit wrench to their own use the lantern of Aladdin? What is the economic bottom of it and of them? For there is an economic bottom to the matter, a tragic truth, which justifies, because it proves necessary, the sweat of the delvers. . . .

Beyond a certain distance on the road to destitution, there is a vanishing point for self-respect. "Physical disgrace" and social meanness are at once indicative and productive of moral squalor. And therefore the cloistered philosophers erred when they stated with due eloquence that solely in the spirit of a man, and not in his material well-being, manhood consists. To maintain in some sort the reserve of social power which makes possible mental freedom is a just instinct of self-preservation. If bankruptcy, absolute not relative, and including the loosing of each social grip, ensues, what may a man do? For the enmity of the fates is a variable, only the answering force of the man may be built up measure by measure. To build up this force and buttress it with friends and efficiency in work is to attempt to over-top the unknown variable; man can not do more, or know the result before the event. It is only certain that all the advantages and probabilities are with the workers. And though they cannot afford to vaunt their immunities, the Hurstwoods will in comparison forever be unlucky. And if a thousand of them are becalmed in prosperity, and never meet a gale, yet a negative demonstration is of more effect and is not thereby invalidated.

The novel named *Sister Carrie*—Heaven knows why—says these things, and truly.

Albany *Journal*, December 22, 1900.

"Sister Carrie," by Theodore Dreiser, is distinctly a novel with a purpose. It is intensely human and therefore cannot fail to interest. The story deals with everyday people and is well and smoothly told. The heroine is a little country girl, who goes to Chicago to work and failing to obtain it, falls in with a drummer whom she met on the train and follows the usual course revealed so shockingly in the daily press from day to day. She goes to live with the drummer and afterwards meeting another man whom she likes better, lets herself be led away by the latter. He is a married man of respectable position, and he forsakes wife and children to go with Carrie, taking a large sum belonging to his employers while about it. The story of his gradual downfall is piteous. But as he goes down, Carrie having gone on the stage to help support them goes up and earns a name for herself. But she was not happy. "Sitting alone she was now an illustration of the devious ways by which one who feels, rather than reasons, may be led in the pursuit of beauty," and so the author leaves her.

Omaha [Neb.] *Daily Bee*, December 22, 1900.

"Sister Carrie" is the title of a volume by Theodore Dreiser, which may be best described as a novel of city life. It tells the story of a girl who comes to the city from a little country town; how she fails to find employment, finally falling into the hands of a traveling salesman, and details her subsequent life. While it describes unmistakably one side or phase of city life and tells a story that is undoubtedly often repeated in real life in every city, it is not a book to be put into the hands of every reader indiscriminately.

George Seibel. Pittsburgh *Commercial Gazette*, December 28, 1900.

If the function of the novel be to give lessons in the art of life, this book has not been born in vain. There are in it many lessons like the following:

"Well, if I were you," he said, looking at her rather genially, "I would try the department stores. They often need young women as clerks."

Was ever weighty truth enunciated so simply? Anyhow, Sister Carrie, who has come to Chicago to secure work, finally gets it at $4.50 per week. Life has more lessons for her to learn—lessons and temptations. Finally she gets upon the stage, in the chorus, at $12 per week. Here we have the difference between life and art. Carrie has learned her lessons well, and has now a diploma from the university of experience. If you doubt this, or if you doubt the novelist's depth of psychological insight into woman nature, here is a bit that will dissipate the doubt:

"I'll not give him the rest of my

money," said Carrie. "I do enough. I am going to get me something to wear."

Churchman, December 29, 1900.

"Sister Carrie," by Theodore Dreiser, tells a plain, unvarnished tale of the downfall of a poor girl who comes to Chicago for work. The description of the industrial conditions in a manufacturing establishment of the great city is well done and the futile struggle against adverse circumstance is so temperately described as to be effective. But there seems, after all, to be no justification for the book. When one collects and catalogues phenomena, we look for generalization in some conclusion. The work is certainly conscientious, but "to compass sea and land to make one proselyte" and then to really do nothing with him is disappointing to the reader.

"A Feminine Type." San Francisco *Chronicle*, December 30, 1900.

"Sister Carrie," by Theodore Dreiser, is a narrative of the career of an attractive and ambitious girl of 18, who visits her married sister in Chicago, and makes her way in the world by methods not always discreet or reputable. . . . It is a long and complicated narrative, that is well handled and the chief character, though unlovely, is a distinct type.

"A Novel of To-day." *Recreation*, January, 1901.

Under the non-committal title of "Sister Carrie," Theodore Dreiser has written a remarkable novel. He cuts loose from all preconceived, conventional ideas and paints with a strong, fearless touch a picture of startling intensity. That which the world calls sin he sees to be, in a woman, often only a love of what seems to her to be beauty; and because she reaches out for her ideal, false though it be, the sin itself scarcely touches her. The working out of this truth in Carrie's life is unique.

The scenes are laid in Chicago and New York, both of which Mr. Dreiser knows thoroughly and paints graphically.

Litte [William Marion Reedy]. "*Sister Carrie:* A Strangely Strong Novel in a Queer Milieu." St. Louis *Mirror*, 10 (January 3, 1901), 6.

A novel that a man will read through at one sitting is, in these days of novels *ad nauseam*, a rarity, and yet the writer found one the other day,— a novel that has been neither extensively advertised by its publishers, Doubleday, Page & Co., nor enthusiastically reviewed, if, indeed, it has been reviewed at all, in any of the journals of criticism. The title of the novel is "Sister Carrie."

The author is Theodore Dreiser.

Now, it isn't at all a nice novel. Neither is it nasty, which is supposed to be the antonym of nice. It is a story of the seamy side. It deals with the "fall" of a girl who goes to Chicago from a little Wisconsin town, and, strange to say, though the situation is treated with a calm frankness of tone, the fall is a fall upwards. The author writes with a startling directness. At times this directness seems to be the frankness of a vast unsophistication. Without any brutalities whatever, he is, nevertheless, intensely realistic in his painting of the methods which are employed, circumstance and temperament assisting, in the luring from sordid and dull and wearisome loneliness of innocence a girl by a flashy and flighty drummer. The peril of the girl who ventures into a great city to earn a living, without any training or moral preparation for the ordeal, is shown with a simplicity and strength that are the more impressive for being recorded in the strain of one who thinks the incident quite a frequent and a natural, though regretable, occurrence.

The scenes of the book are laid always among a sort of people that is numerous but seldom treated in a serious novel. And, for all its easy acceptance of the situation, this novel, "Sister Carrie," is a very serious production. Its veritism out-Howells Mr. Howells and out-Garlands Mr. Hamlin Garland. One would think that, with a factory girl for a heroine, with a fatuously empty-headed drummer for a leading figure and with a manager of a fashionable saloon for the dominating male character, such a novel would descend to depths unplummeted even by Mr. Albert Ross. But the book doesn't plunge into the obscurely salacious at all. It is, in spite of veritism, very much restrained. It is photographically true and yet there is an art about it that lifts it often above mere reporting. And there grows upon the reader the impression that there lurks behind the mere story an intense, fierce resentment of the conditions glimpsed.

The girl's experiences in a shoe factory, her life in a small, dismal flat, and her easy surrender to a tawdry masculine charm and a coarse kindness, are revealed with a convincing truth to character and to conditions in a great city like Chicago. The vain, silly, kindly drummer introduces the girl to the saloon manager *Hurstwood,* who wins her by his superior personality and, finally, after quarrelling with his wife and taking $10,000 from the safe of his employers, forces her to accompany him to Montreal, where he "marries" her, without the formality of divorcing his wife. The manager returns the stolen money, is not prosecuted, and the pair go to New York, where he becomes a partner in another saloon. Wrong as all this is, the girl always has something sweet and fine in her character. She is hardly to be called by as harsh a word as vulgar. She is even good, though in a negative fashion. She is not glorified in the least, not a particle idealized and yet she holds one's sympathies with a strange security. She has a natural talent for the stage, unwittingly discovered at an Elks' entertainment, though, in New York, she settles down to a quiet domesticity, all ignorant of her supposed husband's peculation or the truth of his departure from Chicago.

Hurstwood, however, fails, and it is in the delineation of the man's gradual sinking or slinking into degradation that the author shows his real power. The slow slackening of will, the subtle growth of indecision and self-abandonment, the loosening of all manly fibre, the crumbling, rotting of character in a kind of narcotic procrastination touched with fitful gleams of paretic, puling pride, until he comes to beggary on the streets, and final rest in a fifteen-cent room with the gas out but turned on—all this is shown with a power which no endeavor to keep awake a critical attitude can resist. The terrible slowness of the ruin of a man, the descent marked by the clever, casual bringing to light of little, obscure symptoms, is hideously oppressive—all the more so that the man was only a saloon manager and a character, in the beginning, conceived upon so high a plane of attractiveness as to verge closely upon the absurd. The narrative of *Hurstwood's* progress down hill is, in what some would call, "journalese," but it is a tale with no abuse of words, and with no over-use of detail. Vulgar as the fellow *Hurstwood* was at first, vile as he was, even, there is that tragedy in his descent of the Avenues of failure which moves the heart. *Carrie,* forced to earn her living in the chorus, becomes, finally, a comic opera "queen," and her star rises in glory as *Hurstwood's* goes out in the dark.

The woman, *Carrie,* is a reality all through the book, as real, to be paradoxical, as she is, to a certain extent, shadowy. The drummer you have met often, and liked, with a touch of contempt. The scenes in which the drama works out are all well realized. The separation of the drummer and the girl, when he discovers *Hurstwood* has won her affection, acutely develops the strong hint of the pathetic in *banale* situations which is more frequent than is often imagined. Indeed this queer, *banale* atmosphere hanging over the story is of the essence of the fascination of the volume. The tragedy and romance is of the commonest kind of common people, yet the spell is there. There are times when the tale seems to lapse into the veriest bathos of the cheapest sort of novel, but so sure as this is imminent the indeterminate somewhat in the writer suddenly bursts forth and informs the characters with a vivid vitality. The book is, as one might guess from what has gone before, very uneven, but the best of it is undeniably worth while and the worst of it seems, in some inexplicable fashion, to be a support to the best. At times the whole thing is impossible, and then again it is as absolute as life itself. The writer errs frequently in the selection of the material for his pictures, the incidents that he portrays, but the story, as a whole, has a grip that is not exercised upon any unwholesome taste. You read it through with interest and a stirring of the emotions, and when you sit down to write a criticism of it you find yourself trying, as it seems, to write and analyze the charm away. But you cannot. The charm, despite violence to taste and hovering intimations even of absurdity, remains superior to and defiant of analysis.

New Haven [Conn.] *Journal Courier,* January 12, 1901.

"Sister Carrie," by Theodore Dreiser; published by Doubleday, Page & Co., New York, is a strong story of American life. It is, moreover, extremely interesting. The writer shows a keen insight into human nature and the characters of the three chief persons of the book, those of Sister Carrie and of Hurstworth [sic], the business manager, and Drouet, her lovers, are most skilfully drawn. There is a depth of insight into human character evidenced, which has a touch of Balzac's strength and penetration. One of the most affecting passages is where Hurstworth falls, ruined, disgraced, by an accident when at the moment of intended restoration of the funds, which in a terrible stress and crisis in his moral life he had taken. No American writer has more successfully depicted the type of character represented by Drouet, and the author's handling of his theme in relation to the erring and bright young woman in the case is highly artistic and refined. Circumstances, including an uncongenial and unloving wife and family, seem to combine for his downfall. Hurstworth's enforced flight from Chicago and the irony of fate which tinged his subsequent sad career, down to his final ineffectual struggles for bread, and his last days and bitter end in New York, are deeply impressive. The book is one of the most powerful of the past year in all respects, and the author has manifested ability as a writer of a high order.

Indianapolis *Journal*, January 14, 1901.

It is a difficult task to write a book dealing in lax morals and keep all vulgarity out of it, at the same time maintaining the irresponsible, happy-go-lucky point of view of the ignorant little shop girl. In "Sister Carrie" Theodore Dreiser has done this. While the story is not one to put into the hands of the young girl, it is not one either which grates upon the sensibilities. The heroine, Carrie—Sister Carrie her own family call her—drifts from hard work into the care of a Chicago drummer who establishes her in what is to her the lap of luxury. Later on, she has another lover, George Hurstwood, the manager of a very prosperous Chicago barroom, who throws away his fortune, honesty and family for the girl. The many vicissitudes of his downward course, the loss of ambition, pride, independence—all that had heretofore made him a man, are admirably depicted. It is a very readable book, entertaining and remarkably clever in never swerving from the lower middle class standpoint. But it would have been a much stronger story if it had been condensed into half its present length.

Chicago *Chronicle*, January 14, 1901.

"Sister Carrie," by Theodore Dreiser (Doubleday, Page & Co., New York), is the story of a girl of 18 leaving her Wisconsin home to try her fortune in Chicago. . . .

The story is so plainly told that it seems actual fact without the least touch of romance. Names of Chicago streets, business houses and proprietors are given so definitely that the reality of it all is unconsciously forced upon the reader. It is a story that every girl in Chicago who is making her own living might well read to advantage. There is little art in the book. It is a photograph of life in a large city with its cold, hard, forbidding side and its brilliant, alluring attractions.

George Horton. "Strong Local Novel." Chicago *Times Herald*, January 16, 1901.

Another novel of extraordinary merit, dealing with contemporary American life, or life of a few years ago, has appeared. Perhaps it is possible to call Theodore Dreiser's "Sister Carrie" a great book and still keep safely within the bounds of judicial reserve. So true a picture of lower and middle class life in Chicago has not been hitherto achieved. It is relentlessly exact in all details, and consequently possesses an intensely human interest.

When the public once understands how true a picture is contained in this book its sale will commence. The characters are such as every man about town knows. They act and talk so naturally that one fancies he knows them, and attempts to identify the models which Mr. Dreiser has used, and will often believe that he is on the right track. The hero, Hurstwood, the manager of the popular eating and drinking resort, can be seen to-day in the office of one or more of Chicago's leading refectories.

The realism of Mr. Dreiser's characters is almost uncanny. They do not seem at all like people in a book; they are so genuine that they produce that queer feeling which one sometimes experiences when listening to a phonograph. You are certain that the human being must lie just a little back of the talk.

It was the great good fortune of THE TIMES-HERALD to call the attention of the public to the uncommon excellence of Maurice Thompson's "Alice of Old Vincennes," and the public has liberally responded, corroborating the estimate set upon that work in this column. With equal confidence we now advise lovers of good literature to turn their attention to "Sister Carrie." They will not find any scenes of intense dramatic interest; there are no theatrical effects, there is no brilliant dialogue—such as ordinary people never attain to. . . .

No review or synopsis can do justice to this book or give any idea of the intensity of its realism or its fascinating nature. Here, at last, is, in its field, a great American novel. It is hard to see wherein Mr. Dreiser, in so far as he has gone, is inferior to Zola. Why a firm that can get hold of such literature should expend all their resources in pushing such cheap and trite clap-trap as "An Englishwoman's Love Letters" must remain a puzzle to everybody not in the publishing business. "Sister Carrie" (Oh that it had another name) is one of the big books of 1900, and will respond, both in quality and quantity, to any amount of booming.

Denver *Republican*, January 20, 1901.

Vice is triumphant and virtue finds the potter's field in "Sister Carrie," by Theodore Dreiser. The author calls his work a novel of city life, but he might have been more descriptive had he called it a novel of the worst side of city life. . . .

The chief merit of the book is its photographic descriptions of character. Scenes and incidents are freely localized. The book is unhealthful in tone, however, and its literary quality is not high enough to cover its faults of theme.

Seattle *Post Intelligencer*, January 20, 1901.

The author of "Sister Carrie" is a new writer with endowments of a most unusual order. It seems not unlikely that, if himself so wills it, he can stand at the head of American novelists. To sum up his most striking qualifications briefly one may say that he unites a vivid realism with a remarkable selective power and a profound conviction that idealism is the only thing in the world worth while. The combination is a most unusual one, and should carry far.

His book in itself is, frankly, an unpleasant one. Its theme is the evolution of a little girl from the country who comes to Chicago to live with her sister and find some kind of work to do. Carrie is a harmless little thing without principles or convictions. Her one characteristic is that she involuntarily reaches out after the thing that seems to her "next best." Her first conscious yearning appears to be for a silk petticoat. The incidents of the story, considered in themselves, are squalid and revolting, but in spite of his realism the author handles them with a dryness and delicacy which would sterilize the most bacterial theme. What he is seeking to set forth is his perception of the fact that the salvation of the individual is in his discontent, in his vague reaching forth after something a little better than anything yet within his reach. It may lead him through strange morasses, but it is the path to perfection in the end. The demonstration is made upon a humble plane. There is nothing very remarkable about the girl's achievements in the end except the fact that she has come through degradation apparently unharmed by virtue of her insistent, almost automatic outreaching for something a little better than the thing she has. She is still climbing when one leaves her, while the character with which her own is chiefly contrasted, the man who is a complete materialist, without even Carrie's slight hold upon the immaterial universe, goes down into the pit almost without a struggle. There is hardly such another picture anywhere of the man who has lost his grip, the man who disintegrates utterly in the face of adversity. He had all the adventitious aids to development and good behavior. Carrie had none of them, but he goes down and she rises, the writer would have us believe, the one because he is a materialist and the other because, no matter how vaguely and feebly, the tentacles of her spirit are always reaching out for the great something else.

The philosophy of the book is very clear and very interesting. Its incidents, the squalid plane upon which its development takes place, will naturally prevent it from achieving a marked popularity. Even Mr. Dreiser's antiseptic style cannot make it anything but a most unpleasant tale, and you would never dream of recommending to another person to read. Yet the fact remains that as a work of literature and the philosophy of human life it comes within sight of greatness.

Minneapolis *Journal*, January 26, 1901.

It takes some 550 pages for Theodore Dreiser to tell his story, "Sister Carrie." He tells it pretty well, but it is too long. Carrie had a better fate than most pretty country girls who go to a large city to get work; find drudgery, get tired of it and become the mistresses of unprincipled men, beguiled by fine dresses, comfortable quarters and plenty to eat. Carrie becomes an actress and rich, is charitable and lonely, and—well, the story leaves a very unpleasant impression.

Wallace Rice. Chicago *American*, January 26, 1901.

Just who Theodore Dreiser is, I do not know. His first published book is, however, dedicated to Arthur Henry, once a Chicago newspaper man and latterly the city editor of the Toledo Bee. This book is sufficiently remarkable to deserve attention, as well for the errors in it as its manifest excellences, bearing in mind the fact that all the mistakes, numerous as they are, can easily be corrected, while the real ability which brought forth the book can be retained. . . . it may be said that within no broad limits [Dreiser] has left three or four characters clearly outlined, that his pages contain a convincing account of the manner in which stage success may be attained by a friendless woman of ability and adaptivity and a no less convincing account of the manner in which a man may lose his grip on the things of this world and sink down to complete and hopeless ruin, and that the atmosphere of materialism which envelops so many Americans is vividly reproduced throughout the work. Dealing with a class in society which has escaped the attention of American novelists, who have either gone above or below it, he has fixed his members in his book as types, and Carrie Madenda [sic] will be recalled by lovers of character drawing along with Daisy Miller, Selma White and one or two others, though the utter truth of portions of the book will keep it from attaining any very wide popularity.

Syracuse *Post-Standard*, c. February, 1901.

With more than enough realism and less than a sufficient sense of humor, Theodore Dreiser tells us in "Sister Carrie" that a country girl without money and without what we call bringing up, once came to Chicago, failed to find work which suited her, went to live with a drummer, abandoned him for a handsomer man, though married, and finally drifted into an artistic career on the stage. Mr. Dreiser aims to depict the sordidness of municipal life and the artistic yearnings. I imagine that he would be flattered by being called the Zola of the United States. He is so realistic that he gives the street and number of his characters, adopts their slang for his own, and fills pages with conversation in which the heroine says chiefly, "Oh, I don't know." This is a very usual and harmless remark in conversation, but it does not lend much zest to fiction.

With a generous adoption of the principle of absorbing whatever you want wherever you find it, Mr. Dreiser in describing the drummer in the early part of the story, clips a page entire from Mr. Ade's "Fables in Slang," namely, the description of the ways of Gus of Milwaukee with the women. Occasionally Mr. Dreiser's language is ridiculous, as when, describing Carrie's feelings when a nice young man has left her, he remarks that "the coach seemed lorn."

Yet, on the whole, there is something about "Sister Carrie" which deserves to be talked about. Mr. Dreiser has served a useful apprenticeship as a newspaper man in various cities of this country. He knows the aspect of the hopeless granite wall that seems to surround the unsuccessful in a great city. The decline of Hurstwood, Carrie's second venture, who comes to New York without a reputation, and drifts downward from the position of a small business man to that of a vagrant, finally dying miserably, is touching, and, no doubt, truthful. The description of the street car strike in Brooklyn is better than most of the newspaper reports of the time.

The Interior, February 21, 1901.

Sister Carrie, by Theodore Dreiser, is a bit of modern realism which does several notable things in a slovenly manner. It is evidently the author's first work, and it exhibits all the weaknesses of such a performance. Sophomorical reflections, statements solemnly made which are egregiously incorrect, confusions of fancy and reality which are the death of art, a characterization which follows almost word for word the work of another man previously published, and similar blunders harass the reader and make him wish that the publishers could have provided an editor for the work who had the one qualification of common sense. The English is seldom good and frequently atrocious. But after all this has been said, it is undeniably true that Mr. Dreiser has made a noteworthy addition to American literature, and that the book would have some of the aspects of greatness if sufficient attention had been paid to detail. In the heroine, Carrie Madenda [sic], may be read the manner in which a woman follows out a career which ultimately leads to success upon the stage, and all by way of drifting with the tide, never morally robust enough to assert herself and only wakened out of mental torpor by two brief conversations with an electrical engineer from Indianapolis, whose handling lends an aspect of genius to the work. Of the two men who hold the reader's attention, in the one, Charles Drouet, a commercial traveler, is painted a careless, self-seeking, moralless young business man of a type becoming too common in the world; in the other, George Hurstwood, manager for a liquor saloon, is shown the manner in which a man without seeming bad habits but utterly lacking moral stamina, may go down into the depths and perish. The name of God is not mentioned from cover to cover, a most significant omission. The part the saloon plays in modern city business life is graphically told—for the first time in American fiction, we believe, and the atmosphere of Chicago and of New York is well indicated. Another book from the same hand will be awaited with impatience.

Louisville *Courier-Journal*, February 23, 1901.

Mr. Theodore Dreiser has done some clever work in literary fields, but nothing that can compare with "Sister Carrie: A Novel of City Life," that has recently been issued from the house of Doubleday, Page & Co., New York. In some respects the book is remarkable. It works out cleverly the character of a young American woman, whose career can almost be paralleled by that of a million others in large cities of our country.

It is to be noticed that the same subtle quality or perception of the motives of the average woman determined to rise in the world is shown in this book that is so strong in Judge Grant's novel "Unleavened Bread."

Mr. Dreiser has taken life as he finds it in "Sister Carrie." It is the only tolerated realism—that of truth and actual conditions. The principal characters are most representative ones. Drouet, the "drummer" and "masher"—there are no other good English words to describe him—is one of the best. The general manager of the great clothing firm, Hurstwood, is quite as strong, but so pathetically tragic is his reward for sin that his shortcomings and weaknesses are forgiven. The minor actors in this drama of life have their full value. Of ordinary existence, to-day's existence, the writer has made an artistic play, a dramatic truth.

"Sister Carrie" is an effort to set out clearly the social feminine vagrant of American life, she who goes on and up and achieves without the handicapping of family, conventional ties or an undue regard for others. There is no question of morality aroused by the story. It is a study, and a very strong one, of the development of a soul that seeks the unattainable, whose goal flies before it.

"Among the New Books." Chicago *Tribune*, February 25, 1901.

Transgressing the literary morality of the average American novel to a point that is almost Zolaesque, Theodore Dreiser's "Sister Carrie, a Novel of City Life" is still a powerful and convincing tale of Chicago and New York, destined to take rank as a truthful and artistic depiction of contemporaneous life in the heart of American civilization.

At the same time, it is to be said that it abounds with annoying anachronisms and blunders in English, which reflect quite as much discredit upon the publishers for permitting such easily removed blemishes to stand, as upon the inexperienced author for making them in the first place. The fastidious will find almost every page marred by an error of style, yet the book is sufficiently painstaking to have carried more errors, had more been possible.

Yet none of these things goes to the heart of the book, which is such a presentation of the godless side of American life as has been waited for through many years. Not once does the name of the Deity appear in the book, except as it is implied in the suggestion of profanity. The heroine, a mere country girl, budding into the late womanhood of the American at the opening of the story, knows no law beyond her own convenience; and her two companions, Charlie Drouet and George Hurstwood, are equally the creatures of their own inclinations. An insistent and blind fate seems to urge them on to brilliant success in one case, to a mere holding of one's own in another, and to complete . . . failure in the third. And in each case it is felt that this fate was of the man's own making, that it was not inexorable, that self-discipline and well grounded morals would have avoided every evil, and that man is still the Captain of his destiny, the master of his fate.

There is much more in the book than this, though this is its spiritual lesson. Its pages disclose a panorama of modern life in cities. The workshop, the great store, the saloon and its relation to business life, the secret social order and the diversions of its members, amateur theatricals and their heart-burnings and triumphs, the household of the well-to-do with its unblushing and unconscious materialism, the hotel, the city apartment, the woes of labor wars, the sinking down of men into beggary and helpless pauperism, the glint of the comic opera stage, the successful actress and her duties and pleasures, the action and reaction of poverty and wealth upon social position—all these things have been caught by a firm hand and broad grasp on art, and confined within the limits of a single volume. It is a noteworthy achievement, and Mr. Dreiser's next book will be awaited with impatience.

Needless to say, the book is not a pleasant one to read, if one is to maintain a cheerful optimism. But the author is right in assuming that America needs enlightenment rather than indiscriminate flattery, if the present rate of advance is to be maintained. If unpleasant, therefore, it is none the less deserving of perusal for the sake of enlightenment.

Newark [N.J.] *Sunday News*, September 1, 1901.

Unfortunately the title of this book gives no hint of its interest, and neither does it bear the faintest relation to the story. The heroine is not a nun, nor has her story any family circle for its setting. On the contrary, her life is distinctly nonconventional, and the portrayal of it begins after she has left home.

But the fitting monograph on this suggestive subject of titles has yet to be written.

In the case of "Sister Carrie," the title is the weakest thing about the book. From its first sentence and throughout its most inconsiderable length the story holds the reader. It is one to sit up over late at night and ponder by day. Told with an unsparing realism and detail it has all the interest of fact; and the terrible inevitableness of fact, also. Perhaps no better word picture of a man's downfall has ever been painted than is to be found within these pages. The evolution of the hanger-on, the beggar, the social outcast, here finds its final portrayal. From the successful man of affairs to the beneficiary of city charities; from a respected member of society to the veriest outcast; from a being instinct with energy and ambition to a wretched, broken creature—every step of the long downward course is followed and illuminated as though by a gleaming searchlight. The possibility of it all is horrible; an appalling arraignment of human society. And yet there is here no word of preachment; there are scarce any philosophic reflections or deductions expressed. The impression is simply one of truth, and therein lies at once the strength and the horror of it.

The conception and portrayal of character in "Sister Carrie" would be striking in any case, but for a writer, in his first book, to show this power of individualism so highly developed, is really remarkable. The faculty for character development is shown in the evolution of the outcast from the man of position, and in the evolution of the shop girl into the charming and successful woman. And the sketching in of minor personalities is no less skilfully effected. The Chicago drummer is a living, breathing and talking creature. The reader not only sees him, but actually feels his personal atmosphere. The man Hanson, a thrifty Swede-American, is strangely real, and so is his wife, with her subdued air. Scarce a character, indeed, is introduced who does not justify his presence by lending an added interest to the story.

This talent for character drawing has been altogether devoted to the portrayal of decidedly second-rate people —second rate as to character, mental capacity and culture. There is no strong nor noble nature in the book; neither is there any lady or gentleman. The effect is depressing, and the reader longs for some relief from the commonplace talk, and material standards, and shallow thinking of these very real and convincing people. If they were less real and convincing, the need of relief would not be so great. In the slight sketch of Ames there is just a gleam of something better—far too small a gleam to lighten the general effect, however.

Perhaps this is the most serious criticism to be made upon the book—this, and its utter lack of any approach to a literary manner of diction. The word style is here purposely avoided, because the style is, in many ways, excellent, strong, convincing, clear, at times, even nervous.

But one does not wish to have a writer express himself in the same way as do his somewhat uncultivated characters. For him to do so, robs his work of literary flavor—a thing still precious, and in favor of which there is always setting in a strong reaction, as against the temporary popularity, with some readers, of the manner which repudiates any thought of choice and discretion in the use of words. Among some of the inelegancies (not to say vulgarities) noted, are the following:

"Swashed around with a great air."

"He was crazy to have Carrie alone."

"As he spruced around their chambers."

"He wondered how he would get ahead of the drummer."

Having quoted these examples of illiterate diction, it is but fair to try to convey some idea of Mr. Dreiser's power in portraying emotional situations.

The following bit of analysis, as found in its setting, is admirable:

"He thought he saw in her drooping eye, her unstable glance, her wavering manner, the symptoms of a budding passion."

And who would not recognize the truth of the following touch:

"Now, as he spoke, his voice trembled with that peculiar vibration which is the result of tensity. It went ringing home to his companion's heart."

But good examples of emotional expression abound throughout the book, and, of course, lose their effect when disconnected.

Quite as happy, and possibly more rare, is this writer's ability to suggest those delicate mental conditions in which the thought, or sentiment, of one person reacts silently upon that of another:

"Once or twice he held his peace, hoping that in silence her thoughts would take the color of his own. * * * Presently, however, his silence controlled the situation. The drift of his thoughts began to tell."

"She was listening, smiling, approving, and yet not finally agreeing. This was due to a lack of power on his part, a lack of that majesty of passion which sweeps the mind from its seat."

The multiplication of these interpretations of mood impresses the reader, and gives him penetrating glimpses into the minds of the men and women who figure in the story.

It is somewhat singular that one with so much knowledge of human nature as Mr. Dreiser evidently possesses should fail to appreciate the power and depth of certain feminine instincts. The heroine, Carrie, is a sensitive, rather pure-minded girl, and possessed of the rudiments of the artistic temperament—therefore possessed, also, of capacity for suffering. Besides this, she came from a respectable and sheltered home. Yet, after having yielded up that which woman holds most precious, and for the loss of which nothing compensates her heart, this strange heroine feels but the slightest pangs of remorse or shame. Her mental state finds itself expressed in a very few words by the writer:

"Ah," thought Carrie, with mournful misgivings, "what is it I have lost?" And in the brief depicting of her thought which follows there is an utter lack of intensity. She briefly and "infrequently" repines her lost estate, exactly as the average woman might repine some indiscretion which had temporarily wounded her self-complacence.

The construction of the book is excellent as to management of plot, but somewhat elaborated as to detail. While one cannot find fault with the realistic style as such, yet an undue insistence upon detail may seriously mar the effect and power of a book. In the part of "Sister Carrie" which deals with the financial straits of the heroine and Hurstwood, the prolongation of the agony is somewhat unnecessary, even for realistic effect. Even this peculiarity of parts of the book renders it in no sense dull. One is not tempted to skip a single line. Yet all effect of luminous fusion is necessarily sacrificed to such a minute dealing with detail.

The effects of this book are, upon the whole, secondary, while its merits are those which betray great talent—possibly genius. Certainly the writer whose first book is strong and interesting, both in conception and in development, true to life in its portrayal of character, and powerful in its emotional parts, can have no limits placed by any critic upon his possible accomplishment.

Indianapolis *News*, March 9, 1901.

This oddly named story is pathetically true, to an unhappy side of life, but nevertheless, it tells a common experience, as too often the daily newspapers witness. It is unrelieved by a single ray of sunshine. It reads straight on, as if the author, Theodore Dreiser, were intent on telling a story which he knows to be one of real life, but one which he tells simply to point its moral. Sister Carrie is not willfully evil, but force of circumstances makes her the mistress of one man and them. The wife of another, who deserts his family and becomes a thief for her sake. The end is sad and taken as a whole, it leaves a bad taste.

Scotsman, August 12, 1901.

This is another volume of "The Dollar Library" of American fiction. The story is not concerned with the pleasantest sides of life in the United States. Yet there are aspects of it which give the impression of reality. The account of the conditions of work in some of the Chicago factories a few years ago has a genuine ring about it, while the sorrowful fate which overtakes the manager of one of them, as the result of his "double life," is described with sustained power and remarkable pathos. There may be a good deal of superficiality and tinsel about the poor girl who becomes a great actress, amid the dubious surroundings in which she finds herself as the outcome of her ambition; but the story is neither tawdry nor tiresome.

London *Daily Mail*, August 13, 1901.

At last a really strong novel has come from America; a novel almost great because of its relentless purpose, its power to compel emotion, its marvellous simplicty. If Mr. Theodore Dreiser obtains the success he deserves, then "Sister Carrie" should make the book not of one but of many seasons.

The story is hardly agreeable; nor is Caroline Meeber herself the most artistically satisfactory character. Her rise from Chicago work girl to star of light opera is less convincing than conventional. So negative a nature could assuredly not exert such an influence over a man like Hurstwood, who flings away home, position, honest name, in consequence of this young woman; adding this final villainy that he decoys her to flight. He enters the narrative as the prosperous manager of a famous Chicago drinking saloon. In the picture of this man, from his first appearance in "his fine clothes, his clean linen, his jewels, and above all, his own sense of his importance," through the course of his descent upon poverty and suicide, Mr. Dreiser has contrived a masterpiece. The life that Carrie and Hurstwood lead together in New York is positively haunting. He drags her lower and lower, comes to depend at last on her wages as a chorus girl, until it is not to be wondered at that she resolves to leave him.

No quotation from the book would do justice to it, for the story must be read as a whole to gather any real picture of the tragedy of a bright and active and energetic man deteriorating into apathy and waste. Carrie leaves him, and Mr. Dreiser's art brings it about that we pity him and feel only anger with the woman. The tale is too elaborated towards the finish, ending too insistently, as it seems to us, on the same drab note.

Manchester *Guardian*, August 14, 1901.

The advertisement prefaced to the "Dollar Library" suggests that in the "actual life of America" the young American novelist must look for his opportunity. We may believe that in this latest volume of the series, SISTER CARRIE, by Theodore Dreiser, the author has realised this. Rarely, even in modern work, have we met with characters so little idealised, so patiently presented. There is nothing of the showy development of the worse kind of psychological novel, and so faithful to their types are these products of a fiction that has a real scientific basis that they might seem to have something in common with the unchanging heroes of adventure. Sister Carrie—we hardly know whether to accept the title as irony or symbolism—is a poor girl who comes to stay in Chicago with a married sister and her husband while she looks for work. Perhaps nothing in the book is more admirable than the presentment of the two workers, subdued to their "conservative round of toil," dogged in their pursuit of a material safety, intolerant of the cheap pleasures that lie within their reach. Carrie escapes from their control and falls to the temptations common to her kind. She becomes successively mistress to two men, both of that kind, with the "insatiable love of variable pleasures," which is without a moral basis, with no support but in prosperity. The one is safe in his frivolity of nature, the other has the touch of passion that betrays him. Hurstwood's decline is a faithful and minute piece of work. He is pursued relentlessly, without virulence and with no forcing of the pathetic note. The moral fall is inconsiderable—it is a mere shedding of a few habits and traditions,—but the physical degradation reacts on the woman. Her revolt becomes, in the art of the narration, the hunger for life, the pursuit of beauty which knows "neither surfeit nor content." She presses onward to the light that she can see, while those around her rise or fall in the scales of accident. Mr. Dreiser impresses us by his truthful sequence of events. He is strictly normal, and no fantastic light is shed on the credible steps of vice and crime. He is a faithful student, but his eyes are not fixed dully on the model. He might be called unimaginative by those who see no imagination in the insight which makes its deductions from experience nor in that illuminating intelligence which controls a design. We recall much of particular value—the introduction, in one or two short passages of artistic effect, of the one strong, clean man in the book, the indication of a draggled romance in the passion of Hurstwood, the fine differentiation between Hurstwood and the more volatile Drouet, the grim scenes between Hurstwood and his wife, his experiences in the strike at Brooklyn, his squalid end. The effect of the whole is perhaps a little depressing, and Mr. Dreiser has not much charm of style. He has many happy phrases, but we are occasionally oppressed by such "Americanisms" as "eyes snapping" or "when he went home evenings the house looked nice." His work is faithful, acute, unprejudiced, and it should belong to the veritable "documents" of American history.

Spectator, August 24, 1901.

Unless we are greatly mistaken, the most successful and remarkable study in *Sister Carrie* is a figure which was not intended to occupy the central place. This post of honour was probably intended for the heroine, Caroline Meeber, a girl of blunted moral sense, who, through hatred of poverty, lapses into the relation of mistress to a commercial traveller, is subsequently persuaded by a trick to elope with another lover and finally becomes a great success as a comedy actress. She reaches this last stage only to find, however, that the dazzling position she has longed for all her life is as incapable of making her happy as any other phase of existence. But the really powerful study is the figure of Hurstwood, Carrie's second lover. The picture of the sapping of the man's whole nature by the inertia which attacks him in his weary search for work is most subtly and strongly drawn. The reader follows each weakening struggle to its inevitable defeat with something of the sickening sensation which a real spectator must have felt; indeed, the whole situation is almost too poignant in its hopelessness. *Sister Carrie,* in short, is at once an engrossing and depressing book. Incidentally it gives English readers a curious insight into the rapid turns of fortune possible in America.

"Fiction: *Sister Carrie.*" *Academy,* August 24, 1901, p. 153.

In the prospectus of his "Dollar Library," of which *Sister Carrie* seems to be Number 6, Mr. Heinemann says: "More striking than the greatest of these successes [*Richard Carvel, David Harum,* etc.]—for popular successes are frequently scored by mediocre talents—is the fact that a young school of American writers is pressing for recognition, gifted with the sense of form, and not wanting either in pathos or in humour—real delineators of life and character." We admit we were unaware of the existence of such a school, but *Sister Carrie* has opened our eyes. It is a calm, reasoned, realistic study of American life in Chicago and New York, absolutely free from the slightest trace of sentimentality or prettiness, and dominated everywhere by a serious and strenuous desire for truth. We were impressed on the second page by this description of Carrie as she enters Chicago with the object of extracting a livelihood from the hard-fisted world:

> Caroline, or sister Carrie, as she had been affectionately termed by the family, was possessed of a mind rudimentary in its power of observation and analysis. Self-interest with her with high, but not strong. It was, nevertheless, her guiding characteristic. Warm with the fancies of youth, pretty with the insipid prettiness of the formative period, possessed of a figure promising eventual shapeliness and an eye alight with certain native intelligence, she was a fair example of the middle American class—two generations removed from the emigrant. Books were beyond her interest—knowledge a sealed book. In the intuitive graces she was still crude. She could scarcely toss her head gracefully. Her hands were almost ineffectual. The feet, though small, were set flatly. And yet she was interested in her charms, quick to understand the keener pleasures of life, ambitious to gain in material things. A half-equipped little knight she was, venturing to reconnoitre the mysterious city, and dreaming wild dreams of some vague, far-off supremacy, which should make it prey and subject—the proper penitent, grovelling at a woman's slipper.

We do not remember to have met such a description of an American heroine before, and we were startled into interest. The book is thoroughly good, alike in accurate and synthetic observation, in human sympathy, in lyric appeal, and in dramatic power. We finished with genuine regret this record of the mediocre little creature who chanced to make a hit as an actress in musical comedy, and of her abandoned lover, who, from being the rosy manager of a flourishing "resort," descended to "chair-warming," mendicancy, and suicide. We shall not soon forget the chapter in which George Hurstwood robs the safe of ten thousand dollars, and then lures Carrie away to Canada; nor that in which an afternoon stroll down Broadway first impregnates Carrie with the lust of riches and success. Nor shall we soon forget many brief passages of insight like the following (Carrie has just returned from Broadway):

> The immediate result of this was nothing. Results from such things are usually long in growing. Morning brings a change of feeling. The existent condition invariably pleads for itself. It is only at odd moments that we get glimpses of the misery of things. The heart understands when it is confronted by contrasts. Take them away and the ache subsides.

Mr. Dreiser writes with a painful lack of dignity. His pages are crowded with the latest American slang, and yet he appears to be unable to use even this very piquant slang effectively. We cannot but think, however, that a writer of talent so conspicuous must soon realise the importance of acquiring a style worthy of his matter. If other American novels are being written in the school of *Sister Carrie,* Mr. Heinemann will do well to bring them over here.

London *Express,* August 26, 1901.

Mr. Theodore Dreiser, in "Sister Carrie," has written one of the most painful novels it has ever been our lot to come across. But it is of absorbing interest throughout, and proves the author to be a writer of unusual ability. Carrie is a young girl who is sent by her parents to her married sister's house in Chicago to find work and earn her living. On the journey a man named Drouet speaks to her. Carrie, on arrival at her sister's, finds the new home most uncongenial, and after a miserable time spent in trying to work, she leaves her sister and goes to live in comparative luxury with Drouet. Now Drouet is a bagman, and while on his travels he asks his great friend, Hurstwood, a married man with a family, to look Carrie up occasionally. Hurstwood's visits develop into intimacy, and in course of time Carrie is ready to leave Drouet. Hurstwood, after making off with the cash contents of his employers' safe, induces Carrie by means of a subterfuge to take the plunge and come with him to New York. Here they live for some years, Hurstwood gradually sinking lower and lower in the mire of poverty until Carrie, who has had to take to the stage as a means of support for herself and Hurstwood, and who has begun to have a slight measure of success, deserts him and leaves him in his demoralisation to starve. Carrie "catches on" with the public, and becomes a popular actress; while Hurstwood, after suffering the utmost agonies of poverty in New York, at last commits suicide. The only character in the book that we have any sympathy with is Drouet, who is treated with such base ingratitude by Carrie; and yet it must not be forgotten that, with all his kindness to her, he was the first man to lead her astray. Not that that counts against him much, however, for Carrie was not particular, and she had to live. A more heartless, unprincipled, selfish, and ungrateful specimen of a woman we have never met with, and, indeed, none of the people in the book appear to have either natural affection, religion, or morals. Even Carrie's parents, after parting with her, never troubled their heads as to what became of her, neither did her sister make any inquiry about her after she left her house. It is a cruel, a merciless story, intensely clever in its realism, and one that will remain impressed on the memory of the reader for many a long day.

"American Fiction." [London] *Daily Chronicle*, August 26, 1901.

. . . [Dreiser] draws no moral from the life of Sister Carrie (the book ought only to have been called "Carrie," "Sister" is both superfluous and misleading), the reader may find his own moral—it is no concern of the author's; it is simply a grimly-grey story of life, and life near the bone; in this lies the powerful attraction it holds, and it proves Mr. Dreiser an author to be reckoned with and never to be overlooked—a true artist. Publishers notoriously mis-describe the volumes they advertise, and one would be interested to know how Mr. Stephen Crane's influence is to be traced in the volume before us. Mr Harold Frederic to some extent, the Russian group considerably, and Hamlin Garland's book, "Rose of Dutcher's Coolie," most of all.

Eversham *Journal*, September 7, 1901.

"Sister Carrie," by Theodore Dreiser, is the last addition to Mr. Heinemann's "Dollar Library" of American fiction, and it is certainly the best of the series. It tells how Carrie Meeber, a young girl of eighteen, came up from her country home to Chicago to earn her own living, and how in a brief experience of work in a shoe factory she drifts into a liaison with a commercial traveller, whom she subsequently forsakes for one Hurstwood, the manager of a fashionable "saloon."

Hurstwood robs his employers in Carrie's interests, though not to her knowledge and takes her off to Canada, whence the couple subsequently go to New York. Here Hurstwood, under another name, takes a share in a third-rate saloon. The saloon is a failure, and Hurstwood loses most of his money. He gradually goes from bad to worse till in the end Carrie who has gone into the chorus, to keep the "home" together, declines to help him any more, and after months of begging in the streets, he commits suicide in a cheap lodging house. Carrie, on the other hand, has gone gradually forward—from the chorus to a small part—and finally to the principal part in the smartest New York burlesque house. She is depicted as a quiet unobtrusive girl, the exact opposite of the typical burlesque "star" but for all her success she is not happy. She has longings to do better dramatic work than she is doing, really serious work; but she lacks the energy to attempt it. And on that rather depressing picture the curtain goes down. The story is told throughout with perfect simplicity. There is no straining after effect, no attempt at "elaborate" writing, not a suspicion of a purple patch. But the result obtained is singularly successful. The picture is an admirable piece of fine-etching. Carrie herself, we must confess, is not too convincing. One sees in her no qualities of fascination such as the action of Hurstwood suggests she must have possessed. But in drawing the portrait of Hurstwood Mr. Dreiser has been entirely successful. In few books has the gradual deterioration of a man's character been so cruelly exposed. We cannot say that "Sister Carrie" is a pleasant story, nor is it exactly a dramatic story. But as a presentment of facts, as a human document (we detest the phrase but no other serves) it is beyond question a book to be read.

Theodore Watts-Dunton. *Athenaeum*, September 7, 1901.

This is the sixth of the volumes that have appeared in Mr. Heinemann's "Dollar Library"; and it is the most important. Says the publisher in his advertisement to readers:—

> "Inspired possibly at first by several exceptional men who stood on the threshold of this new literary development [distinctively American fiction], there is now growing up a school of writers of talent to whom respect cannot be denied and whom we can no longer afford to ignore in England."

If Mr. Heinemann has in hand many novels of the solid merit and genuine documentary value that distinguish 'Sister Carrie' his "Dollar Library" deserves success and his rather poorly composed advertisement is more than justified:

> "When a girl leaves her home at eighteen, she does one of two things. Either she falls into saving hands and becomes better, or she rapidly assumes the cosmopolitan standard of virtue and becomes worse."

Thus the author of 'Sister Carrie' on his first page. The book disproves his axiom, for Carrie, whilst avoiding saving hands, and assuming the cosmopolitan standard of virtue with great readiness, does not become noticeably worse:—

> "Self-interest with her was high, but not strong. It was nevertheless her guiding characteristic. Warm with the fancies of youth, pretty with the insipid prettiness of the formative period, possessed of a figure promising eventual shapeliness and an eye alight with certain native intelligence, she was a fair example of the middle American class two generations removed from the emigrant. . . . A half-equipped little knight she was, venturing to reconnoitre the mysterious city and dreaming wild dreams of some vague far-off supremacy which should make it prey and subject—the proper penitent grovelling at a woman's slipper."

This passage is better written than most of the book, throughout which the phrasing is of the streets and the bars—colloquial, familiar, vivid, slangy, unlovely, but intensely real. Of the manner of the book it is not easy to speak favourably; it is strikingly unworthy of the matter thereof. Whilst large, dignified, and generous, the scheme of the story here told is not pretentious, or complex, or ambitious. It is a very plain tale of a plain though eventful life. Between its covers no single note of unreality is struck. It is untrammelled by any single concession to convention or tradition, literary or social. It is as compact of actuality as a police-court record, and throughout its pages one feels pulsing the sturdy, restless energy of a young people, a cosmopolitan community, a nation busy upon the hither side of maturity. The book is, firstly, the full, exhaustive story of the "half-equipped little knight's" life and adventures; secondly, it is a broad, vivid picture of men and manners in middle-class New York and Chicago; and, thirdly, it is a thorough and really masterly study of the moral, physical, and social deterioration of one Hurstwood, a lover of the heroine. Upon all these counts it is a creditable piece of work, faithful and rich in the interest which pertains to genuinely realistic fiction. It is further of interest by reason that it strikes a key-note and is typical, both in the faults of its manner and in the wealth and diversity of its matter, of the great country which gave it birth. Readers there are who, having perused the five hundred and odd pages which go to the making of 'Sister Carrie,' will find permanent place upon their shelves for the book beside M. Zola's 'Nana.'

Liverpool *Daily Post*, September 11, 1901.

"Sister Carrie," by Theodore Dreiser, is the latest addition to the Dollar Library (W. Heinemann), and is a characteristic story of American life in Chicago and New York. The tale is not a pleasant one, dealing as it does with unpleasant happenings to people who hardly excite one's sympathy or interest. Perhaps the author's tendency to accentuate the worst sides of the character of his "dramatis personæ" may be the cause of this, but the fact remains that although its cleverness is undeniable, "Sister Carrie" leaves a somewhat objectionable impression on the mind.

New York *Commercial Advertiser*, September 18, 1901.

Mr. Theodore Dreiser's *Sister Carrie,* which was not only one of the best novels published last year by Doubleday, Page and Company, but one of the strongest and best-sustained pieces of fiction that we have read for a long time, curiously enough attracted comparatively little notice in this country. In England, however, where it has just appeared in Mr. Heinemann's Dollar Library of American Fiction, it is winning golden opinions from the critics. The *Daily News* calls it "a cruel, merciless story, intensely clever in its realism, and one that proves the author to be a writer of unusual ability." The *Daily Chronicle* brackets it with Will Paine's kindred, but less powerful, *Story of Eva,* and says in conclusion: "It is a grimly gray story of life and life near the bone. And it proves Mr. Dreiser an author to be reckoned with and never to be overlooked—a true artist." The opinion of the *Athenæum* is on the whole rather the best of all. It sums the book up as "a creditable piece of work, faithful and rich in the interest which pertains to genuinely realistic fiction," and adds, "it is further of interest by reason that it strikes a keynote and is typical, both in the faults of its manner and in the wealth and diversity of its matter, of the great country which gave it birth. Readers there are who, having perused the three hundred and odd pages which go to the making of *Sister Carrie,* will find permanent place upon their shelves for the book beside M. Zola's *Nana.*"

"Withdrawn Novel Is To Be Given A Second Publication." Chicago *Tribune*, April 27, 1907.

I have before me a book with a curious history. It is a novel called "SISTER CARRIE." The author is an American by the name of Theodore Dreiser. Seven years ago, when the late Frank Norris was reading manuscripts for Doubleday, Page & Co., he read "Sister Carrie" and recommended its publication. Other readers for the house read it and also recommended its publication. It was accepted, put into type, and duly copyrighted. Then the wife of one of the members of the firm read it and condemned it. It was not, in her estimation, fit to print. It had, however, been accepted, and not only that but 500 copies had been printed and bound, and the English rights had been disposed of. So for copyright purposes there was a formal publication made, but the book was not allowed to appear. Copies were sent to a few well known writers, all of whom praised its cleverness, and praised some of its other qualities. It was published in London and highly spoken of by the best reviewers, but it never was really published in this country. In the meantime Miss Flo Mai Holly, who acted as authors' agent, had seen a copy of the book, read it, and thought it too striking a performance to go unknown in its own country. She took it to a young publishing firm, B. W. Dodge & Co., and arrangements were made by which Mr. Dodge bought the plates and the few copies on hand from Messrs. Doubleday, Page & Co. So in the course of a few days the book will be regularly launched upon the American market.

I can readily understand why the wife of a member of the firm of Doubleday, Page & Co., or any other firm, might object to "Sister Carrie," but for my part I would rather be the publisher of "Sister Carrie" than of Mr. Dixon's novels or Mr. Lawson's "Friday the Thirteenth." "Sister Carrie" is strong meat. It is just the sort of a story that I should think would have impressed Mr. Frank Norris. He liked realism, and he liked his realism strong. Stephen Crane published stories which were greatly admired by men of refinement, but which, to my mind, were much coarser than "Sister Carrie." I don't say that I would have published this book, if I were a publisher, but I do say that I would rather have published it than the ones mentioned. This is sincere, at least. The author is writing from conviction.

The scene of "Sister Carrie" is laid in Chicago, but it is not the Chicago of fashion or the Chicago of Bohemia. It is the plain, workaday Chicago, with nothing particularly inspiring. Nothing more or less than the story of a girl of the "plain people" who fell among men of her own class, who saw little of the beauty of the world but much of its pain and sordidness.

Frederic Taber Cooper. "The Fetich of Form." *Bookman*, 25 (May 1907), 287.

Among the books appearing this month is one which is to all intents and purposes a new novel; for the readers who were lucky enough to secure a copy when it first saw light, upward of five years ago, are so few and far between that it might far better not have appeared at all. The book in question is Theodore Dreiser's *Sister Carrie,* and the story of its vicissitudes forms an interesting chapter in the secret histories of books and manuscripts. In America, it is no exaggeration to say that the book never had a fair hearing. In England, its merits were quickly recognised, and sober reviews like the *Athenæum* assigned it a place on the same shelf with Maupassant's *Bel Ami.* To assume from this dictum that *Sister Carrie* shows anything approaching the literary finish of the French master is to court disappointment. Mr. Dreiser is no stylist. He merely writes with great simplicity and quiet force of life as he sees and understands it. The only adverse criticism which it seems worth while to make about a book which on the first reading gripped the present writer with a force unequalled by any other American novel that has appeared within five years of it, is in regard to its rather colourless and misleading title. It has more than once been necessary to explain to friends that the heroine is not a member of a religious order. But there is nothing misleading about the theme of the book. It is simply the direct, unflinching, pitiless history of the physical and moral ruin of one more fool, for the sake of a woman who did not care—a pretty, self-centered, passionless thing, who indifferently suffers his presence while he is useful to her—and then climbs over the wreck of his life in her hasty escape from the mire into which she has helped to sink him. A strong book, yes. An unpleasant book, also, if fearlessness and sincerity are unpleasant. But surely in no conceivable sense an immoral book. Carrie, to be sure, is a detailed, unsparing picture of the representative type of her meretricious class. But Mr. Dreiser does not draw her for the sake of censuring her. He simply sets her before us for what she is, what the world has made of her and hundreds of her sisters as well. But the big achievement of the book is not Sister Carrie, though Mr. Dreiser in his title implies that he thinks it is. The real centre of interest is rather Hurstwood, the man who sinned for Carrie's sake, and slaved for her, and dropped steadily down the social ladder, one rung at the time, suffering a long slow martyrdom, because up to the very last he fails to fathom her abysmal selfishness. In all fiction there is probably no more graphic and poignant study of the way in which a man loses his grip on life, lets his pride, his courage, his self-respect slip from him, and finally ceases even to struggle in the mire that has engulfed him. *Sister Carrie* many not be a book *virginibus puerisque,* but there is more tonic value in it than in a whole shelfful of sermons. It ought to have a widespread hearing.

Harrison Rhodes. "Mr. Dreiser's 'Sister Carrie'." *Bookman,* 25 (May 1907), 298–99.

Sister Carrie, reappearing after a mysterious absence in the limbo of forgotten books, deserves from every one interested in the American novel more than the welcome originally given it. It is a book very much worth reading. But as about a lady one might be excused for noticing that a costume dating seven years back was a trifle out of fashion, so in the case of Mr. Theodore Dreiser's story, one may perhaps be pardoned for feeling strongly, as one begins to read, that the stock tricks of the realistic method, even in 1900 somewhat discredited, now almost fatally fail to impress or to move.

When one was very young—the period suggested considerably antedates 1900—it would have seemed a wonderful thing that as Sister Carrie trod Chicago's streets each should be mentioned by its own authentic and realistic name, and that department stores, newspapers, saloons, and theatres should never elude identification. It would have pleased one to know that when Carrie met her lover in Jefferson Park, Monroe Street, it was an old gardener, not a young one, who was on the lawn with a pair of pruning shears. It would have thrilled one almost that when a man with stolen money in his pocket used a telephone in an all-night drug-store to make preparations for flight to Canada, Mr. Dreiser's poise should be so great that, even though the interest of his story was running high, he could stop to tell us that "it was a famous drug-store and contained one of the first private telephone booths ever erected." But now such gems of realism seem less lustrous. One feels doubtful whether it will ever become necessary to reconstruct Chicago from the pages of this particular book, and, on the purely artistic side, callous to the effect of descriptions so carefully detailed.

This is not an attack upon Mr. Dreiser and his book. He is merely tarred with the same brush as his school. The school itself has partly disappeared; he himself would probably write differently now. But the question as to the ultimate value of local colour is ever present. The magazine and book advertisements of the day are screamingly patriotic; may we not have to learn that all is not necessarily wild that's Western, nor all that is American (in capital letters) inevitably throbbing, vital, and "virile"?

It will perhaps seem ill-natured to add to this that writing which lacks marks of great cultivation is not, just because of that, rugged and picturesque. Mr. Dreiser takes a number of what he might perhaps call "flush colourful" liberties with the English language, but on the whole his style is fairly simple and serviceable. And though his book deals with vulgar people, it is essentially never itself vulgar. It is needlessly prolix, but it is a good book, in some ways a remarkable one.

Carrie Meeber at the age of eighteen comes to Chicago from Columbia City, Wisconsin, to look for work and to live with a sister who is married to an employé in the stock-yards. She finds employment, miserably hard and underpaid; is ill; can find no more work; and at last, instead of returning to the dull home from which she came, puts herself under the protection of a genial, lively "drummer," a "masher" who had made her acquaintance on the train that brought her to Chicago. After a time she comes to accept with pleasure the attentions of an even more elegant man called Hurstwood, the manager of a well-known saloon. When she learns that he is already married and cannot regularise their union, she is angry and inclined not to leave the "drummer." But when Hurstwood, by a trick, smuggled her and some of his employer's money over the Canadian frontier she contents herself with an irregular and bigamous ceremony. Hurstwood changes his name, and, ultimately restoring what he had embezzled, brings Cárrie to New York. There through several years he slips into failure and finally into complete penury. Carrie, when she realises that all is hopeless, leaves him and secures a position in the "Casino" chorus. We see him at the end committing suicide in a Bower lodging-house and her "owning Broadway" as a comic opera star.

So much for the story, not marvelously well invented, and sometimes ill hung together. The first merit of it is that the author, whether because of his realistic method or in spite of it, convinces us that he is showing us the look of things as they are. A greater virtue is the calm, dispassionate, unsentimental way in which he refuses to mould his characters to any supposed exigencies of the plot or of its "human interest," to employ the current cant phrase. Carrie is neither good nor bad in the conventional sense, neither the injured heroine nor the adventuress. She is never in the whole course of the story in danger of falling in love wth any one, but she never consciously does much to make men fall in love with her. She hates work, and she loves luxury. The latter seems to her a reasonable aim in life. She is good natured and kind hearted, but at the same time perfectly selfish. She is unemotional, but relentless. She is never painted in gaudy colours, still she is a little juggernaut on a car. Mr. Dreiser secretly likes her enormously. The intelligent foreigner will find her amazingly typical of his idea of the American woman making her way on the bent shoulders of the subject male.

He would also find her typical of the chill in our national blood. No one need avoid *Sister Carrie* as an "improper" book. When Miss Meeber yields to the blandishments of her "drummer" there was unquestionably—from the point of view of the intelligent foreigner—a *scène à faire.* That Mr. Dreiser avoids it is proof equally of his innate refinement and of the American sense that love involves many things besides physical passion. Indeed, one is tempted for a moment to the reflection that Miss Meeber considered that physical feature of life too unimportant to be worth even avoiding, and one cannot help wondering whether here is any key to some of the questions raised in one's mind by the *cause célèbre* of the spring in New York.

Mr. Dreiser's book is, however, worth reading, not so much for Carrie's story as for Hurstwood's. Into the account he gives of the downfall of the sleek, competent, good-natured manager of the big saloon, of his gradual and merited slide into squalid inefficiency and final starvation, the author has managed to put a strain of gloomy poetry, has succeeded in making one feel something of the sombre march of fate.

Not in single episodes, but through long stretches of narrative like this he moves both the intellect and the heart—a considerable achievement.

"Sister Carrie." New York *Times Saturday Review*, May 25, 1907, p. 332.

Theodore Dreiser's frankly realistic story called "Sister Carrie," originally published seven years ago, is now published by Messrs. B.W. Dodge & Co., and deserves to be received as a new book, for it did not get a chance for recognition when it first appeared. Except for his provincial avoidance of simple and perfectly understandable phrases, Mr. Dreiser writes very well. He tells what happened to a farmer's daughter from Wisconsin who went to Chicago almost as a child, there to seek her level in the world. She had beauty of a mild sort, a natural sensibility, a rudimentary intellect, a liking for fine clothes and silk and soft places, the good nature which goes with the lack of passion, and no particular burden of education or conscience.

To an extraordinary degree the book is a photograph of conditions in the crude larger cities of America and of the people who make these conditions and are made by them. There is no attempt to complicate the facts as they are with notions of things as they should be morally, or as they might be sentimentally or aesthetically. People's feelings are not considered. The author is quite impersonal. Withal, the story is interesting in spite of the commonplace character of the personages and the low plane of the gallery in which they move. Carrie, without a shining quality, with little to say, with almost no initiative, only her second-rate good looks, her first-rate instinct for soft places, her genius for fitting into such places when she finds them—in brief, her rudimentary femininity—gets a tremendous grip upon the imagination of the reader. She is as perfectly simple and human a creature as one sees trapped very rarely between the dry covers of a printed book. It may be added that the story even upon its first publication seven years ago attracted much attention and won favorable recognition in England. We do not, however, recommend the book to the fastidious reader, or the one who clings to "old-fashioned ideas." It is a book one can very well get along without reading.

Agnes Repplier. "Among the Books." Philadelphia *Public Ledger*, June 1, 1907.

"Sister Carrie" is literature of high class. It is of serious purpose, shows keen insight, deep penetration into the facts of life, an unusual power of psychological analysis, and well-trained artistic sense and skill. Mr. Dreiser has the faculty of picturing his scenes so vividly in clear-cut English that they compel an instant and abiding interest; the story once read will be remembered. Above all, the book shows absolute sincerity, and an accurate knowledge and sharp discrimination of the people who come into its pages and the conditions under which they live. The author reveals himself as the social philosopher with the welfare of the race at heart, as well as the gifted novelist. . . .

The story is not a pleasant one. It deals with sordid, reprehensible and unpleasant conditions; but these exist and are to be reckoned with, it is futile to blink them, and in this book they are handled with such delicate skill, with so large-minded cleanness, that the spiritual squalor in which the lives of so many people are cast simply enforces a moral. There is indeed an insistent and very convincing moral to be drawn from this book, though Mr. Dreiser does not preach. The story is sombre, but it is a strong and a notable production, especially for an author's first work of length, and it ought not to be lost sight of.

New York *Evening Sun*, June 1, 1907.

Mr. Theodore Dreiser's "Sister Carrie" has had a curious history. It was published originally in this country in 1900, and withdrawn immediately from circulation. We have heard various and conflicting explanations of this. One was to the effect that some sensitive person, male or female the legend telleth not, persuaded somebody in authority that the story was improper. At any rate American readers did not get a chance to make up their minds about it—a mere detail seeing that the interests of the young person were properly considered in the matter. And do we not all exist for the sake of the young person?

The novel had a great success abroad. One British critic, a novelist and a poet of eminence, indeed no less a person than Mr. Theodore Watts-Dunton, writing of it in the *Athenæum*, said:

> The book is, firstly, the full, exhaustive story of the "half-equipped little knight's" life and adventures; secondly, it is a broad, vivid picture of men and manners in middle class New York and Chicago, and thirdly, it is a thorough and really masterly study of the moral, physical and social deterioration of one Hurstwood, a lover of the heroine. Upon all these counts it is a creditable piece of work, faithful and rich in the interest which pertained to realistic fiction. It is further of interest by reason that it strikes a key-note and is typical in the wealth and diversity of its matter of the great country which gave it birth. Readers there are who, having perused the five hundred and odd pages which go to the making of "Sister Carrie," will find a permanent place upon their shelves for the book beside M. Zola's "Nana."

We quote this passage, not because we want to thrust the opinions of the author of "The Coming of Love" down the throat of any virtuous New York publisher, but for fear anybody should accuse us of being "coarse and vulgar" ourselves, seeing that we too admire this story. And we cannot help saying that we should prefer to be regarded as coarse and vulgar in the good company of the creator of Rhona Boswell than the other thing in the self-satisfied company of other people that we might mention.

"Sister Carrie" is not a pretty story. It is not a story with a moral attached to it. Some even may go so far as to say it is not an entertaining story. Mr. Dreiser's style is far removed from perfection. His reflections are irritating at times, as are his phrases—there are superior and sensitive souls who will shudder when they find the pages defiled with such expressions as "vest," "Prince Albert coat," and so on. We would warn all such to give the book a wide berth.

With regard to another objection it is necessary to go into detail. It is easy to imagine somebody calling it an unnecessary story. Why, it may be asked, should a lot of tenth rate people be put into a novel? A young girl from a country town who "goes wrong" in Chicago and New York, a loud, noisy, "drummer," her first lover; the manager of a fashionable bar, her second lover; her low class sister and brother-in-law, and the other characters and their adventures—why should these be placed before a public that can stand low life in novels or pictures only when it is treated sentimentally?

Unfortunately this argument proves too much. For it would be as destructive in the case of Defoe's "Moll Flanders" as in the case of Mr. George Moore's "Esther Waters." The limitations imposed by considerations of gentility would exclude from literature the story of a maid of all work that was the best thing ever done by the Goncourts, just as they would bar out the book before us. We can imagine critics of this kidney having their doubts as to whether or not "Evan Herrington" was fit for the suburban drawing room table, and then saving themselves by the recollection that the sub-title of Mr. Meredith's novel was "Or He Would Be a Gentleman."

However, let us admit that this book does not deal with the comfortable and the well-to-do, with the virtuous and successful. It does deal with life, and, what is more, without heroics, sentimentalizing or humbug. It is disquieting, because it is true. It is a strong book, not in the mistaken sense of the word, the sense of a bad smell. Amid the thousand of anæmic novels that come out like a flood, written by ladies, for ladies of both sexes, here is a book written by a man, obviously intended for men, and without a thought of that everlasting nuisance, the young person. We know of no novel of which the scene is laid in this town in which certain sides of New York life are set forth incidentally with more force than in this book.

"The Career of 'Sister Carrie'." Boston *Advertiser*, June 5, 1907.

The spirit of Zola and Zola's painstaking style are recalled by Theodore Dreiser's "Sister Carrie," a story which somehow failed to receive due attention when first published, seven years ago. Now a new edition is brought out and discriminative readers are not blind to its merit.

With the air of a mathematician solving some problem Mr. Dressier traces Sister Carrie's career. A country girl, the inexperienced daughter of a farmer, she comes to Chicago to earn her living. She finds work available hard and disagreeable and wages low. In her disappointment the professional "masher," a drummer named Drouet enters, offering with benevolent air pleasures she longs for. We need not trace the affair to its end. Suffice it to say it is followed by her experience with Hurstwood, a man with slightly superior character. He ruins himself and dies [sic] disgracefully in a Bowery lodging house, having lived to see Carrie lost to him. A stage favorite, amid the tinsel and shine of her state she walks unhappy. Not really despondent, however, for she is morally and emotionally deficient. Reviewing her course in the world, we see that she wanted pleasure, she wanted position, and was confused as to their real nature and value. Whenever the kaleidoscope threw a new lustre upon something, it became for her the thing desired—the all. She merely desired to be comfortable. The higher reaches of human aspiration were sealed to her. She was born to be a plaything, the wedded chattel of one man or a woman whose sole source of support is her physical charm.

To some Mr. Dressier's study may seem unpleasantly bald, but he is guiltless of wilful offence. His spirit excuses certain aspects otherwise vulgar. An intelligent reader must find enlightenment in his story.

Boston *Transcript*, June 5, 1907.

The first two things that strike the reader in Mr. Dreiser's very unusual novel are its bigness and its sordidness. The author's large and easy grasp of his subject, his breadth, even in minute analysis, his gifts of construction and characterization, his power to let a nature work itself out and leave it, make it all the more a matter for regret that he should have deliberately chosen to devote his creative energy to a woman and two men who never quicken our nobler impulses.

It must in justice be added that they fail equally to stir our lower impulses. The cleaness [sic] of the book is no less striking than its bigness and its sordidness. To write the story of two such men as Drouet and Hurstwood—whose very sins are commonplace—and to relate in detail and at the same time with cold, impersonal reticence the temptations of a country girl, vain, pretty, unreflective, imitative, eager for the pleasures, ornaments and applause of a city like Chicago, is no small achievement, above all, when the girl becomes through force of circumstances the mistress of one man she does not love, and later of another whom she eventually deserts.

The book in the problems it deals with is of no time or place. In its atmosphere, characters and situations it is essentially American. In neither the one nor the other does it teach a lesson or point a moral. If the author has any intention beyond showing what some part of life has meant to him, it is summed up in the title. Taken commercially "Sister Carrie" as a title is a mistake; in the author's hands it stands, large and significant, for the sisterhood of woman: her temptations and her opportunities, her wrongs and her rights, her obedience to the ordinary demand of the moment, her responsiveness to the appeal of sex, her power to develop out of and above it into independence of thought and action, man's responsibility to her and the part she plays in the responsibilities as well as the pleasures of man's life.

Mr. Dreiser depicts this responsibility and this part with almost impassive aloofness, with dispassionate capacity to see the truth and to tell it without bias of sex or moral standard. Men and women alike follow their natural bent. It is not the woman who tempts the man—both Drouet and Hurstwood are the tempters—except unconsciously by her youth and beauty. Just as she is unconsciously tempted by her longing for happiness—her first fall in its real analysis is simply an effort to get what she thinks constitutes this happiness—so are Drouet and Hurstwood actuated solely by the desire to get what for the moment constitutes for each one his pleasure.

Though Mr. Dreiser uses the commonplace and prosaic in theme, situation, incident and character, he has succeeded in investing them with the dignity of psychological insight and literary perception, and with an interest —often rebellious—which never flags.

Color and atmosphere, whether of Chicago or New York, of the theatre or the strike, is as convincing as it is cold, and the last chapters, which show forth the creeping paralysis of Hurstwood's moral deterioration and Sister Carrie's emancipation from a class into an individual, are a remarkable piece of writing—so remarkable that those of the craft impersonally interested in Mr. Dreiser's literary future must hope that his habit of the split infinitive, his predilection for long words at the cost of literary distinction and finely discriminating shades of meaning, the heavy phrasing that here and there wastes the reader's attention and impedes the movement of the author's thought—indications only of the amateur in his book—are faults that time and study will eliminate from his next novel. For unquestionably there will be a "next novel." The man who is big enough to write "Sister Carrie" will not be content to rest upon an achievement so full of promise, any more than he will be satisfied with that achievement.

"A Plain Tale From The Life." Kansas City [Mo.] *Star*, June 8, 1907.

By sheer force of its truthfulness Theodore Dreiser's story, "Sister Carrie," compels such an attentive reading as rarely is expected for a modern novel, and persists in the reader's thoughts long after the final two pages of interpretation have tinted the picture with a cast of purpose. Told straightforwardly, without a shadow of artistic consciousness, the complete impression it gives, nevertheless, is that a human episode has been faithfully set forth in all its essentials, with the import of each element exactly weighed and without deviation from the inflexible line of verity. It is not a happy story, for its persons never find peace, with all their eager following of the false promises of their desires and all their flights from the menace of their fears. There will be those who, startled by contact with unsanctioned behavior, will proscribe it as "immoral," though it is far from that. It is not even gross, as it inevitably would be were its author less clear-eyed and comprehending, and more of a gloating realist. George Moore, who wrote "The Mummer's Wife," would have made a salacious mess of this story of a girl who unsophisticated, pretty, impulsive and without an evil thought, takes up with a vain and good natured man and turns from him to another. Frank Norris, who wrote "McTeague," would have brutalized it. Theodore Dreiser, calmly, dispassionately, restrainedly, tells a plain tale in such wise that it takes on vividness and leaves an afterglow.

The two men of the story are of ordinary types, neither low nor lofty, but well dressed, conversant with the world, successful within their metier, agreeable, confident. There is a third man, seen but twice, of a finer quality and most skillfully utilized in the parable that the story ultimately exemplifies. Of the first two, one is unscarred by the episode and remains unabashed, self-satisfied, well-dressed, amiable. The other, a stronger man, slowly goes to the devil. The girl, sophisticated at last, faithful to the breaking point of her simple nature, and without an evil thought, attains to the ashes of a great success.

Buffalo [N.Y.] *Courier*, June 8, 1907.

"SISTER CARRIE," by Theodore Dreiser, is no ordinary novel, being a striking and brilliant study of American life in Chicago and New York among the middle classes. It points a strong moral and is dominated by a serious and evidently determined effort to depict the life of a girl in a department store and the pitfalls which are on every side for those whose moral sense is somewhat blunted. Caroline M. Meeber is one of these, and her spectacular and ofttimes pitiful career is skilfully drawn by one who apparently is familiar with every phase of what he represents. The character of Hurstwood is a powerful and subtle piece of delineation, and indeed the seamy side of life is so graphically drawn that, as a piece of realistic fiction, it stands pre-eminent. Not since "The Masqueraders" has any novel so gripped the interest, and it is one that will be widely discussed on account of its marvelous strength and daring pictures from the real life that is everywhere about us.

Newark [N.J.] *Evening News*, June 8, 1907.

It is essentially a serious study that Theodore Dreiser presents in his novel, "Sister Carrie"—so serious, indeed, that the author cannot forbear more or less moralizing as his narrative unfolds. Were it not for this extraneous element of observation persistently injected, the story would make a greater impression, for there is that in it which of itself holds the attention despite certain crudities in the actual recountal of events. It is a sordid enough drama, to be sure, this narrative of the fortunes of a young woman who comes to Chicago to seek employment, and, disheartened by her first struggle with the world, and the repellent atmosphere of her sister's house, takes what apparently is an easy road to comfort and the satisfying of her yet almost dormant ambitions. But, from first to last, the delineation of Carrie Meeber is calculated to create an impression, and what is true in her case is even more marked in the portrayal of one of the men who play their parts in Carrie's life history. Indeed, although this is scarcely in the author's plan, the attention is focused even more directly on the figure of George Hurstwood than on Carrie herself, and there is nothing in the novel more convincing in quality than Mr. Dreiser's sketch of Hurstwood's last days, an outcast and a beggar in the streets of New York. In this particular description he does what we think will be conceded to be his best work. Hurstwood, the man who fails, partly, it may be said in charity, as the result of circumstances that are too much for him, but largely because of an inherent weakness, is a character drawn with that skill which comes only from understanding. He is typical in his heyday as manager of one of Chicago's showy saloons; he is typical on his downward path, and only too typical in his last stages, when Carrie, who had been trapped first into leaving Chicago with him, and later by an illegal marriage, feels that as an act of self-preservation she must leave him to work out his fate alone.

The effect that Hurstwood produces on the reader is due, in large measure, to the fact that the man's pitiful career is allowed, practically, to tell its own story. Carrie is more nebulous, because Mr. Dreiser envelops her to a considerable extent with his own imaginings, which have a tendency to blur what is clear cut in the record of her struggle with the forces surrounding her, and of her ultimate success in her chosen profession—that of the stage. But these imaginings cannot obscure her salient points, nor does the author have any intention of glossing over her mistakes, careful as he is to explain how it is natural for her to make them. It is the ugly truth that Carrie lacks moral fiber in accepting the offer that her first admirer, Charles Drouet makes her, and that she has no scruples in deceiving Drouet, no matter how little she thinks that she owes him. To the end she is strangely heedless of her past—calloused, perhaps, expresses it better than any other word. Intellectually developing, as she does, her moral nature seems to be quite at a standstill, and, although in her vicissitudes she never loses a certain innate reserve and simplicity, her final aspirations, as her first, are inseparably connected with her own well-being. The fine instincts imparted by religion do not touch her life—this explains much—and her relations with humanity are not, it is to be admitted, such as to lead her to an exalted conception of duty. It may be that Mr. Dreiser has in mind the emphasizing of these very lacks. At any rate, his heroine disappears, as she appears, with certain vague longings for happiness, only more conscious that, with the resources at her command, she cannot look for anything approaching complete realization. An analysis of limitations is what the author, to all intents, offers.

"Sister Carrie" is, as has been said, a sordid tale; but in its disagreeable features Mr. Dreiser seeks to appeal to the thoughtful rather than to those persons greedily desirous of the sensational in fiction. There are passages which one more practised in writing would have omitted or modified; still even in these, regrettable as their presence may be considered, it is only fair to recognize that it is not the author's object to provide what is merely unpleasant or suggestive.

Harris Merton Lyon. "Theodore Dreiser's 'Sister Carrie': A Review of a Re-published Book." Houston *Daily Post*, June 9, 1907.

That American readers have paid little or no attention to this work is by no means surprising; that British critics have welcomed it enthusiastically is to be taken as a matter of course. And in France, were Mr. Dreiser's book written in French and about characters which would interest the French, he would probably gain some of the praise and recognition which he justly deserves. He will not, it is safe to say, be applauded by America for some years to come, and then the praise will not be given on account of his "Sister Carrie," but on account of his later and more mature work, if there shall be any.

To me the volume has essential elements of greatness. It is the "biggest" thing I have read in the way of fiction—long fiction, synthetic fiction—since George Douglas' "House With the Green Shutters." The heroine of the book is not a nun, as her title would seem to indicate, but is a simple little Hoosier girl who goes up to Chicago in August, 1889, to seek her fortune. In 550 pages her pitiful moves on the chess board of life are revealed, and at the end of the game Mr. Dreiser leaves us with the question as to whether she has won for herself a victory or not. Ostensibly she has. Has she?

Two other characters in the book are wrapped up in her fortunes and influence her strongly—Drouet, the "drummer," and Hurstwood, the manager of a saloon. At a glance the reader will see that this book is a document concerning the average middle class American; it is an attempt to do, with an Indiana woman, what Flaubert did with a woman of the provinces, though Carrie is by no means a Madame Bovary. It is an attempt to catch, with the spirit and scope of Balzac, the humdrum life of our bourgeoisie. The "drummer," so well has Mr. Dreiser depicted him, would, it is no exaggeration to say, live and be intelligible for all time, were he to be wiped as a class from the face of the earth tomorrow. Hurstwood—as for Hurstwood there is something uncanny about him, he is so true to life. In Mr. Dreiser's hands he is triumphantly analyzed. Hurstwood reminds you of yourself, of each one of your friends. He epitomizes your theory of life. He is the greatest thing in the book, from every point of view.

To tell you the plot of the story would be to destroy for you that inestimable pleasure which comes with perusing any slow revelation of relentless tragic forces, moving with Greek-like logic from cause to effect. Suffice it to say Carrie goes up in the world, Hurstwood goes down, and Drouet, the drummer, does the only thing which he is capable of doing—he stands still. But the whole result is absolutely masterful, ruthless, fascinating. It is as big, as vital, as American as Frank Norris' "Octopus"; only it lies in a far different field. It is more of the color-of-life found in Norris' "McTeague." It is a book that I have read twice and intend to read and re-read. Nowadays in the United States you do not find busy people doing this sort of thing with very many books.

Mention has been made casually of Flaubert, Balzac, and Frank Norris in connection with Mr. Dreiser's work. It is true, I think, that these elements are found there. Flaubert is but hinted throughout, by means of the author's impersonal attitude. Certainly it would be ridiculous to speak of Mr. Dreiser in the same breath with the French master as regards technical finesse. Mr. Dreiser can not punctuate. He knows nothing of sentence and paragraph structure. He sees a scene, a situation, a crisis in huge, massed effects. Details, from their human side, are regarded by him with a painstaking nicety; but from the technical side of the craftsman, the word-artisan, he flouts them and lumbers over them, disdainful, with an uncouth grandeur. The book was first published seven years ago. For a man under 30 it is a most remarkable performance. Yet it is to his lasting discredit that, upon its present reissue, he lacked the energy, the concentration, the pride in his work which should have impelled him to use his more mature powers in correcting his dishevelled youthful technique. He should have edited this new edition of "Sister Carrie" with infinite pains.

"People in general attach too much importance to words," says Mr. Dreiser, somewhere in the first part of his novel. Evidently he doesn't. As a matter of fact, they are the only tools with which he has to communicate his information and his analyses; and it is to be regretted that he allowed himself to be slipshod in his methods. If he had the craftsmanship of Maupassant his "Sister Carrie" would be ten times more powerful.

The Balzac-like treatment, the Balzac-like attitude, is everywhere apparent. Mr. Dreiser speaks of department stores. He is writing for all time. "Should they ever permanently disappear," he adds a complete description of them, tedious but thorough. The art of suggestion is unknown to him. He begins to work out his character of Drouet, the "drummer." "Lest this order of individual should permanently pass," says Mr. Dreiser, "let me put down some of the most striking characteristics of his most successful manner and method." A page is given up to this cause, unmindful of the fact that it, of course, impedes the direct progress of the story. Many of Mr. Dreiser's American critics seizing upon this didactic crochet of his, have concerned themselves solely with this matter, utterly ignoring the great human force of the book. A recent namby-pamby reviewer in that namby-pambiest of molly-coddle literary magazines, the Bookman, was utterly myopic, and hence futile, in this respect. Perhaps this critic was unconsciously celebrating the criticism which the great American public will make upon Mr. Dreiser's work. It is slow; it is devious; and a public used to reading novels of the quick, snappy, rapid order will find "Sister Carrie" a difficult book to skim through. There are innumerable, weighty batches of Mr. Dreiser's philosophy thrown gratuitously about in his work. They clog the dramatic action, but in their way they are germane to his analysis of character, and they are decidedly worth while. If you make up your mind to read "Sister Carrie" make up your mind before you begin that you will conscientiously spend a week in the reading. Read him as you would Thackeray, not as you would read Dumas.

A word about the circumstances under which this book is composed will help to give you an advance estimate of its style and treatment. It was being written at the time when Frank Norris, filled with the abounding roughness and vigor of the West, was electrifying the atmosphere of our literary circles with his study of "McTeague," the huge San Francisco dentist, and with the first novel of his proposed "trilogy," "The Octopus." Norris was young; so young that his great work was loose-jointed. His synthesis was a synthesis of gristle, not of bone. His main ideas were detached from the body of his work, indiscriminate, incoherent. When the young men of the time began to catch the sympathy of Norris' reckless force, they, too, plunged into big things recklessly. Willy-nilly, helter-skelter their dreams took the shape of mal-formed prose. They were so strong that they stood without needing the strong steel understructure of restrained technique, the hidden girder which supports the masterpiece. It was at this time and under these conditions that Mr. Dreiser was working on his book.

"Sister Carrie" is, for today at least, a book for the few; not for the many. It never would have "run" as a serial in the Ladies' Home Journal, or in one of our 15-cent, popular magazines—for the home. It has been adjudged "immoral" by some of our very best citizens. Carrie, while fully meaning to do so, never quite managed to get a proper marriage certificate; and Drouet and Hurstwood, although happy-go-lucky, lackadaisical villains, are nevertheless felt to be villains by the public conscience. There is nothing in the book to offend any serious-thinking person; it is not an esoteric, a lubricious, a salacious book in any way whatsoever. It is simply the calm, impassioned, impersonal statement that such-and-such forces worked thus-and-so about a woman and a man produced such-and-such results. I mention this point to warn those who might read the book and choose to be offended at it, at me, at this journal, and at Mr. Dreiser afterward. It is no more immoral than Pinero's "Iris."

I also mention this because it brings opportunity for me to explain, in part, my interest in such books as "Sister Carrie." I see in "Sister Carrie" one more evidence of a broader American intellectual freedom. Possibly the day may come when George Moore's "Memoirs of My Dead Life" will not have to be expurgated, as for children, when it is being issued in the United States. No wonder England, no wonder France, no wonder Germany looks patronizingly down upon us—a nation of grown men and women for whom publishers must expurgate books before we are allowed to read them! "The land of the free," "freedom of the press"—the words are empty. We are free to swallow literary pudding out of a decidedly tin spoon. England, insular England, speaks contemptuously of our "rudimentary state of civilization." Politically, commerically and otherwise the sneer falls as water upon a duck's back; but, when our continental cousins mean intellectual civilization, their sneer sinks in. The time is coming some day—I care not whether it is within twenty-five years or within a century—when the United States will have to "stand for"—if it comes to the point of compulsion—an American Tolstoi, Turgenieff, Flaubert, Balzac, Nietzsche, Wilde, de Maupassant.

"Sister Carrie," tentative and insecure as it is, is a step in the right direction. Just as are the poems of Mr. Viereck (though in a far different and lesser way) which I reviewed in these columns recently.

"American Realism." Los Angeles *Times*, June 16, 1907.

"Sister Carrie" is a book which must be regarded seriously, whatever opinion of its value and propriety the reader may form. It is somber, powerful, fearlessly and even fearfully frank, and, above all, realistic beyond the usual domain of the American school of realism. There is hardly a kin to it in modern American literature. It is a cousin in letters to Emile Zola's "Nana" and Guy de Maupassant's "Ma Vie." Yet it is no more than a cousin, for there is a relentlessness of purpose in it that is apart from the somewhat morbid moral clinic of the French realists.

The book has had an interesting history. It is a first novel, written several years ago. Mr. Dreiser submitted it to a well-known American publishing-house, where two readers of the firm reported enthusiastically in its favor. One of them was the late Frank Norris, who said: "It pleases me as well as any novel I have read, published or otherwise." One of the members of the firm then read it, and it was accepted. Another member took it home to his family to read. What happened subsequently is not known, but the book was suddenly withdrawn.

Soon thereafter it was published in England. It had a success which must have been gratifying to Mr. Dreiser, for the London Academy, the London Spectator, the London Athenaeum and the Fortnightly Review united in saying that "Sister Carrie" represented a school of American literature which England could not afford to ignore, and that it was a most powerful and admirable work.

It has now been published in America by another firm than that which first accepted it.

"Sister Carrie" is a plain story of American lower-class city life of a form which exists too commonly. Caroline Meeber was a country girl of some beauty, little knowledge and little practical capability. Unsophisticated, emotional, with a mind that felt rather than reasoned, she came to Chicago to get work—not from necessity, but because she wanted better things than she had. She had moral sense—"blunted," a police-court analysis might conclude. It was not blunted, but out of focus. She became the mistress of a prosperous commercial traveler, exchanging her youth and beauty, not for money in hand, but for peace, comfort and a state of mind which it seemed impossible that the long road of honest labor would give her.

Thereafter, the book is a full, exhaustive—almost merciless—vivisection of the "half-equipped little knight's" life and adventures—her struggles with herself and her situation, and her final rise as an actress, by her own resources.

Powerful as is the laying bare of Caroline Meeber's heart, the greatest strength of the story is in the study of one Hurstwood, Caroline's second lover, whom she thought she had married. His home life with his true wife is rapidly and forcefully shown, but his deterioration is still more powerful. This is truly masterful. His whole nature is sapped by inertia, and each weakening struggle, which leads to inevitable defeat, is calmly drawn with a poignancy of hopelessness which is almost sickening.

If it is ever possible to gain vicarious experience, it may be found in this book. The value of it lies in the fact that no one can read "Sister Carrie" without gaining knowledge and sympathy. "Sister Carrie" is not nice, but it is honest, true, without a stain of pettiness or sentimentality. It must be said also that while it is largely analytic, it is also synthetic. It shocks, it takes apart a woman's soul, but it also puts it together again.

In the wealth of material which "Sister Carrie" embraces, there are two things which are of minor import, but deserve especial attention. One is the influence of clothes and of the niceties of dress, which, in less skillful hands than Mr. Dreiser's, might become an obsession. Another is that in Hurstwood's decline, he takes refuge from his conscience in desultory reading. America is a press-ridden country, but few ever put on paper the intellectual excesses and deterioration to which this sometimes gives rise—a thing that college professors might do, from their own observation, if they were so minded.

Cleveland *Plain Dealer*, June 16, 1907.

Caroline Meeber, whose story is told by Theodore Dreiser in his novel, "Sister Carrie," is the most notable woman character in fiction since Hardy's "Tess." She is notable, too, for the same qualities which make the best of Hardy's women so amazingly convincing. She is a mere everyday human being, about whom there is no glamour of romance, whose sins seem but the errors natural to an average woman placed as she is placed, whose virtues are but normal virtues, whose development appeals irresistibly to the reader as the working out of the natural law of environment.

But Caroline Meeber is not the only amazingly fascinating figure in Mr. Dreiser's book. Hurstwood is no less true. It is difficult to determine which of the two figures carries the greater conviction. . . . The stories of Mr. Hardy and Mr. Dreiser are strangely alike in their unwavering study of the development of feminine character under conditions most unfavorable. For both Tess and Carrie there is much more of sympathy than of condemnation. Neither was bad. Relentless force of circumstance shaped the destiny of each.

In style Mr. Dreiser's work is decidedly inferior to that of Mr. Hardy. It possesses the straightforwardness and power so characteristic of the English master, but lacks Hardy's wonderful descriptive quality. But whatever stylistic shortcomings there may be are wholly forgotten in the unremitting intensity of the story.

"Mr. Dreiser and His Critics." New York *Evening Sun*, June 18, 1907.

Young novelists ought not to allow themselves to be interviewed, because they are liable to make as bad mistakes about the nice things said of their work as they are with regard to the warnings addressed to them by kind yet conscientious critics.

Mr. THEODORE DREISER wrote a book called "Sister Carrie" when he was very young. We have never heard his age, and guessed it from his prose. The story was suppressed here because, as was reported, the publisher's grandmother or maiden aunt, or somebody like that, thought that it was in bad taste. Of course it really wasn't. It was simply crude and rough and immature. However, it was republished the other day, and treated very nicely by the reviewers. It was still a powerful story badly told. For, strange as it may seem, Mr. DREISER showed that he was as faulty a critic of his own work in 1907 as in 1900. Indeed, so thoroughly satisfied was he with the book that, as far as we could make out, he had not changed a single word or cut out a line of the childish philosophy contained in the original.

This was bad enough. But it was worse to find that our young friend had lost his temper and was reported as reviling the whole race of critics as follows in the columns of a literary review:

> "Well, the critics have not really understood what I was trying to do. Here is a book that is close to life. It is intended, not as a piece of literary craftsmanship, but as a picture of conditions done as simply and effectively as the English language will permit. To sit up and criticise me for saying 'vest,' instead of 'waistcoat'; to talk about my splitting the infinitive and using vulgar commonplaces here and there, when the tragedy of a man's life is being displayed, is silly. More, it is ridiculous. It makes me feel that American criticism is the joke which English literary authorities maintain it to be. But the circulation is beginning to boom. When it gets to the people they will understand, because it is a story of real life, of their lives."

Charity and real respect for Mr. DREISER as a promising, or at one time promising, young author leads us to suppose that though he writes he does not read much. Otherwise he would be aware that some of the books which have been most "close to life," which have dealt with "the tragedy of a man's life," have been composed with the greatest possible care and with a painful regard for the proprieties of a good style. What is more, his novel, as a picture of conditions "done as simply and effectively as the English language will permit," would have gained vastly by the elimination of all the eloquence and fine writing which we and others found so irritating.

Before Mr. DREISER completes his second book a short course in home reading would be desirable. There is, we think, a translation of the Letters of FLAUBERT. In them he would find an account of how that great man labored to find at all times the fitting word. In the "Moll Flanders" of DEFOE, from whom the sainted R. L. STEVENSON learned how to persuade the American and English public that he was an original genius as a prose writer, Mr. DREISER would learn how to do a thing "simply and effectively." And from the books of Sir HENRY MAINE, an author unfortunately read only by law students, he might find an object lesson in the application to literature of the mathematical process known as the elimination of the constants and learn something of the virtue of austerity.

After such a course we are sure that Mr. DREISER'S gents will cease to be swell dressers, and will give up wearing the pants, vests, prince alberts and tuxedos of the slop shops.

"Triumphant Vindication of a Suppressed Novel." Baltimore *Sun*, June 26, 1907.

Seven years ago Doubleday, Page & Co. copyrighted "Sister Carrie," but no sooner had they arranged for the publication of the novel than for some reason it was suppressed and all plans for its sale abandoned. Without entering into the reason for the withdrawal of the work from the market, we may well say that the novel which the American publishers rejected was brought out in England with the result that it was there hailed as the greatest American novel of the decade. The critical press, with scarcely a dissenting journal, declared the work to be a masterpiece of realistic fiction. This praise from the papers across the water was endorsed by scores of American writers and critics to whom the work strayed. It is then nothing to be wondered at that the present edition, the first authorized American issue, has met with large approval and a most gratifying sale. As the London Athenaeum well points out, the novel is, first, the full, exhaustive story of the "half-equipped little knight's life and adventures; second, it is a broad, vivid picture of men and manners in middle-class New York and Chicago, and, third, it is a thorough and really masterly study of the moral, physical and social deterioration of one Hurstwood, a lover of the heroine." The novel is one that has been illy compared to Zola's "Nana." There is no room for comparison, although the leading woman of both stories is of "blunted moral sense." Perhaps it were better to say of Carrie that she is a type of thousands of women who, because of poverty or of utter loneliness, regard themselves as married, although the bond between them and their male companion is not legalized. But Carrie is not strong enough to be true to her lover, and she leaves him for another. The genius of this village girl lifts her to high rank as a comedienne, and when the world is at her feet she finds that she has gained nothing that will give her happiness. Carrie as a character study is well drawn, but is entirely subordinated to the delineation of Hurstwood, a terribly powerful characterization. If we were asked to compare this book with an existing novel we would unhesitatingly put to one side the analogy between it and Zola's "Nana" and say that in style, if not in incident, it is the equal of "McTeague," by the late Frank Norris. It has the same power and brutality.

Musical Leader, June 27, 1907.

Theodore Dreiser's novel, "Sister Carrie," is enjoying quite a vogue. The book is well written and holds the interest to the end, but the critics are exaggerating the worth of the work. To judge from their frenzied eulogies, the great American novel has at last appeared, whereas "Sister Carrie" is simply a sound piece of work, and sound pieces of work are still fairly common even in these days of "best sellers." Moreover, Dreiser is but an imitator of an imitator, by George Moore, out of Zola. Dreiser will yet give us better work than "Sister Carrie," for he thinks clearly and sees straight. . . .

Chicago *Advance*, June 27, 1907.

A piece of realism embracing life in Chicago and New York. The Sister Carrie of the book is a good looking country girl who becomes a successful actress of a certain stripe. How she does it takes up 557 pages and makes the reader wish she would hurry up and succeed so as to bring the tale to an end. As the author draws her she is a colorless, uninteresting character, one of those lucky female sinners who acquire fine raiment, jewels and lodging at the Waldorf while ten thousand others of her kind land nowhere. The book is not a good or wholesome one for women to read, for

Sister Carrie is not nice or clever or bright or kind-hearted or respectable, or anything much but a kind of puppet that Mr. Dreiser uses to hang the assertion on that all the girls who come from the country do not become "white slaves" or commercial drudges or wives of poor clerks, and that one girl in a million can succeed on the stage. Carrie is assisted in the cast by two male characters, one of whom is drawn in such a convincing manner as to make the reader think. Hurstwood runs off and leaves position, wife and everything for Carrie. Oh how the author punishes him, and he deserves it. He drags poor Hurstwood down to a tenth rate lodging house, where he commits suicide. The descriptions of a "down and outer's" life among the lodging houses of New York city is terrible in its reality. As the author spends so much time on Hurstwood a better name for the book would be "The Fatal Step," or "The Wages of Sin Is Death." For no better sermon could be preached to a man on the necessity of behaving himself, leaving other people's money alone, in particular, than is contained in this book. A volume containing a terrible warning to men and one that women had better not read is *Sister Carrie.*

Frederic Taber Cooper. "The Fallacy of Tendencies in Fiction." *Forum,* 34 (July 1907), 117–118.

Another book which deserves a brief word of commendation is *Sister Carrie,* by Theodore Dreiser, which the London *Athenaeum* placed pretty accurately by assigning it to the same shelf as Zola's *Nana.* When and how *Sister Carrie* came to be written, why it was virtually suppressed in this country almost as soon as published and how it happens to be reissued now, after a lapse of seven years, are a series of interesting questions in the secret history of book publishing. But they have no bearing upon the merits of the story, which for all practical purposes comes before the reading public for the first time. It is an unpretentious book, written without any effort after style, but with a downright sincerity that compels attention. It is simply the history of a young girl who comes to Chicago from a country village, intent on earning her own living, finds the toil too hard, the companionship of her fellow-workers too coarse, and inevitably drifts along the way of least resistance into that Half-World which Anglo-Saxon fiction for the most part chooses to ignore. Some critics have chosen to quarrel with Mr. Dreiser's choice of title; and in a way it is misleading. Yet it was presumably selected for its symbolic sense, as a reminder of the ties of blood between the Carries of this world and their more fortunate sisters, a reminder that we are our sisters' as well as our brothers' keepers. There are two reasons why *Sister Carrie* is a book to be recommended in spite of its boldness of theme. First of all, for the sake of its truthfulness, the frankness of its portrayal of a widespread type: the good-natured, yielding, pleasure-loving type of woman, not emotional, not capable of deep feeling, essentially selfish at heart, who finds it easiest to accept the good things of life as they offer themselves, quite indifferent as to who shall pay for them. And secondly it is a pitiless, unsparing portrayal of a man's ruin. The history of Hurstwood, from the first hour of his meeting with Carrie to the final moment when he turns on the flow of gas in an East Side lodging house and lies down to await oblivion, is fiction of a grim, compelling force that has the value of many sermons. It is the story so often repeated in life, so rarely frankly told in novels, of the man carried away by a foolish passion, and a woman thinking only of herself, her vanity, her ultimate glorification. When Hurstwood has sacrificed for her sake his social and financial standing, his prospects and his honor, and has lost his self-respect and with it his grip upon life, you can see the moral and physical disintegration of the man, from day to day, see his clothes wear shiny, the seams fray out, the buttons fall away—symbols of the permanent wreck of the man's own self-esteem. And over the shoulders of this human wreck, Sister Carrie climbs into public favor, to a brief span of tinsel glory before the footlights, yet finding even in the midst of her triumphs that there is something, she scarce knows what, some indefinable, vital thing, the lack of which robs life of its savor.

Mr. Dreiser teaches his lesson by fearlessly telling the truth.

New Orleans *Picayune*, July 1, 1907.

This book is the strongest piece of realism which we have yet met with in American fiction. It is far more broadly typical of American life than "The House of Mirth," and this essential typicalness is the quality which has made the book appeal so forcibly to the best literary public in England. Its realism lies deeper than that of any story of Mr. Howells for the reason that it deals not alone with the pettiness of human nature, but with its more elemental passions as well. It is the story of the moral descent of a woman, but it has a wider scope than "The House of Mirth," because where Mrs. Wharton is occupied with a differentiated social class this embraces the great mean of human nature. It is even more powerfully the study of the moral descent of a man, since in the man the moral descent is a sheer drop down the face of the cliff until he touches bottom. The woman saves herself on protecting ledges of sentiment. The man is engaged with all the strength of his carnal nature, and his passion is basic; the woman is engaged through her senses and her passion is a thing of the surface. The realism of the author approaches the realism of Zola in such a study as the latter's "Nana," with the difference between the English and the French standpoints. The inordinate eroticism of the Gallic author is missing, Mr. Dreiser's handling of his theme is clean and unpornographic; his men and women are not animals, they are only, like the majority of mankind, creatures of the senses whose intellectuality or spirituality is merely the last flourish added by evolution to their physical natures—the grace note of a comparatively recent psychical development.

Carrie represents, as we have said, the great middle class. "She was an apt student of fortune's ways—of fortune's superficialities. Seeing a thing, she would immediately set to inquiring how she would look, properly related to it. Be it known that this is not fine feeling, it is not wisdom. The greatest minds are not so afflicted, and, on the contrary, the lowest mind is not so disturbed. Fine clothes were to her a vast persuasion; they spoke tenderly and jesuitically for themselves. The voice of the so-called inanimate! Who shall translate for us the language of the stones?" The unusual circumstantialness of this book helps greatly to heighten that sharp impression of reality which it makes upon us. The writer does not shirk details. He makes no use of vague generalities. He names the very shops at which Carrie buys her shoes and her gloves, and jacket. We stand by and read all of her pleasurable sensations in the act. The importance of the episode cannot be exaggerated. It is upon such small pivotal moments that her life turns. And hers is one of the rare instances in which investment in bodily beauty repays tenfold, though in the same coin. The turn of her head, the graceful swaying of her body, the little drop at the corners of the mouth, the trick of the wistful eyelids—upon these is built the success of her venture on the stage. One thing that is brought home to us implicitly and unconsciously by the story is a conviction of the cheapness of the average mimetic art. Of the first imitative peacockings of Carrie before the glass, it is said "as a matter of fact it was nothing more than the first subtle outcroppings of an artistic nature endeavoring to recreate the perfect likeness of some phase of beauty which appealed to her. In such feeble tendencies such outworking of desire to reproduce life, lies the basis of all dramatic art." But this is the most rudimentary groping of the artistic temperament, the lowest reproduction of the life of the spirit.

Carrie, although in the end we leave her with an unsatisfied ache in her heart, was a shallow egotist obeying the first law of self-preservation. Her tragedy is slight compared to that of Hurstwood. Hurstwood is a more forcible delineation than Carrie herself. His is the dominant figure. The last chapter in his degeneration is worked out with somber power. While it is acting Carrie is reading Pere Goriot with superficial sympathy. Yet the catharsis of pity is withheld from us. Drouet, the inimitable drummer, can easily dispense with it, as can Carrie, and Hurstwood is his own victim where he was willing to victimize others. It will sometimes happen that the men who mark out women as their prey have the role reversed and become themselves the quarry. But they are scarcely deserving of our commisseration. Carrie is by no means a type of the conventional adventuress, which is the title with which society invests a reversal of its usual order in the persons of women who make use of men and cast them aside. Mr. Dreiser's is a strong book; it would be a great book if its realism were correlated with that touch of idealism which is essential to greatness. All of its persons are as sordid as they would probably be in life. It is life, but the world is asking something more than life as it is, in the very act of turning to art.

New York *Press*, July 3, 1907.

It is not often nowadays that a novel has so interesting and curious a story of its own as is possessed by Theodore Dreiser's "Sister Carrie." We are informed that it was published originally in 1900 by a local firm, but no sooner had a feminine relative of one of the firm read it than she decreed the book must be suppressed, and suppressed it was, in this country at least. But it met with so favorable a reception from the English reviewers that the author evidently persisted until he found a publisher, evidently with no opinionated feminine relatives, who has just issued it again. After reading "Sister Carrie" we can understand easily the shock it gave the first publisher's relative. But we think the shock might have come from another cause than her reported objection to the moral atmosphere of this "novel with a purpose." We saw nothing particularly objectionable in the frank portrayal of Sister Carrie's living with the genial commercial traveler on his promise to marry her, or in her enforced desertion of him and flight with Hurstwood, the suave manager of the "elegant resort" in Chicago. Those incidents interested us and even more so did Carrie Madenda's [sic] stage life in New York and the gradual tragedy of Hurstwood's decline from a man of affairs to a Bowery wreck, with suicide as his end. Indeed, as a picture of an actress of a certain type, a woman of little intelligence and practically no moral sense, we think Carrie Madenda may take rank with Henry James's heroine of a finer type in "The Tragic Muse" and Anthony Hope's "A Servant of the Public." But we were shocked by one element in this novel and that was the fashion of the writer's English. We cannot recall such vulgar forms of expression in any book we ever have read. As it stands, this novel may remain a minor curiosity of literature, in that its author could have observed life with so much truth and yet could not observe ordinary usages of good English. These solecisms are so strangely out of touch with everyday speech that they give to the book a character that can be described only as naive.

Boston *Journal*, July 4, 1907.

So long as human nature remains what it now is, so long we shall have books which depict the seamy side of life. But not all of them are as strong, vital and effective as this story. The plot is commonplace enough—the story of an inexperienced country girl in a great city, a girl irresponsible and unmoral, dazzled by her first glimpse of luxury and the frivolities of life—but few authors have dealt so understandingly and so strongly with this problem as has Mr. Dreiser. The type is as old as the hills, but the portrayal is fresh and vivid. It is a study of woman, her temptations and weaknesses, her responsibility to man and man's responsibility to her. It is not a pleasant story, but the author's handling of it lifts it from the sordid and makes it an interesting psychological study.

Hartford [Conn.] *Courant*, July 8, 1907.

. . . The author is without a sense of humour or of poetry. He tells what unfortunately is a very possible story of sordid licentiousness and pitiful degredation in Chicago, Montreal and New York. The only startling improbability of which Mr. Dreiser is guilty is in making so insipid a young woman as Carrie a theatrical success.

The only high light in his picture, is

the benevolent work of a salvation army Captain in the dark streets of New York, begging from the passers by the price of a night's lodging for outcasts. The dreary common-place of Mr. Dreiser's style may not refute the comparison of Sister Carrie by some of the critics to Zola's Nana—the realistic detail which the Academicians dubbed "the brutal truth"; but the comparison that has been made with the powerful drawing of Balzac must have been suggested only by the lack of high lights, or by way of contrast.

Washington *Evening Star,* July 20, 1907.

"Sister Carrie" is undoubtedly one of the most important books of the year. It would not be too much to say that, from certain viewpoints, it is the most important novel published in the United States for several years. In plot it is the story of an American woman driven, in part by circumstances and in part by temperament, into a life reprobated by all society. With her career is bound up the downfall of Hurstwood, the second of her lovers. The purpose of the book seems to be threefold: To arraign the social and economic conditions which can produce Drouet and Carrie and Hurstwood; to exploit Mr. Dreiser's own conception of the temperament of the artist, and to present the evolution of two types which every honest-thinking man will admit are but too common to our civilization. In his first purpose it must be conceded that the author has succeeded. No more pitilessly true picture of certain conditions of American lower and middle class life has been presented. To the second purpose—which would make Carrie an exponent of the type of which artists are made—many will take exception. But no one can fail to respond to the unerring realism with which Mr. Dreiser has reproduced the lives of Hurstwood and of Carrie.

The author has explained the infallible instinct with which Carrie chooses the easier, materially comfortable, way in part by the cruelty of economic conditions which make almost impossibly hard the lot of the unskilled working girl, and in part by the fact that she feels rather than thinks, that she has the instinct of the artist in following the lure of beauty. He apparently considers that the artist is all emotion, that he need have neither mind nor will. The discussion of this point brings up the ever-recurring controversy over "the artistic temperament." Mr. Dreiser's position will probably be combatted by those thinkers who hold that art is not art where it is not the expression of an intellectual conception which could be expressed, if necessary, in an algebraic formula. However that may be, Mr. Dreiser has builded better than he knew. For Carrie is not the sport of circumstance because she has certain imitative faculties which ultimate by giving her a vogue on the stage. She yields because she is the feminine exponent of a class of which Hurstwood is the masculine, a class to which belongs the mass of the population which have no moral standards other than conventional and superficial ones, the class which has no moral backbone, from which are recruited the army of suddenly defaulting bank cashiers and the sorry ranks of frail women. She has, as has Hurstwood, on the whole, an inclination toward things that are materially refined and conventionally moral. But she is morally flaccid, she has no power of resistance.

The artistic triumph of the book is the character of Hurstwood. There can be no controversy as to the purport of his life. He is superficially shrewd, imitatively courteous, handsome, devoutly worshipful of the external signs of success, resistless in his bland determination to have what he wants. He is conventionally a husband and superficially a father. The man looms up as a monster because of his vacancy of any trace either of spirituality or of thought. The presentation of the stages of his downfall, following the impulse which makes him give up his solid advantages in pursuit of the latest thing he wants, is masterly. The successive degrees of sordidness into which he sinks with Carrie are inevitable. Out of ruin he vanishes, through stages of starvation, to ultimate suicide; and out of it she rises. And the reason is, not that she is better or greater than he, but that she is twenty years younger. He is unable to recover from the wrench by which he has brought his house of life tumbling about his ears. But she has formed no scheme of life to be shattered, she is untouched because she is flaccid. And her qualities of beauty and light adaptability have a market value on the stage.

Of the minor characters Drouet is as real as are Carrie and Hurstwood. Every one who has observed will recognize the type. There are certain crudities of Mr. Dreiser's diction which are subjective, rather than native to the classes of which he writes. As a whole, however, the book must stand as a painful memorial to the worst tendencies of contemporary American life.

Louisville [Ky.] *Journal*, July 27, 1907.

Every now and then a novel is written that puzzles the reviewers. Personally they like it, recommend it and perhaps reread it for further light; but they are not quite sure whether it ought to be commended unreservedly to the public for fear lest the easily influenced portion may find therein something that may direct in a way it should not go.

Sister Carrie is a piece of realism that gives a wonderful impression of life in certain surroundings. It tells of the pretty country girl coming to the great city to seek her fortune. With no experience, no conviction even in her own mind of what she can do. She only wishes to escape the monotony of a narrow life, wear good clothes and see the world. On the train she meets a drummer who is a typical, good hearted, well-dressed traveling man. She likes him and gives him permission to call on her at her sister's where she will make her home.

But this sister is married to a hard-working foreigner, and her whole life is a thwarted, stunted thing, without variety or brightness. Carrie hates the very thought of it, and feels that she is only welcome there for the weekly stipend she will bring. She seeks work, finds it, punching holes in shoe leather all day long at $4.50 a week, $4 of which goes for board. She needs clothing, a warm jacket, even shoes and she finds that she must go cold and ragged and weary.

In this predicament she meets Drouet, and he offers to lend her money. The drummer, one is told, meant no harm, he was not a cold-blooded scheming villain, but a common type, vain, boastful, but genial and superficially kind. The way of a man with a maid is set forth with forceful truth. Carrie at length leaves her sister and goes to the rooms provided by Drouet. And just here is where the critic is doubtful. It is made so plain, that Carrie cannot be blamed. On the one side she saw the most grinding labor without reward—on the other a life of ease, affection and a promise of marriage.

Carrie, it must be remembered, was simply a type of thousands of girls, she was not a genius, she was simply a pretty little thing fighting to live. Her life with Drouet, with the promise of marriage in the background seemed excusable.

But another man, wealthier, belonging, as she thinks, to the great high world of wealth, sees her and falls in love. She, thinking him a single man, compares him with her genial drummer to the latter's disadvantage, but out of gratitude refuses to leave him.

Here the story begins to reach its highest point. In his portrayal of Hurstwood and his fall the author almost touches perfection. There is sympathy with the fallen, but a warning in every line of his subsequent fate. The same cannot be said of Carrie, who attains the height of her small ambitions, and at the close of the book is left a successful, popular actress. Even though Carrie's experience in life has gradually brought her to perceive that higher ideal, the intellectual; in spite of the fact that she is lonely and unhappy; in spite of her successes, and her real shrinking from vice, the earnest worker for the progress of humanity must see something dangerous in the effect a perusal of Carrie's life must have on the thousands of young girls who resemble her. To the experienced mind the book shows very clearly the wrong conditions of life and it is plain that these must be corrected before the Carries of the world can be either despised or condemned. The Carries will see only the excuse and the glamour; their imaginations will never show them the emptiness of the final state. The book is too true to life.

Indianapolis [Ind.] *Star*, July 27, 1907.

Theodore Dreiser's "Sister Carrie" was first issued by Doubleday, Page & Co. in 1900 and immediately withdrawn by the publishers. It has since been issued in England, where it has attracted considerable notice, and is now brought out by Dodge & Co., in New York. It is a remarkable piece of realism, suggesting comparison with no other American book, but rather with various of the master Europeans. But it is essentially faulty. It lacks ideals. It lacks the high handling, as of an irresistible, somber destiny, a thwarting inherent doom, which gives many of the foreign books of the same character something of the dignity of a Greek tragedy. Just another touch would have made the book into a masterpiece of its kind, but one is haunted by the feeling that the author himself knows little more than poor Carrie of the ideals that are transgressed, of all those higher things of life and feeling that are above and beyond conventions. It is all very well that the groundlings of the theme should know nothing beyond plush and gilding, but one feels that the author should. . . .

San Francisco *Argonaut*, August 3, 1907.

This is a book that will trouble the consciences of those who have not drawn for themselves a clear and intelligent line between the moral and the immoral in literature. Carrie Meeber's surrender in her distress and despair to the temptations offered by the pleasure-loving and prosperous Charles Drouet, will be instantly condemned by those who carry a stock of adhesive labels ready for instant application to the conduct of others. When she eventually leaves Drouet and allows herself not quite unwillingly to be abducted by his rival, Hurstwood, a special scarlet label will describe the book as an immoral one, quite unsuited to the perusal of the young person and the boarding-school miss. But these critics will have little to say in condemnation of the immorality of a commerical system which offers to young girls a wage of three or four dollars a week in payment for labor as destructive to the mind as to the body.

The modern writer is under no compulsion to write with an undivided eye to the young person, nor is he blameworthy if he write what it would be better for her not to read. We have a right to ask him not to write in such a way as to make vice seem attractive or to promise that happiness can come out of misconduct. The book that does this is immoral and is to be condemned. But it is not immoral to describe the allurements that await the young girl in our overcrowded cities, so long as it shows that no breach of the moral law ever did or ever can result in happiness.

Therefore Sister Carrie is not an immoral story, because it shows bitterness and disillusion at the end of the path. With Drouet discarded and Hurstwood a worthless wreck, Carrie Meeber discovers her dramatic ability and becomes a star and the very child of fortune. But there is no happiness for her in any of the things for which she pined, and in her splendid luxury she almost regrets the work-bench in the Chicago factory. "In your rocking chair, by your window dreaming, shall you long, alone. In your rocking chair, by your window, shall you dream such happiness as you may never feel."

Paris Modes, September, 1907.

The vicissitudes that attended the prenatal history of Theodore Dreiser's novel are sufficiently remarkable to bear retelling. It appears that the manuscript of "Sister Carrie" was accepted for publication by Doubleday, Page & Co. in 1900, and that then having received the disapproval—so the story goes—of the wife of one of the members of the firm, who reserves the right of censorship on all fiction which they publish, it was withdrawn from their presses. The author was not content with this unexpected suppression and took his book to England where, on being published, it enjoyed a measure of success. He then brought it back to America, and found another publisher for it over here. It has received some praise and much condemnation, but it is certainly not a pleasant book to read. Why a sordid, selfish, uneducated mite of a girl, whose overweening vanity makes her an easy prey to the schemes of certain low-minded men, and who would rather live in sinful luxury, if fine raiment is hers, than engage in any sort of independent toil, should be considered a suitable subject for a lengthy novel passes comprehension. From the feminine standpoint the girl is not even interesting, and her story is immoral and inane. Can any one explain why such a story—calculated to be harmful in the hands of the young—should ever have been deemed a worthy *motif?* It may be "relentless truth," but why tell it?

John Horner Coates. " 'Sister Carrie.' " *North American Review,* 186 (October 1907), 289.

Quite apart from its intrinsic merit as a work of literary art, "Sister Carrie" has, for the discriminating, in a marked degree the special interest which any writer's first novel possesses in proportion to the peculiarly individual power it may show as a promise for the future. In this, Mr. Dreiser's book is especially noteworthy, since rarely has a new novelist shown so singular a power of virile earnestness and serious purpose with unusual faculty of keenly analytic characterization and realistic painting of pictures. His people are real people; he compels you to know them as he knows them, to see the scenes amid which they move as he sees them. He shows absolute sincerity, he plays you no tricks; he is rigidly uncompromising, he scorns to tamper with the truth as he knows it, he refuses any subterfuges or weak dallying with what, to him at least, are the crucial facts of life. One may not always accept his philosophy fully and without reserve, but he always believes in it. That is the general impression the book creates, and he possesses, therefore, a compelling individuality which is bound to make its mark.

The story is of Caroline Meeber, a girl of eighteen bred in a small country village where her father is a miller, who comes to Chicago to seek an independent livelihood by the work of her hands. She has never been away from home before; she knows nothing about the life of a great city, so strange and marvellous to her inexperienced girlhood. She has come, impelled by some restless but vague and as yet unconscious craving for happiness; and happiness in her crude and immature imaginings is confused with pleasure and the sensation of the stir of life as it is with so many of her brothers and sisters the world over. This impressionable girl, unsuited for any successful struggle with hardship by temperament or training, is thrown into the whirlpool of city life during the years when character is beginning to form; and she is weighted by a soft attractiveness of face and gentleness of heart. In the opening chapter, on her way to Chicago she meets Drouet, a travelling salesman, who greatly influences her career. Later, she met Hurstwood, the manager of a fashionable drinking resort and in his way a man of respectable position. The conditions under which she comes to live are not justified, nor excused, by any acceptable code. But they are not uncommon, and Mr. Dreiser handles them with such delicacy of treatment and in such a clean largeness of mental attitude, that they simply enforce an impressive moral lesson. The inevitable growth of her initial yielding softness into a hard cold selfishness at the last, but which yet fails to escape from the power of unsatisfied longing, is traced with much skill and with a logic which seems unanswerable. And the parallel working out of Hurstwood's character is surely a convincing piece of literary art.

"Sister Carrie" is a sombre tale. It does not leave you with a bad taste in the mouth, as one says, but with something very like a heartache; an effect even more pronounced here than in Mrs. Wharton's powerful novel, "The House of Mirth," to which it bears a notable similarity in the underlying theme, although widely different in most else. Mr. Dreiser belongs to the realistic school much more distinctly than Mrs. Wharton; he falls below her in grace and beauty of style and in her own characteristic literary art, but he gains in power and in vividness perhaps. The stories told are not the same, the methods of telling differ, but the *motif* in each is at the root of it essentially the same; the tragedy of human beings who, in our present social order, do not escape the crushing weight of a surrender to primal human impulses. The two books seem inevitably in the same class; they enforce a like moral. One is the complement of the other, with little or no superficial resemblance between them other than that each is of great and sombre power and deals with the same theme—the aberrations of social mankind, in America, in its search for pleasure and in its attempts at some basis for sex relations. In the two books the practical difference is only in the variables, the theme itself is constant. Mrs. Wharton works out her problem on one side, the complex laborious pleasure-seeking cult among that small and comparatively insignificant group, the idle rich; Mr Dreiser is concerned with the greater and far more important class, the working-people from whose ranks it is that the upper strata of the future are to inherit character; for in this country, at least, the proletary of to-day begets the leader of tomorrow. It is the great lower and middle classes, if there are such things, that count.

Human nature is a tolerably constant quantity; men and women are pretty much alike in all times and places, and in all environments. Class distinctions, so far as the humanity of their elements is concerned, are more apparent than real; men are of the same nature everywhere. To find a great difference in essential quality between the very rich and the very poor, the very good and very bad, the very cultured and intelligent and the very ignorant and stupid, we must, after all, take our measurements with a micrometric scale, so to speak; if we attempt to gauge these human differences by the finger of God, they are hard to find. No doubt, one bacillus differs from another in length, but you cannot mark it by a yard-stick. So that the "drummer" and the saloon-keeper who are arbiters of destiny for Sister Carrie are essentially of the same sort as the men who riot in "The House of Mirth," except that they appear to have retained more human quality of redemption; and the Lily Barts of the world of fashion are but Sister Carries after all. Indeed, the title of Mr. Dreiser's book is, no doubt, intended to suggest the kinship of the world.

And in these days, perhaps more markedly in America, the process of breaking down the class barriers, of interfusion of the social strata, is taking place with notable distinctness. Not only are the upper social ranks, or what passes for such, being constantly recruited by those who have lately risen from the lower stratum, but the economic change in industrial conditions is more and more bringing all humanity into closer touch; with the result that the high and mighty influence, as never before, the desires and the ambitions, the passions, too, of those who are low in social degree. As Mr. Dreiser puts it:

> "The great create an atmosphere which reacts badly upon the small. This atmosphere is easily and quickly felt. Walk among the magnificent residences, the splendid equipages, the gilded shops, restaurants, resorts of all kinds; scent the flowers, the silks, the wines; drink of the laughter springing from the soul of luxurious content, of the glances which gleam like light from defiant spears; feel the quality of the smiles which cut like glistening swords and of strides born of place, and you shall know of what is the atmosphere of the high and mighty. Little use to argue that of such is not the kingdom of greatness, but so long as the world is attracted by this and the human heart views this as the one desirable realm which it must attain, so long, to that heart, will this remain the realm of greatness. So long, also, will the atmosphere of this realm work its desperate results in the soul of man. It is like a chemical reagent. One day of it, like one drop of the other, will so affect and discolor the views, the aims, the desires of the mind, that it will thereafter remain forever dyed. A day of it to the untried mind is like opium to the untried body. A craving is set up which, if gratified, shall eternally result in dreams and death. Aye! dreams unfulfilled—gnawing, luring, idle phantoms which beckon and lead, beckon and lead, until death and dissolution dissolve their power and restore us blind to nature's heart."

So that, from the sociological point of view, the study presented in this book of existing conditions operating on human impulses which are inextinguishable, and often dominating, is of timely import. There are signs that the future of the race in this country may be more perilous than its past has been; it is possible one of those racial crises which are constantly recurring in the history of mankind, may be on the way. "Sister Carrie" is a book to be reckoned with, just as the social conditions—or defects—on which it rests must be reckoned with.

A. Non. *Musical Leader*, November 28, 1907.

Some of my professional brethren are objecting that Theodore Dreiser's novel, "Sister Carrie," is not a "pleasant book." It is not, for it is written with a pen dipped in wormwood. Nevertheless, wormwood, though bitter, *is* medicinal.

Akron [Ohio] *Journal*, November 30, 1907.

Demurely bound and well illustrated is the book, "Sister Carrie," by Theodore Dreiser. The embellishments are undoubtedly calculated to deceive the public into reading what is between the covers. The book is a dangerous one, the story of lives steeped in sin and degradation. There is not one sentence to redeem the sordid tale of the sickening life of men and women who pass before the public eye as honored members of society. All that is low in the theatrical life has been raked up and put into this story. The whole thing is immoral and disgusting. Such books are to be shunned, and it is to be deplored that publishers will accept this kind of work from authors when there is so much in the world that is fresh and clean, elevating little stories, that, while simple in the happening, are well worth the telling.

Checklist of Additional Reviews

New York *Tribune*, November 3, 1900.
Publisher's Weekly, 58 (November 17, 1900), 1925.
New York *Sun*, May 11, 1907.
New York *Herald*, May 19, 1907.
St. John *Globe*, May 25, 1907.
Syracuse *Post-Standard*, May 25, 1907.
Indianapolis *Star*, May 27, 1907.
New York *World*, June 1, 1907.
Reedy's [St. Louis] *Mirror*, June 6, 1907.
Buffalo *Times*, June 6, 1907.
Hartford [Conn.] *Courant*, June 7, 1907.
Buffalo [N.Y.] *Courier*, June 8, 1907.
Newark [N.J.] *News*, June 15, 1907.
"Otis Notman." "Mr. Dreiser." New York *Times*, June 15, 1907.
Buffalo [N.Y.] *Times*, June 16, 1907.
Baltimore [Md.] *American*, June 17, 1907.
Louisville [Ky.] *Times*, June 19, 1907.
St. Louis *Republic*, June 22, 1907.
Chicago *Post*, June 25, 1907.
Boston *Globe*, June 27, 1907.
Indianapolis [Ind.] *Star*, June 29, 1907.
Denver [Col.] *Republican*, June 30, 1907.
Detroit *Tribune*, June 30, 1907.
Current Literature, 43 (July 1907), 109–110.
Style and American Dressmaker, July, 1907.
Riverside [Cal.] *Enterprise*, July 4, 1907.
San Francisco *Bulletin*, July 6, 1907.
New York *Dramatic Mirror*, July 6, 1907.
New York *Herald*, July 7, 1907.
New Orleans *Statesman*, July 7, 1907.
Denver *Times*, July 15, 1907.
Denver *News*, July 15, 1907.
New York *Tribune*, July 23, 1907.
Lewiston [Me.] *Journal*, July 27, 1907.
Washington [D.C.] *Post*, July 27, 1907.
Chicago Evening *Post*, July 27, 1907.
Harrisburg [Pa.] *Star-Independent*, July 31, 1907.
New York *Press*, July 31, 1907.
Los Angeles [Cal.] *Express*, August 3, 1907.
New York *Globe*, August 7, 1907.
Syracuse *Herald*, August 7, 1907.
Detroit *Journal*, August 10, 1907.
San Francisco *Town Talk*, August 10, 1907.
New Orleans *Times-Democrat*, August 25, 1907.
Boston *Herald*, September 14, 1907.
Mobile [Ala.] *Register*, September 15, 1907.
Life, October 10, 1907.
Atlanta [Ga.] *Evening Journal*, November 16, 1907.
Milwaukee *Evening Wisconsin*, November 22, 1907.
Akron [Ohio] *Journal*, November 30, 1907.
New York *Standard*, January 2, 1908.
Springfield [Mass.] *Republican*, August 21, 1908.
Philadelphia *Item*, August 22, 1908.
Cleveland *Plain Dealer*, August 23, 1908.
New York *Evening Mail*, August 29, 1908.
Boston *Advertiser*, November 27, 1908.

Further Reviews: *Bibliographical Information Incomplete*

Advertiser and Union, ca. November, 1900.

Sunday Dispatch, June 10, 1907.

JENNIE GERHARDT

A NOVEL

BY

THEODORE DREISER

AUTHOR OF

"SISTER CARRIE"

HARPER & BROTHERS PUBLISHERS

NEW YORK AND LONDON

M - C - M - X - I

Jennie Gerhardt

"Realism." New York *Daily Tribune*, October 21, 1911, p. 8.

More than ten years ago Mr. Dreiser published "Sister Carrie," a novel that once attracted the attention and won the praise of a small number of literary critics and lovers of serious fiction. So far as the general reading public was concerned, however, the book was practically stillborn. An enviable "succes d'estime" was its fate. It had its faults, grievous faults, all of them technical—lack of style and proportion, baldness and common-placeness of diction—but in this case utterly inadequate literary means were justified by the end, by the production of a deep impression. "Sister Carrie" remains to this day one of the most powerful productions of uncompromising realism in American literature.

"Jennie Gerhardt" reveals the fact that Mr. Dreiser has learned nothing since the days when he wrote "Sister Carrie," but it proves also that he has forgotten nothing. The parallels that might be drawn between the earlier and the later tale are not, as might be considered at first sight, a matter of repetition, but of the author's unaltered, gloomy philosophy of life. He is a determinist; life is to him a matter of blind chance. This is also the ruling viewpoint of the modern German novelists whose leader is Herman Sudermann. Students of evolution have long known that the fittest who survive are not always those most worthy. Jennie Gerhardt is doomed by the very qualities of gentle womanliness, of unselfishness and readiness to serve and give happiness to others that should have won for her a better fate. Her story has not the compelling power of Sister Carrie's, its outward incidents are not so dramatic, its tragedy is of the inner far more than of the outer life; but none the less it deserves to be read, especially if it leads its readers back to the pages of the earlier book.

Kansas City [Mo.] *Journal*, October 22, 1911.

. . . "Jennie Gerhardt," which has just found its way to the book counters and has been received within the past week by several of Mr. Dreiser's Kansas City friends, is no milk for mollycoddles. It might be described as a sort of post-graduate product of the reporter's art, free alike from a perfumed apology for facts as they exist and that overt suggestiveness which American readers are wont to associate with what they sometimes call the modern French school. It is the story of a woman who sinned and succeeded and finally suffered in the midst of success. There is nothing forced, nothing artificial about it. Dreiser seems to be as incapable of nerve-racking plot as nature herself, but the calm certainty with which he paints his characters is just as gripping as life.

The book neither is moral nor immoral—it is art. Its logic is that of the mountain, which speaks from crude and solemn peaks, saying: "I am here; who shall deny me?" And the critics are just now of the opinion that while the public may be able to scale or tunnel through or go around the book, it never will be able entirely to ignore it. One describes it as "grim, gaunt, mirthless, shapeless" and of course as "gripping."

The newspaper man's attitude crops out in the book everywhere. The author neither condemns nor approves. He merely pictures. The tragedy is real—that of one who has struggled and fallen and risen, and come at last, in the realization of her dreams, to unhappiness.

Evidently, like Flaubert, Balzac, Hugo, and in a lesser measure Dickens, Dreiser cares nothing for the literary traditions of his day and has profited by that indifference. If the book is of any school it belongs in a class with the all but incomparable "Madame Bovary" and "Eugenie Grandet." The chief difference in "tone" between the American and the French products is a little grain of Puritan conscience in the former. But this the average reader will welcome, rather than object to. . . .

Edwin Markham. "Theodore Dreiser's Second Novel." New York *American*, October 25, 1911.

Theodore Dreiser's first novel, "Sister Carrie" (a somber history of a Chicago working girl), was a novel which had a curious experience. It was practically suppressed by the repentant American publisher who had accepted it. Yet in England it was acclaimed and widely read and when it came back to America on the rebound it was widely read and discussed at home.

Mr. Dreiser (who, by the way, Arnold Bennett reckons one of our most distinctive novelists) has just issued another unusual story, "Jennie Gerhardt." A girl of the poorest working class is again the heroine, a girl of honest, sober, industrious German stock, with a strain of the old German sentiment and poesy that the grind and grime of life cannot obliterate. Gentle and yielding, the native iron of Jennie's spirit is never wrought and tempered to the steel that would protect her from the harshness of the world and the ravening of men.

Mr. Dreiser has again shown himself master of a pen that etches with power the dark side of poverty with all its cares and despairs.

The pathetic girl living always on the negative, shadow side, her patient, drudging mother, her pious, slavish father and the two worldly-wise, half pagan, thoughtlessly generous and thoughtlessly swinish betrayers [sic]—all of them step out of the book as well defined as the figures on a screen rounded out by the play of light and shade.

The comfortable, pin-saving school of economics tells us that prosperity follows, nay chases, those who slave and save; still the fact remains that under the present order of industry a family like the Gerhardts may sweat and scrimp and scrape, foregoing the joy and beauty of life, and yet be overtaken and hag-ridden by poverty that they can never shake off.

Jennie Gerhardt, pretty and pleasing, coming from a bleak, unbeautiful home, where coal and clothes and food are never sufficient, is an easy prey for a certain type of self-indulgent, sentimental men. Innocent of evil, eager for beauty, craving for affection, she goes out on her humble, eager quest for work. Under the dastardly plea for helping her hungry, workless family, these men tempt the tenderhearted girl more than once, and she falls. It is the tragedy of Sudermann's Lily in "The Song of Songs"—a girl with no strength of character in fighting temptation, a girl with an unusually affectionate disposition who goes the easiest way to comfort and shelter.

Jennie, through all the indignities of fate, through all the careless, irreverent bandyings of the two men she trusts, through all the infamy they idly thrust upon her, never becomes wholly degraded in spirit, as does the girl in Reginald Kauffman's "House of Bondage" She gives love, no matter what her return. She does not lose her sense of the beauty and wonder of life; and this untaught, unguarded, sore-tempted daughter of the scrub-woman and chore-man (in spite of all the dishonors and disasters of her career) develops into a forgiving and ministering woman.

Admitting the invertebrate character of the girl as a defender of herself, and casting no stones at her, Mr. Dreiser aims to show the closing around her of fate in a world ruled seemingly by chance and chicanery. The softest side of her nature, the side that would aid and comfort her family, that would live in harmony with beauty, that would trust all men as honorable—this is the immediate door to her undoing.

The defect in the whole under-structure of the girl's character is that the girl forgets the reverence that she owes to her own womanhood. One can be sweet and forgiving and yet have it all spring from flabbiness of spiritual fiber. Jennie is no model for any girl who sees life on all sides. Every girl should put a high price upon herself: the price of the woman is the man.

The book raises another question: Is a woman ever justified in smirching her womanhood, in staining her virtue, in order to help her relatives—even to save them from starvation? This must be answered with an iron "No" by all who take a deep look into life. The wise are aware that there are some misfortunes that are worse than starvation.

New York *Herald*, October 28, 1911, p. 8.

About a generation ago—perhaps it was even longer—a book called "Sister Carrie," by *Theodore Dreiser* was published. So far as the general run of novel readers went, it had no vogue to speak of, but there were discerning ones who saw in it qualities of striking significance. Since then Mr. Dreiser has contented himself chiefly in the production of ephemeral magazine work, but at last he has returned to his earlier style with "Jennie Gerhardt." This is the life story of a girl who belongs to what might be called the middle class German-American. Persons of aristocratic or fashionable tendencies probably will call it common, or even vulgar, but the discerning ones mentioned will be more deeply moved than they were in the first instance. "Jennie Gerhardt" is a story wrung from the heart strings and dripping with vitality. It should have been written by a Flaubert. It has the inexorable simplicity and reality of which only the French seem to be capable. George Moore might have done it, but no other writer in English. Jennie is the victim of a relentless destiny. She is born for sacrifice. The braver her fight against the ironic whim of circumstance the quicker her vanquishment. Naturally virtuous, tender and pure minded, she is pursued by this malicious fate, but even with a nameless child she remains pure. Can such a paradox be understood in 1911? It is not necessary to go into the plot. In fact, there is none to speak of. It is life—big, inscrutable, crushing. It is the life with which we are in collision every day, if we but knew it. There will be various opinions about this book. One that may or may not be of value is that it comes near deserving that abused word "great."

New York *Globe and Commercial Advertiser*, October 28, 1911.

More than one of the famous English novelists who have been visiting us lately has been reported as asking, "What is Dreiser doing?" and as being surprised when asked in turn, "Who's Dreiser?" It appears that in England Theodore Dreiser's first novel, "Sister Carrie," is regarded as about the best novel that has ever been written in America. Here in this country, however, it had only that most discouraging of successes, the success of esteem. Those people who read "Sister Carrie" realized it came very near to being a great story. But most people didn't read it.

Well, now, anyway we know what Mr. Dreiser has been doing, for the Harper's publish "Jennie Gerhardt," a remarkable feat in realistic writing, like its predecessor, but whether it is the great American novel we don't know. We doubt whether we should recognize the great American novel if we should see it. Much disappointment makes a man wary. "Jennie Gerhardt" is the story of a poor girl in Columbus, Ohio, in whom Fate or the novelist shoots one arrow after another until she is as bestuck as Saint Sebastian, but as that seraphic young man is most often represented in art, still smiling. Greek, we believe it is called, this willy-nilly way of things happening when people simply stand and take what's coming to them. This is what Jennie does. She is the coolest, most passive, thoroughly static heroine we have ever come across in fiction. She resents nothing. We were almost going to say she feels nothing, but we remember Dr. Dreiser says her feelings are so deep they rarely come to the surface.

Jennie's troubles begin when she goes to the hotel to get the washing of the great Senator Brander. They seem to be reaching a climax when the senator dies before her child is born. But there is more, much more, to come. She has that about her, a certain softness and womanliness the author describes it, that apparently attracts men to her and that makes her unable to stand out against them. Another man has only to come along after Jennie's one disastrous experience, and say, "You're my girl, Jennie. You belong to me," then she belongs. When after living together for years, the man decides to leave Jennie and marry, she doesn't even make one little protest. When he is dying and sends for her, she goes.

Jennie at fifty is apparently the same Jennie she was at twenty. She is always unselfish and self-sacrificing, responsive to goodness and not resentful of wrong. There is not a character in the book who completely wins the reader's sympathies. Perhaps Jennie's father, in his old age, comes most nearly to it. The hard-working mother ought to, but she doesn't quite. Mr. Dreiser draws a distressing picture of the family's poverty and mean struggle, and the general unloveliness of their lives and characters. For the most part, his narrative is as plain and straight as a gingham apron. But at times he lifts it up into poetry. It is a remarkable story on many counts. But that it enlightens, enlivens, points a moral or will adorn a shelf, we are not so sure.

H.L. Mencken. "A Novel of the First Rank." *Smart Set*, 35 (November 1911), 153-155.

If you miss reading "JENNIE GERHARD," by Theodore Dreiser, you will miss the best American novel, all things considered, that has reached the book counters in a dozen years. On second thought, change "a dozen" into "twenty-five." On third thought, strike out everything after "counters." On fourth thought, strike out everything after "novel." Why back and fill? Why evade and qualify? Hot from it, I am firmly convinced that "JENNIE GERHARDT" is the best American novel I have ever read, with the lonesome but Himalayan exception of "Huckleberry Finn," and so I may as well say it aloud and at once and have done with it. Am I forgetting "The Scarlet Letter," "The Rise of Silas Lapham" and (to drag an exile unwillingly home) "What Maisie Knew?" I am not. Am I forgetting "McTeague" and "The Pit"? I am not. Am I forgetting the stupendous masterpieces of James Fenimore Cooper, beloved of the pedagogues, or those of James Lane Allen, Mrs. Wharton and Dr. S. Weir Mitchell, beloved of the women's clubs and literary monthlies? No. Or "Uncle Tom's Cabin" or "Rob o' the Bowl" or "Gates Ajar" or "Ben Hur" or "David Harum" or "Lewis Rand" or "Richard Carvel"? No. Or "The Hungry Heart" or Mr. Dreiser's own "Sister Carrie"? No. I have all these good and bad books in mind. I have read them and survived them and in many cases enjoyed them.

And yet in the face of them, and in the face of all the high authority, constituted and self-constituted, behind them it seems to me at this moment that "JENNIE GERHARDT" stands apart from all of them, and a bit above them. It lacks the grace of this one, the humor of that one, the perfect form of some other one; but taking it as it stands, grim, gaunt, mirthless, shapeless, it remains, and by long odds, the most impressive work of art that we have yet to show in prose fiction—a tale not unrelated, in its stark simplicity, its profound sincerity, to "Germinal" and "Anna Karenina" and "Lord Jim"—a tale assertively American in its scene and its human material, and yet so European in its method, its point of view, its almost reverential seriousness, that one can scarcely imagine an American writing it. Its personages are few in number, and their progress is along a path that seldon widens, but the effect of that progress is ever one of large movements and large masses. One senses constantly the group behind the individual, the natural law behind the human act. The result is an indefinable impression of bigness, of epic dignity. The thing is not a mere story, not a novel in the ordinary American meaning of the word, but a criticism and an interpretation of life—and that interpretation loses nothing in validity by the fact that its burden is the doctrine that life is meaningless, a tragedy without a moral, a joke without a point. What else have Moore and Conrad and Hardy been telling us these many years? What else does all the new knowledge of a century teach us? One by one the old ready answers have been disposed of. Today the one intelligible answer to the riddle of aspiration and sacrifice is that there is no answer at all.

"The power to tell the same story in two forms," said George Moore not long ago, "is the sign of the true artist." You will think of this when you read "JENNIE GERHARDT," for in its objective plan, and even in its scheme of subjective unfolding, it suggests "Sister Carrie" at every turn. Reduce it to a hundred words, and those same words would also describe that earlier study of a woman's soul, with scarcely the change of a syllable. Jennie Gerhardt, like Carrie Meeber, is a rose grown from turnip seed. Over each, at the start, hangs poverty, ignorance, the dumb helplessness of the Shudra—and yet in each there is that indescribable something, that element of essential gentleness, that innate, inward beauty which levels all caste barriers and makes Esther a fit queen for Ahasuerus. And the history of each, reduced to its elements, is the history of the other. Jennie, like Carrie, escapes from the physical miseries of the struggle for existence only to taste the worse miseries of the struggle for happiness. Not, of course, that we have in either case a moral, maudlin fable of virtue's fall; Mr. Dreiser, I need scarcely assure you, is too dignified an artist, too sane a man, for any such banality. Seduction, in point of fact, is not all tragedy for either Jennie or Carrie. The gain of each, until the actual event has been left behind and obliterated by experiences more salient and poignant, is rather greater than her loss, and that gain is to the soul as well as to the creature. With the rise from want to security, from fear to ease, comes an awakening of the finer perceptions, a widening of the sympathies, a gradual unfolding of the delicate flower called personality, an increased capacity for loving and living. But with all this, and as a part of it, there comes, too, an increased capacity for suffering —and so in the end, when love slips away and the empty years stretch before, it is the awakened and supersentient woman that pays for the folly of the groping, bewildered girl. The tragedy of Carrie and Jennie, in brief, is not that they are degraded but that they are lifted up, not that they go to the gutter but that they escape the gutter.

But if the two stories are thus variations upon the same somber theme, if each starts from the same place and arrives at the same dark goal, if each shows a woman heartened by the same hopes and tortured by the same agonies, there is still a vast difference between them, and that difference is the measure of the author's progress in his art. "Sister Carrie" was a first sketch, a rough piling-up of observations and impressions, disordered and often incoherent. In the midst of the story of Carrie, Mr. Dreiser paused to tell the story of Hurstwood—an astonishingly vivid and tragic story, true enough, but still one that broke the back of the other. In "JENNIE GERHARDT" he falls into no such overelaboration of episode. His narrative goes forward steadily from beginning to end. Episodes there are, of course, but they keep their proper place, their proper bulk. It is always Jennie that holds the attention; it is in Jennie's soul that every scene is ultimately played out. Her father and mother, Senator Brander the god of her first worship, her daughter Vesta and Lester Kane, the man who makes and mars her—all these are drawn with infinite painstaking, and in every one of them there is the blood of life. But it is Jennie that dominates the drama from curtain to curtain. Not an event is unrelated to her; not a climax fails to make clearer the struggles going on in her mind and heart.

I have spoken of reducing "JENNIE GERHARDT" to a hundred words. The thing, I fancy, might be actually done. The machinery of the tale is not complex; it has no plot, as plots are understood in these days of "mystery" stories; no puzzles madden the reader. It is dull, unromantic poverty that sends Jennie into the world. Brander finds her there, lightly seduces her, and then discovers that, for some strange gentleness within her, he loves her. Lunacy—but he is willing to face it out. Death, however, steps in; Brander, stricken down without warning, leaves Jennie homeless and a mother. Now enters Lester Kane—not the villain of the books, but a normal, decent, cleanly American of the better class, well to do, level-headed, not too introspective, eager for the sweets of life. He and Jennie are drawn together; if love is not all of the spirit, then it is love that binds them. For half a dozen years the world lets them alone. A certain grave respectability settles over their relation; if they are not actually married, then it is only because marriage is a mere formality, to be put off until tomorrow. But bit by bit they are dragged into the light. Kane's father, dying with millions, gives him two years to put Jennie away. The penalty is poverty; the reward is wealth—and not only wealth itself, but all the pleasant and well remembered things that will come with it: the lost friends of other days, a sense of dignity and importance, an end of apologies and evasions, good society, the comradeship of decent women—particularly the comradeship of one decent woman. Kane hesitates, makes a brave defiance, thinks it over—and finally yields. Jennie does not flood him with tears. She has made progress in the world, has Jennie; the simple faith of the girl has given way to the pride and poise of the woman. Five years later Kane sends for her. He is dying. When it is over, Jennie goes back to her lonely home, and there, like Carrie Meeber before her, she faces the long years with dry eyes and an empty heart. "Days and days in endless reiteration, and then—"

A moral tale? Not at all. It has no more moral than a string quartet or the first book of Euclid. But a philosophy of life is in it, and that philosophy is the same profound pessimism which gives a dark color to the best that we have from Hardy, Moore, Zola and the great Russians—the pessimism of disillusion—not the jejune, Byronic thing, not the green sickness of youth, but that pessimism which comes with the discovery that the riddle of life, despite all the fine solutions offered by the learned doctors, is essentially insoluble. One can discern no intelligible sequence of cause and effect in the agonies of Jennie Gerhardt. She is, as human beings go, of the nobler, finer metal. There is within her a great capacity for service, a great capacity for love, a great capacity for happiness. And yet all that life has to offer her, in the end, is the mere license to live. The days stretch before her "in endless reiteration." She is a prisoner doomed to perpetual punishment for some fanciful, incomprehensible crime against the gods who make their mirthless sport of us all. And to me, at least, she is more tragic thus than Lear on his wild heath or Prometheus on his rock.

Nothing of the art of the literary lapidary is visible in this novel. Its form is the simple one of a panorama unrolled. Its style is unstudied to the verge of barrenness. There is no painful groping for the exquisite, inevitable word; Mr. Dreiser seems content to use the common, even the commonplace coin of speech. On the very first page one encounters "frank, open countenance," "diffident manner," "helpless poor," "untutored mind," "honest necessity" and half a dozen other such ancients. And yet in the long run it is this very *naïveté* which gives the story much of its impressiveness. The narrative, in places, has the effect of a series of unisons in music—an effect which, given a solemn theme, vastly exceeds that of the most ornate polyphony. One cannot imagine "JENNIE GERHARDT" done in the gipsy phrases of Meredith, the fugual manner of James. One cannot imagine that stark, stenographic dialogue adorned with the brilliants of speech. The thing could have been done only in the way that it has been done. As it stands, it is a work of art from which I for one would not care to take anything away—not even its gross crudities, its incessant returns to C major. It is a novel that depicts the life we Americans are living with extreme accuracy and criticises that life with extraordinary insight. It is a novel, I am convinced, of the very first consideration.

Floyd Dell. "A Great Novel." Chicago *Evening Post Literary Review*, November 3, 1911.

"JENNIE GERHARDT" is the new novel by the author of "Sister Carrie." To some readers this will mean a great deal. To such it is only necessary to say that the new book is a bigger, finer thing even than the old.

There is reason that it should be bigger and finer; it is the work of a man some ten years older, who has lost none of the creative vigor of his twenties. Accordingly it is done with a surer hand, a wider vision, a subtler art. The episode of the going-to-pieces of Hurstwood was, after all, the best thing in "Sister Carrie"; Carrie herself, for all the objective faithfulness with which her career was depicted, showed only the faintest glimpses of her inner life. This new work is above all things the history of a woman's soul.

Jennie Gerhardt, for whom the present book is named, is a girl whose life is lived outside the pale of the conventions. Her story is one easy for a writer to tell sensationally, or is one easy to libel, easy to mistakenly glorify. In taking such a person as his subject, Mr. Dreiser has selected a theme of first-rate importance. In succeeding with it, he has done something which is of profound significance to American literature.

In the columns of a contemporary a judicious critic, Mr. H. L. Menken, has attempted to evaluate this book. I am in entire accord with his opinion, which puts it at the head of American fiction. But "Jennie Gerhardt" is a book which one would really prefer not to assess in set terms. Anybody may say of any book that it is the "great American novel," and everybody else may treat that statement as incompetent or insincere. What one would like to do is this: To write soberly about the book in such a way that the reader must himself feel what the critic omits to say as to its absolute worth.

But the very quality of the book makes description difficult. One can only say: Here is a story, a rather unusual story, told in an extraordinarily lucid and sympathetic manner. There are no surprises, no shocks, no bits of splendid writing—just the tale of a woman from girlhood to middle age, in her relations with her mother, her father, her lovers, her child. For perhaps half the volume it is only very interesting. And then it comes upon one that a wonderful thing is being accomplished.

This novelist is dealing with a dozen human beings; and he has very quietly revealed every one of them to us. They live. We know them intimately. And yet there have been no dazzling pages of psychological analysis. There is no brilliancy of character-study. The book is as devoid of this as it is of amazing feats of realistic description. The story moves on, without any straining for effects, without a sign of effort. There is page after page of utterly simple narrative.

And about the middle of the book there comes this sense of the power behind this quiet narrative—the sustained strength, the penetrating vision, the boundless sympathy, the nobility of soul. It is not by minor writers, or by merely clever writers, or by "promising" writers, that such things are done.

Mr. Dreiser is not, in fact, a clever writer. He is weak in the very thing in which a clever writer is strongest—in verbal taste. This was pretty uncertain in "Sister Carrie," in which he would use such phrases as "cultured humans." And the chapter headings, as a distinguished admirer of Mr. Dreiser's regretfully pointed out to me, are what I should call the limit. The present book shows a great improvement. But on the very first page there are phrases which an infinitely lesser writer with a keener taste in the matter of words would have excised with a blush for their banality.

And yet on that same page there is a sentence which is such as to signify a great deal to the discerning reader. It is of Jennie's mother: "Her eyes were large and patient, and in them dwelt such a shadow of distress as only those who have looked sympathetically into the circumstances of the distraught and helpless poor know anything about."

That sentence signifies that Mr. Dreiser has at his command the power to bend language to the spirit of its content: to call forth a subtle and sympathetic prose music. This power is different from the artificial eloquence, the prose-poetry, which some writers affect: it is, as these are not, a sign of the born artist. I have compared as carefully and fairly as I could certain passages of Mr. Dreiser's writing with certain passages from the writing of one of the most notable of his English contemporaries; and despite its obvious faults it seemed to me that Mr. Dreiser was inherently the better writer.

Be that as it may—Jennie Gerhardt is the daughter of a poor German woman who gets work as a scrubwoman in a hotel at Columbus, Ohio, and who takes home the washing of one of the hotel's guests, Senator Brander. Jennie's father is a glassworker, now out of a job. When this 18-year-old ingenuous girl takes Senator Brander's washing to his room she attracts his attention, and an acquaintance begins, which on the man's part slides rapidly down the scale from paternal benevolence to amorous rashness. He thinks of sending the girl to school, and then marrying her. But he dies suddenly, and Jennie is left with the burden of a fatherless child. She leaves home, and goes to Cincinnati, Ohio, where she is employed as a maid. In this aristocratic home she again attracts the attention of a man, and soon, hoping to relieve the terrible economic situation of her family, becomes his mistress. He is rich and good-hearted, and she hopes that some day he may marry her; so she does not tell him about her child. She lives with him for years, and gains his whole respect. Nevertheless, under pressure of circumstance, he leaves her. Her child dies. She is left neither rich nor poor, neither happy nor miserable, neither rewarded as for heroism nor punished as for sin. That is the story. It is inconclusive, true; but its inconclusiveness is part of its interest.

The book has a theme: and this theme, again, is difficult to describe by virtue of its simplicity. Starkly put, it is the beauty, and the helplessness, of a generous soul. The whole book is the explication of the inevitable defeat of a woman who asks only to give; and of the loveliness of that doomed nature. It sounds, perhaps, absurd. We have not much sympathy with unselfish people in books. They are either prigs or fools, or both. That is when the author attempts to make a virtue out of a temperamental necessity. Mr. Dreiser makes no such mistake. He looks with a philosophic eagerness upon the spectacle of human life; he sees Jennie, an essentially unselfish girl in a world of essentially selfish people; he knows that she will be exploited, that she is bound to be exploited: and he shows how it happens—that is all.

He does not blame Jennie's exploiters; nor does he defend them. Selfishness is human. Selfishness can be noble. And even the everyday selfishness of the people among whom Jennie's career unfolds itself is shown to have its aspects of beauty. None of these people were brutes. There was something fine, because it was warm-hearted, instinctive, about the selfishness of the man. Senator Brander, who first took this poor washerwoman's daughter in his arms. There was something exalted about the cruelty of the girl's Lutheran father, when he tried to put her out of his life as hopelessly wicked. There was something beautiful, because violent and daring, about the selfishness of the man, Lester Kane, who made this girl his mistress. And there was something attractive, because frank and open, about the ruthlessness of the society woman who took this man away from the girl at last.

But more beautiful than these aspects of their selfishness, because rarer and more passionate, is the girl's generosity. When she yields to Senator Brander in her innocent gratitude for the love of such a wonderful man; when the desperate poverty of her family compels her to accept the relation of mistress—a relation instinctively desired but dutifully refused at first—to Lester Kane; when she gives loving service and companionship to this man, who carelessly postpones the legalization of what he has come to consider a real marriage; and when she finally sends him away so that he may not be disinherited—in all this there is an elemental, natural, human quality. It is a positive, not a negative thing; a strength and not a weakness. Jennie never suppresses herself; by such actions it is that she expresses herself.

But in Mr. Dreiser's novel this never becomes abstract: it is always exhibited in a flowing stream of natural events. Jennie goes to Chicago with Lester Kane. The existence of her child is discovered, and the menage for a time is threatened with disruption. Jennie's mother dies. Her father, believing Jennie and Lester are married, comes to live with them. Vesta, the little girl, goes to dancing school, much to her grandfather's dismay. The old man worries because Lester wastes so many matches—five or six to light a single cigar, by chops! It is along this stream that the reader is borne—a journey whose end one foresees, but of which one would not lose a moment.

The melting mood: this, which has been said to be the sign of great art, is what this book continually evokes in the reader. How it is done I do not know; a great part of the effect must be due to the long-sustained simplicity of the narrative, rather than to the quality of any certain passage. Quiet sympathy, it seems, can be prolonged until it reaches the breaking-point of poignancy. . . .

Mr. Dreiser writes of meetings and partings, festivities and funerals, as though no one had ever written of them before—freshly, yet without any straining after novelty of effect. The life of Jennie and Lester together is as familiar as a sunset—and as perpetually interesting. He sees everything eagerly, clearly, without prejudice.

When Lester leaves Jennie, when he married the cultivated woman of whom he has always been fond, the author does not depart from his attitude of impartiality. It was inevitable. He did not love the girl enough to make this last sacrifice for her. It is true, if he had married her in the beginning, he would not have been put in such a position. But there was no way of knowing what was to come. He had behaved rather sensibly. He had never expected that the affair would have such elements of permanency. And he had behaved rather kindly, too; but his amour propre was offended by the discovery that Jennie had been keeping a secret, the secret of her child, from him—after that, could he marry her? And when he has left her, he is not visited by remorse. He is happy with the other woman—for after all she is of his world, can talk his language. But he is no happier than he was with Jennie; perhaps—he concludes at last—not so happy. His wife is in

Europe when a fatal illness overtakes him; he sends for Jennie, and she comes, glad to be able to be of some final service to him. "You are the only woman I ever really loved," he tells her. There is some satisfaction in that confession to Jennie. She knows that he did not love her enough. But he loved her that much, and she is glad.

Meanwhile, Jennie has been left in a gathering of loneliness. Her mother had died, and her father. Her lover has gone away. Her little girl succumbs to the typhoid. She is left alone, sad, perplexed, wondering now and then what it all means.

What does it all mean? Mr. Dreiser doesn't say. Life seems to him to justify itself. He does not point to a mistake in Jennie's life or in Lester Kane's, and say that the trouble lay there; that if they had done the right thing there, everything would have gone well. There is no right thing to do. People act according to their natures, and the end makes their actions seem wise or foolish; but there is no way of knowing at the time. There wasn't any mistake in Jennie's life; she lived it well. And the end proves nothing—except that what is going to be, is. Only there is a great sympathy which envelops the history, a sympathy which bathes every incident with a tender light and brings out clearly the tragic outlines of the whole.

Tragedy? The word is loosely used nowadays. It means—what? "Pity and terror" are said to be the emotional effects which distinguish it. "Sympathy and awe" would perhaps be a better rendering of the Greek idea. A Tragedy is the representation of a defeat which brings out the inherent nobility of the defeated one. Nobility is various; it is of one sort in Prometheus, of another sort in Hamlet, of another in the heroine of "The Tragedy of Nan." And Mr. Dreiser's Jennie has an authentic nobility no less—a nobility which nothing but utter defeat could bring out.

Have I conveyed any sense of the power, the truth, the inspiration of "Jennie Gerhardt"? Then perhaps I may say, without saying it in vain: this is a great book.

Edwin L. Shuman. Chicago *Record Herald*, November 4, 1911.

Theodore Dreiser's "Jennie Gerhardt" is one of the few American novels to which one may without hesitation apply the epithet great. It is not a book that will appeal to the mere entertainment seeker, for it compels thought rather than feeling; the sentimentalist will not like it, for it deals with disillusioning truths of life and human nature; the moralist may condemn it because it preaches no sermon, the optimist because it contains no laughter, the romanticist because it strikes no note of wonder or surprise; but those who can appreciate Hardy and Balzac will find in "Jennie Gerhardt" one of the best realistic novels produced in recent years in any country.

"Jennie Gerhardt," like Mr. Dreiser's former novel, "Sister Carrie," is the story of a woman gone wrong, so far as the marriage law is concerned; but Jennie's character and motives are of a higher, less selfish type than those of her predecessor, deserving, in all personal essentials, her stern and honest father's dying admission: "You are a good woman, Jennie, a good woman."

Yet at that moment Jennie was living

with Lester Kane without being married to him (a fact her father did not know) and was the mother of a nameless child. Her goodness lay in her tender motherhood and in her self-sacrifice, both for her parents and for the man who ought to have had the manliness to marry her, but had not. She was one of those soft, yielding, childlike women whose deepest need is to have affection and to give to those she loves. She was sinning against society—a fact the author might have made clearer than he does—while she yet remained unspoiled in heart.

In its larger lines the book is an imposing drama of the hopeless struggle of honest poverty against dominating wealth, but Mr. Dreiser leaves that looming in the background and concentrates our attention upon the two or three individuals whose faults and virtues are contorted into unexpected shapes by the impact of these social and economic forces. All the large events of the latter half of the story take place in Chicago. Not since "The Pit" has this city been the scene of a novel of equal caliber.

Jennie is the oldest daughter of a poor German glass worker in Columbus, Ohio, and the story opens upon a scene of dire want in the Gerhardt household. The girl's first downfall is at the hands of a senator who helps the family and means to marry her, but dies and leaves her disgraced. The main story, however, has to do with her relations with Lester Kane, member of a wealthy Cleveland family of carriage manufacturers, with an office in Chicago.

Lester is as vividly depicted and analyzed as Jennie herself. A strong man, unmoral, ruthless in a way, yet kind, generous and considerate in other ways; a man forceful, stubborn, dominant, yet at heart a drifter, he typifies a large class of the business masters who are shaping American affairs at the present moment.

In many thoughtful passages Mr. Dreiser is a philosophical realist, following the method, though not the manner, of George Meredith. In the main, however, he is a pure realist after the style of Hardy; indeed, "Jennie Gerhardt" is in some respects an American "Tess of the D'Urbervilles," though it is calmer, less tragic—and more absolutely true to life. The influence of Balzac, of course, is apparent in Mr. Dreiser's method and rather hopeless philosophy, but still more marked is the influence of Flaubert's "Madame Bovary," with its stippled pictures and psychological analysis. "Jennie Gerhardt" is not as great a novel as "Madame Bovary"—nor as unpleasant —but every character in it is alive and amazingly natural in every word and gesture.

The extreme simplicity of the author's style has a somewhat banal effect in the first chapters, and toward the end he strikes a discordant note with a hint of "new thought" mysticism, which consorts ill with the stark realism of the rest of the book; but the fact remains that the novel leaves a powerful impression, while Jennie lingers in one's memory almost as distinctly as Camille, Tess, Emma Bovary and Anna Karenina. Though written with admirable reticence, the book is not one for immature readers. It is one, however, likely to be widely discussed, condemned, extolled—and remembered.

Detroit *Free Press*, November 4, 1911.

The author of "Sister Carrie," a story of sordid, sorrowful lives and of woman's downfall, writes another powerful but sad story in this biography of Jennie Gerhardt. . . . The author reads no moral into his book; he simply tolls a straightforward story, repugnant to all our ideals and standards—as "Sister Carrie" was—and yet one that has been lived many times and will be lived many times more. It is not a book one enjoys, it is too bald and naked, yet there is nothing sensational in it. There is simply no need that it should have been written. It can do no good; it may do harm, for in spite of Jennie's immoral life, we can hardly condemn her as unmoral.

Frederic Blount Warren. New York *Telegraph*, November 5, 1911.

That an American author should write a novel containing no germ of the terrible literary disease known as "adjectivitis" affords sufficient excuse for dragging him forth that his fellow men may gaze upon him in all his bold shamelessness.

Theodore Dreiser has done this. He has written "Jennie Gerhardt," which the Harpers have published. In the months to come you will hear much about Jennie Gerhardt. There will be sharp divisions of opinion over her. Already one critic usually noted for his rationalism has thrown discretion to the winds and termed it the greatest novel ever written in America. In this he is wrong, though he has justification for his enthusiasm.

In point of literary craftsmanship Mr. Dreiser has produced a book that will make him a permanent reputation. Without knowing what books have contributed to his literary diversions, a reviewer would infer that he had kept a faithful eye upon the Germanic authors, rather than the French. He is even more direct than Sudermann, and his characters in this new novel represent themselves most of the time and their author rarely ever. He is less florid than Hauptmann and less given to repetition.

"Jennie Gerhardt" gives us an accurate, painstaking picture of a life, though it cannot be said that it portrays many lives. In New York or any of the larger cities we are familiar with a type known as the "kept" woman. In ratio to the population of this or any other city she represents but a minute fraction of 1 percent of the total population. There will be many persons who will differ over the propriety of making her the central figure in a novel, since she is such an infinitesimally small social unit. . . .

In time it is fair to expect that Mr. Dreiser will write the big story that is in him. He will not find one fair book reviewer ready to belittle the skill and ability he has shown in the writing of this work, but he ought to choose a bigger theme than the story of a kept woman.

Elia W. Peattie. Chicago *Tribune*, November 11, 1911.

Theodore Dreiser, having emerged from the chaste precincts of the Butterick Publishing company—where, indeed, he bore something of the appearance of a pirate selling ribbons—has written his second novel "JENNIE GERHARDT." The memory of his first book "Sister Carrie" had persisted through many years in spite of the troubled career of that fictional venture and it is with expectation of reading a significant story that "Jennie Gerhardt" is opened.

It strikes one upon perusal as bearing a certain resemblance to a number of memorable stories—to "Esther Waters," by George More; to "Tess of the D'Urbervilles," by Thomas Hardy; and to "Hilda Lessways," by Arnold Bennett. It is, indeed, a tepid and completely modern version of the Faust story. But there are two Fausts, neither of them interesting, and the Gretchen remains sane and thrifty and grows a trifle stout.

Gretchen, otherwise Jennie Gerhardt, had—inevitably—golden braids coiled about her head. Her eyes were blue and childish; her face dewy and provocative. She was the eldest child of a glass blower who has six children and who was bitterly poor. Jennie was a loving soul with poor powers of reflection. She had no more resistance than a down pillow and was the easy and immediate prey of the two men—both men of wealth and position, who made love to her. Oddly enough, they made love precisely alike. They saw Jennie and accosted her with: "Girl, you are mine." And she is. Nothing could be easier. She loves them both; accepts money from each of them, even at the beginning of her acquaintance, and lavishes this money upon her desperately hard pushed family at hand.

Mr. Dreiser means to convey the idea that the girl is born with the brooding mother passion; that to provide for her loved ones is her first instinct; that, having nothing else to sell, she sells her little white self; that she remains untroubled by remorse because her soul was suffused with love, and that at the last, when one paramour was in his grave and the other had decently pensioned her and married another woman, finding her tenderness and instinct for providence still unappeased, she adopted two orphan children and gave them the rich remainders of her heart.

But a book must be judged by the impression it leaves upon the mind, and judged by this standard, Mr. Dreiser's book falls short of what might have been expected of him. That he has had great literary models before him, that he possesses artistic courage beyond most American writers, I would be the last to deny. But his heavy and carnal men, his fluffy little sofa cushion of a woman, his detailed account of offensive amours, pall at last. It is really difficult to feel grieved over a plump little lady who settles down on an investment of a hundred thousand or two.

It was not so that Tess did; not so that Gretchen did. Their love was as a flame which purified while it consumed. Mannon Lescaut was as a wandering star that burst into flame in midair. . . .

" 'Jennie Gerhardt' a Great Book." Kansas City *Post*, November 9, 1911.

"Jennie Gerhardt," by Theodore Dreiser, published by Harpers, is a great big book by a great big man. For nine years the literary world has been awaiting the publication of "Jennie Gerhardt" and now that it is out the reviewers and critics proclaim it the greatest novel of a generation. And they are not far from being right. "Jennie Gerhardt" is the life story of the daughter of a German glass blower. Being a story of life there is no plot and to tell the nature of the contents would be to tell the story. The book takes hold in the very first pages and moves forcefully and resistlessly through each succeeding chapter and time and again the reader will close the book for a minute as the force of it strikes him in its quiet dramatic intensity and he will bite his lips to hold back the burst of feeling it arouses. . . .

"Jennie Gerhardt, one of the Most Distinctive Novels of the Year." San Francisco *Evening Bulletin*, November 18, 1911.

Among the hundreds of novels published each year there are a very few that stand out distinctly—very few indeed, which will live in the memory of the reader; therefore, such a story as Theodore Dreiser's "Jennie Gerhardt" may be justly regarded as one of the rare exceptions. Here is a novel that will not only hold your "undivided attention," but its heroine cannot fail to enlist your sympathy, even though you may possess certain Puritanical ideas concerning morality. In the usual sense of the term, Jennie Gerhardt is immoral. It is well to make this frank admission at the outset, lest someone should make her acquaintance through this review and thus be inexpressibly shocked. There are those who might leave Jennie at the beginning of the story, for fear of contamination, yet it is safe to say that the great majority will recognize her whole-souled, generous nature, even though she breaks the moral code, and will be quite ready to sympathize with the girl, whose innocence proves her downfall, yet whose unselfishness and womanly sweetness make her a truly lovable character.

Mr. Dreiser has done his work well. There is no evidence of haste in the building of his story. The people he has created live and breathe, move and have being. One has no doubt of their human qualities, and fiction has never presented a more lifelike picture than that of Jennie Gerhardt. . . .

Mr. Dreiser is an author who "says things."

While he may jar one's notions of propriety at times, one is forced to pause and reflect and mayhap wonder if our moral code is based on equity and justice as it affects the lives of those caught in the chains of circumstances. "Jennie Gerhardt" is a novel that will make you think.

"Theodore Dreiser's Second Novel." New Orleans *Times-Democrat,* November 19, 1911.

It is more than a decade since Theodore Dreiser's remarkable book, "Sister Carrie," appeared, and was immediately smothered under a "conspiracy of silence." But, as another proof that truth crushed to earth will rise again, the book still lived, and found a few appreciative readers. Now comes his second novel, "Jennie Gerhardt," which, while it has no episode so powerful as the recounting, in "Sister Carrie," of the downward career of Hurstwood, is yet a more finished and coherent piece of work. . . .

In the character of Jennie, Mr. Dreiser has depicted a woman who remained honest in the midst of an irregular position, though he does not bedeck the circumstances of the case with romance or sentimentality. There was nothing of the wanton about Jennie. Her loss of virtue was due to the accident of her helpless poverty, not to any native bent towards vice; and the author makes us recognize what is the truth,—that we cannot place in one class all women who have "fallen," as the phrase is. Such a woman as Jennie, being by nature sincere and loyal, will remain as true to the man she loves as though there were some legal bond between them. In her heart, he is her husband. . . . Let no one turn to "Jennie Gerhardt" with the expectation of finding scenes of passion. The author is essentially reticent in dealing with the great facts of life. Though he has no graces of style,—in fact, his phraseology is sometimes absolutely crude,—the story seems somehow told in the manner that suits it. In its truth, simplicity and sobriety, "Jennie Gerhardt" is a remarkable book.

"Jennie Gerhardt On a Big Canvas." New York *Times Book Review,* November 19, 1911, p. 728.

. . . [Dreiser's method] is remarkable for the utter lack of artificial carpentry of modern letter-craft. It abhors overemphasis with almost the same cloister severity of Nature's hatred for void. There is no display of cleverness one can resent; not even the gilding of slang and brogue, which is not quite as precious as diamonds and rubies in these our glorious catch-as-catch-can days of literary industry.

I do not say that the author is the master of the art that was Flaubert's or Tolstoi's. But, honestly, do not "Sister Carrie" and this present new novel, "Jennie Gerhardt"—for it is a novel, not by courtesy—make one think of the works of Russian and French painters of life? And that fact alone is a rather far cry from the boast of some of the best sellers as we all know.

Neither is the author a finished stylist in prose. His pages do not even recall those of Daudet or of Anatole France.

"I want a canvas big as the back of a church, you know," he told me one day.

He deals in big things bigly. If he does

not "chisel like a jeweler" he certainly "builds like a giant."

"Jennie Gerhardt" is not a "gem." It is, in reality, a chunk cut out of life of today, and the author cuts it out with no pink, manicured hands. He must have sailed in like the far-famed and very old Chinese Panku who chopped out the sun, the moon, and the earth and the rest of the universe with his sledge hammer. Perhaps I am a bit off in comparing Theodore Dreiser to the old gentleman of China. The comparison, which, as usual, is odious, holds nevertheless one point good—that both the Chinese author of the universe and the author of Jennie went at their jobs with about the equal absence of false modesty, with the equal amount of courage.

It is a naked picture, this story of Jennie, but no one can for a moment question that the real life about us is much more naked than the story. For in spite of all the broad, and sometimes rugged, portrayal it is clothed with much art. . . .

Peoria [Ill.] *Herald-Transcript*, November 19, 1911.

. . . Mr. Dreiser's novel shows a woman's heart in the midst of a broad picture of modern life which is full of contrasts and of vivid characters—the life of rich and poor, the factory and the magnate, the social butterfly and the drudge, the stern fanatic and the epicurean. It is not only Jennie who lives with us, but also her brooding father and contrasting types of men and women following out a mysterious destiny.

It is a book which does not preach a moral, but makes one felt—a moral dealing with questions actively in our minds today. It is a book of humanity—of real men and women. Mr. Dreiser's manuscript has been read by many men and women, both professional, literateurs and others. In not one single instance has the reading failed to elict the tribute of absorbed interest and enthusiastic praise.

Dallas [Tex.] *News*, November 20, 1911.

"You're sweet, all right, but you need courage and defiance." In these words Jennie's lover sums up her character, and so she will appear to the reader. She is not unmoral; she knows the right, and left to herself would follow it. She is not immoral, in spite of the fact that her life is lived contrary to social conventions. She simply yields to the stronger will, to force of circumstances, to the pressure of poverty, to the dire extremity of a family buffeted by relentless fate. It is a sad story, powerfully told. Mr. Dreiser is a disciple of the Russian school of fiction, and paints in detail. One may well question the ethics of the revelation. Though he presents life in a big, masterly way that rings true, one feels that there is nothing gained when all is said—only a feeling of hopeless depression that such things can be. It is like gazing helplessly at humanity being tortured.

Waterbury [Conn.] *Democrat*, November 25, 1911.

"Jennie Gerhardt" is the best book from the facile pen of Mr. Dreiser since he wrote his famous book "Sister Carrie." No end of time and preparation have been expended by the popular author on this book to make it a success. It deals with the life story of Jennie, who is unselfish, sweet and refined, but who has an unsatiable desire for affection. However, as the rule goes Jennie meets with a disastrous end. She loses the man she loves and he having married a girl whom he thought in his own station of life is bitterly disappointed by this butterfly woman. Eventually he yearns for Jennie, his first love and just before he answers the trumpet's call, he sends for Jennie, who with unabating devotion even to the end comes and comforts him in his last hours. This story full of pathos deals with the ups and downs of the rich and poor contrasted under various circumstances. It takes in a most broad scope, from the factory to the drawing room, and describes in minute detail the life of both the poorest and the richest in the land. "Jennie Gerhardt" is a book which leaves an after taste in the mind of the reader and forces him to look much more humanely upon poor, weak, frail mankind.

New Haven [Conn.] *Courier*, November 25, 1911.

Theodore Dreiser, whose remarkable novel, "Sister Carrie," published a few years ago, created a sensation, and was frowned upon occasionally by public libraries as unfit, and proclaimed by many critics as a literary achievement of surpassing merit, has, after a long silence, produced another novel of great power in his "Jennie Gerhardt." Like his "Sister Carrie," it is highly realistic. It is no problem story; it points no moral, although the lesson to be drawn is obvious. It is simply a case of straight, simple, but powerful, story telling. It gives a strong picture of modern life, with its contrasts—the life of the meritorius rich and the poor, honest, struggling factory worker and the board of directors, the social butterfly and the judge. While the bursts of eulogy the work has evoked in a few instances are extravagant, the great artistic merits of the book are apparent, and are recognized by leading authorities, both here and abroad. . . .

Washington *Evening Star*, November 25, 1911.

The reader closes this book strengthened in her belief this world is no place for women. Youth, beauty, innocence and poverty make a complex upon which life bears brutally and irresistibly. Charles Dickens could not have shown the Spartan resistance that Theodore Dreiser here maintains toward his subject. Had Dickens written the story of Jennie Gerhardt time and again would he have sent her from the stage that he himself might take it to make impassioned pleas for her or to hurl maledictions upon a world that could produce a Jennie Gerhardt. But Mr. Dreiser, behind the scenes, takes no concern save to spread his story in the pattern of exact truth. With rare fidelity to the character that he has set —that of a good, unselfish and beautiful girl; with complete knowledge of human nature, both in the individual man and in the whole worldly lump of men named society; with never a turn toward overstress nor any single move made for effect alone, the true and tragic story grows in the exact similitude of life. At its close one cries, out of an absorbing urgency to help: "Everybody must read this book!" Then in a minute one settles back. What is the use? Who can help Jennie Gerhardt? No one. Men cannot; their help always hurts. Women will not. In 10,000 years from now, Mr. Dreiser, when the animosities of sex, mayhap, are somewhat mollified, put out this book again. Then we shall see what can be done for your Jennie Gerhardts.

Calvin Winter. "Theodore Dreiser's 'Jennie Gerhardt.' " *Bookman,* 34 (December 1911), 432–434.

Readers familiar with modern Italian fiction are aware that several years ago Giovanni Verga, author of *Cavalleria Rusticana,* planned a series of five novels which, while unrelated in theme, social environment or caste of characters, were nevertheless grouped under one comprehensive title, *The Vanquished,* and had in common this basic idea, that in all the different social strata there seem to be certain individuals and certain families that, while apparently as well fitted as the others for survival, are nevertheless doomed in advance to failure, destined to suffer a slow and inevitable disintegration. Mr. Theodore Dreiser has nowhere specifically expressed any similar social or artistic creed; and yet, in reading his *Jennie Gerhardt,* one's thoughts inevitably go back to Verga's doctrine of *The Vanquished;* in following the slow breaking up of the Gerhardt family, we see again in memory the dissolution as a social unit of Verga's *I Malavoglia,* and realize that, however far apart these two authors may be in the theory and practice of their art, they have a rather curious mental kinship in their outlook upon life.

Jennie Gerhardt is a novel possessing an interest outside and beyond the specific story it has to tell; it contains an answer to the not unimportant question raised by Mr. Dreiser's earlier volume, *Sister Carrie,* "What are the mental and moral measurements of this author? Has he reached the limits of his powers, or is he destined to go further, much further, into the higher altitudes of fiction?" The question is an interesting one because there can be little doubt that if the world at large had discovered promptly, instead of after a delay of nearly seven years, that *Sister Carrie* was a volume of some importance, we should not only have had *Jennie Gerhardt* a decade sooner, but other volumes besides of similar substance and intent.

A careful reading of *Jennie Gerhardt* is consoling to this extent: it does away with the illusion that Mr. Dreiser has or ever had much greater altitudes to scale; it shows more fully than his earlier book the whole gamut of his powers and his limitations; it is, of the two, a more ambitious effort, a more complex picture drawn on a wider canvas,—and its defects are proportionately more numerous and more apparent. Both books are stamped with a certain crudity, both in literary style and in the specific things which certain characters say and do: over and over again the reader finds himself involuntarily echoing Assessor Brack's familiar expostulation, "But people don't do such things!" And because *Jennie Gerhardt* has a more crowded canvas than *Sister Carrie;* because also, in a measure, certain characters are higher up in the social scale, the things that people do not do stand out rather more frequently and more obviously.

Nevertheless, *Jennie Gerhardt* is a rather big book,—not a great book, not a book worthy to stand,—as an enthusiastic English reviewer once said of its predecessor,—on a shelf between *Madame Bovary* and *Nana;* but a big book, undeniably, full of a rugged sincerity, a fearless devotion to the truth, and undisguised pity for the impotence of human nature under its double handicap of heredity and environment.

Jennie Gerhardt is one of those novels of which it is extremely hard to give the right sort of impression in a review, without letting the review run to altogether disproportionate length, because the specific story that it has to tell is one which necessitates a possession of all the facts before one may judge it fairly. In this respect it resembles life,—and the judgment of the hasty reader, who merely skims its pages, will also resemble the hasty judgments which in real life are passed upon the human derelicts that from time to time pass for a moment under our notice. Full knowledge means full sympathy, Mr. Dreiser would seem to say,—and to this end he multiplies little details unweariedly, endlessly, until there is at least one character in the story whom we know with something approaching the intimacy with which we know ourselves. And since this particular character is one foredoomed to be swept under in the current of life, the pervading atmosphere of the book is, as in Arnold Bennett's *Clayhanger,* a wonderfully sustained sense of greyness, a fatalistic acceptance of the inevitability of human tragedy.

Mr. Dreiser himself has defined his new volume as "the life story of a woman who craved affection." Jennie and Carrie, in the opening chapters of the respective volumes, are sisters in misfortune and in weakness; both have been born to a life of toil and temptation; both of them hunger for something different; and both of them, when temptation comes, succumb to it. But from this point onward the two stories are a whole world apart. And the difference lies in the characters of the two heroines who, if all womankind could for the sake of convenience be divided into two groups, would stand as representatives of these opposite types, the woman whose pleasure lies in receiving, and the woman whose joy it is to give. Carrie Meeber lived for herself alone. She yielded to temptation, not through love, or gratitude, or because it was a means toward helping others, but simply because she craved a winter coat, new shoes, gloves and ribbons, the petty vanities of a young woman who has awakened to a realization that she is good to look upon. Jennie Gerhardt has the inborn instinct of motherhood; she must have, always, something or somebody to whom she may make sacrifice. In her case, it is no vulgar, flashy drummer who brings temptation through appeal to her sex or her vanity, but a man of importance, a mature and dignified United States Senator, whose attentions mean the lifting of a cloud of despair from the shoulders of an overworked mother and a sick father, food and clothing for half a dozen needy brothers and sisters. The senator has been attracted by the girl's beauty while staying at a hotel in which she is employed; and at first his interest in her is, or at least he cheats himself into thinking that it is, merely paternal. It is Jennie's own gratitude, when the senator crowns his many kindnesses by saving her brother from prison, that brings about the initial tragedy of her life. And when, shortly afterward, the senator dies, and Jennie finds herself facing the world single-handed, with the added burden of a nameless child, she is still unchanged, still the woman who will always pay in full for the privilege of a kind word, always sacrifice herself to the uttermost for the sake of those who are dear to her.

The main substance of Jennie's story, however, deals with that part of her life which follows upon the death of the senator, and after another man comes into her life, to whom she is able to give not merely gratitude but a mature woman's love,—the one and only love of her life. That a girl like Jennie could throughout a series of years live more or less openly with a man of such social and financial prominence as Lester Kane, travel with him as his wife, visit fashionable summer resorts in his company, and finally take a house in one of the city suburbs and be for a time on terms of intimacy with the neighbours, to whom she is known as Mrs. Kane,—all of this without exciting gossip, or arousing suspicions, or disturbing the tranquillity of her austere old father, who at this time lives with her,—is almost too much of a tax upon the reader's credulity. But, if we accept the situation, then the underlying tragedy of it, the abiding sense that it was foredoomed not to last, the daily lengthening shadow of the inevitable sacrifice she must sooner or later make for the best good of the man she loves,—all this is given to us with an assured touch, showing with quite wonderful insight how relentlessly the consequences of human errors tread on one another's heels. Over and over the story of Jennie makes the reader's heart ache with the helpless pity of it all. Yet at the same time, and this is perhaps the highest tribute that can be paid to Mr. Dreiser, and in a measure offsets the strictures and reservations of an earlier paragraph,—it never occurs to the reader to ask, "Oh, why did he do it? Why was he so needlessly cruel?" One feels, on the contrary, that the cruelty in this book is not of Mr. Dreiser's making; it is the cruelty of life.

" 'Jennie Gerhardt' Is Sordid Realism." Philadelphia *Press*, December 2, 1911.

From a perusal of his new book, "Jennie Gerhardt," one might well imagine that Theodore Dreiser has reached that time of life when to some temperaments the whole scheme of things as they are appears simply the result of a gigantic mistake, due perhaps to the slipping of a cog in the machinery of the universe, and significant of nothing. An atmosphere of pessimism pervades the story that is even more intense than in the author's former work, "Sister Carrie," published several years ago and appreciated by a few. Mr. Dreiser evidently wishes to convey the idea that life is but a useless thing, inconsiderable in its brief duration, and inconsequent in its outcome. He tears down, but offers nothing in place of what he destroys; criticises without suggesting; and writes of grim realities in such a manner as to leave a nasty after taste in the mind of his reader. In his earlier work Mr. Dreiser evinced a stern dissatisfaction at the bitter sordidness of life as he found it, but without the extreme note of despair for better things found in "Jennie Gerhardt." Indeed, it appears that this writer is imbued with Schopenhauer's doctrine to the effect that nothing is positive but pain; and that happiness is negative, and can only be measured by the relative absence of suffering. . . .

Here we have a sordid enough tale, told in a manner of almost brutal simplicity and realism. Suffering is depicted in all of its grim detail, from the first page wherein are set down the trials through which Jennie's family pass in their efforts to obtain enough bread, until the final chapter, when we leave Jennie in empty unhappiness. The author is successful in his picturing of the nasty side of life as it is, but he is not a literary artist, and consequently his work falls short of being satisfying. Other pessimistic novels, dealing with the miseries of an ordinary life, have been written without a painful sacrifice of art. Indeed, De Maupassant's "Une Vie," which is certainly pessimistic enough in tone, is considered one of the most artistic of his works. But in Mr. Dreiser's book there is none of that delicacy of handling of an unpleasant subject, which in the hands of a writer possessing more literary facility would have made a truly powerful novel.

San Francisco *Chronicle*, December 3, 1911.

Admirers of "Sister Carrie," and they are legion, will find "Jennie Gerhardt" all that they had a right to expect. Theodore Dreiser has the happy knack of taking the best out of half a dozen good novels and piecing them together in a way that never suggests sufficient of any particular source to arouse the suspicion of plagiarism. As a matter of fact, he does not plagiarize, but rather remembers too much and too vividly. One is frequently reminded of "Esther Waters," George Moore's heroine, who was wooed by a parson and a bookmaker, but who wanted a husband who was not all parson and not all bookmaker, and yet beyond Moore's influence it cannot be said that any particular parts of "Esther Waters" or "Evelyn Innes" are incorporated in "Jennie Gerhardt." However, if we could treat Dreiser as the higher criticism has treated Shakespeare and trace each borrowing to its source, he would be none the less Dreiser. Better a brilliant composite than a dull original all of a piece. Then, again, apart from the characters and situations, our author possesses that rare distinction of saying many things of his own in a way of his own. The style has many blemishes, but they are not so pronounced as to be unpleasing. And his realism, though at times bordering on the brutal, generally gives the impression of having emanated from one who, in the language of Gilbert, hesitates to be very terrible. All of which says nothing very definite about Jennie, the poor, hard-working girl of Columbus, O., who is loved first by a Senator, who dies before the child is born or the marriage ceremony performed, and then by a youth penalized for his affection by disinheritance. The fact that she accepts money from both her lovers may be taken as argument against the heroine, but, on the other hand, she should be credited with spending the coin upon her poor relations. In a final note "In Passing," the author warmly defends Jennie, who loved, and, loving, gave. "This daughter of the poor, born into the rush and hurry of a clamant world—a civilization, so called—eager to possess itself of shows and chattels." This defense is both defective art and defective ethics. Jennie acted logically in accordance with her particular nature, and not because she was a daughter of the poor. Daughters of the poor who have not her particular type of nature are under no compulsion to follow her particular course of conduct.

Baltimore *Evening News*, December 5, 1911.

To read a small part of "Jennie Gerhardt," by Theodore Dreiser, is to read it all, in that there is no new aspect of life here, either in its individual nature or human nature generally. "Jennie Gerhardt" is the non-creative photograph of the same pretty, weak, receptive young woman who has figured in countless novels of "Life" since books began to be written. While accurately told, nothing more can be said for the book, as from beginning to end there is no noble philosophy, no outlook, no manliness in the man's character. It is the well-known story of a weak and pretty girl who, for her family's sake and because of dire poverty, yields to those who work upon her will. No fresh gleam of insight relieves it, nor any spiritual sense. Jennie's father dies, her mother dies, her child dies, and finally, while her lover is dying, the words put in his mouth by the author show without any need of comment the book's lesson—a lazy and materialistic lesson it is: "After all," says this man, who has lived as he wished to live, "life is more or less of a farce. It's a silly show. . . . it doesn't appear that integrity has much to do with it." If the book can be said to hold any philosophy, this decadent expresses it.

Independent, 71 (December 7, 1911), 1267.

This story of a beautiful young girl who begins life as a scrub-woman, will remind the reader, curiously, of many other heroines. Moore's Esther Waters was also a servant girl, and Zangwill's "Merely Mary Ann" scrubbed floors and stairways for her living, but Jennie Gerhardt resembles them distantly. Lily in Suderman's "Song of Songs" has much of Jennie's pathetic gentleness of nature, making each the easy prey of better instructed selfishness. DuMaurier's "Trilby," too, had so little of self in her makeup that she lacked the protection of self-respect. Jennie's story of self-forgetful sacrifice is told with the baldest simplicity, with no tragic hightening of the situation. It is like a gray day—all the landscape keyed low, and not a gleam of cheerful sunlight anywhere. It has the sort of fatalism which grows out of character. Jennie is weak and gentle, with a passion for self-immolation, and that makes her tragedy not a red tragedy of hate nor a black one of despair, but the gray commonplace one of a woman whom the world has cast out as a sinner, yet who never feels herself quite vile, because her impulse had always been to love and to serve those around her. Poor Jennie is morbidly grateful to those who help her family, and she does not stop to scrutinize the motives of her benefactors. She is a dreamer, too, living in a world of her own—which was necessary if she were to live at all. Two men make her the victim of her own pity and generosity; yet, tho they are admittedly evil, the author sees each situation from their point of view, so calmly that he seems unduly cold-blooded. We miss the warm indignation that should fire his heart at sight of their cruelty. Several of the characters in summing up Jennie say: "She is a good woman," but we wonder if so much soft-heartedness is really "good." Jennie's wretched story might have been so different if at any crisis of it she had had more sense and less sweetness. The novel begins with sorrow and ends with an interrogation. The lives it has passed in review seem all so futile and meaningless. There is no lift to the spirit, as when we read of suffering bravely borne to some end, however dimly apprehended. The author is either a fool or a genius. At first we were annoyed by his failure to make the most of his situations, and by his repeatedly missing, apparently thru mere stupidity, opportunities for fine dramatic climaxes. But gradually the possibility dawned upon us that the author was deliberately keeping down the emotional tone and that he was exercising as great art in avoiding sensational scenes as other authors do in contriving them.

New York *Evening Mail*, December 9, 1911.

Theodore Dreiser's novel, "Jennie Gerhardt," is a very unusual American story. It is unusual in its simplicity, its naturalness, its deliberation, its promotion of plain truth above every consideration of artifice. It is unusual also in its refusal to make its bad people wholly bad, or its good people purely good. . . .

"Jennie Gerhardt" is not "good art." Mr. Dreiser's homely style of narration is bald and dry. A little fire—a little something internal and subjective to Dreiser—would be appreciated now and again. Not infrequently the author employs the cant phrases of newspaper reporting. No matter; his novel is so strangely true to the whole life which he has depicted, so philosophically sound, so calmly reserved, so natural, that it is entitled to the wide attention that it has received.

"Jennie Gerhardt" is not a moral book in the Sunday school sense, but it is broadly moral nevertheless. No girl will be tempted to follow Jennie's example by this narration of her experiences. She has a hard life, with very little happiness in it. The picture of Jennie's poor old father, the German immigrant, is most pathetic and admirable. He is real and true in every line, from his wrath at the first to his tame submission at the last.

Utica [N.Y.] *Press*, December 15, 1911.

. . . The novel is intended to tell, and doubtless it does tell with considerable accuracy, the temptations which attractive girls who are poor have to contend with and the temptations they meet. At best it is not a pleasant story. It is exceedingly well written and indeed is one of the novels which can be characterized as strong. The fault which suggests itself at once is that it glosses over the immorality which it narrates and the heroine leads a perfectly happy, comfortable, enjoyable life, attended by disappointment, to be sure, but the sins of all concerned are not emphasized as sins. While social evil is not extolled, it is not condemned, and no one would claim that it teaches a moral with any great force. While the story may be fascinating in a way, it can afford the reader little or no pleasure other than the admiration excited for its literary merit.

New York *Press*, December 23, 1911.

Several years ago Theodore Dreiser wrote a realistic novel, in the manner of Zola at his worst, called "Sister Carrie." It suffered the unusual experience, for an American work of fiction, of being suppressed before publication, although subsequently Dreiser had it published through another house. Nothing could well have been more true to life than the tale of Sister Carrie, who was a young woman that persons much broader than Mrs. Grundy would not approve of. Yet few stories could be drearier than that tale or more repellent in its groveling in the gutter of life. One thing at least this author learned out of that experience, and that was if you want a book to sell in this country you have to eliminate the "strong" scenes. And so in "Jennie Gerhardt," the sweet narrative of the career of a young woman with absolutely no strength to withstand the passions of men, he glosses over the scene of his heroine's ruin with a quotation from an English classic. This photographic narrative of the career of a young woman who puts herself beyond the pale of ordinary life, photographic except where past experience taught the author to fog his plates and be smugly proper and vague, has been talked of as "the greatest American novel in years." This is literary bravado of the cheapest sort. As a matter of fact, the story is gross in matter and morals, it is written in indifferently bad English, and it is inartistic for the reasons we have pointed out. No, Theodore Dreiser's shabby story will not wipe out readers' memories of "Silas Lapham," "Through One Administration," "A Little Journey in the World," nor "The Awakening of Helena Richie."

New York *Call*, December 24, 1911.

This is the story of a daughter of the proletariat whose moral downfall is occasioned by poverty. That is the one great fact that should recommend the book to Socialist readers. It is the terrible economic struggle of her family, to whom she is devoted, that places her in the position where she is victimized by

Rich Man No. 1, the United States Senator.

Jennie's father is a glassblower, who, when the story opens, had for some time been without a job through illness. Jennie, aged 18, is the oldest of six children. There is no food and no clothing and no coal in the home and Mrs. Gerhardt takes Jennie to see if they can't find work in one of the hotels of their city. Among other things, they get Senator Brander's washing to do. Jennie, who is trusting and innocent, gentle, refined and pretty, calls at the Senator's room for his wash and returns it to him. And that is the beginning of the end.

The Senator, who is a kind-hearted man, according to bourgeois and capitalist ideals, showers money on Jennie's poverty-stricken family, thereby winning the warm gratitude of Jennie, which she expresses by yielding to his passion.

It is true, he says he intends to educate her and marry her, but since she is only a working class girl, he does not consider the formality of the wedding ring necessary before entering in the marriage relation with her.

Imagine a United States Senator "engaged" to a girl of his own social sphere and forcing himself upon her before the marriage ceremony has been duly performed! But, of course, there are no classes in "democratic" America.

Well, the Senator dies suddenly before he has a chance to marry Jennie, leaving her pregnant. Her father, a reactionary German, of the stern Luthern type who never so much as heard of the class struggle, puts her out of the house.

The comfort enjoyed by the family through the Senator's bounty having ceased, economic necessity drives the family apart, and with the father gone, Jennie leaves her baby with her mother and goes to another city with one of her brothers to find work. On the strength of their meager wages, the family follows them and are soon in a condition of the direst poverty once more.

Now appears Rich Man No. 2, who visits in the house where Jennie ie employed as maid at $4 a week. He wants her and must have her. That's all there is to it. Why, what else can there be? Isn't he a millionaire and she a common girl of the lower classes? And, mind you, he knows nothing whatever of her former experience. The fact that she is of the proletariat is quite enough for him.

"You belong to me," he says in his very first conversation with her, "remember that. I've been looking for you, and we might as well understand each other right now."

Well, he promises a fine house and garden and plenty of money for her desperately poor family, and saying to herself that nobody would marry her now anyway, after her other experience, she agrees to become his mistress —for her family's sake.

This second man is also depicted as kind and generous to a fault. It certainly makes us blush for bourgeois standards of nobility. He is constantly overcome with surprise that Jennie is capable of big attitudes of utter unselfishness; that she loathes dress and show and loves all things refined as well as beauties of nature. "She is a 'good' woman," he keeps saying over and over again, each time in utter astonishment that so low a creature could exhibit virtues which should belong by rights to his class alone.

How he lives with her for years, thinking the world of her; how his family finally threaten to deprive him of his fortune if he will not take the necessary steps to rehabilitate himself in the eyes of "society" (nobody, of course, gives even the slightest thought to the rehabilitation of Jennie in the eyes of society); how, after all those years, he brutally leaves her and marries a fabulously wealthy woman of his own class; and how, on his death bed, he sends for Jennie and tells her that he should never have left her, but should have married her, as she is the only woman he ever really loved—all this we leave the prospective readers of this novel to find out for themselves.

The point of the book to be brought out—and it seems only the Socialist can do that, judging by the other reviews we have read—is that poverty, UNESCAPABLE POVERTY, was the whole cause of Jennie's wretched wasted life. The crux of the whole problem is expressed in the touching letter written by her to this man, when she decides to leave him for the sake of HIS future. She says:

". . . . I didn't see just how I was to get away from you. Papa was sick at home that time and there was hardly anything in the house to eat. We were all doing so poorly. My brother George didn't have good shoes and mamma was so worried. I have often thought, Lester, if mamma had not been compelled to worry so much she might be alive today. . . . You know you told me right away you would like to help my family, and I felt that maybe that would be the right thing to do. WE WERE SO TERRIBLY POOR."

The book is written throughout most simply and sympathetically. While it does not aim to teach or to solve, it should, however, make those points it seeks to make more vigorously. This is the great weakness of the book. It is too gentle and the result is that the average reader will not take away from it all that he could, were the book more tellingly and emphatically written.

The reason for this grave shortcoming is not hard to find. It is that the author took for his theme a subject of graver and deeper import than he knew, and that his understanding of it is not big enough or scientific enough to make his work of any permanent value.

As a sign of the times, however, and for the other reasons above stated, it is well worth a reading.

Chicago *Advance*, January, 1912.

—Theodore Dreiser has a way of heading up a book "Sister Carrie" or some other little sister and then sketching with a remarkably clever pen his male characters, while the leading lady does not exactly impress us with her reality. "Sister Carrie" by this author, made a strong impression because it told so forcibly of the awful downfall of a man and the rise to success of a rather ordinary type of a girl, a little soldier of the footlights. In his latest "little sister" installment, *Jennie Gerhardt,* Mr. Dreiser introduces us to a much less interesting female character. Jennie, another poor girl who manages to climb from the ranks of the poor and oppressed, to a good resting place on the golden ladder, which all women seem to be climbing or attempting to climb these days, does not convince the reader of her genuineness. She does not seem like a real person but the author's dream girl flitting through hardships, down the pages to wealth and opulence, which she cannot enjoy. But again in this book as in his other, Mr. Dreiser's men are sure men and the kind not hard to find along the everyday road. His leading male character is a rich man's son, and a rich man's son all right from start to finish no reader will deny. . . .

The book is full of tragedy and the cold heartlessness of the well-to-do and a feeling of sadness possesses the reader as he comes to the last page. The author's leading character does not impress us as do the women of some other writers.

Craftsman, January, 1912, p. 458.

"A Book of Humanity" is the subtitle of Theodore Dreiser's recent novel, "Jennie Gerhardt." Perhaps without meaning to, Mr. Dreiser has made a very interesting and subtle distinction between humanity and society. Evidently to present humanity truly and feelingly is in his mind a matter of understanding, sympathy, imagination. And without comment he seems to lead you to believe that this is a much more worth while occupation than to write of the little doings of society. For as Mr. Dreiser must know and as we all know, in the last analysis, society is but the crust which convention forms over humanity. And but little is known or understood of real humanity except as the crust is sometimes broken, through tragic upheavals, through the fire and the flood of sorrow and wretchedness. "Jennie Gerhardt" is unquestionably a more finished production than Theodore Dreiser's first novel, "Sister Carrie," and yet one still sees in the English papers and hears from the English critics the widest appreciation and sincerest understanding of the big quality which made "Sister Carrie" a book of international importance. William J. Locke, while in America, asked the writer why he (Locke) did not hear more in our literary circles of Theodore Dreiser. "In London," he said, "we consider 'Sister Carrie' the most significant American novel that has come to us. I do not mean," he continued, "of course, that it is the most perfect presentation of American life, because I do not know American life. But I am sure that it is as sincere an understanding of human conditions as could be presented of any life."

The plot of the story of "Jennie Gerhardt" is laid in Chicago, as was that of "Sister Carrie," a Chicago which Mr. Dreiser knows by heart. Eventually the story touches New York and foreign lands, but the bigness of its development depends upon the environment which Mr. Dreiser knew as a young man and boy. In "Jennie Gerhardt" as in "Sister Carrie" you have essentially the Teutonic type of woman. It is the old world Teuton who though transplanted has still the overwhelmingly feminine quality, the gentleness, the maternal instinct, the need of love and guidance. Both women led the unconventional life, not through love of unconventionality or display, or the dramatic phase of life, but through that far greater need, affection. In both instances there is almost always suffering in the lives of the women, and in the life of the bigger woman, *Jennie Gerhardt*, there is of course greater suffering. It is quite extraordinary how in this recent story, utterly without the sharper lights of melodrama, the deeper sympathies of the reader are illuminated. One reads from page to page with a certain dry-eyed sorrow, that the more flamboyant tragedy would not win. And the whole book is logical, the psychology true, and the sorrows which result from opposing society worked out with inevitability. The tragedies which come to *Jennie Gerhardt* are not those inevitably of her own temperament, except as tragedy must always follow weakness; they are rather the tragedies which come where society is not recognized quite heartily enough and bowed before quite humbly enough. In no part of her life was this kindly, friendly, conscientious woman other than unselfish, helpful, tender, devoted. But not having the dominant qualities which would force into channels of self-satisfaction the events of her life, others of less goodness were able to control her, while she in the long run alone paid for the wrong done to herself. And yet perhaps it is scarcely fair to say that she alone paid, for the man who put her out of his life for the sake of greater self-satisfaction slowly disintegrated from the time that her unselfish influence left his life, and the woman who forced the separation of *Jennie* from the man whom she loved, also disintegrated, as supreme selfishness and self-satisfaction must disintegrate. In fact, the development of every character is the development which a knowledge of human motives alone could make possible. These men and women progress or retrograde according to the very essentials of their own character. Mr. Dreiser does not build up puppets and talk through them and play with them, putting in their mouths risqué conversation which has no relation to their environment, but which means an appeal for the public and flamboyant advertising for the publisher. The people in this little book, the good, hard German father, the overworked, heartbroken German mother, the man of wealth, and with the deterrent weakness of inherited wealth, the working girls and the sad children, each one lives or dies through inherent characteristics, inescapably driven by inherited traits. Not only are the characters worn by contact with the hardness of life, but by contact with each other. It is indeed a presentation of real humanity, a closely woven, beautifully rounded, sincerely told story of the lives of very real people. The writer of this review has read the book twice without finding a false note. The emotion left is a sense of knowing life better and of seeing the great things of life more clearly, the same feeling that was evoked by the reading of Balzac's Comédie Humaine. And it is literary art of a high order that not only enlarges your knowledge of the fundamentals of life, but your vision of what such fundamentals should be.

"The Realism of Theodore Dreiser." *Metropolitan Magazine*, January, 1912.

MR. DREISER is one of the most sincere, serious, and restrained of American writers, and the reputation which he gained from his former novel is certain to be increased and widened by the one just published. "Jennie Gerhardt" is a much better piece of work than "Sister Carrie." The years have taught him to eliminate all that mass of verbal underbrush, the so-called effective, but really uninspiring and obstructive, detail, of which every follower of George Moore and Mr. Howells is enamoured when young, to the pitch of feeling it mysteriously inseparable from his mission to write the actual truth. Another pitfall he avoids, although not completely—unfortunately not in the particular instance where it was most important to do so; I mean the false supposition, or unconscious belief, that for fiction one person is as good a subject as another—that verity of treatment is the great thing and about all that counts. Jennie's father, with his stark heroism applied to a miserable hole-in-corner existence, his intimate, strong personal convictions, is an admirable example, and Lester Kane, whose character more words would be needed to describe, but who is distinctly a portrait, and an excellent one, of a very interesting sort of American man, is a still better example of the use of an artist's judgment in the selection of personages. But Jennie herself, the heroine, the figure upon whom are lavished the greatest pains, and upon whose final appeal to the sympathy of the reader the lasting worth of the story must depend, is insufficiently realized, at best suggesting a mere average type, with strikingly few traits of her own. It is as though the author, having called her feminine, and being absolutely assured in his own mind as to her predestined fate in a world where pretty daughters of the poor are eagerly disposed of in a certain way, ceased to think of her as an individual possessing an inner life and effective promptings of her own. He looks at her position most sensitively, but not at her, and the result is an unavoidable monotony and the absence of charm and vitality in certain portions of the story.

It is with no lack of admiration for Mr. Dreiser's method and spirit that this detraction is made. It would be impossible not to write what one thinks about a work of his. His method is the best for his purpose; perhaps nothing more. But his intention and spirit are things in themselves satisfying and noble.

J.B. Kerfoot. "The Antics of Maiden Aunts." *Life*, January 4, 1912.

. . .although the author of "Jennie Gerhardt" has not altogether outgrown the crudities that sometimes almost suggested illiteracy in the author of "Sister Carrie," the last trace of adolescent rancor and belligerent championship has departed from his attitude. He returns, from we know not what journeys of the spirit, to bring to us in this history of a technical outcast—a history so commonplace as almost to appear common, and so revealatory of reality as almost to seem like mere "realism"—the ultimate message of all travel—that true beauty often lies close at home, unnoticed, and that we often draw aside our maiden auntish skirts as we pass it—and the eternally restated message of art—that life's deepest meanings are often hidden from us by our ideas of life. But these messages are not spoken. They are implicit. And even to put them into words is perhaps to do the story an injustice. Let us rather say that in "Jennie Gerhardt" Mr. Dreiser has striven, with a simplicity of purpose that awkwardnesses of performance occasionally mar but never defeat, to place before us that most humdrum and homely, yet most romantic, of all histories and that most obscure yet most pregnant of all messages, the unbiased and unadorned story of human life.

Roswell Field. "Dreiser's Novel Nearly Great." Chicago *Examiner*, January 4, 1912.

. . ."Jennie Gerhart" [sic] narrowly escapes the distinction of classifying as a great story. Mr. Dreiser lacks the emotional quality so necessary to a work of distinguished merit. The fact that he writes as a most proficient stenographer rather than as a sympathetic observer is fatal to a description of life, however accurate the description may be. The leader pities Jennie with a sort of dumb pity, and reflects intelligently on the hardness of her lot and the pathos of her life, but at no time is he moved to any emotional fluttering or profound feeling. He is at all times interested but at no time stirred. He follows Jennie in her helpless subserviency to man's domination from Columbus to Cleveland, to New York, to Chicago, and on to her littleWisconsin haven. He knows that she is the innocent victim of a strange and relentless fate—for the author concedes to her all the virtues of innocence and right motive—but he is forced to study her as an abstract quantity, not as a concrete being, and at the last his only regret is that so good a girl should suffer so cruelly, the good girl being not Jennie, but any girl in Jennie's place. Such is the astonishing result of Dreiser's mechanical methods.

The entire absence of humor in the 425 pages seems only to intensify the sordidness of the story while, in the opinion of the realists, it may augment the realism.

At the best it is a pitiful tale, showing strength, cleverness of story-telling, and at the last an unwritten moral which would be spoiled by words. It is dramatic in its suggestion rather than its telling, absorbing more as a written report than as a moving chronicle of life, and it is entitled to consideration for the qualities it has, notwithstanding the vital qualities it lacks. Among the painstaking and earnest disciples of realism in its naked truth, the pitiless photographers and cold and relentless chroniclers, Theodore Dreiser is a distinguished force.

Minneapolis *Bellman*, January 6, 1912.

Theodore Dreisler's [sic] remarkable novel, "Jennie Gerhardt," reads curiously like the work of a foreigner translated into English. Indeed the book might have been written by a Gogol or a Dostoevsky, and we would not have lifted an eyebrow of inquiry. Stiff and awkward, the style has neither the smoothness nor the freedom of one who writes in his mother tongue. And the *milieu* in which the author has set his people is untouched with Americanism. Had he placed them in St. Petersburg, Berlin or Copenhagen, they would have fitted equally well into their surroundings, for though one of his heroes is an American United States senator, and the other a Chicago manufacturer, they are such admirably drawn types of a class of man who, in a sense, is the typical man of the world, that either might speak any tongue or claim any country and be accepted as true.

Nowadays, when a novelist sets out to tell the story of the character Mr. Dreisler has chosen, he has a purpose up his sleeve. He tells it to excite sympathy for the unfortunate or to suggest subtly the evil of wrongdoing, or he is deeply pessimistic and would show the hopelessness of a struggle against fate. Of course now and then there are decadents like the authors of "Madame Gervaisais," but generally even with Suderman and the realists, we know that they write with motive to prove a state of society.

In this brilliant book, which depicts the most hideous of situations, the aloofness of the author from passion, from prejudice, his power to show the man's side of the question (both men are "good fellows," though they do not pretend to be gentlemen), sets him in a category by himself. Jennie, a servant girl, ignorant, modest, loving her starved and wretched family with the utmost unselfishness and devotion, is no "Esther Walters." She is just poor and humble, and charming in her poverty, for she is the very embodiment of femininity. For herself poverty has no terrors; gladly would she have cooked, mended, watched, as wife and mother. Riches bewilder her; hers is the nest-making, home-creating soul. What she felt, "Sweet Alice" felt: "She blushed with delight when you gave her a smile and trembled with fear at your frown." . . .

Never is "Jennie Gerhardt" pleasant reading, but never is it commonplace, vulgar or dull. Even when treating of sordid conditions, or when treating of situations in which frankness of speech is necessary, the author's aloofness is felt. He is never one with his characters, but he sees them in the atmosphere in which they lie and he paints solidly. The story comes with great force. There is no trace of sentimentality or moral reflection. Lester has his code of honour, as Brander had his. Jennie would have been the ideal wife to either. Her affection was always maternal to her lovers, more maternal perhaps than that she first felt for her child; and to the type of man whom she attracted, this trait was her abiding charm—this, and her power to make them comfortable. One touch of the other quality, and she could have bent Lester's will to hers and taken the place she humbly craved.

In Mr. Dreisler's writing all notes of extravagance and weakness are absent. His is a presentation of life, not an interpretation. Interpretation is the reader's task. The author's facts are homely, almost vulgar, but the subjective side of the business has an extraordinary light.

"Current Fiction." *Nation*, 94 (January 11, 1912), 34–35.

In "Sister Carrie" Mr. Dreiser aspired to be an American Balzac; in "Jennie Gerhardt" he has contented himself with being an American Sudermann. Sister Carrie herself was the American equivalent of that debonair and amiable epitome of Parisian success, Rastignac; Jennie Gerhardt is a debrutalized Regina—a Regina intelligibly transposed into terms of American life. The cross-section of American society placed before us in "Sister Carrie" was fresh, containing types and relationships never before seriously recognized in an American novel without some display of phariseeism. It was handled without either squeamishness or effrontery, and from this suspension of moral judgment we hoped great things. From this present espousal of the perverted ideal of feminine character which naturalism has fathered in the earnest German mind, much less is to be hoped.

Docile, submissive, and exquisitely tender-hearted, physically beautiful and strong, Jennie Gerhardt is the perfection of passivity. Early in the story a definition of virtue is propounded which shall precisely fit this predestined victim of masculine selfishness—"virtue is the wishing well and the doing well unto others. Virtue is *that quality of generosity which offers itself willingly for another's serivce.*" Then, provided only that opportunity shall always coincide with some other exigent family plight—a brother arrested, the father incapacitated by accident—the sensual complaisance of the German immigrant's daughter easily assumes the guise of "generosity," or even of that sterner virtue, "self-sacrifice." Mother of an illegitimate child at eighteen, and subsequently the sharer for many years of a second illicit union, she steadily gathers strength and sweetness under the burden of her false position, and eventually emerges from those dubiously shadowed experiences with all the gentle dignity of self-abnegation. Even granting the "natural refinement" of which no American novelist has yet been rude enough to deprive a heroine, and which Mr. Dreiser has taken care to include in Jennie's equipment, we still mistrust this conclusion.

"Recent Fiction." *Dial,* 52 (February 16, 1912), 131–132.

To those who have read "Sister Carrie," Mr. Dreiser's new novel, "Jennie Gerhardt," will appear one of the more significant books of the year. It has the same homely quality, and exhibits the same type of realism, as the earlier work, and is infused with the same sort of quiet and deep human sympathy. It is the story of a woman, more sinned against than sinning, whose lot falls among the outcasts, yet who remains in most of the essentials a good woman, and whose errors, although technically serious, are attributable to circumstance and environment rather than to anything vicious in her nature. . . . This is a very moving story, gravely proceeding to what, given the conditions of the existing social order, is its only possible logical termination, and leaving the reader with a deep sense of the pity of it all, and a stirring wonder whether in some finer scheme of things, such a soul as Jennie's, even with her succession of haps and mishaps, might not work out its salvation in honor and peace. It offers one of these special instances which seem to defy the application of all the general principles of conventional morality, and which puzzle the mind that would base its sympathies upon a clean-cut distinction between what is right and what is wrong. "Jenny's case, " in this modern presentment, does not seem nearly as clear as the moralist would like to view it.

Newark *Evening News*, March 16, 1912.

The new novel, "Jennie Gerhardt," from the pen of Theodore Dreiser, appears several years after the publication of his widely discussed story, "Sister Carrie." Mr. Dreiser is deliberate about what he does—something that, of itself, differentiates his work from that of many a present day writer. His former novel was not thought out nor was it put together hastily, and the book at hand represents, it is easy to see, the same careful methods. The author evidently has put the best of himself into the narrative; it is a serious setting forth of what he has observed, and, incidentally, of what he thinks.

As in "Sister Carrie," Mr. Dreiser here holds to that realism which is closely related to photography. He desires to make his scenes, and his people, too, perfectly intelligible. He insists upon detail. So insistent is he that he over-emphasizes. Fearful of telling too little, he tells too much, with the result that not infrequently he becomes tiresome. If he were content with trying to establish fewer points, he would make a greater impression. Still much may be pardoned to earnestness, and Mr. Dreiser, above all, is earnest. A fault less pardonable is a tendency, now and again, to moralize, to bring in his own reflections. To wind up a chapter with a couple of paragraphs of quotation capped with several lines of his own, approaching rhapsody, is not good art. It is irritating, also, to find a chapter beginning in this fashion: "In this world of ours the activities of animal life seem to be limited to a plane or circle, as if that were an inherent necessity to the creatures of a planet which is perforce compelled to swing about the sun."

But, with comment made, as it must be made, on these features, the fact remains that Mr. Dreiser has succeeded in presenting compellingly another of the unfortunate characters who so engross his attention. Jennie, in the last analysis, is a figure as understandable as she is pathetic. Her pitiful story is brought home to the reader. It is something more than a surface story. The author has been able to get the girl's viewpoint at different stages of her career and he mirrors her feelings. One comes to appreciate just what Jennie is, her weakness and her strength, her capacity for joy and suffering, just how far she is herself an influence, and just how far she is the creature of circumstance. This is no mean achievement. It lends a distinction to the book, it gives the book a human quality. Mr. Dreiser shows a decided advance over his former novel in the way of rounding out his episodes, and in following out, in so far as occasion requires, the fortunes of his people. "Jennie Gerhardt" is therefore more complete and more satisfactory than "Sister Carrie." The side of life with which the author is concerned is, very emphatically, not a pleasant one, the novelist is under no illusions, nor does he wish his readers to be.

Lexington [Ky.] *Herald*, March 24, 1912.

The criticisms of this story have been most flattering the advance notices say, "Mr. Dreiser's manuscript has been read by many men and women, both professional and literaturers and others, in not one single instance has the reading failed to elicit the tribute of absorbed interest and enthusiastic praise." This leaves one, after reading the book, unable to formulate any phrase other than the ancient and honorable, "What t' 'ell?"

It is a long, full and unreserved statement of the lower motives and baser instincts of the worst order of human animals. The unfortunate woman in the case is a German-American girl, with natural enough desires for the things that make life easier than taking in washing, for instance. So with the connivance of her over-worked mother, she succeeds in outwitting her hateful, but honest father, and keeping herself and family well supplied with the bread of shame. That is pitiful enough, horribly, unutterably pitiful, when the cry of brothers, sisters and even her own mother drove her to it, yet she goes to the bad with all these dreams of purity and happiness, without even a semblance of feeling, simply a non-moral, semi-idiotic creature, and the men are deliberate and open and uninteresting boasts. Even suggestion and delicacy of language is denied the reader. There is not one alleviating circumstance, not one chapter that is not unutterably base; every line is upon such a low plane it is hard to believe that this is all. The afterword is one of the strangest ever written. "It is useless to apostrophize such a soul as Jennie's" (that is perfectly true) "which has reached the full measure of its being," (which was about the calibre of dumb driven cattle), "Shall you say to the blown rose, 'well done.' " Consider the insolence of an author who asks that of an intelligent reader when infinite mercy can say only, "Let him who is within sin, cast the first stone,"—and to the victim of life's stress, "Go and sin no more."

But the author ends, "Jennie loved and loving gave. Is there a superior wisdom," forgetting that she gave most and first not for love but utter need of money, for her brother, it is true, but she did not specially care. It is as base and wrong-headed a volume as ever was written.

Musical Leader, May 2, 1912.

If "Jennie Gerhardt" is the most popular novel of the day, as its publisers assert, we know of no more biting comment on the worthlessness of current fiction. Its author's first book, "Sister Carrie" was a notable novel, but "Jennie Gerhardt" is merely a warmed-over rehash of Carrie of Chicago.

Rowana Hewitt Landon. Columbus [Ohio] *Dispatch*, May 11, 1912.

The social question presented by Theodore Dreiser in the most significant fiction he has yet written—probably his crowning life work—the novel "Jennie Gerhardt"—is as old as civilization, an in its geographical application as wide as is the sweep of the intelligent nations. . . .

If you are wedded to the letter of the law, which killeth, do not read "Jennie Gerhardt." It will offend you. If you cherish the promise that it is the spirit which maketh alive, and hold that the greatest of human virtues is charity, and believe that human wisdom should judge not lest it, too, be judged, then will Jennie Gerhardt grow into your understanding as an illumining revelation, convincing in its inescapable truthfulness; saddening in its photographic realism in the portrayal of existing social conditions; leaving as its final impress a message—not to despair, but one rather of renewed hope that somehow as "the thoughts of God reveal themselves in the slow history of their ripening," good shall be the final goal of the present American social ills.

What constitutes greatness in a novel? If it be a vitally human motif, wrought into adequate literary form, then is "Jennie Gerhardt" but entering into a deserved inheritance of fame destined to prove abiding.

Checklist of Additional Reviews

"Jennie Gerhardt's Love." New York *World*, October 21, 1911.

New York *Evening Post*, October 25, 1911.

Publisher's Weekly, October 28, 1911.

"Another 'Real Story.'" Syracuse *Post Standard*, October 28, 1911.

Des Moines [Iowa] *Midwestern*, November, 1911.

Philadelphia *Telegram*, November 1, 1911.

Detroit *Journal*, November 4, 1911.

Columbus [Ohio] *Journal*, November 5, 1911.

Burlington [Vt.] *Free Press*, November 7, 1911.

New Orleans *Times-Democrat*, November 10, 1911.

Nashville *Tennessean*, November 19, 1911.

"Study of Femininity." Boston [Mass.] *Globe*, November 11, 1911.

Chicago *Journal*, November 11, 1911.

"The Bookshelf." Birmingham [Ala.] *Age Herald*, November 12, 1911.

New Orleans *Picayune*, November 12, 1911.

Philadelphia *Telegraph*, November 15, 1911.

Chicago *Continent*, November 16, 1911.

Chicago *Inter-Ocean*, November 18, 1911.

Henry Haynie. Boston *Times*, November 18, 1911.

Burlington [Ia.] *Saturday Evening Post*, November 18, 1911.

Pittsburgh *Press*, November 18, 1911.

"In the Realm of Imagination." Boston *Herald*, November 18, 1911.

Los Angeles *Tribune*, November 19, 1911.

Buffalo *Express*, November 19, 1911.

New York *Daily People*, November 20, 1911.

New York *Call*, November 20, 1911.

New York *Sun*, November 21, 1911.

Denver *Times*, November 23, 1911.

Rockford [Ill.] *Republic*, November 24, 1911.

Rochester [N. Y.] *Herald*, November 24, 1911.

Publisher's Weekly, November 25, 1911.

New York *World*, November 25, 1911.

New York *Amsterdam*, November 25, 1911.

"A Bold, Pitiful Story." Brooklyn *Standard Union*, November 25, 1911.

St. Paul [Minn.] *Pioneer Press*, November 26, 1911.

Christian Science Monitor, November 27, 1911.

H. L. Mencken. "The Free Lance." Bal-

timore *Evening Sun*, November 27, 1911.
Grand Rapids [Mich.] *Press*, November 27, 1911.
Minneapolis [Minn.] *Tribune*, November 29, 1911.
Boston *Herald*, November 29, 1911.
Cleveland *News*, November 29, 1911.
"Theodore Dreiser's Second Novel." Los Angeles *Examiner*, December 2, 1911.
"Stories of Two Women." New York *Herald*, December 2, 1911.
"New Books: Realistic and Sad." New York *Sun*, December 2, 1911.
"A Luckless Woman." Boston *Daily Advertiser*, December 2, 1911.
Edwin L. Shuman. "Best of Recent Fiction." Chicago *Record Herald*, December 2, 1911.
New York *Call*, December 3, 1911.
Boston *Evening Transcript*, December 6, 1911.
Cleveland [Ohio] *Observer*, December 8, 1911.
Philadelphia *Inquirer*, December 9, 1911.
"Realistic Novel of Present Time." Philadelphia *American*, December 9, 1911.
Trenton [N. J.] *Advertiser*, December 10, 1911.
Columbus [Ohio] *Journal*, December 10, 1911.
H. L. Mencken. "Jennie Gerhardt." Los Angeles *Times*, December 10, 1911.
Brooklyn [N.Y.] *Citizen*, December 10, 1911.
Portland [Me.]*Express*, December 13, 1911.
Chicago *Press*, December 15, 1911.
Hartford [Conn.] *Times*, December 15, 1911.
Philadelphia *Record*, December 16, 1911.
Kansas City [Mo.] *Independent*, December 16, 1911.
Newark [N.J.] *Call*, December 17, 1911.
Lincoln [Neb.] *Star*, December 17, 1911.
Hartford [Conn.] *Post*, December 17, 1911.
Charleston [S.C.] *News*, December 17, 1911.
Baltimore [Md.] *Sun*, December 20, 1911.
Buffalo [N.Y.] *Times*, December 26, 1911.
Omaha [Neb.] *Bee*, December 30, 1911.
New York *Satire*, December 30, 1911.
Pittsburgh [Pa.] *Index*, December 30, 1911.
Oshkosh [Wis.] *Northwestern*, December 30, 1911.
San Francisco *Argonaut*, December 30, 1911.
"Recent Fiction and the Critics." *Current Fiction*, 52 (January 1912), 114.
Everybody's Magazine, January, 1912, p. 284.
Review of Reviews, January, 1912.
Chicago *Evening Post*, January 5, 1912.
New York *Evening Bell*, January 6, 1912.
Portland [Ore.] *Telegram*, January 10, 1912.
James Edward Leslie. "Book News." Pittsburgh *Dispatch*, January 14, 1912.
Publisher's Weekly, January 20, 1912.
New York *Evening Post*, January 27, 1912.
Curtis Lublin. "The Case of 'Jennie Gerhardt'." *Town and Country*, February 3, 1912.
Brooklyn *Times*, February 10, 1912.
Musical Leader, February 15, 1912.
Chicago *Evening Post*, February 23, 1912.

Boston *Evening Transcript,* March 2, 1912.
Brooklyn *Eagle,* March 9, 1912.
Indianapolis *Star,* March 10, 1912.
Cleveland [Ohio] *Topics,* March 16, 1912.
Life, June 13, 1912.
"A Few Books of Today." *Outlook,* 102 (November 23, 1912), 650.

Further Reviews: Bibliographical Information Incomplete

"Jennie Gerhardt." *Reedy's Mirror.*

THE FINANCIER

A NOVEL

BY
THEODORE DREISER
AUTHOR OF
"JENNIE GERHARDT" "SISTER CARRIE"

HARPER & BROTHERS PUBLISHERS
NEW YORK AND LONDON
M - C - M - X - I - I

The Financier

" 'Traction' Interests." New York *Tribune*, November 2, 1912, p. 11.

Mr. Dreiser's artistic limitations and shortcomings were sufficiently discussed on the appearance of his first two novels. They will be found again in this third book from his pen—his indifference to the right word and the right turn of phrase, the flatness of his descriptions, which does not even spare us, in the present instance, the crowning half inch of the stature of his characters. Method he has, a plodding method, which piles detail upon detail, but which is justified by the cumulative effects obtained. We must accept him as he is; he has imposed himself upon our current fiction. His is a reportorial, rather than a literary talent—but what a painstaking talent it is!

"The Financier" is a study of the birth of "traction" interests in Philadelphia before the outbreak of the Civil War. It is a photographic panorama of the beginnings of "big business," of increasing corruption in city and state, of the use by politicians of municipal funds, of the manipulation of stocks, of "wash sales" and "bearing" and "bulling"—of all that underground system which, in its later and perfected state, has been exposed again and again. Here, indeed, lies the difference between Mr. Dreiser's story and the many novels of frenzied finance of the last decade or so: he goes back to the beginnings. He spares us no detail, every cog and wheel of the dishonest machinery is described and shown to us in action, and the result is clarity, and an undeniable interest. There is picturesqueness, also, in the pictures of the period when railroads had but just emerged from their infancy, when no cable linked the Old World to the New, when the telegraph was the only means of rapid communication, and the telephone was not yet dreamt of. It was the closing period of the old, simple order of things, the opening hour of the opportunity of the shrewd and unscrupulous few. Mr. Dreiser takes us through two panics, that caused by the Chicago fire, and the greater one of 1878, in which the house of Jay Cooke & Co. went under. And as the earlier disaster broke the growing fortunes of his protagonist, so did he rise with the later one to greater power and wealth. But the author, having devoted pages and pages to his financier's shipwreck, to his desperate attempts to evade it, deals but briefly with his reemergence. Even the longest of novels must have an end.

This financier is a born, a predestined money maker. Gold lures him from childhood; the intricacies of finance are to him as an open book the moment his father, who is a bank cashier, begins to unfold them to him. He starts his career in a commission house; he perceives that he is but a middleman, that others stand between him and power through wealth. He becomes a stock broker, and again he finds himself only an instrument, kept away from the centre of things. Note brokerage brings him nearer to it; then, by way of the city treasury, he begins his direct operations. Without scruples, without enthusiasms—the Civil War is to him only a danger to business—he carries into private life the same coolness of purpose, the same callousness. He marries; there are glimpses here of the difficult social rise of the financial newcomers in those more static days. Then he falls in love with the daughter of one of his early political and financial sponsors. It is a sordid affair. Such things be. No moral can be drawn from them. Their contemplation is unprofitable and unpleasant.

The realism is photographic. He who is so minded may look for hidden identities. Mr. Dreiser fills his picture well: his endless details have the ultimate value of mass. He tells us nothing new; he merely takes us further back into our financial past than his predecessors in the field have done. The book is a monument of patience and industry.

"A Hero of High Finance." New York *World*, November 2, 1912.

Forsaking the paths of suggestion in which he found "Sister Carrie" and "Jennie Gerhardt," Theodore Dreiser has taken his pen of realism into the field of frenzied finance. From reading the book which follows the change we rise impressed rather by Mr. Dreiser's industry, patience and perseverance than by the quality of interest which he inspires. He has told a very long story, undoubtedly true to life, justified in the facts of financial history, describing what would have been considered once upon a time a marvel of fortune-building, but containing for the reader of the present moment not a throb of agitating concern. Perhaps he meant this to be so. Possibly he has aimed to induce thoughtfulness by a cold recital rather than thrills by a pulsing tale. At least his work lacks nothing of the detail essential to a complete picture of the world of money-madness as it is dominated by method. . . .

"The Financier" gives evidence of a careful study of the monetary period in which it is placed. Famous names are mentioned, such as those of Jay Cooke and the Drexels; quotations are given from the stock-lists of the times; not only the Chicago fire, but the panics of '57 and '73 are among the money influences cited, and there is a graphic description of Jay Cooke's failure following his Northern Pacific enterprise. These things justify our note on Mr. Dreiser's diligence. They do not make a book capable of appeal on deeper grounds than the Cowperwood cash account affords.

Brooklyn *Eagle*, November 2, 1912.

The time has already arrived in the literary career of Theodore Dreiser when the publication of a new novel by him may be called an event. The event took place last week. It is called "The Financier." The work is characteristic of this author as we have become acquainted with his methods and style in "Sister Carrie" and "Jennie Gerhardt." Whatever the reader many think of it, there will be no doubt in his mind that he has read a great work even if he thinks that it is marred by the representation of sexual passion.

The scene of the novel is laid in Philadelphia and there can be little doubt but that a study of that group of financiers and of politicians which grew to such power and wealth in that city inspired the author to the task of which he has acquitted himself so greatly. But this is not to say that any one of them individually, or collectively, has had his picture taken. No one will be able to say that such and such a character stands for So and So. But the events of the days when the Philadelphia group grew and flourished and the practices of these men, by no means well known at the time of their occurrences, but now well understood, do stand in the book even if fictitious characters work the one and move about among the other. . . .

As was said above, the book is characterestic of the author. His style is as simple and direct as that in his former works, which elicited such high praise from the critics. Perhaps it is because he deals with great events of a public nature that his work can be said to be more dramatic. There is nothing that can be now recalled that is stronger and more vivid than the description of the panic days that followed the fire or of the struggle of an able, resourceful and courageous man to stem the tide of disaster as it rolled in on him. But far greater is the dissection of this man's character. This is a wonderful piece of work, absorbing and gripping. Nor is the work of characterization confined to this one person. Every figure is a real person of flesh and blood and when you have finished you have added to your list of acquaintances the characters of this book, whom you know as well as you do those with whom you have come into personal contact, perhaps better because you have come to knowledge of them through the wonderful keenness of the author.

The work is frank to a degree that may bring it into condemnation in certain quarters. A spade is a spade and the author says so without reserve. The relation between the girl and this married man is told with a candor that may give offense. The telling of the truth seems to be the aim of the author, without fear of consequence. All the same, it is a great book.

E.F. Edgett. Boston *Evening Transcript*, November 6, 1912.

Words are many in the novel Mr. Dreiser has chosen to write as the successor of his "Sister Carrie" and "Jennie Gerhardt." And since behind them are ideas, and the ability to weld them into the unity of a well-constructed work of fiction, the reader need not be daunted by the task that confronts him as he turns the leaves of "The Financier." He will find there a bulk that is astonishing even in this era of much writing, and he will doubtless derive some interest from a survey of its mere material statistics. "The Financier" reaches to 780 compact pages, printed from a clear and readable type upon paper of a weight and thinness that keep the book within easily portable compass, and it contains nearly three hundred thousand words, thereby extending to more than twice the length of the average long novel. These facts in themselves are significant of Mr. Dreiser's serious realization of his mission as a writer of novels that deal in abundant detail with the realities of those phases of life that he studies so deeply and conscientiously. . . .

As may readily be imagined during the progress of so long a story, its pages are filled with a multitude of characters. Some of them appear and reappear frequently throughout its course; some are seen and heard at long intervals; others come forward for a moment and then vanish. Personalities and firms well known in the history of the country as well as in the local repute of Philadelphia—the Drexels, Jay Cooke & Co. among others—are mentioned by Mr. Dreiser without fear and trembling, and so closely does he tread to the march of actual events that he brings into his story and gives names to the mayor and the treasurer of Philadelphia, to the governor of Pennsylvania, and to numerous other officials who are all more or less the creatures of the political machine in control of the government and all its resources. He moreover places the incidents of his story exactly to the year, the month and the day, and by so doing he is certain of involving himself in the meshes of considerable argument as to the artistic justification of so extraordinary a realistic method. But perhaps "The Financier" is more history and biography than we so far away from Philadelphia can see. In that case it will be something especially for Philadelphia and the Philadelphians to read and discuss.

The moral aspects of the story need not be enlarged upon. It takes life as it is found, and it describes life exactly as Mr. Dreiser finds it after energetic study and many-sided investigations. Frank Cowperwood is revealed simply and faithfully as a man who relies solely upon himself for his standards of conduct. The story is told wholly from his point of view. In the old-fashioned novel he would be presented and condemned as the married man who basely seduces a beautiful young girl and induces her to become his mistress. But "The Financier" is nothing if not new-fashioned, and therefore Aileen Butler's love for Frank Cowperwood is emphasized, as is also his love for her, and we find them at the close of the story beginning a life together in the far West. But this does not happen until Cowperwood has fallen from his high estate as a financier and until after he has been made a scapegoat through the political power of Aileen's father.

Unfortunately Mr. Dreiser's style still lapses into amazing rhetorical vulgarities. He is apparently unaware of the exact meaning of many English words, his most grievous offence being the persistent misuse of the verb "locate," his misunderstanding of the significance of the word "transpire," and his use of the phrase "from whence." These are merely examples of numerous offences that show his need for study of the graces of the English language. But we forget all this in the face of his amazing imaginative vigor and his astounding realistic truth. "The Financier" is in many ways crude, but there is a greatness in its crudity.

"An Unsuccessful Financier." New York *Evening Mail*, November 9, 1912.

Theodore Dreiser's new novel, "The Financier" is not as solid work as either his "Sister Carrie" or his "Jennie Gerhardt." He has attempted to handle material which is not his to command. . . .

Mr. Dreiser's "hero" is a money-making genius of the most repellant type. The strange part of the matter is that the author himself seems to admire him and to regard him as "clean cut" and "manly." His hero has no more conscience or decency than a pig. His eventual financial downfall is inevitable. In the treatment of the financier's checkered sexual relations Mr. Dreiser is more successful than in the financial parts. The picture of his liaison with a "red-blooded" Irish girl is cleverly drawn. In the depiction of affairs of this sort Mr. Dreiser is particularly strong.

The whole book suffers from a prolixity of detail. No reasonable critic can object to the multiplication of details which are necessary to the relation of a strong story or to the development and unfolding of character, but many of Mr. Dreiser's details are redundant from any point of view. The wearied reader is forced to skip what the author should have cut out with a blue pencil.

H.L. Mencken. "Dreiser's Novel the Story of a Financier Who Loved Beauty." New York *Times Book Review*, November 10, 1912, p. 654.

Theodore Dreiser's new novel, "The Financier," shows all of the faults and peculiarities of method that gave a rude, barbarous sort of distinction to his "Sister Carrie" and "Jennie Gerhardt," those arresting tales of yesteryear. The man does not write as the other novelists of his day and generation write, and, what is more, he does not seem to make any effort to do so, or to have any feeling that such an effort would be worth while. You may read him for page after page, held spellbound by his people and their doings, and yet not find a single pretty turn or phrase, or a single touch of smartness in dialogue, or a single visible endeavor to stiffen a dull scene into drama, or any other such application of artifice or art.

For all the common tricks of writing, in truth, he reveals a degree of disdain amounting almost to denial. He never "teases up" a situation to make it take your breath; he never hurries over something difficult and static in order to get to something easy and dynamic; he never leads you into ambuscades of plot or sets off stylistic fireworks; he never so much as takes the trouble to hunt for a new adjective when an old one will answer as well. In brief, his manner is uncompromisingly forthright, elemental, grim, gaunt, bare. He rolls over the hills and valleys of his narrative at the same patient, lumbering gait, surmounting obstacles by sheer weight and momentum, refusing all short cuts, however eminently trod, as beneath his contempt, and turning his back resolutely upon all the common lifts by the way.

But do I give the impression that the result is dullness, that all this persistent, undeviating effort leads to nothing but a confused and meaningless piling up of words? Then I have described it very badly, for the net effect is precisely the opposite. Out of chaos, by that unceasing pounding, order finally emerges. Out of the disdain of drama comes drama stirring and poignant. Out of that welter of words step human beings, round, ruddy, alive. In other words, Dreiser accomplishes at last, for all his muddling, what men with a hundred times his finesse too often fail to accomplish, and that is, an almost perfect illusion of reality. You may say that he writes with a hand of five thumbs, and that he has no more humor than a hangman, and that he loves assiduity so much that he often forgets inspiration altogether, and you may follow up all of these sayings by ample provings, but in the end you will have to admit that Carrie Meeber is far more real than nine-tenths of the women you actually know, and that old Gerhardt's veritable existence is no more to be doubted than the existence of Père Goriot.

If "The Financier," on a first reading, leaves a less vivid impression than the two books preceding it, then that apparent falling off is probably due to two things, the first being that its principal character is a man and that in consequence he must needs lack some of the fascinating mystery and appeal of Carrie and Jennie; and the second being that the story stops just as it is beginning, (for all its 780 pages!) and so leaves the reader with a sense of incompleteness, of a picture washed in but not wholly painted. Final judgment, indeed, will be impossible until the more important second volume is put beside this first, for it is there that the real drama of Frank Cowperwood's life will be played out. But meanwhile there can be no doubt whatever of the author's firm grip upon the man, nor of his astute understanding of the enormously complex interplay of personalities and events against which the man is projected.

This Cowperwood is meant, I suppose, to be a sort of archetype of the American money king, and despite a good many little deviations he is probably typical enough. The main thing to remember about him is that he is anything but a mere chaser of the dollar, that avarice as a thing in itself is not in him. For the actual dollar, indeed, he has no liking at all, but only the toleration of an artist for his brushes and paint-pots. What he is really after is power, and the way power commonly visualizes itself in this mind is as a means to beauty. He likes all things that caress the eye—a fine rug, an inviting room, a noble picture, a good horse, a pretty woman, particularly a pretty woman. There is in him what might be called an aloof voluptuousness, a dignified hedonism. He is not so much sensual as sensitive. A perfect eyebrow seems to him to be something worth thinking about, soberly and profoundly. The world, in his sight, is endlessly curious and beautiful.

And with this over-development of the esthetic sense there goes, naturally enough, an under-development of the ethical sense. Cowperwood has little more feeling for right and wrong, save as a setting or a mask for beauty, than a healthy schoolboy. When a chance offers to make a large sum of money by an alliance with political buccaneers, he takes it without the slightest question of its essential virtue. And when, later on, the buccaneers themselves lay open for pillage, he pillages them with a light heart. And as with means, so with ends. When Aileen Butler, the daughter of his partner and mentor, old Edward Malia Butler, the great political contractor—when Aileen comes his way, radiant and tempting, he debauches her without a moment's thought of consequences, and carries on the affair under old Butler's very nose.

The man is not vicious: a better word for him would be innocent. He has no sense of wrong to Aileen, nor of wrong to Butler, nor even of wrong to the wife of his youth. The only idea that takes clear form in his mind is the idea that Aileen is extremely pleasing, and that it would be a ridiculous piece of folly to let her charms go to waste. Even when he is the conquered instead of the conqueror, not much feeling that an act of conquest can haye a moral content appears in him. Old Butler, discovering his affair with Aileen, knocks over his financial house of cards and railroads him to prison, but he shows little rancor against Butler, and less against the obliging catchpolls of the law, but only a vague discontent that fate should bring him such hardships, and take him away from beauty so long.

This term in prison is a salient event in Cowperwood's life, but it cannot be said that it is a turning point. He comes out into the Philadelphia of the early seventies with all his old determination to beat the game. He has been defeated once, true enough, but that defeat has taught him a lot that easy victory might have left unsaid, and he has full confidence that he will win next time. And win he does. Black Friday sees him the most pitilessly ursine of bears, and the next day sees him with a million. He is now on his feet again and able to choose his cards carefully and at leisure. With the utmost calm he divorces his wife, tucks Aileen under his arm, and sets out for Chicago. There, where the players are settling down for the wildest game of money ever played in the world, he will prove that luck in the long run is with the wise. And there, in the second volume of this history, we shall see him at the proving.

An heroic character, and not without his touches of the admirable. Once admit his honest doubts of the workaday moralities of the world, and at once you range him with all the other memorable battlers against fate, from Prometheus to Etienne Lantier. The achievement of Dreiser is found in this very fact: that he has made the man not only comprehensible, but also a bit tragic. One is conscious of a serene dignity in his chicaneries, and even in his debaucheries, and so his struggle for happiness becomes truly moving. I am not alluding here to that cheap sympathy which is so easily evoked by mere rhetoric, but to that higher sympathy which grows out of a thorough understanding of motives and processes of mind. This understanding Dreiser insures. Say what you will against his solemn and onerous piling up of words, his slow plodding through jungles of detail, his insatiable lust for facts, you must always admit that he gets his effect in the end. There are no sudden flashes of revelation; the lights are turned on patiently and deliberately, one by one. But when the thing is done at last the figure of the financier leaps out amazingly, perfectly modeled, wholly accounted for.

So with the lesser personages, and particularly with Aileen and her father. Old Butler, indeed, is worthy to stand just below the ancient Gerhardt, by long odds the most real of Dreiser's creatures, not even excepting Carrie Meeber and Hurstwood. You remember Gerhardt, of course, with his bent back, his squirrel's economies, his mediaeval piety and his pathetic wonderment at the deviltries of the world? Well, Butler is a vastly different man, if only because he is richer, more intelligent, and more powerful, but still, in the end, he takes on much of that reality and all of that pathos, raging homerically but impotently against an enemy who eludes him and defies him and has broken his heart.

And so, too, with the background of the story. I can imagine nothing more complex than the interplay of finance and politics in war time and during the days following, when the money kings were just finding themselves and graft was just rising to the splendor of an exact science. And yet Dreiser works his way through that maze with sure steps, and leaves order and understanding where confusion reigned. Of tales of municipal corruption we have had a-plenty; scarcely a serious American novelist of to-day, indeed, has failed to experiment with that endless and recondite drama. But what other has brought its prodigal details into better sequence and adjustment, or made them enter more vitally and convincingly into the characters and adventures of his people? Those people of Dreiser's, indeed, are never the beings in vacuo who populate our common romances. We never see them save in contact with a vivid and fluent environment, reacting to its constant stimuli, taking color from it, wholly a part of it.

So much for "The Financier." It is the prologue rather than the play. The real tragi-comedy of Cowperwood's struggle for power and beauty will be played out in Chicago, and of its brilliancy and mordacity we have abundant earnest. Dreiser knows Chicago as few other men know it; he has pierced to the very heart of that most bewildering of cities. And, what is more, he has got his secure grip upon Cowperwood.

"Theodore Dreiser's New Novel." New York *Evening Sun*, November 11, 1912.

A novel of almost 800 pages is a portentous publication. Mr. Theodore Dreiser makes heavy demands on the patience and loyalty of his admirers by the painful fidelity to fact with which he has loaded "The Financier." Nevertheless, they will assert, and it will probably be admitted by all who read this new tale of the most substantial of our realistic writers of fiction, that it is a worthy successor to "Sister Carrie" and "Jennie Gerhardt." If Mr. Dreiser has at any time been concerned in trying to prove anything except that life is a tremendously interesting and puzzling affair to all who go through it open-eyed and anxious not to deceive themselves, it has never been apparent in his novels; the parables with which "The Financier" concludes completely define his artistic attitude.

One of the distinguishing characteristics of the Dreiser novels is their utter lack of any brutal indication that the non-platonic relations of men and women are dealt with therein just for the sake of dealing with them. In "The Financier" Mr. Dreiser has chosen to consider these things in the part which they play in the life of man, not of a woman—the first time he has focussed his attention chiefly on men while relegating women to subordinate roles. . . .

It suffices to say that every hope and expectation heretofore based on Mr. Dreiser's promise of artistic achievement are convincingly justified by the third and best novel that he has so far written.

Philadelphia *Press*, November 16, 1912.

That particular sort of "bigness" which results from heaping small details mountain high exists in abundant measure in Mr. Dreiser's new novel. Its extreme length and laborious method of procedure amply attest the tireless industry of the author of "Sister Carrie" and "Jennie Gerhardt." Its sentences are imposed upon one another with the even progress of bricklaying, and with much the same effect upon the reader.

There is neither quickening nor slacking of pace, nothing ornamental, nothing illuminating. Each description of person, incident, mood or motive is set before the reader to the last detail. Effects produced by the art of suggestion are apparently disdained by the author, and yet, through the very hardness of the style, reality and force are attained, and the interest is held by the complex drama of life that emerges from the maze of affairs. . . .

Carl T. Robertson. Cleveland *Plain Dealer*, November 16, 1912.

It is not without reason that British critics exclaim that Theodore Dreiser is the greatest of contemporary American novelists. Of course Howells is excepted; his masterpieces find no counterpart in the output of today; but by these critics, it seems, Howells is accounted a novelist of an earlier generation. This reviewer will not venture the dictum that Dreiser is the best America has to offer today; but he will timidly, and at the same time with a righteous consciousness of being in good company, assert that one of Dreiser's books seems worth more to him than a large granary tightly packed with promiscuous selections from the American fiction of the present decade.

In the first place Dreiser is a man who magnificently scorns artificialities. He is like Thomas Hardy. But he is unlike Hardy in that he even scorns the beauty of background. Hardy will give you plenty of pretty scenes, and in these landscapes he will present the deformities of humanity—till you hate men and love trees. Dreiser does not supply the trees.

He takes places like New York and Chicago—especially Chicago—and shows humanity under localized influences. If Hardy makes the folk of rural England, the folk of the eternally lovely woodland, sordid and too human, what can be said of Dreiser, who with the same relentless veracity depicts of the very common people of a dirty and unbeautiful American metropolis?

Whoever has read "Sister Carrie"

need only be told that a book by Dreiser is in the market.

Whoever has read "Jennie Gerhardt" will merely feel an added incentive to delve into this man's wondrous mine of dross.

It is a mine of dross; there is little gold there.

But it is true humanity.

Most of the other novelists are separating the gold from the dross, and reveling in the gold.

This Dreiser takes American mankind as he has found it, and his people are of the ninety and nine per cent; they are indubitably of the dross.

In the last book he has sent out, "The Financier," Dreiser has taken a man for his central study. Hitherto he has dissected a woman. He now shows that he knows masculinity as surely as femininity. His Cowperwood is a living and wonderful man; a man who is wicked and good; mostly wicked; as most human being are. But dominantly he is human.

There will not be here the most meager hint of the story of "The Financier." Suffice it, for those who have read Dreiser's other novels, to say that there is a new Dreiser novel on the book shop shelves. Suffice it, for those who do not know Dreiser, to say that "The Financier" is the really notable work of American fiction for the autumn of 1912.

Herbert Bashford. " 'The Financier': Theodore Dreiser Writes Another Big Novel." San Francisco *Bulletin*, November 16, 1912.

America has at least one novelist who takes himself seriously and whose novels may be spoken of in the same breath with those of the great European realists. His name is Theodore Dreiser. He is the author of "Sister Carrie" and "Jennie Gerhardt." Neither of these two studies of the eternal feminine has been numbered among the "six best sellers." No such doubtful recognition has been accorded one of Mr. Dreiser's novels to our knowledge, yet each story is a "slice of life" in the full meaning of the term. Of course, Mr. Dreiser's uncompromising realism is not in public favor as compared with the chocolate-coated bunch of sentiment which passes for fiction and is eagerly devoured because of its saintly sweetness and utter inocuousness.

Whatever may be said of this novelist, it is certain that as a psychological analyst he has no equal among contemporary authors. He has never shown his ability as a literary vivisectionist to better advantage than in his latest novel, "The Financier," which is masterly in conception and brilliant in execution—a big, keenly interpretive, wonderfully virile study of an aspiring Napoleon of finance. . . .

St. Louis *Post-Dispatch*, November 16, 1912.

The sort of American life that is depicted in Theodore Dreiser's latest novel is the life of the jungle, where men as keen as hawks and as ferocious as tigers rend and despoil each other, even as jungle beasts do. Sometimes, surfeited, they spare, but only as gorged wolves spare, putting by for the gratification of another day's whetted gluttony and greed.

Humanity is presented on the zoological plane, dumb driven by murderous natural law, finding its inspiration and justification in the chicanery and cruelty of the lower orders, reading altruism out of the universe, introducing morality but little better than that of the rabbit burrows, blighting family life and only dimly glimpsing at the last such retribution as resides in the dead desire of satiety. All this is presented, not as an unrepresentative and exotic phase of American life, but as life in the large, not only through the characters of the story, but more subtly through the cynical asides of the author.

Greed and graft are glorified, conservatism in morals caviled at, the "grasping legality of established matrimony" contrasted rather unfavorably with illicit love that is not tainted with guile or gain.

Frank Algernon Cowperwood is the capitalist. He runs his ruthless career in Philadelphia before and during and after the war. He is a financial genius, a supreme egotist, dynamic, acquisitive, vital, an opportunist, having no morals, bowing only to the expedient and not often to that, recognizing only strength and weakness in the universe, using his strength zestfully to wrest gain from weakness, living richly, fulsomely, and finding joy in achieving, prevailing, dominating, crushing when need be. "I satisfy myself" is his motto and he satisfies himself, without heed to the laws of God or man.

Immensely imaginative and facile in finance, he achieves dubious greatness and large wealth in stocks and bonds, establishes a profitable alliance with the city treasury through devious political channels, falls when days of panic come, is sent to the penitentiary, from which barefaced lying cannot save him, and after his release wrests another fortune from another day's panic.

Married to a woman older in years, but younger in mentality than he, and the father of two children, he tosses aside their claims upon him when he is attracted to the sybaritic daughter of a political boss who has befriended him. As the author finds no scheme in nature for the unity of two beyond the temporary care of the young, he has the financier rail at the Christian effort to compress the world into the one-life, one-love idea and repudiates it, invoking chemistry and physics to the annulment of moral law, lives a double life, is ultimately divorced and marries his mistress.

There are 800 closely printed pages of this and although it is an unlovely phase of life that the story presents, and it is a libel in so far as it pretends to be more than a phase, that phase is presented with skill, certainty, mastery. Cowperwood is clearly and consistently, not to say ruthlessly, drawn. The author does not yield to the temptation to woo the reader's favor by giving the unheroic hero something noble and unselfish to do. He is strong and forceful and resourceful, splendidly potent, and that is all. For that matter, one does not readily recall at the end anything noble or generous that anyone has done in the story's unfolding. Lacking the noble even as a foil to the ignoble, lacking complexity of plot, though not of plottings, lacking elements of surprise and dramatic climaxes, the story nevertheless is such a compelling revelation of the American fight for gold and power and lawless love that it will take high rank in the lists of modern fiction.

Providence [R. I.] *Journal*, November 17, 1912.

The story is less important than Mr. Dreiser's way of telling it. We hardly think he has justified the 780 substantial pages to which his book extends. In the first place he has no charm of style to relieve the tedium of such a journey. He writes well enough, but there is no touch of imagination, In the second place, he cumbers the narrative with huge masses of irrelevant details. He describes minutely every one of Cowperwood's "deals." He explains with careful exactness every process of banking or stock gambling. The book might almost be a treatise on "How to Speculate." He cannot introduce even a subordinate character with an illuminating phrase or two; he has to check the current of the story while he goes into family history. These are obvious defects, both of method and of execution. Mr. Dreiser is as voluble and diffuse as the late Frank Norris without his gift for picturesque color. It will be a very conscientious reader indeed who does not skip something like one in three of these 780 pages. Yet the novel is so sincere an attempt to deal with a large theme that it demands respect. What the author needs is the power to arouse enthusiasm as well. Aileen is the most compelling personality in the book, and she fails to charm after a time.

San Francisco *Chronicle*, November 17, 1912.

In "THE FINANCIER," Theodore Dreiser has written a powerful and well-constructed story, which, despite its 780 compact pages and all the many details it contains of the intricacies of high finance, holds the reader's interest throughout. The book is a drama of the lust for wealth, and almost, one might add, the lust for love. In its scope and power it is a greater novel than either of the author's other efforts, "Sister Carrie" or "Jennie Gerhardt."

Social, business and political life in Philadelphia during a period of some twenty years before, during and after the Civil War makes up the atmosphere of Mr. Dreiser's book. And his sketch of his hero, Frank Cowperwood, seems to be literally a biography. Public characters and business firms well known in Philadelphia history are mentioned freely by the author, and so closely does he seem to tread the path of real events that he does not hesitate to name the Mayor and various public officials of Philadelphia, the Governor of Pennsylvania and machine politicians of more than merely local note. Many events which actually happened are introduced into the narrative, with the exact dates of their occurrence and the names of prominent participants.

The life story of Frank Underwood [sic], the future "financier," is taken up when he is a boy and early discloses the genius for making money which brought about his subsequent rise and fall. Through it all the sympathy of the reader is with the hero, whether the path which he treads is a straight or a crooked one. Here the genius of the novelist is well shown, and makes Mr. Dreiser's novel a really great example of modern fiction.

Many characters find their way into the pages of "The Financier," as is not unnatural in the course of so long a story. Not all of these remain for a long time, but all seem essential to the narrative and each is clearly drawn. The story takes life as it is found and supplies an insight into large phases of its evolution in America. It is a man's story for men, whereas the author's other stories have been mostly of a particular woman from a woman's point of view.

Cleveland [Ohio] *Leader*, November 18, 1912.

Theodore Dreiser is the American Balzac in the minuteness of his writing; its faithfulness to detail; its patient building up of a scene, a plot or a character by infinitesimal pieces.

He did this in "Sister Carrie" and "Jennie Gerhart." It is even more in evidence in his latest novel, "The Financier." I haven't the book by me to note the number of its pages but there are enough to make two average sized novels owing to this carefulness. . . .

Like Balzac, too, Dreiser makes a man's nature—his fleshliness count in the final reckoning, just as it does in real life. The amour of Copperwood is sordid and dishonorable; he robs a benefactor of his daughter. And it is told with a bluntness that is a blot on the tale. There is no disguise; no mincing. It is bald and bold.

But the story itself is strong and attractive in its final essence. Good art, though untouched with anything imaginative. It is the best thing Dreiser has yet done.

Lucian Cary. "A Big Novel." Chicago *Evening Post*, November 22, 1912.

An ordinary novel runs for from 50,000 to 100,000 words; one of Mr. Wells' "dreadnoughts" runs for, say, 175,000 words; and even Arnold Bennett has not written as long a novel as this of Mr Dreiser's. It runs to nearly 300,000 words, and it is only the first volume. It is already as long as three average novels. This is not stated as an objection but as a significant fact. It was the admirable and acute Bennett who said that only reviewers object to long novels.

These 300,000 words signify that Mr. Dreiser has taken the means necessary to do what he proposed. He wanted to set before us, against a background of American life, the growth of a boy who from the first desired to be a financier, into a full-grown man. He wanted to give not a sketch but a portrait, and a portrait in the Dutch manner. He has done this. I believe he has done it as it has never before been done in America.

Of course space, essential as it is to such a performance, is not everything. The fact that the amount of space Mr. Dreiser has chosen to give himself is very unusual is first-rate evidence that novelists generally hold that space is dangerous. But Mr. Dreiser has more than the courage to write as fully as he pleases.

He has, in the first place, a philosophy of a sort which, so far from coloring everything he sees, rather incapacitates him for coloring anything. Perhaps this philosophy might be described as the absence of a philosophy; but it would be truer to say that it is characterized by the absence of dogma: it is not a system. He is not certain that the ways of nature are undiscoverable; he is merely certain that they are undiscovered. In a large way he is impatient with the various attempts which have been made to explain the universe. He would be contemptuous of such codes as men have formulated—he regards the ten commandments as quite too rigid for human beings—were it not that he is a person of keen sensibility, of wide sympathy. He cannot be completely contemptuous of anything which has cost as much in human pain as have "morals."

It is clear that a man of such a philosophy has a great advantage over the dogmatist as a novelist. He would have no such advantage as a pamphleteer. Effective argument can be built only on a platform. No man can debate effectively who does not know exactly what he believes and who does not believe something exact. But a novel is another matter. A novelist is dependent on his reader's acceptance of his facts, and readers are suspicious of the novelist with a dogma. They suspect him always of manipulating life to fit his theory of it. Thus Thomas Hardy held to a theory that chance, not to say unfortunate coincidence, is pretty nearly the largest factor in human life. Those who do not agree with his theory feel that in ordering the lives of his people on this principle he has been untrue. They do not question one mischance, but they question one mischance after another; and from discrediting the repeated coincidences of mischance they come to discredit him rather generally. A man who believes that virtue is its own reward can write a really convincing and satisfying novel only for those who believe that virtue is its own reward.

Mr. Dreiser has no dogma to uphold, no thesis to prove, no rigid generalization to illustrate. He looks upon life and tells us what he sees. The fact that he has no codified and articulated ethic may alienate some of those who have, but not many. I cannot follow Mr. Dreiser's metaphysics, but I do not find him even so much as irritating—only interesting, immensely interesting.

In the second place, Mr. Dreiser has a vast fund of knowledge. He knows the complex and fluid life of the Philadelphia to which he introduces us, the Philadelphia of the period from 1837, when Frank Cowperwood was born, to 1873, when that remarkable person left his birthplace for Chicago. He knows the business and the politics and the society of this town; he knows the houses and the furniture and the clothes which these people know; he knows the degree of their sophistication in morals and in art. But more than all this, he knows how men and women think and act and feel. He is a mine of information on human beings.

Finally, Mr. Dreiser has achieved a technique which is peculiarly suited to his capacities and to his purposes. His style, except occasionally, is excellent. I am aware that there are some who would insist it is no model for a college student of English Composition, and that there are others who would dismiss it as an abomination. No one who is satisfied with Robert Louis Stevenson's style will be satisfied with Theodore Dreiser's. But Mr. Dreiser's style comes very near to being a clear reflection of what is going on in Mr. Dreiser's mind, and what is going on in that mind is rather more than worth while. The fact that Stevenson would now be forgotten if he had written only the sort of phrases which Mr. Dreiser writes is not a reflection on Mr. Dreiser's style but a reflection on Stevenson's mind.

The great virtue of this plain, homely way of speaking which is Mr. Dreiser's is that it is so honest, so forthright, so completely without affectation. He has no purple patches. He makes no attempt to lure the reader with words. And so the reader is lured by what he has to say.

This style is of a piece with his method. He depends on facts and more facts. He does not sketch in a story and attempt to resolve it by one high light. He gives not only climaxes but all that led up to them. He dramatizes only in the sense that he lets things happen—which turns out to be ever so much more dramatic than when things are arranged

It may be objected that it is the business of the novelist to choose from a mass of details those which are significant and, in rendering, to arrange them. Of course Mr. Dreiser does choose, does arrange. He seems to tell everything only when he is compared with the ordinary novelist; he only seems to let episodes fall where they may. But this carrying of the realistic novelist's method several steps farther than it usually is carried produces an effect which is its own. One reads on and on in this history of Frank Cowperwood without skipping—it is very difficult to skip the details even of tremendously involved financial transactions—but asking oneself how much of this wealth of information one is going to carry in one's head and answering that one is going to remember very little of it. But this answer, though a true one, does not invalidate the method. Somehow or other it is the significant details one remembers. Those that do not count gradually drop out of one's mind after they have contributed to his understanding of the others. One may remember only a few episodes of Cowperwood's boyhood, but one would not understand that boyhood so well nor find it so convincing if only those episodes were given

The story to which Mr. Dreiser applies this equipment of his appears to be that of the late Charles T. Yerkes. Indeed, he has paralleled that person's career very closely in minor details. Frank A. Cowperwood was, like Yerkes, born in 1837 in Philadelphia; he failed in 1871, as did Yerkes; he was charged with larceny of city funds, as Yerkes was charged with "misappropriating city funds"; he was sentenced to the penitentiary for four years and six months, as Yerkes was sentenced to two years and nine months; he was pardoned in thirteen months, as Yerkes was pardoned in seven months; he married in Aileen Butler some such woman as Yerkes married in Emily Grigsby; he came to Chicago to start over, just as Yerkes did. To cap off, Mr. Dreiser remarks that Cowperwood's study of the stars while he was in prison resulted later in his giving a great telescope to a university.

But Mr. Dreiser is far from requiring any such adventitious aid as this identification of his hero with a man who went through very much the same sort of experience. One who had never heard of Yerkes would be quite as convinced that Cowperwood actually regained his money and his prestige after leaving the penitentiary. Mr. Dreiser may never have met Yerkes, may know very little more about him than can be found in the Encyclopedia Britannica, but he knows Cowperwood through and through. And he makes his reader know Cowperwood.

Of course Mr. Dreiser has created characters before. Hurstwood, in that first novel, "Sister Carrie," is thoroughly real, completely convincing. He is not only a real and a convincing character: he is a changing character. He is one man at the beginning and another at the end. That makes him the achievement he is. One has only to think back over the novels one has read, over the best of them, to recognize how rare an achievement he is.

Cowperwood is such another. This book, or this volume of the complete work, leaves him when he is 36 years old, and merely foreshadows the career which awaits him in Chicago. But one knows the man so well that the foreglimpse Mr. Dreiser gives of him is unnecessary. He is made on a larger scale than Hurstwood, a figure of tragic altitude, less simple, and hence more difficult to put before the reader in the round. But Cowperwood is always Cowperwood from the day he is introduced as a boy to the day he leaves for Chicago with his second fortune. He develops, but he develops in character. . . .

Hartford [Conn.] *Courant*, November 28, 1912.

Mr. Dreiser's "inflexible realism, psychological insight, literary perception, bigness" have received almost fulsome recognition from leading critics: Arnold Bennett considers him "a leading representative American novelist whose work truly reflects current literary tendencies." The publishers announce this novel as "a great book in its scope and power—broader and deeper than anything which Mr. Dreiser has done." Well, as far as Mr. Dreiser's ability is in question to perform a great literary feat, let us not dispute it. His new novel is a very thorough and complete representation of a life of greed of money; of display; and of women (not love, though it is called that); of the ways and means by which stocks, bonds, banks and corporate franchises were manipulated to the making of private fortunes and the lasting disgrace of Pennsylvania and, in great measure, of the whole country. This great performance founds its claims to be literature by centering in the intimate biography of Frank Cowperwood, a tale minute and psychological. Frank begins his acquistions at fourteen. He is athletic, handsome, no end ambitious in a "business" way, plucky, alert, selfishly and always prudently amorous, a high school and office first in mathematics and book-keeping. Not a romantic hero: hardly an interesting figure of a youth in his teens.

There is a sort of excitement, possibly romance for those whose fate is sounded, in the ticking on the tape and the scuffles of the stock exchange. There may be romance in moving into large and larger houses, in giving balls, in buying Chippendale, in keeping a second establishment with a handsome and stupid mistress of it.

Save for such interludes realism does not make a slip in Mr. Dreiser's faithful charge. Boyhood and youth extend to middle age while the Cowperwoods grow more and more sordid, more corrupt and finally, in a pinch, criminal. Nothing is more realistic than Frank's trial, prison life and pardon.

"One of the great examples of modern fiction" is fictitious only in giving a name and a personality to unprincipled greed and lust of possession whether of money or a friend's passionate daughter. The book is powerful by reason of its careful accuracy and minuteness, chiefly by its patient persistence—something less than 800 pages which in the ordinary type and spacing given to novels should be 1,500. However powerful and exact the protracted and minute reproduction of him may be, a bore is a bore.

D.S.K.
Boston *Times*, November 30, 1912.

One of the notably strong novels of the year is "The Financier," by Theodore Dreiser, author of "Sister Carrie" and "Jennie Gerhardt." It is dramatic, gripping, realistic, powerful. It presents phases of American life during the last half century with a mastery of portrayal which is seldom equalled. As its title indicates, "The Financier" is the story of the lust for wealth, the story of financial success and power. It is a big story—big in its incidents, big in the minuteness of detail. The author reveals exceptional knowledge of the processes of financial and political achievement, and has woven them together in a way to give them pulsing life. The scene is laid in Philadelphia—a city whose political and financial history has had few if any moments of dulness; and the period begins before the panic of 1857, which, with the Civil war, the Chicago fire and the Jay Cook failure, makes a group of events which lend themselves readily to the purposes of an author who is developing the life success of a money maker.

From the opening line Frank Algernon Cowperwood has personality. As a boy he won his fight with a bully, grasped an opportunity to make money at an auction sale, and got an insight into how life is organized from watching a lobster and a squid from day to day in a tank outside a fishmonger's. The lobster gradually wore down the squid's endurance, and finally got him. The squid wasn't quick enough, for one thing; he couldn't kill the lobster, for he had no weapon; the lobster could kill the squid, for he was heavily armed; the squid had nothing to feed on, and the lobster had him as prey—in time. The squid didn't have a chance, and there was only one end. Young Frank had been puzzling over the riddle of life, and this incident impressed him greatly. "Things lived on each other—that was it." . . .

"The Financier" is absorbing, thoroughly interesting in its realism, in its all too true description of one kind of American success. The reader admires Cowperwood's indomitable will, his keenness, his mastery of men, and now and then there flashes through the mind a feeling of envy of those who gain so much so easily when the many obtain so little with such difficulty. But the glamor is not real, and the lesson underlying Mr. Dreiser's novel is an abiding one. . . .

"The Bookshelf." *Harper's Monthly Magazine*, December, 1912.

The extraordinary vitality and realism of Theodore Dreiser's new novel, *The Financier*, will surprise even the warmest admirers of his art. Not even the many notable critics and writers who bestowed so much extravagant-seeming praise upon *Sister Carrie* and *Jennie Gerhardt* could well have seen in these books the promise of such a novel as *The Financier*. For here is such an understanding of character and of life such as we hardly expect to find short of Balzac and the very greatest realists, and here also is a bigness of theme that gives the truly epic quality to a story which is at the same time convincingly faithful to the things of every-day existence—to the little significant events and feelings that count tremendously to the individual and to the hopes and plans and personal force that make the individual count tremendously in the world. From the beginning the reader feels the inevitableness of the career of Frank Cowperwood. The son of a commonplace Philadelphia bank-clerk, born before the Civil War, he is gifted with a mind predetermined for finance, and his life falls in a time full of financial opportunity. The temperament that goes with the mind is revealed to us with a naturalness that fairly stops the mouth of praise or blame. Cowperwood fighting his first fight with a young tough and winning, praised by the leader of the gang to which his adversary belongs, but too cautious to involve himself with low associates and too tactful to give offense in shunning them—seems admirable. We are off our guard and begin to idealize him; later we are inclined to judge him harshly; soon we see that we can do neither. He is as far from delighting in cruelty for its own sake, as far from the abnormality of vice, as a tiger. On the whole we are obliged to admit that his attitude is sensible and good-natured. With extraordinary candor and clearness he sees life as a struggle for existence, and in this struggle he is wholly absorbed. Which of us, we ask ourselves, having his intellectual power and his temperament, would have thought or acted otherwise? It is remarkable that we feel all this in Cowperwood as a boy. We are compelled to regard him as a tremendous force—a force to be reckoned with, not reasoned with—and at the same time we cannot help thinking of him as a human being, if anything more normal in mind, more sentient, more alive than ourselves.

His tremendous career unfolds itself as naturally as the experiences of boyhood. In Cowperwood's progress from one financial position to another, his experience with a commission house, in a brokerage firm, as a note-broker—always the human side is emphasized: we see the everlasting distinction between the merely shrewd man and the man of real foresight, between the man adapted to his environment and the man who has the power to adapt himself. In this novel big men and little men—men of all degrees of bigness and littleness—shoulder one another, and there is no confusion of types; we learn to know them for just what they are. Even the least of them are vital in their way—vital in their cowardice, in their rough-and-ready efficiency, in their limited shrewdness. Each has qualities that in real life would have to be recognized and dealt with; and so we feel at every moment that the story has its setting in the real world. . . .

Through this story flows the tide of life in all its apparent strength and cruelty. We see the workings of impulse and temperament, mysterious and powerful. The narrative thrills with raw human emotion, with undeniable pathos, with the excitement of great endeavor. Yet it is not primarily a story of passion or pathos or ambition, but a story of life. Everywhere there is a wonderful mingling of truthful description and truthful insight. We see the courtroom with strange distinctness, and we are shown the real mental processes of jury, lawyers, and judge. Whatever our convictions about realism as opposed to romance may be, we must admit that *The Financier* is a tremendous book of its kind—a book for mature minds, of course, plain-speaking, and picturing evil as it is, but far too big, too significant, to be thrust aside as realism of the useless, dreary sort. It is not that; it is a portrayal of life-compelling interest, upsetting theories, provoking thought.

Frederic T. Cooper. "Theory of Endings and Some Recent Novels." *Bookman,* 36 (December 1912), 435–436.

. . . The type of story that [*The Financier*] represents is one that has become fairly frequent since the novel of the business and financial world has come into vogue. It is the type that follows the hero through a promising career, as he rises through spectacular strokes of fortune to a dominant position, and then suddenly by one fatal blunder sends the whole carefully built structure tumbling, card-like, to the ground. This was the formula of *The Pit,* by Frank Norris; it served the purposes of Robert Herrick and David Graham Phillips, in a modified form, for more than one of their volumes—in fact, a representative list of recent novels in which it forms the main structure would seriously encroach upon available space. And the noteworthy point about this formula is the nature of the ending which it foreordains. The hero, having learned his lesson and suffered bankruptcy, sometimes only of fortune, but in other cases, of love and honour as well, is supposed to have learned his lesson; and the implication of the closing pages is, that in a new environment and with a chastened spirit, he will begin over again and eventually achieve victory. But to give the impression that Mr. Dreiser's novel belongs undistinguishably to the rank and file of its class is to do him grave injustice. *The Financier* is a very unusual piece of work, a social and economic picture of American life that, in spite of certain crudities, must be recognized as a novel of the first magnitude. Its one real fault is that it is unwarrantedly long. Through nearly eight hundred pages of rather fine print, it surges forcefully on, in a mighty tide of words that the author himself seems to have been impotent to stay. Not that the structure of the story is loose and rambling, nor that the episodes are irrelevant or lacking in interest. It is simply that for the purposes of a clear, forceful picture, he has given us too much. That Mr. Dreiser should himself know all he has told us about his principal characters, and perhaps a good deal more, is as it should be; but he would have gained by practising a more rigid elimination. If Mr. Dreiser's structure had been of an epic variety, if it dealt with the destinies of a race, or summed up the psychology of an epoch, then space and amplitude, and crowding throngs of characters and incidents would all contribute quite properly toward the needed impression of vastness both of theme and of setting. But *The Financier* is distinctly the story of a single character, a certain Frank Algernon Cowperwood, from the time when as a small boy, he bought castile soap at auction and resold it to his father's grocer at one hundred per cent. profit, until a day twenty years later, when the doors of the penitentiary open to give him freedom, and he starts once more to take up the broken threads of his life. In a certain broad sense, the book does give us, in addition to this central character, a picture of American business life, as it was during the Civil War and the reconstruction period, and in a veiled way it is a criticism of the same conditions, on a larger scale, existing in the financial world of to-day. But all this seems to interest Mr. Dreiser only as background. There is no dominant central symbol, like Wheat in *The Pit,* by Norris, or the Bourse, in Zola's *L'Argent.* The dishonesty of the local political ring in Philadelphia during the sixties and seventies, the juggling with city funds, the grabbing of street-car franchises, all of these things concern Mr. Dreiser only to the extent to which they react upon the character and the fortunes of his hero. And for that reason, the sheer mass of detail, the cumulation of names and incidents, people and situations glimpsed only for an instant, in a swift, bewildering panorama of life, have the effect of obscuring, instead of helping us to see. None the less, the personality of Cowperwood, born manipulator of money and colossal egotist, is a portrait not easily forgotten. From early boyhood, he knew precisely what he wanted, and he got it. He never was satisfied with what he had, but was always looking ahead and above for something better and bigger. There was no limit to his ambitions: wealth, position, influence, luxuries of living, a beautiful home, a beautiful wife: all these come to him, one by one, and fail to satisfy his insatiable demands. When he cannot amass fortune quickly enough in an honest way, he cajoles the city treasurer into gambling with the public funds; when the attractions of his lawful wife begin to wane, and his eye falls upon Aileen, favourite daughter of the Irish political boss, old Butler, who has largely made young Cowperwood what he is, no sense of gratitude or loyalty prevents him from reaching out and taking unlawful possession of Aileen, and no flash of intuition warns him that by doing so he is laying the fuse to his own destruction. After this events follow swiftly; the Chicago fire precipitates a panic, in which Cowperwood becomes dangerously involved; yet he might have weathered the storm, had it not happened that, at this fatal hour, old Butler learns the truth about Aileen, and wreaks his vengeance by prosecuting Cowperwood for his irregular dealings with public funds. A term in state's prison sends him forth a wiser but apparently not a sadder man; and as the story closes, his first wife has divorced him and he has repaired his wrong to Aileen by making her his second. Mr. Dreiser, in taking leave of the couple, starting anew in another city, implies that Cowperwood has learned his lesson and is a changed man. But the reader knows better. Cowperwood is the type that does not change; he learns the wisdom of avoiding certain specific mistakes; he will never again be convicted of juggling with city funds; but to the end, he will always be as dishonest as the subtleties of the law allow; and when Aileen's charms begin to fade, his second marriage bonds will hold him no more tightly than did his first. That is why the point at which Mr. Dreiser interrupts his story is not a logical end, but merely a convenient stopping-off place: some of the most crucial chapters in Cowperwood's life are yet to be told.

"A Strong Novel of Finance by Theodore Dreiser." Baltimore *Sun*, December 1, 1912.

It has been said that court records can furnish more remarkable plots for the writer of fiction than the unaided mind of man could conceive, and Mr. Dreiser, in his powerful and dramatic story of Philadelphia finance and politics from 1860 to 1881, has evidently borrowed, as a basis for his narrative, the spectacular, and phenomenal financial rise, fall and commercial re-establishment of the late Chicago traction magnate, Charles T. Yerkes. Probably no attempt is made to portray in the personality of Frank Algernon Cowperwood (the financier of the story) Charles T. Yerkes as a man, but many incidents of the American capitalist's life are introduced as the history of the hero. His birth and residence in Philadelphia, his education at a local high school, his early commercial training in a grain and flour commission house, his entrance upon a stockbroker's career and specializing in bonds, his business assignment in 1871, also, his subsequent trial and conviction by the Philadelphia courts upon charges of misappropriation of public funds; his pardon after serving a short term of imprisonment, the ultimate re-establishment of his business affairs, and his sudden accession to wealth through a series of successful investments at the time of the Jay Cooke failure in 1874. The story closes with the financier's removal to Chicago as a place of residence and foretells as "in a glass darkly" a further life of financial success, patronage of art and boundless riches, but honors that, according to the glass, ring as hollowly to their possessor as did the crowns of Macbeth and Lady Macbeth seated upon their troubled throne.

In the personality of Frank Algernon Cowperwood, the author disclosed an unscrupulous, strong and utterly selfish character that is a law unto itself. A man who in childhood ponders over the unavailing struggle of the weak against the unscrupulous strong. The spectacle of a squid and a lobster in a tank—the squid gradually harried and finally devoured by the lobster—furnish him an example of what he accepts as the law of life—the certainty of conquest on the part of the daring and strong—the inevitable failure and destruction of the weak. Upon this philosophy he shapes his career, and well equipped physically and mentally proceeds to take what he desires, yet with outward seeming of financial integrity and a pretense of personal honor. As a character study the literary creation is most remarkable in its absolute consistency from first to last. Here is a man as subtle and unscrupulous as he is capable and strong. In his lexicon there is no such word as fail, and in spite of calamities that would have wrecked forever a less resolute nature, he rises from the ashes of defeat to still greater worldly achievement. What he is in business he is also in passion. A man of strong sensual impulses controlled by will and wholly selfish in this as in all else. A man who enters a benefactor's house to dishonor it and is not overwhelmed by the whirlwind of deserved wrath that strikes him as a result.

As a picture of Philadelphia financial, political and social life during the period represented, the author is unerring in his revealing of municipal fraud and the endless ramifications of a system of graft and spoliation that cloaked itself with the habiliments of legal financial transactions. The endless chain of personal manipulation and investment of public funds is described with a degree of knowledge that is wide and exact.

Of literary beauty the book has none. Conversations are inane, love-making, utterly without inspiration. It is a sordid story, sordidly told. The reiteration of the word "Honey," addressed to Aileen by her lover, gets horribly upon the reader's nerves, but the author visualizes his characters so that they stand out as in strong sunshine, and his descriptions of Aileen's family, especially of her good-hearted Irish father, are among the finest touches of the book. A ward boss the father is, yet a fine example of the loving, protecting parent, whose daughter's dishonor arouses all his strong nature to battle.

The construction of the story is strong and its unfolding direct. A bewildering number of people are crowded upon the scene, but beyond and above them all move, distinctly and sharply outlined, the central figures of the narrative.

A second Lady Macbeth, unscrupulous but deeply loving, is Aileen—a woman meant for better things, but hypnotized by the attraction of sex and governed in action by recognition of masculine strength, coupled with blindness to the hard and unscrupulous nature behind such fair showing.

The author does not hesitate to class his hero among the successful finance operators of a system only too well known at the present day. Speaking of the hero's financial actions, he says: "Manipulative tricks have always been worked in connection with stocks of which one man or one set of men has had complete control. It was no different from what has since been done by the Erie, Standard Oil, sugar, wheat and what not. Cowperwood was one of the earliest and one of the youngest to see how it could be done."

H.H. Peckham. "Theodore Dreiser Scores a Success." Raleigh [N.C.] *Observer*, December 8, 1912.

Among the contemporary American novelists who write really significant books must certainly be mentioned Mr. Theodore Dreiser. And be it further mentioned that his latest book, "The Financier," is by no means his least significant.

"The Financier," as the title clearly indicates, deals with the career of a man who handled money in large sums; but the scene is not, as might be inferred, laid in present-day Wall Street, but in mid-nineteenth-century Philadelphia.

When Mr. Dreiser wrote "The Financier," he ought to have borrowed one of Thackeray's ideas and called his tale "A Novel Without a Hero"; for if ever a hero (?) was lacking in all the essentials of true heroism, it is Frank Cowperwood, chief personage in "The Financier." Admire him for his cleverness, ingenuity, and business acumen, we must; but sympathise with one so conscienceless as he, we cannot. Not that Cowperwood is so desperately bad—many a man with very good intentions commits as great sins as he,—but in his guilt Cowperwood is utterly unashamed, utterly devoid of heart. . . .

And the deplorable thing about the whole matter is that experience does not chasten Cowperwood, does not perceptibly alter his character.

But he is interesting, grippingly interesting, from the time when as a precocious boy of thirteen he speculates in Castile soap, to the day when he lands in the penitentiary for making illegitimate use of city funds. Nor do the facts that he marries a pretty young widow, subsequently deserts her, and with the coolest heartlessness seduces the handsome young daughter of one of his best friends serve to render him a dull character.

There is nothing pretty or romantic about "The Financier"—nothing to make it otherwise than revolting to the reader of dainty tastes. But the admirer of frank realism can scarcely fail to recognize its bigness, its fearlessness, its vitality. The lover of homely philosophy, too, will find in the book much that is worth while, as note the following apt dictum: "When a high-stepping girl that ought to be wearing a check-rein and a Mexican bit gets so she thinks she can drink booze with the fellow that is keeping her company, she needs her mother, a spanking, and a life-preserver. The first glass of wine for that kind of a girl, whether she's up in G or only a working-man's daughter, is right at the top of a toboggan-chute that has hell at the bottom."

Adverse criticisms which may be made against "The Financier" are that it is about twice as long as it ought to be, and altogether too full of insignificant details; and that its literary style is generally crude and often obscure.

Des Moines [Iowa] *Register Leader*, December 14, 1912.

One of the really vital and appealing novels of the season is "The Financier," which is fascinating in spite of a certain crudeness and its almost revolting materialism. The character of Copperwood the keen, self-contained money-maker, is excellently portrayed. The analysis of motives, of the psychological significance of his actions, is admirably done. And the story maintains a strict unity of interest about the big central figure, at the same time suggesting a background of consistently complex human emotion. This singleness of impression is one of the strong things about the book. Yet the author has related his hero accurately and with unusual fidelity to the whole of life, the underlying pathos or humor or tragedy of it all. . . .

"No Hero Stalks Through His Pages." Kansas City [Mo.] *Journal*, December 17, 1912.

That old proverb concerning a prophet's honor in his own country has been first exemplified and then knocked into a cocked hat by Theodore Dreiser, former Missouri newspaper man. It was Mr. Dreiser's first novel, "Sister Carrie," that brought him a circle of admirers in London, facetiously called the "Sister Carrie Society." That book made him the head of a sort of literary cult, to which no less persons than William J. Locke, author of "Septimus," H. G. Wells and Arnold Bennett, three of the most virile literary figures of the day, were proud to subscribe. Now "The Financier," just off the presses of Harper & Bros., is bringing to the reporter of yesterday an American endorsement of the London verdict. And the London verdict was that Dreiser is in many ways the most significant American author.

When Theodore Dreiser was a reporter for St. Louis newspapers some years ago he contracted the habit of seeing things as they are and of telling the truth about them. "The Financier" is essentially a reporter's novel, and it is the longest one written by an American in recent years. It is also, according to a certain considerable number of critics who do not live in dove cotes, the most masterly study of American life ever written, and the best study of life in any country since Dickens and Thackeray. It is to be remembered that Dickens also was a reporter and Thackeray a journalist. Both had the habit of seeing things as they are and of telling the truth about them. The dove cote critics confess that they don't quite comprehend a novel without a hero and one of the dove cote imitators has called Mr. Dreiser's book "brummagen," having first carefully looked up the definition of the term in the dictionary. A considerable controversy has raged about the novel in the few brief weeks since its publication, but the champions of Mr. Dreiser are quite willing to support their contentions with the verdict of the English authors, who several years ago placed the American in the front rank of those who write the English language.

The book is a terror to hesitant critics. In the first place it has 780 pages, which is too many for a critic but not too many for Dreiser's readers. Again, it paints life as one sees it in the pages of the newspapers and magazine articles. There is no hero, for Mr. Dreiser does not believe in picturing heroes unless they exist. But there is a real man in the book, who has a trick of getting out of the print and walking about the room and going down into the street and doing things. Frank Cowperwood grows from vigorous, independent boyhood to commanding manhood; wins a fortune, loses it, goes to jail, gets out and gets his money back; loves, hates, sins, suffers and goes about his business just as strong and none too conscientious men do every day. He is never a hero and never wholly bad. He is human at every stage of his development. There are several women in his life and some of his relations to them are none too creditable, while his relations to others are all that can be desired. His business life is all of a piece and as natural as the rest of it. No phase of his character is exaggerated to give color or to compromise with the reader's preconceived notions. As for the critics, they are utterly disregarded—neither style nor structure is vamped to please them.

Cowperwood is utterly human, and all but an inconsiderable minority of the critics agree that he will live. With him will live that faithful picture of American life which is the background of his activities.

Beside this novel, rich in its multitudinous detail, with every touch contributing to the thoroughly unified whole, the works of most of Mr. Dreiser's contemporaries seem thin and unsatisfactory. It has a mouth-filling taste and "body" that few books have. No man who looks on life with wide open eyes can fail to catch its significance.

For all its 780 pages, "The Financier" does not finally dispose of Cowperwood, and the reader will be glad that it does not. The story is complete in itself, but it leaves a lingering appetite for the second volume, which will complete the chronicle of the master of finance.

"Current Fiction." *Nation,* 95 (December 19, 1912), 589-590.

Turgenieff dismissed a pair who prospered on the fruits of iniquity with this observation: "Everything in the world, both good and bad, is bestowed upon a man, not in accordance with his merits, but as the result of some unknown but logical laws which I will not even take upon myself to indicate, although it sometimes seems to me that I dimly discern them." These laws Mr. Dreiser is prepared to declare unto us. Scanning the phenomena of success afforded by our national life, he selects a typical career to illustrate their workings—a perfect specimen of the American financier whom he represents as having lived in the Philadelphia of two generations ago.

Briefly to summarize the achievements of thirty-odd years, this genius of finance made a fortune in local speculation; saw it wiped out in the collapse of the market caused by the Chicago fire, and his share in the time-honored traffic in city funds thereby brought to light; paid the penalty of this exposure by a year in prison; and, a few months subsequently, having recouped himself to the extent of $100,000, carried his new-made fortune West. From the time when young Cowperwood took his first object-lesson from an aquarium tragedy, watching an unwilling squid appropriated bit by bit by a relentless lobster, to the day when in the fulness of his powers he migrates from his native habitat to a freer field of development, the study leaves little to be desired from a biological standpoint.

To our thinking, Mr. Dreiser is far and away the ablest humanologist at work in the American field. True, much that is fine slips through his net. But that in itself is no cause for dissatisfaction. Other novelists who have had anything like his power of analysis have been uniformly predisposed to confine themselves to what is choicest and most attenuated in our national life. We rejoice that Mr. Dreiser is not too dainty in his selection, especially since his grasp upon what he has apprehended is so stout. The collection of types in this case is remarkable, both for its representative completeness and for the consistent individuality of each character.

Still more remarkable is the singleness of intention with which they are analyzed, and as it were, comparatively estimated. Who is fittest to survive amid the forces of man's own creating? The answer is, for this *milieu* as for the jungle, he who is most vigorous, most acute, and most intelligently selfish—in a word, Cowperwood. He is the standard. Other characters are measured thereby and their fates justified. Small pity is wasted on those who fall by their deficiencies, as Stener, the flabby-minded city treasurer, who paid the natural price of being other men's tool, and the temperamentally unresponsive wife of whom Cowperwood quietly rids himself. Whatever sympathy Mr. Dreiser permits himself is expended on those who fail by the superabundance of their endowment—a superfluous capacity for other motives than self-interest. The reader's cordial partiality is enlisted for Butler, the old Irish contractor and politician, whose daughter becomes Cowperwood's young mistress. He is vulnerable in his large, fatherly heart, and the retaliation which his strength renders so disastrous to Cowperwood is still more fatal to himself. Aileen herself, though we leave her in the ascendency of her youth legally established as Cowperwood's wife, shows doubly marked for later discard by the ineradicable crudity of her taste and the uncontrollable force of her affections.

It is in his *exposé* of character and relationships and his constructive feeling for human drama that Mr. Dreiser is distinguished. His literary imperfections are many and glaring. He only speaks right on—interminably, diffusely, redundantly, with no stylistic guide beyond a warm feeling for an apt phrase. His attempts to identify his story with a definite period in the past are strangely intermittent.

Even more exasperating are his rambling incursions into the field of ethical speculation. The ease with which he walks through the things he does not see is certainly extraordinary. But he is merely out for exercise—nothing so stern as pioneering. Those who accompany him most willingly will soonest perceive that they are coming back in the end to the point they started from. To the best of our discernment, the three essays in unconventional morality which he has already accomplished in "Sister Carrie," "Jennie Gerhardt," and "The Financier," have not yielded one conclusion that seems to him worth a whole-hearted defense. Obviously, until his own convictions have clarified, he can do little to inform our understanding of right and wrong.

"The Literary Show: A Great American Novel." *Town Topics*, December 19, 1912.

When the news is broken to you that Theodore Dreiser's new novel, "The Financier," runs to 780 pages, your first impulse, I dare say, will be to run shrieking from the scene; but if you value my advice you will throttle that impulse and read the book, for it is one of the most painstaking and searching stories of this our degenerate day. The newspaper reviewers, for a month or so past, have been printing pretty pieces proving that Dreiser has no sense of form, that he doesn't know the precise meaning of certain English words, that he is a poor grammarian, that he has no gift for the dramatic, that he plods along at one unvarying, exasperating pace, up hill and down dale. So much they allege and prove. But to what avail? In answer to them I offer you the book. Read it and puzzle the thing out for yourself. How, with all these faults, does he get such astonishing effects? How does he compound such vivid colors out of drab and gray? How does he achieve so nearly perfect an illusion of reality in the end?

The central figure of "The Financier" (you may call him hero if you choose) is a stock operator who hammers his way to riches, taking all sorts of hammering in return. The scene of his exploits is the Philadelphia of war time and after, and when we leave him at last it is still far back in the 70s. The atmosphere is heavy with politics and finance, and both sciences are breeding their first genuine professors. *Frank Cowperwood* (for that is our hero's name) plays one against the other. As financier he operated through politicians, and as politician he operated through financiers. The result is a quick success, but perils go with it, for the public is not yet educated up to the dizzy legerdemain of later years.

It is not, however, an outraged populace that brings *Cowperwood* down, but an outraged father, old *Edward Malia Butler*; to wit, an eminent contractor and speculator. *Cowperwood*, a married man, makes the tactical blunder of seducing *Butler's* daughter, and *Butler* pays him up for it by railroading him to prison, and there he spends a bleak, sad year. But when he comes out at last it is not as a chastened man, but as a determined man. He will win back his lost money; he will get his revenge. And, what is more, he actually gets it. When the curtain falls he has a round million in negotiable securites—and *Aileen Butler* is tucked under his arm. The two turn Westward; it is in Chicago that the second act of the drama will be played out.

Thus a crude outline of the story—too crude, alas, to give you any notion of its incisive reality, its overwhelming piling up of detail, its amazing air of cold-blooded, unadorned truth. It is not, indeed, a story at all, at least in the conventional sense, but an infinitely elaborated character sketch, an incredibly minute and convincing picture of one man. You come to know that man from head to heels, and you must inevitably conclude in the end that he is worth knowing. An ardent chaser of the dollar, he is yet something vastly better than a money grubber. The thing that lures him on is not even a lust for power, but rather a lust for beauty. He thinks of wealth only as a means of attaining to beautiful things—fine pictures, good horses, rare old furniture, pretty women. A perfect eyebrow seems to him to be something worth sitting down and wondering at. The world, in his sight, is endlessly curious and beautiful.

The achievement of Dreiser lies in the fact that he has made this man perfectly comprehensible, and, as they say on the stage, entirely sympathetic. As the scroll of his acts and motives slowly unrolls, one begins to perceive a serene dignity in his chicaneries, and even in his debaucheries. He evokes, in brief, that solid and well-considered form of sympathy which has its roots in understanding. And this understanding is the product of Dreiser's unflagging patience and industry. Say what you will against his labored piling up of words, his dogged plodding through jungles of detail, his ascetic renunciation of all the common tricks and short cuts of writing, you must always admit that he gets somewhere in the end. You wonder, for page after page, if there is any actual end to get to, and then of a sudden *Cowperwood* emerges from the maze, superbly modeled, perfectly colored, as wholly alive as Tom Jones or Barry Lydon.

And in the background of the story there is the same justification of Dreiser's onerous method. The task before him is to give order and direction to an extraordinarily complex muddle of events, stretching over half a lifetime and involving not only the acts of *Cowperwood, Butler, Aileen* and other individuals, but also the acts of great masses of people. And yet he never falters and never fails. Step by step he works his way through that welter of politics, finance and intrigue, leaving sequence and causation where only confusion was before. Here, in brief where inspiration would have left unreality hanging in the air, the mole-like industry of this American Zola produces an almost uncanny illusion of reality.

William Marion Reedy. "Reflections: Dreiser's Great Book." *Reedy's Mirror*, 21 (January 2, 1913), 2.

If you read novels, let me recommend Theodore Dreiser's "The Financier." It's big—physically and intellectually. It is bigger than his powerful books, "Sister Carrie" and "Jennie Gerhardt." Bigger as man's sphere of action is bigger than woman's. It is passionate with a passionateness of more than sex love, with the passionateness, the intense, undeflectable, remorseless passion of American business, of power. There's sex passion in it, too, and it partakes of the same *idee fixe* quality of the passion for success. Mr. Dreiser's book reminds me of Flaubert's "Sentimental Education" for realism, but that book of Flaubert's is dull. Dreiser's detail is all alive. It is more alive than the detail in Arnold Bennett's "Old Wives' Tale," or "Clayhanger." It is more simple. It has the supreme vividity of good reporting in the days before yellow journalism murdered style and ostracized facts. The story is that of a man bent on limitless success in finance. He plays the game. He plays men as pawns in the game. He has no scruples. He is not immoral, only unmoral. *Frank Cowperwood*, the hero, goes in for financial power and gets it by hook or crook. He doesn't do anything his rivals and associates do not do. He does it more daringly, more brilliantly, with a sort of icy brilliancy. Comes the Chicago fire and a panic and Philadelphia, the scene of *Cowperwood's* activities, is squeezed. *Cowperwood* is caught too much extended. He can't meet his obligations. He has used official tools to enable him to use city moneys and he uses city moneys that he should not have used. Dreiser gives all the details of the transactions—all heightened with marvelous photographic character-sketches of all the men *Cowperwood* deals with. These men, bankers, brokers, bosses, understrappers, brokers' clerks, stand out with a lifelikeness that is more than cinematographic. You can see back of them, around them, *into* them. The old boss, *Butler*, is wonderfully done. You can hear his brogue.

Cowperwood is a thoroughbred in his way, a clean-cut fellow. He never loses his nerve. He exhausts every resource to save himself, but the time, the circumstances are against him and he goes to the wall—and to the penitentiary. Through all the maze of financial intrigue stands out character—the book reeks with it. *Cowperwood* dominates all the others in his cold, keen, well-groomed, alert fashion. But underneath the cold runs a smouldering flame, a flame repressed. *Cowperwood* meets boss *Butler's* daughter, loves, is loved, and seduces—I am not so sure he is not seduced by—her. She's a red-headed girl and a wonder. She reminds me of that red-headed Irish girl in Harold Frederic's "The Damnation of Theron Ware." She is a woman of will-power. She is not afraid of wrong. She knows *Cowperwood* is married. She knows *Cowperwood's* wife. She will give herself to get *Cowperwood*. And she does it right regally, accepting, nay inviting the consequences. No whimpering for her. She goes to her man and does it defiantly, even though it breaks the stout heart of her father whom she loves. *Aileen Butler* is a Superwoman, beyond good and evil. Not oversexed, mind you: her passion is as intellectual as carnal. She is the daughter of a man of power and she worships power in the mate she has found for herself. When her father finds her in an assignation house with *Cowperwood* the scene is tremendous—though without a loud word, a shriek, a scream. The terror, the horror, the ethicless splendor of it lie in the simplicity of the telling. Phryne before the judges was not more supreme in assurance of her own matchless power. *Cowperwood's* wife has to go by the board: at best she was only a respectable person whom *Cowperwood* had married, as a young widow, for no other reason, apparently, than propinquity and a complacent conformity to what was, at the time, expected of a young man bent on getting along. *Cowperwood* "does his time," his wife is divorced, he comes out to freedom and he and *Aileen* go to Chicago, where Dreiser leaves them, married, living in a sort of splendid, lonely misery. You can't help recalling somewhat the real-life-story of the late Charles T. Yerkes. I've given the story in foreshortening. I cannot give you any impression of the crowdedness of Dreiser's canvas—crowded, but without confusion. I cannot convey to you that smouldering glow in the story that now shows through the texture of Dreiser's words like the absinthean, opalescent color in favrile glass, but often and again flames up into diamond brightness. The whole story is so fused and fluid that it's not like a story at all. It's like nothing in the world but life. And there play through it some glories, many meannesses, sordidities, occasional fantasticalities of character. It's a great story of Self in a half hundred manifestations—Self bent on Self's ends to the end of everything. That is the demiurgue of the tale. It is the passion behind all passion, the flame into which all minor flames burn. You not only read the narrative. In quite a wonderful way you are of it, and when you are at all conscious of Mr. Theodore Dreiser it is only in a dim, faint fashion, as if you heard his voice as he guides you through this hell which is only the life of Self. For it is a hell. There are splotches of pale happiness in it that make you think of St. George Mivart's queer conception—for which Rome damned him here and hereafter—of happiness in hell, or more vividly of Shelley's line—"Hell is a city very much like London."

For London write Philadelphia or—St. Louis. Finally, "The Financier" has an odd effect, which I think stamps it with something of greatness. You close the book hating no one, but sorry for everyone in it. Yes; Dreiser's like James Clarence Mangan: "He too has tears for all souls in trouble, here and in Hell."

Charlotte [N.C.] *Observer*, January 12, 1913.

No one book of recent months has been more written of than "The Financier." Its forcefulness and various merits have all been brought before the light of criticism. There is not one dissenting voice as to the author's wonderful comprehension of and his description of things, his fearless analysis of the struggle and weakness of men and women.

The book is absorbing in interest and the style is such as to make things seem all too real. But the tremendous danger that lies in his reasoning and philosophy concerning life and the relations of life is not considered in any way. Flagrant sin we all abhor and avoid, but the subtlety of reason in Mr. Dreiser's views appeal so strongly to those who are all too willing to be upheld in their defiance of conventionality. For downright evil suggestions, for plainness of detail concerning things unspeakable and unwritable, he rivals Balzac or Daudet, or any of the French school of realism. He shows so plainly that Christianity and religious teachings after all have little to do with the control of passion and morality generally.

The man, whom he makes his hero, by sheer struggle and selfishness, overcomes difficulties that would crush the average man. Go your own way, be strong enough and there is nothing you may not accomplish. This is a dangerous precept for ordinary men, those who do not view life with the progressive mind of a scientist. There is one thing that life and experience teaches us all: an outward show of perfect success does not mean happiness. There is always the flaw in the crystal, the ashes of dead sea fruit. In our tremendous effort and self-concentration, we lose the power to live, to feel. We have to enjoy as we go, or we lose the ability; we become less than human.

Life is finely adjusted and easily unbalanced. This must be the moral of this unusual book, or it has none.

I.E.M.
"Vanity of Vanities." Chicago *Tribune*, January 19, 1913.

Now that David Graham Phillips is gone, Theodore Dreiser is perhaps the most realistic of America's younger novelists. He not only presents his characters without gloves, but does not trouble much about washing their hands. He is quite as downright as Phillips, but not so vivid, and, at least in his latest book, not so entertaining. Phillips never allowed his affection for the god-of-things-as-they-are to interfere with his story-interest; Dreiser becomes prosy often through an overplus of detail. In "The Financier" he traces the life of one of those remarkable American boys who are born to finance as the sparks fly upward. This child, Frank Algernon Cowperwood, puts us in mind of the Father Goose rhyme to the effect that "each American boy is a king," said young Hoy, "for a crown always grows on his head."

. . . He is a man who craves love. It is not the kind of love one reads about in Sunday school books; it is of the earth, but he is of the earth, too, and he needs it. He marries the wrong woman, although she does very well until he tires of her and sees someone younger and fresher. Then he has two wives, and doesn't feel any more sensitive about it than would a Mormon. This part of the story is so very plain that one forgets to be shocked. It is not suggestive, and therefore is as clean as such things can be—in fact it rather bores one. The moral of the whole thing is that all is vanity. He gets what he wants, only to find that he doesn't want it, and one is left wondering what he can find to buy "one-half so precious as the thing he sells."

San Francisco *Argonaut*, January 25, 1913.

Before estimating the ethical values of Mr. Dreiser's latest novel—indeed of any of his novels—it is well to discriminate between successful ambitions and happiness. After all it is happiness that we are all looking for. The attainment of ambitions may seem the most desirable road to happiness, but shall we rightly ascribe success to him whose ambitions are triumphant, but who finds that they do not lead to happiness? It is significant of much of Mr. Dreiser's work that his heroes get everything they want except happiness. They win money, power, and the love of women in unstinted quantities. But they leave the stage with downcast faces, drearily, and to slow music.

This is true of Frank Cowperwood, hero of "The Financier." He is force personified. His morality is the business conventions of the day, no more. He makes a fortune, loses it, goes to jail, recoups himself, and settles in the West. He once saw a lobster devour a squid, methodically, remorselessly. He determines to be the lobster and the business world his squid. He succeeds because he is efficient and because he absorbs or destroys every inefficiency in his path. When he meets Aileen Butler he absorbs her, too, however willing a victim she may have been. He has a wife already, but what of that? Cowperwood and Aileen are wholly conscienceless, knowing no law but their own desires, no restraint but the public censure that is bad business. Unthinkingly we may say that we have here a type of success and a map of the roads that lead to success. That will be true enough, but we may still ask if success is an end in itself, or merely a means to happiness. For certainly Cowperwood is not happy. Nor is Aileen. Nature has given them everything they asked of her, but they are left to find that happiness is not included in this prodigality of attainments. They have confused the means with the end.

Mr. Dreiser writes much as one would write a private diary, careless of style, and with a tendency to disquisitions upon things that do not matter. He seems anxious to formulate an ethical idea and to state it succinctly, but without a clear idea of what it is or enthusiasm in its defense. But the ethical idea is in the story itself. It is the disillusionment that follows success. His last chapter leaves us with a sense of the pity of it all, the futility of the efforts even of Titans who win the whole world and lose their own souls.

St. Joseph [Mo.] *Press*, January 31, 1913.

There ought to be a law requiring young men of the acquisitive temperament to read Theodore Dreiser's latest book, "The Financier." The youth who begins his career with the idea that money is the only thing worth while is likely to find, in the end, that he has harvested a lot of Dead Sea Fruit. Most people who endeavor to teach this lesson, by means of novels, essays or sermons, do it drearily and tediously, and fail to make the desired impression. Frequently the people who would teach us spend most of their time in the pursuit of wealth; so we listen to them politely and then go chasing dollars with the usual enthusiasm.

Chasing dollars is all right if a man doesn't lose his sense of proportion, if he can avoid the conclusion that the dollars are the only things worth chasing. That is the evil the acquisitive young should guard against, and "The Financier" will be a great help to him. . . . There is no expounding of moral lessons in any part of the book. The story is told with a realism that reminds the reader of Zola, and the reader may extract his own moral.

It is a splendid picture of American life, or that phase of it which deals with stocks and bonds and speculation. There is no careless work in any part of it. There are dozens of characters in the story, and each one is a living, breathing human being, as much so as any man you know in real life. There are no dummies from first to last. The descriptive work is remarkable. Whether the author is describing a scene on change or the furniture of a new house, he writes as though he had made a life study of the business; and the story of Cowperwood's admittance to the penitentiary, and of the soul disturbing experiences he had there, will stick to the memory a long time. The story has no plot, and reads more like a biography, compiled from accurate data, than a novel, but it gains rather than loses dramatic force from the author's method. It is a story that will make even the thoughtless or calloused reader spend an occasional hour communing with himself.

"The Financier," *Book News Monthly*, February, 1913.

Mr. Dreiser is taken very seriously among English authors and readers. His American public grows more slowly. Ten years ago *Sister Carrie* sank into immediate oblivion, to be resurrected when *Jennie Gerhardt* appeared, something over a year ago. *The Financier* is as great a book as either of the earlier two, but we question its ability to win appreciation among more than a fastidious few. And even these will likely deplore the continued tendency on Mr. Dreiser's part to deal with some of life's most unpleasant and unfortunate aspects, and to deal with them in a manner so frank and matter-of-fact as to be more than a little disgusting.

The Financier has its scene in Philadelphia, in the years preceding and during the Civil War, in those years when American finance received its greatest impetus and big fortunes began in small ways to be made.

The small boy who becomes the tale's

hero is pictured with strong, sympathetic touches that immediately dispose the reader in his favor. His rapid development, his sturdy independence of thought and action, his genius, as early discovered, promise a high man and a fine man, as well as a successful man.

Frank Cowperwood grows rich fast. People like him, his colleagues recognize his talents, his enemies respect them. He marries decently and in order and has children; but as events show, he marries too soon. His wife proves to be the wrong woman, and from the time that he finds the right one the reader is subjected to the perusal of a series of entirely unpleasant and wholly unnecessary episodes. Mr. Dreiser has no hesitancy in revealing his hero to be as mad in the pursuit of passion as in the race for wealth, and as altogether unscrupulous in his method of acquiring both. The situation verges on the dramatic, but it has little to recommend it otherwise.

In all, for a writer so evidently gifted, Mr. Dreiser presents a point of view by no means wholesome or uplifting; to create a man as immoral and as unmoral as Frank Cowperwood is not an achievement, even if created for the purpose of showing what a man who starts right may become. Mr. Dreiser could do things that would make his work far more effective among the great circle of readers who wait eagerly for the tale that makes life seem a better than a worse thing.

Edwin L. Shuman. Chicago *Record-Herald*, February 1, 1913.

It is evident that Theodore Dreiser has taken the early financial career of the late Charles T. Yerkes as the basis for his long new novel, "The Financier." Frank Cowperwood is Yerkes, so far as the latter's Philadelphia business career is concerned, including his early years in the grain commission trade, his success as an exchange broker, his early bond deals, his dabbling in street railways, his spectacular failure in the panic caused by the Chicago fire, his imprisonment, his pardon and his departure to begin a new career in Chicago.

Upon this foundation Mr. Dreiser has built up an elaborate, painstaking, infinitely detailed and at times decidedly wearisome study of this masterful type of American financier and of the political conditions that foster such growths. The style is plain, without humor or sparkle. The psychological analysis is minute and masterly. Cowperwood and his methods are discussed with the same keen discernment and fearless truth that Mr. Dreiser exhibited in "Sister Carrie" and "Jennie Gerhardt." You come to know Cowperwood from the inside even more intimately than he knew himself—and he knew himself right well.

Around this dominant, unscrupulous, yet not altogether bad or unlovable figure Mr. Dreiser has created a little world of imaginary but very real men and women, including the whole corrupt clique of politicians who buzz like bees around the city treasury of Philadelphia. Most interesting and most innocent of these is an Irish contractor named Butler, whose daughter, Aileen, falls under Cowperwood's baleful fascination and becomes the foremost feminine character in the story. It is the financier's illicit relations with Aileen, even more than his use of the weak city treasurer as catspaw, that causes his dramatic downfall and imprisonment.

An immoral sex relation is the center of every one of Mr. Dreiser's novels, and "The Financier" resembles the others in its unmoral yet absolutely true and human portrayal of such a situation. Cowperwood is married and has two children, but the buccaneer is not content, so he captures the love and person of Aileen Butler. The story of their life in a secret house is handled with about the same degree of reticence, if not skill, that Flaubert shows in "Madame Bovary"; which is equivalent to saying that "The Financier" is fundamentally a moral book, if read by mature people, but that it is doubtful whether it should go indiscriminately into public libraries.

In some respects "The Financier" is a great novel. It conveys the sense of infinite numbers and vast human horizons. In the creation of vital and natural—but never admirable—characters, Theodore Dreiser is among the foremost of living American novelists. Both his merits and his faults suggest Balzac. The masterful qualties of Cowperwood, the pathetic figure of the father he drags down to ruin, the outraged paternity of Butler, the intense femininity of Aileen; the putty character of Stener, the sleek rapacity of the silk-hatted politicians who are making a tool of him —every one of these phrases will recall a living person to those who have read "The Financier."

On the other hand, Mr. Dreiser's realism is defective in its almost total lack of ideals. It would be unfair to say that he is without moral sense, but this sense is like Mrs. Cowperwood's temperament—lymphatic, to use the author's own word—and contents itself with philosophic apologies for the evil portrayed. "These men and women are made thus," he says in substance, "and who are we that we should condemn them?"

His literary method, too, has an inherent weakness that makes some dull pages in "The Financier." The massing of infinite details is interesting so long as the details deal with the human soul, but when applied to the explaining of financial methods they become wearisome. Cowperwood and his doings are not worth 780 closely printed pages, and the book would be better if it were shorter by at least one-third. At the same time the reader who wades through "The Financier" will have an illuminating insight not only into a complex type of perverted genius, but into a whole phase of American life.

William Morton Payne. "Recent Fiction." *Dial*, 54 (February 1, 1913), 99-100.

Mr. Theodore Dreiser has been long-winded enough in his two previous performances, but in his third novel, "The Financier," he has carried analysis and amplification to an extreme hitherto unattained. There are nearly eight hundred pages in this book, and the story that they tell might have been more effectively set forth with half the number of words. He cannot introduce a new character, of however minor significance, without telling us all about him, or a new situation without enveloping it in a cloud of comment and exposition. The details of Cowperwood's stock manipulations are explained in a manner that may be interesting to stockbrokers, but are unspeakably wearisome to the reader who is impatient for action and results. When the financier is on trial for embezzlement, we are given all the steps of the legal procedure, and even the twelve good men and true who act as jurors in the case are individually characterized. The fault of over-elaboration is much more grievous than it was in the case of Mr. White's "A Certain Rich Man," which the present novel resembles in both theme and construction. Mr. Dreiser gives us truth, no doubt, and in that fact is the defence of his method, but it is truth in conglomerate chunks such as the literary artist is under bonds to dispense with. . . .

Audrie Alspaugh. "Dreiser's 'Financier,' a Big Theme." Chicago *Tribune*, February 1, 1913.

Theodore Dreiser's third book, "THE FINANCIER," is a very creditable accomplishment that will undoubtedly add to his literary reputation, for it is a big theme handled in a most finished fashion. It is not a pleasant book, but it is admirable, carrying a powerful impression yet built up with the amazing minuteness of the realist who almost records the number of buttons on one's shoe or of the hairs along one's part. The theme is the big one of love of money and of love with the role it plays in American life, localized in this instance in Philadelphia along in the forties. . . . The book is plain life with no glamour about it—a little too plain, for there is none of the saving poetry of youth, but it strikes the right tone for its theme.

It is without doubt a big thing—this book—a bitter and a distasteful thing, but healthy in its effect; it won't reform politicians nor give morals to the moralless, but it will arouse in many a reader a keener sense of civic duty and of human fraility and perhaps stir in some a protest against their own normally selfish lives.

Los Angeles *Graphic*, February 15, 1913.

There is no doubt that Theodore Dreiser holds high place in the ranks of American novelists, for he covers a wide scope in his writings; showing a power of deep thinking that is all too rarely evidenced in our literary output. His previous novels have won him attention from the reading public, as well as raising dissension among the critics, who either condemn or lavishly praise. It is to be feared that his latest novel will receive more condemnation than commendation. While it is typically American, with the spirit of strife and an intricate financial problem, and while its character delineation is par excellence, Mr. Dreiser has so obviously striven after effect that there is a hallow echo to his work. He is not hesitant in calling a spade a spade, but he does it so unbeautifully that it is revolting, nauseating, and certainly inartistic. Mr. Dreiser is graphically analytic, but he carries this power to too great a degree in "The Financier," so much so that the plethora of detail becomes wearisome. After all, art in writing is in suggesting to one's readers with a few words all that an author wishes to convey. There seems no wisdom in dwelling overlong on this phase or that phase of a character's moral nature. Cowperwood is a financier, born of a commonplace family, with a talent for handling money that amounts to genius. He is not the usual figure of fiction; for while cast in a heroic mould, he differs vastly from the "never-do-wrongs" that find so much favor with most writers. Mr. Dreiser makes him far more contemptible than interesting. His eagerness for love is as great as his eagerness for wealth, and upon this side of his nature the author lingers to the point of distraction—so that the reader turns over many pages to escape from the harrowing details. Cowperwood's negative wife; his vivid, passionate mistress, Aileen Butler, are as distinct in the mind as creatures of flesh and blood; and Aileen's father, the sturdy Irish financier, whose Aileen is the flower of his heart, is a far bigger character than that of Cowperwood—the best thing in the book. The story is unclothed in any beauty save that of the language in which it is couched. The finale, however, is truly artistic—for it ends with a picture of not the failure of poverty and lost love—but the failure of success which is ashes in the mouth.

"Mr. Dreiser's Financier." *Independent,* 74 (February 27, 1913) 470-471.

It is the easiest thing in the world to point out Theodore Dreiser's shortcomings. His tedious convolutions, his circuitous manner of telling a story, his crudities of style, his inability to crystalize an emotion in a phrase or a scene in less than a chapter—these are the most obvious externals, and therefore need not detain us. For there must be something indefinably powerful about an author whose Complete Works consist of only three painstaking novels and yet are reckoned "a force and a fresh impetus" wherever Literature is known; whose first book, *Sister Carrie,* was refused by almost every publisher in this country, and yet, upon its appearance in the meanest of paper and typography, was ranked as one of the greatest pieces of work ever produced in America; a man whose name was unknown by the book-devouring public at the very time it was being hailed by such a variety of critics as Arnold Bennett, Frank Harris, John Galsworthy, Floyd Dell, and the unusually caustic H. L. Mencken. And this bigness that smothers all petty criticism is the man's vigorous sincerity. No craftsman living today, no matter what his art man be, has less of artifice than Theodore Dreiser—in fact, from a standpoint of outward beauty and esthetics, much of his work would be improved were there more of it.

On the very first page of the new novel, for example, is this passage:

> Young Cowperwood's father was a bank clerk at his birth, and ten years later, when young Cowperwood was turning a very sensible, vigorous eye on the world, his father was still a clerk, altho a much more trusted and desired one, and was so near a tellership that there was not the least doubt in the world that he would get it.
>
> The next year, because the president died and the vice-president became president, the cashier was made vice-president, and Mr. Henry Worthington Cowperwood was moved into the place vacated by the promoted teller. He was a happy man. It meant the munificent sum of thirty-five hundred dollars a year, and he decided, as he told his wife joyously the night he heard it, that he, or they, rather, would now move from Number 21 Buttonwood Street to Number 124 New Market, where there was a nice brick house of three stories in height, as opposed to the one of two stories which they now occupied.

Taken from its context this fragment may seem unimportant, but it has the same value that a single drop of blood may have under the microscope. Here is the author's almost ridiculous love of detail, his much too careful eye for truth, his meticulous preciseness of incident—and underneath it all is the honesty and power of his vision. Mr. Dreiser calls on no exterior glamor for aid; the Fact is glorious enough for him; it is the beginning and the end of his art; it is his all in all. He is no doctrinaire; he has no economic axe to grind; no panacea to relieve the ills of the world; no mental Balm of Gilead to smear unctuously over the perplexed soul. He voices a frank but jubilant materialism; he is concerned but little as to the justice of things—whether they are good or bad interests him less than whether they are. With all its contradictions and muddled tragedies Life is to him a very moving and noble thing; he sees no reason why he should color it, distort its values or eliminate any part of it—if it is worth while living, it is worth while writing about. He does not even seek to dignify the commonplace; he finds it glorious and romantic enough. Every incident, every casual interchange of thought is to him a vital thing—and so the tale of half the life of Frank Cowperwood (from his youth to middle-age) consumes seven hundred and eighty closely printed pages—the other half is still to be told!

And it is just because of this insistence on the value of life's minutiæ that Dreiser's work is so often powerful rather than final; big without being great. A greater artist would choose from this welter of facts, would eliminate, condense and give us the essentials in a less tortuous manner. Dreiser's method of approaching a point may be described as an ever-narrowing spiral. But it is this very circumlocutory process that enables him to display his most effective gift—the building up of character. No living author has a sense of characterization more keenly developed; possibly no one since Balzac has drawn such amazing portraits as old man Gerhardt; as the pathetic Jennie, floating thru life, unable to strike out for herself; swept on by whatever waves carried her; the pitiful spectacle of Hurstwood; the brilliant and blind strivings of Carrie Meeber—these are all etchings none the less beautiful because they are laborious. And now comes Frank Cowperwood, the "Financier"; an arresting, and to many, an irritating figure; an unmoral, capable, generous, shrewd, ambitious manipulator, taking what he wants, untroubled by codes, ethics or conscience. From the moment when, at the age of thirteen, he makes his first "deal" in soap, one sees in him the outlines of something unquestionably big.

Aileen Butler, with whom he falls in love, after ten years of vapid wedlock, is not so fully drawn—but her development in the forthcoming sequel will be interesting. It is this genius for character, together with the power for revealing the chaotic surge of life, that will reward the reader for plodding thru the many tedious intricacies of banking, politics, and a court trial. One wishes at times for more sensuousness, more refinement of expression and less baldness of narrative, but once in the midst of the story one feels that the charm of such prose as, say, Meredith's, Moore's or Wells's would be out of place here; one is satisfied to find beauty in what Mr. Dreiser says rather than in how he says it. A gaunt beauty, perhaps, like a bronze of Rodin's or a wild tone poem of Richard Strauss—but it is a moving beauty, even if it moves with its power instead of its poetry. *The Financier* must be ranked as one of the finest contemporary novels, even tho Mr. Dreiser has the instincts of a portrait painter rather than a novelist. It is above all a splendid life-size portrait of a man ("in the Dutch manner," Lucian Cary says) against the vast background of America —tremendous, in spite of (or, possibly because of) the fact that it is often as vague, as tedious and as formless as life itself.

Gardner W. Wood. "Books of the Day." *McClure's Magazine*, March, 1913, p. 231.

"The Financier," the latest production of Theodore Dreiser, is printed in small type and fills 780 narrow-margined pages. It also by this fact fills the average reader with horror—we have yet to find any one who has had the courage to finish this monumental collection of quaint and simple Dreiserian words.

For two years Mr. Dreiser has been the mode, ever since the publication of "Jennie Gerhardt," whose instant success served to resurrect "Sister Carrie," his previous story, for a larger and more generous reading and appraisal. "Jennie Gerhardt" was proclaimed, albeit, with rather apoplectic enthusiasm, as the greatest book of the decade. Many a critic nailed his flag to the mast with that statement.

Very naturally, then, the appearance of Mr. Dreiser's third book, "The Financier," was eagerly awaited—and has been greeted with mingled emotions. One faction has asked itself, "Was our claque a little too loud when 'Jennie Gerhardt' made her bow?" The others, disappointed but still hopeful, feel that if he learns his lesson Mr. Dreiser will do better next time. We hope so, too. . . .

With Mr. Dreiser's characterizations there is little fault to find. They are done with minute precision, and have the same sharp brilliance that dazzled the readers of "Jennie Gerhardt." Cowperwood himself, old man Butler his patron, Aileen the feminine firebrand are splendid drawings. The story is, or would be if it were not swathed in a winding-sheet of words, a gripping drama. But Mr. Dreiser has overdone the thing that had distinguished him.

He is like a dredge scooping its way across country. Everything is brought to the surface: mud, water, stones, organic life, sticks, tadpoles, old shoes—everything; and left open to the startled vision of man. Nothing escapes the automatic Mr. Dreiser, and it all goes into his book; leather chairs, "stained glass of a soothing key," politicians innumerable, turgid and frequent philosophizing, boodle, intrigue of all known varieties, Gothic architecture, black silk stockings—an unending hodge-podge of detail, gone over and over with iteration and reiteration until the weary brain reels and shrieks for relief.

Perhaps after this gigantic effort Mr. Dreiser will amend his ways and his diction. There is such a thing as overestimating the quantity of one's own quaint qualities and misdirecting one's directness.

Ainslee's, April, 1913.

Theodore Dreiser's last book, 'The Financier," published by Harper & Brothers, is the most important work he has done, so far.

This time he has taken a more varied and stirring theme, and has devoted himself to the study of a man instead of to a "Sister Carrie" or a "Jennie Gerhardt." Like Balsac, he has a taste for a big canvas, and he paints upon it boldly the figure of Frank Cowperwood.

But although he bestows any amount of study and analysis upon the type of man he seeks to present, his background apparently interests him quite as much. He sees an infinite wealth of detail, a crowd of people, and it all seems important to him, a part of the composition; but much of it, although interesting, and often valuable, is almost wholly extraneous.

It may be that, in the future, an epic of American history will be written of the genius and development of a group of financiers, the conditions that created them, and the marvels they accomplished. Mr. Dreiser has seen this opportunity, and seized it. He shows, dramatically and, one feels, truthfully, the ideals and desires that animated Cowperwood, the circumstances and environment that molded him. He has depicted every step of his hero's rise, of his fall, and of his phoenixlike emergence from his ashes. He has portrayed the part women played in his life—a not inconsiderable part, by the way—and in this carefully worked-out novel has shown sincerity, and a distinct, although certainly not overwhelming, power as a novelist.

"Recent Reflections of a Novel Reader." *Atlantic Monthly*, III (May 1913) 689–691.

. . . *The Financier* is an imposing book, both in intention and execution. If it resembles a biography more than a work of art, that, doubtless, is an aspect of the matter with which the author deliberately reckoned before he began. The critic is entitled to ignore it in view of Mr. Dreiser's success in presenting an intimate picture of the development of a man of financial genius whose kind is only too common in America. Should the type become extinct (Heaven speed the day!) and the novel survive, our descendants will have in it the means of reconstructing for themselves the business life and immorality of a whole period.

The book details with endless particularity, but forcefully, the character and career of Frank Cowperwood, a Philadelphia boy: his rise in the financial world, his rocket-like descent to the status of a convict, and the means by which he, later, recoups his fallen fortunes. The picture includes his business associates, alleged friends, entire family connection, and the family of the girl whom he finally marries after a long *liaison,* wrecking a first marriage. The author has all these threads of his tapestry well in hand, and no less clear is his presentation of the ins and outs of Philadelphia politics, and the opportunities they afforded for unscrupulous money-making. So painstaking, so lavish of detail, so determined to cover the large canvas closely, is he, that he seems to propose to himself the feats of an American Balzac. If this is the case, he has made a good beginning and is alone in a field that is ready for harvest.

Perhaps the most extraordinary quality of this unusual book is the dryness of its atmosphere. We are reminded of those caverns where nothing ever decays, where all dead things lie mummified, retaining the outward aspect of life for centuries. This effect is, in part, intentional. I do not make out to my own satisfaction whether it is wholly so. Certainly Mr. Dreiser wishes us to feel the extreme aridity of nature in a man like Cowperwood, who sees life under the categories of strength and weakness, and in no other way; certainly also it is hardly possible to overestimate the desiccating effect of absolute materialism in a man of his ability; doubtless, too, the environment and relations of such a man would inevitably tend to grow more and more arid. Still, one would like to ask the author if, as a matter of technique, this juicelessness of the money-maker might not have been brought out more poignantly by the introduction into the book of somebody with a soul—somebody, that is to say, who sees our existence under the categories of good and evil, right and wrong. This is the chief thing that gives atmosphere and perspective to life. Lust and greed, the pride of the flesh and the joy of life, are not shown in their proper values unless they are contrasted with something quite different. This something different, the spirit-side of life as opposed to the material side, is wholly omitted from *The Financier.* As the book stands, the part of foil is played by a hard-headed old contractor and politician, the father of the girl with whom Cowperwood becomes entangled. Butler is a soft-hearted parent, and is sufficiently shocked and vindictive on learning of the illicit relation in which his daughter exults. He is more nearly human than any other character of the tale, but even he fails really to touch the reader.

Since the death of Frank Norris, no American novelist has attempted anything on the scale of *The Financier.* Far apart in temperament and method, the two writers are alike in the resolution to do a big thing in a big way. For the novelist, I apprehend that the biggest way of all is one which is, as yet, closed to Mr. Dreiser by his philosophy. One must not be rash in formulating this philosophy, but it seems to be negative, to consist in the belief that life is an insoluble problem, and that the existence of predatory types in nature and society justifies us in indicting that dark Will which places man in a universe where 'his feet are in the trap of circumstance, his eyes are on an illusion.'

Whatever the truth of such a philosophy, one thing is certain: the consensus of men's opinions through the centuries has demanded a different basis from this for the enduring things, the great things, in literature. And the long consensus of opinion is our only real criterion. But to quarrel with Mr. Dreiser upon this point is, after all, to praise him, since it makes clear the fact that his achievement must be looked at from the highest ground.

A man's philosophy is determined in part by his length of days. Knowing nothing as to the fact, I would place the author of *The Financier* near forty-three—too old for the optimism of youth, too young for the optimism of late middle life. If the horribly cold and insanely bitter realism of Strindberg melted at sixty, under the impact of life, into a believing mysticism, who can say what insight and tenderness, what softness of atmosphere and richness of feeling, a dozen years may not add to the already very notable performances of Mr. Dreiser?

Checklist of Additional Reviews

San Francisco *Evening Post,* September 13, 1912.

Bookseller, September 15, 1912.

Chicago *Evening Post,* September 27, 1912.

Pittsburgh *Post,* October 26, 1912.

H. L. Mencken. "Today's Book." Baltimore Evening *Sun,* October 28, 1912.

Terre Haute [Ind.] *Star,* October 28, 1912.

Boston *Advertiser,* November 1, 1912.

Syracuse *Post Standard,* November 2, 1912.

Publisher's Weekly, November 2, 1912.

New York *Globe and Commercial Advertiser,* November 2, 1912.

New York *American,* November 2, 1912.

James L. Ford. New York *Herald,* November 2, 1912.

San Francisco *Evening Post,* November 2, 1912.

Salt Lake City [Utah] *Tribune,* November 3, 1912.

Youngstown [Ohio] *Vindicator,* November 4, 1912.

Portland *Oregonian,* November 10, 1912.

"Of an Early Financier." Buffalo *Express,* November 10, 1912.

Waco [Tex.] *Times Herald,* November 14, 1912.

Chicago *Continent,* November 14, 1912.

Baltimore *Evening Sun,* November 15, 1912.

San Francisco *Bulletin,* November 16, 1912.

Salt Lake City [Utah] *Republican,* November 16, 1912.

Portland [Ore.] *Telegram,* November 16, 1912.

Baltimore *Evening News,* November 16, 1912.

"A Philadelphia Novel." Philadelphia *Inquirer,* November 16, 1912.

Detroit *Free Press,* November 16, 1912.

Philadelphia *North American,* November 16, 1912.

C. T. Jewett, Terre Haute [Ind.] *Star,* November 18, 1912.

New York *Press,* November 18, 1912.

San Francisco *Zion's Head,* November 20, 1912.

Grand Rapids [Mich.] *Press,* November 21, 1912.

Kansas City [Mo.] *Star,* November 23, 1912.

Washington [D.C.] *Evening Star,* November 23, 1912.

Publisher's Weekly, November 23, 1912.

Boston *Globe,* November 23, 1912.
Kansas City [Mo.] *Post,* November 23, 1912.
Savannah [Ga.] *News,* November 25, 1912.
Dallas [Tex.] *News,* November 25, 1912.
"Cowperwood the Primitive." Boston *Advertiser,* November 28, 1912.
New York Morning *Telegraph,* November 30, 1912.
W. C. Lengel. Wichita [Kan.] *Beacon,* November 30, 1912.
"Literature and Art." *Current Literature,* 53 (December 1912), 696–697.
New York *Times,* December 1, 1912.
"Fiction Built on Fact." Minneapolis *Journal,* December 1, 1912.
Chicago *Banker,* December 7, 1912.
Chicago *Record Herald,* December 7, 1912.
New Orleans *Times Picayune,* December 8, 1912.
H. L. Mencken. " 'The Financier' Powerful Novel of Modern Commerce By Theodore Dreiser." Los Angeles *Times Magazine,* December 8, 1912, p. 6.
Newark *Call,* December 8, 1912.
Trenton [N.J.] *Advertiser,* December 8, 1912.
Kansas City [Kan.] *Gazette Globe,* December 11, 1912.
Good Health Clinic [Syracuse, N.Y.], December 12, 1912.
"Strong Novel of American Life." Philadelphia *North American,* December 14, 1912.
Lansing [Mich.] *Journal,* December 14, 1912.
Bookseller, December 15, 1912.
Hartford [Conn.] *Post,* December 15, 1912.
Mobile [Ala.] *Item,* December 15, 1912.
Charlotte [N.C.] *Observer,* December 15, 1912.
Augusta [Ga.] *Chronicle,* December 15, 1912.
Trenton [N.J.] *Advertiser,* December 15, 1912.
Hartford [Conn.] *Times,* December 19, 1912.
"Current Fiction." New York *Evening Post Saturday Supplement,* December 21, 1912, p. 5.
Burlington [Ia.] *Saturday Evening Post,* December 28, 1912.
H. L. Mencken. "Again the Busy Fictioneers." *Smart Set,* 39 (January 1913), 153, 155–157.
Shan F. Bullock. "London Letter." Chicago *Evening Post,* January 3, 1913.
New Orleans [La.] *Times-Democrat,* January 12, 1913.
Brooklyn *Times,* January 18, 1913.
Newark *Evening News,* January 18, 1913.
Denver [Col.] *Times,* January 25, 1913.
Denver [Col.] *News,* January 27, 1913.
"The Financier: Modern and Brutal." Chicago *Mutual News,* February, 1913, p. 12.
American Review of Reviews, February, 1913.
Fort Worth [Tex.] *Record,* February 2, 1913.
Pittsburgh *Dispatch,* February 2, 1913.
"Finance in Days of Panic." Pittsburgh *Press,* February 26, 1913.
New Haven [Conn.] *Journal Courier,* February 17, 1913.
Burlington [Va.] *Free Press,* February 26, 1913.
Chicago *Public,* February 28, 1913.
Delineator, March, 1913.
Building Management, March, 1913.
St. Louis *Star,* March 3, 1912.
Coningsbly Dawson. "A Row of Books." *Everybody's Magazine,* April, 1913.
Vogue, April, 1913.

New York *Cotton & Finance*, April 5, 1913.

Edith Delong Jarmuth. New York *Evening Globe*, April 11, 1913.

"A Novel of Serious Strength." Springfield *Republican*, May 3, 1913.

Margaret Anderson. "Literary Aftermath." *Trend*, November, 1913, p. 367.

A TRAVELER AT FORTY

BY

THEODORE DREISER
Author of "Sister Carrie," "Jennie Gerhardt," "The Financier," etc., etc.

ILLUSTRATED BY
W. GLACKENS

NEW YORK
THE CENTURY CO.
1913

A Traveler at Forty

E.F. Edgett.
Boston *Evening Transcript*,
December 3, 1913,
p. 24.

Blessed be the writer who in telling of his travels can rob them of the sting of the conventional and the terrors of the commonplace. . . .

Whither may we go for the novelty of travel in a book? From the North Pole to the South, from Perry to Amundsen and Scott there is no corner of earth left unexplored. The novelty must therefore be sought in the adventurer's own mind, not in the scenes he sees and describes. Therefore, to repeat ourselves, blessed be the writer who in telling of his travels can rob them of the sting of the conventional and the terrors of the commonplace. Blessed then be Theodore Dreiser, who in visiting England, France, Italy, Germany and Holland follows main-travelled roads with a seeing eye, an observant mind and a wide-awake energy that takes immediate and constant control of the reader. As in "Sister Carrie," in "Jennie Gerhardt" and in "The Financier" Mr. Dreiser was no ordinary novelist, so in "A Traveler at Forty" he is no ordinary tourist.

The success of Mr. Dreiser in telling the tale of his first trip to and through Europe comes from his writing of it as if he were writing a novel. He allows his imagination full play and he gives his enthusiasm no restraint. He writes no bald chronicle of places seen and people met. He creates his characters, he makes them the participants in happenings, and he places them against a background of scenes that all seem to have sprung forth from the originality of his mind. He himself is its protagonist. Everything in the story, and it may be read as a story rather than as a book of travel, is his own. The reader feels as if he were Mr. Dreiser's inseparable companion and friend, as if he were touring Europe under his guidance, and as if at every stage of the journey he were communing with him upon life in all its multitudinous aspects as it confronts a worldly and experienced man who is seeing for the first time a new world and a strange people. . . .

Each country through which Mr. Dreiser travels is viewed with the same combined air of ingenuousness, naiveté and sophistication. As in his novels, his style is at times deplorable. He still rides in a "taxi," talks over a "phone," says that a man or a thing is "located" here or there, and adorns his pages with such extraordinary words and phrases as "caravanserai" and "in evidence." But nevertheless we repeat: Blessed be the writer who in telling of his travels can rob them of the sting of the conventional and the terrors of commonplace.

Israel Solon. "A Novelist in Europe." Chicago *Evening Post,* December 5, 1913.

The fact that is to be borne in mind when reading Theodore Dreiser's "A Traveler at Forty" is the age of the author. That Mr. Dreiser is in his forties must not be forgotten. In no other way is his somewhat strange book to be clearly understood. Once this is understood, and due allowance made, there is nothing to prevent our whole-hearted enjoyment of it. Let me try to make my meaning clearer:

Supposing that the reader were to disregard Mr. Dreiser's age; supposing, that is to say, the reader were to consider this book as a self-sufficient work of art; supposing, in short, that he were to do just what I did at first—what would result? I can best answer this by relating my own experience:

Page after page for some sixty or seventy pages, I was charmed, delighted thrilled. Mr. Dreiser had manipulated words, sentences and paragraphs not merely as a means to an end, not merely as vehicles for his ideas, but also for their color and form, for their own values, their values to the human tongue and ear. An uncommon quality nowadays. His mood, his attitude toward life, likewise charmed me. It is peculiarly engaging. The spread of common-school education and typewriters brought with it a herd of dull, leaden-witted writers whose view of life is depressingly naive and smug. Mr. Dreiser's sad and quizzical attitude toward life proved to me quite refreshing. I bade it welcome.

To be sure, I had long felt a mild resentment. It was a vague, inarticulate awareness that all was not quite well with Mr. Dreiser. I felt that he was too much the Stoic, or, more properly, the Hindu; that he was too contemplative, insufficiently active. I believed that he was altogether too willing to leave bad enough alone. A writer fully aware of the present possibilities of life ought to be more Shavian, I thought. He ought to be aiming "blows at human noses for the good of human souls." Still, knowing that the pragmatic view of life is not the only possible one, I not only allowed Mr. Dreiser his own view of life, but I admired him for it. He further secured my friendship by defying conventional taboo. I thought him heroic.

But as I read on in this book of his I finally found it too much to let pass unchallenged. What is one to say of an author who wishes to understand Europe that he may tell the rest of us about it, but who confines his observations to the cafe life of European capitals after midnight? (His other observations are altogether lost in the mass of details about his half-world.)

Syndicalism stood threatening France and Italy while Mr. Dreiser was in those countries. But of course he tells us nothing of it, never a word. How could he? If he was to clink champagne glasses with the ladies of the half-world he had to do so after midnight, and do his sleeping during the day, of course. A gigantic strike held England paralyzed during the time that Mr. Dreiser was there. He was chatting pleasantly with a little Welsh girl that he had picked up in Piccadilly one evening, and so could do nothing else. At the very time that

Mr. Dreiser was there, England was engaged in the most momentous political revolution of its history. But you would never suspect it from reading Mr. Dreiser's volume.

He judges women at the footlight value. His opinion of them is that of the Tired Business Man. Over and over and over again he shows us that he thinks of women as things, more or less expensive. And he bemoans the fact that you can have no assurance that you will get what you pay for. He tells us, in fact, that we never do get what we pay for. Women are inferiors! . . .

And he tells us this at the time, and from the place where thousands upon thousands of women walked from out their homes, warm, soft, man-protected homes, and flung their frail selves against the mighty men of England, and demanded in one voice: Acknowledge our right to equal human dignity or we will force you to become our executioners!

But I recalled that Mr. Dreiser was in his forties and in the company of women of the underworld. I could hardly keep myself from laughing at his notions of good in children. A really good child, according to Mr. Dreiser, is, as it were, a young adult. It talks beautifully, and only when it is spoken to. It is never, never dirty; with the added advantage that you can order it about, call it into your superior presence, dismiss it, deck it out as you will and parade it about where everybody will know that it owes its all to you. . . .

And when we remember that he is in his forties we cease to marvel at the colossal mental laziness which forced him to employ "lovely" and "nice" as descriptive adjectives over and over, in every sense but the right one; and "so" and "such" in every schoolgirl sense, thruout the volume. And it is because of this same laziness, due to the same cause, that he employs such rubber-stamp phrases as "The peace that passes all understanding," "The rest is silence." And, also, his calling on Merciful heavens! and Great God! whenever he wants to tap the deepest wells of our emotions, even after he had again and again informed us that he does not believe in Him.

And when we learn that "there is in me the spirit of a lonely child somewhere and it clings pitifully to the hand of its big mama, Life, and cries when it is frightened; and then there is a coarse, vulgar exterior which fronts the world defiantly and bids all and sundry to go to the devil," we cannot help feeling for him. And then he adds: "It sneers and barks and jeers bitterly at times, and guffaws and cackles and has a joyous time laughing at the follies of others." We now know that he still finds it needful to confess to some one. And it ought to surprise no one if, sooner or later, he learns that Mr. Dreiser had made his peace with the Church into which he was born and attained peace of soul.

It is more than likely that Mr. Dreiser will yet do his best work. When a few more years will have passed he will have attained outward calm and inward peace. He should then be able to do good work, better work than ever before. We may see some signs of it in this very volume. The last chapters, those dealing with Germany and Holland, are perhaps the best in the book. I believe it to be due to the fact that he felt more quiescent because of his fever having abated. The Voyage Home, the last chapter of the book, relates the feeling among the passengers at sea when they learn of the sinking of the Titanic. It is terribly moving.

"Mr. Dreiser Travels." New York *Evening Globe*, December 6, 1913.

To enjoy Theodore Dreiser's description of his first trip abroad, called "A Traveller at Forty," you must try to get into the mood of Mr. Dreiser and his monocled English friend "Barfleur," who personally conducted him and arranged all the details of the trip, from securing the inevitable seats at the captain's table and introducing him to the actresses (what would shipboard be without actresses?) to buying the waistcoats he should wear in London and the socks he should display on the Riviera. Marvellous man, Barfleur!

To Mr. Dreiser and Barfleur it is a matter of tremendous importance that the author of "Sister Carrie" should at the age of forty for the first time be going to Europe. No mother watching her babe walk for the first time could be more anxiously beaming than Barfleur over this trip of Dreiser's, and no babe, it may be added, was ever more crowingly pleased over its first steps across the great spaces of the nursery floor than Dreiser over his first crossing of the Atlantic.

He is naively thrilled (and communicates some of the thrill to you) over the ship's life, from "dressing for dinner" to talking to the actresses—who found him intellectual but not handsome. In England, he likes the way the servants say "Yes, sir," and "No, sir," and their quiet and efficient, and automation-like service. He admires the orderliness of English life, and is greatly stirred when in his friend's house dinner is served to him alone, even to coffee, in the drawing-room, with as much state as if a big company had been present.

We have often thought that if a man could write about something that had never been written about before he might produce a book worth reading, no matter what it was. Well, Mr. Dreiser succeeds in large measure in writing about things "as if" they had never been written about before. And this we maintain is no small feat. In fact, we are not sure but that "A Traveller at Forty" is Mr. Dreiser's best book—even his best story. . . .

Philadelphia *Record*, December 6, 1913.

Theodore Dreiser does not fall into the usual error of travelers and give us merely prozy detailed descriptions of places. He is primarily interested in people and he writes down even the very conversations he had with his fellow-traveler "Barfleur," and all the other people with whom he came in contact. The result is a book of travels that is as diverting as a novel. Living personalities crowd the canvas; the author lights up all the scenes with the glow of his intellect. The reflections on life, religion, marriage and other important topics give the work a great literary value. It is a refreshing treat to know the exact ideas that float through the brain of the author of Sister Carrie and Jennie Gerhardt. The point of view may at times shock the conservative, but it is usually sound and original. . . .

No doubt many will dislike the Nihilistic note in many of Dreiser's reflections. Others will claim that he is always uttering unpleasant truth. If he does have one fault it may be that he has little faith in humanity or ideals. He has the Machiavellian viewpoint; he sees hypocrisy everywhere. . . .

Nevertheless, this is surely one of the great works of American travel writing. A more striking book of this sort has not appeared probably since Hawthorne's travels. The only English work of travel that bears an affinity to it is the late Samuel Butler's profound "Alps and Sanctuaries."

Dreiser has shown us, as did Goethe, Heine and Brandes before him, that a book of travel can be literature. The style is also superior to that in "Sister Carrie."

San Francisco *Bulletin*, December 6, 1913.

Theodore Dreiser, author of three novels which rank with those of the greatest of modern realists, has made his first trip abroad, and in "A Traveler at Forty" he records his experiences and impressions in that candid, straightforward style which we might expect from the biographer of "Sister Carrie" and "Jennie Gerhardt."

Humanity has been Mr. Dreiser's absorbing study. He is far more interested in men and women than in musicians and cathedrals, and while in this narrative he pays his respects to certain edifices and public buildings, he devotes more attention to the people and their characteristics, the way they live, etc. Mr. Dreiser's insight into human nature and his ability to portray character is recognized by all critical readers, therefore when he pictures European manners and customs with his keen sense of humor and boldly disregards the conventions that he may give an accurate report of things as they are and not as they seem to the average tourist, who seldom departs from the beaten paths, we are afforded an unusually interesting narrative—one both instructive and entertaining.

Mr. Dreiser expresses his mind frankly, and where some have been greatly impressed by old world shrines and somewhat awed by ceremonials and the power and display of royalty, his critical mental attitude is always apparent—he is never afraid to say what he thinks. Doubtless there are those who will be shocked by his seeming lack of reverence when describing his visit to Rome, but he has the courage of his convictions, at any rate, and the fearless writer usually commands our attention, particularly if he startles us with sudden flashes of original thought as Mr. Dreiser is wont to do. . . .

George Hamlin Fitch. "Impressions of Europe." San Francisco *Chronicle*, December 7, 1913.

Probably no magazine feature in recent years excited more general interest than the series of articles in the Century Magazine, in which Theodore Dreiser related his impressions of Europe. These aritcles now appear in book form, under the title, "A Traveler at Forty," which is brought out by the Century Company, with some good and some very bad sketches by W. Glackens. Mr. Dreiser writes in the first person and his book primarily is a collection of personal impressions and is concerned far more with the people of the different countries than with the places that he saw. He had evidently read a good deal about the various cities, but not too much, and, although he had a fair grounding in history, he more than once expresses regret that he did not know more intimately the history of places that had a special appeal for him. Taken as a whole, the book gives the impression of rare honesty and extreme frankness. This man, who has written three novels of strong realistic force, was given suddenly an opportunity to take this European tour. The man who opened the door for him he calls Barfleur, an Englishman with a monocle and most of the insular traits. Much of the charm of the first third of the book consists in the pen pictures of Barfleur and his managerial ways. He stage-manages the trip for Dreiser and apparently he gets fully as much satisfaction out of the strong first impressions of the American as Dreiser did himself. Extremely sophisticated as he is, this Englishman's only chance to enjoy the thrill of the novice is to travel with him and absorb some of his rapture. And this Barfleur does, with a rare geniality and charm.

One who has visited most of the places which Mr. Dreiser describes will be amazed to see how faithfully he has reproduced the charm of famous cities and buildings of historical interest. No effort is made to give facts or to provide a guide for any traveler; but extreme care is taken to record first impressions and to get at the life and character of the various peoples. . . .

The book invites to frequent quotation, for the author sees things with his own eyes and he is terribly frank in his revelations of social hypocrisy and religious cant. It is a book to take up frequently and read a few chapters, for it will endure many readings. With the single exception of Price Collier's books, it is the best record of recent travel impressions.

Charles E. Hasselgrave. "A Holiday Trip Into the Land of Books." *Independent,* 76 (December 11, 1913), 507–508.

A Traveler at 40. What an enticing title! We respond with avidity to the thought of wandering over seas with one old enough to perceive the essentials of culture and disentangle them from the complexity of the passing show, and yet not so old as to have dulled the edge of his enjoyment and interest in the follies and foibles of his fellow-creatures. But some disappointment awaits us on our first venture. Mr. Dreiser, indeed, gives us to understand that he is quite sophisticated, even if this is his first voyage across the Atlantic, and we are led to expect some shrewd observations on men, women and things. Altho he visits the familiar places of the tourist, his related experiences are not those usually recorded. Many of them, we are bound to say, are not worth recording. In his struggle to achieve the unconventional he often falls into the insignificant or wallows in the unsavory. As the reader follows the photographic descriptions of the author's doings and feelings, he is struck by the incoherency and lack of point in the detached scenes and impressions. There is no subtle integration thru the touch of strong personality, of idealism, of interpretation in the light of some worthy philosophy of life. The straining for effect has vitiated the judgment and destroyed the perspective, while the book is full of valuable crude materials. . . .

"Views of People in Strange Lands." Philadelphia *North American*, December 13, 1913.

A first trip abroad, at 40, by Theodore Dreiser, author of "The Financier," "Jennie Gerhart" [sic] and other works of American fiction, has resulted in a travel book quite out of the ordinary run—dealing with people, rather than places; life comparisons, rather than social institutions. . . .

Intimacy in description extends even to inconsequential details of trips and hotel experiences, and is carried far in occasional studies of real life, interspersed between pages on pages of frank and unconventional comment and comparison. Mr. Dreiser sought out types of common humanity, talked with them and sought to understand them and their immediate vicinage and atmosphere—a far better thing than any hasty survey of old world wonders.

There is novelty and interest enough in his viewpoint and his methods of observation to warrant additional studies of kindred sort. Methods of jurisdiction and social demarcation yield only to leisurely and studious inquiry; but Mr. Deiser found right at hand all necessary materials for instant and intelligent estimate. He heard the common people gladly, that is all. . . .

Boston *Globe*, December 13, 1913.

Comfortable in the enjoyment of his pleasing royalties from "Sister Carrie," "Jennie Gerhardt," "The Financier" and other novels, Theodore Dreiser naturally made a trip to Europe, and as naturally he has written a book about it.

In "A Traveler of 40" he tells of his experiences on his first trip abroad frankly and unconventionally and with much detail, extending his narrative of the journey to England, France and Italy, across Switzerland to Germany and Holland, back to Paris and home again, to fill something more than 500 good-sized pages.

The book is out of the ordinary, as books of travels go, being rather a record of personality than a description of the ordinary sights. Mr Dreiser writes with frankness and freedom about the people that he met, the characters that he saw, the life of the dwellers in the different countries that he visited, and the idiocyncracies of his traveling companions, two of whom, a litterateur and an Irish knight, a patron of art, made a large part of the journey with him.

Mme. Grundy would perhaps be shocked at the freedom of his chapter about "Lilley, a Girl of the Streets," in London, but it is a realistic study of life at first hand, and there are few of those who take up the book who will not read every word of it with attentive interest. Full of fascination, also, is Mr Dreiser's story of his search for Mayen—not Mayence—in Germany, where his father came from, and his amusing experiences in the fascinating little old town when finally he found it.

Altogether, the book is one telling of

experiences and impressions rather than the sights of travel—although the sights and scenes are not neglected—and it is full of the philosophy of the novelist, to whom the study of human nature is the occupation and the chief end of life. It is a book to be read in a leisurely way, not hurried through, and the attention it gives to commonplace things and the views it presents of life abroad in various relations, and particularly of home life in England, give it a special value and cannot fail to interest the reader.

Nation, 97 (December 18, 1913), 591–592.

For various reasons, Mr. Dreiser's grand tour was postponed beyond the fame of three novels and the age of forty. It is an age at which, without much abatement of enthusiasm, open-mindedness begins to be possible, and understanding is quickened by a sense of the swiftness of the years. As to open-mindedness, it was already Mr. Dreiser's forte, and the trip gave him abundant opportunity to open his mind still further. In England and France he was personally conducted by an admirable gastronome and manager-general. Except when he slipped the noose, Mr. Dreiser was chiefly limited to disillusioned England and dissolute France. In Italy, Switzerland, Germany, and Holland he went his own gait and took his impressions a little easier.

In the pursuit of knowledge Mr. Dreiser showed enterprise. His London contacts were carefully arranged, but he managed to quiz a street-walker on his own account. At Paris such investigations were naturally part of the programme. Into all his observations Mr. Dreiser carries a keen, quiet curiosity that is pretty close to sympathy. There is an odd reverence about what can only be described as prying tactics. The style is fumbling and uneven, glancing at things, quitting them, and returning for a new try. The dialogues, which might irreverently be called "heart to heart" talks, are of a queer baldness and rawness. We have to do with either the complete absence of literary technique or with a rather special technique which is hard to classify. Since the chapters are undeniably interesting and the passing people often vivid, the effect obtained with the hesitant, half-nonchalant manner which is familiar to readers of "Sister Carrie," we may suppose that a special technique is involved.

As a matter of fact, we have to do with an attitude and a style allied to Russian realism. Absence of prepossession, desire to move with the material, an almost mystical respect for all expressions of temperament—one who has these qualities in high degree may hope to achieve a myopic humanitarianism. This, indeed, is Mr. Dreiser's personal note. He adores temperament in all its phases. A hot-headed and violent labor leader is admirable, so is a winsome degenerate of the Paris cafés. Temperament he will have, if only retrospectively. How otherwise explain the lugging in of Lucrezia Borgia at many pages of length?

Now, this kind of myopic humanitarianism makes an excellent observer for certain men and matters. It would be hard to make more of Parisian café life than Mr. Dreiser has made. There is just the right blend of sympathy, with detachment. Most chroniclers of the theme are cynical—which Mr. Dreiser never is—or sentimentally fulsome, or morally scornful.

But certain visions, rather worth while in their way, are denied to the myopic humanitarian. So far as knowing the France that was and is the fertile mother of great ideas, the new Hellas of the world of letters, Mr. Dreiser might just as well have stuck to Broadway. Again, his notion of the great art patrons of Florence is that they were "ambitious, struggling, vain-glorious men." The element of taste and discipline that made these patrons true fellows of the great artists is ignored, for the sake, of course, of a fuller display of temperament. In short, distinction of any sort, especially intellectual distinction, eludes this sort of approach. Distinction is not casual, and may not be casually apprehended.

Mr. Dreiser, both in his novels and in these travel sketches, is perhaps quite logically the foe of distinction, except in its aberrations. Distinction means hardness and discipline, restraint of temperament. Too much distinction would destroy utterly Mr. Dreiser's favorite world. For resolving the undistinguished flux into its palpitating human elements he has a rare gift. If he is less than the great Russians whom he recalls, it is because of smaller moral grasp. His readings of life stop at a sense of flux and a ready compassion. His subjects are chosen as fluid and pathetic. Of humor there is nothing in him, and next to nothing of philosophy. The less meaning there is in a person or an incident, the better he treats it. He prefers it should have no meaning. Let it be a casual reverberation of temperament, and for his purposes it is all the better.

It is a peculiar art, for the artist is both in and out of his material; difficult to locate. That the art has an odd fascination, almost hypnotic in its way, is undeniable. Yet the perusal of this singularly open-minded book awakens in at least one reader a keen desire for prejudice, conviction, point of view. All narrow stable sentiments gain a new impressiveness after sufficient reading of Mr. Dreiser's patient, languid phrases. Why are Mr. Glackens's illustrations so refreshing in the setting of Mr. Dreiser's prose? Because they have sardonic humor, are brusque and superior. Their incisive, prejudiced touch leaves Mr. Dreiser's universal sympathy with a maundering aspect. The word is too harsh, but it does emphasize both the quality and the defect of his point of view, and naturally of his literary procedure.

Providence [R.I.] *Journal*, December 20, 1913.

The title of Mr. Dreiser's latest book is far more attractive than those of any of his novels. Mr. Dreiser proves that the man of forty may be as avid to receive impressions as the man of twenty. The book gives evidence of a truly youthful enthusiasm. It is to be noted, however, that Mr. Dreiser's enthusiasms are mostly for things tangible and visible. He appreciates London, is delighted with Paris, admires Rome, and is rapt at Venice—but when he talks of men and women, the glamour is gone; he becomes disillusionized, sophisticated, and we remember that he is the author of "Sister Carrie" and of "Jennie Gerhardt." Although his criticisms of life are very shrewd, very clever, very ironical, most of us will prefer the descriptive portions of the book to those which strive to be analytic. . . .

Washington *Evening Star*, December 20, 1913.

That which makes "A Traveler at Forty" more interesting than many—even than most—travel books is that in its making Mr. Dreiser assumes, and rightly assumes, that what proved interesting to him on this his first trip to Europe is more than likely to be interesting to the great majority who have not yet been to Europe at all. And so, instead of writing eulogies on more or less of the great dead-and-goneness of the old country, Mr. Dreiser, under the capacious and capable wing of a certain English "Barfleur," goes to London teas and talks to the ladies, makes week-end visits into the country, browses about odd corners of London, stays out o' nights making copy of "Lilly, a Girl of the Streets," and, in a word, opens up every sort of opportunity for getting next to the live folks of every grade and degree, remaining curiously insensible meanwhile to the usual excitements of sightseeing. And so it is in Paris and through Italy and Switzerland, Germany and Holland. There is no other travel book just like this one. At first, too, you resent it, wondering if Theodore Dreiser thinks you care to read about his not very exciting excursions into London society in the role of a small domestic lion. You miss the tower and the houses of parliament, the galleries and the Nelson column, Richmond, Hampton Court and the rest of it. But by the time Paris is reached, or before, you begin to wake up to the people. Without saying anything in particular about it Mr. Dreiser makes anything that is alive and around seem more worth while than things that are dead and shut up somewhere in crypts. And so you join with him in the hunt for the human, declaring loudly, like all converts, in the betweenwhiles of the pursuit that this is probably the only contemporaneous travel book in existence.

"Sincere and Sparkling," Chicago *Record-Herald*, December 20, 1913.

Theodore Dreiser waited until he was 40 to go abroad. It is doubtful whether the event had much significance in his intellectual development. Mr. Dreiser was thoroughly prepared to see just what he did see, and he appears to have been a little indifferent as to those things for which his preparation was less thorough.

Mr. Dreiser is a connoisseur of cities. The connoisseur of wines may know much about wines; his greatest obvious utility is that he is able to distinguished their flavor and bouquet. Mr. Dreiser does the like for cities. He may be only dimly aware of the profound and still life going on under the surface, but he is quick to seize the atmosphere and the savor of life in the capitals of Europe and to place them before us with no less of color and movement. The impressions may have a facile air, but they are genuinely observed—not the deepest truth, perhaps, but an undeniable kind of truth, none the less.

Like many travelers who are compelled to take a bird's-eye view of strange countries, Mr. Dreiser fixed his eye on extremes, because extremes are easy to see and become dramatic without much working over. If the drama is a little crude so much the better; it is the more obvious. Mr. Dreiser sought his extremes in the slums of manufacturing centers and in the glittering cafes of Paris and Berlin. Historic Europe, the Europe of museums and picture galleries, did not hold his attention. "A Traveler at Forty" is emphatically a book of the present. Mr. Dreiser may say that the Europe of memories and of social movements has already, in the artistic sense, been sufficiently "done," but if he had felt the tone of these things a bit more he would have written a different book. As it is we have glimpses mainly of the night life of Paris and London, with its resplendent ladies of the half-world, who know the secret of dressing and charming, and who are withheld by no inconvenient pride from taking themselves at about their escorts' valuation. Mr. Dreiser is profoundly interested in this life; he finds drama in it. So there is; but it is drama that is just a little obvious perhaps. In such circles Mr. Dreiser has great confidence in his savoir-faire. Though his friends will regard this as a rank heresy, one must record an honest doubt as to whether his confidence is completely justified.

But Mr. Dreiser writes freshly and entertainingly and, above all, with a most engaging candor. He dislikes shams; he is ready to tell you what he thinks about almost everything under the sun, and he does you the honor to assume that you will take what he says in the right spirit. There is quite as much about Theodore Dreiser in this book as about Europe—perhaps more. As a picture of one man's mental attitudes, presented without reserve, the book is distinctly interesting. One wonders while reading it why literary sincerity is so very rare in our day.

Edwin Markham. "News of the Latest Books." New York *American*, December 20, 1913.

Theodore Dreiser, whose novel, "The Financier," may be set down as one of the best that have appeared for some time, diverges into the field of travel and, modestly acknowledging to 40, gives us an account of wanderings in a vein all his own.

His newest book, "A Traveler at Forty," might well be studied by those who travel to write, for it bears unique marks of individuality emblazoned with keen comment and is alive with real persons.

Mr. Dreiser wanders through Germany and France and Italy and England, where hundreds of thousands of others have preceded him. What he sees now they have seen, and yet it is as though his eyes were trained to see the things that have escaped them—as though his ear were tuned to sounds too high-pitched for the ordinary ear.

Nor is he afraid of life as he finds it; and, not being afraid, neither is he afraid of telling what he does. He dines with a woman of the street, and he gambles, and he is none the worse for it, since he does what he does in the spirit of those who would see.

It is more than possible that good people who live by rule and preconceived conceptions may object to many of his descriptions . . .

But one can't please everybody. Mr. Dreiser's book is more than a book of travel; it is a book of reflection, a book of observation, mental, moral and spiritual, and altogether the most satisfying thing of its kind that has appeared in many a long day.

W.J.C.
Detroit *Tribune*, December 21, 1913.

A most unusual book of travel, Mr. Dreiser has made a place in American letters for himself by his "Sister Carrie," "Jennie Gerhardt," and "The Financier," but this is his first book outside the realm of fiction. A man of ability—especially ability in observing and recording his observations—could hardly miss saying something worth while if he had turned 40 before taking his first trip abroad. The trip was made possible by a friend of the author, who was intensely interested in seeing what Europe would do to Dreiser, and in turn what Dreiser would do to Europe.

And this is a book of travel—with the emphasis on the "travel." The author does not catalogue cities and "sights." Some of the most exploited "sights" of Europe leave him very cold. A line disposes of many anciently worshiped "wonders." But everywhere he is interested in people, and the lives they lead, from the night moths of Parisian restaurants to the mill hands of smoky England.

His observations are delightfully fresh and frank. His own impressions become facts quite as much to be reckoned with as the objects which create them. To follow him through the more than 500 pages of this book is to travel indeed—and, better still, to travel for the first time. The atmosphere of changing places and peoples pervades his every page. He says precisely what he thinks, about pope or peasant, and some of his sayings are a bit disconcerting, but, strange to say, one has the feeling just what oneself would say if one were honest enough. Dreiser nowhere subordinates his actual sentiments to the conventional ones that certain places or personages are supposed to invoke.

The book—goes. It holds one like a story. It simply illustrates once again what service a fresh and honest mind can render the rest of the world.

"Mr. Dreiser."
New York *Times Review of Books*, December 28, 1913, p. 763.

It is only a very big man who should risk taking nothing but himself to Europe, and we should not allow Bennetts or Barfleurs to deceive us as to our real proportions. Mr. Dreiser, at the age of 40, has just been taken abroad by Mr. Barfleur for the purpose of having some sensations and publishing them. The idea in view was an entirely new sort of travel book. Take a man with the ability to write and the courage to see the plain facts of life, but a man as yet unspoiled by cosmopolitanism or the ravages of an Old World culture, give him his first glimpse of Europe and let him write frankly what he thinks about it. Above all, keep him from reading or hearing what other people have been saying through the centuries about Europe. The result, argued Mr. Barfleur, would be a "document," a fresh and unhackneyed presentation of a familiar subject. To this end Mr. Dreiser came up out of Manhattan and scuttled through the regulation schedule—England, France, Italy, Germany, Switzerland, and Holland, and "A Traveler at Forty" is the product.

We trust Mr. Barfleur realizes his mighty error. We are confident that Mr. Dreiser doesn't, for Mr. Dreiser's creed of late years has come to be the deification of the commonplace, and the commonplace quite divested of what the Lake poet chose to call the shaping power of the imagination, and which Mr. Dreiser labels hypocrisy, pose, and sham, forgetting his excellent employment of that power in his excellent "Sister Carrie." Mr. Dreiser took Mr. Barfleur's advice about avoiding second-hand knowledge of Europe, dropping in upon it totally unprepared, with the unfortunate result that he has delivered just about all the stock remarks which are made by every first-time traveler. The chief difference is that Mr. Dreiser and the Century Company have had the courage to put them into print, whereas the average traveler releases them for the immediate family only. Illinois and England are two vastly different propositions. One of those unafraid souls, close to life's crudities, can look life in Ohio squarely between the eyes and write a "Jennie Gerhardt." But Paris and Perugia, London and Berlin, these demand something more than a valiant stare; they require sympathy and a delicacy of imagination born of a cosmopolitan culture, of a contact with art and literature and quiet Old World civilization rather than with "life."

Mr. Dreiser, however, has fancied that the chronicle of his intimate daily life would be a sort of novelty to our jaded tastes. Hence he scrupulously records everything—the size of the tips, the cost of the champagne, the exact weather of every day, whether or not he received mail that day, what he wore, what he ate—in short, Mr. Dreiser's narrative is worse than sheer photography; it is photography with the assumption of a witness possessed only of a retina and an optic nerve.

Much of it is as bad as that, though not all of it. At times when he loses his self-consciousness in some of the few interesting people who decorated his trip abroad he gives the reader a flash of something less dull and less trite. It is people, above all, who hold his attention, and here and there are vivid flashes, a picture of the women in a London washhouse, of the audience at the Vatican awaiting the Pope, of Italian women leaning out of their windows, of the cabaret dancers at the Abbaye Thélème. It is women, above all, who interest Mr. Dreiser, and, among women, the demimondaine especially. The lady of the half-world has a value for publication only if treated from one of two points of view—as an economic fact, or as a subject requiring sentiment and imagination. Mr. Dreiser fancies that by treating her bluntly and realistically he is accomplishing something ultra-modern; yet his chapter on Lilly, the little girl of the London streets, lacks all that makes Rosetti's "Jenny" endure, and his pictures of Paris cafés seem tritely unsympathetic beside the brilliance of Mr. George Moore. Moreover, what Mr. Dreiser finds in the various people of his acquaintance seems most insignificant. Take, for example, one of the several conversations with his companion in the next steamer chair, a gay little actress.

> "I wish my path in life were as white as that and as straight," observed Miss X, pointing to our white propeller-churned wake.
>
> "Yes," I observed, "you do and you don't. You do, if it wouldn't cost you trouble in the future—impose the straight and narrow, as it were."
>
> "Oh, you don't know," she exclaimed irritably, that ugly fighting light coming into her eyes, which I had seen there several times before. "You don't know what my life has been. I haven't been so bad. I have done the best I could, considering."
>
> "Yes, yes," I observed, "you're ambitious and alive, and you're seeking—heaven knows what! You would be adorable with your pretty face and body if you were not so—so sophisticated. The trouble with you is—"
>
> "Oh, look at that cute little boat out there! I always feel sorry for a poor little thing like that, set aside from the main tide of life and left lonely—with no one to care for it."
>
> "The trouble with you is," I went on, "you're romantic, not sympathetic. You're interested in that poor little, lonely boat because its state is romantic, not pathetic. It may be pathetic, but that isn't—"

It goes on like that for several pages. At another point Mr. Dreiser prepares us for an acquaintance with a very beautiful lady associated with a small white donkey, and when we finally encounter the lady she only smiles, and assures us that she doesn't like the idea of her children's toys being made in America. The justification for the inclusion of the lady and her conversation is that they both really happened, and it is this naïve attitude which has led Mr. Dreiser into making a book.

"Philandering Abroad." New York *Press*, January 11, 1914.

On page 339 of Theodore Dreiser's "A Traveler at Forty" the author writes apropos of a couple of married compatriots he met in Rome: "There is something so childlike and pure about the attitude of many strong, able Americans that I marvel sometimes that they do as well as they do. Perhaps their very innocence is their salvation. I could not have told this man and his wife, for instance, anything of the subtleties of the underworld of Paris and Monte Carlo, as I encountered them and if I had he would not have believed me; he would have recoiled from it all as a burned child would recoil from fire."

In view of this tender solicitude over the feelings of these natives of Tennessee one may well wonder how Mr. Dreiser fortified himself with courage to set down the record of his philanderings abroad in cold print for the delectation of the rest of us Americans, who are so innocent, childlike and pure? It is not an uncommon experience for a man traveling en garcon to meet women of dubious morals, but it is not the usual course for such men to narrate their indulgences of this kind before their mothers, sisters or in a mixed company. Yet meetings of this sort are not an inconsiderable part of this author's narrative; for we read of the dubious women he met on the steamer, in London, Paris and Monte Carlo, and he takes a kind of pride in describing them, never once failing to inform his readers just how immoral they were, and reporting their stupid, wearisome colloquies with an apparent sense of enjoyment in his task.

It is a sincere pity that he should have marred his pages with these noisome things, for he approached Europe in the spirit of one to whom everything is absolutely novel, with no preconceptions to speak of, and in a state of abysmal ignorance of its social and national traits.

Mr. Dreiser is always naive in his writings and never more so than when he describes the conventions of English social life as he saw them through the courtesy of his inimitable friend and guide, Barfleur. But when one says this one has done everything in the way of praise for this narrative. Elsewhere it is blotted by a willful ignorance and vulgar attitude toward the Catholic Church and its artistic monuments and personages that sinks to its lowest ebb in his description of an audience at the Vatican in which he saw the Pope. It was shameful for any one to have written such a passage and it is shocking for any one to have printed it. Such a thing is offensive not only to Catholics but to thousands of other readers who revere the Pope for the holiness of his life as a man, even if they are not concerned with him in religion.

Christian Intelligencer, January 21, 1914.

Mr. Dreiser was forty before he visited Europe. His trip was all arranged by an English literary friend. The purpose of the trip was a book of travel. The literary friend did not confine Mr. Drieser's trip to places of memory and eminence but included the temples of vice and excitement. And Mr. Dreiser went off on his own account here and there in order to investigate the zone of shame. Thus in London he hazards the perilous experiment of accompanying a woman of the street to her secret lair in order to get her story. In Paris Mr. Dreiser and Barfleur, the literary friend, hit the high spots like the man who tried to discover how close he could walk to the edge of the precipice without falling over. Of course these trips were in the interest of a book and Mr. Drieser makes it clear that the life of Parisian cafes is not to his liking. But he knows the art of cocktail drinking and speaks freely of habits and actions which certainly do not commend him. And, therefore, his views lose weight, too. Indeed, it is soon evident that Mr. Dreiser is none too friendly to established religions. He boasts that he does not believe any creed, but shortly after he says, "[I] acknowledge the Furies. I believe in them. I have heard the disastrous beating of their wings." He tells later that he was born a Roman Catholic but that he soon outgrew it. He speaks of "what is true in the teaching of Jesus" and would turn some of the European cathedrals into museums if he had his ways. Nor do his views on marriage and divorce and the home commend themselves to us. If people make a mistake in marriage, the mistake should be made easy of amendment by an easy divorce. Mr. Dreiser seems to think only of making the correction of such a mistake easy; he does not give his attention to the matter of preventing such mistakes nor of the disruptive results of a system of easy divorce. By the same token he does not consider the value of discipline, but seems to want to make it easy for everyone to do as he likes. It must be possible, according to Mr. Dreiser, for the individual to throw the harvest of his misdoing on the state and to find some other affinity as if nothing had happened. It is evident what manner of a man and what manner of writer Mr. Drieser is. He is a man of the world and he writes of that world with as great a degree of daring and boldness as conventional standards allow. What we take exception to is the views he advances on many matters in which the public needs sound instruction and also the lurid descriptions of that world of sin and shame where the lust of the flesh, the lust of the eye and the vainglory of life hold sway. But all this is not to say that Mr. Dreiser's book is base and worthless. On the contrary, it is a book of fascinating interest and sterling values. His descriptions of the different countries he visited are unusually original and real; he reveals the very atmosphere and time-spirit of each country so effectively that the reading of his book is like a trip abroad. What Mr. Dreiser speaks of as "places of eminence and memory" are dealt with in a manner of compelling interest. Mr. Dreiser, remember, was forty before he went to Europe. He took with him a fine equipment of knowledge and experience with which to form judgments of weight and value. His power of description is charming. The reader will, therefore, find this a rewarding book, full of mature wisdom, and if he will only remember that Mr. Dreiser is not an expert in religion, and that his flings at Christianity are perhaps worse in expression than in motive, he will find much in this travel book to inform and give pleasure. We are sorry that Mr. Dreiser met so many pale people abroad, especially in England. Pale seems to be a serviceable adjective with him.

Life, January 22, 1914.

If we are like the Greeks in nothing else, we are true habitues of the Acropolis in our eagerness (if one may Yankee-ize the Scriptures) to "hear tell some new thing." And there is therefore a real drag upon our interest and a real fillip for our curiosity in the announcement that Theodore Dreiser, the intent, saturnine author of "Sister Carrie," "Jennie Gerhardt" and "The Financier," having recently for the first time in his life visited Europe, was publishing a book about the adventure, "A Traveler at Forty." But the book dashes the expectations which it raises. It is, indeed, intensely interesting in places —when Dreiser the novelist, analyst and observer is talking about that extremely curious and convenient object of study, Dreiser the unfamiliar traveler and old-boy-out-of-school. But it is also deadly dull in places—when Dreiser the rubber-neck is talking, say, about Perugia. And in a gradually cumulative, rising tide sort of fashion, it is repellent—because of the preponderantly sensual nature of its concentrations and of the essential crassness of its response to such stimuli.

D.S.K. Boston *Times*, January 24, 1914.

If it is true that there is nothing new under the sun, it is equally true that there is no part of the world that has not been written up again and again. The remote Arctic region long had its literature in goodly quantity, and the Antarctic is accumulating a collection that will, no doubt, equal it in a few years. One would need a large room to contain all the books that have been written about Africa, and still they come from the press, but when one gets down to modern Europe, England, France, Germany, Italy and the other countries, he is literally swamped with volumes that have been presented to the attention of the public. Under these conditions it is not to be wondered at that many might look upon Theodore Dreiser's new book, "A Traveler at Forty," without enthusiasm.

But only for the moment; when he has read the first chapter he begins to become interested and his opinions quickly change. He reads on and on as if he had never before heard of the places visited, and if he, too, has traveled abroad he reads because the author has seen so many things that the reader did not see. There is nothing of the commonplace, for instance, in the descriptions by the author of "Sister Carrie" and "Jennie Gerhardt," as there was nothing commonplace in those popular novels; and what is more, he does not describe the places and things we have been wont to expect in a book of travel. Only think of an author who visits England and does not speak of Stratford-on-Avon, does not wander about literary and historical London with a guide book, or even mentions Westminster Abbey! In place of these well-worn subjects we have delightful chapters of English country life, such as Christmas in England, scenes and people in the rural districts, the social life of London; and to show the frankness of the author, he devotes one chapter to Lilly, a Girl of the Streets." And it is a mighty interesting chapter, too. In fact, the people the author meets seem to interest him greatly as types of the countries and places. His style is that of the novelist, one seems to be reading a story in which are incidental descriptions; and with all else, he is not afraid to express his opinion freely, whether he is dealing with the condition of society, art, or the government. . . .

The reader of "A Traveler at Forty" feels that the author and his friend "Barfleur" would make most delightful traveling companions, and we congratulate Mr. Dreiser on having given us such a very interesting book of his own experiences.

Hartford [Conn.] *Courant*, January 31, 1914.

It is a pity that Mr. Dreiser did not see Europe earlier, before he had been stuffed with adulation for his incomparable humanology. It is true that he has an unusually penetrating mind, is outspoken, disregards conventions and writes an unusual book. It is also true, that his pessimism makes him a malinger. It is not true that on the whole: "life is literally compact of make-believe illusion, temperamental bias, false witness, affinity." And "the so-called standards of right, truth, justice, law," are more than "the wire netting of a scene through which the water of life rushes almost uninterrupted." One would think Mr. Dreiser had been unfortunate in his acquaintance. But he had companions of his choice with him; and he did see many things that charmed him and has a happy faculty of talking familiarly about them. There is a way, Mr. Dreiser ought to know, of seeing a foreign city—or your own—

without having one's eyesight dazzled by the demi-monde.

Indianapolis *News*, January 31, 1914.

Theodore Dreiser, whose work has already commanded attention and admiration, especially in his two realistic novels "Jennie Gerhardt," and "Sister Carrie," is an Indiana man, though he has not lived in his native state for years. In reading these two novels one has been proud of the fact, proud of his courage and his workmanship. In reading his book of European travels this pride is tempered to a noticeable extent. Here is another man, indeed. Some one has spoken of Mr. Roosevelt's "enthusiasm over his discovery of the ten commandments": it is here equalled by Mr. Dreiser's enthusiasm over the discovery of Europe. He begins his narrative by a frank confession that he has just turned forty, and he tells us briefly some of the accomplishments he had succeeded in during the later years of the forty. Then comes the introduction of his friend Barfleur, who is a man with "wide wisdom, rare selection, discriminating taste," and a monocle in his right eye. This gentleman persuaded Mr. Dreiser to take the trip to Europe with him. Both were convinced that he was the very person to write an original book about this hackneyed subject, since he had never been there, could view old scenes and different peoples with an unprejudiced eye, and could write in a realistic way these impressions.

Now the thing that strikes unpleasantly upon the reader's intelligence is that even if a great many people have never been to Europe, they have read more or less widely and have an excellent idea about it, anyway. And when they do go finally, they have too much regard for the public and too much awe of publishers to inflict their naive surprises upon us. Mr. Dreiser, if one would believe this book, never has read anything that prepared him in the slightest detail for his experiences. So he takes us solemnly on board the Lusitania, tells us about the stewards and how he was obliged to tip them, details the inane conversations of the parvenues who sat next him on deck, then just as solemnly escorts us through England and the continent, with the same naive comments. One's feeling is chiefly one of amazement. Barfleur's discriminating taste and rare selection seem to have been at fault for once. And most astonishing of all, Mr. Dreiser puts down all the astonishing lapses of his table manners—tells us, for instance, how Barfleur was obliged to rebuke him because he put his own spoon into the jelly, and how that monocled cicerone took away the sandwiches his Indiana friend was eating on the Oxford streets. One is almost afraid to turn the page, lest this unsophisticated traveler be found eating with his knife and gravely recording the fact.

All this does not prevent a great deal of interesting comment on places and events. There are chapters, like the one on "Lilly," a poor waif of the London streets, where Mr. Dreiser's real power shows itself. He likes women, likes to study the underworld women especially, and is at his best in their portrayal; but "Jennie Gerhardt" has ill prepared him for the sophisticated ladies of continental Europe, for the delicacy and smooth surfaces of European society. He can describe places well, sometimes, but then so many people have done it so much better that it is hardly worth while to spend time over these pages. The idea was all right, doubtless; if Barfleur could have found a real philosopher, a cultured student, even if he hadn't seen the world. But one is sorry to conclude that Mr. Dreiser seems what the untutored Hoosier calls "green." Glackens' pictures are singularly appropriate, for Glackens, while humorous, never gives the faintest hint of beauty—he too is naive.

H.L. Mencken. "Anything But Novels." *Smart Set,* 42 (February 1914), 153–154.

. . . Dreiser's volume is an astounding mixture of the commonplace and the unprecedented. On the one hand he fills a long and gloomy chapter with the story of the Borgias, apparently under the impression that it is news, and on the other hand he enters into highly intimate and diverting discussions of the persons he encountered in his wanderings, not sparing either the virtuous or the aged. The children of his English host at Bridgely Level strike him as fantastic little creatures, even as a bit uncanny—and he duly sets it down. He meets an Englishman on a French train who pleases him much, and the two become good friends and see Rome together, but the fellow's wife is "obstreperous" and "haughty in her manner" and "so loud-spoken in her opinions" that she is "really offensive"—and down it goes. He makes a mash on a Mlle. Marcelle in Paris, and she accompanies him from Monte Carlo to Ventimiglia, and there gives him a parting kiss and whispers, *"Avril—Fontainebleau"* —and lo, this sweet one is duly spread upon the minutes. He permits himself to be arrested by a fair privateer in Piccadilly, and goes with her to one of the dens of sin that suffragettes see in their nightmares, and cross-examines her at great length regarding her ancestry, her professional ethics and ideals, and her earnings at her dismal craft—and into the book goes a full report of the proceedings. He is entertained by an eminent Dutch jurist in Amsterdam—and upon the pages of the chronicle it appears that the gentleman is "waxy" and "a little pedantic," and that he is probably the sort of "thin, delicate, well barbered" professor that Ibsen had in mind when he cast about for a husband for the daughter of General Gabler.

In brief, a boyish and innocent frankness runs from end to end of the book —that curious *naïveté* which is half the charm of "Sister Carrie" and "Jennie Gerhardt." Dreiser had never crossed the Atlantic when he set out upon this pilgrimage: he had forty long and hard-lived years behind him before he saw his first cathedral and took his first sniff of Paris air and got his first glimpse of the Italian sun. One might reasonably look for a certain immovable calm, even for a downright emotional anesthesia, in so mature a traveler; but there is no trace of it in the record. He reacted wholly youthfully to the stimuli of a new world, and out of that fact, perhaps, arose the obviousness which gives so quaint a flavor to parts of his story. That English houses are chilly, that the Thames at London is "utterly delightful," that the gaming tables at Monte Carlo are piled high with glittering coin, that the Italian hill towns are lovely at sunset, that Paris guides are a fraudulent and verminous lot—one scarcely looks for such immemorial facts in a book otherwise the very antithesis of hackneyed. But, after all, such empty impressions of the touring novice do not obtrude: outnumbering and outweighing them are the pregnant observations of an old hand at looking, the sharp remarks and annotations of the creator of Hurstwood, Cowperwood and Père Gerhardt. Here the book rises completely out of the commonplace, and becomes something new, illuminating and heretical. It differs enormously from the customary travel books: it is not a mere description of places and people, but a revelation of their impingement upon an exceptional and almost eccentric personality. Whoever has got civilized pleasure out of the Dreiser novels will read it with joy. It is, in a sense, a free commentary upon those novels, a sort of epilogue in mufti. It makes a bit clearer the Dreiser philosophy, the Dreiser view of life. . . .

Henry Langdon Stuart. "Theodore Dreiser's 'A Traveler at Forty.'" *Bookman*, 38 (February 1914), 673–674.

Epicures affirm that our American dishes are but partly cooked and swim in a good deal of water. Our American travel books may likewise be said to be so often half-baked and served with a good deal of diluted language. Our public seems exceptional in having a fondness for voyaging volumes written by persons avowedly ignorant of their subject. Offered an informed tourist book and an uninformed one, the Yankee is quite likely to choose the latter, seeing perhaps a chance for more heedless diversion in it. To readers knowing nothing of Europe nor wanting to, but wishing to know about Mr. Dreiser, his imposing-looking volume will strongly appeal. He professedly carried little across the waters and brought it somewhat laboriously back. At least one may say that the reader is not greatly enlightened or inspired. The author has merely written of himself *à propos* of Italy, Germany and so on. The indications here about his own original personality overshadow the features of his European scene.

Such a frankly superficial volume helps contribute to the generally uninformed and inartistic state of our gulping-down reading public. To stir about among parboiled facts and in half-stewed impressions, leaves our western world as ignorant about and prejudiced against things foreign and foreign life as it was beforehand. To visit Italy without poetry or imagination, Germany without music, Holland without art, France without gayety and humour, is to start with a strong handicap. Features to be regretted may be shown by the two following small examples. We are told that the Seine at Paris is "not so wide as the Harlem River, which makes Manhattan an island." The significant fact is that the Seine is considerably narrowed by splendid embankments to deepen it for an immense volume of commerce of which our Harlem stream is almost as innocent as its banks are bare of civilised attention. Again, in Germany. "I should say that any nation that to-day chose to pick a quarrel with Germany on her home ground would be foolish in the extreme. It is the beau ideal of the aggressive, militant, orderly spirit and, if it were properly captained and the gods were kind, it would be everywhere invincible." This is a neglected array of English that sounds at first like meaning something worth the time, but in reality is not even resonant emptiness. Of course Mr. Dreiser, in his serious intellectuality, is not properly here. But the above instances illustrate the misfortune of the considerable production of our tourist books by greatly advertised writers who have not lived with their subjects, but whom the public is none the less importuned to read. There is nothing more likely to be misleading than first impressions, yet it is a popular American fallacy that somehow because an author is little educated in his theme, he is therefore at least innocent of harm.

To speak of something more vital, Mr. Dreiser exemplifies his German origin, it would seem, by being drawn to consort in Europe with the underside of life, as so many German and Russian writers have accustomed us. Instead of bringing to notice men who are worth while or entertaining, he acquaints us rather with those who can guide through night haunts of immorality, have sex on the brain or desire to "lick" foreigners. And for the women of Europe we are freely offered examples from the various tenderloins who, even for their class, do not propose much in the way of edification or esprit. With his oddly oblique look toward life, desiring to know of vice neither for the purpose of reforming it nor for dissipation, Mr. Dresier appears here as a victim of a morbid curiosity which is never satisfied because never fully gratified. While he mentions on the ground, in passing, names great in art, what his readers feel he is really thinking about at the time is whether some ordinary lady of the pavement is waiting for him and diagnosis around at the public bar. Not that he is to leave her or himself any worse. Nor any better, it must be added. And he has come away from Europe without apparent regret or consciousness that he missed the fine flower of those civilisations. It is partly because the destructive forces—the forces of evil—so strongly attract him.

Due to his burdened German air of unhopefulness, his best art as a prominent and promising novelist is born of the obliquities of his nature, his viewings through thickened colours, the characteristically *gauche* and discouraging formlessness of his circumambient world. His mind suggests the idea of an imposing darkened interior of a vague edifice where the light comes in coloured or gloomy. The superb brilliance of noontide, the noble loftiness and wholesome charm of sightly human kind and human endeavour out in the open, are likely to be lost to view for him in the shadows of a haunting, creeping, slouching night. His frankness and honesty in the present volume are virtues, but virtues which are not unmixed sources of pride or satisfaction. What he observes that is not helpful or beautiful serves small purpose save as an outlet for the course of his own inclinations. In his dominant inbrooding, his first law is unto himself. He is a moraliser recognising secondarily an obligation to society or his fellow-men. It is natural to such a temperament that destruction figures distinctively. Unfortunately, the habit of enlarging on the uncomplimentary phases of foreign life only aids in keeping nations apart and mutually contemptuous. To seek out and exploit much of the undesirable in foreigners, is to encourage the curse of high and ever-widened national barriers. To cultivate and proclaim the best in other peoples, is to bring all a whit closer together in a worthy entertainment of sympathy and enlightenment.

Floyd Dell. "Mr. Dreiser and the Dodo." *Masses,* February, 1914, p. 17.

Theodore Dreiser is an interesting example of an intellectual species that is fast becoming extinct. His attitude toward the world has become so rare among thinking people that one comes upon it with a sense of awe, as one would meet a megatherium in a park. Mr. Dreiser is impressive in all his books, and not least of all in his new one. It is an account of a trip through Europe, and it shows, even more clearly than his novels, the philosophy of—what shall I call it?

There is a philosophy which disposes of revolutionists more completely than any other. It disposes of them, not by hating them, or by ignoring them, but by accepting them as Interesting. According to this philosophy, the revolutionist is a part of life just as much as the artist, the fine lady and the prostitute. They are all interesting. This man's zeal for revolution is an expression of temperament—and nothing more. As such it is admirable. He plans his utopias, the artist paints, the fine lady dresses for the ball, the prostitute smiles invitation to a new man . . . and life goes on. It has always been so, it always will be so. A mad world, my masters, but an interesting one!

This is the philosophy of Theodore Dreiser. It is a philosophy which has been apparent in all his writings. In his novels he has given a broad and impartial account of life as he has seen it lived. Nothing has been too common or mean to escape his observation, nothing too ugly or evil to arouse his scorn. He has described the just and the unjust with a calm and even balance. He has looked on our enthusiasms and our disappointments, our dreams and our lusts, as might some cynical and compassionate god: and we have been properly awed.

It was Theophile Gautier, about the middle of the nineteenth century, who started the idea that the Gods were cynical about human affairs. The idea was characteristic of the period. Cynical? Not so the Gods of the Greeks—they descended *ex machina* in their Godlike anxiety to see that things were right on earth, and the noise of men's quarrels reechoing through Olympus testified to the importance of human affairs. Not so the God of Job, who answered him categorically out of a whirlwind. And not so the God of Bernard Shaw, who waits on his servant to find truth and establish it. Anyone who believes in his own power will have a powerful God—or a philosophy of revolution: it is the same thing. But the Mid-Nineteenth Century—

It was a period dominated by what was called Darwinism—the idea that change came into the world with a tragic tardiness, and that the only way to help the process was to let it alone.

People sometimes talk as though Darwin put the idea of evolution in people's heads. He did establish a mechanical and deadly conception of evolution. He made people think of change as something outside human effort. With the chill of his doctrine he froze the blood of revolution for a generation. Darwinism descended like a blight upon the world and upon men's minds.

Conceive yourself in the Darwinian frame of mind. Forget all you have ever learned in histories about the past, and all you have learned in dreams about the future. Then look about you—see how the fly is devoured by the sparrow, and the sparrow by the shrike (whatever that is), and the shrike probably by the cat. That is "natural selection," and it results in the "survival of the fittest." Then observe the same process going on in the industrial world: No, no, don't interfere because it would spoil the natural condition of "free competition"; and, besides, it wouldn't be any use to try, on account of the "iron law of wages"! . . .

Nothing is more certain than that we don't live in that kind of world now. We know better. We have revised our notions of biology to take revolution into account. And we have dislodged enough sticks from the woodpile of economics to know there is a nigger in there somewhere. Besides, we just can't look on while the process is processing. We have to do something about it ourselves, even if it is only to pull judiciously at other people's coat-tails.

Mr. Dreiser calls this, when he runs across it in his travels, the efflorescence of a temperament. It is more than that: it is the solemn knowledge that according to whether you lift your hand or stay it, the world will be different. We have seen changes in machinery, and changes in institutions, and changes in men's minds—and we know that nothing is impossible. We can have any kind of bloody world we bloody want.

We are in the twentieth century. Mr. Dreiser is still in the nineteenth. For purposes of fiction that is all right. It is absurd to quarrel with an artist about the means by which he achieves his effects. "Sister Carrie" justifies mid-nineteenth century pessimism; a book as good would justify Swedenborgianism, or the theory that we live on the inside of the earth. But when Mr. Dreiser comes to write about modern Europe he needs a modern mind. Sympathy isn't enough; it takes understanding. And Mr. Dreiser simply doesn't understand the most outstanding features of contemporary European life. Firm in the impression that things are to-day essentially what they were yesterday, he dwells upon those aspects of social life which might well have attracted an observer of forty years ago. He draws it, while yet it is there to draw, with vivacity and charm: but he does not see ten minutes into the future. And he conceives the past so naively in terms of the mid-nineteenth century, that he talks of the Renaissance as though Lorenzo the Magnificent were a kind of Charles T. Yerkes.

All passes. Lorenzo the Magnificent is gone, and gone that magnificent curiosity about life which created the Renaissance. Gone too is the mid-nineteenth century, and gone the stark grandeur of its philosophic pessimism. One representative of that period remains, one only, the last survivor of a great and pitiful race. And through his eyes we can take one last look at mid-nineteenth century Europe—a Europe of streetcorners and drawing-rooms, cafés and cathedrals, repartee and women, and over all a sense of lovely futility as of flowers and toys.

J.M. Lee.
Book News Monthly, February, 1914.

This personal narrative in which Mr. Dreiser has set down his experiences and impressions of his first trip abroad will surely interest the reader of forty. Its publishers assert that Madame Grundy's conventions have been disregarded and hence we suggest the reader might well be of her age or at least that of the author.

Frankly, we do not care a "hang" about Miss E or Miss X and their silly twaddle, but when the author leaves them to their laces and frills and goes with the chief engineer through the engine-room of the ship he gets interesting.

The chapter, "Lilly: A Girl of the Streets," seems to us a waste of space. And male reader can duplicate the experience in practically every detail should he care to take a stroll along the red-lighted streets of any American city. Why go to Piccadilly?

On the other hand, "A Trip to Marlowe," one of the best chapters in the book, is an exceptionally fine piece of literary craftmanship. In it one catches an actual glimpse of a quaint old English town which is soon to exist only in fiction. To us, the commercial traveler met in the Marlowe inn is a more agreeable companion than Mlle. Rillette, "The Poison Flower" of "Gay Paree." We are more interested in learning about the curious costumes of the English Knights of the Grip than in being told that certain types of women in Paris use "powder and paint for the face, belladonna for eyes, rouge for the lips, palms, and nails." Need we go to Paris to learn the latter facts? A trip along the Great White Way will suffice.

Fortunately, there are in the book trips well worth taking. "The Stop at Pisa" will not soon be forgotten. "The First Impressions of Rome" are indelibly impressed on the memory. "A Night Ramble in Florence," "Entering Germany," "On the Way to Holland," etc., are sure to be enjoyed. The "Spotless Town" (Haarlem) is something more than an advertiser's dream. Any one of these brief excursions is worth the cost of the fireside trip to which Mr. Dreiser invites us. *A Traveler at Forty* abounds in human interest because more attention has been paid by its author to people than to places.

Town & Country, February 7, 1914.

. . . A few years ago Mr. Dreiser wrote "Jennie Gerhardt," and we took occasion to praise it in these columns. The heroine is a working girl who trades her virtue for a protected life, on the whole with fair success. In a story of that kind it is always a question whether it is written frankly for the element of concupiscence and the ready financial reward which such tiltillation of public desire promptly brings, or in a sincere wish to portray contemporary conditions, with an eye towards amelioration. We gave Mr. Dreiser the benefit of the doubt at that time and hailed him as one who had a new message, some skill in its delivery, and a style which bore ripe promise for the future. In fact, as a result of that book Mr. Dreiser has become one of the important figures of local American literature. The effect upon us of "A Traveler at Forty," however, is so distinctly different from what we assumed it would be, that we are now anxious to re-read "Jennie Gerhardt" and find out what it was we liked, appreciated and praised in that earlier volume—which is the most extraordinary comment we have ever made upon a recent book. The very tone of "A Traveler at Forty" is irritating and unfortunate. Mr. Dreiser's style has been an intensification of the commonplace; now it has fused into smugness. Mr. Dreiser has not yet reached that pinnacle where he can pat "Dickens, Thackeray, George Eliot, Charles Lamb and that refined company of English sentimental realists" patronizingly upon the head before consigning them to the limbo of imperfections from which he himself has been delivered. It almost reads as if Mr. Dreiser had lost his head. The avowed plan of the volume is simple enough. On the one hand is Mr. Dreiser; on the other Europe. Bring the two together and publish the results. This purely physical feat Mr. Dreiser has accomplished to the extent of exactly five hundred and twenty-six pages of text—all of them strangely familiar to anyone who has ever been bored by a returning friend's descriptions of foreign places. We are unwilling to devote space to details; but, in the lump, Mr. Dreiser has seen and described just about what everybody else has seen and described. When we add to this the air Mr. Dreiser has adopted of conferring a favor upon humanity by publishing these commonplaces, the volume comes perilously near being a gigantic, but wearying, hoax.

Sinclair Lewis. "Intimate Travel Talks by World-Famed Writers." St. Louis *Republic*, February 21, 1914.

Three famous novelists, Howells, Dreiser and Bennett, have written three books of travel, in which they so mingle observations of foreign lands with glimpses of their own selves that the reader needs but little imagination to fancy himself traveling with them. . . .

Theodore Dreiser, whose "Sister Carrie" was widely hailed as the largest fruit of American realism, has in "A Traveler at Forty," by far the most intimate of these three books. Not for a second does he write just travel only. He writes of Dreiser apropos of servants' buttons and Monmartre and Sir Secrop, the art critic. He is chatting familiarly with you all through the book. And this quality, precisely, has caused "A Traveler at Forty" to be ridiculed and praised about equally. One reviewer of some fame—at least among reviewers—declared that "Dreiser writes what the average Cook's tourist would like to describe and can't."

Actually, Mr. Dreiser is about as different from the average tourist as his "Jennie Gerhardt" is from the average ribbon-decked romance. For everywhere he goes he watches people with a terrible intentness and a curiosity about them that never rests until he has their secrets.

He watches the stewards on the steamer. He finds out why their manners are so sandpapered smooth. He watches Sir Scrop, and gauges the amount of normal human good fellowship that is hidden within his delicate criticisms of all the beautiful things that have no relation to real life. He watches a typical well-bred English family at their Christmas dinner. He seeks through the tiny German village that was the ancestral home of the Dreisers for traces of his forebears, and presents the town to us just as it would seem to us on a like errand—not as it would seem to some professional travel-book maker, with his knowing little references.

Dreiser has made one reader, at least, disembark at Fishguard and whirl off south to magic London. Dreiser has taken him to Italy and Switzerland and France. Dreiser has walked with him for hours in a sleepy English village and, while not forgetting that the thatched roofs are picturesque and quaint and all the rest of those good old property adjectives, has made earnest inquiry as to the real nature of life in this town that life has forgotten. . . .

Kansas City [Mo.] *Star*, May 16, 1914.

In "A Traveler At Forty" Theodore Dreiser has done something unique in travel books. It is unlike anything else of its kind, because nobody else ever wrote exactly like Mr. Dreiser. If anyone had, Dreiser doubtless would have written in still another fashion. The very title is a reflection of the book's peculiar excellence. The author has avoided the ordinary error of egotism by being thoroughly egotistical. The volume doesn't pretend to tell about the conventional "grand tour" of England and the continent; it leaves that to the guide books and to authors who know no better.

It is a book about a more or less candid Theodore Dreiser and what he thinks about what happened to him in England, France, Germany, Italy and Holland and some other localities which he saw for the first time just as he had turned 40. Therefore any errors of appreciation or criticism that he may have made come charmingly home to be acknowledged.

He is immediately acquitted, brutally frank though he has been, of pillorying this or that city or nation. But this point of view has accomplished something even more surprising than an escape from the common fate of men who see, write and confound themselves. It has made a great book, a vital, vivid volume through which one lays hold of the life of the author among the scenes which afford the setting, and through that life, with the people and peoples who make up the kaleidoscopic procession that marches through the pages.

"A Traveler at Forty" is what might have been expected from the author of "Sister Carrie," which in London, has its select circle of admirers generally referred to as "the Sister Carrie Society," and of "Jennie Gerhardt" and of that stupendous old and new fashioned analysis of a familiar type, "The Financier."

Indianapolis *Catholic*, March 17, 1914.

Of Theodore Dreiser's book "A Traveler at Forty," there is but little to be said, unless one feels inclined to enter into a quarrel with the author and to devote a lot of space to the refutation of errors and calumnies against the Church, which would be quite out of keeping in a book column. Mr. Dreiser, a native of Terre Haute, long a resident of New York, and the author of several books of fiction which drew much antagonistic criticism because of their unconventionality (to use a polite term), saw Europe for the first time at the age of forty.

He describes the people he meets, and from the standpoint of good writing describes them unusually well. For the most part he tells us what we want to know about Europe, not what we can glean from any book of general travel, or Baedeker. On the whole, his chapters devoted to England are delightful. His descriptions of France are marred because they deal principally with the demi-monde; but his Italy is genuinely offensive.

Mr. Dreiser acknowledges himself to be a fallwn-away Catholic, and he reveals the fact that his laxity in matters of religion is not one of mere indifference. He is a bigot of the first water, a hater of the Church, and he devotes page after page to citing those lies and errors of history upon which every bigot bases his claims to wisdom. Many of them could be refuted by a child equipped with the knowledge to be gleaned from the penny catechism. All of them may be refuted by anyone having a half knowledge of Church history. The present day author who charges the Church with frowning upon education; who speaks of the "greediness" of the Papacy; who sets up the claim that there was neither Pope nor bishop, priest nor altar, until three hundred years after the beginning of the Christian era, makes himself a laughing stock.

Delightful as this book is in parts; much as we expect of it when reading the earlier chapters; unusual as is the author's style and the method he employs of recording his impressions, it is not to be recommended. It is a breeder of bigotry, the outpouring of the bitter spleen of one of those unfortunates who has denied his birthright, and, failing to find a heart balm in this world equal to that which God has given us in religion, is attempting to overcome the realities of this life by plunging headlong into its materialistic and fleeting pleasures.

Checklist of Additional Reviews

Chicago *Evening Post,* September 12, 1913.

Bookseller, September 15, 1913.

New York *Post,* November 19, 1913.

Savannah [Ga.] *News,* November 22, 1913.

St. Louis *Globe-Democrat,* November 29, 1913.

Buffalo *Commercial,* November 29, 1913.

Boston *Traveler and Evening Herald,* November 29, 1919.

Ethel M. Colson. "Gossip Out of Bookland." Chicago *Record Herald,* December 5, 1913.

Portalnd [Ore.] *Telegram,* December 6, 1913.

New York *Chronicle,* December 7, 1913.

Buffalo [N.Y.] *Express,* December 7, 1913.

Pittsburgh [Pa.] *Chronicle Telegraph,* December 8, 1913.

"Travel and Nature Studies." Chicago *Continent,* December 11, 1913.

"Mr. Dreiser Abroad." New York *Tribune,* December 13, 1913, p. 9.

New York *American*, December 13, 1913.

Indianapolis [Ind.] *News*, December 13, 1913.

Houston [Tex.] *Post*, December 14, 1913.

Albany [N.Y.] *Argus*, December 14, 1913.

Madison [Wis.] *Journal*, December 20, 1913.

New York *Morning Telegraph*, December 20, 1913.

Brooklyn *Eagle*, December 20, 1913.

"A Dispassionate Observer." New York *Post Saturday Supplement*, December 20, 1913, p. 4.

Hartford [Conn.] *Post*, December 21, 1913.

Savannah [Ga.] *News*, December 22, 1913.

Portland [Ore.] *Express*, December 27, 1913.

American Review of Reviews, January, 1914.

Edwin Markham. "The One Thing Drudges in Factories Learn." New York *American*, January 1, 1914.

H.L. Mencken. "Dreiser in Foreign Parts." Baltimore *Evening Sun*, January 3, 1914.

San Francisco *Argonaut*, January 3, 1914.

"The New Books." *Outlook*, 106 (January 3, 1914), 48.

Louisville *Courier-Journal*. January 5, 1914.

"A Self-Centered Traveller." New York *Evening Mail*, January 10, 1914.

Chicago *News*, January 15, 1914.

"A Traveler's Impressions." Philadelphia *Public Ledger*, January 24, 1914.

Dallas [Tex.] *News*, January 26, 1914.

Christian Advocate, January 29, 1914.

New York *World*, January 31, 1914.

Building Management, February, 1914.

E.F.A. New York *Travel*, February, 1914.

Philadelihia *Book News Monthly*, February, 1914.

Vogue, February 1, 1914.

Milwaukee *Wisconsin*, February 13, 1914.

New York *Spur*, February 15, 1914.

Real Estate Management, March, 1914.

New York *Watchman Express Examiner*, March 12, 1914.

Minneapolis *Bellman*, March 21, 1914.

Everybody's Magazine, April, 1914.

Binghamton [N.Y.] *Republican Herald*, April 9, 1914.

Literary Digest, May 9, 1914.

New York *Craftsman*, June, 1914.

Boston *Congregationalist*, August 20, 1914.

Further Reviews: Bibliographic Information Incomplete

George H. Fitch. "Impressions of Europe." San Francisco *Chronicle*, December, 1913.

Jeannette L. Gilder. "Mr. Dreiser on His Travels." December 3, 1913.

Notes

THE TITAN

BY

THEODORE DREISER

AUTHOR OF
"THE FINANCIER," "SISTER CARRIE,"
AND "JENNIE GERHARDT"

NEW YORK: JOHN LANE COMPANY
LONDON: JOHN LANE, THE BODLEY HEAD
TORONTO: BELL & COCKBURN MCMXIV

The Titan

"The Eighteen-Eighties." New York *Tribune.* May 23, 1914, p. 11.

While Robert Herrick is still pleading for greater freedom for the American novelist, Theodore Dreiser long ago took it, and by the mere weight of his ponderous talent imposed himself upon our literature. Others had done this, and continue to do it, in minor measure, but he is our arch-realist, unrestrained and unafraid. It is well for American fiction that he has been accepted; it is, perhaps, as well that opposition to him continues. In fact, at the present stage of his career opposition may do him more good than harm. He gave us the full measure of the matter and the manner of his art in his first book, since when he has neither progressed nor retrograded, so far as the essential quality of his novels is concerned. He has broadened his canvas, he has come to deal with far more vital social forces than in "Sister Carrie," but his conception of men and women has remained fundamentally the same; and he has continued to take them from approximately the same social stratum. He does not see American life whole; and, so far as he sees it steadily, he is becoming increasingly preoccupied with one phase of it, whose importance he exaggerates. This over-emphasis is the weakness of realism in its reaction from the sentimentality and pink-and-gold unreality and timidity of the average of our immature fiction.

Love and passion are legitimate subjects for the novelist who addresses himself to mature readers, provided always that he recognize their idealism, their beauty and romance as well as their tragedy. Neither the beauty nor the tragedy is found in this second volume devoted to the career of Frank Algernon Cowperwood. He has not the eye to see them, he has not the temperament to create them. He merely obeys an impulse; his passing amours do not interest us, except where they threaten to interfere fatally with his business interests, a danger that he often incurs with no perceptible excuse of a really great passion. In his love affairs he is decidedly not a "Titan." He is very commonplace, and the most that one can say is that he runs after women as a puppy runs after chickens, because it is his nature. There is not even the strong touch of a deliberate defiance of society in his furtive intrigues.

This is all of a piece, it is true, with his turnings and twistings, his chicanery and dishonesty and treachery as a Titan of finance. The character study is consistent. But that, even as realism, does not satisfy us any more than does a faithful photograph of a particularly uninteresting subject. The title of the book does not fit its hero, except in so far as his acquisition of a gigantic fortune is concerned. And here, indeed, we find the true merit of the book. It is a stupendous picture, built up ponderously, detail upon detail, in the Zolaesque manner, of the period in which gigantic fortunes were created out of public utilities, out of gas and street railways, and the formation of the first trusts; the period of the wholesale corruption of city councils and state legislatures, of bought and stolen franchises and elections, of the control of politics by big business.

The struggles for control, for the spoils, the hidden and open fights, the personal quarrels that are transferred to the financial arena, all this is vivid reading. Had Mr. Dreiser called his book "The Titans," no objection could have been made to his title. The late Frank Norris drew in "The Octopus" the picture of one of these giants of an earlier generation, and, crowning triumph of his book, when at last the reader came face to face with this superman of transcontinental railroad building, he found him to be a Titan indeed, irresistible as a force of Nature. Compared with him Mr. Dreiser's Cowperwood is not even clay; he is slippery, common city mud.

The scene is laid in the Chicago of the eighties and nineties of the last century. The author's pictures of the city's "society" of the period may be left to the Chicago reviewers for comment and criticism. They are pungent; so, no doubt, will be the critics. So far as Mr. Dreiser even considers this phase of American life at all, he looks at it through the eyes of the Ishmaels his leading characters always are. In conclusion it may be said that this picture of an era in our financial and industrial evolution has serious socio-historical value.

Baltimore *Evening Sun*, May 23, 1914.

An epoch in American fiction is created by Theodore Dreiser's novel "The Titan," just out today.

No statement which stops short of that is adequate to describe the significance of the book to those who take the novel seriously as an interpretation of life and times.

In it we find at last a man with a sufficiently strong, masculine mind (too big, thank Heavens, for cheap tricks of romance!) to seize the life today and stamp it upon the printed page undecorated; with all its toil and sweat, its raw light, its aspiration, and its cruel failure. And the life which Mr. Dreiser elects to portray is the life of a financial Titan—a figure which the evolution of the race has just cast—new and totally unlike anything seen before—out from the whirl of human affairs. In "The Financier" Mr. Dreiser laid his hand to this work, but it was only the dim lines of the figure emerging under his touch that one saw in that book. In this the figure stands completed—with the robustness of absolute truth. Other novelists have tried Mr. Dreiser's field, Frank Norris the most conspicuous and the strongest of them. But all of these have been betrayed into the weakness of decorating, of dressing, their theme. Mr. Dreiser's volume is as real as the chart of a fever patient, as matter-of-fact and as full of elevations and depressions, since it is life. The book has faults, but its virtues are such that one becomes absorbed in them to the forgetfulness of blemishes . . . .

No author has ever before so laid hold, by the scruff of their necks as it were, of the saloonkeeper, the ward leader, the political boss, the City Councilman, the Mayor, the Governor, the corporation lawyer, the banker—all those people who make America—and made them walk through the pages of a book to show what American life is. The firm, dead-sureness of his grip upon his characters never relaxes for a minute. The progression from cause to effect in the life of Cowperwood and his associates never drags behind reality, never trots ahead. Characters troop into the story in the crowding numbers in which they troop into life, stay for a time long or short and move on. Yet the speech of every one of them rings as true as good coin flung on marble—as consistent to himself or herself. Behind them is the background of Chicago and New York, and weaving them together are the countless little things—from the ward leader who stands at the door of his saloon on a summer evening and greets his followers to conferences behind closed doors of the bankers who hold the pursestrings of cities—which weave men together in the whirl of time and produce the event. In this novel the great event is a city gone mad over the accumulation of things which one man has done until his interests reach into the pockets of the whole populace. Few things in fiction are better than the staring white reality of a city moved by a single thought which Mr. Dreiser drives into the pages of his book when he shows the Titan engulfed by the very forces he had set in motion now arisen to a tidal wave and encompassing him. Nothing like it has ever been attempted in American fiction.

The faults? One grows weary of Cowperwood's illicit love affairs and thinks that the author could have found a more heroic figure among the Titans who have made an industrial civilization if he had selected one who now and then quickened in affection to his fellow-man.

But the great virtue of the book is its illusion of reality, and perhaps it would have been less real if it had been anything other than it is. One could forgive Mr. Dreiser much more than the faults of this book for the eye-assaulting reality which he gives here. The two volumes are reported to follow the career of Yerkes, the Chicago traction magnate.

It is said that a third volume is planned. One is inclined to think that "The Titan" will remain tremendously bigger than that which may come after, as it is tremendously bigger than that which went before.

E.F. Edgett. "Dreiser and His Titan." Boston Evening *Transcript*, May 23, 1914, p. 8.

Voluble as Mr. Dreiser has been in "Sister Carrie," in "Jennie Gerhardt," in "The Financier," these novels have been the height of reticence compared with the license of incident and speech with which he has filled "The Titan." The second volume in "a trilogy of desire," it continues the record of Frank Algernon Cowperwood's exploits in love and finance. That hero, it will be remembered, found himself in prison towards the close of "The Financier" as the result more of a political conspiracy against him than of any wrong-doing, and it is his life following his emergence from about a year's confinement that Mr. Dreiser recounts in "The Titan." Fortune came to him again in response to the touch of the novelist's magician's wand, but since he was not looked upon fondly by the social and financial hierarchy of Philadelphia, he considered it wiser to seek other worlds. He chose Chicago and in the five hundred and more pages of "The Titan" we are told how he came, how he saw, and how he fought and conquered. With him also went the beautiful Aileen Burke, once his mistress and soon to be his wife after he had secured a divorce from the first wife whom he had deserted for her.

The gift of verbiage is certainly Mr. Dreiser's to command. He seems able to write of everything earthly with a hand that is unrestrained by any sense of the eternal fitness of things. He sees men and women, but he does not see them completely. He sees scarcely anything but the evil in them, and the pages of "The Titan" therefore becomes merely a record of the adventures in vice of Cowperwood and the creatures of both sexes with whom he surrounds him. He lays equal emphasis upon the vices of politics and business and the vices of sex, and he makes Cowperwood an adept in both. His story is built up of alternate layers touching now upon Cowperwood's conquests in high finance and now upon his successes with women. It is in fact substantially two separate novels, and they could be easily separated and with but a few changes become independent stories.

The path of Cowperwood through the twenty years or so of his life upon which the story is founded is strewn with the relics of his personal dishonor. He can be true to no man and to no woman for even a moment. At times the novel becomes a list of his successes in business by means of bribery; at other times it is a catalogue of his triumphs over women. He seems to be an all-conquering hero to the novelist who created him; to many of his readers he is nothing more than an unmitigated scoundrel. He attacks both the strong and the weak; the wives of men he despises and the daughters of his associates in business are alike his victims. Mr. Dreiser represents them as more tempting than tempted, but his attitude towards all mankind seems to be that there is no virtue in either man or woman. He seeks to show us not merely a fragment of the world in which evil is rampant; he endeavors to convince us that there is nothing but evil in the whole world and in all men and women. His Chicago is even worse than his Philadelphia; it is a hotbed of business crime and of social vice. His men have in them no good that Mr. Dreiser is able to discover.

A one-sided, serious view of life such as this betrays a lack of balance on the part of a novelist. However true it may be, it is not the whole truth. Such men as Cowperwood exist, but all men are not such men as he. The reader is certain, unless he happens to be a devotee of pornography for its own sake, to become utterly disgusted at the recital of Cowperwood's affairs with women, and he will search his vocabulary and easily find words wherewith to express his opinion both of the character and of the novelist. It is not of course the slightest use for us to seek or to find, or to use these words. They would defeat our own purpose. We leave them to the reader.

In spite of its tremendous shortcomings, "The Titan" nevertheless commands admiration and respect. Mr. Dreiser's knowledge of affairs in the world of business and society is remarkable. He is never at a loss for a scheme wherewith to explain Cowperwood's methods, or with his explanation of them. His pictures of the time and the place are vigorous and graphic. . . .

With all his experience, with all his undoubted descriptive powers, with all his voluminous writing, Mr. Dreiser is unable to rid himself of the use of words and phrases that are an offense against good taste and the dignity of the English tongue. He persists in saying that a building is "located," in using the impersonal "one" as the antecedent of the personal "they," in placing something on "either" side when he means both sides, in "alluding" to an object or person that he specifically mentions, and in a thousand and one other tricks of speech that are the faults, doubtless, of the careless facility with which he writes. Whole sentences, too, may not infrequently be found that are sublime in their egregiousness, as "she stockinged her legs in brown silk," or "the colonel, who had a small, gray goatee and sportive dark eyes, winked the latter solemnly."

Understanding life so thoroughly, it is a pity that Mr. Dreiser cannot see all sides of it clearly. "The Titan" is a big book in size and intellectually, but it is by no means a great novel. It lacks the discretion, the restraint, the good taste, the normality essential even to an approach to perfection.

"Financier Becomes Titan." New York *World*, May 23, 1914.

We have to acknowledge again our failure to find enthralling the personality or the career of Mr. Frank Cowperwood.

This gentleman was introduced by Theodore Dreiser nearly two years ago through the agency of a novel called "The Financier." Acquaintance is pushed some degrees further now, in the many, many pages of "The Titan," and we observe with apprehension the symptoms of Mr. Dreiser's intention to convert his enterprise at some future date into a trilogy.

Cowperwood was of Philidelphia in the first instance. He accumulated sudden wealth in the Quaker City and added eventually, through force of circumstances, bankruptcy and a brief term in the penitentiary. Under the dictates of discretion, opportunity and, perhaps, Mr. Dreiser's demand for fresh scenes of action, he removes to Chicago, and there we have him through the principal portion of "The Titan." It is significant that toward the end of the book he builds him an extravagant mansion in New York.

Reviewing "The Financier," on its publication in November, 1912, we paid tribute to Mr. Dreiser's industry, patience and perseverance rather than to his power as a gripping story-teller. The same testimonial must obtain after a reading of "The Titan." Cowperwood's manipulating process with Chicago gas, rapid transit and city fathers is followed in dry detail, with even less illumination than as if an enterprising reporter had written the story from the sessions of an investigating committee; but to write it even so has required, on the part of the author, a great deal of labor on the spot, as it were—an intensive cultivation of facts, methods and local history. No real names are mentioned, such as those of the Drexels, Jay Cooke and others in "The Financier," but there are numerous strong indications of Dreiser fiction merging into Chicago truths. . . .

"The Titan" is unillustrated. Nor does one see it in pictures after reading it.

Hildegarde Hawthorne. "Mr. Dreiser's Trilogy." New York *Times Review of Books*, May 24, 1914, pp. 241–242.

This is the second part of Mr. Dreiser's "Trilogy of Desire," taking up the life of Frank Algernon Cowperwood when he emerges from the penitentiary, where his operations as "The Financier" in the first book had landed him. He comes out with a second fortune in his possession, and fully prepared to conquer the world which has downed him. Mr. Dreiser intends to present him as a giant among men, commanding every one by the immense force and charm of his personality, winning out against whatever odds by sheer strength of intellect, magnetism, and daring; creating hate, certainly, but never indifference; loved by all women and successful with all.

We say "intends," because Mr. Dreiser "has bitten off a lot more than he can chew." Whatever Mr. Dreiser's intentions, the Cowperwood of his book is very far from the titanesque. He neither charms nor compels, but appears as an ordinary man given to questionable business methods, and common intrigues in which the suggested note of passion is more talked about than present.

There is nothing the matter with Mr. Dreiser's idea, which is to present one of those bucaneers of the last generation who saw far and saw big and whose rule of life was "everything for me." He sets this figure in Chicago, the Chicago of the seventies, booming after the fire, utterly corrupt in its government, utterly unbounded in its confidence and energy. Beside him is the woman because of whom he has been divorced by his wife, and to whom he is now married. Aileen is beautiful, unintelligent and socially ambitious, in love with and dominated by her husband, who soon begins to weary of her.

Surely a typical American situation, full of possibilities.

Unluckily, Mr. Dreiser, instead of dealing in large masses and broad sweeping lines, loses himself in a mesh of petty detail and endless repetitition. Nothing salient emerges. It's all about it and about. [sic] His most successful effect is produced in his portrait of Aileen, of her gradual degeneration under the poison of her union with Cowperwood. This delineation, repellant though it may be, is masterly, conveying something of the pathos of ruin and waste in character, always pitiful, however slight the original beauty and fineness.

The story fluctuates between Cowperwood's dealings in business with men and his love affairs with women.

These latter are endless, common, and detailed. To be sure, once in a while the author runs over a list of Dorothys, Jessies, Tomas and Hildas, saying they shall be names only. But usually these affairs are related in full. Apparently they are intended to indicate a boundless vitality, a huge, generous, glowing temperament. But they remain simply sordid and animal, evoking a sort of casual disgust in the reader rather than any stronger emotion. Never does the author succeed in creating the impression that here, truly, was a man whom women might love. One feels sure, on the contrary, that he would have bored them inexpressibly.

The book is crowded with characters, and many of the briefer portrayals are vivid and interesting. Our first meeting with most of the men with whom Cowperwood comes into contact is always the best. They stand out, for the moment, real, alive, and various. But after that they flatten and fade, receding into the fog of words within which the story indistinctively moves. Of distinction of style Mr. Dreiser has nothing; he even descends to such constructions as "Quite like a character in a Japanese print might be." "She was probably something like her own mother would have been." "If any one fancies . . . they but little," & c. He also inclines to the use of words like cognoscenti, illuminati, with a result not unlike what might be produced by a tramp in a silk hat. He has, however, his felicities, for instance this paragraph describing the boss:

> There is a kind of nature, not artistic, not spiritual, in no way emotional, nor yet unduly philosophical, that is nevertheless a sphered content of life; not crystaline, perhaps, and yet not utterly dark—an agate temperament, cloudy and strange.

To be sure, the subsequent filling out of McKenty's outlines does not illustrate this adumbration of him, but the picture has been produced.

Cowperwood, between his amours, piles one fortune on another in Chicago, though he fails to achieve "society." Toward the end he comes to New York, building a house even grander than his Chicago residence. Here his wife endeavors to commit suicide, on finding that the move has been inspired by his last infatuation, a girl called Berenice, daughter of the keeper of a house of ill-fame who has been brought up in ignorance of her mother's profession—shades of Bernard Shaw! Berenice brings the hero's philanderings to an end, for to her plea, "And there aren't to be any other ladies," he replied, "Not another one, as I hope to keep you." Here the book ends, so that we feel Berenice is safe—at least until the start of the third part of the Trilogy.

Berenice only consents to come to Cowperwood when failure overtakes his last big scheme in Chicago, an outraged populace and frantic newspapers having shrieked him down as scoundrel and robber.

> Rushing like a great comet to the zenith, Cowperwood did for the hour illuminate the terrors and wonders of individuality. But for him also the eternal equation—the pathos of the discovery that even giants are but pigmies, and that an ultimate balance must be struck. . . .
>
> So the author. As for the reader—

The main trouble with the book is that Mr. Dreiser does not get inside his hero's skin. He tells us about him, and we feel that what he tells is heresay. It is something like the report a blind man might be expected to give of a sunset which had been carefully described to him. Mr. Dreiser's mind is rather reportorial than creative, and he lacks discrimination. Everything goes in. At times the result is happy, and certainly the reporter has his uses. But the book fails of its declared attempt. Here is no vision of a mighty phase of the American spirit, mingled of good and evil, welding and breaking. Here is instead a lot of little people doing a lot of little things, often interesting, occasionally amusing, at times dull and distasteful. If some one asserts, "but this is life," it is fair to retort, "a commonplace view of life, lacking dignity and perspective, more like a crowd in the street seen from a window than the intimate understanding and experience of a human being at grips with circumstance and existence."

William Marion Reedy. "Reflections: Dreiser's 'Titan'." *Reedy's Mirror*, May 29, 1914, p. 3.

Theodore Dreiser's novel, "The Financier," was a big success to which a sequel was promised. The sequel was written and sent to Harper and Brothers who had it set up in type. Then they refused to publish it. Almost the same thing happened in the case of Mr. Dreiser's first novel, "Sister Carrie:" the publishers withdrew it from sale. Now John Lane has published the sequel to "The Financier." It is entitled "The Titan." It is sexy—very; but not more so than "The Financier" and "Jennie Gerhardt." It tells the story of the hero of "The Financier" in Chicago, after he settled there with his mistress, whom later he married, after the collapse of his career in Philadelphia and his release from the Pennsylvania penitentiary. *Frank A. Cowperwood* is the key-name for Charles T. Yerkes. He is taken through his spectacular career of operations in gas and street railway franchises in Chicago. He is a genius in finance, in the manipulation of men. Likewise he is a connoisseur of art—and of women. Mr. Dreiser tells this man's story with a detail more minute than Flaubert's in "Sentimental Education," with a wealth and complexity of incident worthy of Dostoievsky. And the author philosophizes as he goes along, though not superciliously. His philosophy is that such men, such things are. They are part of the pattern of life, and if they are unbeautiful it is only as parts; in the whole they may contribute to the beauty of the scheme. But in "The Titan" there is something mellower than in any of its predecessors. It is a more urbane, more cultured book. The author has been touched by the appeal of art, by the influence of tradition. Every page shows the effect upon him of those experiences he told us about in his book, "A Traveler at Forty." The "grand tour" has softened him and his art. There is no plot in this story. It is a straight story of splendid crookedness by a man of power. It ranges among the turpitudes of high finance and the villainies of politics. It shows corruption at its highest efficiency. It takes us into what Mr. Dreiser doesn't quite venture to call high society. We are brought into the sanctum of venal journalism. And it is all true, terribly true. *Cowperwood* varies his existence with *liaisons* with women. The book names, I think, seven women, maids and matrons, whom he seduced. Privilege is his vocation, but his avocation is the enjoyment of his prowess as a "parish bull." He has two or three women at a time, not counting his wife, with whom, as his leman, he left Philadelphia and his first wife. This second wife is beautiful and gorgeous, but she doesn't belong. She can't make good as he does. And she loves him too much. She pays bitterly for what she did to the first wife and sinks to assignations and high balls. Author Dreiser is great on describing women. He introduces us into a splendidly variegated harem, and he is so frank a guide he does not offend. The women are highly incidental. *Cowperwood* fights for power. He fights so well that the other big brigands combine against him. We know them all under their disguises—Marshall Field, Armour, Cudahy, just as we recognize Mike McDonald, Bath House John and Hinky Dink McKenna among the politicians. These big business men, in fighting *Cowperwood,* are driven to such argument as means the end of them all. The attack on *Cowperwood* makes for a municipal ownership sentiment. He wants to consolidate all the railroads under a fifty year franchise. The fight ranges from Chicago to Springfield—at the latter place he meets an honest man; we know him as Altgeld. Finally *Cowperwood* is beaten. The roads are consolidated but with Chicago getting a big share of the earnings. Somewhat sex-jaded, *Cowperwood's* lust is excited by a girl to whom he becomes guardian, the daughter of a fast woman from Kentucky. She has quality in everything. He educates her. She learns about her mother and is disillusioned, but she remains cold. The night that all his street railway plans are ruined she comes to his arms right regally. And the book closes with a clairvoyant glimpse of a future in a New York art palace, where the sodden neglected wife lingers for a while, tolerated, pitied; with visions of promotorial struggles in London; with a premonition of a procession of kept odalisques in other European capitals. Another sequel is to tell us all about these, and the comic-opera rapacities after *Cowperwood,* or Yerkes, has gone down to death. Strange to say, the book is not depressing, even in its details of financial or legislative battles. One does not tire of the women. And finally the book leaves the impression that this big, bad man wrought in his own way, all blindly, for good. We don't meet many good or even respectable folk in the book, but as Dreiser introduces the people there are, he makes them ingratiate themselves with us, for all their meanness. *Cowperwood* is large-looming. He's ruthless but he's kind, too. He has a contempt for men but likes them. Women—they comfort his body and cause a glow in what he would call his soul. *Cowperwood* is an artist in evil. He obscures, for Dreiser, the people in the mass whose blood and sweat made the glory for which *Cowperwood* fought and bribed his way to—defeat. But Dreiser is big because he has no philosophy, no economics, no sociology, no tradition, no background, no learning to stop him from boldly picturing and saying things so obvious no cognoscenti of letters would venture upon them for fear of being accused of banality. If he should get a little more "art," Dreiser will become a "literary" novelist and then he'll be a "goner," not fit even to be damned. Let us hope and pray that he'll keep clear of coteries and not learn to show off himself instead of his characters.

Frederic Tabor Cooper. "Summer-Time Fiction." *Bookman*, 39 (June 1914), 447.

Whatever value we may place upon Mr. Theodore Dreiser as a novelist, he is certainly not one whose works may be dismissed lightly. That he is tremendously in earnest, is obvious. That an amount of patient toil and endeavour goes into each and every one of his volumes is evidenced by the crowded detail, the tumultuous activity, the multitudinous sequence of episode, the whole effect of thronging humanity, the ceaseless storm and surge of existence. And yet, in his later books he fails to produce the effects that he secured by far simpler means years ago in *Sister Carrie.* There was no confusion of many characters and many incidents in that volume, no overcrowding of the canvas. It was all quite direct and elemental, and poignantly true. The reader took sides keenly, glowing hot and cold alternately, with the surge of personal sympathy,—because every character in the book was a personality, some one whom we could have loved or hated in real life in a frankly human fashion. The new volumes are vastly more elaborate: one feels that Mr. Dreiser has studied and toiled and striven, before reaching the minute understanding of business and finance, monopoly and graft that makes books like *The Titan* and *The Financier* read like the concentrated extract of a whole world of bribery and corruption. And yet, by the very force of iteration, the wearing action of endless repetition, they deaden their own effect; the sheer volume and extent of the detailed schemes pall upon us and leave us indifferent. In *The Financier,* it will be remembered that Cowperwood, Frank Algernon Cowperwood, having defied gods and men once too often, was borne down under the wreckage of his own vast schemes and landed for some thirteen months in the Eastern District Penitentiary in Philadelphia. *The Titan* takes up his subsequent career from the date of his release, witnesses his achievement of a fresh fortune, his removal to Chicago and his ambitious plans for effecting a consolidation of the city gas companies, with the ulterior design of controlling the monopoly himself. Incidentally, the volume is a detailed, minute and rather sordid secret life of a modern Don Juan. Cowperwood is not content to divorce his patient, long-suffering first wife and marry his mistress in her stead; but he seems temperamentally unable to look upon any woman without desire. Mr. Dreiser spares us none of his many gallantries. They become wearisome, repellent, almost nauseating from the sheer monotony of their endless sameness. It is all, no doubt, true to the actualities of a certain side of life, although one wonders at times how any one man could always have the luck of such seemingly easy conquests; the law of probabilities would point at least to an occasional rebuff. But, be that as it may, Mr. Dreiser might have been content to give us a few specimen cases and let us conjecture the rest. Infidelity following infidelity, discovery following discovery, husband and wife both hiring detectives to spy out their respective rendezvous, hair-pulling, face-scratching and torrential outpourings of billingsgate invective do not make pleasant reading when extended over upward of five hundred closely printed pages. The reviewer's quarrel is not with the author's method, nor with his outlook upon life, but merely with his sense of proportion and quantity, his tendency to overstate his case so vastly. Cowperwood's first few lapses from virtue compel our attention, but the time comes when we merely say wearily, "What, not another one?" And the only relief from this obsession of women is an equally tiresome obsession of monopoly, Gas Company shares, street-railway shares, bills, ordinances, injunctions, the whole machinery of legal and legislative chicanery. Undeniably, the book has a certain bigness, it is cast on broad, bold lines, and incidentally it strips a human soul bare of its last remnant of covering. But it is not enough to tell the reader the truth, the whole truth, and nothing but the truth; it is necessary also to hold his interest,—and to do that, an author must be careful not to try the reader's patience too far nor too long.

Louisville *Courier Journal*, June 1, 1914.

It may be that there is no such thing as the man's, or the woman's point of view since each man or woman has an individual viewpoint, but it seems certain that no woman could have written anything even remotely resembling "The Titan," Theodore Dreiser's second volume of the "trilogy of desire," of which "The Financier" was the first. Perhaps it is difficult for a woman even to judge such a book based as it is upon the principle of masculine individualism running riot, unrestrained by tenderness, compunction or honor.

Frank Cowperwood might have been understood and admired by such conscienceless men as the Chicago politicians who are represented as his tools in this epic of graft and license, but Mr. Dreiser has left slender hold for the sympathy of the average reader. The average feminine reader must regard this wrecker of women with as much angry repugnance as his political and financial rivals viewed the wrecker of fortunes and the people's rights. . . .

Allan Updegraff. "Theodore Dreiser's American Superman." Baltimore *News*, June 3, 1914.

Mr. Dreiser's new novel, "The Titan," is written around a large and unpleasant personality, a personality in many ways as unpleasant as Napoleon Bonaparte's, and in many ways as interesting. Frank Cowperwood is the type of conquering individualist, of ruthless superfinancier, that America produced in such number in the last two or three decades; in fact, the character is said to follow closely that of a Chicago magnate who died not long ago.

Mr. Dreiser has been hailed abroad as the most significant American novelist and the most American of our novelists. There is something that might be called national in his creation of the character of Frank Cowperwood, and in his feeling for the Chicago background against which the drama of Cowperwood's financial and love intrigues is played out. America, and a prominent American ideal, are in a way put up for inspection and judgment. The presentation is made in a sustained, powerful, somewhat bitter narrative that rises at times to genuine poetical inspiration. Mr. Dreiser's big, square sentences were never piled upon each other to better effect than here.

There is frank realism, relentless sincerity in all that has to do with the dealings of the central character; practically all of the Ten Commandments, and particularly the Seventh, are broken as often as a man like Cowperwood would break them. He is unscrupulous and socially poisonous in nearly all his activities, and yet he is huge, human and genuine as well—a tremendously significant man.

Taken with Mr. Dreiser's preceding novel, "The Financier," in which Cowperwood figures, we have here a good part of the epic of a modern Major General of finance. It will not make good reading for those who have not "the interests and values of maturity," but for those who have it offers entertainment as vital and interesting as are the Cowperwoods still in our midst, and as the conditions of whose real meaning Cowperwoods are the human expression.

Brooklyn *Eagle*, June 6, 1914.

American business take note. Theodore Dreiser's "The Titan," one of the widely applauded (by its publishers) romances of the day, is nothing more or less than a moralized, highly dramatic, fictionized story, based (with a good many of the incidents left the same), on the exploits of the great Charles T. Yerkes of Chicago. Mr. Dreiser need not contradict us. We have him. We know as well as if we had been sleuthing him just how he wrote these pages from the life of a big American business man. He has waded through some friendly newspaper "morgue," has borrowed, adopted, rewritten, revised, changed, romanticized thousands of clippings. Every paragraph of "The Titan" shows it.

This way of gathering material, though unusual, is perfectly legitimate. Mr. Dreiser, out of his spoils, has made one of the best books of American fortune amassing yet written. There will be people that do not know the ins and outs of unscrupulously acquiring gigantic properties. Dreiser may not know how it is done, either, but he has been wise enough to get perfectly good, raw material and fashion it together.

There was romance in the Yerkes' policy, a vast and splendid drama. Here, changed here and there, and with stories of illicit passion freely invented and added, it has worked splendidly into modern fiction. Dreiser took a giant for his hero. Never mind the moral side at the moment. The giant was there. Dreiser makes us see him and feel him. He has built up chapter by chapter a real Titan, a man so resourceful and able that no one can beat him in the marts of trade.

There is your story, big and terrible, the biggest of all situations in American life. It is almost Norse drama, but with this difference, no retribution comes, evil is not punished or avenged, no calamity falls. The Titan goes on heaping up his millions. Not only does he get these, but there is no lack of "lady loves," impressionable young women who are fascinated by his personality and will, with slight persuasion, be "his."

Thackeray called his "Vanity Fair" a novel without a hero. Theodore Dreiser might easily call "The Titan" a "novel with two score heroines." There is a new heroine every score of pages. The Titan specializes in securities and also in hearts. He divorces his wife in Chapter I, and gets a new one. That poor woman finds she has countless rivals.

To get at the inner life of the American of today, some of its most disagreeable aspects, certainly, but those that are true and real, that make a lesson for us all, read this book of Dreiser, "The Titan."

Boston *Times*, June 6, 1914.

Mr. Theodore Dreiser, who is already widely known as an author on account of his early novels, but more especially on account of "The Financier," which he wrote in 1912, and which both at the time and since has always been considered a book of rare merit, and the reading public has anxiously waited for his next novel and it has now appeared and its title is "The Titan." It is really a sequel to "The Financier," and in it Mr. Dreiser presents a story of rare interest. As a novelist he is deeply in earnest and writes seriously and does not hesitate to attack the large issues of life with force and as a consequence all of his productions are well worth reading. Every character he presents is necessary to make his story complete, and the whole book is good solid reading. From the beginning the interest in it continually increases and even the ordinary reader does not wish to leave it for a moment even if things more important present themselves. He compels attention and makes you feel the importance of each and every one of his characters and to accept his ideas of them and of what they do.

Its treatment of things financial are clear and incisive and there is no misunderstanding as to what he has to say or of the ideas he wishes to convey. In "The Titan" he has introduced business, politics, love and many other things in which every one is interested. The character of Cowperwood is prominent in the story. He is a man of strong passions and whatever he attempts to do he invariably does it. His love conquests are numerous and in this line he may well be styled a conqueror, for he wins and relinquishes many ladies and seems to have no scruples as to whether the world approves his acts or not.

It is said that Mr. Dreiser is to write another volume in which Cowperwood will figure quite prominently, and it will surely be eagerly awaited by all who have read "The Titan," and those who have not already done so should read the volume at once.

Chicago *Journal*, June 6, 1914.

Theodore Dreiser's new book, "The Titan," is now on the market and exciting unusual interest among Chicagoans, as it is a novel of Chicago life, the second volume of business fiction based on the life of Charles T. Yerkes. It is a difficult task for a prejudiced critic to review a book fairly and the writer is deeply prejudiced in Dreiser's favor through the wonderful work he did in Sister Carrie and Jennie Gerhardt.

Somehow or other it is very difficult to consider Dreiser's novels as fiction. There is a reality and a human note about them that makes one forget it is merely a story. Mr. Dreiser is a big man, judged by his writings, a tremendously big man. Apparently he has undertaken the task of making the greatest American interest, business or finance, the subject of romance—a difficult task. He has taken one of the most picturesque characters in the high finance of America and traced his career through Philadelphia and a term in prison to Chicago and the street railway manipulations which are still a vital part of Chicago's life.

Surely no greater theme for fiction could be found. The facts are as strange as the strangest fiction, and somehow or other Dreiser's book doesn't read like fiction. One unconsciously takes it for fact, forgetting that it is fiction founded on fact.

Dreiser has made his novel, "The Titan," almost biographical in the telling. He has pictured his hero, Cowperwood, as a strange combination of cold-bloodedness and eroticism. The novel will be severely criticized by those who are not quite sure of the purity of their minds and fear to take chances of contamination. There will be much raising of hands in holy horror over the incidents told in "The Titan" of Cowperwood's relations with divers and sundry women, having, at the same time, a wife of surpassing physical charm, who had previously been his mistress.

If the novel had been written by a Frenchman it would be read eagerly and the author excused because he was French and couldn't help his state of mind. Being written by a healthy, virile American, who scorns subterfuge and calls that useful implement, a spade, by its real name, the small-minded will protest.

There are some wonderful bits of writing in "The Titan." The characterization of Chicago is, perhaps, one of the finest bits of descriptive and rhapsodic writing Dreiser ever did—and he isn't given much to flights of fancy and picturesque imagery. He tells his facts and the facts are sufficient to wring the heart in Sister Carrie and Jennie Gerhardt.

After these two masterpieces, "The Financier" and "The Titan," are disappointments until the reader adjusts himself. Then the wonderful versatility of the man commands admiration. If genius is an infinite capacity for taking pains, Dreiser is a genius. The book reveals tremendous study and research, a marshaling of details nothing short of wonderful. Again we are taking a novel for fact. But there must have been a vast array of fact as a basis for the fiction.

There is not a stranger character in fiction than Cowperwood, not a lovable character, not an admirable character at any stage, yet a character of compelling interest. Perhaps no character has been so clearly, concisely, and minutely analyzed since Balzac's human comedy. It is strangely real. A city editor read the book and mistook it for news. . . .

It is the story of a soul corrupted, overwhelmed, destroyed by lust, lust for money first, lust for women afterward, a description of unparalleled selfishness that he who reads may be warned. A powerful sermon if properly taken. After reading "The Titan" one can not help but feel how little a part of real life the pursuit of money is, how apart from the real soul of man commercialism is removed. It seems an artificial, destroying passion. If it was the author's intention to point this moral, he has done his work wonderfully well. But the writer does not believe that

Dreiser wants to point any morals. He wants his readers to point their own. He has given them material with which to work upon their own individual consciences. His books are books that can not be forgotten. Somehow or other they stick in the mind.

If he wades through mire, it is in order that cleanliness may look brighter and altogether desirable by comparison. The comparison can not be avoided in "The Titan."

Rochester *Post-Express*, June 8, 1914.

. . . Mr. Dreiser certainly gives promise of force as a writer and, if he but exercised the power of selection, he might yet succeed in establishing a reputation as a novelist. He paints on a broad canvas, but why paint only bad men and foolish or fallen women? He writes as though he believed all who do not fit into these two categories are hypocrites. His hero in "The Titan" has willpower and amasses millions—but the root of Cowperwood's nature is untamed brutality. One might as well glorify a callous murderer. The novel is the second portion of a "Trilogy of Desire," as Mr. Dreiser calls it. One sincerely wishes that so vigorous and talented a writer had not embarked on such an undertaking. Life, as it is presented to us in his pages, is a loathsome thing—it recalls what Matthew Arnold says of the "dark pagan world" in which sated cruelty and luxury made a hell of earth.

"Books of the Day - - The Current Novels." New York *Post*, June 6, 1914, p. 5.

Mr. Dreiser continues his notable study of the predatory genius of the market introduced in "The Financier." The present scene of operations is Chicago of the eighties and nineties, where gas and street railways spelled golden opportunities. Cowperwood, who in true outlaw fashion establishes and maintains himself in the field by sheer craft and audacity, remains from first to last an interloper, waging his campaign singlehanded against the coalition of local capitalists. The spectacle has so fascinated Mr. Dreiser that he has turned Roman historian, sketching in every figure of any importance in this fight for plunder, following all the moves and countermoves with smiling pagan veracity. Witness the protestations of the two ward leaders who had sold out to the enemy everything but their own seats in the City Council:

> "Look at meself! I only won by 300 votes," archly declared Mr. Kerrigan. "By God, I almost lost me own ward!"
>
> Mr. Tiernan was equally emphatic. "The police was no good to me," he declared firmly. "They let the other fellows beat up me men. I only polled 6,000 . . ."

and the ferocious ultimatum of Cowperwood in parley with his enemies who have thought to take him unprepared on the eve of a financial crisis:

> "If you open the day by calling my loans, I'll gut every bank from here to the river."

A whole epoch of American history could be reconstructed from these two incidents alone; its end, too, foretold from the night when a formidable army with banners camped round about the City Hall while boodling aldermen inside, heckled by a galleryful of resolute constituents, reluctantly voted down the fifty-year renewal of Cowperwood's franchises. For it is not the superior strength of his antagonists or any weakening of his own powers that finally determines this battle of giants, but a change of popular temper so profound as to mark the dawning of a new social era. So much for the application of evolutionary principles by our social historian.

In this volume, however, the emphasis is no longer meant to be upon Cowperwood's business operations, but upon his self-realization—rapacity is a plainer word—in quite another line. " 'I satisfy myself,' was his private law," and the consistent individualist must be expected to satisfy himself with many women. These appear in due succession, this one requiring several chapters, that one accounted for in as many paragraphs, a half dozen others listed and disposed of in a line apiece—maids and matrons of outward respectability, all too willing to be properly classed as victims. Mr. Dreiser, who seldom understands when the way to completeness is through elimination, has felt obliged to include them all in order to illustrate authentically the promiscuity of the man who "had little faith in women aside from their value as objects of art," and at the same time can afford to cultivate a very fine taste. It is a pity, since many readers are sure to judge the book entirely by their own disposition towards episodes of this character, whereas what Mr. Dreiser offers to our contemplation is in no sense a rake's progress, but the detailed process of the ripening of appetite into taste. . . .

Mr. Dreiser is no longer, as in "The Financier," an altogether scientific analyst rejoicing in the striking exemplification of a natural law in an unusually fine specimen. He has become more the interpretive philosopher. And his conception of a nature emancipated from fear of consequences by its own exceptional capacities, and maintaining itself at the expense of others, in defiance of the social order, a triumphant though lonely outlaw, would have excited a lesser moralist to indignation and an anxious haste to see justice done.

Ethel M. Colson. "Realism and Romance." Chicago *Record-Herald*, June 13, 1914.

Theodore Dreiser's new story, "The Titan," is no more a novel than a moving picture scenario is a drama or the most romantic of biographies an actual romance. It is, in fact, an almost literal transcription of the meteoric career of a certain street car magnate who used Chicago as the scene of his middle life struggles and triumphs, retiring to Europe to solace his social and political defeat. As to the justice, the good taste, the decency, even, of thus making literary capital out of all but living tissue there are, of course, differences of opinion. The "art for art's sake" enthusist will proclaim the right of the artist to take where he can find, congratulate him upon the discovery of material so easily worked and promising; the humanist, on the other hand, will deprecate such use of a man's life story, at least while its memory still is warm among his fellows. In any event, Mr. Dreiser's wholesale borrowing has not resulted in any great gain to literature. "The Titan" is vigorous, virile, sensational, arresting, but it is neither finished nor fine. . . .

There is a moral to this story, although Mr. Dreiser, who believes that "the world is dosed with too much religion" and that "the professional moralist is at best but a manufacturer of shoddy wares," probably would be slow to admit it. Cowperwood, throughout, is calmly, carefully lawless. But life, despite Mr. Dreiser's retrospective conviction that it is to be "learned from life," exacts stern payment for moral lapses both conscious and unconscious, and the lesson of "The Titan"—all the more impressive for being rather against the author's will—is inevitably that deduced from the history of that other monumental light o' love and leader whose career closed so sadly on St. Helena's lonely isle.

It is well, perhaps, for Mr. Dreiser that he does not live in Chicago, as that many of the old-time residents of the city are no longer living. The earlier Chicago that he paints is immoral and sordid to blackness, and there are few redeeming features. The only touch of anything like goodness in the narrative, indeed, is the devoted, heart-hungry loyalty of Aileen, and even this is of frankly peccable origin. The style is businesslike, the conscientious chronicling of events and episodes intrinsically dramatic but intrinsically repugnant to the clean-minded; recurrently distinguished by an outspokenness reminiscent of the profane youngster who believed in calling a spade a spade even if it were a condemned old shovel, and marred by occasional mannerisms that smack of careless revision. Mr. Dreiser, for example, is almost as fond of "rich" as Henry James is of "wonderful." One of his characters takes "rich" strides, another experiences "rich" thrills, another feels things "richly." The book is overweighted with grime and gloom from start to finish. But all these matters would be as naught, in face of the author's evident earnestness and desire to translate life for his fellow livers, were it possible to see what real purpose is served by such stories. Realism has its wide place in literature, pure romance must fight its own battles. But why, in a world full of mixed good and bad men, women and conditions, refuse to recognize the faintest peep of light?

"A Master of Immorality." Providence [R.I.] *Journal*, June 14, 1914.

In the paper cover of "The Titan"—which is, by the way, by a singular stroke of ineptness, bound in the shade of blue generally associated with virginity—the publishers assert that the author "is the one novelist who has his finger upon the pulse of our national life." There is much more of that style of criticism which Mr. Gelett Burgess has so perfectly epitomised in a single word; but it is with this especial statement that we are most closely concerned. Here is a book in which there is not a single decent woman, and by "decent" we mean not merely conventional or respectable but possessing the fundamental essentials of a clean outlook upon life and love—a book in which there is not a man to whom the god of money is not the only god who can exact tribute. Do debauchery and blind greed represent the heart of American ideals of living? Is there in this body corporate of a great nation only a festering mass of gilded impurity? No one denies that there is such an aspect of our American life. No one denies that the conditions that Mr. Dreiser describes exist. That there are and have been such men as Frank Cowperwood everyone at all familiar with certain great figures in the financial world knows. What then? Is this the whole story? the half? the fourth? or rather a still smaller fraction?

It is not merely as Americans or as would-be impartial censors of ethical conditions in America that we quarrel with the picture presented by Mr. Dreiser in this utterly dreary book. As an artistic performance "The Titan" can only be regarded as a travesty. A book which consists in equal layers of the history of the Chicago stock market —as "arranged" by Mr. Theodore Dreiser—and the history of the kept women of Frank Cowperwood—with "variations"—forms an aesthetic mélange calculated to disgust the most robust appetite. Mr. Dreiser can not for all his particularity succeed in putting flavor into either section of his ill-conditioned feast. It is difficult to say which is the more distasteful, whether Mammon or the god of the "yellow ticket" is the more revolting. One thing, however, is clear. This is the story, so far as it is a story, of a satyr not a titan. Copwerwood is not a demi-god but a demi-beast. Mr. Dreiser has not succeeded, though one does not fail to recognize the sincerity of his attempt, in making his hero's brutal strength outweigh his brutal weakness. Cowperwood is an animal swayed by his own desires rather than a juggernaut moving by immutable law. And all the details—details elaborated almost beyond belief—of his operations in making himself a master of millions do not convince us of his power. It is not because Cowperwood was devoid of conscience that we turn with an inalienable consciousness of the pathos of unrealized artistic purpose from "The Titan" it is because he is devoid of charm.

Unhappily the pathos of the book lies not merely in the failure of the author to achieve his end, despite a sincerity of intention, an ability stultified by spiritual—or, if you like, artistic—limitations rather than by lack of intelligence, and an industry which apparently knows no bounds. It lies also in the fact that it is going to be accepted by hundreds, perhaps by thousands, of thoughtful readers for what it is meant to be and is not—a picture of American life. There is much to lead the uncritical to such a point of view. There is, in the first place, the consciousness that such men and women as those depicted do exist and play their part in the American maelstrom. Truthfulness is the most specious argument that can be offered to prove truth; but Mr. Dreiser's public does not recognise this basic axiom of life and art. The public will doubtless welcome with a measure of intellectual avidity a novel that is both profoundly immoral and profoundly inartistic. Never was the Spanish proverb more forcibly illustrated than in the case of "The Titan"—for of the good intentions of Mr. Dreiser there can be no possible doubt. There is only one thing that may possibly frustrate the harm which a book of this kind may do—its almost unbelievable dullness.

Lucian Cary. "Recent Fiction." *Dial*, 56 (June 16, 1914), 504.

The distinction, so commonly attempted in newspaper offices, between reporters who "write" good stories and reporters who "get" good stories is often applied to novelists. And though to press the point is to divorce form and material to a degree altogether misrepresentative of the facts, the distinction is a useful one. It was not artistry that made "Uncle Tom's Cabin" the flaming document it was. Mrs. Stowe had a thumping story to tell, a story that circumstance had made so good that only her limited skill was needed to render it effective. On the contrary, it was artistry that made "Mademoiselle de Maupin" the book it was, and is. The story was nothing, or would have been nothing in the hands of a lesser writer than Gautier.

The case of Mr. Dreiser's new volume, the second of his "trilogy of desire," is as far as possible from that of "Mademoiselle de Maupin." My first feeling was that Mr. Dreiser had as good a story as Mrs. Stowe's, and one a good deal more to my own taste, without the art to tell it. But the truth is that Mr. Dreiser has, in the slang of the city-room, "fallen down on the story." He wanted to give us, against the background of that great, new, struggling Chicago of the eighties and nineties, the figure of an adventurer without master or scruple, a Superman. He has all the facts. I do not doubt that he could give names and dates for every incident in the book. Indeed, any one who knows Chicago could come very near doing it without any assistance from him. The story is always dangerously close to actual event; dangerously close because Mr. Dreiser has depended on this actuality to convey reality. He has so many facts that he supposes he has done enough when he has set them down. But outward facts are significant only when they are the sign of an inward meaning. And Mr. Dreiser simply does not know the inward meaning. He has never for a moment stood in Frank Cowperwood's shoes and looked out upon the Chicago of twenty-five years ago with Frank Cowperwood's eyes. The result is that though Frank Cowperwood conquers a woman or a financier in every other chapter, he is no more a Superman than the barber around the corner.

But if Mr. Dreiser has failed to draw his figure he has done some astonishing things with his background. No other writer's view of Chicago is so individual or so effectively presented. I confess, also, to enjoying his ironies at the expense of the pillars of society, though it is silly to pretend that the *liaison* was as well established in the Lake Shore Drive of 1886 as it was in the French farce of the same period and tiresome to read so many pages about dull creatures like Stephanie Platow.

New York *Evening Sun*, June 22, 1914.

Theodore Dreiser has published another book. We have just perused "The Financier" and give it as our opinion that in that book Mr. Dreiser mauls and mutilates the English language with more brutal carelessness than any literate person we have ever known. His dull spots are duller than the dullest stretches in the *Congressional Record.*

And yet in spite of this we read "The Financier" through in two evenings, because there is not a character in it that is not essentially alive and solid to the touch; the author has both insight and power and makes you feel it; he has thought deeply and has the native force to impose his point of view on you, at least, while you read. It is astonishing that a man with so much to say and with such a strong conviction that it needs to be said should be content to say it with such utter absence of distinction. There are not very many American fiction writers who are even trying to do large, serious work right now, and a man as good as Dreiser should be better.

Louisville *Post,* June 27, 1914.

In some respects—or, to drop a trite phrasing, in some respects, or in what we may term "literal sections"—this book is a big novel, or, at least, very near to bigness. That Dreiser is aiming at that quality is evident from the title of his book as well as from other evidences noted in the very beginning. Big subjects demand big treatment—and Frank Cowperwood, is at once elemental and modern, a curious mingling of the simple and the complex, a spirit of the mid-nineteenth century, with all the individualism of that period, yet with all the desire for life, the joie de vivre, the hedonism that is marking the twentieth century. The conception itself we call "big;" we do not call it "large"—and the reason for this distinction is very clear. It is big, indeed, with a certain brute force and vitality and a certain quality of the intellectual and emotional which verges upon the tremendous. Yet large the thing is not, either in conception or in execution—for "large," as we understand it, implies a certain uplift, a certain ability to translate and glorify, or, at the least, to lead one on to a sense of the spiritual, to something—call it Force or Life or God—which directs the world of men yet, apparently, permits it a measure of liberty. It is so that certain of Shakespeare's tragedies are large, and certain dramas of Aeschylus and Sophocles, and a few very notable pieces of fiction, such as "The Scarlet Letter." The synonym, of course, is "great"—and "The Titan," we repeat, is big but not large, not great. . . .

Cowperwood, it is constantly brought home to us, is a very strong example of the exuberance which is possible to the mental and physical nature of man—though he, by his very exaggerations, proves himself a remarkable exception. He is a man who is full of what we used to call "red blood," a phrase which is now out of fashion and which, indeed, should never have been so used as it has. In the end we have no dead level either of failure or of achievement, for the man is left as a big dynamo, still working, still radiating energy.

As to the raison d'etre, we are not quite sure that we like it. It would seem to be merely good photography—and photography, we hold, is for little things, not for Titans. There is a lack, here, of the constructive feeling which goes to the making of great novelists—the ability to see something more than the fact, to be "cognizant of life beyond this blood heat." It is all too black and white, the terms are too clear, too lacking in the penumbra of the spirit. Mr. Dreiser is a remarkable photographer; a great, synthetic novelist he is not. "The Titan" is a terrible story, with only too much of truth in it—but we miss that finer hand, with a keenly spiritual touch, which we have learned to look for in really great fiction.

"Amorous Money-Maker." Los Angeles *Times*, June 28, 1914.

Mr. Dreiser has made a mistake in the title of this, the second volume in his "Trilogy of Desire," of which "The Financier" was first. Frank Algernon Cowperwood, who emerges from prison to sustain the leading role in this book, is not a "titan," and should not be designated as such.

He is an unscrupulous, corrupt money-maker with a passion for the other sex, and not at all particular about the caste, complexion or build of the woman he breaks on the wheel of his lust.

Mr. Dreiser writes with force, at times with brilliancy; but we do not think the so-called "titan" nearly so powerful, so masterful, so overwhelming as the author has intended to represent him. Time and again the author iterates in effect: "What a great man is this! So Cyclopean in intellect and passion!" But when Cowperwood speaks or acts for himself he falls below the expectations we have of him.

But the book, considered without introspection for titanic qualities, is startling, brutal, graphic. Only those whose virtuous sensibilities are insulated would do well to approach it, for Mr. Dreiser is not affected by any weak regard for conventions. . . .

The character of Cowperwood is not pleasing; he is a typical money-making, licentious blackguard—but, as such, he stands a distinctive, a remarkable creation.

DeWitt C. Wing. "An Unreeling Realist." *Little Review*, 1 (July 1914), 49–51.

Theodore Dreiser possesses none of the standard qualifications for the art of fiction writing. He is not imaginative but inventive; he is not clever but clear; he is not excited but calm. Whatever the flaws in his considerable body of work no fair-minded reader may say that it is made to catch popular applause. Its tremendous distinction is sincerity. Another characteristic which his novels exhibit is resolute purpose. Dreiser is aiming at something, and in *The Titan,* the second book in an unfinished trilogy, he takes a long if wobbly step toward it. Previously to the publishing of this volume he had not even hinted at what he intended to work out. One thing was certain: he was not a trifler; he was not trying to write best sellers; literary success was not in his mind. He had set out seriously and indefatigably to write, not so much what he felt and thought, as what he saw. Some day he would try to get at the realities that lay back of their representations. He would probably undertake to reveal the soul of the American nation. He would pass through the growth stages of a nation, and achieve some kind of spiritual national life. In the last two pages of *The Titan* this guess at his purpose receives appreciable encouragement. Moreover, it is made evident for the first time, in these concluding paragraphs, that Dreiser's prosaic realism springs not only from a vague, deep idealism but a large, hidden spirituality. For at the core of him Dreiser is a profoundly religious person.

Neither his style nor his stuff is far above the dead level of mediocrity; in fact, Dreiser's rhetoric is often inexcusably atrocious—intentionally crude, one is tempted to assert. Obviously he is not interested in style; he is conscious of something bigger than that revealing itself in a huge, ugly, unfinished moving picture—a net result symbolical of a young, raw, riotous, unsynthesized national life. One is therefore tempted to say that Dreiser, more than any other author, is the personification of America. He represents the composite personality of Uncle Sam.

After reading *The Financier* and running far into the interminable pages of *The Titan* I felt that in the absence of cameras, kodaks, Baedekers, and historians Dreiser would be worth while. His endless reels of pictorial facts did not impress me as possessing sufficient animation successfully to compete with these odd rivals, but I admired his consistent sincerity and simplicity and felt that something important was promised by the mere unfinishedness of his pictures. I was sure that he did not write as one inspired, and certainly not as one fired. And after finishing *The Titan* I felt that here was a work having the aspects of a seriously performed duty, exacted by fidelity to some personal theory of industrial change. I could not imagine the author happy as an artist is happy in his creative work; he was too conscious of service to a cause. But in the last paragraph I discovered a big, personal note which introduced an attitude that extends beyond the borders of materialism. It presented another Dreiser—an author who was much more than a cinematograph, snapping superficial impressions of a vast panorama. Two years ago I should not have attributed the following words to Theodore Dreiser:

> In a mulch of darkness is bedded the roots of endless sorrows—and of endless joys. Canst thou fix thine eye on the morning? Be glad. And if in the ultimate it blind thee, be glad also! Thou hast lived.

After laboring through arid deserts of description, this memorable passage, fraught with recognition, satisfaction, challenge, hope, and promise, stands out as an oasis.

The Titan, by virtue of its bold, graphic strokes, loses its identity as a tree, with sharply defined individual characters, and represents the forest. It is more like a jungle, and the jungle is our national life, into which the morning sun inevitably will shine.

Pittsburgh *Sun,* July 10, 1914.

The second volume of Theodore Dreiser's "Trilogy of Desire"—of which the first was "The Financier," serves only to strengthen our belief that this writer is one of the most significant in modern American letters. The book fulfills the promise of the first, and stands, independent of it, an imposing expression of the American capitalist, a detailed revelation of financial and political methods in the last quarter of the nineteenth century.

Mr. Dreiser triumphs with ease over his one shortcoming, the slovenliness of his style. So broad is his vision, so penetrating his analysis, so realistic his expression, that very often this very defect serves rather to enhance than to detract from the effect he seems to be laboring mightily with his pen. But in the summing up, one finds he has obliterated all thought of his style, and that instead his characters stand out with surprising vividness, his incidents with convincing detail. . . .

The manipulations of Cowperwood in politics, in seeking concessions, franchises, privileges for the growth of his interests, are told with an intimacy which betrays, in Theodore Dreiser, a most astonishing knowledge of the methods of the eighties. Few more frank exposes of these methods have been written, and this novel should stand as a unique record of an interesting period in city government in the United States, a period from which we have not long emerged.

"Mr. Dreiser's New Novel." *Newark Evening News*, July 18, 1914.

. . . Mr. Dreiser professedly is a realist—a cool, impartial, scientific observer of life, to whom facts are all important, and in whose observations no preconceived notions must interfere. In actual working he is no such thing, and here comes the contradiction. His observations evidently are to emphasize his own ideas. These observations, one must conclude, are not directed at obtaining the truth of life, but at proving his various theses. He forces the society he observes, the people he depicts, the events he chronicles into the mold of his theories. Mr. Dreiser is a poor realist because he is a partisan, and a poor philosopher because he is both superficial and antiquated.

It cannot be said that Mr. Dreiser has succeeded, to any marked degree, in depicting American character or life. He does bring in local color with more or less effect, and it is apparent that he seeks to introduce as many "types" as possible. But there are faults in his realism and in his characterization. As to Cowperwood, whatever basis of fact may be in the portrayal, the man, as a whole, cannot be accepted. No man however possible of the type of Cowperwood would be tolerated for a twelve-month in any American community. Mr. Dreiser makes Cowperwood's activities as outrageous as possible in order to show how he can dominate all, can crush opposition no matter how determined. But the opponents of Cowperwood are men of straw.

One must note the purely mechanical character of the novel's construction, and, too, the mechanical construction of not a few passages. Mr. Dreiser also is mechanical in that he attempts to secure reality by introducing into his story actual persons under very thin disguises, and actual incidents garnered from the newspapers without any attempt to adapt them to the circumstances. There is felt, throughout, the presence of the bulky notebook employed with dull persistency.

People with old-fashioned ideas of grammatical construction may be bold enough to criticize Mr. Dreiser when he speaks of "one or two others whom he felt sure would come." There is a rather irritating repetition of such words as "chemic" and "trig." But in a story of such length some words are certain to be overworked.

H.L. Mencken. "Adventures Among the New Novels." *Smart Set,* 43 (August 1914), 153–157.

After all, Dr. Munyon is quite right: there is yet hope. Sometimes, of course, it is hard to discern, almost impossible to embrace. Sweating through the best-sellers of the moment, shot from the presses in a gaudy cataract, one can scarcely escape a mood of intense depression, a bleak esthetic melancholia. What is to become of a nation which buys such imbecile books by the hundred thousand, and not only buys them, but reads them, and not only reads them, but enjoys them, gabbles about them, takes them seriously, even pays reverence to them as literature?

Publishers get rich printing that sort of "literature," and then use their money to bludgeon and browbeat all authors who try to do anything better. Imagine a young American bobbing up with a new "Germinal," or a new "Lord Jim" or a new "Brothers Karamazov": what a job he would have getting it between covers! But let him rise shamelessly out of the old bog of mush, dripping honey and buttermilk, and at once there is silver in his palm and praise in his ear. The Barabbases fight for him, playing one another all kinds of sharp tricks; the newspapers record his amours, his motor accidents and his table talk; the literary monthlies print his portrait (in golf togs) opposite that of Gerhart Hauptmann; the women's clubs forget Bergson and the white slave trade to study his style. In the end, he retires to Palm Beach or Tuscany with a fortune, and so becomes a romantic legend, half genius and half god.

But, as I started out to say, there is yet a glimmer of hope. A small class of more civilized readers begins to show itself here and there; a few daring publishers risk a dollar or two on fiction of an appreciably better sort; the literary monthlies forget their muttons long enough to say a kind word for Joseph Conrad; now and then a genuine artist is seen in the offing. Fate, alas, conspires with stupidity to keep the number down. Frank Norris died just as he was getting into his stride; David Graham Phillips was murdered by a lunatic at the very moment of his deliverance; a dozen others, after diffident bows, have disappeared in ways just as mysterious. But there remains Theodore Dreiser, patient, forthright, earnest, plodding, unswerving, uncompromising—and so long as Dreiser keeps out of jail there will be hope.

Four long novels are now behind him, and in every one of them one sees the same grim fidelity to an austere artistic theory, the same laborious service to a stern and rigorous faith. That faith may be put briefly into two articles: *(a)* that it is the business of a novelist to describe human beings as they actually are, unemotionally, objectively and relentlessly, and not as they might be, or would like to be, or ought to be; and *(b)* that his business is completed when he has so described them, and he is under no obligation to read copybook morals into their lives, or to estimate their virtue (or their lack of it) in terms of an ideal goodness. In brief, the art of Dreiser is almost wholly representative, detached, aloof, unethical: he makes no attempt whatever to provide that pious glow, that mellow sentimentality, that soothing escape from reality, which Americans are accustomed to seek and find in prose fiction. And despite all the enormous advantages of giving them what they are used to and cry for, he has stuck resolutely to his program. In the fourteen years since "Sister Carrie" he has not deviated once, nor compromised once. There are his books: you may take them or leave them. If you have any respect for an artist who has respect for himself, you may care to look into them; if not, you may go to the devil.

In all this, Dreiser runs on a track parallel to Conrad's; the two men suggest each other in a score of ways. Superficially, of course, they may seem to be far apart: the gorgeous colors of Conrad are never encountered in Dreiser. But that difference lies almost wholly in materials; in ideas and methods they are curiously alike. To each the salient fact of life is its utter meaninglessness, its sordid cruelty, its mystery. Each stands in amazement before the human tendency to weigh it, to motivate it, to see esoteric significances in it. Nothing could be more profoundly agnostic and unmoral than Conrad's "Lord Jim" or Dreiser's "Jennie Gerhardt." In neither book is there the slightest suggestion of a moral order of the world; neither novelist has any blame to hand out, nor any opinion to offer as to the justice or injustice of the destiny he describes. It is precisely here, indeed, that both take their departure from the art of fiction as we of English speech commonly know it. They are wholly emancipated from the moral obsession that afflicts our race; they see the human comedy as a series of inexplicable and unrepresentative phenomena, and not at all as a mere allegory and Sunday school lesson. If art be imagined as a sort of halfway station between science and morals, their faces are plainly turned toward the hard rocks of science, just as the faces of the more orthodox novelists are turned toward pansy beds of morals.

Conrad tells us somewhere that it was Flaubert who helped him to formulate his theory of the novel, with Turgenieff and the other Russians assisting. The influences that moulded Dreiser are not to be stated with such certainty. Here and there one happens upon what seem to be obvious tracks of Zola, but Dreiser, if I remember rightly, has said that he knows the Frenchman only at second hand. Did the inspiration come through Frank Norris, Zola's one avowed disciple in America? Against the supposition stands the fact that "Sister Carrie" followed too soon after "McTeague" to be an imitation of it—and besides, "Sister Carrie" is a far greater novel, in more than one way, than "McTeague" itself. Perhaps some earlier and lesser work of Norris's was the model that the younger man followed, consciously or unconsciously. Norris was his discoverer, and in a sense, his patron saint, battling for him valiantly when the firm of Doubleday, Page & Co. achieved immortality by suppressing "Sister Carrie." (Some day the whole of this tale must be told. The part that Norris played proved that he was not only a sound critic, but also an extraordinarily courageous and unselfish friend.) But whatever the fact and the process, Dreiser has kept the faith far better than Norris, whose later work, particularly "The Octopus," shows a disconcerting mingling of honest realism and vaporous mysticism. In Dreiser there has been no such yielding. His last book, "THE TITAN," is cut from exactly the same cloth that made "Sister Carrie." Despite years of critical hammering and misunderstanding, and a number of attacks of a sort even harder to bear, he has made no sacrifice of his convictions and done no treason to his artistic conscience. He may be right or he may be wrong, but at all events he has gone straight ahead.

"THE TITAN," like "Sister Carrie," enjoys the honor of having been suppressed after getting into type. This time the virtuous act was performed by Harper & Brothers, a firm which provided mirth for the mocking back in the nineties by refusing the early work of Rudyard Kipling. The passing years work strange farces. Today the American publisher of Kipling is the firm of Doubleday, Page & Co., which suppressed "Sister Carrie"—and "Sister Carrie," after years upon the town, is now on the vestal list of the Harpers, who bucked at "THE TITAN"! The grotesque comedy should have been completed by the publication of the latter work by Doubleday, Page & Co., but of this delectable fourth act we were unluckily deprived. Life, alas, is seldom quite artistic. Its phenomena do not fit snugly together, like squares in a checkerboard. But nevertheless the whole story of the adventures of his books would make a novel in Dreiser's best manner—a novel without the slightest hint of a moral. His own career as an artist has been full of the blind and unmeaning fortuitousness that he expounds.

But what of "THE TITAN" as a work of art? To me, at least, it comes closer to what I conceive to be Dreiser's ideal than any other story he has done. Here, at last, he has thrown overboard all the usual baggage of the novelist, making short and merciless shrift of "heart interest," "sympathy" and even romance. In "Sister Carrie" there was still a sop, however little intended, for the sentimentalists: if they didn't like the history of Carrie as a study of the blind forces which determine human destiny, they could wallow in it as a sad, sad love story. Carrie was pathetic, appealing, melting; she moved, like Marguerite Gautier, in an atmosphere of agreeable melancholy. And Jennie Gerhardt, of course, was merely another Carrie—a Carrie more carefully and objectively drawn, perhaps, but still one to be easily mistaken for a "sympathetic" heroine of the best-sellers. Readers jumped from "The Prisoner of Zenda" to "Jennie Gerhardt" without knowing that they were jumping ten thousand miles. The tear jugs were there to cry into; the machinery seemed to be the same. Even in "The Financier" there was still a hint of familiar things. The first Mrs. Cowperwood was sorely put upon; Cowperwood himself suffered injustice, and pined away in a dungeon.

But no one, I venture to say, will ever make the same mistake about "THE TITAN"—no one, not even the youngest and fairest, will ever take it for a sentimental romance. Not a single appeal to the emotions is in it; it is a purely intellectual account, as devoid of heroics as a death certificate, of a strong man's savage endeavors to live out his life as it pleases him, regardless of all the subtle and enormous forces that seek to break him to a rule. There is nothing in him of the conventional outlaw; he does not wear a red sash and bellow for liberty; from end to end he issues no melodramatic defiance of the existing order.

The salient thing about him is precisely his avoidance of all such fine feathers and sonorous words. He is no hero at all, but merely an extraordinary gamester —sharp, merciless, tricky, insatiable. One stands amazed before his marvelous resourcefulness and daring, his absolute lack of conscience, but there is never the slightest effort to cast a romantic glamour over him, to raise sympathy for him, to make it appear that he is misunderstood, unfortunate, persecuted. Even in love he is devoid of the old glamour of the lover. Even in disaster he asks for no quarter, no generosity, no compassion. Up or down, he is sufficient unto himself.

The man is the same Cowperwood who came a cropper in "The Financier," but he has now reached middle age, and all the faltering weakness and irresolutions of his youth are behind him. He knows exactly what he wants, and in the Chicago of the early eighties he proceeds to grab it. The town is full of other fellows with much the same aspirations, but Cowperwood has the advantage over them that he has already fallen off his wall and survived, and so he lacks that sneaking fear of consequences which holds them in check. In brief, they are brigands with one eye on the *posse comitatus,* while he is a brigand with both eyes on the swag. The result, as may be imagined, is a combat truly homeric in its proportions—a combat in which associated orthodoxy in rapine is pitted against the most fantastic and astounding heterodoxy. The street railways of Chicago are the prize, and Cowperwood fights for control of them with all the ferocity of a hungry hyena and all the guile of a middle-aged serpent. His devices are staggering and unprecedented, even in that town of surprises. He makes a trial of every crime in the calendar of roguery, from blackmail to downright pillage. And though, in the end, he is defeated in his main purpose, for the enemy takes the cars, he is yet so far successful that he goes away with a lordly share of the profits, and leaves behind him a memory like that of a man-eating tiger in an Indian village.

A mere hero of melodrama? A brother to Monte Cristo and Captain Kidd? A play-acting superman, stalking his gorgeous heights? Far from it, indeed. The very charm of the man, as I have hinted before, lies in his utter lack of obvious charm. He is not sentimental. He is incapable of attitudinizing. He makes no bid for that homage which goes to the conscious outlaw, the devil-of-a-fellow. Even in his amours, which are carried on as boldly and as copiously as his chicaneries, there is no hint of the barbered Don Juan, the professional scourge of virtue. Cowperwood pursues women unmorally, almost innocently. He seduces the wives and daughters of friends and enemies alike; there is seldom any conscious purpose to dramatize and romanticize the adventure. Women are attractive to him simply because they represent difficulties to be surmounted, problems to be solved, personalities to be brought into subjection, and he in his turn is attractive to women simply because he transcends all that they know, or think they know, of men. There must be at least a dozen different maids and wives in his story, and in one way or another they all contribute to his final defeat, but there is nothing approaching a grand affair. At no time is a woman hunt the principal business before him. At no time does one charmer blind him to all others. Even at the close, when we see him genuinely smitten, an easy fatalism still conditions his eagerness, and he waits with unflagging patience for the victory that finally rewards him.

Such a man, described romantically, would be undistinguishable from the wicked earls and seven-foot guardsmen of Ouida and the Duchess. But described realistically, with all that wealth of minute and apparently inconsequential detail which Dreiser piles up so amazingly, he becomes a figure astonishingly vivid, lifelike and engrossing. He fits into no *a priori* theory of conduct or scheme of rewards and punishments; he proves nothing and teaches nothing; the motives which move him are never obvious and frequently unintelligible. But in the end he seems genuinely a man—a man of the sort that we see about us in the real world—not a transparent and simple fellow, reacting docilely according to a formula, but a bundle of complexities and contradictions, a creature oscillating between the light and the shadow, a unique and, at bottom, inexplicable personality. It is here that Dreiser gets farthest from the wallowed rut of fiction. The Cowperwood he puts before us is not the two-dimensional cut-out, the facile jumping jack, or the ordinary novel, but a being of three dimensions and innumerable planes—in brief, the impenetrable mystery that is man. The makers of best-sellers, if they could imagine him at all, would seek to account for him, explain him, turn him into a moral (*i.e.*, romantic) equation. Dreiser is content to describe him.

Naturally enough, the lady reviewers of the newspapers have been wholly flabbergasted by the book. Unable to think of a character in a novel save in terms of the characters in other novels, they have sought to beplaster Cowperwood with the old, old labels. He is the Wealthy Seducer, the Captain of Industry, the Natural Polygamist, the Corruptionist, the Franchise Grabber, the Bribe Giver, the Plutocrat, the Villain. Some of them, intelligent enough to see that not one of these labels actually fits, have interpreted the fact as a proof of Dreiser's incapacity. He is denounced for creating a Cowperwood who is not like other capitalists, not like other lawbreakers, not like other voluptuaries—that is to say, not like the capitalists, lawbreakers and voluptuaries of Harold MacGrath, E. Phillips Oppenheim and Richard Harding Davis. And one hears, too, the piping voice of outraged virtue: a man who chases women in his leisure and captures a dozen or so in twenty years is ungentlemanly, un-American, indecent—and therefore ought not to be put into a book. But I do not think that Dreiser is going to be stopped by such piffle, nor even by the more damaging attacks of smug and preposterous publishers. He has stuck to his guns through thick and thin, and he is going to stick to them to the end of the chapter. And soon or late, unless I err very grievously, he is going to reap the just reward of a sound and courageous artist, just as George Meredith reaped it before him, and Joseph Conrad is beginning to reap it even now.

Berenice S. Skidelsky. *Book News Monthly*, August, 1914.

He who has never read any of the Dreiser novels, but is lured by Mr. Dreiser's enviable reputation into picking up *The Titan* in pleasurable anticipation, is doomed to dismal disappointment. Here is no great work of a master, but only another of the many hundreds of books which yearly come forth, live their little hour, and sink into oblivion.

The book is a tale of business and love; loves, we might better say, for Frank Cowperwood's affairs of the heart are legion. It dizzies one to try to keep up with the kaleidoscopic shift of his emotions. "He was too passionate, too radiant, too individual and complex to belong to any one single individual alone," says the author; but the reader wonders whether it was not rather that he was too egoistic, too wholly materialistic, to recognize any law outside his momentary inclination—too fundamentally limited, indeed, to have any needs in his nature outside of that. We are given a picture of the whole sickly fabric of "social ascendancy"; and Cowperwood and his wife are frankly of that pitiable class that give their lives and ambition to the phantom-pursuit which is social climbing. To be ignored by the Hyphenated-Joneses is tragedy; to be smiled upon by the Compound-Smythes is the ultimate realization of mundane well-being. The unfortunate part is not that Mr. Dreiser portrays this human weakness, but that he succeeds in conveying the impression that to his way of thinking the game is worth the candle.

But after all the test of a novel is not what has been done, but how it has been done. The characters in *The Titan* are not sufficiently complex, not well-balanced, and therefore not real. It is rather that in a given situation Mr. Dreiser has need of a certain human trait; he brings it forth, incarnates it, and asks that you accept it as a flesh and blood reality. We are frequently feeling that effects are aimed at, but missed; and this applies both in situation and character delineation. The bits of abstract philosophy introduced here and there are for the most part platitudes over-elaborately dressed. Emerson was not the first nor the last to discover that there is nothing new under the sun; but granting the fact does not prevent us from demanding the atmosphere of revivification which is only another term for good writing.

An element of humor has been unwittingly introduced in some of the descriptions of feminine garb. We are a little dubious about some of them; but when we are told of one woman that "her black hair was caught by a childish band of blood-red ribbon. . . . her lithe body . . . was clad in an apple-green bodice and a black skirt with gussets of red about the hem. . . . her stockings were apple-green silk," it conjures up too startling a picture for perfect gravity.

The book's main charm is in the spell which is always woven by the presentation of long years crowded with incident. It is the second of Mr. Dreiser's "Trilogy of Desire," of which *The Financier* was the first; and while we have not read the first, nor do we especially admire the second, we will be tempted to read the third when it appears, because we have seen so much of the career of Frank Cowperwood that we have had roused in us a curiosity to learn what further might befall in his eventful life. And there are occasional touches of real merit which lead us to hope that the present book is not Dreiser at his best, and that he will redeem himself in the next one.

"A Note on Theodore Dreiser by a Man." *International,* August, 1914, p. 249.

A man's novelist has arrived at last.

Now that the appearance of "The Titan" renders possible a judgment upon the work of Theodore Dreiser as a whole, one begins to understand the magnitude as well as the nature of the service he has renderd to American literature.

He has rescued that literature from the feminization to which it had so long succumbed.

It will no longer be possible to affirm that contemporary fiction is never read by masculine persons. The feminization of American literature has caused the decay of nearly every periodical in the land except those which make women a source of income. Theodore Dreiser has effected enough of a revolution to bring men back to literature.

This explains the horror with which he is regarded by elderly spinsters who, in order to eke out inadequate stipends, do a little book reviewing for preposterous, although great newspapers in New York and Chicago. Theodore Dreiser being masculine, his supremacy threatens the vested interests that have been built up in the publishing world on the basis of contracts for face powder advertising. His hero is the sort of man whom none of the "sissies" in editorial chairs would introduce to his stenographer. The wife of that "sissy" would meet Theodore Dreiser's hero clandestinely. This is a cryptic mode of pointing out that Theodore Dreiser understands woman. Her slyness is an open book to him. Her healthy contempt for the man who reveres her is equalled only by her adoration of him who holds her with a high, hard hand. Every woman one encounters in the pages of Theodore Dreiser's novels is feminine. That is why the editors of literary columns dislike Dreiser's novels. Those editors are feminine leaders of the feminine.

Dreiser does more in his fictions than expose the imbecility of woman. He reveals how constructive her viciousness is. He explains that viciousness by his proof up to the hilt that the American man does not know how to make love. True, the American woman is not lovable. Dreiser shows us that. But he brings out with dazzling clarity that if one could love an American woman in the tremendous sense, one would not know how to make love to her because our American atmosphere is fatal to love. Cowperwood, who figures so freshly in Dreiser's chapters, was an American who could woo. He had the women of Chicago pretty much to himself in Chicago. He was a man. The average American woman never meets a man. There are none, as a rule, in her family.

Greater than any other single quality exploited in the novels of Theodore Dreiser is his humor. It is large, elemental, seemingly unconscious It has escaped the ladies who review "The Titan" for newspapers, because those ladies, apart from the fact that they lack the sense of humor, know beforehand what they must say about a great book, and they take pains to say it badly. Here is a key to the mystery which makes contemporary reviews of Theodore Dreiser's last book so like the report on Gulliver submitted to the King of the Lilliputians. The phenomenon is on too vast a scale for the local perspective, the very bigness of Dreiser comprising his crime. What humor he has! The highest tribute one can pay to it is to say that it is not typically American. It has too many characteristics in common with the humor of Shakespeare, of Rabelais even, of Moliere.

The Dreiser philosophy of life looms greatly behind the characters in his tremendous stories. To Dreiser there seems no God in the intimately personal Christian sense. He begins an impressive chapter with an exposition of what morality meant to his hero Cowperwood. It was a morality based on might. All is permitted. It is not a gratuitously brutal absolutism that Dreiser glorifies or seems to glorify as he takes his hero from one triumph to another. Cowperwood will destroy no one for the mere satisfaction of playing the bully. Cowperwood has the soul of the artist. He has evidently heard what Keats has to tell us about beauty being truth and truth beauty. He is capable of artistic strokes of generosity. Look, for instance, at the honest governor. He had foiled Cowperwood. On the edge of beggary he received a large sum and was saved. Cowperwood did this noble thing, when the honest governor could be of no service to him. One is reminded of Mark Antony sending the treasure of Enobarbus—was it Enobarbus?—after him to the enemy's camp.

In his study of character, Dreiser places himself on a level with Balzac. Like Balzac he has his difficult places. One must work one's way through some chapters, yet one does it hopefully, like Cortez traversing the Mexican desert because the treasures of Montezuma await him. Dreiser's dialogue is never overdone. It invites slow and repeated persual, seeing that every word he puts into the mouth of an Aileen or of a Kerrigan enlarges one's own knowledge of human nature, making people more interesting. "I like life as it is." Theodore Dreiser said that once to an interviewer. His novels force one to share that liking. He has no style in the literary sense of the word. Only at long intervals does a reader find a passage arresting for its manner apart from its matter. The author of "The Titan" is not an artist like Stevenson, but Stevenson was not a giant like Dreiser.

Life, August 13, 1914.

There is a clever woman—a specialist on the social geology of Cook County, Illinois—who contributes to one of the Chicago papers, over the signature of "Madame X," occasional articles on local society history, ancient and modern, sacred and profane. Madame X's omniscience is fallible but fascinating. She is an expert at tempering the tact of the dove with the *savoir-faire* of the serpent. She is neither a garnerer of gossip nor a digger-up of dry-as-dust, but a sort of sublimated avatar of the Oldest Inhabitant. And one cannot but hope that she will take an early opportunity to read Theodore Dreiser's "The Titan" and will thereafter translate for us, into plain Chicago history, the hieroglyphic identities of its many characters.

"The Titan" contains the second half of the life story of Frank Algernon Cowperwood, begun in "The Financier"; and together these novels offer us what is undoubtedly, in several important respects, the nearest approximation yet arrived at to that figment of our fictional dreams, the Great American

Novel—the novel, that is to say, which is some day to imprison between its covers the soul-symbol and essential spirit of America. The spirit of America is indeed the theme of Mr. Dreiser's two novels here considered—the spirit of the America of the Nineteenth Century, incarnated in one of its sons. And when we look back upon the dual work it is not Cowperwood himself, nor the mass of secondary characters clustered round him, nor even the ruthless unromanticism of the author's philosophy of human motives, that stands out clearest and most significant in the retrospect of our realization; it is a spiritual synthesis that we see; the soul of America—seeking. . . .

Audrie Alspaugh. " 'The Titan' a Record, Not Literature." Chicago *Tribune*, August 22, 1914.

"The Titan," the second book in Theodore Dreiser's pretentious trilogy, is at hand for general consumption, heralded by the publisher. John Lane Company, as "a masterful book by the most significant American novelist," and fanfared as a convincing rebuttal to Robert Herrick's assertion that the American novel is weakly sentimental. . . .

The book's main hold is through its historical minutiae showing the development of Chicago's transportation facilities, with an analysis of the political cloud that shadowed their origins. The general assumption that the central character is a lay figure for the personality of Charles T. Yerkes is made quite obvious by the inclusion of the observatory presentation at Lake Geneva. For a leisurely reader, with time to corroborate, the many references to past events would be interesting to trace.

These things, however, are outside the realm of fiction judgment. The book tells a story, a sordid, disagreeable one, so overwhelming in its materialism as to lose moral force, in a crudely direct fashion, with no pleasant turnings for style, with many blemishes of split infinitives, unnecessarily coarse speech and rough colloquialisms. That seems too bad, for Mr. Dreiser can create interesting phrases, he can put words together to make clear-etched pictures, but he makes no effort in this volume, which reads like the first draft gotten out by a very efficient but a very busy man. It is a record, not literature.

Milwaukee Wisconsin September 22, 1914.

The publisher introduces this book with a quotation from a well-known novelist and critic to the effect that virile literature must represent both a man's world and a woman's world. Certainly the author has attempted to represent two distinct sides of life, but each is a man's world—one the world of a man among men, the other of a man among women. "The Titan," intended as the second of a trilogy of which "The Financier" was the first, is to an unusual degree a book of one character. This is Frank Cowperwood, who, quitting his Eastern home under a cloud that shaded his personal character and his business integrity, finds a new field for exercising his unique powers in Chicago. It is doubtless true that during the early seventies Chicago, like the rest of the world, had a code of business and political ethics which Twentieth century society finds rather primitive. It is equally true that as regards personal morality Chicago, like the rest of the world, was considerably closer to Puritanical than it is today, a fact of which Mr. Dreiser does not take account. Among the group of business men who are making Chicago great, some of whom are so gauzily disguised as to make the old settler sit up, Cowperwood achieves colossal success. Among the ladies he is not less invincible. We can't see how he does it or what of it, anyhow. We have to take the author's word for that! The list of Cowperwood's mistresses is nearly as long as Homer's famous catalogue of ships—and about as exhilarating! The tiresome part of it is that not one of these frail ladies seems to have left the slightest impress on Frank Cowperwood's nature; to chronicle his cups of coffee would be as significant. We strongly object to this book; not because of its morals, for neither vice nor fraud are made attractive, but because it is so inartistic. A naughty book, if clever, is more than forgivable; a stupid book must be tolerably virtuous to pass muster. And this book is not merely gross, but stupid. It leaves us quite incurious about the concluding volume of the trilogy. Rather more than his other novels, "The Titan" reveals the self-made quality of Mr. Dreiser's style.

"Recent Reflections of a Novel-Reader." *Atlantic Monthly*, 114 (October 1914), 523.

Certainly there are no faintest traces of anything like salvation in such a typically modern character as *The Titan*. In this book Theodore Dreiser pursues the history of Frank Cowperwood, introduced to us in *The Financier*. The latter was absorbing and indubitably great; its continuation is neither. One does not make out whether this is partly Mr. Dreiser's fault, or wholly that of his hero. *The Financier* was kinetic. Cowperwood developed before our eyes from a shrewd lad into a financial magician. He rose, then fell, melodramatically, into prison, only to rehabilitate himself again. The author scorned the element of contrast, and gave us no character to admire or love, but he took infinite pains to show the zest of youth and crescent experience. What feeling the book contained was genuine and strong, though lawless and primitive.

The Titan is static. Here Cowperwood is an established magnate, an established libertine. He but adds million to million and seduction to seduction. In both cases the details are infinitely dreary. Like taking candy from a child is the process of diverting other men's gains to his own purse, while the wives and daughters of his associates are such easy captives of his magnetism that it becomes nauseating. Were there, then, no virtuous women or able men in Chicago? As Cowperwood becomes less and less human, the reader becomes more and more impatient. The framework of the story rises to an appropriate climax, but the reader's imagination refuses to rise with it. We are asked to believe that Cowperwood at fifty conceives so disinterested a passion for a young girl that he considers her an *objet d'art* and is willing to house and provide for her indefinitely as such. After living for some years upon his bounty she chooses to come to him with the offer of her heart and life in the hour when he has just met his most serious financial defeat.

Here is sentiment, not to say sentimentality. Probably Balzac, with the French genius for 'slush,' could have made us feel the situation sympathetically. But Mr. Dreiser is not in such thorough accord with his hero as to be able to do this. He knows perfectly that Cowperwood's heart has by this time about the freshness and value of a sucked orange-peel kicking about the dusty street, and he knows readers do not yield sympathy to sucked orange-peel. Therefore he does not, perhaps cannot, try his hardest to convince. What he tells may be entirely true to fact, but it also fails entirely of that deeper reality which alone holds our interest. So we come back to the query—is Cowperwood or Dreiser to blame?

On the one hand, Cowperwood's historian is certainly a little afraid lest he be caught moralizing, or deviating from a tolerant, man-of-the-world attitude toward his subject. Now, the artist must not be moralist first or chiefly; nevertheless a failure in moral perception is ultimately a failure in both psychology and art. No writer, realist or not, can afford this.

On the other hand, could any writer possibly make the middle age of a Cowperwood appetizing? The inner life of the strong man who takes for motto '*I satisfy myself*' lacks that element of struggle which the dullest audience demands in its drama. How make a hero of a monster? Here is no success other than the success of a gorged animal in obtaining its prey. However, *The Titan* is only the second volume of a proposed trilogy. It is too soon to speak with finality either of Cowperwood or his chronicler.

Seattle [Wash.] *Post-Intelligencer*, October 17, 1914.

If one were to describe in one word Theodore Dreiser's latest novel, "The Titan," that word would be "tiresome." "The Titan" takes up the career of Frank Algernon Cowperwood where "The Financier" dropped it, leaving an interval of a little more than a year, which was spent by Cowperwood in a penitentiary as the result of his financial breakdown. After Cowperwood is released from prison he goes to Chicago, where he builds up a new fortune in gas. Here the author gives in detail a story of financial and political crookedness that, if such a thing were possible, surpasses that in "The Financier." Incidentally there is rather too much of the details of Cowperwood's private life as a modern Don Juan. Mr. Dreiser spares his readers none of the disgusting details of Cowperwood's adventures with women. They are set forth ad nauseam. So with Cowperwood's financial and political rascalities. The reader literally is overwhelmed with them. In fact, the author, in the white heat of his own emotions—more or less simulated—seems to forget that something more than force in a novel is necessary to hold the attention of a reader. Mr. Dreiser has worked himself up to a frightful pitch, but he overdoes the thing. There is too much of it, and it is all of one piece of cloth. "The Titan" is muckraking in literature run mad, and literary, like political, muckraking is somewhat passe at the present moment.

Checklist of Additional Reviews

Arkansas *Democrat,* May 20, 1914.
Llwellyn Jones. "Realism of the Chair." Chicago *Post,* May 22, 1914.
New York *Globe,* May 23, 1914.
Philadelphia *North American,* May 23, 1914.
Buffalo *Times,* May 23, 1914.
Terre Haute [Ind.] *Star,* May 25, 1914.
Milwaukee [Wis.] *Sentinel,* May 25, 1914.
Akron [Ohio] *Journal,* May 27, 1914.
San Francisco *Bulletin,* May 30, 1914.
"A Nasty Novel." St. Louis *Post-Dispatch,* May 30, 1914.
John Macy. "The Titan: Mr. Dreiser's New Novel." Boston *Herald,* May 30, 1914.
"The Titan: A Business Novel." Philadelphia *Public Ledger,* May 30, 1914.
Publisher's Weekly, May 30, 1931.
Parkensburg [W. Va.] *News Dispatch,* May 31, 1914.
Charleston [S.C.] *News,* May 31, 1914.
Rev. Charles Graves. "Among the Books." Albany [N. Y.] *Knickerbocker Press,* May 31, 1914.
"Dreiser Does More Reporting." Minneapolis *Journal,* May 31, 1914.
Battle Creek [Mich.] *Enquirer,* May 31, 1914.
Book Review Digest, June, 1914.
Bookseller, June 1, 1914.
Magazine of Wall Street, June, 1914.
Memphis [Tenn.] *News Scimitar,* June 2, 1914.
Philadelphia *Evening Star,* June 3, 1914.
Cincinnati *Enquirer,* June 6, 1914.
Cleveland *Plain Dealer,* June 6, 1914.
Boston *Times,* June 6, 1914.
St. Louis *Republic,* June 6, 1914.
Edwin F. Bowers. New York *Call,* June 7, 1914.
Chicago *News,* June 9, 1914.
Hartford [Conn.] *Courant,* June 10, 1914.
"Current Fiction." *Nation,* 98 (June 11, 1914), 697-698.
The Scoop [Chicago], June 13, 1914.
New York *Sun,* June 13, 1914.
S. C. Williams. "A Mirabeau of Finance." Boston *Advertiser,* June 17, 1914.
Life, June 18, 1914.
H. L. Mencken. "Dreiser and His Titan." *Town Topics,* 43 (June 18, 1914), 17-18.
Indianapolis *News,* June 20, 1914.
Kansas City *Star,* June 20, 1914.
Richmond [Va.] *Times Dispatch,* June 21, 1914.
San Francisco *Chronicle,* June 21, 1914.
Springfield [Mass.] *Republican,* June 23, 1914.
New Orleans *Times Picayune,* June 23, 1914.
"The American Business Pioneer." St. Louis *Pioneer,* July 26, 1914.
Puck, June 27, 1914.
"Literature and Art." *Current Opinion,* 57 (July, 1914), 47-48.
Bond Buyer, July 4, 1914.
"Loves and Labors of a Business Titan." New York *Sun,* July 4, 1914.
Newark *Evening Star,* July 11, 1914.
Pittsburgh *Post,* July 11, 1914.

Rochester [N.Y.] *Democrat Chronicle,* July 17, 1914.
San Francisco *Argonaut,* July 25, 1914.
Birmingham [Ala.] *Herald,* July 26, 1914.
St. Louis [Minn.] *Pioneer,* July 26, 1914.
Vanity Fair, August, 1914.
Craftsman, August 1914.
Rochester [N.Y.] *Herald,* August 1, 1914.
Vogue, August 1, 1914.
Portland [Ore.] *Telegram,* August 1, 1914.
New York *Evening Sun,* August 1, 1914.
C. K. J. Los Angeles *Graphic,* August 8, 1914.
Lewiston [Me.] *Journal,* August 15, 1914.
Philadelphia *Record,* August 15, 1914.
New York *American,* August 29, 1914.
McClure's Magazine, September, 1914.
"A Story of Chicago." St. Louis *Globe Democrat,* September 6, 1914.
New York *Evening Mail,* September 10, 1914.
New York *Independent,* September 22, 1914.
"The Failure of Success." *Independent,* 80 (October 12, 1914), 63.
Rochester [N. Y.] *Union & Advertiser,* November 20, 1914.
Chicago *Examiner,* December 13, 1914.
Columbus [Ohio] *Dispatch,* January 9, 1915.
Spartanburg *Herald,* February 7, 1915.
Louis Gannett. "A Gossip on Criticism." *Atlantic Monthly,* 117 (February 1916), 182-184.

Further Reviews: Bibliographic Information Incomplete

"Rabid Realism." Philadelphia *Press,* May, 1914.

Notes

THE
"GENIUS"

BY

THEODORE DREISER

NEW YORK: JOHN LANE COMPANY
LONDON: JOHN LANE, THE BODLEY HEAD
TORONTO: S. B. GUNDY :: MCMXV

The "Genius"

The Scavenger. "The Dionysian Dreiser." *Little Review*, 2 (October 1915), 10–13.

Theodore Dreiser is the greatest novelist in America. It is not a distinction. He has written poor novels. His latest novel, "The Genius" [sic] published by John Lane Company is loose in parts. It limps. It loses its breath. It grows thin. But it is a novel of sweep and magnitude, of sledge hammer blows and fine chiseling. In the caramel chorus of America's chirping fictionists Dreiser raises the smooth, virile voice of an artist. And there is no voice like his in America.

I prefer to write of what Dreiser has done in "The Genius" than to tell in detail of what it is about. Calmly, aloofly with a consummate dispassion Dreiser has thrust his magic pen home into the heart of American Puritanism. God forgive him. God forgive the publishers. God forgive everybody who reads the book and forgive me who write about it. For American Puritanism is a sacred thing, as sacred as the gilt on the cathedral altar places, as hallowed as the bathroom in a bawdy house. And Dreiser has peeled off the gilt and ruthlessly thrust open the door. May he be cursed with the wrath of an avenging public conscience. May he be made to wither under the distinction of being a maniacle sensualist, a libidinous ruffian, a lascivious distiller of corrupting langours. Amen.

Against the gray-dirt background, the shallow-hued smears of his many contemporaries, Dreiser's book stands forth like a red cry of truth. It is not the book of a man enraged with the narrowness of a country, sputtering against the inspidity of its composite ideals. Dreiser never descends to the punitive hectoring of a Robert Herrick. Nor does he join the plaintive assaults upon the pusillanimous conventions which characterize the "advanced" fiction of the country. He does not make his men and women vehicles for the antiquated day dream of brotherhood bosh. He does not prostitute his work in dramatizing the current quibbles, marketing asinine public convulsions in the literary capsules so commonly compounded by our quack "creators." All these things he does not do and if the reading public of today will not reward him, the God of Dostoevsky, Flaubert, Huysmanns, Shakespeare and Ambrose Bierce will.

What Dreiser does do is tell a straightforward story, tell it with all the painstaking genius of the old Flemish painters. And he uses for his background not the isolated strata of any single calling, but a country—your world and mine and our neighbor's. Life is greater than any of its truths, sings Theodore Dreiser. There are many kinds of good, many kinds of standards and many kinds of virtue. There is the virtue of farmer Blue, the solid, masculine, clear and open virtue rooted in the laws of the land and the rigamarole of society; thriving on the long, brown roads, the ploughed fields and the homely beauties of existence. And there is the virtue of Eugene Witla, the aesthetic, vibrating pursuit of beauty rooted in the soul of the artist, thriving on the illusive lust of women, the intangible urge of inspiration; spitting in the face of laws unnatural to it and the fallacies that would be its fetters. Yes, says Dreiser, (I do not quote him), life is a wide field bearing on its bosom beautiful flowers that do not resemble each other and that require widely different care and nourishment. To think that such commonplaces should be distinctive notes in the art of a country! But they are. If you have read these things into novels before you have not read them into American novels. I do not recall a single hero in American fiction, who is not a Puritan, who does not suffer when he sins, whom the indulgence of his desire for women does not inspire to repentance and "reform" and success as the blue literary laws of America demand. . . .

On this broad canvas of thought it is that Dreiser works. In his new novel he begins in a little town in Illinois. Out of the midst of a mediocre family living in the concentric provincialism of the middle west he launches his young hero Witla—a lad suffering from dreams and stomach trouble and a vague distinguishing unrest. His types are masterpieces. His style, shorn of pretentious reticence or rhetorical pomp, is the painstaking and poetical diction he revealed in Jennie Gerhardt. But he is not infallible. There are sentences, paragraphs which jar. Although his strokes in delineating character and situation are swift and certain, his language often seems lame, his words watery, his phrases trite. But these are as the flaws of a panoramic pen crowded at moments to a point of impatience and not the faults of a weak writer. The effect is untouched. His people breathe out of the pages. They are personalities. From beginning to end Dreiser reveals a psychology of character amazing in its range and detachment. Witla as a boy lives in Alexandria, Illinois. Dresier traces the development of his soul and sex and struggle out of the blanketing bourgeois of his birthplace. The young 'Gene answers the call of beauty, without knowing what it is that calls him. He comes to Chicago. He is a laundry wagon driver, a collector for an installment furniture house, a student of the old Art Institute, a worker in the art department of a newspaper. Dreiser traces him out of the half way stratas of Chicago to New York, to success, and then through a labyrinth of incidents all interesting and big. He follows him through one development after another until Witla, the painter, realizes himself. I cannot begin to tell what the book is about. It is partially a depiction of the struggle between an artist husband and a "good woman" who is his wife, partly the struggle between the flesh and the spirit of the same husband and the tale of their final adjustment. It is an Odyssey of a type of man in whom the future of the arts rest as they always have rested. In the 736 pages there are persons of every type. You will meet everyone you have known and many you have dreamed of knowing. Every shade of womanhood flashes between the covers. It is as a novel should be—complete. It tingles with the quick spasmodic life of the city. of the country, the factory, the field, the drawing room. And above all, it breathes the atmosphere of America's art life, the lively, struggling workers of the studio.

Witla, however, remains Dreiser's calm, masterful argument against the one-sided perversions of the Puritan. Witla is a genius. What are you going to do with him, you proselyting blue stocking? Such a detached study in perfideous polygamy is enough to damn the very printers who set the type for the book. Here is a man of strong ideals, great productive talent, an indispensable contributor to life, who naively considers setting up an establishment for his pretty model just after he has proposed matrimony to the woman he loves at the time with all the finest desires of his nature; a miserable fellow who ruins and ravishes without compunction every shapely creature who crosses his path. He is without even unconscious morality, innate morality. Woman is beauty when she is anything and to posses beauty is the motive force in his life. His eye possesses the beauty of the city's filth and dirt, the beauty of landscape, his mind possesses the beauty of books and talk and other minds, and his body the beauty of passion wherever he encounters it. Logical, natural, primitive and entirely artistic. But immoral? God, yes. No one woman can satisfy a man unless he deliberately stunts himself, is the Dreiserian Gospel. A man needs blonde women, brunette women, short ones and tall ones, radical ladies and conservative creatures—that is, a man like Witla does. And is Witla a supreme type, a distinctive Sanine sort of fellow? Not a bit of it. Whether Dreiser thought he is, I don't know. He doesn't say. But he isn't. He is man and not artist in his "sins."

There is naturally more color to his escapades, to his "pursuit of beauty," for he is the "genius" with an eye to shades and a soul for nuances not possessed by his more hum drum brothers. To him matrimony is naturally a pit, a degradation, a series of cages, for he is the eternal masculine. But how many men are there who have always been faithful to their wives? What? I do not know of a single one. In his high lighted type of Witla, Dreiser tells of this rudely, brutally and beautifully—with the indifference of a Juggernaunt and the cunning of a magician.

Really, you of the firm-fireside-faith, what is there to be done? Here is the Dionysian dastard who dares proclaim that life is a decent, orderly routine and that life is also a wild, warm passionate thing; that it is also a flame in which there is only one color, the red, golden color of youth.

And the answer is—howl. A howl will go up, I swear it. It will start from the critics.

I can almost read their forthcoming reviews as I close my eyes.

"A sensually depraved and degenerate type."

"Striking at the bed rock of public solidarity, of home happiness, of everything decent and worth while."

And America's reading public—"Horrible, filthy."

Howl, you who have stultified your artists and buried them under the gingerbread morality of your own monotonous lives. Dreiser is the one novelist being published in America today who doesn't listen to you, who describes you at your various bests, who wrings the pathos and joys out of your little worlds; who paints in with the brush of a universal art what you and I are doing in Alexandria and Chicago and New York and all the milk-station stops between.

I am not a disciple of the Dreiserian Gospel. I would like to argue with him the certain superiorities of monogamy for the artist. But he has limned a hero who is not a sugar-coated moralizer. He has ignored superbly the mob-begotten mandates of literary excellence. Whatever his faults of composition or construction, and there are not so many as his friends endeavor to make out there are, he has magnificently booted the reading public, the morally subsidized critics and the very publishers in the coarsest regions of their bodies—their souls.

And for these things I hail him as the greatest novelist in the country. I acclaim him as the only real, uncontaminated genius of these States and pray to God that my friend Sherwood Anderson will hurry up and get published so that there will be two of them.

Bookseller, Newsdealer and Stationer, October 1, 1915, p. 394.

The "Genius," by Theodore Dreiser, is perhaps the most remarkable study in emotional temperament that any modern writer has given. In more than seven hundred pages we have the life development of a Western middle class man, gifted artistically, who is a slave to beauty; and his liasons before and after marriage are the ebb and flow of his genius, as it were. It is a story at once repelling and compelling—a brutally frank and insistently vivid portrayal of a man brilliant and weak, who is selfishly obsessed with and driven by the sense of beauty. The woman he married is a splendid example of the mismated faithful wife, jealous beyond measure, yet so in love that she endured everything to keep him. Vivid scenes are laid in and about New York, and the climax is reached when, after giving up his career as a struggling artist, he becomes the manager of a great publishing house, doing business with books and magazines on a salary of twenty-five thousand a year. Then he meets a girl of eighteen—he is then forty—and he braves everything to win her love and does. How this is treated shows the author an artist. The frenzy of a great passion, the strength developed by opposition, the instability of human emotion overfed, and how one emotion crowds out another, is shown in a way that leaves its impress. No other writer has felt called upon to bring to his art the realistic description of child-birth to drive home to a man the sense of his own unworthiness. It is one of those stories that will cause infinite discussion and will sell by the impetus of its own life force.

New York *Tribune,* October 2, 1915, p. 8.

. . . This is a prodigiously long novel—over 700 closely printed pages. Mr. Dreiser is a master of the ponderous realism that piles fact upon fact, detail upon detail, without ever losing control of the cumulative effect of the whole. He is a philosopher of civilization rather than of life; the phenomena, the symptoms, are more to him than the causes, which he accepts, than the verities, which he leaves unplumbed. Still, this "genius" of his, without the training of home or a formal education, uncultured beneath the thin social veneer he acquires, unable to think logically, his mind a jumble of unsystematic, fragmentary occasional reading which leads him to think that he thinks, gropes in his confused way toward Christian Science. The author leaves him subdued rather than reclaimed by the price he has paid, the suffering he has undergone and caused, with a daughter who awakens in him a deeper feeling.

"Mr. Dreiser's 'Genius'." New York *World*, October, 2, 1915.

"The Genius," by Theodore Dreiser, the story of an artist who goes in for advertising and the pursuit of women, is 736 pages long, weighs nearly a pound and three-quarters, and contains approximately 350,000 words.

It would be better if it were less by about 350,000 words, lighter by nearly a pound and three-quarters, and shorter by 736 pages.

Mr. Dreiser should get over the idea that because he was successful with two novels of sex, he can keep on, world without end, filling thick volumes with the emptyings of passion.

Beneath all the inconsistencies of such a character there is an admirable consistency of treatment. The man is never in revolt against society; he merely follows his own impulses, unable to reason from cause to consequences. He has no theories of a "higher" moral law; he runs after youth and beauty as a puppy runs after chickens. In the same uncalculating, impulsive way he pursues material success in the business world and attains it, to see the results of all his weaknesses converging in the great crash. It is his art, which has kept itself alive with only intermittent nourishment from him, that gives him, sobered and calmed down by the storms of his early years, his final chance of rehabilitation.

Long as it is, the book is crowded. There is a constant change of scene and interests. From the little Illinois town of the "genius's" birth to the art school in Chicago and the life of its students; thence to New York and the struggle for a footing, with the youth's first glimpses of the city's artistic and professional life, of keen, alert, cultivated men and women. Then his progress from an advertising agency to the offices of a great Philadelphia publishing house, and back to New York again as the editorial manager of an even more ambitious venture—all this throbs with the busy life of the day, and is closely linked to actual enterprises and real leaders. There is more than a hint here and elsewhere of the "roman a clef." The women whose beauty lures this man on his way to his undoing are touched in with all the painstaking elaborateness which their significance in the story requires. Mr. Dreiser proves himself once more a master realist. We must take him as he is; he has imposed himself upon us by mere ponderous strength of talent. He may, he does offend at times —he has *les défauts de ses qualités*— but he is a great, a very great artist. In a season remarkable for its excellent fiction this new book of his immediately takes its place in the front rank.

Ethel M. Colson. Chicago *Record Herald*, October 2, 1915.

. . . There is little of salacity in this strange and audacious story, although it plays about the pathological danger point like lightning. The author is no more indecent in his ruthless exposure of Witla's sorry soul than in his unsparing description of the dread operation ending Angela's piteous, tragic career. He merely sets down dispassionately the sad and shocking facts conducive to full understanding of his purpose. But from the lay viewpoint much of his material is highly unnecessary and regrettable, while the cross section of modern life so richly, rarely presented loses in value for lack of proper proportion. The evil of the tremendous tale too markedly predominates; it is scarcely to be believed that wanton women so abound in supposedly decent circles, even when these circles are infested by such creatures as Witla. But the depressing book in many ways is a great one. Its people live, its lesson is all the more forceful for the author's consistent refusal to press it. Yes, Mr. Dreiser indubitably is an artist. It would be interesting to note his handling of characters conventionally good.

William Marion Reedy. "The Genius of Theodore Dreiser." *Reedy's Mirror*, October 8, 1915, p. 166.

Seven hundred and thirty-six pages are required to tell the story of "The Genius" the last number of Theodore Dreiser's "Trilogy of Desire," the other two being "The Financier" and "The Titan." Desire and its gratification, sexual desire and its satiation or defeat constitute the *fugue* in this as in the other works. The genius is *Eugene Witla*, the artist, born in a small town in Illinois, finding his *metier* in newspaper illustration in Chicago, moving to New York, achieving a success with his pictures and becoming a great art director and general manager of a noted publishing concern. *Witla* has a love of beauty and an ingratiating personality not only with women, but with men. He rises to affluence and social distinction, with women and women, like roses, all the way—a laundry girl, an artist's model, *Angela*, whom, later, he marries, a singer, the fast wife of a gambler, and, finally, *Suzanne*. Never was there a more detailed, documented, fictional biography. Mr. Dreiser tells everything in minutiae. His method would be a frightful bore but for the genius of him. The book has a fierce pulse of energy and a hungry zest of life and action. There runs through it a warmth that fuses its mass into a glowing colorfulness. The book is full of people, all of them vividly alive. Mr. Dreiser builds up character by indefinitely multiplied touches, like the *pointillists* in painting. So, too, he paints the setting of his characters until he impresses you as an inspired cataloguer not only of life but of still life. This method is applied to the details of passion not less than to the detail of business. In "The Genius," as in "The Titan" we have another *"Ars Amoris,"* without the Ovidian lightness of treatment, but with a steady, sombre seriousness of treatment almost scientific. Dreiser can draw a woman. No doubt about that. But clearly, Dreiser sees woman as an incident on a man's way to his goal. Successively, different women appeal to *Witla*. Each serves to bring him out, to stimulate him on his way. With each he has at least one grand scene of passionate surrender to his will. These are restrained at exactly the right point, and so far as they go, they are as intense in fervor as anything in Zola. With *Christine*, the genius has a week of idyllically lawless love that recalls "The Lovers of Orelay" in George Moore's "Memoirs of My Dead Life." The seduction of *Angela*, whom, later, he marries, is a marvel of narration without telling too much. The affair with the fast wife of a gambler, in her mother's home, is pictured with a Gallic fidelity to the artistry of intrigue, that is piquant even if a bit cheap. These women affairs are bright beads strung upon the story of *Witla's* rise in the world. Dreiser handles business and high life with the same meticulous specification of the little things that he employs in describing life in a country town, or in the position of a collector for a laundry, or in the doings of students and artist colonies of Bohemia. His treatment of painting and music, when they enter into his scheme, is copiously particularized, but his eager lust of the play of life fuses all this particularization into a consistent blend of values and tones and hues, transmutes drab burlap, as it were, into a magnificent tapestry. . . .

"The Genuis" is a work of art to which Dreiser has risen from mere works of devoted craft. It lives, perhaps more with the heart's blood of the women devoured and drunk by the "hero" than with blood of *Witla* himself, who is best realized for us when his sensual egoism goes to pieces.

"A Genius and Also a Cur." Brooklyn *Eagle*, October 9, 1915.

. . ."The Genius" is not a story for young readers, and it would probably do more harm among boys than among girls, to whom at least it conveys a warning to beware of fascinating married men who seem straightforward and friendly. It is a question for a time whether the book is fit reading for anybody, the first section called "Youth" being pretty nearly an orgy of lust. The thing that saves it from the condemnation which falls on some classic recitals of the same sort is the emphasis which Dreiser puts on the mental side of Witla's various fascinations. That attitude, coupled with what follows, shows that the author is trying to make an honest, though exceedingly frank, picture of a man in whom the love of beauty flowers into both good and evil, and to trace the complex convolutions of a plant which bears such diverse fruit. The portrait has the strength and the convincing quality which finally won for "Sister Carrie" recognition as literature after its first suppression as filth. There will be the same confusion of judgment about this story, but its strong and impressive ending will win for it acceptance as literature by the people who regard Balzac as the greatest novelist of the Nineteenth Century, and who should be able to keep an open mind in regard to his American disciple.

Mr. Dreiser takes 735 pages to tell his story and it is idle to try to offer an epitome of it in a column. Readers who wish to know what happened to Witla and how he saved the remnant of his life from a ruin which promised to be Samsonian in its completeness, will have to go to the book. Mr. Dreiser has told it in what seems quite unnecessary detail and the reader for review becomes thoroughly convinced that the story would be clearer and stronger if there were 200 pages less of it. But that same complaint has been reiterated to weariness against both Balzac and Wagner, so we need not take it too seriously. The fact is that when you meet genius you have to take it on its own terms or let it alone, and Theodore Dreiser is quite clearly a genius. Whether his artistry is at all commensurate with his great native endowment is another and a much more open question. Dreiser makes his strongest impression by his pictures of everyday life, couched in the language of the street and the store. The style utterly lacks distinction, but it achieves a sense of reality. That, together with the conviction that Dreiser was trying to paint life whole, rather than to emphasize that side of human nature which has made the popularity of Elinor Glyn and her school, won acceptance for "Sister Carrie."

In "The Genius" he follows the same method, but he includes now too much homely detail, so that his scenes sometimes turn from conviction to weariness. It is those redundancies which give the irritating impression that the book is too long. If an energetic blue pencil had been used to remove all those touches which are not essential to the picture the length of the volume might not have been greatly reduced, but the sense of repetition and surplusage would have been avoided and with it an irritation which is now inevitable. . . .

E. F. Edgett. Boston *Evening Transcript*, October 9, 1915, p. 9.

No restraint of words or ideas limits Mr. Dreiser when he sets himself to the writing of a novel. In "The Financier" and "The Titan" his energies expended themselves at extraordinary length, and now before he has completed that trilogy upon the life of Frank Cowperwood he has written another novel in which he goes to even greater realistic extremes. As he tells the story of the life of Eugene Witla from boyhood to middle age, his readers accompany him through more than 700 pages and 330,000 words, and into personal details that even a Zola would avoid. But to Mr. Dreiser everything human seems important, and therefore when we have closed the last page of "The Genius" we lack no knowledge of its hero's most intimate mental and physical processes. . . .

Throughout the story we are spared no phase of life encountered by Eugene Witla. His successes and failures are all described with an unprejudiced hand, and in a style of verbal extravagance that does violence to every law of the English language. Ten years of writing have not mended the error of Mr. Dreiser's ways of language, and he still lacks as much restraint in the use of words as in his descriptions of character. He glibly mentions "phones" and "photos" and "autos," evidently laboring under the delusion that since these words are used in the rush and hurry of conversation they are acceptable to the eye on the printed page, and at the same time his distortions of the English language glare at the reader again and again. "Frank Bangs, who was a practical man, as well as firm believer in Christian Science because of his wife's to him miraculous healing from a tumor several years before." "The Dale home, or homes, rather, were in several different places." "After paying for endless repairs, salarying a chauffeur wearisomely, and meeting with an accident which permanently damaged the looks of his machine, he decided to give it up." "Because of his art work his art connections had revived considerably, and he had heard again from such men as Louis Deesa, M. Charles, Luke Severas, and others who now knew where he was and wondered why he did not come back to painting proper." These are merely a few of Mr. Dreiser's infelicities. Yet for all of them, and for all its verbosity, "The Genius" is something more than a mere novel of words, words, words.

St. Louis *Republican*, October 9, 1915.

"The 'Genius,'" by Theodore Dreiser, proves once more that its author is head and shoulders above all the other novelists of the younger school in America—that he possesses a quality which entitles him to rank with the most vigorous novelists of Europe.

This statement remains none the less true when it is added that Mr. Dreiser seems further away than ever in his new book from those refinements and subtleties of art which are the stamp of the real masters of realistic fiction.

This serious-minded author cares no more for the conventionally correct forms in English than a steamboat clerk; and it does not seem an unwarrantable statement that "The 'Genius'" might have been confined to half its length without losing an ounce of force if its author had conquered the slovenly habit he has of being verbose rather than incisive—of including the impertinent and insignificant in the matter of detail, in the effort to effect a truly realistic effect.

As against this failing, there must be set several extraordinary merits. Mr. Dreiser manifests a wonderful knowledge of the details of American life in its practical aspects. He knows cities intimately; he is as familiar with real estate schemes as if he were a specialist in that line.

He has a photograph knowledge of the workings of a railroad camp. He knows the real financier, the real laborer, the real artist, the real newspaper office. He is an expert photographer of women. He is not, we think, a great portrait painter in this relationship. . . .

Mr. Dreiser is more than bold in his methods sometimes. His lawless love scenes are occasionally superfluous to say the least. His final hospital scene, where his wife ceases to be a weight upon him, is so unrestrained that it makes the realism of Zola seem almost mild by comparison.

A big book, this; a powerful book. The pity is that a writer possessing so unhackneyed and vigorous an outlook upon life might not pay more heed to the more reasonable rubrics of art. There is so much in "The 'Genius'" which one would recommend unreservedly to all discerning readers—and yet so much that one cannot so recommend.

"Three New Novels of American Life." New York *Times Book Review*, October 10, 1915, p. 362.

Once more Theodore Dreiser has chosen an abnormal character and written an abnormally long novel about him. "The Genius" fills 736 closely printed pages, all about Eugene Witla, his ambitions, amours, marriage, and adventures in lawless passion; his rise to a high pinnacle of success, and his swift and tremendous downfall. In a way it is a study of the artistic temperament, but really of only one abnormal weakness, that of ungoverned sexual passion and its effects on the life and work of an otherwise great artist. . . .

It is all very realistic—and very depressing and unpleasant. Eugene's infatuations for pretty women are incorrigible, and the author relates his experiences at interminable length and with wearisome iteration. The scene changes from Illinois to New York, to Paris and back again, but Eugene's fickleness never changes. First it is Stella, then Margaret, then Ruby, Angela, Christina, Frieda, Carlotta, and so on until the affair with Suzanne comes to cap the climax and lay the whole structure of his worldly success in ruins. . . .

"Mr. Dreiser's Latest Novel." Providence [R.I.] *Journal*, October 10, 1915.

When a man calmly sits down and writes a novel of considerably over seven hundred pages one of two things is to be presumed—either that he is sure of his public or that he deliberately ignores the question as to whether his book is to have—in the ordinary acception of the term—any public at all. Frankly, in the case of Mr. Theodore Dreiser's latest offering, we are uncertain whether the public library or the literary museum is the author's objective point. In its present form one finds it difficult to understand how "The 'Genius'" can make any appeal either to the general reader or to the aesthetic critic. From the point of view of the former it is insufferably dull. From the point of view of the latter it is insufferably bad—bad, that is, regarded by any criterion by which Mr. Dreiser, presumably, wishes to be judged. . . .

Mr. Dreiser has sought to depict a genius and he has only succeeded in depicting a man who has an abnormal personality—abnormal in the strength of his passions and equally abnormal in the corresponding weakness of his intellect. Set a thief to catch a thief may or may not be a good motto; but in this case a parody of its sentiment inevitably occurs to the mind—and Mr. Dreiser is, as he has emphatically demonstrated in his latest work, not a genius, but a writer of some talent, rather conspicuous ignorance as to the fundamental principles of art and a total lack of humor. If one ever had any hope that Mr. Dreiser would outlive the vulgarities and weaknesses which marred his earlier books, although they did not totally obscure an ability which it has been the pleasure of a certain cult greatly to exaggerate, that hope is dispelled by "The 'Genius.'" The most arresting characteristic of this presumably mature expression of Mr. Dreiser's powers is its puerility.

If the author's aim has been to make his readers despise Eugene, he has succeeded thoroughly. The affair develops into a battle royal between Suzanne's mother on one side and the infatuated pair on the other, and it ends in a crash dramatic enough almost to justify even the inordinate length of the book. But when it is all over a bad taste remains in the mouth of the reader, and he closes the volume wondering whether so despicable a character was worth portraying with such infinite care.

Mr. Dreiser is one of the few significant American novelists who cling to the European methods of realism. His work reminds one at times of Zola, or Balzac, and of Tolstoy; but he lacks the reticences and the deep moral convictions of the Russian, and the artistic deftness of the Frenchmen. In "Sister Carrie," he did a memorable piece of work, but his later novels, like Zola's, are rendered unwieldy by excessive masses of philosophic and material detail. He gets powerful effects, but heavily, unpleasantly. "The Genius" has about the same degree of force as "The Financier." In its moral effects, however it is much more deleterious.

In its philosophical aspects "The Genius" is a quest after the meaning of life, and the author's answer is that life is a vain and meaningless chaos, in which the human will is powerless. Eugene Witla's own philosophizings are a jumble of hedonistic theories, moral anarchism, mechanistic science, and Christian Science. The last named element figures largely in his later life, and the author seems to be considerable impressed with it. But the final impression of the novel is that nothing in this world is worth while.

Washington [D.C.] *Evening Star*, October 13, 1915.

Mr. Dreiser's new novel is quite Russian in its tedious prolixity. 736 pages are required to set out here the multitudinous love adventures of its hero in the fullness of realistic detail that this patient and conscientious writer considers to be their just due. Having religiously followed the course of this story from cover to cover, one finds out that this is not at all the proper way to read it, since time does count even with the most negligible of us. A far better way is to open the book at random—now here, now there, and again in another place. In each and every case one finds the "genius," Eugene Witla, at a most perfervid crisis of passionate love. Each attack is an exact pattern of all the others, save that the object of Witla's devotion changes from Stella to Ruby, from Ruby to Angela, from Angela to Carlotta or Susanne, or another. Along near the middle of this series, one of the girl's becomes the wife of Witla, but this formality hardly serves to interrupt the procession of female loveliness that this artistic temperament finds quite too much to withstand. As a study of masculine vanity and egotism, as an analysis of the male under the urge of beauty hunger and love hunger, the book is German in its quality of thoroughness, in its mastery of infinite detail. As a story, as dramatic fiction, it is tediously long, loose, diffuse, with much the larger part of its characters below the level of personal charm and appeal.

H.W. Boynton. "Varieties of Religious Experience." *Nation*, 101 (October 14, 1915), 462.

Requiescat Dchenieff! He has lived under a heavy handicap, for was he not an artist, of that celebrated tribe born without backbones and seldom achieving them? At least he lived long enough to see himself for what he was. We may rightly prefer him to Mr. Dreiser's "genius," who, reduced from the multitudinous facts in which his author envelops him, is a bounder pure and simple, a genius by sheer assertion. Often as, in the course of these seven hundred closely printed pages, we are assured of Eugene Witla's brilliant mind and charming manner; there is nothing that he says or does which enlightens or fascinates us in the smallest degree. If a duller fellow ever lived in a book, we have never met him. As for his character of Lothario, it would be hard to imagine a practitioner of more primitive methods: he is a drummer in a frock coat, a Don Juan of the streets. On the whole, his morals are less distressing than his manners, since he is supposed to be a gentleman, or as near as we can get to it in America. His father, to be sure, is a sewing-machine agent in an Illinois town; but this author believes him to have outgrown that, early in his career. The course of that career we cannot here trace in detail—it has been done by Mr. Dreiser, Heaven knows! Eugene Witla has an early knack at drawing. While still a boy he goes to Chicago, and presently becomes staff artist on a minor newspaper. His editors and associates tell him how remarkable he is and urge him to find something bigger in New York. He consents, and has not been in New York long when he wins fame as painter of a series of city scenes. He is hailed as a genius, and his road to success appears secure. But in the meantime (after, and contingent with, several amours) he has married, and his sexual life saps his powers. He becomes a neurasthenic, can do no work, and as a last resort becomes a manual laborer at 15 cents an hour. A year or two later he is able to draw again, and finds a position with an advertising "firm"; one step leads to another, and in no time at all he is in control of a great publishing business at a salary of $25,000. Unluckily, he always has an amour or two in hand, and presently one of them threatens a scandal, and makes him neglect his business; so he loses the job. His wife dies in giving birth to a daughter (all recent records in obstetrical data are here broken). We leave him sentimentally dallying with Christian Science, mysticism, fatherhood, and art. "What a sweet welter life is," he murmurs, as for the last time he runs his hand through his hair, "how tender, how grim, how like a colorful symphony." Welter is the word for such life as is here painted—and romantic welter, that is the funny thing. Stripped of their patiently amassed and chiefly meaningless details, these pages give a record of the paltry business and sex adventures of a common little hero of amatory romance. Far enough this from the sincere realism of a "Sister Carrie" or a "Jennie Gerhardt," in which Mr. Dreiser was working upon his own last.

Edgar Lee Masters. "An American 'Genius'." Chicago *Evening Post*, October 22, 1915.

"The Genius," by Theodore Dreiser is not the third part of his trilogy of desire, tho it is so designated in some critical quarters. Yet it is a story of desire, the delineation of a man who simulated a genius, but was not one. The author puts the word genius in quotation marks, thereby conveying an intimation of his own judgment; at least by that method leaving the question to the judgment of the reader. In this book Dreiser's clear eye and patient, accurate hand display themselves in all the elaborateness that we have been taught to expect in his work. All his books, beginning with "Sister Carrie," have this quality; and together they form a remarkable record of what a man of large experience and deep sympathy with his fellow beings has gleaned at first hand from a world that enthralls his imagination and bewilders his thought. As history these books are valuable—more valuable than the histories we have. For Dreiser knows Illinois and Indiana, Chicago and New York. He knows America, and he knows the people in villages and cities. He understands what a man almost a genius must contend with in this disorderly land of rhetorical freedom and societal tyranny and banality. He knows that the American soil is not productive of genius; and hence Witla, the hero, a name which connotes witless, goes thru the experience that would come to a genius, but fails in the main thing as a genius would not fail. Yet, so far as a chronicle of as well as against America is concerned, Witla suffices. The theme is bigger than Mr. Howells' "A Modern Instance," and Dreiser has gorged the book with things intimate and subtle and true to the life we know. His unique intellectual gifts show nothing more conspicuously than a zealous interest, a primal wonder, concerning the ironies and grotesqueries of life.

Over the book one can hear at times Gargantuan laughter; at other times a trembling sensitiveness seems to vibrate thru the pages. Life's phantasmagoric procession passes before his eyes. He sees its tragedies clearly; its comedies, fundamentally speaking, do not escape him. But ever he asks why should this be and what is the end? What makes the machine run? Who is running it and why? He is therefore never done with explaining, and adding in touches and bringing forward facts. The reader must see what he sees. Nothing must be omitted, lest the picture lose the fidelity that he would portray—lest some less discerning eye fail of comprehension of the whole. Boundless curiosity, passion for life, immense strength and patience carry him beyond Browning in the endeavor to make the record complete. But, unlike Browning, Dreiser has no philosophy, unless it be a philosophy to see a cosmic force which concerns itself with great events, and cares nothing for the human souls bobbing like corks in its current, whirled here to transports of brief happiness, carried here thru unmitigated trial to sorrow, but to failure in either case at the last. America should awake to the significance of the fact that Dreiser is not striving for popularity or to make money. He is not writing to propitiate American standards. He does not see a power for righteousness moving thru the world, tho he is bound to see laws at work in every domain of human life, more clearly than he has seen them thus far. But he is admirable and to be acclaimed because he looks for truth and tells the truth. If America can boast of a novelist now living of greater power, insight, imaginative sweep, let him step forward and claim the laurel wreath. He seems to me our greatest novelist now writing, and destined in the wise judgment of posterity to be given a place among the noteworthy writers of this age.

Witla the "genius" is in truth a pathetic character. He was born in a little town in Illinois, the son of a sewing machine agent. His youth is faithfully depicted, its inner and outer realities; we all know the town, the people, the household. He is a boy enraptured of beauty. His boyish dreams center about the lovely little girls of his acquaintance. There's Stella Appleton with her braids of golden hair, even as Becky Thatcher captured the heart of Tom Sawyer. But Witla does not even as a boy remain innocent. Havelock Ellis would understand him. He might get a psychopathic classification at some hands. For soon Margaret Duff, a laundress, figures in his life. Witla is sexually precocious. And this predisposition germinates the events of his life all along. But other things modify the general results. For one thing the American atmosphere stunts his unfolding; for another his nature is unstable, his ideals shift and fade from vision; for another the love of money-making diverts his attention from art. The denoument discloses eroticism and its consequences in spiritual and physical exhaustion, weakness of will, disappointment at the reception accorded his work, even speculation, as the forces which undermined him. Is this not an American story? Compare it with Wilhelm Meister or Jean Christophe to get the difference between an atmosphere stimulating to genius and one that freezes it. We see clearly that Witla was doomed from the first. We feel that had he gone from the provinces to Paris, instead of from Alexandria, Ill., to Chicago, he might have become an artist—a genius.

Instead he came to the Art Institute and went thru Chicago's drabby Bohemia. He painted pictures in New York, had an exhibition, sold some of his work and went to Paris. He married at this time Angela Blue, the daughter of an Illinois farmer. Shortly after he was stricken with nervous prostration. He returned to America and became a day laborer, could do nothing now with his art. Newspaper illustrating next came to hand. Finally he worked up to be managing director of the United Magazines Corporation at $25,000 a year. He was now prospering, but what of art? He embarked on land speculation at this time. And Susanne Dale came into his life. Nine women, including his wife, figure in the story, Susanne ended him. She absorbed his strength and distracted his attention from the magazine corporation. The ground began to slip from under his feet. The land speculation blew up: he lost his position. At this juncture, Angela, his wife, theretofore childless, became with child. She could not give it birth: a Caesarian operation was performed. The mother died, the child lived. And Susanne's mother, who had undermined him with the magazine, had taken Susanne away. He is now alone. These chapters, the last three of the book, are unendurably poignant. He stands by his wife's bedside thinking over his selfishness, his sensual pursuits. His thoughts mock him, they mock the dying wife. Penitent, almost terror-stricken, Witla watches the death throes. Over his shoulder leers the diabolical face of twenty years; satiety has entered his blood like a septicemia. A great fatigue has him in its grip. He is not a genius—he is a failure. Inevitable laws working in his nature demand the price of folly, instability, lust; and things for which he was in no wise responsible demand their price, too. Indeed, Witla is responsible for none of the results, for no man can supervise with wisdom which is not his. He goes out under the stars and the mystery of life comes over him. He had done this years before on a perilous night with Angela during the courtship.

And here the work ends after more than 700 pages. The tragedy seems too much for the weak back which bore it; but that's the way generally with tragedies. Witla is just a cork on the cosmic stream. Life has been a Dionysian festival, its wine has gone to his head. Great vital forces, sex, love of art, beauty, ambition, have swept him along. Down the stream he has gone. Like a tale that is told—"a schoolboy's tale the wonder of an hour"—life has gone. He is only 38—but what can be the continuation of the epos? Consciously or unconsciously Dreiser has recorded the definite figure of a man moving thru an America that required strength of the first order to overcome, if any strength could do that. In texture, in detail, in color, this is a trustworthy record of American characters and circumstances of this day. Like "The Titan" and "The Financier" it will furnish future generations with material for understanding of our era. It is a greater book than any he has written—for its theme is great—the defeat of a soul, self-defeated it may be—and the author has not only resumed the artistic mood that created Sister Carrie and Jennie Gerhardt, but he has refined and enriched his style.

Mr. Dreiser can be glad, if he will, that he has revolutionized American fiction. It can never return to the old standards of reticence about life. But he has not reached the climax whither his genius inevitably tends. That climax must come. It cannot come now in the fierce heat of Dostoivesky; rather it may be expected in a mellow glow, a calm flame of transfiguration. That book when it shall be written will be shorter than this one. It will be more quintessential.

The last look that one has of Witla leads one to believe that he is nearer to becoming a genius than at any time in his life. He is now intellectually and emotionally hard. His soul has reached a static equilibrium, but in the realm of bio-chemistry that is the stage of being which just precedes union with other forces, resulting in disruption of old cohesions and the creation of new ones in the process of evolution. He is still following the lure of sex with poetasters and varietists, but he is really sick of the chase. His child evokes emotions he has not known before. Philosophy, speculation on the vastness of life, enters his thought. And mysticism raises a not ineffectual appeal. This novel might have been called Ixion, for Witla clasped the cloud of ideal beauty, lost the embrace and was pinned upon a wheel of fire. The author leaves Witla in a sort of Tartarus befogged and quieted. Another book might show him incandescent with creative force, a genius indeed.

"A Riot of Eroticism." St. Louis *Post-Dispatch*, October 23, 1915.

Theodore Dreiser has given us another erotic story in his latest output "The 'Genius.'" The central figure of this book, like those of some of his other books, is a man who can not rest until he possesses every woman who attracts him. He has no moral sense and never sees in a woman a human personality. To Eugene, as to the wretched hero of the same author's "The Titan," women are mere playthings.

There is little use relating the story even in part. It is all a huge orgy of the flesh without the slightest touch of the divine. If the story is meant to indicate that sex attraction without the divine spark is evil, it would be worth while reading it. But Dreiser never indicates things of this sort in his work. He seems to delight in delineating characters who do not know anything about the moral sense.

His Eugene Witla but faintly and distantly appreciates the pure and normal in woman. In fact, he touches purity to sully it. The author himself seems to gloat over the "conquests" his hero makes with women. His Eugene betrays any and all trusts. He has immoral relations with one woman while making love to another and being engaged to a third. He remains a contemptible cur to the end.

Only persons bent upon indulging in the reading of erotic stuff care to go through the closely printed 700 pages of Dreiser's latest book. Such books can not benefit anyone except their author, and only benefit him in a financial way. From the point of view of life they are worthless, even when written as well as Dreiser writes. The more is the pity that his gift is not used for human service.

C. W. "Genius and Today." New York *Call*, October 24, 1915.

. . . "The Genius" is a splendid story. Interest is maintained throughout its vast reach of over 700 pages. The feeling of variety is always present. Theodore Dreiser does not distort life; he does not whitewash it, nor present it as dirtier than it is. He will grow to a deeper knowledge of the motives underlying the actions of men and women; but he cannot reproduce their actions more accurately. In detail he is arresting, sympathetic; in the treatment of the broader trends of life—of the adolescent civilization of our vast Western land, of the splendid crest of the life-stream in the Eastern metropolis, of the quieter and older life of London and Paris—in all of this, he shows a clean vision to us. The book serves to establish still firmer his place as one of the most significant novelists of this land—of this age.

"The 'Genius'." Louisville [Ky.] *Courier-Journal*, October 25, 1915.

In "The Genius" Theodore Dreiser fills 736 pages with the life-history of Eugene Witla, who is only a potential genius, as the author indicates by quotation marks. Although Witla is described as an artist of some power, it is in the business world that he attains his greatest success. As advertising manager of the United Magazines Corporation and as stockholder in the Sea Island Realty Company he would have been financially secure, but for the anti-social forces of his emotional temperament. The development of his artistic talent was sidetracked at the first opportunity which presented itself to exchange the work of newspaper artist for that of art director of an advertising company. Mr. Dreiser has shown in his previous novels, "The Financier" and "The Titan," that his ideal of masculine leadership is apt to clothe itself in the form of business ability, and Witla's prompt willingness to abandon his artistic career betrays the author's lack of sympathy with it. His sympathy with and admiration for his hero is betrayed constantly—nowhere more strikingly than in the almost savage delineation of the character of poor Angela, Eugene's wife, for whose torture and death in the effort to regain her husband's love there is only a fleeting pity. The author's sympathy is apparently with his hero in the storms of his married life also, although these are without exception the result of Witla's infidelities.

Mr. Dreiser's method, like that of Witla, the artist, is uncompromisingly realistic. He does not intend to convey an impression of what he likes, but of what is. . . .

It is a sad, sordid story. As the author says of the marital relations of Eugene and Angela: "It was one of those pitiless, scandalous situations in life which sicken us of humanity." Yet even such brutal revelations of life and human nature doubtless have their uses. There is an ominous lifelikeness in the character of Eugene Witla which may well depress the idealist and the moralist. "Thus it is," says Mr. Dreiser, "and thus and thus—" and the heart sinks with conviction. "How does the incorporation of such a figure within book covers affect its possible existence in life?" the moralist will ask. But that is not a question for the reviewer, nor, some will claim, for the novelist. In the meantime Mr. Dreiser and his masculine outlaws loom large in American literature.

N.P. Dawson. "Books of the Week." New York *Evening Globe*, October 30, 1915.

. . . "The Genius" is probably Mr. Dreiser's most subjective work—and it is the ugliest. It is true that what interest the story has is pathological. One may be sorry for a man who sees nothing in life but girls, an unending procession of girls, hardly more to be differentiated than the Pink Leg and the Blue Leg of the chorus. For such a man life must be one long musical comedy; and one may understand how at the end he should become (almost!) a Christian Scientist.

Professor William Lyons Phelps, endeavoring to distinguish between "realism" and life and reality, has illustrated by saying that when Zola gazed upon a dunghill he saw and described a dunghill and nothing more; while Rostand, looking at the same unlovely object, beheld the vision of Chantecler. But Dreiser would never see Chantecler; only the dung—and the Hens!

We understand that the Tauchnitz publications are about to be resumed, following an interruption made by the war. We hope that "The Genius" will immediately appear in a German translation. That's how kindly we feel toward the Germans!

John Cowper Powys. "Theodore Dreiser." *Little Review,* 2 (November 1915), 7-13.

. . . In *The "Genius"* Theodore Dreiser has achieved a very curious and a very original work. In doing it he has once more made it clear how much more interesting the quality of his own genius is than that of any other American novelist of the present age.

The "Genius" is an epic work. It has the epic rather than the dramatic quality; it has the epic rather than the mystic, or symbolic, quality. And strictly speaking, Dreiser's novels, especially the later ones, are the only novels in America, are the only novels, as a matter of fact, in England or America, which possess this quality. It is quite properly in accordance with the epic attitude of mind, with the epic quality in art, this reduction of the more purely human episodes to a proportionate insignificance compared with the general surge and volume of the life-stream. It is completely in keeping with the epic quality that there should be no far-fetched psychology, no quivering suspensions on the verge of the unknown.

Dreiser is concerned with the mass and weight of the stupendous life-tide; the life-tide as it flows forward, through vast panoramic stretches of cosmic scenery. Both in respect to human beings, and in respect to his treatment of inanimate objects, this is always what most dominatingly interests him. You will not find in Dreiser's books those fascinating arrests of the onward-sweeping tide, those delicate pauses and expectancies, in back-waters and enclosed gardens, where persons, with diverting twists in their brains, murmur and meander at their ease, protected from the great stream. Nobody in the Dreiser-world is so protected; nobody is so privileged. The great stream sweeps them all forward, sweeps them all away; and not they, but *It,* must be regarded as the hero of the tale.

It is precisely this quality, this subordination of the individual to the deep waters that carry him, which makes Dreiser so peculiarly the American writer. Perhaps this is one of the reasons why he has had a more profoundly appreciative hearing in England than in the United States. It was so with Walt Whitman in his earlier days. To get the adequate perspective for a work so entirely epical it seems necessary to have the Atlantic as a modifying foreground. Americans—so entirely *in it* themselves—are naturally, unless they possess the Protean faculty of the editor of Reedy's *Mirror,* unable to see the thing in this cosmic light. They are misled by certain outstanding details—the sexual scenes, for instance; or the financial scenes,—and are prevented by these, as by the famous "Catalogues" in Whitman, from getting the proportionate vision.

The true literary descendants of the author of the *Leaves of Grass* are undoubtedly Theodore Dreiser and Edgar Masters. These two, and these two alone, though in completely different ways, possess that singular "beyond-good-and-evil" touch which the epic form of art requires. It was just the same with Homer and Vergil, who were as naturally the epic children of aristocratic ages, as these are of a democratic one.

Achilles is not really a very attractive figure—take him all in all; and we remember how scandalously Æneas behaved to Dido. The ancient epic writers, writing for an aristocracy, caught the world-stream from a poetic angle. The modern epic writers, writing for a democracy, catch it from a realistic one. But it is the same world-stream; and in accordance with the epic vision there is the same subordination of the individual to the cosmic tide. This is essentially a dramatic, rather than an epic epoch, and that is why so many of us are bewildered and confused by the Dreiser method.

The "Genius" is a long book. But it might have been three times as long. It might begin anywhere and stop anywhere. It is the Prose-Iliad of the American Scene; and, like that other, it has a right to cut out its segment of the shifting panorama at almost any point.

And so with the style of the thing. It is a ridiculous mis-statement for critics to say that Dreiser has no style. It is a charming irony, on his own part, to belittle his style. He has, as a matter of fact, a very definite and a very effective style. It is a style that lends itself to the huge indifferent piling up of indiscriminate materials, quite as admirably as that gracious poetical one of the old epic-makers lent itself to their haughtier and more aristocratic purpose. One would recognize a page of Dreiser's writings as infallibly as one would recognize a page of Hardy's. The former *relaxes* his medium to the extreme limit and the latter *tightens* his; but they both have their "manner." A paragraph written by Dreiser would never be mistaken for anyone else's. If for no other peculiarity Dreiser's style is remarkable for the shamelessness with which it adapts itself to the drivel of ordinary conversation. In the Dreiser books—especially in the later ones, where in my humble opinion he is feeling more firmly after his true way,—people are permitted to say those things which they actually do say in real life—things that make you blush and howl, so soaked in banality and ineptitude are they. In the true epic manner Dreiser gravely puts down all these fatuous observations, until you feel inclined to cry aloud for the maddest, the most fantastic, the most affected Osconian wit, to serve as an antidote.

But one knows very well he is right. People don't in ordinary life—certainly not in ordinary democratic life—talk like Oscar Wilde, or utter deep ironic sayings in the style of Matthew Arnold. They don't really—let this be well understood—concentrate their feelings in bitter pungent spasmodic outbursts, as those Rabelaisean persons in Guy de Maupassant. They just gabble and gibber and drivel; at least that is what they do in England and America. The extraordinary language which the lovers in Dreiser—we use the term "lovers" in large sense—use to one another might well make an aesthetic-minded person howl with nervous rage. But then,—and who does not know it?—the obsession of the sex-illusion is above everything else a thing that makes idiots of people; a thing that makes them talk like Simple Simons. In real life lovers don't utter those wonderful pregnant sayings which leap to their lips in our subtle symbolic dramas. They just burble and blather and blurt forth whatever drivelling nonsense comes into their heads. Dreiser is the true master of the modern American Prose-Epic just because he is not afraid of the weariness, the staleness, the flatness, and unprofitableness of actual human conversation. In reading the great ancient poetic epics one is amazed at the "naivete" with which these haughty persons—these gods and demi-gods express their emotional reactions. It is "carried off," of course, there, by the sublime heightening of the style; but it produces just the same final impression,—of the insignificance of the individual, whether mortal or immortal, compared with the torrent of Fate which sweeps them all along.

And the same thing applies to Dreiser's attitude towards "good and evil" and towards the problem of the "supernatural." All other modern writers array themselves on this side or that. They either defend traditional morality or they attack it. They are anxious, at all costs, to give their work dramatic intensity; they struggle to make it ironical, symbolical, mystical—God knows what! But Dreiser neither attacks morality nor defends immorality. In the true Epic manner he puts himself aside, and permits the great mad Hurly-Burly to rush pell-mell past him and write its own whirligig runes at its own careless pleasure. Even Zola himself was not such a realist. Zola had a purpose;—the purpose of showing what a Beast the human animal is! Dreiser's people are not beasts; and they shock our aesthetic sensibilities quite as often by their human sentiment as they do by their lapses into lechery.

To a European mind there is something incredibly absurd in the notion that these Dreiser books are immoral.

Unlike the majority of French and Russian writers Dreiser is not interested in the pathology of vice. He is too deeply imbued with the great naive epic spirit to stop and linger in these curious bye-paths. He holds Nature—in her normal moods—to be sufficiently remarkable.

It is the same with his attitude towards the "supernatural." The American Prose-Epic were obviously false to reality if the presence of the supernatural were not felt. It is felt and felt very powerfully; but it is kept in its place. Like Walt Whitman's stellar constellations, it suffices for those who belong to it, it is right enough where it is—we do not want it any nearer!

Because the much-tossed wanderer, Eugene Witla, draws a certain consolation, at the last, from Christian Science, only a very literal person would accuse the author of *The "Genius"* of being a convert to the faith. To omit Christian Science from any prose-epic of American life would be to falsify the picture out of personal prejudice. Dreiser has no prejudices except the prejudice of finding the normal man and the normal woman, shuffled to and fro by the normal forces of life, an interesting and arresting spectacle. To some among us such a spectacle is not interesting. We must have the excitement of the unusual, the shock of the abnormal. Well! There are plenty of European writers ready to gratify this taste. Dreiser is not a European writer. He is an American writer. The life that interests him, and interests him passionately, is the life of America. It remains to be seen whether the life of America interests Americans!

It is really quite important to get the correct point of view with regard to Dreiser's "style." The *negative* qualities in this style of his are indeed as important as the positive ones. He is so epical, so objective, so concrete and indifferent, that he is quite content when the great blocked-out masses of his work lift themselves from the obscure womb of being and take shape before him. When they have done this,—when these piled-up materials and portentous groups of people have limned themselves against the grey background,—he himself stands aside, like some dim demiurgic forger in the cosmic blast-furnace, and mutters queer commentaries upon what he sees. He utters these commentaries through the lips of his characters—Cowperwood, say, or Witla—or even some of the less important ones;—and broken and incoherent enough they are!

But what matter! The huge epic canvas is stretched out there before us. The vast cyclopean edifice lifts its shadowy bulk towards the grey sky. The thing has been achieved. The creative spirit has breathed upon the waters. Resting from his titanic labor, what matter if this Demiurge drowses, and with an immense humorous indifference permits his characters to nod too, and utter strange words in their dreams!

The carelessness of Dreiser's style, its large indolence, its contempt for epigrammatic point, its relaxed strength, is not really a defect at all when you regard his work from the epic view-point.

There must be something in a great cosmic picture to take the place of the sand and silt and rubbish and rubble which we know so well in life, under the grey sky! And these stammered incoherences, these broken mutterings, fill in this gap. They give the picture that drab patience, that monotonous spaciousness which is required. Symbolic drama or psychological fiction can dispense with these blank surfaces. The prose-epic of America cannot afford to do without them. They suggest that curious sadness—the sadness of large, flat, featureless scenery, which visitors from Europe find so depressing.

Well! Thus it remains. If one is interested in the "urge—urge—urge," as Whitman calls it, of the normal life-stream as it goes upon its way, in these American States, one reads Dreiser with a strange pleasure. He is no more moral than the normal life-stream is moral; and he is no more immoral. It is true the normal life-stream does not cover *quite* the whole field. There *are* back-waters and there *are* enclosed gardens.

There was a Europe once. But the American prose-epic is the American prose-epic.

Frederic Taber Cooper. "Some Novels of the Month." *Bookman*, 42 (November 1915), 322–323.

Mr. Theodore Dreiser is a figure which refuses to be ignored in contemporary fiction. He has an undeniable strength of a certain sort, and he carries on some of the distinctive features of the French naturalistic school in a decade when they are in danger of becoming a lost art. And yet his volumes, especially the later ones, leave behind them a sense of disappointment, a feeling that somehow or other they have just fallen short of being really big. There are, to be sure, big pages, even big chapters here and there. He has the gift of taking the human animal and turning him inside out pitilessly, and then seeming to say sardonically, "There, whether you like it or not, that is what men and women are really like!" He can do this sort of thing with such unblushing thoroughness that there are times when the reader has a sense of physical discomfort in the presence of humanity stripped so bare. The tendency to depict this side of life seems to have grown upon him, reaching, let us hope, its culmination in *The "Genius."* The central character, Eugene Witla, is defined by the author as "an artist who, pagan to the core, enjoyed reading the Bible for its artistry of expression, and Schopenhauer, Nietzsche, Spinoza and James for the mystery of things which they suggested." But a pagan may still sense the joys of living; he may have deep-rooted passions for the beautiful and the true; he may worship faithfully at some single shrine,—but not so Eugene Witla. He thinks that he loves, not one but many women, successively, simultaneously, as it may happen: but of fidelity he does not know even the definition. He has the promiscuity of a Turk, and the callousness of a slave-driver. Women are pretty toys, to be taken up, played with and tossed aside, when his mood has cooled. To one girl only, Angela Blue, he gives the semblance of loyalty; yet after keeping her waiting year after year for him to fulfil his promise of marriage, he does not scruple to seduce her under her own father's roof. And the only reason why he later redeems his promise and makes her his wife is not from any sense of pity or remorse, but from cowardice, —she has threatened to drown herself, and his artistic soul shrinks from the thought of how her dead body would look in the water. It is quite possible that Mr. Dreiser meant to depict a somewhat different character from what he has actually done. It is equally possible that the reviewer has failed to interpret him correctly. The trouble may be partly that he has shown us his hero a little too intimately, and thus has bred the proverbial contempt. It is not unlikely that he has meant him for a sort of American substitute for Maupassant's Bel-Ami,—but there is a gulf between them. The Frenchman understood the great value of reticence and implication. We do not know how many other women than those mentioned in his pages figured in the butterfly life of his amorous hero; but we sense the abiding memory of their vanished faces, the echo of their bygone tears and laughter. Mr. Dreiser gives us no chance for flights of fancy. All the women, and there are throngs of them, who figured in Eugene Witla's life are recorded with the fidelity of a dictograph; one affair endures for seventeen days, another for a specified number of weeks,—passion reduced to the prose of daily entry bookkeeping. As has already been admitted, there are some quite wonderful pages on certain subjects, as for instance the mixed emotions of a young art student the first time that he draws from a female model in the life class, and again, later in the volume, a child-birth scene unequalled in frankness since Zola wrote *La Joie de Vivre.* But episodes of this sort do not in themselves constitute great fiction; they are merely pardonable if the fiction is of big enough magnitude to be its own justification.

Addison Lewis. "Dreiser's 'Genius'." Minneapolis *Bellman*, November 6, 1915.

. . . "The 'Genius' " is remarkable propaganda for realism, yet I am afraid it is not realism in the highest sense, if Mr. Dreiser means to give us American realism. The hero is no more the average American, or the average American artist, than the man in the moon. His women are real, but he carefully holds all their qualities in leash to their passion or their "deadness" to it.

The book is powerful and interesting, but very unpleasant, and will make most men who read it resentful that such an unworthy representative of their sex as its hero should creep into fiction.

Los Angeles *Graphic*, November 6, 1915.

Realism gone to seed is the predominating characteristic of "The Genius" by Theodore Dreiser. Realism should develop vivid, living, human characters, should make the reader see clearly the workings of the human mind, should increase one's knowledge of personality, but here, for more than seven hundred closely-written pages are petty, trivial details—how much a man gets for selling a sewing-machine, the exact size of a studio, particulars as to a woman's sufferings in childbirth, the traits of individuals who play no important part in the story, pages on pages of hopelessly uninteresting and entirely irrelevant matter. Meantime, the important topic, the character of Eugene Witla, artist and principal person in the book, is allowed to drift along without development. The reader is assured that he is a clever man, but in the entire seven hundred and thirty-six pages he does not say or do a clever thing. He is reputed witty, but the remarks at which other people in the book laugh, are so puerile as to bore a fifteen year old boy. He is declared to have become a gentleman and received into the best society, but from the numerous samples given of his uniformly bad manners, no self-respecting hosteler would tolerate his company. That he is a cad, a gutter Don Juan, a false lover and husband would be neither here nor there were he portrayed convincingly; but in the maze of details obstretical and otherwise, the author has failed completely to make his "genius" ring true. There is Mr. Dreiser's word for it that Witla is clever, witty, commanding, attractive to men and women, but then the "genius" proceeds to deport himself in a way that would disgust one begging for alms. Sympathy for Witla, for his wife, for his amoratas is impossible because none of them is real and living—and, besides, the reader needs to save all his sympathy for himself if he intends to read the entire seven hundred and thirty-six pages of small type. It seems a pity that an author who could conceive so powerful and vivid a personality as "The Titan" should follow that remarkable book with so weak and unconvincing a volume.

"Too Much Genius." *The Independent*, 84 (November 8, 1915), 237.

If Theodore Dreiser had made two novels of his latest book, *The "Genius"*, one containing the work-history of the great artist he seeks to depict, and the other his love-life with its wearying succession of emotional episodes, and then had found the courage and good taste to burn the second volume, the reader would have been spared much *ennui*, and the author would have enhanced his reputation.

Life, November 11, 1915.

Sex-land uber alles would seem to be Theodore Dreiser's national anthem. Let's see, there was "Sister Carrie," "Jennie Gerhardt," "The Financier," "The Titan," and at no time, in any of them, was it ever very far to Tipperary. But now, in "The Genius," he actually goes into action on a fictional front of seven hundred and thirty-six pages singing "sex-land" in close formation of fine type all along the line! Puritanically speaking, the book takes the offensive in the first chapter and never surrenders it. Yet this history of Eugene Witla—country lad from Illinois, newspaper illustrator in Chicago, artist and plunger in New York, spiritual cross between a vampire and a steam roller everywhere and always—is in some ways the most fully realized thing that Dreiser has done. The trouble with it is not that, in itself, it is sex-ridden, but that it is its author's third all but identical handling of the same sex-ridden theme. "The Genius" is better done than either "The Financier" or "The Titan," but it is a virtual repetition of them. Alone, it would be an achievement. Together they amount to a habit.

Albert Mordell. Philadelphia *Record*, November 13, 1915.

Theodore Dreiser's new novel, "The Genius," shows him at the height of his powers. The same absorbing interest, the same mastery of dialect, the same powerful delineation of passion and character, pervade this novel as they did his earlier novels.

Dreiser traces the career of Eugene Witla, artist, from his boyhood days to his manhood. We have an account of his rise till he commands a salary of $25,000. But, more interesting than the story of his various occupations as advertising manager, art director, etc., is the story of his amours. In short, Witla is another Frank Cowperwood, but he is an artist instead of a business man. Moreover, he is not so conscienceless a sinner as the financier.

If Dreiser is master of one kind of literature, it is of that which tells of the amorous entanglements into which a married man may fall. Let anyone read the last portion of the book, which tells of the affair with Suzanne. The sorrows of the wife Angela are graphically described. The devotion of Suzanne, her clash with her mother for her proposal of carrying out an unconventional arrangement with Eugene, and her final desertion of him, are well told. The prior affair with Charlotte Wilson and the wife's discovery of it are grippingly and intensely narrated. Dreiser can write about a love affair, and this is a novelist's most important function. His English at times might be actually horrible, he may go off frequently into unimportant details, yet the power and interest as a whole are there. We cannot help admiring the courage, boldness and frankness of the author. He is erotic, but life is often, most often, so. He dwells on tragic situations, but only because life abounds in them. . . .

"The Genius" may be too long, but it holds one's interest and ranks as high, at least, as any other Dreiser novel, with a possible exception of "Sister Carrie."

Randolph Bourne. "Dreiser as Hero." *New Republic*, 5 (November 20, 1915), Fall Literary Review, pp. 5–6.

The insistent theme of Mr. Dreiser's work is desire, perennial, unquenchable. The critic who would discuss him takes his life in his hands. He must either be denounced as an advocate of prostitution, or an admirer of that second-rate pseudo-passion which Mr. Hearst and his able fictional lieutenants have made it their business to introduce to our American consciousness. A public which uses the word "sex" as indiscriminately as it does would be very hard to talk to on the subject of desire. As currently used, sex has a subtly derogatory sense. What it really means is, "We have no intention of making primary the values and implications which cluster around desire." A recent naïve critic expressed it exactly when he preferred Booth Tarkington to Tagore and Artzibashef because Tarkington makes business the master-motive of life, to which religion and sex are incidental. One simply takes them for granted in a turmoil the vortex of which is professional or business action. Of course no great Continental novelist ever believed this, Rolland or Dostoevsky or Tolstoi or Frenssen or Nexö, and it is in this contrast of values that we get our American uniqueness in the imaginative world. The major motive of these Continentals is almost always the inexorable desire of life, a desire which is no more physical than it is spiritual, a desire which consists often of walking in the mud with the face towards the stars. This push and yearning is what makes for religion and art in a kind of insatiable straining towards realization and perfection. The East has too much of it and tries to put it to sleep. The West in the last century had almost too much, but struggled nobly to make something out of it. That struggle, embittered by a new knowledge of how meanly constituted the world was, produced modern literature.

No matter how badly Mr. Dreiser might do his work, he would be significant as the American novelist who has most felt this subterranean current of life. Many novelists have seen this current as a mere abyss of sin from which the soul is to be dragged to the high ground of moral purpose and redemption, but this will not quite do. The great interpreters see life as a struggle between this desire and the organized machinery of existence, but they are not eager, as we are, to cover up and belittle the desire. There can be little creative imagination as long as we regard the motion-picture trappings and action of life, the safe running in social harness, as "realer" than primeval or almost subconscious forces.

That Mr. Dreiser is our only novelist who tries to plumb far below this conventional superstructure is his great distinction. We have enough "red blood" in our fiction, but too much of it is patently compounded of carmine and water. And if we are to talk of bestiality, there is nothing more bestial than the romantic love of the conventional novel. What Mr. Dreiser has discovered is that "libido" which was nothing more than the scientific capturing of this nineteenth-century desire. You may come away from the Freudians and the Jungians chagrined at their technicalities and horrified at their phenomena, but you can scarcely deny that they have found and interpreted a central *leitmotiv* of our human living, which is immensely to illuminate our understanding of ourselves and the world about us. What Mr. Dreiser seems to me to do is to give us a crudely impressive fictional portrayal of this motive. His hero is really not Sister Carrie or the Titan or the Genius, but that desire within us that pounds in manifold guise against the iron walls of experience. Sister Carrie was a mass of undifferentiated desire, craving finery and warmth and light and sympathy quite as much as satisfied sex. The masculine Titan appeared in unpleasantly crystallized form of physical passion. In the Genius the libido takes the form of an insatiable desire which is sexual and yet incurably aesthetic. In his world, genuine spiritual monogamy would be an *idée fixe,* a kind of pathological petrifaction of desire. Here it is always overleaping the particular, seeking something elemental, almost metaphysical, that eludes the individual woman. The "Genius" himself calls it Beauty, and perhaps that is as good a word as any. Some magical manna he seems to seek in the women he is mad about. As they pass from his sight, that spirit merely becomes incarnated in another form. To those who would dismiss a character like Eugene Witla, the "Genius," as a beast, such an interpretation will seem over-idyllic. But he eludes moral capture. From Mr. Dreiser's first chapter we are out on a wider and more perilous sea.

Mr. Dreiser carries his hero over a restless field of adventure. From his boyhood in the Illinois town he takes him to Chicago and little jobs, until he discovers artistic talent and is drawn to the dazzling life of New York. (Mr. Dreiser never quite gets over this dazzle.) Studio life, exhibitions, social intrigue, come to a halt in nervous collapse and the effort to recover through hard physical labor. When the Genius's career revives, it is in the form of advertising art and the dizzy directorship of the United Magazines Corporations. Ultimately his good art reasserts itself, and he regains his place in the world. Through all of this runs the tragic stream of incontinence.

Mr. Dreiser writes of the erotic with an almost religious solemnity. There is something crudely massive about such a long epic of desire. There is a touch of the same Greek tragic note which vibrates through "Spoon River Anthology." The Genius, swept away by girlish beauty, is himself bewildered by the vehemence of the Unknown Eros within him. That experience of such thrilling loveliness should end in such bitter and humiliating woe! Like Medea's "O wrath within me! Spare my children!" he feels himself haunted by this power not himself which makes for unrighteousness. The storms of angry chagrin which his unfaithfulness excites in his wife Angela bring him only the most undisguised astonishment. There is almost Greek irony too in the fact that the only good, responsible and dutiful act which he performs—his marriage to the devoted Angela—precipitates many of the horrors. When her child finally releases her in death from a purgatory of agonized jealousy, we are left with the unquenched Genius, worn but not repentant, restored to his painting and reconciled in a devotion to his unwelcome little daughter.

This does not pretend to be a solution. Through the chaotic welter of his artistic, business, and social career, the Genius wearily seeks a guiding thread which does not emerge. His researches in Herbert Spencer, cosmic philosophy, and Mrs. Eddy, are curiously typical manifestations of the libido. Mr. Dreiser seems to take them all very seriously, but he is honest in not making them points of satiation for weary desire. Very true also is the contrast between the Genius's hard and realistic art and his supersensuous life. He never becomes integrated, because with talent and passion and intelligence he yet finds himself in a world which is too diverse and too big for him. He is on a sea which is full of cross-currents where he cannot steer. The major current pulls him where he would not go. And the sea opens so far on every side that he does not know in what direction he wants to steer. One feels that this chaos is not only in the Genius's soul, but also in the author's soul, and in America's soul.

Mr. Dreiser compels and convinces almost entirely in spite of his method. He has no distinction of style. His conversation is negligible, and at times falls even below the level of cheapness. He is portentously wordy. He has no humor. And yet one reads him. In the 736 pages, one skips only the business and social details—which are too minute to be even good photography. One reads him because he never forgets that he is talking about life as it is lived, and because he takes it seriously. Even scenes of freezing realism like the birth of Angela's child do not offend as they might. He is always saved by a plodding sincerity. His people are rarely desirable or interesting. Yet they live and you cannot escape them.

And, for all its dull and rather cheap texture, the book is set in a light of youthful idealism. Nobody but Mr. Dreiser could manage this fusion, but it is there. For the Genius the golden glow shines from everything. Always there is a sense of the miraculous beauty of girls, the soft clinging of charming atmospheres. Of sordid realists Mr. Dreiser is certainly the most idealistic. You cannot disillusion him. He still believes in, and still gives, a sense of the invincible virginality of the world.

I trust that the quotation marks in the title indicate Mr. Dreiser's realization that he has created only a second-rate personality, that he never, indeed, creates any but second-rate personalities. In the Genius he has made, however, a grandiose caricature of the masculine soul. And his real hero, anyway, is not his second-rate personality, but the desire of life. For this, much shall be forgiven him.

James L. Ford. "The Sex Question Dominating Theme In 'The Genius'." New York *Herald*, November 20, 1915.

Just now a great many of those persons who think they think, and a few who really think, are reading Theodore Dreiser's "The Genius," and asking themselves and their friends whether or no it is a novel of genuine value.

Certainly Mr. Dreiser gives his readers their money's worth in space, if in nothing more, for the book consists of more than seven hundred pages, and is closely printed at that. Moreover, every one of its chapters literally rings with what is nowadays termed "the sex question" and which used to be called something else when it was spoken of at all. . . .

It is all very sordid, but unquestionably true—that is to say, true in detail. Mr. Dreiser is an extremely observant writer. Nothing that is not worth talking about escapes his eye, and everything that catches his eye finds a place in his story. Of humor, satire, the spiritual or poetic quality, there is no trace whatever in his chapters, but he has given us a clear vision of the sort of material from which a certain kind of artist is made. The women are truthfully portrayed, too. We can see them all in either the crosstown or the Third avenue car at any hour of the day, and after seeing them it is pleasant to observe life in a Fifth avenue omnibus, which is at least five cents higher than the other in social degree.

Story telling is something more than a mere recital of facts and incidents. In its best form it contains those qualities of imagination and wisdom which underlie good writing, and in which Theodore Dreiser is sadly deficient. But as a hundred reel film of everything that might actually happen to a young man during the early years of his life "The Genius" leaves nothing to be desired.

"Very Artistic Temperament." New York *Evening Post*, November 20, 1915.

In his first two books Theodore Dreiser told a plain, unaffected story of moral deterioration. In "Sister Carrie," the chief interest lay in the detailed record of the career of a girl of the lower middle classes, led into vice by her love of pleasure. In "Jennie Gerhart," while a broader theme was supplied in the contrast between the fortunes of two immigrant families, German and Irish, the one sinking and the other rising, the central study was of the succumbing of Jennie to the temptations offered by the son of the Irish family, who was drawn to typify the vices and dangers of our materialistic social organization. The trilogy which he has lately finished may, from the fact that it was in part built upon the career of an actual figure, be looked upon as an interlude in Mr. Dreiser's development. "The 'Genius' " can then be taken as evidence of a progressive preoccupation with moral disease on the part of the writer, of a progressive tendency to exploit the animal streak in humankind. Its hero is introduced as an artist in possession of the type of "artistic temperament" that displays itself in ruthless disregard of the interests and feelings of others. He is a "genius" (it is impossible not to believe the term used with sarcastic intent) whose great passion is the realization of hedonist ideals of life.

The action lies in this hero's, Witla's, amorous adventures with many women, several sometimes occurring simultaneously; and he is shown as a positive prodigy of faithlessness, tossing one girl aside after the other. A semblance of devotion to one woman of rural extraction, Angela Blue, he does retain, but it is only a semblance. The novel carries him through a varied artistic and business career, culminating in entire worldly success, and its catastrophe comes when, following his marriage with the rural heroine, she dies in childbirth, while he is estranged by circumstance from the one other woman he has ever loved with anything like genuineness of feeling. It is as the portrait of a personality that the novel is presented, and it cannot be denied that the presentation is done with remarkable vitality—with a wealth of detail and of ideas that leaves the sensation of great vividness. But the portrait has little excuse for being, and in the very vigor of its execution we feel that the author strives after "bigness" without the fundamental profundity of conception that must underlie anything really big. Sweeping mastery of incident, detail, and psychology, unusual boldness and realism in describing the events of a very disagreeable story, are made to serve no real end. Honesty is a keynote of the book, and there are scattered pages of impressive writing, as the description of an art-class at work, and the picture of a surgical operation at the end. But it is honesty without conception of the literary value of reticence or of arrangement, an honesty without style or construction, and an honesty based on the assumption of the weakness or viciousness of the group of characters with which the book deals. Both in the large and the narrow sense of the word, the novel is utterly inartistic.

H. L. Mencken. "A Literary Behemoth." *Smart Set*, 47 (December 1915), 150–154.

On page 703 of Theodore Dreiser's new novel, "THE 'GENIUS'," the gentleman described by the title, Eugene Tennyson Witla by name, is on his way to a

Christian Scientist to apply for treatment for "his evil tendencies in regard to women." Remember the place: page 703. The reader, by this time, has hacked and gummed his way through 702 large pages of fine print: 97 long chapters: more than 300,000 words. The stage-hands stand ready to yank down the curtain; messieurs of the orchestra, their minds fixed eagerly upon malt liquor, are up to their hips in the finale; the weary nurses are swabbing up the operating room; the learned chirurgeons are wiping their knives upon their pantaloons; the rev. clergy are swinging into the benediction; the inexorable embalmer waits in the antechamber with his unescapable syringe, his Mona Lisa smile. . . . And then, at this painfully hurried and impatient point, with the *coda* already under weigh and even the most somnolent reaching nervously for his goloshes, Dreiser halts the whole show to explain the origin, nature and inner meaning of Christian Science, and to make us privy to a lot of chatty stuff about Mrs. Althea Johns, the lady-like healer, and to supply us with detailed plans and specifications of the joint, lair or apartment-house in which this fair sorceress lives, works her miracles, trims her boobs, and has her being!

Believe me, I do not spoof. Turn to page 703 and see for yourself. There, while the fate of Witla waits and the bowels of patience are turned to water, we are instructed and tortured with the following particulars about the house:

1. That it was "of conventional design."
2. That there was "a spacious areaway" between its two wings.
3. That these wings were "of cream-colored pressed brick."
4. That the entrance between them "was protected by a handsome wrought-iron door."
5. That to either side of this door was "an electric lamp support of handsome design."
6. That in each of these lamp supports there were "lovely cream-colored globes, shedding a soft lustre."
7. That "inside was the usual lobby."
8. That in the lobby was the usual elevator.
9. That in the elevator was the usual "uniformed negro elevator man."
10. That this negro elevator man (name not given) was "indifferent and impertinent."
11. That a telephone switchboard was also in the lobby.
12. That the building was seven stories in height.

Such is novel-writing as Dreiser understands it—a laborious and relentless meticulousness, an endless piling up of small details, an almost furious tracking down of ions, electrons and molecules. One is amazed and flabbergasted by the mole-like industry of the man, and no less by his lavish disregard for the ease and convenience of his readers. A Dreiser novel, at least of the later canon, cannot be read as other novels are read, *e. g.*, on a winter evening or a summer afternoon, between meal and meal, travelling from New York to Boston. It demands the attention for at least a week, and uses up the strength for at least a month. If, tackling "The 'Genius,'" one were to become engrossed in the fabulous manner described by the newspaper reviewers and so find oneself unable to put it down and go to bed before the end, one would get no sleep for three days and three nights. A man who can prove that he has read such a novel without medical assistance should be admitted to the *Landwehr* at once, without thesis or examination, and perhaps even given the order *pour la mérite.* A woman of equal attainments is tough enough to take in washing or to sing Brünnhilde. . . .

And yet, and yet—well, here comes the inevitable "and yet." For all his long-windedness, for all his persistent refusal to get about his business, for all his mouthing of things so small that they seem to be nothings, this Dreiser is undoubtedly a literary artist of very respectable rank, and nothing proves it more certainly than this, the last, the longest and one is tempted to add the damnedest of his novels. The thing is staggering, alarming, maddening—and yet one sticks to it. It is rambling, formless, chaotic—and yet there emerges out of it, in the end, a picture of almost blinding brilliancy, a panorama that will remain in the mind so long as memory lasts. Is it necessary to proceed against the reader in so barbarous a manner? Is there no way of impressing him short of wearing him out? Is there no route to his consciousness save laparotomy? God knows. But this, at all events, is plain: that no other route is open to Dreiser. He must do his work in his own manner, and his oafish clumsiness and crudeness are just as much a part of it as his amazing steadiness of vision, his easy management of gigantic operations, his superb sense of character. One is familiar with stylist-novelists, fellows who tickle with apt phrases, workers in psychological miniature, carvers of cameos. Here is one who works with a steam-shovel, his material being a county. Here is a wholesaler in general merchandise. Here, if such a fellow as Henry James be likened to a duellist, is the Hindenburg of the novel.

And what have we, precisely, in the story of Eugene Tennyson Witla? A tale enormous and indescribable—the chronicle, not only of Witla's own life, but also of the lives of a dozen other persons, some of them of only the slightest influence upon him. And what sort of man is this Witla. In brief, an artist, but though he actually paints pictures and even makes a success of it, not the artist of conventional legend, not a moony fellow in a velvet coat. What the story of Witla shows us, in truth, is very much the same thing that the story of Frank Cowperwood, in "The Financier" and "The Titan," showed us, to wit, the reaction of the artistic temperament against the unfavorable environment of this grand and glorious republic. If a Wagner or a Beethoven were born in the United States to-morrow it is highly improbable that he would express himself in the way that those men did; if a Raphael or a Cézanne, it is even more unlikely. The cause thereof is not that we disesteem music and painting, but that we esteem certain other arts infinitely more, particularly the art of creating vast industrial organisms, of bringing the scattered efforts of thousands of workers into order and coherence, of conjuring up huge forces out of spent and puny attractions and repulsions. Witla, as I have said, tries conventional art; he even goes to Paris and sets up as a genius of Montmartre. But his creative instinct and intelligence are soon challenged by larger opportunities; he is too thoroughly an American to waste himself upon pictures to hang upon walls. Instead he tackles jobs that better fit his race and time, and so, after a while, we see him at the head of a mammoth publishing house, with irons in half a dozen other fires—a boss American with all the capacity for splendor that goes with the species.

The chief apparent business of the story, indeed, is to show Witla's rise to this state of splendor, and its corrupting effect upon his soul. To this extent

Dreiser plays the moralist: he, too, is an American, and cannot escape it altogether. Witla mounts the ladder of riches rung by rung, and at each rise he yields more and more to the lavishness surrounding him. He acquires fast horses, objects of art, the physical comforts of a sultan. His wife, out of Wisconsin, is hung with fragile and costly draperies; his home is a thing for the decorator to boast about; his very office has something of the luxurious gaudiness of a bordello. Bit by bit he is conquered by his pervasive richness, this atmosphere of gorgeous ease. His appetite increases as dish follows dish upon the groaning table that fate has set for him; he acquires, by subtle stages, the tastes, the prejudices, the point of view of a man of wealth; his creative faculty, disdaining its old objects, concentrates itself upon the moulding and forcing of opportunities for greater and greater acquisitions. And so his highest success becomes his deepest degradation, and we see the marks of his disintegration multiply as he approaches it. He falls, indeed, almost as fast as he rises. It is a collapse worthy of melodrama. (Again the moral note!)

I say that this rise and fall make the chief business of the story, but that, of course, is only externally. Its inner drama presents a conflict between the two Witlas—the artist who is trying to create something, however meretricious, however undeserving his effort, and the sentimentalist whose longing is to be loved, coddled, kept at ease. This conflict, of course, is at the bottom of the misery of all men who may be truly said to be conscious creatures—that is, of all men above the grade of car conductor, barber, waiter or Sunday-school superintendent. On the one hand there is the desire to exert power, to do something that has not been done before, to bend reluctant material to one's will, and on the other hand there is the desire for comfort, for well-being, for an easy life. This latter desire, nine times out of ten, perhaps actually always, is visualized by women. Women are the conservatives and conservators, the enemies of hazard and innovation, the compromisers and temporizers. That very capacity for mothering which is their supreme gift is the greatest of all foes to masculine enterprise. Most men, alas, yield to it. In the common phrase, they marry and settle down—*i. e.*, they give up all notion of making the world over. This resignationism usually passes for happiness, but to the genuine artist it is quite impossible. He must go on sacrificing ease to aspiration and aspiration to ease, thus vacillating abominably and forever between his two irreconcilable desires. No such man is ever happy, not even in the moment of his highest achievement. Life, to him, must always be a muddled and a tragic business. The best he can hope for is a makeshift and false sort of contentment.

This is what Eugene Tennyson Witla comes to in the end. Women have been the curse of his life, from the days of his nonage onward. Forced into their arms constantly by an irresistible impulse, an unquenchable yearning for their facile caresses, he has been turned aside as constantly from his higher goals and led into smoother and broader paths. Good, bad and indifferent, they have all done him harm. His own wife, clinging to him pathetically through good and evil report, always ready to take him back after one of his innumerable runnings amuck, is perhaps his greatest enemy among them. She is always ten yards behind him, hanging on to his coat-tails, trying to drag him back. She is fearful when he needs daring, stupid when he needs stimulation, virtuously wifely when the thing he craves is wild adventure. But the rest all fail him, too. Seeking for joy he finds only bitterness. It is the gradual slowing down of the machine, mental and physical, that finally brings him release. Slipping into the middle forties he begins to turn, almost imperceptibly at first, from the follies of his early manhood. When we part from him at last he seems to have found what he has been so long seeking in his little daughter. The lover has merged into the father.

It is upon this tale, so simple in its main outlines, that Dreiser spills more than 300,000 long and short words, most of them commonplace, many of them improperly used. His writing, which in "The Titan" gave promise of rising to distinction and even to something resembling beauty, is here a mere dogged piling up of nouns, adjectives, verbs, adverbs, pronouns, and particles, and as devoid of æsthetic quality as an article in the *Nation.* I often wonder if he gets anything properly describable as pleasure out of his writing—that is, out of the actual act of composition. To the man who deals in phrases, who gropes for the perfect word, who puts the way of saying it above the thing actually said, there is in writing the constant joy of sudden discovery, of happy accident. But what joy can there be in rolling up sentences that have no more life or beauty in them, intrinsically, than so many election bulletins? Where is the thrill in the manufacture of such a paragraph as that I have referred to above, in which the apartment-house infested by Mrs. Althea Johns is described as particularly as if it were being offered for sale? Or in the laborious breeding of such guff as this, from Book I, Chapter IV:

> The city of Chicago—who shall portray it! This vast ruck of life that had sprung suddenly into existence upon the dank marshes of a lake shore.

But who protest and repine? Dreiser writes in this banal fasion, I dessay, because God hath made him so, and a man is too old, at my time of life, to begin criticizing the Creator. But all the same it may do no harm to point out, quite academically, that a greater regard for fairness of phrase and epithet would be as a flow of Pilsner to the weary reader in his journey across the vast deserts, steppes and pampas of the Dreiserian fable. Myself no voluptuary of letters, searching fantodishly for the rare titbit, the succulent morsel, I have yet enough sensitiveness to style to suffer damnably when all style is absent. And so with form. The well-made novel is as irritating as the well-made play—but let it at least have a beginning, a middle and an end! Such a confection as "The 'Genius' " is as shapeless as a Philadelphia pie-woman. It billows and rolls and bulges out like a cloud of smoke, and its internal organization is as vague. There are episodes that, with a few chapters added, would make very respectable novels. There are chapters that need but a touch or two to be excellent short stories. The thing rambles, staggers, fumbles, trips, wobbles, straggles, strays, heaves, pitches, reels, totters, wavers. More than once it seems to be foundering, in both the equine and the maritime senses. The author forgets it, goes out to get a drink, comes back to find it smothering. One has heard of the tree so tall that it took two men to see to the top of it. Here is a novel so huge that a whole shift of critics is needed to read it. Did I myself do it all alone? By no means. I read only the first and last paragraphs of each chapter. The rest I farmed out to my wife and children, to my cousin Ferd, and to my pastor and my beer man.

Nathless, as I have before remarked, the composition hath merit. The people in it have the fogginess and impenetrability of reality; they stand before us in three dimensions; their sufferings at the hands of fate are genuinely poignant. Of the situations it is sufficient to say that they do not seem like "situations" at all: they unroll aimlessly, artlessly, inevitably, like actual happenings. A weakness lies in the background: New York is vastly less interesting than Chicago. At all events, it is vastly less interesting to Dreiser, and so he cannot make it as interesting to the reader. And no wonder. Chicago is the epitome of the United States, of the New World, of youth. It shows all the passion for beauty, the high striving, the infinite curiosity, the unashamed hoggishness, the purple romance, the gorgeous lack of humor of twenty-one. Save for San Francisco, it is the only American city that has inspired a first-rate novel in twenty-five years. Dreiser's best books, "Sister Carrie," "Jennie Gerhardt" and "The Titan," deal with it. His worst, "The Financier," is a gallant but hopeless effort to dramatize Philadephia—a superb subject for a satirist, but not for a novelist. In "The 'Genius' " he makes the costly blunder of bringing Witla from Chicago to New York. It would have been a better story, I venture, if that emigration had been left out of it. . . .

Elia W. Peattie. "Mr. Dreiser Chooses a Tom-Cat for a Hero." Chicago *Tribune*, December 4, 1915.

No novel of the year has aroused so much discussion as Theodore Dreiser's "THE 'GENIUS'." John Cowper Powys, writing in The Little Review, refers to it as the American prose-epic. Randolph Bourne, in his article in The New Republic, says that it is Dreiser's great distinction that he is the only novelist who tries to plumb far below our conventional structure down to the subterranean currents of life. He declares that Mr. Dreiser's hero is not Eugene Witla, but that it is Desire itself. He adds that the major motive of continental writers is almost always "the inexorable desire of life, a desire which is no more physical than it is spiritual, a desire which consists often of walking in the mud with the face toward the stars. This push and yearning is what makes for religion and art in a kind of insatiable straining toward realization and perfection."

To those who have not read the book, let me say briefly that writing with complete absence of melodrama, and in a manner which he purposely permits to be sloven and casual, Mr. Dreiser unfolds the life of a country boy of talent who goes first to Chicago and then to New York that he may get into the stream of life, and incidentally that he may develop his talent. This talent might have taken any one of several directions, but Witla decides to be an artist. He is one who keeps step to the bugle notes of beauty, and who thrills to it whether he sees it in a mass of smoke stacks rising against the swarthy Chicago sky, or in a young laundry maid who looks at him with desire and expectation in her eyes. But obviously a man can do little with smoke stacks, whereas a young laundry maid's curved lips hold promises. For such promises Witla was keen. The enchantments of women dimmed all other delights. He followed them with an unrivaled zest, bringing woman after woman into his life. At last he married, but even as he did so he was wondering if he would be able to support two households, for he had no idea of relinquishing his avid mistress for the chaste embraces of a wife who believed in the arranged program of life. . . .

But I wish to say that the book does not seem to me to even faintly resemble the great American prose-epic. An epic, as I understand it, is a narrative of elevated character describing the exploits of heroes. It is bold in action; imposing. In other words, it is something to lift the mind and soul and to enable one to tread with prouder step.

Then I have to say that if this book is an epic, it is the epic of a human Tomcat. It is back fence narrative. It describes a youth who was the slave to lust at a very early age, who went from mistress to mistress till he was threatened with locomotor ataxia, who knew neither self-control nor compassion, who longed for the death of his wife, who went into poor men's homes to betray their daughters, and who had no intention of ever changing his ways. If ever a man messed along through life, serving no one, injuring many, belying the spirit within him, and letting his talents rust, it was this man. I repudiate it as the American prose-epic. I have not yet lost my patriotism, and I will never admit such a thing until I am ready to see the American flag trailing in the dusk dark with stains of my sons, and the Germans completing their world rule by placing their governor general in the White House at Washington. I feel just that strongly about it. I protest against this hypnotism which is going on in art, in which whatever is opposed to the righteous forces of the will is celebrated, and whatever recognizes the dignity and powers of mastery of the soul is regarded as banal and juvenile.

Here is a book which is called epic because it is not dramatic; which is called true to life because it is false to conscience. It is said to be above good and evil. Do not believe it. They will tell you it is a piece of magnificient objective exposition of a second rate soul, and will call attention to the fact that Mr. Dreiser has placed quotation marks around the word "genius." No book is ever objective. I tried for a long time to believe that it was possible, and that Mr. Wells and Mr. Herrick and others could really write objective books. I have learned that it is not so. A book is an emanation of personality; it is the exudation of the soul; it is the mind's product solidified into a tangible thing. In other words, it is an involuntary confession of faith. Mr. Dreiser regards the life of Eugene Witla as typical; he gives it his sympathy and indubitably he regards his hero, with his love of natural and artistic beauty and his moral idiocy, worthy to be talked about for over 700 pages. Frankly, I do not agree with him. . . .

Mr. Bourne, the critic in the New Republic, is right when he refers to Dreiser as the one who has felt most the subterranean current of life. That is true. Let him have the credit of it. No record so remarkable has been written of the nonmoral man. Mr. Dreiser, says Mr. Bourne, "writes of the erotic with an almost religious solemnity." So he does. It is well. The erotic has its enormous place in life. I would not deny it its importance, its delights, or its penalties. I have known a few men of great talent who would refuse themselves nothing. Desire was like a symphony to them, besides which all other sounds were feeble and meaningless. One of these men—he was a poet and a critic of great beauty of mind—died in a madhouse. Another, with talents hardly less, committed suicide. Another is the shame and byword of those who hoped for great things for him. This is realism. This is the debacle of those who know no self-control. But to follow these careers to their logical conclusion is thought parochial. Besides, as Mr. Dreiser would no doubt inquire, why not die in a madhouse? Why not commit suicide? What not be a byword?

I'll tell you why not. It is because the "urge, urge, urge" of which Whitman wrote, and which these defenders of the subterranean in man are forever quoting, impels normal souls to honest achievement. It does not alone demand that the life instinct shall be satisfied, but it clamors for the elevation of personality. It splendidly includes love, but it does not set sexual indulgence above other things. The normal souls grows upward even as the trees of the earth grow heavenward. One attains to something at the last—after the follies and blunders and sins. One gets at least as far as understanding that one must not wreck the happiness of others. When formulated religion has gone, and friends have failed and lovers forgotten, when one's talents seem no more than tatters and faith in humanity is as dead as any Belgian babe in the debris of its shattered home, still one clings to the spar of essential integrity in the soul.

It is true. You know it, you many thousands of men and women who read this paper. Some light which you cannot define directs you to use your powers of resistance, to cultivate your self-control, to prepare yourself for that Further Adventure which may come. The Tom cat variety of fiction will not prevail with you, no, not even though the particular Tom cat under discussion loved beauty. Indeed, all Tom cats howl most eloquently when the moon shines bright. The American prose-epic does not set itself to such a theme! Imagine the resounding laughter of Lincoln at such an idea. Yet he knew love and temptation, indecency and low jests—knew life. But he didn't permit his ideas to get mixed. He wasn't hypnotized into thinking those the great events of life. He might have written a book with an erotic egotist for its protagonist, but he wouldn't have done so without depicting that great element of good faith and integrity of purpose which arises like a background to all living creatures. If he had been a critic he would not have mistaken such a book for the American prose-epic. Would he?

Albrecht Monteglas. "Dreiser's 'Genius'." Chicago *Examiner*, December 11, 1915.

In "The Genius" Theodore Dreiser has proven that he is the greatest living American epic writer of life as it is. That he represents only one phase of this life matters not. That he has chosen in this novel to picture a life that is hardly worth while—not to the man that lives it, as he realizes in the end, and not to humanity, which owes Eugene Witla little outside of a few paintings—all that can not change this judgment. And therefore my quarrel is not with Dreiser, but with his critics.

Dreiser, like his hero, Eugene, is "so keenly interested in life as a spectacle" (page 144) that he has not time to sympathize or to moralize. The critics who find fault with Dreiser for his lack of an aim or because of his choice of subject show that they do not understand this fundamental principle of epic art. Also they forget that a literary critic as well as an art critic steps out of his sphere of jurisdiction so to speak when he criticises the subject of a work instead of the work itself.

But worse than the critic who finds fault with Dreiser for the reasons just mentioned are the ones who eulogize him for choosing as his subject a life that to them is a "masterful argument against the one-sided perversion of the Puritan" (The Little Review, vol. II., 7, page 12). What rot! As if painting a nude figure necessarily raised the painter into the highest sphere of art. Again it must be repeated that in literature as in art, and as in everything else for that matter, the thing important is not what you try to do, but how you do it. And those enthusiastic radicals are not right in their assumption. Dreiser's "Genius" an argument for freedom in sex relations! Is it indeed? How about the author's own reasonings put into Eugene Witla's self-dissection (page 394), that "idlers had nothing as a rule, not even the respect of their fellow men;" that "the licentious were worn threadbare and disgraced by their ridiculous and psychological diseased propensities;" that "one had to be strong, eager, determined and abstemious if wealth was to come"—(he might have put success in any line of endeavor for "wealth")—that "otherwise one became much what he was now, a brooding sentimentalist—diseased in mind and body." Could one express more strongly the condemnation of the Witla type? Its utter uselessness to a world that calls for strong men and women in its needs, and therefore the justification of this world to ignore it, yes, to ruthlessly thrust it aside?

And those critics have the naiveness to ask the world: "What is there to be done?" (Little Review, ibidem.) As if Witla mattered. I say these critics are worse because through their inane "howling" (ibidem) they put the other critics on the defensive and have actually succeeded in making them take up the challenge. And in the general discussion of the merits of a life like Eugene Witla's, or of its presentation in a seven hundred and thirty-six page book (critics are petty sometimes) the merit of Theodore Dreiser's art of observing and expressing the observed is almost forgotten. And a foreigner, an Englishman, must come and bring American critics who cannot see what they have in their American Dreiser to their senses! (John Cowper Powys, Little Review, Vol. I., 8).

To anybody who reads "The Genius" in the spirit it was written, as a record of a life; who opens his mind to the views that pass as to the scenes of a panorama, there must come the conviction that Dreiser has succeeded with a realism that is astounding and almost frightening in its veracity, to picture the life of a talented dilettante with a weakness for beauty in woman and of the characters of women who are attracted to such a type. If Dreiser had tried to picture a real genius he might have failed. Very likely he would have, because his force is observation, not imagination. But he did not try. Why, therefore, tell him he should have? Why belittle his work because he did not aim higher in the selection of his hero? Why be unfair and compare "The Genius" to Werther or even to Jean Christophe, when Dreiser is neither a Goethe nor even a Rolland?

Rather show us an American writer that can do better, yes, that can do as well as Dreiser; dissect human emotions, lay them bare and make us shudder at the thought of the forces that we feel are at work in every one of us? There are other human emotions, lay them bare and dealt with by Dreiser [sic], but there is no other American author to-day who can like Dreiser put them before our eyes, neither the same emotions nor any of the many others! And that is the point! That is the reason for Dreiser's, not absolute, perhaps, but relative greatness among American authors.

I repeat, Eugene Witla is not a genius. He was born a sentimental man with these brilliant talents all but wasted in an undiscipلied dilettantism. But there are men like that and like every other type of which this world of ours is made up. Whether farmer or financier, bootblack or scientist, he is part of this world and as such worth to be recorded by a master pen.

Floyd Dell. "The 'Genius' and Mr. Dreiser." *New Review*, 3 (December 15, 1915), 362-363.

I have always admired the builders of Babel. They said: "Come, let us make a city and a town, the top whereof may reach to heaven."

Mr. Dreiser has said to himself, "I will write a novel which shall be founded deep in the mire of fact, whose boundaries shall include vast territories of human striving, and with a tower of hopes and fears that shall pierce the heavens of illusion."

In the Babel project God found a certain lack of modesty, of good taste, and though the Bible does not mention it, probably a lack of finish in the minor architectural details. More pleasing to him was the humbler but more perfected work of the other builders of the period, who carved their cornices with utmost care, and put a high polish on the handles of the big front door. In this respect certain contemporary critics resemble God, and have confounded the presumptous Mr. Dreiser with the confusion of their tongues.

Mr. Dreiser's theme was in itself vast enough. His theme was the life of one of those persons who are called, and who believe themselves to be, "geniuses"; who indubitably possess some form of artistic ability, and along with that a peculiar organization of nerves, which makes them the strangest, most alluring, most unstable, and most troublesome of all living beings. He wanted to show the growth of this odd, attractive and vexatious being, his triumphs in art and his failures in life, his preposterous and malignant effect upon the lives of others, chiefly women, his vanity, his rapacity, his cruelty, his folly, his overweening selfishness, his blind graspings at happiness, his tumble into the gulfs of despair, almost of insanity, his twilight wanderings in the region of doubt, his pitiful recuperative beliefs by which he aspires upward toward the sunlight. But this is only the theme.

Mr. Dreiser's book being a novel, it was to be expected that he would represent the drama of his hero's life in some detail, physical and psychological, in front of a living background of American fields, streets, studios, offices, houses. Human knowledge being limited, and human energy more limited still, it was inevitable that some part of this huge story should be passed over lightly, suggested rather than described. But Mr. Dreiser was not content to do that. Nothing would satisfy his pride but he must tell it all, from beginning to end, not neglecting a single economic fact nor a single scrap of background, nor a single incident, nor a single thought of any of his characters which would serve to illuminate his theme or contribute to its solid reality. In this he had the precedent of Tolstoi and of Zola, to be sure. But Tolstoi did not try to put in *everything;* and Zola never had much of a story to hamper him in the amassing of materials. But Mr. Dreiser tried to put in everything and make it part and parcel of a gigantic and moving story, which should break the heart with pity and terror. It was a task requiring superhuman energy and superhuman taste. A being who possessed the powers of Dostoievsky, Defoe and Aeschylus might have accomplished it. Mr. Dreiser undertook the task.

The result shows that Mr. Dreiser possesses superhuman energy, if not superhuman taste. He has written a great and splendid book which contains many dull pages. He has given such a picture of American life as no American writer besides the late Frank Norris ever tried to give. He has written with sympathetic insight a convincing account of one of the most complex and unpleasant characters that fiction has ever dealt with. He has staged a dozen powerful dramas with beauty, sincerity and tragic force. He has exposed the depths of the human soul with a kind of relentless awe.

He has done all this in spite of a carelessness in the execution of details of which anyone else would be ashamed. In the end, one forgets those imperfections. In the shadow of these gigantic pillars one forgets the flaws of workmanship in the masonry. But God, and certain God-like critics remember them, and pour forth the vials of their wrath.

As for me, I have another quarrel with the book. I do not mind the sentences, which serve after all to convey a tremendous story. I do not even mind Mr. Dreiser's lack of a certain intellectual sophistication; what though Mr. Dreiser thinks, like his hero, that Bougereau was a great painter, or, knowing better, fails to tip you the wink when his hero stands in open-mouthed awe before the Bather with her polished toe-nails? Or what though Mr. Dreiser appears to take seriously the jejune philosophisings of his hero? It is the privilege of novelists to be mistaken or inept about things which do not, after all, matter to the art of fiction. Nor do I care greatly that Mr. Dreiser neglects to mention through three fourths of his book the sufficiently obvious fact that his hero is a cad, a vulgarian and a coward, as "geniuses" are only too likely to be. The thing that really concerns me, and the only serious flaw that I find in this story, is the author's apparent unconsciousness of the fact that his hero is an ass.

It is, I am well aware, no part of Mr. Dreiser's intention to pass judgment on his character. The tremendous impressiveness of some of his stories is due to just this, that he tells them without moralistic comment. It is an attitude that has been called Olympian; but if it were Olympian, that is, remote and aloof, it would be offensive. However, it is not that Mr. Dreiser is too far away from his story to care about its moral values, it is rather that he is too immersed in it to know. His faithful attention to exterior detail leaves an erroneous impression at times of his real preoccupation, which is precisely with the souls of his characters. And the soul, that underground world where in darkness are generated the events which afterward appear in the world of action, is one in which there is no such thing as good or evil—there are only conflicting impulses, mysterious desires. To attempt to judge these impulses by moral standards is like trying to cut an atom with a knife; for, as someone has said: "In the world of knives there are no atoms, and in the world of atoms there are no knives." In the world of action there is good and evil; but not in the hidden world of impulse. Over the entrance to that obscure world, as over the gate of Dante's hell, might be an inscription: "Abandon judgment, ye who enter here."

But when all is said, and the high credit given that is Mr. Dreiser's due as an explorer of these shadowy realms, it remains true that half of his story takes place, not in the world of impulse but in the clear daylight of the world of action, where it is difficult if not impossible to abstain from judgment. Mr. Dreiser abstains, considering it none of his business.

Mr. Dreiser tells all the facts about his hero. He suppresses nothing. But the case needs more than candor; it needs as heightened a sensibility on the part of Mr. Dreiser to comic fact as he has to tragic fact. Mr. Dreiser lacks that sensibility. When Mr. Dreiser was born, fairies came with many gifts, but among those conspicously absent was the fairy with the gift of humor. Now humor is a thing that a great poet may get along without, but a great novelist needs it badly. It is only after we have been allowed to laugh at what is ridiculous in his characters that we can begin to like them. The hero of Mr. Dreiser's book is not so utterly different from us his readers that we might not like him a little and be sorry for him a great deal if we were first permitted to laugh at him. To laugh is to forgive. But we do not forgive Mr. Dreiser's hero, we detest him.

For example: Eugene Witla, the "genius," while studying art in Chicago, becomes engaged to Angela, a country girl who lives in Wisconsin. He really believes, however, that she is his "inferior," and postpones the marriage while he conducts a series of love affairs; reluctantly marrying her at last, he proceeds to conduct more love-affairs in a spirit partly of self-righteous revenge against her for marrying him. A seeker after beauty, he descends to the most sordid intrigue, justifying himself in whatever he does, in the manner of "geniuses" and common people. Now if one had known this Eugene Witla personally, one would not necessarily have despised him; his wobblings and straddlings and subterfuges and hypocrisies and above all his solemn self-justifications, would have seemed both comic and pitiful, and when the thunderbolt came that ripped his life to pieces and left him shattered, one would have been really sorry for him. But with entire gravity, Mr. Dreiser records the gyrations of this Charlie Chaplin of the emotions, until the suspicion that Mr. Dreiser actually thinks him an admirable personage comes near to wrecking the effect of the story. Happily, there is only one genius in the book, and the women with whom Eugene's life is implicated are such that the grave and tender portraiture of Mr. Dreiser does justice to their docile charm and their passionate generosity.

These women are of all sorts and various ages, though Eugene preferred sugared sixteen; they are so different, and so admirably drawn in their differences, one wonders that they should have all possessed the same weakness, the weakness for Eugene. This, in spite of Mr. Dreiser's explanation, remains a mystery.

One knows, however, that the love of women bestows itself most bounteously, in life as in this book, upon those men who are perhaps of all mankind the most certain to abuse the gift. And it is an account of how that gift is given by women and treated by a "genius" that Mr. Dreiser's book is most tragic and most true.

Kansas City [Mo.] *Star*, December 18, 1915.

Adverse criticism and approval locked horns in mortal combat when Theodore Dreiser wrote "Sister Carrie" and "Jennie Gerhardt," which have been followed by so many other street-girl stories. When he wrote "The Financier," first of "A trilogy of desire," his admirers' ranks wavered, and "The Titan," second of the trilogy, following up with the various amorous and financial-political intrigues of Mr. Dreiser's superman, put some of his warmest admirers to rout. But it remained for "The 'Genius,'" Mr. Dreiser's 736-page latest novel, to set forth the culmination of the type he makes his principal and unprincipled chief character. The type has become an obsession with him—a habit.

In the two volumes of the trilogy the type of man he portrayed was modeled somewhat on the career of Charles T. Yerkes of Chicago, and portrayed somewhat of the inside history of that city, contemporary with the attempted bribery of Governor Altgeld. So, with such wonderful city-painting as Mr. Dreiser at times did, the unpalatable matter of the "The Titan," even, might have been passed over. But with the present novel, "The 'Genius,'" the reader is plunged into a turmoil of unbridled emotions, and beholds a procession of sordid philanderings—which, since the book is twice the length of the preceding ones, is nearly twice as dragged out and certainly doubly emphasized.

There need be no belittling Mr. Dreiser's ability or significance in passing a criticism on him for the repetition with such emphasis and detail of "affair" after "affair," wherein Eugene Witla, small town Illinois boy, rises to fame as an artist and business man and sinks correspondingly to infamy as a rational purposeful human being. There need be no denying his insight into the character he has created and the needs of various types for each other. It is the method he has chosen for his medium, and within it he works strenuously, undeviatingly, hugely.

But the question arises after the first few hundred pages of this encyclopedic work, whether he does not defeat himself by his own method, wearying the hardiest by over-emphasis of the points he makes, by analysis of Witla's character which always leads to the same results, by emphasizing the search for "the impossible she"—and ever and again bringing Eugene back to a whining "what's the use—what is the good of it all?" A country girl, a model, a school teacher who has never had her chance (she marries him and loses all chance of happiness), a musician, a gambler's wife —so the list runs. And the maddening thing is, that Eugene, in all his stumbling and failings and breakdowns—*never learns.*

Mr. Dreiser has done great work—verile, significant, valuable work. But his first and most stanch admirers are unable to voice approval of the tone and weary iteration and reiteration of "The 'Genius' " with anything like enthusiasm. And its very bulk and ponderousness adds to its unsuccess. It is too gross, in several senses of the word.

"Our American Balzac." Minneapolis *Journal*, December 19, 1915.

Theodore Dreiser's *"The Genius"* (the quotation marks are his own) has been hailed as "the American epic" by those reviewers who regard DREISER as a lesser BALZAC. But Mrs. ELLA PEATTIE, reviewing *"The Genius"* in the *Chicago Tribune,* remarks that if it is an epic, it is the epic of the human tom-cat. That about disposes of *"The Genius,"* we fancy.

BALZAC, like SHAKSPERE before him, was interested in the history of a passion. The passions he depicted were not all erotic. He made studies of jealousy, of envy, of ambition, of vanity, of the meanness we Americans denominate "pure cussedness," of acquisitiveness, and also of pure love, of unselfish devotion, of renunciation, of beauty, of religion. One meets in the pages of BALZAC characters of austerity and of various idealities. BALZAC'S women are not all essential courtsans, and his men not all various kinds of tom-cats. He depicted erotic passion faithfully, without slurring a stroke. But he was not himself enamored of eroticism, although he was curious.

For our lesser BALZAC it is asserted that he is non-moral, as Nature is, that he is content with presenting the truth, that is, the facts. But the great BALZAC was not non-moral, although to a Victorian Puritan he might seem to be immoral. BALZAC did not neglect the moral world—he could not with that comprehensive vision of his. BALZAC, moreover, was sensitive to the beauty and order of the moral world, as he was sensitive to the ugliness and discord of what the churches call sin. No intelligent student of BALZAC, but is confirmed in the wisdom and distinction of the moral life—we do not mean the respectable life—and in the folly of the life of evil.

DREISER, however, possesses no moral sense; he doesn't love virtue, he doesn't hate vice. He is engaged in portraying life as it is, without reprehension or commendation. And he succeeds in portraying life as it isn't, or he indulges in the fallacy of assuming what he portrays is broadly typical of life.

There have been great writers—IBSEN, for one—who delighted in showing up respectability for what it is, in proving that what struts as virtue and is accepted as virtue isn't virtuous. BERNARD SHAW has enjoyed that sort of employment. But we shouldn't say that SHAW hadn't a passionate love of justice, that he had a doting weakness for foul things—neither should we say that of his master, IBSEN, nor of the supreme satirist, SWIFT, nor of the MOLIERE, whose special business was the exposing of vice. A man doesn't have to be a Puritan to be a moralist. A physician doesn't have to be enamored of the disease he investigates. To flout the Pharisee and to shock the prig is all very well; but to gloat over the fact that life is pretty foul and human beings pretty mixed is to be not the American BALZAC, but a literary Caliban. Compare the character of Falstaff with this "Genius" of DREISER'S, and this point will appear. The drama of Falstaff is comedy; the fiction of *"The Genius"* is a dull copy of uninteresting fact.

Berenice C. Skidelsky. Philadelphia *Book News Monthly*, January, 1916.

To one who several months ago deplored in print the commonplaces of *The Titan*, by Theodore Dreiser, and expressed a hope that in his next effort he would make better showing, *The Genius* comes as a delight. Therein the author shows himself one of those who understand and interpret life, not in its obvious aspects, but in those elusive, delicate shadings that lend themselves to formulation only by the gifted of the earth. There are so many Europeans thus gifted, and so few Americans; that is why a kind of literary patriotism hails *The Genius*, since it is from an American pen, with a two-fold joy. . . .

The reader's personal reaction to the Eugene Witla type of man and the situations in which he is placed is a matter entirely outside the merit of the work. If the reader feels himself steeped in a morbid abnormality of atmosphere by the over-sexed nature of the man, and has an impulse to get out into the sunshine and the air for the drawing of an untainted breath, it in nowise alters the fact that nature, with her magnificent recklessness, frequently "over-endows" with sex, as she does with genius, with tendency to crime, with charm of personality, with beauty, with ugliness, with lack of intellectual capacity or strength of it, with the countless qualities good and ill that appertain to human beings. Aristotle's advocacy of the nicely balanced mean is all very well for man—but nature dearly loves extremes! It is not the business of the reader—indeed, it is not the wish of the intelligent reader who says, with Lord Bacon, that he has taken all knowledge to be his province—to question the particular human type which the author has selected for treatment. The reader's concern is with the nature of the treatment; Eugene Witla is justified in literature because he is flesh and blood. Theodore Dreiser has produced a masterpiece of psychology which is sure of a hearty reception among all lovers of realistic literature.

"A Genius and A 'Genius'." *Harper's Weekly*, January 1, 1916.

The Genius is a chunky little volume of some seven hundred pages, detailing mostly the amours of one Eugene Witla, painter, poet, and business man. Mr. Dreiser, chronicler of vulgar American types, has failed dismally with his genius. To be sure, one does not expect a genius to go always about, like an animated Roman candle, shooting off epigrams in every direction,—but somewhere, one fancies, the divine gift must come to light in a flash of poetry, a touch of wit, if only the slightest. Mr. Witla is about as witty as an operetta librettist, and not half as poetic. "Nix" is his favorite negative, and his "line of talk," an expression he himself would relish, fills me with a sort of yearning; it is so like the conversation I used to write in "English 12" stories.

Mr. Dreiser's book, apparently intended as the subtle interpretation of the "love life" of a man of temperament, is only the bald, passional record of a man as intemperamental as he is intemperate. Mr. Dreiser has powers. No one who has read *Sister Carrie* or *The Financier* can doubt that . . . but they are not subtle powers. I sometimes think of him as a sort of denatured Zola. His grasp on reality is powerful, brutal, never fine.

There are traces of Mr. Dreiser's better manner in *The Genius* enough to make it passably worth reading. Some of the earlier, less sophisticated women are admirable studies, and a scene of child birth towards the end is terrible . . . but on the whole, one gets an impression of misguided efforts, wasted powers. I might add that the book is disfigured throughout by traces of carelessness, including vulgarities of diction.

Vogue, February 1, 1916.

. . . As usual, Balzac is Mr. Dreiser's inspiration. He is as merciless in detail as Balzac himself, and if possible more tedious. Indeed his abuse of dialogue is unpardonable. Like Balzac, also, he cares nothing for style, apparently knows nothing of style except the excellent rule of directness. He employs habitually in the body of his text the cant of any trade with which he is dealing. He thinks "individual" a synonym for "man"; such phrases as these are frequent: "salable art feature," "society man," "as low as could possibly be figured," "Eugene 'stated' to Colfax," "exclusive restaurant," "he must behave himself," "a record price." Several of the characters talk like muckers; not one has the speech of a gentleman. Mr. Dreiser seems to have acquired about all that a brilliant man can acquire except taste.

Checklist of Additional Reviews

Leonard Baird. New York *Morning Telegraph*, October 2, 1915.

St. Louis *Globe Democrat*, October 2, 1915.

Cincinnati *Commercial Tribune*, October 3, 1915.

Chicago *News*, October 6, 1915.
Chicago *Evening Post*, October 8, 1915.
Detroit *Free Press*, October 9, 1915.
"New-Century Life Study in Dreiser's 'The Genius'." Philadelphia *North American*, October 9, 1915.
Joseph M. Quentin. Portland *Oregonian*, October 10, 1915.
Salt Lake City [Utah] *Herald Republican*, October 10, 1915.
Francis P. Biddle. Philadelphia *Public Ledger*, October 13, 1915.
Boston *Globe*, October 15, 1915.
"An Amorous Specimen of Genius." Boston *Herald*, October 16, 1915.
Springfield *Republican*, October 31, 1915, p. 15.
San Francisco *Bulletin*, November 6, 1915.
Buffalo *Express*, November 7, 1915.
San Francisco *Chronicle*, November 7, 1915.
Cleveland *Plain Dealer*, November 10, 1915.
Edward E. Hale. *Dial*, 59 (November 11, 1915), 422.
San Francisco *Argonaut*, November 13, 1915.
Publisher's Weekly, November 20, 1915.
"A Good and Realistic Tale of Vast Extent." New York *Sun*, November 20, 1915.
Albany *Telegram*, November 21, 1915.
Boston *Herald*, November 27, 1915.
Atlanta [Ga.] *Constitution*, November 28, 1915.
Alexander S. Kaun. "Choleric Comments." *Little Review*, 2 (December 1915), 22-24.
William C. Lengel. "The Genius?" *The International*, December, 1915, pp. 382-284.
Cincinnati *Times Star*, December 6, 1915.
Town & Country, December 10, 1915.
Newark *Evening News*, December 18, 1915.
Minneapolis *Journal*, December 26, 1915.
"Literature and Art: The Massive New Novel by Theodore Dreiser." *Current Opinion*, 60 (January 1916), 47-48.
Philadelphia *Telegraph*, January 14, 1916.
Alexander Kaun. "Homo Americanius." Daily *Maroon*, January 19, 1916.
Rochester [N.Y.] *Democrat-Chronicle*, January 21, 1916.
Ithaca [N.Y.] *Daily News*, January 22, 1916.
Denver *News*, January 23, 1916.
Lewiston [Me.] *Journal*, January 29, 1916.
Lawrence Gilman. "The Biography of an Amorist." *North American Review*, 203 (February 1916), 290-293.
Springfield [Mass.] *Republican* February 5, 1916.
Puck, February 12, 1916.
"Amatory Adventures." Philadelphia *Press*, February 27, 1916.
Chicago *Record Herald*, March 14, 1916.
The Continent, March 16, 1916.
Brooklyn *Daily Eagle*, March 18, 1916.
Floyd Dell. "Talks With Live Authors." *Masses Review*, August, 1916.

PLAYS *of the* NATURAL *and the* SUPERNATURAL

BY

THEODORE DREISER

AUTHOR OF "THE TITAN," "THE GENIUS," ETC.

NEW YORK: JOHN LANE COMPANY
LONDON: JOHN LANE, THE BODLEY HEAD
MCMXVI

Plays of the Natural and the Supernatural

Ethel M. Colson.
Chicago *Herald*,
February 26, 1916.

Whatever may be thought of Theodore Dreiser's spiritual atmosphere—and to many of us he mainly is an immoral pestilence, no less!—his artistic endowment is beyond question. The seven one-act "Plays of the Natural and the Supernatural" just published, although some time since announced, alone would sustain high contention in this regard.

The plays are not, as might be supposed, divided into two distinct classes; three, "The Girl in the Coffin," "The Light in the Window" and "Old Ragpicker," are staged on the material plane only, but even these have an evasive aroma of that which cannot be weighed or measured, and in all the rest the element of the supernatural, so-called, is treated as simply and naturally as the wind or the weather. The Shadow, Demyaphon, "an element of chemistry," Alcephoran, "a power of physics," spirits, wraiths, "The Rhythm of the Universe," "The Ghost with the Red Eyes," a faun, hama-dryads, etc., are described and employed in just the same matter of fact way as the labor leaders, the police officers, the railway engineer or the organist. Only, they play their several parts sensed rather than seen of men.

"The Girl in the Coffin," first and perhaps strongest of the poignant dramas, deals with a striking workman whose daughter lies dead for the saddest of reasons, and who, when the play begins, cannot be induced to address his expectant fellows, according to schedule. To this man, William Magnet, comes John Ferguson, the organizer who fears failure without Magnet's assistance, and who, as presently devolves, has his own bitter grief to bury deep under stern fortitude and courage. The reader, sharing the grim secret hidden from the victim's father, still cannot condemn Ferguson entirely. To say that this play is like life is to water truth with convention. It is life—life in the bleeding, the raw.

"The Blue Sphere," in which a beautiful Shadow lures beneath the fast mail the infantile monstrosity loved but dreaded by its parents, and "Old Ragpicker," also stark and relentless in its arraignment of social conditions as yet seemingly irremediable have the same flavor of intrinsic but impersonal bitterness. "Laughing Gas," paralleling the astral-earthly experiences of an eminent physician who all but loses his life through hospital inefficiency, is masterly in the quiet realism of manner superimposed upon material of such widely different order. In this mood, this manner, this apparently unstudied welding of attributes and forces ordinarily considered antagonistic if not irreconcilable, this calm acceptance of phases and hypotheses at present unverified by science, lies the root of the author's conviction. In the face of his certainty, his ease—as far removed from faith as fancy—responsive acquiescence seems the only normal course open. "The Spring Recital" and "The Light in the Window" are less effective, though more closely allied to everyday situations and minds.

Of course, there's no happiness in these plays, written rather to be read than to be acted. Mr. Dreiser, it would seem, has not yet realized simple, unheralded happiness as a distinct if not too general factor of human existence. But there is no lack of low-lying sweetness, of sympathetic insight, of philosophy keenly constructive and stimulating, of psychology wonderful as even Henry James or a college sophomore would have it, of power to move the heart and spirit like a living flame. Moreover, and here's a significant feature of perhaps Mr. Dreiser's most significant achievement, there's no immorality dragged in solely for its own sake. Alike in good and evil, in sin, sorrow and synthetic co-ordination of physical and psychic phenomena the strange, vivid, brilliant and touching plays ring true.

N. P. D.
"The New Books."
New York *Globe and Commercial Advertiser*, February 26, 1916.

If a perfectly harmless uncle will put on a fur rug and get down on his hands and knees, and growl sufficiently ominously, there are children who will shriek with terror, even while knowing all the time that it is only Uncle. In like manner, if a writer will put on a sufficiently strange garb, and lift up his voice in a strange manner, there are people who will talk of art and metaphysics, and who will be almost persuaded that the man is a genius, even while knowing he may be only—Theodore Dreiser!

Mr. Dreiser has written seven short "Plays of the Natural and Supernatural." They are unlike any plays ever written before. The comforting thing about them is that, with possibly one exception, they do not seem intended to be played, but to be kept strictly to one's closet. The most skilled play producer of our day would hardly know what to do with characters like Alcephoran (power of physics), and Demyaphon (nitrous oxide).

In addition to such reassuringly familiar friends as policemen and respectable grocers and quarrelling marital pairs, Mr. Dreiser has introduced into his plays a truly remarkable conglomeration of natural and unnatural characters. There are fauns—horned fauns with gay white teeth—that say "Tra-la-la"; cats that go "Pfhst-s-st"; and dogs that howl; child monstrosities with big, wabbling heads that gurgle "Ah-da-ooblub"; fast mail trains that roar "Oooooo-ee! ooh-ohh"; the Rhythm of the Universe that sings "Om! Om!" wraiths and spirits and dead girls in coffins; ghosts with red eyes and ghosts with hard, green eyes; Alcephoran (as we have said) and likewise Demyaphon; a monk of the Thebaid, A.D. 300, and three priests of Isis, B.C. 2840; and, to bring this strange company to a close, "clouds of Hag and Wastrel, and persistences of Fish and Birds and Animals, and various living and newly dead spirits."

The titles of the plays are "The Girl in the Coffin," "The Blue Sphere," "Laughing Gas," "In the Dark," "The Spring Recital," "The Light in the Window," and "Old Ragpicker." "The Girl in the Coffin" is the most "natural" of the plays. It portrays with a good deal of strength a dual tragedy of labor and of the individual. It is striking, has well-sketched characters, a little mystery and gruesomeness, and an effective stage setting—in short, the things that go to make up a play. But even here there are doubtless people who would be squeamish about seeing the coffin in full view on the stage. Mr. Dreiser insists that the coffin, with the girl's pale face and dark hair, shall be in view of the audience all the time. His explicit stage directions are that when any one goes to stand by the coffin he shall stand behind it. . . .

At least the compact, dramatic form keeps Mr. Dreiser within bounds. There is no space for his tongue-lapping lust for detail. And, unlike his novels, his plays are chaste enough—so far as we know what they are about. At least, they are not, like his trilogy, a "septet of Desire." But they are abnormal. They reveal the author more than ever as a literary Monstrosity, arousing curiosity and even wonder, perhaps, but not admiration.

"Word Pictures of Life of Working Class Thrill." St. Louis *Globe Democrat*, February 26, 1916.

There probably is nothing in the American drama quite like these plays, so realistic, so true to nature, and yet so suggestive of those spiritual undercurrents that are the real factors in the problem of existence. . . .

The pictures of life are quick, sudden, sharply defined, taking your breath away for the moment, in which you become conscious of their full significance, and the supernatural have the same forceful effect, the real combining with the unreal in a manner sometimes quite shocking, but always artistic.

Pittsburgh *Dispatch*, February 26, 1916.

A book of one-act plays by the author of "The Genius," "Sister Carrie," etc. Into the "natural" plays the writer injects an undercurrent of psychology which lifts them from the realm of reportorial realism and places them in the profounder category of achievement. The causation of human striving and aspiration is made of intense human interest. In the "supernatural" plays Mr. Dreiser has co-ordinated the real and the unreal, the physical and the metaphysical, making their interdependence visible and coherent. They are neither symbolical nor esoteric, but they set forth the fundamental synthesis which exists between the material and the immaterial. They are as interesting as they are startling, and will be a boon to all who delve into the radical problems of life.

San Francisco *Call*, March 4, 1916.

Theodore Dreiser has poured his disordered particularity into a new mold, that of the one-act play. The seven in this volume range from drama, drawn as surely from the souls of the characters as any action of his novels, to transcendental philosophizing in which the characters include the "Rhythm of the Universe." "The Girl in the Coffin" is genuine drama, done realistically—a situation made up of flesh and blood, hope, love and sorrow. "Laughing Gas" has for hero Demyaphon (nitrous oxide), an Element of Chemistry.

In his novels Dreiser has laid himself open to the charge of over-emphasizing criticism; here his fault is a mysticism combined of Shelley and a spectral Zola. There is poetry in "The Spring Recital," yet the dominant note of reality is given by the cat (no less a character than the ghosts), which pounces, fails, and marks for another time the church mouse. The cat overshadows even the two lovers listening to the organ music whose vibrations attract the spirits of priests of Isis, a monk of the Thebaid, a barrel house bum who has been dead only twelve years. Others, too: Dreiser has shown a predilection for the Weird Sisters since his apostrophe to Macbeth-Cowperwood; here one meets the Weird cousins and aunts as well.

And the lesson of their experience and philosophizing seems chiefly to be this: It is better to be alive than dead; for the rest, enigma. . . .

When not Buddhisitic thus Dreiser the playwright, is evasive or indecisive. The pull of life keeps spirits to the earth —and there is love. Six plays aren't required to say this, and America might find more like "The Girl in the Coffin" to be a needed tonic.

"Mr. Dreiser's Plays." New York *Sun*, March 12, 1916.

It cannot be said that THEODORE DREISER, in his new book of one act plays, *Plays of the Natural and the Supernatural* has opened up any new field of dramatic possibilities. On the contrary what one feels is that Mr. Dreiser has read his Ibsen and his Strindberg and has decided to go forth and do likewise. Unquestionably the best play of the seven contained in the book is one which falls under the heading of "Natural," namely, "The Girl in the Coffin." This play is indeed fairly impressive. Mr. Dreiser has learned the modern method of putting minutely detailed description as well as thumb nail sketches of character into his stage directions. Since plays are written nowadays, not necessarily for the stage but also for the reading public, the dramatist is learning to do away with whatever reminds the reader of the accessories of the theatre. In the first play Mr. Dreiser has used this means of making his play readable with excellent technique. The play is also a good example of the maintenance of all the unities. It takes place in a single room, within an hour and with only seven characters. . . .

Apart from false standards and superficial thinking this play is technically well made and dramatically intense.

It is when one comes to the supernatural plays that Mr. Dreiser falls down. They are very, very funny. Indeed, one wonders why Theodore Dreiser, who of all writers writing to-day is perhaps the most claybound, the most earthy of all the earthy, should have tried a flight into the supernatural. These plays are evidently not intended for the stage at all. One character in "The Blue Sphere" is "The Fast Mail," supposed to play its part, sometimes at one hundred and fifty, sometimes seventy-five and sometimes fifty miles distant. . . . Also it would be difficult on the stage to carry out the following directions: "The arc of his spirit's flight bisects the first of a series of astral planes." This sounds like Marie Correlli at her worst. Indeed we have long suspected that Theodore Dreiser was Marie Correlli's American counterpart.

The four plays, "The Blue Sphere," "Laughing Gas," "The Spring Recital" and "In the Dark," seem to have been inspired by that bold Stratfordian lady writer.

"The Light in the Window" is sordid and tawdry, but at least possible as a presentation of life. "The Old Rag Picker" has some humanitarian value. Thus far, however, Mr. Dreiser, though he has studied Strindberg and read Ibsen, is not quite in the ranks of the modern dramatists.

D. L. M.
"With the Supernatural." Boston *Evening Transcript*, March 18, 1916.

The group of one-act plays which Mr. Dreiser has included in this volume of "Plays of the Natural and Supernatural" opens up a new vista in American play writing. We do not need to be told that American playwrights have been very prone to confine themselves to certain types of experience and certain characters and parts of the country. In these plays, Mr. Dreiser, with his usual independence of mind, refuses any limitation of time or place. He even transcends the earth plane and has his characters fully cognizant of a fourth dimension. The result is startling. There is, however, even in these plays which take us furthest into the supernatural, an innate realism which distinguishes them. They never pass beyond the point of probability. On the contrary, they leave us with the feeling that we have been enabled to grasp a little more clearly the inner meanings of life and the subtle dependence of the material on the immaterial. . . .

In the midst of the undeniable impression which Mr. Dreiser's plays make upon us, we come face to face with the vital problem of the literary play. Has Mr. Dreiser been right in putting these problems of his in play form? They are not straight acting dramas. While they vary, we can say for the group that they possess too little action to take their place as anything except literary plays. In the repertory of the "little theatres" it is admitted that some of them at least could take their place, because there we have an audience who are willing to help furnish the illusion. On the other hand, it seems questionable, whether the author has gained anything by making them plays instead of short stories, because the public as such is not yet fully accustomed to the play as a type of literature to be read rather than acted. That there is room for such a literary form, and that it is already fairly well established among certain classes of readers, it is permissible to believe. It is undeniable that Mr. Dreiser makes distinct progress in the form and that he reveals both an artistic and a philosophical unity which is noteworthy. Mr. Dreiser's previous work has shown him to be a significant figure in contemporary American literature, and these plays serve to emphasize the importance of the fact.

Brooklyn *Daily Eagle,* March 18, 1916.

Theodore Dreiser's realistic novels have had such a success that his publisher has persuaded him to ransack his desk and bring out a lot of studies in dramatic form, which read as if they were written in the period when Dreiser was feeling his way and before he achieved the certainty and distinction of "Sister Carrie." The volume is "Plays of the Natural and Supernatural." The publishers say that Dreiser "has opened up an entirely new field of dramatic possibilities." It would have been much nearer the fact to say that he had "opened up an entirely new field of dramatic impossibilities," but even at that Strindberg was ahead of him, and Strindberg's supernaturalism seems more poetic and effective than Dreiser's. One of these little plays, "The Girl in the Coffin," is a vivid and ghastly piece of naturalism and ought to make an effect in vaudeville with actors like Frank Keenan or Wilton Lackaye. "The Blue Sphere" mingles naturalism and supernaturalism, but it does not seem possible for the stage or worth while for the reader. "Laughing Gas," with its footless attempt to relate the visions of anesthesia with the material world and with unknown mysteries of science is even worse.

Mr. Dreiser does not have to do this sort of thing. He has a field in which he is without serious rivalry at present. If he wishes to make experiments in other forms of art, let him burn them when they fail. Put out in book form they invoke the judgment of Don Marquis on a Georgia genius, that his poetry was "like jelly that didn't quite jell." The new poets turn out enough of that kind of stuff, without help from an artist who has mastered one field.

Los Angeles *Times,* March 19, 1916.

Mr. Theodore Dreiser, he of the realism that will not be placated, the Balzacian chronicler of marital infelicities and the adulteries of millionaires, has turned to the dramatic form, and with characteristic indifference to such little things as technique, tradition and limitations, has adapted but few of the seven plays to the dramaturgical form. In other words, five and probably six of the plays could not be played without even more "wizardry" than Belasco has yet shown.

The natural plays are a bit clumsy, especially "The Girl in the Coffin;" and

"Old Ragpicker," though an artistic study of a feeble-minded derelict, is without the dramatic theme—"action," it is sometimes called—that is, whether rightly or not is another question, required on the stage. "The Light in the Window" is the least dramatic in form, being constructed with soliloquies and segregated dialogue to show how people err in associating happiness with wealth.

The worst has been said. Meeting Mr. Dreiser on his ground, and every artist has the right to choose his medium, we must tear down the curtains between our material and the dimensionless world of those who have died, and let in a number of ghosts. This is required in all the "supernatural plays."

Mr. Dreiser remains essentially the novelist; his belong to narrative rather than to drama; they are scarcely narrative, either, but rather mordant, fanciful studies interpreting what he has conceived as the way invisible spirits might view and influence our lives.

The most dramatic is unquestionably "In the Dark." Because all of the "supernatural" plays have been called fanciful studies does not imply that they are weaklings; though they have vividity rather than what is usually meant when a play is said to have dramatic strength. . . .

In "The Spring Recital" Mr. Dreiser's fancy is impressive, but there is reason to suspect that if he did not do so naturally he would deliberately inject something irreverential, a little of that uncouthness and shabby brutality which realists of his type seem to think essential to all comment and pictures of life. Stress on outcasts and derelicts may as easily become an affectation, pronounced and unattractive as the now much-laughed-at love-sickness of the Victorian novelists and poets. And among the stately ghosts of Egyptian priests, monks and others, who come as shadows to listen to the organist, disgruntled at the few people in attendance and unaware of his invisible audience, comes also the bum; and this bum supplied a comic relief, not greatly dissimilar to the comic tramp of melodrama. It would be going wholly outside of critical jurisdiction to say the play is "spoiled" by it, but the impressiveness of the piece is lessened by the inevitable and not unamused attention given to this eccentric and insolent ghost.

The plays are unique, especially among "supernatural," a sustained and uniform attitude is shown; they are something more than eccentric, than the bid of novelty for attention. Back of them, back of the words, back of the stories, is an idea; and the ideas have been worth the variations Mr. Dreiser has used.

G. D. "Fourth Dimensional Dramas." San Francisco *Chronicle*, March 23, 1916.

Theodore Dreiser, author of that truly remarkable story, "Sister Carrie," breaks entirely new ground in "Plays of the Natural and Supernatural," a series of seven dramatic monstrosities, some of which are absolutely unplayable. Indeed, they might without any great exaggeration be called fourth dimensional dramas. The laws of time are shown some respect, but the laws of space are put into the discard. Everything is present and before the reader, though some of the incidents and conversations are occurring hundreds of miles away.

This is particularly true of "The Blue Sphere," a very short play in which the dramatist sets aside all the limitations of his art and embraces those privileges of the novelist by which space is annihilated. In the novel the reader expects to be moved all over the globe if necessary to the telling of the story. In one chapter we may be in New York, in the next in Russia, and in the third back in New York again or here in San Francisco. The dramatist may also move from act to act, but there is something uncanny about hearing a conversation in a grocer's kitchen interrupted by the dialogue of an engineer and his fireman one hundred and sixty miles away. And they are not asides—not the remarks of a chorus stepping before the curtain to enlighten us as to the action. The author sees and hears everything material to his purpose and sets it down precisely in order, but the whole could never be presented except by dissolving pictures thrown on a screen and helped out by voices from the wings.

For the rest the thing is simplicity itself. Indeed the work is so simple as to become obvious. A monstrosity is born to a grocer and his wife. It has a head almost twice the size of a normal one, but though three years old can neither walk nor talk. The father thinks that it would be much better if the child should die and the mother has her temporary leanings to the same thought. But they are only temporary and she is really fond of it. The Shadow dances before the child's eyes, luring it away from home by enticing it to crawl after the blue sphere. This imaginary being also whispers to everybody passing through the gate to leave it open. The fast express keeps coming on and the engineer and his fireman break into the dialogue every ten miles or so. There is no escape from the conviction that when the train reaches the immediate scene that it will run over the infant. It does, and that tragedy is really the happy ending of the play.

Is this a valuable or an impossible form of the drama? Is it not going the limit in the movement for the play for reading only, and if plays are for reading only then why bother to preserve any stage traditions? Why not frankly interrupt the dialogue with straightforward descriptions and character portraits and dispense with the custom of directions printed aplogetically in italics? Far better to be frankly fictional in form.

The publishers are correct in saying that these plays possess "that artistic and philosophic unity which takes them at once outside the realm of reportorial realism and places them in the profounder category of achievement where one becomes conscious of the motivating impulses of existence, of the psychological undercurrents of causation, of the great flux and reflux of human striving and aspiration." They possess all these things, but that does not make them drama. A statue hollowed out in such wise as to accommodate a phonograph and fitted with movable lips to give the illusion of life would be a monstrosity, and so is a play which is partly novelistic and only partly dramatic. Genius never complains of the limitations of its art, but, recognizing them, manifests itself in triumphs over them. The painter is confined to one surface, but he creates the appearance of depth; the sculptor is restricted to an even color, but he makes it vivid by the eloquence of form; the dramatist is hemmed in by the requirements of the stage, but if he have genius, we are made to feel the world behind the scenes.

Llewellyn Jones. "Men and Ghosts." Chicago *Evening Post*, March 24, 1916.

Taking Mr. Dreiser's own division of the seven plays in this volume, let us deal first with the plays of the "natural." Some of them, such as "The Girl in the Coffin" and "Old Ragpicker," are actable, but others, like the supernatural plays, use the dramatic form simply for its literary value, and thoughts are expressed which the characters do not put into words, and changes of scene are made in such a way as to make actual staging of the plays impossible. In these cases, however, the author justifies his novel use of the dramatic form by the effects he is thus able to produce.

Mr. Dreiser, of course, is a realist and enough of his opinions have been expressed in interviews for the announcement of such a volume as this to excite unusual curiosity. What possible interest can he have in the supernatural? we can imagine many a reader of the title asking. The book, however, answers that.

The "natural" plays treat life as one would expect Mr. Dreiser to treat it in the form he has here chosen. There is the same honesty of presentation we have seen in his novels, the same disillusionment, and, in addition, a kindliness in the depiction of weak and abused characters that is sincere and native. This last quality shines out particularly in "Old Ragpicker," which is a study of a derelict who was once a rich factory owner, but who has now lost everything —wife, friends, money, home, even the memory of his own name. Such of his pitiful story as is given us is elicited thru the conversation between themselves and the questioning of the derelict by two policemen, and the reactions of the policemen are especially well done and most revelatory of that careless kindliness, atrophied, however, when it comes to doing anything, which characterizes most people in this world in which kindness is such an expensive virtue. "The Girl in the Coffin" may also be mentioned as a pathetic study in the dangers and pains which involve lover and loved one in a world which subordinates love to alien necessities and taboos.

But why should Mr. Dreiser write supernatural plays? The answer is plain in "The Spring Recital," for here he uses the supernatural in one of its minor but legitimate roles—social criticism. To an organ recital in an old New York church various presences from fauns and their ilk to a bygone minister of the church and ancient priests and a monk are attracted. They converse, and thru their remarks Mr. Dreiser is enabled to satirize many things from religion to love.

But there is a more serious use for the supernatural in literature, and in the attempt to achieve this we cannot see that Mr. Dreiser answers the above question satisfactorily. There are certain feelings and associations of place, certain kinds of fears, vague emotions, emanations of the soul, which come from and appeal to the marginal parts of our being, from the childish parts or the intuitional parts of the total consciousness, from the echoing corridors of early or even ancestral memories, perhaps, or from recollections of those loved but now dead. To express such phases of life as those, the supernatural in art is legitimate whether we believe in an objectively real supernatural world or not. . . .

Now, our objection to Mr. Dreiser's use of the supernatural is that it is all machinery; and the other name for machinery is mechanism; and mechanism is a philosophy of the world which absolutely shuts the door on supernaturalism. For even if, on the mechanistic principle, ghosts were proved to exist, they would be reduced to phenomena, subsumed under some new law or other, and lose at once their ghostly freedom, their "uncontrollable mystery" and their power to raise the dickens with our nerves. . . .

There are certain things which Mr. Dreiser can do excellently well: some of those things he does in this volume, but his exploration of the extra-mundane abysm of being is emphatically not one of them.

Buffalo *Express*, March 26, 1916.

This series of studies, stripped of every unnecessary line by their presentation in dramatic form, reveals their author in a new guise and, incidentally, opens up a new field of dramatic possibilities. The plays for the most part are not actable, unless, perhaps, in a house given over to stage studies that are somber and harrowing, but they are plays to be read, analyzed and pondered on. . . .

In his supernatural plays Mr. Dreiser has co-ordinated the real and the unreal, the physical and the metaphysical in such a way that their interdependence is made visible and coherent. They are as interesting as they are startling, and, because of their verity, are of the utmost significance to those interested in the basic progress of art and in the radical problems of life.

Jack Barrows. Denver [Colo.] *Times*, April 5, 1916.

Mr. Dreiser's plays are not meant to be acted. Only two of the seven contained in this new volume could be acted and in one of these the action is centered about a coffin, in which a corpse reposes. But Mr. Dreiser's plays are meant to be read and they will bear reading. By the sharp, dramatic style, with its ghostly characters, brief description and staccato speeches, Mr. Dreiser brings out in naked form weird ideas that would be far less interesting in literary clothing. It is a volume of the greatest interest.

The ghostly forms of troops of spirits make the work fascinating. Mr. Dreiser's religious beliefs, if he has any, are evidently strictly original. We have in one play the rhythm of the universe, saying endlessly, "Om! Om! Om! Om! Om!" in another, a red-eyed ghost that dotes on blood; in another, a spirit with a blue sphere, who leads a malformed child to death; in another, the spirits of priests and clergy of times separated by many centuries, discussing the delusions they pursued on earth.

It is all deeply interesting and unmarred by a single long speech or long sentence. Surprises are numerous. It seems to be a new departure in imaginative but graphic literature. . . .

Girard [Kan.] *Appeal to Reason,* April 15, 1916.

This book of one-act plays is by the author of "The 'Genius,'" a novel which was reviewed in this column recently. Mr. Dreiser, we believe, is a writer of great importance. In his novels he strikes an original note. He pictures life sincerely; his realism is inexorable. Mr. Dreiser, in these seven plays, has done work which should attract serious thinkers to this most delightful form of art.

Dreiser's plays are very readable. The first, "The Girl in the Coffin," is a labor play, the reading of which is a pleasurable experience. In fact, it is one of the best one-act labor plays we have ever read. Its action is lightning-swift, but at every moment it is convincing and sincere.

The mad tumult of existence is never chaotic to this graphic, vigorous writer. He understands life; he sees its drama, its pathos, its grim despair and troubled mien.

We were moved by the last play, "Old Ragpicker." Here is an old, bleareyed victim of capitalist society who has been crushed so heartlessly that he is no longer a human being. When asked what his name is he cannot answer; he has forgotten. After a great effort, "Old Ragpicker" says his name is "Ragpicker." He cannot think of any other.

We heartily recommend this striking book of plays to our readers. If only "The Girl in the Coffin" appeared between its covers we would be as firm in our praise. But here you have seven plays—a treat indeed!

American Review of Reviews, 53 (May 1916), 634.

Theodore Dreiser's "Plays of the Natural and Supernatural," are as gripping as the work of Galsworthy and Synge. The "Natural" plays are realistic dramas. The "supernatural" might be called metaphysical dramas in that they are dependent upon the essential nature and relations of those realities of being that lie beyond the domain of the senses. They are startling, significant episodes of life wherein the most of the action takes place in the unseen world, yet so closely coördinated with actual physical reality is the play of beings and forces in the unseen, that the reader may hardly know where the one ends and the other begins. . . . Everyone who is interested in the progress of the American drama will welcome this new departure in the field of dramatics.

Montrose J. Moses. *Book News Monthly,* May, 1916.

It was said of Baudelaire that he tried to create a new shudder; and there is no doubt that in this respect Mr. Theodore Dreiser has come under the decadent school of symbolistic playwriting. Yet none the less has he produced a most remarkable volume, which he has rightly called "Plays of the Natural and Supernatural," and which he has connected closely with the life of his own time and of his own locality. It is surprising that, with his realistic tendencies, he should so successfully mingle realism with what one might almost call a super-symbolism, and produce such definite psychological effects. He has not only made use, as Maeterlinck made use in "The Interior," of hidden forces, but he has likewise utilized that element of distance and that quality of the passing of time which Henry James once claimed were so difficult to reproduce in literature.

Mr. Dreiser's seven plays are all of them disagreeable, not in the sense that Shaw's plays are "unpleasant," but through the sheer story they have to tell, rather than because of the condition they might criticise. As a playwright, Mr. Dreiser does not stand in the position of the critic. He photographs the condition as he sees it and, having an X-ray attachment to his artistic camera, he at the same time gives us the drama of unseen forces playing about his characters.

There is only one play which, in its unity of time and place, is suitable for stage production. This is the one—"The Girl in the Coffin"—which Mr. Emanuel Reicher was to have produced had his theatre been as long as the public announcements of his cause. Though the plot of this play is very evident, it is to be warmly noted because it is a sincere attempt to bring upon the stage a life which is close to the soil. No one but Mr. Dreiser so far has been conscious of the fact that what the theatre needs is to be kept close to the soil. Over in England we get that soil quality in Masefield, in Housman, in McEvoy, in Mrs. Havelock Ellis but in this little one-act play, Mr. Dreiser does psychologically what Mrs. Wharton has done in such a close study of New England life as "Ethan Fromme."

Quite remarkable in its effect is "The Blue Sphere," wherein a whole village life is reflected and disaster cumulates in the shape of an approaching train. In "Laughing Gas" we get the fight with death that a patient makes on the operating table, and we are fully conscious not only of the operation but of the subconscious state of the man under the influence of an anodyne. "In the Dark" reflects the furore in a locality where murder has taken place, and the final hunting of the murderer to his lair. And so we might go on with these little impressionistic sketches, giving a bald description without fully indicating the interesting technique Mr. Dreiser has employed.

What we are anxious to find out is whether Mr. Dreiser, whose interest is evidently centering upon the theatre, will be able to write a play subject to the conditions of the playhouse. He has produced in this volume a restlessness which, on the stage, would scarcely be permissible throughout an entire evening's entertainment. His cleverness in this book lies in the fact that he almost hypnotizes his reader into the nervous state he desires; but in the theatre there must always be a conservation of energy, and from that standpoint none of Mr. Dreiser's seven little plays will stand the test.

It strikes us that this volume is an experimental one with him, and we are wondering whether he will be as successful in creating cheerful moods as in creating a type of shudder not often repeated in American literature since the day of Poe. To readers of his novels this volume will come as a surprise. To the critic it comes as a distinctly new element in playwriting in this country. But the volume must not be taken too seriously as a contribution to the theatre. Mr. Dreiser will have to travel a long road—as Maeterlinck traveled it after writing his "marionette dramas"—before he has mastered the technique of the theatre. His little pieces now published for the first time consist of panoramic states of mind centering on a main story. I do not see how they could be whipped within the confines of the proscenium arch and the footlights. They are moving pictures in dialogue form.

Indianapolis *News*, May 20, 1916.

In a group of seven extraordinary fantasies entitled "Plays of the Natural and the Supernatural," Theodore Dreiser has struck chords of elusive and unknown harmonies which are none the less beautiful and haunting for all their unfamiliarity. But Mr. Dreiser has drawn upon every conceivable sphere of existence and nonexistence for his characters and moves with absolute nonchalance from plane to plane without regard for the exigencies of scene-shifting and other such details connected with the production of plays. As fantasies of spirit, earth, heaven and hell, these are interesting reading; as plays they are not possible save perhaps the "Girl in the Coffin." There is not enough unity of place in the entire volume to make a good-sized comic opera book. Mr. Dreiser might have done well to have selected another title for his book.

Springfield [Mass.] *Republican*, May 28, 1916.

In another field Theodore Dreiser has written a book that should have the recognition of his "The 'Genius,'" but probably will not—"Plays of the Natural and Supernatural." Some of the plays of the natural are apparently mere sketches, but each of them has a bit of the vital that makes it more important than its material. This vitality is, of course, the Dreiser in them and it is what makes the book of plays worthy of a place alongside of "The 'Genius.'" The author is voluminous in stage directions and thus ekes out the bald outline of dialog. Whether this artifice is responsible or whether, as he undoubtedly has, he has succeeded on making the characters autophotographic through the magic of the English he has put into their mouths, the fact remains that Mr. Dreiser has produced a book of plays that stands head and shoulder above the books of plays of a season that has been replete with them. Principally because of existing traditions and conventions it will be recognized by the reader that there are difficulties, in the way of production of these plays, but that is a far cry from saying that they lack dramatic qualities. . . .

H. L. Mencken. "A Soul's Adventures." *Smart Set*, 49 (June 1916), 154.

Of the current play books, the only one that interests me is "Plays of the Natural and the Supernatural," by Theodore Dreiser, a volume containing seven pieces, four of which have been printed in THE SMART SET. Of the seven, that which shows the best promise of popular success is "The Girl in the Coffin," a somewhat obvious piece of realism but with saving overtones. The four plays of the supernatural are: "The Blue Sphere," "Laughing Gas," "In the Dark," and "The Spring Recital." In each of them Dreiser tries to depict dramatically the blind, unintelligent, unintelligible forces which lie behind all human motives and acts. Superficially, they may seem to reveal an abandonment of his "chemic" theory for mysticism, but that seeming is only seeming. The two are really no more than diverse aspects of a single philosophy. That philosophy, like Joseph Conrad's, has for its central idea the fortuitousness and inexplicability of human life, and you will find it running unbrokenly through all of Dreiser's books, from "Sister Carrie" down to this last one. The criticism which deals only with externals often praises him for making Carrie Meeber so clear, for understanding her so well, but the truth is that his achievement in his study of her consists rather in making visible the impenetrable mystery of her, and of the vast complex of muddled striving and aspiration of which she is so helplessly a part. It is in this sense and not in the current critical sense that "Sister Carrie" is a profound work. It is not a book of glib explanations, of quasi-scientific cocksureness; it is, beyond all else, a book of wonder.

Dreiser's characteristic lack of technical cunning is plainly seen in some of these plays. "The Girl in the Coffin," for example, is too long. Its content and doctrine would be better discerned if it were not so heavily blanketed with words. Again, "The Spring Recital" seems but half worked out, and "The Light in the Window," in more than one place, comes perilously close to banality. But these defects are more than made up for by the photographic observation shown in "Old Rag Picker" and by the disarming plausibility and impressiveness of "The Blue Sphere" and "In the Dark." If these pieces had been done by Maeterlinck or by some fantastic Russian, the noise of their celebrity would be filling the ears, but with Dreiser's name upon them, I doubt that they will arouse much enthusiasm among the lady critics, male and female, of our fair republic. These pious numskulls, in truth, seldom consider him as an artist; they almost always content themselves with belaboring him as an immoralist. The reviews of "The 'Genius'" themselves reviewed, would make a curious contribution to Puritan psychology, and if my health holds out, I may attempt its confection later on. The book was read with a salacious eye, as Sunday School boys read the Old Testament, and then denounced pontifically as naughty. I wonder what the smut hounds will find to shock them in his plays!

"Seven Plays By Dreiser." Philadelphia *Press*, June 18, 1916

Dreiser, in these new plays, has written a most remarkable volume in the symbolical school of playwriting, in which he connects closely realism and symbolism, and, in the mingling, produces definite and unusual psychological effects. He has opened up an entirely new field in dramatic possibilities. In the "natural" plays, he portrays more than the mere accurate transcriptions of life,—they possess an artistic unity, which takes them out of the realm of repertorial realism, and places them in such a way that one becomes conscious of the motivating impulses of existence, —of the psychological undercurrents of causation.

In the "supernatural" plays, Dreiser introduces a novel element into dramatic effort. He has combined the real and the unreal, the physical and the metaphysical, in such a way that their interdependence is made visible and coherent. They contain, what might be called, for want of a better term, the "fourth dimension."

None of the plays are pleasant, because of the story they tell. They create a shudder, as did Edgar Allen Poe. . . .

This is Dreiser's first attempt in the dramatic, and although the impossibility of staging these plays is evident, still, considered as a piece of literature, the book is most excellent, and it is to be hoped that more of the same style will be forthcoming from the author's versatile pen.

William Marion Reedy. *Reedy's Mirror*, July 14, 1916.

There's one bit of drama in Theodore Dreiser's "Plays of the Natural and Supernatural" that has not yet been surpassed in one-act plays by any American writer. It is "The Girl in the Coffin." I shall not tell its theme, its very tragic theme of a "sinful" love that was yet a happy, noble one. The action moves in speech about the girl in the coffin whose love yet lives. There's a stern, almost Roman duty-theme involved in the love-affair; an exaltation of a cause above personal grief or revenge or regret, and there's a faith and trust that make conventional moralities meretricious. Mr. Dreiser's play is terribly condensed and intensified. He is as sparing of words in his little plays as he is lavish of them in his novels. His motive simply burns through his rather spare method. In the realm of the supernatural, "The Blue Sphere" in this volume is a high achievement. Here is mysticism brought into a highly plausible relationship with our modern, materialistic world. It is, if not superbly imaginative, at the very least the highest reach of the finer fancy. "The Ragpicker" is another bit of fanciful reality that in a remote and not imitational fashion, suggests the attitude, as distinct from the method, of Maeterlinck. In these plays Mr. Dreiser is more the artist and less the reporter than in his fiction. He is more concerned with spiritual substances than with material superficies. One rejoices over Dreiser's emancipation from the catalogic.

Philadelphia *Public Ledger*, July 15, 1916.

Is it a limitation of the English language, or the elasticity of the dramatic form that leads the writer, anxious to convey his impressions of humanity, to classify them under the title of "Plays"?

In Theodore Dreiser's volume, "Plays of the Natural and Supernatural," are seven so-called plays, but with the exception of the first, entitled "The Girl in the Coffin," they are formless impressions of human phases. . . .

But in each of these fantastic sketches lurks an idea worthy of expression. The author has given us accurate impressions of life, experience and human character, and it is not to be wondered at if, in an effort to link the realism of these impressions with the overpowering sense of the unseen forces that control human life, Mr. Dreiser has found the dramatic form inadequate.

Whether these subtle and powerful reflections belong in a metaphysical treatise, in a poem, in essays, in fiction or in movie scenarios it is hard to say. At any rate Mr. Dreiser has something worth while to tell us, and so long as he expresses himself in the form in which he has scored such a brilliant success, our literature will be enriched by his work.

Bruce Bliven. "Some Spooky Drama." *Outlook*, August, 1916.

Theodore Dreiser is determined to startle. After wearying us with the interminable pages of his "Genius" he publishes a thin little volume of one-act plays which are the apotheosis of condensation. Moreover, he invents an entirely new technic, whereby he shifts his scene from one point to another as rapidly as motion pictures do; and further complicates his surprise by introducing a strong undercurrent of mysticism of an unclassifiable sort. Add to this the fact that he includes among the characters introduced into the dialogue spirits, voices, subliminal selves, chemical elements, physical powers, and even the rhythm of the universe, and you get an interesting potpourri.

Only one of these plays, "The Girl in the Coffin," could be put upon the stage; and it is perhaps the least interesting in the book. The fact that these plays are unactable does not, however, keep them from being dramatic. Every one of them is calculated to produce a shudder—or at least, a chill; and one or two of them are horrible. They show characteristics of Mr. Dreiser which even his faithful followers since the days of "Sister Carrie" can hardly have suspected; and they will surely afford thoughtful hours to every student of the drama.

"The Understanding of Mr. Dreiser." *Nation*, 103 (October 12, 1916). 355.

In the mud and scum of things something always sings to the not over-nice ear of Mr. Dreiser. Relentlessly pursuing the ugly, he has bagged in these seven short plays: a death through an illegal operation ("The Girl in the Coffin"); the death of an idiot struck by a railway train ("The Blue Sphere"); the removal of a tumor ("Laughing Gas"); the murder of an Italian gambler by his brother, the fruit-peddler ("In the Dark"); the drifting of pagan priests, monks, hags, wastrels, nymphs, and fauns through a city church ("The Spring Recital"); a domestic row and smash-up—we use the words for their "connotative" value—in the "best residence section of an old but fashionable district in the heart of a great city" ("The Light in the Window"); and the dribbling and decay of a ragpicker ("Old Ragpicker").

Those whose appetite for this sort of thing is not yet equal to one of the author's immense novels may well be recommended to try his flavor here. Though, of course, without the massiveness of his narrative fictions, these little dramas give a very fair impression of his surly sincerity and crude power. No one can question his ability to use his physical eyes and ears, and to find words for the sensational life. His minor personages in particular—policemen, workmen, street Arabs—fairly reek with actuality; and more elaborate studies like the labor leader in "The Girl in the Coffin" and the ragpicker have an advantage over the heroes and heroines of the novels in being presented without explicit "philosophical" commentary. Any one who has had the pleasure of lying on an operating table under an anaesthetic may repeat his sensations at leisure, and, on the whole, without very serious after-effects, by reading "Laughing Gas." The subject seems perhaps slightly "rococo"; yet, as in these days of facile surgery almost every one has had the experience, it may be said to possess one requisite of a classical theme—universal interest.

The well-written advertisement on the jacket of the volume advises us the plays "possess that artistic and philosophical unity which takes them at once out of the realm of reportorial realism and places them in the profounder category of achievement where one becomes conscious of the motivating impulses of existence, of the psychological undercurrents of causation, of the great flux and reflux of human striving and aspiration." We fail to discover much in them—or in Mr. Dreiser's other works, for that matter—of essentially human "striving and aspiration"; but the rest of the statement is sound enough. Through his piquantly original dramatic persons—chemical elements, voices, phantoms, and squalid human creatures—Mr. Dreiser does manage to express his curious gloomy bewilderment about the universe, his sense of the hollow hypocrisy of religion, his conviction of the impotence of ideas and the omnipotence of animal and mechanical forces, his somewhat sardonic satisfaction in brutality, his aesthetic pleasure in what he conceives to be man's natural tendency to degradation.

Horridly interesting, original, and, we believe, honest, work like this reminds one in a roundabout way—undoubtedly Mr. Dreiser intended that it should—of certain ancient saws about the function of art: "Through the contemplation of works of art, to keep alive in the mind a high unapproachable ideal"; or "The highest aim of art is beauty, and its last effect the feeling of pleasure"; or "The object of art is to raise man above common life and to waken in him a sense of his divine origin." These are rather pretty and winsome notions; one clings to them. Before one who has pleased one's self with them can yield to the seductions of Mr. Dreiser's art and his philosophy, one wants to be assured that one cannot help it. One wants to be certain that Mr. Dreiser has seen all and said the last word. It would be a great satisfaction to know, for example, what none of his works betray, that he thoroughly understood some of the genuinely fine products of civilization—for instance, a lady or a gentleman.

Detroit *Times*, February 19, 1917.

These plays of Mr. Dreiser can easily take their place beside those of Isben, Brieux and Maeterlinck. They are radical in their social lessons, exquisite in their depth of feeling and symbolic like those of the great Belgian. Just how any virile mind can consider that Mr. Dreiser is a harmful factor in the country, it is difficult to imagine. The case of "The Genius" is now being tried in the courts, and the Author's League of America as well as the foremost writers of Great Britain are behind the author.

The present volume contains a play which for pathos and dramatic power can only be compared with the "Maternity" of Brieux. From a literary standpoint, it is perfect. It is called "The Girl in the Coffin," and each character is a very cosmos of the emotions of the universal life. The entire life of "the girl" is felt by a few words from those about the coffin and the most perfect touch is that of the little, simple, old woman who feigns complete ignorance while knowing the entire story.

Mr. Dreiser is an artist. He is one of the very few Americans who sees American life as it is and is able to find a soul in the hard, commercial tawdryness of it all. His is the magic touch which transforms the common, ordinary, daily struggle of men and women into something heart-breaking, noble and divine. There is no circumstance so sordid but Theodore Dreiser can see beneath it the cause, the excuse and the possible good. His is a big soul, and America would better recognize her geniuses than wait until Europe has shown them to her. It was not until England had found Poe and Whitman that we were able to understand that here, at last, we had produced a poet.

Checklist of Additional Reviews

Boston *Herald,* February 26, 1916.
Detroit *Free Press,* March 5, 1916.
Detroit *News Tribune,* March 7, 1916.
New York *Evening Sun,* March 11, 1916.
Elia W. Peattie. Chicago *Tribune,* March 18, 1916.
Los Angeles *Graphic,* March 18, 1916.
Saturday *Evening Post,* March 25, 1916.

New Orleans *Times Picayune,* March 26, 1916.

Kansas City [Mo.] *Star,* April 1, 1916.

Bookseller, April 1, 1916.

Denver *News,* April 2, 1916.

Milwaukee *Evening Wisconsin,* April 4, 1916.

Book Review Digest, May, 1916.

Bougar *Daily Commercial,* May 6, 1916.

Louisville *Courier-Journal,* May 8, 1916.

Cincinnati *Times Star,* May 8, 1916.

Book Chatter, June, 1916.

"Music and Drama." *The Independent,* 86 (June 26, 1916), 554.

Detroit *Saturday Night,* July 22, 1916.

New England Magazine, August 1916.

Vogue, *October,* 1916.

"Plays to Read." Providence [R.I.] *Journal,* December 24, 1916.

Homer E. Woodbridge. "Some Experiments in American Drama." *Dial,* 62 (May 17, 1917), 440

Theatre, July, 1917

A HOOSIER HOLIDAY

BY

THEODORE DREISER

WITH ILLUSTRATIONS
BY FRANKLIN BOOTH·

NEW YORK: JOHN LANE COMPANY
LONDON: JOHN LANE
THE BODLEY HEAD
MCMXVI

A Hoosier Holiday

H. L. Mencken. "The Creed of a Novelist." *Smart Set*, 50 (October 1916), 138–143

The similarity between the fundamental ideas of Joseph Conrad and those of Theodore Dreiser, so often exhibited to the public gape in this place, is made plain beyond all shadow of cavil by the appearance of Dreiser's "A Hoosier Holiday." a volume of mingled reminiscence, observation, speculation and confession of faith. Put the book beside Conrad's "A Personal Record" (*Harper, 1912*), and you will find parallels from end to end. Or better still, put it beside Hugh Walpole's little volume, "Joseph Conrad," in which the Conradean metaphysic is condensed from the novels even better than Conrad has done it himself: at once you will see how the two novelists, each a worker in the elemental emotions, each a rebel against the prevailing cocksureness and superficiality, each an alien to his place and time, touch each other in a hundred ways.

"Conrad," says Walpole (himself a very penetrating and competent novelist), "is of the firm and resolute conviction that life is too strong, too clever and too remorseless for the sons of men." And then, in amplification: "It is as though, from some high window, looking down, he were able to watch some shore, from whose security men were forever launching little cockleshell boats upon a limitless and angry sea . . . From his height he can follow their fortunes, their brave struggles, their fortitude to the very end. He admires that courage, the simplicity of that faith, but his irony springs from his knowledge of the inevitable end.". . . Substitute the name of Dreiser for that of Conrad, with "a Hoosier Holiday" as text, and you will have to change scarcely a word. Perhaps one, to wit, "clever." I suspect that Dreiser, writing so of his own creed, would be tempted to make it "stupid," or, at all events, "unintelligible." The struggle of man, as he sees it, is more than impotent; it is meaningless. There is, to his eye, no grand ingenuity, no skillful adaptation of means to end, no moral (or even dramatic) plan in the order of the universe. He can get out of it only a sense of profound and inexplicable disorder, of a seeking without a finding. There is not only no neat programme of rewards and punishments; there is not even an understandable balance of causes and effects. The waves which batter the cockleshells change their direction at every instant. Their navigation is a vast adventure, but intolerably fortuitous and inept—a voyage without chart, compass, sun or stars . . .

So at bottom. But to look into the blackness steadily, of course, is almost beyond the endurance of man. In the very moment that its impenetrability is grasped the imagination begins attacking it with pale beams of false light. All religions, I dare say, are thus projected from the soul of man, and not only all religions, but also all great agnosticisms. Nietzsche, shrinking from the horror of the abyss of negation, revived the Pythagorean concept of *der ewigen Wiederkunft*—a vain and blood-curdling sort of comfort. To it, after a while, he added explanation, almost Christian—a whole repertoire of whys and wherefores, aims and goals, aspirations and significances. Other seers have gone back even further: the Transcendentalists stemmed from Zeno of Elea. The late Mark Twain, in an unpublished work, toyed with a characteristically daring idea: that men are to some unimaginably vast and incomprehensible Being what the unicellular organisms of his body are to man, and so on *ad infinitum*. Dreiser occasionally dallies with much the same notion; he likens the endless reactions going on in the world we know, the myriadal creation, collision and destruction of entities, to the slow accumulation and organization of cells *in utero*. He would make us specks in the insentient embryo of some gigantic Presence whose form is still unimaginable and whose birth must wait for eons and eons. Again, he turns to something not easily distinguishable from philosophical idealism, whether out of Berkeley or Fichte it is hard to make out—that is, he would interpret the whole phenomenon of life as no more than an appearance, a nightmare of some unseen sleeper or of men themselves, an "uncanny blur of nothingness"—in Euripides' phrase, "a tale told by an idiot, dancing down the wind." Yet again, he talks vaguely of the intricate polyphony of a cosmic orchestra, cacophonous to our dull ears. Finally, he puts the observed into the ordered, reading a purpose in the displayed event: "life was intended as a spectacle, it was intended to sting and hurt" . . . But these are only gropings, and not to be read too critically. From speculations and explanations he always returns, Conrad-like, to the bald fact: to "the spectacle and stress of life." The bolder flights go with the puerile solutions of current religion and morals. Even more than Conrad, he sees life as a struggle in which man is not only doomed to defeat, but denied any glimpse or understanding of his antagonist. His philosophy is an agnosticism that has almost got beyond curiosity. What good would it do us, he asks, to know? In our ignorance and helplessness, we may at least get a slave's comfort out of cursing the gods. Suppose we saw them striving blindly too, and pitied them?

The function of poetry, says F. C. Prescott, in "Poetry and Dreams" (a book so modest and yet so searching that it will be years before the solemn donkeys of the seminaries ever hear of it), is to conjure up for us a vivid picture of what we want, but cannot get. The desire is half of the story, but the inhibition is as plainly the other half, and of no less importance. It is this element that gives its glamour to tragedy; the mind seizes upon the image as a substitute for the reality, and the result is the psychical *katharsis* described by Aristotle. It is precisely by the same process that Dreiser and Conrad get a profound and melancholy poetry into their books. Floating above the bitter picture of what actually is, there is always the misty but inordinately charming picture of what might be or ought to be. Here we get a clue to the method of both men, and to the secret of their capacity for reaching the emotions. All of Conrad's brilliant and poignant creatures are dreamers who go to smash upon the rocks of human weakness and stupidity—Kurtz, Nostromo, Lord Jim, Almayer, Razumov, Heyst, even Whalley and M'Whirr. And so with Carrie Meeber, Jennie Gerhardt, Frank Cowperwood and Eugene Whitla. They are not merely vivid and interesting figures; they are essentially tragic figures, and in their tragedy, despite its superficial sordidness, there is a deep and ghostly poetry. "My task," said Conrad once, "is, by the power of the printed word, to make you hear, to make you feel—it is, above all, to make you *see.*" Comprehension, sympathy, pity—these are the things he seeks to evoke. And these, too, are the things that Dreiser seeks to evoke. The reader does not arise from such a book as "Sister Carrie" with a smirk of satisfaction, as he might from a novel by Howells or James; he leaves it infinitely touched. . . .

Mr. Walpole, in his little book, is at pains to prove that Conrad is neither realist nor romanticist, but an intricate combination of both. The thesis scarcely needs support, or even statement: *all* imaginative writers of the higher ranks are both. Plain realism, as in the early Zola, simply wearies us by its futility; plain romance, if we ever get beyond youth, makes us laugh. It is their artistic combination, as in life itself, that fetches us—the subtle projection of the muddle that is living against the orderliness that we reach out for—the eternal war of aspiration and experience—the combat of man and his destiny. As I say, this contrast lies at the bottom of all that is vital and significant in imaginative writing; to argue for it is to wade in platitudes. I speak of it here simply because the more stupid of Dreiser's critics—and what author has ever been hoofed by worse asses!—insist upon seeing him and denouncing him as a realist, and as a realist only. One of them, for example, has lately printed a long article maintaining that he is blind to the spiritual side of man altogether, and that he accounts for his characters solely by some incomprehensible "theory of animal behaviour." Could one imagine a more absurd mouthing of a phrase? One is almost staggered, indeed, by such critical imbecility, even in a college professor. The truth is, of course, that all of Dreiser's novels deal fundamentally with the endless conflict between this "animal behaviour" and the soarings of the spirit—between the destiny forced upon his characters by their environment, their groping instincts, their lack of courage and resourcefulness, and the destiny they picture for themselves in their dreams. This is the tragedy of Carrie Meeber and Jennie Gerhardt. The physical fact of their "seduction" (they are willing enough) blasts them doubly, for on the one hand it brings down upon them the conventional burden of the pariah, and on the other hand the worldly advancement which follows widens their aspiration beyond their inherent capacities, and so augments their unhappiness. It is the tragedy, too, of Cowperwood and Witla. To see these men as mere melodramatic Don Juans is to fall into an error almost unimaginably ridiculous.

The salient fact about them, indeed, is that they are *not* mere Don Juans—that they are men in whom the highest idealism strives against the bonds of the flesh. Witla, passion-torn, goes down to disaster and despair. It is what remains of the wreck of his old ideals that floats him into peace at last. As for Cowperwood, we have yet to see his actual end —but how plainly its shadows are cast before! Life is beating him, and through his own weakness. There remains for him, as for Lord Jim, only the remnant of a dream.

With so much ignorant and misleading criticism of him going about, the appearance of "A Hoosier Holiday" should be of service to Dreiser's reputation, for it shows the man as he actually is, stripped of all the scarlet trappings hung upon him by horrified lady reviewers, male and female. The book, indeed, is amazingly naif. Slow in tempo, discursive, meditative, it covers a vast territory, and lingers in far fields. One finds in it an almost complete confession of faith, artistic, religious, even political. And not infrequently that confession comes in the form of somewhat disconcerting confidences—about the fortunes of the house of Dreiser, the dispersed Dreiser family, the old neighbors in Indiana, new friends made along the way. As readers of "A Traveller at Forty" are well aware, Dreiser knows little of reticence, and is no slave to prudery. In that earlier book he described the people he encountered exactly as he saw them, without forgetting a vanity or a wart. In "A Hoosier Holiday" he goes even further: he speculates about them, prodding into the motives behind their acts, wondering what they would do in this or that situation, forcing them painfully into laboratory jars. They become, in the end, not unlike characters in a novel; one misses only the neatness of a plot. Strangely enough, the one personage of the chronicle who remains dim throughout is the artist, Franklin Booth, Dreiser's host and companion on the long motor ride from New York to Indiana, and the maker of the book's excellent pictures. One gets a brilliant etching of Booth's father, and scarcely less vivid portraits of Speed, the chauffeur; of various persons encountered on the way, and of friends and relatives dredged up out of the abyss of the past. But of Booth one learns little save that he is a Christian Scientist and a fine figure of a man. There must have been much talk during those two weeks of careening along the high-road, and Booth must have borne some part in it, but what he said is very meagrely reported, and so he is still somewhat vague at the end—a personality sensed, but scarcely apprehended.

However, it is Dreiser himself who is the chief character of the story, and who stands out from it most brilliantly. One sees in the man all the special marks of the novelist: his capacity for photographic and relentless observation, his insatiable curiosity, his keen zest in life as a spectacle, his comprehension of and sympathy for the poor striving of humble folks, his endless mulling of insoluble problems, his recurrent Philistinism, his impatience of restraints, his suspicion of messiahs, his passion for physical beauty, his relish for the gaudy drama of big cities, his incurable Americanism. The panorama that he enrolls runs the whole scale of the colors; it is a series of extraordinarily vivid pictures. The sombre gloom of the Pennsylvania hills, with Wilkes-Barré lying among them like a gem; the procession of little country towns, sleepy and a bit hoggish; the flash of Buffalo, Cleveland, Indianapolis; the gargantuan coal-pockets and ore-docks along the Erie shore; the tinsel summer resorts: the lush Indiana farm-lands, with their stodgy, bovine people—all of these things are sketched in simply, and yet almost magnificently. I know, indeed, of no book which better describes the American hinterland. Here we have no idle spying by a stranger, but a full-length representation by one who knows the thing he describes intimately, and is himself a part of it. Almost every mile of the road travelled has been Dreiser's own road in life. He knew those unkempt Indiana towns in boyhood; he wandered in the Indiana woods; he came to Toledo, Cleveland, Buffalo as a young man; all the roots of his existence are out there. And so he does his chronicle *con amore*, with many a sentimental dredging up of old memories, old hopes and old dreams.

Strangely enough, for all the literary efflorescence of the Middle West, such pictures of it are very rare. I know, in fact, of no other on the same scale. It is, in more than one way, the heart of America, and yet it has gone undescribed. Dreiser remedies that lack with all his characteristic laboriousness and painstaking. When he has done with them, those drowsy villages and oafish country towns have grown as real as the Chicago of "Sister Carrie" and "The Titan." One sees a land that blinks and naps in the sunshine like some great cow, udders full, the cud going—a land of Dutch fatness and contentment—a land, despite its riches, of almost unbelievable stupidity and immobility. We get a picture of a typical summer afternoon; mile after mile of farms, villages, little towns, the people sleepy and empty in mind, lolling on their verandas, killing time between trivial events, shut off from all the turmoil of the world. What, in the end, will come out of this over-fed, too-happy region? Ideas? Rebellions? The spark to set off great wars? Or only the silence of decay? In Ohio industry has already invaded the farms; chimneys arise among the haystacks. And so further west. But in Indiana there is a back-water, a sort of American Midi, a neutral ground in the battles of the nation. It has no art, no great industry, no dominating men. Its literature, in the main, is a feeble romanticism for flappers and fat women. Its politics is a skeptical opportunism. It is not stirred by great passions. It knows no heroes. . . . What will be the end of it? Which way is it heading?

Save for passages in "The Titan," "A Hoosier Holiday" marks the high tide of Dreiser's writing—that is, as sheer writing. His old faults are in it, and plentifully. There are empty, brackish phrases enough, God knows—"high noon" among them. But for all that, there is an indeniable glow in it; it shows, in more than one place, an approach to style; the mere wholesaler of words has become, in some sense, a connoisseur, even a voluptuary. The picture of Wilkes-Barré girt in by her hills is simply done, and yet there is imagination in it, and touches of brilliance. The sombre beauty of the Pennsylvania mountains is vividly transferred to the page. The towns by the wayside are differentiated, swiftly drawn, made to live. There are excellent sketches of people—a courtly hotel-keeper in some God-forsaken hamlet, his self-respect triumphing over his wallow; a group of babbling Civil War veterans, endlessly mouthing incomprehensible jests; the half-grown beaux and belles of the summer resorts, enchanted and yet a bit staggered by the awakening of sex; Booth *père* and his sinister politics; broken and forgotten men in the Indiana towns; policemen, waitresses, farmers, country characters; Dreiser's own people—the boys and girls of his youth; his brother Paul, the Indiana Schneckenburger and Francis Scott Key, author of "On the Banks of the Wabash"; his sisters and brothers; his beaten, hopeless, pious father; his brave and noble mother. The book is dedicated to this mother, now long dead, and in a way it is a memorial to her, a monument to affection. Life bore upon her cruelly; she knew poverty at its lowest ebb and despair at its bitterest; and yet there was in her a touch of fineness that never yielded, a gallant spirit that faced and fought things through. *Une ame grande dans un petit destin:* a great soul in a small destiny! One thinks, somehow, of the mother of Gounod. . . . Her son has not forgotten her. His book is her epitaph. He enters into her presence with love and with reverence and with something not far from awe. . . .

In sum, this record of a chance holiday is much more than a mere travel book, for it offers, and for the first time, a clear understanding of the fundamental faiths and ideas, and of the intellectual and spiritual background no less, of a man with whom the future historian of American literature will have to deal at no little length. Dreiser, as yet, has not come into his own. In England his true stature has begun to be recognized, and once the war is over I believe that he will be "discovered," as the phrase is, in Germany and Russia, and perhaps in France. But in his own country he is still denied and belabored in a manner that would be comic were it not so pathetically stupid. The college professors rail and snarl at him in the *Nation* and the *Dial;* the elderly virgins of the newspapers represent him as an iconoclast, an immoralist, an Anti-Christ, even a German spy; the professional moralists fatuously proceed to jail him because his Witlas and his Cowperwoods are not eunuchs—more absurdly still, because a few "God damns" are scattered through the 736 crowded pages of "The 'Genius.'" The Puritan fog still hangs over American letters; it is formally demanded that all literature be made with the girl of sixteen in mind, and that she be assumed to be quite ignorant of sex. And the orthodox teachers sing the hymn that is lined out. In Prof. Fred Lewis Pattee's "History of American Literature Since 1870" (*Century*), just published, there is no mention of Dreiser whatever! Such novelists as Owen Wister, Robert W. Chambers and Holman F. Day are mentioned as "leaders"; substantial notices are given to Capt. Charles King, Blanche Willis Howard and Julian Hawthorne; five whole pages are dedicated to F. Marion Crawford; even Richard Harding Davis, E. P. Roe and "Octave Thanet" are soberly estimated. But not a line about Dreiser! Not an incidental mention of him! One recalls Richardson's "American Literature," with its contemptuous dismissal of Mark Twain. A sapient band, these college professors!

But the joke, of course, is not on Dreiser, but on the professors themselves, and on the host of old maids, best-seller fanatics and ecstatic Puritans who support them. Time will bring the Indianan his revenge, and perhaps he will yield to humor and help time along. A Dreiser novel with a Puritan for its protagonist would be something to caress the soul—a full-length portrait of the Eternal Pharisee, a limning of the Chemically Pure, done scientifically, relentlessly, affectionately. Dreiser knows the animal from snout to tail. He could do a picture that would live. . . .

E. F. Edgett. "Theodore Dreiser on a Hoosier Holiday." Boston *Evening Transcript*, November 15, 1916.

Several years ago Mr. Dreiser took a journey eastward to Europe, and shortly thereafter he wrote a book about it called "A Traveler at Forty." Recently he went westward to the scenes of his boyhood in Indiana, and as might be expected, the result is another book embodying his observations and impressions. In everything he writes Mr. Dreiser is nothing if not voluminous, and whether his subject be the life of a Jennie Gerhardt, or a Frank Cowperwood, or his own personal adventures, he may be depended upon to leave no important portion of the tale untold. It is largely as a stickler for detail that Mr. Dreiser has become the most discussed and most assailed American novelist of the present day.

Out of the story of his wanderings to and through his native Indiana, Mr. Dreiser has made a portentous book. It is a stout and heavy volume of five hundred pages, and they are alive with the mingled imaginative feeling and sturdy devotion to facts that have given a vigorous realistic atmosphere to all of Mr. Dreiser's novels. From the outset of the chronicle the reader finds himself in the grip of a thorough master of the art of story-telling, and he accompanies Mr. Dreiser through every stage of his journey with an enthusiasm akin to his feeling for a hero of fiction. In brief, Mr. Dreiser has the knack of writing fiction as if it were fact, and an ability to make fact seem like fiction. . . .

No one who knows Mr. Dreiser through his novels . . . will imagine for a moment that the story of his travels is confined to a mere record of the places through which he passed. In it, as in his novels, he has written a study of his own soul and has given many views of his outlook on life. We may read it to know something of Indiana, and the country on the way there from New York, but we may read it also to discover something of the vigorous intellectual equipment of a writer of apparently limitless imagination. And the subject of sex. Of course Mr. Dreiser cannot overlook that all-absorbing topic!

Henry Blackman Sell. Chicago *News*, November 22, 1916.

The faithful who for many years have gazed toward Theodore Dreiser as the novelist of the times and who have acclaimed his every production as The Great Interpretation (censors, conservatives, et al., to the contrary notwithstanding) may for the time being lay aside their defiant expressions. Their leader has written such a book as those who admired his singular powers, but could not subscribe to certain phases of his philosophy, had begun to think him incapable of writing, to wit, a book in which the sex urge does not reign supreme.

What power of mind or spirit has contrived to free this truly inimitable artist from the sex lunacy which has seemingly possessed him we do not pretend to know—in the ecstasy of welcoming him back to sanity we do not care; what concerns us here is his return.

Never—a word used after deliberation—has there been a more incisive and yet just criticism of America and Americans written in this country than "A Hoosier Holiday," Dreiser's latest.

Dreiser has the remarkable faculty of making fiction read like fact and fact read like fiction. Add to this his almost uncanny "nose for news"—to speak in journalese—and you have something of the strangely fascinating style which has apparently drawn to this unusual writer the largest and in some ways the most loyal audience in this country despite the depravity of much that he has written.

"A Hoosier Holiday" has for its excipient a journey—via motor and in company with Franklin Booth, the noted illustrator—from New York city to the author's boyhood haunts in central Indiana. A less original writer would have offered the narrative to us in the form of a diary, for such is its character.

The route of this sentimental journey is by no means hackneyed—beaten paths and "cities of importance" were carefully avoided—nor are the observations by the way of the usual sort.

Dreiser has a fierce, brave hatred of sham, dogma and empty living; a keen appreciation of sincerity wherever it is found; an exquisite feeling for beauty; and exceptional understanding of humanity and human endeavor and a saving grace of humor that makes his comment on the most trivial or the most important sight, happening or condition well worth reading.

A glance at [his] biography . . . will assure the reader of Dreiser's peculiar fitness to undertake the task of critical commentary on these United States and the inhabitants thereof. As has been intimated he fulfills that task past all expectations.

A rounded critical work must have its unpleasant as well as its pleasant phases; "A Hoosier Holiday" is no exception to that rule. It contains many irritating fatalisms and pessimistic observations which need not be taken at their face value if one chooses to disagree. Dreiser has lived deeply—at times violently. He has forsaken much that many intelligent persons hold as sacred ground. He has found knowledge in ways which seem strange even to the radical mind, but his sincerity is not for a moment to be questioned, nor is the total of his findings to be denied as a comprehensive basis for life interpretation.

The book will especially recommend itself to his admirers as an incomplete autobiography. The ideals and ambitions of his youth and early manhood are here dramatically suggested as is the philosophy which has occupied his much discussed condemned and praised novels.

As a book "A Hoosier Holiday" is one of the most satisfying volumes of the year. The heavy olive board covers, soft sepia paper and large clear type only accentuate the charm of the text. Books are often disgracefully shabby in paper and type. The John Lane company has occasionally been an offender in this respect, but all is forgiven in admiration of the present volume.

Prophecy is a vain occupation, but we venture to indulge in it occasionally. "A Hoosier Holiday" will outlive Theodore Dreiser and all his former works.

New York *Globe and Commercial Advertiser*, November 25, 1916.

One way to look at it is that Mr. Theodore Dreiser never gives his readers a fair chance to judge him fairly. His books are so long that a reader gets groggy before half through. Mr. Dreiser's latest book, "A Hoosier Holiday," sounds innocent. But the first line trenches of Hoosierdom are not reached until page 256, and it is not until page 283 that we read the welcome words, "Warsaw at Last!"—where Mr. Dreiser first was kissed!

There are more than five hundred pages in all, not counting some omissions, due to a censorship ("Out upon the swinish mass!" as he now says), or to a discretion that is sometimes preferred to valor, or to simple error, we are unable to say. But it is exasperating on page 315, for example, when in the middle of one of Mr.Dreiser's thoroughgoing descriptions of a kiss—the glowing and shivering and response of atom to atom —to have the pages suddenly skip to 321. Let us hope, however, the omitted pages are due to inadvertence. Instead of censoring or expurgating Mr. Dreiser's books, the same result may surely be attained, and more simply, by letting everybody read them—all of all of them.

For Mr. Dreiser can be depended upon, if given sufficient white paper to wear out the most valiant of his readers. His literary or writing method suggests the old writer who put all his punctuation marks at the end of his book, with advice to readers to pepper and salt to suit themselves. Mr. Dreiser jumbles everything together (bad eggs as well as good) and leaves to the reader to select and harmonize and interpret to suit himself; in other words, to sink or swim in the deluge of print indiscriminately provided.

Perhaps if a reader were patient enough, out of these more than five hundred pages describing Mr. Dreiser's automobile trip from New York to his native Indiana, with Mr. Franklin Booth, his illustrator (and host), could be built up a picture of life and scenes along the route. At least there is no difficulty in building up a life-size portrait of Dreiser himself, and as in the puzzle picture, after you have once seen the man in the tree you can't see anything else—except the ladies. . . .

In "A Hoosier Holiday" Mr. Dreiser's writing style is as undistinguished as ever. Details are indiscriminately scraped up and shovelled out as realism, an apparently innate and repellent coarseness is set up as a noble truth telling, while the commonplaces of thought are paraded as philosophy, and crude apostrophe is made to do scant service for profound reflection. Mr. Dreiser apostrophizes everything from Love to Terre Haute. Chapters end with "Even so! Even so!" and there are as many "alases" in the book as in the girl's obituary poetry which Huck Finn was fired to emulate. . . .

New York *Sun*, November 26, 1916.

Readers of "The Genius," "Sister Carrie," "Jennie Gerhardt" and the other books of THEODORE DREISER may learn what manner of man this author is in his latest volume, *A Hoosier Holiday*. His book is four books: the record of an automobile trip from New York to Indiana in company with the Hoosier artist Franklin Booth, whose drawings adorn the volume; a criticism of America's democracy, with special attention to the mingling of native and alien elements; an autobiography and a philosophy of life. For any one of these Mr. Dreiser's readers must explore the whole volume. . . .

The interest of this book is not the Middle West, not the sights along the road, not the cooking and the clothes, the restaurants and hotels, not the morals and manners of the people, but Theodore Dreiser, dropping sharp words about women and religion and life—and about Theodore Dreiser. The pages flash and sparkle. They also rumble and sometimes explode. They change the subject as often as the dictionary does, but preserve some sort of a balance by running Theodore Dreiser through it all. Some of it is pure fake; some of it is genuine—genuine joyousness, genuine indigestion of the spirit. The pages about the old home smile through tears. The autobiographical paragraphs are almost too interesting; the autobiography of a novelist must be. Altogether a big, blazing book. Whether the glow comes from fires of genius or from dry reeds kindled may be found debatable. . . .

"Travel in America." *Dial*, 61 (November 30, 1916), 474.

After an absence of nearly three decades Mr. Theodore Dreiser was moved to revisit the scenes of his early life. The journey was pleasantly made in the motor car of his artist friend, Mr. Franklin Booth, these two with the chauffeur composing the party. "A Hoosier Holiday," written in Mr. Dreiser's well-known manner of mingled description, anecdote, dialogue, and philosophic reflection, details the incidents of the summer outing in a highly readable manner, while Mr. Booth's frequent drawings by the way—sketches of a pleasant softness and dreaminess, done in charcoal or crayon—add charm to the whole. For a man not very much over forty, Mr. Dreiser is perhaps unduly fond of assuming the part of the world-weary, the disillusioned, the *blasé* (the one best word for it all), as if life and love and all the delightful possibilities of the future held nothing further in store for him. One reads him always with enjoyment, but this same Hoosier-holiday narrative might have been made equally interesting and equally true to the facts without any indulgence in what at times savors of a contemptuous superiority to the innocent and simple joys of human existence. If one has outgrown these joys, it is a misfortune, not a thing to be paraded with complacency. Perhaps a few more decades will work a change and make Mr. Dreiser as young in heart as he now is in years.

Brooklyn *Eagle*, December 2, 1916.

. . .For that considerable body of readers who care little or nothing about Indiana, but who have read Mr. Dreiser's novels, and who have tried to believe that an American Balzac had thrust his head above our horizon, this book may be interesting for a certain light it throws upon Mr. Dreiser's intellectual processes. Whatever difference of opinion there may be about the power or the truthfulness of Mr. Dreiser's novels, there is no disputing the fact that they are fearfully long-winded and overlaid with detail. The same thing is true of Balzac, and in the novels of both men you try to believe that the multiplication of detail is necessary to make the realistic picture for which they are aiming. An artist is largely a law unto itself as to method so long as he produces truthful and artistic results, and there is no questioning the truthfulness of much of Dreiser's detail.

But when it comes to travel a writer has no such leeway on the score of artistic necessity. Any man who can be trusted with a typewriter can write a book of travels if he has seen the country, and some men manage to do it from bunches of picture post cards supplemented with a gazateer. Also he can make his account long or short to fit the patience of his readers or the requirement of his publishers. There is no question that Mr. Dreiser's book would have been more readable if it had been only half as big. Details are piled up here to wearisomeness, just as they are in the novels, and now without the excuse of having to register a character or a mood. They are included simply because Mr. Dreiser sees things in full detail instead of by outlines, and because, apparently, like Richard Wagner, he is vain enough to believe that anything he has written is important just because he wrote it. Frankly, there is a great deal of this book which is not important, and which would have adorned the waste basket much more effectively than it does the printed page. . . .

"Mr. Dreiser Goes Traveling." Chicago *Tribune*, December 2, 1916.

Though the more especially fanatical worshippers within the inner holy of holies of the Theodore Dreiser cult will no doubt pronounce the book a masterpiece, the fact remains that Dreiser's "A HOOSIER HOLIDAY" is a case of verbiage—words! words! words!—rather than anything else. The volume's publisher describes it on the over cover as "a vivid picture of the middle west," "a criticism of America," "a confession of faith," "a personal record," and an account of "the author's own youth and early aspirations."

But to one who is neither the book's publisher nor a fanatical Dreiserite it seems on the whole a mass of radical cant of the platitudinarian variety of shallow if frequently true enough observations, and of nowise strikingly original criticism—the whole being done in characteristically Dreiserian worse than slipshod English. . . .

"Theodore Dreiser's New Book Affords a Near View of American Scenes." New York *Herald*, December 2, 1916, p. 7.

Theodore Dreiser revisited the scene of his birth in Indiana and has written a book about the journey. He calls it "A Hoosier Holiday," and it is published by the John Lane Company. These facts may not sound as startling as an announcement of a new sex novel by Mr. Dreiser, but the new book is a larger contribution to American literature than any of his previous offerings. In a way the book is revolutionary, for its author has discovered that the American hinterland is an unexplored field of tremendous wealth, which may be garnered by anybody who can describe it. . . . [Mr. Dreiser] has introduced philosophy, wit, philistinism, iconoclasm and perhaps a bit of egoism into his vivid chronicle until it has become as interesting as a novel. The book is the best writing that has been done by an author who will be appreciated more in the future.

Philadelphia *Press*, December 3, 1916.

Theodore Dreiser's books have been given the uninvited advertising of the purity leagues. Unjustly, most of us reviewers think. But whether or not you like his books, you are sure to like Theodore Dreiser, unless of course you prefer mummified human nature. He tells about himself in this book. Not so much as you might like to know, once you have been permitted a glimpse of some of the pages of his life, but enough to show him as a frank, speculative and dreamy chap who looks at life with the seeing eye and fearlessly sets down what he has seen. . . .

Mr. Dreiser loves life. He loves all the wonder and the maze and the drive of it. He possesses a pity for error and suffering that is profoundly moving. He is tolerant with exceptions. When he meets with dogma and institutionalized religion and sex suppression and the money grubbing, tawdry-minded middle class he slashes at it with impetuous wrath and vigorous invective.

Had Mr. Dreiser merely written the record of a 2000 miles auto ride the book might have had little more than passing interest. The drive was tame and tepid. The most intense excitement of the journey was the occasional blowout, the author's hunt for banana pie and Booth's wail for more musk melons. But he has etched into this route all his fancies and forebodings; the vivid beauty of mountain, hill and glen and starlit nights and delectable days. The route cut open to Mr. Dreiser's view a cross section of American life and drove straight into the heart of the Middle West. Stirred to describe it and comment on it, he has spread through these pages, acute and keen passages on the trend and direction of American life, and in turning up the things which struck his mind he plumbed deeper, elucidating his thought on the infinite and eternal and the passion and position which shapes his own career.

From the foregoing it is seen that the volume defies definite classification. But altogether it is a captivating book, scintillating with beautiful description of nature, shot through with the observations of a trained and sympathetic mind, reflecting thoughtfully and sharply the life and aspirations of the American people—a book which has something in it to hold readers of nearly every taste. . . .

New York *Evening Sun*, December 9, 1916.

It does not thrill us ecstatically to learn from the jacket that Theodore Dreiser's "A Hoosier Holiday" contains that author's confession of faith. Readers of Mr. Dreiser's previously published books have learned much of his faith both in the lines and between them. It is a powerful faith and a sincere one, but few of us find it sympathetic.

It is more hopeful to learn that this large and attractive volume of over five hundred pages will give a vivid picture of the middle West. It fulfils this promise manfully. It is an account of an automobile trip across the States which lie between New York and the Hoosier country to those old haunts in Indiana where the author was born and where he spent most of his youth. It is more or less a labor of love, therefore, and the journey a sentimental and most reminiscing one. Something of a pot pourri (it is kinder to use the foreign term), it leaves, in the end, the pleasant impression of a fragrant but indiscriminate and mediocre dish.

It is interesting to know of Mr. Dreiser's youth, as it is interesting to know the youth of every man whose work has brought him forward into the light. In some of his descriptions of home—the one he left and the one he came back to —he achieves a distinction of style which heretofore has been always missing in his work. But most of the book has his faults—overlengthiness and heaped-up inconsequentials—and here they seem twicefold swollen. He sprinkles it all with a humor which is not quite sharp enough to give it a tang, and at times his ruminations by the wayside fall into the dull whine of a complaint that makes for nothing at all. . . .

Los Angeles *Times*, December 10, 1916.

. . . "A Hoosier Holiday" is a peculiar book. Perhaps but few people will find the whole of it interesting, but none should fail to discover much that is absorbing. It is a curious conglomeration. Excepting "A Traveller at Forty," with its marked lack of reticence, this is about the only directly personal writing that Mr. Dreiser has given to the public; and it is much like his novels—intense where it is not listless; wordy; philosophical in spots; always veering from anything that looks like it might have the popular viewpoint; and most of it sicklied o'er with the pale cast of melancholy thought—when not flaming and rebellious.

"Theodore Dreiser Revisits Indiana." Indianapolis *Star*, December 11, 1916.

It is a queer sort of book that Theodore Dreiser offers in "A Hoosier Holiday." Though Dreiser is an Indianian, having been born in Terre Haute and received his education at Warsaw and Bloomington, he is not commonly counted among the authors of the state probably because he has not lived within its borders for half a lifetime, and his literary reputation has been the product of his later years. Last year, in company with Franklin Booth, the illustrator whose parental home is at Carmel in Indiana, just north of Indianapolis, he made a motor car trip from New York and revisited the scenes of his youth. This book is a record of the tour, but it is more than a mere description of places. He incorporates in it his philosophy of life and discusses social problems. He presents in a scattered way a sort of confession of faith, and it is easy from these discourses to see that the peculiar characteristics of his novels are presentations of his personal views. The sex element, for example, which, in his fiction, has brought so much criticism upon him is explained by his ideas on the subject clearly set forth in the book and by a relation of his own thoughts and experiences showing his possession of an abnormal sex consciousness. His comments on the young women encountered while on his tour indicate this.

Mr. Dreiser has made a volume of more than 500 pages in describing his holiday, but does not reach Indiana until the 256th page. Then he comes to Warsaw and goes back across the border of boyland and indulges in many personal and sentimental reminiscences. He is extremely frank in regard to his family and it is conceivable that any member who may be living will look upon his disclosures of their poverty and their disagreements with displeasure. Families of schoolmates and early associates, some of whom, he finds, have gone to the bad, will hardly enjoy his free setting forth of the information he receives. In numerous cases he gives the names of the persons asked about. Some of his reminiscences are of the grim sort that suggest the unpleasant realism of the Spoon River graveyard.

He devotes two or three chapters to Warsaw—mainly to recollections rather than present conditions. He finds the changes rather melancholy, as returned natives usually do, even though many improvements may have been made. From Warsaw they took their way south, through the "chautauqua belt"—North Manchester, Wabash, Peru, Kokomo and finally Carmel. At the last-named place he spent three days with the Booth family, then continued his tour, going to Terre Haute, then south to French Lick, Evansville and back to Indianapolis. He comments but briefly on the capital city. He sees nothing distinctive about it and says: "There is a river there, the White, with which nothing seems to have been done, except to build factories on it at one place; but, on the other hand, a creek called Broad Ripple—pretty name that—has been walled and parked and made most agreeable to look upon."

Terre Haute, the city of his birth, had a mournful fascination for him and he offers another chapter of depressing family reminiscences, as well as some of more pleasing character.

As in his novels, Mr. Dreiser is altogether too much given to detail, but the comments made mainly in a friendly tone, on his home state and its towns are interesting. The book will doubtless do more to make Indianians acquainted with Mr. Dreiser than his novels have done.

William Marion Reedy. *Reedy's Mirror*, December 14, 1916, pp. 839–840.

At the risk of being accused of "slopping over," I will say here that one of the best American books in I know not how long is "A Hoosier Holiday," by Theodore Dreiser. You may not care for Mr. Dreiser's novels, "Sister Carrie," "Jennie Gerhardt," "The Financier," "The Titan," "The Genius." Even you may sympathize with the moral boneheads who have been trying to get the authorities to suppress the latter novel. For myself I think there are very decided elements of greatness in Dreiser's novels. They are elemental and yet they have an art of their own as well. He may be called indiscriminating in choice of material, but he is not, actually. He is trying to grasp the American in all his multifariousness, trying to give us the big chaotic effect of American life. And he does it—does it better than anyone among us who is writing to-day. If you want to find Dreiser as he is, you should go to his book, "A Hoosier Holiday." There you will discover, too, his philosophy. There also you will discover the United States more honestly limned, yet lovingly withal than in any other book I can recall. You will find things in the book raw and crude. But even as the big volume is made beautiful by the drawings of Franklin Booth, the artist who accompanied Dreiser on his "Hoosier Holiday," you will discover the crudities of the narrative turned to something rich, rare and delicate by the very genuine sympathy of Dreiser. He tells us of an automobile trip through New York, Pennsylvania and Ohio to his boyhood home in Indiana. He leaves nothing out. His record is a glorified guide-book, but into all that he sees Dreiser puts Dreiser. And if Dreiser does take himself seriously, nevertheless he is a good, honest, sound-hearted and direct thinking Dreiser. If you have ever been an American boy brought up in a small town and you do not find yourself touched to something close to tears by the way in which Dreiser visualizes in retrospect his youth, there is something wrong with you. Here and there are flashes of bitterness of memory, but they do not last for long. They melt into a beautiful sympathy for all American life, for its lack of aesthetic value, for its unilluminated materialism, for its deprivation of culture, for its lack of vision. Dreiser is beauty-hungry. He craves for the beauty of life. He is a sort of behemoth raging that he did not and does not live in a Renaissance. His esurience positively burns in these pages. For a page or two he breaks forth into what seems like contempt, but the mood passes and the people whose sodden contentedness he condemns are spoken of in terms of endearment. All this accompanies a most microscopic observation. Nothing is too small to escape record, and when recorded, philosophizing thereon.

As you get along in the book you find in Dreiser a Superman. He has not much faith in anything. He admires idealists but dismisses them with a sad smile. He cannot see any order in the scheme of life. So far as I can make out, he thinks that everything and everybody are moved by some incomprehensible life-force—some force which, according to our view, is little short of insane. Possibly we are working out into a new race which shall have no trace of ourselves. Dreiser doesn't know. But he cares. He cares that we miss so much of the joy and beauty of life as we go along from darkness to darkness. It is this true philanthropy of his that saves his—what shall I call it?—atheism from being utterly horrible. I gather from Dreiser and all his works, and especially "A Hoosier Holiday," the same impression I get from Gobineau's "The Renaissance." The Superman may be all right, but eventually democracy or the ochlocracy "gets" him. The Supermen are all failures in the long run. Dreiser is a superman but he cannot be happy for thinking of the piteous plight of the epigoni. Dreiser is ambitious, but he knows ambition will not bring him what he wants. He wants something that is not here at all, or at least is not here in any satisfying measure—as Walter Pater says. It would not surprise me if Dreiser should go back to the Roman Catholicism from which he emerged and for which, now, he has anything but reverent or kindly feeling. Dreiser seems to me to be a spiritualist without exactly knowing it. This I believe must be apparent to any serious student of his work. He seeks and seeks in the material, the sensual, something he does not find. He worships success, yet knows it is nothing. Possibly he dreams of himself or another, some day, moulding this American mass into something like a Great Race, but his dream ends in wistful weariness.

His book indicts the American people on scores of counts, for sins against taste and crimes against the larger life. He cites things innumerable in proof. But cheerfulness will break in upon his moroseness, and every little while, the sight of a beautiful bridge, the prospect of some city as he approaches it, the gleam of aesthetic yearning in some girl briefly met, the politeness of some hotelkeeper makes him lift up his heart and go singing along his road. Dreiser has a grudge against our puritanism. He loathes the way in which we shut our eyes and harden our hearts against such a fact as sex. He despises as heartily as William J. Bryan, the false god of greed. He has no patience with reform, but plenty of sympathy for the honest reformers who are inevitably destined to defeat. Dreiser thinks a great deal, but much of his thinking is done with his emotions and, to tell truth, is no worse thinking for that, in my opinion. He is not quite a democrat, but he is not much of an aristocrat either. He looks over his America and broods and broods—and ends upon an interrogation point. He seems to appeal to a heaven in which he does not more than half believe. He has even a half hope of the people themselves, or so it appears to me. I know he is not quite so Leopardian as Edgar Lee Masters, for Masters is possessed of a cynic mysticism or a mystic cynicism. Dreiser is more of a Platonist. The stuff that was put into him in his early days at a Catholic school in Indiana is not deracinated. All this, however, may not appeal to many readers. For such as care not for philosophy there are in "A Hoosier Holiday" pages and pages of extremely good writing, descriptive, analytic, humorous, poetical. Dreiser is at his best. He "lets himself go." And he is a self whom it is good to know. He seeks the best there is in American life—and finds some of it. American life and, oh, most emphatically, American letters, would be the better for a few more Dreisers, or failing that, more of this frank and fearless and incurably-fond-of-humanity Dreiser, who gives us among other unforgettable things such a powerful picture of the Dreiser family in his boyhood days.

Ethel M. Colson. "Holiday Jaunt With Theodore Dreiser." Chicago *Record Herald,* December 16, 1916.

"Murder will out," and so will the moving springs of human nature. "A Hoosier Holiday," Theodore Dreiser's latest venture, is offered as a sort of intimate travel study or jaunting car chronicle; the volume's paper jacket describes it as "a vivid picture of the middle West, a criticism of America, a confession of faith and a personal record," adding that "the author's own youth and early aspirations are in it." All this and more spells the simple, sparkling account of an automobile trip from New York to Warsaw, Ind., in company with Franklin Booth, whose characteristic sketches provide pleasing illustration. But the note of sex is sounded as insistently as in any of the Dreiser novels. Directly and indirectly, through description, allusion, suggestion; seriously and in a spirit of jesting, the reader perpetually is reminded of sex instincts, effects, appeals, allure and reactions. "The first girl who ever kissed me and the first girl I ever ventured to kiss" figure (not figures) on the fourth page of the narrative; a college reminiscence of none too delicate order is offered close to its conclusion. And whatever the nature of the incident or occurrence narrated Mr. Dreiser, as always, is amazingly frank.

The travel phase embodied, though interesting and usually piquant, is by no means remarkable; its vehicle cannot always be classed as impeccable English. But keen wit, shrewdly varying philosophy and sword-like perceptions alternate with indubitable reverence for beauty, and if Mr. Dreiser now and then indulges in unhallowed bitterness he provides abundant food for thought of diverse and not commonplace order. . . .

New York *Evening Post,* December 16, 1916.

Mr. Dreiser's motor trip from New York to Indiana with his friend and illustrator, Mr. Franklin Booth, was in the nature of a sentimental journey to the State of his birth. His record of it is a full and animated one, with charmingly poetical descriptions of places, supplemented by personal incident and anecdote, and autobiographical reminiscences overlaid by the characteristic Dreiserian philosophy. An engaging charm of manner, the artist's sense for poignant detail, and a keen appreciation of the "spectacle of life," lend animation to his pages, while his sophistication serves as an effective background for the simplicity which he has chosen to portray.

His narrative moves with swiftness and sparkle, picturing with equal lightness of touch a Jersey countryside, a Pennsylvania manufacturing town, and a mid-Western village, pausing here for a tale and there for a characterization, wandering off into the byways of philosophy, or returning to some bit of personal history. The author's idealism, as well as his frank eroticism, his sympathy for the workingman and his opposition to capital, his love of democracy and his faith in America, all find frequent opportunity for expression. His parents, his boyhood homes, and his youthful experiences furnish the matter for the specifically Hoosier part of his chronicle, and the occasion for considerable sentimentalizing. Despite its graphic qualities, the book is over-long, and much of its philosophy and moralizing will doubtless win no more general approval than when offered through the medium of fiction. Its felicity of style, however, and the delightful freshness of its descriptions cannot fail to make appeal. . . .

"Most Outstanding American Novelist Reveals New Vein." San Francisco *Bulletin*, December 30, 1916.

Whether or not you may have read Theodore Dreiser's great novels—the word "great" being used advisedly—you will enjoy his "Hoosier Holiday" just the same, but that your appreciation of this chronicle will be heightened greatly by a knowledge of the author's ability to make his works of fiction throb with the pulse of life, there can be no doubt.

Mr. Dreiser is one of our few novelists whose work is vitalized after the manner of the European masters. His novels possess significance. He is a psychologist —a vivisectionist who lays bare our hypocrisies and our social shortcomings. Dreiser abhors sham and pretense. He attacks our most revered conventions and those who have read his "Jennie Gerhardt," "The Titan" or that remarkable study, "The Genius," will find "A Hoosier Holiday" of especial interest, not only for the very charming way in which he describes this sentimental journey, but for the philosophy it contains—a philosophy upon which his novels are based and which gives us a better understanding of the man and his ideals. Doubtless there are those in sympathy with the views of New York's vice commission, which condemned "The Genius," who would not attribute to Mr. Dreiser any idealism whatsoever, but he is not only an idealist, but a poet as well. There are certain descriptive passages in "A Hoosier Holiday" which challenge comparison with the best the "free verse" writers have given us.

Beauty and tenderness and sympathy add to the charm of this narrative, which tells of the author's return, after many years, to his native State and to the little town where he was born and where he first attended school. . . .

Throughout this story of his return to the old home there are pertinent observations and comments, bits of philosophy inspired by some gossip of the neighborhood, flashes of imagery, sentimental reveries and poetical descriptions of old scenes now viewed through the mists of years—memories of joys and sorrows, pleasures and pains that go to make up the sum of life. On every page is the human touch—that indefinable something that brings you in close relationship with a great soul.

Washington [D.C.] *Evening Star*, January 14, 1917.

Publisher and author and artist come together here with fine effect. An elaborate holiday is planned and carried out by Mr. Dreiser. A car, a driver, a friend with sketchbook in hand and an amazing gift of artistry to go with it, and Mr. Dreiser himself, also with notebook in hand—these are the factors contributing to that enviable motor tour from New York to the writer's old home in the Hoosier state. The journey turns out to be a glorified vagrancy. These are tramps on wheels, whizzing from one point of lure to another along this stretch of beautiful country. They loaf and work, and soak themselves in a thousand views. They take notes and make pictures, and, under the soft seductions of out-of-doors, they grow expansive with theories of society, and industry, and art and life itself. Reaching the old home state the leader of this vagrant band goes from one point of disillusionment to another, to the old places where he used to live, to the old times that had suffered an astonishing shrinkage in the intervening years, to the old neighbors the most of whom were gone. Yet, it was, after all, a happy holiday with melancholy and gladness hobnobbing together as they are bound to do when folks go a-hunting for the dreams of childhood. Vivid pictures by the score, from both writer and artist, accumulate here, and many inside glimpses of the two come to the surface under such evoking circumstances. Back to their starting point, it then becomes the business of the publisher to put the results of this expedition into the past into a suitable dress. It is a very beautiful book, one with which both Mr. Dreiser and Mr. Booth should be as pleased as the reader is with the work of everybody having part in it.

Clement Wood. "The Stuff We Are Made Of." New York *Call*, January 14, 1917.

Fact is not usually held to be as engrossing as fiction. But this is the unusual book. And no matter how entertaining and searching a novel Mr. Dreiser may produce hereafter, he will have to go far to exceed in interest this account of a trip which he and a friend took to his boyhood home in Warsaw, Indiana.

Good people, like the late unlamented Mr. Comstock, and his Elisha, Sumner, are wont to picture Mr. Dreiser as the very devil of the Apocalypse, with horns and hoofs and an apparent brimstone Greenwich-Villagey smell. Here we have revealed his true picture of himself; and we find him merely a likeable man, groping earnestly after the truth. He decides to make a leisurely trip to his childhood haunts, and to write the impression they make upon him after he has passed the fourth decade of his life. The trip is a sort of epic of the eastern half of the continent; he finds time to tell us his impressions of each of the places he passes through. We recall no book which bares so mercilessly the sham of American life, the pitiful small town's aping of the hideous brightlight and sky-scrapered Manhattan, the melancholy littleness of contemporary individualities in this focal spot in the world's trying-out of democracy. Along with this goes a kindly humor, a tolerant recognition of the occasional bright spots in the dingy totality of the effect of contemporary American life upon the honest observer, which is refreshing and encouraging. The book photographs American life as no fiction we have yet come across has done.

And it goes beyond this. It gives a big man's groping for an amelioration of this drab present; it gives the credo of a great novelist, based upon the facts of life. No character that the novelist has sketched is so big nor so true to life as this self-portrait, the portrait of a man sound at the core, subtle at points and humanly obtuse at others, but always driving toward a deeper understanding, a mellower acceptance of life.

The telling is as memorable as the tale. Clever critics profess themselves stumped by Mr. Dreiser's over-abundant use of words in his fiction; here the story is told simply, with a profusion of beautiful poetic passages such as that concluding "The Genius." And this simple telling is intensified by the splendid illustrations of Franklin Booth which have caught the spirit of the landscapes that Theodore Dreiser uses to hang his story upon, and reflected them, truly and adequately.

G.D.
San Francisco *Chronicle*, January 14, 1917.

Even a genius can prove a tedious companion on an automobile tour, especially if it lasts for many days, and you allow him to keep talking all the time. Theodore Dreiser badly needed the vacation, which he describes in "A Hoosier Holiday." Any man so much abused by narrow-minded people as was the author of "The Genius" requires an outlet for his pent-up anger, and when we come to think of it, a speeding auto is an excellent means of blowing the cobwebs out of one's brain. You literally feel the sense of leaving the world behind you as you speed past village after village, and throw her into the high after slowing down to meet the requirements of cities big enough to have ordinances, traffic regulations and the necessary policemen to enforce them.

But having thus ridded oneself of the mustiness of incompetent comment, it is not necessary to write a book about the experience, or if one does, one should be sufficiently considerate of the reader not to extend it over 500 pages, many of which are redolent of wrath.

There are many good things in this book, quite enough to repay the reading, but it would have been greater had it been less, and the parts to have been omitted are those which should have been linked together and published as a separate philosophy and reply to criticism.

Unfortunately for his many defenders, Dreiser does lend color to some of the charges against him in this volume. Things said by others and as incidentals to the story in "The Genius" are here repeated and emphasized with the freedom of an autoist traveling so rapidly that even the chauffeur in front may not hear.

He does not seem to have nursed his grievance against those who debarred his recent novel from certain libraries, but he does not forget them, and whenever there is a favorable moment he explodes with Carlylian anger. . . .

For all this, it would be unjust not to mention the many excellent descriptive passages, and those delightful character sketches and entertaining anecdotes which make up the larger portion of the book. Then, too, it should be remembered that not all the comment is irritating. Our author is an entertaining philosopher when he chooses to figure in that role. He is also readable as a critic. He spares no one. From Billy Sunday to Elbert Hubbard and all round he hits with the vigor of a literary pugilist. . . .

L.J.
"Mr. Dreiser's Soul."
Chicago *Post*,
March 2, 1917.

To read Theodore Dreiser's holiday wanderings is to recognize once more that the genius is primarily a child. He sees things naively and logically and not thru the eyes of practical consideration. To him to tell the truth is natural, and to dream is natural. But some children even learn by sad experience to hold their tongues, and in the man of genius there may be inhibitions against overmuch speech. But Mr. Dreiser represents the sort of genius who is not troubled with inhibitions. What is in him comes out. Even now his friends tell stories—and the legend will grow—of the length of his books. Those exceedingly long novels of his are really only the butchered remains of immeasurably longer manuscripts.

The reader of "A Hoosier Holiday" can well believe that there is some truth in the legend, for this book—and before saying that it is really a worth while document and interesting and the work of a genius—runs to 513 large octavo pages. And it contains everything—travel, philosophy, biography, hopes and fears for art, guesses at the future, Franklin Booth's theory as to why a chicken always crosses the road in front of the automobile, Theodore Dreiser's reception of the theory, the chauffeur's lack of interest in it, an automobile flirtation that came to nothing and the fact that one of the Beach family of Sullivan, Ind., had gone into the hardware business—at least Mr. Dreiser inferred that this might be the case from the fact that the name of Beach was mentioned on a hardware sign that he saw when he first entered the town (and the inference is certainly a most reasonable one).

But that is Mr. Dreiser's method, and it would be as absurd to quarrel with it as it would be to ask a child to blue pencil its narrative as it tells of its day's adventures. And Mr. Dreiser's adventures are worth telling because he does see things artistically—that is naively, as they are, not as use would have them to be. His recollections of childhood, and of his mother especially shine with this naive expressiveness and the darker experiences of his childhood, his parochial school experiences, the lack of freedom in his life, are told with a clear understanding of their genesis. . . .

Altogether the book is one that no other American man of letters could possibly write—tho if other men of letters were as honest with themselves and the world as Mr. Dreiser is a number of such books would be the most valuable kind of psychological document. But such naive self-relevation as this is possible only to the greatest men, and it is characteristic of men who could achieve it that they will pile insight on platitude and platitude on insight and never know the difference. So it is with Mr. Dreiser's book. It throws everything out pellmell and, behold, illuminating them as the soul of a child—

the sort of soul that alone can be weighed against the world.

"Mr. Dreiser's Favorite Hero." *Nation,* 104 (March 8, 1917), 268–269

Mr. Dreiser, novelist, with Mr. Booth, artist, and Speed, chauffeur, drove a Pathfinder car from New York to Indiana to revisit the scenes of the author's early life. Mr. Dreiser describes with occasional Whitmanesque rhapsodies the sights and smells and sounds and the "feel" of cities, countrysides, summer resorts, mines, bridges, hotels, drug stores, saloons, garages, "resorters," farmers, clerks, barkeepers, policemen, hotelkeepers, and waitresses. Mr. Booth contributes some thirty soft, smudgy, sympathetic charcoal sketches, including a view of Wilkes-Barre, a coal-breaker near Scranton, a Buffalo grain elevator, an Ohio wheat field, the main street of Indianapolis, French Lick, and roads, rivers, houses, and mills of Indiana. Speed adds his shrewd young personality and some beguiling stories. The publishers have put all this into a tall, handsome volume of 513 pages, and have summarized the result as follows: "a vivid picture of the Middle West," "a criticism of America," "a confession of faith," "a personal record," "the author's own youth and early aspirations."

It is very much like a Dreiser novel without a plot—the same slice of life, the same sense of cutaneous contacts, the same aspersion of law and morality and religion, the same barnyard notions of "love," the same sentimental Caliban philosophizing, the same genuflections before the mystery of physics and chemistry, and the same difficulties with English grammar. Like many other representatives of the naturalistic school, Mr. Dreiser is ashamed only of being ashamed. Until he wrote "The Hoosier Holiday," "The Genius" and "Jennie Gerhardt" might have passed as fiction, as works of the imagination. He has done in this last book what he could to reveal their intimate and vital connection with the Dreiser family. About himself he has confessed nothing that is not patent or easily inferrible in his previous writings, and we see no serious objection to his establishing the fact that he is his own favorite hero. He has now, however, exposed the badly soiled linen of his relatives and friends with a brassy impudence which we can only trust meets with their entire approval. "Personally," he says, "I am by no means a conventionalist." Truer word was never spoken. He is outside all the conventions and decent loyalties of the society which he professes to represent. Apparently he has never been inside them. Obviously he knows no more of the significance of the Middle West than he knows of the mountains of the moon.

The whole truth about our traveller is that he was an ill-bred, undisciplined child, and that he has never grown up. If the truth seems less harsh in his own words, let us have them: "Life was a strange, colorful, kaleidoscopic welter then. It has remained so ever since." If there is one thing which life isn't to the convention-loving, purposeful, progressive, scientific Middle West, it is a "strange, colorful, kaleidoscopic welter." To our feeble sense it is not at all clear why we should concern ourselves with a "criticism of America" from a critic who resides at the heart of a "kaleidoscopic welter." Yet the so-called "critical" element is really the piquant and amusing novelty in this huge book. Leaning out from his colorful welter, Mr. Dreiser exclaims with his characteristically Teutonic choiceness of phrase: "Dear, crude, asinine illusioned Americans! How I love them!" And again: "Dear, kind heaven, how shallow some people are!" And once more: "Kind heaven, what is the matter with a country where such things can be? What's the trouble with their minds anyhow? What a deadly yearning for the commonplace and crude and offensive possesses them!" This last effusion rushed to our observer's lips at sight of a brick and plaster mausoleum connected with a crematory in Ohio. This note of disgust with his fellow-countrymen for their addiction to the "commonplace," the "crude," and the "offensive" is, we say, piquant from the author of "The Genius." It is Mr. Dreiser's new note. It is the one falsetto note in an author whose sole virtue has been to reproduce without discrimination the "sensory sting" of life. For our author's true individual note we may turn to an excerpt from the dialogue between him and an Erie policeman:

> "Get out of here!" he shouted angrily at one street corner, glaring at us, "sticking your damn noses into everything!"
>
> "What the hell ails you anyhow?" I replied, equally irritable. . . .
>
> "Well, you can't come in. Get out!" and he flicked his boot with his hand in a contemptuous way.
>
> "Ah, go to hell," I replied angrily, but we had to move just the same.

When one tries to harmonize Mr. Dreiser's aesthetic falsetto with his naturalistic bass, one recognizes that life is indeed very complex. One repeats his own profound exclamation, "Oh, to escape endless cogitation!" One yearns to flee away from the colorful welter. To one's mind recurs his own exquisite and haunting image of the buzzard winging its way on wide pinions through the blue, seeking, seeking —what?

Susan W. Ball. [Terre Haute, Ind.] *Saturday Spectator,* March 24, 1917.

Have you read Theodore Dreiser's book "A Hoosier Holiday?" Hoosiers will read it. It is not often that we have a well known novelist tour the state and write a big book, handsomely bound and illustrated, about his old haunts in Terre Haute, Sullivan, Evansville, Warsaw. The intimate personal manner of recording the holiday makes its appeal. Then the fact that the book is sold at $3.00 in this day of cheap books gives distinction to the volume.

Everyone knows of Paul "Dresser" (as he chooses to spell his name), who wrote "On the Banks of the Wabash Far Away." Theodore Dreiser is a younger brother. Why Paul changed the spelling of his name when he became a song writer is not explained.

The reader is told, in the beginning, that Franklin Booth, an illustrator, asked Dreiser of New York, to come to Indiana in his car, promising that he would take him to all the places associated with his early life. Booth is an Indiana man, living at Carmel, near Indianapolis, but who has a studio in New York. Three men, including the chauffeur, who also was a native of Indiana, started on the motor trip from New York.

The story of the happenings are those that would appeal especially to men. The chapters on Terre Haute are perhaps the least interesting of the book. Probably because the author was only 7 when the family moved to Sullivan and also that when they lived here the desperate straits, financial and otherwise of the family, as known to Theodore later, tinged everything with a sadness felt by his readers. The author speaks of Chauncey Rose wanting to help his father financially, but that he declined the aid.

The opening chapter, entitled 'The Rose Window," is a poetic memory of the author's early life in Indiana, in which the painful experiences are thrown into the discard and only the high lights of his dream youth are woven into a rose window of prismatic hues.

When the party reaches Terre Haute, they go to the Terre Haute House, because the mother and sisters had found work in the hotel. Dreiser describes the Deming as the usual "largest" hotel in the city, quite like all such in every other city of the same size. He describes Terre Haute as being something different from the other towns of the state. "It has a young, hopeful atmosphere. I like it."

The book is filled with beautiful descriptions of scenes that suggest strains of philosophic expression. The tributes to his mother are touching, exquisite, and might make a souvenir brochure on mothers in general. One wishes Mr. Dreiser had left out some things in the book, a confession of faith, or rather lack of it, and his avowed free love advocacy. Confessions are the order of the day but they can be carried too far. Some things ought never be confessed, at least in printed, irrevocable form. His father's fanatical Catholicism drove him from the church leaving him stranded with what seems to some of us a false philosophy as a standard of conduct. If he were younger (he is 44), one might excuse his easy dismissal of monogamy marriage. He says "Monogamy is good—nothing better for its purpose—but if all did so, where would be a story like Carmen or an opera like Tristan and Isolde, or I Pagliacci, or Madame Butterfly, or Louise?"

Much of the book is an autobiography and quite without egotism; still one gets the impression that Theodore was a "dear" in his childhood and youth. His one year at the University at Bloomington was through the efforts of a former school teacher. This woman sought him out in a Chicago wholesale hardware house and insisted upon his accepting $300 and going to the University. She thought the warehouse life would crush his spirit and knew he had a poetic temperament and a mind to imbibe an education.

One of the most vivid impressions left on the mind after reading this book is of how a boy can rise from the most discouraging environment to one of literary and social prominence. The Dreiser family had other impediments besides poverty to their standing in this region.

Irregularities in the standardized respectable conduct of some of the members of the family of 13 added poignancy to the situation.

Paul, who rescued the mother and her smaller brood, had been driven from home for offenses the writer says he will not recount. Later he came back a rich minstrel song writer and took care of the family. The author enveiging against large families, his parents having 13, says "Governments love large families; they recruit large armies and navies. They fill the gaping maws of factories. The churches love large families, for they bring recruits to them. But if an ordinary working man, or one without a serene and forceful capacity for toil and provision, could see the ramifications and miseries of birth in poverty, he would not reproduce himself so freely."

The author's experiences as a reporter on a St. Louis paper, the Cleveland Blade and others, are vivid pictures. He says of reporters: "To this day, though I have been one in my time, I stand in fear of them. I never know what to expect, what scarifying question they are going to hurtle at me, or what cold, examining eyes are going to strip me to the bone—eyes that represent brains so shrewd and merciless that one wonders why they do not startle the world long before they usually do."

One is given the impression that Mr. Dreiser is a bachelor, but he is said to have a wife "somewhere." She doubtless does not sympathize with his advanced theories on the narrowing effect of monogamy. One speculates on why he does not tell us of his later love affairs since he is frank about earlier ones.

With all his reading, his keen analysis of character, one feels he has not yet really found himself. He is pessimistic about this republican form of government and prophesies it will fail. In the closing chapter, in summing up, he says, "Oh, the wondrous memory of it (The Republic.) For these days were free, because they imagined they were free."

Indianapolis *News*, May 26, 1917.

. . . Mr. Dreiser's book is remarkable in many ways. Sometimes he is so irritating that one feels like calling him names, if it weren't so impolite. The one name one wants to call him oftenest is "smart aleck." And then, when this impulse has passed, one feels greatest admiration for his shrewdness, his penetrating analysis, his wonderful little pen pictures of people and places. His references to his mother are numerous and as touching as the memories of a man visiting his old home and recalling his childhood usually are. She was so kind, so sensible, so loving, holding her little family together, sacrificing and toiling, loving and understanding that it is no wonder the man's heart should be full as he comes to a deeper realization of what such mothers mean to boys and girls, no matter what age or what region produced them. Striking are his descriptions of his early schooling, and his breaking away from the Roman church in which he had been trained. Striking are his revelations of his thoughts about love, sex, human impulses in general. Whether his friends who entertained him and gave him the best they had will be pleased to behold themselves thus named and described so frankly is a question.

All in all, Mr. Dreiser is much happier and more likable in this volume of travel in homely places than he is in his "Traveler at Forty," which he must frequently wish he hadn't written. It is good for us to see ourselves from a new angle, sometimes, and this new angle Mr. Dreiser furnishes in this volume. His critical observations on Elbert Hubbard and East Aurora, which the party visited on its way out west, show that he can be very severe indeed when he doesn't like certain people. One might take the severity of his criticisms a little more seriously, perhaps, if he were not so frequently guilty of such grammar as this: "There were a choice array of those peculiar bindings, etc."

Marion Tucker. "Out-of-Door Books." *Churchman*, 115 (May 12, 1917), 551.

Mr. Dreiser takes an automobile trip from New York city to Indiana in company with his friend, the illustrator, and fills a ponderous volume of over five hundred pages with an account of what he saw, felt and thought during the two weeks, and also of what he had seen, felt and thought during the first twenty-five years of his life. Ostensibly the journal of a short tour, the book is in effect an autobiography. Apparently a great deal happened between New York and Warsaw, Indiana. The bursting of a tire became an event, the sight of a pretty face a greater event. But Mr. Dreiser is a close observer with a picturesque vocabulary; and he makes us see with him the panorama of life as it unfolds through a thousand miles of forest, stream, and hill, farms, cities and towns, beauty and ugliness, presenting here and there a vivid characterization or a human picture. In this he is at his best. His often half-baked philosophy of life is not so acceptable. Mr. Dreiser is a professional rebel against the accepted religious, economic and social order. He says many new things which are not true and many true things which are not new. We prefer his descriptions to his meditations. The book abounds in sharp criticisms of persons, uttered apparently without malice, but in doubtful taste; in egregious egotism which, though in equally bad taste, almost disarms through its frankness; and in constant and wearying obtrusion of the over-emphasized sex element. The style, at times striking and even happy, is on the whole extremely bad. Yet, for all its monumental faults, the book embodies at least one great redeeming virtue: its picture of the vigorous Americanism, its faith in the happy, prosperous democracy of the Middle West has its value in these times of national questioning.

Checklist of Additional Reviews

Bookseller, November 15, 1916.

Portland *Oregonian,* November 19, 1916.

Publisher's Weekly, November 18, 1916.

"Theo. Dreiser on Wheels." New York *World,* November 19, 1916.

Rochester [N.Y.] *Democrat Chronicle,* November 19, 1916.

W.R.Rose. "All in the Day's Work." Cleveland *Plain Dealer,* November 22, 1916.

Book News Digest, December, 1916.

New York *Sun,* December 2, 1916.

"Mr. Dreiser Undertakes a Motor Tour." Boston *Herald,* December 2, 1916.

New York *Hebrew American,* December 3, 1916.

"The New Books." *The Independent,*

88 (December 4, 1916), 409.
Indianapolis *Times,* December 8, 1916.
Pittsburgh *Dispatch,* December 9, 1916.
Seattle [Wash.] *Post,* December 10, 1916.
Chicago *Record Herald,* December 10, 1916.
Louisville *Courier-Journal,* December 11, 1916.
Chicago *News,* December 13, 1916.
Springfield [Mass.] *Republican,* December 31, 1916, p. 15.
A.M. Chicago *Examiner,* January 6, 1917.
Salt Lake City [Utah] *Herald Republican,* January 7, 1917.
Fayette [Ind.] *Review,* February, 1917.
Book Review Digest, February, 1917.
Milwaukee *Evening Wisconsin,* February 13, 1917.
"Priggish and Ponderous." Minneapolis *Journal,* February 13, 1917.
Life, February 15, 1917.
Denver [Col.] *News,* March 11, 1917.
Lewiston [Ma.] *Journal,* March 17, 1917.
[Terre Haute, Ind.] *Saturday Spectator,* March 31, 1917.
"Girard's Topics of the Town." Philadelphia *Public Ledger,* May 4, 1917.

Further Reviews: Bibliographic Information Incomplete

Binghampton [N.Y.] *Press,* March-April, 1917.

FREE AND OTHER STORIES

BY THEODORE DREISER

AUTHOR OF "SISTER CARRIE," "THE HAND OF THE POTTER," "JENNIE GERHARDT," ETC.

BONI AND LIVERIGHT
NEW YORK 1918

Free and Other Stories

Boston *Post*, August 24, 1918.

When Theodore Dreiser looks around to get material for a novel, he usually sees too much. His long stories are appallingly long. Perhaps it is the war that has distracted his attention and made him give us, in "Free and Other Stories," a book that is very unlike what we expect from him. In this collection of 11 tales, the author's passion for minute details is decidedly curbed. And there is nothing in it that would have disturbed the late Anthony Comstock, who was a good deal worked up over some of the things that Mr. Dreiser's sorry heroes used to do in their successive philanderings.

There is about everything except boisterous humor and the conventional love story in Mr. Dreiser's latest book. Ardent maidens and youths in their budding affections and reflective wives and husbands are studied with a ripe observation and a grim irony. These are noted in the author's best vein. More unlikely [sic] his usual fiction and more conventional but holding the reader's interest because of the swift action are stories of a lynching and of a newspaper rivalry to pull off a real "scoop."

Seven of his stories are sincere and effective studies of American life as it recurs again and again in our cities. The other four reveal unsuspected angles of the author's mind. One is a pleasant tale of New York in 1801, when people lived on Wall street and lovers sauntered under the shade of the trees that overhung the Bowery, when the merchants laughed at the mad inventor who had dreamed that a ship might move without sails through the water, and dandelions and wild roses bloomed on the lane called Broadway. There is a mild fantasy in the story of the workingmen who played that their shop was a boat and a wild fantasy of ant life and its warfare that is not so very different from our disordered world of today. And, perhaps best of all, is the tale of "The Lost Phoebe," an idyl seamed through with poetry. The book is one of varied, honest and sincere achievement.

E.F. Edgett. "Theodore Dreiser and the Short Story." Boston *Evening Transcript*, August 28, 1918, p. 6.

. . . Despite all his many deficiencies, temperamental and otherwise, it is undeniable that Mr. Dreiser is a modern master of the novel. He is prolix, his style is frequently crude and unfinished, he unduly emphasizes the sordid elements of humanity, he dwells persistently and with constant reiteration upon sex relations, rarely seeking to throw the glamour of romance over them that gives them the genuinely poetic quality of love. At times, and many times, he seems to see nothing in men and women beyond the ineradicable sex instinct, and he makes all of their actions and thoughts dependent solely upon this one physical and intellectual attitude. To read "The Financier" or "The Genius" is to be enshrouded in the befogging atmosphere of a persistent sexual immorality.

For his eleven short stories, Mr. Dreiser has gone to other fields for his plots and his characters. They are of varying lengths, one being as brief as twenty pages, another extending to eighty, and the rest ranging between those extremes. Some of them are filled with movement and dialogue, some are direct narratives of a logical course of events, and others are wholly analytical studies. In fact, some of them are not short stories at all, but merely fragmentary sketches or psychological impressions. . . .

Unfortunately Mr. Dresser still persists in misusing the English language. With him events transpire, and such constructions as "in the as yet bright study" seem to allure rather than to repel him. It is extraordinary that a writer who is frequently able to make such excellent use of English can scarcely less frequently maltreat it so vigorously. The one thing he needs most is expert training in the cultivated writing of his mother tongue.

"Book of the Day." Philadelphia *Inquirer*, August 29, 1918.

Theodore Dreiser, who has distinguished himself with the long story and with other forms of literary expression, is represented in a book of short stories which is published under the title of "Free," which is the caption of the first tale in the volume. There are eleven stories in all and they are about as different as it would be possible for that many stories to be, and yet be the product of the same writer. . . .

Taken in their entirety, these stories may be more regarded as character sketches than tales with plots—not that some of them have not good plots, but rather that they deal with the mental attitudes of the characters. They all show an intimate knowledge of life, and whether we agree or disagree with the philosophy of life expounded by the author we must admit that he writes as one who knows what he is doing. Some of the tales are rather slight, and suggest that they might be the by-product of his apprentice days, but taken all in all they will repay reading by the discriminating lover of good literature.

"Stories By Dreiser." Louisville *Courier Journal*, September 2, 1918

In his new book, a collection of short stories, Mr. Dreiser varies his theme in nearly every instance from the "jungle-motive" of the predatory male on which "The Titan," "The Financier" and "The Genius" were based. . . .

The collection, on the whole, indicates that Mr. Dreiser's spirit, or whatever takes the place of spirit in the anthropology of the materialist, is marching on. He has not exhausted himself upon his Titans and unleased financiers; he has escaped the meshes of a facile mysticism. There is breadth and amazing energy in the man, and the end of his development is not yet in sight.

Leonard L. Cline. "Dreiser Tries Short Stories." Detroit *News*, September 8, 1918.

For all of his latest book, "Free, and Other Stories" Theodore Dreiser continues to be the great enigma of American literature. Indeed this volume positively fortifies him in that position. For if ever his novels were clumsy, prolix, unorganized, dispassionate and unsympathetic, utterly without a palpable charm, certainly these stories are equally so, proving that the author is not a master of one more literary form. Here, as in the novels, is the supreme sloven of contemporary letters—often shockingly ungrammatical, careless of his facts; the hasty builder who cannot wait for specifications, and is compelled too frequently to hold up construction while he goes back to the very foundations to repair or strengthen or complete a step in the job that had been left unfinished in the headlong scramble to get it done. Indeed, some of these short stories are not short stories at all, but in substance entire novels and in treatment amorphous; one is inclinced to put them down for rapid studies preliminary to some other extended work.

Certainly the astounding applause his performances evoke from critics and intelligent people generally is in spite of his craftsmanship; there is no such wretched artisan in letters. I conceive that it is because of two qualities. The first is his straightforward freedom from any bias, his bold clarity of vision, and the second is his painstaking analysis of psychological processes. There is the substance of these qualities in the short stories. . . .

Mr. Dreiser appears so much of a scientist that he cannot wholly forget that role, when he poses as artist. Undoubtedly his reputation rests on the quality of keen analyst, but he might very well buttress it with some literary craftsmanship. His unwillingness to do so has alienated many readers of his novels, and he does not reconcile them in these stories, which one reads with protest. Their bigness is notwithstanding the author.

"Short Stories." New York *Evening Post Book Section*, September 14, 1918, p. 2.

Dreiser is one of the problems of contemporary fiction. He has his ardent admirers, and, by way of compensation, an equally large public which refuses even to consider his work literature. "Sister Carrie," his first important novel, took the public more or less by storm. There was pretty general agreement as to the novel. But as to everything else he has written the differences of opinion are pronounced, and one might say, almost embittered. The present volume of short stories illustrates all the traits that earn Dreiser both his critics and his admirers. Vulgarity; lack of precision, color, intuition, a sort of moving-picture touch throughout, here also will turn many against him. He attempts a great variety of genres, in these tales, the O. Henry, the Barrie, the Bret Harte, and even Allegory of the Swift types, and in all he displays the same clumsiness of technique.

And yet, despite everything by bull-headed persistence, by repetition of crudity, by a sort of slam-dash of audacity, he nearly always manages to save himself from the commonplace. "Will You Walk Into My Parlor?" a story of cheap political blackmail, quite ordinary in its substance, gradually grows into a kind of reality because of the length to which it is drawn out and the painstaking detail of its telling. It ends by becoming fairly amusing. The same might be said of "The Cruise of the Idlewild," a thoroughly Barrie conception, but without a spark of Barrie's genius. For sentiment and whimsicality, Dreiser substitutes a make-believe joviality; for New York argot, something that is neither New York nor Chicago nor even small-town lingo. Nothing could be more irritating than these attempts at a dialect which he does not know and which he is too indolent even to try to keep up consistently. Nevertheless 'The Cruise of the Idlewild" is by no means a failure nor unamusing. It is like the rest of the stories in this volume; it leaves Dreiser as great an enigma as ever.

"Dross and Gold." Philadelphia *Press*, September 14, 1918.

There are many surprises in this volume for the numerous admirers of Mr. Dreiser's uncompromising art. Perhaps the greatest surprise is that he, the writer of so many interminably lengthy —too often unnecessarily lengthy novels—can express himself so satisfactorily in the short story form. Almost equally surprising is the revelation that the sloppiest stylist in American letters can write so superbly when he chooses to.

Save for these reservations the book can be pronounced typical of Dreiser. It has all his maddening faults and all his perverse and monumental talent. It bites deeper into life than most writers can or dare; it is as bitter, as meditative, as profoundly sincere as anything he has done. Much dross must be wallowed through before the gold is found, but the gold is always there. Trite people, incredibly trite dialogue, intentionally trite situations move across his pages; yet behind them there is always the idea, the golden idea.

And yet not always. Two of his stories are frank melodrama, "A Story of Stories" and "Will You Walk Into My Parlor."... In this field Mr. Dreiser does not shine. One other, "When the Old Century Was New," is a mere picture of Colonial life in New York City, superbly done as a portrait of manners in a bygone year and forcible in its suggested contrast with Metropolitan life of today, but remarkable chiefly for the ease and grace with which the usually heavy-handed Mr. Dreiser has executed it. The imagery and beauty of "McEwen of the Shining Slave Makers" is another example of uncommonly fine writing.

But the other stories are faithful to Mr. Dreiser of "Sister Carrie," "Jennie Gerhardt," "The Genius." The furtive, unexpressed hope of a man past middle age that his sick wife would die and leave him free is the basis for a searching psychological study in the title story. The details of a lynching bee, the dangers of the innocent girlhood in the slums of New York, the drab domestic tragedy of a girl who was jilted—these are some of the themes he illuminates by the X-ray method of his which sees everything, rejects nothing—not even the irrelevancies.

All in all the book is not up to the best Dreiser standard. Despite his unsuspected facility for handling the short tale, his true medium still appears to be a novel.

"Latest Works of Fiction." New York *Times Book Review.* September 22, 1918, p. 398.

Mr. Dreiser's latest book is a volume of short stories—or perhaps it would be more accurate to call them sketches. The first, and the one which gives its name to the book, is a very long and very minutely detailed analysis of the thoughts and feelings of a man whose wife is so seriously ill that there is only a slight chance of her recovery. But a chance there is, and it is this fact which makes all the trouble. For the hero, Rufus Haymaker, an architect, now about 60 years old, did not love the wife he had married some thirty-one years before, because, having become engaged to her when little more than a boy, he felt it his duty to carry out his compact. He was faithful to her, though she bored him dreadfully. His varying moods, his desire for the death which will set him free, and his horror of his own desire, are carefully recounted. But the idea which finally comes to him, and which is the real climax of it all, is concerned with a truth so entirely obvious that the reader cannot help feeling that any one possessed of ordinary human intelligence would have seen and realized it with considerably less tardiness.

"Married" also analyzes the thoughts and feelings of a man wedded to a wife as unsuited to him as he is to her. "McEwen of the Shining Slave Makers" is a sociological study, the story of a man who dreamed he was an ant, and thereby learned to understand something of the "worlds within worlds, all apparently full of necessity, contention, blinding emotions and unities" which exist now and will continue to exist until this "odd, strange thing called life has ended." A different lesson, the eternal truth that it is impossible to punish the guilty without bringing suffering to the innocent, is the one taught the cocksure young newspaper man who is sent to report the case of "Nigger Jeff." The tale of a lynching, this story has a well-drawn picture of a mob, excited and irresolute until a leader appears. Follows "The Lost Phoebe," which is the best story in the book. Although it is overdetailed, and the effectiveness of many of its incidents lessened through their being dwelt upon too long, there is a touch of real pathos in the sketch of the old farmer, the range of whose interests and activities had been measured by "the orchard, the meadow, the cornfield, the pig pen, and the chicken lot," searching with distraught mind for the dead wife who had been his constant companion for nearly half a century.

"The Second Choice" is the story of a girl who, being unable to get the man she wanted, took the man who wanted her. Then comes another tale of newspaper experiences, the story this time being that of the struggle between two rival reporters, ending with the defeat of the superior brain by the "gross savage desire * * * to win" of the coarser-fibred man. "Old Rogaum and His Theresa" tells how a dictatorial father locked out his disobedient daughter, and one tragedy prevented another. It pictures a situation unfortunately only too familiar to all those who have ever taken any part in what is called social work. The longest narrative in the book, "Will You Walk Into My Parlor?" is semi-political. Edward Gregory had been busying himself for some time "ferreting out and substantiating one fact and another in regard to the mismanagement of the city" preparatory to the Fall campaign and the hoped-for defeat of the Mayor and his "ring." This was not the safest of employments, and more than one friend warned Gregory that the political gang would "get him" if he was not extraordinarily careful. But Gregory, who was not, it must be admitted, either a very strong or a very intelligent man, braved the perils of a Summer hotel, and there encountered the young woman who played spider to his fly.

Dorothy Scarborough. "Dreiser's Vignettes of States of Mind." New York *Sun*, September 22, 1918.

The stories in *Free,* Theodore Dreiser's first volume of short stories, are cleverly written and are interesting from the standpoint of psychology, but they are unsatisfying. The style is that of an artist in some of the stories at least, and the insight into human nature is searching and revealing. Yet the effect of the book as a whole is depressive. The reader does not feel spiritually enriched by the reading.

There is too much that is morbid in situation and too much that is sordid in character. There is overmuch grayness of soul and of destiny, unrelieved by beauty. You feel that among the number of characters Dreiser has here pictured there should surely be at least a few who are noble, who rightly win your respect. Even in a muddy gutter one may see the stars reflected. But the only character for whom the reader is likely to feel genuine respect is an ignorant old man who has lost his mind. . . .

Albany [N.Y.] *Knickerbocker Press*, Setpember 22, 1918

This collection of Dreiser's short stories was published in August and has already gone into a third edition. There has been no Comstockian protest against its circulation, nor will there be, for the simple reason that the book contains nothing the most rabid puritan could object to. We may even hope that at last a Dreiser book may find a place in the catalogue of every public library in the country and the general reader be given some encouragement to taste of his quality. There are eleven stories in this volume and they bear witness to the versatility of their author's genius, and are proof positive of the ease with which he might long ago, had he so desired, have enriched himself with the spoils of a second rate success. For here are stories to suit all tastes; perfectly good and conventional short stories, some of them, such as Richard Harding Davis might have written or any other popular magazine writer; others there are less ordinary; and one, at least, of a much higher type and unmistakably Dreiserian. There is nothing of the potboiler about "Free," the first story in the book. It is an intensely subtle psychological study, a literal turning inside out of the mind of a man about to be set free by the approaching death of his wife from a yoke that has secretly galled him for more than thirty years. It is a wonderful piece of writing. But if psychology bores you, turn to "A Story of Stories," a racy tale of a cub reporter and the scoop that he didn't quite land; or "Old Roguam and his Theresa," a Bowery police court tale. And for those who prefer something less strenuous there is "The Cruise of the 'Idlewild,'" a delightfully imaginative and quietly humorous little narrative, or "When the Century was New," a dainty love story, an idyl of New York City in 1801. As a matter of fact I doubt if you could find a more varied collection of short stories by any living author. If indeed, you have hitherto known only what Van Wycks Brooks calls "those vast literary pyramids of Mr. Theodore Dreiser, those prodigious piles of language built of the commonest rubble and cohering, in the absence of any architectural design, by sheer virtue of their weight and size," you will no doubt marvel at the neatness and verbal economy with which the author of "Sister Carrie," "The Titan" and "The Genius" can tell so simple and frail a little story as "The Second Choice." . . . "Free and Other Stories" is far more eloquent of its origin than the casual reader might suppose who had merely been told that it was the work of the foremost American novelist of the day.

Springfield [Mass.] *Republican*, September 22, 1918.

Theodore Dreiser's realism has been the subject of much nonsense and, it must be added, much legitimate criticism. His most conspicuous book has been barred from several public libraries and then hailed by critics as a great work of art largely because of its having been banished from the libraries. "Free, and Other Stories" does not approach the crushing unloveliness that makes "The Genius" regrettable to so many readers. There is, within the narrow limits between which Mr. Dreiser chooses his material, hard realism and unrelenting accuracy, but there is nothing to which the most ardent watch and ward committee could object. . . .

In all these stories—which are told without exceptional art—Mr. Dreiser takes greater account of life's unknown quantities than of the established facts. Indeed, he does not seem sure that there are any established facts, save possibly discontent and misapprehension.

Richmond [Va.] *Journal*, September 23, 1918.

Why Theodore Dreiser chose "Free" for the initial offering and title role of his volume of short stories is difficult to determine, for it is less artistic and not so interesting as many of the subsequent ones. . . . Among the more interesting of the eleven offerings are two newspaper sketches, one dealing with the rivalry between two reporters on morning dailies and in which an ambitious young "cub" is sent to cover a lynching case. There is zest and balance in these. Perhaps, most readers would choose "The Lost Phoebe." Herein are depicted a lonely old couple living out in an isolated corner, deserted by their children, who have grown up and left for the busy marts of life. When the woman dies her life-long partner is desolate, although he used to quarrel, occasionally, in an ineffectual way. From loneliness and grief his mind soon becomes affected and he wanders about the neighborhood for years searching for his Phoebe. "When the Century Was New" gives a charming picture of New York in the days when it was Nieu Amsterdam and the founders of many great Knickbocker houses were testing the power of steam for the first time. Frankly, Mr. Dreiser makes stronger appeal in his novels, although this is not to say that his short stories are not worth reading.

Los Angeles *Times*, September 29, 1918.

What Theodore Dreiser has tried to do in "Free and Other Stories" I frankly confess not knowing, but it is suspiciously like an effort to write popular stuff. The adjective sentimental has been applied to but one class of fiction; but a story can be sentimentally morbid as well as "sweet," and there is a sentimental morbidity in many of these stories which are conspicuously lacking in force. They appear very much like the result of a floundering effort to hit on a method of writing short stories. And that Mr. Dreiser, who flung the banner of sex from his pyramidical novels, should lower that flag in his briefer, but not brief, tales is somewhat disconcerting to a few of us who have defended his courage, his faithfulness, to ideals as he saw them and joined with him against the censor.

Dreiser is not an artist in the artistic sense. He made what friends and enemies he had by the sex-challenge; and here he appears to be compromising with the censor and no doubt expects his friends to value a collection of stories in which there is nothing for them to admire, since they do not even contain a challenge to smugness. . . . A poor lot, all of them.

Frank Harris, "Books Worth Reading." *Pearson's Magazine*, October, 1918.

It is some eight or ten years now since Mr. Arnold Bennett declared that there were half a dozen English writers who were as great masters of the short story as any in France; and here is now an American to add to the list. I have swallowed half this volume by Dreiser in one short evening, have been interested, stirred even, and am eager to go on and finish it. Thinking back over what I have read, I remember five stories—and there were only five—every one made a definite impression on me and the first and the last, I believe, are going to remain with me.

"Free" is the story of a man of sixty whose wife is ill and likely to die. The doctor condoles with him, and the husband realizes that he won't be sorry if his wife does die, that he has never loved her much, and that whatever love he had for her is long ago worn out and dead. He has had dreams, too, in his dull forty years of married life, wild dreams of love, dear dreams tho' fleeting as shadows on glass, and if he were "free" he might yet realize one of the entrancing desires. But when his wife does die he just understands that he is old and tired: "Free, I am free now at last! Free! Free! . . . Yes—free . . .to die."

It is a sad story, a page of real life torn out of the great book, difficult to forget, and yet more difficult to read again. Why? Why should it be impossible to read again?

First of all, it is a little too long; there are wearisome repetitions; no crescendo of interest, and on almost every page there are blunders or at least carelessnesses of phrase—feelings clumsily expressed. Sometimes the mistakes are American, the frequent use of "will" when "shall" is obligatory, as on page 45, where Mr. Haymaker muses: "Now she will really get well. I *will* never be free. I *will* never have a day—a day!"

Frequently, however, the fault is in the writer. Dreiser writes what first comes into his head, without a second thought. Take perhaps the best passage in this story, when, just before the end, Haymaker realizes that he is "old, weary, done for, a recluse and ungainly."

Dreiser goes on: "Now the innate cruelty of life, its blazing ironic indifference to him and so many grew rapidly upon him." What dreadful writing! The whole sentence is, of course, Dreiser, and not poor dull Haymaker at all; then take the phrase "blazing ironic indifference"; does Dreiser mean "blazing indifference"? No! Plainly he means the blazing irony of nature's indifference, and even then how bad is "blazing," for if you please "it grew rapidly upon him!"

The last story, "The Second Choice," is better still: it is about a young girl's love, has a thrill in it and is relentlessly true to nature to boot. Dreiser is a magician when he treats of love: he might, one imagines, write a world-masterpiece on that theme; but even then he should be forced to rewrite it at least half a dozen times. Tolstoi, who is a great writer, confesses at the end of his life that he often rewrites a story ten or twenty times—that's the true artist's spirit. Masterpieces never come to the birth without labor and pain.

Rochester [N.Y.] *Post Express*, October 15, 1918.

The short story needs a different sort of fictional faculty from the novel. Theodore Dreiser has written novels which may be pornographic but which, at any rate are—novels. But he cannot write a good short story. The art of which Guy de Maupassant was the great master—even in a higher degree than either Balzac or Flaubert—is apparently beyond the reach of Mr. Dreiser. The tales in the collection entitled "'Free' and Other Stories," just published by Boni & Liveright, lack unity of impression—a thing indispensable in every short story. . . . They are all failures as short stories, although passages in them display both cleverness and knowledge of the complex civilization of the United States.

Mr. Dreiser should confine his efforts to the production of novels. He is a realist who, in order to succeed at all, must paint on a broad canvas. He is not a writer who has yet done anything great, but he is ambitious to differentiate himself from the herd of manufacturers of commonplace fiction. But his powers are not such as to admit of conciseness or concentration. He has not a jot of Gallic refinement and he cannot produce that "nervous thrill" which Flaubert considered one of the triumphs of fiction.

David Karsner. "Theodore Dreiser's Short Stories." New York *Call Magazine*, October 27, 1918, p. 11.

Dreiser not only fascinates you and grips your attention; he makes you think. That is where his power lies. I have read everything Dreiserian, from "Sister Carrie" to "A Hoosier Holiday," and the more I read him, the more I want to read him. In Dreiser's writing there is a peculiar homeliness, a fine realism, that one is led almost to contemplate the situation or the circumstance, yet there is charm and beauty and poetry and art and truth running all through his work.

Dreiser has been written about quite a great deal, but scarcely any two persons have agreed about him. He is mysterious in his books and stories, just as he is mysterious in the flesh. He lives very close to the thing we call life, yet he confesses he understands it not at all. Who does? Who can plumb its depths? Who knows anything about it at all, except that it is, as Jack London once stated it, "a ferment"? There is no humbug about Dreiser. He is not in any sense an intellectual cheap skate, word monger or paragraph pander.

No matter whether a fact of life be pretty or ugly, Dreiser takes it up and runs it to the earth, until he has revealed its secret. You never lose the artist in the philosopher when you read him, nor the poet in the mathematician. It may be that Dreiser's power lies in the fact that his characters are breathing beings. Should you read his stories or his books, you will know some one in your own circle that would fit one or more characters to a "T." You would imagine that Dreiser knew your friend, and wrote of her or him.

In this book, which runs to 369 pages (there are no little books in the Dreiser output) there are 11 of his best stories. Each one is powerful, the work of a master. Dreiser is a born artist. I have heard it said that he began writing novels by accident. It is doubtful that any man with Dreiser's ability is an accidental artist.

In these stories, beginning with the title one, "Free," there are all the qualities that have given Dreiser a vogue. He is so far above his fellow craftsmen that he must be intellectually lonesome. There is growing up a Dreiser clan in America. It was inevitable. Many of his contemporaries have turned him down. Many critics fly into a white-heat rage when his name is mentioned. But Dreiser smiles, plaits his handkerchief and writes another book just for luck.

"Why should people read my books when they can come to my rooms and throw a stone at me through the window?" he once remarked. Dreiser does not conciliate his readers or the market. He does not write anything he does not believe.

Dreiser's short stories are as interesting as his novels. The only disappointment one might point to in them is that at the end one wishes the story were longer.

H.L. Mencken. "Dithyrambs Against Learning." *Smart Set*, 57 (November 1918), 143–144.

The eleven pieces in "Free and Other Stories," by Theodore Dreiser, are the by-products of a dozen years of industrious novel-writing, and are thus somewhat miscellaneous in character and quality. They range from experiments in the fantastic to ventures into realism, and, in tone, from the satirical to the rather laboriously moral. The best of them are "The Lost Phoebe," "The Cruise of the *Idlewild*," "The Second Choice" and "Free." The last-named is a detailed and searching analysis of a disparate marriage that has yet survived for forty years—an elaborate study of a life-long conflict between impulse and aspiration on the one hand and fear and conformity on the other. Here Dreiser is on his own ground, for the thing is not really a short story, in any ordinary sense, but a chapter from a novel, and he manœuvres in it in his customary deliberate and spacious manner. "The Second Choice" is of much the same character—a presentation of the processes of mind whereby a girl deserted by the man she loves brings herself to marriage with one she doesn't love at all. Those of the stories that are more properly short stories in form are less successful; for example, "A Story of Stories," "Old Rogaun and His Theresa" and "Will You Walk Into My Parlor?" The true short story, in fact, lies as far outside Dreiser's natural field as the triolet or the mazurka. He needs space and time to get his effects; he must wash in his gigantic backgrounds, and build up his characters slowly. The mountebankish smartness and neatness of the Maupassant–O. Henry tradition are quite beyond him. He is essentially a serious man, and a melancholy. The thing that interests him most is not a deftly articulated series of events but a gradual transformation of personality, and particularly a transformation that involves the decay of integrity. The characters that live most brilliantly in his books, like those that live most brilliantly in the books of Conrad, are characters in disintegration—corroded, beaten, destroyed by the inexplicable mystery of existence.

In the midst of many reminders of his high talents, Dreiser's worst failing as a practical writer appears with painful vividness in this book. I allude to his astonishing carelessness, his irritating slovenliness. He seems to have absolutely no respect for words as words—no sense of their inner music, no hand whatever for their adept combination. One phrase, it would seem, pleases him quite as much as another phrase. If it is flat, familiar, threadbare, so much the better. It is not, indeed, that he hasn't an ear. As a matter of fact, his hearing is very sharp, and in his dialogue, particularly when dealing with ignorant characters, he comes very close to the actual vulgate of his place and time. But the difficulty is that this vulgate bulges beyond the bounds of dialogue: it gets into what he has to say himself, unpurged by anything even remotely resembling taste. The result is often a series of locutions that affects so pedantic a man as I am like music on a fiddle out of tune, or a pretty girl with beer-keg ankles, or mayonnaise on ice-cream. . . .

"Dreiser's Short Stories." Nashville *Tennesseean*, December 8, 1918.

Theodore Dreiser's new book, "Free," contains eleven short-story masterpieces, each a brilliant bit of literature, making up a book of supreme interest and value. For each contains the heart of a romance in itself. Probably no recent collection of short stories contains so much of human life, or so many really significant stories, so uniformly readable and suggestive. Life in several of its phases is depicted with the genius of a man who has mastered the story-teller's art. Whether telling the story of a rivalry between reporters on the two newspapers of a small city, or the near-tragedy of "Old Rogaum's Daughter," there is evident everywhere the pure story-telling instinct that never leaves a sentence incomplete or a detail of the word-picture unpainted. Characters are drawn in bold strokes, with never a line too much or a detail too highly filled in. Those familiar with Dreiser's previous writings will expect much of these stories, but not more than will be realized in reading them. Whether one claims to like short stories or not, he will be inevitably charmed with these.

William Marion Reedy. "Dreiser's Short Stories." *Reedy's Mirror*, December 13, 1918, p. 641.

I don't think Walt Whitman was a whit more American than Theodore Dreiser, nor in some respects a whit less *naïve.* I knew Walt's brother "Jeff" when he was water commissioner of St. Louis, and about the same time I used to talk with "Jeff," or "Tom" as we knew him, Theodore Dreiser was working here on the *Globe-Democrat,* as a reporter. Theodore was a serious boy, bent on doing something big in letters. Well, he has done it in his novels. He does it something as Walt did his big things, by putting everything in. Theodore is unselective, but the man has a passion for life that does now and again fuse his *omnium gatherum* into a life other than merely photographed fact. Dreiser piles up his facts until they sometimes glow as by spontaneous combustion from their pressure upon one another. You may rage at Dreiser's unmorality, at his unaesthetic or whatever, but he does give you great gobs of life and he puts pity and love into his work. Those are things that will save much worse work than his. I think "Sister Carrie" and "Jenny Gerhardt" are books of pity and of power and there are splendid splashes in "The Titan" and "The Genius." So I find high merit in "Free and Other Stories." If "Free" isn't a good story of marriage and its *ennui* I don't know a story when I see it, and if it isn't well done, with cumulative touches of ironic pathos, I have no conception of the writing art. "The Lost Phoebe" is a beautiful story of an old man's delusion and "The Cruise of the Idlewild" is a piece of humor that has tenderness in it too. Dreiser makes a shuddery tale of the lynching of Nigger Jeff and he transforms a man into an ant, with a great deal of the quality of the stuff we find in Henri Fabre's books. A little tragedy of the commonplace in "Old Rogaum and His Theresa" comes out on the comedy side of the ledger, but it is good realism all the way through. There are social studies more ambitious in the book, if not so surely handled, but nothing in it is unworthy of the intense and painstaking Dreiser. The "Story of Stories" is the tale of a newspaper scoop in St. Louis, the hero being drawn from the late Red Galvin and the incident built up on the item about a lone bandit holding up a Missouri Pacific train and being reported by the state officials aboard the train as a whole robber band. It is a good newspaper story showing how the roughneck reporter outwits a high-brow reporter in getting the captured bandit's photograph. This book of short stories is not as good stuff as Dreiser's plays of the natural and supernatural, but they are interesting chips from the workshop whence he has turned out big work and will turn out greater. For Dreiser, crude though some call him, has a devotion and desire to work that cannot fail of strong achievement. He may not strive for beauty as some interpret it, but he does strive for truth and—well, we all know what Keats has said of truth and beauty.

"Dreiser Again." Minneapolis *Journal*, December 20, 1918.

On the cover of this book is an impressionistic representation of what we take to be a highly sophisticated gentleman in the last spasm of matrimonial breakdown. It might represent a scarecrow in a cherry orchard, but we hold to our first guess because it seems to tally well with Mr. Dreiser's chief obsession. He is fond of dealing with marriages made unhappy by the smashing of a certain commandment.

But, for the moment at least, let's not hold either the cryptic picture or the obsession against Mr. Dreiser. At his best he can certainly write, and though he is perhaps too much given to identifying realism with nastiness, his ability to see through those situations which he chooses to treat is extraordinary.

There are 11 stories in the present collection and each is noteworthy in its special way. . . .

Whether or not one approves of Dreiser's themes or his outlook on life, one cannot deny his power.

Dial, 65 (December 28, 1918), 630, 632.

Mr. Theodore Dreiser may always be depended upon to show his readers what an essentially commonplace and fatuous thing life is. His novels—from the really exceptional Sister Carrie to that ponderous commentary on Weininger's Sex and Character, The "Genius"—abound in situation and auctorial asides on the extreme, irremediable banality of man in conflict with himself, his fellows, and with the universe. This attitude, which is the logical conclusion of the realist (or perhaps one should say the naturalist) philosophy in literature, sits upon Mr. Dreiser's bowed shoulders like the mantle of a prophet; and this prophet delights to utter his mournful, harpy-like lamentations at the impoverished banquet of existence in a tone whose skepticism is a little too like self-impotence always to convince. In the present volume he deserts the novel for the short story, but he still wears the mantle and executes the familiar gestures of realism. These eleven tales are not only so many Zolaesque slices of life of the most drab content, but in structure and style they are deplorably inadequate. Quite aside from the author's frequent perversions of good English—especially his irritating habit of splitting infinitives—the development of practically every story in this book obeys the prescriptions not of art but of journalism. A police-court reporter with a modicum of culture and literary aspirations could do no worse. And even Mr. Dreiser, whose claims to literary ability have received the confirmation of more than one genuine achievement, could scarcely do worse.

The fact is that Mr. Dreiser, in this book, has committed the ultimate blunder: in his worship of the trivial he has taken up the position of supposing that the mere "presentation" of the insignificant is enough to render a story "vital." Accordingly he insists upon eliminating from his situations and characters every hint of those incalculable factors which lend dramatic power to the lives of even the sorriest peasant and charwoman. It is not, be it understood, that Mr. Dreiser lacks feeling for real character and psychology—Jennie Gerhardt proves the contrary—it is just that in these rather colorless tales he has failed in responsibility to himself and to his artistic ideals. With the exception of The Lost Phoebe, a really charming study in the pathos (and pathology) of old age, and in the sketch of a village Bovary, The Second Choice, the sensitive reader would find it difficult to distinguish between these awkwardly written footnotes to a thesis and, say, the "sobstuff" of some exceptionally clever journalist. As an example of what real genius might have done with such material as this book contains read the Dubliners of James Joyce. Any reference to Tchekhov or Garshin or Galsworthy would perhaps be spreading it on too thick. Free and Other Stories is a book Mr. Dreiser will have to live down. It mars his reputation as an exact, patient student of the prosaic, offends by its unpardonable uncouthness of style, and seems conclusive evidence that its author will never master the difficult, heart-breaking technique of the short story. Yet, in the two exceptions above mentioned, there is indisputably a spark of promise for Mr. Dreiser in this field. Now if he will just fan this spark into a flame for us . . .

John Nicholas Beffel. "Dreiser's Story Book Is Sad Assemblage." Chicago *Herald & Examiner*, April 3, 1919.

Whenever a writer of reputation dies all of his writings are gathered up regardless of quality, and are foisted on a trusting public by publishers who want to clean up on a ready market. Some of Jack London's inferior stories were recently put between covers, and Morgan Robertson's death was capitalized for all it was worth.

But here is Theodore Dreiser, alive and well. What shall we say when a book of his short stories, most of them amateurish and worthy of a high school girl, is advertised as a great work? Shall we blame the publishers or the author? Or shall we pity them?

My impression on reading "Free and Other Stories" was that Dreiser had been induced to dig up whatever short stories he could find in his trunk, and that the eleven least worst had been put into the book.

This is not a condemnation of them all. "Free," the title story, is a fine piece of work, a powerful commentary on life as it is lived by unnumbered husbands and wives. "The Lost Phoebe" and "Old Rogbaum and His Theresa" also are big stories.

"Nigger Jeff" is a masterful description of a lynching. It is not a short story in the usual understanding of that term, yet I have no quarrel with its inclusion in this book, for it is literature of permanent worth.

The seven other stories, however, are sorry stuff. In "Will You Walk Into My Parlor?" Dreiser uses seventy pages to tell a blackmailing story that could have been told in twenty. "Married," "The Cruise of the Idlewild" and "When the Old Century Was New" are not short stories, but sketches. "The Story of Stories" is the kind of rot new reporters write.

Checklist of Additional Reviews

Publisher's Weekly, August 31, 1918.

Brooklyn [N.Y.] *Library News*, September, 1918, p. 137.

"Books and Reading." New York *Evening Post*, September 3, 1918.

New York *Evening Globe*, September 14, 1918.

Buffalo [N.Y.] *Express*, September 22, 1918.

Baltimore *Evening Sun*, September 28, 1918.

American Review of Reviews, 58 (October 1918), 445.

A.L.A. Booklist, October, 1918, p. 29.

Utica [N.Y.] *Observer*, October 3, 1918.

"One Hundred Leading Books." New York *Times Book Review*, October 13, 1918, p. 434.

Boston *Herald*, October 19, 1918.

Cincinnati *Times Star*, November 1, 1918.

Boston *Evening Transcript*, November 5, 1918.

"Dreiser's Short Stories." Indianapolis *Star*, November 6, 1918.

TWELVE MEN

By THEODORE DREISER

AUTHOR OF "SISTER CARRIE," "THE HAND OF THE POTTER," "FREE AND OTHER STORIES," "JENNIE GERHARDT," ETC.

BONI AND LIVERIGHT
NEW YORK 1919

Twelve Men

H. L. Mencken.
"H. L. Mencken Tells of Dreiser's New Book."
New York *Sun,*
April 13, 1919,
p. 4.

From the highest swing of Theodore Dreiser to his lowest stoop there is a distance so great that it seems almost fabulous—the distance, to wit, which separates all that is rarest and soundest in our literature from all that is shoddiest and most trivial. Such a book as *Jennie Gerhardt* is so brilliantly vivid, so profoundly moving, so spacious and dignified, that one turns from it with a sort of dismay to such a book as *The Genius,* with its tedious pedantry, its interminable inconsequence, its childish and irritating flatulence. It is as if Joseph Conrad, quitting a *Youth* or a *Heart of Darkness,* should proceed to a sentimental serial for shopgirls and fat women; it is almost as if Brahms should rise up out of hell to write patriotic ballads for vaudeville.

The phenomenon, unluckily, is not unmatched in our beautiful letters. The late Mark Twain, in the intervals of challenging Swift and Rabelais (and, somewhat behind the door, Nietzsche), often leaned down to challenge Artemus Ward, Charles H. Hoyt and M. Quad; it was his own incurable weakness, indeed, and not the mere imbecility of press agents, that bred the astounding doctrine that Irvin Cobb is his heir and assign. The causes of this disconcerting wabbling, though they are instructive, I need not go into here. I have touched upon them elsewhere, and shall expose them in detail in a forthcoming work. More important to the present purpose is one of the effects. It is this: That one approaches a new book by Dreiser as one always approached a new book by Mark, with a certain uncomfortable uncertainty—with one's aesthetic heart in one's mouth. It may be a new *Sister Carrie* or *Jennie Gerhardt* or *Titan* or *Hoosier Holiday,* and so praise God!—but on the other hand, it may be a new *Traveler at Forty* or *Hand of the Potter* or *Genius,* and so a thousand damns!

Well, here is *Twelve Men,* just off the press. To which of these categories does it belong? Let all cognoscenti be of cheer! Not to the second, surely! But to the first? Almost I am tempted to say clearly to the first. The high swing is undoubtedly there, and though there are also occasional dips to much lower levels the general effect is that of Dreiser at his most penetrating and persuasive. In more than one way he has done nothing better since *The Titan.* It shows, with a few unimportant breaks, a deliberate return to his first manner—the manner of pure representation, of searching understanding, of unfailing gusto and contagious wonderment. There is no banal philosophizing. There is no torturing of flabby theory. There is, above all, no burden of ethical purpose, no laboring of a duty to be performed. Instead there are simply a dozen sketches of character—rotund, brilliantly colored, absolutely alive. The thing is done capitally, and, at its top points, superbly.

Most of these dozen men are real—perhaps all. The author's brother Paul—the famous Paul Dresser, author of *On the Banks of the Wabash* and *Just Tell Them That You Saw Me*—appears in his proper person. Others—for example, Muldoon, the trainer; Harris Merton Lyon and Dreiser's father-in-law—are easily recognized. But this actual reality has little if anything to do with the reality they show upon the printed page. That reality is due altogether to the extraordinary skill of the man presenting them. What he produces is not merely an objective likeness; it is a searching and at times almost shameless inner genuineness. He gets into them; he understands and interprets them; he turns them inside out. And always in a way that somehow seems casual—always with a guileless and offhand air. Not once is there any creaking of literary blocks and tackles. Not once is there a formal vivisection. It is ever a picture he presents, not a diagram.

And what a gaudy and diverting picture it often is! Consider, for instance, the chapter devoted to Dresser-Dreiser, the song writing, tear squeezing brother—the Indiana Rouget de Lisle and Francis Scott Key. Intrinsically, he was an intensely interesting man, huge in body and yet ready to weep like a flapper, a fellow of remarkable talents and yet as devoid of elementary taste as a green grocer or a Congressman, a great success and yet a pathetic failure. But even more interesting than the man himself was the world he moved in and the culture he represented—the world and culture of the old Broadway, of vaudeville theatres, of the spangled demi-monde, of facile friendships, maudlin sentiments, gross revels, shady enterprises, stupid and hoggish folk. In such scenes he was a man of mark. He was the peer and intimate of other men of mark. He drank, drabbed and whooped 'er up with the best of them. But all the while he was something far finer than the others—a man of feeling, a dreamer of grotesque dreams, almost a poet. It was the contrast that made him salient and memorable, and it is the deft and poignant evocation of that contrast that makes his brother's portrait of him so brilliant and so excellent.

Muldoon is done almost as well. He remains at the end a sort of mystery, a man essentially inexplicable, but it is a mystery mellowed and humanized—one recognizes him and takes joy in him without precisely understanding him. So, again, with the forlorn, preposterous evangelist of *A Doer of the Word*—an astonishing creature indeed, a Christian actually devoted to the practice of Christianity, but somehow made credible. So, finally, with Lyon, with the queer Admirable Crichton of the sketch called *Peter* and with the venerable White, the author's father-in-law. In each of these men there was something fantastic. Each was a neglected alien in a nation of the undistinguished. It is Dreiser's feat that he has displayed that oddity vividly without the slightest touch of caricature—that he somehow convinces us of their general humanness, and gets into his portrait of each something of the universal human tragedy.

In brief, this is a book of extraordinary qualities—novel in plan, sound in structure, and, barring a few smears of feebleness, highly adroit in execution. As I have said, it goes back to the manner of *Sister Carrie* and *Jennie Gerhardt*—a variety of representation that has room for the profoundest feeling, but is yet rather aloof and unimpassioned. It projects human existence as the greatest of spectacles, thrilling, harrowing, sometimes downright appalling, but never hortatory, never a moral tale. The trouble with Dreiser in, say, *The Genius*, was that this manner had slipped away from him—that moral pressure had forced him, on the defensive, into a posture not unlike that of the pulpit. *The Genius* presented life less as an engrossing and inexplicable spectacle than as a somewhat mawkish document against comstockery and the Methodist revelation of God. To that extent it wabbled and was flabby. To that extent Dreiser made a mess of it.

But in *Twelve Men* he has his old tools in hand and is back at the trade he knows so well. His hacking is still often crude. He has his old weakness for phrases that outrage the sensitive ear like successive fifths. He must wallow, anon, in his banalities. He must give the English language a clout or two over the head. But the work that finally emerges from his inept striving is work that bears every mark of a first rate artist, save only that of style. It is solid and soundly organized. It has a sort of rough grace. It conveys its idea massively and certainly. It is a good job.

One wonders what the campus pump critics will make of it. One wonders still more how long they will cling to the delusion that the way to get rid of an artist beyond their comprehension is to invent the hypothesis that he doesn't exist. The saddest business of our literary artists is to prove, over and over again, that the academic Schlegels and Brandes of the land are idiots. Poe did it. Whitman did it. Mark Twain did it. And now Dreiser is doing it again.

Heywood Broun. "Theodore Dreiser at His Best in His New Book, 'Twelve Men'." New York *Tribune*, April 26, 1919, p. 10.

Most the admirers of Theodore Dreiser are poor press agents. I had heard enough about his painstaking and literal realism to keep me miles away from all his books. In fact, I pictured him as the sort of man who says "one" when he puts a nickel in the window of the subway ticket seller. Then "Twelve Men" came into the office and was tackled solely in the line of duty, but I found it by far the most readable and interesting book of all the late spring output.

It is probably true that Dreiser carefully avoids writing as well as he might. When he makes up his mind to split an infinitive he does it with a swagger and opens a breach for battalions. Thus, we get things like "to swiftly and agilely take a bath." Also he uses "outre" to an extent which would seem to indicate a desire to annoy his readers. But none of these things stand up against the fact that most of the sketches in the new volume are told with an eye to true, fascinating and essential details. There is no waste effort [sic]. Dreiser not only sees his subjects with extraordinary clarity, but he makes just the right selection of things out of the whole picture when he comes to jot down his impressions. The form is in general a middle ground between the short story and the short biography, although one or two of the sketches might well be classified as stories. The book is not uniformly good. "The Mighty Rourke" seems to me the best and "'Vanity, Vanity,' Saith the Preacher," the worst. The latter is almost in the form of a magazine article for "The New York American." Mr. Dreiser seems unduly impressed with a "large nickeled ice tray on wheels," which he encountered at a swagger reception. It was "packed with unopened bottles of champagne and you had but to lift a hand or wink an eye to have another opened for you alone, ever over and over. And the tray was always full." . . . Whatever faults may be found here and there, it seems to me that "Twelve Men" is an interesting and readable book, and an exceptionally fine piece of work as well. . . .

Newark *Evening News*, April 26, 1919.

Theodore Dreiser seems to have found a method perfectly suited to his type of mind and manner of writing in "Twelve Men." These "twelve men" are all real persons, to whom Mr. Dreiser acts as Boswell. They will scarcely seem disguised to those who knew them. . . .

It is an interesting book, although there is the temptation to say that this is so almost despite the author. There is Mr. Dreiser's style, for example. He writes with all the distinction of phrase, all the beauty of diction, of a machinery catalogue. Then there is Mr. Dreiser's occasional attempt at sentiment. These attempts remind the reader of nothing so much as the inept and sugary lyrics of which Paul Dresser was guilty. Then, again, there are the unsavory details with which Mr. Dreiser, in his intense, if mistaken, longing for truth, feels bound to indulge the reader, although, fortunately, such details are much fewer in the present volume than is usual with the author of "The Genius."

Yet, as has been indicated, despite all these faults, despite writing that is at times crude and never very impressive, Mr. Dreiser manages to "get there." The reader will like these men, most of them marked by admirable traits of character, and he will like Mr. Dreiser the better because he has perceived these admirable traits and himself feels respect for them.

New York *Globe*, April 26, 1919.

There is disappointment upon learning that Theodore Dreiser's new book is a series of biographies of "Twelve Men." Mr. Dreiser is most interesting when writing about one man. Fortunately for the enjoyment of the book, however, it might more accurately have been named "Twelve Men and Myself," or even the other way around.

In the first biography of "Peter," for example, Mr. Dreiser early has to pull himself up to say, "But I was talking of Peter." Talking of Peter, or anybody else, inescapably makes Mr. Dreiser think of "myself." "Like myself, Peter was raised a Catholic," or "Unlike myself, Peter had not the slightest trace of any lingering Puritanism." Peter had a "great stomach for life," whereas "I was a poor spindling, prying fish anxious to know life," but afraid. Peter was not afraid. He took a lusty delight in a certain "black house of prostitution," which proved him the "bigger" man, "saner, really more wholesome." Peter was "strong, vital, and unafraid, and he made me so." Mr. Dreiser is "grateful" to Peter, especially for the black house of prostitution. It is an interesting sketch of "Peter and Myself."

The most vivid portrait in the collection is "My Brother Paul," who called himself Dresser instead of Dreiser, doubtless to avert the nickname of "Dutchy" that was fastened to Theodore. Paul wrote "On the Banks of the Wabash" and many other popular songs. He was end-man in the minstrel show, and member of a patent medicine travelling troupe. He also had a great stomach for life, and especially for ladies. To take the walk up Broadway with Paul and Theodore is to revisit the heart of the old Tenderloin, beginning at Twenty-ninth street and stopping in every hotel, theatre, and bar, and talking with every hotel clerk, box-office man and bartender on the way until the Metropole is reached. The sketch has all the value of an old colored print, with bright spots of color in the "hot" socks, loud clothes, and flashy jewelry of the men and gay apparel of the ladies. The scene is not unlike one of those old English print series of high jinks in low places, some Nick or Dick or another making rough-house in a cellar or cave. This is an excellent sketch of "My Brother Paul and Myself."

But, speaking of myself, it was unfortunate that Paul was not fitted "intellectually or otherwise to enjoy high forms of art and learning," and did not understand "even in later years (long after I had written 'Sister Carrie,' for instance) what it was that I was attempting to do; he never did." Poor Paul, it must be confessed, was distinctly "middle class" —"and I say this in no lofty, condescending spirit, by any means."

We have lived in fear that Theodore Dreiser would some day smile, which would spoil everything. It might be advisable for John Shand to smile, as wife Maggie said. But for Mr. Dreiser to smile and take himself any less seriously than he does would be as fatal as it would be if the great Buddha should smile, thus revealing to his worshippers that he is only human like themselves. Mr. Dreiser almost smiles in several of these sketches of men who have been his "most gorgeous rapprochements" (even more than women, he says), but in each case saves himself in time.

Can it be that after all it is his middle-class morality that saves Mr. Dreiser, even his middle-class sentimentality? Contrary, perhaps, to popular belief, and contrary to what he may think himself, he is as "full of middle-class romance and tenderness" as his brother Paul. Peter, with all his great stomach for life and the black house of prostitution, is strong for the "home stuff," too, and marries the little German girl and proudly totes around the baby, which moves his friend to unexpected deeps of sentiment. Mr. Dreiser is apparently moved by the same tenderness that leads the lady to carry flowers to the prisoner; that uncovers in the criminal a tender spot for home and mother. "Peter was as much thrilled and entendered by the brawling strumpet in the street or the bagnio as by the virgin with her starry crown." Mr. Dreiser does not say in this case "like" or "unlike myself," but he may be depended upon to imitate Peter in his catholicity of taste.

No one should avoid "Twelve Men" under the delusion that Mr. Dreiser is not as busy and inquisitive here in examining his marvellous reactions and gorgeous rapprochements as when he was a Traveller at Forty. Peter and Paul are the most interesting of the "Twelve Men." "Culhane, the Solid Man," is almost amusing, with its description of the ex-prize-fighter head of the sporting sanitarium (where Mr. Dreiser went to be cured of a "psychic depression") screaming at his shocked and shivering gentlemen patrons to wash their toes and soap their legs. Most of the other biographies are tiresome, perhaps because they have less of Dreiser in them.

"Twelve Men." New York *Times Book Review*, April 27, 1919, p. 234.

So far as one can discover, Mr. Dreiser's predominating theory in writing these studies of "Twelve Men" would seem to have been simply this: if it is well to say a thing once, it is better to say it twenty times. He elaborates, and explains, and expounds, and describes every detail of every one of these twelve men, illustrating his explanations and descriptions with anecdotes and more or less philosophical comments; and when he has finished, his characters have about as much life in them as so many waxen figures set up in the showcase window of a department store. They are carefully costumed, and painted, and barbered, and arranged in appropriate attitudes; but the breath of life is entirely absent. And despite the natural irritation which results from being profoundly bored, one cannot help feeling sorry that this should be so, for in the lives of these dozen men—several of them individuals easily recognized by the circumstances surrounding them, and only slightly disguised under an initial or an altered name—there was evidently much material which, had it been better handled, would have proved very interesting. Indeed, there are moments in the study of "Culhane," owner and manager of a famous sanatorium in Westchester, which afford hopes that now at last we are to meet a real human being—hopes quickly swamped beneath a flood of verbiage.

The same comment applies to the study called "De Maupassant Junior," which tells of a young writer named L——. He wrote short stories, some of which appeared in magazines "excellent enough to have but a small circulation," but he presently compromised with "that curse of all American fiction, the necessarily happy ending," and the results were disastrous. Here again there are moments of interest, and again they are overwhelmed by the author's determination to use just as many words as possible. It would be pathetic, even sad, to see so much effort wasted, so much twisting and turning, dressing and redressing of the waxen figures, were it not for the author's apparently complete satisfaction with his own performance, from beginning to end.

This beginning is with a man he calls "Peter," a newspaper artist connected first with a St. Louis and later with a

Newark paper. Next comes "A Doer of the Word," this being an ex-fisherman and builder of model yachts, with a pronounced religious streak. He is followed by "My Brother Paul," composer of "On the Banks of the Wabash" and other popular songs. "The Country Doctor" is described as living up to the best traditions of his profession. The sketch of "Culhane, the Solid Man," already alluded to, comes next, and "A True Patriarch," who had a good deal of political influence, follows him. "The Village Feudists" tells of a groceryman living in a Connécticut fishing town who was convinced that his interpretation of the Bible was the only right and proper one, while succeeding it comes the study of a multimillionaire of the get-rich-quick variety. "The Mighty Rourke" is an Irish foreman given to vigorous speech, and "A Mayor and His People" is an account of an unlucky reformer. "W. L. S." is an illustrator with ambitions and plans, left unfulfilled by his early death. It will be seen that the volume has a sufficient variety in its types, if not in the author's treatment of them.

David Karsner. "Theodore Dreiser's 'Twelve Men'." New York *Call Magazine*, April 27, 1919, p. 10.

Those persons who are only luke-warm toward Dreiser, and there are probably many if his reviewers and critics are a criterion (which they are not), will find in his latest book elements of Dreiser's genius that will certainly put to rout whatever amount of skepticism that may still be lurking in their minds. If Dreiser had not written "Sister Carrie" and "Jennie Gerhardt" his "Twelve Men" would win him place and power in the realm of letters that the first two named books had already earned for him.

In point of literary construction, manner and mood "Twelve Men" is easily Dreiser's best book since "Jennie Gerhardt," with "The Titan" and "The Financier" running a close second and third respectively. It is so much superior to "The 'Genius'" and "The Hand of the Potter" that one almost wonders if the same author wrote those books. This only proves the many sidedness of Dreiser's character and power which tomorrow might lead him into the production of an essay, the day after a Cowperwood novel, and the day after that another play, one act or four, depending entirely upon Dreiser's mood.

These Twelve Men are characters whom Dreiser has met and had social intercourse with at some time or other. In revealing them he has revealed himself, and in this sense the book contains a large amount of autobiography. Yet Dreiser is seen only as a sculptor at work in his studio, modeling his object. The object is the thing, after all, and Dreiser steps aside from his finished work with the modesty of the true artist. Any person who can read this book, or any single one of the dozen character sketches in it and still say the figures portrayed are "waxen and lifeless" does not know how to read a book, let alone criticise one. He should go way back to the nursery and play with toy balloons and a train of chu-chu cars. . . .

It cannot be said that the men whom Dreiser has chosen to write about are "exceptional." Indeed, they are very ordinary human beings for the most part, for twelve men are still nothing more than twelve men. Twelve others would be just as interesting to Dreiser and the rest of us. He has proved that human life, wherever it is found, is most precious, most fascinating, most true, most dear. That any story, thesis or theme built upon it is interesting and charming.

"Twelve Men" is a permanent book. Its appearance is an event in the year's literature, and Theodore Dreiser, as its author, has earned one more gold service stripe in literature.

E.F. Edgett. "Theodore Dreiser Dissects Humanity." Boston *Evening Transcript*, April 30, 1919, p. 6.

While fifteen years or more of practice find Mr. Dreiser still unwearied in the midst of his realistic literary efforts, the progress of time has nevertheless somewhat modified or lessened his enthusiasm. In his first novel, "Sister Carrie," he revealed a fondness for the consideration of sex problems, and in "Jennie Gerhardt," "The Financier" and the tales that followed he left nothing undone and no word unsaid to emphasize his belief in the fact of the overwhelming influence for good and evil of the relations between men and women upon the entire course of their lives. He has been, moreover, from the first a believer in the value of elaborate detail, and the result has been a series of novels that are remarkable for their length as well as for much else. Indeed, he set out to tell the story of Frank Cowperwood's life, from boyhood onward, in three volumes, but it remains incomplete and with no successor yet in sight to conclude the tale begun in "The Financier" and "The Titan."

Long experience both as a magazine editor and novelist has not given to Mr. Dreiser the power of self-criticism. Although his "Twelve Men" is not pervaded with so many verbal perversities as his other fiction, it contains many banalities and shortcomings of style. In all of his novel may be found sentences that set one's teeth on edge. For a novelist to write in perfect seriousness that "they carted him off to the hospital," or "she is a good-looker," displays a crudity that admits of no excuse. Furthermore, Mr. Dreiser's misuse of words is suggestive of the yellowest of yellow journalism. He apparently is ignorant of the meaning of "locate," "allude" and "transpire"; he uses the phrase, "from whence," he uses the impersonal pronoun "one" as antecedent of the personal "they," he speaks of "either" side when he means "both" sides, and in many other expressions he violates even the most elementary canons of good taste and dignity.

Less offense of this sort is to be found in "Twelve Men" than in some of his other fiction. In the first place, it is not a long novel, but a collection of impressionistic and realistic sketches of personality, many of them drawn from life and from Mr. Dreiser's actual contact with the people he describes. The tales have, therefore, a compact brevity, a directness and a convincing power not to be found in his longer and more pretentious work. Each of his personages obviously steps forward into his pages from real life and in every instance they are closely companioned by Mr. Dreiser. In fact, the stories contain frequently as much of their author as of their subject, and whether he refers to himself or not, we feel his continual presence, for we are watching his friend Peter, his brother Paul, the mighty Rourke, the country doctor, and all the others as they react upon himself. We see each of them through Mr. Dreiser's eyes and with his mind, and they are persistently very keen eyes and a very alert mind.

The identity of several of these "Twelve Men" is easily discernible to the casual reader, and of course to Mr. Dreiser's personal friends they are doubtless all familiar. The two best known and most significant figures are of course Paul Dresser, his brother, and William Muldoon, whom he disguises not at all under the designation of "Culhane, the Solid Man." Perhaps the best of all these sketches is "My Brother Paul," because of his closeness to him through many years, but in its way the story of Muldoon is a marvellously accurate feat of pen portraiture and dissection, while the human qualities of "A Doer of the Word," "A True Patriarch" and "The Country Doctor" show the extent of Mr. Dreiser's sympathetic observations. The only sketch approaching failure is that of "A Mayor and His People." . . .

M.A.
"Theodore Dreiser."
New Republic, 19 (May 3, 1919), 30–31.

A fairly respectable biography of Theodore Dreiser might be concocted with no other bibliography than his Twelve Men and an American Who's Who. For the round dozen of them are manifestly real folk the author has known more or less intimately at different stages of his career, and we glimpse him through his contacts with them. We learn, for example, that he grew up in a stringently moral home in the middle west, and that his coming to New York was hastened by the undeniable fame and fortune his brother Paul was accumulating there as the foremost writer of popular songs. It comes as news that Theodore (and not Paul) wrote the first stanza and the chorus of On the Banks of the Wabash just to show his brother how these things should be managed. It would be possible to piece together the facts of his connection with many newspapers and magazines, the details of a "psychic breakdown" necessitating a sanatorium, an adventure in labor as a member of a railroad gang, and an astonishing prestige as editor of magazines for women, such as the Delineator.

The style of Twelve Men differs from that of The Genius in being fairly simple, with only occasional inextricable meanings. It lacks as did The Genius and all its predecessors, the finish that might have given resonance and carrying quality to what is said. Only a man as thoroughly sophisticated as Anatole France could use a medium of expression so loose as this without drifting once in a while into inanity. And he would not use it. But Mr. Dreiser is not sophisticated. He is easily disgusted, easily moved to tears. He writes "my dear brother" a little too often, and regrets Paul's eastern burial in the sentence, "It was so cold and dreary there, horrible."

The most acid realism may sometimes represent nothing more than a self-conscious sentimentalism dodging itself, if one judge from the following, hard to ascribe to any realist: "Ah, Broadway! Broadway! And you, my good brother! Here is the story that you wanted me to write, this little testimony to your memory, a pale, pale symbol of all I think and feel. Where are the thousand yarns I have laughed over, the music, the lights, the song? Peace, peace. So shall it soon be with all of us. It was a dream. It is. I am. You are. And shall we grieve over or hark back to dreams?"

But this lack of style, whether it be flaw or virtue, is only one angle of a general and real lack of philosophy. Theodore Dreiser is a conscientious and competent observer, but an observer galled and limited in range by strands of old repressions, angered to find himself bound by an inculcated morality in an age when others have fought free. He is constantly at war against his Puritanical instincts, with the result that he is never sure of his own boundaries. He can assume no consistent attitude, can put no coherence into the way he says his say about American life.

There is, strangely enough, a kind of consistency in the lives of the twelve men he has chosen to represent. No less than six of them were men of great promise who died without achieving the things they seemed fitted to do. And four, perhaps five, can be put down as minor philanthropists, men who, because of some religious or personal bias, have found their happiness in serving others. For Dreiser it is a remarkable collection. In all of them the element of selfishness is reduced to a minimum; it is as if he had said to himself that he had been confined too closely to the hopeless, that he would now make a study of the creative spirit and eternal kindliness in men. He succeeds rather indifferently with the humanitarians. For them he seems to have only a mild and artificially exaggerated sympathy; and his misunderstanding of them verges in some instances on complete bewilderment. With the young journalists, artists and publicists he was in closer touch; catalogues of peculiarities occur, but vivified by inner acquaintance. Peter, who opens the book, assumes life and charm from the beginning.

It was evidently Peter who first woke Theodore Dreiser from his middle-western sleep to a realization that the world and its possibilities were wider than had been allowed to appear on the surface, and much wider than his education. With Peter he went about St. Louis for the first time. "As I view myself now, I was a poor, spindling, prying fish, anxious to know life, and yet because of my very narrow training very fearsome of it, of what it might do to me, what dreadful contagion of thought or deed it might open me to! Peter was not so. To him all, positively *all*, life was good. . . . When I look back now upon the shabby, poorly lighted, low-ceiled room to which he led me 'for fun,' the absolutely black or brown girls with their white teeth and shiny eyes, the unexplainable, unintelligible love of rhythm and the dance displayed, the beating of the drum, the sinuous, winding motions of the body, I am grateful to him. He released my mind, broadened my view, lengthened my perspective. For as I sat with him, watching him beat his drum or play his flute, noted the gayety, his love of color and effect, and feeling myself *low*, a criminal, disgraced, the while I was staring with all my sight and enjoying it intensely, I realized that I was dealing with a man who was 'bigger' than I was in many respects, saner, really more wholesome. I was a moral coward." There are many instances of their common adventures, told with the same directness, and indicating in a similar fashion the influence of Peter in opening the eyes of his companion, not only to the dives of the city, but to the religions, arts, and philosophies of the earth. Probably it was these peregrinations that temporarily smothered the sentimentalist—the song-writer—in Dreiser.

As an experiment in literary form the book is only a passable success. Interesting as many of the figures are, they interest only in themselves, and not in the sketches to follow. There is nothing in Peter to prepare us for the sudden change of atmosphere in A Doer of the Word, and though the autobiographical thread exists it runs in tangled convolutions. There comes a time when the momentum is insufficient to carry over. To be sure there will be those who overcome the inertia, and turn the page, remembering that this man Dreiser never puts his best foot forward, never seems to be going to get anywhere, and yet somehow, after a good deal of fuss and bungling, sometimes does.

Burton Rascoe. "Dreiser Gives Us His Best Effort in 'Twelve Men'." Chicago *Tribune*, May 3, 1919.

I am sorry that the Urbana grammar teacher who set the mob at the heels of Theodore Dreiser no longer has a place to hang his critical hat. For I should like to hear what he has to say about Dreiser's new book, "TWELVE MEN." The most persistent, lusty, and ingeniously sadistic among Dreiser's persecutors, it was he who invoked the lynch mania against Dreiser with cries of "animal behavior," "sex obsession," and "barbaric naturalism," uttered with all inflaming ardor of meaning by these words, rape, arson, murder and treason.

I say I am curious to know his opinion because Dreiser's new book is such a flat and final refutation of the charges to which he gave general currency. Here are portraits of twelve men, several of them readily identifiable, in which there is scarcely any mention either of sex or of women. The reason is not that Dreiser has abandoned a former method of writing or yielded to Puritanical dictates; but the simple reason that in the lives of the men with whom he is here concerned erotic desire is either sublimated or unimportant.

When Dreiser wrote of Cowperwood in the two books of his incompleted trilogy and of Witla in "The 'Genius,'" sex was prominent because sex occupied the real determining feature in their lives. He attempted conscientious, full length portraits, and for him to have shirked the importance passion played in shaping their careers would have been to present crude and false semblances of these men. He worked from documentary evidence and from personal observation. He saw "nature through a temperament" as clearly as it was given him to see, and he recorded his impressions with the utmost fidelity possible to a humanly limited endowment of omniscience. Beyond this no artist in any medium can hope to go.

Thus also is his method in "TWELVE MEN" one of profound curiosity and diligent scrutiny. He has sought to present these men as he saw them, from every angle of observation of which he is capable. He has tried to get at the bottom of their thoughts and motives, their aspirations and their vanities, their attitude toward life and their manner of facing it. He has found in his twelve characters twelve amazingly divergent philosophies of life, all of which he presents without criticizing, blaming, or moralizing. He does not, to quote the historian, "propose or impose," and, if he does not thoroughly expose, it is because a certain overwhelming human pity and sympathy makes it impossible for him to do so.

"Pity and sympathy"—those are words which Dreiser's detractors would never think of applying to him; and those are the words which really characterize him as an artist. Nowhere is he gay hearted or facetious, cynical, thoughtless, or indifferent toward human life. He is haunted always with the tragic inexplicability of destiny, the aberrant cruelty of fate, the seeming indifference of the Infinite to the pitiable human struggle. Life's questions torture him, and no slight, irreverent gift of humor saves him from the pain of them.

Seldom has there appeared in print a more moving tribute than Dreiser's to his brother, Paul Dresser, who is one of those portrayed in this book. This elder brother, a massive compound of fatness, joviality, gross tastes, liberality, tenderness, and sentiment, enjoyed in his time the fleeting adulation of the populace. He was a minstrel end-man, a jokesmith, and a writer of popular songs, who achieved by degrees the fame of favorite in the tinsel playworld of old Broadway, New York.

Dreiser portrays this elder brother with evident honesty and an affectionate touch. We see him, the author of "On the Banks of the Wabash" and other sentimental ditties, an affable, appealing figure, blubbering profusely over his own compositions, the victim of his own generosity and compassion, something of an angel and something of a rake, nursing in an atmosphere of facile success and flashy pleasures a certain flicker of high purpose and retaining against all rebuffs of men and fate a fine unselfishness and beauty of character. It is a rounded and admirable portrait, tender, truthful and human.

So, too, with his story of Harris Merton Lyon, "De Maupassant Junior," an abrupt, self-centered, censorious, highly talented youth who struggled with a fixed purpose, fought to impose his artistic ideas upon a sentiment loving people, compromised, became a personage, lost his ideals in an excess of vanity, regained them, and died, just as he promised to become one of the important figures in American literature.

You will recognize under the thin disguise of another name, Muldoon the far-famed trainer, that modern Spartan, whose rigid self-discipline enabled him to triumph over the inadequacy of his education and low beginnings of his career, until with a mingled envy and contempt he could dominate and rebuild the physical failures who conquered in the world either by fact of birth or by mental energy.

There is an admirable sketch of "The Contented Man," a strange being, actually living the gospel of Jesus, a believer in the goodness of mankind and the clemency of God, a witness to miracles, and a doer of beautiful deeds. Then there is a fascinating portrait of a newspaper artist, interested in everything under heaven, a genius of a thousand accomplishments, a connoisseur and an inventor, a dilettante extraordinary who accepted life without question and for all it offered—a clean minded, efficient, high principled man, whose sudden death filled Dreiser with bitter anger and despair for months.

In all these portraits there is that same sincere attempt to present these men as they are—the modern Heliogabalus, and the modern ascetic, the section boss, and the village patriarch. Here is wondrous, inscrutable, fascinating life as revealed in the diversity of twelve marionettes of the Great Impresario. It is one of the most unusual books in our literature, and certainly one of the best books that Dreiser has given us.

New York *Morning Telegraph*, May 3, 1919.

There are more things in Heaven and earth than are dreamed of in my philosophy, and I sincerely hope that I never get to the point where I am unwilling to admit it. The unexpected, almost the incredible, has happened. I have read a book by Theodore Dreiser and liked it. Its title is "Twelve Men."

For some time I have entertained a prejudice against Mr. Dreiser's writing which I have not hesitated to express in song and story. Stephen Leacock's burlesque on "The Genius" filled me with joy, and I envied the Canadian professor for having written it. I revelled in Mr. Stuart P. Sherman's chapter on Dreiser in "Contemporary Literature," because it reflected my own views in language so beautifully academic. Mr. H. L. Mencken, who reviewed "Twelve Men" most ably for the Sun, would, of course, call Mr. Sherman a "campus pump critic." By the same token, he would call me an "old maid." But he professed curiosity as to what such inferior intelligences might think of "Twelve Men." In all justice, I am obliged to state that I think well of it. And so will you, Gentle Reader.

"Twelve Men" is a series of pen portraits dealing with a dozen types of American masculinity. That they are taken, in the main, from actual individuals is beyond doubt, in spite of the traces of fine fictionizing which appear here and there. Some of the men are easily recognized. One chapter is devoted to the author's brother, Paul Dresser, who wrote "On the Banks of the Wabash" and "Just Tell Them That You Saw Me." I like this sketch best of all. "The Mighty Rourke" comes second; "De Maupassant, Jr.," third.

Mr. Dreiser supports his main strokes of characterization with an abundance of detail and anecdote which adds greatly to the interest of his work. He has written an engaging book which does him credit. "Twelve Men" is a good literary performance.

C. B.
"Dreiser's Rare Genius Is Shown In 'Twelve Men'." Baltimore *Evening Sun*, May 3, 1919.

About a month ago I was so much interested in an article in the current number of La Mercuri, one of the foremost French journals of literary criticism, that being imbued with the sense of the missionary spirit, I pestered the editor to allow me to translate it for THE EVENING SUN book page. It concerned modern American literature, and as I don't suppose any one read it (for who ever reads book reviews or news), I will not hesitate to quote again from it.

> Dreiser is certainly the most important novelist in the States today. Without any particular effort to invent animated scenes, he shows us the real American that one meets on the streets, in shops, in "pensions de famille," while traveling.
>
> Dreiser is far from being a perfect artist; his superiority is largely due to his subject. He writes so badly and has so little the power of selection that his recent book, "The Genius," is difficult to read. . . . But "Sister Carrie" and "Jennie Gerhardt" remain to his credit. If anyone should wish to translate one of the best modern American novels let him choose one of these two.

Last week there came off the presses of Messrs. Boni and Liveright the first copies of a new book by Theodore Dreiser. After the somewhat deplorable slump of the "Genius" and the "Book of Plays," many former admirers may have vowed themselves to abstention of Dreiser and all his recent works. To them particularly I could say that "Twelve Men" is a really fine piece of work, not exactly to be compared with the novels, for its form is different, but most certainly to be placed on the same level of excellence. In some ways its appeal is wider and will probably be as immortal as such things can ever hope to be, for these 12 men are in their several ways typical of their epoch. They are not literary puppets answering stiffly to the jerky twangings of their author. They are pictures of men who have actually lived and in so doing have added their contribution of widow's mite, or titan's gift, their fragment of sadness, mirth, poverty or wealth to the period in which they lived. It is certainly a great relief to read about and browse among, actual Americans, instead of the usual alternatives of villainous or pious "Captains of Industry," "athaletic" heroes on football teams and those even more impossible people either in real life or fiction, leaders of society in the monde or demimonde. . . .

I can only reiterate that by some God-given miracle Dreiser has up his sleeve the incomparable art of picturing people that you may love, despise, hate or admire, but to whom you cannot remain indifferent. In some extraordinary way he seems able to select significant phrases or incidents that reveal all sorts of intricacies and simplicities of their minds; and here I disagree with the writer in the Mercuri who accuses him of lacking the power of selection. At times his writing is jerky, and he never rises to "flights of eloquence," conventional or otherwise. It is not the way he says things that fascinates, but that he has real things to say: real insight, real understanding and real feeling for and with the troubles and joys of his fellow-men. I do not mean by this that he ever descends to "sob stuff" or sloppy sentimentality, but merely that he seems possessed of the chameleon-like quality of putting himself in the other fellow's place and seeing the world through his eyes. He never moralizes, he merely presents. I have been told that he is a man of great feeling, always indignant about something or pitying some one. While that is a very questionably comfortable temperament to have, certain advantages do go with its obvious drawbacks, and "Twelve Men" seems to be the very direct result of those advantages. Personally, I am extremely grateful to Mr. Dreiser for some hours of considerable enjoyment, and I hope that for once I may have stepped out of my role of being the exception to prove the rule.

"The Phenomenal Dreiser." New York *Evening Sun*, May 10, 1919.

Theodore Dreiser is a remarkable phenomenon. There is only one of him; there never was anybody quite like him before, and although it is rash to forecast the future one feels reasonably sure that he is not likely to happen over again in our time. He is something of a *lusus naturae*, a "sport"; not catalogued or easily placed among the known varieties. Or, it may be more exact, under the circumstances, to call him a human *'aepax legomenon,'* an embodied word that occurs but once.

Here is a writer, novelist, essayist, editor, and miscellaneous man of letters who positively cannot write English—and yet does it, and "gets away with it," with obvious success. He cannot produce a page of type without committing mayhem on the tough and long suffering language. His eccentricities rival Mrs. Partington. He is capable of writing such sentences as this: "Then, not incuriously, seeing the affectional tie that had held us, he wanted to see me."

One remains "not incurious" as to the genesis of such a misunderstanding of words. . . .

Let us admit the brutality of reference to his derangement of epitaphs, but it is justified by the value and fine qualities of the rest of him. It would be cruel and beyond forgiveness if there were no more of him. But there is such a lot! He has ideas; he sees things, and has something positive and upbuilding to say of them. He is a Personality, with a large P. Articulate, but sometimes verging on the incoherent.

His newest book, "Twelve Men," is by far the most important thing he has done. It has all the good qualities, and all the strange defects, of his emphatic personality. It is full of "blazing indiscretions," and, perhaps, owes some of its values to the naiveté that leads him to commit them. Interesting indiscretions are always attractive, especially when the subject matter is fairly fresh in the minds and experience of its readers.

The book is a series of portrait biographies of a dozen men, most of them easily to be recognized; by their neighbors, or, in some cases, by the larger public. Each sketch is "convincing," drawn from the living model by one with a seeing eye, though sometimes the result suggests something of a caricature, an overemphasis on some chosen element in the character.

But there you have him: the seeing eye. Mr. Dreiser is valuable as an observer; a man who sees into the corners and is as interested in the heaps of dust swept under the sofa as he is in the well arranged parlor table or the graven images on the mantelpiece. Such an inquisition is useful, entertaining, and something of a stimulant.

But—and it is rather a pity—one recurs to the manner of it, and wonders whether that does not, in itself, imply a certain obliquity of vision. "Do I seem to rave?" he asks on page 3, and one is constrained to answer—well, yes; sometimes.

There is a horrid fascination in studying it. One may forgive the split infinitives—he makes a helpless victim learn "to swiftly and agilely take a bath"—as minor eccentricities. There is a ghoulish savor to such coined words as "entendered." But it leaves a bewildered wonder as to how any one could have written so much, with such a real perception of facts, such sound feeling for color, and values, and significances, and still mouth it so. It is a living contradiction of the critical maxim enunciated—was it by Pliny the Elder?—*rem tene; verba sequantur.* Mr. Dreiser has a solid grip on the things, and the words follow, but they step on each other's feet unaccountably and bring along many strange words that exist nowhere else. . . .

But these "intimate" portraits of real people have a curious attractiveness. It is built, really, upon the absolute sincerity of intent, coupled with a keen perception of the realities and true meanings of character. And to do that is a triumph, however peculiar the mode of expression.

Providence [R.I.] *Journal*, May 11, 1919.

Mr. Theodore Dreiser may be taken as an example of a case where a smattering of Gallic penetration has been grafted upon a mind utterly unsuited to the treatment. Of Mr. Dreiser's considerable ability in the writing of fiction there can be no question. Has he not himself loudly and insistently proclaimed his genius? And who should know better?

In the volume of short stories called "Twelve Men" Mr. Dreiser has, in certain respects, done some of the best, the most sincere, work of his literary career. He has taken a round dozen of typical Americans and made pictures of them—pictures which are in the main true to life. The fault of the book—aside from the vulgarity which disfigures all Mr. Dreiser's work—lies in the fact that the portraits never step out of their frames. We grant the likeness; but we do not feel the personality.

Even so fine a sketch as that of "The Country Doctor" or in that equally admirable one of quite another character, "De Maupassant, Jr.," the artificiality of the form of construction is apparent and dulls the interest of the reader. Yet, Mr. Dreiser, although he is far from being "poor in ideas but rich in power," should have been the very one—judged from one point of view—to come across successfully with the short story. That he has come very near to doing so and has given us an interesting though not tensely absorbing gallery of character-studies is indeed a remarkable exhibition of what an artist who lacks one of the supremely necessary qualities of art, a sense in some sort, of humor, may do when he sets out to tackle literature with a bludgeon.

" 'Twelve Men'." San Francisco *Chronicle*, May 14, 1919.

It is a quite unusual book that Theodore Dreiser has written in "Twelve Men." Some of the studies are manifestly direct portraits, but others leave the reader guessing as to whether they are fact or fiction. We may be sure that "Culhane, The Solid Man," is a moving picture, plus a phonograph record, of the proprietor of a famous health resort much patronized by American celebrities of all classes. Often as this worthy has been described, he never really lived on the printed page until placed there by Dreiser. . . .

There are passages in the book which suggest that the writer is feeling the restraint of a possible censorship, then all of a sudden he lets go and we get that nearest thing in American letters to the immortal Frenchman whose name is still the byword for that which the Puritans tell us we ought not to read.

As separate sketches these chapters are works of art; as a whole they are the product of genius, for only genius could sustain itself in the same masterly manner. Some of the people may not be worth while—that is viewed as possible realities—but as figments of the imagination they reveal the creative brain at its maximum of productiveness. Never has Dreiser done better nor more daring art, and if he is "getting by" the censor it is perhaps because he is not thinking of him.

"Twelve Portraits By Theodore Dreiser." Philadelphia *Press*, May 17, 1919.

The best and the worst of Theodore Dreiser are represented in this book. And speaking of the best of Dreiser means something so singularly strong and searching that the worst is readily to be tolerated for its sake.

His twelve men are real men, men he has known intimately, some of them of such prominence that they are easily to be recognized behind the fictitious names he has given them. There is a study of Muldoon, the famous trainer and wrestler; one of Harris Merton Lyon; one of Dreiser's own father-in-law and another of his brother Paul. The identity of the others is not as clear, but they are none the less interesting personalities on that account.

Interest is precisely the quality that dominates the book. Sometimes it is akin to the spell that absorbing fiction casts upon a reader, sometimes a sheer gossipy brand of interest in the affairs of other people's lives, but always it is an interest keen, sustained and vivid. Undoubtedly it is evoked by Mr. Dreiser's profound sincerity. The most loosely written of his pages, the most banal of his preachments are animated, curiously enough, by the infectious fire of his sincerity. . . . to faithful readers of Dreiser this book will be a revelation of how astonishingly many episodes of his novels—and particularly "The Genius" —are based upon personal experience.

More than this, the twelve portraits in their wide variety and uncompromising candor, comprise a striking incidental picture of American life. It is precisely this quality which distinguishes the writing of Dreiser from the average of his contemporaries. Irregular as is his workmanship, tiresome as his occasional moral "lags" may be, in the end he has shown you truth unadorned and unmistakable.

Baltimore *News*, May 18, 1919.

Displaying the meticulous care in characterization, the subjective insight and that curious, ever-present element of blind power that mark his past works, Dreiser's new book not only commands attention for its expected qualities, but also does it quicken interest by reason of traits not before disclosed in any considerable degree.

To think of him as writing to please or to delight would be to invest him with a willingness for compromise, and it must be said that this is not at all indicated by his latest effort. His style is still devoid of "charm," but there are in this book touches of tenderness and humor that reveal an unfamiliar phase of his temperamental equipment.

The incidents on "Culhane, the Solid Man," an account of a celebrated "renovator" of alcoholic and other wrecks, for instance, are extremely amusing in themselves. In the hands of a professional humorist they would be screamingly funny.

The tenderness referred to is chiefly apparent in "My Brother Paul," a very beautiful recital of the life of Paul Dreiser, better known as Dresser, composer of such popular song hits of the past as "The Banks of the Wabash" and "Just Tell Them That You Saw Me."

"Twelve Men" is a book that unflinchingly holds the attention of the reader who appreciates skill in projecting full-length studies "from life" that besides accurately depicting physical superficialities, delves deeper and reveals soul. These are literary portraits in the truest and most convincing sense of the term. The types are vastly varied and in his record of them Dreiser gives many autobiographical facts and presents what in collective significance really amounts to a striking picture of the times.

Summing up, "Twelve Men" ranks with the very best things of its kind that have recently appeared. It is another fine achievement of a writer whose work, for all its "unattractiveness," all its palpable faults, yet bears the hallmark of real greatness.

"American Types." *Nation*, 108 (May 24, 1919), 838.

The work of Theodore Dreiser has been, from time to time, the subject of a controversy not lacking in heat. Both parties to this quarrel have fixed their attention upon his preoccupation with sex, and the reactions of both have been a trifle strained and morbid. Mr. Dreiser is, of course, not really more preoccupied with that single theme than is the conventional novelist. But there are precisely two ways of interpreting life through literature. Either you assume antecedently that all people are, even in their lapses, spiritually identified with the dominant social morality of their group and age, or you do not. Mr. Dreiser does not. Observation and experience have led him to conclude, as they led Samuel Butler to conclude, that a great many people have never so identified themselves with group morality, that their conformity is born of fear or the web of circumstances, and that thus there arises a very acute and significant conflict. To call these people of his "bad" or to stigmatize their behavior as "animal" is perfectly justified from the point of view of an idealistic ethics. It is also perfectly sterile. Life is terribly concrete and insistent, and in all questions of human conduct an idealistic nominalism seems to serve no end save to arouse agreeable if not always charitable emotions in the philosophic breast.

A fruitful attack upon Mr. Dreiser's substance can be made only by invalidating his facts. But this no one has sought to do. What has constantly impressed good judges who were neither among his friends nor his detractors is the man's massive knowledge of those phases of American life with which he has chosen to deal. His powers of observation and of vicarious experience are of the first order. By virtue of them he ranks among the major novelists. His personal philosophy may be negligible, but so was Balzac's. His concrete subject-matter is marvellously varied and abundant. And the concrete, if it be adequately represented, points symbolically, as Goethe said, to the totality and the meaning of things.

If it be adequately represented! Here one comes upon the source of Mr. Dreiser's weakness. His substance reaches us despite his form. His structural technique is sound enough. In his longer stories he produces an illusion which shows him sensitive to the rhythm of life; in "Twelve Men" he experiments not unhappily in a new mood of narrative. In the narrower sense, however, he cannot write. No man of equal power has ever written so poorly. Even Balzac's French is more attractive and finished than Mr. Dreiser's English. He has moments of homely strength. But these are very brief, and he quickly returns to his masses of blunt and lumbering verbiage. His insensitiveness is partly linguistic, partly cultural. He is capable of constantly using "betimes" as though it meant "at times," and of bracketing "Salammbo" and "Quo Vadis" as works equal in kind and quality. And yet, somehow, his substance does reach and impress and profoundly move us. So that one finally gains a vision of him as of a giant in chains. In chains, indeed, but a giant none the less.

His new volume, "Twelve Men," consists of interpretative character sketches of real people. These pieces are so built as to suggest the progression of a spiritual drama, which usually ends upon a tragic note. The men are all men whom Mr. Dreiser has known and lived with, who have engaged his affection or admiration, and whose fate has induced in him a characteristic brooding over the strangeness of mortality. And they are nearly all people in whom great energy and vividness of mind and character came to a but broken and futile end. Such was his brother Paul, such the late Harris Merton Lyons, the financier in "Vanity, Vanity," and the artist W. L. S. Such, too, among humbler folk, were the impressive shop-keeper in "The Village Feudists" and the social reformer in "A Mayor and His People."

It is notable that the interest of sex is entirely absent from this volume. But, indeed, every attentive reader of Mr. Dreiser's work must have known that love is to him but the great anodyne that soothes, at moments, the ache of life and hides its futility. It is no less remarkable that the only ones among these narratives that sound a note of peace and reconciliation are those that treat of simple men who deliberately make their lives a round of

> "little, nameless, unremembered acts
> Of kindness and of love."

But these, too, fill Mr. Dreiser with a sense of keen pathos, a pathos not always rigidly enough guarded from the confines of sentimentality. Even so, it is but just to say that the Virgilian *nos mortalia tangunt* accurately renders the mood and burden of these portraits.

They have another value. Most of these men belong to vanishing types. Or, at least, the same types assume a very different guise today. And Mr. Dreiser has projected them, at times with an ease and fluidity unusual to him, at others through the torment of his amorphous manner, but always with a final effect that is massive and vivid at once. Thus they give one a very deep sense of American life—its feverish energy, its crude force alternating with sentimentality, its kindliness and its hostility to distinction and veracity. If it is the aim of imaginative narrative to clarify the soul by enlarging our experience of human life and character, Mr. Dreiser has once more vindicated his imperfect art and emphasized his station among our novelists.

"Dreiser's Portraits." Springfield [Mass.] *Republican*, May 25, 1919.

Whatever one may think of the artistic purpose of Theodore Dreiser's novels, the purpose which has inspired his "Twelve Men" is not only sound but valuable. He has undertaken to give balanced and lifelike sketches of 12 real men about whom there was something curious or significant. Some Americans must have lamented that the characters of their fellow-countrymen in fiction are so often less interesting and less characteristic than many persons whom they see daily, or who are to be seen somewhere if one has the password that admits to their presence. In the offices of large cities and in hundreds of country villages there are personalities so individual and so many-sided that they dwarf the ordinary creations of fiction. Too often the young novelists appear to have begun to write without having first richly and widely observed the life about them. And they remain hopelessly behind it, never overtaking more than some small section to which they are drawn by affinity of taste.

Two outstanding faults of Mr. Dreiser's sketches are that they are self-conscious and that their language—never very finished language—is abstract. "I was staring with all my sight and enjoying it intensely." "I was a moral coward," "I was becoming both amused and interested," "I was sensible of being in contact with some one who was really in touch with life in a very large way" —these are a few sentences of the illusion-killing kind. They interpose Mr. Dreiser between the reader and the subject of the sketch. Vividness vanishes before it is fairly caught.

In the portrait for which the famous Muldoon was the original, we come upon the following sentences: "And yet really, at that moment he reminded me not so much of a man, in his supremely well-tailored riding costume, as of a tiger or a very ferocious and yet at times purring cat, beautifully dressed, as in our children's storybooks, a kind of tiger in collar and boots. He was so lithe, silent, cat-like in his tread. In his hard, clear, gray animal eyes was that swift, incisive, restless, searching glance which sometimes troubles us in the presence of animals."

But how little we are inspired to read on. The description is sodden and unrevealing. It is labored and abstract. In a word, it is dull. Now it is not the use of impressions that is itself at fault, for impressions may be subtle and suggestive. It is rather that Mr. Dreiser's impressions are not interesting or imaginatively phrased.

L. J.
"Twelve Men as Seen by Dreiser."
Chicago *Post*, June 13, 1919.

The academic critics who have been summing up Mr. Dreiser—and rendering a hostile verdict—ought really to have waited until "Twelve Men" was published. For here the impersonality of the fictional artist is abandoned and Mr. Dreiser speaks in his own person. And that person is much more human than such critics as Stuart Pratt Sherman would lead us to imagine. The twelve men of whom he discourses are alike only in that they exhibit significant aspects of American life during the last thirty years, each of them having been a friend or associate of Mr. Dreiser, and, altho he gives most of them fictitious names, it is likely that the reader will recognize more than one of the individuals portrayed.

Perhaps the story most revelatory of Mr. Dreiser is his account of his brother Paul—Paul Dresser, the creator of those once popular songs, "On the Banks of the Wabash," "The Blue and the Gray" and others. Paul was Theodore's elder brother, and took an almost fatherly interest in him after he had persuaded him to try his fortunes in New York. Mr. Dreiser returned his brother's affections to the full, and is yet able to stand off and view his personality and achievement in relation to its time and its surroundings. He is able to see the pure gold in his brother's character and yet estimate at its real lack of permanent value the easy sentimentality that went into his songs and his choice of associates, into the ease of his good nature and the facility with which he fell into the manners and customs of his set and his day. In fact, that sketch and the sketch of "The Country Doctor" reveal in Mr. Dreiser himself a sensitiveness to those emotional states that may eventuate in either sentiment or sentimentality that some of his critics have denied him. Indeed, one suspects at times that Mr. Dreiser's often-emphasized ruggedness and brutality is but a slowly deposited "exo-skeleton" to protect very sensitive nerve endings from what he takes to be—and with good reason—a very brutal and callous world.

But, apart from the revelation of its author, the book does exhibit a surprising number of aspects of American life. From the surroundings and "mores" of Dr. Gridley and his Indiana neighbors, to the bacchic dances and other studio and country-house revels of the since imprisoned millionaire with whom Mr. Dreiser associated for a time, there is a wide gamut. And occasionally Mr. Dreiser comments on his characters with real philosophic insight. For instance, his account of the methods and personality of the ex-prize fighter who runs a "repair-shop" for worn-out highbrows and bankers and rich young rogues is well worth reading not only for its amusing dialog and incident but for its study of conflicting ethics—that of the man who can control his own body and that of the weak teacher or minister who has to submit to Culhane's profanity and abuse while he is under his care—an abuse in part due to the fact that Culhane knows the clergyman or editor despises him for being an ex-prize fighter, and knows equally well that the other's scheme of life has broken down for him—or else he would not be the victim of ill health and the patient of the big, strong, self-confident man whose revilings and sarcasm are part of his method of cure.

Mr. Dreiser is quite successful in making his stories interesting and vital, but, of course, he writes in his own way, and if occasionally he is verbose and repetitious, we must forgive the blemish, remembering the writer's method. As a stylist he is still an individualist. All he wants to do is get the thing written down, and if the result is like this—

"It was airy and well-appointed, with, on the ground floor, a great gymnasium, containing, outside of an alcove at one end where hung four or five punching bags only medicine balls"—it is apparently quite satisfactory.

But let the reader say that sentence very quickly and see what a most extraordinary effect will be produced.

But, after all, to a man who wrestles with life as Mr. Dreiser does, it would probably seem a mere waste of time to fiddle too delicately with mere words. Mr. Dreiser's value lies not in any constructed artistic effects but in his removal of clothes and lids. He gains his effects by exposing to us things which cowardice and conventionality and interests of various kinds—to say nothing of stupidity—have hidden. He spades up evidence, and it matters not to him whether he actually uses a spade or a barrel stave—whichever he can get hold of with the least delay. Keeping that in mind, Mr. Dreiser's use of his instrument—our language—is at its most grotesque only the more fascinating. Heaven forbid that he should ever try to improve it.

Frank Harris. *Pearson's Magazine*, July, 1919, p. 422.

This book of Dreiser's is a sort of experiment; something the same sort of experiment that I made when I began trying to write "Contemporary Portraits," only I had the advantage of picking distinguished men about whom everyone was curious. Dreiser takes people of no particular interest to the general public and gives portraits of them in their habit as they lived. I should have expected him to emphasize the sex-urge of their lives; he has not done so; indeed he has left the sex-drive rather out of the picture; yet three of the twelve stories seem to me extremely well done.

Perhaps the best of all of them is the one he calls "My Brother, Paul." Paul is astonishingly realized from several sides. So long as he is successful and admired by men and petted by women Paul is delightful, but as soon as his song-writing fails and "the goldheaded cane and silk shirt and smart suit vanish," he gets depressed and discouraged. Dreiser meets a doctor who says, "Paul cannot live; he has pernicious anæmia; he is breaking down inside and doesn't know it; he can't last long; he is too depressed." And on the next day he dies; a blood vessel has burst in his head, and Dreiser writes of him these words that reach the very heart of pathos:

"Ah! Broadway! Broadway! And you, my good brother! Here is the story that you wanted me to write, this little testimony to your memory, a pale, pale symbol of all I think and feel. Where are the thousand yarns I have laughed over, the music, the lights, the songs?

"Peace, peace. So shall it soon be with all of us. It was a dream. It is. I am. You are. And shall we grieve over or hark back to dreams"?

Then there is a picture of the true Christian under the title "A Doer of the Word"—a carpenter who might have been the direct descendant of Him of Nazareth; also an admirable sketch. And then the last story in the book entitled. "W.L.S."

W.L.S., Jr. was an illustrator, it appears, and also a most astonishing mechanical engineer. He could build engines and battleships and make the battleships steam and fight; and not only did W.L.S. touch life from two such opposite poles but he had all sorts of accomplishments and sympathies. He was "an expert bicyclist and trick rider and could use a camera in a way to make an amateur envious." He had a fine tenor voice and was an architect as well.

Suddenly W.L.S. tells Dreiser that he is going to Tampa; the Spanish-American war has broken out; he will be away some three weeks. The next thing Dreiser hears is that Louis is dead; died suddenly of fever. Here is Dreiser's comment:

"It seemed *to me* that a great tragedy had happened—he was so ambitious, so full of plans. His dreams were so near fulfillment.

"I saw the little grave afterward and the empty studio. His desks revealed several inventions and many plans of useful things, but these came to nothing. There was no one to continue the work.

"My feeling at the time was as if I had been looking at a beautiful lamp, lighted, warm and irradiating a charming scene, and then suddenly that it had been puffed out before my eyes, as if a hundred bubbles of irridescent hues had been shattered by a breath. We toil so much, we dream so richly, we hasten so fast, and, lo! the green door is opened. We are through it, and its grassy surface has sealed us forever from all which apparently we so much crave—even as, breathlessly, we are still running."

Why didn't he end this at "eyes" instead of "running"?

I had written this when I suddenly heard that Dreiser had had an automobile accident. I made inquiries and found that he had been injured but was getting well. I hope it is nothing serious. Anything that retards his writing would be an injury to American letters. He is one of the two or three writers in this country today who count. I can only wish him with all my heart a speedy recovery.

"A Reader's Notes." Indianapolis *Star*. July 14, 1919.

People may or may not like Theodore Dreiser's novels, but his severest critics do not deny his power of vivid delineation or that when a story is laid aside its characters stand out clearly and are remembered, or that they are remembered because they are recognized as transcripts of life. . . .

This power to depict character is one of the indispensable qualities of the best novelists. To be able to portray imaginary personages so that they seem real shows, not only a gift for close observation of living men and women, but an insight into their motives, their characteristics, an understanding of the cross currents of their inner lives. It is a talent that should be equally good in life portraiture, an art that is biography, but something more. Theodore Dreiser has proved his ability in this line in his "Twelve Men."

The volume, so called, is made of descriptive and analytical studies of twelve men Mr. Dreiser has known. He names none of them but his brother, Paul Dresser, but the identity of two or three others may easily be discovered, and there must be many who would recognize all the men described. Some of the studies are plainly labors of love, as "Peter," the opening sketch; "My Brother Paul," "A Doer of the Word" and "A Country Doctor." These are of men for whom he had a personal affection or in whom he was somehow specially interested. Other sketches are of men in whom he discovered unusual qualities that attracted his attention and whom he evidently deliberately studied in order to get the secret of their peculiar qualities or characteristics. The first series is of higher interest than the other because of this personal element, but each sketch has the interest of a piece of fiction because each life depicted has its story. Mr. Dreiser illustrates in these life portraits the truth of the assertion often made that the story of every human life is worth the telling, if a narrator who can discern the romantic, the dramatic or the tragic elements in what to dull eyes is commonplace can be found. . . .

John Cowper Powys. "Real American Book By Genius Is Star In Literary Heavens." San Francisco *Bulletin*, August 23, 1919.

At last it has really reached our Pacific Coast, the genuine "American Scene," by a genuine dyed-in-the-grain American! Oh, how long we have waited for this book, fed by tantalizing rumors of its appearance from one after another of all the progressive reviewers of the East!

Like the telescopes of expectant astronomers, the eyes of our best critics have been long scanning the literary sky, vaguely aware that such and such an abyss of darkness must contain a stellar body of just this sort. But the planet they looked for seemed so long in manifesting itself that many of them were tempted to deny that it existed at all.

Well! We have it now; and it is all, and more, than we hoped for. Theodore Dreiser, the novelist, has had the proverbial difficulty in being acknowledged for what he is among his own. In England he has been recognized, by those who have intelligence in such matters; nor are the French unaware of his existence; but in this country there has been something like an organized puritanic and academic campaign against him which is not creditable to our mentality.

The importance of this book, now at last in our hands, cannot be overestimated. It is more than a personal achievement. It is a landmark, a memorable mile-stone in the history of American literature. For in this book, Theodore Dreiser, the most American of literary Americans, has really found himself. . . .

And "Twelve Men" is a masterpiece of what might be called Imaginative Realism. At last Dreiser has found the "psychic clue," the spiritual "note," that gives rhythm and harmony to the discordant elements of his demonic energy.

A novel written in the style of "Twelve Men," and in the intellectual and emotional atmosphere of "Twelve Men," would certainly be a novel that would establish without question its claim to be a "classic." For in these apparently easy and careless sketches we have as large, as genial, as wise an outlook upon life as the present reviewer has had the good luck to happen upon anywhere in these questionable days.

And with this gentler, but not less penetrating, philosophical outlook, an outlook which has the "humanity" of Jenny [sic] Gerhardt, the drastic formidableness of "The Titan," the imaginative mysticism of the Plays, together with something that emanates freshly and newly from the author's vision, there has come into existence the thing above all things that lovers of Theodore Dreiser have prayed for . . . a genuine charm of style.

Something of the sort we noted in that book of his called "A Hoosier's Holiday." The loose, free, diffusive manner of "The Genius" was, no doubt, as he revised it and worked upon it, obscurely moving towards this. But this is the thing itself. This is the style of Theodore Dreiser expressing the vision of Theodore Dreiser. This is, for all its unobtrusive and unassuming form, a work of art of a high order. . . .

Rebecca Drucker. "Dreiser and O'Higgins." New York *Tribune*, November 29, 1919, p. 10.

. . . There is no glibness or facility in "Twelve Men." Dreiser plows heavily across the field of living, but he turns up rich furrows of reality. The man is not at ease in life, in a social sense. He is esthetically insensitive. He is provincially agape at the glitter of wealth. But the breadth and variousness of his vision are astonishing. He sees man not only in relation to his social scheme, but in relation to the larger cosmic scheme.

He writes as if with stiff fingers. There are passages in which it would be a pleasure to prompt him to an easier turn of phrase. Not only is there phrasing that makes one writhe, but an ineptitude like this stands as a gibe at fine writing: "My first recollection of him is myself as a boy of ten and he a man of twenty-five (my oldest brother)." Yet this inarticulateness seems the will rather to err on the side of sincerity than on the side of literary posing. In no necessity does Mr. Dreiser's equipment fail him to set down amazingly fine and powerful and subtle distinctions.

The sketch of his brother Paul, the famous song writer, who was the author of "Just Tell Them That You Saw Me" and "On the Banks of the Wabash," has no suavity. In an awkward way, the more touching for its awkwardness, there is presented a poet of the streets. Dreiser has a great stomach for life—a great feeling for the wonder and romance that lurk in the common thing. In Dreiser it is proved that a realist is a poet who finds life greater than any symbols.

At least four of these sketches are sympathetic pictures of religionists. Dreiser, who is himself bitten deep with intellectual pessimism, seems profoundly touched by the impulses that urge men to dogmas. "A Door of the Word" renders quite literally Dreiser's encounter with a man who stood literally on the Bible's injunction to love your neighbor. Make what you like of this uncommented interview. It has in it a perception of essential greatness. . . .

There are artistic sins and to spare in "Twelve Men." The first sketch in the book, that of the newspaper artist, shows not the slightest sense of selection. One perception painted over another finally blots out the picture. But at their best these things transcend pictorial values. They have an immense subcutaneous vitality. These twelve men are three-dimensional. They prove that realism is something more than a new treatment of surfaces.

Checklist of Additional Reviews

Doris Webb. *Publisher's Weekly.* 95 (March 15, 1919), 822.

"Groups of Short Stories." *The Independent,* 97 (March, 1919), 414.

"About a Dozen." New York *Herald,* May 4, 1919.

"A Dozen Personalities." New York *Review,* May 10, 1919.

"Dreiser and Just a Dozen." Boston *Herald,* May 10, 1919.

Grand Rapids [Mich.] *News,* May 10, 1919.

Philadelphia *Public Ledger,* May 10, 1919.

"In the Cheerful Key of G." Chicago *Musical Leader,* May 15, 1919.

Brooklyn *Eagle,* May 17, 1919.

Los Angeles *Times,* May 18, 1919.

New York *American,* May 18, 1919.

Washington [D.C.] *Star,* May 18, 1919.

Springfield *Republican,* May 25, 1919, p. 17.

"A Baker's Dozen of Dreiser's Portraits." *Current Opinion,* 66, (June 1919), 389–390.

Review of Reviews, June 1919.

"Dreiser Remembers His Brother." New York *Clipper,* June 4, 1919.

Toledo *Daily Blade,* June 7, 1919.

Edgar Lee Masters. "Books of the Year." New ,York *Sun,* June 15, 1919.

A.L.A. Booklist, 15 (July 1919), 397.

Literary Digest, October 11, 1919.

Heywood Broun. New York *Tribune,* September 15, 1919.

North American Review, 210 (October 1919), 567–568.

Birmingham [Ala.] *Age Herald*, October 26, 1919.
Cleveland *Open Shelf*, November, 1919.

Further Reviews: Bibliographic Information Incomplete

Charles J. Finger. "Out of the Grip." *Reedy's Mirror*, pp. 373–374.

The HAND *of the* POTTER

BY

THEODORE DREISER

A Tragedy in Four Acts

BONI AND LIVERIGHT
NEW YORK 1918

The Hand of the Potter

"Tragedy and Trifles." *Nation,* 109 (September 6, 1919), 340.

The proper character of the tragic hero has long been a fruitful subject of critical controversy. One recalls the old formula of the schools: he must not be ignoble, he must not be guiltless, he must occupy a reasonably important station in human society. In brief, he must be Œdipus, Macbeth, Wallenstein. Let us look at Mr. Dreiser's protagonist. Isadore Berchansky is the son of a Jewish peddler of thread and needles. He was born in an East Side slum. There were ten children. Four are dead. Of the six who survive four are normally energetic and decent people. But poor little Masha (who has the most sensitive soul) is a cripple, and Isadore a psychopathic degenerate. Twice, then, the hand of the Potter shook: From the point of view of the police records Isadore is a loathsome criminal. But in Mr. Dreiser's portrayal of him his struggle against his ghastly infirmity is not wholly ignoble; his guilt is merged into social and, in the last analysis, into cosmic forces; his importance is in his character as representative of the tragic consequence of ignorance, poverty, and oppression. He is not ignoble, he is not guiltless; he is important. To realize thoroughly the new meanings that here attach to the old form of words is to have grasped the fundamental change in thinking about human life which is the very soul of the age in which we live, an age in which so many new things are still known by old words and consequently hardly known at all. For it is not only the political map of the world that we must study anew. Ethical frontiers are also subtly shifting before our eyes.

Mr. Dreiser's dramaturgic structure is a little clumsy, a little awkward and helpless. The fourth act is plainly unnecessary. But in the three preceding acts there is such characterization and such a projection of the interplay of character through dialogue as we shall seek in vain in any other American play. The delineation of the Berchansky family is not less than masterly. The brothers and sisters could have been but of one blood; they could have been the children of no one but these parents; yet each is, in addition, a definite and peculiar personality. Best of all is the father, Aaron Berchansky. Mr. Dreiser, as he showed in the character of old Gerhardt, has always had a deep sense of the pathos of old age, of a genuine if rigid righteousness that has lost the battle and is stricken at the evidence that righteousness alone avails so little against the vast forces of the world. Berchansky, assuredly, has a tragic quality and appeal that belong to no age. He has them when he turns to the District Attorney: "If I had been a better fader maybe dis would not happen"; he has them, above all, when he silences the nagging landlord in words as characteristic as they are beautiful: "Vy pull at de valls of my house? Dey are already down!"

R.D. "Grim Play by Dreiser." New York *Tribune*, September 6, 1919, p. 9.

The younger dramatists' protest that more of life is legitimately the stuff of drama than was ever admitted by the older dramatists is a fine and courageous insurgency. By searching in obscure places for what is rich and strange and moving in human conduct they have magnificently extended the frontiers of drama. Nevertheless in "The Hand of the Potter" Theodore Dreiser has gone adventuring down a strange path.

It has led him to the laboratory of the pathologist and to dramatizing a clinical report of abnormal psychology. He has built the play around a creature degenerate and mad—the deformed son of hard-driven people who have brought ten children into the world and given only three a reasonable chance for life.

It is not because this is what unimaginative people are fond of calling morbid, unpleasant, material that the play seems to us to fail, although the sight of a human being helpless in his distintegration is really too monstrous and terrible a thing to stir the imagination. It is because there is nothing here of universal experience in which it may strike root. The well-springs of conduct are here, after all, distorted mental processes to which only a handful of psychiatrists may have the key. If there is any validity in the old dramatic law that drama is man's conflict with his destiny, it would seem to require as its first condition that the struggle should be on some sort of representative terms. A madman in the grip of his madness represents no conflict. Indeed, whatever the catastrophe still to come, the struggle has already been fought out, the leaden weight of doom hung around the protagonist's neck before he has so much as lifted a finger.

Dreiser has done some things in this play with extraordinary and searing vividness, though with no sustained skill. The first act, showing the Berchansky household—the beaten parents, the hard, knowing sister, the mad boy just returned from prison for assault on a little girl, the callousness or helplessness of all to the mounting tragedy, carries with it undeniably the conviction of pure horror and truth. The following scenes beat weakly on dulled nerves—the scenes of court inquiry and testimony, the scenes of discussion and even the final catastrophe, are as heavy as routine pieces of reporting.

One foresees that there will be rampant ones complacent over the failure of the public to appreciate so courageous a piece of work—regarding the coldness to it as another manifestation of Philistinism. But what courageousness this play represents is of a purely literal sort—the deductions it affords are singularly obscure. By the bitter, satiric line which prefaces it, "What did the hand, then, of the Potter shake?" there is manifest the impulse here of the agnostic, the gesture of pity and terror over the incomprehensible. It is this intention, only incompletely evident in the play itself, that marks it from those more rudimentary forms of the theatre. So far from blazing out a new trail of dramatic expression, Dreiser has reverted to the showmanship of the Grand Guignol, the medical museum and the freak show.

Indianapolis *News*, September 16, 1919.

Theodore Dreiser has come in for some sympathy and the American public for some ragging through a story to the effect that the novelist has written a great play which no manager would produce because of hurting the tender susceptibilities of the public. What appears to be the play in question has just been received from the publishers. After reading it one has more sympathy for the producers who shy at "art." Any man who attempted to put the Dreiser play on the stage would risk physical as well as financial injury. The audience, more than likely, would call for the author and then call the police, if the latter had not already stopped it. The play is a dramatization of the most abominable sexual perversion. Several scenes in it are so revolting that if presented with the vividness of stage projection they would horrify and physically sicken any audience.

And the play is weak in reasoning and blows up with stupid and peurile propaganda in the last act. It is not even convincing as a study of degeneracy, though there is in it one fine and pathetic portrait of an old man whose son's sins is his tragedy. Some of the other characters are drawn with the fidelity and clearness that distinguishes some of the Dreiser novels, and the drama is powerfully moving at times, but on the whole, how futile, how exasperatingly perverse!

"Super-Dreiser." New York *Evening Sun*, September 20, 1919.

The jacket on Theodore Dreiser's play, "The Hand of the Potter" asks: "Do you want to read a tragedy stark naked unashamed?" Well, that depends; but generally speaking no. Certainly not unless it has some valid artistic excuse for parading in that undraped state. There is no objection to nudity merely as such, but the kind that exists in the dissecting room or the hospital has no real place on the stage or in fiction.

This play is dramatic enough, in part, though the last third of it is out of proportion and an anticlimax, but its subject matter belongs to the clinic, or to medico-legal literature: the murder of a child by a degenerate, whose malady rises to active criminal insanity, told with a devoted fidelity to detail. One must, however, do Mr. Dreiser the justice of admitting the sincerity and conscientiousness of his motive. The result remains, none the less, an error in judgment and instead of being uplifting is merely repulsive.

"Books of the Fortnight." *Dial*, 67 (September 20, 1919), 276

The Hand of the Potter . . . a "tragedy" in four acts, should suffice, by its incredibly inept construction, to remove the last doubt whether its author is capable of mastering any existing technique. Upon an authentic background of East Side family life he has presented a courageous and understanding picture of a certain kind of erotic pathology—and then has squandered his materials in a sensational plot that is as clumsy melodrama as it is arbitrary tragedy.

Albany [N.Y.] *Knickerbocker Press*, September 21, 1919.

. . . With characteristic courage Dreiser has tackled a dreadful theme. Young Isadore Berchansky is a born degenerate and he commits a fiendish crime. Dreiser tells his story to prove that the boy is neither a fiend nor a criminal, but the helpless victim of heredity and environment. The first and second acts in the Berchansky home are masterly. We find it difficult to believe that they can fail to be effective in the highest degree upon the stage. Particularly the awful climax to the first act and the scene at the close of the second in which the old people realize that the crime has been committed by Isadore. And Dreiser has surely never done anything better than his characterization of the Berchansky family. The third act, in which the scene shifts to the courtroom, may act more convincingly than it reads. Isadore's death scene in the fourth act is too long drawn out. But it is utterly pathetic. Moreover, it is the logical conclusion of the play. The debate between the newspaper men in the scene that follows is an anti-climax of the worst description. The purpose of the play is clear as daylight without any such tub-thumping. The fact that "The Hand of the Potter" is Dreiser's first long play is probably responsible for the over-emphasis that mars the concluding scenes. There is so much that is truly great in the whole conception, so many flashes unmistakable genius, such genuine tragedy, that its technical imperfections are, in comparison, trifles light as air.

Washington [D.C.] *Star*, September 21, 1919.

Theodore Dreiser here makes use of a four-act play to crystallize the tragedy of a pervert. An east-side Jewish boy—Isadore Berchansky—set upon by himself and goaded to desperation by the sex-lure of the open streets, runs amuck, and in his madness makes a little neighbor girl his victim. The missing girl, the finding of her body, the man hunt, the dawning fear of the Berchansky family that Isadore might have done this thing, their pathetic efforts to deceive themselves and others, their examination in the courtroom—these are the steps by which the play rises to its climax, when Isadore—starved, hiding, hunted, hated—slips finally out and away through the friendly offices of an open gas jet and an arm's length of rubber tubing. That is the play. Without an extra word and with never a stepping aside from the straight course of stark portrayal, the author, with a new austerity of spirit, in a rigid economy of gesture, sets the hideous thing out nakedly. Is it a reform performance? Not at all. If reforming measures should come out of this play they will come by virtue of the fact that readers must get together for their own peace of mind to help the unfortunate. Dreiser is not thinking about social amelioration—that is, not to the extent of deforming his play. He is tremendously busy painting the thing as it is. And how helpless one is, after all. What is it about? What is one's own part? What can he do? What are the forces—sinister and beneficent—that mix themselves so inextricably in each one of us? A terrible play—and terrible because it impels one to look into his own depths and because it leads him to realize his own nothingness in the hidden motives of the grand whole.

George Jean Nathan. "Dreiser's Play—and Some Others." *Smart Set,* 60 (October 1919), 131–133.

It is called "The Hand of the Potter." Announced for production by the Coburns, it remains still between book covers. Arthur Hopkins has said that it is the best American play that has been submitted to him and that he would eagerly have produced it had not Dreiser imposed upon him so many bulls, caveats and salvos. Mencken, Dreiser's most faithful critical mount, private shimmy dancer and rajpoot at large, says that Hopkins is crazy and that it is one of the worst American plays he has read. Burton Rascoe, Chicago's leading journalistic professor of the arts, informs me that it has made a considerable impression upon him; Tarquinius Ramgunga Smith, erudite *sposo* to the *Century,* has said the same; the theatrical producers, aside from Hopkins, to whom the manuscript was submitted have observed that it is, in their estimation, largely whim-wham. It has given birth to boisterous palm pounders, tin-sheet shakers and shillabers on the right hand, and to nose wrinklers, tongue stickers and loud sneezers on the left. I find myself occupying a position in the no-man's land stretching between the two camps—but rather far to the left.

The story of a victim of a certain phase of Kraft-Ebbing demoralization—one has a sneaking suspicion that the late Leo Frank case may in a general way have suggested the theme to the author—Dreiser has written a play whose chief merit (as it is ever one of Dreiser's most notable assets) consists in the achievement, in the very teeth of life's low derisory comedy, of a poignant and tragic pity. This deep compassion, this summoning forth, honestly and soundly, of forbearance, this is the note Dreiser can strike as few other Americans can strike it. Out of the tin of the grotesque, the ignoble and the mean, he can evoke the golden E flat of human frailty and charity as few modern Europeans can evoke it. And yet with never a suspicion of the bogus "heart interest" that passes promiscuously for the currency of art, with never a suspicion of slyly studied fact blue-pencilling or of self-compromise. From "Sister Carrie" down through "Jennie

Gerhardt" and, with but a few skips, on to "Twelve Men," one encounters always this grim and understanding heart upon a hilltop, at once moved and immobile, at once condemning and forgiving: without sentimentality as without imperturbation. You will find it, perhaps at its most eloquent, in his chapter, "My Brother Paul"—"And you, my good brother! Here is the story that you wanted me to write, this little testimony to your memory, a pale, pale symbol of all I think and feel"—a really first-rate, immensely realistic and affecting arrangement of the jigsaw of the eternal marriage of the ridiculous and the gentle. And though the amalgam of heart and eye, the one warm and the other cold, dresses his play not so convincingly, it is yet there to breathe into the work a something that in its absence would have left the play a mere third-rate Third Avenue melodramatic mossback diddler not much above the quality of such dime magnets of yesterday as "Devil's Island."

The dramatist Dreiser is the precocious bad boy of the novelist Dreiser: that offspring of the artist who looks upon the stage as a neighbour's apple orchard wherein to penetrate by night enveloped in a bed-spread, scare off with sepulchral groans the watchful Spitz, and make away with the pippins. The bed-spread and the groans are apparent in each of the various short plays that Dreiser has written, as they are doubly apparent (Dreiser has doubtless grown tired of waiting and wishes to "knock 'em off their seats" now or never) in this, his first long play. The girl stretched out in the coffin, the fourth dimensional dramaturgy with its divers laughing gases, the violent sensationalism of the defloration of eleven year old Kitty Neafie by the degenerate Berchansky—this is the crescendo Dreiser box-office attack; the last in particular the do-or-die dive against the Rialto show pews. And what is more, if the Coburns put on the play down in the Greenwich Village Theater—away from Broadway—I somehow feel that its scandalous air will presently draw to it enough of jay Broadway to make Dreiser the money upon which he had his eye when he wrote it. For that Dreiser wrote the play with a Rolls-Royce in view seems to me as certain as that he writes his novels with nothing in view but the novels.

"The Hand of the Potter" has three extremely effective theatrical scenes: the attack scene at the conclusion of the first act (in effect similar to the scene at the conclusion of the first act of a prize play of twenty years ago called "Chivalry"); the scene in the second act wherein the suspicions and fears of the mother and father of the demented boy tremble upon their lips; and the scene wherein the crazed, pursued pervert closes the door against the child Hagar and demoniac temptation. I am probably unfair to Dreiser when I bluntly characterize these scenes as mere stage melodrama: there is something more to them than merely that. But that they were initially conceived less for their intrinsic relevance and integrity than for their more obvious yokel-power, I somehow can't disbelieve. Conceived otherwise, their brazen baldness, for all the well-known stubborn and eccentric hand that executed them, must have taken on at least a show of the reticence that is currently nowhere visible.

The balance of the manuscript reveals here and there a touch or two of moderately good characterization, but little more. The structure of the play is disjointed and awkward. The third act, jumping á la Hal Reid from the Berchansky flat to the grand jury room of the Criminal Courts Building, invades the continuity of the action: the third act might better have followed up the action of the preceding act after a slight lapse of time, in the locale of that act. The long monologues of the insane boy, though logical and sound enough, are repetitious and tiresome. The German dialect of such a straight character as Emil Daubenspeck—"ich vuss by a liddle chob in Sixty-fift' Sthreet und vuss going down troo der lot py Fairst Affenoo back of mein house da"—smacks rebelliously of Sam Bernard, as the "I can't give you her exack langwidge . . . she was kinda nervous an' a-fidgitin' with 'er hands this-a-way" of such a straight character as Rufus Bush smacks of William Hodge and as the Irish McKagg's "divil a bits" and "sure, ye'll be afther sayin's" suggest the Russell Brothers and the Yiddish Berchansky's "oi, oi's," "ach's" and sedulous use of the "v" sound suggest Ben Welch.

The play, in brief, though probably a financial success if handled with a sufficiently cunning showmanship, falls short on a score of counts. It has a touch of the great and gorgeous pity; it has twenty touches of the great and gorgeous whangdoodle. It belongs very largely to the Dreiser who writes for the Saturday Evening Post and goes to see Henry B. Walthall in the moving pictures; it is not the work of the Theodore Dreiser who has written some of America's finest novels. *That* Dreiser could never seriously have written such an idiotic scene, for example, as that of the newspaper reporters' colloquy in the last act: not unless he appreciated the idiocy of a Broadway theatrical audience as well as I.

"Hand of the Potter." *Outlook*, 123 (October 1, 1919), 191.

This play is classed by its publishers as a tragedy. It is, indeed, a tragedy that any writer of Theodore Dreiser's technical attainments should be so warped in his outlook as to regard the theme of this play as a fit subject for anything except a medical treatise.

Jesse Lee Bennett. "The Incomplete Sceptic." *New Republic*, 20 (October 8, 1919), 297–298.

Despite the pessimism of all his books and the tediousness of many of them; despite the censorship of publishers, libraries and vice societies; despite the bitter onslaughts of conventional critics; Theodore Dreiser moves ponderously but steadily into place as one of America's outstanding literary figures, and for this there are many reasons but two of them would suffice. He is intellectually honest. And he is incredibly typical of the average American of today.

No wonder he is esteemed abroad. To a detached social philosopher who desired to understand the human actuality underlying the unconvincing surface manifestations of contemporary America, Dreiser's characters and Dreiser, as expressed in those characters, would come like a ray of light. Seeking to understand America, we picture such a philosopher studying The Saturday Evening Post, Harold Bell Wright's lububrations, Christian Science, strikes, far-sweeping generalizations of American statesmen, the Woolworth Building, the Ford plant, our movies and many another manifestation. And over all of them he would shake his head. These things are of the surface. What is the actuality underneath? What are the actual thoughts and acts of the actual human beings who read or produce or are, unconvincingly, mirrored by these things? Our philosopher would know that there must be something less definite, less standardized; more animal, more illogical, tangled, muddy and perplexed below all these evidences of vigor and normality and surface life. And in Dreiser he would find what he sought. He would find a picture of the mental and emotional spasms which the average American undergoes in the contemporary chaotic welter of experiences. He would find the doubts, the despairs, the uncertainty bound to exist in a great polyglot nation where the discipline of the past had been destroyed and no new discipline had yet come to replace it. Above all, he would find an incomplete scepticism which, growing out of a good heart, leads to gnawing doubts and a hopelessness more forlorn and passive than bitter and dynamic.

Older civilizations have come through the mental state which Dreiser depicts so convincingly because so unconsciously. Their complete scepticism has crystallized into a solid core from which radio-active energies, expressed in cooperation, discipline and determination, are shot off. Their bitterness has lead to a determination to accept the inexorable and to make life better by the use of human will and intelligence

It was one Frenchman who said to an American woman:—

"I, Madame, believe in everything. I am a sceptic."

It was another Frenchman who said:—

"The universe is unquestionably the project of some great Architect who died before it was finished."

Mr. Dreiser depicts the incomplete sceptics who believe in nothing—very long. And—trusting and kindly hearted, hopeful and with bits of orthodoxy remaining—he cannot bring himself to believe that the Architect of the universe has died. He insists that life must have a meaning, a meaning which we can understand. Since he cannot find the meaning, he despairs in multitudinous pages.

Conrad is a more complete sceptic—the product of a more finished civilization. Conrad insists that we live in "a spectacular, episodic universe," that life is but a succession of unmeaning spectacles and episodes. But Conrad boasts "I am a disciplined man." Mr. Dreiser has come to believe in an episodic universe. He has not yet boasted that he is a disciplined man. Yet if he ever comes to realize that it is somewhat immature and sophomoric to inveigh against the inexorable, and much wiser and much manlier to take life just as it is; accept the conditions and, by will and intelligence expressed in discipline, cooperation and loyalty, mould it closer to the heart's desire; he will probably cease writing such books as have thus far come from his pen and American literature will, accordingly, lose something which expresses America amazingly.

Dreiser's four-act play called The

Hand of the Potter has just been published. Its cover inquires:—

"Do you want to read a tragedy—Stark—Naked—Unashamed—Tender—Intensely Pathetic—A True Tragedy? Then read this!"

Well, The Hand of the Potter is a tragedy, a grim tragedy. And, because it is sincere and because one feels that it bruised the heart of the man who wrote it, it is worthy of all praise. An abnormal boy who has been in prison for injuring one little girl assaults and kills another little girl on his release. He is not a brute but a defective. He is depicted as having many kindly impulses and good traits but he is helpless because of psychopathic derangement. His father and mother are Russian Jews caught in the maelstrom of New York and unable to influence and direct their children as they would. The boy commits suicide under sensational circumstances and the old man, a pathetic figure for whom life has proved too much, closes the play by saying to someone inveighing against him for not bringing the boy up better:—"Vy pull at de valls of my house? Dey are already down"—his efforts and struggles and dreams have proved unavailing against the resistless, the incomprehensible, the terrifying, the illogical tides of the thing called life. The title of the play is from the quatrain of Omar Khayyam which asks:—"What, Did the Hand then of the Potter shake?" and implies that the abnormal boy was a mistake of God's.

But how naive this is, after all. It is a phase of adolescent Weltschmerz; it is much the same refusal to accept life as it is, that defenders of Dreiser bring as a charge against his opponents. It is the childish, incomplete scepticism which has come only to the brink of the abyss of meditations. Just as the play—for all its sincerity—fails of being an authentic work of art because the writer has to editorialize in his last act through the medium of two reporters who drag in Havelock Ellis and Kraft-Ebing and moralize in lengthy dialogue. Any French writer of the first rank would have made the thing as impersonal as a death certificate, and, so have enhanced the indictment of life.

But then no Frenchman of the first rank would have been so incomplete a sceptic. Can it be that Dreiser has never read Octave Mirbeau or even Barbusse? Can it be that he does not know that the great literatures of the world are filled with tragedies all the more truly human and tragic because they start with no thought of a fathering divinity?

Burton Rascoe. "Dreiser Shakes the Potter's Hand." Chicago *Tribune*, October 11, 1919.

I had been getting conflicting reports of the new Dreiser play for more than a year. In incompleted manuscript it had already estranged Dreiser adherents, provoked innumerable ructions [sic] in literary camps, and led to bitterness and enthusiasms without end. It had been refused by publishers and rejected by producers. It had set the Comstocks on Dreiser's trail, with seizure warrants and writs of execution in their pockets. It was to make him, and it was to break him. All this I heard.

"It is bawdy, disgusting, obscene," said some. "It is a poignant masterpiece," said others. "It is Dreiser the bragging toreador of literary freedom waving the scarlet cape before the Puritan bull," said yet others. "It is the greatest play ever written by an American." said still more.

H. L. Mencken told me, with tears rippling down his neat Van Dyke, how he had vainly pleaded with the obdurate Dreiser to burn the manuscript before it was too late. "It is not art, or drama, or literature, or even good theater," he wailed, "it is pure muck, cheap and revolting. It is just the thing that Sumner and his gang are waiting for from Dreiser to pin him down on a charge of outraging decency. And for once they will be almost right. The play, if produced or published, will ruin him."

And when I saw George Jean Nathan he was yet in a state of suspended judgment over the matter, but rather inclined to think that Mencken had miscued the play. He had received highly favorable reports of the drama from Arthur Hopkins, who, it seems, approved the piece almost to the point of delirium for a play producer.

So then, my reading of the published version, which reached me this week, was not deferred. I emerged from the ordeal, not considerably refreshed to be sure, nor yet cleansed by that catharsis which the Greeks held to be the peculiar function of tragedy, but astounded that Mr. Dreiser has written so dignified and impressive a drama upon so treacherous a theme, and pointedly regretful that he had almost completely nullified the effect of the three excellent preceding acts by a nonsensical, irrelevant sermon as a fourth.

The play is concerned with a pervert whose crime bears a close analogy to that recently given so much space in Chicago newspapers. Succinctly, a mentally diseased youth who had previously been convicted of an attempted assault upon a young girl, returns home, attacks and murders another child, and slashes her body into threads. He disappears. After desperate efforts of the family to protect the boy, of whose guilt they are certain, the father breaks down on the stand and confesses. Meanwhile, further crazed by his act and its consequences, the youth commits suicide.

That is the ghastly human tragedy which for three acts Mr. Dreiser handles with superb restraint, convincing sincerity, and no little technical art. And it is this ghastly human tragedy which he mulls over with a clumsy hand in the fourth act. For three anguished and almost perfect scenes, there are evoked the profound emotions of tragic pity and terror in a manner which no other American writer seems capable of doing. There are three glimpses arranged by an humble sorrowing, honest, and resourceful artist, at the woeful spectacle of botched lives. It is an artful wringing of impressive drama out of one of life's hideous accidents.

Then something happens to cause you to suspect that this extraordinary performance is the peddler's deft and ingenious prelude to attract the crowd; that when interest is assured out will come the pink pills for human ills; that after showing you a highly creditable chamber of horrors the attendant in charge is going to whisper admonishingly that you had better drop in on the quack upstairs and have him look you over.

Your suspicions are confirmed. When the play is done there is appended another act. In the mouth of an absurd reporter—who, in actual life would long ago have been back to his office whipping out the melodramatic details of his "story" on a typewriter—in the mouth of this reporter Mr. Dreiser puts a long disquisition voicing his own opinions on the case at hand, his vague and facile philosophy of chemical compounds, and his curious jumble of current theories of perverts in general.

The dramatic text from Rubaiyat about the Potter's hand shaking as it thumbed this and that wet clay, is carefully, movingly expounded for three acts. Thereafter it is not so much that the Potter's hand shook, but that it is Mr. Dreiser who shakes it.

That's the trouble frequently with Mr. Dreiser as an artist—he usurps the function of the Deity, and he is so tiresomely and uninterestingly moral. Contrary to the current opinion, he does tear at holes in life's foundations; he is really forever putting chinks in the holes which already exist. He is more militantly moral than the most pious ecclesiastic. He cannot resist a temptation to preach, to advise, to comment.

This tendency bungled "The Genius," and defaced "A Traveler at Forty"; it weakened some of the stories in "Free," and led him astray in other fictions. He is a tragic optimist, trembling with profound pity over the dismal contortions of life, but ever hopeful that somehow, some time, man's burdens will be lightened and his afflictions stilled. That consummation, it appears, he believes might be affected, not in the orthodox manner, but if every one read and took to heart the words of Voltaire, Robert Ingersoll, Ernst Haeckel, Krafft-Ebing, Havelock Ellis and Carl Snyder.

For the rest he remains the sincerest novelist America has of late produced, the one who touches most unerringly the mainsprings of American life, who illustrates, records and represents our strange spiritual welter and gropings and disorders and despairs most accurately. And it is this sincerity and honesty of treatment that makes "The Hand of the Potter" in the main excellent drama.

Mr. Dreiser's power as a dramatic technician are evident in the suspense and outcome of the scene where the perverted youth approaches, hesitates and sends from him the temptation in the form of the innocent little girl who brings him an apple; again, in the scene where the family accepts slowly and terrifyingly the evidence that the boy has committed a hideous crime; again in the scene in the courtroom where they attempt to protect him; and again in the scene where the boy writes the disjointed letter about himself.

The tragedy actually is concerned less with the degenerate boy than with his poor, simple, harried parents. For him, I, for one, had neither hatred, sympathy, disgust, nor compassion—only a mild and somewhat unconcerned pity, an easy gesture which we grant offhandedly to cripples who pass us in the street. For the parents, though, there is an imponderable concern, an emotion sharing sympathy with their plight, and it is this quality in "The Hand of the Potter" which atones for the atrocity of the last act and for the trick dialect of the third.

Baltimore *Sun*, October 11, 1919.

In his grimly tragic play entitled "The Hand of the Potter," Theodore Dreiser has taken the sort of theme which the newspapers of any great city furnish every day. But he has dealt with it in such masterly fashion as to produce a tragedy which is singularly moving and affecting—a tragedy of the righteous forsaken. A degenerate boy has assaulted a little girl and been sent to prison. Upon release he assaults and kills another little girl, then flees and hides and, eventually, commits suicide. He is depicted as a congenital defective, incapable of mastering his impulses, yet with many qualities of kindliness and with desire to do the right thing. His father and mother and sisters are the chief characters and are masterly depicted. The old father, particularly, one cannot soon forget. He has tried so hard to do his best. He has sought to bring his children up as they should be brought up, but poverty and New York streets have proved too much for him. His efforts are unavailing and the walls of his house topple down upon him. Mr. Dreiser spoils the effect of his play somewhat by the too-lengthy dialogue between the newspaper reporters in his last act—an act not really necessary in any case. But this play is certainly the sort of thing American literature needs as a reaction against the Pollyanna school of art. A homely tragedy. The sort of thing which happens every day, yet given an eternal value by being dealt with grimly and vitally. One may feel that the life of the average man is too short for him to give his time to concern with one tragic experience out of all the millions of tragic experiences which every day brings to the sons of men. And one may feel that Mr. Dreiser sees life somewhat lopsidedly. But all art and all artists down the ages have been open to such criticism. "The Hand of the Potter" is literature. And we need literature.

John T. Stone. "Choice of Material Spoils Dreiser Play." Detroit *Sunday News*, October 12, 1919.

Theodore Dreiser's new play, "The Hand of the Potter," will help many people to make up their minds more definitely as to the right and wrong of the famous Dreiser controversy. It defines the issue more sharply than ever. Probably it will alienate many of his supporters, and it may find for him a few new ones on quite different grounds.

The Dreiser controversy has raged along three lines: his artistic competence, his moral sincerity, his right to his choice of subjects. This play wil help establish his artistic competence and his moral sincerity, but it will find few to defend it on the question of material. I believe the commonest verdict will be that Dreiser is not so bad morally as he used to be thought, but that he is vastly more mistaken that he has any right to be.

With regard to moral sincerity. There has always been a well-founded feeling that Dreiser chooses his subjects because of a morbid curiosity, because he has a narrow-gauge, distorted mind that finds allure in the ugly, the deformed, and never balances it in the slightest by an interest in the normal or the beautiful. His revelation of life has been as false as that of the most arrant romanticist in spite of his realism of treatment. Too, he has always seemed to champion the right of the individual to live his life according to his impulses, regardless of his effect on society as a whole or even on the lives of those nearest to him.

For two acts "The Hand of the Potter" runs along much the usual Dreiser lines, dealing with the sordid life of a Jewish family in the New York slums. The third act presents some slight rise in the moral reactions of the family, and the fourth climbs straightway to emotional heights, a real, passionate conception of the moral qualities of his materials. It has, too, a point of view that is new to Dreiser, a balancing of his claims of the twisted, misguided individual against the claim of society to be protected. It looks as if Dreiser has acquired some social sense and some ability to be lifted out of the slime by a moral passion. Thus far to his credit.

Artistically, he has made great strides. "The Girl in the Coffin" foreshadowed a care for technique which "The Hand of the Potter" has nearly perfected. It is an artistic accomplishment in addition to its moral sincerity.

But—

Is anyone going to admit Dreiser's right to his choice of material? "The Hand of the Potter" is a study of one of the most revolting types of mental twists that society has to meet. Is such a subject material for art!

Many theorists say it is not, on purely artistic grounds. Hatred, they say, is a literary emotion, but physical repulsion, nausea, is not. One has to give his own answer to such questions.

But there must be an absolute answer to the question as to whether the general discussion of such problems is to the advantage or disadvantage of society. There is a valid objection to it. There is nothing that the public can do about such cases. Enlightened public opinion would still be worlds behind the actively concerned public agencies that are carefully working out their policies in the matter. If Dreiser thinks that the police and the charitable agencies are too slow, he should know that they are slow only because it is imperative that they should be right before they take too decided steps. The psychological experts who work for our great civic agencies are thoroughly alive to the problem. Dreiser can add nothing to their knowledge or the moral breadth and alertness, and nobody but they can do anything worth considering to help. Moral and mental defectives are recognized early, and they are being dealt with as early as it is safe to deal with them and not work injustice to them. In the meantime they are carefully watched. Society is as carefully safeguarded as is consistent with the rights of the individual. And nobody who has the mental equipment and the training to deal with such problems is morally asleep. Therefore "The Hand of the Potter" is a well-nigh useless book, and, quite innocently I believe, a potentially harmful one. The power of suggestion on ill-balanced minds is not a force to be trifled with.

Dreiser must be credited with great artistic progress in the handling of material. I believe he has raised his reputation for moral sincerity, but he has mistaken the moral good to be accomplished, if he has not mistaken the artistic possibilities of his material. The book should be only in the hands of specialists. But it will not do great harm anywere probably because it is written in such a way as to preclude all possible allure for morbid minds. Probably it will accomplish less harm than many a salacious best seller, because it will prove deadly uninteresting to the type of mind it would most inevitably harm.

Nevertheless, I wish Dreiser had written something else with the same art and the same passionate sincerity.

Denver *Mountain News*, October 12, 1919.

Here is a tragedy in four acts, based upon the sort of tragedy that recently occurred on our own North side—an assault upon a little girl by a defective.

Mr. Dreiser has done a remarkable realistic job of it—so realistic that I doubt if any American manager will ever care to put the play on the boards. . . .

Had any other man written this play it would have been taken as a thesis play, as an argument in dramatic form for the study of the individual delinquent by alienists with a view to social phophylaxis. But Mr. Dreiser would surely never condescend to write a thesis play, and besides that, the thesis is admitted, and such work, subject to the limitations, is being done. It must, therefore, be the drama of the thing that appeals to Mr. Dreiser, the spectacle of human futility and the stupidity of human comment on it—as exemplified in the least sympathetic of the reporters. But such a case as Isadore's can hardly be called universal, and so our reaction to the tragedy is far fom that classic purgation associatied with the genre.

"A Play By Theodore Dreiser." Indianapolis *Star*, October 19, 1919.

"The Hand of the Potter," by Theodore Dreiser is a tragedy in four acts. It seems unlikely that it will be produced on the stage, for its theme is too repellent, though it must be said that the author has handled it with as much delicacy and reserve as the subject will permit; but it is a striking production that could only be properly presented by high-class actors. If Dreiser had written nothing else this would establish his reputation as a writer of power. . . .

Trenton [N.J.] *Times*, October 19, 1919.

Theodore Dreiser has few living equals in the power of character delineation and finished diction. He has produced some admirable literature in magazines and between book-covers, but it is to be regretted that he displays a fondness for the exploitation of the seamy side of human intercourse. "The Hand of the Potter," in the form of a play, deals with the shameful career of a degenerate who, having served time for assaulting an innocent young girl, is unable while on probation to resist his base nature and involves his unfortunate old father and mother anew in disgrace and brings himself to a suicide's grave. Realism has its place in the novel, and the drama, but there are limits which decency and good taste set up to guide the writer and to protect the public.

"A Dreiser Play." New York *Post*, October 25, 1919, p. 11.

There is no real literary or dramatic value in the so-called four-act tragedy,

"The Hand of the Potter," of which Theodore Dreiser is the author. To the title of tragedy it has no pretensions. At best it is very sordid melodrama. As a reflection of poverty-stricken conditions and of speech and manners in East Side districts it is, in a sense, veracious, but the realism is unrelieved by any redeeming touch of imagination. It rehearses in baldest fashion the murder of a child by a criminal degenerate, who thereafter commits suicide and becomes the subject of a post-mortem discussion among reporters, who reach the profound conclusion that sexual maniacs may be largely irresponsible for their actions and ought to be kept under watch and ward. The whole thing reads like a collection of extracts from penny-dreadfuls and official police records. Of dramatic structure it exhibits no trace. That it contains bait that might be attractive to one sort of audience is likely enough, but nothing in it is worthy of preservation in print.

Alexander Woollcott. "Hand of the Potter." New York *Times Review of Books*, October 26, 1919, p. 598.

"The Hand of the Potter," the tragedy of one marred in the making, is the name of an interesting and occasional dramatic narrative in play form by the author of "Sister Carrie." It tells, often in passages of great pathos, the story of a congenital degenerate's helpless battle with a tempting and uncomprehending world into which he does not fit. There is rehearsed then such a squalid and repellent murder as the sensational newspapers gloated over about a decade ago, when the body of little Ruth Wheeler was found.

However, it is not merely the fact that the story is hideous that makes Mr. Dreiser's play in its present form unsuitable for the theatre. It is also because he has written it with the spendthrift novelist's ignorance of the dramatist's enforced economy of means, relying lazily on long and archaic soliloquies to make himself clear, and indulging in his last act in such a symposium of windy and anti-climactic discussion as an older and better playwright named Shaw would have carefully put first and called a preface.

It is conceivable, however, that a neater artisan could prune the play into actable shape. He would begin by lopping off the last act, and it may be said that a play which can lose its last act without regrets is a defective play. The publishers of "The Hand of the Potter" bill it somewhat meretriciously as "Stark naked and unashamed"; but it really ought to be ashamed of its last act.

Ralph F. Holmes. Springfield [Mass.] *Morning Union*, October 26, 1919.

Theodore Dreiser has let himself in for another drubbing by the publication, through Boni & Liveright, of a four-act play entitled "The Hand of the Potter." And the defenders of Mr. Dreiser, if I mistake not, are going to be few in number and feeble in voice, for he has written a play which is not only unimaginable on the stage but almost impossible to read, so grim, so hideous and so true it is.

It is one thing to tell the story of a girl who triumphs over her surroundings at the expense of what the world likes to call the moral self, to picture the financial rapacity of a man of wealth, the amorous adventures of a man of genius—these things are not only true but they are typical. But is is quite another to go down into the dark and fearsome depths of abnormal psychology and bring forth to view on the printed page the tragedy of an ill-born youth who commits the most unspeakable of social offenses, the attack upon children.

This is the kind of horror with which newspapers willingly harrow the hearts of eager readers whenever the opportunity offers, but that it constitutes legitimate material for the artist is going to be hotly denied, and by many who would resent being classed as conservative critics.

Any review which a commentator attempts to offer of this book must be regarded almost as a warning, for I think it is frankly the duty of the reviewer, in this case, to strive as far as possible to prevent the book falling into the hands of anyone unprepared to receive it, quite as much as it is his duty to urge it into the hands of all who have staunch hearts in their contemplation of life, and that high degree of optimism which does not flinch or despair at the naked truth. . . .

Providence [R.I.] *Journal*, October 26, 1919.

Why is "The Hand of the Potter?" After reading it we might with equal disgust and indignation ask, "Why is Theodore Dreiser?" His play, "The Hand of the Potter" is one of the most appallingly repulsive plays ever written, not alone for its subject, but because it has been clumsily and awkwardly treated. The author not only reveals himself as a violator of the rules of good taste, but as a crude worker in the art of dramatic construction. From any point the play must be considered inexcusable. Drama, whether tragedy or comedy, implies a conflict of some sort, a struggle between man and man, or man and his nature. "The Hand of the Potter" has no struggle or conflict of any sort. Its moving character is a degenerate of the worst kind, a lunatic, and, consequently, unable to rule his own actions. To say that he comes in conflict with the world outside the asylum he has left, is a specious and puerile argument. There is no drama in watching a lunatic run amuck. Mr. Dreiser with equal effect might have taken us to an insane asylum and asked us to watch through a key hole the painful and distressing scenes. That is all his play affords.

San Francisco *Chronicle*, November 15, 1919.

Theodore Dreiser at his best writes stories and passages that rank with the best of things in our contemporary American literature. A perusal of his play, a so-called tragedy in four acts, forces the conviction that at his worst he can seriously write stuff as sordid and mediocre as the copy of any uninspired reporter. "The Hand of the Potter" concerns the murder of an eleven-year-old child by a criminal degenerate, and narrates with interminable prolixity of evidence, the trial of the youth before the bar of justice. The fourth act is clearly superfluous, and is added on for the sake of the naive comments and tepid moralizing of the courtroom officials. Yet it is not conceivable that the excision of the last act would improve the play at all. It is weak melodrama, lacking in plot, devoid of structure, without feeling and imagination, and without any discernible trace of literary or dramatic value.

Philadelphia *Press*, November 22, 1919.

Mr. Dreiser's theme in "The Hand of the Potter" is the disagreeable one of criminal insanity. His chief actor is a mentally diseased youth who attacks female children and who, tracked by the police after a revolting murder, resists the impulse to attack yet another child, and commits suicide in a wretched boarding house. For all that theme is handled with a certain dignity and with rare dramatic skill it is mainly disappointing. Mr. Dreiser could not resist the temptation to moralize. After sticking nobly to his artistic job in the first few acts he gets sentimental in the third and makes a tedious sermon of the fourth. And Dreiser is never so trite and dull as when he turns reformer.

Baltimore *News*, November 29, 1919.

In "The Hand of the Potter," Theodore Dreiser has produced a work that, from the standpoint of literary craftsmanship, further strengthens his undeniable position as one of the foremost American writers of the day.

This is a four-act play—a tragedy that is almost unbearably revolting in its nature with sexual degeneracy as the theme.

Dreiser handles his material supremely well. That is one reason why the effect is so appalling, for if the thing were badly done it would not even receive scant attention.

Indeed, as a matter of technique, Dreiser, generally speaking, in this work shows a real mastery of dramatic form. The play is splendidly constructive, the scenes being cumulative in their effect, the characters are vividly and truthfully portrayed and beneath the terror and horror of it all there is a heartbreaking pathos.

It is only in the last act when the newspaper reporters engage in a pseudo-scientific discussion that the dramatic values are at all weakened. This episode is entirely irrelevant and is moreover improbable. Fancy the star men of big metropolitan journals wasting their time, while gathering detail of a very yellow story, by starting a psychopathic symposium! In the first place, it's rare to find any of them with enough sense to make such an undertaking plausible, and in the second place, nobody cares a hang what their opinions are anyway. This last act, then, is only strong in its opening, when the ravings of the criminal maniacs are recorded, and in the closing when the old father finds the body of his son.

David Karsner. "A Tragedy." New York *Call*, December 6, 1919.

Dreiser has dramatized a sensational newspaper story in which a Jewish youth, living with his family in a tenement on the upper East Side of New York, assaults a little Irish girl who came to his house to seek a playmate, kills her and buries her body in a vacant lot near his home, where it is soon found, hides in the big city for some days while the newspapers and detectives search for him, and finally commits suicide by inhaling gas in a poor lodging house.

Isadore (he didn't like the name; so he changed it to Irving) Berchansky was what the police would call a "nut," a magistrate would say "sexual pervert," a district attorney would define him as a "lust-murderer," and all three definitions would come somewhere near identifying him, but none would explain him. Look at two apples on a limb of a tree. One grows green and dwarfed, the next is perfectly rounded and rosy. The same sun shines on both, and both are nurtured from identical roots. It is not true that we are born equal, nor is it true that having been born our "rights" are "unalienable." These are myths invented to comfort the weak, but they do not comfort; they only accentuate the torture of obvious inequalities.

Isadore's subnormality ran to sex. He had tried to "get smart" with his sister. She rebuffed him and slapped his face, saying, "Let go! What's the matter with you, anyhow? Don't try to pull that stuff on me. You nut! Whadda ya think I am? Another 10-year-old?"

Isadore whines: "Gee, I must be crazy. I don't seem to be able to stand anything no more. You look so nice, that's the trouble. Don't say anything to the folks, will you, Rac? I ain't quite right, I guess. Ain't I suffered enough? Don't you know what I'm up against, havin' the feelin's I do? I ain't so bad. I just can't stand things, that's all. It's just their pretty faces, an' their mouths, an' their shoulders, an' the way they fix their hair."

In most newspaper offices the beginning of summer is spoken of as "the silly season." We are regaled with the most lurid details of sex crimes in all stratas of society. The newspaper reading public follows the details of these episodes and crowds into the courthouses if there should be a subsequent trial of the person who has offended the moral and criminal codes. Yet the public is ignorant of the subtler inferences, the congenital weaknesses, the pathological side of cases of this nature.

Ten or twelve years ago a bright young man was haled before a police magistrate in Chicago. The charge was burglary. The magistrate heard the policeman's story of the capture of the culprit and listened attentively while a butcher told how the young man had brazenly walked into his house at 3 o'-clock in the morning. The offender was bound over to the Grand Jury in heavy bail, and it was not until his case came into a higher court that he had a chance to prove he was a somnambulist and not a burglar. I heard the youth's story when he first told it to the ivory-headed police judge, and later interviewed his mother, and I had every reason to disbelieve the burglar tale. If society must have courts let them be presided over by mental doctors, for most people are not criminals, but society is plumb crazy, and it is small wonder that some of its weaker members succumb to sad fault.

Dreiser's treatment of this important subject—sex perversion—or subnormality, is neither frivolous nor flippant. His particular story is by no means an isolated case. He has put the setting in a poor East Side home, but that was done for character study and effect. Otherwise it might fit Fifth avenue just as well. His chief characters are Jewish. They could just as well have been Germans, Irish, Chinese or Americans.

I have watched the reviews of "The Hand of the Potter." Many of them deprecated the theme. Others attacked Dreiser for writing it. Yet the newspapers idealize the "juicy murder" and feed every detail to their readers in four or five daily doses. The average newspaper reader reads two things in his paper—"juicy" stories, meaning tales flavored with sex, and the sport page. Yet when he makes a gift of a book it will be Shelley's poems (which he never read).

Dreiser has done much better writing than is presented here. There are parts that are long and windy, the philosophical observations of newspaper reporters, for instance. Reporters don't often become philosophical. Especially not on such occasions.

Old man Berchansky, he who peddles needles and thread, and who knows little of life, what a sad, melancholy figure he is! Dreiser's old men are wonderfully real. This book followed eight or nine volumes by Dreiser. I would have said that Dreiser had about shot his bolt in this, if he had not followed it with "Twelve Men," a twentieth century classic which starts Dreiser anew again.

As a play to be produced, I don't believe the American public would stand for it. It is too horribly real. Its lights, when they do shine, are a melancholy yellow. The picture is too gruesome, yet it is commonly true.

"A Pathological Play." *New York Medical Review*, March 6, 1920, pp. 431–432.

Incest, rape, murder and suicide follow each other with startling rapidity in the pathological drama which Dreiser so realistically portrays in *The Hand of the Potter.* From the literary point of view the work is excellent. The members of the family group and the home life are painted carelessly and yet with an insight akin to that of Dostoievsky—an insight that overlooks no detail. All this makes interesting reading, but in reaching his conclusions the author draws upon old line psychology and failure results. Cause and effect are bandied about in a superficial manner and no successful sifting is accomplished.

The chief actor in the drama is a youth distinctly marked with a tic. His downfall is attributed to hormones which make him more sensitive to the appeal of women. He is excited by their filmy waists, their painted mouths, their hair, by the way they walk. . . . These are forces over which he has no control. This is all important enough, but why not get to the bottom of the question? Here is a delicate theme—a series of themes, if you please—carried out in fearless fashion; why not the conclusions?

Most of us have come to realize the workings of the œdipus complex in our dream life, where incest and parricide are the unwelcome visitors which the censor has so carefully suppressed in our conscious minds. Behind all this there is the sex drive pushing us on, suppressed through centuries of civilization, reaching out for the nearest object in our early environment. This is so universal that it can no longer be considered as abnormal, but merely as unfortunate. It may be looked upon as the necessary progression of narcissism, homosexuality, and finally the complete heterosexual development. It is only when the evolutionary process is arrested and a holdover continues for an unusual length of time that the condition must be considered pathological. For the interests of the herd and for the common welfare of the individuals comprising the herd, it is necessary to have either a direct normal sex outlet or a creative, sublimated substitute. Suppression is necessary for selfpreservation. In reaching the higher levels of sex expression and turning from selflove to a complete heterosexual desire, a transference is made from the mother object to another female who answers more fully our sex wants.

In the character Dreiser has portrayed this evolutionary process is checked. In an infantile manner the boy reaches out for the sex object nearest at hand; his mental status prevents him from adjusting himself to the more elemental demands of society. It is interesting to follow the story of the trial in the courts of law. The clever prosecuting attorney is unable to confuse the loyal family group who try to save the life of the uncaught culprit. Only when the father, urged by his conscience, reveals the plot of the family to save the boy's life by concealment and lies, are they able to fix the guilt upon his son.

Every physician or student of psychology who is interested in psychopathological conditions will find it worth while to study this book, even though some of the conclusions are not as fundamental as they might be.

Checklist of Additional Reviews

St. Louis *Republican*, September 9, 1919.

New York *Review*, September 13, 1919.

"Another Striking Book by Dreiser." Cincinnati *Times Star*, September 11, 1919.

New York *American*, September 14, 1919.

"A Dreiserian Play." Boston *Evening Transcript*, September 17, 1919, p. 4.

Pittsburgh *Dispatch*, September 25, 1919.

Philadelphia *Inquirer*, September 27, 1919.

Chicago *Tribune*, October 5, 1919.

Springfield [Mass.] *Republican*, October 26, 1919, p. 16.

"Dreiser's Play." Philadelphia *Evening Ledger*, June 5, 1920.

Further Reviews: Bibliographic Information Incomplete

Pittsburgh *Gazette Times*.

Chicago *Post*.

W.P.B. "The Pervert." Syracuse *Post Standard.*
Los Angeles *Times.*
K.M.G. *Social Hygiene.*

HEY RUB-A-DUB-DUB

A BOOK OF THE MYSTERY AND
WONDER AND TERROR
OF LIFE

By THEODORE DREISER

AUTHOR OF "SISTER CARRIE," "THE HAND OF THE POTTER,"
"FREE AND OTHER STORIES," "JENNIE
GERHARDT," ETC.

BONI AND LIVERIGHT
NEW YORK 1920

Hey Rub-A-Dub-Dub

"Theodore Dreiser Writes a Modern Prose Rubaiyat." Philadelphia *North American*, March 13, 1920.

No minister will need to read more than a few pages of "Hey, Rub-a-Dub-Dub" by Theodore Dreiser to spring to the edge of his pulpit and utter denunciation of the tub into which the writer puts the men and women of his observations.

The book of essays, varied with a play or two, which is published by Boni and Liveright, describes too many of the actual reasons for pessimism, and pessimism isn't a permissible theological attitude of mind; not for a Christian.

The volume "strikes at the very foundations" of the average sermon, and yet —there is little in the book that can be denied its truth. It is the Rubaiyat of Dreiser. It is his confession of an unanswered quest. It goes further than old Kahyam. Even wine cannot minister to this discouragement. The misfortunes, the insignificance, the delusion, the cruelties of man are confronted and there is no light of faith and hope in the seeing eye. There may be some purpose in it all, says the writer, but if so, can the purpose be anything much?

Divine and natural shortcomings are recognized with a gloomy nod. Social and economic conditions are considered with a frowning, alien gaze but there is no senseless, unavailing revolt expressed in spite of the appaling prospect, until the subject of literary censorship is encountered.

Dreiser maintains a detached, critical, almost humorous attitude until this crops up in his mind. Then it is apparent that the suppression of his book "The Genius," left a reservoir of excusable bile. It vents itself in a brief pungent protest, the mildest sentence from which asks: "When will we lay aside our swaddling clothes, enforced on us by ignorant, impossible puritans, and their uneducated followers, and stand up free-thinking men and women?"

"Art is the stored honey of the human soul, gathered on wings of misery and travail," he adds. "Shall the dull and the self-seeking and the self-advertising close this store on the groping human mind?" The philosophy of his book answers his question. It could indicate that the answer is "Yes."

Some will call the book "horrible." Others will read it with a very keen and lasting appreciation. Whatever else it may be it is real. Whatever his philosophy Dreiser is one of the real thinkers of present-day America.

Chicago *Tribune*, March 14, 1920.

Under the intriguing title of "Hey Rub-a-Dub-Dub," Theodore Dreiser has collected his thoughts about American life. Bernard Shaw has one of his characters in "Antony and Cleopatra" say "The crowds along the Appian way are ever the same age." Theodore Dreiser's book recalls that memorable phrase. Mr. Dreiser seems suddenly to have discovered that fundamental fact. He seems to have extricated himself from the crowds and to have suddenly turned upon them the eyes of a man who was but lately one of them.

He was for a few years the bright light on the American literary horizon —he was in the flow of American life. He was one of the eternal youths of the Appian way. He wrote books which had the quality of what Waldo Frank might call the rhythm of America. And then suddenly he stopped to look in a toy shop window, perhaps, and became so fascinated by the highly sensitized mechanical dolls that the boisterous, buxom, sometimes blowzy crowd seemed unreal to him.

"Hey Rub-a-Dub-Dub" is his attempt to analyze that crowd. It is a book of undeniable facts about human nature—a restatement of the injustices of life, of the unfair distribution of wealth, of the law's unfairnesses, of the wrongs of the ballot, of the injustice of the price of living, of the cruelties of the Negro question, of the autocracy of the government during the war, of the morbid Puritanism of America, of the unbeatitudic attitude of the press, of America's signal failure to realize her ideals. But that is all it is, just a statement of cases. There is no vision, no passionate hope, even, of a change. It is just the picture of the crowds. Waldo Frank in "Our America" really has a vision. He sees where the crowds might go when they have ceased wandering up and down the Appian way, when they have grown beyond the "ever the same age" period. Theodore Dreiser does not.

R.F.H. Detroit *Journal*, March 17, 1920.

Theodore Dreiser has arrived at that interesting and dangerous point in his career where he has succumbed to the temptation to set down upon paper the fatal words "I believe."

An interesting point to his readers, many of whom have undoubtedly been rather more than mildly curious as to just what Dreiser does believe, but dangerous to Mr. Dreiser because now, having foresaken the role of artist for that of philosópher, he has given his detractors a stationary target at which to aim.

And it is a target of no small dimensions, either, for what Mr. Dreiser believes is hardly what the orthodox believe, and what he suggests as a remedy for present conditions and for the personal guidance of others goes counter to the current social and moral code.

On the other hand, to be sure, what Mr. Dreiser believes is totally without novelty or thrill to those who have worked out for themselves much the same conception of existence as he sets forth in "Hey, Rub-a-dub-dub," and their only feeling regarding the work will be one of regret that under Mr. Dreiser's pen these convictions lack a brilliant advocate—an Anatole France, a Remey de Gourmont. For Mr. Dreiser in this volume runs true to form and presents just the same lumbering, stumbling, half articulate figure as a philosopher that he does as a novelist.

But for my part I have a suspicion that this same incoherent formless, ambling, rambling, redundant manner of his, this total lack of anything we mean by style, might prove the greatest resource of this book in some hands.

Brilliance, with a certain type of mind, is suspect. The Shaws, the Frances, the Menckens, the Chestertons—all those who send their shafts out barbed, are distrusted.

Here, on the other hand, is a man who speaks the vernacular, who, so far as I know, has never written a brilliant line in his life, has never committed an epigram, who does not pack his sentences with meat so that one must needs keep on the edge of one's intellectual seat to catch every shade and depth of meaning. He gets an idea and mulls it over, paws it around, tears it apart leisurely, puts it together slowly. If you miss his point on page one, you needn't worry because you will find it reaffirmed—on page five or seventeen or oftener.

The great difficulty about this method is that the readers more at home with loose and leisurely methods of expression are not apt to be those interested in the subject matter of Mr. Dreiser's essays, or, if interested, sufficiently liberal to tolerate his conclusions.

A writer who declares himself convinced that the individual is of no concern to Nature, that there is no deity to whom one may turn for protection, that there is no hereafter to which we can look for the adjustments of the malorganization of this world, is apt to find himself alone, save at the extremities of the social order, the highly sophisticated intellectuals (even the so-called intellectuals) at one end of the scale and with the illiterate natural philosophers who have had their theories of existence smashed into them by the heavy hand of experience at the other end. The well-fed, the well-housed and the well-entertained intellectual middle classes will have none of such "pessimism" or worse. For them a God of Wrath and Righteousness, concerned with the fall of the sparrow and the souls of individuals and equipped with heaven, hell and purgatory as the machinery of ultimate justice.

"Battling Dreiser—and Less Striking Writers." New York *Evening Post*, March 20, 1920.

. . . It is, to quote the jacket, "A Book of the Mystery and Terror and Wonder of Life." It is the mature expression of his beliefs and theories about existence in general and America in particular. What do we find? That truth is beyond the consciousness of man, that American financiers are inclined to be ruthless, that life is vain, that sex repression is one of the harmful features of our national life; this and much more of the same sort, written wretchedly and full of vain iterations like an old man's gossip before the fire. Nothing that has not been said before; nothing that men as diverse as Dewey, Bergson and H. L.

Mencken have not expressed more forcibly.

Scattered through the volume are a number of extravaganzas in the Smart Set manner but without the cleverness that makes the Smart Set readable if not palatable. One finds in the other chapters many high-sounding phrases about biology and chemistry and a great deal of second-hand materialism, pragmatism, skepticism, empiricism, so confused that a candidate for a Sorbonne Ph.D. would have a hard time untangling them. While Dreiser says much that is indubitably true and his sincerity is painfully apparent, he is both dull and repetitious.

However, let us return to the jacket; the publisher's praise is often more revelatory than one would expect. "If Philosophy can ever be made exciting," says the blurbist, "Mr. Dreiser has here achieved that feat. Here is Life—mysterious, terrible, wonderful—and Dreiser looking at it unafraid."

One has the vision immediately of two champions stripped for the prize ring. Life is a big old man, with a harsh voice and a scrubby chin. In the opposite corner sits Battling Dreiser, contender for the championship. The first round begins; on each side there are a few blows and much vituperation. Life hasn't much wind, you surmise, and Dreiser is going to outtalk him by the third chapter—I mean round—the audience has fallen asleep; they wake every few pages and yawn to find the struggle going on as before. The last I remember, Life had become pretty groggy, but I fell asleep again in the last chapter and I really can't tell you how the battle came out.

Dreiser will publish a new novel some time during the year. I shall read it to learn the results.

Philadelphia *Press* March 21, 1920.

The essay form suits Theodore Dreiser perfectly. That didacticism which marred so many of his novels finds a perfectly natural outlet in "Hey Rub-A-Dub-Dub," the collection of his miscellaneous writings which Boni and Liveright have just published. For when a novelist preaches he is only a bore; but an essayist may sermonize to his heart's content provided only that he be convincing.

And Dreiser in the main is very convincing. It is the driving, sorrowful earnestness of him that convinces. He means what he says so intensely you cannot be indifferent to his views. Life interests him so profoundly. He preceives [sic] the "mystery and terror and wonder" of it so acutely . . . It is only a pity that the beauty of it so often eludes his vision.

In the first essay he sits and looks at New York City from the opposite bank of the Hudson and wonders if there be not "some great elemental spirit" controlling and ordering the mad procession of life. But he is not sure: "Illusions hold too many; lust and greed, vast and blear-eyed, dominate too many more. Ignorance vast and almost unconquerable, hugs and licks its chains in reverence. Brute strength sits empurpled and laughs a throaty laugh."

With the same inconsolable pessimism he examines the art, the economics, the social order, national traits, science, "big business" and many other aspects of America. There is nothing startlingly new in his analyses, but even the most commonplace of them is redeemed by a quality of vehement sincerity which, in Dreiser, ever burns like a fever. Grateful memories of "Sister Carrie" make one hope that, having delivered himself of all these purposeful sermons, Mr. Dreiser will not feel constrained to preach again in his forthcoming novel, "The Bulwark."

"Books of the Day." Philadelphia *Enquirer*, March 23, 1920.

Mr. Theodore Dreiser has stopped writing stories of sexual moment to appear in the role of a social philosopher. Apparently he is now trying to formulate into a system the views which he has expressed in his novels which have had unusual themes for exploitation and which are of all varieties of merit. One or two might be mentioned which seem to be as fine specimens of realism as this country has produced and with a resulting flood of light on social matters of a constructive variety. Others have been of less value and some seem hardly worth printing let alone reading.

"Hey Rub-a-Dub" is his latest volume, which consists of a series of essays on varous topics dealing with sociology, capitalism, injustice, shams and the like, which sound much more like productions of a Russian brain than those of an American. Mr. Dreiser is a writer of jeremiads in these days. He is seldom constructive in any possible way. Naturally he has his ideas of remaking the world, but few of them are practical. One might think from reading this book that there was little of love, joy and progress in life, but rather that the human race had become decadent.

Whether Mr. Dreiser is the voice of a prophet crying in the wilderness or a closet philosopher, gone mad over things which displease him, the future must determine. What he says differs little from what has been said of society for at least four thousand years of recorded protests, and the same thing may be expected for milleniums to come. Nevertheless his views now, as always, are worth reading. He always says things in an impressive way.

"Brave Mr. Dreiser." New York *Review*, April 24, 1920.

Mr. Dreiser is getting more and more philosophical as he becomes more and more middle-aged. He is not so keen now to write *Sister Carries* and *Geniuses* and have Puritans condemn him as immoral, and censorial societies give him free advertising.

In this new volume we are told that Mr. Dreiser has shown his fullest reaction to life as it is lived and prostituted under his observation. Mr. Dreiser has had his eyes and ears open, both the eyes and ears of the body and of the spirit, and what he has seen and heard has shaken him to his foundation: he can't make out what it is all about, with its contradictions, incongruities, abnormalities and monstrosities.

Among the things which Mr. Dreiser has heard and read about most are right, truth, justice and mercy. The newspapers are full of the words, the pulpit and the forum are eloquent with them, individuals spout them upon all occasions. But when Mr. Dreiser looks about him he can see none of these qualities or its result. All that meet his eye and ear are wrong, falsehood, injustice and cruelty—crime, recrimination, backbiting, malice, hypocrisy, hatred, lust and selfishness.

Beholding all these things, Mr. Dreiser is sore amazed, not to say disturbed, but he is *not afraid.* We are assured by the jacket of *Hey-Rub-a-Dub-Dub* that Mr. Dreiser positively is not afraid. Others may blanch and quake at the horrors of the world, but not Mr. Dreiser. He faces Life, mysterious, terrible, wonderful, without a tremor of fear. Still he is troubled, and he writes many frank pages trying to figure out the riddle of it all and come to some definite conclusion about it. That he does not solve the question should not be held against Mr. Dreiser. Others more far-famed have failed similarly—take Plato, for instance, and Voltaire. So Mr. Dreiser is not to be scorned for failing to touch the bottom of the unfathomable.

He does sound some of the depths, however, and it may be said unequivocally that his book is mighty interesting reading, showing deeper thought and more powerful grasp upon modern social and civic problems and tendencies than most works upon the subject, and having behind it a genuinely impressive personality, and being expressed in a rough and ready but effective style.

J.B.
"Dreiser's New Element." Brooklyn *Eagle,* April 3, 1920.

Theodore Dreiser . . . abandons the sphere of fiction and devotes himself to essays in his new book, "Hey, Rub-a-Dub-Dub." This volume comprises a series of papers on life in general and American life in particular. Mr. Dreiser is much happier in this branch of literature than in those he has previously embraced—and he is much pleasanter as well as more beneficial reading. There are many questions asked in this book. Indeed, it is one collossal interrogation. Mr. Dreiser is impatient with our ways and weaknesses. He flaunts our inconsistencies, he punctures our complacencies. Yet all is not irritant here, for he is constructively critical. He wants a greater America, he wants a truer, happier America. There is the urge of the poet in his intolerance. There is the inspiration of the pioneer in his plea for the abandonment of false standards and social superficialities. He is less a cynic in this new book than in anything he has yet written. "Change," one of the most significant contributions, is a composite of question and answer. He queries, he explains, and then he joins with us in marvelling over the whole. "The Toil of the Poet" is quick with color, intensity, significance and sincerity. Not in the entire volume is there anything so appealing. True, it is less logical than many of the other papers. It possesses, however, a spiritual depth that lifts it in this sphere far above its fellow contributions. "Hey Rub-a-Dub-Dub" is a cold shower bath on a January morning—it is a smart, stinging slap in the face—it is an imperative reveille.

Jackson D. Haag. "Frank Exposition of Dreiser's Philosophy." Detroit *News*, April 4, 1920.

Theodore Dreiser is an irritating individual who writes what he thinks so convincingly that a reader prejudiced against him finds his previously firmly grounded convictions slipping away and being replaced by iconoclastic theories that really shock by their frankness if not their novelty.

Mr. Dreiser's latest offering in the way of disturbing literature is "Hey-Rub-A-Dub-Dub." This is a collection of some 20 essays on a wide variety of subjects that extend from "Some Aspects of Our National Character" to "Life and Art." In each is the Dreiser philosophy brought forth in dress that shocks, surprises, pleases or gratifies, but never is it paraded without some emphatic effect which rather leads one to the conclusion that something substantial exists in this Indianan's belief in men and things.

Dreiser is not a master of a brilliant or striking style, nor one that is effective in producing startling or bizarre effects, or which will permit a sentence being lifted from the text as an example of trenchant expression. His is pure narration, such as characterizes the talk of the average well educated man—an easy flow of words that fit so snugly into the places they occupy and express the author's meaning so well that the general reader seldom questions their right to be there. No single word or expression growls at one as one passes from page to page. We may not agree with the would-be tearer down of temples and cleaner of stables that the world is awry and that the majority of humankind is built on the bias; but he does have a way of making the uninteresting interesting; of almost persuading that his theories of life are logical and, consequently, acceptable. From the opening essay in this volume, in which he thinks and talks through a fanciful foreigner whom he locates in a squalid section of Jersey, across from New York but within sight of the great skyline and the wonderful river, to the closing fanciful conceit, the book shows matured thought.

In some of Dreiser's stories we are treated to ideas hurled out of a printed page without unnecessary clothing, so to speak. In the essays one encounters the same thing, but here they seem less offensive or showy and the reader can not refrain from wondering if he has grown used to the Dreiser method or if the age has advanced since the days of "Sister Carrie," or if we have become inured to nudity of thought through encountering so much of the physical variety on the stage. Anyhow, Dreiser goes ahead in his own way, and in substance he says, "If you don't like what I say, I'm not even sorry—unless it be that you are suffering because you are so mentally hidebound that you can't see the truth as I do; it is all so clear and unmistakable."

But the freedom he advocates would be good only if the world were populated with just the right types of human beings—the kind that Mr. Dreiser and those of his ilk might select. The rein of restraint might then be tossed on the neck of the body politic, and the community rest assured that thought and action would be directed toward the betterment of humanity. Unfortunately, however, if the Dreiser system of philosophy were to become the governing law of the land, unbridled license would quickly trample conservatism in the mire and "the greatest good to the greatest number" would be nothing more than a mouthful of sophistry.

It is in such essays as "Life and Art," wherein the personal phase of life is touched upon, and from which viewpoint, even with a touch of vanity, that Mr. Dreiser appears at his best. The personal pronoun in his mouth doesn't strike the reader as being in the least offensive, and seldom does one catch oneself finding fault with the author because he holds up some of his Indiana experiences as a sample of life as it is lived. Introspection and self-analysis can easily become obsessions and militate against a writer's effectiveness, but thus far with Dreiser the habit has the effect of a counter-irritant in relation to the radicalism of the doctrines he preaches.

Burton Rascoe. "The Books of the Week." Chicago *Tribune,* April 10, 1920.

The title sketch in this volume is one of the finest, most moving, and most poignant things Mr. Dreiser has ever written.

To read the rest of the pieces in the book is to understand the curious mental processes which are at the base of his work as a novelist. He is essentially emotional and imaginative. A conflict goes on in him always, a conflict between his almost infantile attempts at rationalization and his morbid consciousness of sin, between his vague intellectual concepts and his much more deeply rooted Puritanism and sentimentalism.

Dreiser is a moralist if there ever was one, a moralist of so complete a lack of skepticism that were he less intelligent and less an artist he would, probably, be preaching some terrifying gospel of hell fire and damnation in some frontier pulpit. The mood of heavy sorrow and troubled forebodings never leaves him. The sight of young men and women enjoying themselves at a dance fills him with misgivings: he reacts to spontaneous pleasure like a Holy Roller. But therein, I think, lies the secret of his power as an artist; he expresses a phase of American life and temperament with a sincerity and veracity almost unknown before him: he has recorded our growth and groping with profound fidelity.

Benjamin De Casseres. "Mr. Dreiser Talks of Many Things." New York *Times Book Review,* April 11, 1920, p. 167.

In the midway of this his mortal life, having found himself astray and gone from the path direct, Mr. Dreiser utters the curious onomatopoetic yawn, "Hey Rub-a-dub-dub!" Psychologically, Hey rub-a-dub-dub is the very opposite of the syllable Om, which repeated by the Yogi over and over lands him in Nirvana, where the human race ceases from troubling and suppressed desires are at rest.

Mr. Dreiser's ejaculation is one of weariness, a puzzled weariness. It is American for Voltaire's Why is anything? and Montaigne's What do I know? Mr. Dreiser has pondered on everything from the birth of Brahma to the Lusk raiders; he has digested history, chemistry, Nietzsche, Carlyle Harris, evolution, the Woolworth Tower, Sam Gompers, Ashtoreth, the hypocrisy of Nature and Mayor Hylan's Theory of Buses—vanitas, vanitatum, all is Hey rub-a-dub-dub!

Then he bethought himself of a "book of the mystery and terror of life," a sort of *Apologia pro vita swat.* Whatever may be said of life, the book does not inspire mystery, terror or wonder. It is good, solid, ponderous, bourgeois skepticism, with a tremendous piece of satiric buffoonery at the end called "The Court of Progress," which is worth all the rest of the iterations of the obvious that precede it.

The "jacket" of "Hey Rub-a-Dub-Dub" tells us that the essays in the book are the mature expressions of Mr. Dreiser's beliefs and theories. But of theories and beliefs we find none. The author of "The Genius," so far as we can see, never had any beliefs of theories. He is an inarticulate Walt Whitman. He may be a Balzac who cannot visualize. He is a vast, clumsy shadow moving in words unrealized. He is potentially a mystic, a realist, a romantic, an ironist—but only potentially. He has hewed many trails, but prefers to climb up the trees and study the landscape before finishing them. After all, why not? Are not horizons the end of every man's desire?

These essays concern "Change," "Some Aspects of Our National Character," "The American Financier," "Personality," "The Toil of the Laborer," "The Reformer," "Marriage and Divorce," "Life, Art, and America," "Neurotic America and the Sex Impulse"—there are twenty of them, written in the painfully authentic Dreiserian manner. Mr. Dreiser's style always reminds us of a college professor who has been "fired" for trying to make his pupils think. He emits endless commonplaces with the air of having discovered something new. He is pedantic before the threadbare.

He finds that the reformer in all ages is a reaction against the *status quo;* that the American financier is necessary at his worst; that nothing is true but change; that nature and man are necessarily hypocrites in the struggle for existence; that life is tragic; that the introspective being who spends the whole day from his window in Bayonne looking at the Woolworth Tower will never get anywhere. These commonplaces can be done over and over again by a genius; but of genius in his style Mr. Dreiser has not a flake. "I indicate." "Consider." "Will it?" "I admit that—" "I would like to present." "Who can help it?" It is the pathos of the unexpressed by the unilluminated.

"Phantasmagoria" splits the book in twain. It is a little cosmic drama in three scenes—"The House of Birth," "The House of Life," "The House of Death." It is the *via dolorosa* of the "Lord of the Universe," his agglomeration, effulgence in life, and his ingression. A titanic theme, splendid in conception, prosily executed. This sort of thing must be done by a poet—a Flaubert, a Victor Hugo, a Swinburne, a Shelley. It has been done by the Hindus a thousand times—and who shall do it again? The speeches in the mouths of Beauty, Ambition, Pity, Love, Hate, &c., are almost journalistic. Endless repetitions and a cabalistic and recurrent Oh, ho, ho, ho, ho! from the lips of the Eternal. After Victor Hugo's "Legend of the Centuries"—what! Dreiser?

In "The Court of Progress" Mr. Dreiser has written one of the most drastic satires ever written in this country. This ought to be printed separately and distributed by the million. All the stupidities of the present time are doused in vitriol in this burlesque on "progress"—which in America today is the very opposite of "civilization."

It purports to be the record of the doings of the Federated Chairman of the Post Federated Period of World Republics (2,760–3,923). The Court of Progress, held in South Africa, is presided over by Noxus Podunkus, Grand Rerefendunce of the Federated Musnud of the World. The world has become perfect, pure, moral, sleepy and stupid. This phantasmagoria is a celebration of the triumph of humanity over poets, cigarette fiends, saloon keepers, madams, socialists, Holy Rollers, artists and the like. Ralph Waldo Trine, Harold Bell Wright, Gene Stratton Porter and others are the revered names. Nothing that exists today is spared. In that far-off divine event the world is ruled by Zanys, Nizys, Dizzards, Loobies, Hoddy-Doddys, Gaberlunzies, Fuddys and others. It is a carnival, a charivari of color such as seldom has ever got on paper.

In "The Court of Progress," Mr. Dreiser has answered himself. All the question marks and pathetic yowls before life, nature and society in the rest of the book come to judgment in this cosmo-comic spectacle—it is to laugh!

Chicago *News*, April 14, 1920.

Theodore Dreiser's new book, "Hey Rub-A-Dub-Dub," is much better than its title, but its subtitle, "A book of the mystery and terror and wonder of life," is a misnomer. The book performs two functions: First, it provides a text for serious minded men who wish to reflect on life and conditions in America; secondly, it lays bare the extent of Dreiser's thinking on these subjects. This is rather unfavorable to Dreiser, for it discloses that on many subjects he is as ill informed, superficial and illogical as many of his countrymen whom he ponders about. It is difficult to quote instances that come to mind; Dreiser comments on every manifestation of life and a statement picked at random would not be an adequate example. The best chapters in the book are entitled "The Toil of the Laborer" and are narrative rather than argumentative. As I went through the book I found myself saying, "That is right," and again, "That is wrong," "That is a fact," and "That is wholly opinion." If a friend should ask me, "Would you advise me to read Dreiser's book?" I should reply, "Yes, even if you differ with him; it will stimulate your own thinking." Dreiser's attitude is a continuous quarrel with things American. But he does not say what his own idea of heaven is like.

P.E.M.
"Theodore Dreiser, Philosopher."
The Review, 2 (April 17, 1920), pp 380–381.

The editors of the *Review* are great jesters, though this is a secret not commonly known, and it was in a moment of unseemly merriment that they asked me to write an article on the views of Mr. Dreiser as expounded in his volume of essays entitled "Hey Rub-a-Dub-Dub." Now, as these same editors probably suspect, I have never been able to read to the end of one of Mr. Dreiser's novels, and shall never again try to read one; but under their cynical compulsion I have read these essays, and, to tell the truth, have been rather interested by them. The publishers, Messrs. Boni and Liveright, kindly inform all prospective buyers or critics of the book just what to expect. "If philosophy can ever be made exciting," they announce on the jacket, "Mr. Dreiser has here achieved that feat. Here is Life—mysterious, terrible, wonderful—and Dreiser looking at it unafraid" (as one can see him in the photograph furnished with the book). Well, these publishers, like their friends the editors, are great humorists, and it is their jest to evoke the picture of Mr. Dreiser, in a Jersey City bedroom, confronting Life, the mysterious and terrible, and staring the monster out of countenance. And Mr. Dreiser himself, who may or may not have provided the publishers with the notion of his heroic eye-duel, has his funny side. For instance, he has a humorous way of dealing with Logic. "In England," he writes, "they hung men for sheep-stealing a few hundred years ago, and yet sheep were and still are stolen in England. It is death to kill your neighbor, and yet when did man ever cease killing his neighbor?" Argal, the statute books are void of effect and human conduct is governed solely by "the first or pyknotic law of energy as laid down by Vogt."

A good deal of amusement might be got out of Mr. Dreiser's logic, his pyknotic scraps of learning, and his portentous solemnity. But *cui bono?* Probably he would not laugh at his own jests, and I certainly should not. And so I prefer to take him rather seriously as a sign of the times; his originality and egotism are a mere pose, while in reality he is voicing, somewhat hoarsely, the sentiments of a large class of men who take their uneasy muddle of ideas for philosophy. He says it himself: "Philosophers have dreamed, poets have written; and I, mussing around among religions, philosophies, fictions, and facts, can find nothing wherewith to solve my vaulting egoism, no light, and no way to be anything more than the humblest servitor."

He is a "servitor" in two things. In one mtood he is the voice of Nietzscheism: "The race has always been, and will so remain, of course, to the swift, and the battle to the strong. . . . The best that can be said for the theories laid down in the American Declaration is that they do more credit to the hearts of those who penned them than to their heads." Nietzsche is right, and no truer book than Machiavelli's "Prince" was ever composed. Even the masses of men, dull as they are, yet know in their hearts that they are of small importance here or there. Our captains of industry, as we name our "blond beasts," have been cunning and greedy and relentless; they have bought legislatures and robbed the people; they have been a failure in so far as they have not realized their mission to create the genuine superman; yet, after all, they are the best we have, and out of their slyness and ferocity are produced whatever scant gleams of art and beauty have fallen to our lot in a democratic country.

All this is harshly expressed by Mr. Dreiser and with a needless swagger, but in fact it is a view of Life more commonly held, though often inarticulately, by poor as well as by rich than we like to admit.

And so Mr. Dreiser, swimming with the tide, is a Nietzschean—on one page. On the next you will find him the sleek and orthodox humanitarian; and why not? He has worked as a day-laborer at the building of a railroad, and been promoted to foreman of a gang; and in both positions he has revolted from the grinding burden imposed upon the masses, while, as it seemed to him in the trenches, their employers were wallowing in slothful ease. And so, in a moment of pity and dejection, he threw up his job of driving foreman, with a cry of bitterness against the injustice of life. One is rather drawn to Mr. Dreiser by this honest report of his experience; whatever one may say of his philosophy, he put into personal practice the sympathy which generally exhausts itself in vague whimperings or wild threats or attempts to reform somebody else.

This, I should say, is the distinguishing note of the book, this oscillation between a theory of evolution which sees no progress save by the survival of the rapaciously strong and a humanitarian feeling of solidarity with the masses who are exploited in the process. It even looks occasionally as if Life had called Mr. Dreiser's bluff.

The remarkable thing is not that Mr. Dreiser should be intellectually in this state of unstable equilibrium, but that he should pose, or be posed by his publishers, as an original thinker. The fact rather is that, like a good many other vociferous egotists, he is merely tossed about by the contrary currents of popular opinion. In his chapter on "Some Aspects of Our National Character" he has written rather a telling indictment of the "psychological flounderings and back somersaults" of the American people before and during and since the war. For instance, we went into the war under the plea that the world had to be made "safe for democracy," yet once in the war we, the people, submitted to an autocracy worse than that of Russia, and so on, and so on. The account is brilliant, and humiliating; but, oddly enough, Mr. Dreiser never seems to guess that the flounderings of democracy—as democracy now is—are the sure result of just this polarization of the popular temperament between Nietzscheanism and humanitarianism of which he himself is a conspicuous example. Nor does he see that this swaying from one extreme of emotion to the other follows naturally on the denial of all those laws of moral accountability and the abrogation of all those spiritual values which we sum up under the name of religion.

Oh, I know that Mr. Dreiser, like others of his kind, has a good deal to say about balance and equilibration and that sort of thing. But if there is no purpose in the unfolding events of creation, no certain law of justice perceived by faith and truer intuition through the apparent chances of life, no incorruptible tribunal, no inner rewards and penalties besides those which a man can grasp in his hands and feel in his flesh, no ideal world of which this material world is the illusory shadow; if man is nothing more than a product of chemic and mechanic forces, a blind cog in a blind machine, if the great achievement of philosophy is "to rid the human mind of all vain illusion concerning things spiritual," if life is a mere "social or chemic drift," to be reckoned in the end only "errant and nonsensical," if "so-called vice and crime and destruction and so-called evil are as fully a part of the universal creative process as are the so-called virtues, and do as much good"—if these things are true, what compelling power is there in such fine words as "balance" and "equilibration" and the like, and what remains to save a man from oscillating restlessly between the poles of his temperament, practising a more than Nietzschean hardness when his cupidity is excited, urging an indiscriminate humanitarianism when his sympathies are touched without too much cost to himself? I do not mean to imply that mankind in general to-day would assent to the blatant logic of materialism which glares in Mr. Dreiser's eyes when he confronts Life; but it is true, nevertheless, that he is symptomatic of social disease, in so far as masses of mankind have lost their hold on any save materialistic values. Just to this extent democracy has in fact become a victim of evolutionary philosophy, and Mr. Dreiser is a victim of democracy. But I for one refuse to believe that the equation of democracy and materialism is necessary.

In one respect Mr. Dreiser has outstepped the popular mind, though in this, too, the multitude may soon be at his heels. I refer to his unmitigated allegiance to the theories of the man whom our inquisitive college youth are beginning to speak of reverentially as "Frood." Mr. Dreiser has much to say about the "shabby little pinchbeck repressions" of the moralists. "In no law code and in no religion of any nation," he declares, "has the sex question, the need of moderation, duty to family and the like, been ignored; but in all that time the social expression of sex has never been so much as modified, let alone done away with." (His facts are as false to history as his logic is funny; but we pass that.) And then to illustrate this truth, as he holds it, he paints a lurid, and, alas, not wholly falsified, picture of the inconsistency of one of our traditionally Puritan towns, where a lofty code of ethics is still preached officially and decreed legally, while in practice the literature, the movies, the dancing, and the women's dress are all devised to keep the sexual emotions in a state of excitation. The actual results as he sets them forth in "Neurotic America" are not pleasant reading—except to the author. A reasonable man might suggest that the way out of such a morbid dilemma would be, not to repudiate all laws of repression, but to look to the imagination, where alone restraint can be normally effective; and this reform in the realm of imagination, he might add, is impossible until men have been taught again the reality of those values which are not of the body. But Mr. Dreiser, naturally, will have none of this; he admits, in fact, no quarrel with neuroticism, but only with those who reject the full consequences of Freudianism for some antiquated folly of faith and decency.

We are told that Mr. Dreiser has made philosophy "exciting" and has confronted Life unafraid. Perhaps he has only sunk down in terror of true life into the currents of decomposition that have been flowing in dark, ill-smelling places from the beginning of time.

H. L. Mencken. "More Notes From a Diary," *Smart Set*, 62 (May 1920), 138–140.

It is easy enough to understand the impulse which prompted Dreiser to write *"Hey Rub-a-Dub-Dub,"* his new book, of essays and fulminations all compact. There come times in every sentient man's life when he must simply unload his ideas, or bust like a star-shell in the highroad. If he is at that end of the scale which touches the rising ladder of the *Simiidae* he becomes a Socialist on a soap-box or joins the Salvation Army; if he is literate and has a soul he writes a book. Hence the great, whirring, infernal machines which chew up the forests of Canada, now and then salting the dose with the leg or arm of a Canuck. Hence the huge ink industry, consuming five million tons of bone-black a year. Hence democracy, Bolshevism, the moral order of the world. Hence sorrow. Hence literature.

In every line of "Hey Rub-a-Dub-Dub" there is evidence of the author's antecedent agony. One pictures him sitting up all night in his sinister studio down in Tenth street, wrestling horribly with the insoluble, trying his darndest to penetrate the unknowable. One o'clock strikes, and the fire sputters. Ghosts stalk in the room, fanning the yellow candle-light with their abominable breath—the spooks of all the men who have died for ideas since the world began—Socrates, Savonarola, Bruno (not Guido, but Giordano), Ravaillac, Sir Roger Casement, John Alexander Dowie, Dr. Crippen. Two o'clock. What, then, is the truth about marriage? Is it, as Grover Cleveland said, a grand sweet song, or is it, as the gals in the Village say, a hideous mockery and masquerade, invented by Capitalism to enslave the soul of woman—a legalized *Schweinerei*, worse than politics, almost as bad as the moving-pictures? Three o'clock. Was Marx right or wrong, a seer or a mere nose-puller? Was his name, in fact, actually Marx, or was it Marcus? From what ghetto did he escape, and cherishing what grudge against mankind? Aha, the Huneker complex: *cherchez le Juif!* (I confess at once: my great-grandpa, Moritz, was rector of the Oheb Shalon *Schul* in Grodno). Three o'clock. . . .

Back to Pontius Pilate! *Quod est veritas?* Try to define it. Look into it. Break it into its component parts. What remains is a pale gray vapor, an impalpable emanation, the shadow of a shadow. Think of the brains that have gone to wreck struggling with the problem—cerebrums as large as cauliflowers, cerebellums as perfect as pomegranates. Think of the men jailed, clubbed, hanged, burned at the stake—not for embracing error, but for embracing the *wrong* error. Think of the innumerable caravan of Burlesons, Mitchell Palmers, Torquemadas, Cotton Mathers. . . . Four o'clock. The fire burns low in the grate. A gray fog without. Across the street two detectives rob a drunken man. Up at Tarrytown John D. Rockefeller snores in his damp Baptist bed, dreaming gaudily that he is young again and mashed on a girl named Marie. At Sing Sing forty head of Italians are waiting to be electrocuted. There is a memorial service for Charles Garvice in Westminster Abbey. The Comstocks raid the Elsie books. Ludendorff is elected Archbishop of Canterbury. A poor working-girl, betrayed by Moe, the boss's son, drowns herself in the Aquarium. It is late, ah me: nearly four thirty. . . . Who the deuce, then, is God? What is in all this talk of a future life, infant damnation, the Ouija board, Mortal Mind? Dr. Jacques Loeb is the father of a dozen bull-frogs. Is the news biological or theological? What became of the Albigenses? Are they in heaven, in purgatory or in hell?. . . . Five o'clock. Boys cry the *Evening Journal*. Is it today's or tomorrow's? The question of transubstantiation remains. There is, too, neo-transcendentalism. . . . In Munich they talk of *Expressionismus* . . . Poof! . .

It is easy, as I say, to imagine a man beset by such reflections, and urged irresistibly to work them out on paper. Unluckily, the working out is not always as simple a business as it looks. Dreiser's first impulse as novelist, I daresay, was to do it in novels—to compose fictions full of ideas, saying something, teaching something, exposing something, destroying something. But the novelist also happened to be an artist, and at once the artist entered an effective caveat against that pollution. A work of art with ideas in it is as sorry a monster as a pretty girl full of Latin. The aim of a work of art is not to make one think painfully, but to make one feel beautifully. What is the idea in "Jennie Gerhardt?" Who knows but God? But in "Jennie Gerhardt" there is feeling—profound, tragic, exquisite. It is a thing of poignant and yet delicate emotions, like Brahms' Fourth symphony. It lies in a sort of intellectual fourth dimension. It leaves a memory that is vivid and somehow caressing, and wholly free from doubts, questionings, head-scratchings . . . So Dreiser decided to make a serious book of it, a book of unalloyed ratiocination, a book in the manner of Herbert Spencer. The result is "Hey Rub-a-Dub-Dub"—solemn stuff, with never a leer of beauty in it—in fact, almost furious. Once or twice it grows a bit lyrical; once or twice it rises to the imaginatively grotesque. But in the main it is plain exposition—a book of speculation and protest. He calls it himself "a book of the mystery and terror and wonder of life." I suspect that he lifted this subtitle from an old review of H. L. M. If so, then welcome! From him I have got more than is to be described in words and more than I can ever pay.

But what of the thing itself? Is it good stuff? My feeling is that it isn't. More, my feeling is that Dreiser is no more fitted to do a book of speculation than Joseph Conrad, say, is fitted to do a college yell. His talents simply do not lie in that direction. He lacks the mental agility, the insinuating suavity, the necessary capacity for romanticising a syllogism. Ideas themselves are such sober things that a sober man had better let them alone. What they need, to become bearable to a human race that hates them and is afraid of them, is the artful juggling of a William James, the insurance-agent persuasiveness of an Henri Bergson, the boob-bumping talents of a Martin Luther—best of all, the brilliant, almost Rabelaisian humor of a Nietzsche. Nietzsche went out into the swamp much further than any other explorer; he left such pallbearers of the spirit as Spencer, Comte, Descartes and even Kant all shivering on the shore.

And yet he never got bogged, and he never lost the attention of his audience. What saved him was the plain fact that he always gave a superb show—as good, almost, as a hanging. He converted the problem of evil into a melodrama with nine villains; he made of epistemology a sort of intellectual bed-room farce; he amalgamated Christianity and the music of Offenbach. . . . Well, Dreiser is quite devoid of that gift. Skepticism, in his hands, is never charming; it is simply despairing. His criticism of God lacks ingenuity and audacity. Earnestly pursuing the true, he too often unearths the merely obvious, which is sometimes not true at all. One misses the jauntiness of the accomplished duellist; his manner is rather that of the honest householder repelling burglars with a table-leg. In brief, it is enormously serious and painstaking stuff, but seldom very interesting stuff, and never delightful stuff. The sorrows of the world become the sorrows of Dreiser himself, and then the sorrows of his reader. He remains, in the last analysis, the novelist rather than the philosopher. He is vastly less a Schopenhauer than a Werther.

But a book by Dreiser is a book by Dreiser, and so one reads it with curiosity if not with delectation

---

"A Word to Dreiser." *Pearson's Magazine*, May, 1920, pp. 902–904.

Many years ago now, as we men measure years, Heinemann, the most intelligent of English publishers, sent me a copy of "Sister Carrie," the first novel of an unknown man, Theodore Dreiser, and asked me to say what I thought of it. After a week's reflection I praised the book enthusiastically as about the best first book I had ever read and I bought fifty copies of it and sent it out to all and sundry, English writers chiefly, who I thought might be interested in a good novel which is after all probably the highest form of art.

From that time on I have read every book of Dreiser's and have not spared praise of his work when I thought it was deserved. But now he has written a dozen or more books, must be nearing the summit of his powers and as yet he has produced nothing as good as "Sister Carrie."

After the first book came "Jennie Gerhardt," almost a replica of "Sister Carrie," though the heroine was better painted; but it was the gradual deterioration of the protagonist Hurstwood that made "Sister Carrie," and there's no Hurstwood in "Jennie Gerhardt." Next appeared "The Financier" remarkable not for the millionaire hero, for he was hardly more than a lay figure, but for a love-story of astonishing imaginative charm. Then "The Titan," a poor replica of "The Financier" and since then nothing of any moment.

It was with some uneasiness, fear, almost, that I picked up Dreiser's latest book.

The title is not inspiriting or even engaging, and alas the book is worse—mere journalism.

On the jacket the publisher tells us that "this volume is the mature expression of Mr. Dreiser's beliefs and theories about life in general and America in particular. If philosophy can be made exciting, Mr. Dreiser has here achieved that feat. Here is Life-mysterious, wonderful, terrible," and so on and so forth;

not a truthful word in the whole farrago of nonsense which is to be debited I devoutly hope to the publishers Boni and Liveright, for it is unworthy of any writer of Dreiser's position and power. But let us get to the book.

Here are the first two sentences:

> "I have lived now to my fortieth year, and have seen a good deal of life. Just now, because of a stretch of poverty, I am living across the river from New York, in New Jersey, in sight of a splendid tower, the Woolworth Building on the lower end of Manhattan, which lifts its defiant spear of clay into the very maw of heaven."

With a gasp of sheer pain I cry involuntarily, "Could any writing be worse?"

Why the pleonastic "now" in the first sentence, which is repeated and used with true effect in the second? Why should the white Woolworth Building be likened to a "defiant spear of clay" when it is not like a spear but is square-topped and is of marble, white and not of clay at all; and why, oh why, is the illimitable blue skyscape called "the maw of heaven . . . the very maw of heaven?" when it's not like a maw and could never under any circumstances suggest a maw to any pair of human eyes!

This dreadful first page with its "splendid tower" and "splendid masses" and its "if I go of a Sunday," instead of "on Sunday" made me throw down the book, and I only took it up again weeks later from a sense of duty.

When Mr. Wells went on writing drivel about God as "the invisible King" and bishops and all such rot, spewing out the lees and dregs left in his spirit by the indefensible war that he had tried to exalt into a crusade, I warned him that if he contined he would choke off one good reader at least and no author can count on more than a dozen or so.

Now I must warn my friend Dreiser; the world doesn't want any one's journalism, not even Shakespeare's. "The Merry Wives of Windsor," written in a fortnight to Queen Elizabeth's order, is almost worthless; save for a phrase or two of personal self-revealing sheer drivel that we should have been better without and Dreiser is not Shakespeare by a long, long way. We don't want your journalism, Dreiser, good as some of it is; it should only appear in ephemeral newspapers or magazines; but in your books we want Dreiser at full stretch, Dreiser doing his damndest, turning out the best in him, minting the ore into golden forms of gods and goddesses as perfectly as he can do it.

Or else we shall conclude that it was by mere chance that for once you put beside the pulsing youthful figure of the American girl, Carrie, the played-out disillusioned business man voluptuary Hurstwood and so came near writing a masterpiece.

Now you give us this so-called "Phantasmagoria" of yours with its characters or rather names such as "The Lord of the Universe," "Beauty," "Ambition," "Pity," "Love," "Hate," "Despair," and the rest, and not one sentence worth reading in the twenty pages, or do you really think that when you make the Lord of the Universe cry: "Thou dearest Death! Bring thou me heaps of dead —the endless slain! Breed winged and forked things, horrors all! . . . Rank thou me them, rank on rank . . ." you can by your exclamation notes turn rant into literature?

And when you create "Beauty," and describe Beauty as a woman "Pink-limbed and perfect" do you imagine that you enthral or astonish us? In one phrase of Bacon there is more thought, more magic of expression than in this whole book; Bacon, too, had thought of Beauty; thought and thought of it, till at length the magical phrase sprang from his travail. "There must be something strange in any excelling beauty."

Think of it, Dreiser; think of it, side by side with your "pink-limbed and perfect!" Compare it with your "spear of clay" which is white and square, or with your "maw of heaven!" Man, man, what are you about?

Yet Dreiser is one of the half dozen best produced in these hundred million of Americans in this generation; alas, alas! Now we have to write for a living and the fool-public will pay more for a dozen mediocre books than for one good book, though the good book is deathless and costs years of thought and years of work and years of blood and tears; *these come not out,* says the Bible, *but with "tears and fasting!"* . . .

I have already spoken of Dreiser, the stylist; now with the sad superiority of the senior I wish to give him one word of advice. He has as vivid a sense of human passion as Rodin himself; but Rodin was a master-craftsman who was as articulate in bronze as Michel Angelo himself, and Dreiser is only half-articulate; but he has a great knowledge of certain sides of American life. Let him take a girl that attracts him and put her on the paper especially dwelling on the trivial little nothings that characterize her and give her sex-attraction, individuality and persuasion; then let him take say one of his masterful millionaires and one of his weak but sensual, smooth-tongued assiduous fellow artists and tell us of the pursuit of the girl and the ultimate conquest or tell how she is seduced by the artist-wheedler and betrayed and is finally taken by the rich man who thinks she is his and his alone, only to discover later that he, the cheat, has been cheated. With some such material Dreiser might write a book that would live, a greater "Sister Carrie!" But he must do his best and not his second best.

Van Wyck Brooks "According to Dreiser." *Nation,* 110 (May 1, 1920), 595–596.

The Dreiser who emerges in these essays is anything but the pachydermatous animal that has caused so much alarm in respectable circles. He is very like a perplexed and weary child, dazzled by a kaleidoscope in which he is able to discern no thread of meaning. One receives the impression of an essentially passive, diffident, and highly sensitive spirit that has been hurt by life and is yet perpetually charmed anew by its "active, dancing, changeful" beauty. "Personally," he says somewhere, "I stand with the fools of love, because I think for all their follies and errors and Lear-like end, they are happier." He ranges himself, in short, with the Sister Carries and Jennie Gerhardts of his own creation.

And the view of life which he presents is just such a view as Jennie might have held, amplified, articulated in a measure, but still dark, jumbled, limited, instinctive, and sentimental. He likes life, "this sharp, grasping scheme of things"; he likes "Mr. Woolworth's splendid tower"; he likes everything that is "vivid, colorful, human"; he likes change and believes in it—"for by change have come all the spectacles, all the charms, and all the creature comforts of which our consciousness is aware." Furthermore, he likes the American Financier and writes a chapter to show that although Russell Sage and Jay Gould were probably unacceptable in polite society, and might have done much more for art, they at least achieved that "avid forceful expression" that so delights "God, Good, Nature, Force, the Universal Substance." Isn't that Jennie all over? If Jennie had been appointed foreman of a railway gang she would have resigned, too, and for just the reason Mr. Dreiser gives in The Toil of the Laborer: "Not to drive where I could not ease, not to urge where I could not repay, not to be a tool in the hands of their indifferent masters who could not or would not interest themselves in them, was something, even though my ceasing could not relieve them of their toil." Jennie knew quite well that the race is to the strong and that it is mere rubbish, the theory of the uplifters that all you have to do is to reach out and Take the World and It's Yours. As for Secrecy—Its Value, another of the Dreiserian themes, Jennie never had a doubt of that. "The charm that would disappear with the arrival of absolute frankness, the mystery that would go! . . . We do not know [the creatures of the earth]; we do not understand them; we wonder at their states, their thoughts, their moods, what they will do, which way turn when attacked, whom attack, whom deceive, whom praise, whom reward. Secrecy—secrecy—mystery. If it were gone the illusion of life itself, which is all that it is, would be gone also. And we are cautioned to love truth and to say truly and to our own hurt if necessary!" Can't you hear Jennie saying that? Add the obsession of sex; an extreme skepticism on the subject of permanent unions ("Does the average strong, successful man confine himself to one woman? Has he ever?"); a conception of reformers, saints, and messiahs as magnified vice investigators, equally futile if not equally impertinent; a general surrender to Nature because Nature wins anyway; and a view of life as the "mere idle rocking of force in one direction or another"—and you have the complete *Weltanschauung* of, well, one of the most beautifully and tenderly drawn women in American fiction.

In his novels Mr. Dreiser seems very much the thinker. One is astonished, consequently, to find how unsublimated a product he is of the benighted environment he describes in his last essay when he has no characters through whom to express himself. Very simple and almost purely emotional is the reaction upon life cloaked in the scientific verbiage of this book. One asks oneself whether the soul of Jennie Gerhardt is not really the soul of Mr. Dreiser himself and whether that doesn't explain the ceaseless thrill with which he has felt the magnetism of all those agents of "avid force," those dinosaurs of the dollar he so loves to track through the American jungle. One thing is certain: he is far more interesting as the painter of Jennie's life than as the recorder of Jennie's views.

Francis Hackett. "Mystery, Terror and Confusion." *New Republic*, 22 (May 26, 1920), 423–424.

Mr. Dreiser calls this "a book of the mystery and terror and wonder of life." It is, in a way, his profession of faith. In form it moves from pseudo-autobiography to direct preachment, and from preachment to dramatic dialogue,—a collection, in fact, of divers papers but all mainly concerned with the problem of good and bad. The manner is loose, with occasional rhetorical gestures, but the mood is almost unrelievedly serious. The point of view is, on the whole, a queer combination of scepticism and humaneness and egoism.

Most writers who affect this sort of discussion come to it with a certain grace. Mr. Dreiser has practically no grace. His road is a flat, dusty road. He has hardly one glint of humor in the whole book. He has hardly a touch of fancy. He drives along like a springless truck, sparing neither himself nor his passenger. And yet, heavy and turgid and monotonous and sensuously obtuse as he seems to be, he makes his discussion interesting. He is himself sincerely interested, and he is writing because he has something to communicate. His manner is blunt and his method cumbersome and confused, but there is in him a persistent force which refuses to stop or be turned aside. Whether he is discussing life or art or Nature or God or sex or industry or Puritanism or marriage, he produces views which are patently his own views, and in that important respect authentic. His sincerity is the salt of his nature. It makes even of his manner a sort of virtue. It redeems him even when he is saying that "Brute strength sits empurpled and laughs a throaty laugh."

This sincerity is goaded from Mr. Dreiser particularly by the moral pretensions of America, and a great part of his book is rage against the moralist and the religionist. Rage is perhaps too spirited a word. What Mr. Dreiser seems to do is to beat with arms of stone the mush-headed American philistine. Calmly enough he can say at times, "My observation and experience lead me to believe that there is scarcely a so-called 'sane,' right, merciful, true, just, solution to anything." But from this despair of any moral objectivity, which is arguable enough, he moves on to berate everything ethical as "silly illusion." "Nothing is fixed," he proclaims as if it were in itself moral carte blanche, and he follows up with such jaded cynicism as "it is useless to say to the average American that democracy is a dream and can never be realized." Yet when these formulae accumulate to the point of boredom, Mr. Dreiser inserts a confession to the effect that he, for one, could not exploit his fellow-man. To which he appends immediately some utterance to the effect that "Nature, or God, or what you will, showed that it cared no whit, not a snap of her or his fingers, what becomes of man or an American with his theories, religious or otherwise, unless he was able to protect himself."

To understand Mr. Dreiser it may be forgivable to start with this sentence, "Because my father was a Catholic and I was baptized in that faith, I was supposed to accept all the dogma, as well as the legends, of the Church as true." Hey Rub-A-Dub-Dub is full of the unfortunate after-effects of Catholicism. Chief among these is Mr. Dreiser's resentment that the rest of America, if not of mankind, is obsessed by otherwordly assumptions. He insists that people cling "fatuitously" to "the idea that there is some fixed idyllic scheme or moral order handed down from on high, which is tender and charitable, punishes so-called evil and always rewards so-called good." This defunct notion excites him seriously, and in his anxiety to destroy it he is practically ready to destroy every distinction between good and bad, right and wrong. Like many ex-Catholics, indeed, he has got rid of his religion with considerable detriment to his ethics, and has never spent much apparent effort in examining the claims of ethics as independent of religion.

Hence, following the various jabs he gives to God and certain other tall conceptions, Mr. Dreiser proceeds to repudiate moral objectivity. "Life seems to prove but one thing to me, and that is that the various statements concerning right, truth, justice, mercy, are palaver merely, an earnest and necessitous attempt, perhaps, at balance and equation where all things are so very much unbalanced, paradoxical and contradictory—the small-change names for a thing or things of which we have not yet caught the meaning."

In the same vein he writes elsewhere. "For my part, I am convinced that so-called vice and crime and destruction and so-called evil are as fully a part of the universal creative process as are all the so-called virtues, and do as much good—providing, as they do, for one thing, the religionist and the moralist with their reasons for existing. At best, ethics and religion are but one face of the shield which is essentially irreligious and unethical as to its other face, or the first would not exist."

What Mr. Dreiser means by the "universal creative process" is utterly bewildering. We hear of blind Nature and of nature purposeful, of ruthless change and of "the law of balance or equation which governs in all processes." But the purport of his argument in this direction seems merely to be that "One thing we do know: our impulses do not always accord with moral or religious law, the so-called will of the Creator here on earth, and yet our impulses are assuredly provided us by a Creator, if no more than the mechanistic one of the chemists and physicists." To get rid of "commandment from on high" haunts Mr. Dreiser like a bad dream.

And possibly because he is so haunted, or possibly because he is muddled, Mr. Dreiser is an egoist. It is this egoism which, for me at least, gives a rather rancid flavor to his book. Why don't mothers ignore their children? Mr. Dreiser explains that they are subject to a "chemic necessity." Does any man put the general welfare of the state above affection or passion? That is because "thousands of people are by temperament sacrificial, one might almost say masochistic. They never put themselves first, and that for the very simple reason that their emotions or desires do not compel them so to do." Similarly Buddha, Christ, Confucius, St. Francis, Luther, Mohammed, are of the type that "seeks to readjust conditions as he finds them to something more in accord with what is agreeable to him, and who accordingly . . . seeks to represent himself to himself as a world need." Thus egoism is universal. "There is much talk of charity and the beatitudes, but let one lose an arm, a leg, an eye, a hand. Practically the entire world shudders and withdraws." But we are not to blame. "Man does not make or regulate Nature. Nature makes and regulates man, and She makes him any way She pleases—vile, lovely, strong, weak, simple, complex, and so on." Shall we then worship the strong, the successful, the sons of wise Nature? Well, "I beg to call attention to the fact that Nature, or God, or the biologic process, or what you will, is no better planner or executor of any given theory or scheme it may have in mind than man himself."

So, at the crucial point, our egoist seems to falter. And, catholic as he is in his acceptance of Titans and Geniuses, "unethical forces, subtlety, craft," Rockefellers, Morgans, Goulds, and in general people who get away with it and are a law unto themselves, still, he has his own indignation against certain cruelties and brutalities, even if "forceful, vigorous, natural." He reproaches England, for example, with conquering the Boers. He reproaches America with its treatment of the Negro, its slavish press, its lack of culture and intelligence. "The darkest side of democracy, like that of autocracy, is that it permits the magnetic and the cunning and the unscrupulous among the powerful individuals to sway vast masses of the mob, not so much to their own immediate destruction as to the curtailment of their natural privileges and the ideas which they should be allowed to entertain if they could think at all—and incidentally to the annoying and sometimes undoing of individuals who have the truest brain interests of the race at heart, vide Giordano Bruno! Jan Huss! Savonarola! Tom Paine! Walt Whitman! Edgar Allan Poe!"

The truth seems to be that Theodore Dreiser's mind is formless, chaotic, bewildered. He has never thought through to any real conclusion about egoism, but has simply rushed into egoism to escape the unreality of edifying Christian talk. Similarly, he does not appear to have conceived of any moral objectivity except as propounded from on high, and so he is driven to fill up the void with a "law of equation or balance" which has less than no meaning. In short, our leading novelist is intellectually in serious confusion, and needs a deeper philosophy than—hey rub-a-dub-dub.

"America Gives the World Nothing Spiritual, Says Dreiser." New York *Tribune*, Magazine and Book Section, July 4, 1920, p. 11.

Theodore Dreiser is a solitary figure in literary America. With no tribal affiliations to give him safety and definition, with no derivation from a school or group to mark his place, he remains largely unassimilated in our American literary scheme. It is possible that he confuses the radicals a little more than he does the conservatives. They, being more orderly-minded, are the more easily upset by Dreiser's apparent contradictions.

"Hey-Rub-a-Dub-Dub" is seemingly the rag-bag into which he has thrown everything that has engaged his mind in recent years—all the philosophic speculations and beliefs and impressions with which his mind has adventured. These essays represent a curious mixture of the philosophic and pseudo-scientific and merely journalistic. They are often confused and contradictory, vague and naïve, but they have in them the drive of a strong and restless mind. There is no doubting the vigor of Dreiser's imagination and the extent to which he is occupied with the social phenomenon.

In his perception of the narrowest social milieu there is an active sense of the cosmic background, of the biological processes that have gone into its making. It is a view of life which turns the scientific conception of the universe to an essentially romantic purpose. He sees life as something fluid, mysterious and ungovernable. In Dreiser's decalogue the primary virtue is to be alive—and the intensity of vitality in a men is the measure of virtue. That is why his imagination is so deeply stirred by our Titans of finance. They are figures of heroic force, and he comes close to the pagan in his worship of natural force.

But though he is immensely critical of the form to which these Titans have pressed our civilization, he bewilders and irritates the radical as much as the conservative. For if he scorns the bourgeois ideal, neither does he subscribe to radical idealism. His quarrel is precisely with the illusion of idealism, with the faith that men can be sublimated by the mechanistic process of any phrase. In the idealism of the radical and the morality of the conservative he sees the same assertions of finiteness—a finiteness which life denies at every turn. Nature is ruthless and endlessly experimental, and so is society, though if its creed is otherwise that conscious creed is, as he regards it, a sort of escape from the evidences of life.

Nowhere are these assertions of idealism and morality more arbitrary than in this country, and nowhere is raw force so abundant and all-conquering. "Here in America, by reason of an idealistic constitution, which is largely a work of art . . . you see a nation dedicated to so-called intellectual and spiritual freedom, but actually devoted with an almost bee-like industry to the gathering and storing and articulating and organization and use of purely material things. In spite of our bass-drum announcement of our servitude to the intellectual ideals of the world (copied mostly, by the way, from England) no nation has ever contributed less philosophically or spiritually to the actual development of the intellect and the spirit. We have invented many things, it is true, which have relieved man from the crushing weight of a too-grinding toil, and this may be, perhaps, the sole mission of America in the world and universe—its destiny, its end."

"Hey-Rub-a-Dub-Dub" is an indiscriminate, unassorted, heterogeneous mass of impressions and reflections, which frequently contradict each other. It is a curious mixture of the journalistic and the philosophic. It is sometimes crude and sometimes finely poetic. It is full of large, vague, floating speculations of the nature of man and the universe. But these are in a sense the background. The true preoccupation of all these essays, the core of this diffuse mass, is its preoccupation with the social spectacle, the "fierce, rudimentary mass mind that is America." Here his mind grows sharp and hard and bright. Here Dreiser is the real critic—perhaps the only critic of it. And he is the best critic of this America because he is bred of it, because he feels its responses in himself, because he is as intense and concentrated an expression of its genius as its Titans.

W. W. B.
"Who Ever Saw Dreiser in a Sportive Mood?" Baltimore *News*, July 31, 1920.

Anybody who picks up "Hey-Rub-a-Dub-Dub" and is beguiled by the title into thinking he is going to perform the miracle of discovering Dreiser in a playful, cavorting mood, is going to be sadly disappointed.

The more one reads of the man whom Arnold Bennett proclaimed the most distinguished of American contemporary writers, the more one thinks he never learned how to play, the one more is mortally certain that he could not cavort to save his life.

"Hey-Rub-a-Dub-Dub," instead of indicating the fiendish enthusiasm of a boy when driving his elders mad with a drum, is rather a sort of bally-hoo announcement of heroic agonizings in the slough of despond that is Dreiserian philosophy; it is full of the moanings and groanings over life's desperate futility and hopelessness, of a spirit unillumined by the slightest glow of a sense of humor.

The book, however, is interesting in many ways and there is much about it that challenges attention and that cannot be gainsaid. For Dreiser is an exhaustive and frequently a profound thinker and even if, as has been claimed for him, one of his "glories" is a complete lack of style, he can write very powerfully. In fact, there are times when he suggests nothing so much as some strange natural force functioning in spite of itself.

In his latest work he abandons himself without reserve to the essayist's task and fairly gloats over humanity's incurable wrongs, the bitterness of life's inevitable banality, its "essential tragedy" and the general wretchedness of conditions "here below."

What strikes the broad-minded, tolerant soul as being a bit unfair is that he "localizes" ills in the poor old United States that belong to all mankind without respect to nationality. Is not Nietzsche's "Human, All Too Human" axiom an explanation that, if it inspires no hope, at least is sufficiently illuminating?

Dreiser is extremely material and wholly destructive in his reasoning. His system of philosophy knows not the value, apparently, even of a sardonic smile. It bears, but it does not grin. It is forever and ever tearing apart the old "myths" concerning human conduct, ripping away with savage butchery the cherished illusions and offering for them—what? Well, after all, what does most philosophy offer? Is it not possible that disillusionment itself may be only a form of illusion or rather delusion?

Dreiser's attitude toward life reminds one of that of a surgeon who, with his sleeves all rolled up, his professional scimitars and javelins shined and sharpened cruelly, and the patient stretched unconscious before him, shakes his head and announces to the relatives sadly that there is no hope because the case is inoperable.

Agnosticism is the very breath of life in the nostrils of such a man. The only belief he can hold is in unbelief—all else is fallacy. His remarks concerning the Deity are calculated to bring keen delight to the heart of the theologian, though the terminology is a bit confused and mixed. In one place we find Nature, God and the "biologic process" used as synonyms, and the Creator is referred to once (the author admits "crudely") and [sic] a "sideline manufacturer."

Such a book as this is apt to prove most depressing and in this respect it has an effect on the intelligent reader quite as marked, for instance, speaking antithetically, as "Pollyanna." It is valuable, however, because of its neutralizing powers as an antidote to such works as the chef-d'oeuvre just mentioned.

Who knows? Perhaps it is one of the unescapable things that tend to balance the "equation" that Dreiser himself is eternally talking about. The chapter on "Life Art and America" stirred us up so tremendously that we do not dare to go into details concerning it. Why? Because it contains the most scathing, the most, etc., etc., criticism of newspaper criticism imaginable. And we cannot forget we indulge in newspaper literary criticism ourselves and also that the world would know little of Mr. Dreiser and his associate artists, perhaps, if it were not for the abhorred, dissolute press. But, then, what would you? Nothing is easier than to create one's own criteria of distinction.

"Briefer Mention." *Dial,* 69 (September 1920), 320.

HEY RUB A DUB DUB holds American life under a competent but somewhat foggy microscope, disclosing its artistic shortcomings and its social defects with literal accuracy. Democracy, art, sex, labour, newspapers, and millionaires come successively under the lens, while Dreiser sets down his findings with all a greengrocer's assiduity, and not a little of a greengrocer's unimaginative painstaking. Here is a surprising absence of the creative instinct in a creative writer. Even iconoclasm is entitled to its exhilarative intervals, but Dreiser dons the cowl of a carping critic, and makes such a solemn business of his expostulation that he might well pass for one of the puritans whom he abjures. If he had left out some of the lengthy passages in which he reiterates what every one concedes, and replaced them with a vital, creative impulse, woven out of artistic experience, his book would be closer to kindling the imagination, and further from kindling the furnaces of the Philistines.

"Dreiser's Latest 'Shocking' Book." Cincinnati *Star,* September 4, 1920.

Theodore Dreiser has achieved notable success as a shocker. Any little thing that he may write is sure to shock some one. He takes delight in his ability to shock, and probably would consider that he had failed if any performance of his should not give a shock more or less severe to some one. Dreiser shocks because he rides rough shod over platitudes, worn out conventions, ancient hypocricies and modern subterfuges. The most shocking part of it all is that Dreiser is so nearly right all the time.

He has a peculiar faculty for getting at the real truth, not what has heretofore been held up as the truth. His latest shocker is "Hey Rub-a-dub-dub," in which he discusses persons and things as he finds them in life to-day, and shows that many of the complacently accepted ideas are so far from the truth as to have no connection with it. "Hey Rub-a-dub-dub" is an arresting sort of book. It awakens the mind, stirs the emotions and gives one a new view of life.

Checklist of Additional Reviews

Baird Leonard, "The Book Market." New York *Telegraph,* March 20, 1920.

New York *Sun,* March 21, 1920.

"Dreiser's Beliefs in New Books." New York *American,* March 21, 1920.

Providence [R.I.] *Journal,* March 28, 1920.

R.F.H. "Musing With the Muses." Detroit *Journal,* March 31, 1920.

"New Books in Brief." *Current Opinion,* 68 (April, 1920), 570.

R.F.H. "Musing With the Muses." Detroit *Journal,* April 3, 1920.

Washington [D.C.] *Star,* April 4, 1920.

R.F.H. "Musing With the Muses." Detroit *Journal,* April 7, 1920.

Ben Macomber. "Dreiser Likes the Noise His Thwacking Cudgels Produce." San Francisco *Chronicle,* April 18, 1920.

Guy Bogart. "A Propagandist's Desk." Seattle [Wash.] *Crucible,* April 18, 1920.

Catholic World, 3 (May 1920), 260.

Springfield [Mass.] *Republican,* May 2, 1920, p. 13a.

Anne Nathan Meyer. "Mr. Dreiser's Battle for Truth." *The Review,* May 8, 1920.

Grand Rapids [Mich.] *News,* June 28, 1920.

Evansville [Ind.] *Journal* July 4, 1920.

"A Reader's Notes." Indianapolis *Star,* April 18, 1921.

Further Reviews: Bibliographic Information Incomplete

New York *Globe and Commerical Advertiser.*

Literary Lounger, n.d., p. 24.

Marion Latour. The Burlington Iowa.

Notes

A BOOK ABOUT MYSELF

THEODORE DREISER

BONI AND LIVERIGHT
PUBLISHERS NEW YORK

A Book About Myself

Edith Leighton. "Literary Confessions." *Bookman*, 56 (December 1922), 497–498.

Theodore Dreiser has written up a straightforward sketch of his experiences in newspaper work and filled it full of real people and events under their own names. Every line is vibrant with life seen through the prism of personality; it is an orderly arrangement of facts, viewed in perspective from a distance of time. Mr. Dreiser can treat even himself with a large impersonality and a quiet sense of humor that establishes our faith in anything and everything else he has to say. One feels above all that the breadth of his experience is due wholly to himself. Other men have been reporters and have seen fires and accidents, society balls one hour and sordid murder scenes the next, or interviewed all sorts and conditions of men —politicians, archbishops, train robbers —but what gives this book its particular quality is the depth of the author's insight and the sympathy of his understanding. It is a sympathy that identifies him with his experience for the time being and, through his power of vivid word picturing, is handed on to his reader. Despite his difficulties one always feels that this man is a success. The years of which he writes are those of his early twenties, but he has already come close enough to life to judge of its real values. Despite his blundering escapades with women, his sentimental streaks and his lost jobs, one has perfect confidence in the outcome. His is a big personality, and so, by the laws of literary equation, his is a big book.

"Theodore Dreiser Looking Backward." New York *Times Book Review*, December 24, 1922, p. 14.

An infant at a certain period of life manifests a profound absorption in the contemplation of its toes. Perhaps this is indicative of the dawning of conscious mind. It may be that from this study of his pedal extremities is derived the child's first conception of numbers, his first perception of color, his first realization of individuality. On the other hand, this absorption may indicate nothing more than mental vacuity. In the flood of biography and autobiography now pouring forth from American publishing houses—a flood which must have been let loose in response to a popular demand—there is something remotely suggestive of the above infantile occupation. America is examining its toes.

If the desire for this intimate study of the prehensile nether members will stimulate the growth of national consciousness, if it will develop a more clearly defined and a more vital national individualism, and if it will stimulate and clarify our understanding of national forces and national needs, we cannot have too much of this biographical output. We have the right, however, to protect ourselves from inundation by demanding that the facts of a man's life be of sufficient importance to justify their being paraded in public.

Theodore Dreiser is justified in presenting us with a book about himself, though scarcely justified in filling five hundred pages in bringing us merely to the point where his career as a novelist begins. The importance of the volume would be more apparent had it been less minute. Often the reader fails to see the forest because of the trees. But the volume is important, for in it is seen in the making a novelist who has brought Americans face to face with vital facts and vital forces. In this history of Dreiser's early career as a newspaperman one beholds the furnace in which the creator of Sister Carrie was forged.

Dreiser says somewhere in the volume that he is a sentimentalist in his thinking but a realist in his writing. The former is open to question. The title, "A Book About Myself," is so instantly suggestive of Rousseau's "Confessions" that the reader is prone to expect outpourings of the same romantic and sentimental sort. But he will not get them.

It is not meant by this that Dreiser is at all reticent in talking either of his ambitions or of his love affairs. His hatred of sham and hypocrisy, which flames out from one end of the narrative to the other, makes it as impossible for him to do his love making behind window shades as to take a bribe to hush up a news story. The reason for the slighting of his emotional experiences is to be sought elsewhere. Dreiser's interest in life, in his surroundings, in himself, in women is fundamentally an intellectual interest. His analysis is that of the sociologist or the psychologist—that is to say, of the scientist. He falls in love with a girl whom he calls Alice, but he knows that it is not love, merely desire. The man who knows that—at least, the man who knows it at the time—is not even thinking sentimentally.

The reader who wants sentimentalism may as well turn aside from Dreiser's volume, for it is realism from the first page to the last, written for the most part in a hard, reportorial style. . . .

His real feelings are often concealed under the reportorial manner of his writing, but the reader never fails to feel Dreiser's reactions to his experiences. The pages live. Through poverty and disappointment and joy in little things a soul is seen emerging. Dreiser's experiences are worth receiving vicariously by the reader. They are a stimulus to thought. One is not likely to regard many things with complete complacency after reading this book.

Burton Rascoe. "The Interesting Dullness of Dreiser's Life." New York *Tribune Book News and Reviews*, December 31, 1922, p. 17.

The most interesting thing about this interesting autobiography is the singular uneventfulness of Mr. Dreiser's youth. Nothing in particular happened to him. He had his sweethearts; but what youth has not, and with more rapid frequency, greater moonshine, happier novelty and more signal success than had Mr. Dreiser? During all his years as a newspaper reporter, in Chicago, St. Louis, Pittsburgh and New York, he seems to have had but one adventure, to have been witness to or assigned to cover but one catastrophe and that quite by accident. You have but to remember that he was a reporter in Chicago during the wide-open days following the World's Fair, in Pittsburgh when that city was just reaching its apothesis as a community of steel and poverty, in New York when Richard Harding Davis, David Graham Phillips, Arthur Brisbane, and Samuel Hopkins Adams were on the rise as newspaper men, to wonder what Mr. Dreiser was doing when a great deal of interesting hell was popping all about him.

There is an unconscious irony in these revelations. Or perhaps the irony is conscious. There was never a youth who started out in life with a more grandiose impediment of romantic illusions; and there was never a romantic youth who encountered fewer dragons to slay, fewer maidens to rescue and fewer varlets to put in their place than Mr. Dreiser. He had almost no fun at all. He held hands here and there; he missed, he tells us, one or two opportunities; having his breakfast in a diner once he had the momentary satisfaction of an aristocrat when a yokel on the platform of a bleak way station gazed upon him in saucereyed envy and admiration; he bought a Stetson hat broad-brimmed enough for Buffalo Bill and a military coat long enough to fit the late Grand Duke Michael Michaelovitch to go courting in; he played up to his relatives once far too effectively for solvency as a man of mark, position and salary; Arthur Brisbane was once kind to him; and he chaperoned a delegation of school teachers on a visit to the World's Fair. But the unexpected, serio-comic, ludricrous-pathetic, Rabelaisan escapades and adventures the cavaliesi reporter is usually heir to, Mr. Dreiser never had. His brother, Paul Dresser, had them and he was not a newspaper man. One gets an impression of Theodore as a moony, much-troubled poetic, shy and diffident young man stumbling dreamily, vaguely through the murky streets of Chicago and Pittsburgh, transferring the self pity of his poverty into an easy and comforting pity for the people of the slums, challenging the God of his pious German Catholic parents to answer for the miseries of the world and his own, finding a momentary solace in the flattery of a smile or a kiss, catching a fleeting glimpse of beauty in a sunset, the shadows of a city street, the foliage of a city park, the trim body of a pretty girl, or of a campanile against a winter sky. But his adventures were those of the spirit, not of the flesh.

That is why it was on the calendar

that Mr. Dreiser should become a novelist and not a great newspaper man. All the factors of his early life, which may be discovered in the frank and beautiful pages of "A Hoosier Holiday," "A Traveler at Forty," and the chapter on his brother Paul in "Twelve Men," tended to mold him into a man of dramatic imagination, romantically inclined. And life is not dramatic; only art is that. Life is melodramatic, with elements of low comedy relief; and to be a good journalist, a good reporter, one must recognize this truth. Mr. Dreiser was not a good reporter: he might have made a fair to middling editorial writer or a Sunday feature man, for he thought in dramatic terms, with wistful overtones of criticism and of wonder; but he had not the equipment to see events in a cynical, cool light as a spectacle, amusing, pathetic, ephemeral—as ephemeral as last year's great murder mystery. He had much, far too much soul.

It must be a cause for pain and chagrin to Mr. Dreiser's detractors as a novelist, who urge against him the single score of immorality, to read this book. On the face of it this self-revelation is frank and sincere. Mr. Dreiser has the conspicuous virtue of all great confessors: he does not hide the truth even when it makes him ridiculous. For certainly he is in turn pathetic and lovable, sublime and ludicrous. He is, like the George Moore of "Hail and Farewell," much and often a booby; he is, like the St. Augustine of the "Confessions," much and often a noodle; he is, like Rousseau, much and often an ass; he is, like Casanova, much and often a vain and comical boaster; he is, like Bunyan and Dickens, in frequent bad taste; but he is forever and always frank, honest, and sincere. He blurts it all out, "Here I am," says he, "in all my nakedness, I have tried hard, desperately hard, to find some meaning, some symmetry, some meaning to life. I have thought as much as it is in my capacity to think; I have felt as much as it is in my capacity to feel; I have experimented, struggled, fought, argued to the limit of my capabilities that those who come after me may know something more of life than I. I have learned little; damned little. My impressions are as confused and disarranged as the life I have seen and experienced. I have a theory, from some scientist or philosopher with whom I could agree, about chemical reactions, laws of attractions and repulsion, the mating force, the instability of dogma, the anachronism of monogamy and all that. I may be wrong. But I am telling you, frankly, fully, sincerely, what my life has been; what I have thought and experienced. Make what you can of it. I am impelled to write it out of the same inner necessity that dictated 'Sister Carrie' and 'The Titan.' If it is valuable to humanity, I am glad. If it is not, well and good; I have had my day."

And what is that life and what has it to say? In a small industrial Indiana town Theodore Dreiser was born of poverty-stricken, pious, German-Catholic parents. There were far too many children; they had early to shift for themselves without adequate training and education; there were the bickerings and family quarrels incident to insecure, precarious domestic life. Among the children there were definite evidences of a heritage of talent, even of genius. Paul was a musician by instinct, an amiable and talented man, generous, sentimental, childlike; he became a notable figure of his time upon Broadway as a variety entertainer and as the author of "On the Banks of the

Wabash." There was another brother who had the sensitive equipment of a poet and for whom life proved to be too great a strain: he flared brilliantly for a moment and died abjectly in a house of prostitution.

Theodore was, curiously or significantly enough, the Parsifal, the Galahad of this family group. It was upon him that the family teaching and training had settled most definitely. To this day he does not drink or smoke and his language is free from profanity or obscenity. He was and is tender, affectionate, still a little credulous and sentimental. His autobiography is an analogue of the spirit of his time. He went like a boy hero out of a Horatio Alger jr. novel, to Chicago to seek his fortune. His ambitions, as he states them, were definitely material. He wanted to cut a figure in the world. He wanted rubber-tired carriages and fur coats and pretty women in beautiful gowns to admire and love him. There settled upon him the spell of what the psychologists, since the time of the debut of Jules de Gaultier, have called Bovarysm; he eagerly sought to be something quite otherwise than what he was. He was (or rather thought himself to be, for he is really handsome) an ugly, ungainly and unattractive man; and so he wanted women to fall for him in windrows. No one was more surprised than he when, in a measure, they did. A smile swelled his chest, a kiss vastly reassured him, a conquest set him up, made him proud. Utterly without vanity, greed, or aggressiveness, indeed a humble, grateful compound of sentimentalism and idealism, it is amusing to consider the gossip and criticism which have made of him an ogre, a Machiavelli and a terrible Don Juan. It was after more than a year of ardent courtship that "I reached a place where I could hold her hand, put my arms about her, kiss her; but never could I induce her to sit upon my lap. That was reserved for a much later date."

In his other contacts with life he was no less ill at ease and without assurance. The office boys in the outer corridor of the editorial rooms of "The World" treated him so rough and disrespectfully that he has not to this day got over it. He pays tribute to their bad manners to the extent of five pages. He was buffeted at every turn by life, by reality; he was sensitive with the sensitivity of an artist; by instinct tolerant, kind, gentle, self-effacing, but no less giving the full meed of his admiration to the dashing, aggressive, successful figures of American life. A saving sense, not of humor, but of intelligence, made him see these men in their proper perspective; it was this sense plus the endowment of his romantic imagination which enabled him to create Frank Cowperwood and Eugene Witla, which stand as authentic and carefully realized figures in American society during its great epoch of industrial democracy. He had, it appears, during the years recorded in this autobiography but two or three literary enthusiasms, Dickens, Hugo and Balzac. It was Balzac whom he wished most to emulate; and it was not, interestingly enough, out of worship of Balzac as an artist. It was frankly because he wanted to know as much of American high life and to mingle in it as Balzac appeared to know. He tells us he loved and suffered and lived with Balzac's heroes and heroines, that they were to him as real as any people he knew. It was such a world that he lived in. No wonder he failed as a newspaper man, for in newspaper reporting there is little room for imagination—life is much too stridently colored for that—and became a novelist. And it is little wonder that he has begun to write his reminiscences out of a failure fully to have his say in fiction, and that he has given us here a book of tenderness and truth, humbly and sincerely told, the poignantly interesting history of a not unusual life, which in its very commonplaceness may serve as a representative record of the barrenness of the average life in elements of adventure and ecstasy.

E. G. Potter. Chicago *Tribune* [Paris Edition], January 1, 1923.

Unlike most authors Theodore Dreiser has chosen to give to the world the story of his immature years of journalistic struggles rather than an account of the ripened period of his successful literary work. "A Book about Myself" although running through five hundred pages gives but a fragment of the author's life, covering scarcely four years.

It presents, however, a period full of significance in its influence on his later writing:—these were years of youthful ambition, hard work, disappointment, and minor successes—when in the school of experience he was learning the lessons which later made him a successful magazine editor and writer.

The author does not burden us with details of his childhood but plunges into his story at the time when as a lad of nineteen he secured his first position on a Chicago newspaper. With pleasing frankness we are told of the conceits and subterfuges of these immature years, of his disrupted home life, of his youthful love affairs and his gradual advancement in journalism.

The personal "myself" which dominates the early part of the book reaches out, in the latter pages, to a broader horizon giving glimpses of various phases of life touched by a newspaper reporter. We hold our breath as we follow the story of the attempted "Scoop" of the train robber's story, and smile over the chagrin of the young journalist as he reads in a rival newspaper that a certain theatrical troupe, whose evening performance he had described in detail, had failed to reach the city because of a washout.

Through these pages we glimpse the inside machinery of the newspapers of Chicago, St. Louis, Pittsburgh, and New York, and see these cities as they appeared in the early nineties. With a few bold strokes he pictures the inhabitants and the throbbing life of the streets and exposes some of the sore spots of the time.

The book calls for a sequel. The interest aroused by the author's early struggles demands that in fairness to his readers, he carry his autobiography to the fuller years of successful achievement.

"New Books at Random." Washington *Star,* January 16, 1923.

This has been called an honest book. It is. Honesty, however, is not the motive power behind it. Self-absorption is the driving force of the story. And a perfect abandon of self-disclosure delivers it. Honesty is a mere accident in this passion for self-expression, where nothing pertaining to the writer is negligible, where everything is vital. Inevitably an author in this state of being runs to words. Mr. Dreiser does. He here gravely offers a 500-page volume to project the content of a four-year period of his, to him, momentous daily existence. Only that innocence of mind possessed by children alone—children and a few Mr. Dreisers—could, in sober earnest, achieve this gesture. His painstaking devotion to all the multifarious details of himself contains a glint of humor for the reader, while to the writer it is obviously up to the last letter a most serious business. And to be sure, everybody is to himself a serious business. Fortunate the one, however, who learns to laugh a little now and then over the fix he is in. This is the fix that we are all in. Mr. Dreiser is one of the unlucky who never for an instant sees the joke of himself.

If the author were to build a house in the manner of his building this book any one qualified to pass upon his work would say, right off, that he was no architect; that he had not the ghost of a notion of those proportions upon which any structure depends for much of its beauty and for the most of its stability. And Mr. Dreiser would say that he knew this very well; that he was not trying to create architectural units, but that, rather, he was following the plan of the Almighty, who never takes the trouble to show to man any complete and rounded aspects of life, but leads him instead through a hit-or-miss welter of events, which He suddenly shuts off squarely before one can gather even a hint of general design or purpose or of his own individual part in working out some special pattern. God, and the Russian writers, and Mr. Dreiser, all work that way.

Tramping the Chicago streets on the trail of news, this overgrown, unwaywise boy became an explorer, an avid youth hunting life. And he came upon wonderful things. Overjoyed, he found out that the big city was of itself a personality, with hours of bewitchment upon it—the night, the brooding dawn, the open day. Amazed, he discovered much about the sublimate chemistry of all creation—man, human life, so beautiful and so terrible. These contacts soaked through his senses down into his emotions. The boy became overcharged and was likely to explode with the wonder of its existence. A little part of this he came gradually to let out on paper for newspaper print. Much the larger part of it, however, went into romantic philanderings, tenuous and unreal as dreams. The lovely chin and throat curve of a girl, or sheen of hair, or lure of glance, would send him off into some impossible seventh heaven. He mouthed queer things—some of it poetry—and worked out social theories of his own—marriage a mistake; too many delays about it, the delay of courtship, the delay of engagements, the delay of the marriage ceremony itself: better to seize life hot off the fire than to wait till it has grown clammy and tasteless like a cold pancake. He is vain, absurd, bombastic, grotesque, inordinately proud of his small advances in the press game. For he did advance. A little of this surge got into his writing and the powers caught the difference between his copy and that of the more sophisticate. They thought, guardedly, that it might go, that they might give the fellow a little more rope now and then. The basic fact at this point is that the youth was suffering a belated and painful adolescence—crazy and dazed with himself and with life a large part of the time. And he tells all he knows right in this book—at any rate, one hopes that he knows no more than he has told here.

The newspaper proved finally not to be his medium. The story, he felt, would make a better channel for him. So he fell to reading the best of our story-writers—Howells and the rest. No, no: none of this would do—pretty, polite, polished things, but not real, had nothing at all to do with life. At the most these were but variants of the old fairy tale. Then he came upon Balzac and ate him up. Here was the very stuff of life, and here was the way to put it across. And by and by there will emerge Theodore Dreiser, writer of sprawling, cumbersome novels that are, nevertheless, acutely conscious of the ways of the human heart, hand in glove with the contradictions and vagaries of human behaviors. To go back to the book in hand, here is a big, bewildered, groping, persistently groping, human, infinitely pathetic, not in himself alone as Theodore Dreiser, but as a human implication in the wilderness of life. A lovable person, too; but he would not care a straw for that.

Terre Haute [Ind.] *Tribune*, January 19, 1923.

Under the title of "A Book About Myself," Theodore Dreiser has just issued a fragmentary autobiography of himself.

Right on the heels of Harry Kemp's "Tramping on Life" comes this autobiographical essay of Dreiser's, and the reviewer is forced to compare and contrast the two books, whether he would or no. There are points of similarity; there are tremendous differences. Dreiser is a more important literary figure than Kemp; Kemp is a more entertaining personality than Dreiser. The "tramp-poet's" life has been full of incident and adventure; the novelist's career, as set down in his book, has been drab and commonplace.

But Theodore Dreiser's book about himself has this in common with the other—that in spite of its length it is fascinating. It has the personal and human interest, and it has a distinct historical value, too. We see the last decade of the nineteenth century through the eyes of a serious minded and introspective newspaper reporter. Chicago before and during the world's fair; St. Louis at about the same time; a passing glimpse at Toledo, Cleveland and Buffalo; an unforgetable sketch of Pittsburgh as it was after the Homestead riots, and finally a description of New York as it appeared to a stranger in the days before the subways.

The veteran newspaper man recognizes many of the figures in Dreiser's narrative; and the author makes doubly sure of that by using their real names. There is an interesting sketch of his brother, Paul Dresser, Terre Haute's beloved bard. And other Broadway figures now faded to traditions. And the Herald Square theater, and Brown's chop house—all gone now.

All this in such a deadly serious vein; poetic, at times, in spite of Dreiser, but humorless as always. There is a ray of light; it seems as if Dreiser were, by sheer volume of work, at last learning a decent English style. There are fewer marks of prodigious and awkward effort in this book than in the novels. Perhaps it is his subject that makes it easier for him. One of the mysteries of contemporary literature is how this man can be one of our few great novelists, think like a philosopher, observe like a genius, and write like a cub reporter.

But if you want to know all about Dreiser, you will find it in this book. He drops the narrative at the period before he began to write fiction; perhaps he intends to issue another book about himself.

Richard Le Gallienne. "Certain Literary Sins of Theodore Dreiser." *Literary Digest International Book Review*, February, 1923, pp. 10–11, 70–71.

This is a dull, distasteful and quite unnecessary book. Mr. Dreiser has wasted valuable time in writing it, when he might have been giving Mr. Sumner, at least, new food for thought with a new novel. Nor can young or old who has yet to read any of the great and entertaining masterpieces of the world's literature afford the time to read it, unless their time is paid for, as reviewers. Five hundred and two large pages! Boswell's "Life of Johnson"—really a more entertaining book, in spite of its being a classic—is, I suppose, about twice as long. Either it or, say, Benvenuto Cellini's Autobiography might well have the benefit of the time saved from reading Mr. Dreiser; and from those or any other such inspiring autobiography (what about "The Education of Henry Adams"?) the reader would have risen quickened, instead of deadened and disgusted. For, to be frank, and, quoting a jest of Mr. Charles Hanson Towne à propos Mr. Dreiser's other voluminosity, "I rise from reams" of "A Book About Myself" with some such feelings. The book has some good spots to which I shall presently do justice, but, in the main, to read it is "on this short day of frost and sun" "to sleep before evening."

If a dull book can have any *raison d'être,* one might find it in the importance of the writer. But is Mr. Dreiser important enough as a novelist to justify him in thinking that the world has "awaited" from him such confessions as these? Had he concerned himself chiefly with his processes as a novelist, the case would have been somewhat different, tho even so, he is not so distinguished a master of his art as to make such confidences of any great importance. I would be the last to deny that he is a conscientious workman of the realistic, documentary school; even in America, however, that school already has at least one far more significant representative, Frank Norris, to wit. Had Norris told us about the writing of "McTeague," we should have been glad, even eager, to listen. But Mr. Dreiser has brought us nothing to match "McTeague." Norris had something of the originality of genius, in spite of his affiliations with the realistic "naturalistic" school. But Mr. Dreiser is only one industrious member of that school, and his prominence is less due to any individuality of talent than to the themes with which the society now represented by Mr. Sumner caused him some time ago to be publicly identified. "Sister Carrie" achieved "greatness" rather, so to say, "by position" than by its intrinsic merits. It was a famous *casus belli* between a stupid Puritan censorship and the representatives of literary freedom in this country, and the part played by it in our subsequent comparative emancipation from such illiterate control of letters deservedly won for Mr. Dreiser the sympathy of his fellowcraftsmen. But even a police-court prosecution can not take the place of genius, tho the newspaper publicity involved is sometimes mistaken for fame.

Mr. Sumner may be a poor judge of literature or anything else you please; but certain publishers and authors are surely unfair in regarding him as their enemy. Some recent occurrences, indeed, have proved that, however involuntarily, they have no better friend. Without his aid, does any one suppose that "Jurgen," or "Women in Love," would have undergone the disgrace of being "best-sellers?" Mr. Cabell would have continued in his sacred seclusion as a purveyor of imitation caviare for the dilettanti, and Mr. Lawrence's genuine neurosis would have attracted only those readers similarly afflicted. As it is, thanks to Mr. Sumner, both these writers are eagerly ransacked by readers who must have great difficulty in knowing what they are all about, but who persevere in the hope of rooting up those choice morsels which have given the books their police-court immortality. Mr. Sumner, too, as well as the authors involved, deserves well of all lovers of literature because the fight against prurient ignorance parading as moral censorship has thus been brought out into the open, and a way been thus cleared for a freer and saner expansion of the literary art in this country. As a pioneer in this fight, Mr. Dreiser deserves our respect and support, and he has had both to something like excess. He has attained to something like a position in the literary martyrology of America, and the value of his work has been exaggerated in consequence. Probably it is for this reason that he considers himself sufficiently a national figure to write "A Book About Myself." . . .

The greater part of Mr. Dreiser's volume is made up of this newspaper apprenticeship. When we close the book his career as a novelist is yet to begin. On page 502 he half suggests a sequel "under some such title as 'Literary Experiences.' " One is inclined to wish that he had written that sequel first. For these newspaper experiences are spun out at far too great a length, nor are they either in matter or manner sufficiently novel or striking to justify the inordinate demand they make on the reader's time and attention. Mr. Dreiser has nothing like the vivid, selective dramatic art of another recent autobiographer, Mr. Harry Kemp, whose recent "Tramping on Life," whatever faults it may have along with its very great excellences, has not a dull page in it. Fault has been found with Mr. Kemp for the frankness of his amatory recollections. The most serious one of them it is, indeed, hard to condone, but, for the most part, there is a naïveté about them, even sometimes a touch of romantic beauty, which earns him absolution. It is the outspokenness of young blood. Now Mr. Dreiser has his amatory recollections, too, and, if his newspaper experiences are for the most part dull, it has to be said that, in his shabby recollections as a sort of Chicago Don Juan, his naïveté, if such it can be called, has no saving grace of poetry or romance. Distasteful and underbred are hard words, but surely they are too mild for this paragraph with which his book closes. To praise the opening pages of his book is but justice as well as a pleasure. But something like "Jersey justice" seems to be called for by the hard unchivalrous tone, not to say cynical brutality, of this concluding "N.B.":

> N. B. Four years later, having by then established myself sufficiently to pay the rent of an apartment, secure furniture and convince myself that I could make a living for two, I undertook that perilous adventure with the lady of my choice—and that, of course, after the first flare of love had thinned down to the pale flame of duty. Need anything more be said? The first law of convention had been obeyed, whereas the governing forces of temperament had been overridden and with what results eventually you may well suspect. So much for romance.

One might possibly have overlooked what went before, but what must one say of this? Did a writer ever more deliberately leave his reader with such bad taste in the mouth? And what went before was distasteful and unnecessary enough. "Alice" is the name of the lady who bears the brunt of most of Mr. Dreiser's cubbish philanderings. But there was a "Scotch girl," too, who paled her uneffectual fires when Alice came on the scene. "The thing that troubled me," says Mr. Dreiser "was what my Scotch girl would think if she found out (which she never would), and how I could extricate myself from a situation, which, now that I had Alice, was not as interesting as it had been." The world of Mr. Dreiser's early gallantries was not a very courtly one—for which, of course, he was nowise to blame. It was a world where wooing is done by pressing the lady's toe "in an open, foolish way," and such like advances. Here is a typical scene:

> I was alone with her in the front room, looking over the family album. I realized that by now she was as much drawn to me as I to her, and that, as in the case of my Scotch maid, I was master if I chose so to be. I was so wrought up in the face of this opportunity, however, that I scarcely had courage to do that which I earnestly believed I could do. As we stood over the album looking at the pictures, I toyed first with the strings of her apron and then later, finding no opposition, allowed my hand to rest gently at her waist. Still no sign of opposition or even consciousness. I thrilled from head to toe. Then I closed my arm gently about her waist, and when it became noticeably tight, she looked up and smiled.
>
> "You'd better watch out," she said. "Some one may come."
>
> "Do you like me a little?" I pleaded, almost choking.
>
> "I think so. I think you're very nice, anyhow. But you mustn't," she said, "some one may come in," and as I drew her to me she pretended to resist, maneuvering her cheek against my mouth as she pulled away. . . .
>
> Was I in love with her? No, as I understand myself now. I doubt that I have ever been in love with anyone or with anything save life as a whole.

There is nothing here or anywhere in the book for Mr. Sumner. But even flaming sensuality, with which the modern reader is all too well acquainted, would have some "relish of salvation in it" compared with such drab silliness, such chronicling of five-and-ten-cent-store philoprogenitiveness. Why should a grown-up writer, in the maturity of his gifts, think it worth while solemnly to make such commonplace revelations? The time is long past when it was necessary, in the interests of the veracious representation of life, to deal frankly with the usual sexual experiences of human beings. Since Whitman defiantly announced his intention to "make illustrious" "that of myself without which I were nothing," "tho I stand sole among men," sex has certainly been made as "illustrious" as need be. There is surely nothing more to learn about it and no necessity for our being told it all over and over again. The purpose of Whitman's protest has been served. Prurient hypocrisy has had its death-blow. Now one would be glad of a few veils once more, so that the romance of sex be saved for us, after all the demonstrations of clinical realism. The romance of it is just as real, and spiritually more important, than the physiological, not to say pathological, "facts." Mr. Dreiser adds nothing to our knowledge. He only makes a beautiful thing silly and distasteful, and his literary exhibitionism only serves to class his book with the mawkish pages of Rousseau, and Hazlitt's unfortunate "Liber Amoris."

One says nothing of "taste." There is no such thing, we are told, nowadays. It has been sneered out of existence in the general Bolshevism of the times. To express oneself is all—whether that self be worth expressing or not. Yet, however deep the present occultation of the finer standards of life and literature, no one acquainted with human history has any fear for their endurance. Honor and reverence, taste and breeding are qualities the world is too wise ultimately to throw away. In fact, it evolves them constantly in spite of itself. Standards of life and literature may change for the better, but never for the worse; and, momentarily eclipsed or not, there are still standards by which that last paragraph in Mr. Dreiser's book must be judged an unpardonable offense, the more regrettable because it does an injustice to Mr. Dreiser's usually genial and humane personality. To much else in it, too, there applies a saying of Napoleon which comes to me by way of a writer for whom, I presume, Mr. Dreiser has respect, Stendhal in "Rouge et Noir": "There are some things which are not written."

H. W. Boynton. "Der Arme Theodor." *The Independent*, 110 (February 3, 1923), 99–100.

This book, like every new book of Mr. Dreiser's, has been greeted with hemming and hawing on one side of the critical camp, and with nodding and chortling on the other. Everything he does is more or less patently a manifesto of anti-Puritanism, which greatly pleases the professional anti-Puritans and has to be made a note on by the rest of us—earnest, conservative (and hypocritical) souls that we are. More justice might be done such books, on both sides of the camp—they might at least be taken more easily and profitably—if we could rid them of the living personal consideration. A realist is always half-autobiographer when he writes a novel, and half-novelist when he writes an autobiography. If in reading Mr. Dreiser's various utterances which are professedly about himself, we could think of "himself" as a third person, a "hero" under literary treatment, we might be meeting such utterances more fairly, as pieces of writing, than we can by everlastingly dwelling on the identity of the writer and his central figure. "A Book About Myself," like Hamlin Garland's "Son of the Middle Border" and its sequel, ought to be read as a novel if we are interested in it as literature. For the right attitude we need only take the writer at his face value: as a disinterested chronicler of events which have hardly more to do with his present entity or self than with our own.

This is the story of a few years in the life of a youth named Theodore. The place, at the beginning, is Chicago, the time 1890; he is nineteen years old. Theodore's father is a German, apparently a step above the laboring class. He is a good man and an ardent Roman Catholic. He has no knack for "success," and is not a dominant figure even in his own house. It is the mother of the family who has made the home. From the moment of her recent death the family life has been fast disintegrating. For some little time its outward bonds hold. Four grown children continue to live in their father's house and do their share towards maintaining it. But there is small love lost between them. Theodore's feeling for his brothers and sisters ranges from distaste to hatred. The poor old father can only shake his head, when the inevitable break-up comes, and murmur sadly, "I'm sorry, Dorsch. I done the best I could." And after a few "pointless insincere phrases," as the grim chronicler hath it, our Theodore turns from the old man to his own new ways among the glorious regions of youth. For this Theodore is a dreamer and sentimentalist, and all things are glorious to him at this time. He plies the dingy trade of collector for a credit-giving furniture house; but the sights and sounds of great Chicago entrance him: "As I walked from place to place collecting, I began to improvise rhythmic, vaguely formulated word-pictures or rhapsodies anent, these same and many other things—free verse, I suppose, we should call it now—which concerned everything and nothing, but somehow expressed the seething poetry of my soul" . . . "For myself, life was at the topmost toss. I was like some bird poised on a high twig, teetering and fluttering and ready for flight." . . . "Joy was ever before me, the sense of some great adventure lurking just around the corner."

Meanwhile, to the eye of ordinary observers, he is an overgrown, awkward, and nearly inarticulate lad, full of German sentimentality, and disposed to find the world a beautiful place so long as it continues to seem worthy of that sentimentality. There is a Mädchen of his dreams, and there are American girls who more or less plausibly represent her, and more or less warmly respond to his fumbling approaches. At this early time there has been one who is merely called "my Scotch girl," and whom he is embarrassed to find on his emotional hands when an Alice turns up. Alice is a shop-girl, a friend of Theodore's shop-girl sister. When Theodore meets her, she is engaged to a worthy middle-aged clerk. But she prefers our hero, and, if we are to take his word for it, she is ready to become his mistress as a step towards becoming his wife. He is greatly touched by her devotion, and is vastly fond of her in a condescending way, but not even the coddled sentimentalism of this period demands of him the ignominy of marriage. He philanders with Alice till she wearies him, and then turns his back on her, and she marries her middle-aged suitor and departs into the outer darkness of a Theodoreless existence.

Before this romantic exit takes place much has happened to Theodore in other than amatory paths. The milk of his sentimentalism has been curdled by eager drops of knowledge from several quarters. Even before he abandons the job of collecting "instalments," his eyes have been sadly opened. The following is characteristic of his ingenious habit of thought: "I was tired of collecting—the same districts, the same excuses, the same subterfuges. By degrees I had come to feel a great contempt for the average mind. So many people were so low, so shifty, so dirty, so nondescript. They were food for dreams; little more. Owing to my experience with the manager of the Lovell Company in the matter of taking what did not belong to me I had become very cautious, and this meant that I should be compelled to live from week to week on my miserable twelve dollars." Surely this must be taken as a triumph of ironic humor on the part of Theodore's chronicler. Theodore resolves to leave collecting because of (a) its monotony; (b) its meanness and its unpleasant effect on his view of humanity; and (c) its inconvenience for an enterprising young collector who might have lived comfortably enough if he could have safely stolen part of the moneys collected. As for the experience with the Lovell Company, it has been charitably recorded on an earlier page. "From this firm, having been hard pressed for a winter overcoat the preceding fall, I had abstracted or held out twenty-five dollars, intending to restore it. But——" The short of it was that before he could restore it, he was found out. The manager of the company, "who had seemed to take a fancy to him," let him off with a reprimand. . . . The odd thing about the episode as recorded is a certain squeamishness inconsistent in a chronicler of Mr. Dreiser's highly accredited realism. Theodore didn't steal, he "took what did not belong to him"; there was a twenty-five dollars which he happened on occasion to "abstract" or "hold out." We note further that it is not the experience of his own dishonesty which disillusions him, but the spectacle of other people's dirtiness and shiftiness. Thus ever with sentimentalists!

So Theodore leaves collecting, and finds a foothold in newspaper work. He aspires to write, and the business of reporting appeals to him as a career of glory. He becomes a reporter, succeeds in the newspaper world. . . . Alas! Again dust and ashes in his tender mouth. The newspaper world proves to be a world without moral principles and of no generous quality whatever. It believes in nothing and nobody, it uses any sort of method to attain its mean ends: "Most of these young men looked upon life as a fierce, grim struggle in which no quarter was either given or taken, and in which all men laid traps, lied, squandered, erred through illusion: a conclusion with which," says our chronicler with his best put-this-in-your-pipe-and-smoke-it accent, "I now most heartily agree. The one thing I would now add is that the brigandage of the world is in the main genial and that in our hour of success we are all inclined to be more or less liberal and warmhearted. . . . But at this time I was still sniffing about the Sermon on the Mount and the Beatitudes, expecting ordinary human flesh and blood to do and be all those things. Hence the point of view of these men seemed at times a little horrific, at other times most tonic."

However the mature anti-Puritan may affect to rejoice in disillusionment, it is a serious business for youthful Theodore. There is now a hole in the dyke of his emotional optimism, and the rest is but a matter of time. It is everything or nothing with him. If this is indeed not altogether a world of rosy virtue and delight, then it must be ignoble, inane, an object to be tolerated with a sort of weary distaste. In Chicago, in St. Louis, in Pittsburgh, in New York, he finds political corruption, venality of the press, immorality in high life, dishonesty in business, the foul unregarded debauchery of the slums. Well, then, if this is what the world is made of, it is no kind of a world to be alive in. Now and then he looks back with mournful regret to the better sort of world in which he once believed. So it is when he visits the country home of his beloved: "We Americans have home traditions and ideals, created as much by song and romance as anything else: 'My Old Kentucky Home,' 'Suwanee River.' Despite any willing on my part, this home seemed to fulfill the spirit of those songs. There was something so sadly romantic about it. The shade of the great trees moved across the lawn in stately and lengthening curves. A stream at the foot of the slope leading down from the west side of the house dimpled and whimpered in the sun. Birds sang. . . . To me it seemed that all the spirit of rural America, its idealism, its dreams, the passion of a Brown, the courage and patience and sadness of a Lincoln, the dreams and courage of a Lee or a Jackson, were all here. The very soil smacked of American idealism and faith, a fixedness in sentimental and purely imaginative American tradition, in which I, alas! could not share. I was enraptured. Out of its charms and sentiments I might have composed an elegy or an epic, but I could not believe that it was more than a frail flower of romance."

In short, young Theodore (no longer quite so young), since he is condemned to the pains of unbelief, wishes to reap its pleasures also in this idyllic spot. To his lifelong resentment, he is balked of his wishes. Apparently he lays the fiasco of his later marriage to the beloved of this episode, to her folly in resisting nature, as embodied in his desires, at this time. The whole narrative is concluded by this dry and sardonic, and interesting, if not superfluous postscript: "N. B. Four years later, having by then established myself sufficiently to pay the rent of an apartment, secure furniture, and convince myself that I could make a living for two, I undertook that perilous adventure with the lady of my choice—and that, of course, after the first flare of love had thinned down to the pale flame of duty. Need anything more be said? The first law of convention had been obeyed, whereas the governing forces of temperament had been overridden—and with, what results eventually you may well suspect. So much for romance."

So much for romance: as who should say, "Here lies young Theodore, definitely done for, and with him all the youth and beauty and virtue of the world!" The epitaph, we must think, is too sweeping, the world not being totally or even chiefly composed of embittered sentimentalists, Teutonic or other. . . . Dreiser's great powers of observation and description are of course fully shown in these pages. His slow and not always distinct drone is broken by moments of extraordinary brilliancy; and now and then the Herr Doktor fairly bursts into song. Those parts of the narrative which deal with newspaper life have been widely commented on. The book as a novel would rank not with the two Dreiserian masterpieces, "Sister Carrie" and "Jennie Gerhardt," but rather with studies of the blundering male like "The Titan" and "The Genius."

Ben Macomber. San Francisco *Chronicle*, February 4, 1923.

In "A Book About Myself," by Theodore Dreiser, you will find something rare enough in biography, still rarer in autobiography. You will find what seems to be complete honesty.

In Dreiser's book about himself you will find autobiography without concealment, without smoothing things over, without alibis, without self-deception, without cant.

At any rate he is so frank in what he has told that certainly he could have no obejct in concealing anything else. He has written about himself as objectively and as dispassionately as though this Theodore Dreiser, who is his subject, were a man on Mars whom he had watched and studied through some super-telescope with an all-revealing lens. To check up on this book I imagine one would need to know as much about Dreiser as he does himself. . . .

The book is a brilliant picture of newspaper life in those days, about 1890 to 1898. But it is much more than that. It is a vivid and moving portrayal of the progress of an ambitious, very human and very imperfect young man; of the jolts and jars, seldom gentle touches, of his contacts with other human beings and with the facts of life; of the development of a man who from the vantage point of newspaper work, matchless for the purpose, learned to see things as they are and not as the Sunday School books assume them to be.

It reads like a novel. Yet one sees that Dreiser had no more remarkable experiences as newspaper man than dozens of those you meet every day. But with such objective realism he has used them and his other experiences at the time to throw light upon himself and others as exemplars of human nature and upon the facts of life in this world, that it is sometimes necessary to remind one's self that the chief figure of the book is a veritable person now moving about the precincts of Los Angeles.

It is told with a simplicity that makes the style beautiful. There are only two words in the book that a schoolboy might need to look up in a dictionary.

Dreiser is a thoroughly disillusioned man. But in the stage that the writing of this book represents he is neither bitter nor cynical. With only a great calmness he recognizes frankly that human beings and human society in general are deeply disappointing in comparison with what children and sheltered persons are led to believe. His sincerity appears in the use of himself as an example.

In some other of his books Dreiser has swung a heavy club and growled and roared as though in a rage with society. Apparently he has developed out of that stage. He has not changed his opinions, but in advancing them hard and bitter words are no longer his tactics.

The result is a great advance in Dreiser's artistry. "A Book About Myself" is a very fine book indeed.

David Karsner. "Here and There and Everywhere." New York *Call*, February 10, 1923, p. 8.

In many things I am not neutral. I am certainly partisan toward food, clothing, shelter, books and politics. It will not be necessary for me to continue the list of partisanships. Suffice it to say that I am partisan toward Theodore Dreiser and thoroughly enjoy, admire and appreciate 90 percent of his literary product. I make a reservation for the 10 per cent, and that allows me to be critical when I feel like it, though I have not so far felt like it.

I have observed that many professional critics do not like Dreiser's latest volume, "A Book About Myself." Fortunately I had read the book before a shameless culprit stole it from my desk. And now comes Richard Le Gallienne in a criticism in the Literary Digest International Book Review to inquire: "Is Mr. Dreiser important enough as a novelist to justify him in thinking that the world has 'awaited' from him such confessions as these? . . . Had he concerned himself chiefly with his processes as a novelist, the case would have been somewhat different, though even so, he is not so distinguished a master of his art as to make such confidence of any great importance."

Such nonsense! What gives Le Gallienne the idea that Dreiser thought the world was waiting for his book? Le Gallienne has written and published enough himself to have learned by this time that a real poet and a real novelist are not imbued with the silly notion that the world, or any part thereof, or any person therein, is "awaiting" their poetry or prose. A man who has a poem in him writes it because he can't help it, and a man who has a novel in him does likewise. Poems and novels that are written "for the world" are not the best in literary art and when they appear and enjoy their first flare (if they ever do) they are soon offered "as the alms of oblivion," to borrow a neat phrase from the precise and poetic vocabulary of Frank Harris, who, by the way, found it necessary to go to Nice to write his memoirs, so unfriendly was the American attitude toward him and his work.

Le Gallienne says that Dreiser is only one industrious member of the "realistic, naturalistic" school of fiction "and his prominence is less due to any individuality of talent than to the themes with which the society now represented by Mr. Sumner caused him some time ago to be publicly identified. 'Sister Carrie' achieved greatness, rather, so to say, by 'position' than by its intrinsic merits." From which it is quite evident that Le Gallienne doesn't like Dreiser's books, and will have nothing to do with him as a literary figure, whether or no. And in that sense I gather that Le Gallienne is also a partisan, though not to Dreiser.

The point then resolves itself into the speculation that whereas Theodore Dreiser offers strong meat for strong people, Le Gallienne prefers charlotte russes capped with a Maraschino cherry.

Evidently referring to the numerous dismal sessions that either Dreiser or his agents have had with the literary suppressionists from the time that "Sister Carrie" appeared some 20 years ago down to and including "The Genius" in 1915, Le Gallienne observes that "even a police court prosecution cannot take the place of genius, though the newspaper publicity involved is sometimes mistaken for fame."

Other writers in this country have had to run the gamut of police court prosecution and worse. For example, James Branch Cabell, on account of his "Jurgen," which surely would never have gone beyond the first edition of that book (which was bought up by the dilettanti) save for the fact that Sumner informed all those afflicted with genuine neurosis that here was a book to appease at least some of their inhibitions. Has Cabell's day in the Sumnerian court increased the public's interest in his work? How many people have read "The Rivet in Grandfather's Neck"? Did another of Cabell's titles, "Beyond Life," reach anything like the popularity of "Jennie Gearhardt"? What of Dreiser's "The Financier" and "The Titan," its sequel, both of which caused the fiction-reading public to clamor for the third of the trilogy, "The Bulwark," which has not appeared?

Le Gallienne complains that Dreiser "has nothing like the vivid, selective dramatic art of another recent autobiographer, Mr. Harry Kemp, whose recent "Tramping on Life,' whatever faults it may have along with its great excellence, has not a dull page in it." Le Gallienne will, I am sure, be glad to know that he has a first-rate second for this observation, the same being Kemp himself.

For myself, I would only add to this note that I wish the crook who stole Dreiser's "A Book About Myself" had instead swiped "Tramping on Life." I would also add this, that if Le Gallienne has a first edition of Dreiser's latest book I will be glad to give him my "first" of Kemp's memoirs in exchange for it. I will do even better than that; will throw in for good measure a copy of "Pilgrim's Progress," "Robinson Crusoe," "The Sermons of Drummond" and the "Life of Henry Ford."

H. L. Mencken. "Adventures Among Books—III," *Smart Set*, 70 (March 1923), 143–144.

The Dreiser book, a tome of more than 500 large pages, is the second volume of what is projected as a three-volume autobiography. It deals with the author's years as a newspaper reporter, and, despite his usual discursiveness and undistinguished English, it is a work full of fascination. Here we see the beginnings of the Dreiser novels and of the Dreiserian philosophy of resigned pessimism. That philosophy is not the fruit of a native sinfulness, as Prof. Dr. Sherman would have us believe; it is the fruit of an extensive and laborious observation of the human farce from a singularly favorable grandstand. While Dr. Sherman was an innocent child in Iowa, and familiar with blood only as it issued from the cut necks of domestic fowl, Dreiser was serving as a reporter at Bellevue Hospital and along the waterfront of New York. That service knocked all the ethical cocksureness of the prairie out of it, and put pity into him. He is today perhaps the only American novelist who shows any sign of being able to feel profoundly, and he is surely the only one who can arouse genuine feeling in his readers. There are plenty of others who far surpass him in technical facility, in humor and in ingenuity, but there is none who comes near him in the primary business of a novelist, which is to make the transaction depicted seem real, and important, and poignant. His poor drab, Jennie Gerhardt, is perhaps the most unattractive woman ever put into a novel as heroine. She is dull, helpless, and without imagination, and it is hard to think of her save as a frump. But Dreiser somehow makes a tragic figure of her before he finishes. In the sordid, commonplace story of her life there is a presentation of the universal misery of man. To do that is to accomplish a very rare and difficult business. The only other American novelist who seems likely ever to achieve it is Miss Cather.

Dreiser's career as a reporter was not distinguished, and the tale he has to tell is thus not very startling. He covered the usual assignments, met the usual public frauds, saw the usual horrors, diverted himself in his scant leisure with the usual carnalities of young reporters. I doubt that his newspaper writings, though they were regarded as masterpieces by the staff of the Pittsburgh *Dispatch*, had any actual merit as journalism. He is quite without the journalistic talent for superficial vividness; he must have room to manouevre. In "A Book About Myself" he gives himself this room, and the result, despite some windy excursions, is a volume that probably gives a better picture of the life of a young reporter than any that could be written by a better journalist. I need not add that absolutely nothing is left out. We have meticulous reports of conversations carried on 30 years ago; voluminous discussions of obscure and forgotten personalities; laborious accounts of banal love affairs. It is, on the surface, obvious, unimportant, dull; it is, underneath, full of a strange eloquence.

May I. Baym. "On Dreiser." Detroit *Free Press Book Review*, February 25, 1923, p. 4.

. . . I consider this book a veritable American document. The whetting of a knife against a huge stone must needs produce sparks of fire and screeches of friction along with the increased sharpening of the implement. Theodore Dreiser started out with a passion to sharpen his intellect against that chemic mystery called life. Dreiser is not ashamed of showing his passions, just as Rousseau wasn't, just as St Augustine wasn't. And his passions are always in a major key—strong, open, fearless. His expression, therefore, of the adventures of his soul is saturated with that sense of reality which readily communicates itself to the intelligent reader. Theodore Dreiser does not contemplate life in a passive manner. Rather does he direct life's currents to pass through him, and as they pass, he makes a supreme, virile attempt to intuit their meaning, to grasp their inner stuff. If it be true that at times the mystery is too much for him and leaves him baffled as a child, it is equally true that he makes an adult attempt not to allow the mystery to germinate in him a new cycle of fetiches. He call this mystery the Chemistry and Physics of life. And in this expression we have at once the admission that life is ever evasive and yet subject to a certain amount of analysis. In this point of view we are removed at least one stage from the savage's fear and worship of the mysterious.

In talking about himself, Dreiser really talks about America, for through him courses the whole tide of humanity, especially that part of it which is America. . . . In reading the story he sets down each one of us may read, with variations, the fable of his own life.

Dreiser gives us the story of his years as a journalist even as he gives the story of Eugene Witla's early adventures as an artist—here lyrically calm, there tragically stormy, and sometimes merely boring with inconsequential details. And yet, in the light of the inevitable interconcatenation of things and events, one acquiesces even in the presence of these details. All the while, as day by day, year by year is recounted, one feels that the manifold of life did not slide over the novelist's shoulders like so many drops of rain over hard, impenetrable slate; but, that these drops—the hours, the weeks—fell upon fertile soil, that grew warm and furtive with each additional drop. Life sang to him and he yearned over its melody. Sometimes he grew pensive and disconsolate, just like the small-town Indiana boy that he was. At other times he merely listened but sternly set his breast against the oncoming tide of struggle, like a true Weltmensch.

E. G.
Freeman, 7 (March 21, 1923), 46.

"A Book About Myself," is concerned with but three years of the author's life, years of his early twenties when, as a newspaper-reporter, he roamed through Chicago, St. Louis, Pittsburgh, and New York. This is disappointing, for one of the chief interests of autobiography is that it enables the reader to follow the author's development to a more or less definite conclusion. During these years Mr. Dreiser does not appear to have grown very much. His circle of experience was enlarged, permitting him to reach a few axiomatic generalizations about life and a gradually clarifying knowledge of himself and his desires; but the latter he is only beginning to evolve when the book closes, and of his final expression of himself as a novelist there is no hint. From the bulk of the book, one is led to conclude that Mr. Dreiser regards the experiences of these years not only as important to himself but as unique; and one must wonder at a *naïveté* that, thirty years later, can so look upon the aspirations, despairs, and ecstasies that all talented and ambitious youth has in common. These moods are indulged with a seriousness too deep to be retrospective; they are, one feels, the moods of the author's entire life—the manifestations of an adolescence that has been prolonged into middle age. On the other hand, none of his novels has afforded Mr. Dreiser a better opportunity for his gift of portrayal and description. He writes here as always of what he has seen and felt, and, in the writing, vigour of reaction becomes vigour of expression.

Theodore Madowsky. "A Book About Myself." *Forum*, 69 (April 1923), 1472–1473.

"All ye who novelists would be"—does that leave anybody in America out?—"hearken!" For here is the stuff of which novelists are made. Not that Theodore Dreiser in his "A Book About Myself" tells step by step how he became preeminent in the profession of novel-writing (how could he when at the very end of the book he does not know what kind of job he is to get next?), but he tells what he saw, what happened to him, and how he reacted to these influences during a few of the formative years of his life, so that those who read may—run. Yes, run; for who would willingly suffer? And Dreiser certainly did suffer.

Perhaps it is an old story that every fine artist suffers; yet when it is continually being impressed on us through five hundred and two closely printed pages, we may finally be convinced. Possessed of a sensitive soul and an inquiring intellect, he could not help but be abashed by this world. It was not so much that there were "whole streets of degraded, dejected, miserable souls." What troubled him was the why of it. "Why didn't society do better by them? Why didn't they do better by themselves? Did God, who, as had been drummed into me up to that hour was all wise, all merciful, omnipresent and omnipotent make people so or did they themselves have something to do with it?" Ah, there's the rub.

You cannot shunt him off by accusing him of being a fool, a mope, an ascetic. Being human he desired worldly things very strongly and was willing to work hard to attain them. He admits there were moments when he was happy, but these moments were all so fleeting as to have vanished before one could drink of them to the deep. His deepest despair, moreover, is hardly ever caused by his own ill-fortune but by that of others. In Pittsburg he was greatly moved by the condition of the steel workers, which prompted him to make this astute observation: "There was constant palaver about the equality of opportunity which gave such men as these" —Carnegie, Frick, Phipps—"their chance, but I could not help speculating as to the lack of equality of opportunity these men created for others once their equality at the top had made them." Nor does he hold a much milder brief for the journalistic Jehovahs—"The Boy Grew Older," notwithstanding—for of Joseph Pulitzer, founder of the *World*, he writes: "The man, because of his vital, aggressive, restless, working mood, and his vaulting ambition to be all that there was to be of journalistic force in America, was making a veritable hell of his paper and the lives of those who worked for him."

In that, as well as in many other notions, we may be shocked. But Mr. Dreiser has tried to be honest and could not be concerned with whether he might upset us. Unlike the autobiography of a distinguished dramatic writer published recently, Dreiser does not take the attitude, "Well, now I am a great man, and if anything I did in my youth seems menial, you should remember it was necessary as a step to the heights." He is genuinely modest and so does not have to apologize for every incident he relates. He covers only five years of his life, from nineteen to twenty-four years of age, but he does it thoroughly and sincerely, and since, as Carl Van Doren said in a recent lecture, "It is really only from autobiography that you learn anything," it is impossible to see how anyone with any pretensions to a serious purpose could fail to wish to read this book.

John D. Barry. "Living This Life." Minneapolis *Tribune*, April 14, 1923.

In some ways it's a pity reviewers should be so irresponsible. They can say pretty much what they please without being called to account. However, on the whole, in manners they've improved. They're not nearly as savage as they used to be. But they are often incomptent and unfair. For instance, there are the notices of "A Book About Myself," by Theodore Dreiser. Before I read it those that I saw were discouraging. Some of the reviewers professed to be shocked at exposures so egotistical. Some gave the impression that there were revelations deplorable, of matters usually kept private, sex! They took a superior tone, sometimes patronizing as well.

Now that I've read the book I think I can see how incompetence and injustice worked among those reviewers. In some instances, I imagine, they began with a prejudice against Dreiser. Perhaps they thought the title was prejudicial. . . . Dreiser is fearless. He isn't afraid of saying "I" or "me" when he means "I" or "me." And the words don't stand for a great person, different from every one else in the world and played up as such. They might be "you" or "me." They stand for a human being that goes through an experience very like what millions of human beings are going through at this minute. To call the narrative egotistical is absurd. Egotistical is exactly what it is not. It has a quality that is universal, and this quality gives it its chief value.

There's a big difference in the way "I" and "me" can be used. Howells used to use them a good deal. His autobiographical writings are extraordinarily voluminous. But even in the days when it was the fashion to disparage Howells no one accused him of egotism. He wrote about himself because he was one he knew best and because in himself he reflected a multitudinous human experience. He wasn't merely himself. He was every man. And it's as every man that every writer of autobiography has his greatest contribution to offer the world.

In a very true sense "A Book About Myself" isn't merely about Theodore Dreiser. It's about youth, and it's about Chicago and St. Louis and New York, and it's about complicated human relations, and it's about poverty and longings and thwartings and dreams, and it's about despair and the bitterness of disappointment and the sense of futility. In other words, it's about life as most human beings who have gone into the middle years have known it and it's put down there with the insight and with the loyalty to truth of an artist.

As for the impropriety of the book, perhaps my sense of impropriety is blunted. Though I have carefully read every word, I haven't found what I should call impropriety anywhere. On the contrary, there's the seemingly unconscious revelation of a life much better than the lives led by the average youth thrown on his own resources and living for the most of the time away from home. I suppose that like the rest of us, Dreiser prides himself on having certain virtues. But I doubt if he prides himself on his youthful respect for the proprieties. Yet here we have the amazingly frank reflection of a mind intensely preoccupied with worth while interests and unaware of being controlled by certain homely principles of self-restraint and conderation for others.

However, frank as Dreiser is, I don't believe that, in spite of his impersonal attitude toward himself, he has told all the truth. I doubt if anyone ever does. I doubt if Rousseau did, staggering as he was in his candor. Nevertheless, Dreiser has told enough to make us see that, in spite of being a pretty good fellow, he was distinctly every man. He has very little mercy on himself. He is merciless even in describing his personal appearance. He tells things that most people would hesitate to tell about themselves the things we find discreditable in others and regrettable but excusable in ourselves. He isn't interested in excuses or in blaming. He's interested in what is. He shows how close scientist and artist can be to each other.

What to me is most remarkable about the book is that its material should be what a great many readers and writers, too, would consider commonplace. I can imagine many a writer looking back on that dreary youth and saying, "Hopeless stuff. Nothing there worth writing about." But everything there was worth writing about. What lay beneath the apparently commonplace surface was the fire of life, flaming high with youth.

Some people, of course, would find the incidents of newspaper work absorbing. And yet there used to be a tradition that stories about newspaper work had no appeal for the public. Dreiser makes them seem interesting because he makes them so real. He looks them straight in the face and writes about them as they present themselves to his imagination. He's never tempted to dress them up. He isn't concerned with mere effects. He finds effects enough wherever he looks. He's a realist who celebrates the marvel of reality, the splendor, the poetry, the drama.

"Dreiser's Notable Autobiography." San Francisco *Call*, May 5, 1923.

The author who gave the world Sister Carrie, Jennie Gerhardt, and other immortals has given us Theodore Dreiser.

Some five hundred pages there are in this new publication—"A Book About Myself"—by Theodore Dreiser. And at that, this volume reveals only one of the selves of Dreiser—the self that struggled through young manhood on Middle Western newspapers and went down to defeat in the first battle with the New York press. His other selves—Dreiser, the editor, and Dreiser, the novelist, are promised in further revelations.

Many men have professed to affirm the self in autobiography form. One can see them sitting at their desks saying this is the sort of man that I am in spite of what my enemies say of me and this true self will I reveal; this is the sort of man my children would like to think that I am; or this is the sort of man that my wife pretends to herself that I am and it's only fair to her to put over that image; this is sort of man that my friends would have me write about.

Dreiser writes without any concern of family, friends or bystanders. It is an autobiography that does not spare Dreiser nor any one else. It moves through the ugly places, the barren place, the ecstatic places, the dumb places, the anguished places in his life with no concern of the light in which it places him.

Squeamish persons will complain. But unless an autobiographer can be as impersonal as Dreiser in his personal revelations why enter the field of autobiography? . . .

Back of the grotesque, the humorous, the exciting incidents that crowded his life, one feels the struggling intensity with which Dreiser viewed life. He was never the debonnair reporter skimming the surface.

Nor was he the sort of determined realist bound by some strange, secret compact he had made with himself to find only the ugly, the sordid things of life.

He was what he was—the Dreiser who had come to manhood with certain possibilities. And he shows simply and relentlessly what life does to those possibilities and what he does with life—shows it through incidents and people who move through the autobiography with that lumbering sort of boldness which somehow holds the swift attention of the reader as the facile author never holds it.

Dreiser does not build a false facade to hide behind. He gives you himself as he finds himself. All the other people in the book are real people, not paper phantoms perforated along conventional lines.

Those who place Dreiser first among contemporary American novelists will rejoice in the realism of the autobiography. Those who insist on the romantic novel will find the autobiography as untouched by the romantic school of literature as the Dreiser novels. . . .

Edwin Seaver "Theodore Dreiser Himself." *Advance*, June 15, 1923, p.6.

The most interesting parts in Theodore Dreiser's "A Book About Myself" are those which do not concern him at all, or only incidentally, as one character in a scene. Personally I don't care whether Dreiser had a scrap with his sister in 1890 and so came to live apart from his family. I do care, though, to know something about that mad, feverish, cruel, scoundrelly, sentimental, commonplace world that was America in 1890 and after, and there is no one writing in this country today who can tell it better than Dreiser. As a newspaper reporter on a grand scale he is superb. As a great artist, a man who has lived much, thought much, presumably, and should therefore have much to give us, he is in no way extraordinary.

When Dreiser reflects he is a child. Or rather, without the spiritual innocence of a child, he is a half-baked cynic who has a tremendous appetite for life but whose stomach can not assimilate all that he devours. There are hundreds of newspaper men in this country to day, up to their eyes in the muck of what is called news, who have as broad an outlook on life as has Dreiser, as deep a vision. Keen, shrewd, gifted with a facility to write down whatever he saw, and without any ideas about what life ought to be or might be, he was bound to make a name for himself in an age which was too busy living to think much about life. No wonder H. L. Mecken, that prodigy of the commonplace who poses even today as a great critic among undeveloped minds, should have been the first to hail Dreiser as master!

Reading "A Book About Myself" it is easy to understand the mental and spiritual bankruptcy which America finds herself in today. This intense interest in every passing detail of life, with no thought to the power which pulls the strings, this constant search for facts, facts, facts, with an ever ready sneer at a possible truth behind all these facts, this rudder-less scramble for every chance happening in the name of the great god news, could bring nothing in the end but chaos. Dreiser tells in several places of friends of his who committed suicide, and expresses wonder that they should have done so when they were in a fair way to becoming successful. Yet that is the most natural thing to do in circumstances such as they found themselves in, for if you plunge headlong into the whirlpool of life and then happen to be flung up on the shore with yourself a moment, the whole game of life is bound to look like an unbearable mess. Unable to exist except in the herd, the only logical thing to do when the herd passes you by, is to blow out your brains.

All that activity, that intense thirst for accomplishing things, that mad scramble for success, to get somewhere in the world, which made America spread from coast to coast, in so short a span of years, is symbolized in Theodore Dreiser. He is the spiritual brother of P. T. Barnum, who announced that there was a sucker born every minute, and went ahead to fleece people on his theory. Dreiser is different only in the fact that he has the insight to realize that Barnum, too, was a sucker. Mankind is a pretty hopeless lot, in his opinion. Maybe it is, but we don't need artists to tell us what we already know and have experienced. Aren't artists supposed to be ahead of the rest of us, searching far a new truth, new beauty, carrying on whatever of mobility there is in mankind? Isn't that why common people look with such reverence upon great artists? Or am I am wrong about that?

Checklist of Additional Reviews

E. F. Edgett. Boston *Evening Transcript*, December 30, 1922, p. 4.

Edmund Lester Pearson. "New Books and Old." *Independent*, 110 (January 6, 1923), 25.

Joseph Wood Krutch. New York *Evening Post Literary Review*, January 20, 1923.

Catholic Review, March, 1923.

David Karsner. "Here and There and Everywhere." New York *Call*, March 20, 1923.

New York *Evening Post,* August 6, 1931.

New York *World Telegram,* August 12, 1931.

Further Reviews: Bibliographic Information Incomplete

Thomas F. Ford. "Mr. Dreiser Tells the World." Los Angeles *Times.*

Ames Kendrick. "Even the Poets Join Attack on Dreiser."

Notes

THE COLOR OF A GREAT CITY

THEODORE DREISER

Illustrations by
C. B. FALLS

BONI AND LIVERIGHT
PUBLISHERS :: :: NEW YORK

The Color of a Great City

"As the Uncommercial Traveler."
New York *Times Book Review*,
December 23, 1923,
p. 7.

There have been many attempts to catch the light and shade of the City of New York and to transfer it to the written page, as in this new book by Theodore Dreiser. It is a fascinating subject, this vast city, which in every way but governmental is the capital of the Western World. Its life is as colorful as the life of Bagdad in the famed, and largely legendary, days of Haroun al Raschid, and infinitely more varied. And if New York is not ruled by a tyrant who chops off the heads of his subjects without notice, or orders them sealed up in sacks and thrown into the river, there is a tyranny of the city itself, albeit exercised in a more subtle manner, which is none the less heavy, its sentences no less severe, or their execution slower.

No writer has as yet done justice to New York; probably none ever will. The field is too vast for any single mind to comprehend it in its entirety or with that critical discrimination which is necessary to recreate it as a living whole. O. Henry, despite the fact that his eyes were a bit dazzled by the sun of romance, will always remain as the most successful and best-beloved interpreter of that portion of Manhattan's life stream on which he focused his attention. And perhaps O. Henry's success was due in no small part to the fact that he adopted as his watchword what has become New York's best-known slogan—"Watch your step!"

Dreiser has not always watched his step, and the book is uneven. In places he has missed the color he sought for the reason that his eye was not trained to perceive the tints and shades of that locality, or that phase of Manhattan life. But these failures are few. For the most part the author walked familiar ground and interpreted what he saw with authenticity and emotional appeal. Like O. Henry, Dreiser came to New York from another part of the country, so that he was able to view the city's varied and frequently puzzling phenomena with the detachment of an outsider. And in another way, also, he was more than well qualified for the task of this sort of a book: Theodore Dreiser, before he turned novelist, had been a newspaper reporter for many years, having learned this trade in Chicago and St. Louis, and "The Color of a Great City" is written throughout in the easy, reportorial manner that makes for pleasure in reading.

It is impossible to record here the

many aspects of New York life on which Dreiser turns his penetrating glance. He ranges from a vanished seaside resort, namely, Manhattan Beach, in the days of the Oriental Hotel, to "Hell's Kitchen"; he writes vividly of the waterfront, of the pigeons in the parks, of the wonder of the ever-flowing rivers that embrace Manhattan Island; he catches the color and the laughter of "Little Italy"; he realizes the pathos of the Bowery Mission, and of the men and women who are ever looking for jobs, who strive valiantly for awhile, and then succumb eventually to the weight of the city—its unseen tyranny—perhaps to give their bodies over at last to the keeping of one of those same rivers. There are thirty chapters—thirty pictures—in the gallery of Dreiser's book, and offering sufficient variety to please any reader.

The keynote of the book is struck in the opening passage of the first chapter, which the author heads with the caption "The City of My Dreams."

> It was silent [he writes], the city of my dreams, marble and serene. It was an amazing city, so far-flung, so beautiful, so dead. . . . And then, after twenty years, here it stood, as amazing almost as my dreams, save that in the waking the flush of life was over it. It possessed the tang of contests and dreams and enthusiasms and delights and terrors and despairs. Through its ways and canyons and open spaces and underground passages were running, seething, sparkling, darkling, a mass of beings such as my dream city never knew.

And this is the charm of Dreiser's book—it was always the life of New York which interested this precocious young reporter from the West. But he did not merely view this life, he undertook, in a measure, to live it. "Hell's Kitchen," for instance, he was unable to accept as the sink of the world merely because it was generally so regarded by city editors, on the word of the police. Dreiser went to live in "Hell's Kitchen." Perhaps Dreiser was unfortunate in the time of year he chose for his sojourn; it may have been that the gangsters were tired of murder and had postponed their pastime for a season.

> But why they chose to dub it "Hell's Kitchen" I could never discover. It seemed to me a very ordinary slum neighborhood, poor and commonplace, and sharply edged by poverty. But just life and very human life at that.

There is one notable chapter in which the author turns from life to revel in color and action, a chapter in which he describes a fire among the tall buildings of Manhattan. But mostly he is interested in life. It may be that many readers—since the book is a picture and not a tract—will feel that the author concerns himself too much with the bread line, the unemployed, the pushcart peddlers, the frequenters of the park benches. But it is a book that makes excellent reading; and it is immensely humane. And the illustrations by C. B. Falls are excellent.

"The New Books." *Outlook*, 136 (January 9, 1924), 70.

New York City changes so rapidly that sketches dealing with its life a quarter of a century ago seem like ancient history. But to persons whose memory goes back so far, Mr. Dreiser's accounts of that old life are full of charm. They are written by a real lover of the city, though they seldom touch on the higher or more aesthetic aspects of the metropolis. The political boss, the Bowery, the bums, the water-front, the push-cart man, the police, the rowdies, the firemen—these are the subjects that interest Mr. Dreiser, and they are treated in a reminiscent style that is wholly attractive.

H.L. Mencken. "Mencken Becomes Reminiscent Over Dreiser's New York." Baltimore *Evening Sun*, January 12, 1924.

The New York that Dreiser deals with in this stately book (tall, blackbound, creamy paper; sketches in brown ink by C. B. Falls) is not the city of today, but that of two decades or more ago. In one of his chapters he speaks of himself somberly as a man of 32; he is now 54. New York, I fear, has changed a great deal more in those years than he has. Most of the color has gone out of its life. It is bigger than ever, and richer, and more debauched, but it is no longer rakish and picturesque. What has happened to it is what has happened to every other town in America; it has been standardized, regimented, ironed out. There is now no more difference between the Bowery and One Hundred and Twenty-fifth street than there is between Forty-fourth street and Forty-fifth. Hell's Kitchen is gone; Harlem is gone; the Five Points are gone. And with them have gone their peculiarly barbarous and charming fauna.

In his preface to his book Dreiser mourns this passing of all the heroes and villains of the old stock company. "Who recalls," he asks, "Steve Brodie, McGurks, Doyers street, or Chuck Connors?" Or Big Tim Sullivan? Or Little Tim of that ilk? Or Dry Dollar of the same? Or Michael J. Powers? Or Chief Croker, not the Tammany boss, but his nephew, the fire chief? Or Captain Schmittberger? Or Dr. Parkhurst? Or Monk Eastman? Even the theatrical district, once so gay with birds of brilliant plumage, is now dull with third-rate and anonymous men. Bim the Button Man has had no successor. Nor has Diamond Jim Brady. Nor has Wilson Mizner. Nor has Paul Armstrong. The Forty-second Street Country Club is now a drug store. Rogers' is closed forever. So is Sherry's. So is Delmonico's. The old theaters have new and undistinguished names. Charles Frohman is forgotten. And so, I fear, is Dreiser's brother, Paul, the peer of them all.

Prohibition has hurt New York more than it has hurt any other American city, save perhaps San Francisco. It is not that drinking has ceased there, or even appreciably diminished. Far from it, indeed: the old saloons are now all legging the boot, and there are few big restaurants whose head waiters cannot supply anything that is ordered. It is simply that the old innocent communal guzzling has been replaced by furtive solo guzzling—that the picturesque, amusing life of the old-time drinking places, East Side and West Side, has been stamped out.

There were saloons in New York that were more celebrated than any cathedral in the Western Hemisphere, and bartenders whose eminence compared to that of archbishops and admirals. They are all gone, alike from the Bowery and from Fourteenth street, from the region of Wall street and from that of the Rialto—and if they are not actually gone, then they are denaturized.

Where do the district leaders of today hold their courts? Are there, indeed, any district leaders left? If so, then they are as anonymous as the fire chiefs, the police captains and the theatrical managers. New York now goes to the movies, like Bucyrus, O., and Roanoke, Va. It has become Americanized.

Dreiser hints that the subways have had something to do with this change. They have broken up all the old neighborhoods. The people of Grand street are now but 10 minutes from Times Square and but half an hour from Columbia University. The New York that Dreiser describes is the New York of my own first memories. It was then a serious business to go down to Lüchow's or to Little Hungary. Now it is a matter of a few minutes from the uptown hotels.

But I forget: August Lüchow is dead and Little Hungary is closed. So are two-thirds of the old French and Italian *table d'hôte* joints: dinner with wine, 60 cents. So are the German *Bierstuben*. So are most of the Irish chop-houses, though Dinty Moore still holds on. So are the oyster-houses and the Beefsteak Johns. New York begins to eat in cafeterias. It has been made safe for Y. M. C. A. secretaries. That is, on the street. Behind the door—but that story I reserve for another day.

Dreiser, as everyone knows, is not much interested in gilded revelries. It is the life of humble folk that attracts him. Here he presents it in his patient, painstaking manner, as it was at the turn of the century. It is not a very exciting book, but there is in it something of the glamor and something of the poetry of the New York that is no more.

David Karsner. "Dreiser's Tableaux." New York *Tribune, Magazine and Book Section,* January 27, 1924, p. 19.

"If I were a painter one of the first things I would paint would be one or another of the great railroad yards that abound in every city, those in New York and Chicago being as interesting as any. Only I fear that my brush would never rest with one portrait."

In this way Dreiser achieves the opening of his sketch on "The Car Yard," and it has been chosen for the opening of this review because of the reviewer's wonderment that a man like Dreiser (as if there are any like him) should express a half wish that he were a painter after accomplishing a panoramic canvas of New York in thirty-eight sketches. I doubt if New York has ever been done this way by a writer. Some of our painters have captured a facet here and there of this swirling city and many writers now and then have acquainted Palm Beach and the residents of our hinterland with the cliff dwellers of the Bronx and the pushcart men of Rivington Street. But the throb of this town, the push and the go of it, its masks and its mush, its sheer beauty and its unforgettable ugliness, its romance and its tawdry compromise between the real and the ideal—the bruised and battered heart of this town which never misses a beat for those who live on its fat, or for those who drink its blood, or for those whose sense of inner sight and sound is dimmed and dulled by the crashing grind of their own lives —I say that heart and the throb of it has rarely been registered in the deep tones of grays and glints that Dreiser presents.

This book will scarcely interest those who desire a guide manual of "interesting places." Such a directory used to be sold down on Park Row for 10 cents. Maybe the fakers are selling them now for 15 or 20 cents because, of course, interest in a place usually increases. Moreover, those who are not acquainted with New York might never locate the places and scenes Dreiser describes. They are not always visual. They are envisioned. Their mystery, romance, song and tears are felt with a sense that a person either has or has not, but may not be imparted. Probably half, certainly a third, of New York's six millions could walk over the Brooklyn Bridge in the dusking twilight from Manhattan's side and never turn their heads to glimpse the wonder of the skyline dotted with diamonds, whose luster lends beauty to those majestic commercial cathedrals. There are a few others, such as Dreiser, who see not only the obviously beautiful, but who may stand for hours looking at a barrel house, or who will capture the whole revelation of a sooty little tug plying up the East River past those gray, forbidding buildings standing on what is known as Welfare Island.

Dreiser gathered these impressions of New York—at least many of them in his very early years of residence here—some of them during that period when he failed to make good as a reporter for that noble institution which seeks to impart the knowledge of journalism to gifted young men through the processes of higher learning on Morningside Heights. Another young man who saw life with his inner eyes likewise failed in the more practical test of reporting faithfully that which happened instead of turning in to his city editor a brilliant sketch on the significance of the event that might have happened. One thinks of Stephen Crane. Other names occur. Richard Harding Davis, David Graham Phillips and Frank Ward O'Malley were counted as ideal reporters, in that they did not diffuse what was in their minds with what was going on in the church, the political meeting, the prize-fight ring or the funeral parlor. There used to be a newspaper in Chicago whose editors would not permit their reporters to write what is called a straight-away news story. It had to have a "feature" or it didn't get in. I recall one of its subordinate editors who had a rasping voice and a poetic eye lash a cub reporter who had turned in a story freighted with statistics accepted as a rule by meticulous minds as irrefragible facts. The reporter could not comprehend that he was expected to write, say, a coal production report after the manner of De Maupassant as against a convincing anlysis that might earn him a bonus from Mr. Babson's bureau. I have often wondered if there are not, after all the statisticians are through and their tables carefully burned, only two facts in the world—male and female, and that all else that is and appears to be is nothing more than argumentative paraphernalia relating to and issuing from those two facts.

Small wonder that Dreiser and Crane went speedily into fiction without graduating from those austere preparatory schools whose pupils and faculty (reporters and editors) solemnly estimate the world each drifting hour on the basis of a coroner's verdict or a statesman's pledge. There is nothing as sure as that in "The Color of a Great City." . . .

Many of these sketches which, as Dreiser states, have accumulated in his workroom these last score of years or so, were first printed, some of them, in various publications. They seem to have been written with Dreiser's sheer joy of writing, and all of them are authentic and bear the impress of a man alive and responsive to the cacophonies of his swirling city. It is true that by far the majority of them were gleaned from those dark and drab passages in our labyrinthine life, but a great deal of Dreiser's writing is the product of our darksome side. Have any seen "a glad book" of his? For this much there is everything in "The Color of a Great City" to please the Dreiserians and nothing to annoy the Watch and Ward Society, nothing even to satisfy the chemical curiosity of those who linger over "purple patches" in literature and who stand a quarter of an hour of a winter's night before the window of a "novelty" store exhibiting 50-cent nudes for people who could never understand the stark beauty and import of Walt Whitman's "Children of Adam" poems.

"Recent Books in Brief Review." *Bookman*, 59 (May 1924), 353.

Theodore Dreiser's "The Color of a Great City" is a realist's picture book of New York in the first and second decades of this century. Sombre in tone and sometimes labored as to style, the thirty eight sketches that comprise the volume form a pattern of despair that belies its title. Of the mad, clashing, ever whirling spectrum of the city there is little here. Pessimism, like the darkened eye of the camera, has silhouetted these figures against a doomsday sky: sandwich men and pushcart pedlers, bums and roustabouts of the waterfront, the now vanished bread line and the old style ward boss, stunted child laborers in the slums and the stiletto-marked amours of Little Italy. In his introductory chapter, Dreiser describes these things as of the very substance of the city he knew in his early adventurings in it. Glimpses of a crumbling substratum of hopelessness that served O. Henry for copy spell out for him the whole riddle of existence—youth stripped of its illusions and old age barren of comfort. But underneath this intent and characteristic preoccupation with the dull, monotonous lives of drab people smolders a desire to lay hold on beauty. And it is this desire, breaking into occasional exquisite flame, that brings his latest book up to and above the level of Dreiser's best work. Things seen before as through a glass darkly are suddenly bathed in light. The aching loveliness of pigeons in flight, the eternal freshness of the universe, the city he dreamed of before he knew its sordidness—"so far-flung, so beautiful, so dead"—even the inscrutable wisdom that moves behind the Bowery Mission: these mark a realist's progress beyond the realms of personal bitterness and the dreary, humorless saga of the underdog.

R.B.
"Mr. Dreiser at Home." *Christian Science Monitor*, May 24, 1924, p. 8.

Mr. Dreiser has assembled 30 or 40 sketches or impressions—both terms are here to be taken for serious and noteworthy contribution to art and literature—of people and places in New York between 1894 and 1914 or 1915. The volume has also its interest in showing how the writer found material for his novels.

Throughout the book Mr. Dreiser's sense of the significant is an important asset. Take, for example, the little seamstress "who occupied a tiny hall-bedroom in a side-street rooming house, cooked her meals on a small alcohol stove set on a bureau, and who had about space enough outside of this to take three good steps either way."

" 'I would rather live in my hall-bedroom in New York than in any 15-room house in the country that I ever saw,' she commented once, and her poor little colorless eyes held more of sparkle and snap than I ever saw there, before or after. . . . The color and noise and splendor of the city as a spectacle was sufficient to pay her for all her ills."

She was part and parcel of the thing that interested Mr. Dreiser in the great city—"the sharp, and at the same time immense, contrast it showed between the dull and the shrewd, the strong and the weak, the rich and the poor, the wise and the ignorant."

Or again, the sandwich man on whom Mr. Dreiser once tried an experiment to determine how far another observer was right in thinking that sandwich men are without emotions. "I stopped before the first old wizened loiterer I met, his sign hanging like a cross from his gaunt shoulder, and before his unsuspecting eyes lifted the half-dollar. Who could be offering him a half-dollar? His eyes seemed indifferently to ask at first. Then a perfect eagle's gleam flashed into them, old and dull as they were, and a claw-like hand reached for it. No thanks, no acknowledgement, no polite recognition—just grim realization to get it. What possibilities that half-dollar seemed to hold to that indifferent, unimaginative mind at that moment! What it suggested, apparently, of possible comfort! Why? there, because life meant nothing? Not in that case, surely. A whole epic of failure and desire was written in that gleam—and we speak of them as emotionless."

A book, in short, that presents vividly the New York that Mr. Dreiser explored, and sometimes lived in, "fascinated by the problem of life itself, the riddle of its origin, the difficulties attending its maintenance." The reader, as the chapters accumulate, may well find himself very solemnly contemplating this same puzzle. Tragedy and comedy, grim realism and beauty in unexpected places, yet the book, in its composite effect, is not pessimistic.

Thomas F. Ford. "Old New York's Seamy Side." Los Angeles *Times*, June 15, 1924.

Is Theodore Dreiser inherently a sentimentalist, masking his weakness in a pose of cynicism, or is his cynical attitude toward life the result of honest doubt? Those familiar with Dreiser's work will, I am sure, upon reading this book, admit that this is a pertinent question.

In his foreword Mr. Dreiser says: "My only excuse for offering these very brief sketches of the city of New York as it was between 1900 and 1914 or '15 or thereabouts, is that they are the very substance of the city as I knew it in my early adventuring in it." In this series the author waxes sentimental, satirical, ironical, but mostly it seems to me, sentimental.

The sketches deal in the main with the submerged portion of New York. This probably explains their general trend. In these sketches Mr. Dreiser has caught every fugitive glint of light and every passing shadow playing about that vast conglomeration of heterogenous humanity living on the East Side of New York. We are given a picture of its comings and goings, its births and deaths, its weddings and holiday feasts, its loves and hates, triumphs and tragedies.

Here in his picture of New York in the sketch entitled, "The City of My Dreams:" "And have I not felt the glamour of it myself? And do I not still? Broadway, at Forty-second street, on those self-same spring evenings when the city is crowded with an idle, sightseeing cloud of westerners; when the doors of all the shops are open, the windows of nearly all the restaurants wide to the gaze of the idlest passer-by. Here is the great city and it is lush and dreamy. A May or June moon will hang like a burnished silver disc between the high walls aloft. A hundred, a thousand electric signs will blink and wink. And the floods of citizens and visitors in summer clothes and with gay hats; the street cars jouncing their endless carloads on indifferent errands; the taxis and private cars fluttering about like jeweled flies. The very gasoline contributes a distinct perfume. Life bubbles, sparkles; chatters gay, incoherent stuff. Such is Broadway."

Is this picture he gives us of a "bum," for instance, a real picture, or is it Mr. Dreiser's notion of what he himself would be, were he reduced to the social status of the genus he describes? Did Mr. Dreiser's contact with bums enable him to penetrate the inner being of the class of which the nondescript described is typical, or is Mr. Dreiser merely a clever but unscrupulous reporter, filling a difficult assignment and in the absence of tangible facts, "faking"—that is employing his imagination—or is he unconsciously merely giving us his subconscious reactions, honestly believing them to be well documented and authentic facts? Sentimentalists, under stress of their emotions, do that.

When Mencken reads the sketch entitled "The City of My Dreams," or "The Track Walker," I'd forego a shot of Old Taylor for a glimpse of his face or to hear a few of his verbal explosions. Are these the outpouring of a cynic soul? Well, hardly. Mr. Babbitt never rose to loftier or more incoherent heights of emotion in his contemplation of the glory of "Floral Heights" in his beloved city of Zenith. No social Messiah of the nineteen hundreds ever waxed more eloquent or sentimental over the woes and the wrongs of the lowly worker than does Mr. Dreiser. He fairly hurls upon the unprotected head of that nebulous thing called society a searing stream of vitriolic denunciation for its neglect of one who, though performing a great and useful service, is paid but a scant 35 cents per hour.

Now, in much that Mr. Dreiser presents here there is vast truth and great beauty—mankind's nobility, shown so clearly in the sketch entitled "Hell's Kitchen," but it is all so foreign to Mr. Dreiser's cynical attitude that one can not help but wonder.

There is little artistic detachment in these sketches, written mostly for newspapers, but there is a wealth of passionate protest, biting satire, at times an almost satanic irony. But always the question arises, "Is Dreiser a sentimentalist or a cynic?"

Austin [Tex.] *Statesman*, June 21, 1924.

In "The Color of a Great City" Mr. Dreiser has succeeded admirably, so far as an outsider is competent to judge, in reconstructing the New York of the early years of this century. This is not a collection of premature jottings brought out and published after the fame of later writings has made them salable; rather it is work in which experience and memory have revived the freshness and vitality of early observation. . . .

Many of the sketches are essays in form, discussions of such topics as "Bums," "On Being Poor," "Characters," and the like. Others are descriptive, vivid pictures of "The Fire," "The Car Yard," "The Bread Line," "Christmas in the Tenements," and of such less obvious things as the awakening of the city and its appearance at 6 o'clock in the evening. There are a few bits of narrative, of which "The Log of a Harbor Pilot," "The Michael J. Powers Association," and "Hell's Kitchen" are most prominent. Any classification of the sketches must be suggestive rather than definite, for there is much overlapping. The narratives, for example, abound in descriptive and reflective passages which add both beauty and interest.

The New York that Mr. Dreiser presents in this book is more somber than we generally conceive the metropolis to be. That is due, in part, to the fact that conditions are different, if not better, than they were in the time of which he is writing. There is besides, in this work of Mr. Dreiser's a deep sympathy for those who represent the seamy side of life. He suffers a genuine, not an assumed or professed, grief at the lot of the men who compose the bread line or sleep in "flop houses." This may be accounted for by the fact that, at the time of which he writes, Mr. Dreiser himself was making the acquaintance of poverty, so that he was able to share more completely the feelings of the failures who form such an important though usually inarticulate part of the city's population. It is in the accurate and poignant portrayals of those individuals who slink through New York streets like the human driftwood they are, that "The Color of a Great City" reveals its highest accomplishment and its chief value.

Abraham Resika, "Once Over." 7, *Liberator* (July 1924), 31.

It was a young Dreiser who wrote the series of sketches, character studies and mood impressions, gathered between the covers of this book. But it was a Dreiser with an ear delicately attuned for the song of the city, an eye expressive to its many varied colors, and a youthful soul, leaping and buoyant in its reactions to the poetry and music and tragedy found everywhere within a great city.

These sketches, being short in structure and written in an intimate style, do not possess that ponderousness so commonly associated with Dreiser's longer novels. But, in common with his novels, they lack in that one quality so essential to universal greatness in an author. There is no humor in Dreiser's studies.

W. O. Babb. "New York's Color." Dallas *News,* July 26, 1924.

"The Color of a Great City," by Theodore Dreiser, contains a series of more or less related sketches of New York, some of them having been written ten to fifteen years ago and published in a New York newspaper. The sketches possess a subjective realism and the lyrical beauty and colorful imagery of some of Amy Lowell's poetry. The scenes that Dreiser depicts are those of the tenement district and the wharfs, the bread line, the bums in the parks, the immigrants, and the home of the seamen who are too old to go to sea. Not once does he invade the habitat of the wealthy and luxurious on Fifth avenue and Wall street.

The scenes are both whimiscal and ironical, and deftly interpreted. He paints the settings and tells the stories with the skill of an artist, and with the tractability of a realist who has grown old. He is the observer who is tired of being the critic. It is from these scenes, he admits, that he has drawn many of the characters portrayed in his novels. In writing these sketches Dreiser is as a child lying flat on its back in the sand and looking at the sky and saying: "The sky is blue like a violet, and the clouds are soft like a kitten's fur."

Yet, what he has written is of the New York of fifteen years ago, and would scarcely be recognized now.

Betty Adler. "Book Reviews." Davenport [Iowa] *Times,* July 26, 1924.

A distinctive contribution to our best American literature is Theodore Dreiser's new book, "The Color of a Great City." In this he enriches the portrait gallery of our memories of Little Old New York. They are pictures from the kaleidoscope of life in the metropolis gleaned during the last decade of the last century and the first decade of this The New York of from 1890 to 1914 according to the author, has disap peared. The East Side and the Bowery of those days, crowded areas of poverty and squalor, contrasted with the brilliancy, the splendor of Fifth avenue of that period, are no more. Then it was he came to New York, a young writer, keen for the adventure of living, and the city left these pictures indelibly etched into his mind. In them you will find studies that recall those that Balzac wrote of Paris, so keen, so analytic, so moving has he made these sidelights on bygone days, that were not without romance, often piquant and picturesque, as they appeared to him in the impressionable years when he was struggling for recognition.

No matter how well you may think you know New York of that period, you will find in these sketches an amazingly interesting retrospect. No matter how many sandwich men you have met on Broadway it is probable you never saw this bit of human wreckage from the angle of this author, who is today counted among America's foremost writers. He takes us to the depths of the city's poor and forsaken, to where the breadline waits in helpless patience for the morning loaf; he shows us bums and pushcart characters, the sweatshop worker and the tenement's worst and yet there is nothing morbid about it. For Dreiser believes that the direst poverty, the most-to-be-pitied poverty is poverty of mind; this he calls "the true misery, the freezing degradation of life." And so wedged in between studies in somber drabs there is such a chapter as "The Flight of Pigeons" as they "rest upon the bosom of a breeze or run down its curving surface in long flights."

To those of us from the Hinterland to whom New York means bright lights, the theatres, Broadway, the Fifth avenue shops this book opens another world. . . .

As you read on you enjoy Dreiser's point of view. You see with him the colonies of foreigners from many countries who "add rich, dark, colorful threads to the rug or tapestry that is New York," and the masses from the surrounding territory as they trickle cityward when the metropolis awakes every morning. He causes you to understand the satisfaction of the ragged old snow shoveler on clutching his $1.75 for a day's hard labor shoveling snow from the city's streets; you sense the discontent of the old tars housed magnificently in the Sailors' Snug Harbor, chafing at the monotony, irritable at the institutional routine; he makes you see Hell's Kitchen, the toughest part of the city a quarter of a century ago, and he even acquaints one intimately with the feuds of Little Italy, from the heart side of the triangle love affairs instead of from the police blotter.

In his limpid, clear English, with keen, incisive contrasts he pictures the waterfront life, the East Side boss, an old box car in the car yards. He gives an illuminating etching of the "Track Walker," the man who walks the tracks examining bolts that millions may ride in safety, and who, for a beggarly pittance, hourly takes his life in his hands. "The day's work is the thing" he tells us in the sketch entitled "Six O'Clock," when he shows the city's workers laying down their tasks for the day. "At six o'clock the rank and file are through . . . it is for them that the six o'clock whistle blows . . . it is for them that the evening lamps are lit in millions of homes."

The vanished glories of Manhattan beach, that one time rival to fairyland, is a colorful chapter. The lodging house, and the Bowery mission are graphically pictured as is the man on the park bench, together with the hundreds awaiting before dawn the early edition of a morning paper to scan the ads for a job. And then, if you want to feel your heartstrings vibrate, read his "Christmas in the Tenements." . . .

Yet not all dark or tragic are these portraits. "Whence The Son" has to do with the authors, singers and publishers of song hits of those days and the ups and downs of the ballad writer and the variety star.

If you want to know old New York as you never could otherwise, you will read "The Color of a Great City." The book is beautifully illustrated by C. B. Falls who has caught the atmosphere of the times so vividly portrayed in the text.

Checklist of Additional Reviews

S. L. C. Boston *Evening Transcript,* January 9, 1924.

R. L. Burgese. San Jose [Cal.] *Evening News,* March 26, 1924.

Arthur Bartlett Maurice. "The Splendid Quest for Bohemia." *Literary Digest International Book Review,* April, 1924, pp. 378, 380.

Further Reviews: Bibliographic Information Incomplete

Terre Haute *Tribune* [Quotes Fanny Butcher's review in Chicago *Tribune*].

Leonard Stallings. "The First Reader: An Anglophile's Confession."

Stanley E. Babb. "Book News and Book Reviews." Galveston *Daily News.*

Notes

AN AMERICAN TRAGEDY

BY

THEODORE DREISER

VOLUME ONE

NEW YORK
BONI AND LIVERIGHT
MCMXXV

An American Tragedy

Mary Rennels
"Be Normal."
Cleveland *Topics*,
January 2, 1926.

Knowing the old wag that resolutions are made to be broken, nevertheless I have gone ahead and solemnly resolved never to commit murder.

This decision is not based on reading the crime stories in our daily journals,—but it arises from a saturation in the latest literature of the hour, "An American Tragedy" by Theodore Dreiser.

Much comment has been passed here and there about this latest work from the pen of Dreiser,—but I wonder how many have read word by word, the two volumes that comprise it? I, for one, might have skimmed the surface and given a snap opinion, were it not for the cold that forced me into the easy chair and turned me to Dreiser for forgetfulness and surcease. Two volumes are nothing to start at for an hour's pastime, —you will admit,—but for a whole day —bliss!

The first volume has to do with the adolescence of Clyde Griffiths whose parents are street singers and mission owners,—because they are fevered with the word of God and find in the occupation a haphazard sort of living. Clyde resents singing in the streets and longs for the broadminded existence of boys with wealth and experience. There is a recording of sordid happenings to a daughter in the family and the awakening in Clyde the knowledge of the dangers of sex,—not to mention its lures.

He finally becomes a bellhop in a hotel in Kansas City. And in this section of the work, Dreiser has done an excellent piece of writing, his observations of the actions and attitudes of travelers, the bellhop's estimate of the characters by the amount of the tip or the manner in which they offer it; their delight in the clandestine affairs arranged by couples seeking oblivion in the bustle of a large hotel. It is like having your own thoughts laid bare, those thoughts that are true but unkind and which are the knowledge that eventually destroys one's pleasure in life as well as one's ability to play or enjoy.

As the first volume closed I had about decided that the great American tragedy was sex. The book was heavy with it but not given over to it entirely as I realized in retrospect. As I got on to the second book I could see there was no hope for Clyde. He was a boy who envied, desired and received many times, at the hand of Chance,—but he lacked a sense of direction, was like water coursing through the grass of life.

Finally, he became involved with one of his workers and Dreiser has painted in detail the actions and reactions of this affair. Then the boy, with no moral stamina to begin with, but with a handsome face and appealing air, is picked up by a flighty society girl and has his head turned with the idea of riches,—how he could engage her in marriage and reach the pinnacle of his desires.

But Clyde has no finesse. He had become too involved with the little factory girl to make a graceful exit and his desire for the wealthy girl destroyed his ability to think sanely on the subject.

He contemplated murdering his sweetheart because of a suggestion given him by a newspaper account of an unexplained drowning of a couple on a lonely lake. He schemed and planned and finally made up his mind to do the dire deed.

What happened to this mental and moral coward is for the reader to find out. However, to Theodore Dreiser I owe my resolution,—never to commit murder and to let sex have its place with the rest of the normal things of life.

Stuart Sherman. "Mr. Dreiser in Tragic Realism." New York *Herald Tribune Books,* January 3, 1926, pp. 1–3.

What is comedy?

A selection of truths about the follies of 1925.

What is tragedy?

The whole truth about the follies of 1925. That is the subject of this book.

Many of the younger novelists in these whirling days speak of Theodore Dreiser reverently, yet retrospectively—much as free verse writers ten years ago used to speak of Whitman. Youngsters who think to shelve him with the retiring title of "the grand old man of realism" reckon without his large, stolid, literary ambition, which, to my mind, is his most salient and admirable moral characteristic. As a novelist he has been silent these ten years. Yes, but with a brooding and pregnant silence! In silence and isolation he has been industriously harvesting, like some old bear of the mountains cleaning up a great thicket of blackberries. And now with his familiar huge plantigrade tread he comes lumbering down the trail with a massive 800-page American tragedy which makes the performances of most of his rivals and successors look like capering accomplishments of rabbits and squirrels.

I shall not quarrel with any one who contends that "An American Tragedy" is the worst written great novel in the world. There are few forms of bad writing which it does not copiously illustrate. Every horror which the schoolmarm teaches the fourth-grade pupil to avoid the "Father of Modern American Realism" riots in: "illy-dressed," "eventuate," "demeaned," in the sense of degraded; "enthused," "different to," "emasculate structure" of an anemic young girl, "via marriage," "via her determination," "the mentating section of her brain," an "ideational lake," scraps of all technical jargons, all varieties of journalese, French tags, queer coinages, and long wallflower words of Greek and Latin origin, serving purely decorative purposes.

Nor are these the most serious defects of Mr. Dreiser's style. There are chapters in which he is slower and more difficult than Proust. In dialogue and exciting narrative passages he often achieves simplicity and fair speed. But the moment he begins to "psychologize" he flounders in a morass of parenthetical and concessive clauses, slovenly beyond belief with repetitions, and infuriatingly clogged with "connective tissue"—"At the same time," "Also that despite," "And although, because of it," "And although, according to," "And in spite of the fact that"—till one is ready to yell with the torture of it.

And yet a most impressive novel. One has to take it seriously, if one takes it at all. Somehow—astonishing to relate—I feel as if this book had been very expressly left on my critical doorstep. I am not at liberty to think that Mr. Dreiser wrote it to please me. But in more than one way it does please and encourage me. It cheers me especially by demonstrating that a novelist need not stop growing at forty-four and work thenceforward on the formula which he adopted at thirty. Mr. Dreiser is taller and broader than when he wrote "The 'Genius.'" This new book marks a long stride toward a genuine and adequate realism. In order to indicate clearly the direction of his development I must briefly review his position up to 1915.

From "Sister Carrie," 1900, to "The 'Genius,'" 1915, Mr. Dreiser wrote fiction from outside American society, looking in. There were both advantages and disadvantages in that position. At his point of view, he was almost completely insensible to the force and validity of multitudinous complex powers which constantly operate within the social structure. He was incapable of understanding, for example, that etiquette has as much tensile strength as Bessemer steel. In compensation, he was able to observe the operation of other large powers of which the insiders are often unconscious, as they are of the diurnal and annual movements of the earth. He began his literary career with an overwhelming impression of what the sun, the moon, gravitation and a Cave Man ancestry were doing to him and to the captive animals inside the flimsy cage called civilization. The intensity of his vision of natural forces blotted out, for him, or reduced to insignificance, human efforts to introduce art and design among the gigantic conflicts of nature.

Born in a Mid-Western German Catholic family, Mr. Dreiser had accepted, he tells us, till he was well on in his adolescense a conventional account of society and a religious picture of the universe. Then came awakening experience with numerous girls of a sort, with numerous newspapers of a sort, politicians of a sort, captains of industry of a sort, and one thing and another—including browsing in Haeckel, Darwin, Spencer, etc. In consequence of this experience, with which he was quite unequipped to deal critically, he rushed with journalistic speed and violence to the conclusion there was nothing solid or real in this religious, legal and conventional account of the world and the societies of men. From end to end it was a romantic fiction, such as he himself was accustomed to fabricate by way of a news story for unscrupulous editors. Or it was merely a dull sham, maintained by hypocrites with smug faces and starched shirtfronts.

The real world, he concluded, after considerable introspection and reportorial looking in at the windows of several cities—the real world was composed of money-hungry and sex-hungry males and females, who, so far as the heat of their blood supported them, seized what they wanted and ran off with it, or rushed upon one another in carnal rages under the impulse of forces which they were helpless to resist—the devil taking the hindmost.

The only laws which enforced themselves in this real world were biological, physical and chemical. Accordingly, these became the only laws which commanded his respect. Whoever conformed or attempted to conform to a religious or moral "code" he was inclined to rate as a coward, a fool, or a "ragbag moralistic ass." He embraced "realism"; it offered an escape from the inferiority of a class subjugated by its morality. The successful, enviable, admirable denizens of the real world, he opined, were the Cowperwoods and the Witlas—as long as their luck lasted. The truly "virtuous," he held, were those whom nature had made strong and ruthless in the eternal struggle for the fierce pleasures and the unconscious biological ends of the animal creation.

Ten years ago, in an article subsequently included in "On Contemporary Literature," I carefully examined Mr. Dreiser's work up to and including "The 'Genius.' " It appeared to me then that he was the outstanding representative in American fiction of a point of view which I then considered, and still consider, tragic, disastrous. It was easy to show that the informing spirit of his work was naturalism rawly conceived—the crude "jungle" philosophy which I have just outlined. I thought the logical issue of such philosophy was tragedy—such tragedy as the nations of Europe were then staging in the name of "realistic" politics. It struck me that this philosophy was nowhere near so realistic as its advocates tried to make it out. It seemed to me inadequate—inadequate as a guide to civilized conduct, inadequate as an explanation of the behavior of men and women when they were civil. I suggested that a more adequate designation for it would be "barbaric naturalism."

There was, I say, no difficulty in showing the pervasive presence of it in Mr. Dreiser's novels. Up to that time he had not attempted to imitate the artful and deceptive "objectivity" and "impersonality" of the Flaubertain technique. He was a propagandist in the open, and very much bent on letting his readers know what he was driving at. His novels were elaborate documentations of a preconceived thesis. He was not pursuing truth but browbeating it into the service of a crude theory. His naïve naturalism shaped his plot and colored his characterization. But it also protruded defiantly above the surface of his narratives. It was explicit in little dissertations which a reader blind to its presence elsewhere could not fail to plump against.

In the decade since "The 'Genius,' " Mr. Dreiser has been observing, meditating and revising his views of American society, the nature of reality and the nature of realistic fiction. He has put forth several plays, two books of observation—"A Hoosier Holiday" and "The Color of a Great City"—a collection of moral ruminations in "Hey Rub-A-Dub-Dub" and a highly illuminating autobiographical work, "A Book About Myself," 1922.

This piece of autobiography is as valuable to the student of Mr. Dreiser as "A Story Teller's Story" is to the student of Mr. Anderson. It substantiates the impression which one receives from the novels. It lays before us the elementary psychological stuff out of which Mr.

Dreiser has molded his heroes and his heroines as well. Comparison of the autobiography with the fiction indicates, I think, that this author has little power of penetrating antipathetic types. He specializes in the primary instincts. But he understands himself pretty well and he constructs his men and women out of parcels of himself.

In his years as a newspaper reporter, between 1890 and 1894, he developed, if we may believe him, from an unlicked bear cub, an untrained, inexperienced, formless and hungry youth, into an impecunious Don Juan, sentimental, inflammable, vain and greedy for the luxuries which insulted his poverty—in the street, in the hotel lobby, in the ornate barroom; the flash of studs and stickpins, the rustle of silk, the shine of patent leather shoes, the distinction of tailor-made coats, the glitter of glass and the rich harmony of potted palms and mahogany.

In "An American Tragedy" Mr. Dreiser presents the life history of much such another youth—a youth, however, who never got past the passion for girls and stickpins to the larger and more engrossing passion for understanding how he came to be what he was, and why he did what he did.

I think this story must have originated in the "tragedy" itself. I conceive that Mr. Dreiser began with the tragic fact and worked backward, with no thesis whatever, with no ulterior purpose beyond the complete uncovering of all the intricate network of causes which led to the event.

Mr. Dreiser has either renounced or effectually suppressed the naïve naturalism of his previous novels. There are no interspersed philosophical dissertations here. There is no special pleading, no coloring of the news, no studied continuous aspersion of the customs and habits of men in civil or religious societies from the untenable point of view of "barbaric naturalism."

No; Mr. Dreiser has changed both his method and his point of view. He has withdrawn to a position of far more complete artistic "detachment." He gives me now for the first time an impression of "impersonality," "objectivity," "impartiality." He appears to me now for the first time in his fiction to be seeking sincerely and pretty successfully to tell the truth, all the relevant truth and nothing but the truth—and with such proportion and emphasis that every interest involved shall feel itself adequately represented.

Clyde Griffiths is the "hero." He is the son of itinerant evangelists who sing and march and pray in the streets of Kansas City. Clyde is ashamed of his parents, of their piety, and their poverty, and of the dreariness of life in the Bethel Independent Mission where they dwell. They have exchanged animality for hymn books and a spirituality so thin that it is a dubious bargain. Christian nurture has not sunk in. Enviously he looks upon the advantages enjoyed by unconsecrated society: "Oh, the fine clothes, the handsome homes, the watches, rings, pins, that some boys sported; the dandies many youths of his years already were! Some parents of boys of his years actually gave them cars of their own to ride in. They were to be seen upon the principal streets of Kansas City flitting to and fro like flies. And pretty girls with them. And he had nothing. And he never had had."

Clyde gets a job, first as a soda fountain clerk in a drug store, and then as a bellboy in the Green-Davison Hotel. The first book of this novel, running to 148 pages, might be called "A Bellboy's

Romance"; and there Mr. Dreiser skirts one of the great possibilities of fiction: the corruption of the lower classes by the upper classes. Clyde is a selfish, vain, greedy little beast, and quickly learns to lie to his mother about his wages, to dress with some "elegance," to drink, to feast and to play with girls of about his sort. His sister "gets into trouble." His mother comes to him for pecuniary help. He wants his money to buy his girl a fur coat. But, becoming involved in a serious and disgraceful automobile accident, he evades all his problems by running away from them. The whelp is selfish and a coward to the marrow of his bones.

After an interim of wandering and of rehabilitation as a bellboy in the Union League Club of Chicago Clyde makes a fresh start in the cotton mills of a prosperous uncle in Lycurgus, New York. Here his ignorant amorousness soon gets him deeply involved with a hitherto respectable girl employed in his department. If you will compare Mr. Dreiser's romantic glozing of Jennie Gerhardt's predicament with his exhaustive and astoundingly intelligent study of the shame and misery and torment of Roberta Alden in being pregnant, penniless, without a husband, and dependent on a resourceless sneak, you will readily recognize that Mr. Dreiser's ability to see all the elements in a situation has grown enormously since he published that earlier sentimental tale.

While surreptitiously carrying on this affair Clyde's snobbishness and his lust for luxurious living lead to an attachment in the "higher circles" of Lycurgus society. Mr. Dreiser's women generally have no individuality beyond their physique, their softness, and their clothes. If he has met with a feminine intelligence, he has made no boast of the encounter. This girl of the upper circles, Sondra, has impressed me mainly, as she did Clyde, by a tailored suit which followed her form exactly and which was enhanced by a small dark leather hat, pulled fetchingly low over her eyes. In addition, there was a leather "belt" of the same color around her neck. Note also that by a leather leash she led a French bull. To Clyde, "youth and beauty in such a station as this represented the ultimate triumph of the female." I have forgotten to mention that in her more tender moments this leather-panoplied creature called her lover "Clydie Mydie," and so on.

Well, Clyde has $25 a week and a girl who is about to become a mother; and he is attempting to maintain social relations with the sons and daughters of the mill owners. *That* in a sense is his tragedy, and Mr. Dreiser most impressively lays it bare. But out of Clyde's economic and moral predicament a death results, for which he is held criminally responsible, though perhaps he is technically innocent, yet not without murderous malice aforethought.

There is a pretty situation for dramatic treatment. Mr. Dreiser makes the most of it. His exhibition of the antecedent and attendant circumstances is complete and convincing. So is his analysis of the psychology of Clyde and the working girl. It is of a masterly exhaustiveness. The reader is put in possession of everything relevant. Then through the greater part of the second volume we attend a long drawn-out trial, in the course of which we hear everything that public opinion and the law can say for and against Clyde. Then we get the verdict of the boy's mother and of his latest sweetheart and of the court of appeals and of the Governor of the state and of a sympathetic, intelligent and conscientious clergyman, and finally of Clyde himself. The law, the gospel, and the individual conscience all have a fair hearing. For Mr. Dreiser, sternly detached, lets every fact and opinion speak for itself.

I have not the slightest intention of offending the author by suggesting that he has become a sound moralist. I imagine that is quite unintentional. All that he has sought is comprehensive veracity. But only this morning I assured a young woman that if she would read Mr. Dreiser's latest novel it would permanently deter her from folly. I showed her the book. "Yes," she replied with an appraising glance at the two volumes, "but by that time it would be too late."

In its larger features the construction of "An American Tragedy" is as solid as a bank building. It is very long, to be sure, but there is little in it which is not functional, not a part of Mr. Dreiser's ponderous design. I was very nervous for fear the roof would fall during a couple of sagging chapters early in the second volume; but, no, he slowly swung his heavy timbers into place, restored his tension and maintained it to the end. The structure of a novel he has mastered. It is the structure of the sentence which remains a mystery to him. Often he plunges into a sentence head foremost, "trusting to God Almighty to get him out of it"; and is vouch-safed no divine aid. And yet the work as a whole is massively impressive. I do not know where else in American fiction one can find the situation here presented dealt with so fearlessly, so intelligently, so exhaustively, so veraciously, and *therefore* with such unexceptionable moral effect.

Julia Collier Harris. "Dreiser's Long Expected Novel Depicts the Turmoil and the Tragedy of Youth." Columbus [Ohio] *Enquirer Sun*, January 3, 1926.

Theodore Dreiser's latest novel, *An American Tragedy*, just published by Boni and Liveright, might have been appropriately called *A Tragedy of Youth*. . . . [It is a] novel which is likely to rank not only as one of the most important of Dreiser's books, but as one of the most powerful and moving stories ever given to American readers by an American. The cumulative effect of this tragedy of youth's longings, turmoils and rebellions is overwhelming. Without dogmatizing or sermonizing, without rancor toward the existing social order, without sentimentalizing, without any of the tricks of the sensationalist, though the material of the story is compact with the sensational—Dreiser builds up the structure of this every-day tragedy as Hardy might have done or even as *Macbeth* was built. Indeed, not even the mental processes of Macbeth or Lady Macbeth are more surely or inevitably developed than those of Clyde Griffiths, from the moment he discovers the dilemma of Roberta, a disaster for which he is only partly resonsible since she not only yielded to him in love but was a woman full two years his senior, but which nevertheless threatens the destruction of all his hopes and ambitions.

Here is a youth of attractive, even of

endearing, traits, full of the ardor and romance of a dreamer, sensitively alive to the charm and beauty of woman, and of life's joyous and highly-colored aspects—a refined, imaginative boy who, under happier circumstances might have created something delightful or contributed something gracious to the sum of things. Yet because of a lack of wise training or sympathetic direction in his early years, or a suitable outlet for his emotions during his adolescence, gone down to his ruin, thrown out on the scrapheap. And in his fall dragging down others, young and misdirected like himself. How deeply Dreiser makes the reader feel the waste of it, the pity of it. How he moves one by his picture of the betrayal of sacred, beautiful youth—this destruction of a priceless golden treasure by the corroding acid of neglect, ignorance and indifference.

In spite of the heavy, graceless, involved style of the author—a style which irritates those who love the beauty and rhythm of words set in a pattern of symmetry and persuasiveness—in spite of this and of a multiplication of trivial details which often weary and irritate, the bigness of soul and the clearness of vision in Dreiser compel unwavering admiration. Himself the victim of many an injustice, many a deprivation and misunderstanding, and of hounding at the hands of muddle-headed censors and bigots, he is never bitter or petulant, nor is his understanding obscured by personal prejudice or grievance.

For example, Dreiser can have no jot of sympathy with the fanaticism of Clyde's parents, with their literal interpretations and their narrow outlook. Yet what a sympathetic characterization is that of Clyde's mother! Perhaps the most complete and touching portrait in this gallery of Americans is that of Elvira Griffiths, who is shown as so honest and humble in her primitive, superstitious faith that we respect her and feel for her, while at the same time realizing her tragic lack toward her children. For after all it was this salvationist milieu of drab fanaticism and complete misunderstanding of youth's needs which was as responsible for Clyde's tragedy as his own weakness and wilfulness. Yet the author, with large sympathy and admirable impartiality brings out all that is strong and touching in the narrow and deluded religionist, especially in her relation to her son after he is imprisoned. How differently would a lesser talent have dealt with Mrs. Griffiths. Picture such a character in the hands, say, of the author of *Main Street.* His satiric preoccupation would have blinded him to any claim for tolerance and he most likely would have pictured her as mean and contemptible.

An American Tragedy is a big book and there is much that should be said about it in a review. One might lay emphasis on the surpassing skill with which Dreiser has worked out the latter part of the story, that part which deals with Clyde's prison life and the details of his trial. It is likely that this portion of the novel will make the widest appeal to readers. Or one might note with enthusiasm the true and subtle way in which the author defines Clyde's reactions to the three women who in turn absorb his interest. Certainly the analysis of his passional life in each case is done with astonishing insight.

But that quality in *An American Tragedy* which most impresses and moves me and which will cause the book to live in my memory is the author's comprehension of the fever of youth and his genius in delineating its reckless, foolish, sublime and palpitating orders. This type of clairvoyance is one which he has in common with other masters of the novel—with Hardy, Meredith and Tolstoi, and it compensates largely for his utter lack of aesthetic background and his indifference to stylistic grace. His wise and tender sympathy with the dreams and turmoils of life's spring-time invests the present work with an emotional beauty which reconciles one to many tedious and pedestrian pages.

Sherwood Anderson. "Dreiser." *Saturday Review of Literature*, 2 (January 9, 1926), 475.

Theodore Dreiser—what a man—what a huge figure on the American scene.

There are certain American men I myself have met and am glad to have met, Mr. Dreiser, Henry Mencken, Clarence Darrow, Stark Young, Alfred Kreymborg, Alfred Stieglitz, John Marin. There are a dozen others, all notable American men to me.

America has many men of note just now, walking about, doing their work, helping to mold our minds. How clearly Dreiser stands out among them all. There will not be another like him here. He is to my mind the biggset, most important American of our times. As a writer the man is often crude, dull sometimes with unbelievable dulness, honest, tender. His tenderness is the finest thing of all. How can anyone—a writer like myself—help being sorry his tenderness does not run out more directly toward words? Surely the man does not love words as words. He is so often unbelievably brutal with them. I pick up this new, big novel of his, "An American Tragedy," and on every page there are sentences that make me cringe, words that make me cringe.

It is Christmas morning in New Orleans and I have been all morning reading Dreiser's new novel and Amy Lowell's "John Keats"—going from one to the other. They are both unfinished as I sit writing. What a fine sensual love of words in Miss Lowell. What a lack of it in Dreiser. But what corking American writers. American writing was never so fine as it is now. Do you believe with me that Mr. Theodore Dreiser is more responsible for that fact than any other American? I get it very keenly as I sit writing this article. Miss Lowell of Massachusetts—Dreiser of Indiana.

In New Orleans—in the poorer section where I live—the neighbors all get drunk on Christmas. A drunken man, in sport, has just taken all his wife's best clothes down into the yard and soused them in a washtub. Now she will have to stay home all day and take care of him. He laughs hoarsely. The wife laughs and swears.

These are Dreiser's kind of people—these in their grim and gay moments. Common Americans, undistinguished. What a lot of them. How the man Dreiser has loved and understood them.

And yet look what the man does. Right at the beginning of this new big book—on page ten—read this. He is describing his hero's father:

> To begin with, Asa Griffiths, the father, was one of those poorly integrated and correlated organisms, the product of an environment and a religious theory, but

> with no guiding or mental insight of his own, yet sensitive and therefore highly emotional, and without any practical sense whatsoever.

"No guiding or mental insight of his own." Great God! One's mind jumps away to other fellows of the ink-pots—say George Moore in the "Brook Kerith," Stark Young's jeweled clearness, Henry Mencken's gay word rattling, Mr. Stuart Sherman's solid prose.

Plenty of word lovers in the world, loving words, slinging ink. But Dreiser isn't one of them. If you look for word-love in his book you'll get left. Love of human beings you'll find. It's a finer attribute in the end. Lay your Dreiser book over against the book of any of the modern "smarties" among our writers and you'll understand. You'll understand also why all men here who care about writing care so much for Dreiser.

You go on for endless pages of dulness with Dreiser, like walking on the prairie, say of the Dakotas or in the desert country, endless piling up of heavy cumbersome sentences, something level and low, with a dreary sameness you think at first will drive you mad.

If you think you are going to escape Dreiser by realizing he can be dull you are mistaken. He'll get you in the end. Buy this book and read it all. Don't be finicky. It will reward you as every book of Dreiser's always does. You'll never get the beauty of the prairies or the desert by being mincing and finicky. They are beautiful. So is Dreiser and his work. You have to pay for beauty. Pay for it in Dreiser by going right on through with him. Take along water, bread, and wine. Prepare for a journey you'll never forget. Take a day off, two days, a week. Go up into the country for a week-end alone—take Dreiser's two volumes with you on a train journey. Find out, once for all, the difference between a human flesh and blood, male man, full of real tenderness for life, and the smarties, the word slingers, the clever fellows, the nasty cocksure half men of the writing world.

All that Dreiser misses in feeling for words, sentences, the page of the book, he pours out into tenderness for people. He goes with his people into every little detail of their lives. The drama grows slowly bigger and bigger. A Dreiser book—Dreiser's people—you never forget. That's a lot. That's everything. That's what makes Dreiser what he is—the most important American writing. More than that—the most important man writing English.

I'll not go on any more about Dreiser's bad sentences. You'll find them on every page of his book like sage brush on the desert. You go around anywhere in America where men and women who care about writing get together and you'll hear the same thing. Everyone begins by speaking of the terrible sentences of Dreiser. Then they speak of other things for a time and come back to the man Dreiser. Tenderness creeps into voices. Every writing man and woman in America who really cares about writing loves this man. And it isn't Dreiser, the human social being, they love. He keeps himself to himself, is that odd thing among writers, a truly modest man. What other American writers love is Theodore Dreiser the writer as he is in "An American Tragedy," with all of his sins on his head, just as he always is.

I am not going to try to talk of these two new volumes in detail. Frankly I haven't had time to read them enough for that and I won't be hurried. And anyway, you can't get at Dreiser that way. Buy and read "An American

Tragedy." Stand the two volumes upon your shelves. An American library without Dreiser complete is just no library at all—at least not an American library.

It comes to this—that the great human tenderness of Dreiser, that has got into his work in spite of his word heaviness, is in "An American Tragedy." There is no smartness, no cleverness. There is just the man we American writers love and respect above all other writing artists here—the biggest man we've had. And that's enough.

Get and read "An American Tragedy" for yourself if you have any feeling for American writing. That's all I can say.

Maxwell Bodenheim. "On Writing." *Saturday Review of Literature*, 2 (February 13, 1926), 562. [Letter in Response to Above Review by Sherwood Anderson.]

To the Editor of *The Saturday Review:*
Sir:

After I had read Sherwood Anderson's review of "An American Tragedy," in your issue of January 9th, I determined to write the present letter, not from any feelings of personal enmity toward reviewer and author, but because the matter extends far beyond Mr. Anderson's accuracy in the specific review, or Mr. Dreiser's fame.

Mr. Anderson begins by admitting that Theodore Dreiser is often crude, unbelievably dull, and cumbersome—a writer of "terrible" sentences and awkwardly misused words. However, these defects are of no importance to the reviewer, and he goes on to lavish the highest of praise upon the tenderness of the author, and his love of human beings, and his "beauty"—that impressive, overused word, which is easy to mention and harder to prove—and his compassionate attitude toward common people. As a background for this eulogy, the reviewer cites writers whom he describes as "the smarties, the word-slingers, the clever fellows, the nasty cocksure half men of the writing world."

One cannot fail to notice a curious, underlying harmony between most modern critics of literature in this country—they have not the slightest interest in literature itself! They insist that the art of writing—it was generally supposed to be an art once upon a time—should become a steam-shovel, or a toothpick, or a kiss and a handkerchief for the lips and eyes, or a sermon, or a jug of molasses, or anything except a skilful and distinct combination of words used for the purpose of symbolizing thoughts and emotions. I knew an old negress in my boyhood days in the South, who was filled with valid tenderness and with a largely inarticulate but sincere love of human beings—that softly decayed, nearsighted, naked simplicity, in which the mind is scarcely more than the browbeaten servant of limited emotions. If you listened to her for ten minutes, she was piquant and warmly droll in her mingled caresses and stupidities, but after an hour had elapsed she became boresome, and monotonous, and over-transparent. Apparently, American critics can never have too much of these latter three qualities, because literature to them is a pretext—a medium which they heed only when it entirely confines itself to an expression of the few, broad, emotional attitudes commonly reiterated in life. When the author is more subtle, varied, thoughtful, and searching, and when his emotions use words in a delicate experiment with questions, and uncertainties, he is dismissed through the use of reliable but rather unsubstantiated nouns and adjectives—word-slinger, tenuous—must one have the heaviness of an elephant to be important?—artificial, precious, clever, word-juggler, stilted trifler—and the process reminds me of school-boy throwing epithets at the English-teacher who persists in correcting his "tender" but bungling compositions. If literature is to be rated solely on the basis of its loving and serviceable attitude toward men and women, and if all matters of style, and dexterity, and depth of thought, and gracefulness, and clarity are to be dismissed as obnoxious trivialities, then I would seriously advise every sympathetic, tolerant, and compassionate bricklayer, merchant, and lawyer, to apply himself immediately to the writing of fiction, and to proclaim himself as one of the foremost American writers. Such minute things as the proper use of nouns, adjectives, and adverbs would not have to worry these beginning writers, for they could instantly gain the praise of seven-tenths of the existing American critics and book-reviewers.

MAXWELL BODENHEIM.

New York.

Burton Rascoe. "An American Tragedy." New York *Sun Saturday Book Reviews*, January 9, 1926, p. 10.

. . . Dreiser has never been guilty of an epigram; he has never been facetious; he has never been humorous at the expense of the human soul. If he has prejudices against people in his contacts with life or when he forsakes the role of novelist for that of essayist, he has none whatever when he sets to work to present a character to his readers. . . . Clyde Griffiths, the hero of "An American Tragedy," is the least heroic of all the main characters in Dreiser's novels. It could seem that Dreiser had deliberately taken almost the least interesting and the least sympathetic character he could imagine in the American scene in order to show his power to hold one's attention through two volumes each over 400 pages long. I say that it would seem so, but that is not Dreiser's method, not his purpose in life as he sees it, not his conception of the dignity of the novelist as a truth teller. . . . [*An American Tragedy*] might be accepted as the great American novel if Dreiser had not already written at least two novels that may lay equal claim to such distinction—"Sister Carrie" and "The Financier." As in those two novels, "Dreiser has told a story in "An American Tragedy" that is peculiar to the American milieu. Murders happen in other countries, certainly, even murders of sweethearts by young men (though, to be accurate,

Clyde did not actually commit the murder he premeditated but allowed the girl to drown in an accident without going to her aid); but all of the social forces leaning up to the tragedy are special to the contemporary American scene. . . .

[*An American Tragedy* is a] novel of such breadth, depth and significance as only Dreiser could write. He is the most honest of all the realists I have ever read, not excluding Flaubert. Let others reiterate the stereotyped criticism that Dreiser writes badly because he uses such words as "chemism," "via" and "anent," lumbers along slowly when he is not narrating action or writing dialogue, but is merely about his ordained business of shirking no detail of his presentation of truth. Then let them read what every French critic and every eminent English critic of French literature, including Saintsbury (who translated Balzac) and Lytton Stachey has had to say about the style of Balzac. Finally let them read the pages describing the fatal automobile ride and the last chapter of the book and ask themselves if they know of any one who writes any better. Dreiser's already towering stature among modern realists increases with this tragedy.

Robert L. Duffus. "Dreiser's Undisciplined Power." New York *Times Book Review*, January 10, 1926, pp. 1, 6.

If any less well established writer than Mr. Dreiser had brought the manuscript of these two volumes into a publishers office it is easy to guess what would have happened to him. He would have been told that his work was very promising indeed, and asked to take it away and cut it in half. The story is far too long, and there are scores of copy readers in newspaper and magazine offices who could shorten it and make it better. Mr. Dreiser not only reports his hero's love affairs in full, even in those details in which love affairs do not greatly differ, but he documents every other incident as carefully as a biographer endeavoring to establish a new conception of a famous character. He describes a murder trial as though he were a star reporter who had been told by his editor to take all the space he needed.

Sometimes this superfluity of details dulls the interest and sometimes it does not. Among his other qualifications Mr. Dreiser is a good reporter—a far better one than certain newspaper executives had the good sense to see when he attempted journalism in New York thirty years ago. He does not write of anything he does not know about. His description of the life of a bellboy in a big hotel or of the processes by which collars are made is quite as interesting as the ordinary magazine article on such subjects. When he wanted to place a part of his action in the death house he took great pains to visit a prision and familiarize himself with every incident of the State's system of torturing and finally killing its condemned prisoners. The result is something that every believer in capital punishment ought to read.

But whether Mr. Dreiser's 840 pages ought to be 420 is a vain question. Nothing that can be said to Mr. Dreiser or about him will in the past alter his artistic method. He has written "An American Tragedy" at this length and in this form because he cannot possibly write it in lesser length or other form. And this obstinacy, if it is that, is the defect of his strength. His name is well known today, and will continue to be known to all who are seriously interested in American literature, very largely because of the very fact that he would not listen to reason. Reason would have demanded in the 90s that he conform to the romantic requirements of the period. Reason might now demand that he consider the profits of serialization and motion picture rights. But he has the unreasonableness of an author afflicted with a certain touch of genius.

The question must be whether the genius breaks through the defects of form, whether it survives the dilution of the flood of words. Has Mr. Dreiser created character? Has he dramatized a significant situation? One feels that he has. The story of "An American Tragedy" seems at times as shapeless as clouds blown in the wind or shadows from a flickering fire but the reader who surrenders himself to it will be aware of a steady and inevitable movement. There are a number of ways in which Mr. Dreiser has no kinship with the Greeks but the machinery of his tragedy is as authentic as that of Aeschylus himself. The end comes out of the beginning just as relentlessly as a new automobile comes out of the steel, rubber, leather, nickel and stove polish that is fed into the yawning mouth of a Ford factory though there is no doubt that Mr. Ford could give Mr. Dreiser pointers in methods of routing.

Clyde Griffiths becomes a living figure—there can be no doubt that Mr. Dreiser meets that test. He is as much alive as Sister Carrie, more alive, possibly, than Jennie Gerhardt. He is the obverse of the Titan, a weaker and less appealing brother of Eugene Witla. Perhaps he may be regarded as the protagonist of Mr. Dreiser's changed conception of American life—a creature helpless in the grip of forces and circumstances which few individuals can master. Clyde Griffiths dreams, as all Mr. Dreiser's heroes seem to do of love, social position and power. A world of supreme happiness exists, if only he can force his way into it. But he has not the will or the self-control that such a victory demands.

The skeleton of the story is such as may be found, by a sufficiently astute reader, in almost any morning's newspaper. Clyde Griffiths is the son of a street preacher in Kansas City—a beaten, nondescript, shambling person. The mother is of stronger fibre, but her world is bounded by the Bethel Independent Mission. Youth will not be pinched within such narrow walls. Clyde's young sister meets a handsome actor and falls by the wayside. Clyde himself, at 16, breaks away and becomes a bellboy in "the very finest hotel in Kansas City." A few drinks, a visit to the tenderloin and a scrubby love affair, and the process of sophistication is complete. An escapade with a borrowed motor car, ending in tragedy, forces him, as he thinks to leave the city. A chance meeting with his father's brother, Samuel Griffiths, a wealthy collar manufacturer of Lycurgus. N. Y., seems to promise a reversal of fortune. The uncle gives him a small place in the collar factory and despite the opposition of his cousin Gilbert, Clyde sees the road to wealth and position opening before him. He even manages to make headway with Sondra Finchley, daughter of one of Lycurgus's upper-class families. And then what visions fill his somewhat ratlike brain!

Unfortunately he has been injudicious enough to enter into an affair with Roberta Alden, one of the operatives in the collar factory, and by the time he is tired of her it is clear that she is to become a mother. Clyde has no sense of responsibility, yet if he abandons Roberta she will expose him and he will lose Sondra. On the hook of this dilemma he is impaled. His mind has become fastened upon Sondra, and all that she represents, with the fatal tenacity of an obsession. He has the incurable selfishness and lack of imagination that sometimes does produce success. But he lacks the intellectual strength to extricate himself. He sinks in deeper and deeper. A chance newspaper clipping puts a gruesome idea in his head. Suppose a man and a girl go out in a canoe. Suppose the canoe tips over and only one returns. He finds himself led on, almost without willing it, into plotting murder.

From this point on, for some 120 pages, Mr. Dreiser gives us as fine and haunting a study of crime and punishment as he or any other novelist has written in America—a passage so penetrating, so poetic and of such weirdly dramatic power that the remaining 247 pages are something in the nature of an anti-climax. We see a vapid but not really evil little soul becoming, by easy steps, blood-guilty; it is almost as horrible as watching a vivisection.

And then once on the water again—about 500 feet from shore, the while he fumbled aimlessly with the hard and heavy yet small camera that he now held, as the boat floated out nearer the centre. And then, at this point and time looking fearfully about. For now—now—in spite of himself, the long-evaded and yet commanding moment. And no voice or figure or sound on shore. No road or cabin or smoke! And the moment which he or something had planned for him, and which was now to decide his fate, at hand! The moment of action—of crisis! All that he needed to do now was to turn swiftly and savagely to one side or the other—leap up—upon the left wale or the right, and upset the boat; or, failing that, rock it swiftly, and if Roberta protested too much, strike her with the camera in his hand, or one of the oars free at his right. It could be done—it could be done—swiftly and simply, were he now of the mind and heart, or lack of it—with him swimming swiftly away thereafter to freedom—to success—of course—to Sondra and happiness—a new and greater and sweeter life than any he had ever known.

At the last there is a moment of hesitation. Did he mean to strike her with the camera? Did he commit murder? Perhaps no jury of readers would vote to acquit him, and yet there remains a doubt.

In all this Mr. Dreiser does not appear as special pleader. It is Roberta, not Clyde, who appeals to one's sympathies. But he does succeed in conveying an understanding of Clyde—an understanding so terrific as to give the reader an uneasy sense of shame and guilt. The book clings to reality, yet takes on a nightmarish quality. We see the hounds baying on the trail, the frantic efforts of the fox to escape—the spectacle of society hunting down its chosen victim. Yet here, too, the complexity of human motives is shown. The prosecuting attorney is the fiercer in his pursuit because he is trying to fight down a sense of inferiority arising from a broken and disfiguring nose: he weeps honest tears over Roberta's pathetic letters, but realizes also that if he can convict an unpopular criminal his chances for the Judgeship to which he aspires will be improved. His assistant threads two of the dead girl's hairs into the camera by way of strengthening the case. It is not exactly justice that we witness—it is a comedy of crime and violence and double motives on all sides.

Mr. Dreiser's patience with details is endless. He pauses to give us in brief the life story of the district Attorney, Mason—material for a novel in itself. He outlines with bold strokes the attorneys for the defense, Belknap and Jepson—pure Dickens with a blend of the sinister. Even in the death house he pauses to sketch in the Rev. Duncan McMillan and the prisoners, those other rats in the same trap, who pray and groan and play cards and go mad and walk through the little green door in the end. There is little of the sentimentality which crept into Mr. Dreiser's previous work. He has achieved what may be described as an ironic pity. He has approached a little nearer to the mind of Thomas Hardy.

H. L. Mencken has said of Dreiser, in a sentence quoted on the jacket of these volumes: "He stands isolated today, a figure weatherbeaten and lonely. Yet I know no American novelist who seems so secure or likely to endure." There is obviously at least this amount of accuracy in the statement: Mr. Dreiser is not imitative and belongs to no school. He is at heart a mysticist and a fatalist, though using the realistic method. He is a totally undisciplined, unorganized power—yet, on the evidence of this novel alone, none the less a power. "An American Tragedy" is not to be recommended as fireside reading for the tired business man: yet, as a portrayal of one of the darker phases of the American character, it demands attention.

John W. Crawford. New York *Sunday Book World,* January 10, 1926.

Theodore Dreiser leaves an enormous, almost unwieldy, deposit in the reader. He has passed under review an entire epoch and contributed to the illumination of a whole phase of the national life.

He has been from the start a figure of protest. He was a gusty, marrowful reaction against the cerebral tepidity of a whole generation of phantom-thinkers, of stereotyped romancers, of sterile celebrants of a quaintly trivial "local color" cult, of timid anatomists of a nonexistent code of manners. In the nature of things, he has been a powerful, invaluable agency of destruction. He has broken up preconceived notions, brought alien matters into the novel.

A penalty common to the pioneer has been exacted of Mr. Dreiser; he has been forced to ignore method for the sake of his content. In detail, he writes as badly as ever in "An American Tragedy." There are the same slipshod sentences, the bulky paragraphs, the all but unleavened chapters. Nevertheless, there is the inescapable sense of an imperceptible drift in his narration, the slow, irresistible movements of a boundless, untamed energy. This has always lifted and carried on a captivated attention; it performs the same function in "An American Tragedy."

Further, Mr. Dreiser has been too

busy clearing the way to give much thought to his ultimate direction. He has admitted to American fiction an entire range of motive which was previously ignored. In so doing he was, it seemed, less convinced of their intrinsic validity than persuaded of their efficacy in disproving the more favored tenets in conventional circles as to the mainsprings of human conduct.

His essentially agnostic attitude, his insistence upon the concrete manifestations of character cannot but be regarded as wholesome in its relation to American literature, but it cannot be evaded that Mr. Dreiser often found himself at work within a field as limited as the area which he had forsworn.

"An American Tragedy" marks a distinct advance. Mr. Dreiser has discovered memory and the static conflict of an immediate moment as modifying agents of human behavior. In addition, he has found the emptiness in his "rich, material living." There were times when Mr. Dreiser appeared to be falling a victim to the irresponsible, grandiosely vulgar fantasies of the prosperous, traveling salesman. The reader detected the accent of special pleading in the pictures of saloons and hotel lobbies, of sybaritic week-ends in the Long Island homes of millionaires, of triumphs on stage or in factories. Mr. Dreiser seemed to be indulging in a sort of inverted evangelism.

"An American Tragedy," if it is nothing else, is a tacit record of a parching absence of beauty in the common life, "rich and material," or religious. Mr. Dreiser nowhere states conclusions. He has assembled such a mass of evidence, if you will, that inference is unavoidable.

The scene is presented throughout by means of the life and personality of Clyde Griffiths. The drama never transcends the author's integrated, devious, far-reaching conception of Clyde. The environment which has produced Clyde is false and wasteful and criminally inert. The distortions of Clyde's native bent toward health and usefulness are inherent in a warped scheme of things. Clyde's heredity, too, is made to contribute toward his weakness and downfall. Mr. Dreiser's triumph, however, is the fixing of Clyde's share of individual, inevitable, personal, peculiar responsibility.

Mr. Dreiser has been prodigal with his material. He might have fashioned a grand murder mystery by starting somewhere near the beginning of the second volume, with the death of the despondent girl. All the melodramatic circumstances, in their unevaluated form, could have been detected and linked together by the sterling honesty of the rural District Attorney, with the flatteringly breathless co-operation of the reader.

Mr. Dreiser never lets go his hold for a minute, all through 800 pages. He clearly demonstrates his mastery of the measured, implacable tracing of a disintegrating personality which was earlier indicated compellingly in the portrait of Hurstwood in "Sister Carrie."

"An American Tragedy" is not without its many minor defects, and a few serious deficiencies. American literature, however, is not sufficiently rich in big, comprehensive personalities, in dogged devotion to a vision of truth, in unrelenting effort toward a profound articulation of that vision, for such considerations to be permitted to cloud the name of Theodore Dreiser. "An American Tragedy" is a sound and vigorous achievement in pushing out the boundaries of thought.

Clarence Darrow. "Touching a Terrible Tragedy." New York *Evening Post Literary Review*, January 16, 1926, pp. 1–2.

I finished Theodore Dreiser's latest story just before going to bed last night. I assume that I must have had some sleep during the troubled hours through which I tossed and dreamed after laying it down. But the haunted face of a helpless boy, strapped to an iron chair at Sing Sing, and the wan form of a dead girl floating on a lonely black lake surrounded by tall pine trees in Northern New York still were haunting me when I awoke. I presume the feeling will slowly fade from my consciousness and be blended with the other experiences, painful and pleasant, which make up life. I hardly can think of the eight hundred pages of "An American Tragedy" as a book. It does not leave the impression that goes with reading a story; the feeling is rather that of a series of terrible physical impacts that have relentlessly shocked every sensitive nerve in the body. . . .

"An American Tragedy" is a somber, gruesome tale. It is not relieved by a single flash of color or light of joy. Dreiser carries the story straight, honest and true to the inevitable end. One thing, at least, is sure: it is deadly interesting from the beginning to the last word. One hardly stops to realize that he is gripped in the hands of a master. Such a master of technique and tragedy as the world has seldom known. One is not reading; he is living—and dying! He is held in a spell from the first page to the eight hundred and thirty-fifth. When he has finished the book it lingers and haunts and plays with his emotions as few books have ever done.

Whether this book will sell, I cannot guess. In this weary world people want to be amused. They like pleasant pictures, however fantastic or impossible they may be. They do not dare to look at life. Mr. Dreiser will not lie. He will not use his marvelous powers to trick, deceive and please.

It is useless to discuss what form art should take. This depends on the artist. The crowd will turn to Harold Bell Wright and the rest. They wish to be fed on lies. Mr. Dreiser could no doubt do this if he would. For his honesty and fidelity the world will never give him a cash return. He must know this better than any one else. "One cannot eat his cake and keep it too." Even though Mr. Dreiser may live and die poor and neglected: even though his art and work may be criticized and derided, still that part of the public which thinks and feels will understand his fanatical devotion to truth and will recognize Mr. Dreiser as one of the few real writers who has never wavered nor been afraid; and he will one day be acknowledged one of the master artists of the world.

W. Elsworth Lawson. "Book-Land Glimpses." Foxboro [Mass.] *Reporter*. January 16, 1926, p. 4.

Within the compass of two narrow columns it is impossible to say all that ought to be said of a novel of such depth, sincerity, passion, magnitude and massive impressiveness as Theodore Dreiser's "An American Tragedy" recently published by Boni & Liveright in two volumes. In creative energy and vitality it surpasses anything the author has hitherto accomplished. Although the story consumes 840 pages in getting itself told, there is none of those deserts of argumentative exposition that so irritated us, for instance, in that fine book, "The Genius." Here there is an unbroken sequence of circumstance, character, will, deed and catastrophe that marks the greatest tragedies of the past. Here, also, as in no other of his novels, Dreiser's inspiration and careful craftsmanship go hand-in-hand. In only one instance (his handling of Myra and Bella Griffiths, the rich cousins of the hero) does his inspiration appear to falter. They exist in the story as channels through which Clyde Griffiths comes to know Sondra Finchley. Once that purpose is served, the two girls drop back into very minor characters and have no further appreciable influence on the course of events, although our expectations had been aroused especially by the delightfully vivid presentation of Bella's personality. But what Mr. Dreiser has done in this novel is so great that what he has left undone is of comparatively small moment.

Crowded as this book is with characters, alive, vital, interesting and important in themselves, the story fulfills one significant function of pure tragedy in being pre-eminently the story of one person—Clyde Griffiths—the hero. . . . Oh, it is a painful story, a harrowing story, relentless and awful in its inevitability; yet no one, unless he be a literary moron, can deny its tremendous power. The author's apprehension of this tragic world is so intense and over-powering that we feel sometimes as if the hero were being hounded to his ruin by an ineluctable fate. But there is nothing here that simply happens, nothing that can truly be called fatalistic. The whole story moves from the actions of the hero. Without any fumbling with reality, it is a revelation of the tragic depths of life. The peculiar up-bringing of Clyde Griffiths, the formative influence of his various companions, the cold attitude of his rich relatives, the loneliness in which they left him, the atmosphere of the factory, the two stratas of society in which he finally moves, the conflict and contrast of his love for Roberta and Sondra, the problem which the factory girl's condition evokes—all these are indispensable elements in the tragedy; but they are never overstressed, and we are never once allowed to feel that these events, circumstances and persons have released Clyde Griffiths from his responsibility for the problem that faces him, and his power to act rightly towards it.

The careful emphasis Dreiser lays on the conflict of spiritual forces within Clyde—his passion, vanity, aspirations, doubts, scruples, ideas and fears—is enough to prove that the main action of the story is essentially the expression of character. Thus and thus it happens, because Clyde Griffiths is this and that.

From the moment when the hero, enmeshed in the subtle net he has woven by his own acts, comes upon the newspaper account of an "accidental double tragedy at Pass Lake," we hold our breath in fear. For myself, I could scarcely continue reading. It was as if an ice-cold hand had clutched my heart, and I watched Clyde Griffiths harrowed and torn by the monstrous temptation that seized him. Nothing that I have ever seen on the stage, nothing that I have read for thirty years affected me as those masterly pages where the crisis of the tragedy comes in sight. I was shaken with pity and terror. They are overwhelming in their truth and fidelity. In this tragic world things like that are always happening. Just when he is least fitted to face it, in the hour of his utmost perplexity and weakness, when his whole being is infected with the virus of fear, that newspaper comes into his hand and the doom of Clyde Griffiths is already foreshadowed.

"Accident," you say. "No mere accident should be admitted into a tragedy." Yet Shakespere did it. Juliet waked an instant too late. An insignificant delay cost Cordelia her life. Desdemona lost her handkerchief at the one moment that was fatal to her. In the case of Clyde Griffiths, Dreiser makes it perfectly plain that personal responsibility and capacity to act remained with the boy. The conflict that followed the reading of the story can have no meaning otherwise. Stricken with horror of the thoughts that storm his brain, he yet plays with them and, although the horror never lessens as the days go on, it is a being whose conscience is awake and aware who lays those lividly ludicrous plans to escape detection of his contemplated deed which nevertheless lead him to his lurid catastrophe. It is also true that, when Clyde and Roberta are finally canoeing on Big Bittern, he found he could not do the deed his tormented mind had planned, and the actual drowning of the girl was brought about by her own sudden rising in the canoe. Yet here again is no mere accident, no fatalism in its primitive, crude form. Mr. Dreiser is too finished an artist to have recourse to such simple expedients. Responsibility still remains with Clyde Griffiths. The tragic fact of the drowning was the inevitable culmination of a long and tortuous course of events started by Clyde which he could neither calculate nor in the end control. And that is pure tragedy.

The 300 pages that follow the story of Roberta's death are, in the truest sense of the term, a superb climax. I have not space here even to give an idea of the dramatic quality of Dreiser's narrative of the trial. It is a triumph in itself that would make the reputation of a dozen lesser novelists. Nor can I show how, in spite of the multitude of new characters that appear in this last section, our interest still centers in Clyde Griffiths—his thoughts, evasions, hopes and fears, spiritual struggles and final calmness. "An American Tragedy" must be read, it must be studied. I have had to content myself here with the central character alone, although the story is crowded with people and scenes that one can never easily forget. The poetic treatment of the tragic theme, the vividness and reality with which the various characters are invested, the atmosphere in which they all move and the fusion of intellect and feeling make this transcript of modern American life the most notable literary achievement of this century.

V. L. O. Chittick.
"The Work of Ten Years." *Sunday Oregonian*, January 24, 1926.

. . . It is doubtful if any novel of equal pretension to serious consideration and of equal seriousness of intent has ever been written so completely devoid of literary charm as this one. Throughout the whole of its enormous length—it appears in two volumes of more than 400 closely printed pages each—there is not a single sentence which one would care to reread for its stylistic excellence. Every infelicity of faulty diction and unidomatic phrasing is illustrated in the course of its knotted and twisted rhetoric. In this connection it may be of interest to recall that H. L. Mencken (feelingly referred to in some quarters as the Baltimore anti-Christ, and hence, as one might suppose, in most respects poles asunder from Mr. [Stuart] Sherman, though on this point they are in entire accord) has had to say of Mr. Dreiser's writing: "It is flaccid, elephantine, doltish, coarse, dismal, flatulent, sophomoric, ignorant, unconvincing, wearisome." Mr. Mencken was speaking of "The Genius," and while Mr. Dreiser has never again penetrated to the depths of auctorial ineptitude reached in that grotesque compilation, he is still sadly deficient in what are generally accepted as the rudiments of elementary composition.

Happily, the claims for urging "An American Tragedy" upon the attention of the reading public can be based on something more enduring than virtuosity of style. The book deserves all the profound interest it undoubtedly will arouse because of the importance of its content and the soundness of its structure. Its theme is not different from that which Mr. Dreiser has repeatedly made use of before, but he has varied its development in a manner unusual to him. In volume one he masses his data for not justifying the ways of God to man; in volume two he denounces man's inhumanity to man.

In both volumes he keeps his attack indirect by relying solely upon the device of implication already referred to. Fundamentally, his two problems are identical, but there are surface distinctions between them, and these he evidently determined to carry in mind while working out his dual division.

In brief, his narrative recounts the life history of one Clyde Griffiths, a youth of a "temperament as fluid and unstable as water . . . not any too powerful physically or rock-ribbed morally or mentally," from the time of his boyhood amidst surroundings of humiliating poverty and fanatical religiosity, through his various nondescript attempts to earn a living that would both relieve him from poverty and enable him to pursue the primrose pathway of hitherto forbidden pleasures, to the fateful moment when, having seduced his sweetheart and made her his mistress, and having, as the saying is, "got her into trouble" and refused to marry her because of his insane dream of completing another and more desirable conquest, he goes to his abject and miserable death in the electric chair for having plotted a cold-blooded murder, which, owing to the strange, though not incredible coincidence of a drowning accident, and the loss of his nerve, he never actually committed.

A thoroughly worthless and despicable creature, this Clyde Griffiths, truly. "Then why inflict his story upon a long-suffering world?" might be asked fairly enough. "Because," doubtless Mr. Dreiser would reply, "it serves to bring sharply into focus certain effects of a so-called civilization allowed to evolve by what seems to be only a 'vast imbecility'."

"But since nothing can be done about it . . ." his interrogator might begin in further dissent. To which Mr. Dreiser, not waiting to hear the plaint out, would very likely retort, "If that indeed be true, then we had better commence right away to revise our current social and moral philosophy." Quite possibly he would be altogether and hopelessly wrong; but it would be an exceedingly difficult task to convince anyone under the potent spell of his book that there was a flaw in the argument upon which he bases his contention. Certainly no conceivable defect in his colossal arraignment of the universe could be traced to failure in documentation. He has fortified his charges with informing detail of every sort, biological, erotic, anatomical, contraceptual.

The first part of the novel is devoted to presenting those features in the life of the adolescent Griffiths beyond the youngster's personal control, his heredity, upbringing and early environment. Like the typical Dreiser narration, it is dull dreary and long drawn out. But the whole of it is essential to the conduct of the rest of the work.

Having established his case against God (or nature or fate) at the outset, Mr. Dreiser goes on to establish his case against man in the sequel. Here his grip on his readers' interest intensifies. To an extent never essayed in his previous volumes he complicates his plot and multiplies his characters. But he succeeds notably in sustaining one's curiosity as to the outcome of it all until the very end. Nor does he allow his unwonted wealth of action and dramatic personae to weaken for an instant the cogency of his central thesis.

In that stage in his unheroic hero's development when he might be expected to display some relative power over the hardships of existence he is shown more helpless than ever, since the hand of everyone he encounters is, either actively or passively against him. Not a person, not an institution, not an ideal comes clean from this devastating revelation of humanity's conscious or unconscious inhumanity. The method, as always with Mr. Dreiser, is that of ironical juxtaposition, with, for the first time in his career as an author, any tendency to indulge in derisive or pitying commentary rigorously suppressed.

The climax in the succession of disillusioning contrasts is reached in those sections of the book in which he exhibits a number of practices alleged to be peculiar to that procedure commonly known as "the administration of justice." Their disclosure comes about in the course of an account of the arrest, trial and conviction of Clyde Griffiths on the charge of murder. Neither the prosecution nor the defense was undertaken or carried on with any primary concern in the actual guilt or innocence of the accused. The attorneys both for the people and for the prisoner were actuated in their zeal, the one group for conviction, the other for acquittal, solely by political and pecuniary motives.

Both sides resorted to chicanery and

downright falsehood to attain the verdict desired. But the irony of the victim's plight was not complete until he had undergone a two years' incarceration in the deathhouse of an up-to-date "model" penitentiary while awaiting the result of an appeal for retrial, which was being urged so half-heartedly, since there were no fees forthcoming substantial enough for its being urged otherwise, that there was not the slightest chance of its being acted upon favorably.

In this ghastly chamber the living conditions were such that on each prisoner was placed "the compulsion of enduring all the horrors of all the vicious, morbid or completely collapsed and despairing temperaments about him. No true privacy of any kind. By day, a blaze of light pouring through an overarching skylight high above the walls; by night, glistening incandescents of large size and power which flooded each nook and cranny of the various cells.

The crowning torment of all arose from the fact that these same remorseless lights were three times momentarily dimmed on the occasion of all executions, which were not infrequent —"an idiotic or thoughtless result of having one electric system to supply the death voltage and the incandescence of this and all other rooms." Can the limits of modern ingenuity in the infliction of legal torture be extended farther in the direction of diabolism?

Mr. Dreiser has spared no effort to make his double indictment complete. He has delved painfully, laboriously, interminably through top soil, buried springs, quicksand and hardpan, down to solid bedrock. Upon that he has laid a foundation of reinforced concrete. And upon that, in turn, he has erected a structure durable, massive, foursquare.

Like a gigantic monolith it dominates the landscape in the midst of which it stands, a thing to marvel at if not to delight in. Like a monolith, too, it will continue to stand, indubitable evidence that some elemental state of mind or feeling, no matter how naive, has mysteriously demanded and at length secured the unique artistic form needed to express it. In the case of Mr. Dreiser the inward compulsive force has been his primitive, brooding tenderness. By giving expression to this, his most characteristic mood, in "An American Tragedy" he has done himself infinite credit.

Abraham Cahan. "Dreiser's New Novel and What the Critics Say About It." *Jewish Daily Forward*, January 24, 1926, Section 1, p. 3.

I am reading Theodore Dreiser's new novel, "An American Tragedy." It is in two volumes, 838 closely printed pages, about three times the size of the usual modern novel. I haven't reached the end of the first volume yet, and it is impossible as yet to write of the book as a whole, but it isn't the book itself that I want to discuss today but, chiefly, the attitude of the critics toward it, or, rather the spirit in which they approach it.

Many of the reviewers are in ecstasies

over the novel. Others welcome it with reserve. Still others treat it with a compound of half-hearted approbation and ill-concealed enmity. But there is something which is common to all of them and which strikes me as quite out of the ordinary in the daily run of contemporary newspaper criticism.

An unusual tone, a unique manner characterizes all the reviews of the book that have so far fallen under my notice. They make one feel as though all other novelists, good or bad, are to be grouped in one category while Theodore Dreiser constitutes a class of his own. It isn't a question of rank but of kind, as if their art and his represented two distinct vocations.

There are novelists who have received a more generous measure of praise. Certainly few books that have attracted wide attention during the past ten years have been condemned so heartily and so generally for infelicity of phrasing and vocabulary. And yet none has really been taken quite so seriously as has Dreiser.

The appearance of "An American Tragedy" is an event of first-class importance in the history of American letters; this is the spirit in which the novel is received by the critics. Whether they put it in so many words or let you infer it from their general manner one is aware of it, even in the case of those who have a good deal of adverse criticism to offer and whose appraisal is marked by not a little irritation.

Nor is this all. Other books have been acclaimed as lasting contributions to American literature. The characteristic thing about the way Dreiser's latest offering has been received, to my mind, is the fact that it is held first of all as a portrayal of American reality and that as such it is taken far more seriously than any other novel of recent origin, not excluding the marvellous works of Sinclair Lewis.

One can name any number of authors who are handier with their literary tools than Dreiser, authors who are endowed with a greater facility in using language than he. Also one may name a long list of novelists whose efforts are more liberally adorned with what is generally termed cleverness and brilliancy. But this sort of superiority vanishes the moment you think of fiction as an art whose business it is to present men and things, human character and human motive, in a way to make them convincingly true. It is an art that calls for gifts of which your brilliant writers can rarely boast.

To picture things as they are is supposed to be an achievement of commonplace merit, something within the ready reach of every person who knows how to write decent English. This is one of the widespread superstitions of which American literature is a victim. The truth is, of course, that to portray life with fidelity and artistic sincerity and to give the reader a sense of being in the presence of living men and women is a task requiring the highest and rarest sort of talent to be found among writers. The essence of life, the soul of an incident, is the most elusive thing with which a story-teller is called upon to grapple. In the great majority of cases it escapes his sensibilities the moment he sits down to his desk, leaving him in a haze of distorted impressions and false notes. It is as though the pen and ink he uses had a paralyzing effect on his imagination, turning men and women into paper dolls and events of throbbing import into the subject matter of fairy tales. In this respect Theodore Dreiser is one of the very few exceptions in the literature of the world and the only one in his own country.

Dreiser has the great gift of retaining his vision, an undimmed memory for things, while he writes. He has the art of making men, scenes and occurrences as actual as they are to him, not as a story-teller but simply as a living creature with eyes to see, ears to hear and a mind to register impressions.

Barring poetry of great original force and beauty, no other kind of novel-writing really matters, not at least as a heritage for future generations, and this is what all the critics are apparently aware of, consciously or otherwise, when they speak of Dreiser's ing his vision, undimmed memory new novel [sic].

This is the kind of literature that is really taken seriously and has lasting merit as a work of art. Other works of fiction may possess ever so many virtues and achieve ever so large a measure of success, but they are mere toys doomed to mere ephemeral glory.

The strength of a book like "An American Tragedy" is something above brilliancy and cleverness. It is a quality for which a compliment of this kind would be an insult. It is something infinitely more intrinsic, infinitely more vital.

"True to life" is one of many misleading terms current in the literary jargon of today. Anybody can make a statement that is absolutely true to life but mere truthfulness is not enough to raise a story to the dignity of Art. *A work like Dreiser's is not merely true to life. It conveys the illusion of being Life itself.* Nor is life alone enough to be art. The multiplication table is life. Your laundry bill is life. In like manner there are novelists whose stories are true to life but that leave you cold. They do not inflame your imagination, whereas truth in the form of art does. It sets your heart palpitating with a sense of witnessing a drama alive with the red-hot blood of human conflict.

Dreiser's novel contains the story of a murder trial, and even his bitterest opponents are forced to admit that it is the most profoundly truthful and effective description of a murder trial ever offered to the American reader. It is not a question of depth of insight but of overpowering artistic truth. You seem to have known everything he tells you, before you read it. If he shows you a person or a situation you feel as if you had come across someone or something like it in real life. It is as though you were continually exclaiming in your heart: "Precisely! That's it!" Whereas in the case of other novelists, no matter how dazzlingly brilliant, you are mutely saying: "After all, it is only a story."

A word about Dreiser's style. The critics find it, at times at least, rather lumbering and slovenly and they quote words like "anent," "via," which sound natural in court papers or other official documents but which are out of place in literature. I might add that there are words and phrases which Dreiser uses rather too lavishly, so much so that in some cases they pall on the reader.

Then there are long drawn-out, involved sentences which might be cut and recast to advantage. So far as a paragraph here and there is concerned, this is true. But passages of this kind are, after all, mere exceptions. On the other hand there are whole pages in which the English is not only thoroughly readable but, in an important sense, an example of what fiction writing should be. Its simplicity, directness and *stylistic sincerity* are part and parcel of the simplicity, directness and that *artistic sin-*

cerity which is the highest merit a novel could boast. There are thousands of words and phrases which indicate a subtle understanding of a situation, a mood or a character and which bear evidence to the profound earnestness which the artist brings to his work. In no place do I find anything like parading or flirting with the gallery. Most novelists gain cheap applause by appealing to a cheap taste for a happily turned phrase.

Talking of the gallery. There is, indeed, more than one gallery among the novel-reading public. There is the ordinary mass of intellectual minors who are hungry for the kind of dime-novel that sells for two dollars, and there is the highbrow novel-reader, in many cases university-bred, who mistakes unhackneyed phraseology for art, though in many cases unhackneyed quality spells lack of clarity, directness and genuineness. Dreiser takes his art too seriously and too honestly to stoop to salesmanship of this kind. He is too deeply absorbed in the character and situation at hand to have time for trifling with words.

John Maxwell. "An American Tragedy - - By Dreiser." Indianapolis *Sunday Star,* January 31, 1926.

Theodore Dreiser, one time of Terre Haute, Ind., but in more recent years of New York, has written a new book, "An American Tragedy," his first novel in a number of years. The novel is in two volumes, 840 pages. Mr. Dreiser himself feels that "An American Tragedy" is his premier work of fiction. . . .

Taking it all in all, while "An American Tragedy" is a dark, pessimistic story, yet it is extraordinarily faithful to the literary ideals set by Mr. Dreiser long ago and continuously espoused by him in an extended literary career. May it not be justly said of Mr. Dreiser that he is the first truly great American realist. Let him be the literary vivisectionist that he is, he is not vulgar with it all. Imagine him clad in the spotless operating robe of the physician, bending over the patient with knife in hand, deftly tearing nerve and tissue, eagerly bent on probing the mysteries of soul and life. Dreiser is just as coldly scientific in his literary method. He may seem cruel in his delineations, but he is not, but just true, faithful to the last detail to the art of the grim realist. We regret the painful gloominess of Mr. Dreiser's method, we wish that his method might be a happier one, some of us will not be content to dwell long on the picture which he presents, but who can deny his honesty, who can deny admiration for this extraordinary insight into the action and reaction of the human mind.

Mr. Dreiser seeks to lay bare the human soul; he writes not primarily for money, to amuse, or entertain. When he describes the operation of the Lycurgus collar factory, one is quite sure that Dreiser has been personally on the scene and has made a study of the workings of such a factory. When he describes the gruesome machinery connected with death in the electric chair, the last sad moments of the condemned, etc., we are quite sure that Mr. Dreiser has personally visited a prison and made an investigation of the atmosphere and paraphernalia attended with official executions—which,

In fact, Mr. Dreiser did. He writes after the manner of Victor Hugo, who before he could portray the desperate plight of John Valjean in the sewers of Paris, was compelled to make a personal visit to these deep, unsavory recesses of the ancient capital.

Therefore, length constitutes no valid objection to Mr. Dreiser's two-volume soul study. One might as well criticize "Les Miserables" or the "Count of Monte Cristo" for the same reason. It is the literary craftsmanship shown, the faithfulness to detail, the vigor and genius displayed that really go to make up the verdict. Mr. Dreiser may truly be said to have built a great book from the peculiar Dreiserian viewpoint. Whether the viewpoint and style are to give Mr. Dreiser the permanence, the outstanding literary immortality predicted for him by Mencken and others only the furure will tell.

Donald Davidson. "Theodore Dreiser." Nashville *Tennessean*, January 31, 1926.

Theodore Dreiser's new novel is in two volumes, with fine print, some eight hundred pages in all. But to those who have the wisdom and the courage to undertake it, the reading will bring an unforgettable experience. It is a complete presentation, methodical, unsparing, and yet somehow tender and pitying, of a being who could perhaps exist at this time in no land but America, yet who is so fully and poignantly imagined that he partakes of universality. Clyde Griffiths, Mr. Dreiser's hero, is a weakling, a trivial worm crawling vainly through a complex morass of social and moral forces that he cannot understand, forces which rule and blind and bewilder and finally kill him. But he aspires, this poor worm, in his fumbling and uncertain way. He dreams eagerly of some state better than his trodden wormhood, and would rise, treading down other worms in his turn. The dream brings disaster, and at last death to which he goes with dignity yet with wonder that the immutable laws of the universe can inflict such extinction on a being so conscious of life's warmth, its brightness, its beauty.

Therefore *An American Tragedy* is, in a sense, a moral and spiritual allegory depicting man as the victim of the complicated civilization he himself has made. But of course it is not actually an allegory. It will generally be put in the class of "realistic" novels. Such in truth it is, and as such it has in it material enough for a dozen or so sociological treatises. It has all the defects of Dreiser's work—uncouth, rambling sentences, prosiness, lumbering, dry, matter-of-factness; enormous masses of details apparently trivial. Yet really nothing is trivial in this book. Nobody but Theodore Dreiser would have had the courage and patience to write it. The very multiplicity of detail arises from an honest and sympathetic desire to allow nothing pertinent in this man's life to remain undiscovered. Nothing, absolutely nothing, must be shirked which will disclose him and the society in which he moves. And even the gawky, sprawling sentences may be the product of the same unflinching honesty. Artistic effects? Artistic selection? Let all be abandoned for the sake of the truth. And Dreiser, so far as he is concerned, is right. The result is an overwhelming book; a book convincing, terrible, and true; a book that tears you away from whatever you are doing and incorporates you into itself; a massive and pitiful document of human verity; a book from which may be gained, as from George Eliot's *Romola*, an overpowering sense of the reality of evil. . . .

To summarize the story . . . is really to give no idea at all of the book—its masses of psychological detail and inquisition; its host of minor characters; its relevation of the inner workings of American social life from higher to lower strata; its tremendous dramatic moments such as the scene on the lake when Clyde takes the innocent Roberta to her doom, and his last hours when he is facing, in the death house, the remorseless fact of the waiting electric chair. In his study of motives, especially, Dreiser is amazing. What is there, I ask myself, that this man Dreiser does not know about human beings? Clyde turns and twists from subterfuge to subterfuge, always justifying himself while he is acting, yet always repentant for his errors when they are at last evident. Even in the death house, when tragedy has finally achieved its purgation, his mind still puzzles over the question of his guilt. To save his soul (literally, for he faces the problem of religious salvation) he cannot decide whether he really was guilty or not, in the ultimate sense. He has a feeling that he has somehow been wronged, though he has undoubtedly done terrible things. He thinks of all the people who condemned him as a monster.

> He had a feeling in his heart that he was not as guilty as they all seemed to think. After all, they had not been tortured, as he had, by Roberta with her determination that he marry her and thus ruin his whole life. They had not burned with that unquenchable passion for the Sondra of his beautiful dream as he had. They had not been harassed, tortured, mocked by the ill-fate of his early life and training, forced to sing and pray on the streets in such a degrading way, when his whole heart and soul cried out for better things. How could they judge him, these people, all or any one of them, even his own mother, when they did not know what his own mental, physical and spiritual suffering had been?

At the last he had his moment of dignity, when word comes that the Governor has refused to pardon him—

> So they've decided against me. Now I will have to go through that door after all—like all those others. They'll draw the curtains for me, too. Into that other room—then back along the passage—saying good-bye as I go, like those others. I will not be here any more.

It is, after all, the universal human exit. Those words are fraught with a symbolism; we are all pressed toward that Door—all of us poor puzzled creatures, born will-nilly into a world we do not understand and forced to leave it before we have really had a chance to understand it, not always perhaps like Clyde Griffiths, with innocent blood on our hand, but certainly, like him, finding it terrifyingly difficult to adjust ourselves and our fine dreams to all its complex forces. That is the tale told by Dreiser in this great and powerful book—a sombre tale of an ignoble and curious creature, that paragon of animals, that quintessence of dust, Clyde Griffiths, or in other words, "Homo sapiens."

Herbert S. Gorman. "A Canvas of Living Figures." *Book Review,* February, 1926, p. 19.

An American Tragedy" is Theodore Dreiser's first novel in ten years and it s his best work. Through the eight hundred pages that make up the two-volume bulk of this book, a theme disturbing in its acrid comments on a ertain phase of American life becomes manifest. It is impossible to circumscribe the thesis (if so impartial a preentation may be called a thesis) within the confines of a sentence, for it is not nough to assert that this novel is a painstaking and comprehensive elucidation of a morally-weak youth's disastrous attempt to lift himself from one plane of living to another. This Clyde Griffiths, the son of itinerant street-preachers, who comes to his rich uncle n Lycurgus, New York, and tastes there the heady sweetness of a social plane far above his own, is a somewhat specialzed case. He sees all the finer aspects of iving personified in Sondra Finchley, ut he is tied to Roberta Alden, for Roberta is to bear him a child. The tragic significance of his position is eepened by the cowardice of his weak ature and, as we follow the various teps that lead him to the electric chair, dozen and one contributing causes ender his tragedy all the more certain. Clyde Griflths becomes an aspect of living as well as an individual. He is incoerent ambition struggling in a menally defective nature. He is a victim of circumstances induced by a weak will and so we see him finally like some pathetic and cornered little rat fighting in a bewildered manner against a gigantic juxtaposition of the Fates.

This book is written on a major scale. As far as the prose goes, it is fumbled badly for Dreiser seems unable to comb his periods or escape the most obvious of clichés and the most wandering of constructions. And yet a vast and glacier-like force, advancing sluggishly part of the time, moves steadily forward to the one inevitable conclusion. Dreiser is like a behemoth doggedly pushing his way through the enormous jungle of words that makes up "An American Tragedy." Badly written as this book is there is not a moment when it sags and not a moment when the reader does not carry on with the author. It is deliberate, sometimes stemmed by an over-expansiveness, and yet its vitality is never concealed, for in all essentials it is a novel in the best sense of the word. Here is a vast section of American life torn crudely, perhaps, from its whole, but yet unquestionably authentic in its implications.

It will, of course, be inferred that "An American Tragedy" is based in part on an actual murder trial that was once a country-wide sensation and this is true. One has but to go to the yellowing files of old newspapers and read there of the Chester Gillette-Grace Brown tragedy at Big Moose Lake in 1906, to discover where Dreiser found the inception of his book. But the author has taken this actual story and transformed it to a significant exposition of a phase of American life. He has lifted it to the heights of tragedy by building up the character, which is based on Chester Gillette, into the weak-willed vacillating person that is necessary to the theme. "An American Tragedy" may be badly written insofar as prose construction goes, but Dreiser shows here most unmistakably that he has conquered the novel-form and that he has reached that plane that was Flaubert's ambition—a colossal impartiality that presents facts for what they are. Because of this his book is a huge canvas of living figures.

Charles R. Walker. "Dreiser Moves Upward." *Independent*, February 6, 1926, p. 166.

. . . The "American Tragedy" is, first, intensely American, and beyond that, I believe, universal in its humanness. It is the story of Clyde, the son of an evangelistic street preacher, who began as a bell hop in a Kansas City hotel and finished his life in the electric chair. The boy's character, though not inherently weak, was thoroughly malleable. The early environment of a hand-to-mouth existence, supplemented by a great many Bible texts and a rigid and unilluminated morality, left him both sensitive and exceptionally eager for the privileges of life, especially the material and sensual ones. Except for this he was much like any other youngster, and through his eyes we see the life of an American city. Every bell-hop emotion is here: there is the talk and the petty graft of hotel life, there are liquorish bell-hop parties, and there is a mooncalfish love episode with a self-centered office flapper, which is abruptly terminated by an automobile accident with a stolen car. While he is joy riding home from an all-night party, the car
runs down and kills a child. Clyd
leaves town, vagabonds for a year, an
ends by going to work in the collar fac
tory of a rich uncle. Here the work o
the factory, Clyde's ambition to rise an
to share in the social life of Lycurgu
New York, and his love for two girls ar
the complications. One of the girls, wh
works in the stamping department wit
him, he loves madly—only for a time
but long enough to make her yield t
him completely. Then by luck and con
trivance he begins to emerge from th
"poor relation" status given him by hi
uncle's family and to meet some of th
"upper set." When he falls in love wit
one of the town's social elect, life, h
finds, has become complicated by th
announcement that the other girl is "i
trouble."

A newspaper furnishes him with th
story of a girl who was drowned whe
the canoe in which she was riding wit
a young man was upset. How conve
nient, how wonderful—almost—h
thinks, if fate allowed such a thing t
happen to him and to the girl who i
embarrassing his career! He fights o
the horrible idea, but eventually th
thing does happen—they go canoein
together, he plans to kill her, but at las
after he has lost his nerve, by sheer acc
dent, she is drowned. There is arrest, o
course, a long, long trial, conviction
and death by the electric chair.

Here is a pretty simple, somewhat ob
vious, and very terrible story. It re
quires an enormous amount of detaile
knowledge and an almost faultless psy
chology to make it a living novel. Bu
the difficult mental transitions in th
story leave no doubts in the reader
mind. He knows it must have happene
that way. The compound of bravad
curiosity, passion, and fear that le
Clyde with his bell-hop friends into
house of prostitution in Kansas City, de

pite his earlier training; the slow, hesi-ating, confused, half-irrational process hat led from the first newspaper read-ng of the accident to a decision to lrown his sweetheart—did he ever eally decide it?—up to the drowning tself: but wasn't it half an accident? The days of the trial, the long weeks in he death house, those hours in which Clyde was led by the Rev. Duncan McMillan to accept faith in God and to ay that he had found peace. And yet ad he really accepted faith? Had he eally found peace? As in the long ac-ount of the murder trial, the evidence s piled up every hour, more damning, nore fatal—so the whole story from its ery beginning moves steadily, relent-essly, inevitably toward its almost un-earable catastrophe. This novel is a ragedy in the great sense. Few Ameri-ans have written with such unfailing urpose.

In past years, Dreiser has been as vio-ently attacked for the leaden mediocri-ies of his style as for his immoral episodes. "An American Tragedy" is inmistakably Dreiser, but it is written n a smoother style than any of his pre-ious novels; the structure is done in loser mesh; there is a tendency to oil he ways with participial constructions n the long passages of emotional con-lict and transition. He still keeps his old acophonies, his abominable *clichés*, is newspaper manner. But, sometimes ecause of these, sometimes in spite of hem, he has built up a great novel that s profoundly tragic and intensely American.

Joseph Wood Krutch. "Crime and Punishment." *Nation*, 122 (February 10, 1926), 152.

Mr. Dreiser's new novel is the crowning achievement of the work which he began a quarter of a century ago. To him it seemed then the novelists had lost themselves in their own refinement, that, enamored of moral delicacy and psychological subtleties, they had forgotten the simple motives by which the vast majority of mankind are moved; so with a single shrug he sloughed off once and for all the implications of the theory that man is primarily a moral animal and he did this much as the behaviorists in psychology sloughed off the soul. Let us, he said in effect, take life as I have observed it and let us see if it may not be explained upon the basis of what was afterwards called, in a brilliant analysis of his world, "a theory of animal conduct." Thus he began and thus, with a dogged insistence almost unmatched in literature, he has continued, unshaken by vituperation or neglect and unchanged by a growing fame; content to interpret an ugly world in terms of an ugly theory.

It is not, be it understood, that he denies the existence of delicate feelings or of moral restraints. The present book begins with a scene in which the family of Clyde, the hero, send up from a street corner the plaintive wail of a hymn which beats against the wall of a skyscraper and loses itself in the passing throng. Clyde himself is not unaware of the moral precepts which his parents have inculcated, nor is he unmoved by the thought of another's pain. But these things are pale shadows in comparison with needs and lusts which are nourished not by ideas and habits but by blood. They may go forth to battle but they never win; they may haunt the mind like overtones or like ghosts but they never direct a crucial action. Given a man strong enough, the lust for flesh and for power will lead him, if chance happens to favor, through the career of "The Financier"; given a man weak as the hero of "An American Tragedy" and, fortune against him, he will end with murder and the electric chair. One may revolt and rage if one likes; one may deny to Dreiser any universality for his philosophy; but one may not deny him his novels. He himself may choose what stories he wishes to tell, and no one can question either the ring of truth in the incidents or the adequacy of the motives assigned. Thus and for these reasons murders are done.

Dostoevski told once and for all the story of a metaphysical murder; he showed how an idea born of logic and carried through to a logical conclusion might lead a man by a series of reasonable steps to take a life. But murderers are not ordinarily moral philosophers, and Dreiser has told with almost equal finality the story of one of those more typical murders which merely happen. He has shown a young man, neither better nor worse than thousands, led step by step into a situation from which it seems that murder alone can furnish an escape. He has shown him caught in a web of pleasant little sins committed at the behest of the common desires indulged by half mankind, and he has shown him so little plotting with deliberate malice that at the instant of the crime itself he had not yet made up his mind whether he would commit it or not. Then, relying still upon the simplest of motives, he has shown how a district attorney with his eye upon coming election brought Clyde to tri before a jury anxious to wreak its ver geance upon a representative of th privileged class and how thus a fat driven criminal is brought unjustly t justice. At no point in all the vast an closely woven story does any motiv based upon moral, social, or religiou abstractions count. Clyde may be ex plained without them and so, wit equal completeness, may those wh happened to be in the position to er force the law against him.

Had Mr. Dreiser substituted for th indefinite "An" of his title the definit "The" he would not have been wholl unjustified, for his story implies, with a the force of a concrete example, th tragic failure of this, the most preter tiously moralistic nation of the world, t live in the main by any law but the la of the jungle. Clyde, born into a famil which preached tenets of a fanatica religion and a puritanical morality, ob served as no intelligent person can hel observing the hopeless inapplicabilit of that religion and that morality to th world as he found it. He cast them off t live by the commandments which hi desires dictated because they alon had, in his experience, any real authen ticity; and though a little knowledge o experience of the world as it is migh have saved him, no amount of conven tional moral instruction or religiou training could have done so. Born a animal into an animal world he wen clumsily to work to win for himself th satisfactions which all about him wer winning and for his clumsiness he wa punished; but the civilization in whic he found himself was one which ha offered him no choice save that be tween a feebly sentimental religion an a disastrous experiment in anarchy. H had, in a word, the misfortune to b orn in a country which offers in a hundred thousand churches to teach how to enounce life but which considers it ighly immoral to teach how to live.

Unfortunately there is no space in a eview so brief as this must be to decribe the excellences which make this ovel a complete justification not only f Mr. Dreiser's theories in so far as they pply to the milieu which he has chosen ut of his art as well; it must suffice to ay that the story, continuously interesting and continuously terrible, marches orward with a resistless energy. Incilent is piled upon incident and fact ipon fact, but never—and this distinuishes the present from all the other ong novels of the author—does the tructure grow unwieldly or the interst falter. Nor, it must be added, do the nuch-advertised faults of Mr. Dreiser's tyle come between the reader and the vents which he is following; for so aborbing are the things communicated hat one forgets completely the manner n which they are communicated—a act which must mean, I take it, that Mr. Dreiser's style is, for his own purpose, erfect. "An American Tragedy" is, in ine, the greatest of its author's works, nd that can hardly mean less than that t is the greatest American novel of our eneration.

'After Long Silence Dreiser Writes Two-Volume 'American Tragedy'." Dallas *Morning News,* February 14, 1926.

Theodore Dreiser, according to a large nd probably growing body of opinion, is the dean of American novelists. For more than ten years he has been content, apparently, to rest his reputation upon the half-dozen volumes of fiction with which he slowly forced himself upon the public attention, a process that was not lacking in incident, for many of the battles over what should and what should not be printed in a book have been fought with one or another of Mr. Dreiser's novels as the case in point. Now, after these years of silence, so far as novels are concerned, it appears that Mr. Dreiser has not been content to let his claim to fame rest upon the books already written, but rather it seems he has been storing up ideas and maturing his observations for a magnum opus.

The new work is "An American Tragedy"—two volumes, nearly nine hundred pages, in rather fine print. . . .

No thoughtful reader, I believe, will be able to read this novel without being deeply impressed by the fundamental honesty of the novelist. He has highly resolved to see accurately and to report accurately. An occasional bit of a mannerism may be noted, perhaps, but in the main the purpose to tell the truth about American life is so strong, so passionate, the novelist is not even tempted to stoop to artifice to make his story novel-like. And, indeed, he does not need to. The truth has a hold more compelling than art; or that is the effect. Of course that is art, high art. The result is here a tale that fascinates because it is true: it will take a hardened reader of fiction to remember always that there is no need to pity the poor sufferers in the story, because, after all, they never lived. The impression is very strong that they did live. And perhaps they did, and do.

This praise is more for the conception

of the narrative than for its execution; at least, so far as the writing of words and sentences is concerned, for I do not remember when I have been more annoyed by ineptitude of word and phrase than while reading "An American Tragedy." The frequent lapses seem unnecessary, if not downright gratuitous and willful. Let me insist at once that I am not squeamish about colloquialisms, slang, coinage, or an occasional solecism for which no authority may be found in any dictionary. I am willing for a writer who is as much in earnest as Mr. Dreiser is to take some liberty with the language. If he is happy in his defiance of the rule, I should applaud and maybe plagiarize his defiance. But these circumstances are not of that sort. Mr. Dreiser gets hold of a novel usage that pleases him by its freshness of effect and tries it on every page for chapters on end, until the ear is weary to hear it and the eye weary to see it. He undoubtedly can count many staunch friends among the writers and critics, and why he did not find some one who would read some of these blunders out of his proofs is hard to imagine.

Although I am entirely serious in protest against this "modern" writing, I do not wish to leave the impression that on the whole the novel has left a bad taste in my mouth. For a long time, I have been complaining that our American novels do not truly picture our life. More than any that I can at the moment recall it seems to me this one does. I read once that an Englishman had remarked: "No classes in America? We have three classes in England; in America you have a hundred." And there is this greater difference: in England people are pretty well content to stay in the class into which they are born, while i America everyone counts any year failure that has not witnessed his pro gress upward through half a dozen o these classes at least. Of course, no on will admit this. Is not this a democrati country?

And so I think the Clyde Griffith o this novel is nearer the average Ameri can than Dr. Kennicott, or Carol, o Babbitt, or any other of the character of recent fiction that are considere "good" because typical. Most of th Clydes in real life escape, by acciden rather than by desert, the tragedy tha overwhelmed Clyde Griffiths, bu though they avoid his fate, enough o them practice his psychology.

It is especially interesting to me tha Dreiser, who is often considered the fa ther of the young generation of pagan who are flouting the churches and de crying their Puritan ancestry and it art-killing, gloomy asceticism, shoul have written just this novel, which is i truth not much more than an evange listic illustration—in excelsis—of wha happens when pleasure-seeking yout leaves the straight and narrow path. am not sure that the pulpit could eve argue the young pagans down; the would still be talking, I think. But thi novel will be a poser.

When I look for the avenue of escap for the Clydes of the present day I can' see it in paganism. I should soone try asceticism of the worst kind— puritanism, if you please. This nove is more than art to me. It is grisl warning.

Ieywood Broun. 'It Seems to Me." New York *World*, 'ebruary 20, 1926.

You have not said anything about 'heodore Dreiser's 'An American 'ragedy,'" writes John Macy. "Will you et me say something? I am an old cau-ious critic not given to a rash use of uperlatives. So I mean much when I ay that "An American Tragedy" is the Iount Everest of American fiction, and t is one of the high hills in all the fiction f the world. A word about its faults—o be over and done with them. Dreiser s clumsy, verbose, tangled in his syntax. would flunk a college freshman guilty f some of his sentences. He is often ulgar, even cheap, in his expressions. I tch for a blue pencil to cut and correct im. I would slaughter every 'former' nd every 'latter" and no less than 10,-00 'no lesses.'

"But! I was once arguing about Dick-ns with a man of exquisite taste." He ointed out that Dickens was often rude and slovenly and that he lacked he finer instincts of the artist, and so n. And rather hotly I answered that a iant can bear the burden of a thousand ins. It is so with Dreiser. He is so strong hat his faults do not count. Even when e is weak and inarticulate, he compels ou to see, to hear, to feel, to under-tand. And what are surface blemishes n a story whose essential structure is olid as the roof of the Grand Central tation? The journey of that poor weak-villed boy from childhood to death was nevitable as the passage of the sun rom dawn to darkness. And all the peo-le simply *are*. There is not an unreal person in the entire book, not an episode but must have happened so.

"Dreiser does not weep over his characters or laugh at them—he has very little humor—he presents them, gives you their thoughts and actions. Just and so it was, no less. And you believe him, you have to, you cannot get away from him. I warn you that he will kill two nights, one for each volume. That is what he did to me, to whom most of the accepted great novels of the world are old stories.

"Well, here is a new one. We never had anything like this before. The fundamental thing that holds you is the old, old stuff, humanity. Dreiser, for all his detachment and refusal to take sides, is a man of immense sympathy. See with what delicacy, what infinite pity, but without the slightest touch of sentimentility, he handles the girl, Roberta. You did not know there could be an epoch in a collar factory as well as on a battlefield? Read, and see for yourself.

"One thing more. Who else is there that gives you such a sense of a whole city? It may take an hour to read through one of Dreiser's cities, but when you have read through, you have been there. It is a great book. Yes, I said it, I'm not afraid of the word when it is properly used—great."

Gretchen Mount. "Theodore Dreiser Surpasses Even Himself." Detroit *Free Press*, February 21, 1926.

And now, ladies and gentlemen, let us waste no time beating the tomtoms and ballyhooing for the sideshow, but pass immediately into the Big Top.

For Mr. Theodore Dreiser has come again into the arena from which he has been absent for ten years and the entertainment he offers may be catalogued very simply: " 'An American Tragedy,' the best novel yet written by the greatest of American novelists." It has the same extraordinary completeness of detail which has characterized all of his books. It has a frankness which, recalling the supression of "Sister Carrie" and "The Genius" makes this unchallenged publication another irony of our ridiculous censorship. It is even more massive than its predecessors, two volumes—840 pages:—of solid reading matter. And yet not an extraneous chapter, not an incident which fails to take its place as a vital and illuminating factor in this complex cross-section of the world's social and economic problem at the point where it impinges with tragic consequence upon the individual. . . .

When you have read this chronicle of a humble and unimportant life you will understand Clyde Griffiths, and your emotional founts will be emptied of tears in the agonizing process of understanding. You will not admire Clyde Griffiths; you will not even approve of him; but you will be desperate in his desperation and, defenseless as he, you will seek as eagerly to break through the thin wall which keeps him from his happiness. While society tosses him about, while individuals play with his feelings and with his life, as pawns gambled in a game concealed from him, you will stand by literally in horror. You will live with him through those awful days of the trial; you will share with him the hideous nightmare of those two years in the death house, and then you will go with him to the place where they bathe him and shave him carefully, put o
him the white shirt with the conver
iently open collar, slit his trousers le
for the electrode and start out to ki
him—with two preachers for compan
trying to salve with temporary opt
mism the muddle their sectarian opt
mism has been unable, after twent
five hundred years, to ameliorate.

But you will not pass with Clyd
Griffiths into that peace which th
world cannot give. You will be left in
welter of inquietude and pity, bewil
dered as the wise and compassionat
have always been bewildered by the vi
olence which is as necessary to virtue a
it is to vice. But for what may well b
the first time in a placid existence yo
will understand an ignorant sensualist
a sly wastrel riding on a chip throug
the torrents of life, a weakling capabl
of the futile, terrible crime of murder

Yes, you will understand!

I have said that Mr. Dreiser is ou
greatest American novelist, and by tha
is meant no canting reviewer's com
monplace. For me at least, this is a ver
dict cool of enthusiasm. Nor is it base
upon any consideration of magnitud
or density. All his later books are hug
indeed, and "An American Tragedy" i
the hugest of them all, the most densel
populated, by far. It is, perhaps, almos
as voluminous as the evidence upo
which a mortal jury years ago hange
the poor Gillette boy, whose sorry his
tory is its basis. Yet its voluminosity ha
that greater inclusiveness and dispas
sion which a god might require befor
arriving at a just decision.

But Mr. Dreiser's greatness as a nov
elist does not depend upon his being
reporter for the gods. He is our fines
realist because he is the most under
standing. The structure of our social or
ganization and the pressure of its mas

pon the individual is clearly understood by him, yet understood in no abstract way. He visions the individual as n individual, the residual Adam stirring in him still, and he presents him in is own ego and in his secret difference rom all others. Above everything else, e presents each in his own emotional nilieu, for the humanist in him always vercomes the realist and the scientific esearcher into the springs of action. So, hough there is no concern in his pages vith esthetics or with the creation of eauty, those pages are overwhelming n their emotional quality. Some gift of he spirit is upon them, and although he ompounds his heavy sentences out of he commonplace facts of ordinary ives, they are transmuted by some alhemy into tears and heartache and ompassion.

And therefore for the third time I reeat that Theodore Dreiser is the greatst American novelist. And his present chievement is all the greater in that he as surpassed even himself.

Delos S.
'A Masterpiece."
New York *World*,
February 21, 1926.

. . This reviewer does not propose to lefend Dreiser for writing "An American Tragedy." Such a defense would be s side-splitting as the antics of the half akes who denounce him for writing it.

It would be difficult to prove that "An American Tragedy" is superior to "Siser Carrie" or several other of Dreiser's vorks. Yet on the other hand it would e difficult to prove that "Sister Carrie" s superior to "An American Tragedy." Simply, Dreiser's last is Dreiser at his very best. Some call his style rough and "rugged," but, as a matter of fact, he is crude in the handling of English and the construction of sentences. But that can be forgiven, not because it is Dreiser but because it is a man who can write as fine novels as "An American Tragedy" and "Sister Carrie." . . .At first glance the plot seems morbid and uninteresting. But under the masterful hand of the artist, Clyde Griffiths, (the offspring) is as real as a mole on a spinster's chin. He is not a hero by any means. He is merely a character whom Dreiser chooses to toy with, bait him along through page after page, to finally plop him down in the death chair. But always there is that undercurrent of irony; that feeling of stark tragedy; the absolute realism of a master of realism. There is no mercy in Dreiser. He plays with a character like one would play with a dancing toy. He dances all his springs will allow. Then all there is to do is to look after the matter of a proper disposal.

Of course "An American Tragedy" is padded. Dreiser cannot write unless he uses a lot of unnecessary words. The book drags in places, but again that is as much Dreiser as his oldest pair of socks. It is as much Dreiser's style to write crudely and interestingly as it is Carl Van Vechten's style to write cleverly and interestingly about nothing at all.

One reads "An American Tragedy." First one rather sympathizes with Clyde Griffiths, then one is seized with the desire to give him a good resounding kick in the pants. One is amused and disgusted in turn. One wades through page after page of dull, uninteresting tripe, to suddenly run smack against a dramatic situation that is completely devastating in its effect. That is

Dreiser's gift. He baits his readers along just like he does his characters. He makes them think it is rather dull, then he crowns them with a crowbar.

"An American Tragedy" is contained in two volumes, running something over 800 pages. Some say it is too long. Yet could the story of Clyde Griffiths be told in fewer words? Would the great scenes in the novel be as real and as thrilling as they are if it were not for the careful and painful leading up? The continual repeating of certain things so as to clearly show Clyde Griffiths as Clyde Griffiths, so the reader can better see why Clyde Griffiths reacts as he does in the high moments.

Try to find a more dramatic situation than the one in the boat where Clyde has lured his sweetheart, Roberta, out on a lake with the long-planned intention of drowning her. The moment has arrived; he must do it now or never, but, alas, he is a coward, he hasn't the courage. Then accident intervenes. The boat overturns and Roberta is drowned. The situation in itself is a wonderful piece of work, but the ironic twist at the end is like a dash of cold water in a Turkish bath.

Buy and read "An American Tragedy" by all means.

H. L. Mencken. "Dreiser in 840 Pages." *American Mercury*, 7 (March 1926). 379-381.

Whatever else this vasty double-header may reveal about its author, it at least shows brilliantly that he is wholly devoid of what may be called literary tact. A more artful and ingratiating fellow, facing the situation that confronted him, would have met it with a far less difficult book. It was ten years since he had published his last novel, and so all his old customers, it is reasonable to assume, were hungry for another—all his old customers and all his new customers. His publisher, after a long and gallant battle, had at last chased off the comstocks. Rivals, springing up at intervals, had all succumbed—or, what is the same thing, withdrawn from the Dreiser reservation. The Dreiser cult, once grown somewhat wobbly, was full of new strength and enthusiasm. The time was thus plainly at hand to make a ten strike. What was needed was a book full of all the sound and solid Dreiser merits, and agreeably free from the familiar Dreiser defects—a book carefully designed and smoothly written, with no puerile clichés in it and no maudlin moralizing—in brief, a book aimed deliberately at readers of a certain taste, and competent to estimate good workmanship. Well, how did Dreiser meet the challenge? He met it characteristically, by throwing out the present shapeless and forbidding monster—a heaping cartload of raw materials for a novel, with rubbish of all sorts intermixed—a vast, sloppy, chaotic thing of 385,000 words—at least 25,000 of them unnecessary! Such is scientific salesmanship as Dreiser understands it! Such is his reply to a pleasant invitation to a party!

By this time, I suppose, you have heard what it is all about. The plot, in fact, is extremely simple. Clyde Griffiths, the son of a street preacher in Kansas City, revolts against the piety of his squalid home, and gets himself a job as bellboy in a gaudy hotel. There he acquires a taste for the luxuries affected y travelling Elks, and is presently a eader in shop-girl society. An automo- ile accident, for which he is not to lame, forces him to withdraw dis- reetly, and he proceeds to Chicago, where he goes to work in a club. One lay his father's rich brother, a collar nagnate from Lycurgus, N. Y., is put up here by a member, and Clyde resolves o cultivate him. The old boy, taking a hine to the youngster, invites him to ycurgus, and gives him a job in the actory. There ensues the conflict that nakes the story. Clyde has hopes, but ery little ready cash; he is thus forced o seek most of his recreation in low life. But as a nephew to old Samuel Griffiths he is also taken up by the Lycurgus *haut ton*. The conflict naturally assumes the orm of girls. Roberta Alden, a beautiful emale operative in the factory, falls in ove with him and yields herself to him. Almost simultaneously Sondra Finch- ey, an even more beautiful society girl, alls in love with him and promises to narry him. Clyde is ambitious and de- cides for Sondra. But at that precise mo- nent Roberta tells him that their sin has found her out. His reply is to take her to a lonely lake and drown her. The crime being detected, he is arrested, put on trial, convicted, and elec- trocuted.

A simple tale. Hardly more, in fact, than the plot of a three page story in *True Confessions*. But Dreiser rolls it out to such lengths that it becomes, in the end, a sort of sequence of serials. The whole first volume, of 431 pages of small type, brings us only to the lamen- table event of Roberta's pregnancy. The home life of the Griffithses in Kan- sas City is described in detail. We make intimate acquaintance with the street preacher himself, a poor fanatic, always trusting in the God who has fooled him incessantly, and with his pathetic, drab wife, and with his daughter Esta, who runs away with a vaudeville actor and comes home with a baby. There ensues a leisurely and meticulous treatise upon the life of the bellboys in the rococo Green-Davidson Hotel—how they do their work, what they collect in tips, how they spend their evenings, what sort of girls they fancy. The automobile accident is done in the same spacious manner. Finally, we get to Lycurgus, and page after page is devoted to the operations of the Griffiths factory, and to the gay doings in Lycurgus society, and to the first faint stirrings, the pas- sionate high tide, and the disagreeable ebb of Clyde's affair with Roberta. So much for Volume I: 200,000 words. In Volume II we have the murder, the ar- rest, the trial and the execution: 185,- 000 more.

Obviously, there is something wrong here. Somewhere or other, there must be whole chapters that could be spared. I find, in fact, many such chapters—lit- erally dozens of them. They incom- mode the action, they swamp and con- ceal the principal personages, and they lead the author steadily into his weak- ness for banal moralizing and trite, meaningless words. In "The 'Genius' " it was *trig* that rode him; in "An Ameri- can Tragedy" it is *chic*. Did *chic* go out in 1896? Then so much the better! It is the mark of an unterrified craftsman to use it now—more, to rub it in merci- lessly. Is Freudism stale, even in Green- wich Village? Ahoy, then, let us heave in a couple of bargeloads of complexes —let us explain even judges and district attorneys in terms of suppressions! Is the "chemic" theory of sex somewhat flyblown? Then let us trot it out, and give it a polishing with the dish-rag! Is there such a thing as sound English, graceful English, charming and beautiful English? Then let us defy a world of scoundrels, half Methodist and half aesthete, with such sentences as this one:

> The "death house" in this particular prison was one of those crass erections and maintenances of human insensibility and stupidity principally for which no one primarily was really responsible.

And such as this:

> Quite everything of all this was being published in the papers each day.

What is one to say of such dreadful bilge? What is one to say of a novelist who, after a quarter of a century at his trade, still writes it? What one is to say, I feel and fear, had better be engraved on the head of a pin and thrown into the ocean: there is such a thing as critical *politesse.* Here I can only remark that sentences of the kind I have quoted please me very little. One of them to a page is enough to make me very unhappy. In "An American Tragedy"—or, at all events, in parts of it—they run to much more than that. Is Dreiser actually deaf to their dreadful cacophony? I can't believe it. He can write, on occasion, with great clarity, and even with a certain grace. I point, for example, to Chapter XII of Book III, and to the chapter following. There is here no idiotic "quite everything of all," and no piling up of infirm adverbs. There is, instead, straightforward and lucid writing, which is caressing in itself and gets the story along. But elsewhere! . . .

Thus the defects of this gargantuan book. They are the old defects of Dreiser, and he seems to be quite unable to get rid of them. They grow more marked, indeed, as he passes into middle life. His writing in "Jennie Gerhardt" was better than his writing in "The Genius" and so was his sense of form, his feeling for structure. But what of the more profound elements? What of his feeling for character, his capacity to imagine situations, his skill at reaching the emotions of the reader? I can only say that I see no falling off in this direction. "An American Tragedy," as a work of art, is a colossal botch, but as a human document it is searching and full of a solemn dignity, and at times it rises to the level of genuine tragedy. Especially the second volume. Once Roberta is killed and Clyde faces his fate, the thing begins to move, and thereafter it roars on, with ever increasing impetus, to the final terrific smash. What other American novelist could have done the trial as well as Dreiser has done it? His method, true enough, is the simple, bald one of the reporter—but of *what* a reporter! And who could have handled so magnificently the last scenes in the death-house? Here his very defects come to his aid. What we behold is the gradual, terrible, irresistible approach of doom—the slow slipping away of hopes. The thing somehow has the effort of a tolling of bells. It is clumsy. It lacks all grace. But it is tremendously moving.

In brief, the book improves as it nears its shocking climax—a humane fact, indeed, for the reader. The first volume heaves and pitches, and the second, until the actual murder, is full of psychologizing that usually fails to come off. But once the poor girl is in the water, there is a change, and thereafter "An American Tragedy" is Dreiser at his plodding, booming best. The means are often bad, but the effects are superb. One gets the same feeling of complete reality that came from "Sister Carrie," and especially from the last days of Hurstwood. The thing ceases to be a story, and becomes a harrowing reality. Dreiser, I uppose, regards himself as an adept at he Freudian psychology. He fre- quently uses its terms, and seems to ake its fundamental doctrines very eriously. But he is actually a behavio- rist of the most advanced wing. What nterests him primarily is not what peo- ple think, but what they do. He is full of a sense of their helplessness They are, o him, automata thrown hither and hither by fate—but suffering tragically under every buffet. Their thoughts are muddled and trivial—but they can feel. And Dreiser feels with them, and can make the reader feel with them. It takes skill of a kind that is surely not common. Good writing is far easier.

The Dreiserian ideology does not change. Such notions as he carried out of the experiences of his youth still abide with him at fifty-four. They take somewhat curious forms. The revolt of youth, as he sees it, is primarily a revolt against religious dogmas and forms. He is still engaged in delivering Young America from the imbecilities of a frozen Christianity. And the economic struggle, in his eye, has a bizarre sym- bol: the modern American hotel. Do you remember Carrie Meeber's first en- counter with a hotel beefsteak in "Sis- ter Carrie"? And Jennie Gerhardt's dumb wonder before the splendors of that hotel in which her mother scrubbed the grand staircase? There are hotels, too, and aplenty, in "The Ti- tan" and "The 'Genius' "; toward the end of the latter there is a famous de- scription, pages long, of the lobby of a New York apartment house, by the Waldorf-Astoria out of the Third ave- nue car-barn. It was a hotel that lured Jennie (like Carrie before her) to ruin, and it is a hotel that starts Clyde Griffiths on his swift journey to the chair. I suggest a more extensive exami- nation of the matter, in the best Dreis- er-Freud style. Let some ambitious young *Privat Dozent* tackle it.

So much for "An American Tragedy." Hire your pastor to read the first volume for you. But don't miss the second!

R. N. Linscott. "The Atlantic's Bookshelf." *Alantic Monthly,* 137 (March 1926)

Dreiser's method of creation resembles that of the oyster. The flashing and predatory career of Yerkes, the traction magnate, was the hard, sharp grain of fact about which grew *The Financier* and *The Titan.* From certain episodes of his own life were evolved *The Genius.* And now a forgotten murder of the last generation, smoothed, ag- glutinated, worked over for a decade, has been transformed into the two im- posing volumes of *An American Tragedy.* . . .

For the telling of this story, Dreiser has taken 840 closely printed pages. He has included a more detailed, absorb- ing, realistic account of a murder trial than has hitherto found its way into fiction. He has documented the tale with even greater thoroughness than the career of Copperswood in *The Fin- ancier* and *The Titan,* omitting no inci- dent, no thought even, relevant to a full and precise understanding of the case that he puts before the reader. And by making his protagonist a typical Ameri- can youth, and his opponent the com- plex and unconquerable forces of heredity and environment (the modern equivalent to the Fates of Greek tragedy), he has translated this story of a weak and commonplace boy into an American epic comparable in power and understanding to *Jude the Obscure* or *The Brothers Karamazov.*

Too much pity, too little style—these are the barriers that have stood between Dreiser and a place among the world's greatest novelists. These barriers he shows signs of surmounting. His passages of exposition are still clumsy, but his narrative is now, for the most part, simple and straightforward, a competent piece of honest reporting that interposes no verbal window between the reader and the scene described. And, what is more important, he no longer turns aside from the course of his story to give tongue to those cries of compassion or despair which so often, in his earlier novels, were evoked by the sufferings of his characters. The result is Dreiser's greatest novel, and an impressive achievement to be reckoned with in any history of American literature.

"Dreiser's'The American Tragedy'." *Argonaut,* March 6, 1926, p. 5.

Theodore Dreiser has been an agitating element in American letters. Outside Walt Whitman, no native author has aroused more vehement controversy, caused such critical cleavages. Hostile camps are in agreement only in their common admission of Mr. Dreiser's gifts. There is no gainsaying the power of his pen, however invidious the inkwell wherein it is dipped. It is a quarte century now since the writer flew th defiant colors of "Sister Carrie" an pursued by the privateers of censo ship, was brought to port like a picaroo craft of the Spanish main. Nothing i the way of whilom Comstockian cru sade called forth the hubbub of that no vel's suppression nor did more, per haps, to bring about the reactions whic today express themselves in the wide armed reception accorded Mr. Dreise and his newest production, "Th American Tragedy," which, as was wel surmised, is no woolen sock of a re formed pirate's knitting needles.

That Mr. Dreiser has at last come tri umphantly into his own and enjoys th hearing to which his talents entitle him is in great measure due to the mighti ness of H. L. Mencken. He has so sermo nized on him, pounded his pulpit wit such fiery fist of championship, that no to acknowledge Mr. Dreiser's head and-shoulder superiority to other con temporary American fictionists and ac cept him in those issues of his art whic were most disputed, would be as hereti cal as the rejection of him was once th proof of unvitiated belletristic taste. S much has the tide finally turned in fa vor of one whom even Mr. Mencken i apparently compelled by candor t designate as "the vulgarest voice ye heard in American literature."

The voice of Mr. Dreiser is not no ticeably vulgar in "The America Tragedy"; or it may merely be that on is more attuned than formerly to suc inflections in fiction. What impresse one, first of all is the bulkiness of th book, which runs to near 900 pages o long primer: a rival almost of old-tim three-deckers; and as a laborious task i in itself a possible explanation for th fact, rather stressed by Mr. Dreiser' publishers, that it is the author's first novel since 1915. There is ample proof, besides its verbal abundance, that this is no light effort of Mr. Dreiser's seasoned talents. There is careful finish to the style, and something close to perfection in its proportioned, intricate architecture, that is a testimony to the seriousness with which Mr. Dreiser takes literary art, and intimates that he has meant "The American Tragedy" to be his most momentous contribution to it.

There is no doubt that the novel challenges high comparisons. One can't read it without having Dostoievsky's "Crime and Punishment" come to mind as a measure of its American parallel. It is not that the crude mentality of a Clyde Griffiths even impinges on the complicated, finely evolved psychosis of a Raskolnikov, any more than the former's egotism resembles the morbid mind-functioning of a Julien Sorel in Stendhal's "Rouge et Noir" or expresses the intellectual selfcentered cynicism of the youthful seducer of "the Disciple," by Paul Bourget; though it is conceivable that these and sundry notable examples of the sort of thing Mr. Dreiser gives us in "The American Tragedy" have provided their suggestions. The common equation is found in the elaborate search after cause and effect; the probing into psychological depths; the unremitting attempt in every case to present in the completest, fullest form the machinery of motivation directing the individual presented; to stop at nothing less than his ultimate, innermost solutions.

It is indisputable that Mr. Dreiser has done this in his Clyde Griffiths—done it quite as thoroughly, most persons will concede, as Dostoievsky has plumbed his Raskolnikov—and if one is less content with "The American Tragedy" than with "Crime and Punishment" it can only be perhaps from one of two reasons or because of both. In other words, it is a matter purely of values, of the comparative interest to the reader of the portraits, together with what importance he attaches to the surplus philosophy he gets from the Russian masterpiece, wholly lacking in Mr. Dreiser's work. Dostoivesky is moralist; and in the conclusion of "Crime and Punishment" he converts the spiritual travails, life's miseries and sufferings, he has depicted into illuminating terms of hopefulness. Mr. Dreiser acknowledges no ethic aims. He paints life and its bald facts as he sees them, and then puts aside his palette. The finish of "The American Tragedy" leaves one figuratively, as well as literally, in a death-cell; leaves one there to one's own deductive resources, to make what one can out of the whole pitiful affair. The difference between the novel and "Crime and Punishment" is a difference that involves the fundamentals of art itself; the question what are, after all, the responsibilities of art, what its truest, highest ends. . . .

T. K. Whipple. "Theodore Dreiser." *New Republic*, 46 (March 17, 1926), 113–115.

Dreiser is one of those writers who are said to have historical importance, one of those trail-breakers, that is, who make a deep impress on their own time and who are known to later generations by reputation, but by reputation only. Dreiser's force and originality—greatness is not too strong a word—must become only more obvious with the passage of years; but surely that greatness will be taken more and more on faith. The labor of reading him, with the sense it brings of a grinding despair, as of being pursued in a nightmare over endless wastes of soft sand, is an experience, however profitable, that is too painful to be sought out by normal humanity.

To take the full measure of Dreiser's achievement, one must remember that Sister Carrie appeared in 1900 and Jennie Gerhardt in 1911, and that among the most popular and typical novels of those years were When Knighthood Was in Flower, Graustark, and Rebecca of Sunnybrook Farm. No wonder that from the first Dreiser was treated either to invective or to apologetics, and that his apologists dwelt on his intentions and on his personal qualities almost to the exclusion of his work. At least, at a time when fiction was a kind of confectionery, he was not facile, conventional, pretty and optimistic: at least, he meant well. And the critics who approved of his purpose—to tell the whole truth about American life as he saw it, even though he saw it as unpleasant—could not afford, in the bitter war being waged with the censors and the moralists, to question his literary success. Furthermore, his granite-like steadfastness and integrity, his insistence on seeing for himself, were so striking and so admirable that it was natural to praise the man and forget the novelist.

All Dreiser's virtues are as evident as ever in An American Tragedy; if they no longer shine quite so brilliantly and all-sufficingly, it is doubtless because the contrasting background has disappeared, owing in part to the lesson which Dreiser has himself taught. Fifteen years ago, An American Tragedy would have been a portent; now it is another of Dreiser's novels, much like its predecessors. More successful than The Financier, The Titan, and the "Genius", less successful but also a more difficult undertaking than Sister Carrie or Jennie Gerhardt, it marks a return rather than an advance, a return from high finance and high society, from elaborate études de moeurs and minute accounts of social machinery, to the sort of topic which Dreiser is best fitted to handle: the sordid and pathetic story of a midwestern boy of the lower middle class whose weakness lands him in disaster. It shows development only in that Dreiser tries to reach higher emotional levels and greater intensity than he has attempted heretofore. Otherwise, it is another manifestation of his familiar merits and defects: in other words, it is a novel no other living American could have written—and also, probably, one which no other would have written.

An American Tragedy could have been written only by a man of unusual power and magnitude. Even on the harshest critic Dreiser's novels must leave an impression that the author has a kind of greatness. The cause of this impression and the source of Dreiser's greatness I take to be his emotional endowment—not so much an intensity as a tremendous, steady, unfailing flood of feeling. He is distinguished from ordinary men by extraordinary strength and volume of passion. Chiefly it shows itself in his tragic sense, in his profound consciousness of the tragedy inherent in all existence, in the very scheme of things—tragedy inescapable, essential, universal, perceived by man, but by very few so overwhelmingly felt. His brooding pity penetrates all life as he sees it, touching every human being, from the most glittering superman to the forlornest prostitute, as in An American Tragedy it touches everyone from the bellboys of the Green-Davidson Hotel in Kansas City to the rich and beautiful Sondra Finchley, social leader of Lycurgus, New York. Especially acute is his perception of man's endless capacity for suffering, a trait which lends dignity to even the weakest and most contemptible of Dreiser's creatures, even to the elder Griffiths, the streetpreaching derelict who is the hero's father in An American Tragedy, just as Clyde's mother, for all her grotesqueness, in her grief for her son illustrates Dreiser's saying that "sometimes even the mediocre and the inefficient attain to a classic stature when dignified by pain."

Dreiser's emotional capacity shows itself not only in his tragic sense but also in his zest, his unflagging relish for actuality and his feeling of its mystery. His is a romantic love of reality, charged with wonder and awe. His love of life, good or bad, beautiful or ugly, is omnivorous; because it is all strange, to him it is all exciting. To a curiosity so voracious and an interest so insatiable as his, nothing whatever seems dull or tiresome. Hence come his amazing faculty of observation and his relentless heaping up of detail; hence also, therefore, the epic sweep often and rightly attributed to his novels, which have the range and vastness pertaining to any minute record of an enormous area of human life. This gusto, however, not content with imparting scope to his work, leads him into trouble, for because of it he can resist no temptation to wander off into by-paths and tedious digressions. Because he can bring himself to leave out nothing, he piles up mountains of pointless minutiae, irrelevant and insignificant, and produces an intolerable tedium. He can never learn to omit, for his latest novel is as overweighted as his earlier; on page 78 of the second volume Clyde commits the murder which really ends his story; he is captured on page 145; his trial drags along to his conviction on page 330; and his execution takes place on page 405. Not even The Financier so abundantly illustrates Dreiser's ability to make ten pages do the work of one. His emotion, when it shows itself as all-inclusive love of reality, is a source of weakness as well as of strength.

Yet even these vast talus-heaps of detail are stirred by the tides of passion which surge under them. Somehow, in spite of everything, Dreiser manages to communicate something of his feeling, which burns, though dimly and feebly, even through the slag and dross of his writing. If many readers regard his emotionality as merely sentimental, it is partly because the childish crudity of his expression lends an appearance of falsity. When the "Genius" exclaims "What a sweet welter life is—how rich, how tender, how grim, how like a colorful symphony" and the author adds "Great art dreams welled up into his soul as he viewed the sparkling deeps of space," it is difficult, but also I think necessary, to believe that words so inadequate and so false could be called forth by true emotion. An American Tragedy contains some two hundred pages like the following:

> But, God, what was that?
> Oh, that terrible sound!
> Like a whimpering, screeching spirit in this dark!
> There!
> What was it?
> He dropped his bag and in a cold sweat sunk down, crouching behind a tall, thick tree, rigid and motionless with fear.

That sound!

But only a screech-owl! He had heard it several weeks before at the Cranston lodge. But here! In this wood! This dark! He must be getting on and out of here. There was no doubt of that. He must not be thinking such horrible, fearful thoughts, or he would not be able to keep up his strength or courage at all.

But that look in the eyes of Roberta! That last appealing look! God! He could not keep from seeing it! Her mournful, terrible screams! Could he not cease from hearing them—until he got out of here anyhow?

Finally the author's agitation grows insufferable in the chapters devoted to Clyde's experience in the death house, which rival a Hearst paper's account of a popular murderer's last agonies. Dreiser's understanding of Clyde, his pity and sympathy, his remarkable imaginative power, are rendered all but vain by the terms in which they are expressed, terms which disgust fully as much as they move the reader.

Most of Dreiser's warmest champions, such as Mencken, grant that he cannot write, grant that he has no narrative sense and no sense of words or of style, that he is prolix and irrelevant, that his sentences are worse than chaotic, that he violates English and even American idiom; these foibles, however, they regard as but petty irritations which must be overlooked. But how can such writing be negligible? Dreiser could not write as he does, mixing slang with poetic archaisms, reveling in the cheap, trite and florid, if there were not in himself something correspondingly muddled, banal and tawdry. Futhermore, since a writer works through words alone and words are his only means of communication, a failure in writing is necessarily a failure in communication—and of Dreiser's failure the best that can be said is that it is incomplete. Somehow he contrives to give a sense of reality and veracity, as of a tremendous story which actually happened told by an inept, loquacious stutterer, himself deeply stirred, who sometimes unintentionally misrepresents the facts. In An American Tragedy he has particularly difficult problems in carrying the reader's belief—that so feeble a creature as Clyde would prove a social success and carry out a murder. I cannot doubt Clyde's story in the main, but I cannot believe that it happened precisely as Dreiser has recounted it.

Dreiser's characterization suffers, and must inevitably suffer, from his incapacity to handle words. As in The Financier and The "Genius" he asserts that his heroes are brilliant and irresistible, yet shows them as vulgar dullards because he is unable to write good conversation, so in An American Tragedy he misses success because he cannot so use language as to communicate intense feeling. Not that the reader is unaffected—but the disparity between the author's perturbation and the inadequacy of his expression is almost grotesque. If Clyde and Roberta and the rest were not half concealed by a deluge of inept verbiage, An American Tragedy might well be one of the world's great novels.

Perhaps Dreiser's incompetence in the management of his medium is partly accounted for by the striking resemblance of his writing to the world which he depicts, a world chaotic and tawdry, without plan, purpose, or sense, lacking even the rudimentary organization of a wolf pack, a world offering no valid reasons for living, no reward which would appeal to a rational or civilized being, no prize save an economic success which can buy only physical luxury, inane display and vulgar snobbery. It is a brutal world, a free-for-all of personal aggrandizement, no more humane than the aboriginal jungle of sabre-toothed tiger and woolly elephant, a world seeking meretricious and gaudy in the absence of genuine satisfactions. Not only futile and wasteful, it is also tragic and passionate, for its inhabitants are endowed with desires and possibilities for which it affords no possible means of fulfillment. The strongest and coarsest are dissatisfied victors; the weak mill helplessly about, kicked and trodden upon. Dreiser's books are the stammering utterance of this pathetic and flashy disorder trying to speak.

Similarly, one might say that Dreiser's philosophy is this world trying to think. Being able to conceive nothing else, he assumes that human life everywhere has always been and must always be like the life he has himself known at first hand. His thought is simply a formulation of the beliefs which he has discerned in the practice of those about him. The official and avowed creed of his world—the taboo morality and silly ostrich-like optimism with which it oils the wheels of progress—he never tires of attacking; but the creed implicit in its actions he has exalted into universal philosophy. He regards human existence as inevitably a bestial anarchy never under any circumstances capable of yielding better gratifications than the joy of fighting, sensual pleasure, and the parade of money. For all his onslaughts on the pious camouflage with which his compatriots conceal their motives and doings even from themselves, he has essentially accepted American life as he found it in the midwest of his younger years. He has felt and experienced his world too fully to be able to detach himself from it and try it by any other standards than its own. He has identified himself with it, and the union has brought forth the misbegotten Leviathans of his novels. Through this union he has taken into himself and so into his art the anarchy and the cheap barbarity of his surroundings.

Yet what a tremendous emotional pressure has gone into this identification, what power of realization! Of that power, the basis of life as well as of literature, surely Dreiser has more than any other living American. Furthermore, in the making of this vital contact with American life, Dreiser was the first, the pioneer. Herein lies the debt which all other writers owe to him—herein lies his greatness and his significance. No doubt it was necessary that someone should be sacrificed by being merged and sunk, and that he was chosen was Dreiser's fortune and misfortune. His real achievement is to be found in the work of others, work which he has helped make possible. And his contribution is not to literature alone; he has done more, directly and indirectly, than any other individual to rouse Americans to a consciousness of what American life is like and if an American civilization ever emerges, Dreiser's share in its making will not be small. That is what it is to have historical importance. Perhaps it is more than being a good novelist.

Henry Miller "Dreiser's Style." *New Republic*, 46 (April 28, 1926), 306. [Letter in Response to Above Review by T. K. Whipple.]

Dreiser's Style

Sir: In his review of Dreiser's American Tragedy, Mr. T. K. Whipple raises an interesting problem in the art of the novel, in his discussion of Mr. Dreiser's style. "Dreiser could not write as he does," says Mr. Whipple, "mixing slang with poetic archaisms, reveling in the cheap, trite and florid, if there were not in himself something correspondingly muddled, banal and tawdry . . . a failure in writing is necessarily a failure in communication." This is all very true when the thing to be communicated is an abstract idea or philosophy. The novel, however, is effective because of images and emotions and not because of its abstract ideas. Mr. Whipple's error lies in applying intellectual criteria such as logic and profundity to art, which affects us by its vividness or beauty.

From this point of view it becomes evident that Mr. Dreiser's effects are not achieved in spite of but because of his style. The "cheap, trite and tawdry" enable him to present a world which a more elegant and precise style could only hint at. He uses language, consciously or not, in the manner which modern writers, notably Joyce, use deliberately; that is, he identifies his language with the consciousness of his characters. Mr. Whipple evidently expects all writing to conform to the "mot juste" technique of the Flaubert school. But fortunately style cannot be prescribed by rule.

HENRY MILLER.

New York, N. Y.

William Lyon Phelps. "As I Like It." *Scribner's Magazine*, 79 (April 1926), 431–438.

. . . And now let me tackle that two-handed engine of naturalism, Theodore Dreiser's "An American Tragedy," where we follow the fortunes of a nincompoop from childhood to the chair. What A. E. Housman told in a page Mr. Dreiser tells in two volumes. Yet his steam-roller method gains, I suppose, by crushing out all this accumulated mass of detail. The style is clumsy and awkward; it has as much grace as an ichthyosaurus in a quagmire. But it is all true, unanswerably true. It is the naturalistic method of Zola. And if the novelist chooses to select from life a hero without brains or backbone or charm, and depict his unimportant career with patient microscopy, and bring in hosts of other characters none of whom one would ever wish to know in real life, that is his own affair. There are plenty of such persons and I suppose they spend their days in the manner herein described. One may justly admire Mr. Dreiser for sticking to his own theory of art, and for his dogged and truth-loving patience not in writing jewels five words long, but in scraping together pebbles and more pebbles.

It is properly called an American tragedy not because of the unfortunate career of his particular protagonist, but because he represents many Americans who lead equally tragic lives although not meeting an equally tragic end. The very commonplaceness of the vast number of characters in this story makes their representative quality more depressingly impressive. They are, alas, samples.

Yet it is strange that in this work and in others of the same author there should apparently be no hint that every town in America contains individuals of nobility, unselfishness, and idealism, people of intellect, resolution, and charm, who find and help to make life a splendid adventure.

The last thing Mr. Dreiser would wish to be called is a moralist or a preacher; yet this vast book resembles not a little the obvious sermon of Hogarth's Idle Apprentice.

It is quite easy for me to see and feel the qualities emphasized by his adorers, such as Mr. H. L. Mencken, Mr. Burton Rascoe, and the latest convert, Mr. Stuart Sherman. I remain outside this kneeling group, sceptical and unconvinced. For two reasons:

First, all great novels should have the element of transfiguration. People who are poor in health and brains and money may still be rich in significance. I would not be fair to compare Mr. Dreiser with Dickens; but it is easy to imagine how splendidly Dickens, with a knowledge of the seamy side of life fully equal to the American's, and with as much studiously realistic detail, would nevertheless have breathed into this ash-heap such a glow of life that it would have made a conflagration unquenchable by time. It would not be fair to compare Mr. Dreiser with Dickens, because Dickens was a man of genius. Let us then compare him with Mr. Arnold Bennett, who has perhaps no genius, but who is a literary expert, who has mastered the art of the novel, who is a shrewd, hard-bitten man of the world, and who loves life with a fervor both chronic and passionate. Compare "An American Tragedy" with "The Old Wives' Tale," or with "Riceyman Steps." Mr. Bennett has transfigured the lives of the commoplace and of the downtrodden with a veritable glow of creative power, with the gift that belongs only to the true artist. Now if Henry James complained that Arnold Bennett's novels were simply an accumulation of bricks without ultimate significance, if what should have been the means had become the end, what would he say to "An American Tragedy"?

Furthermore, the great preservative is *style.* There *is* a literary standard, there is a difference between good writing and bad. I cannot believe that this work, hampered by such clumsy composition, will be read in the next century. To use William Sharp's phrase, it will float around awhile, a colossal derelict on the ocean of literature, and will eventually sink.

John Cowper Powys. "An American Tragedy." *Dial,* 80 (April 1926), 331–338.

The fact that Theodore Dreiser's new novel seems likely to leave many readers repulsed and many critics confounded does not detract from its value.

Its cold Acherontic flood pursues its way, owing little, if anything, to the human qualities that disarm, endear, or beguile, owing nothing to the specious intellectual catchwords of the hour. The pleasure to be derived from it is grim, stark, austere, a purely aesthetic pleasure, unpropitious to such as require human cajolery in these high matters.

To use the expression "objective" with regard to it is only illuminating if what one means is that the writer's energy is so powerful that his vision of things is projected to a certain distance from himself; to such a distance, in fact, that here are no trailing and bleeding fringes left to tug at his vitals or to hinder him from taking up his load and going on his way. In this sense the book is certainly a planetary projectile. It lives, if it lives at all, by its own revolution on its own axis. Its creator has written no *apologia*, no consolatory interpretation, on the sky of its orbit.

But what chasms and crevasses, what dark cavities worse than lunar craters, have we to enter, in order to geologize and botanize among the lava-cracks and the grey moses of this scarcely congealed metallic microcosm! One reads somewhere that certain aboriginals of North America used to murmur of mysterious presences they named *manitou, wakanda, orenda.* The Bantu Africans whisper too of an invisible essence called *mulungu.* These primordial emanations do not appear to have been exactly divine or exactly diabolic. Rather do they present themselves as diffused magnetic dispersions, thrown off by the motions of primal Matter, as it stirs in its sleep, groping forward from the inanimate towards the organic. Some such *orenda,* some such *mulungu* seems to be the motive force and indeed the subject-matter of An American Tragedy; only in this case the mysterious effluence is given off rather by psychic than by physical forces. But to catch, out of the "palpable obscure," these secret stirrings and to follow them in their furtive motions a writer has to break many rules of language.

Perhaps the *Introibo ad altare* of any scrupulous initiation into the Dreiserian cult is to put one's finger upon the "blind mouth" of the historical method and wash one's hands clean of all rules, standards, conformities, traditions.

An American Tragedy certainly justifies its title. It is not merely American in its external stage-sets and the superficial idiosyncrasies of its characters. Plenty of American novels offer these allurements and yet remain as much afloat and deracinated as drifting seaweed. This extraordinary creation is American in its bones and blood and entrails. It is American in the heave of its breath, in the swing of its stride, in the smoke of its nostrils. Its Atlantean shoulders are American; so are its portentous buttocks. Its solemn wink, its shameless yawn, its outstretched, nonchalant limbs, all betray the sardonic sentiment, the naïve brutality, the adamantine stoicism of that organized chaos whose event is "in the hands of God."

The greatness of this work lies in the fact, among other things, that it covers so much ground. Some of the most arresting of Mr. Dreiser's contemporaries are vigorous and convincing enough when on their own particular native soil. But where these "localists" lose their plumage is when they leave home and like all ill-advised migratory birds settle and chatter upon alien rooftops. No one except Dreiser seems strong enough to swallow the whole chaotic spectacle and to disgorge it into some form of digested brain-stuff. His alone is the sprawl and the clutch, his alone the gullet and the stomach, competent to make away with such a cantle! On their own immediate ground these other writers can be suggestive enough. Off their ground they are nothing at all. But to be off the American of Dreiser's saturation you would have to take ship; and even then you would be miles out at sea ere that voice of Polyphemus fell upon silence or that Cyclopean eye, along with the light-ship of Sandy Hook and the search-light of Alcatraz, sank below the horizon!

An American Tragedy begins in Kansas City, the geographical navel of the land, moves thence to upper New York State, and terminates with the execution of its hero in Sing-Sing; but the psychic chemistry, of which it captures the *mulungu,* has its body and pressure in every portion of this country, and needs no map nor chart. This would hardly have been the case had what interested Dreiser most been those particular idiosyncrasies of our common nature that require a local habitation for their richest efflorescence. His Ygdrasil, his occult World-Ash-Tree, straddles its roots from coast to coast; finds nourishment as easily from the sands of Arizona, as from the red soil of the Carolinas; and it can do this because its roots are not really in the earth at all but in a vast diffused life-illusion, rising up like a thick mist out of a multitude of defrauded souls. This accounts for the fact that An American Tragedy is so lacking in what is soothing and healing to the mind, so sombrely naked of the kind of charm which pastures upon old usages, grows sweet and mellow upon the milk of ancient fields. Bell-hops, store-keepers, drummers, lawyers, sheriffs, politicians, factory-owners, factory-managers, factory-hands, stenographers, policemen, ministers, waiters, crooks, doctors, newspaper-men; all these, together with their counterparts in the residential sections, are perpetually throwing off, from Portland, Oregon to Portland, Maine, from Duluth to Miami, a cloud of invisible eidola, airy images of their grosser desires; and these are the filmy bricks of which Dreiser builds his impregnable dream-world.

It needs something thaumaturgic in a writer to enable him to separate this *mulungu* of accumulated life-illusions from the rest of the cosmic spectacle. But what Dreiser has done is nothing less than this; and we are compelled to accept as reality the "grim feature" thus starkly presented; although we cry to it in our dismay—"Hence, horrible shadow, unreal mockery, hence!" For it is as if, in Dreiser's work, *America itself* —the "commensurate antagonist" of the old civilizations—*saw itself* for the first time; cast a sly, shrewd, exultant, inquisitive look at itself; and turned away with a sardonic shrug.

Why is it that agriculturists and seafaring people play so small a part in Dreiser's books, though both Witla in The Genius and Clyde in this story find their friendliest sweethearts in a farmhouse? Is it not because the doom is on him to recreate just that particular life-dream which cannot co-exist with any close contact with earth or sea? The traditions of earth-life and sea-life surround the persons committed to them with all manner of magical encrustations such as have the power to reject and ward off that garish hubbub, that crude hurly-burly, of an existence dominated by "modern improvements."

The very fatality of this spectacle, as Dreiser half discovers and half creates it, is something that sets its rhinoceros-horn, rampantly and blindly against all that is quaint, delicate, subtle in human nature. And yet throughout those scenes in the Kansas City hotel, throughout the coarse duplicities of the boy's first infatuation, throughout the scatter-brained jovialities in brothel, wine-shop, and automobile, throughout the rough-and-tumble on the frozen river—so like a picture by Teniers or Jan Steen—throughout these pathetic struggles of Clyde and Roberta to outwit the vulgar respectability of Lycurgus, New York, one grows increasingly conscious that, rank and raw as it all is, there is something in the relentless and terrible *gusto* of the author's relish for what he is about which rises to the height of a monstrous sublimity.

It seems a strange use of the word "realistic" to apply it to this stupendous objectification of the phantasmal life-dreams of so many tin-tack automatons of a bastard modernity; but when one grows aware how Dreiser's own Deucalion-like mind murmurs, weeps, laughs, and gropes among them, a queer oppression catches at the throat and a kind of grim hypnosis—as if a beast-tamer were luring us into his cage of snouts and tails and hungry non-human eyes—makes us almost ready to cry out, in kindred delusion, "It's the truth! It's the truth!"

An American Tragedy is the other side of the shield of that "plain democratic world" whereof Walt Whitman chanted his dithyrambic acceptance. And we may note that just as Whitman took ordinary human words and made them porous to his transcendent exultations, so Dreiser has invented a style of his own, for this monody over the misbegotten, which is like nothing else in literature. I think it is a critical mistake to treat this Dreiserian style as if it were a kind of unconscious blundering. If it is unconscious it certainly could find a very sophisticated defence; for who is not aware to-day of many recondite craftsmen who make use of the non-grammatical, the non-rational, and even of the nonsensical, to most refined aesthetic results?

It is much easier to call Dreiser naïve than to sound the depths of the sly, huge, subterranean impulses that shape his unpolished runes. The rough scales and horny excrescences of the style of An American Tragedy may turn out to be quite as integral a part of its author's spiritual skin as are the stripes and spots and feathered crests of his more ingratiating contemporaries.

The subject of the book, this tragedy that gathers and mounts and accumulates till it wrecks the lives involved, is the tragedy of perverted self-realization, the mistaking of the worse shadow for the better. All are shadows; but the art of life is still in its infancy when we make the mistake that this poor Clyde Griffiths made. But, after all, such in its own day and place was the tragedy of Macbeth; such, with yet insaner convolutions, the tragedy of Raskolnikoff. One has to take refuge in a different world altogether, in a world that has vanished with the philosophy of the ancients, to find an ignoble mistake of this kind unworthy of the ritual of Dionysus. Certain it is that with the exception of the unfortunate Roberta, not a character in this book wins our deeper sympathy. Clyde is pitiable, if we renounce all craving for mental and moral subleties, but we pity him as we would pity a helpless vicious animal driven to the slaughter-house, not as we pity a fully conscious human intellect wrestling with an untoward fate. And yet the book produces a sense of awe, of sad humility, of troubled wonder. How has this been achieved?

No one but Dreiser, as far as I know, could take a set of ragamuffin bell-hops, scurvy editors, tatterdemalion lawyers, greedy department-store wenches, feather-weight society chits, "heads without name, no more rememberéd than summer flies," could thrust into the midst of these people an ill-starred, goodlooking weakling like Clyde; and then, out of such material—surely more uninspiring than have ever been selected by the brain of man or artist—set up a colossal brazen-ribbed image, which the very wild geese, in their flight over the cities of men, must suppose to be fathom-based upon reality!

To taste the full flavour, the terrible "organic chemical" flavour, like the smell of a stock-yard, which emanates from this weird book, it is necessary to feel, as Dreiser seems to feel—and, indeed, as we are taught by the faith of our fathers—that the soul of the most ill-conditioned and raw-sensed of our race, gendered by man, born of woman, has a potentiality of suffering equal with the noblest.

Thus in place of the world we know there rises up before us Something towering and toppling and ashen-grey, a very *Balaena Mysticetus* of the abyss, riddled with devouring slime-worms. And we ourselves, so great is this writer's power, become such worms. It is a formidable achievement, the creation of this "empathy," this more than sympathy, in the case of such unfortunates; and to have brought it about is, say what you please, a spiritual as well as an aesthetic triumph. To watch the death-hunt of the faltering Clyde is to watch a fox-hunt in the company of some primordial Fox-god, who knows as you cannot know, both the ecstasy of stealing into the hen-roost and *what it is* to feel the hot breath of the hounds following your flying tail!

Balzac used to throw his protean magnetism into the urge of the most opposite obsessions, becoming sometimes an angel and sometimes a demon; but Dreiser does something different from this. He overshadows his herd of hypnotized cattle in the totality of their most meagre and petering-out reactions, meditating upon them in an ubiquitous contemplation that resembles the trance of some "astral body" of iron and steel and paving-stone, some huge impalpable soul of the inanimate, yearning in sombre tenderness over its luckless children. And yet it is not really out of the elements of the earth that Dreiser—moving like some vast shepherd of Jotunheim-flocks, among his rams and ewes—erects his sorrowful sheep-fold, but rather out of the immaterial hurdles and straw of their own turnip-tasting dreams.

The portion of the story that deals with the murder itself is so imaginatively heightened as to cast a Janus-like shadow backwards and forwards over the rest of the book. What the boy sees and hears as he sits in the train that is bearing him towards his victim; the "supernatural soliciting" that calls to him out of the air; the spasm of panic-stricken weakness that distorts his purpose at the supreme moment; his convoluted doubts, after the event, as to his actual guilt; these passages, like the dark waters of the lake where the girl is drowned, possess so much poetic porousness and transparency that they make the earlier and later portions of the work seem like an opaque face, of which they are the living and expressive eye.

Dreiser has always been a mystic. Only a mystic could capture the peculiar terror of *Matter become a ghost to the mind*, as he captures it, so as to be a veritable confederate with the Chthonian divinities. Only a mystic could ponder so obstinately upon the wretched pulse-beats of a scamp like Clyde, till they respond to the rumble of Erebus, till they rise and sink in ghastly reciprocity with the shadow-voices of Typhon, of Loki, of Azazel, of Ahriman!

We can protest—and here, as I pen these lines in the very hotel where Clyde served his transients, I do most heartily protest—that there are aspects of human nature entirely obliterated from this gregarious shadow-dance. But such protests must conform to aesthetic intelligence. An American Tragedy is the tragedy of only such aspects of mortal consciousness as can get themselves objectified in such a psychic panorama. An artist, a mystic, a prophet if you will, must be allowed to *isolate his phenomena.* Dreiser's phenomena are not lacking in their own inherent contrasts. Compare the letters of Roberta, for example, so poignant as to be almost intolerable, with the baby-talk in the letters of Sondra, so intolerable for the very opposite reason! Sondra is one stage further removed from nature than Roberta; but the genuineness of her infatuation for Clyde is not lost in her queer jargon. Infatuated young persons, of both sexes, do babble in this unpleasant way when they are devoid of all critical alteregoism. Like some gigantic naturalist studying the twitchings and turnings of a crowd of shimmery-winged dung-beetles Dreiser has been put to it to invent human sounds such as shall represent the love-cries and the panic-cries of these husks of inane rapacity.

Had any of his rampaging bell-hops, his crafty lawyers, his sly department-store ladies, his bouncing society-chits, shown too marked a tendency to emerge into a more appealing stratum of consciousness, a certain formidable unity of "timbre" would have been lost to the book, a consistency of rhythm broken, a necessary pressure removed. Composed of everything that prods, scrapes, rakes, harrows, and outrages an intelligent organism the environment, to which these creatures of Dreiser's contemplation respond, itself mingles with their lamentable response. It is out of this appalling reciprocity of raw with raw, that the mass and weight and volume of the book proceed. And this accumulated weight—so terribly mortis'd and tenon'd by its creator's genius—has its own unparalleled beauty, as pure an aesthetic beauty (almost mathematical in the rigidity of its pattern) as the most purged and exacting taste could demand. Thus is brought about through the mediumship of this omophagous intellect, the only escape from the impact of a certain horrible dream-world which a lost soul can find; the escape, namely, of giving to the Chimaera itself the lineaments of a work of art. To the unhappy wretch by the wayside whom Zarathustra found with a snake in his gullet was uttered the magic formula—"Bite and spit!" This is what Theodore Dreiser has done; and the result is An American Tragedy.

In Plays Natural and Supernatural this same author bestowed an articulate voice upon that thundering ox-bellow of the American Locomotive (so different from the thin whistles of European trains) which, reverberating across a continent, sounds the modern tragic chorus to so many broken-hearted vigils. In this same book there reaches the brain of a patient under laughing-gas a monstrous voice, repeating the syllable Om! Om! Om!

Such, it seems to me—that moan of the freight-train as you hear it in the night and that *other sound* which few have the ears to hear—is the only adequate commentary that can be made upon the temptation and crime and punishment of Clyde Griffiths, bellhop of Kansas City! Not for nothing has this unique book gathered itself about the mystery of evil.

Every imaginative writer is doomed sooner or later to become a scape-goat; doomed to take upon himself, in a strange occult fashion, "the Sins of the World." And as one ponders upon the figure of Dreiser, moving in sombre *bonhomie*, humming and drumming, across the literary arena, one cannot fail to note that he also has had to balance that pack upon his shoulders.

His vision of things blames no one, lets no one off, reduces all "benevolence and righteousness" to sorrowful humility; pitiful, patient, dumb. For at the back of the world, as he sees it, is neither a Devil nor a Redeemer; only a featureless *mulungu*, that murmurs forever "Om! Om! Om!"

Carl Van Doren. "Beyond Good and Evil." *Century Magazine,* 111 (April, 1926), 763–765.

The place of Theodore Dreiser in American literature must always have been for him a trying one. His earlier novels were met either with the calm of neglect or with storms of abuse. Then came the battles in his behalf led by H. L. Mencken, and sooner or later joined by almost every critic strong enough to lift a pen. While the war was on, it was for many readers more thrilling than the debated books themselves. And when it was ended and, on the whole, won, Mr. Dreiser had so long been talked about that his name had the familiar ring which led him to be somehow taken for granted. Moreover for the past ten years he has published no new novel until now. Consequently his works have stood rather too silently upon their shelf. Whether dishonored or honored, they have not been read as they deserve. Too long an outcast, he was too suddenly made a classic.

The publication of "An American Tragedy" has revived the question but not the quarrel. Virtually all the soundest opinion is as much in Mr. Dreiser's favor as it can be, or as it dares to be in the light of this or that record. In the circumstances, the friends of "Sister Carrie" and of "Jennie Gerhardt" may be tempted to rest their case, merely allowing the new novel to speak for itself. This it of course can do. At the same time it is important to insist that the qualities for which Mr. Dreiser is now praised are precisely the qualities which he has always had, and for which he should have been praised long ago as well as now.

It may be admitted that "An American Tragedy," being on so large a scale, exhibits certain of Mr. Dreiser's traits with an increased clarity. In particular, it once for all answers the charge that he has an inadequate sense of the interwoven fabric of human lives for the reason that he is too much interested in Nietzschean creatures who make their own way without considering or even noticing other men and women. This new story is knit as close as canvas. Clyde Griffiths, the muddled and doomed hero, tries to rise from the ranks of a mean poverty into the world of ease and power which calls him with such an irresistible allurement. The son of a street preacher in Kansas City, he has as a child not been permitted even the comfort of obscurity, but has been dragged out wincing every day to help his father and mother make a doleful noise before the Lord. When from this he escapes to what seems the freedom of well paid work as bell-boy in a hotel, the burden of his family is still upon him, and, as the consequence of a thoughtless prank, he is involved in the dangers of the law, from which again he has to flee. Taken up later by a wealthy uncle in Lycurgus, New York, Clyde is put in the difficult situation of being regarded by his uncle's household as hardly more than one of their workmen, and by the workmen as hardly less than one of their employers. The situation is too difficult for Clyde. He oscillates and clutches in both directions. Love draws him to Roberta Alden, a girl in the collar factory. Ambition draws him to Sondra Finchley, a member of the Lycurgus aristocracy. Once more divided between love and ambition, as in Kansas City, he bungles again, but this time his bungling is criminal. And with what remorseless eyes and hands the law runs him down! No other trial in fiction, so far as my knowledge goes, more tremendously emphasizes the fact that men are forever tangled in their societies. Clyde has thought that he moved about almost invisibly, but he finds instead that he has left traces wherever he has gone. Nor does Mr. Dreiser merely make a statement to this effect. He follows the evidence through all its windings, almost without comment. When he has finished, the network of society is no longer an abstraction but has been made real.

If society is real in "An American Tragedy," the individual is no less so. Never before in America has the impulse to success been handled with such penetration. The hero is not indeed one of those glib and slick young men who in the most popular national sagas run lightly up the slopes to triumph. The world to which Clyde aspires is forever a shining blur to him. From his dull routine he lifts his eyes to the only splendors that he knows: the splendors of life as led in buzzing hotels and quiet Pullman cars and curtained drawing-rooms, of life as led along summer lakes and on tennis-courts and golf-links and country-club verandas, of life where there are leisurely men and pretty women. His vision of these things is tawdry enough, but it is all he can piece together out of his own snatches of observation and the elaborate distortions of the newspapers. His vision is, I suspect, exactly what swims before the gaze of every ordinary youth who sees the rich at work or at play, but sees them from a distance. But whereas most such youths never have the opportunity to draw nearer to these scenes, Clyde accidentally has it, and then his occasion gives his tragic weakness a chance to assert itself. His weakness lies in the vagueness of his aspiration. If he were more complacent or clear-cut, he would know better how to choose what he most wants, and how to go about winning it. As matters stand, he has only the philosophy of success, without the technic. For every American with that technic, there must be thousands with that philosophy. This Mr. Dreiser knows, though again he does not say it too explicitly. He is content to make his point as unavoidable as the Rocky Mountains, and to let it go at that.

What makes the mountainous "American Tragedy" so disturbing is the pity which runs through its whole bulk as unbrokenly as if it were a brief tender idyl. That pity lifts the book above all partisanship. Mr. Dreiser might have thought it necessary to condemn Clyde for the drifting selfishness which brings him to his bad end; he might have lost himself in sympathy for Clyde as the victim of a law which, as administered, cannot look too long into delicate motives but must judge offenders by their actual deeds. Either of these attitudes seems trivial beside the attitude which Mr. Dreiser takes. In the truest sense of a phrase often confused, he is beyond good and evil. Such distinctions, applied to the story, have an academic sound. As if he were a man strayed among aminals, this novelist has strayed among men, studying their behavior. He leaves it to others to assess blame or reward. He wants only to observe and to understand how certain actions come about. His novel seems somehow like the unedited material of life. Nevertheless it is edited with a vast slow patience. Only "Moby Dick" among American novels moves with the same fateful tread, carrying all its documents on its back, and yet never seriously delaying. To read it is to want to resist its march, to turn aside into a sunnier, more hopeful direction, but to find it impossible to do so. Large hands have planned the caravan. Long foresight has chosen the road and the destination. A powerful will urges the narrative forward, as a glacier is urged. Yet in the midst of this advance, the observer, though his mind appears never to be made up for him, is permitted and obliged to ponder upon all the follies and sins of mankind. His emotions are wrung; his judgment is tried. With the broad world before him, as it seems, he realizes that he cannot ever pronounce verdicts upon his fellows with the brisk confidence which the ignorant enjoy.

Ernest Brennecke, Jr., *Commonweal*, 3 (April 28, 1926), 696-697.

Facing you across a rough table—a table embellished with whiskey bottle and glasses—sits a hard-boiled newspaper man with heavy features. He is telling you a story, a true one, obviously drawn out of his journalistic experiences. He tells it in a curious jargon of his own invention: a mixture of newspaper English, medical English, business English, legal English, psycho-analytical English—of almost everything but pure and simple English. But even while you are repelled by the sloppiness of his language, you are never in doubt as to his meaning, which is itself fairly simple and earthly.

The story rolls on for hours and hours.

The heavy narrative, unrelieved by humor, wit or irony, ploughs and churns its way steadily into your brain, keeping you wide awake in spite of yourself and the whiskey. You have learned that one Clyde Griffiths, the son of an unordained street preacher, has been harried through a series of most miserable experiences, stirred as he is by biological and ambitious impulses of which he has the faintest possible understanding. Clyde is weaker than water, and the eager prey of every variety of temptation. He has been a bell-hop (the bell-hop's life, including a memorable episodic visit to a brothel, has been set forth with meticulous and vivid accuracy) a joy-ride accident has forced him to flee from Kansas City to Chicago, where he has come to the notice of his uncle, a successful collar-manufacturer with a factory at Lycurgus.

Slowly Clyde has made his way, or rather has been propelled, into the social life of the younger smart set of Lycurgus. He has fallen in love with Sondra, an ornamental upper-crust flapper; she proves willing to marry him, and such a marriage will satisfy (he thinks) all his unrealized desires—for position, money, beauty (as he conceives it) and passion. But Roberta, a factory girl whom he has seduced, stands in the way; she is soon to have a child, and demands marriage. The situation is too much for Clyde's ignorance and lack of will. After a short period of fatal inaction, he takes Roberta to a lonely lake, intending to drown her. He bungles the job very badly. At the crucial moment his courage fails, the girl notices the agony written in his features and upsets the canoe in her excitement; Clyde instinctively lunges at her, strikes her with a camera, and swims ashore, leaving her to drown. He is speedily arrested and tried for murder. He is himself undecided as to his own guilt.

So far the story has wormed its way under your skin. It is legitimately depressing, ghastly in its convincing naturalism. Nothing is unexplained. "There, but for the grace of God, go I," you feel. You submit. But soon a new note is heard. The narrator grows more eager, and you are more unwillingly fascinated by his manner. He really seems to be having such a good time! The whole drab tale is unnecessarily retold in the full reproduction of the attorneys' harangues, the examination of witnesses, the interviews, the comments in the courtroom. Clyde is at length found guilty, and with savage delight the narrator takes you to the death house at Auburn.

Now the Sadistic spirit of the whole performance begins definitely to repel you. For hours you watch (you no longer live) the life of the condemned, and you instinctively fight against the endless and purposeless bombardment of mental horrors. The story is now too long. But soon all this must end; and at the conclusion you are listening politely and unabsorbed. Clyde goes to the electric chair, the narrator goes on his way —you to bed, battered, and very, very weary.

Such is the general initial effect of this latest novel of Mr. Dreiser's, a huge work which has already collected unto itself a vastity of unbelievably extravagant critical encomiums and a volley of diatribes against its aesthetically abominable length, style, and structure. As to its sheer strength, the adverse criticisms are scarcely tenable. Surely a novelist who aspires to a position in the line established by the authors of Tom Jones, Vanity Fair, and The Egoist need not apologize for a work which runs to a mere 800 pages of 8-point type. As to its general structure, there is really very little cause for complaint. The preliminary motivation, elaborate and extended as it is, is surely necessary; and the cumulative effect of the connected, undiscrete episodes makes for a unity of real power.

The style is another matter. There can be no possible pardon for a writer who can permit himself to spew forth (nor for a copyreader who can let pass) violations of the most elementary grammatical decency such as "he was still convinced that he had no skill with or charm where girls were concerned"; or maddening repetitions of "all this," "in the interim," "via," "chemic," "chic," and "libido"; or endless chains of dangling participles and of split and shattered infinitives; or such unthinkable ponderosities as:

"There are moments when in connection with the sensitively imaginative or morbidly anachronistic—the mentality assailed and the same not of any great strength and the problem confronting it of sufficient force and complexity—the reason not actually toppling from its throne, still totters or is warped or shaken—the mind befuddled to the extent that for the time being, at least, unreason or disorder and mistaken or erroneous counsel would appear to hold against all else."

Even the terrible-tempered Mr. Mencken, perhaps the most ardent and articulate of the whole tribe of Dreiserites, has confessed that such imbecilities on every page of An American Tragedy made him very unhappy.

The mere outrage to the reader's aesthetic sensibilities is a minor matter beside the final intent. As a satirical novel, An American Tragedy fails most miserably. Mr. Dreiser's feeble satirical juices are the only digestive influences that are here applied to the crude stuff of the story. The stuff remains coarse, unilluminated, without a single seizable significance. Any good newspaper story covering any current brutality will present just as much and just as good stimulation to an imaginative person as he can find here.

The work seems to present just another mass of evidence in favor of the old critical contention that a bad style inevitably accompanies or indicates a vital and serious short-coming in the author's view of the world. Here the shortcoming is a definite lack of any kind of philosophy. Mr. Dreiser looks at the tragedy of life, not through it.

E. M. Kayden. *Sewanee Review*, 34 (October 1926), 495-497.

After ten years of silence, Dreiser has returned from themes of high finance to populated towns and streets he loved to explore in the earlier days of *Sister Carrie* or *Jennie Gerhardt*. His new novel, *An American Tragedy*, is the bulkiest among his bulky works, and it has all the familiar defects of size, formlessness, and clumsiness of style. And one hears again the echoes of familiar but thoughtless complaining that he is so unbeautiful. We do not like the springless wagon-ride behind oxen on rutted country roads. There is no speed, no glamor, no humor, no cadence, no crushed perfume, and no cool refuge for the heart's refinement in Dreiser's style. But as for me, he holds me steadfast to the end, fascinated, this steadfast ox-cart driver with his story so authentic and inevitable, so complete of integrity with itself and the materials, so tragic in its nerveless gestures. It is not a story of smiling cultivated fields and of trim secluded gardenplots, nor of a land with tamed, channeled rivers sparkling in the springtime sun. His is primitive prairie; a dark continent; a muddy, sprawling, untameable Mississippi, carrying the life of farm and forest on its vast expanse, unmoving if one watches it at one point, yet majestic, rude in its passion, and steady in its power and magnitude if one looks at it, Father of Waters, from the north to the Gulf. Then it seems no longer still and muddy; then it has color, persuasiveness, ease of force.

A dark continent. A brutish, planless life of cities, grand hotels, factories, clubs. The inheritance of lawless traditions of getting on in the blood. Predatory man, with murder in his heart, unassimilating the symmetry and beautiful ordering of his delicate machinery, and so breaking and ravishing the root-ends and the root-needs of life. Passionate, personal success. Mawkish sentiment. Optimism. And the human wolf-cub fed on hypocrisy, squalid ambitions, and the vulgar pap of evangelism, avid for ready cash and the things cash buys. Clyde Griffith—one of millions spawned of a vast industrialism, trivial bits of humanity living extinguished lives before the sun is at midday, left with nothing save the ambition to get on and to possess, dreaming of the beauty of girls and money, money which will buy position and beauty and meaning of life perhaps. Clyde is legion—wolf-weaklings entangled in the little sins and desirings, committing murder in their hearts every day; wolf-weaklings who can neither wholly will nor act, whom passion finds defenceless and unprepared, but leading them on just the same and just as inevitably to kill the dead unstruggling prey. A lawless order, strong in possessions. A lost, bewildered man-cub. Murder. . . . Who is the murderer?

Millions murdered of spirit, and millions murdering at heart, this is the American tragedy, the universal tragedy of a sweating, on-getting, incoherent, moralistic industrialism, the muddy current of our untamed and chaotic existence. The claws of the beast are in our souls. And Dreiser is touched by the tragic failure of our being in its innermost relationships, moved by the strangeness of life, and the sanctities of our human contacts floundering in the brutal mass of matter. He loves life, insatiably, in all its significances and irrelevancies, the whole wealth of life he cherishes, the mighty current surging around and under all the agitated particles of mankind carried resistlessly on, massive, always terrible. Whither? There is no answer. We move darkly on the boundless current of life—victims, victims all: Clyde, his mother, Roberta, Sondra, doctor, factory hands, foremen, bellhops, the powerful collar-magnate, the frail and the competent, all unimportant, without the strength to put meaning in life, and so without the truth of life by which man lives. Occasionally a gleam of beauty and tenderness—O Clyde and O Roberta in the brief moment of love under the dark-blue sky—and then swallowed by darkness and driven to inevitable doom; again unmeaningness, again helplessness. And humbly, kindly, helplessly, the genius of Dreiser is looking on, touching every one with his pity, condemning no one, ridiculing nothing. And what he sees he tells honestly, brokenly, as a man reeling and befuddled by the terror of things seen. Murder, in fact, and greater murdering of the human spirit. Here one goes puzzled to die in the electric chair; one will return to preaching on street-corners; one to the manufacturing of more collars, more collars. . . . And the heart trembles in the unrelenting grasp of some ancient god. . . .

Checklist of Additional Reviews

"With a Bookworm." Minneapolis *Journal,* January 3, 1926.

Chicago *Journal of Commerce,* January 4, 1926.

Sidney Williams. Philadelphia *Inquirer,* January 9, 1926.

"Dreiser's Novel." San Francisco *Bulletin,* January 9, 1926.

E. F. Edgett. Boston *Evening Transcript,* January 9, 1926.

George Currie. "Passed in Review." Brooklyn *Eagle,* January 9, 1926.

"Dreiser's Novel at Last." *Morning Court,* January 10, 1926.

G. D. E. New York *Morning Telegraph,* January 10, 1926.

West Virginian. January 12, 1926.

New York *Graphic,* January 16, 1926.

Oliver M. Sayler. *Footlight and Lamplight,* 21 (January 21, 1926).

John Gould. Wichita *Daily News,* January 24, 1926.

G. D. E. "Merrily He Whirls Around." New York *Morning Telegraph,* January 24, 1926.

Isaac Goldberg. "In the World of Books." *Haldeman-Julius Weekly,* January 26, 1926.

St Louis *Post-Dispatch,* January 30, 1926.

H. K. Ellingson. "Literary Notes." Colorado *Sunday Gazette and Telegraph,* January 31, 1926.

Jim Tully. "Mr. Dreiser An American Tragedy." *International Book Review,* 4 (February, 1926), 167, 169.

Phil Townsend Hanna. "An American Tragedy." *California Sports,* February, 1926, pp. 28, 38, 42.

Henry Bellaman. "The Literary Highway." *Sunday Record,* February 7, 1926.

Edmund Pearson. *Outlook,* 142 (February 10, 1926), 22-223.

"More About the Heavy Tragedy Called American." San Francisco *Chronicle,* February 13, 1926.

El Paso [Tex.] *Times,* February 14, 1926.

Dallas [Tex.] *Morning News,* February 14, 1926.

Saturday Review of Literature, 2 (February 20, 1926), 569-570.

St. Albans *Messenger,* February 20, 1926.

Victor Schultz. "Dreiser's Powerful New Book." Des Moines [Iowa] *Sunday Register,* February 21, 1926.

George McCrossen. "Books." *Boulevardiers,* March, 1926, pp. 11, 23.

Wisconsin Library Bulletin, 22 (March 1926), 109.

C. M. Morrison. Newark *Public Ledger,* March 6, 1926.

America, March 6, 1926.

Vogue, March 15, 1926.

Atlanta [Ga.] *Journal,* March 21, 1926.

Springfield *Republican,* March 21, 1926, p. 5.

Springfield *Union,* March 21, 1926.

"The Bookshelf of a Workingman." *Weekly People,* March 27, 1926.

Booklist, April, 1926, p. 295.

J. F. "The Fiction Reader in the New

Season." *Bookman,* 63 (April 1926), 202.
Cleveland *Open Shelf,* April, 1926, p. 53.
Industrial Pioneer, April, 1926.
Kenelm Digby. New York *Evening Post,* April 3, 1926.
Karsten Roedder. "The Book Parade." Brooklyn [N.Y.] *Citizen,* April 10, 1927.
Minneapolis *Tribune,* April 11, 1926.
New York *Sun,* April 12, 1926.
Minneapolis *Tribune,* April 18, 1926.
Paul Francis Webster. "Book Reviews." *New York University Daily News,* April 28, 1926.
Trenton [N.J.] *Times,* May 1, 1926.
Camden [N.J.] *Courier,* May 13, 1926.
Chester Dirgin. "The Band Wagon." Long Island *Daily Press,* May 22, 1926.
A. R. New Haven [Conn.] *Union,* May 23, 1926.
Henry Longan Stuart. "Fifty Outstanding Novels of the Last Six Months." New York *Times Book Review,* June 27, 1926, p. 3.
Simeon Strunsky. "About Books, *More or Less:* Prose Poems," New York *Times Book Review,* June 27, 1926, p. 4.
Heywood Broun. "It Seems to Me." New York *World,* September 8, 1926.
Billingham [Wy.] *Revielle,* September 26, 1926.
William J. Robinson. "An American Tragedy." *Critic and Guide,* 25 (October 1926), 391-398.
Emily Newell Blair. "Some Books Worth While." *Good Housekeeping,* October, 1926.
I. F. D. "A Tremendous Book." Evanston [Ill.] *News Index,* January 6, 1927.

Further Reviews: Bibliographic Information Incomplete

Alfred Wood. "Agates and Migs." Springfield *Union.*
V. F. Calverton. "The Greater American Tragedy."
George Douglas. "Dreiser's Novel." San Francisco *Bulletin.*
Sidney Williams. "Mr. Dreiser's 'An American Tragedy.' "
Lillian Ford. "Dreiser's American Tragedy." Los Angeles *Times.*
Mark De W. Howe. "An Epic Written in Diggerel." *Harvard Advocate,* p. 52.
Eloise Campbell Long. "Dreiser's Novel on Crime and Punishment a Sound Achievement."
P. A. Kinsley. "Of Youth's Greatest Folly Is 'An American Tragedy.' " Tulsa [Ok.] *Tribune.*
Sunday *Advertiser,* February 14, 1926.

Notes

· CHAINS ·

LESSER NOVELS
AND STORIES

BY

THEODORE DREISER

BONI & LIVERIGHT · NEW YORK

· 1927 ·

Chains

H. W. Boynton. "Dreiser Broods Again." New York *Sun*, May 14, 1927.

As a "forward" to "Chains" Mr. Dreiser offers this aphorism: "The inevitabilities of our fate are: Love and hope, fear and death, interwoven with our lacks, inhibitions, jealousies and greeds." Nobody takes up Theodore Dreiser with the idea of having a cheery time. He is a disillusioned dreamer, a Teutonic idealist who cannot forgive fate for having cheated him and all mankind with the semblance or promise of a happiness that never really comes off. The spectacle of human frailty and folly gives him none of the satisfaction experienced by jauntier or gloomier souls. He wishes the inevitabilities of fate were kindlier; but there the odds remain 3 to 1, love and hope forlornly opposing all those other unfriendly comers. The best we can do is to acknowledge the truth and make the best of it. Though commonly bracketed with Sherwood Anderson, Dreiser has less in common with that bitter Scotch mystic than with, say, the late W. M. Thackeray. Remove a few literary inhibitions and all graces of style from the creator of Becky Sharp, and you have, or may have, the creator of Sister Carrie and Jennie Gerhardt.

The fifteen tales and sketches in "Chains" pretty well cover the Dreiserian range. In them we are taken behind the scenes of a dozen of those human actions which are implicit and utterly unintelligible in the news items of any morning's newspaper. A street woman finds sanctuary behind the walls of a religious sisterhood. What is her story? For Dreiser it has two parts, first the facts of her experience, unbelievably gross, and then their meaning. And the net effect of it all is an effect not of contempt but of pity and understanding. So it is with "The 'Mercy' of God" and "Typhoon," further studies of the hapless lot of potentially happy, normal women. In the first named a homely spinster attains to happiness by going a little mad. The illusion that she is beautiful and desired is a kind of compensation—"a beneficent illusion, a providential hallucination." Or is it just an accident? "I could not judge and did not. Truly, truly, I thought, I wish I might believe." "Typhoon" is the inner story of a case of seduction, murder and suicide—another loving girl gone to ruin and despair.

Three or four of these tales are studies in the slavery and indignity of love as infatuation, plus habit. "Chains" tells the story of a marriage in terms of a man's undercurrent of thought and feeling during a short journey by rail. He has a flashy young wife whom he distrusts and dotes on, and the whole course of their relation passes through his consciousness while his surface mind is occupied with trivial things. These surface impressions are interjected in short italicized passages with singular effect. The same method is used in "Fulfillment," which gives almost the same picture in obverse from the woman's side. Here also are a number of other forms of slavery dwelt upon, slavery to convention, to the past, to fear. . . .

"A Dreiser Group." Springfield [Ill.] *Journal*, May 15, 1927.

It is difficult to imagine Theodore Dreiser as a writer of brief stories. None of these tales are short in the general acceptance of the term. His shortest stories are little more than episodes, ponderously told. But to this reviewer's notion, they show more the true Dreiser than any of his other works.

In all, the group contains fifteen stories, each of which might be said to set forth a distinct phase of this thing we call Life. There's a heavy air of hopelessness about many of them. Some of them do little more than relate incidents, which if submitted to a magazine by some unknown writer would be promptly rejected. And, if accepted and published would not, in themselves, win any more than passing notice. But as a group they combine to produce an excellent panorama of life, as seen through Dreiser's eyes. . . .

There is not a truly happy story in the collection. All of them are a trifle depressing, a bit too gloomy for general consumption. That they portray life is admitted, that they might include a bit of sunshine likewise is extremely plain. This reviewer believes that there is some happiness to be found about him, but he has yet to find any of it in Dreiser's writing. Some day, we hope to find a smile in one of his lines. Until we do, he remains a doleful artist.

Henry Longan Stuart. "As Usual, Mr. Dreiser Spares Us Nothing." New York *Times Book Review*, May 15, 1927, p. 2.

One of those clever Frenchmen whose perceptions every one is glad to remember, but whose names every one is resigned to forget, has told us that, in literature, all styles are permissable except one—the boring style ("sauf l'ennuyeux"). No critic with any self-respect, it may be stated at once, is likely to take shelter behind any such aphorism. In the first place, it strikes at the root of his own reason for being. In the second, it leaves the judgment of what is possible or impossible writing too nakedly at the mercy of an individual appetite for coarse fare. People exist, some of them very finicking over their own production, who make no shame in owning to an occasional relish for the corn beef and cabbage of letters. It is not by what readers will resign themselves to on occasion, but by what ey would be content, at need, to live ith, that a standard of taste is to be dged.

Even Mr. Dreiser's most ardent adirers, one presumes, would be preared to admit some very serious isabilities in their idol. To begin with e has no perceptible sense of humor. he spark that can be struck out by the ontact of two minds moving on differnt planes of intelligence and which is e most fertile source of the ludicrous, out of his ken. He writes with no apreciable relish, being perhaps the ost eminent drudge among our native ractitioners. Syntax is continually preenting him with difficulties, as whom oes it not? But instead of solving them s they arise with the contrivances out f which style is hammered, he has reourse to sorrowful expedients that ing Lardner at his happiest could not etter.

Yet it would be both unjust and aburd to deny that with all these faults oes an equipment that many a felicious writer must envy. His patience is ntiring. No one has written more conincingly of a man or woman thinking nd brooding, because no one can more aïvely and convincingly cling to the rail of a thought, discarding nothing, electing nothing, but following each ad convolution into its innermost reesses and blindest alleys. In this repect he has all the candor of George Moore, whom one suspects he follows in is own leaden-footed fashion, without he occasional frivolity of the Irish maser. And only a prodigious memory, a aculty for impressibility that never lets he sharp edge of what has once been bserved be dulled, can account for his ncanny power of so taking over the ensory apparatus of his characters that ne cannot read his criminal trials without sharing in some degree the vertigo of the man in the dock, nor his murders without every silly, vulgar hue and cry registering upon exasperated nerves, nor of death in a tunnel accident without feeling the slime and ooze and drip underfoot and overhead.

One is hardly well started on "Chains," a series of fifteen "lesser novels and stories" by the author of "The American Tragedy" without being plunged in a sea of slovenly writing. "Sanctuary" is the story of a sensitive tenement child born amid foul smells and fouler language, who falls into prostitution, is "reformed" in a home conducted by gentle nuns, leaves it to become the prey of a pimp and bully, and creeps back to it convinced that what has been assigned her as punishment is really the only condition under which life is possible. As we read it wonder grows that it can be humanly possible, talent apart, for any practicing writer to advance to where Mr. Dreiser had advanced, while retaining a construction and syntax that would bring down the blue pencil in any composition class in a high school. Worse even than the flaws in syntax are vulgarities of diction repeated over and over again so unbelievable in a writer of the slightest distinction that one asks one's self whether Mr. Dreiser may not perhaps be hovering on the brink of a new literary experiment and striving to convey banality of mind by banality of phrase.

> . . . One of those suave masters of the art of living by one's wits, with a fortune of looks, to whom womanhood is a thing to be taken by an upward curl of a pair of mustaches, the vain placement of ringed locks, spotless and conspicuous linen, and clothes and shoes of a newness and lustre all but disturbing to a very work-a-day world.

Where all is so precious it is an ill task to pick out any one gem of language, but surely "all but disturbing" deserves mention.

"Chains," the story which gives the collection its title, affords Mr. Dreiser's talent its happiest chance. The musings of an elderly and doting husband, returning to a young wife whom he has married in an afterglow of passion and against all sense and reason, are retailed for us with unsparing deliberation. No one of the illusions at which men snatch under such circumstances to allay the intolerable bitterness of jealousy fails to find a place. The strange faculty of jealous and hapless lovers gradually to build up for themselves a picture of what they suspect, image upon image, and at the very moment that the phantom is taking on reality to recoil and fly back to the old drug of self-deception, has never been more convincingly identified. On this one essay Mr. Dreiser, it seems to us, might base a claim to be not only an investigator but to some extent a pioneer in a field that might be called sentimental pathology. . . .

It is not likely that "Chains" will unsettle the reputation of the author of "An American Tragedy" with those who hold a belief in his excellence an article of national faith, nor improve it with those who believe his reputation to be a victory won by sheer bulk and persistence and regard the place given him as not much short of literary imposture. Every writer has the faults of his qualities. What is most exasperating about Dreiser's faults is that they are not a part of his qualities at all. They are gratuitous ugliness and slovenliness, poor literary manners that have been suffered to persist (just why is his own secret) from 'prentice days, and to mar a thought which is, on the whole, fin austere and pitiful. Their danger re sides in the bad example they affor through the very eminence of the ma who insists on practicing them. Nothin worse could happen to the America novel, already subject to dange enough at careless and disingenuou hands, than a belief that genius can dis pense with taking pains.

Ruth Lechlitner. "A Pachyderm Needs Room to Turn In." New York *Evening Post Literary Review*, May 20, 1927, p. 3.

The dozen or so tales that compromis "Chains" are rather weak links at bes They are quite correctly subtitled "Th Lesser Novels and Stories of Theodor Dreiser." I do not know which of the are recent, and which may have bee written some years ago, to appear no in book (or possibly printed) form fo the first time. However that may be they are a rather heterogeneous bunc having for the most part neither th courage nor simplicity of "Jennie Ger hardt" and "Sister Carrie," nor the pon derous cumulative intensity of "Th Genius" or "An American Tragedy. They more nearly approach the statu of journalistic featurewriting than th short story; of social sermons, rathe than the exploitation of character an situation purely in the interest of ar

"Chains," the longest of the pieces, i probably the poorest. The theme is or dinary and harmless enough; the thin s poor work almost wholly because of he method. Dreiser employs a sandwich method, alternating the immediate present with events of the past. The portions representing the present in thought and action are too meager to have true psychological effect, and too interspersed with exclamation points to achieve anything but an absurdly melodramatic quality. There is not one jot of dramatic relief in the whole narration. It is full of what might be called the 'those eyes! those noses!" business. Adelle and the husband narrator and other characters mentioned are convincing enough; but they, poor lambs, are lost in the Dreiserian jungle.

The story "Fulfillment" unfortunately follows the same method, this time with a woman as narrator, and is even less successful, if possible, than the longer tale.

Then there are a number of stories obsessed with some sex theme. "Sanctuary" is one of these: a nice sob-sister tale about Madeline, the poor little poor girl raised in the tenements, and hence gone wrong, but eventually to be redeemed by the institutionalized chastity of the Sisterhood of the Good Shepherd. "Typhoon" is an "American Tragedy" in a little briefer form. The harrassed girl about to become a mother shoots, Frankie-Albert fashion, the man who betrayed her, and she might live happily ever afterward if her conscience didn't bother her. But she chooses to think about it a while and then walk into the river. With plodding, humorless doggedness, Dreiser drags the story to its pseudo-dramatic conclusion of blood, tears and broken hearts; from a "Christ I'm shot" to a "sinking beneath the surface without a cry."

There are three or four good "stories" in the lot; and the best of these is "St. Columbia and the River." It's the narrative of McGlathery's part in the construction of the Hudson tubes, and in it there is the real atmosphere of underground, under-water engineering; you can feel the slimy darkness of the walls of the tunnel, the super air pressure, the immense power of the overhead river. The story holds interest because it rises to a series of three climactic episodes, each of peril and imminent of loss of life, the final one an adventure for McGlathery, which loses nothing by an absurdly humorous ending. With a skillful blending of superstition and humor, Dreiser thoroughly succeeds in characterizing McGlathery, the Irishman. A man's story of a man's work, told with unusual dramatic power and conviction. . . .

C.B.B.
"Life's Ironies."
Detroit *News*,
May 20, 1927.

Rhetorical finesse—even rhetorical decency—is a thing which at odd and unlooked for times seems utterly beyond Theodore Dreiser. This is so much the case that the reader who knows him well sometimes wonders whether his gaucheries are not malice aforethought.

Take for instance the opening sentence in "Phantom Gold," perhaps the best single story in "Chains":

"You would have to have seen it to have gathered a true impression—."

Now how can anybody do that unless he tries? It is the last word in awkwardness. A rhetoric instructor would grit his teeth if he saw it in a freshman composition.

Yet, paradox though it be, what a writer this man is! What a photographer of the human scene! What a master of the essentials in human drama! What a sculptor out of the very stuff of reality!

Such stories as "Phantom Gold" and "Convention" in this new volume may be "only chips from his workshop," as Mr. Harry Hansen says, but they gleam nevertheless with the fine gold of his material, and they live in the mind with a poignancy and vivid certainty that few if any of his contemporaries achieve.

William Hazlitt said of Shakespeare that his tragedies were greater than his comedies because tragedy is greater than comedy. Perhaps that is the secret of Dreiser's supremacy in American letters. He holds to tragedy—humor he has practically none, and satire is too shallow for his genius.

With Thomas Hardy silent in the shadow of many years, he stands as the world's chief interpreter of its sorrows, since by some magic, after his clumsy quill has moved over many pages, Humanity and Sorrow stand revealed past any question of their identity. Soaring rhetoric has often failed to make these things live—but Theodore Dreiser has succeeded. . . .

Carl Van Doren.
"Lesser Novels."
New York *Herald Tribune Books,*
May 22, 1927,
pp. 3–4.

Reading Theodore Dreiser is like looking at a very large picture or a large actual landscape. When you come closer to a part of either of them you are likely to wonder a little at the illusion you had when you were at the proper distance. The texture seems coarse or the details seem to be arranged without any striking order. So with a Dreiser novel. The scale is an element which can rarely be left out of account. There is sure to be an extensive general design, but the parts themselves are executed with reference to their share in that design rather than to the effects which they are individually to make. Whether this is Mr. Dreiser's intention does not matter. It is the impression his work gives.

The largeness of his conceptions, being sustained by him with such force and persistence, tends to give a sense of largeness to each part. When, however, he is not working upon a large scale he loses that advantage. Then his detail has to be viewed by itself, without the significant shadow thrown by a large design. Only in his studies of particular persons, as in "Twelve Men," does Mr. Dreiser succeed with briefer pieces. And that book is hardly an exception, because the attitude which he takes toward the human race hangs over it much as if it were a general design.

The fifteen stories in "Chains" are by no means so uniformly successful as the studies in "Twelve Men." There are two stories with Arabian scenes and characters which look somewhat strange among the American stories, but which show no very marked talent in the "Oriental" direction. There are stories which venture into the field of psychopathology, stories which are presented as mere streams of reverie in the minds of single personages, and one story which is ostensibly a collection of edited documents. These variations, however, of subject and technique need not notably change the reputation which the art of Mr. Dreiser already had. He is best when he is plainest and bluntest, as in "Convention," "Typhoon," "Phantom Gold," "The Shadow"—especially in "Phantom Gold."

This last is a story in which there are none but primitive instincts and in which all the ingenuities of the plot are mere bargaining over money. A farmer, selling a farm which has mineral deposits on it, wants to keep as much of the money as he can from his wife and children, whom he hates. He hates them so much that he overreaches himself and in the end they get what the farm brings, while he loses his mind. The story exhibits no subtleties of character, nor needs to, for there are none to exhibit. It does not call for much speculation about mankind in general, because greed is too simple and too obvious. It does not call for penetrating observation; the actions of the narrative are as simple and as expectable as if the people in it were animals. What it calls for, and what it gets, is that patience with the human race in which Mr. Dreiser surpasses almost all novelists. He tells the story with a kind of patient candor which somehow raises the mean events to a plane of importance. These are, it is true, animals, but they are also human beings. Reading the story you are surprised to see how far your interest in the race can go. Why on earth should it go so far? That question you cannot answer. The answer is a part of Mr. Dreiser's secret.

Possessing that secret, he is able at times to dispense with the neatness and knowingness which are ordinarily indispensable to the writer of short stories. But, of course, he can do this only when the material is suited to his capacities—that is, when it is solid, real and specific. He cannot pack a world of subtle observation in a sentence nor turn the lightning of swift insight upon a set of circumstances. His movement is too slow for that. Nor is he ever happy when he tries to generalize, as in his Foreword: "The inevitabilities of our fate are: Love and hope, fear and death, interwoven with our lacks, inhibitions, jealousies and greeds." Doubtless this is true enough, but it is much too vague. It has to be spelled out, and no two of those who spell it out can possibly agree what it means. It is not a proverb; it is a puzzle. Mr. Dreiser makes his points when he tells his stories.

H. K. Ellingson. Colorado Springs *Telegraph*, May 22, 1927.

In "Chains," a collection of 15 of Dreiser's shorter stories, is presented a marquetry fully as complete in the matter of design as any of Dreiser's novels. Considered singly, many of these stories are nothing short of powerful in their dramatic effect; but considered collectively, they are virtually overwhelming in their power to render the reader aware of the utter cruelty of mankind.

Harry Hansen. "The First Reader." New York *World Book Section*, May 22, 1927, p. 8M.

Theodore Dreiser's new book, "Chains," is described on the cover as "lesser novels and stories," and this is accurate—we may even say that this book is made up of chips from the novelist's workbench. For here are the germs of longer stories and again here are short digressions which remind us of novels that are already on our shelves. Theodore Dreiser thinks in one way, writes after one manner.

The forward may be considered as a sort of keynote of these stories. It reads: "The inevitabilities of our fate are: Love and hope, fear and death, interwoven with our lacks, inhibitions, jealousies and greeds." Here we have the Dreiser text—and it is upon this text that these stories are written.

Dreiser's work, like that of Balzac, deserves to be considered as a whole. Only in that way can we get an adequate idea of the importance and the scope of this man's production. In that way, too, we rise above mere criticism of his uneven utterance. It stands to reason that he will never be held up as a master of style by rhetoricians who publish fragments of prose in anthologies for secondary schools. Every sentence, every paragraph, almost makes him a bad example. Yet the sum total of his work cannot be overlooked by any one who considers seriously the literature of our time and who looks for the influences that have shaped it.

"Chains," taken as a whole, gives us a glimpse of this author's relentless peering into life. He finds this or that emotion, this tragedy, worth study. He plays with the skeins of fate—sees where they lead. He tries to be above sympathy—remembering, perhaps, that he is an objective story teller, setting down life as it appears to him, and yet by his very selectivity and his caressing of poor harassed creatures, betraying his heart and hand. . . .

H. R. Pinckard. "Short Stories By Dreiser Are Above Average." Huntington [W. Va.] *Advertiser*, May 25, 1927.

These are all moderately short stories, some of them done in that confident, meticulous style that has marked Dreiser's recent books and others in an experimental, almost indifferent vein that seem to have been included largely to fill up space. Nevertheless they are all well above the average American short story.

One of the outstanding features of the collection is the variety of plots and styles included. No two are similar and there are fifteen in the book. Of them all the first, "Sanctuary," is perhaps most typical of Dreiser. It is of Madeleine Kinsella, a girl of the tenements, who drifts from kitchen work to prostitution, thence to the house of correction and back to the streets again. The pathetically dwarfed life of Madeleine, er timid and impotent efforts to find ome small "sanctuary" in a sordid, inlifferent world are developed with the ireless patience that only Dreiser, of all merican writers, seems able to muster. In a few pages Dreiser brings the eader back into the brooding mood he upplied you in "An American Tragdy."

"Chains," from which the volume akes its name, we did not particularly ike. It was one of those apparently writen in the most difficult method imaginable simply to test the author's veratility. Except for the climax and the rst paragraph or two the entire story is vritten as the thoughts of Upham Garison during a train ride from a neighoring city to his home. Italic paragraphs, bringing the reader and the 'medium" back to realities of the preent, are inset copiously and the combiation is not pleasing.

Of all the stories "Phantom Gold" is probably the best. It has to do with an gnorant, unbelievably disgusting famly of farmers, living on a small plot of ocky, sun-baked ground, where even veeds will not flourish. When it is disovered that the rocks that make the arm virtually unfit for agricultural puroses are practically virgin zinc, the elfishness and innate meanness of hese people is revealed. . . .

Dreiser's short stories, to judge simly by this volume, are above the average, but not as strikingly so as are his novels. He seems less sure of himself in he short story field. Essentially a careul (some readers say tiresome and vordy) writer, he has not the freedom vith which to develop his characters, nd certainly the development and nalysis of characters—better say of living people—is Dreiser's chief claim to genius.

Personally, we believe that claim to be very secure. To those who find him wordy and tiresome we would say: don't read him. By no means attempt to skim through his works.

There are artists in every line who seem able to accomplish an end with the least apparent effort and in manner frequently unconventional. Dreiser is not one of those. With meticulous care he arranges every sequence, every thought, in the most natural and convincing manner. If the whole does not seem to convey forcefully enough the impression he seeks to make he is not discouraged, but, at least so it seems to me, rips the whole structure and then painstakingly weaves it together again, achieving a co-ordination and brute force that simply overwhelms the reader.

You may not like to read Theodore Dreiser, but, if you've ever read "The Genius" or "An American Tragedy" you're bound to admire him.

Walter J. Auburn. "Lesser American Tragedies." Chicago *News*, May 25, 1927.

In the wake of "An American Tragedy" comes this series of lesser tales and short novels, in rapidly dissolving views of pathos, guilt, sorrow, hatred, unrequited love and abandoned hope. They all bear that quality of reality so difficult to transmute from everyday sordidness to an adequate word picture. Deranged mental processes, neurotic tendencies, supersition, fear, and other mental disturbances are drawn without sentimentality, but Dreiser paints no description of revolting ugliness or horror. That is because his skillful narration dispenses with everything but the stark tragedy and its causes and effects in the method of a calm but intent surgeon concerned solely with the action before him and uninterested in the petty details that cloud the main issue. . . .

In all these tales a rich experience of life allays their tragedy, but a spirit of sadness lingers in their telling, possibly because human nature stands revealed as it so often is, base, selfish and cruel. The only criticism is against the over-burdening detail, in evidence here as in "An American Tragedy."

J. E. T. Washington [Del.] *News*, May 26, 1927.

With Dreiser, there seems to be no middle road of appreciation. Readers either love him for his ruggedness or hate him for his verbosity. Love or hate. There is no single tolerant pleasure to be obtained from reading him. One either reads hungrily or fascinated by the man's sincerety, or one throwns away the book from sheer boredom.

Those of us who love Dreiser's style—or lack of style—of genious, will be a little pained at reading "Chains." There is of course that lumbering, sombre, and above all sincere, photographic writing which is so essentially Dreiseresque; but there is also too great a play of force in too small a scope. There is something so appealing about Dreiser's complete lack of sophisticated smartness, something so invigorating about his great hulking phraseolgy, something so almost pathetic in his naiv seriousness and child-like love of mel drama, that it seems tragic to attem their use in a literary form to whic they are so evidently not adapted.

None of the short stories in "Chains are sensational; they all have a psych logical twist; some are vitally interes ing; a few are infinitely boring. "Sanct ary" and "Chains" seem to me to b among the best with the "Mercy c God" running a close second. One ca ignore "Khat" and "The Old Neighbo hood" and miss nothing.

Despite the touches of genius in th volume, I cannot see how the storie contained therein will greatly en chance the reputation of the autho "The Genius" and "Jennie Gerhardt. Writing a short story calls for more sty lism, more finesse, than Dreiser seem to possess. He is a painter of giganti canvasses which awe by their very im mensity. When he attempts to use th same brush strokes in a vignette, th result is not happy.

William R. Langfeld. "Theodore Dreiser in Abridgment." Philadelphia *Record*, May 28, 1927.

Theodore Dreiser is an author wh works on a large scale, who produces hi effects partly by the cumulative pres sure of piled up detail, who convince partly by mass of evidence. His shor stories in "Chains" to an extent reflec the same trait, but to an extent als suffer from lack of it. While the boo will be interesting to any intelligen reader, while most of its contents mus ertainly be included among the better :ories of the day, as honest portrayals ır removed from the mechanical fforts which crowd our magazines, hey cannot be classed with a book like The American Tragedy." A few of the tories fall below the average, but in eneral "Chains" will neither detract rom nor enhance Dreiser's reputation.

Dreiser has softened with the passage f time. His former novels, as "The Tian," "The Financier" and "The Genius," exalted the superman, or at east explain him on the theory that life vas a necessary struggle, that wealth, voman and power constituted unescaable human motives. In his later works ne finds an increasing note of pity for uman frailty. There is a sympathy, a leep tenderness, in such stories as that f the poor waif who finds life too hard struggle in "Sanctuary." The tragedy, he pathos, of well-meaning but illnated couples who cannot be helped nd cannot be condemned finds expression in "Marriage for One," "The Shadow" and partially in others, as "Chains," dealing with the older man nd younger woman, and "Fulfilment," n which the theme is supplemented by brief love idyll on the part of the voman which contains more romance han is usual with Dreiser. . . .

Dreiser has used a different techique in some of his tales, two of them eing in the form of continued reverie nd retrospect and one a series of reports. Many of them are really sketches, engthy outlines of plots, raw material uch as he has used as a subject matter or an entire novel.

Dreiser sees life as fatalistic, its tragelies as inevitable. The forces of envionment and of human temperament annot be evaded. He reflects the modern cry, "What is the reason for it all? Why and for what do we live?" But he sees less of the triumph and more of the pathos than formerly. He was always observant and sincere. Without losing his power, he has added a touch of deep humanity.

Karl Schriftgiesser. "Theodore Dreiser in His Minor Mood." Boston *Evening Transcript, Book Section,* June 11, 1927, p. 2.

The fifteen "lesser novels and stories" of the latest volume from the typewriter of a leading American novelist are crumbs from a rich man's table. Caught up in one receptacle they fail completely to satisfy one who is used to dining from a full board. They are minor efforts, with one or two exceptions, and one who is willing to concede Dreiser's peculiar ability as a novelist must point out that this ability does not serve him in his shorter stories. Nor is the marked genius of "A Traveler at Forty," "Twelve Men," or even of "Tales of a Great City" [*sic*], noticeable in this collection. It is Dreiser in a minor mood; at best this is a notebook of a man with a remarkable power of observation. It is not the Dreiser of "Jennie Gerhardt," "Sister Carrie," or "An American Tragedy."

There are of course some crumbs of cake as well as of bread. One particularly rich (one hesitates to carry the simile so far as to call it sweet) is a peculiarly Dreiserian tragedy called "Sanctuary." In this, which must have been written a long time ago, one feels the Dreiser of that period when he was telling his tales of a great city. In the book of that name, now but seldom read, I remember particularly a sketch of Hell's Kitchen written in what, for want of a better term, might be called the Sunday supplement style. One felt that in it Dreiser was but skimming surfaces, that he felt deeper than he told in cold print. Now one realizes that he was making observations, as he was in other sketches in that earlier book, which were to serve him in his task of short-story writing. Remembered and thoroughly observed events of the beer-can era, when slums were slums, and there was more mystery to all life, go into "Sanctuary." I feel convinced that despite the sentimentality, or perhaps because of it, this story is as good American writing of the first half of this century as anything of Dickens's (say "Hard Times") was of his generation. The sordidness of city life is well described in this short story and an understanding of the dreams of dwellers of the half world is as well set forth as anywhere that I can remember.

I should like to speak here for a moment of Dreiser's sentimentality, something which has been neglected by the critics who have been overcome by his blundering and utterly frank realism. At times, as "Sanctuary" proves, Dreiser allows himself to become the sob sister. In this story he recounts the life of the frail daughter of a drunken father and a mother who would never be given the white ribbon for her abstaining powers. A hovel is home, blows and cuffs and curses are a part of everyday existence. The inevitable life of the street walker faces the daughter and, because she sees in that life the possibilities of love and a lightness not known in the slums, she surrenders. A detective, or plainclothesman, one night accosts her. She thinks he is a man who wears his heart on his sleeve instead of one who wears his badge on his vest. Result: court, a sentence to a Sister's home. Here at last is peace and release from an utterly sordid world. But she cannot stay there forever. When she gets out a man marries her and then uses her as a tool for his nefarious practices. Because she cannot produce enough for his easy life he kicks her out of the rooms they occupy. She goes to her "sanctuary," bleeding in heart and body, and asks to be taken back.

Dreiser perhaps has never written more poignantly than here. "She urged her very gently to enter and then tucked the covers about her, laying finally a cool, wrinkled hand on her forehead. For answer Madelaine seized and put it to her lips, holding it so.

" 'Oh, Mother,' she sobbed as the Sister bent over her, 'don't ever make me go out into the world again, will you? You won't, will you? I'm so tired. I'm so tired!"

" 'No, dear, no,' soothed the Sister, 'not unless you wish it. And now rest. You need never go out in the world again unless you wish.'

"And withdrawing the hand from the kissing lips, she tiptoed silently from the room."

Dickens, we now know, was not always the sentimentalist. Nor is Dreiser always the realist. He can sob with the rest of the tribe and just as tearfully. But luckily it is only at times. Even in "Sanctuary," the supreme example of Dreiser the sentimentalist, there is power and a certain loneliness of spirit that makes us recall the term of "weatherbeaten figure" once applied to him by, I think

I. L. Mencken. I have yet to read any f Dreiser's fiction in which there has ot crept a note of weariness, a note eminiscent of the days when he was ot acclaimed but was writing by himelf, for himself, and was neglected by ditors and public alike. In the short tory "Chains," whence derives the tile of this book, where Dreiser is writng not of the slums, not of the life he evealed so movingly in "A Book About Ayself," not of such characters as made 'Sister Carrie," a novel which, once ead, cut itself into one's soul, this oneliness crops up. Here it is manifesed by his utter inability to make his haracter (there is only one major charicter therein) living and understandable. This story is of the love worries of Babbitt who has married a woman who cares little for him but who, depite his knowledge that in doing her oid he is being made a fool of, can bend im thoroughly to her will. It is a story with a great deal of truth in it, but to me at least it is lacking in something vital. Dreiser, either because he is writing of a man not of his own class, or because he has been influenced by something foreign and is endeavoring as it were to be "arty," has deadened his effect. I cannot help feeling that if he had been telling of a Chicago bill collector rather than of a wealthy business man with a social position in his home town his story would have come off much better.

Now in "St. Columbia and the River," the tale of an Irishman, with a mortal dread of water, who goes to work under the harbor, helping to dig a tunnel, Dreiser has got nearer to his level. I do not mean to infer that Dreiser is more at home with ditch-diggers than with gentlemen—except when it comes to the writing of fiction. In "An American Tragedy," had he selected, for example, the Hall-Mills case rather than the Chester Gillette case as a model, I am convinced he would never have produced a masterpiece. Theodore Dreiser, as "A Book About Myself" proved, is of the common clay, but that common clay, as one knows from reading "Twelve Men," can be excellent building material. When he tries (and it is a natural thing to do) to be of good rich soil, it is easy enough to see that he isn't, that he cannot be, sincere. That is why "The Hand" fails to click and why "Sanctuary" is the best in this collection.

Style is an important matter—with all but Dreiser. One does not expect the prose of a George Saintsbury in a novel dealing with a harlot knocking at a convent door, perhaps, but even in a story of such brutal realism as "An American Tragedy" there is no reason why clauses shouldn't fit, and phrases go where they belong, and the pronouns be understandable. This is an irritating, and one might say inexcusable fault. Because of this one is apt to miss much that is good in a book, or even in a short story. In "The Shadow" I thought for a long time that the "her" to whom he was referring was an automobile, but later it turned out that it was a woman. Going back to the beginning, it was only after effort that I saw why my mistake had been made. Well, all of us make mistakes in rhetoric and grammar, but Thomas Hardy has proved that one could be a realist and still have a schoolboy's respect for one's native tongue.

Somewhere in this book I ran across this phrase: "The cruelty and inscrutability of life," and I thought, as I jotted it down, how well that explained what interests Dreiser the most. I am not sure whether it is the cruelty, or whether it is the inscrutability, that the more surely holds his attention. Both absorb him always. Life is a cruel thing in his eyes and most of what he has written has been colored with the cuts and the bruises which it has given him. From his German Catholic boyhood, through the stair-climbing days in Chicago before newspaper work called him, and after recognition had come to him and he had traveled in many lands, life always seemed to be cuffing him in the face. Or if it wasn't his own face that got slapped, he has always been unable to refrain from wincing as he saw so many faces all about him getting slapped all the time. It is the cuffs and the slaps and even the cruel kicks of life that have made him write the stories which are to his everlasting credit. Hurstwood (and he was all cuffs and slaps and kicks) would never have been written about if life had taken Dreiser for one of its pets.

One must not forget, however, the word inscrutability in that phrase which I quoted. The cruelty of life alone did not make Dreiser a genius. He learned very early that life is one grand slam in the jaw, but I don't think he ever learned why. The combination of knowing and wondering has made him a great novelist. The latter explains the undoubted mysticism that is evident in such stories as "The 'Mercy' of God" and "The Prince Who Was a Thief." These are decidedly lesser stories and while they may be read with interest they are at best but sidelights on a great career. The psychologist may make use of them in an endeavor to understand Dreiser, for a complete study of this man cannot neglect his mysticism, but the average reader will not read them for that purpose. And the average reader does count somewhat.

"Chains" (the book) on the whole, as hitherto suggested, is Dreiser in distinctly minor mood. But all of the fifteen stories in the collection are part of his creed, part of that "cruelty" and "inscrutability" that mean so much to him. All, in varying degrees of success fit in with his "Foreword," which is "The inevitabilities of our fate are Love and hope, fear and death, interwoven with our lacks, inhibitions jealousies and greeds."

That is a succinct foreword, typically Dreiserian, and it sums up what he is trying to tell us in 425 closely printed pages.

William McFee. "Americana." *New Republic,* 51 (June 15, 1927), 104.

. . . The reviewer with any modesty in him at all will feel a certain nervousness on approaching the work of Mr. Dreiser. There has been built up around this novelist a mysterious structure whose portals are guarded by certain eminent critics. It seems to be almost *lèse-majesté* for the ordinary mortal to express an opinion. The foolish mortal who wants a novel to read which will interest him is warned off with shot-guns. Dreiser is, or was, not for him. In the old days, we are given to understand, nobody except radicals and intellectuals read him, yet everybody knew he was a great novelist. Dreiser, in short, was talked about. This reviewer, who is neither a radical nor an intellectual, once spent two consecutive voyages reading the works of

)reiser. The opinion he arrived at on eaching port once more has not been nodified by "Chains." Mr. Dreiser, he elt, had an uncanny genius for writing bout intensely interesting people in an ntensely uninteresting way. The)reiserian enthusiasts are apt to say, 'Ah!" and look knowing when this view s advanced, but they fail to offer any atisfactory rebuttal of it. "Chains" consists of collected short stories, called, for ome reason or other, "lesser novels," vhich have appeared in magazines over a long period of time. The story entitled "The Hand" must have been ead by this reviewer many years ago in The Smart Set. One of the best—indeed, Dreiser at his best—is "Convenion," of a much more recent vintage. There are several oriental stories included here, which are curious experinents for Dreiser and show the slant of is mind. "Sanctuary," in any other ands, would have been a beautiful tory. By Dreiser, it is a piece of pahetic reporting.

Here, in fact, if one would sum up a nan's life work in a phrase—and no one s more aware of the injustice of such a umming-up than this reviewer—one is compelled to say that for beauty Mr. Dreiser cares not at all. He is preoccupied with what he calls truth. But he as chosen the wrong medium. The novelist who seeks truth save through the beauty of words, the beauty of tructure and selection, the beauty of haped phrases, will discover, sooner or ater, that what he thought was truth is only a grimace on the features of numanity. He will discover that what ne sought has eluded him. The methods of science in the novelists work-room are, if the truth be blurted out, unsuccessful. If we have learned anything at all in our long pilgrimage from Smollett and Fielding to Ring Lardner and Ernest Hemingway, it is that we know nothing about men and women save what we discover in ourselves.

"The Book Table." *Outlook*, 146 (June 22, 1927), 258.

Each of these long "short stories" presents a study of one moving element in human nature—ambition, hatred, greed, faith, sex-urge, and so on. Mr. Dreiser, as always, is thorough and stolid in proving his case by every art of realism. We respect him and his work enormously, but a touch now and then of dramatic fire, of spontaneity, would send his reader away enthusiastic as well as convinced.

Gorham B. Munson. "Odds and Ends." *Saturday Review of Literature.* 3 (June 25, 1927), 928.

Unlike "An American Tragedy," "Chains" will not add to Mr. Dreiser's reputation. It is a collection of odds and ends of short stories and novelettes, the quality of which is distinctly below Mr. Dreiser's best as seen in "Sister Carrie," "The Titan," "Twelve Men," "Free and Other Stories," not to mention "An American Tragedy" once more. . . .

The writing is as wasteful and cumbersome as ever, though it is not often pointed out that in the first place Mr. Dreiser writes a banal sentence as though *he* had discovered it and, secondly, that he generally escapes utter deadness of diction by using here and there a word or phrase that is so precise or forceful or weighty that the entire passage is barely lifted by its energy. Paradoxically, it is the defects of his prose that give it what positive character it has, for these defects stem from his own habits of experience—which is perhaps why he has been deaf to all exhortations to improve his style.

Two things are curious about this book. One is Mr. Dreiser's very simplified adaptation of certain advanced technics of the day. There is in the title story the chain of Garrison's emotional associations with his wife and his reflections on them during the course of a railroad journey home. These associations give us the story of his previous married life. But interspersed and set in italics are the comments Garrison's mind makes on the passengers, progress, and incidents of the trip, and these form a narrative of the present which runs parallel to the past. Both narratives coalesce when he reaches the house and finds his wife absent. The other curious element is Mr. Dreiser's excursion into Oriental tale-telling on two occasions and the strange fact that he writes more correctly in these than is usual in his wrestling with syntax and rhythm and exactitude.

One of the best stories is "St. Columba and the River." We read Dreiser—many of us at any rate—because he has a tenacious memory for the dramatic and fascinating schemes of American life (*e.g.*, political and financial schemes) and the working out of these, no matter how crudely written, carries us to the conclusion. In "St. Columba and the River" the real drama is supplied by the progress of the engineering scheme to tunnel beneath the North River. The workman, McGlathery, and the heavy fun Mr. Dreiser pokes at his religious superstitions, are incidental to our main interest.

Philadelphia *Public Ledger*, June 25, 1927.

One continues to hear that Theodore Dreiser is preoccupied with sex in his stories—the implied notion being that his stories are "raw"; that he has no style (Whatever the word means as a generalization!); that he cannot write English, and that he is dull. The first statement is absurd, of course, to anyone who has read Mr. Dreiser's stories and the other three are less critical than they are very personal expressions of individual taste.

It is true that those who find Mr. Dreiser one of the most impressive and certainly one of the best story tellers of this country are those who accept him on his own terms. Readers have no other approach to him. They must anticipate his courageous willingness to find his tales anywhere—his "heroes" are as likely to be sandhogs as multimillionaires, his heroines drabs as society beauties; they must anticipate his unwillingness to evade any human problem or character; they must be ready to accept his ponderous and often inept methods of piling detail upon detail, of repetition, of unhurried penetration; they must be prepared to follow sentences too honestly eloquent to be decorative or graceful. These are his terms. He offers with them a representation of life.

And his stories successfully represent life—without humor for the most part, it is true (and humor of one sort or another is essential to the greatest stories), but gravely, grimly, and yet not without the deepest sympathy and understanding.

His "Chains," a collection of fifteen stories, is not a book for readers who thrive best on romance, swift, easily followed, and not too sad. "Chains" would surprise even those readers, however. For in his shorter tales, Mr. Dreiser is not infrequently capricious—and there is a light play of humor (I've no doubt it's humor) in his story of the sandhog who fears water, and in his Oriental improvisation, "The Prince Who Was a Thief." Surprising, too, his shorter tales, for all their truth, are now and again artful—shall I say, self-consciously devised?—which is certainly not true of his longer stories, whose slow natural movement and whose credible development are not the least of their power.

Marian Gerber. "Gold in the Ore." "Asheville [N.C.] *Times*, July 24, 1927.

Although the third of this remarkable collection of stories is the only one to be specifically entitled "Chains", yet are they all concerned with human bondage. The author's foreword contains the kernel of his philosophy: "The inevitabilities of our fate are: love and hope, fear and death, interwoven with our lacks, inhibitions, jealousies and greeds." Before us are unrolled fifteen dramas in this vein, for Mr. Dreiser's literary creed is the truthful representation of life, the study of which has convinced him that "the race is not to the swift nor the battle to the strong."

Despite this similarity of outlook, each story is a world in itself, distinct, profound, disturbing. . . .

Unhappily, the same crudity of form that characterizes Mr. Dreiser's greater works mar the beauty and power of these lesser novels and stories. One struggles drearily through a sixteen line sentence only to confront pages with scarcely an honest period among them. There are reflexives instead of personal pronouns, dangling participles and split infinitives, and an irritating reiteration of faddy words—for example, intriguing, which serves as an adjective a dozen times in the course of one short story.

On the other hand, Mr. Dreiser can suggest an unforgettable poem in a few words, such as: "To the east (of the convent) rocks and the river, a gray expanse in winter picked over by the gulls, mourned over by the horns of endless craft." He can demonstrate as well as write that "circumstances are stronger than personalities, and the impotence of individuals is the tragedy of every day life."

Vogue, August 1, 1927.

Chains is the title given to a volume of fifteen short stories published by *Boni and Liveright* and written by Theodore Dreiser, best known as the author of AN AMERICAN TRAGEDY. This title might apply also to some of these stories, for even when they do not end in disaster, misfortune surrounds most of the characters in them or, at the best, sadness hangs like a veil over their lives. This being the case, it is hard to understand the pleasure one feels as one reads; but pleasure there certainly is, and to us it arises from the simplicity and straightforwardness of Mr. Dreiser's style. He has none of the involved would-be subtlety in which one sometimes finds a small kernel of idea voluminously wrapped; he has a tale to tell, in most cases, and he sees it clearly and puts it into plain English, though not always the very purest. He abounds in detail, but this does not check the pace of the narrative, and one feels, as in a well-constructed play, that every phrase of the dialogue helps the movement of the action. . . .

"The Bookshelf of a Workingman." *Weekly People*, August 6, 1927.

Reviews of Theodore Dreiser's works have ever amused us. They are either unqualified laudation, "the Titan of American letters" being the favorite phrase, or else they are a series of unqualified damns—not of the conception indeed. We have never yet seen a damner that dared to tackle that but only the style. The style is awful! It is mere newspaper reporting, so runs the running comment. The other day we came across a reviewer of "Chains" who wanted to say the same thing but felt called upon to say it differently. He made it: I never knew anyone who could write so uninterestingly about such interesting people. We had another smile coming when we wondered who or what made the Dreiser gallery interesting if not Dreiser and his pen? And so we wondered if it might not be perhaps that the modern pure "stylists" on the one hand and the stereotyped plottists, something-doing-every minutes with a happy ending as a matter of principle and sales necessity on the other, had not succeeded between them in reducing to a minimum the readers who could extract pleasure and profit from a story that relates in a somewhat commonplace manner the troubles and tribulations of commonplace people.

Anyhow we have found Dreiser well worth the effort of his company. Sometimes a little fagging and wordy, as most friends are apt to be when they get agoing on a favorite theme, oftentimes very stimulating company, and in spots even inspiring. That we feel is about as much as anyone ought to expect of any so-called realistic author, an author who leads us ploddingly and on foot through the avenues and bystreets of our own society; who does not aim to split our sides with laughter nor to carry us off on a magic carpet of hair-raising adventure.

The present volume is a collection of novelettes, most of which have no doubt from time to time been published in some magazine or other. The title to the volume is given by a story of an ill-mated marriage in which the chains are still too strong for the injured, chafing party to break. While we do not consider this the most outstanding story of the volume, nevertheless the name is well chosen. Chains run through the whole collection, chains to habits, conventions, superstitions, property, incessant toil, chains forged by humanity for humanity in the welter of the society in which we live.

It is a varied procession of strangely commonplace people that pass in review. The girl of a New York slum unable to fight the battle of a cruel and selfish and oppressing world; a miner who murders his partner when success is at hand, too greedy to share it, and is choked to death by the dead man's hand—on his conscience; a superstitious son of Erin who comes through the tunneling under the river by the aid of politics, science, Irish luck—and constant offering to his patron, St. Columba; a timid soul who dared taste life for a moment and lived happily with his wife ever afterward—having been beaten into conformity by a job and the social conventions; a family of worked-out and starved-out western farmers turning greedily on each other and fooling themselves individually and collectively when the fields suddenly turn out to be a rich zinc mine—and so on and so forth, fifteen stories in all, miniature portraits of our ugly and harassing society painted with the painstaking, detailed Dreiser technique.

Checklist of Additional Reviews

Alceste. "Recent Books." *New Yorker*, 3 (May 28, 1927), 88.

Booklist, November, 1927, p. 68.

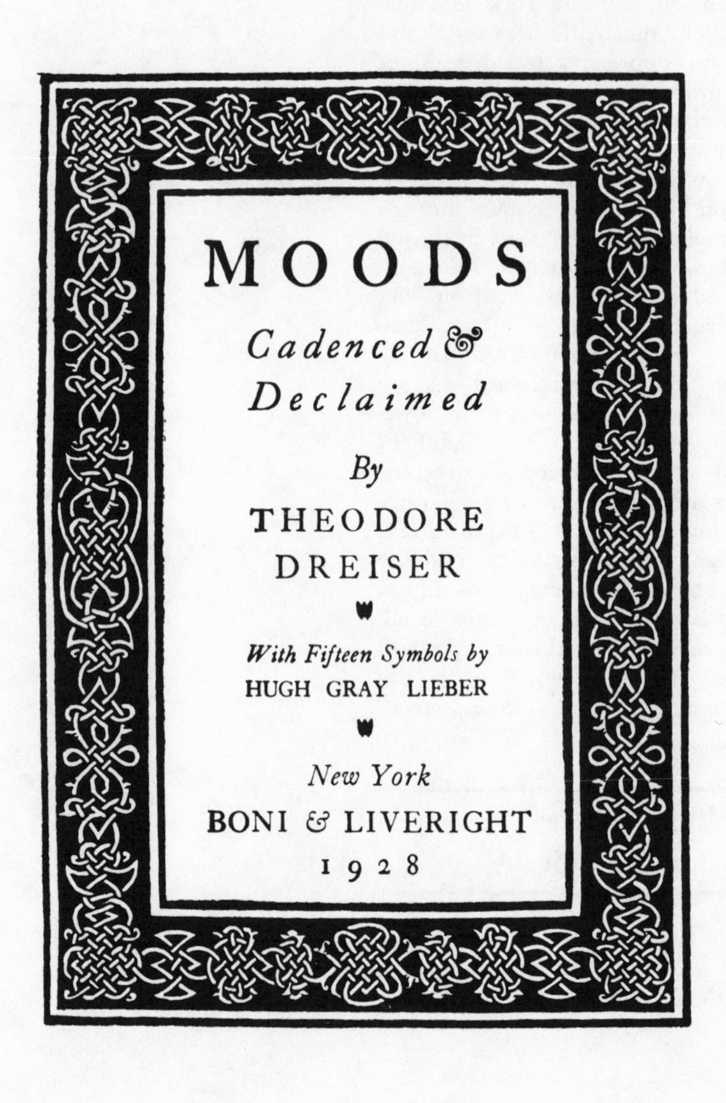

MOODS

Cadenced & Declaimed

By

THEODORE DREISER

With Fifteen Symbols by

HUGH GRAY LIEBER

New York

BONI & LIVERIGHT

1928

Moods, Cadenced and Declaimed

Harry Hansen.
"The First Reader."
New York *World*,
August 9, 1928.

Theodore Dreiser's practice of setting down in rough, poetic form the thoughts and moods that come to him has yielded a large collection of these fragments. Some have appeared from time to time in magazines. In the spring of 1926 his publishers gathered them into a large book under the title "Moods Cadenced and Declaimed," and published it as a limited edition. The large demand for this book now prompts Horace Liveright to issue an edition for general circulation.

Like Sherwood Anderson, Mr. Dreiser employs a method that may be called free verse, but in reality has little relation to poetry. The word poem, as a matter of fact, does not occur in the description of this book, and the publisher speaks of "these pieces" as the "free expressions, often lyrical, often poetic, of a complex and many-faceted mind; often too nebulous and brief for a more extended form, often too lyrical for prose, yet never actually falling into poetry." This seems to fit the case and may stand as a description of the contents of the book.

There are 206 of these moods, and they cover every conceivable subject, revealing irony, sentiment, social criticism and plain observation. They are never elaborate either in imagery or in expression, and frequently deal with the obvious. They do more for the man Dreiser than for literature. They reveal the sensitive novelist, the man who, irritated at social injustice, "exhausted by the savage contests of this world," takes refuge in dreams.

All the questions that Theodore Dreiser has asked in his novels may be found in these moods. His impatience with dogma, his contempt for bigoted authority, his conviction that life needs to be lived wholly to be wholesome, that restraints blunt its fineness; his recurrent sympathy for the under dog and acknowledgment that victory often carries with it unfair advantage, injustice and insensitivity to suffering; his irritation at the stupidities of men—all these are repeated here. But also there is a preoccupation with nature, which refreshes him, and with the evanescent influence of sound, color, flowers, trees, rain and the subtler forces of nature.

Alone amid nature he feels himself shielded "from the irritations and miseries of a world that I disdain."

Inasmuch as Mr. Dreiser is not experimenting with words but actually revealing his moods and his feelings, the following fragment, called "The Humanist," may be thought to have autobiographical significance:

> You carved, intaglioed ivories of speech!
> You graven and minted words!
> You groined and silent sanctuaries of thought,
> Agleam with jeweled images—
> How before your pinnacled altars of phrase and line
> Have I not stood agape,
> How marveled at the care,
> The pain,
> And yet—
> And yet—
> How before the thinly candled effigies
> Of those who felt
> Have I not knelt and prayed!

As a matter of fact, the whole book is autobiographical, and probably the best service that it performs is to reveal the author's mind. He turns out to be rather a mild philosopher, sorrowing over the ways of men, but never growing very indignant about them. Even his most emphatic passages show him as turning from the scenes he derides with a forlorn contempt and an air of hopelessness, never getting very violent. His remarks about beauty are quite conventional; when he says that the "Last Voice" records "Beauty, its worship shall never die," he is as much a modern as Celia Thaxter. But there are some fine lines in the collection, and the simplicity and directness of the moods enhance their value. It would be inaccurate to say that they are not rhythmic. "The Victor" and several other compositions have definite rhythms that may almost be called conventional.

Walter Yust. "Of Making Many Books—?" Philadelphia *Public Ledger,* August 10, 1928.

Two years ago Horace Liveright published Theodore Dreiser's "Moods: Cadenced and Declaimed" in a limited and signed-by-the-author edition of 500 copies. This week he brings out a second edition. How generally known "Moods" is I've no way of determining, but the fact that Mr. Dreiser has occasionally dropped into what might be called poetry is no longer news. His pieces have appeared now and again in the magazines.

In the broadest meaning of the word, poet signifies a creative artist in any medium. And on the evidence of his tumultuous novels, Theodore Dreiser is one of the three or four significant contemporary American poets. In "Moods," this same poet—no other—comes to grips with life, and the volume —characteristically thick—is, consequently, important. Whether it is poetry or not is another thing again.

For "poetry" owns to very limited prescriptions and, inasmuch as Mr. Dreiser doesn't care a hang about them, it will be impertinent to start a row over the, under the circumstances, fairly unimportant question whether Mr. Dreiser can write poems or not. He is a poet because he is sensitive enough to know and tell how it feels for him to be alive, and "Moods" is a collection of his notes, his impressions, freely written and yet held to loose form by the idea and the rhythm of the idea.

Sherwood Anderson gives us pieces such as these in his "Testament," and holds to a Scriptural, paragraph form. Mr. Dreiser, in the main, dresses his moods in long, narrow columns, two to six words a line; more often than not, only one word, (which isn't a matter of weight or worry; I'm merely trying to describe the book). The pieces are not striking for originality, but they are as profoundly and industriously honest as any of Mr. Dreiser's novels. I like him less, however, when he is declaiming, and least when he troubles his fine old head over cadences. One word to a line from Mr. Dreiser of all writers is somehow incredible.

N. E. A.
Denver [Col.] *News*, August 14, 1928.

It seems that Theodore Dreiser, who finally became generally recognized thru his "American Tragedy," has had about 365 pages of varied moods scattered about his study. These he jotted down in the staccato, unrhymed verses. About two years ago they were published in an edition limited to 500 copies, and named "Moods."

A strange book it is, and at times an interesting one. It can hardly be classified as poetry, tho it is sometimes rythmic.

Oftimes it seems autobiographical; oftimes a sort of confessional. Certainly one gets a close picture of the inside man from reading his moods. It is possible to trace even the major arguments of most of his books and catch a recurrence of their themes.

One feels the presence of a great undercurrent of sorrow; a grief for the stumbling hopelessness—even despair. He does not make the effort to wrangle with mankind or grow indignant over their fumblings; he views them with a sort of pity.

There are few subjects he doesn't tap in the course of his moods and he reveals his rebellious impatience against dogma, bigotry and hypocrisy such as can be found around every corner.

Brooklyn *Eagle*, August 15, 1928.

Mr. Theodore Dreiser, the poet, in "Moods, Cadenced and Declaimed," now published in a popular edition, offers the children of his muse with no fantastic preface, such as so many of our poets are addicted to. Consequently, what he thinks about critics is a matter between him and his God.

One is constrained to deal gently, therefore, with his work upon the lyre. He has mastered a certain lively line which gives his verse the appearance of virility. But Mr. Dreiser, as might be expected, is a blunt poet, who shrinks from pretty circumlocutions. His expression in meter is, in the very truth, moody. And he has the moods of a man who has not learned patience.

The consequence is that while one is struck forcibly by his lines one is also disappointed. His whole book of verse is a veritable winter of discontent. His is sardonic where others are sentimental, sentimental where others are cynical, cynical where others are simply silent. One catches the impression of a tempestuous sole [sic] walled in by the simple necessities of living. Even as he writes his novels without the slightest ray of hope, so, too, he writes poetry. His life, one fears, is intellectually, a single, long-drawn rebellious sigh. . . .

His psychic detachment is enough to keep him from becoming offensively personal, so that he escapes the blight of a Beaudelaire [sic]; but the same weary seeking and failure of questing runs throughout his poems. His world persists in leaving undone those things which ought to be done and there is no health in us. Perhaps these scraps and lines and fancies are more revealing than all his published prose. Certainly a good many of them would appear to have been set down in unguarded moments. And the poetic expression is always more naked than a novel. The Dreiser enthusiast may not consider himself thoroughly acquainted with his author until he has dipped into "Moods."

Arthur J. Gorman. "Dreiser's Moods Are Published." Pittsburgh *Press*, August 18, 1928.

A lugubrious philosopher is Theodore Dreiser as he reveals himself in his latest book, "Moods Cadenced and Declaimed," which has just been brought out in a general edition by Horace Liveright. The novelist's feelings on almost every phase of life are set down in a rough kind of free verse that at times attains rhythm, but more often does not. By what name the form Dreiser here employs is to be known is a subject for speculation and has already produced a number of widely varied suggestions. The publishers and one critic whose word carries much weight, discern lyrical and poetical thoughts unpoetically expressed. Others see a likeness to the subjectless and predicateless sentences of Sherwood Anderson, while still others contend that there is an undisputable resemblance to Dreiser's prose style.

With this last the reviewer disagrees. There is, however, a very obvious reiteration of the themes that made Dreiser's novels famous. He is once more the superb aesthete; super-sensitive to beauty in any form, anxious for life, impatient with frustration, unsentimentally sorry for human stupidity, and never rid of a sense of futility and mortal insignificance.

Here he is as sincere an enemy of dogma, bigotry, hypocrisy, and folly as Erskine Scott Wood or Mencken, but he is too pessimistic to be pugnacious, too resigned to believe that vociferation will make man see the error of his ways.

The fact that many of the fragments are autobiographical and that throughout there is an ingenuous outpouring of Dreiser's innermost thoughts, will be of added interest to the admirer of his novels. For the utmost enjoyment, we recommend that it be read concurrently with his "A Book About Myself."

"Dreiser Credo Index to His Character." San Francisco *Bulletin*, August 18, 1928.

Carlyle, preaching the gospel of silence in 17 volumes, and Dreiser, explaining himself in almost as many, suggest yet other comparisons. One might say that Theodore Dreiser is the American Thomas Carlyle without Carlyle's sense of righteousness, but then without that sense of righteousness, what is there left of Carlyle? Perhaps the resemblance is no more than that of seeming to hew their sentences with an ax instead of carving them with the point of a pen. Some say that Dreiser cannot help himself and that Carlyle could, as witness certain fragments of finely turned verse, but here is Dreiser with "Moods, Cadenced and Declaimed," and coming much nearer to poetry than most of our free verse bards.

We refrain from the unfriendly temptation to say that Dreiser's verse is his best prose, but do not hesitate to say that it contains some of his most effective writing. There are moods in this volume that seem trivial; others that lack distinction of expression and some that are strangely depressing, but in many there is more significant emotion significantly sounded than in whole carload lots of contemporary verse.

Dreiser is not a poet, but he has the poet's gift of values; of elaboration and elimination. He can build a forest out of a blade of grass or reduce a forest to a leaf. From anywhere he can go either way to the infinitely great or the infinitely small. He is the center of a universe as much of his own imagination as though he had created it. Often he is the dissatisfied creator, but sometimes even Dreiser looks upon his work and finds that it is good. . . .

But what a lonely creator and what little lasting comfort he finds in his own creations. With all its defects it is to the world of reality, to our world and to our illusions that even he must turn for the worship that shall never die—the worship of beauty. Beauty almost makes of him a poet.

We have said that there is much that might have been omitted. The greatest mind is liable to mistake an incomplete for a completed note, but as mental and emotional autobiography this book fully deserves the public edition in which it is now issued. It may be read and perhaps appreciated by many that find a difficulty in what Carlyle, speaking of Bartram, called "a floundering eloquence."

There is the sage of Chelsea creeping in again, but no more frequently than he comes to mind when reading Dreiser's everlasting why—not his Everlasting Nay, but his everlasting why. Not "whence" so very often but "where," "whither" and "why" are his recurring queries.

Here is no best seller, nothing to challenge the popularity of "An American Tragedy" and not a toehold for a movie scenario, yet it is almost everything that is significant in the life and mind of an outstanding figure in contemporary letters. It is the scenario of the soul of Theodore Dreiser. They are kind to posterity that write such testaments. Kinder than those that leave no key to their work. The critic of an after century coming upon this book will be able to decide in few pages whether to explore or to forget the small library that is now Theodore Dreiser.

H. W. Boynton. "Cadences of an Exile." New York *Sun*, August 18, 1928.

The first thing you notice about any work of Dreiser's is its physical bulk. Always he offers himself in hunks and masses, every book like a clumsy bowlder of low-grade ore which you must crush and smelt for yourself. Its bulk is what makes it worth handling—if you have patience and the right method. And whatever profit you wring from it is a sign of prowess. You marvel at your own admirable achievement, and think quite well of the fellow who blasted out the bowlder.

Some such effect or reaction as this explains Theodore Dreiser's steadily widening audience. Poor old chap, he doesn't write so awfully well, but he does what he can, and you and I, fortunately, are able to do the rest! Besides, most writing nowadays is wearisomely clever, and the man's very ungainliness is restful.

We suspect that this impression of him amuses Dreiser. He began life as a reporter and was long successful in newspaper work. He has been an editor and knows quite well the virtues of compactness. But he knows also what he has to say and he knows how he, Dreiser, ought to say it. Small scale and dainty touch are not for him. He builds up his effect by steady, small accretions (so much less haphazard than they look), and to this method bulk is essential.

We are not surprised to find it even in a book so unlike the usual Dreiserian product as "Moods Cadenced and Declaimed." This is not a new book. A limited edition was sold out before publication, in the spring of 1926. A list of the original subscribers would be interesting. How many of that 500 were bookdealers or collectors begging a new "item," and how many were devoted readers, willing and able to pay the price for this new utterance of the master? To his larger constituency it is now made available in this portly volume of nearly 400 pages. It is adorned, or perhaps defaced, by fifteen queer "symbols," drawn by Hugh and Gray Lieber. We can't help wondering if the frontispiece gentleman with the breastpin, the cauliflower ear, and the vegetables sprouting from his cerebrum is a symbol of our author.

The title warns off any reviewer from comment on the poetic character or quality of the book. The eye gives evidence, however, that its substance is at least not prose—an absence if not a negation of prose is indicated. The pages are divided into lines which bear no mechanical relation to meaning or sentence structure. Nor do they relate to meter. They must therefore be determined by the author's sense of rhythm or "cadence." It follows that the reader's first duty is to try to get the swing of this rhythm and some sense of it as a true medium or vehicle of the writer's moods. A kind of natural pitch or wavelength, to which the soul of one Dreiser is emotionally attuned.

This is made more difficult by apparently arbitrary whims of typography. Here is a representative number called "Days." Printed simply, it reads:

"Days, days, under clear skies—under dark skies. Days exposed to winds from every quarter, to sobs, trills from every instrument.

"Days when accumulated disaster rolls over one like the thundering wheels of a conquering army—the floundering wheels of a defeated one.

"Days that rise upon one faint, hushed, impalpable, tremulous with the light that is hidden within the lips of pearl.

"Days that spring like demons bony fingered and gaunt,—that dawn like disaster itself and mutter and curse and gibber of ill or hatred.

"Days that are lions and rip and wound. Days that are wood doves mourning, mourning, or skylarks singing.

"Days that soothe and heal. Days that spin or flicker, make clear or confuse, yet vanishing in song or shadow, never, never to return.

"Days. Days. Days."

This method of printing (which retains the original punctuation) brings out the full rhythm or cadence. The book gives sixty-one lines and three pages to these same words, as thus:

> "Never
> Never
> To return.
> Days.
> Days.
> Days."

Chopped up that way, it sounds, or looks, less like Whitman but not recognizably more like Dreiser. There is much Whitmanic cataloguing and apostrophizing in these pages. But Dreiser's habitual mood is more like Heine than Whitman. He has none of Walt's zest and exultation. The keynote of his dominant mood is the good old German *Sehnsucht.* Always he has yearned for ideal beauty—still he yearns for it despite his reason, which tells him what a sham and mockery life is. . . .

"Dreiser Finds His Voice." Cincinnati *Times Star,* August 18, 1928.

In 1926 a collection of two hundred or more of Theodore Dreiser's poems was published in a small, limited edition. A beautiful new volume for the first time places these poems before Dreiser's vast circle of readers. The occasion is important. It marks not only a new development in the genius of America's foremost novelist, but a memorable date in the history of American poetry.

Judgments on Dreiser as a poet have thus far been tentative. We have caught occasional glimpses of his work in the magazines, but the creator of those huge, laborious novels does not "take" well in miniature. Here his mood flows freely, changefully, and at length. The "Moods" sweep the scale of human emotions—pity and scorn, tenderness, irony, resignation and defiance—all are there. And over all broods a sense of loneliness and an age-worn disillusionment.

The "Moods" will probably be compared to the "Leaves of Grass." The verses have something of Whitman's large sweep and too much of his irritating habit of cataloguing. But in outlook they are poles apart. If Whitman is the sprawling, optimistic youth of modern American poetry, Dreiser represents a weary maturity. In its curious phrasing and somber thought Dreiser's poetry recalls that of Thomas Hardy—the work of one who came to poetry not to sing, but to express his reflections upon life in a lasting form.

The career of Theodore Dreiser has

been a constant inner struggle. From his early days as an inarticulate reporter on an Indiana daily to his crowning success in "An American Tragedy," he has sought release from the weight of a bitter human experience—freedom through self-expression. Expression has always been torture to him. But in some of the poems—not in all—he breaks free, and finds the perfect words that have so long eluded him. The crude chunks of tragedy which he carried about with him in "Jennie Gerhardt," "Sister Carrie" and "An American Tragedy" are here refined into a series of moving and often wonderfully beautiful verses.

It is difficult to classify the form of the poems. They are done in a free verse, but of a kind quite unfamiliar. Single lines fall into the cadence proper to their mood. But the rhythm of the whole, which the individual lines should compose as a mosaic, escapes him. Perhaps he deliberately avoided any highly wrought form. Certainly in these irregular cadences his spirit moves more easily than in the more logical medium of prose. . . .

But in poetry, as in all the arts, it is not enough merely to feel. The shorter the work, the greater the artistry that must fashion it. In his novels Dreiser's sentences may halt and stumble, and his pseudo-scientific jargon fall harshly upon the ear. But he is an artist of the fundamentals. He sees his work clearly to the end, his structural design is right. On the other hand, any hackneyed thought or phrase, any drop into bathos —and there are many of both in these "Moods"—will mar the texture of the poem.

But when the mood is strong and pure, what a fine ecstasy sustains him! . . .

The finest things in the volume, however, are the many sad, intensely personal lyrics, where we are ushered into the darkest chambers of Dreiser's soul.

Some of the moods are cadenced and declaimed in pure prose. But what there is of superb and poignant poetry ranks with the best that America has produced in many years. And even when he fails, Dreiser's failure is somehow significant; for it brings us nearer to the most powerful, sincere and moving artist of America today.

Don Howard. "Looking at Literature." Salt Lake City *Telegram,* August 19, 1928.

Theodore Dreiser, one of the most accomplished novelists in America, has shown himself to be one of the country's worst poets. His book of free verse, "Moods Cadenced and Declaimed," has just been published by Horace Liveright. It reads like Cubist painting looks, and like that bastard art, is devoid of beauty. It is monotonous, unoriginal, at times humdrum. Most of the things Dreiser has said in his poetry have been said before by better poets. The author of "An American Tragedy" evidently knows but one form for poetry. That consists, mostly, of one or two words in each line, each line apparently having nothing to do with the preceding line. "Moods Cadenced and Declaimed" contains 385 pages of this. There are so many repetitions that they add to the monotony of style, making the volume unbearable after the first hundred pages.

There is no denying the power and

magnitude of Dreiser's poetry. But it takes something more than power and magnitude to make sound poetry. There are few and far-between places in "Moods Cadenced and Declaimed" where Mr. Dreiser achieves an undeniable beauty in theme and expression. His book would constitute a more far-reaching effect on American poetry if the few good pieces had been issued in, say, a hundred page volume instead of piling the whole works in one four times that big; Dreiser is at his best, what little there is of it, in his "Moods," in his shorter poems.

San Francisco *Chronicle*, August 19, 1928.

By what a man does or says we have a standard by which we appraise him. By these "Moods: Cadenced and Declaimed," we get to know something about Theodore Dreiser's mind, but the result does not enable us to class it as poetry, or even verse or prose. Perhaps the title describes it best. These writings are moods, expressed as they came, with something of the spontaneity of emotion, and little caring what sober thought might consider their intellectual value.

Dreiser is a versatile literary man. He has eccentricities of manner that cause many persons to put him in the class of genius.

The volume is finely made. The design of the pages; the laid paper; the clear type and the board and half-cloth binding make it a fine book souvenir of this notable American writer. A complex mind is shown in these lyrics, and the gleams from it often strike fire with their piercing vigor.

Roy Robert. "Theodore Dreiser Again In His Strange Attitudes With 'Moods'." Atlanta *Sunday American*, August 19, 1928.

"Moods, Cadenced and Declaimed," by Theodore Dreiser, published by Boni & Liveright, is a typical Dreiser book, even though it is, according to the title, cadenced. An unusually large book, it contains much that appeals to those who enjoy Dreiser in his strange attitudes that set him out as a distinct angle of American literature.

A first reading of most of these poems will leave the reader feeling that the author could have done much better with his interesting reflections. However, a more careful study of them reveals a depth of feeling and passion.

"Sinuously weaving in and out among themselves
Under bright lanterns."

Dreiser seems to have cadenced personal messages that leave nothing of that detached air that one would naturally expect to find in his free verse.

It seems to us that the symbolic illustrations by Hugh Gray Leiber contribute as much to the volume as does the verse of the author. They are passionately contorted into lines that surprise even the ultra-modern desire for exotic strangeness. The 15 drawings alone would make the book a very desirable addition to anyone's bookshelf.

All told, Moods is strictly worthwhile—creating a heavy simplicity that Wagner would have done had he written "Lohengrin" as a poem.

St. Louis *Daily Globe-Democrat*, August 25, 1928.

Theodore Dreiser as a poet! Well, not exactly, not in the sense ordinarily accepted; and the likelihood is that he would be the first to disclaim such a distinction. But this big book certainly doesn't look like prose. The lines are broken up into initialed shorts of uneven length and presenting the appearance of what is called, loosely, free verse. For that matter, the Dreiserian offering on the whole is far superior in poetic content to most of the collections of hashed-up prose posing as poetry.

Mr. Dreiser is just as serious-minded in these "Moods" as in his tremendous novels. There is nothing of the play boy in Dreiser, whether he expresses himself in prose or what-not. Many of the brief pieces in this volume—there must be nearly 200 in all—are provocative of profound thought. It is well known that Mr. Dreiser takes a somewhat somber view of the universe. This view occurs and recurs here, time and again. Yet occasionally the lighter colors prevail, so that after all the man is not to be set down as a pessimistic mouther against fate.

There are lines and passages of some length in "Moods" which flash the true poetic fire. These happen when the subconscious Dreiser breaks through the murk. There are other pieces, such as "The Dreamer," which are slightly autobiographical of the Dreiser commonly known to his public. . . .

Cincinnati *Commercial Tribune*, August 26, 1928.

. . . This extraordinary book was published in a very limited edition in the spring of 1926. It was far over-subscribed long before publication. It went out of print almost immediately, and admirers of Dreiser were temporarily denied access to one of his most engaging works.

Now, in response to public demand, the publishers have issued a trade edition of this book, prepared in a beautiful format, interestingly decorated by Hugh Gray Lieber, but within the means of the book-lover as well as of the professional book collector.

It is a signal service to the public, as it is a service to Dreiser.

Dreiser is a poet, and a very good one. He is master of delicacy as well as strength in imagery, and the most objective novelist in America finds verse a natural and responsive medium for introspection.

"Moods" is a record of many days, in which Dreiser records impressions, asks questions, gives voice to protest, and sets in articulate form the half-hidden, fears, hopes, sorrows, joy, wonder and worship of a rich and colorful emotional and spiritual life.

It is one of the most intimate books in the language, and reveals Dreiser the man as no previous work of his has done. This is really an emotional diary, and it is natural, therefore, that the verse form should reflect the characteristic diary impulses. It takes a structure which is closely allied to imagist free verse, but denies the usual substance of that school. There is in Dreiser's mind no substitution of image for reality, and as he is obviously trying to set his impressions to the most tangible form for his own satisfaction, he makes them conclusively clear for his readers. Throughout the most profound problems in religion and metaphysics, which occupy his attention, as well as the exposition of his personal philosophy of mechanistic pessimism, there is not a line which is one whit more obscure than his description of a blade of grass.

Now, when such absolute clarity is added to sharp poetic observation and accurate skill in the record of impressions, the effect is splendid. . . .

He is at home in the most poetic of embellishments, but is not afraid to use Anglo-Saxon monosyllables.

This is one of the great secrets of Dreiser's charm. He illustrates admirably that a man can be a man and still be a poet and a philosopher.

It is not our function to examine his philosophy. It bears the stamp of a great sincerity and a great sensitivity and has inspired him to great beauty in its expression. That it will impress many people as futilistic is neither here nor there. Better futilism than fatuity in modern verse!

Theodore Dreiser is one of the most eminent of living Americans. It will behoove all lovers of literature to make his personal acquaintance in this charming volume.

Samy. "Book Worm." Muskogeen [Okl.] *Democrat*, August 31, 1928.

The compelling power of Theodore Dreiser is one which has interested this critic since the publication of his American Tragedy, which changed the little-known literary light into a popular novelist. Dreiser's style is terrible, but he seems to overpower his reader with his omnipotence. He circles around his subject, slipping up on it a little at a time and dashing little rays of light which show the way, and finally when he gets his fangs on a character, he tears it wide open and lets you see what makes it tick. . . .

Dreiser has now become so valuable that Liveright has even collected 365 pages of fragments of writings which he produced during the past dozen years or so and printed them under the title of "Moods."

A strange book it is, and at times an interesting one. It can hardly be classified as poetry, though it is sometimes rythmic.

Oftimes it seems autobiographical; oftimes a sort of confessional. Certainly one gets a close picture of the inside man from reading his moods. It is possible to trade even the major arguments of most of his books and catch a recurrence of their themes.

One feels the presence of a great undercurrent of sorrow; a grief for the stumbling ways of man; a lumbering hopelessness—even despair. He does not make the effort to wrangle with mankind or grow indignant over their fumblings; he views them with a sort of pity.

There are few subjects he doesn't tap in the course of his moods and he reveals his rebellious impatience against dogma, bigotry and hypocrisy such as can be found around every corner.

"Dreiser Tries His Hand at Brevity." Chicago *Post*, August 31, 1928.

The reputation of Theodore Dreiser could hardly be said to rest upon the beauty or loveliness or fragility of his writing, and when he turns to that mode, as in the present volume, the rugged strength that shines thru his prose, which has been called heavy-footed and awkward, but is, nevertheless, magnificent in its way, dissolves. The quieter, more gentle moods become trivial, and the larger, more vital ones lose their stature in a formless rush of not too carefully chosen words and inexplicit gestures.

All of Mr. Dreiser's "moods" seem to be very much alike; they are all but slightly different facets of his central difficulty, the despair and questioning of one of unphilosophic temper at the fate of "those who go the common way." He does not find splendor in life, but cries out for a splendor he believes life might have.

"Moods" is much akin to that great heavy volume which explains the wherefore of all his writing, "A Book About Myself," which marches along, I think, as do none of his others. But the earlier book was more articulate, more rounded; there is little music in this writing, and a mood, a cadenced mood, must sing. Awareness of this, and a straining after fringed words impinges on the directness of the thought. Many of the verses are several pages in length, but it is in the shorter ones that he is best. . . .

There is much that is formless and slightly obscure, but if it falls below the level of his better-known writing, it is priceless for an understanding of the man himself. . . .

M. L. P. Syracuse [N.Y.] *Post-Standard*, September 2, 1928.

These verses of Theodore Dreiser were published in the spring of 1926, in an edition limited to 500 copies. That edition is out of print; and the poems are now published in an edition available to all. In this collection, as the publisher states, are gathered together moods, as felt and written from time to time by the author of "The American Tragedy."

They achieve a form that does not readily fall into any classification that might arbitrarily be set for them. In subject matter they are as varied (sometimes important, sometimes inconsequential) as the moods of such a man as Dreiser must be. Sometimes they are lyrical, sometimes poetic, yet never exactly falling into poetry. . . .

There are some hundreds of these "moods" in the book—some, as has been said, evanescent and unimportant, but many of them with an echo of true beauty and tenderness. To many, it may be, they will more fully and earnestly interpret Theodore Dreiser.

Pueblo [Colo.] *Star Journal*, September 2, 1928.

It seems that the author of "American Tragedy" went rambling, mentally, whilst writing many of his literary works, with the result that he went poetic—almost to a fault.

A strange book is the outcome. We understand that the opus was first published two years ago in limited edition. It has come to the attention of the reading public when Dreiser became generally known thru his "American Tragedy." While not exactly poetic, it has rythmic qualities at times. The popular supposition is that Dreiser jotted down in staccato verse things that bothered his train of thought as he sat in his study laboring over some other more definite effort. The result was that his desk was cluttered with these more or less unrhymed verses.

The whole thing is strange—and interesting, at times.

Is it a confession? An autobiography? There is no doubt but that perhaps the brain child reflects the inner man—his struggle with the literary work in hand at the time. Often the recurrence of a theme in one of his books can be caught.

One feels a despair, a sadness, hopelessness for the manner in which man lives—all this an undercurrent. It is not critical, just a sort of sympathy for man's bigotry and hypocritical way of living.

The sort of a thing to make those who ARE different rather agree with Dreiser—"there's a man that knows whereof he speaks."

The exception is that one is inclined to be indignant with the hypocrites, while Dreiser is not. But then he is in a position to pity.

John G. Neihardt. "What Happens?" St. Louis *Post-Dispatch*, September 3, 1928, p. 17.

There never should have been any argument over the value of free verse as a medium of expression on a higher plane of feeling and thought, for, as nearly everyone knows, much of the greatest poetry has been expressed in loose rhythms. To value the various technical devices and strategies of the regular forms does not imply a condemnation of free verse as such. All that can reasonably be asked of poetry is that it be poetry and have some recognizable value for human beings.

The trouble with the free verse movement in our day is not to be found in the medium employed, but rather in the fact that it has been of a nature to encourage ridiculous insincerities, grotesque posing and a vague windiness of expression. . . .

In striving to read Dreiser's "Moods Cadenced and Proclaimed," it is difficult to realize that the author of the Dreiser novels is the writer. The book is a large one, but it would be a small one if the space on the page had been utilized. Instead, the following arrangement of words is common:

> Never
> Never
> To return.

Days
Days
Days.

It is not easy to fake up any justification for such a typographical arrangement. Surely no meaning or emphasis of any sort would be lost by writing: Never, never to return. Days, days, days. The same is true of the following:

You will be interested
You will be amused
For I have devised
A most surprising
A most engaging
Toy
And game.

So it goes on, yard after yard, and hardly ever is anything expressed that could do credit to a man of Dreiser's generally admitted powers.

If the following was worth saying, why was it not frankly written down as the utterly dull prose that it obviously is?

I examine myself, and I discover
Many defects.
I am he who
In my greatest power,
Appointed C———,
And others like him,
To office,
Without carefully examining
Into his conduct.

There is another peculiarity about free verse as generally practiced in our day. The conspicuous lack of integration is not in the medium alone, but in the very ideas that are expressed, as a rule, when definite ideas are discoverable. Things are not seen together in a large, organic way, but in fragments; and the world-view implied, when it is possible to discover any indications of such, is generally of a very low order.

What is it that so often happens to otherwise intelligent men and women when they are persuaded to write free verse?

Isaac Goldberg. "In the World of Books: Theodore Dreiser as Poet." *Haldeman Julius Weekly*, September 8, 1928.

Most poets write good prose. That is, they write prose that is guided by an ear for rhythm and cadence; at times their prose may be swollen with ornament, or may weigh upon one like a drugging incense, but usually it will have melody and grace. Not all writers of good prose, on the other hand, are gifted poets. And certainly, on the evidence of this book, Dreiser, who does not always write good prose, is not a significant poet. True, he has not aimed high; the collection—first issued in the Spring of 1926 in a limited edition of 500 signed copies, and now for the first time made accessible to the purse of the average reader—is entitled "Moods," not "Poems." If there is any special significance to the presence of the word "Cadenced" in the title, I fail to discover it. As for "Declaimed," unfortunately it is more than justified. Perhaps, in his own way, Dreiser had meant to emit yawps more or less barbaric; certainly these verses often betray a diluted Whitmanism, but never come within miles of the grandeur, the ecstasy and the sweep that the good grey Walt could conjure out of words. From cover to cover, the Dreiser book is filled with statement, not with experience. He apostrophizes, n a rather dull succession of undifferen-iated strains, the Capitalized Com-nonplaces of experience. We crush hese alignments of words, and ink, not blood, spurts from their veins. Every-where is the sign of a groping, stum-bling, clumsy, mumbling intelligence. What a welter of rhetorical phrases! Dreams, souls, hungers, needs—all the worn counters of poesy. Where is the author of "An American Tragedy"? Not here, surely.

> If you but knew.
> If you but wished.
> If but your one art were poetry.

So begins his Mood entitled "Sanctu-ary." But his one art is not poetry. If one were to accept this single book as the mirror of Dreiser's mind, one would find oneself adrift in the sea of sopho-moric memoranda. . . .

I persisted to the last page because, to me, nothing that a great man does can be without interest, if not for one rea-son then for another. Dreiser was not made for the free cameos that he has tried to carve in "Moods." Here, he is a bull in a China shop. He needs the vast background of a novel, against which and through which he may stumble on his path to beauty. Give him elbow room, and he'll find it.

Kansas City [Mo.] *Journal*, September 9, 1928.

. . Like Sherwood Anderson, Mr. Dreiser employs a method that may be called free verse, but in reality has little relation to poetry. The word poem, as a matter of fact, does not occur in the description of this book, and the pub-lisher speaks of "these pieces" as the "free expressions, often lyrical, often poetic, of a complex and many-faceted mind; often too nebulous and brief for a more extended form, often too lyrical for prose, yet never actually falling into poetry." This seems to fit the case and may stand as a description of the con-tents of the book.

There are 206 of these moods, and they cover every conceivable subject, revealing irony, sentiment, social criti-cism and plain observation. They are never elaborate either in imagery or in expression, and frequently deal with the obvious. They do more for the man Dreiser than for literature. They reveal the sensitive novelist, the man who, ir-ritated at social injustice, "exhausted by the savage contest of this world" takes refuge in dreams.

All the questions that Theodore Dreiser has asked in his novels may be found in these moods. His impatience with dogma, his contempt for bigoted authority, his conviction that life needs to be lived wholly to be wholesome, that restraints blunt its fineness; his recurrent sympathy for the under dog and acknowledgment that victory often carries with it unfair advantage, injus-tice and insensitivity to suffering; his ir-ritation at the stupidities of men—all these are repeated here. But also there is a preoccupation with nature, which refreshes him, and with the evanescent influence of sound, color, flowers, trees, rain and the subtler forces of nature. Alone amid nature he feels himself shielded "from the irritations and mis-eries of a world that I disdain."

As a matter of fact, the while book is autobiographical, and probably the best service that it performs is to reveal the author's mind. He turns out to be rather a mild philosopher, sorrowing over the ways of men, but never growing very indignant about them. Even his most emphatic passages show him as turning from the scenes he derides with a forlorn contempt and an air of hopelessness, never getting very violent.

Concord [N.H.] *Independent,* September 22, 1928.

The limited edition of this unusual book, we are told, was subscribed for many times over before its publication in 1926. The present volume has been printed to satisfy a wide demand. Theodore Dreiser stands preëminent as our foremost American novelist. His labored and almost inarticulate genius has achieved a monument in prose to his ability. This book of poems gathered here and there, the expression of all sorts of moods and thoughts, does not fall easily into any poetical category. They are lyric in essence, if not in form —which is free and fragmentary. "Moods" is the marriage of prose and poetry partaking of each. Poems of transitory emotion, they are too unsubstantial for prose, and yet scarcely poetry in their prose rhythms. This collection is rather impressive than moving. "Moods" is more interesting as an expression of Mr. Dreiser's personality than as a volume of independent poetry.

Lucius M. C. Lamar. "Experimental Poetry of Theodore Dreiser Now Issued for Trade." Dallas *Morning News,* September 23, 1928.

"Moods," by Theodore Dreiser, is a hefty volume of poems, privately pub lished in 1926, and now issued in a trade edition. The publishers deny that they are poems, and declare that they "achieve a new and strange form tha does not readily fall into any classifica tion that might arbitrarily be set fo them." But since the father and godfa thers of this novel form have neglectec to christen it, and since I lack both the temerity and the ingenuity, I choose to stick by my orismological guns. "Po etry" I call it, and let who will make definitions.

The appearance in the literary heav ens of a book of poems by Dreiser is ar arresting phenomenon. If in them were to be found the clear essence of his rich troubled and compassionate spirit they were a treasure indeed. If—if in them he could avoid the cliches, the verba improprieties which blot his prose like tin shacks on a mountain side. For po etry, formal or free, demands a high de gree of technical, structural virtuosity In rhymed and measured verse, the structure is apparent on the surface anc comparatively easily attained. Rhyme and rhythm are psychological props for the content, hypnotic devices o proven, though not infallible efficacy Free verse, lacking the support of a for mal, external discipline, must embrace o avoid becoming gibberish or uncom-ortable prose, a relative internal disci-line even more rigorous.

In all except a very few poems 'Moods" is a failure. It is trite, uncom-ortable prose, chopped into arbitrary egments. And a few of them are gib-erish, as these lines from "Geddo Street":

"It knows that it is is,
Antithesis of that—"

Some, such as "Differences," are aboriously metaphysical. The influence of Walt Whitman is strong throughout: n "Related" old Walt speaks at his enu-nerative worst (though Dreiser has ar-anged his enumerations vertically), nd "The Humanist" would do credit to Whitman at his best. Such dreadful lo-utions as "all digits down" are enough o ruin a much better poem than "The Gladiator."

In only about fifteen of the poems numbering in all some 200) does Drei-er's undeniable greatness of heart and nind show forth unobscured by trivial-ty or clumsiness. . . .

. Dana Tasker.
'Dreiser as Poet."
Outlook,
October 24, 1928.

Few books boast as accurate a title as does "Moods Cadenced and De-claimed." And what is even more start-ing, neither Mr. Dreiser nor Mr. Live-right anywhere in the volume attempts o justify these words and lines as au-hentic poetry. These are moods, and nothing more. Sometimes they are ca-denced, but more often they are only declaimed. Surely, one would expect a great novelist to shape his moods into words. Here are the "in-between" mo-ments, aspects of a private life. The form in which these moments are re-corded is something less than good or even acceptable verse—something more or at least something different from good prose. Mr. Dreiser has found expression through a use of language that is unfamiliar; and although that in-vented form is by no means powerful enough to be set up as a fine standard, in this case it is quite satisfactory.

The subjects are widely diversified. They vary from semi-lyrical descrip-tions of city, town and countryside to abrupt, dramatic exclamations on emo-tional and mental attitudes. One of the most interesting studies is "The Far Country," in which the author deplores satiety and yearns again for the hunger and the poverty, for the inconsequence and the loneliness of youth. "The Pass-ing Freight" indicates the imagination of a man who is used to observing life carefully and thoughtfully . . . A good many of Mr. Dreiser's moods are as charming as these two. His book con-tains much pleasant reading and, doubtless, there is a real demand for a new edition.

G. R. B. R.
"*Moods:* Theodore Dreiser's Excursions Into Poetry."
Boston *Transcript*,
November 10, 1928.

A limited edition of Mr. Dreiser's po-ems which appeared in 1926 was exhausted before it left the press. It is now reissued for general circulation. "Moods" is a fitting title, for it is as uneven in theme and in execution as its subject implies. Yet there are two constant outstanding excellences apparent throughout the collection of brief, almost fragmentary "cadenced thought-expressions": one is the unvarying accuracy the author displays in his choice of words, which makes all he has written of such distinctive literary merit, and the other is the equally unvarying sincerity of what he describes, whether it be a man-mood or a nature-mood.

In a way the work reminds one of an artist's note-book; it is full of bits of varying excellence, reflections of a passing experience, and as such it contains more evidence of the artist's genius than a more studied and complicated picture. Mr. Dreiser is of course too much of an individualist to follow any laws of composition, even his own. However, some of the bits here included have a grace, a lyric beauty, an emotional sanity which rank them as lyrics by whatever laws they are judged. . . .

Even where he is bitter there is still the recognition of beauty, but beauty strengthened and ennobled by ultimate and absolute Truth.

Checklist of Additional Reviews

Ann Arbor [Mich.] *News,* August 14, 1928.

Lancaster *New Era,* August 15, 1928.

Canton [Ohio] *News,* August 15, 1928.

Boston *Herald,* August 15, 1928.

Park Island [Ill.] *Argus,* August 16, 1928.

Miami [Fla.] *News,* August 19, 1928.

Columbus [Ga.] *Ledger,* August 19 1928.

Charleston *Mail,* August 19, 1928.

Saginaw [Mich.] *News,* August 19, 1928

Witchita [Kan.] *Beacon,* August 19 1928.

Paterson [N.J.] *Press,* August 19, 1928

Dunkirk [N.Y.] *Observer,* August 30 1928.

Houston [Tex.] *Press,* August 31, 1928

Milwaukee *Journal,* September 1 1928.

Portland [Ore.] *Journal,* September 2 1928.

Chicago *News,* September 5, 1928.

Victor Schultz. "Poems by Two Pessimistic Novelists." Des Moines [Iowa *Register,* September 5, 1928.

Springfield [Ma.] *Leader,* September 9 1928.

Asbury Park [N.J.] *Press,* September 9 1928.

Omaha [Neb.] *World-Herald,* September 9, 1928.

Charleston [West Va.] *Gazette,* September 9, 1928.

Kansas City [Mo.] *Star,* September 15 1928.

"Dreiser Writes a Strange Book." Portsmouth [Ohio] *Sun,* September 16 1928.

Terre Haute [Ind.] *Star,* September 24 1928.

Robert O. Ballou. Chicago *Daily News* September 25, 1928.

Philadelphia *Inquirer,* September 29 1928.

Holyoke [Mass.] *Telegram,* September 29, 1928.

"Theodore Dreiser's Long Awaited Poems." *East St. Louis Journal,* September 30, 1928.

Evansville [Ind.] *Courier,* September 30, 1928.

)klahoma City *Oklahoman,* October 14, 1928.
Forum, November, 1928.
Newark [N.J.] *Evening News,* November 10, 1928.
Poughkeepsie [N.Y.] *Star,* December 8, 1928.

THEODORE DREISER

DREISER LOOKS AT RUSSIA

NEW YORK

HORACE LIVERIGHT · 1928

Dreiser Looks at Russia

Harry Hansen, "The First Reader: Dreiser in Russia." New York *World*, November 10, 1928.

Theodore Dreiser's views on Russia were made public in The World soon after his return earlier in the year; they are being published to-day, more or less augmented, in book form as "Dreiser Looks at Russia." They reveal Dreiser the reporter engaged once more in the occupation that held him in thrall for the years that he paced the sidewalks of Chicago and New York City, years that have been described in "A Book About Myself," during which he wrote some of the sketches contained in "The Color of a Great City."

Traversing Russia, Mr. Dreiser is the open-eyed American who is interested in institutions, external changes, programs, reforms. It is the face that he sees more than the mind of Bolshevism, to borrow a phrase from the title of the new book by Rene Fulop-Muller. And Mr. Dreiser scrutinizes closely. He is eager to look at facts. He listens, observes and lays aside the superior cloak of the American. He had once great hopes for America as a land that had a program. But to-day he doubts that it had any, and he is astonished and happy to find that men in Russia are working not for themselves but for the state, that they have in view an end which shall ameliorate the hard living conditions and make men rich in spirit even when they are poor in material things.

The novelist who broods over erring human nature reveals himself here and there, as when he wonders whether any program which so thoroughly discounts avarice and selfishness can completely rout human nature. But what he sees brings him much hope. Coming to Russia with the average American's views on Mongols, Tartars, Cossacks and the rest, he learns much and imparts what he sees.

If we look in this book for philosophical interpretation and Utopian dreams we shall not find them, for Mr. Dreiser remains rooted to earth and deals with what happens. He finds Bolshevist art difficult and Bolshevist prose and poetry incomprehensible. He tells us that they are saturated with Communist propaganda, and he resents being told that this artist and that is a good Communist, when what matters is whether or not he is a good artist. And, he says, nothing written under Bolshevism approaches the great work of

Dostoievsky, Turgenev and Tolstoy.

Mr. Dreiser is right when he sympathizes with Stanislavsky, who told him that "the white line of art is eternal and passing conditions cannot fundamentally change it." Great political upheavals should not affect the artist, but history proves that they often deflect him from his purpose by filling the air with talk of government and economics instead of spiritual and philosophical matters. The Napoleonic wars were not a period of literary fecundity, but the years that followed brought forth a tremendous outpouring, especially in France and Germany. The ten years that have passed are not enough to tell us what Communism will do for the arts. It is not at all unlikely that drastic regimentation will be followed by a liberation of the spirit, which will soar to heights that none may foresee.

Isabel Paterson. "Books and Other Things." New York *Herald Tribune*, November 13, 1928, p. 23.

Last year Theodore Dreiser went to Russia at the invitation of the Soviet government and was politely taken on a tour. They showed him the new brickyard and gas works and homes of the prominent citizens in the best residential addition and took him to lunch at the Moscow Bankers' Club or whatever. Mr. Dreiser's observations were published here in a series of newspaper articles; and these, presumably with additions and revisions, have been collected in a book, "Dreiser Looks at Russia."

Dreiser enthusiasts will have to have it: and presumably students of Russian affairs. Generally when I see the word "Bolshevik"—or "the New China" or "Germany After the War," I drop the volume hastily and back away. There are said to be people who don't know when they've had enough, and they are welcome to more. Nevertheless, it is a part of Dreiser's peculiar genius that though he can and does write worse than any one in the world even on the most attractive themes, he also invests even the most threadbare topics with something of interest.

Maybe it is his approach. He wants to know and he writes about the things you might want to know yourself, assuming you wanted to know anything at all about Russia. His intention is direct, though his syntax is tortuous.

Dreiser's prose style is really—at last I see where he got it!—it is a verbal pattern corresponding to modes of domestic architectural ornament and furniture which prevailed in the '80s and '90s, Dreiser's impressionable years. It is covered with jig-saw scrollwork, mansard gables and bull's-eye windows, cupolas, iron stags, plush patent rockers with fringe around them, haircloth sofas, gilded rolling pins and golden oak bureaus putting black walnut overmantels out of countenance.

Nevertheless, he gets you. Opening the book at random, I am caught by the information that "there is almost no such thing as good cooking in Soviet Russia." In hotels and restaurants, he adds; he does not answer for home cooking. Still, it seems unlikely that home cooking would be first class, with half a dozen families trying to prepare dinner on one communal stove, as he says they are obliged to do.

Dreiser reports as hopefully as possible of the new Russia. He must have wished to like it, having so often denounced the American social order. But revolutionaries never do like actual revolution, after the first week or two, and they like the results even less. This is natural.

Nobody, of course, could possibly enjoy the results of a revolution which entirely uproots an established social order and substitutes wholly new ideas of government. Nobody, that is, of the contemporary generation. This is largely true even if the old order was iniquitous and the new state of affairs a vast improvement. Men lived through the American Revolutionary War and the turmoil of establishing the United States, without spiritual disaster, because the new thing was really an extension and rectification of the old; self government was already in practice. There was no social upheaval, but a political adjustment to the social conditions then existing. Nevertheless, it took men of stamina. George Washington needed to be six foot two, Jefferson required the physique of a country squire, which he had. Hamilton had the fire of youth in the tough sinews of a fox terrier. Still it wore them out, nearly killed them.

A radical revolution does kill the contemporary generation, including the makers of the revolution. It consumes them, not necessarily by ax or rope, but by nervous exhaustion. They may be willing sacrifices; but even those who survive physically are only half alive. They are done for. The next generation may benefit and be at ease in Zion.

Because we are all geared up mentally to the existing order of things. We like what we are used to, even if we don't like it very much. Our emotions are woven around things as they are. Our ideas refer back to those things, even in disagreement. And the enormous influence of trifles is all against change.

Jeannette Lissey. "The Fly Leaf." Jamaica [N.Y.] *Press*, November 17, 1928.

. . . "Theodore Dreiser Looks at Russia" is a philosophical, economical, and social guide-book to the terror of Europe and the hope of the world, Communistic Russia. For observation purposes, Dreiser uses for his vantage points, the sidewalks, the fauteuil d'orchestre, government chambers, old palaces, hotels and restaurants. Consequently, the descriptions of the apparent changes in Moscow and Petrograd are both vivid and realistic. The Soviets did not limit their invitation to the large cities, and we have a number of short impressions of provincial Russia.

"Being an individualist, I am naturally opposed to Communism," says Dreiser. But throughout, his discussion, he looks at it sympathetically and expresses the hope that some day the entire world will be run on such a communistic basis. He admires the improved condition of the worker and his rise to political power. He is impressed because great wealth is unattainable in Russia and the mad scramble for riches is absent from the civilization. He is enthusiastic about the educational system.

Not entirely blinded by the novelty of the idea, Dreiser sees its defects. He deplores the tyranny of Communism, the filthy and dirty condition of the cities and inhabitants, the sluggish, dreamy Russian personality which impedes their progress, the insidious opposition to Communism in the country itself which seems to destroy it.

Not only are industry, very existence, and religion ruled by the Communistic idea. Even the artistic temperament of the nation must be modeled to fit communistic principles. Thus, must Russian art suffer mediocrity until it is freed from these shackles, thinks Mr. Dreiser. According to his observations, the most advanced form of art in Russia, today, is the Cinema.

He writes in his usual rambling, entangled style, some sentences often covering half a page. As for his sources of information, Dame Rumor hath it that he has copied rather boldly and obviously from Mrs. Sinclair Lewis' account of her travels in Russia. The impression, that Dreiser gives in his description, is that he secured his information from conversations with individuals he met in Russia; Soviet Executives, great theatrical managers, and artists. He says that he visited every spot that was accessible and that could be of interest. Could two people see and hear identical things? Obviously they both could see the same conditions existing on the surface. Perhaps their guides gave them similar impressions because the Communistic regime consciously advertises and propagandises itself.

Clyde Beck. "Tragedy of Empire and the New Russia." *Detroit News*, November 18, 1928.

. . . There is, of course, endless opportunity for comment on such a brilliant and interesting book as this is. It must suffice, however, to say that it is always a fair analysis, even though the author is the prince of individualists. He has sought out the good and emphasized it; he has seen the bad and illuminated it. There is nothing craven about him. It is evident, on the whole, that he considers Soviet Russia a great and noble experiment; that he is convinced of its sincerity and uprightness. When other governments, he infers, can convince the world of theirs, then it will be a better day to condemn.

"Theodore Dreiser Too Individualistic to Stomach Sovietism." Philadelphia *Record*, November 24, 1928.

There still remains to be written an objective account of present-day life in Russia. Certainly Theodore Dreiser who describes himself as an "incorrigible individualist" in the first line of his "Dreiser Looks at Russia," could not do it. A picture of an experiment in collective living, with individualism reduced to a minimum, Dreiser's book on Russia is no more true nor false than a similar volume penned, for instance, by Wil

Rogers. But it is interesting reading and it gets us further away from those early books on soviet life, which were either violently pro or vehemently anti.

When the Russian experiment is further developed we may expect a more objective view of this communist state. Perhaps a well-trained journalist, such as Sir Philip Gibbs, could steer clear of Voks propaganda sufficiently to give us the "low down," but anyone who has been in Russia will testify to the difficulty of getting at facts when apparent realities sound so much like plausible fiction. One wonders whether the Government of the U.S.S.R. itself can fully realize what is going on beneath its ironclad system. Talk to any Government official (and they are still very accessible) and you will soon get the impression that he is indulging in romantic dreams with which the Russian temperament is saturated. The revolution has not changed that, in spite of the evident modification of human nature that it set in motion.

Dreiser, like any other mere tourist in Russia today, must have gotten the impression that he was talking to people living on a remote planet. It crops out in parts of his books. They do seem to have forgotten their individual rights, or selfishnesses, in this new system. They do seem captivated by the dreams of the future which is dangled before them and this seems to compensate them for the evident shabbiness of everybody under their present restricted economy of living. But an incorrigible individualist is the last person to wax enthusiastic over living conditions akin to a goldfish paradise in a bowl. Life in Russia today is too much like an army cantonment, with barrack-like lack of privacy in living and institutions similar to the Y.M.C.A. huts offered for an evening's enjoyment.

It is a shame that Mr. Dreiser did not dig deeper into the educational system, where they are turning out 100 per cent. Reds by the thousands, or into the social welfare program, where they are stepping ahead of the rest of the world in a health and sanitary system from which we will hear much in the future, no matter what the ultimate fate of the communist experiment will be. Nor does he venture much into the intricate workings of a soviet factory, with its committee system and complex working conditions; but all this could hardly attract the attention of an "incorrigible individualist," and hence we must assign this book to the category of just another man's biased view of the oddest nation on the globe today.

G. R. B. R.
"Dreiser on Russia." Boston *Evening Transcript Book Section*, December 1, 1928, p. 7.

Ever since conditions in Russia have become sufficiently normal to make travel there possible, lovers of the unusual have flocked thither to gather material for books on the "New Russia." It would be interesting to know just how many of these have appeared in recent years. The last summer's crop has been particularly heavy. And now comes Mr. Dreiser, self-styled "an incorrigible individualist," invited there by the Soviet government to see what he could see, and having dictated his terms, sets forth his observations and impressions in a manner peculiarly his own, distinguished for its originality and tolerance and above all extremely interesting. . . .

On the whole, the book gives a most compelling picture of conditions in the Soviet Republic.

As Mr. Dreiser warns his readers, it would be unfair to the Soviet regime to assume that so brief a survey would qualify anybody to prepare a sound or complete analysis of the most tremendous governmental experiment ever conducted, but he has gone far towards convincing one that in no case has he gone far astray in his account of the experiences and observations he has recorded.

Alexander I. Nazaroff. "Soviet Russia at the Beginning of Its Second Decade." New York *Times Book Review*, December 2, 1928, pp. 7, 28.

. . . [Dreiser] tells us emphatically that, on the whole he has liked Soviet Russia very much; moreover, he even expresses the hope that "our own country may eventually be sovietized—perhaps in my own day." He earnestly believes that the Soviet régime has greatly improved the welfare of the people. And he believes that it is a very good thing that no person should be permitted to accumulate capital. This, as well as some other such things, he likes so much that he is ready to forgive the Soviet régime for that "inescapable atmosphere of espionage" and "of terror" by which it surrounds all, that misery and decay of intellectual life which he has noticed only two well, and those numerous other things of which he heartily disapproves. He likes it, he weightily repeats. It's a question of taste, after all.

Pittsburgh *Press*, December 8, 1928.

. . . The creator of "An American Tragedy" visited the stronghold of Communism in 1927 at the invitation of the Soviet government. The contents of his book were first printed in the New York World.

Though Dreiser made it clear in advance that he might come to adverse conclusions his Russian hosts accorded him every possible assistance and the result is as clear and concise a summary of the Russian situation as there is in print.

A more competent and careful observer the Soviets could not have chosen. Despite the complicated and many-sided nature of his task Dreiser seems to have thoroughly mastered it. All the important phases—social, political, moral, religious and intellectual are dealt with in his book.

With equal frankness, the novelist sets down both the things that pleased and displeased him about the Russian state. If you are seeking an illuminating treatment of the Russian situation, "Dreiser Looks at Russia" is your book.

"The Bookshelf of a Workingman." *Weekly People*, December 8, 1928.

. . . now that Russia has gone and made a revolution even more revolutionary than the one we presented the world with in the late seventeen hundreds and is emerging out of "barbarism," it may be only fair even if it is foolish that we should rush there and take sweet revenge for the judgment marquises and such once passed on us. At any rate in this age of printed matter the soaplessness and bathlessness and such of Russia make good copy and probably will for some time yet. The latest condescending traveler in Russia is Theodore Dreiser; and of course Dreiser had to write a book. Whether Dreiser had anything to say that hadn't been said better before, or whether he had any light to shed that had not already been shed, made of course no difference. A book on Russia by "the American Titan" was bound to sell—and what other reason is necessary for producing a book!

Dreiser's book of 264 pages has a last chapter called "Random Reflections of Russia." If Dreiser had made that the *first chapter* and let it be the last as well, Dreiser would have written a good and quite sufficient book. Just about all the rest is boredom at its extremest.

Dreiser was invited to come and look at Russia and before accepting the invitation he demanded a free chance to go where he wanted and to say what he wanted about it. It is not that Dreiser has set himself up as a critic that matters; it is that he has set himself up as a critic *without real and essential understanding and without indeed the barest conception of the fundamentals of the thing he undertakes to criticize.* It is this which makes his criticisms not merely valueless, but stupid, irritating in the extreme. Having read just about every book on Russia that has been published in English—and in some other languages too—in the last ten years, we say without hesitation that, barring that last chapter in which Dreiser seems to have dared to let himself go, this is the most useless and provoking, excepting always the effusion of H. G. Wells after his visit a few years ago. Wells came out, we remember, with an irresistible desire to shave Marx (a promise not redeemed yet), but Dreiser appears to be content with irreverently pulling Marx's whiskers. Wells went through Russia whining for his cold morning shower; Dreiser weeps perpetually because a hot bath was not prepared for him from Leningrad to Odessa and all the outlandish places on steppes and tableland east, west and in between. In fact, Dreiser appears to have betaken himself to Russia with a Statler Hotel and tip-top modern duplex apartment standard firmly fixed as the ideal of existence—and Communism being an "ideal state" the shock is tremendous and the disappointment bitter that Statler and duplex hadn't preceded his august person and prepared the way for him. And yet, Dreiser visits the Winter Palace and sees with his own eyes that royalty previous to the revolution took its bath in a bowl with a pitcher of water. Dreiser visits a peasant hut—a relic of Czardom—and finds a family of 'steen, plus cow, sheep, pig and chickens and their mutual "drippings," all occupying one room, and this condition in the worst places not yet remedied or even touched—and yet: The Soviet Government actually has not put in baths from Moscow to Vladivostok, from Archangel to Odessa, for the reception of American scribblers!

It goes—after this—without saying that Mr. Dreiser is constantly irritated by "Soviet propaganda" which meets him everywhere. That that "propaganda" is part of the Soviets' effort—in face of the ninety per cent or so illiteracy that they took over from Czardom—to teach the masses the things they must be taught from the simplest rule of cleanliness as the first prevention against disease and epidemics to the use of modern machines, does not in the least seem to mollify Mr. Dreiser's annoyance. And talk about propaganda—what's the matter with these U.S.A.'s in comparison? Aren't we here propagandized every minute of the day—from the tickets that we vote to the crackers, and pickles that we eat, the soap we use, the brands we smoke? We can't even gaze at the sky any more without being reminded that we should "walk a mile" or that "there isn't a cough." What, we feel, disturbed Mr. Dreiser in Russia was not so much the "propaganda" as the united and organized effort at accomplishing a certain thing—this grated on his boasted "individualism"; he seems to be in a tremendous state of fear and trembling that if misery at the one pole and luxury at another are abolished all color and artistry will go out of life. Poor fellow!

And, of course, being an artist, the art status of Russia concerns him much, even worries him. Imagine the sad state he found—Soviet Russia has not yet produced one single artist of real significance! Curiously enough this was word for word the final condemnation of the United States of America in western Europe on our last visit there in 1910. Our answer was: "Give us time. One hundred and fifty years is a short period in the span of development of a nation. And besides we have been too busy with other things." However, why should not Soviet Russia, aspiring to be an "ideal state," be ready to deliver artistry on the spot and to order! Too much propaganda again! The artists are drawn into the government's utilitarianism! " 'Tis true 'tis pity, and 'tis pity 'tis true." But perhaps America might have "arrived" artistically much sooner than it is doing if our talent had not been so profitably employed, persuading us to eat crackers, pickles, avoid pyorrhea, walk a mile, ride in luxury, "retire," save nerve shocks in walking, etc., etc., etc., from the Atlantic to the Pacific, or to grind out books for a merket on any subject for which the public has been made hungry by much ballyhoo—as for example Russia.

Sometimes it is stupid to be wise. Unquestionably the most stupid thing in the world is to carry the wisdom of one civilization abroad and attempt to apply it to another status of civilization. And this holds good for an American novelist in revolutionary Russia as well as for a French marquis in eighteenth century revolutionary and pioneer America.

E. E. H.
"Dreiser Says His Say on Russia."
Albany [N.Y.] *Knickerbocker Press*, December 16, 1928.

The Moscow authorities extended our Mr. Dreiser, the rank individualist, the last person on earth to lean toward the standardization of human hopes and aspirations, an invitation to visit their Muscovy playground, disect it and report upon it. Whereupon, Mr. Dreiser went to Russia, first stipulating, however, that what he didn't like about the country, he most assuredly would write, or if he didn't feel like writing anything at all, he wouldn't.

Back again in the good U.S.A., he loosens a number of interesting enthusiasms, and also a heavy cargo of sheer disapproval. He doubts the fundamental validity of the Commune idea, hopes it will not exceed the Russian boundaries and he does not believe the Communist regime spells heaven on earth. Of course, Mr. Dreiser predominantly is an idealist and this feeling inevitably creeps into his views. But first and above all, he is a supreme humanist, with a profound sense of human needs and frustrations. Russia, to the author of An American Tragedy, is primarily a problem of human beings merged into a huge adventure. How will they emerge from it and how will it leave them?

Mr. Dreiser gives us a full and fresh report, and we may add, a discouraging one insofar as it relates to the Russian people themselves and what they are getting out of the Communist regime. It is sad to have related that this vast new reading audience, for instance, this presant horde released at last to literacy by the brisk school methods of the Commune, has put its foot on the shoddiest and basest rungs of the cultural leader. Instead of reading the best that their own land has produced—Turgeniev, Tolstoi, Chekhov or Dostoevski, they are reading The Return of Tarzan, Zane Grey, Ethel Dell, James Oliver Curwood and Rex Beach. No new Gogols in letters. No new Tchaikovskies in music. No new culture to encourage them and not much left of the old—not even wreckage.

Of course it is early yet; Mr. Dreiser thinks so; he likes the Communist school system, for instance he would like to see it in force in our own land. And everyone whose outlook upon life goes beyond our own door will find this book profitable, absorbing and thought-provoking, as is the case of most, if not all of Mr. Dreiser's writings.

Lewis Gannett. "Dreiser Gropes in Russia." New York *Herald Tribune Books*, December 23, 1928, p. 3.

Theodore Dreiser went to Russia at the time of the Tenth Anniversary Celebration, in November, 1917, stayed several months, wandered about the country with an interpreter, brooding upon the meaning of life there as he had brooded over the meaning of life in America, and, returning, wrote a series of newspaper articles about Russia. Dorothy Thompson had been in Russia at the same time as Dreiser, but returned sooner. Dreiser read her newspaper articles, and when he came to make his own articles into a book whole sentences out of Miss Thompson's articles, strings of adjectives, successions of ideas, transferred themselves to Dreiser's pages. And since the parallels were discovered, little else has been said about Dreiser's book except that he copied.

Well, he did copy. No one who compares the published parallels can well doubt it; when Dreiser sat down to write he had Dorothy Thompson's clear journalism in the back of his mind. It is impossible to believe that the author of "The American Tragedy," after four months in Russia, deliberately "cribbed"; I leave the explanation to the psychologists. But the impression is abroad that Dreiser's book is like Dorothy Thompson's. Except in a few details it isn't. It is as different as Theodore Dreiser is from Dorothy Thompson. Hers is the clean-cut work of a professional journalist. Dreiser's is the puzzled, bothered stumbling of a man who had groped his way to certain conclusions about men in America, and then had gone to Russia and discovered that his generalizations did not seem to apply.

"Life will not be boxed in boxes," Dreiser once wrote in his "Book About Myself." "It will not be wrapped and tied up with strings and set aside on a shelf to await a particular moral or religious use. As yet we do not understand life, we do not know what it is, what the laws are that govern it. At best we see ourselves hobbling along, responding to this dream and that lust and unable to compel ourselves to gainsay the fires and appetites and desires of our bodies and minds." And then he went to Russia, and found himself on the other side of the looking-glass, in a country ruled and dominated by men without the acquisitive instinct, where the satisfaction of sex was so simple that frustrated sex did not motivate men's actions. He talked with one of the greatest movie directors in the world, who received, and was satisfied with, $150 for the scenario of that superb film, "The End of St. Petersburg"; and he learned that the heroine of the film lived, more or less contentedly, on a salary of $75 a month. And Dreiser did not know quite what to make of it all. Men were hobbling along, moved by different desires, stumbling toward different goals, from those in America.

He wrote a book; but for every conclusion in the book one can find three contradictory conclusions. "Dreiser Looks at Russia" is full of "buts" and "yets." Indeed, it is so full them that I counted the paragraphs beginning with "but," "yet," "on the other hand," and similar expressions. There are 146 of them in 263 pages. Dreiser says nothing which he does not take back. For that very reason his is a supremely honest book. He refuses to make the sweeping statements of the journalist. Life, in Russia as elsewhere, is muddled. Dreiser is not quite sure of anything. He is most definite when he tries to report the organization of the Soviet state or the agricultural situation in Russia; but he is dull as ditchwater when he attempts to be a political scientist. When he gets inside human beings, he becomes the old Dreiser, although still Theodore Dreiser of Indiana, Pittsburgh and Chicago, something of an innocent abroad. He is appalled by the dirt, the lack of bathtubs in Russia; he is amazed at the slowness and incapacity of the plumbers. Yet he also sees in Russia a freshness, a vigor, that inspire him. "Heigh ho!" he cries. "Bully for a new day! Bully for a new idea! To hell with fashion plates, with what the west, or the north, or the south, may think! This is Russia. This is the new, shimmering, changeful, colorful, classless day of a new social order. A new world indeed. A fresh deal. Verily. Selah."

Yet he dreads a new standardization. . . .

So he gropes. Decidedly this book is not like any other book on Russia. For Dreiser is not sure of anything about Russia. And who else has ever written a book about Russia without being abundantly sure? . . .

J.G.C. Erie [Pa.] *Times*, December 29, 1928.

Theodore Dreiser, eminent American novelist, received an official invitation to visit the new Russia and see for himself what went on. Reserving the privilege of writing strictly according to his own impressions, or if he chose, not writing at all, he accepted the courtesies of the Union of Soviet Socialist Republics, and spent eleven weeks in the land the very existence of which is officially unknown to our own enlightened State Department. Then he wrote this book.

But another visitor to Russia was Dorothy Thompson, journalist, who also reported what she saw. Her book was published a few weeks before Dreiser's. When his volume came to the New York Evening Post for review, the editor sent it to Miss Thompson (Mrs. Sinclair Lewis), who had written a series of articles on Russia for that paper, and who might be supposed to know something about the matter. She was astounded to discover a striking similarity of phrases and sentences, even whole paragraphs, between this book of Dreiser's and her own work. The Post published a column or more of "deadly parallels" which made it all too evident that Dreiser had borrowed descriptive matter from the earlier book.

Now in my opinion Theodore Dreiser is not such a fool as to expect to get away with an out-and-out plagiarism, though this is not the first time he has been accused of it. But the similarity is too pronounced to be explained as accidental, or as reliance on similar source materials. Perhaps it is the effect of an unconsciously photographic memory. If this, the kindest as well as the most probable explanation, be accepted, it is still a dangerous sort of mental quirk, and one against which Mr. Dreiser owes it to himself as well as other writers, to take very special precautions.

The book itself is, like most of Russia, chaotic and contradictory. Eleven weeks are time enough merely for the gathering of a vast number of lantern-slide impressions—not for the mature development of a comprehensive picture. . . .

Helen Lohman. "Three Books About Russia After Ten Years of the Soviet." Philadelphia *Inquirer*, January 5, 1929.

Mentally and emotionally "Dreiser Looks at Russia," Theodore Dreiser the artist applauds; Theodore Dreiser the practical citizen sometimes applauds, but often deplores and is oppressed.

In a few words, the net impression to be had from Mr. Dreiser's book is that Sovietism or Communism in Russia is indeed a noble experiment, but literally a reign of terror; that the Russians have exchanged one woe for another, albeit a woe of chains for that of uncharted voyaging, between which there is not exactly equality. For eleven weeks Mr. Dreiser looked, listened—and wondered.

Still, despite the many times that Mr. Dreiser feels impelled to say "I wonder," he states: "I feel that the Soviet form of government is likely to endure in Russia, perhaps with modifications, and not only that, but spread to and markedly affect, politically, all other nations."

Two words stand out in this quotation: "with modifications." From Mr. Dreiser's own report it would seem an obvious necessity that theory and practice draw still closer together if the salvation of the Russian people is to be accomplished. Lenin himself, during his lifetime, realized that he was transferring theories into a laboratory, and that by keeping them fluid they would produce the best results. "With modifications" would still seem to be of paramount importance if Sovietism is to endure, even in Russia; and these modifications may, perforce, lead to some form of compromise with capitalism. . . .

"Dreiser Writes a Russian Tragedy." Chicago *Journal of Commerce,* January 19, 1929.

These were the terms laid down by Dreiser and accepted by the Soviet Government before he went to Russia:

1. Freedom to choose his intinerary and to make any inquiries.

2. Provision of a secretary-interpreter.

3. Acquittal from discourtesy if his conclusions were unfavorable to Sovietism.

4. Freedom to publish or not any report of findings.

In October, 1927, he set out and spent eleven weeks in Russia, leaving Moscow and Leningrad after a time to travel into such inland cities and outlying regions as Perm Novo-Sibirsk, Novorogod, Kiev, Kharkov, Stalin, Rostov, Tiflis, Baku, Batum, and a lot of other unpronounceable places.

This book is his report, a candid and vivid recital of experiences, a series of snap-shots of conditions political, economic, social, industrial, cultural, religious, all presented in the brisk and brutal style of the author of Sister Carrie. He sees the good features of the Soviet system, but he does not agree either with its philosophy or its technique. It is "too much like replacing one dogmatic tyranny with another."

To interpret Russia, or any other place for that matter, an American visitor must make allowance for difference of race and temperament. Dreiser does that. He remembers that Americans are brisk and, shall we say, somewhat limited esoterically, philosophically. Russians, on the other hand, are slow, abstracted, given to reverie, afflicted by a passive weariness, the effect perhaps of their monotonous landscape. Americans are devotees of water and soap. Russians are sluggishly indifferent to these luxuries, and the inquiring reporter shudders as he recalls the dirty floors, dirty windows, disgraceful toilets and frowsy hotel bedrooms.

There is a chapter here on the Soviet

economic plan, with a good description of their all-Russian cooperative stores; another on Communism in theory and practice which includes a drab picture of shabby and shivering officials, uncomfortable housing, high-priced and poor-quality foods, beggars on the streets, and hundreds of thousands of unemployed. He finds their propaganda vastly overdone, their industries directed by foreign, not native technical directors, and too little emphasis on skill and speed in production. Divorce is just as free as marriage, unbridled freedom in sex relationships has led to revolting excesses, and the home is going out of existence in Russia.

Of religion, Dreiser is not equipped to speak. He is himself too violently prejudiced against Catholicism in every form, to appraise the values of the Church of Holy Russia. The chapter on this phase of life, the phase which expresses the profoundest life of the Russian millions, is weak, being given for the most part to the report of an interview with one of the dignitaries of the so-called Living Church, which is, as everybody ought to know, the creation of the Soviet Government and repudiated by the Holy Orthodox Church itself.

Bolshevik art, music, literature, are given a chapter, but perhaps the best part of the volume is "Some Russian Vignettes," where a flashlight falls upon a communal kitchen with its gossipy old women in a back street in Moscow, a street scene in Samarkand, a prisoners' march in Rostov, an abandoned summer-hotel in Sebastopol, a funeral procession in Kiev.

"I saw too much," Dreiser concludes. Well, he did see a lot and undoubtedly much more than he has set down. But what is here sounds like the truth fairly and squarely presented just as he saw it in that "what-the-hell" style of writing for which Dreiser is famous. The one word which he uses at least a thousand times in the book is the mystical symbol which lies like a spell upon any interpretation of Russia, the word "nonetheless." Good features, good ideas, good theory, good practice: "nonetheless," and there follows the messiness, the shabbiness, the dirt, the laziness, the chaos. O there are bad features: the tyranny, the intolerance, the stupidity, the hunger, the cold, the dreariness, the ignorance: "nonetheless," power smoldering fire, potentiality, tomorrow.

This book is by no means a comprehensive study of Russia, but it is a sharp and shrewd and an interesting peek into the conditions as they are today.

Forum, February, 1929.

It was, perhaps, to be expected that the chaos of Russia under the Soviet would appeal to the fumbling, chaotic, yet rugged intelligence of Theodore Dreiser. The title of his latest book, DREISER LOOKS AT RUSSIA, is an accurate description of its content. This is no weighty treatise by a historian or political economist, but rather a jumbled record of impressions, an account of a novelist's reactions to the Communist experiment. Mr. Dreiser likes the principle of work for everybody—but only enough work for each to provide the ordinary privileges and comforts of living. He approves of the new methods of education, the new working conditions, the new status of women under the Soviet régime. On the other hand, he resents the substitution of one tyranny for another, and he has nothing but impassioned bitterness for the filth of Russian hotels and the unpardonable tardiness of Russian trains. His book is a confused but vivid piece of reporting. He pours out his ideas with the utmost frankness—and for his conclusions at least he owes nothing to Dorothy Thompson.

David Cort. "What They Read." *Vogue*, February 16, 1929.

"Dreiser Looks at Russia" is the latest production by guess-who. It is merely a collection of ponderous, and inept, and dreadfully perservering, and perfectly honest, and very shrewd, and getting-there-just-the-same essays about Soviet Russia. The subject-matter is intensely interesting, and it is impossible to say that Mr. Dreiser makes it any the less interesting. "Women in Present-Day Russia" and "Three Moscow Restaurants" are very acute and revealing essays. The book stands up as thoughtful and perceptive sense and truth about a subject that does not yield its truth easily and has had the offices of little enough sense. So much for the book itself. But the really wonderful thing about "DREISER LOOKS AT RUSSIA" is the civil suit that is going on or pending or something or other, brought against Theodore Dreiser for plagiarism by one Dorothy Thompson, who has written something about Russia, too. As a matter of fact, her case is excellent, the papers have quoted parallel passages from her book and Mr. Dreiser's book, which do have a lot in common, even to phrases and sentences. But the essential idiocy, the impossibility, of preferring charges of plagiarism against Dreiser are made only the more overwhelming. And the epic comedy of Miss Thompson's suit assumes the most sublime thick-headedness. An axiom about stealing anything is that the minimum any one can steal is one unit, one molecule that can not be sub-divided any further. But Mr. Dreiser's unit is one-thousand words, this is the least he works with. Give him a hundred units of one thousand words each, and he can get started, he can begin to feel his way and get down a working free-hand draft of what he has in his mind. How, then, accuse him of stealing one-hundredth, one-thousandth, of a molecule? He really and honestly didn't even know it was there. The word, the sentence, the paragraph, what are these trivialia? In the strict sense, Mr. Dreiser has been plagiarizing all his life. What about the time-tables, the minutes of Rotary Club meetings, the Sears, Roebuck catalogues? Intact and *in toto,* they or printed matter very like them have gone into his novels by the gross. It's the way the man works, and, as a lot of people will testify, it has its effect. Mr. Dreiser, it must be clearly understood, never purloins Art from another. The words he borrows are just words, words wholesale, words at so much the thousand, never jewelled words nor precious antiques with fine histories. And surely the articles of this journalist, somebody-named-Thompson, furnished another supply of this vulgar commodity. The devil with the individual word, Mr. Dreiser wanted to say everything, to get it all in, and maybe Miss Thompson had found something he had missed. If she had, the reader had a right to it all in one place, give him all the facts, the truth is what is important, not that's-my-word and that's-your-word. We call this the ultimate honesty. Mr. Dreiser probably hardly realizes the implications of his attitude. If he comes to trial, he may not have any defence, he will probably be glad to go to jail and copy off the scrawls on his cell-wall and publish them and get into some more plagiarism suits at the hands of the former occupants of his cell. Anyway, we're all for him, more than ever all for him. We can't read his books, but he's magnificent. Wonderful Theodore.

"Briefer Mention." *Dial*, 86 (March 1929), 265.

Dreiser Looks at Russia, by Theodore Dreiser, is a book about the originality of which controversy has occurred. It begins to be apparent that just as what one finds in going to Russia depends upon one's equipment, so it is with what one finds in a book about Russia. The present one records irritations, disillusions, angers, enthusiasms, doubts, fears, and a host of incidents upon which these emotions are based. It is possible to find ammunition enough for an old-fashioned Red-hunter's holiday; and also to find background for the profoundest statement yet made about Russia—that by John Dewey, that the Revolution is more important for the release of certain human capacities than for its social and economic policies. The reader is referred to Dr. Dewey's recent series in The New Republic for his exact, and significant, words. It is regrettable that Dreiser should have said in his introduction to THE CRIME OF DR GARINE, by Boris Sokoloff, that "more definitely than in any post-revolutionary Russian play or novel . . . one is permitted to examine, and so sense . . . the pre- as well as post-Revolutionary reactions of the Russians, not only to life but to the Revolution," for this, if true, means that post-Revolutionary literature is utterly contemptible, and gives this slight and unimportant book a position of undeserved prominence. The stories in it are fairly good, conventionally unconventional Russian stories.

Jessie Lloyd. "Two Americans Look at Russia." *Nation*, 128 (March 13, 1929), 317.

In "Dreiser Looks at Russia" and "The Hammer and the Scythe" we see that Russia, the heterogeneous, has succeeded in setting two more critics to contradicting each other—and occasionally themselves. Dreiser says that the art of cooking is unknown in Russia, and the trains are never on time, but he was refreshed by the spirituality and lack of material greed in the Communist soul; while Mrs. [Anne O'Hare] McCormick, who reports the food as uniformly good and the train service as punctual and well-regulated, declares that communism is a war against the soul, "summoning man to a single concentration on the material facts of life."

Dreiser's is a rambling book of impressions, reported in his prosaic style, rarely lighted by imagination. Certain passages which he has been accused of plagiarizing from Dorothy Thompson are strikingly similar to parts of her previous published work, "The New Russia." It is true that these deal with obvious aspects of Moscow and the Soviet system that no visitor could fail to observe; but the presentation of the ideas in the same order and often the same words seems more than a coincidence. Miss Thompson's charges will have to be more adequately answered than they have been yet. Mr. Dreiser, in spite of occasional outbursts of petulance, refrains—more modestly than most transient visitors—from attempting any thoroughgoing criticism of the operation of the system. He is at his best in his understanding of the ideals of this "materialistic" government, and the thinking and striving of the people. . . .

It seems to me that both Mr. Dreiser and Mrs. McCormick overestimate the military danger and the military power of Russia; and neither of them admits the possibility of as much criticism from workers, peasants, and bourgeois as I heard in the year I spent there, perhaps because their inability to speak Russian barred them from experiencing it. Mrs. McCormick's worst mistake, and Mr. Dreiser's greatest bit of clairvoyance, is about Russian materialism and the soul. It will be a great day when somebody invents a word to distinguish between the materialism of the Communists, who say that the soul is matter and spend their time seeking material to educate it, and the materialism of Americans, who say that the soul is spirit, therefore it will take care of itself while we spend our time seeking the latest styles in clothes, cars, and jazz.

G. Vernadsky. "Russia Today." *Yale Reivew,* 18 (Spring 1929), 600-603. [A review of Dorothy Thompson's *The New Russia,* Anne O'Hare's *The Hammer and the Scythe,* Valeriu Marcu's *Lenin,* and *Dreiser Looks at Russia.*]

A Moscow correspondent of the "Berliner Tageblatt" once said to Miss Thompson, author of one of these books on contemporary Russia: "Only two sorts of people can write about Russia—those who stay [in Russia] for years . . . and those who come in for a very short time and leave before the first impression becomes confused." Miss Thompson says she belongs to the second class of observers. Mr. Dreiser and Mrs. McCormick may be ranked among the same group. Dreiser spent eleven weeks in Russia and Mrs. McCormick spent one summer. None of them knew the Russian language, and none of them had been a special student of Russian affairs before making the trip. All were obliged to use interpreters and to rely upon second-hand information for the explanation of things they had seen. It is obvious that none of the three could publish a book which would have the authenticity of a competent, scholarly account, such, for example, as the late Professor F. A. Golder's "On the Trail of the Russian Famine," published last year. Nevertheless, all three authors have succeeded in presenting a vivid picture of Soviet Russia. Their books are brilliantly written and seem to have no bias either in favor of or in hostility to the Soviet government.

Miss Thompson's book presents a rather systematic survey of the Soviet state, while Mrs. McCormick and Mr. Dreiser choose to keep closer to their personal impressions. However, as their points of observation are well chosen, their impressions, on the whole, give the reader a composite picture of life in Soviet Russia.

The reader can find in each of the three books interesting details as well as general characteristics of the Soviet society and state, of Moscow as its capital, of the drift of Communist ideas as well as of the real conditions of life in the country. Their impressions are not always identical—Mr. Dreiser was quite dissatisfied with the cooking, while Mrs. McCormick found it much to her liking. Recently Mr. Dreiser's book has been attacked on the ground of alleged plagiarism by Miss Thompson. It is undeniable that there are some passages common to both books. However, as both are based partly on second-hand information, it is possible that the identity of those passages may be explained by the fact that both authors drew from one and the same source. In my opinion, there are other criticisms which can be directed against Dreiser with more justification. He is inclined to take his informers literally. He states, for example, that the system of pure socialist economy, so-called "war communism," was applied by the Bolsheviks only in view of the civil war in Russia when it was necessary to direct all forces of the state to one aim, and that this system ended immediately after the close of the civil war. This is not correct. The system of socialist economy had been a basic principle of the Soviet government since its formation and was not invented during the civil war. It reached its climax after the defeat of the White armies; and it was only the complete economic inefficiency of the socialist system as it worked out, and the menace of a general peasant uprising, which compelled Lenin to assume the so-called New Economic Policy or NEP in 1921, several months after the defeat of the White armies.

Another of Dreiser's errors is common to many foreign travellers in present-day Russia who are unfamiliar with the country as it was before the Revolution. He seems to think that there was no educational system in Russian villages before the Communist régime, not knowing apparently that the number of village schools had been increasing rapidly in the pre-war Russia under the Duma régime. As a matter of fact, at the end of 1927 when Mr. Dreiser was in Russia, the number of schools in Russian villages was practically the same as it was in 1914.

Miss Thompson's misunderstandings of a similar character are few and incidental as compared with those of Mr. Dreiser, and Mrs. McCormick is the best informed of all three in the achievements of pre-revolutionary Russia. Moreover, of the three writers, Mrs. McCormick seems to have the most sympathetic understanding of what is now developing not only on the surface of Russian life but in the depths of Russian psychology as well. . . .

Checklist of Additional Reviews

"Russia Viewed by Theodore Dreiser." Davenport *Times,* November 17, 1928.

"Mr. Dreiser Sees Things Good and Bad in New Russia." Kansas City [Mo.] *Star,* November 24, 1928.

E.H.W. La Parte *Argos Herald,* November 27, 1928.

Edwin Francis Edgett. "About Books and Authors." Boston *Evening Transcript Book Section,* December 8, 1928, p. 10.

Topeka [Kan.] *Journal,* December 15, 1928.

Wisconsin Library Bulletin, 25 (January 1929), 28.

Pittsburgh Monthly Bulletin, 34 (February 1929), 14.

Notes

A Gallery of Women

THEODORE DREISER

In two volumes

VOLUME I

Horace Liveright · New York · 1929

A Gallery of Women

Grant C. Knight.
"Fiction."
Bookman, 70
(November 1929),
320–321.

Fourteen years ago Stuart Sherman sharply arraigned Theodore Dreiser's naturalism because he failed to accept what every one of the novelist's books declares: that while technically Dreiser is a realist, spiritually he is representative of the romantic Victorian infected with a belief in "chemisms" and natural selection. The man is by race, time-spirit, and inclination an incurable sentimentalist and pagan, but a pagan as far removed from the brittle Twentieth-Century type as Shelley is from Hart Crane. To Dreiser life is still an improvisation to be observed with mingled awe and sadness; the meanest man who breathes can challenge wonder because he is an insoluble mystery. Having read Rousseau at twenty-six, Dreiser is today as much that Frenchman's disciple as he is Balzac's or Zola's.

His latest book—a gallery where for over six years he has been hanging portraits of women he has known or heard about from friends—is testimony to the above thesis. It has little value to the thinker. The one idea on which he strings the stories is a favorite with him: that we are, because of our chemical constituents, the pardonable creatures of vagrom temperaments. And if the idea be comparatively feeble, what can be said for the style, calculated as usual to set the academic's teeth on edge? The seeker will find here no parade colors, no flashing humor, but one epigram. Dozens of lesser men, by refraining from abusing the patience of grammar and by opening their ears to sounds, could fashion better sentences. Yet Dreiser's very clumsiness is an earnest of his peculiar greatness, for we come to realize that his carelessness and absence of manner arise from a profound artistic sincerity, from a concentration upon his subjects. He does not disport himself; he makes us talk and think and feel with these women—most of them unusual, three seemingly commonplace—over whom he broods tenderly. His is not a highly intellectual analysis, not a deeply lyrical compassion, but a healthy, burgher-like sympathy given to those who, for some reason, he believes have been made to bear the burdens of frustration and misunderstanding.

A Gallery of Women is not Dreiser's most important book; that was published in 1925. It is, however, a further revelation of his groping instinct to know all and forgive all, to apprehend if not to unriddle personality. Such stories as "Spaff" and "Ida Hauchawort" convince us that no American writer has equal capacity to reflect the variegated emotional patterns of our current civilization.

Isabel Paterson. "Books and Other Things." New York *Herald Tribune*, November 29, 1929, p. 15.

There are fifteen portraits in Theodore Dreiser's "A Gallery of Women," ranging from a washwoman to the daughter of a Russian nobleman, though the latter is transplanted to a Bohemian atmosphere.

They are strongly differentiated in antecedents and character, yet inevitably they have a kind of family likeness. Whether they have been colored by the author's temperament, or merely selected in accordance with it, it would be presumptuous to say. But their lives exemplify Mr. Dreiser's reiterated inability to discover any ultimate meaning in human life. It appears to him as a succession of fortuitous and incomprehensible episodes leading to nothingness.

Like Jurgen, Mr. Dreiser has followed the Brown Man, Pan, into the woods; but, unlike Jurgen, Mr. Dreiser emerged with no heart for an explicit denial of the revelation of the master realist. Yet in his acts he fails to conform, for he goes on writing the truth as he sees it for its own sake; and what would that matter or how would it be possible to a genuine follower of Pan? "Nothing will come of nothing; speak again."

Mr. Dreiser's purpose is, paradoxically, to proclaim the absence of purpose in mundane things. And the common trait of these ladies in his gallery is their lack of an integrating element. They are drifters. Whatever gifts they have are dissipated in aimless experiments and amatory disillusionments. The happiest are those who do not even try. . . .

Several of the women portrayed are clever Bohemians. They dabble in art, they marry and are unmarried; they love and leave. There are a few earnest radical damsels—one a parlor socialist, one sufficiently energetic to go to Russia and work for the Bolshevik government. There also is a pathetic, cracked creature who had a trick of telling fortunes that came true. Luckily, she could not foresee her own forlorn, unfriended end, dying in a hall bedroom from the fumes of a faulty oil stove.

One does not find fault with a tragic writer for writing tragedies. Mr. Dreiser's unflinching honesty commands respect; his indisputable creative spark compels attention. His ineptitude has a horrid fascination of its own. He writes by main strength and awkwardness and, since he is tone-deaf to the rhythm of English prose and will employ any word he has on hand, regardless of its exact meaning, he is no nearer to a style than when he began to write. To the contrary, for, with time, he has accumulated a larger vocabulary to misuse.

In good faith he can write of Reina: "Grammar was not to be impressed on her, via correction, example or a stick." Hardly "via" such an example. "She could sit in upon the most perfect English spoken by as many as seventeen masters of the art and of a sudden burst in with: 'Whoja think me an' 'Sven seen?' " They musta saw one of our most celebrated novelists at work, proving his mastery via the following example: "And then one day, to greet the new 'in-law' and to see what he was like, of course—came an additional brother-in-law, whom, as yet, I had not seen, that same aforementioned Howdershell, with wife and daughter, the latter a girl between seventeen and eighteen years of age and as pink and laughing and vivacious as one would wish to see. . . . That ringing laugh! That almost deranging sense of health in abundance!" For a nice derangement of epitaphs the same aforementioned paragraph would be hard to beat. . . .

Mr. Dreiser is a curiosity of literature, and he grows curioser and curioser. He cannot write a tolerable paragraph, a passable sentence. He hardly can write a word correctly. But he can write a novel. And he is at his best in portrait sketches, such the "Twelve Men" and "A Gallery of Women."

William Soskin. "Books on Our Table." New York *Evening Post*, November 29, 1929.

The "chemic" reaction upon which Theodore Dreiser builds his literary philosophy of atomic purposelessness may sometimes result in a physical union of elements that produce an artistic and significant whole. There was the great "An American Tragedy." Other "chemic" reactions may produce nothing but a cloud of gas and H^2O. The thick fog which surrounds Dreiser's "Gallery of Women," and the general stupor which pervades it seem to place it in this second category of chemical phenomena.

Dreiser has given us fifteen portraits of various women in this latest book. He has disguised their identity, but it is not difficult to recognize a few of them. I knew some of his subjects. The present characterizations throw little light upon them, except in so far as they are made examples of the futility in which Dreiser basks. And I think I know and have known fifteen women whose lives are far more interesting, more philosophically important and better suited for literary treatment than the gallery Dreiser has assemble. Perhaps, however, in the morass of such blunted intuition as "A Gallery of Women" displays, these women and all women would be reduced to rather pointless existence.

Some 800 pages in these two volumes testify to the fact that Dreiser's creative energy still burns strongly. In almost all of these stories, however, it is dedicated to the proposition that life and lives wander ultimately into the dust. Grant him the hypothesis and he must, by a compulsion of artistry, accomplish one of two things. He must find some area of fertility, some soil thriving in important juices where men act even while they remember their arid destiny. Or he must make so dramatic and powerful a picture of the aimless and dusty journey as to achieve meaning in its own right.

"Sister Carrie" and "An American Tragedy" and "Jennie Gerhardt" and "Twelve Men" recognized that compulsion. "A Gallery of Women" does not.

The ladies of Dreiser's ensemble have, almost all of them, the quality which excites what the author terms a chemical assault on men's sexual hormones. The struggle they wage to make that assault fit rationally or comfortably or happily into their lives is the subject of most of his sketches. Rarely, however, does Dreiser come upon the motivating influences, the denominators of female psychology or the elements of female consciousness which illuminate their behavior.

Reina is the pretty, healthy dumbbell who drifts from her stupid discontent with a tolerable husband into tawdry affairs, shoddy life and good times. Dreiser makes it all sound very bleak, a little pathetic, a little inevitable by dint of the sheer energy of his inarticulate understanding. But Dorothy Parker and Fannie Hurst do such things infinitely better.

Olive Brand is a Bohemian who inspires the intellectuals and artists and radicals of Greenwich Village through the intensity of her enthusiasm, her appetite for living and her intuitive appreciation. She is married to a man who can accept her in that inspirational role, and dies. Neither her village nor her marital career seem particularly important.

Ellen Adams Wrynn is a painter influenced in her art by her lovers. When she becomes no longer attractive to men she loses interest in painting, and her vital talents perish.

Lucia has a "father fixation" which messes up her sex life, causes her to live with an elderly man who stands in something of a paternal relationship to her, brings about a terrific conflict when she finds greater virility in another, and finally sends her off on the inevitable drifting and emotional defeat. That story, I think, is the best of the present collection, but how pale it seems beside such writing about women as Margery Latimer's, or any one of a dozen authors who have given up the futility formula.

And there are many "situations" and "affairs" of marital and extra-marital complexity, such as Albertine's, who makes her husband think her daughter is his own; and Ernita's, whose romance carries her into the service of the Soviet Government and gives Dreiser the opportunity to exploit a bit of Communist color; and Ernestine's, whose career involves orgies in Hollywood.

Out of almost any one them, I believe, Dreiser could build a novel rich in the honest and unflinching tragedy he can create out of the little, seemingly normal, seemingly ordinary materials of ordinary lives. Without the cumulative power of his amassed details, however, and without the mass effect of his little atoms patiently joined together into significance, these stories seem vague and clouded.

Dreiser is willing to recognize, in the course of his story of an old fortune teller, a mystic direction and control and purpose back of the atomic aimlessness of the universe. He cannot seem to reduce that control or purpose to a force within the atoms, within his people, within his stories. Nor, for that matter, within his grammar and syntax.

I am not citing the most flagrant passages in the book when I refer to his description of the illiterate Reina:

"Grammar was not to be impressed on her, via correction, example or stick."

And continues:

"She could sit in upon the most perfect English spoken by as many as seventeen masters of the art and of a suddent burst in with: 'Whoja think me an' Sven seen?"

Poor, illiterate Reina.

Harry Hansen. "The First Reader: Dreiserian Women." New York *World*, November 30, 1929, p. 13.

When Theodore Dreiser was once charged with having written a book with a moral in "An American Tragedy" he replied that if this were the case it must be that life is moral. Strangely enough, the reader of his new book, "A Gallery of Women," which Horace Liveright publishes to-day, is apt to make a similar comment. For life as here exhibited is such a compound of bitter and sweet that only too often happiness seems to lie in the path of restraint and convention.

Theodore Dreiser has not meant to preach, but to present, out of his storehouse of memories, portraits of fifteen women who came across his path. Not necessarily his own, for he makes a reservation now and then that the episode was told by a friend, and as the story-teller he is little more than the neutral interlocutor. Now and then he adds a word to show that he still believes life is largely a matter of chemical reactions, that will power and spirit are slaves of our biological structure.

Thus he observes behavior and comes to certain conclusions about its orgin, giving his sketches the appearance of raw material, of case histories out of which the older novelist was wont to construct a highly ornate structure. This results in a procession of rather drab ladies, despite the author's frequent assurance that this or that heroine was young and beautiful. Neither what they do nor what they say is lifted out of the commonplace, and yet a number of the sketches are decidedly arresting. The reason, of course, is that Dreiser intends these portraits to be realistic, not touched up.

What seems to agitate most of the fifteen women is their approach to the male and their attitude toward what Dreiser calls physical love. The question whether they shall or shall not live with a man, whether they really have the courage to speak out or are too inhibited by family environment and early training to follow their impulses, is often the motive for the action. Describing them rather coldly, Dreiser does not attempt to stir the emotions of the reader. The girl who tantalizes her lover (Rella) does not tantalize the reader; the girl who is unable to tolerate the conventions of Montreal after the liberties of Paris (Lucia) would never strike one as an unusually restless type. To apply Dreiser's words, the book contains "fresh evidence of the blank and humorless clanking of the cosmic urge that had brought . . . so much that is inane or miserable or horrifying on this planet."

Dreiser's approach to human relationships is slightly different from that of the Freudians, although he knows their viewpoint and probably sympathizes with it. He speaks in one place of "any one who postulates the mechanical or chemical origin of life and behaviorism as the path of its development," and this, for the most part, is his approach. The result is that what he writes is not life "seen through a temperament." It is more closely life seen in a mirror, save that the mirror reflects that particular part of life in which Dreiser is supremely interested—the relationships of the sexes, whether tethered or unrestrained.

In the description of a Scotch painter, Keir McKall, in "Ellen Adams Wrynn," Dreiser gives a clue to his own deliberate workmanship. He says that Ellen's work was thrilling in its exotic color and thought, but that Keir's surfaces were deeply and solidly built up. "They were so true. Naturally he avoided with almost religious austerity any suggestion of the sterile eccentricities that spoiled so much of the work of others then, but therein lay his true greatness, which at some time or other must be recognized. Solid paint was what he was after—the solid things behind the paint."

This search for depth and solidity has distinguished Dreiser through the years and makes it possible for readers to overlook the fact that he has no ear for prose. In the present work they must also overlook a wordiness that seems to cry aloud for the blue pencil of the high school English teacher. Surely this book is a monument to the fact that editors do not attempt to change the style of their authors. How else can one explain: "Not that they did not anguish at one and the same time"? Citing the expressions used by a girl, Dreiser mentions that she used "nobby, or, occasionally, the cat's whiskers, or even—I blush to repeat a tithe of all the amazing expressions she used—the cat's pajamas." But that seems little enough reason for blushing.

All of Dreiser's heroines are trying to fit their temperaments to life. Success does not attend them. Whether they restrain their passions, or become "varietists"—pass from one man to another for variety—happiness is not for them. In one instance Dreiser wishes that he could report for once a truly satisfactory denouement, but sadly admits that he can't. Sometimes, as in the case of Emanuela, not even recognition of the devastating effect of inhibitions—the remedy according to Freud—can repair the shattered life of the repressed women. The men are usually enlightened—save for fathers and bankers who have an eye on social position. The others respond eagerly to the advances of the women and grieve when social or personal inhibitions (or "chemisms") make a happy meeting impossible. But even such meetings do not come about in the halo of a glorious sunrise. The forces that affect Dreiserian life turn such delights to vain regrets. Those who live according to society's laws suffer relatively as much as those who break them; life is a game for the cunning, the nincompoops and fools, and human behavior is beyond our jurisdiction.

Such a philosophy of negation emphasizes anew the need for a positive philosophy which believes that besides biologic urges man has within him spiritual treasure that shall enrich his days upon the earth.

Charles Divine. "Dreiser, with Modern Brush, Paints 'a Gallery of Women'." New York *Telegram*, November 30, 1929.

A new book by Theodore Dreiser is an event in American letters. This one, in two volumes, is a series of sketches or life stories of various women, and each might have been a novel in itself. Each is full of the pith and salt of every-day living, its hurriedly snatched joys and its sorrows, and by the outstanding human quality with which Dreiser has depicted these characters he has made the event of his latest book interesting to all lovers of the American scene.

There will be readers, however—as there have been in the past—who will exclaim against his clumsy, uncultured style. They will find it easy picking to select here and there sentences which Walter Pater would never have permitted. This kind of carping has become a cliche in the case of Dreiser. But what the followers of this cliche often fail to see is that Dreiser manages with these words of his, these phrases which annoy some by their awkwardness, to express the very essence of character he is evidently trying to show, to tell the story he wants to tell, and to achieve his aim of communication with the reader.

Simply and graphically he brings before us a semi-literate woman like Reina, who married the honest, industrious Sven and didn't appreciate him; or a sophisticated woman of the artist class, like Ellen Adams. In each case we see and feel the tragedy of it.

Dreiser's way of making us see and feel is done with a warm, homely quality that penetrates to the poignant heart and soul of his people. His power as a writer comes from the fact, so well demonstrated here, that he does not take people for granted.

Characters whom you or I might pass by in life as uninteresting or unworthy of being written about he takes up, lingers over, delves into—and strikes the rich vein of humanity under the surface. Again and again he shows in "A Gallery of Women" that he measures up to Goethe's dictum that a writer proves himself by winning from an uninteresting subject an interesting side.

This power of Dreiser's comes to him partly because of his naive willingness to enter into his characters' thoughts and struggles. To him, too, as he meets these women, there are warm human emotions at work. . . .

Dreiser is a realist who can yet respond to the thing called glamour. But glamour is as real a part of life as any object on the cynical side of the shield, and in "A Gallery of Women" Dreiser convinces you of his ability to present a rounded picture of a human being. Life for these people he pictures is not all smooth sailing. The pictures are not "the smooth, melting, glossy things that fill our galleries," as Dreiser says of paintings when discussing a character who is caught in the first shock of modern art.

"What about these things?" asks Dreiser of the modern pictures then shocking the art world. "Are they not, after all, somewhat in step with what I actually see here and there in life? Not all is as Ingres would do it, say, or Vermeer. There are strange, trying, gloomy, even rancid, effects, on every hand. What about these?" And continuing, he states what is probably his own credo of writing—"and what is it that I personally am trying to do? A smooth countess with a white book in a long green lap? A lady absorbed by a Persian bowl filled with orchids? Not at all! And by degrees I came to see that however offensive (like war, say), here was something new, vigorous, tonic."

"Vigorous" and "tonic" fit Dreiser's own (word) pictures of his women, whether they are young women experimenting with love and sex, or older women who have come to less experimental, less lovely days. Men, too play a notable part in the book, and they are no less well drawn than the women. Both, together with their backgrounds, tell much of American life.

Always extraordinarily sympathetic, always analyzing his people as honestly as he can, and brooding over their troubles like a God of humanity interested in the smallest detail of their suffering. Dreiser makes his book one long, human document rich in its readability.

"Theodore Dreiser in The Maze of Feminine Psychology." New York *Times Book Review*, December 1, 1929, p. 2.

Those who have read Mr. Dreiser's autobiography, "A Book About Myself," realize that he has more than ordinary curiosity where the feminine sex is concerned, and that he feels less restrained than most in recording the results of his observations. This is not adversely to criticize Theodore Dreiser. Science has ever required the devotion of its practitioners, not infrequently even to the point of martyrdom. And perhaps the rest of us are cowards, only too glad to hide behind another's coat-tails and only too willing to exult in secret over the mysteries another reveals. Moreover, it must be noted that "A Gallery of Women" is, in reality, such a collection of material as any writer of short stories would give much to have compiled; such a notebook as Guy de Maupassant might have kept. But because Theodore Dreiser has little skill in the niceties of literary craftsmanship, his successes having been due rather to his two-fisted manner of writing, he could not work this material over into more gracious and ingratiating form. He had to give it forth in lumps or not at all. Hence the many gaucheries are entitled to some measure of excuse.

Seeking a euphemism (although perhaps, in this day none is needed), this writer would slightly distort a line from Goldsmith and say that the theme of Dreiser's work answers the question why lovely woman stoops to folly. But we have done with the eighteenth century, and the line gives a false impression. Let us say, then, that the theme of the book is an answer to the question of why many modern women substitute a single standard for the so-called double standard on which an elder generation relied. Thus we come down to the twentieth century. Moreover, the answer is obtained in the twentieth century manner, empirically, that is through the examination of cases. . . .

Despite the singleness of theme common to most of the stories, there is far more variety than one might expect. For instance, there is the pitiful history of Regina C——, a nurse and head of a hospital staff, who became a morphine addict. This is one of the best told of all the stories. The gradual degeneration of this once beautiful young woman, the lies and the thefts to which she would resort in order to procure the drug, and the friendly care she receives from the physician who once had been her lover, all combine to produce a tale in which mingle pathos and a certain sort of distorted beauty. And there is one picture that of Bridget Mullanphy and her troublesome family, that has even a humorous touch. But it stands alone in that respect, for Mr. Dreiser is not much given to humor. And, indeed, therein lies a telling criticism against "A Gallery of Women," and that is the deadly seriousness of the work. Older writers—who perhaps erred—fostered the delusion that there was something rather beautiful in love, in the relation of men and women. One would not gather this from Dreiser's two volumes. But perhaps the romantic illusion has been dispersed forever, and Mr. Dreiser is not too greatly to be blamed. . . .

What is one to say of the collection as a whole? That the criticism will be severe or laudatory, according to the individual, is certain. It is a daring book, only such a book as one lacking in a sense of humor would write. To those for whom manners still count in the social scheme, the volumes are likely to be less pleasing. For those who ruthlessly place frank investigation of life, buttressed on the somewhat shaky Freudian formulae, foremost, they will seem valuable.

Thayer Hobson. "—And Nothing But the Truth." New York *Herald Tribune Books*, December 1, 1929, pp. 5–6

Deliberately, soberly, without explanation as to what lies over the threshold, a thoughtful man opens slowly the door to a dimly lighted room and steps back for you to cross the threshold. On the walls are portraits, some fifteen, of women mostly, though here and there a man's figure dominates. Behind you the door closes, and you are alone with Mr. Dreiser in his gallery of women, to examine the portraits of those who have interested him. Most of these women he has known himself, a few indirectly. There will be no hurried passing from one to another, no casual observations, no facile comparisons. Mr. Dreiser illumines one single portrait at a time, and you will pause to examine, to study, to think of the woman before you, her character, actions, life, her lovers and friends. At your host's pleasure you will pass on.

They are varied, these portraits, not only in subject but in treatment: from the burly, irrepressible charwoman, Bridget Mullanphy, to the exquisite idealist, Olive Brand; from what is little more than a character sketch with a background of action to scenes of intense dramatic power. Some who study these women will see, or think they see, characters they have known—and be no better off, for all essential vitality is in the portraits themselves. Beauty, ugliness, realism, dreams, purpose, futility are here. Mr. Dreiser has painted from life—"a dangerous, changeful, beautiful and yet deceiving thing, good or worth while or not as chances aid one, yet always fairly endurable even at its worst." But this is perhaps too fair a vision, from one of the more happy of this group.

"You'll meet a character well worth the skill of any portrayer of fact," the author was told before meeting one of these women. *Portrayer of fact.* Dreiser is absorbed in fact, and dominates the reader with fact. He filters life and character drop by drop, and then describes with deadly authenticity. He leaves nothing more to say, nothing else to say. He is, above all, the great portrayer of fact. Search in vain through these two volumes for an imaginative flight, beyond an occasional expression of beauty, for an abstract reflection or groping among the mysteries of life. The most you will find is a conjecture, tentative, almost apologetic.

Those who need life ludwiged may find Mr. Dreiser sometimes dull; those who bow to the irresistible power of truth will marvel at the genius of a man who never betrays the past with a false reconstruction from a vagrant imagination. There could be nothing finer, more completely satisfying, in the real sense of the word, than his study of Emanuela. When it comes to the end—"But from this day to this, I have never seen nor heard of Emanuela. It may be she is dead—although I doubt it"—it is as though a painter left a portion of his canvas unfinished, remarking indifferently, "I don't know about that so I won't paint it." The story of Olive Brand, or of Ellen Adams Wrynn, extending over years, is penetrating, significant, with every glimpse of the woman, every episode in which she is involved, bringing you closer to an understanding of what happened in the pilgrimage which was her life. But there is so much more to know than Mr. Dreiser has given, so much that anyone but Mr. Dreiser would have tried to tell. As the portrayer of fact, he halts before the inviolable shadow of another's inner life. And he is great in so doing; for there must always be something questionable about an exposition in words more complete than ever can be an experience in life itself.

And in addition to being more honest than most authors, Mr. Dreiser is wiser than most men. To read "A Gallery of Women" is to share the experience of a man who at one moment can involve himself passionately with life and the next instant stand aside, aloof, observing coldly, analyzing dispassionately; to share in the reflections of one who has thought deeply of what he has seen and known.

With all his wisdom, what is Mr. Dreiser's attitude toward Woman? I think he would say that there was no such thing as Woman but only women. He has no generalizations with which to handicap the sex. He shows women as intellectually, morally, spiritually the equals of men. In only one respect is there a noticeable change in Mr. Dreiser when he turns from men to women, and that is significant. Rarely the censor, never the judge under any circumstances, it is less disturbing to him to pass over weakness and folly in a woman than in a man. It is not that he expects less of women. He seems emotionally more sympathetic to them than to men, and more tolerant.

There is a price to pay for a visit to this gallery of women. There are passages where you search hopelessly for some interest or significance. There are periods which cause you to pray that Mr. Dreiser may be through with this particular matter and pass on. But in spite of long, arid pages from which you long to escape, you dare not. For you are compelled to read what this man writes whether you want to or not. Here is no Autolycus bearing fardels and ballads. It is Theodore Dreiser, armored with honesty, bearing a shield of wisdom and brandishing a sword of fact. Ponderous, deliberate, inexorable, he confronts you helpless.

Walter Yust. "Of Making Many Books." Philadelphia *Public Ledger*, December 2, 1929.

. . . In these two volumes, Mr. Dreiser memorializes fifteen women who have come under his observation since the days of his early youth. The only unity the volumes have lie in Mr. Dreiser's sane and sympathetic point of view and in the fact that the tales he tells center about one kind of woman or another. The reader, who remembering why Mr. Dreiser was considered beyond the pale before 1925, approaches "A Gallery of Women" in the hope of finding a fair service of eroticism will be sharply disappointed. Most of the problems which dismay Mr. Dreiser's women are problems of love, it is true, but they are dealt with inoffensively. Nobody's going to suppress the "Gallery"; that is to say, nobody who is familiar with the modern popular novel which is not suppressed.

"A Gallery of Women" has the ring of authority about it—authority and consequence. Mr. Dreiser is willing to satisfy the curiosity of readers, but he has come to know how to satisfy their reticence too. This is not to say that Mr. Dreiser has given way to popular taste by refusing to speak of those matters which originally he blurted out. It is to say that discriminating readers of the modern novel are no longer offended so easily, provided they know that a novelist makes no deliberate effort to tease them. Mr. Dreiser plays the game as squarely as ever. He tries to record that which he has seen, as vigorously, as eloquently, as simply, as truthfully, as he knows how.

Once again, you will read here and there that Mr. Dreiser doesn't know how to write, that he is ponderous, awkward, and no stylist. (Whatever that means!) This is a notion with which I have no sympathy. That Mr. Dreiser does not speak in the graceful circumlocutions of Mr. Cabell is no reason for supposing that he cannot write. (Indeed, its absurd. The best proof that he can write are the intelligible words on the thousands of pages he has written.) With football in the back of my head, I think Mr. Cabell as a fast end, and Mr. Dreiser as the plunging linesman. Because they are both craftsmen of special excellence, they both get to where they want to go; Mr. Dreiser, to my way of thinking, getting there more forcefully certainly, and more surely.

Mr. Dreiser's women range from writers, painters, Greenwich Village habitues to old Bridget Mullanphy, scrubwoman and figure of housewifely violence. Most of Mr. Dreiser's women are beautiful, many of them are married and discontented, a number are unmarried and discontented. Love is, chiefly, their peculiar difficulty, which they name by strange names.

Mr. Dreiser stands a little off from all of them and observes them with gentle understanding. Life for him is mystery. He is amazed over the casual manner in which tragedy creeps up upon his people; he is distressed because they often must suffer or express themselves so abjectly, so meanly—especially since life, for all its seeming futility, can become a fine romantic gesture, a brave and noble excursion.

If readers have felt, these many days,

and continue to believe that Mr. Dreiser is a harsh and bitter social historian (and one who has read his novels can never believe he is), "A Gallery of Women" should dissipate the misconception. Mr. Dreiser can be as delicate a reporter of beauty as even Mr. Cabell, give him the chance. You'll search far for a story more beautifully or delicately retold than his chapter called "Rella," or for a woman more kindly celebrated than gaunt, sad-eyed Ida Hauchawout.

As I've said, they are fifteen women, and they offer a broad slice of modern American life in the city, in the country and abroad. For me, these two volumes haven't the sustained power or lift of "An American Tragedy"; but, after all, how could they have? There are fifteen stories here, unrelated, but not one of them in itself uninteresting, and three or four of them regular knockouts.

William McFee. "The Mountain in Labor." New York *Sun*, December 21, 1929.

In a somewhat declamatory announcement on the jacket-flap of this book the publisher informs us that the author is "the rock on which the future of American letters must be raised." The slightly irreverent implications of the metaphor, meaning, if it means anything, that Mr. Dreiser's credentials are of divine origin, are doubtless unintentional and to be attributed to excitement over the large sale of "An American Tragedy."

But those implications do reveal a state of mind for which we have to allow in the admirers of Mr. Dreiser. We are invited to consider him not as a mere writer of books but as a prophet, a seer, a martyr, and we are expected to receive his comments upon "life" and "women" and so forth in awed silence and upon bended knee.

An attentive reading of these two volumes does not confirm the claims made by the publisher's advertisement. Whoever "the selected group of critics" may be who have "returned the unanimous verdict" upon the book, we venture to doubt whether Mr. Dreiser has added "infinitely to our knowledge of women." We would like to have the verdict of a group of women.

"A Gallery of Women" is a series of studies, very much in the note book stage, of various women characters, done in that curious jargon which Mr. Dreiser apparently believes to be the English language and which his publisher also apparently believes to be the rock-like substance destined to support the future of American letters. We may say that, so far as any sane conception of the art of the short story is concerned, an art practiced with certain amount of success by Ring Lardner, Ernest Hemingway, Wilbur Daniel Steel, F. Scott Fitzgerald and Anton Chekov, to name a few, these stories are not any such thing, but are the synopses of stories, with occasional patches of finished work embedded. It is, of course, a thankless task to review the minor works of a man who has, after long struggle, achieved a popular success. "An American Tragedy" told a story, and if we allow for Mr. Dreiser's utter obliviousness to anything resembling conciseness or beauty, told it well. That it was a story destitute of noble characters and depending for its appeal upon the morbid craving that works in most of us to read all about sex murders, that is not to be held against the author. But it does not entitle that author to unload upon the public these crudely constructed monographs as fiction. The pretense that they are, in some way not clearly defined, enormously important revelations of the psychology of women is the purest buncombe. They must stand or fall by their quality as fiction. Mr. Dreiser's much-vaunted "psychology" is that of the tabloid newspaper, his literary art is that of the small town reporter. When Mr. Dreiser's story gets him into a fumbling blind alley of behavior he naïvely solves the problem by hinting at "some Freudian twist" in the woman's nature. Which may sound terrifically learned to the sheiks and Shebas who were entranced over the sad fate of Clyde Griffiths, but it in no way contributes to our knowledge of feminine psychology.

It is time some one protested vigorously against the claims of writers of fiction to be psychologists, or philosophers or social iconoclasts and so forth. Our suspicion is that there is more authentic revelation of feminine character in one of Ring Lardner's swift delineations ("The Love Nest" for example or in "Champion") than in the whole of Mr. Dreiser's two laborious volumes. Compared with Ernest Hemingway, Aldous Huxley and Joseph Wasserman, to take three moderns at random, Mr. Dreiser is not a writer at all. And he is certainly not a psychologist or a philosopher. He possesses an undeviating industry and an unerring instinct for the perfectly inapt and ugly phrase. His courage and persistence far transcend his imaginative powers or his constructive gifts. His significance as an artist is one of those things that have to be accepted, like the Thirty-nine Articles, in blind faith. Criticism that would be applied to the ordinary writer is frowned upon by the Dreiserian cognoscenti. And if "A Gallery of Women" be an authentic example of future American letters, if all wit and humor, all nimble satire, all common and aesthetic sense be taboo in that mournful temple of the arts, then the sooner we know our fate the better. We shall have to import those admirable qualities from Europe, because we cannot do without them.

Meanwhile those who seek startling or shocking revelations about women in this new and formidable work of the master will be disappointed. But any one equipped with normal perspicacity will learn much about Mr. Dreiser.

Allen W. Porterfield. "An American Achievement." *Outlook and Independent*, 153 (December 18, 1929), 628-629.

It is now thirty years since Mr. Dreiser wrote *Sister Carrie*, twenty since the appearance of *Jennie Gerhardt*, and five since that of *An American Tragedy*. This means that for thirty years he has been a figure in American literature, a force for twenty, and a power for five. The two volumes before us, *A Gallery of Women*, increase his stature on every count; they translate him in truth to the realm of the question mark. Having to his credit an achievement of this order, what will he do next?

From the very beginning, Mr. Dreiser, like Ibsen, though the actual influence, of Ibsen on him may be negligibly tenuous, has realized that women always rock the cradle and frequently the boat. He reveals no shadow of inclination to depart from this conviction in the fifteen portraits that make up *A Gallery of Women*, and associated with this gallery of women is a galaxy of men, at the head of which stands Mr. Dreiser himself. He knew these women, or he knew women who knew them, or better still, he knew men who knew them. The study in all its greatness reminds somewhat of an experienced speaker who sits down realizing, to his perturbation and embarrassment, that he forgot the best things he had to say. Mr. Dreiser has had voluminous experience with the exploitation of women as types in fiction. Here he has gathered up the loose ends, noted down the finer points he had previously forgotten, woven the whole into an immense sorority, and laid in the lap of the American people as stimulating a study of American women as has been produced since the first white woman tiptoed around over here in the days of Leif Ericson.

In the story entitled "Ellen Adams Wrynn," Mr. Dreiser says that "you may never have seen a woman or a landscape such as Cezanne shows in his canvases, but after seeing them you can never forget them, for you will see them again in life." It is precisely so with the fifteen portraits here painted. Each is objective, discreet, utterly truthful, quite conservative, and as kind as kind can be. If Mr. Dreiser's women fall, he feels sorry for them; if they win, he ascribes it to their common sense and not to some wild-eyed theory that beset them in their worst days; if they pass out of his life without leaving a syllable of connection behind, he hopes that they eventually come upon good days.

Of the various little novels, "Giff" in the first volume is the queerest while "Bridget Mullanphy," which concludes the second volume, is the most easily located. The Irish of this tale from the ash-can quarter of lower New York is so pronounced that it seems almost out of place along with such creations as "Lucia," "Olive Brand," and "Emanulea." In "Ernita," also a glorious story, Mr. Dreiser makes much out of the fact that in Russia the expressions "It is" and "It happens" are used so solemnly that they come to be looked upon as winged words. It is even so with the vitality, the beauty, the meanness, the ugliness that make up the factual phases of these winning novelettes. Each is; each happens. If you catch yourself reading one story with unseemly dispatch you forgive yourself on the ground that you are merely in haste to see how good the next one will be, the present one being excellent to a most positive degree.

Will Mr. Dreiser survive? Will he be read in the year 2029? If so the Professor will then take him up. Not before. Colleges take up writers after the sidewalks have made them. But suppose the Professor were to take up Dreiser now! How he could comment on his strange language! Mr. Dreiser uses many times the expression "no least." Why did he not say "not the least?" Where did he fall in love with such odd words as "chemism," and "varietistic?" Then there is the unfailing theme of sources. It is much to be doubted whether Mr. Dreiser has read any great writer who is not mentioned by the fifteen women in this museum, or institution; and there are approximately one hundred in all. Mr. Dreiser's "sources" then would make a singularly fruitful theme for search and research and it would be all the more captivating because of his own indurate Americanism. And fancy what a professor of sociology could make out of "Ida Hauchawout!" And if "Reina," "Rella," and "Rona Murtha" were printed separately, what a textbook they would make on the traditionally insubstantial subject of ethics!

A Gallery of Women is in every way a momentous creation; and the most suggestive thing about it is that it should be created just now; for it is written out of American life. If it can now be read into American life with the same sympathetic intelligence that prompted its inditement, the fifty-two per cent of our population that Mr. Dreiser has never been able to leave alone will know more about itself.

Jean West Maury. "A Gallery of Varied Dreiserian Women." *Boston Evening Transcript Book Section,* December 28, 1929, p. 2.

Out of that gray half world into which he goes for much of his material Theodore Dreiser has brought forth most of the characters for "A Gallery of Women." With a few notable exceptions, they are all variants of the egocentric, supremely selfish type of woman who takes what she wants when she wants it, if she can get it, regardless of the suffering she may cause others. The dismal part about it all is that Mr. Dreiser so evidently believes that virtually all women belong to that type. . . . "A Gallery of Women" ranks high in the Dreiser productions. There is as good character-analysis in it as in anything Dreiser has done. Everybody knows he does not try to write pleasant stuff. He takes bi-sections of life, photographs them, and presents them for inspection, the good and the bad, the ugly and the beautiful, the dull and the radiant—whatever shows itself, that he reproduces.

His unfailing appeal is his sincerity. There is, too, something else that shows more in "A Gallery of Women" than in many of his other works—his longing for perfection, his inability to accept as right or beautiful anything that is not up to the standard he has set in his own soul for what is right and beautiful.

Major Alex Well. "Dreiser Pens Realistic Women." Albany *Press,* January 19, 1930.

Yes, this is the same Dreiser who wrote the Titan and An American Tragedy, but somehow after reading A Gallery of Women we feel we know Dreiser better as the author of Sister Carrie. Never a real humorist, always a keen observer of life who records what he sees with camera-like accuracy, Dreiser, a great novelist despite his lack of observance of the niceties of literary craftmanship, has fearlessly told us what he thinks about women, in a group of intensely interesting and human stories.

The power of Dreiser is let loose like a thunderbolt in this series of stories; the procession of women who march across the pages of these two volumes, all different, and yet all the same, all women, all human, and all somehow exciting our deep interest and sympathy, makes one wish that Dreiser would somehow polish up his style just a little now and then.

But this is a modern book, ultra-modern, in fact. If you are wondering why women of today are gradually substituting the single standard for the double one, if you are wondering whether feminine emancipation is killing sex, be enlightened through the charm of Dreiser's powerful pen.

If, like the writer, you are an admirer of Dreiser, if somehow you can never read one of his books without always having before you a mental picture of this fearless man of letters, you will enjoy these stories more than ever. You will see this figure, isolated in the world of literature today, this man who defies all conventions, literary and otherwise, this genius, who despite his lonely position, will remain long after his popular contemporaries are forgotten.

You cannot help but make a mental prophecy as you read this book. You will predict no doubt for Dreiser that some day, perhaps, unfortunately, for such is the say of the world, after he has become dust, literary critics will award him the place alongside of Hardy, Doesteovesky and Conrad that he deserves. You will feel that America is tardy in giving proper recognition to a man who will one day be acknowledged as one of the great writers of the century.

But, and this perhaps is more important, these fifteen women, who stripped of artificiality, pass before your eyes, will give you a keener insight into the influences which have governed Dreiser's writings and of the female background which has made his penetration of the opposite sex and its graphic portrayal in preceding books a possibility. . . .

A.B.C.
Syracuse *Post Standard*, January 19, 1930.

"Gallery of Women" is a good name in these days when a good name is halfway to riches, in the movies, on the stage or on books. It could well have been, and it is probable Mr. Dreiser thought of making it, "Futility of Women."

Picture succeeds picture of woman's failure to achieve by some unexplained and unnamed mental dereliction. The two volumes in which Mr. Dreiser has placed his gallery are not text books in sociology, not analytical studies, but rather case books.

It matters not in what field the characters move; one of them is a scrub woman—and the least irrational of the lot, incidentally—one of them a movie actress, another a moron with no particular connections or ambitions, still another an artist, all of them fail in achieving what they want.

It is a dreary, somewhat commonplace, and interesting procession. It is remarkably worth reading. Its pages may not, perhaps, have the sustained interest of "The American Tragedy," but there is the same dispassionate reporting which is such a valuable part of Dreiser.

What is the common fault which he finds in his women acquaintances and friends, etched so sharply and unsentimentally? A deliberate reading and some thought on the subject brings one conclusion; these women move ahead steadily in careers until they permit their sex to undo them.

As soon as there is some incident in their relations with men which affects their work, in whatever field it may be, the career is lost, gone, utterly lost. The superb skill of Dreiser is shown in the unerring manner in which he brings the idea home without in the least pointing to it and exclaiming, "I told you so."

In each case, the motivating factor in these women's lives is sex relations. Little allusion is made to it, in these days when we expect nothing else, but there it is.

The reader will agree with this theory, or he will not. He will profess to see in these several sketches nothing more than a series of excellent pen drawings of varying types of women. Would Dreiser spend the time on them he undoubtedly has, without some central theme which he is attempting to bring out?

His success is due largely to the honesty which he brings into his work. It appears on the surface to be a mere, bald description of what he has seen and observed. The work is remarkable in its simplicity and finer because of it.

The two volumes, furthermore, deserve reading because of his observations, given with all the skill of a trained reporter, on various tendencies and institutions in modern life. The books alone are worth having for his description of life in the motion picture colonies near Los Angeles, in "Ernestine De Jongh," or of modern tendencies in painting, in "Ellen Adams Wrynn."

H. L. Mencken. "Ladies, Mainly Sad." *American Mercury*, 19 (February 1930), 254–255.

"A Gallery of Women" is a companion to "Twelve Men," published in 1919. There are fifteen sketches, each dealing with some woman who impinged upon the author at some time in the past; if the collection is not quite as interesting as its forerunner, then that is probably because women themselves are considerably less interesting than men. Not one of them here is to be mentioned in the same breath with Dreiser's brother Paul, the shining hero of "Twelve Men," or with Muldoon the Iron Man, who plainly posed for the stupendous Culhane. Perhaps those who come closest to that high level are Regina C——, who succumbs to cynicism and morphine, and Bridget Mullanphy, almost a female Culhane. The rest are occasionally charming, but only too often their chief mark is a pathetic silliness. What ails most of them is love. They throw away everything for it, and when they can't get the genuine article they seem to be content with imitations. And if it is not love, real or bogus, that undoes them, then it is some vague dream that never takes rational form—of puerile self-expression, of gratuitous self-sacrifice, of something else as shadowy and vain.

Dreiser draws them with a surety of hand that seldom falters. He is at his best in just such character sketches, and he has a special skill at getting under the skins of women. In all of his books, indeed, the matter chiefly dealt with is female vagary, and to its elucidation he has brought an immense curiosity and no little shrewdness. As I have said, men are naturally more interesting, if only because they show a higher variability, but women remain more mysterious, and hence more romantic. Why should Regina C—— throw herself away as she does? Why should Esther Norn waste her devotion upon men who have no need of her, and set no value upon her? Why, indeed, should old Bridget Mullanphy stagger through life in shackles to her loafer of a husband and her abominable daughter? The common answer is that there is something noble about that sort of immolation, but Dreiser is too wise to make it. He simply sets forth the facts as he has seen them, and leaves the philosophizing to less conscientious sages. He sees into all these women, but he would probably be the last to claim that he really sees through them. They remain figures in the eternal charade, touching always but inscrutable to the last.

Dreiser's writing continues to be painful to those who seek a voluptuous delight in words. It is not that he writes mere bald journalese, as certain professors have alleged, but that he wallows naïvely in a curiously banal kind of preciosity. He is, indeed, full of pretty phrases and arch turns of thought, but they seldom come off. The effect, at its worst, is that of a hangman's wink. He has been more or less impressed, apparently, by the familiar charge that his books are too long—that his chief sin is garrulousness. At all events, he shows a plain awareness of it: at one place he pauses in his narrative to say, "But hold! Do not despair. I am getting on." The point here, however, is not well taken. He is not actually garrulous; he always says something apposite, even though it may be obvious. What ails him is simply an incapacity to let anything go. Every detail of the human comedy interests him so immensely that he is bound to get it down. This makes, at times, for hard reading, but it has probably also made Dreiser. The thing that distinguishes him from other novelists is simply his astounding fidelity of observation. He sees every flicker of the eye, every tremor of the mouth, every change of color, every trivial gesture, every awkwardness, every wart. It is the warts, remember, that make the difference between a photograph and a human being.

Most other American novelists of his generation have been going downhill of late, but Dreiser seems to be holding on pretty well. The youngsters coming up offer him nothing properly describable as serious competition. They all write better than he does, but they surely do not surpass him in the really essential business of their craft. As year chases year, such books as "Jennie Gerhardt" and "The Titan" take on the proportions of public monuments; they become parts of the permanent record of their time; there is a sombre dignity in them that will not down. The defects that are in them are defects that are common to all latter-day American fiction. They may be imperfect, but they remain the best we have.

Rollo Walter Brown. "Fifteen Women." *Saturday Review of Literature,* 6 (February 8, 1930). 707–708.

Mr. Dreiser has suffered much from the time and place in which he has lived. He came upon the scene when the genteel literature of pre-Civil War days had degenerated into a malarial sentimentalism. While discredited rebels in the academic world were fighting for a less stagnant atmosphere in learning, Theodore Dreiser led a fight in the open field of letters. He wanted people to see that the American scheme was not exactly what the soporific story books had said. He made some of them see. He made them aware of their environment, which he told them shaped their lives more than all the pleasant theories by which they were supposed to live.

He has done much to change environment in America—in one way or another. Yet his environment, directly or indirectly, has shaped him. All the distorting influences which the innovator usually encounters he encountered; and because of theories of social life which he expressed, he encountered special ones. The gauntlet of unintelligent criticism caused him to suffer much in the eyes of the world. He has suffered in this way because certain ones with minds too small to comprehend more than one sentence at a time have found in him only pruriency. He has suffered quite as much from light-headed young lady protagonists who have gone violently forth in various parts of the country proclaiming for Dreiser and Varietism.

He has often been pictured as an isolated figure working conscientiously on some rocky iminence, utterly without regard for the hurly-burly of an unfriendly and trivial world. It is a pleasant picture. And perhaps he has been as nearly able to do that as most men of his time. But no man can remain uninfluenced by the world about which he writes and to which he speaks. If he does not surrender in some degree, he is certain to become too conscious of his position and keep on battling when there is no enemy in the field.

It would not be amiss if Theodore Dreiser should eventually be remembered as the author of "Twelve Men." These twelve have all sorts of interesting vices and aspirations. The sketches of them give the impression of being precisely what they are supposed to be —records of people who by chance came within the author's penetrating view. The facts and the spirit of the facts—the truth—seem to have been set down in honesty, freedom, and directness. The beloved craftsman Peter, A Doer of the Word, My Brother Paul, The Country Doctor, Culhane the Solid Man, a Mayor and His People, De Maupassant Junior, The Mighty Rourke, "Vanity, Vanity Saith the Preacher," and the rest afford as much variety as one could hope for in one volume. They are vivid and stark. Somehow they seem to tell the story.

Naturally an admirer of this volume would welcome the announcement of "A Gallery of Women." But when he takes up the two volumes devoted to fifteen women, he is forced to conclude that Theodore Dreiser has undergone a change since he wrote "Twelve Men."

Anyone who has seen even a little of

the world believes there are all kinds of women in it—all kinds of women with all sorts of preoccupations, just as there are all kinds of men. But a reading of "A Gallery of Women" somehow leaves the impression that Mr. Dreiser believes there is only one kind of woman—the one who is over-troubled with sex. There are a few exceptions—one only in Volume I—but the reader is made to feel that these exceptions were badly off—though they seem to be no worse off in the end than some of the less-repressed. Reina, a pleasantly illiterate barbarian who gravitates to Hollywood and makes hell for a fairly first-rate husband—and for a few others; Olive Brand who came on from the Rockies to New York and "lived a little" while her husband in the West paid the bills—for a time; Ellen Adams Wrynn, a young artist who went from Philadelphia to New York and Paris, sampling the men she chanced to worship; Lucia, a once-repressed boarding-school girl who confessed to the author her earliest—and later—sexual conquests and her sensations at the hymeneal hour; Ernita, who managed to stay with her husband—he was hard to shake—from the Pacific Coast to Siberia only to discover more fully over there how irritating he was, and how fascinating the "untrammeled courtship" of a young engineer; Albertine, who remarked to the man who had given her and her husband an uncontemplated child, that perhaps she would not be disloyal again after her husband's financial reverses, since he seemed "closer, more dependent";—these with Giff, a fortune-teller in tea grounds, make up Volume I.

In Volume II the percentage is not quite maintained. There is a dope fiend; a young girl in Arkansas who ended a young husband's married state and cleared his way to other women; Ernestine, equal to making a reformer divorce his wife in New York, but not so equal to the less restrained competition of Hollywood; Rona Murtha, too orderly to hold a husband; Ida Hauchawout, who had followed the plow and pitched hay for a tyrannous father, rewarded before death in childbirth with a year of relative ease, thanks to a good-for-nothing husband; Emanuela the sex-repressed; Esther Norn, wife of an erratic poet, who took up with an oldish man because, she said, she required the "mental lift" he could give her—and who died in a sanitarium; and Bridget Mullanphy, a refreshing, tongue-lashing Irish-woman from the lower West Side.

Nobody questions the existence of plenty of women who are thus definitely out for blood. But when such an overwhelming number appear in one group, it begins to look less like the chance of observing and more like premeditation. One is not to lose sight of Stendhal's remark that if the writer carries a mirror and it reflects the mud of the road, it is not the mirror's fault. But sometimes a mirror is warped by too much heat, or is wavy, or is written upon in caricature by disrespectful persons with soap, so that the reflection is not adequate. If this is the only kind of women Mr. Dreiser knows, his acquaintance is much more restricted among women than among men. "Twelve Men" seems to tell the story; "A Gallery of Women" does not. It gives the impression that the author is supporting a thesis. And when the reader comes upon a prefatory note which explains that a particular woman among the fifteen was not known to the author, but that the details were provided by a friend, this impression is not diminished, but accentuated. It is accentuated, too, by the author's own occasional self-conscious stepping-aside, as in his account of Olive Brand:

> As to the propriety or worthwhileness of this method, I have this to say. If men and women can enjoy themselves for long in such a whirl, I gather that there must be some natural justification for it. Obviously, Puritanism tends toward the humdrum and the commonplace—the mere breeding of families. And for what? On the other hand, not all men can endure the varietistic woman, any more than all women can endure the varietistic man. And not all can endure humdrum, not even the orderly. Where some are so plainly urged by their own chemisms to spin madly, why not?

In the setting which this Gallery provides, there comes also to be something of overwrought self-awareness in the author's "But hold! Do not despair. I am getting on." . . . "But hearken! Wait! Only see!" and other similar means of maintaining tension.

Individual parts sometimes reveal the author's best power. Where he turns to the hardness of life, to the great tragedy that catches those who must work and suffer, as in the case of Ida Hauchawout, he writes with the authentic quality of "Twelve Men."

Two men from the West sat in the Harvard Stadium and listened to a university band from Indiana that was present to bring courage to its friends and consternation to its enemies. When it played the Hoosier state song, one of the men said, "Wouldn't it be a strange irony if the first stanza and chorus of 'On the Banks of the Wabash,' which Theodore Dreiser was prevailed upon by his brother Paul to write, should outlive all his conscientious labors in prose?" It would be but a slightly greater irony than has overtaken Ben Jonson. It may overtake Theodore Dreiser despite the best he may try to do. But not a few readers will feel that he openly invites such a fate by adding to his published works "A Gallery of Women."

"Dreiser's Portraits." *Plain Talk*, April, 1930, pp. 498–500.

. . . In *A Gallery of Women* there are fifteen portraits, done with patience, exactitude and sympathy. They are of women Dreiser has known and observed. There is something about the man which seems to inspire some women to treat him like a father confessor. Some of the women portrayed in this book have poured out the most intimate details of their lives to him. He has listened, recorded and reported. He does not comment or editorialize or risk conjectures after the fashion of a psychoanalyst as to hidden springs of compulsion.

I beg pardon: he does in one portrait, and makes himself somewhat ridiculous. He desired one woman very much who was unmarried, adult, free, earning an independent livelihood, talented and resourceful. She liked him; but that was as far as it went. He made many attempts to overcome her scruples, some of them rather crude and bumptious, it seems to me. But she positively revolted at the idea of his kissing her and always fended him off. Yet she could not keep away from him and was always asking him to come to visit her or dropping in to see him—to talk. This irritated him and he angrily told her he would see her no more; but each time she managed somehow to see him. Never successful in his efforts to win her, he speculates on the reason why and concludes that her sex life has been frustrated by a too rigid bringing up. In this he reasons like a New Humanist. It apparently never occurred to him that, although she found him charming socially to her he might have been a washout physiologically. It is a situation which occurs now and again. In my younger days I was apprised of this phenomenon on several occasions. It makes me blush for the intelligence of my sex to find men much my elder who have apparently never learned the truth about this, and who fatuously imagine that something must be wrong with any woman who does not respond to their advances. Such a man usually afterwards describes the woman who has told him in a nice way to run along and peddle his papers as "frigid." She is—*to him.*

Dreiser is not as successful in his portraits in *A Gallery of Women* as he is in *Twelve Men.* But that was inevitable. Dreiser is a man, and, say what you will, the minds of men and women differ *in kind.* A woman describing a man must necessarily confine herself pretty much to externals, to observed behavior; and it is the same with a man who is describing a woman. Every woman I know who has read Molly Bloom's internal soliloquy in *Ulysses* says that it is as false as John D.'s hair. They may all be lying. I don't know. I take their word for it. I know what an absurd spectacle May Sinclair makes when she attempts to squeeze her virginal self into the mind of a male character in one of her stories. When she stands outside and observes him and thinks him funny, her caricatures are superb.

But here are fifteen portraits of women, drawn from life, in this, our own time. I found them all extremely interesting, honestly drawn, and drawn with that patience and that sympathy which are among the qualities of genius. Someone will be disappointed if I do not make the usual observation about the clumsiness of Dreiser's style. That someone can go sit on a tack. When Dreiser is tired or phlegmatic from some cause or other, it shows in his writing. He does not grope for the precise word; he uses whatever cliché comes to mind—and he has some tiresome ones—because he is intent on getting what he has to say down on paper and does not wait around until he feels brighter or until the graceful phrase comes to him. He is a worker—a man, curious as it may seem to the dumb, who is under an inner compulsion to get, for good or ill, his vision of life down on paper. He is not a dilettante; he has never compromised. Until he wrote *An American Tragedy* he was persecuted, calumniated and often desperately poor. And remember he published *An American Tragedy* only three years ago. *Sister Carrie* was published thirty years ago. And as to Dreiser's style, it will always be found that his use of words, though sometimes strange, is always uncannily accurate as to definition. F. P. Adams, who had been using the word "betimes" for years in his imitation of Pepys' Diary, encountered the word frequently in *A Portrait of Women* used as "from time to time" or "occasionally," and thought Dreiser did not know what the word meant. He looked it up in the dictionary and found that Dreiser's use of it is not only correct but a more common use of it than employed by Pepys. I don't like Dreiser's use of the words "via" and "anent," but it is because I don't like the sound of the words. I cannot pretend that he has used them incorrectly or that they are not shorter than any of their equivalents.

Checklist of Additional Reviews

John Riddell. "A Gallery of Dreiser." *Vanity Fair*, 33 (February 1930), 58–59.

New York *Herald Tribune*, April 10, 1930.

W. N. Stokes. Dallas *Morning News*, April 27, 1930.

Portland [Me.] *Express*, May 6, 1930.

Further Reviews: Bibliographic Information Incomplete

"Hell Hath No Fury Like a Woman Scorned." Chicago *Daily News*.

"Wise and Foolish Virgins." Fort Wayne *Journal-Gazette*.

Marjorie M. Jacobson. "A Gallery of Dreiser." *Book League Monthly*, pp. 284–285.

Theatre Guild, 1930

Mary Ross. "Women in Fiction." [*Atlantic Monthly*, April, 1930?]

A HISTORY OF MYSELF

DAWN

THEODORE
DREISER

HORACE LIVERIGHT, INC.
NEW YORK

Dawn

Harry Emerson Wildes. "Of Making Many Books—." Philadelphia *Public Ledger*, May 7, 1931.

. . .The Dreiser book will rank, I'm sure, among the classic autobiographies, for he leaves little to be guessed as he looks back upon a life of dramatic incident and of singularly appealing pathos. The book is not a lovely reminiscence of a happy youth; it's not the sort of thing to recommend for Mother's Day next Sunday; it pays no tribute to the idols of our social scheme. Its slabs of raw red meat, its reek of slum-like atmosphere attest its starkly realistic atmosphere.

But Dreiser saves his book from filth and horror by his skill in understanding what the process of his life has meant. It's not alone that he is challenging each reader to match Dreiser's story, incident by incident, with his own vagrant thoughts and happenings; it's not enough that Dreiser throws aside conventional reticence to write an honest story; Dreiser's value as a writer of his autobiography is to evaluate the worth of present social institutions as they impinge upon the consciousness of youth, and as they affect, for good or ill, the artistry and individualty of human units in the social scheme. You'll unquestionably wince at Dreiser's method, you'll shudder at his candor, but you'll find the adolescence of an ignorant and sensual youth set forth in accurate detail. Its honesty may be repellent—as a surgeon's work, a soldier's fighting are detestable to some good people—but his data are indispensable to those who earnestly desire to know the real life of submerged classes. His Aphrodite worship, his complacent boasting of the tremors set up within him by the sight of pretty faces and seductive curves, his setting down in accurate detail of those impulses which lead small boys to chalkmark walls, his budding consciousness of sex could have been guessed by readers of his early novels, but are here set down, in almost psychoanalytic form, for clinical examination.

Don't pick up "Dawn" for light reading, don't regard it as compulsory for literary background, don't read it for pornography; but, for all those whose interest in the psychology of frustrated classes is intense, for those who earnestly desire to know the kind of life led in the "miasmatically puritan and patriotic Middle West" four decades ago, Dreiser's story is a revelation and a memory. . . .

Isabel Paterson. "Books and Other Things." New York *Herald Tribune*, May 8, 1931, p. 21.

Most probably Theodore Dreiser never read the "Confessions" of Jean-Jacques Rousseau. So much the better if he did not. A model might have got between him and the facts of his own experience. As it is he has duplicated Rousseau's feat of candor by holding the same objective in view—the whole truth.

Though it has enormous faults of taste and technique, this record of Mr. Dreiser's childhood and youth is likely to become an American classic of autobiography. He calls it "Dawn" (Liveright). It may become a sort of buried classic, like that curious chapter of Hazlitt's life, "Liber Amoris." But it will be there, built into the foundations of the American literary consciousness.

The faults are in scale, for the book is enormous, unorganized, a chaos out of which a world slowly creates itself. Here is not only Dreiser himself, and his large, strangely assorted family, but the unexplored anarchic fringe of American social life as it existed during two decades.

Flattering or not, this is a purely American chronicle. Even the German origin of Theodore Dreiser's father is representative: he was one among millions of immigrants in process of assimilation. The elder Dreiser may be said to have been destroyed by the process. Born in Germany, of decent bourgeois stock, the man had both the virtues and the defects of his class. He was a weaver by trade and an expert wool buyer. Fortune escaped him by a narrow margin. He had got a good start, owned a woollen mill; it was burned, a total loss, leaving him heavily in debt. His strict honesty made him feel obliged to pay off the money at any cost. And he had not the courage, or the understanding of the new industrial system in which he was involved, to start again on borrowed capital, doubly in debt. He went back to wage working. Of course he had condemned himself to a hopeless undertaking.

This bondage imposed by both his integrity and his narrow views naturally embittered him. Religion was his refuge. He was a devout Catholic and became bigoted through misfortune. It preyed on his mind to see his children escaping from authority in the ferment of the New World. He was an anachronism, and his family learned to disregard him.

The mother, a Pennsylvania girl of the Dunkard or Mennonite connection, was exactly opposite in temperament. A good woman in every sense of the word, sweet-tempered, generous, hard working, she gave her children an inexhaustible affection. Nothing could estrange her love or wear out her patience. Evidently life had so confused her with its manifest inconsistencies between acquired moral platitudes and the way of the world, that she ceased to judge anything or anybody while still exacting from herself the utmost self sacrifice.

This is the background of Theodore Dreiser's writing, an honest bewilderment from which he has been unable to find any philosophical escape. When he comes to the conclusion that the uni 'erse contains no moral principle, there ; still the fact of his mother's pure ;oodness unaccounted for. A world of 'iolence and greed, and of vast imper-onal forces, which includes among its ›henomena the beauty of flowers and he tenderness of maternal love—what ; the meaning of it? Mr. Dreiser does ıot pretend to know. All he could do vas to write down what he saw as he aw it.

The family would defy a geneticist to lassify. Submerged in poverty, they vandered about from place to place, naking forlorn and sporadic efforts to etter themselves. Thirteen children vere born. Ten survived to maturity. 'hey varied extraordinarily. One of the oys was thoroughly worthless, vi-iously he "drank himself into failure, if ot death." One was Paul Dreiser, suc-essful composer of incredibly senti-ıental songs. "The girls, all of them ıarried, but by what devious routes.")ne at thirty-seven, was killed by a rain, another at forty died of cancer.)ne had an illegitimate child, several of hem were "wayward." One at least ıarried prosperously. None of them ame to the conventional bad end pre-icted for bad girls.

Respectability is a precarious affair vith the honest poor. They cannot es-ape at least the knowledge of looser vays. In his growing years Theodore)reiser saw all the "sociological prob-ems" exemplified among his neigh-ors. What he saw didn't give him any elp in charting his own course.

Needless to say, he devotes much pace to his adolescent difficulties with ex. And here he is painfully truthful. 'ot offensively or shockingly so but ainfully. The picture he draws of him-elf, gawky, tongue-tied, snooping, ego-stical hobbledehoy, is embarrassing and repellent. Apparently he had only one thought in his head, girls. And only one thought about the girls. It must be mentioned that he was no youthful Cas-sanova. In his lack of enterprise and of success he was remarkably like Rous-seau.

A chance year in college advanced him very little intellectually. When he went to work, at any odd job he could pick up, he seems to have been dis-tinctly incompetent. The narrative closes before he got his first job as a reporter. If the book had been written in the second person, and offered as fiction, young Theodore would seem ludicrously improbable as a candidate for fame.

All of Mr. Dreiser's notoriously inep-titudes of style are so fully displayed in this book that they seem intentionally comic.

"She has a sensual, meaty attractive-ness," he writes gravely; and it isn't a misprint, for there are other meaty maidens in other chapters. "Eleanor's husband was soi-disant and not particu-larly eager to stay in our home." Soi-disant? Maybe he meant ci-devant or peau-de-soie or sansculotte. They are all very elegant words, too, and would do just as well in the context. "And finally word from Trina, who was also in-trigued, that a freight car was being chartered for the furniture." An in-trigue with a freight car staggers the imagination. "There was some mulch of chemistry that transmuted walls of yel-low brick; and streets of cedar block and horses and men into amethyst and gold, and silver and pegasi, and archan-gels of flaming light." We can't help it—pegasi is what he wrote. Transmuted by a mulch.

Mr. Dreiser's public school teacher once told him: "But, Theodore, dear, you write good English. Your longest sentences and paragraphs are correct and orderly." We don't know what she'd say now, unless what the Scotch mother told her son: "You were aye a pretty baby, but you're mickly altered the noo."

Nevertheless, warts and all, here is a portrait of a man.

William Soskin. "Books on Our Table." New York *Evening Post*, May 8, 1931, p. 11.

Theodore Dreiser gives us a book today. Not the Dreiser who piddled with a collection of studio characters in batik gowns in "A Gallery of Women" nor the Dreiser who looked upon abstractions in Russia. Today we have the writer of mountainous stature, the creator of Jennie Gerhardt, writing of what he knows best—himself. "Dawn" is the title of the first section of Dreiser's history of himself—"Dawn: An Autobiography of Early Youth."

Mr. Dreiser never reads reviews of his books, he says, and so this timorously ventured opinion that "Dawn" is an important addition to American biography, that it is probably the best biography with a background of that peculiar proletarianism characteristic of the lower middle classes in America, will probably never be brought to Mr. Dreiser's attention. I suspect he knows it, anyhow; for Mr. Dreiser is intensely aware of himself and he must recognize the authenticity of this reproduction of himself.

"Dawn" is a story of growth, of the persistent spiritual and physical vitality of a man conquering despite all the accidents of economics and of persona "chemistry" which tended to retar him. The steady ascent of this man is n cheap matter of ambition or greed; i seems to be governed by a principle o growth in the seed from which h came, in the earth which nourishe him.

A growing tree needs no artifice an no explanation. A life such as Dreise has achieved can bear with no concealments. "Dawn," accordingly, is one o the most ferociously frank and sensitively candid biographies I have eve read. Lincoln Steffin's admirable autobiography, for instance, has a sincere honesty about it in its devotion to socia causes, in its depiction of Steffin's youthful career—but it is the honesty of a artist who has rationalized his impulses Dreiser's candor is brutal and deep, th defenseless and strong frankness of man who regards life as an atomi accident and love as a chemical reaction.

Yes, the familiar "chemic" conceptions which have run through most o Dreiser's novels appear again, just a the lumbering prose style and the unfortunate tendency to state easy generalizations are once more in evidence. I the face of a man's life, however, an organically associated with the living processes of his thought, these matter seem somehow all right. The ma dominates his book, his style, hi thought.

Dreiser's story is a whole world— massive, chaotic world through which one may trace the few motivating themes of his life. The man's memory i prodigious. From his early childhood h seems to have been an eager, hungry observer of people and things—an emo tional observer, too—with the result that all the important elements of his life may be traced back to concrete and specific factors.

His father was one of the great horde of German immigrants who were striving to be assimilated in this country some sixty years ago. A weaver by profession, he failed. He thus became a mere adjunct to the Dreiser family that moved from city to city in the Middle West in its heroic efforts to make a living. The father was embittered. His Catholic piety became bigotry. Theodore learned early in his life to distrust religion.

What is more, against the fanatic, narrow ranting of his father, Theodore could contrast the sweet, tolerant, resigned benevolence of a mother he loved and cherished all her life. Like most of the respectable poor she and her brood of ten Dreisers met a great deal of ugliness. They came into contact with the loose, slatternly life of the submerged people who lived opposite roundhouses, above fire-houses, in rows of tawdry coops—and some of the Dreisers found the process contagious.

In this world of greed and strife, however Theodore Dreiser's sustaining interest and passion were an eager sympathy and an intense concern with the living things about him—with stray dogs and cats, and with broken down people, and with flowers and trees living beauty, and with the warmth of his own body and its sexual mysteries.

Out of that profound memory of his Dreiser captures enough of these warm incidents, these scenes that contain the heroism of untutored childhood, these small deaths and these pulsing ecstasies of youth to suffice an ordinary novelist for a half-dozen volumes. The sheer human drama of these incidents seems to wipe out their social pathos. When his family is supported by the "madam" of a house of ill fame, for example, the ignominy of the situation is entirely forgotten in his wide-eyed, lovely interest in the woman, her house, her girls and all the pasty glory of her scene.

The consuming desire for girls, the combination of sickly sentimentalism, introverted agony and forthright lust which make up his passions are quite secondary, I think, to the masterly painting of each romantic incident. The description of his ordeal at a game of "Postmaster," for example, with its feverish rotation from one girl to another, will give readers some of the adolescent pain the actual experience often imparts.

In Sullivan, Ind., in Evansville, in Chicago, working in sloppy restaurants and hardware stores and wherever work was to be found, consuming every aspect of life with a tremendous appetite and a gusto that made him oblivious to most physical hardships, amending his tender, fantastic and ignorant notions of existence as he met hard experience, combining back-alley sexual experiences with his hothouse dreams of romance and retaining through it all the essential nature of a dreamer, a skeptical, pragmatic, but nevertheless persistent dreamer, Dreiser lays the groundwork for the artist he is to become.

I could easily point out to you the ineptitudes of style which mar this book, the references to "pink-meated sirens," the "pegasi" and many other fantastic grammatical conceptions, but that would serve no purpose in considering the value of "Dawn." The book has great power and impressive personality. I pray that Theodore Dreiser may continue and complete his life story with equal effectiveness.

Harry Hansen. "The First Reader." New York *Evening World Telegram,* May 9, 1931.

Theodore Dreiser must have been sitting around one rainy afternoon thinking about the subject that most human beings think about—himself. He must have wondered whether there was anything left about himself that had not been put on paper. And suddenly he recalled that all his autobiographical writing dealt wholly with maturity; that even when adolescence crept into the chronicle, as in "A Book About Myself," it began with his Chicago days, when he first formed an idea of what he wanted to do in life.

And then he called for pen and paper —or perhaps for his secretary—and began to set down the long years that extend from nowhere into somewhere, from birth into boyhood and youth—the magic years which for most of us are a far country which we strive with all our might to leave and which we regret leaving ever after.

"I will not say that this is a true record," writes Dreiser on his very first page. "It must substantiate itself. It is, to the best of my knowledge and belief. . . . I may add, though, that these very sincere impressions and transcriptions are as nearly accurate as memory can guarantee."

And so we get "Dawn," a big, fat autobiographical record of beginnings, of boyhood games and plans, of the vicissitudes of life in a laborer's family, of a boy's interpretation of life and death, of love and ambition and confusion. "Dawn" might have been called "A Middle Western Boyhood," and may well stand as the typical record of the boys of its time. . . .

There never was an autobiography like this. No boyhood was ever described so minutely and so frankly. Some men have told of their boyhood pranks, but always in a spirit of fun. Some have mentioned their bewilderment, their setbacks, but always to demonstrate the beginnings of ambition and courage. But Dreiser tells everything.

He makes no attempt to romanticize the unattractive household in which he grew up. Yet, in spite of his realistic picture, his mother wears a halo. Broken by experience, she toiled and worried, hoping for the best for her brood. What happened to them Theodore makes no bones about. His brother's difficulties, his sisters' amorous misadventures —these are laid frankly before the reader.

When he comes to his own thoughts and experiences he tells everything with the minuteness to which we have long become accustomed. He devotes space to the episode of being kissed by teacher, of playing post office with sh and moody girls, of setting forth to earn a living, of weeding onions at fifty cents a day, of washing dishes in a Greek restaurant in Chicago, of reading books, of meeting girls in an indifferent way, of putting in a year at the State University of Indiana, of finally becoming a collector and trying to hold out money with the idea of repaying it in small amounts —and of being found out and getting completely cured of living beyond his means. An honest record, uncolored and unashamed. . . .

Burton Rascoe. "Dreiser's Early Youth." New York *Sun*, May 9, 1931.

This autobiography of Dreiser's early youth is comparable in many ways to Rousseau's "Confessions." In their youth Rousseau and Dreiser were temperamentally alike. Both were sensual and passionate, yet frustrated, awkward and diffident.

Both of them were plagued by desire and yet were burdened with an overwhelming sense of failure because of their scruples and their fright in the presence of girls and women. For a long time they both remained virginal and prurient; and they experienced the ecstasies of an ideal, unattainable love together with release in crude and obtuse carnalities. They were both brought up in poverty, dependent and living on charity, and they yearned for luxuries and an opportunity to shine in the world. They both had a horror of injustice and an excruciating sense of the inequalities existing in organized society.

Rousseau imagined that he was unique—"I am not made like any one else I have been acquainted with, perhaps like no one in existence"—whereas he was merely the first one completely articulate and profoundly concerned with the nature of his own soul. Dreiser, as a child, was uncomfortably fearful that he alone was "sinful" or "depraved" and his early life was a long and painful experience in teaching him that he was not; his book is a protracted outcry against the bugaboos that haunted his conscience and kept him perturbed, ineffectual, and miserably lacking in courage and self-assurance.

Rousseau, when he started to lay bare his heart, wrote: "Whenever the last trumpet shall sound, I will present myself before the Sovereign Judge with this book in my hand and say aloud, Thus have I acted; these were my thoughts; such was I."

Dreiser says: "I will not say that this is a true record. It must substantiate itself. It is—as they say in law—to the best of my knowledge and belief. I may add, though, that these very sincere impressions and transcriptions are as nearly accurate as memory can guarantee."

After reading Rousseau's "Confessions" and Dreiser's "Dawn" it is impossible not to believe in the honesty and sincerity of their records. They have neither belittled nor exalted themselves: Rousseau's frankness is touching; Dreiser's humility is profound.

Both of them were brought up in an atmosphere of religious piety, and both of them by writing their confessions have attempted to exorcise, consciously or unconsciously, a deep sense of guilt, hanging over from their childhood and adolescence. Indeed, it would appear that we owe the "Confessions" of Rousseau largely to the furies of conscience he bore for so many years because of the beastly trick he played upon the young servant, Marion, whom he accused of stealing a piece of ribbon which he himself had stolen and thus brought about her disgrace and dismissal. We owe "Dawn" to Dreiser's sense of the wonder, mystery, beauty, terror and tragedy of life; but also, perhaps, to his having once been caught embezzling $25 of the funds he collected for an installment house.

Rousseau had his Monsieur de Pontverre, the vicar ("a bigot, who knew no virtue except worshipping images and telling his beads; in a word, a kind of missionary, who thought the height of merit consisted in writing libels against the ministers of Geneva"); and Dreiser had his dogmatic little Bavarian priest who was unfeelingly officious and callous at the death of Dreiser's mother. And these unfortunate brushes with poor representatives of the Catholic Church soured both men unreasonably against the church itself—indeed, helping to make Dreiser (who blames his father's religious mania and idle resignation for most of the family troubles) a fanatical antireligionist.

Rousseau had his unapproachable Beatrice and so had Dreiser (one of the finest and most sympathetic stories of an ideally sentimental attachment is Dreiser's account of his experience in the worship of domnei); and both had their slavies who represented to them profane love. Acutely sensitive to personal slights, indignities, and the handicaps of their poverty and dependence, both men developed adamantine characters which were highly individual, and which carried them relentlessly, stubbornly, uncompromisingly to their high destiny. For good or ill they are pathmakers in literature and they have contributed classics to the language.

Dreiser was one of thirteen children, three of whom died before he was born, whose father was a German Catholic, born in Mayen, fifteen miles from Coblentz, and whose mother was the daughter of a prosperous farmer of the Dunkard or Mennonite faith. Dreiser's father, a weaver by trade, had met the farmer's daughter while working his way from New York to Dayton and after a brief courtship they were married.

Dreiser's tribute to his mother for her tolerance, courage, spirit and love of her children is an eloquent and affecting one, recurring throughout the book. In poverty and disgrace, in sorrow and misery, she somehow kept her family together by superhuman labor, and all of the children, especially the boys, were dependent upon her spiritually and materially. They leaned upon her; she was in a way their hold upon life; they all felt disintegrated and dispersed when she died. Theodore was inconsolable and he faced life without her in greater terror and bewilderment than ever.

In writing this autobiography Dreiser, it would seem, is driven by a compulsion outside himself. He is compelled to set everything down frankly and humbly. He says: "I can feel sorry for him who is so fearful of life and so poorly grounded in an understanding of things that he is terrorized lest some one discover that his uncle was a horse thief or his sister a prostitute or his father a bank wrecker, but I cannot sympathize with his point of view. What has that to do with me? an individual has the right to ask himself. And if he has sufficient consciousness of individuality, it has nothing to do with him. If he is overinfluenced by conditions in which he finds himself, at birth or later, then, of course, they have a great deal to do with him, though it does not follow that they are a cause for shame."

He has spared his sisters public embarrassment by giving them fictitious names and rearranging their chronology, but in portraying them and his brothers he has been as analytical and truthful as with himself. One of the few things in all of Dreiser's work that I had found unconvincing was the seduction of Jenny Gerhardt. Hereafter I shall be less skeptical; for it appears that one of Dreiser's sisters was seduced in precisely that manner. Dreiser's sisters have unburdened their souls to him.

"Dawn" carries Dreiser through his childhood and early youth. It is a record of his associations with people, the trials of his family, the beginnings of his thirst for knowledge and beauty and understanding, his reading and his studies, his odd jobs and his sentimental and sexual yearnings. It is a great book, a memorable and valuable one, destined I believe to become a classic of self-revelation. It has its pages of extremely bad writing; Dreiser's style is often as uncouth as Balzac's and as powerful.

Dreiser reaches no conclusions, except confused and contradictory ones. He recalls for what they are worth certain premonitions others claimed to have had; and he seems to be haunted vaguely by some intimations of a supernatural force, even when he can designate it no more fully than by capitalizing the "N" in Nature. He writes: 'Nature, either necessarily or because spiritually it desires it (and I think the former is the case) is seeking an equation between extremes which would otherwise clash in enormous contests for dominance, the one to the exclusion of the other through aeons of time."

But Dreiser's philosophical speculations are irrelevant to his contribution to life and literature in this book. Here, again, a man, as once did Rousseau, dares to assert the integrity of the soul by displaying it undraped in awful dignity and in humble pride.

Albert Mordell. "Theodore Dreiser Dares to Give Complete Picture." Philadelphia *Record*, May 9, 1931.

"Dawn," the autobiography of Theodore Dreiser's early youth sets down everything that the average writer refuses to tell.

Dreiser is aware of what he is doing and plausibly sets forth his reasons for writing as he does.

He does not hesitate to narrate the struggles of adolescence, and the mental agony connected therewith—because of absurd systems of education and reticence. He is hindered by no filial ties from criticising his bigoted but honest father; he reveals the fact that his sisters followed their own emotions, one of them, for example, eloping with a married man; he tells how his famous brother, Paul, the author of "The Banks of the Wabash," had been in jail, how another brother was a drunkard, how he himself had, while working embezzled, though with honest intentions, twenty-five dollars.

But the reader must not jump to hasty conclusions. For, after all, these episodes do not make up the main body of the book. There is no finer tribute and love in literature than Dreiser's story of his grief-harassed mother. I can think of no work that gives a better picture of the troubles of a poor American family, with their poverty, conflicts, quarrels. There is no hypocrisy, no evading of facts or conclusions.

The volume covers nearly six hundred closely-printed pages and deals with Dreiser's life up to the age of nineteen, that is, up to the year 1890.

There are accounts of characters and personages typical of American life with whom he came into contact. The book is simply (perhaps painfully) fascinating. One wishes it longer and reads breathlessly.

It touches us all, for it records episodes common to the human race. It is a document that should interest educators and should be put into the hands of youths. For the first time in America, we have a life story that is honest, truthful and beautiful without effort to draw absurd conventional lessons. One does not have to agree with the author's conclusions, nor accept his moral standpoint, but one never gets tired of looking at the picture. Incidentally, we learn the springs from which emanated his great novels. . . .

No author that I know has displayed such a powerful memory of the incidents of his youth or shown such genius for observation. No author has revealed the soul of the child so well unless it be Dickens or Mark Twain.

This volume is exceptionally well written. Do not be fooled by those academic critics who tell you that Dreiser cannot write. The style is clear and simple and at times poetic. What though a grammatical error slips in occasionally like the expression "like he did."

"Dawn" is the first volume of a four-volume autobiography to be called a "History of Myself." As a matter of fact the second volume appeared a few years ago, dealing with his newspaper days from the age of nineteen to twenty-three under the title "A Book About Myself." There are two more volumes to appear dealing with the author's literary life.

It is this reviewer's conviction that it is eventually for his autobiographical writing that Dreiser will be known to posterity . . .

In "Dawn" we have the atmosphere of American life in Indiana and Illinois in the eighties; we have the author's frank confession that his interest in girls absorbed him intensely. We get the evolution of his philosophy that man in his moral conduct cannot go against the chemical dictates of his blood, even in response to reason, a conclusion that has, of course, some truth in it, but not as much as Dreiser thinks.

We learn the sources of his occasionally superstitious learnings; these he inherited from his mother (a superstition survives a religion). We see the secret springs of his greatness as a novelist, for he draws no line between art and life; read the poignant account of his mother's death.

The greatest compliment is due the author because he makes the reader forget whether he is really seeing life or reading literature, for here they both merge.

The book should rank with the few great American biographies, "The Education of Henry Adams"; it is superior to the recent autobiography of Lincoln Steffens, though that is a work of a different brand.

Florence Haxton Britten. "When He Was Very Young." New York *Herald Tribune Books,* May 10, 1931, pp. 1-2.

. . . From a literary point of view "Dawn" reveals little about Dreiser

hat his novels have not already in-
licated. Here is a spacious mind, rich
ınd full, and as badly organized as life
tself. Even in his novels he is a reporter
ather than a novelist, with an intense
ınd insatiable interest in the living organisms that surround him. He is too
vise to try to impose upon life a mean-
ng which it has not, but he is not wise
enough to select and subdue his overa-
bundant materials. He must tell us all
hat he knows; must offer us as nearly as
possible literal vicarious experience. In
'Dawn," rather more legitimately, per-
aps, he consents to be a victim of that
ame copiousness that hampers him in
is novels. The autobiography, engross-
ng as it is for the most part, is too liber-
lly upholstered with brief character
ketches—of this playmate who met his
leath in the electric chair or that one
vho died of lockjaw. The vignette is
nost distinctly not Mr. Dreiser's me-
ier; his talent is for the exhaustive
lelineation of character. And he is, in
his volume, most interesting, of course,
vhen he is tirelessly reporting himself.

And how badly he can write! And
ow permanently naïve and humorless
e is. "Dawn" is full of commonplace
ınd vulgar phrases, pointless often: "As
ısual, my tongue began to swell—
wole, swill—which is it?" And these in-
erlarded incessantly with extrava-
antly pretentious writing, with apost-
ophes to the morning, to youth, to
ove, followed by glowing descriptions
f the "meaty" charms of innumerable
vomen. In his frank, almost gro-
esquely uninhibited account of his sex
ife Dreiser has spared neither himself
or his readers.

Yet in "Dawn," as in "Sister Carrie,"
Jennie Gerhardt," "An American
'ragedy" et al., Dreiser is like a robust
ousewife from whose perpetually dis-
rdered kitchen most bounteously satisfying meals emerge. And I for one
should hesitate to exchange the rich
stews of Dreiser with their ungainly
hunks of meat and vegetables and their
other less satisfying ingredients for any
neater literary pastry.

Peter Monro Jack. "Dreiser's Confession of His Early Years." New York *Times Book Review*, May 10, 1931, p. 5.

A considerable part of Mr. Dreiser's maturer years is being dedicated to a chronicle of his life, probably the most minute and circumstantial reassembling of experience ever carried on outside a law court. The decade will presently be brought to its knees by the prodigious burden of this autobiography: "Dawn" is but a beginning, a trifle of a quarter of a million words barely bringing the author out of his 'teens. In preparation are "A Literary Apprenticeship" and "Literary Experiences." Connecting these two with the present volume is "Newspaper Days," presumably a new title for "A Book About Myself," a book in itself, so exhaustive that many vaguely think of it as a life of Dreiser; in fact, it covers four years out of his three-score. If we add the personal material in "A Hoosier Holiday," "A Traveler at Forty" and the rest, and the critical volumes in praise and vituperation, we shall have a library reserve in memory of Theodore Dreiser that only the very hardened reader will survive. In all this we need expect no evasion or ambiguity, no gleanings for research students of the future. We have come to believe, through many ardors and endurances, in the complete integrity of this author. Nor can it ever be said that Stuart Sherman, for instance, has told the worst about Dreiser. Mr. Dreiser will do that himself.

All this was to be predicted. It is right and logical and entirely welcome. His work begins and ends in his unvarying self. Its true import, whether it take the appearance of Sister Carrie or Frank Cowperwood or Eugene Witla, is autobiographical, not dramatic. Indeed, a man with his distaste for ideas, spoiled for religion and unfitted for philosophy, skeptical of social and political theory, unconsoled by the promise of science, is inevitably thrown back on the empirical fact of the individual; his only complete emotional satisfaction is the presentation of his experiences as authentically, as exhaustively, as "sincerely" as it is possible to do. Whatever unity there may be is the unity of self, and this naturalistic history of the ego is the only kind of achievement, one fancies, that Mr. Dreiser would care thoroughly to commit himself to.

The irresistible play of personality, in its uniqueness and continuity, is the theme of his book. By implication and extension it is also a chapter in the American Middle West chronicle, but this we must accept with considerable caution: Mr. Dreiser's youthful eyes see just as much and as little as the bewildered state of his youthful mentality allowed him. His father, who had left Germany in 1844 to escape conscription, settled in Indiana as a weaver, and is chiefly interesting for the unfortunate effect that his religious intolerance had upon Theodore. The son became equally intolerant on the other side, and his scorn of religious faith has left many pages of his books peevish and ill-natured reading, illiberally scattered with "Bunk. Lord! Tush! Tra la! Tra la!" &c. But the father is characterized generally with the objectivity of one who is aloof; it is the mother's personality that is subjectively felt as a deep affection that softens these early recollections with tenderness. Scenes are made memorable and words become tractable and tuneful in a simple kind of prose (how admirable a writer might this author have been!) when his sentiment is touched and quickened by the memory of this lady, evidently brave and understanding, and with a remote suggestion of "orchard and meadow and great fields of grain." Indeed, she is the only person to bring distinction to the book, the distinction of unaffected and disinterested feeling. A chapter which will remain in the minds of many readers is that describing the childish figures of Theo and Ed trudging to their impossibly arduous task of hoeing onion patches in a blazing sun, coming to a close in the homeward journey in a scene that rivals the style and sensibility of the early chapters of Sherwood Anderson's autobiography. Without this tenderness Jennie Gerhardt would never have been created.

The goings-on of the large family are faithfully recorded—that is, as far as young Theodore knew of their goings-on—but perhaps a shade too seriously; the reader at least may be forgiven for taking them less seriously. It was a family of "a peculiarly nebulous, emotional, unorganized and traditionless character," moving from place to place, so that quite possibly no two children were born in the same house, always with rather less money than is comfortable, too often thwarted, repressed and irritable, intermittently fired with new promise of prosperity, but in the end inadequate, as a family, to rise above its own disintegrating individualism. With this shifting environment and in this somewhat shiftless family Theodore Dreiser grew up, without apparent discipline, inadequately educated in the Catholic parochial schools, peculiarly inefficient in the things that boys commonly do, a "dreamy, moony youth," whose dreams were early preoccupied by sex and financial success—the former arising out of a morbid condition, the latter clearly the effect of family difficulties. These two aspirations dominate his early life.

Dreiser is honest with these early years and one can be honest with him. It does not appear that he has added anything, in spite of his candidness, to the physiology of passion. He indulges himself in the recollections of his adolescent obsession with sex, with the pleasures of reminiscence all on his side. Vulgarity and sensitiveness mingle in these descriptions, mawkishness, triviality, eroticism and the ordinary blameless youthful stupidity, and with no particular illumination. The reader is not taking refuge in any dogmatism about reticence in literature; he feels very plainly for himself that the repetition of these scenes and sentiments is tiresome. Acute analysis loses its sharpness in weak and aimless rhapsody; a constant gibing at moralists and scientists settles no problems of morality and biology. And the Myrtles, the Mays and the Mauds soon become indistinguishable, mechanically coalescing into a baroque abstract of "full pink lips" and "swimming eyes," and plump and sensual flesh, like some swirling ceiling by Rubens seen mistily through eyes dazed by too much reading. No one could forgive an autobiographer who ignored this essential part of adolescence; it is simply to be regretted that Mr. Dreiser has written inexactly and inexpertly about a matter in which he is an acknowledged expert.

The narrative moves slowly and corrosively through these sex adventures and his financial misadventures. It is astonishing how many jobs he got and lost. He was a veritable spendthrift of golden opportunities to get on. In rapid succession he was dishwasher in a Greek restaurant, stove-cleaner in a hardware shop, scene-painter's assistant (till he got fired for his garrulity), a small boy in a hardware shop again, railroad clerk, undergraduate in the University of Indiana, real estate clerk, laundry driver, and finally a collector of instalment payments; this ends the last job, and the book, and "with this, as I have always thought, ended my true youth."

This book should be read, and read rapidly, at a single sitting, even the 600 pages. Then one is caught with the animal vigor of the book, the gusto, the insatiable curiosity that races, often stumbling, perhaps, but recovering, through the pages; nor is the tenderness and wistfulness of youth wanting. At a venture one would say that the autobiography will not be as sound a book as "Twelve Men" or as jovial as "A Hoosier Holiday." But in its own way it is a prodigy in confessional narrative, unsurpassed in scope, and quite honestly unabashed at its own revelations. If it fails to elucidate its experience in terms that might reasonably be construed as a broad and responsible philosophy of life, that is because Mr. Dreiser succeeds faithfully in presenting himself. Ultimately one feels that the failure will be acknowledged as a defect, just as we see at the moment that the manner of writing is too often a defect; but a phenomenal book like this will have to rest on its own phenomena. One should add that Horace Liveright has not been the least perturbed in bringing forth this gargantuan volume: it is incredibly light, compact and beautifully printed.

D. W. "Dawn." *Outlook & Independent,* 158 (May 27, 1931), 120.

This is not an autobiography for those who recoil at honesty nor for those who want the facts of life crammed into a nutshell. Employing 300,000 words to bring himself through the miserable valleys of childhood, adolescence and later teens, Mr. Dreiser has neither pussyfooted nor sidestepped. This portion of his projected "History of Myself" might be called a confession of youth; if so it is a confession without apologies or ridicule. Writing with probing power which enhances his remarkable tenderness, Mr. Dreiser not only reveals his own yearning struggle toward daybreak but all that touched it in the haphazard progress through that tatterdemalion realm which was his and his family's in Chicago and other mid-western towns. If this book has it right—and if not, no book ever did—the Theodore of the eighties and nineties was dominated by three forces. There was the oppressiveness of Catholicism, almost the sole heritage from his father ("a narrow, hidebound religionist" who stands in the background, a novel himself) there was the absorbing, terrifying pul of sex, at work on an underprivileged timid, frightened youth, and there was first, last and always, his mother, Dreiser's idol now as yesterday, and well deservedly so. These, as the youth himself may be drawn together loosely but it i questionable that the book loses muc thereby. It does lose, however, by awkwardness running into barbarisms, b too much corner-store philosophy, b too frequent raising of obvious questions. In these respects—probably minor when the book is taken as a whol —*Dawn* cries for scissors and blue-pencils. Yet it is doubtful that any one coul use them to advantage.

Dorothy Parker "Reading and Writing: *Words, Words Words.*" *New Yorker,* 7 (May 30, 1931), 69–72.

There are times when images blow t fluff, and comparisons stiffen an shrivel. Such an occasion is surely a hand when one is confronted by Dreiser's latest museum piece, "Dawn." One can but revise a none-too-hot dialectic of childhood; ask, in rhetorica agressiveness, "What writes worse tha a Theodore Drieser?;" loudly crow th answer, "*Two* Theodore Dreisers"; and according to temperament, rejoice a the merciful absurdity of the conception, or shudder away from the thought

The reading of "Dawn" is a strai upon many parts, but the worst wea and tear fall on the forearms. Afte olding the massive volume for the alf-day necessary to its perusal (well, ook at that, would you? "Massive volme" and "perusal," one right after the ther! You see how contagious Mr. D.'s nanner is?) my arms ached with a slow, nean persistence beyond the services f aspirin or of liniment. I must file this istress, I suppose, under the head of Occupational Diseases"; for I could ot honestly chalk up such a result gainst "Pleasure" or even "Improvenent." And I can't truly feel that Dawn" was worth it. If I must have ches, I had rather gain them in the first ennis of the season, and get my back nto it.

This present Dreiser book is the reord of its author's first twenty years. It equires five hundred and eighty-nine ng, wide, and closely printed pages. Nearly six hundred sheets to the title of Dawn;" God help us one and all if Mr. Dreiser ever elects to write anything alled "June Twenty-First"!

The actual account of the writer's arly life, and of the lives of his mother, is father, and his nine brothers and siss which colored and crossed it, is holly absorbing; but, if I may say so, ithout that lightning bolt coming arging in the window, what honest seting-down of anyone's first years would ot be? And Mr. Dreiser had, in addion, the purely literary good fortune to e a child of poverty—for when, in rint, was the shanty not more glamorus than the salon?

Nor should I cavil at the length, and ence the weight, of the book, were it ll given over to memories, since if a an were to write down his rememrances and his impressions up to the ge of five, much less of twenty, six hunred pages could not begin to contain em. But I do fret, through "Dawn," at the great desert patches of Mr. Dreiser's moralizing, I do chafe at such monstrous bad writing as that with which he pads out his tale. I have read reviews of this book, written by those whose days are dedicated to literature. "Of course," each one says airily, "Dreiser writes badly," and thus they dismiss that tiny fact, and go off into their waltz-dream. This book, they cry, ranks well beside the "Confessions" of Rousseau; and I, diverted, as is ever the layman, by any plump red herring, mutter, "Oh, Rousseau, my eye," and am preoccupied with that.

But on second thinking, I dare to differ more specifically from the booksie-wooksies. It is of not such small importance to me that Theodore Dreiser writes in so abominable a style. He is regarded, and I wish you could gainsay me, as one of our first contemporary authors; it is the first job of a writer who demands rating among the great, or even among the good, to write well. If he fails that, as Mr. Dreiser, by any standard, so widely muffs it, he is, I think, unequipped to stand among the big.

For years, you see, I have been crouching in corners hissing small and ladylike anathema of Theodore Dreiser. I dared not yip it out loud, much less offer it up in print. But now, what with a series of events that have made me callous to anything that may later occur, I have become locally known as the What-the-Hell Girl of 1931. In that, my character, I may say that to me Dreiser is a dull, pompous, dated, and darned near ridiculous writer. All right. Go on and bring on your lightning bolts.

Of the earlier Dreiser, the author of "Sister Carrie" and "Jennie Gerhardt," the portrayer of Muldoon and of Paul Dresser, in "Twelve Men," you don't think I could be so far gone as to withhold all the reverent praise that is in me, do you? But then I read all those hundreds of thousands of words that made up "An American Tragedy" and, though I hung upon some of them, I later read the newspaper accounts of the Snyder-Gray case, and, still later, of the cornering by a hundred or so of New York's finest of the ninteen-year-old "Shorty" Crowley. And I realized, slowly and sadly, that any reporter writes better and more vividly than the man who has been proclaimed the great reporter. It is a quite fair comparison. Mr. Dreiser, with the Chester Gillette case, had a great story; the unnamed men of the daily and the evening papers with the tales of the unhappy Ruth Snyder and the bewildered Judd Gray, and the little Crowley boy who never had a prayer—they had fine stories, too. But they would have lost their jobs, had they written too much.

The booksy ones, with that butterfly touch of theirs, flutter away from Dreiser's bad writing and but brush their wings over the admission that he possesses no humor. Now I know that the term "sense of humor" is dangerous (there's a novel idea!) and that humor is snooted upon, in a dignified manner, by the lofty-minded. Thus Professor Paul Elmer More raises a thin and querulous pipe in his essay on Longfellow—I think it is—to say that there were those who claimed that Longfellow had no humor —of whom I am the first ten. All right, suppose he hadn't, he says, in effect; humor may be all very well for those that like it ("Only fools care to see," said the blind man) but there's no good making a fetich of it. I wouldn't for the world go around making fetiches; yet I am unable to feel that a writer can be complete without humor. And I don't mean by that, and you know it perfectly well, th creation or the appreciation of thing comic. I mean that the possession of sense of humor entails the sense of se lection, the civilized fear of going to far. A little humor leavens the lump surely, but it does more than that. keeps you, from your respect for th humor of others, from making a du jackass of yourself. Humor, imagina tion, and manners are pretty fairly in terchangeably interwoven.

Mr. Theodore Dreiser has no humo

I know that Mr. Dreiser is sincere, o rather I have been told it enough t impress me. So, I am assured, is Mr Kathleen Norris sincere; so, I am in formed, is Mr. Zane Grey sincere; so, am convinced, was Mr. Horatio Alger- whose work, to me, that of Mr. Dreiser nearest approximates—sincere. But will not—oh, come on with your ligh ning again!—admit that sincerity is th only thing. A good thing, a high thin an admirable thing; but not the on thing in letters.

The thing that most distressed me i "Dawn" was the philosophising of i author. His is a sort of pre-war bitte ness, a sort of road-company anger conditions. Once does Mr. Dreise quote a youthful sister: "When me proposed marriage, I found I didn't lik them well enough to marry them, bu when they told me I was beautiful an wanted to give me things and take m places, it was a different matter. When I liked a man, it was easy enough to g with him—it was fun—there wasn really anything wrong with it that could see. Aside from the social schem as people seem to want it, I don't eve now see that it was."

On this the author comments: "A this point I am sure any self-respectin moralist will close this book once an

r all!" But, you know, I must differ. I
on't think that's enough to warrant the
losing of a book by even the most self-
especting of moralists. I think that Mr.
reiser believes that the world is back-
ard, hypocritical, and mean, and so, I
uppose, it is; but times have changed
nd Mr. D. is not now the only ad-
anced one. I think the self-respecting
oralists are much less apt to close the
ook "at this point" than are those that
et a bit squeamish over the authen-
city of a woman who says "Aside from
he social scheme as people seem to
ant it—"

Early in this little dandy, you saw that
had been affected by the Dreiser style.
hat, maybe, is responsible for this ple-
hora of words. I could have checked all
his torrent, and given you a true idea
f Theodore Dreiser's "Dawn" had I
ut succumbed to the influence of the
resent-day Nash and the sweeter-day
entley, and had written:

> Theodore Dreiser
> Should ought to write nicer.

dwin Clark. 'Self-Revelations." *ale Review,* 20 June 1931), 57–858.

. . Dreiser writes here in the manner
f his best naturalistic novels. Without
eticence, but with sombre dignity, he
as produced a book the like of which
as not been seen since Rousseau's
Confessions." A compelling force
eems to have driven him to set down
his revelation of his youth, for he says: "I can feel sorry for him who is so fearful of life and so poorly grounded in an understanding of things that he is terrorized lest some one discover that his uncle was a horse thief or his sister a prostitute or his father a bank wrecker, but I cannot sympathize with his point of view. What has that to do with me? an individual has the right to ask himself. And if he has sufficient consciousness of individuality, it has nothing to do with him."

In this spirit of honesty the history of the whole Dreiser family of ten children, an affectionate and courageous mother, and a fanatic father is recorded in travail. For the Dreiser family, for all their moving, lived on the wrong side of the railroad track and were mired in poverty. The father was a broken man. It was the mother who held the family together, and to whom the children turned with their troubles. To the youthful Theodore, life was full of terror. A timid, shy, diffident boy, he groped his way. Sex and the Catholic church remained maladjusted elements in his life. His sensitivity brought him endless hurts. With all that, he responded to life with gusto—he felt the humble beauty of the Midland, and Chicago he found "a compound of hope and joy in existence."

"Dawn" is a Midland record—a detailed portrayal of a boy growing up with the country. It is colored with the blurred emotions of the "moony" boy Dreiser was, with his urge to understand life, his hankering for beauty, his discovery of books, and his employment with odd jobs. His conclusions, such as they are, are confused and contradictory. In his bitter dislike for the dictatorial German priests, whom he regards as the church, there is nothing more than a mistaking of poor servants for the whole church. His autobiography has the great merit and lapses of his best novels. It has deep feeling, power, and compassionate concern with life and the under-dog. It has pages of moving prose and awkward prose and pages of absurd apostrophes to some little girl whose rosy cheeks and bright eyes held him in awe and enchantment.

Henry Hazlitt. "Another Book About Himself." *Nation,* 132 (June 3, 1931), 613–614.

Surely since the beginning of time no writer has been more impervious to criticism, for good or for ill, than this Theodore Dreiser. In spite of his final popularity his work has never lost any of the merits with which it began, nor, in spite of mountains of adverse and friendly criticism, any of the faults. His style, the despair of all right-thinking people, grows, if anything, worse with each book. In all the 589 pages that make up this autobiography of his early youth, there is not one that will not irritate a reader who has any respect for the common decencies of prose. What an array of verbless, battered, broken-backed sentences! He writes hardly a paragraph that is not stuffed with such amateurish asides to the reader as "you may be sure," or "if you please," or "as you may well guess." He is vague where he ought to be precise and pedantically precise where precision is pointless. He seems to have only the haziest ideas about the meanings of words. He tells us that he was "*literally* blazing physically." He describes masturbation a "this *exotic* practice." His phrases are sometimes downright illiterate: "Hi work was plainly like he was." Often what ought to be simple narrative sentences are so equivocal that one actually cannot tell what he means. Apologists for Dreiser's writing have told u that the man is too passionately in earnest to be bothered with the mere embroidery of style, too concerned with his message to care whether or not he delivers it gracefully. But such an explanation will hardly do. For Dreiser frequently strains for the purple passage—usually of the Ingersoll school (see the paragraph on page 49, for example, beginning: "Come now, let us erect to youth an altar, and against the sapphire sea of time set the scarlet flame of memory!"). He is continually trapped by the pretentious cliché, lured by the falsely elegant. A writer merely unconscious o style does not describe a man as being "frizzled as to his gray hair" or write that a family "laughed and talked and jested betimes with whomsoever would have to do with them." Closely allied to all this is his constant pseudo-scientific jargon. As a child he is afraid to go into the dark woods. "Tell me, oh, physicist and chemists," he apostrophizes, "why so great a fear, so rolling a sensitivity, in a physical chemism four or five years o age?" As a youth, in the presence of a prostitute he finds himself "ecstasized sensorially." And this is what happens when he returns after his first few months at college:

> Approaching Chicago and my own home, I experienced, for the first time in my life, I think, a sense of change in myself—something more toward individuality—the intense centripetal integrality of the same—as opposed to what hitherto migh

> have been looked upon as a merged or group feeling—integrality with the other members of my family and home—my mother, of course, the central centripetal star of the same and one not to be affected, let alone reduced or modified in any way.

One can explain why such a sentence is appalling, but surely not by saying that Dreiser is too unpretentious, too concerned with bald simplicity or common straightforwardness, to trouble about anything so fancy or unimportant as style.

Nearly all critics have regretted Dreiser's prolixity. In the present book the prolixity grows almost fabulous. There are nearly 300,000 words, the equivalent of four or five novels of ordinary size, and they carry his projected autobiography only up to his nineteenth or twentieth year. But Dreiser has carried this vice to so great a length that it becomes one of his outstanding merits. Say what you will, our experiences impress us and remain with us, other things being equal, in proportion to their duration, and no one who has read this book through is likely soon to forget it. In its mere prolixity lies much of its remarkably convincing quality. It is crowded with pointless and irrelevant details and episodes; but so is life. It is enormously repetitious; but so is life. It makes a hundred false starts; again and again we are told of an experience, or of the expectation of an experience, that seems about to lead somewhere, but that in fact leads nowhere—as in life. In his recital Dreiser seems to use no principle of selection whatever. And neither does life. Seeing everything on all sides, and again and again, as the author saw it, the reader comes to feel that he has almost lived through this career himself.

But with this Dreiser has other and less dubious virtues which have always given his work its real distinction—an astonishing memory, amazing eyes for details, for character, and for physical scenes, an immense curiosity and awareness regarding all things of common interest, a profound sense of the wonder and mystery of life. As a boy he seemed to have a "life-hunger" that swallowed everything with indiscriminate greediness. "Would that I were able to suggest in prose," he writes at one point, "the throb and urge and sting of my first days in Chicago." But he does just that. He leaves us a memorable picture of the Chicago of those days, with its streets and sidewalks built up from four to six feet above the land level, the dirty, narrow, and traffic-laden Chicago River, the rats overrunning the city, the slums worthy of the art of a Hogarth, and everything, apparently, "a source of wonder and delight" to him.

To crown all, there is Dreiser's intense sincerity and unparalleled candor, surely the greatest single merit that any autobiographer can have. And in that merit he is comparable to Pepys, Rousseau, and Boswell; certainly his confessions ring truer than Rousseau's. I do not believe he ever attributes any motives to himself loftier than those he actually had, or attempts to make any situation more glamorous than it really was. What we see is a moony boy, not over-fond of work, full of vague day dreams, with no practical or definite aim in life, brought up in depressing poverty, given a hopelessly inadequate formal education, first at various Catholic schools whenever his parents could afford to pay for it, then at public school; later drifting from job to job—newsboy, dish-washer in a filthy Greek restaurant, stove polisher, helper in a large hardware establishment; finally taken out of all this for a year by a Miss Simpson, one of his former public-school teachers who seemed to detect possibilities in him and paid his expenses to the State university; then drifting through various jobs again—real-estate helper, laundry-wagon driver, and instalment collector, a job from which he was dismissed for holding back $25. And always, even as a boy, his great preoccupation, his great obsession, was sex. "The hot fire nature had lighted in my body . . . harried me from hell to hell." For his passion was constantly thwarted—by poverty, by a conviction that his appearance was shabby and unimpressive, by a fixed belief that he had made himself impotent by self-abuse, and by an almost incredible awkwardness, bashfulness, and mental and lingual paralysis in the presence of women and girls.

If Dreiser does not spare himself, neither does he spare anyone else. Few autobiographers, surely, have treated their immediate family as he has. He pictures it as "peculiarly nebulous, emotional, unorganized, and traditionless." His father is everywhere made to appear as a pietistic and conventionally moral Catholic bigot. He tells how his brother Paul, the song-writer, forged a check in his father's name, was suspected of robbing a store, was thrown into jail twice, and later lived with a woman who kept a house of prostitution. He tells of his brother Rome's constant drunkenness, disappearances, and vandalism. To be sure, he changes the names of his sisters, but he tells of the promiscuity of one or two of them, and of how Amy brought disgrace on the family when it lived in a small town by becoming pregnant. Only his mother comes out consistently well by the ordinary moral standards. When he men
tions his own sexual adventures or thos
of others, he almost invariably mention
the real name (so far as the reader ca
make out) of the girl involved, togethe
with her town, her neighborhood, c
the business firm for which she worked
Many of these women are now presum
ably the mothers of grown families: le
us sincerely hope that none of their hu
bands, children, friends, or enemie
chance to read this book. The conver
tional morality which Dreiser so muc
despises calls the man who does this sor
of thing a cad or a bounder; but we mus
remember that in autobiography o
reminiscence the vices of the man ar
the virtues of the writer. It is this unpar
alleled candor, perhaps more than any
thing else, that will keep this book aliv

Dreiser's curiously crude and naiv
philosophy remains as unmodified as hi
style. He cannot help stopping ever
once in a while for a bitter denunciatio
of the Catholic church. He is constantl
deriding "morality," but his own nc
tions on the subject are in the highes
degree vague and superficial. Ethics h
describes as "purely minor group ar
rangements having no relationship t
the larger movements and positive an
dominating forces of the universe." I
by the "larger movements" he is alluc
ing to such things as the orbit of Halley
comet, he is, one can only suppose, cor
rect: but ethics might still have som
slight importance for mankind. At ar
other point his condemnations becom
more sweeping, involving, indeed, th
whole "visible scheme of things.
"What," he shouts, "cooking, eating
coition, job holding, growing, aging, los
ing, winning, in so changeful and pass
ing a scene as this, important? Bunk!
But he does not seem to have trouble
to ask himself, Important to whom? Nc

ɔ that distant cloud of suns called the Ailky Way, perhaps; but reasonably so ɔ ourselves. One is tempted to inquire xactly what Dreiser's definition of importance is. What determines importance? Who confers importance? But ve need not enter upon these metaphysical subtleties, for Dreiser's own uge works of fiction and autobiography are sufficient evidence that he himelf regards even the pettiest details of fe as of immense importance, else he ould not have gone to such pains to ecord them. By "morality," moreover, ne soon discovers, Dreiser means exctly what the man in the street means —conventional (usually Victorian) *sexal* morality. He excuses all sex lapses, o matter what their results, and many hortcomings of other kinds, on the round that men and women are poor, responsible "chemisms." But he is ardly more consistent here than elsewhere, for on his last page he admits hat in the individual's conduct the inerests of "organized society" may ometimes have to be considered, and e speaks of the 50 per cent profit of his nstalment-company boss, and of a petty little beast" of a Catholic priest, n terms that sound to me strangely like hose of moral indignation.

Yet the final marvel, of course, is not hat there is still so much that is crude nd callow in Dreiser, but that, in the eeth of the early environment he pictures here, he managed to survive with he astonishing qualities he has. "I must ave been a very deceptive person," he rites at one point, "seemingly mild, imless, indifferent, dreamy—particuarly in regard to trivial things and maters—whereas in reality, in regard to ny own deepest currents and interests, t least, I could be adamant." And in his Gibraltar-like quality lies the main secret of the stature that Dreiser has attained among American writers.

Robert Herrick. "Dreiseriana." *Saturday Review of Literature*, 7 (June 6, 1931), 875.

Biography is the "revealing" (scandal) type, and now autobiography has become the popular vehicle for exploitation in a "personality" crazed world. "Dawn," the first instalment of Mr. Dreiser's ponderous life story which has already been well worked over in his various novels, may be, as the publishers say, "truly the most intimate confession of youth since Rousseau." . . .

Taste in such matters is, of course, unarguable, but the naked school of self-confessors should be sure before stripping for the public that they have underneath something to reveal which is significant, interesting, at least has some charm of manner if not of substance. Mere nakedness, male or female, no matter how completely exposed, is not necessarily arresting. Nor should the autobiographer resent it if his public deem the show not worth the making. If he "tells all" about himself and his nearest, he must expect to hear quite plain talk in return, as if he had been long dead.

Mr. Dreiser has always written clumsily, badly, even in his best novels, with a verbosity unparalleled in American letters. His style has not improved with exercise, and in this autobiographical volume is at its worst, abounding in tedious iterations of trivialities, Teutonisms, fumbling phrases, journalistic *clichés*, and what is even worse, sentimentalities and rhetorical flourishes altogether unlooked for in one of his literary creed and experience. Too many sentences end in exclamation or question or with an "Oh" *(ach)?*. Such favorite terms as "chemisms," "religionists," "conventionalists," etc., smack of popular journalism rather than of literature. If style is in any degree the man (as some "conventionalists" still hold) there is much in Mr. Dreiser's personality as revealed autobiographically to offend the fastidious reader.

However, nineteen years of a human life (1871–1890) spent in a variety of small and large mid-western American communities as one of a large and varied German-American family, struggling, or fumbling with existence, on the border line of destitution, offers, one might think, an excellent opportunity to a novelist for portraiture, characterization, delineation of social backgrounds. Yet in spite of his proclaimed freedom in dealing with intimate facts Mr. Dreiser has succeeded in hacking out but one distinct character from the family group of ten brothers and sisters, father and mother. That one, his mother, emerges more by force of repetition than from skill in drawing. Indirectly through the impression this woman made on her son and on her other children, the reader creates for himself a large if somewhat blurred image of generalized traits. Never once throughout her tortured and haggard life is she allowed to speak for herself in convincing accents. Nor any of the brothers and sisters: they are presented through the novelist's woolly analyses. It is hard to distinguish them one from another, impossible to remember them. Hence their frailties of conduct as well as their virtues are insignificant.

The Dreiser family had few human relations outside themselves in their years of wanderings through Terre Haute, Evansville, Chicago, Warsaw, *et al.*, singularly few! in which respect their story may be typical of the American process. That sort of nomad existence, moving from flat to small house, from small town to city and back again as "the job" (or restlessness) dictates, would be incredible on any corresponding scale elsewhere in the world. With the advent of the motor car and bus this squirming, rootless form of existence has enormously increased. The mere record of the Dreiser migrations, of their ephemeral possessions (instalment bought), suggests a melancholy commentary upon our American civilization.

Mr. Dreiser dislikes the Roman Catholic faith in which he was brought up and derides it in terms little more tolerant than the mouthings of the Ku Klux Klan. To the poor education received in parochial schools he attributes much of his lack of adaptability to his early environment and his and his brothers' and sisters' ill success in finding and holding jobs. Yet when chance offered him a year at the state university of Illinois he had little more esteem for education of the purest American breed than for that of the parochial school and ridicules his teachers and what they taught as vigorously as Mencken at his crudest. One concludes that the lamentable maladjustment of the Dreisers to their various environments was more personal than social. Nevertheless, it is as a picture of harassed living, of the endless scramble for a sustaining foothold in existence, that "Dawn" presents a single claim for consideration. The chapters dealing with the author's jobs from real estate agent and driver of a laundry wagon to collector of bills are the most interesting, vivid, and credible in the book.

What as a youth he was really preoccupied with, as he reiterates, was sex and secondarily with economic life as a means of satisfying his sexual desires. "Ah! to have money, good clothes, and a girl!" This perpetual sexual day dream may be more characteristic of puberty than our literature has hitherto admitted, but that most youths are so obsessed with erotic impulses even in our tawdry and spiritually starved society as Dreiser was is unlikely: the majority would end in asylums or prisons. He generalizes about this important element in his life as follows:

> For the second, third, and fourth decades of my life—or from fifteen to thirty-five—there appeared to be a toxic something in form itself—that of the female of the species where beautiful—that could effect veritable paroxysms of emotion and desire in me. . . . The mystery! The subtleties of physics and chemistry behind it! . . . We call it love. A word! Any other label that implies that a chemical formula such as a human temperament, embodied as flesh and displayed as a design, can evoke in another such form emotion and so release and exchange tides of desire and sensual relationship, would do as well. The form of a woman is the best expression of that design or geometric formula, and the word "Aphrodisiac" (Aphrodite) the best expression of the power of that form or formula upon its companion formula, the male.

Mr. Dreiser's "philosophy" is exceedingly simple, like that!

> The mental and physical appetites of man alone explain him. He is, regardless of ideals or dreams or material equipment, an eating, savage animal, and in youth, often in age, his greatest appetite sex. . . . There is no other direct first cause for man. Beyond that to be sure may lie other things—electro-physical forces in endless combinations and varieties—but evoking what more than is seen here and where?

As to man's moral sense he reflects thus (apropos of having stolen twenty-five dollars with which to buy a new overcoat):

> I, for one, did not propose that asserted moral law should interfere with my sharp human instincts, and the only thing to do then was to lie and pretend that I was moral, or at least avoid the subject so that I could not be put on record.

In the realm of politics and social organization Mr. Dreiser is equally naïve:

> What I truly believe is that law and all other governing devices and systems can be so calculated, where careful thought is taken, as to achieve the greatest possible latitude for all, consistent with the greatest possible peace and comfort, and each according to his talents.

A simple millenium!

This is the Dreiser faith. He has no other; he ridicules coarsely, boorishly, in the Mencken style, not merely the Catholic faith, but all religions, moralities, traditions, and conventions of belief (except television), with a singular lack of historical perspective for all the voluminous reading and meditation he calls attention to. Mankind is a "chemism" with a sex urge and many looney illusions about himself. Maybe so. But our younger and more radical realists, among whom Mr. Dreiser has long been the bell-wether, might reflect on reading his story how little they have to offer a perplexed world of charm, beauty, significance, for the despised illusions of the "religionists," "moralists," "conventionalists." Not even truth.

H. K. Ellingson. "Theodore Dreiser." Colorado *Sunday Gazette & Telegraph,* June 14, 1931.

The most talked of book in America today is Theodore Dreiser's recently published autobiography, "Dawn," brought out by Horace Liveright, Inc. This talk ranges from the sensible to the most absurd imaginable. Virtually all that I have heard has been utterly nonsensical. For several years I have been an ardent admirer of Dreiser's genius, having decided when I read "An American Tragedy," late in 1925, that America has not, and never has had, another novelist comparable to this great man. Because of my undisguised admiration a large number of persons who know nothing of Dreiser's work, and who could not understand it if they did, take a kind of childish, not to say moronic, delight in criticizing his writings in my presence, for there are a surprisingly large number of persons who think it is smart to sneer and wisecrack at things that lie outside the tiny circle of their understanding. . . .

America is a little nonplussed by "Dawn," for it isn't often that we are confronted by unvarnished truth in this country, everybody being more or less dedicated to the task of concealing the truth. We hide the truth in regard to the motives behind war; we hide the truth in regard to the prohibition situation; we throw a heavy blanket over the truth in connection with politics and religion; we conceal the truth in regard to our education system, and we damn and belabor men who tell even a small part of the truth about industry. No wonder there is a concerted move on foot to belittle Dreiser. A lot of people now think it is smart to join this move.

Even that magazine of cheap sophistication, the New Yorker, has got into the parade and has printed some asininity about Dreiser, a so-called review of "Dawn." But all this is in line with the policy that until recently kept American art in a primitive stage. In the last few years, because of the efforts of a few fearless men, such as Dreiser, Sherwood Anderson and H. L. Mencken, literature in this country has progressed in spite of national opposition.

McG. Dallas *Morning News,* June 14, 1931.

At one point at least, it is impossible to reconcile Theodore Dreiser's art with his philosophy. I remember that when he was in Dallas a year or so ago he fell to talking of H. G. Wells. "Now, Wells is a funny fellow," he commented. "Always toying with some scheme for bettering the human lot. He evidently thinks that mankind is perfectible, rather readily perfectible. If only we made some slight changes in our social arrangements, human beings would behave more decently and be much happier, according to Mr. Wells' idea.

"Now, that's not the way it looks to

me at all," Dreiser went on. "I can't share that beautiful faith. To me man seems to be caught in the web of destiny, and must struggle in vain to extricate himself from his pitiable plight."

That was a fairly accurate statement of the implication of Dreiser's novels. But the very next day at lunch he talked in a different vein. He had been to Russia, and he spoke charmingly of his observations there—indeed, he talked better than he wrote about Russia. Ultimately the world would be a better place to live, and directly as a result of the Russian experiment. Then he fell to dreaming of an American social reorganization, by and bye. It is a bit hazy in my mind just how it was to be, but somehow or other the more intelligent tithe of the population was to take the country over, and run things sensibly and philanthropically—for the benefit of all human kind. The notion was as Utopian as any Wells novel, yet the evening before Dreiser had called Wells quixotic for his child-like faith in human perfectibility.

This same inconsistency may be noted in "Dawn," the new volume in Dreiser's serial autobiography. The years of Dreiser's childhood, which was spent in various Indiana towns, were sordid years, for he and his brothers and sisters were the victims of heredity, of mischance, of unpropitious environment. And as these drab years are recalled, Nemesis stalks the Dreisers as inexorably as in a Greek tragedy or a Dreiser novel. The reader does not feel that things could have been different, or that they will ever be different. Nature seems set against mankind. Still, every now and then Dreiser the philanthropist intervenes to express a hope that in the future better information may put to rout the prejudices and cruelties that made his childhood and youth unhappy.

But this failure to harmonize his intuition and his philosophy does not keep "Dawn" from being a complete and telling personal revelation. The book brings to the reader the very essence of the youth's grapple with his personal problems—his struggles to overcome self-consciousness and timidity; his maladjustment in school, his preoccupation with sex, his stumbling efforts to get an economic foothold. Success in self-revelation comes from candor—there are of course no reticences here; but it comes more from a hypersensitiveness to impressions of whatever sort that has marked the man from childhood until now. When his father's woolen mill burned, and the family fortunes began to slide downhill, the child felt keenly each remove to a smaller house and a meaner street. After more than half a century he recalls the humiliation of picking up coal along the railroad tracks and of having no shoes to wear to school in winter.

Equally vivid are the memories of green lawns, of shadows under the trees on summer afternoons, of rocking in the breeze on pleasant spring mornings. The portrait of his mother, whose memory he reveres, is singularly clear. By nature dreamy and indecisive, still she accepts with fortitude the turns of fortune, and makes a home for her children in spite of everything.

Although "Dawn" is first and foremost a personal testimony, it is an unusual document in social history as well. There are notable etchings of small town life while the Dreisers live in Terre Haute, Vincennes and Evansville. When they move to Chicago the impression of uncouth vitality which stamped the society of the Middle West in the eighties and nineties makes a memorable impression. The Zenith of Sinclair Lewis is a shadowy and underpeopled city by comparison. Chicago is sprawling out over ostentatious wooden suburbs, and along the board sidewalks swarm the jostling immigrants; Germans, Irish, Italians, sweaty with labor, glutting themselves in odorous restaurants; swearing, fighting, getting and spending. Competing laundry wagons rattle over the cobblestones and grocery delivery boys lash their jades into a gallop. Bins are filled and emptied in the wholesale houses that sell hammers, nails and files; men are hired and fired; and in retail hardware stores men strain at heavy stoves. Real estate agents hang out signs of apartments for rent and promotors are "seeing" bankers and city officials about sewers in new additions.

All very American—mobile, unstable, nervous. The social historians a hundred years from now will not neglect this record of the raw and gilded epoch which saw Chicago and Dreiser come of age. But there will be little in this volume for the historian of literature, for it will take a shrewd insight to discover in Dreiser at 19 any indication that he was to be later the foremost novelist of his day. . . .

H. L. Mencken. "Footprints on the Sands of Time." *American Mercury,* 23 (July 1931), 383.

. . . The writing in ["Dawn"] . . . is often dreadful, and various banal clichés (for example, "no less," "of sorts" and "if you please") are worked to death. Nevertheless, it would be idle to deny the fascination of the story. Dreiser commits every variety of literary atrocity, but all the while his narratives move and breathe. Here he shows that he can make of himself as vital and memorable a character as he made of Frank Cowperwood and Carrie Meeber. The period he covers runs from his earliest recollection as a child in Terre Haute, Ind., to his futile year at college. He is brutally frank; he rejects all the ordinary reticences; he is often lost in the dark mazes of his own garrulity. But in the end the record that he produces is seen to have the quality of a really impressive human document. The man himself is extraordinary, and his account of his youthful hopes and agonies is a piece of literature—as bespattered with defects as a farmboy with freckles, but still a piece of literature. One rejoices that it offers new glimpses of his heroic and tragic mother, already seen in "A Hoosier Holiday," and of his incomparable Brother Paul.

Alan Reynolds Thompson. *Bookman*, 73 (July 1931), 533–534.

An autobiography in four volumes, *A History of Myself*, with the publication of *Dawn* is half completed. *Dawn*, however, as the title might indicate, is chronologically the first book. The second, dealing with Dreiser's journalistic experiences, was published by Boni & Liveright in 1922 under the title *A Book about Myself*. The present publisher in his fly-leaf notice of Dreiser's works now lists as the second volume a book called *Newspaper Days*. Evidently he is re-issuing the earlier work under a new title. If such is the case he owes the public a statement of the facts. *Dawn* is a volume of 589 pages. *A Book about Myself* contains 502. If we may expect Dreiser's loquacity to continue unchecked—and we may—the four volumes will run well over two thousand. All told we anticipate by and about Dreiser upwards of a million words. . . .

Few will dispute that he is not only copious but verbose. He tells how during his cubship on a Chicago paper a friendly reporter used to blue-pencil his romantic effusions. He is no longer remantic, at lease in the fashion of his youth; but if he ever learned anything about conciseness there is no indication of it. Besides wordiness *Dawn* exhibits all the other familiar faults of this extraordinary writer. Extraordinary a novelist must be who, possessing rare psychological insight, exact observation and great human compassion, is at the same time so incorrigibly diffuse, so intolerably ignorant of and so grossly tasteless in the use of words, so tiresomely reiterative of pet expressions ("but to return," "redolent of," "smacked of," "too" and "true," "religionists", "sex contracts", "chemisms", etc.), so humourless and heavy, and withal so incapable of the slightest improvement. The ugliness of his writing tends to loom after a time like a monstrous symbol of the ugly civilization which he chronicles. Only by resolutely ignoring the linguistic atrocities, as one does in reading a newspaper, can one get behind the expression to the matter.

That, indeed, is abundant. Like *A Book about Myself*, *Dawn* is crammed with incidents, many of them trivial but all vividly concrete—the stuff of a dozen novels. If only he had spared the reader his ponderous antimoral moralizings! To some it may seem also that he might have spared some of the more childish anecdotes. The adult life of the newspaper man and author is significant enough to justify such fulness; not a commonplace childhood. Of course the memories of his youth are irresistible—to the writer; and Dreiser may have felt that in his case the material was representative of mid-west America as well as psychologically explanatory of the man. We may grant such justifications and still feel that we could do with a deal less of it. It needs much less space to convince us that he has been all his life rebelling against the fanaticism of his "religionist" father, that though frustrated by disillusionments, he still feels the warm sentiments which the boy felt for his mother; and that behind the naturalist's objectivity in telling of love there lurks the romantic sensuality which so engrossed the growing youth.

So far as sensuality is concerned, *Dawn* will no doubt appeal to a large audience of adolescents. The fervor which the father put into a puritanical Catholicism, the son devotes to advocating impure catholicity. In preaching and poetizing sex license he says what instinct is only too ready to accept, and he confesses his sexual experiences with the candour of a Casanova. Unfortunately the maundering, tongue-tied "Theo" was no Napoleon of the couch; and for addicts of the erotic his asinine and ineffectual "contacts" will probably prove as tantalizing as they are ridiculous. Most men are proud of sexual conquests, but it takes an extraordinary man to detail so calmly and copiously his sexual defeats. But with a philosophy like Dreiser's, why not?

As he puts it, "the mental and physical appetites of man alone explain him. He is, regardless of ideals or dreams or material equipment, an eating, savage animal, and in youth, and often in age, his greatest appetite, sex. And from that, as I have always said, and still stand prepared to maintain, arises all that we know . . . houses, temples, arts, travels and dreams of the world, its literature and its seekings. There is no other direct first cause for man." Furthermore, ". . . our follies are our life and what we are most willing to pay for. Yes, yes, yes! A thousand times yes! . . . By our follies . . . and inanities, we come to know what the sting of existence really means." And after all, what does anything matter? "What, cooking, eating, coition, job-holding, growing, aging, losing, winning, in so changeful and passing a scene as this, important? Bunk!"

With which devastating conclusion we may leave it.

Newton Arvin. "An American Case History." *New Republic*, 67 (August 5, 1931), 319–320.

Here is one more of those inordinate novels of Dreiser's, this time in the form of an autobiography—the story of his childhood and early youth. When I say it is one more Dreiserian novel, I of course do not mean that "Dawn" has the earmarks of anything but sober and even humdrum truth: on the contrary, it would have profited, like any of his novels, by being far more simplified, stylized, and hence "distorted," than it is. I mean only that its theme and its tone are very much the same as the theme and the tone of "Sister Carrie" or "The Titan" or "An American Tragedy"; and that, by making himself the protagonist, Dreiser only brings together in one whole those various pieces of himself which formerly did duty as Drouet or Cowperwood or Clyde Griffiths. His subject, in his novels, has always been the familiar American subject, the getting on in the world of an ambitious young man or woman; and that is his subject here. His heroes have varied, not in their aims (they have always been moved by the passion for power over material possessions and physical satisfactions), but only in their ruthlessness, their tenacity and their eventual success. Cowperwood is Dreiser's wishful self-projection: Clyde Griffiths (I leave aside, it goes without saying, his criminality) is the more authentic embodiment of what Dreiser must feel he once came very close to being. At any rate, the "I" of this volume is already an old acquaintance to the readers of his fiction; and "Dawn" is only a yarn about Dreiser's own early hatred of poverty and his first confused struggles away from it.

The book, in consequence, has all the defects and most of the merits of his novels; and it throws additional light on the heavy limitations that have kept Dreiser from true distinction as a writer of prose fiction. Like the novels, it profits up to a certain point by the deep ingenuousness of his mind. Like the novels, it is a document rather than an imaginative performance; and its documentary value—its picture of small-town life in Indiana and of Chicago life, in the eighties—is largely the product of Dreiser's naïveté, his indiscriminateness and his entire want of what is called taste. There are many passages in this book of which one can be tolerant only by remembering the wisdom of Horace Walpole's remark to Mme. du Deffand—that "the bad taste which precedes good taste is preferable to that which follows it." But the sense of style —the "taste"—which is indispensable to an artist, is a dubious advantage to a chronicler; and even Dreiser's exposure of his adolescent sexual life is too much a part of this particular case history to be wished away. How different the novels might have been if it had not been for the harsh religiosity of that early family life, or the combined prudishness and animality of the Chicago-Indiana culture of the eighties! Ignorance and evasion on the one hand, a brutalized laxity on the other: these are all that Dreiser has to record; and he would record them with less historical fidelity if he himself had achieved a third position, more humane and more critical. As it is, one sees with startling vividness the dreary social complex out of which emerged not only the predatory, oversexed Cowperwoods and Witlas, but the Carrie Meebers and the Jennie Gerhardts for whom Dreiser had the models to hand, one now sees, in his own family.

But insistent as the sexual note is in this book—and as it must have been in that society—it is less insistent and less important than something else. This is the note of social envy and social ambitiousness. Here, too, it is Dreiser's ingenuousness that stands us in such good stead. If he belonged less wholly to the life he writes about he would certainly have softened or sophisticated or dramatized his picture of it. But he has no capacity for evaluation, at any point; and hence he delivers his testimony with all the heavy circumstantiality but also with all the oppressive truthfulness of a slow-witted witness under patient inquisition. A greedy society bent on passionate accumulation, obsessed with the ostentation of its comforts and luxuries, ruthless in its contempt for the duffers (like Dreiser's father), jealous of its positions of power: such is the society he lumberingly depicts in these pages. What unifies the whole formless and unselective tale is the central contrast between a poverty-stricken middle-class family, drifting from one small-town or city encampment after another, hounded by economic inefficiency—the contract between this family and the prosperous bourgeoisie of Warsaw and Evansville or the showy wealth of the Chicago industrial barons. A gnawing sense of social inferiority and of personal ineffectiveness seems to have overcast the boy's whole childhood and adolescence: the glimpses that are least easy to forget are the glimpses of an awkward, ill dressed, unprepossessing boy or youth gazing in, with the helpless envy of an outsider, upon the "artistic" comfort of a Warsaw banker's home, or upon the "interesting" hilarity of a Bloomington fraternity house, or upon the "happy affluence" of some West Side Chicago mansion.

In this connection, no passage in the book is more striking than a paragraph or two, in one of the Evansville chapters, describing the appearance at the Dreiser home of a dandified book agent and his display of "the first book that was to influence me"—"Hill's Manual of Etiquette and Social and Commercial Forms." This was the true "Pilgrim's Progress" of Dreiser's "brooding" childhood. Here one hits upon something far more real than anything in those mushy passages of expensive writing in which Dreiser seeks to persuade us of an early penchant for metaphysical speculation or cosmic revery. "To this hour," he says, "I hark back [to "Hill's Manual"] in fancy at times, not to any particular item of its contents but to the wonderful sense of strangeness and mystery and beauty and delight which the most inane things in it evoked in me. . . . Pictures, actual pen-and-ink illustrations, showing the right and wrong way to enter a room, the right and wrong way to make a bow and doff the hat on meeting an acquaintance or your best girl, or on being introduced to anyone, especially a lady . . . pictures of cities and great buildings and of men who began as nothing in this great sad world but rose by honesty and thrift and kind thoughts and deeds to be great." At a later point, in speaking of his omnivorous reading, he tells us that no books made a deeper impression on him than "Water Babies" and "The House of the Seven Gables." Let the analyst make of this what he can. A layman can only confess to seeing singularly few traces in Dreiser's mind or work of either Kingsley's influence or Hawthorne's: the good Hill, on the other hand, whoever he was, has obviously never ceased to exercise his spell.

It is this sort of thing that, in spite of the book's pitiless loquacity, its mumbling monotony of narrative tone, its dank stretches of marshy and undrained prose, gives it a genuine value as sociology and even furnishes the literary student with a clue to the genesis of Dreiser's uncouth fictions. It has always been a question why a man with so little genuine insight into character, so little understanding of social relations, so little command over the grammar of his art, should nevertheless write a series of curiously impressive and partially truthful books. The autobiography explains the writing of the books, explains their quality and explains their immitigable second-rateness. Surely they are the expression of a will to power, a passion for worldly success, which, owing to the man's confessed inefficiency and lack of practical ingenuity, could find an outlet in none of the ordinary functions of a profit economy. If ever creative activity was compensatory, it has been compensatory in this novelist's career: fortunately, that "impure" motivation has kept Dreiser very close to his material, emotionally, and hence the inartistic truth his novels have as documents—hence, too, the tenderness which (a purely personal, not an imaginative tenderness) so many readers have found in them. Of the finer literary truth which a purer inventive motivation would have given them, they have little or nothing. There is a casual, almost an accidental, remark in this book which suggests what I mean. In speaking of a young girl who lived next door to his boarding house in Bloomington, Dreiser observes: "Her family were commonplace, a small-town working-class family. If I were to see her today as she was then, I would probably consider her trivial." "Probably?"—certainly! And this, in one daub of pigment, tells the whole story. If Dreiser has never managed to make his kept women, his salesmen, his Napoleons of finance, his "geniuses," seem anything but essentially trivial, it is, in short, because they are nothing more than that to him. His fancy has been obsessed by values that have nothing to do with personality: his interest in people has never been simple and studious. But, for just this reason, he has been a richly characteristic product of a depersonalized and predatory society; and "Dawn" is only technically a less fictitious account of it than his novels.

John Hermann. "Honest Autobiography." *New Masses,* 7 (September 1931), 19.

The stock complaint against the writing of Theodore Dreiser seems to be that he hits the typewriter keys with mittens on. The aesthetes and Broadway socialists are offended by grammatical slips and lack of poetical and refined metaphor. They are inclined also to raise their noses at the honest and therefore often brutal subject matter of his books.

As long as it is a novel by Dreiser that the arbiters of taste in American reviewing rackets have under their hammers they are able to refrain to some extent from poo-poohing the subject matter. (They, of course, never can stand the way he writes.) But let Dreiser attempt autobiography. Then they rise on their ears.

In *Dawn* Dreiser gives us his childhood and youth, honestly, interestingly and in a style fitted to the period and the story. *Dawn* reeks of the middle-west, of proletarian poor in small town and large city, of attempt to rise from poverty and of the futility of the attempt.

Twenty years ago I know things had not changed much in the mid-west Dreiser writes about, I doubt if there have been any great advances since. There are more families comparable to the Dreisers today in Indiana than there were in his childhood, and their position under this system is more hopeless than ever. All through the middle-west on the outskirts of towns and cities you can still see poor families, licked in the struggle for existence, living in utmost squalor of the kind Dreiser has portrayed. The only difference today is that the back yards of such places are usually encumbered by old broken down model—T Fords.

When a reviewer, who is always a good fellow and very kind to children and animals, is depressed by the subject matter of the book in hand he can easily go into the grammar, syntax, etc. And he can decry the lack of poetic beauty, "Good Taste," interest, etc. (Would the style of Pater with its stupid emptiness, applied to the subject matter of *Dawn,* have made a better book of it? Not a chance. The writing of *Dawn,* with crudity, grammatical slips, redundancy, adds to the power of the book.)

Dreiser's father was forced into the

working class by a failure in business. His religious superstitious Catholicism incapacitated him to regain his former station and drugged him into inability to realize that he was of the proletariat. Theodore was a child at the time of the failure. His early life was the life of a poor child. But what was worse, in his family there was always the hope of regaining a good sound position in respectable bourgeois society. This was denied them. The struggle to appear to be and if possible, to be, more than one is,—that hits off America. *Dawn* is a damn fine book, and has caused a good many readers discomfort.

Dreiser's mind is a questioning one. He gropes after truth because to him truth is elusive and he questions whether there is absolute truth. Man is a chemic being, swayed and ruled by chemical reactions. Love, for instance, is a chemical attraction of beings which can be turned into hatred by the reorganization of the chemical attributes of the body. When Dreiser offers such an hypothesis he lets it be known that it also is open to doubt.

One absolute with the man is that poverty, distress and oppression of human beings causes him both mental and physical anguish of an extreme variety and impels him to give aid to the downtrodden as best he can.

This is apparent not only in his autobiography where he states the fact, but can be seen by a person of average intelligence in all of his novels. That this sympathy for the exploited masses, as Heywood Broun has analyzed it, is a gesture to gain publicity is a damnable libel. It would be more nearly correct to say that Broun ran on the socialist ticket in order to get publicity for his Broadway Bum Wiggle.

In *Dawn* you can trace sources of much of Dreiser's fiction. It impresses one with the fact that Dreiser is a man who writes about things he really knows about. That seems to me commendable. His frankness regarding his family deserves as much praise as his honesty regarding himself. The book comes about as near being honest autobiography as any of the genre I have read. And if he writes with mittens the keys are well spaced.

Checklist of Additional Reviews

Fanny Butcher. Chicago *Daily Tribune,* May 9, 1931, p. 12.

Janette T. Harrington. "Scanning the Shelves." *Ohio State Lantern,* May 14, 1931.

J.T.W. Springfield *Republican,* May 17, 1931.

W.E. Harris. Boston *Evening Transcript,* May 23, 1931, p. 8.

Isabel Paterson. "Books and Other Things." New York *Herald Tribune,* May 18, 1931.

E. Horrwitz. "Witness of Theodore Dreiser." *Dawn,* 1 (June 1931), 342.

Rochester *Times-Union,* June 4, 1931.

John Chamberlain, "An American Record." *Forum,* 86 (July 1931), vi.

Pittsburgh *Monthly Bulletin,* 36 (July 1931), 58.

Further Reviews: Bibliographic Information Incomplete

John E. Drewry. "New Book News."

Notes

TRAGIC AMERICA

BY

THEODORE DREISER

HORACE LIVERIGHT, INC.
NEW YORK

Tragic America

Charles Hanson Towne. "A Number of Things." New York *American,* January 11, 1932.

Theodore Dreiser is not happy over present conditions in these United States. He expresses his unhappiness in no uncertain terms in an exhaustive book, the result of years of study and contemplation. It is called *"Tragic America,"* and Liveright is the publisher. There are 426 pages of fine type, and an appendix. Mr. Dreiser has never been one to shirk a huge task. He has roamed about this country of ours, sympathetic always toward the under dog, fearless in his criticism of systems which crush the poor, eloquent in his righteous wrath.

He holds that millions of people nowadays "live and die without tasting anything really worth while. The average individual today is really tortured; he is so numerous, so meaningless, so wholly confused and defeated." And he goes on to say, in a chapter on our banks and corporations, that "twenty years ago, laborers dreamed of a halcyon machine age, with six or seven hours' work a day. Yet today, with machinery at almost the perfection point, they are beggars, receivers of charity, while 40,000 millionaires bestride the land."

Mr. Dreiser hurls some invectives at the churches, and shows how even these institutions employ press agents; and he shows how offshoots of the churches, like the Lord's Day Alliance and the Methodist Board of Temperance, Prohibition and Morals work at all times in the lobbies at Washington. He paints a sorry picture of these enterprises. One could only wish that in his fervor Mr. Dreiser could have remained a little more calm.

His wrath overwhelms him, when he is given to the use of such childish words as "asinine." They hurt, rather than help, his argument, as the over-forensic lawyer fails to sway a jury when his voice grows too loud.

Yet Mr. Dreiser is always interesting, even when he is not persuasive. His chapter on crime and the reasons for its existence, with individual cases which he has studied, makes one disheartened. Our prisons, he hold, turn out unsalable material. "At Auburn, instead of making only license plates, as is now the case, the men might be kept busy by also being allowed to make all street and highway signs and so possibly arrive at that feeling of efficiency which comes with activity. But no, this is not permitted. Yet I think that all prison industries should be put on a paying basis. Their products should be allowed to enter the open market and the State should be forced to pay the union wage, or nearly so."

The railroads do not fare well at Mr. Dreiser's hands. It costs more to ride from New York to Pittsburgh, for instance, than it would to stop overnight at any first-class hotel in either city. We pay ten cents for a loaf of bread, while hundreds of millions of bushels of wheat lie stored and unsalable. No one can get around these obvious facts.

Toward the end of his volume, Mr. Dreiser makes it clear that America is not the only tragic country. Europe has its Rothschilds and Cortlandts and the Royal Dutch Shell. But he wishes to know if any of the great financiers of our land have yet offered one creative idea for the alleviation of any of the economic ills of America today.

For his own part, he suggests a new statecraft, a reconstruction of our economic life in order to restore the balance of power. He hopes for a day when Aristotle's beautiful dream will come true; a state controlled by and for all and giving equitable honor and recognition, but not wealth, to those most deserving it. He hopes that the ancient philosopher's plan may one day be read weekly in our schools.

Lewis Gannett. "Books and Things." New York *Herald Tribune*, January 18, 1932, p. 11.

Theodore Dreiser replies to Harlan County, Ky., officials and others in America who do not like him in his new book, "Tragic America," published today by Liveright. He does not like them, either. He surveys America, its churches, its schools, its policemen, its courts and its corporations, its slums—like the mine country of Kentucky—and concludes that things are going from bad to worse. . . .

Through most of "Tragic America" Theodore Dreiser writes like a pre-war insurgent Congressman who has not had time to digest the notes prepared for him by his secretary. Occasionally he writes with the fervor of a new convert to the religion of Communism. But in either role, he is a stranger wandering in an unfamiliar labyrinth of economic facts and statistics. Only once or twice does he turn from this undigested book knowledge and speak to the reader through the eyes of a simple human being. He tells of visiting Passaic, N. J., and for a moment the great American novelist, the man with the uncanny gift for making articulate the unarticulate souls of blind, stumbling human beings, speaks to us again. Then he climbs back to his rostrum, and wearily resumes his task of preaching angry sermons from a text of ill-assorted notes. And, in doing it, sounds more like a warm-hearted member of a high school debating society than like Theodore Dreiser, author of "Sister Carrie" and "The Titan" and of "Dawn" and "An American Tragedy." The author of those books knew that even capitalists were variously motivated individual human beings, not mere fat-stomached cartoon figures, with trousers built of dollar signs.

William Soskin. "Reading and Writing." New York *Evening Post*, January 18, 1932.

The theatrical slap in the face which Theodore Dreiser administered to Sinclair Lewis was only one of a series of rather startling events at the since famous dinner for Boris Pilniak given by Ray Long. The newspapers might have reported instead the pointed debate between Arthur Brisbane and Heywood Broun on the value and the permanence of the Russian Revolution. Or they might have reported Theodore Dreiser's announcement before this roomful of distinguished gentlemen of the literary profession that he had decided on Communism as the only sane social and cultural program for the human race.

Since that day Dreiser has received official and high-flown greetings from the Soviet brothers on the celebration of his sixtieth birthday. Since then he has led an economic investigating commission in the coal fields of the South in an effort to crystallize public opinion against the mine operators and to direct attention to the miserable living conditions of the miners. Now he publishes "Tragic America," as iconoclastic an oration as any Union Square soap-box orator has shouted; and in it he calls for an American dictatorship of the Proletariat, to be achieved in the best Moscow manner.

Theodore Dreiser, Communist! It is a little hard to imagine. In my mind the author of "Sister Carrie," of "An American Tragedy" and of an important biographical volume, "Dawn," stands for that gentle, warm, thoroughly disillusioned skepticism which comes of a profound conviction that there is no order, no law, no Divine guidance, no purpose, no evolutionary or God-granted progress for the human race. His compassion is one of sympathy for all men and women in the same, hopeless plight. That is his "chemistry." That is the reason for his explanation of love and the other "romantic" impulses as purely "chemic," to use his own favorite adjective. That, too, is his reason for the final insistence on the rights of the individual and one of the principles of individual freedom—for where is the code or creed sound enough to warrant violation of those rights?

There, I think, was the sincerely felt credo of Theodore Dreiser, novelist. How to fit the Communist doctrine of dictated revolutionary accomplishment, of centralized and highly organized politico-economic action into such a creed? The Dreiserian method is a familiar one. It consists of building up, with the brick-by-brick patience which Dreiser possesses so notoriously in his literary method, a wholesale indictment of the *verdammte Kapitalistische Ordnung* as it functions in the United States; of demonstration a complete stifling of civil liberty, humanitarian progress, economic happiness and social justice in the American Democracy; of indicating that the ordinary ballot box methods and those of political reform can effect no cure; then, of announcing triumphantly "an executive power for the American working masses not unlike the Communist Central Committee in Moscow." Private fortunes and private wealth are to be wiped out. The middle classes must realize that their future lies in the proletariat, and these two groups must join to "build new institutions" and give their Central Committee "the power to confiscate and turn into state property all of the basic industries."

Thus the artist, the individualist, the champion of human liberty maneuvers himself, by social philosophy and by the desperate need of the unbeliever to cling to something, into the Moscow camp. Cheers from the Bureau of Intellectual Welfare, the Bureau on American Propaganda, the Bureau on the Organization of Artists and Writers for the Communist International, and from the offices of a Mr. Stalin!

All right, then. Theodore Dreiser presents a book of social indictment—"Tragic America"—in the role of the political leader, the organizer who wants to bring a message of revolution to his fellow citizens. He is no longer the novelist. He expects to be judged on this new basis. Popularly, of course, his literary reputation will flow over into the political field, and the book will have greater effect than any similar tract by a pontificating, doctrinaire comrade in an East Side Communist local. Actually, Dreiser's book is a persistent, vigorous presentation of all the popular, trust-busting, muckraking, soap-boxing arguments against the American industrial system used for a number of generations.

I am not questioning or considering the value or the truth of Dreiser's arguments regarding Rockefeller's fortune, the American financial oligarchy, the rise of banks and corporations as political dictators, the spread of the American railway system, the loyalty of the members of the United States Supreme Court to their economic masters, the violation of constitutional guarantees of liberty and the pursuit of happiness, the abuse of the individual in the exploitation of police power or the growth of crime under the American penal system. Dreiser draws upon familiar material in his presentation of the questions. He has drawn heavily on the work of Gustavus Myers. His arguments have all the strength of the hackneyed. Nor am I questioning the truth in his demonstration of the ineffectiveness of the American labor movement's tactics in fighting industrial and legal oppression. I do question, however, the effectiveness of Dreiser's performance.

If Dreiser were writing a novel concerning one phase of the social conditions he describes in "Tragic America" (he couldn't deal with all of them), he would apply enough human understanding and a sufficiently realistic psychology to present that problem in many perspectives. He would not write a diatribe. He would not blind himself to every character, every interest and every argument except his immediate one. "An American Tragedy" is proof of that, for it deals with a problem which Dreiser considers in the present work theoretically; and all the pounding of the table, and all the oratorical, pompous, forensic manner, and all the unrelieved *fortissime* of Dreiser's social tract in "Tragic America" are not worth a single chapter of his simple, understanding story of a socially dictated murder in "The American Tragedy."

It is Theodore Dreiser's privilege, of course, to direct his energy and his talent into whatever channels he chooses. He knows better than any one else the importance of his mission as an American champion of the Moscow International. But if that activity makes a mediocre propagandist and a comparatively insignificant sociologist out of an important novelist, the loss is ours. We have everything to lose. Stalin has something to gain.

Harry Hansen. "The First Reader." New York *World Telegram*, January 18, 1932.

Theodore Dreiser's book is called "Tragic America" and is a hodgepodge of abuses, of citations taken from investigations, labor records, personal investigation in mining camps and mill towns and generalizations about the great corporations. The conviction that communism would solve many of the economic ills complained of is deep-rooted in Mr. Dreiser's mind and is the conclusion of his book.

The best thing in the book is the indignation with which the author writes. It shows that he is filled up with his subject, impatient of excuses and no longer confident that capitalism can solve anything. The exploitation of laborers, the low wages paid to workers in industries that have paid tremendous sums in dividends to their stockholders, the misery in mining towns, the unspeakable brutality of State police and men hired to break strikes fill the pages of this book.

Mr. Dreiser makes no bones about names, whether of men or corporations. He sees the government as taking orders from the biggest corporations and banks. He thinks education is warped to keep the status quo. He attacks religion as devoted to upholding the present authorities. Although all denominations get a round volley, he reserves his strongest attacks for the Roman Catholic Church because of its powerful position and its wealth; and for the American Federation of Labor.

With Mr. Dreiser's desire to wake us up I am in complete sympathy and I wish more of us had the guts he has. But when one has read all his specific charges and digested the sum it appears that there is very little in the capitalstic society that he finds praiseworthy. The whole thing, he argues, ought to be scrapped because the ability of private individuals to become immensely wealthy is possible only by starving or exploiting those less fortunate. All great wealth should be confiscated, no great fortunes should be passed on by inheritance and all profits should be for the workers.

Mr. Dreiser's argument is a familiar one and grows increasingly loud as reports of the Russian experiment reach the United States. While his book makes you indignant that there is so much misery in a bountiful land, it remains a one-sided picture. Before anyone can say that Communism is the only remedy he would have to call on Mr. Dreiser to present fairly the other side of the situation.

Mr. Dreiser all his life has been a rebel against conventional living, whether economic or social. When he argued in novel form for the sexual liberty of the individual he let his characters go to extremes that few of his readers would wholly indorse. Yet he was a great influence in helping break down sex hypocrisy and giving us a slightly saner attitude toward such subjects. In the same way his "Tragic America" is overdone, and yet of tremendous importance. It ought to start every reader thinking about his own part in American life, his own responsibility for high-handed methods in industry, corruption in politics, and for the misery and suffering of those who are caught in a treadmill from which they have no chance of escape.

"Predicted Dreiser Book Arrives." Springfield [Ill.] *Journal*, January 19, 1932.

Mr. Theodore Dreiser has published a book incorporating theories on economics, politics and sociology as distilled from his investigation of mine disorders in Kentucky last fall. His book is "Tragic America," adapted from the title of his famous and bulky novel, "An American Tragedy." While he was "investigating" in Kentucky, comment was made that Mr. Dreiser was getting ready to write a book and sure enough, the book is forthcoming.

Strong and bitter language is employed in the book, but that, too, was expected. Dreiser retreated from Kentucky under humiliating and laughable conditions. Smarting under barbed raillery and serious criticism, he has delivered himself of his spleen. He seems to be "agin" everything from the Federal Constitution down.

If Mr. Dreiser fears a "class war" in this country, he is doing nothing to avert it. Rather he is fomenting class hatred. He appeals to passions rather than to sober reason. But hard language sells better than logic and that, after all, may be the reason for writing and publishing the book.

Ben Blumenberg. "Dreiser Indicts Capitalism." *New Leader*, (January 23, 1932), 10.

There are few novelists in the English-speaking world capable of writing a book in the same class as Theodore Dreiser's "Tragic America." This observation at the same time measures the quality of the syrup that oozes from the fiction press. On the whole, writers of novels have no social viewpoint, or, if they have, care is taken to conceal the fact. Like ladies in a certain social strata, they must live. Hence the prevalence of literary house-maid's knee in the ranks of the writers whose work is barren of ideas and of social protest.

"Tragic America" is written with burning passion. Not the passion of the proselyter, but of the philosopher who feels as well as thinks. If most of the pamphlets and books on our social, economic and political affairs which have been written in the past generation are ever destroyed, future readers in possession of Dreiser's book would be able to get a vivid slant at the social system of the present day. In this work there is the same patient searching for facts evident in "The Financier" and "The Titan," the humanness of "Sister Carrie" and "Jennie Gerhardt," the sanity and understanding of "An American Tragedy," the questioning and reasoning of "Hey Rub-a-Dub-Dub." Into "Tragic America" there has been poured thirty years of passionate protest, of unquenchable social revolt and a profound understanding of economic forces.

America's foremost novelist finds our economic system a gummy mess. There are no "ifs" and "buts" about it: the only thing that will clear it up is "Socialism or an American form of Communism. Most certainly one or the other."

If the greatest need of today is the development of a sense of indignation, Dreiser's book will furnish it. Fearlessly and clearly he states the issues that are intensifying the war of the classes in a work written "for those alone who have the patience and desire and will to learn the drift if not the meaning of present day American life." Says the author:

" . . . I am now convinced that this is the one country that, ever since it was conceived as a possibility, has been steadily and deceitfully, as well as fraudulently, shunted along the path of individual and later corporate control, as opposed to its written and widely promulgated determination to make of itself a liberal and helpful democracy in which the individual was to fare more pleasantly and comfortably than ever he had before in the world . . . The petty individual has seen himself more thoroughly coerced, robbed and frustrated, and that always in favor of the cunning individual of capitalistic leanings and with a will to power."

With a wealth of detail we are shown how all the institutions of modern society are used as forces to exploit and oppress the masses. How, when mental chloroform fails, tear-gas, clubs and bullets, deportations and the blacklist follow and how the iron fist of economic and political power shows itself more clearly during the present breakdown of capitalism. The "capitalism that came into the world dripping blood at every pore" continues to perspire freely. Dreiser applies the discovery of Marx to the present economic mess and his facts indicate that radicals are given to under rather than to overstatement.

"Tragic America" will excite controversy among radicals because of the views expressed in its pages on Russia, the sweeping denunciation of the A. F. of L. and "that the old Socialist movement (was) corrupted by capitalistic pacifism."

Socialists will want to know how Dreiser can logically hope for an America which will be "a liberal and helpful democracy," and at the same time urge passionately the emulation of the Russian dictatorship. Dreiser, a recent convert to the collectivist philosophy, may be expected to clarify his views the more he studies their implications. But the great and indisputable value of "Tragic America" is his indictment of capitalism.

It was the poet, Heine who said, "If the people understood the forces which govern them modern governments would not last 24 hours." With this observation some readers of Dreiser's powerful work will be inclined to agree. Others will become "mad"—fighting mad and join forces with those who are working to overthrow our class-ruled society. Greater praise no book can receive.

J. Irwin Boyd. "Dreiser Indicts Leaders but Spies Better Future." Philadelphia *Public Ledger*, January 23, 1932.

Theodore Dreiser, that great novelist and poor writer, has gone economic along with most of the rest of the world. The result is a tome that shows the worst and almost the best of Dreiser, though only the worst of the United States. He has called it "Tragic America," and has summoned from the past and from the press and his own observations of the present an infinitely depressing series of cases to prove the rightness of his title. He would, of course.

No one now sitting in any position of power will like this book, with its 426 pages of fine print, its loosely dictated wordiness, its barbershop hymns of hate against Wall Street and huge corporations, its indictments of churches, politicians, statesmen, labor leaders, grafters and captains of industry (brigands of industry, our author regards them). It will indeed, if they read it, make a lot who don't have any power feel unhappy and nervous, for its cuts down under the schoolgirl complexion of superficial America.

Yet fevers are preludes to healthful convalescence, if not to death. And Dreiser's eye is toward convalescence rather than the graveyard. Therefore he deserves a hearing. He'll get it, too, along with a vast amount of berating and scolding and sneering and ridicule. He'll be charged with goodness knows how many ulterior motives, but, regardless of that, the homeliness, even the carelessness of his book, combined with the ultimate coherence and brief and pointed suggestions of it, indicate to the reviewer the complete honesty and sincerity of his social passion.

In the early days of America a book like this would be given prolonged and excited discussion, as was Thomas Paine's "The Crisis." It might also give its author a decided shove toward an unknown and unhonored grave, such as Paine eventually filled. But it would lead to political and social consequences. It is conceivable (since there exist even now heirs of that American) that this book may have some effect, if not in this decade, then in the decade after next. It is a crystallization of much that is coursing through the minds of a lot of persons who are not great thinkers, but who are perhaps a little less dense than their masters conceive them to be.

Simeon Stransky. "Mr. Dreiser Prescribes for Us." New York *Times Book Review*, January 24, 1932, p. 10.

Escape from the tragic situation in which Mr. Dreiser finds America today must be sought, he thinks, along the road to freedom now building in Soviet Russia. To be sure, this means embarking on a great adventure, but "who is so mean as to fear adventure," particularly when it is inevitable? "Not forever can our capitalists, land trusts and banks continue to aggravate the economic struggle by establishing their scores of mills, their trusts and holding companies, among unknowing people. paying them almost nothing!" Capitalism is a failure in America today, as foretold many years ago by Karl Marx, a man of brilliant attainments whom Mr. Dreiser would put "ahead of such renowned economic philosophers as John Stuart Mill, Voltaire, Rousseau, Fichte and Hegel." The Marxian philosophy was the basis of the old socialism, now corrupted by "capitalistic pacifism," and of the Communist experiment in Russia. Taking the latter for his model Mr. Dreiser proposes "an executive power for the American working masses not unlike the Communist Central Committee in Moscow," a step which involves for the United States a new constitution, "which I feel should supplant the old." A new constitution would seem to be made necessary not only by the failure of the present instrument, to mention anything like a Communist Central Committee but by the fact that Mr. Dreiser contemplates other considerable changes in American society such as the abolition of private property and the disfranchisement of ministers of religion after the Moscow example. Are the American people ready for the change? Our author is optimistic. "Of course, in suggesting such things, any one today is more than likely to be faced in the capitalist press and elsewhere, with the assurance, and without in any way consulting the masses, that the American people don't want these things. But don't they? I rather fancy myself that they do, or will!" So that's that.

Capitalism in the United States is done for because the American people can no longer endure the rule of the corporations. In depicting the part played by the corporations on the American scene Mr. Dreiser draws heavily on the researches of Gustavus Myers in the annals of the gilded age following the Civil War and of Ida Tarbell in the history of the Standard Oil. These studies, with which some of our readers may be familiar, seeing that they were published about twenty-five years ago and have established themselves as a permanent contribution to American history, Mr. Dreiser supplements with a few brief experiences of his own, notably in the Passaic textile strike of 1925. At Passaic he took lodgings with a kindly old German couple, who after a life of self-respecting thrift were forced to let rooms because the husband had been discharged from the mills at the age of 62 without a pension. "Yet the way they met their plight brought to my mind John Newman's words: 'Lead, kindly light, amid th' encircling gloom.' The old man seemed to find some consolation in the evenings spent in the immaculate blue and white kitchen, listening to the zither-playing and singing of their fresh, young German roomers." Of such vignettes and portraits we have only a few in these pages, which bristle instead with figures. Mr. Dreiser reveals a passion for statistics that is almost consuming. We learn that between 1862 and 1882 "Rockefeller's business had increased 14,000 per cent—that is, from a $4,000 to $55,000,000 concern." Readers quick at figures will note that 14,000 per cent, impressive as it is, is not enough. Mr. Rockefeller's business, if the dollar sums are correct, increased 14,000 times, and this means actually 1,400,000 per cent. All through the book Mr. Dreiser is irresistibly attracted by percentages, but seems quite unable to master the technique. In the present instance he understates Mr. Rockefeller's iniquities a hundred fold. In another place he finds that the San Francisco raisin wholesalers selling to the unemployed street vendors make $450 a ton on an investment of $100, thus "taking 45 per cent profit," but, of course, it is 450 per cent profit.

This matter of Mr. Dreiser's faulty arithmetic is not unimportant because the book is full of arithmetic, as one would naturally expect in a comprehensive analysis of the capitalist system in all its ramifications. Is it carping to point out that Mr. Dreiser speaks of 117,000,000 persons in the country "at the time of the World War," although three years later the census of 1920 found only 105,000,000? He finds that if railway rates all over the country were as low as those obtaining on Henry Ford's road the public would have saved $2,000,000 a year; but this is only one-fortieth of 1 per cent of all moneys received by the railroads, and Mr. Dreiser must have meant either $2,000,000 a day or $2,000,000,000 a year. He finds in the chapter describing the unholy alliance between capitalism and the church, and particularly the activity of American missionaries as advance agents of imperialism, that the Methodists—apparently the same group frequently referred to elsewhere as the "Methodist Episcopals"—"have 893,881 in the mission fields (conceive that!) functioning most extensively in China and India." Actually the number of all American missionaries abroad, representing about forty denominations, is something over 8,000 of whom the Methodist representatives would be about 1,900. Mr. Dreiser has thus exaggerated the number of Methodist missionaries about 500-fold, or to put it another way, about 50,000 per cent. . . .

In summary it cannot be said that Mr. Dreiser's incursion into the field of sociological inquiry has been successful. A confused groping toward familiar things, coupled with incredibly bad writing, constitutes his peculiar trademark in American literature. But in the domain of fiction he surmounts his handicaps, he may even be said to profit by them. The basic data of life and emotion can never become too familiar, and people are always groping toward the secret, and Mr. Dreiser's open-eyed wonder in the presence of the catalogue of human experience in the end becomes his greatest merit. Yet it is one thing to stand in awe before the facts that puzzled Job and Ecclesiastes and the author of "Hamlet" and that will continue to fascinate and bewilder the inquiries to the end of time. It is another thing to plunge head first into a mass of chronicle and statistics that, in the first place, may be half a century old, and, in the second place, are sadly misunderstood and mishandled, and in the whole betray an extrordinary blend of ignorance and naïveté. The field of the emotions being his proper field, why should Mr. Dreiser have plunged into the jungle of concrete information where 891,000 Methodist missionaries in China are just as probable to him as 891 missionaries would be, and $2,000,000 a day railroad revenue is just the same as $2,000,000,000, and the American people's readiness for communism is demonstrated by Mr. Dreiser's "rather fancying" that they are?

Stuart Chase. "Mr. Dreiser in a China Shop." New York *Herald Tribune Books,* January 24, 1932, pp. 1–2.

As the depression deepens, competition in my line of business grows daily more keen. Poets, novelists, literary critics, are setting up shop as economists on every Main Street. I give you Burton Rascoe, Matthew Josephson, Edmund Wilson, Henry Hazlitt—and now Theodore Dreiser. The natural tendency of the old guard is to sneer at these upstarts imperiling its majestic traditions, if not indeed its income, but I, as a not very ancient member of the old guard, and never in good standing, find it hard to sneer. I am prone to give the boys a hand. Though they were unable to foot a column of figures twice alike, most of the newcomers possess imagination, a quality which the old guard has conspicuously lacked.

Economics, as every intelligent person knows, is not a science; it possesses hardly a law where the findings of one competent observer can be invariably checked with those of another observer; disagreement on most of its major hypotheses is profound. It is one of my cherished illusions that economics is on the way to become a science, or at least a rigorous art, but to date the territory is lush, virgin and wild. So why shouldn't the poets drive their covered wagons in? They may plant a few seeds of great value in the future development of the territory. Or they may be scalped by the Indians. They must take their chances. Their invasion, furthermore, is implicit in the times. Never before have so many Americans been actively interested in economic phenomena. It is a sore pity that the old guard has so little to tell them.

Theodore Dreiser, his ungainly bulk swaying above the straining mules, with red face, cracking blacksnake, bellowing shout, comes charging athwart the frontler. His wagon is packed with the most amazing conglomeration of economic goods—antique, modern, Baroque, Victorian and totally unclassifiable—ever assembled under one canvas. The old guard will take to climbing trees after one look at the ensemble, and I confess to a certain dizziness myself. With all due allowance for the courage and spirit which animates the driver, the bulk of the freight is pretty terrible. Few worse-written books than "Tragic America" have ever found their way into print, and none to my knowledge has handled quantitative data in so cavalier a fashion. After finding eighteen errors of fact in one chapter. I am almost ready to amend the policy of unrestricted immigration. Poets should be ceded homesteads only for the cultivation of qualitative economics, and economic theory.

"Tragic America" is a four hundred and thirty-five page indictment of the American system, and a few specific—not always too specific—proposals for its uprooting. The general approach is that of the trust busters of the Nineties. We are bedeviled by great corporations, growing ever more huge, profitable, greedy and devouring. The corporations in turn are ridden by a handful of caesars, growing ever more wealthy, grasping and domineering. "In some, I proclaimed the fact that Rockefeller is relatively the present owner of American industry." This contribution to economic thought is followed by a typical Dreiserian sentence, one of many with which I have struggled. "Of course, the conventional capitalist philosophy intended, I believe, to appease labor (cooperation, labor's ownership of stock, etc.), and put forth by all of the high-powered public relations counsels for corporations."

The indictment covers not only industrial corporations, but banks, insurance companies, Wall Street, railroads, express companies, telephone and power companies, the courts—particularly the Supreme Court—"the Constitution as a scrap of paper," the puerility of the American Federation of Labor, the abuse of the police power, the company gunman, the economic causes of crime, the press, the Church, the futility of the ballot, the schools and universities, organized charity. Each is given a chapter, more or less, as full of figures as a dog of fleas.

I may be entirely wrong, but the picture which came to me was this: The author has a fine, full-blooded contempt for the jury system. He was a radical, perhaps a Socialist, in his youth. For the last twenty years he has devoted himself to writing novels. His "Sister Carrie" seems to me one of the greatest books ever penned. He has been following the fortunes of his characters with power, emotion and understanding, having little time to follow or understand the outside economic world. He goes to Russia. His imagination is stirred. Youthful dreams come back. America, too, should be a Socialist state. He goes to Pennsylvania mining towns, to Paterson, and is shocked by industrial conditions. He determines to write a book, exposing these conditions, proclaiming the need for a Red America. Radical friends welcome this decision and pile his desk with documents, reports, court decisions, case material. Though there is neither footnote or bibliography I can name, I think nine out of ten of the standard documents from which he quotes—Myers's "Great American Fortunes," Tarbell's "History of Standard Oil," the Pujo Committee report, the Federal Trade Commission's power hearing, etc.

He takes this statistical tonnage and wades into it, equipped with unlimited enthusiasm but with no technique for either handling or appraising exact fact. There emerge a series of 1890 radical slogans derived from his boyhood, a few penetrating first hand observations of the mature novelist, and a crazy patchwork of copied figures—helter-skelter, inconsecutive, undigested, largely uncomprehended, and frequently grossly inaccurate. "In 1930 the Standard Oil earned $40,000,000, almost the equivalent of 10 per cent on the 17,800,000 shares of outstanding capital stock." The Standard Oil of what? How is $40,-000,000 10 per cent of 17,800,000 shares? The book reeks with stuff like this. I would not on my life dare to use a single figure from it without checking back to the original source.

The Reds will call me crabbed. Perhaps I am. One has to believe in something and I believe in the sanctity of exact fact. I believe Mr. Dreiser would have served his cause better if he had kept his muddy boots out of this chamber. It so happens that his cause is essentially my own. The gory economic system—the word flatters it—is a rotten, cruel, reeking mess. It needs amendment most drastic. No indictment can be too severe against many of its departments. But let us have a true indictment; let us see the system as it really is, debit and credit, especially when we employ a quantitative microscope. How can we repair or rebuild an engine unless first we understand it? This statistical bull charge of Mr. Dreiser only makes confusion more confounded.

If he had given us tragic America in terms of the emotion of a great poet this might have been as fine and permanent a book as "An American Tragedy." It stands a jerrybuilt pile, with still a haunting monolithic grandeur in here a bastion and there a turret. But one cannot fail to salute the spirit behind it; the spirit of one, who, having fame, success, money, is uncompromisingly pledged to the cause of the common man.

Burton Rascoe. "Dreiser Sees Red." New York *Sun*, January 29, 1932.

. . . There are 435 pages of small type in "Tragic America," and I doubt if there is a human brain capable of encompassing the enormous amount of statistics and data, charges and speculations, philosophical asides and rationales, suggestions and plans that go to make up this work. The eloquent wrath, the passionate conviction, the heartfelt grumbling that sustained the labor of compiling this amorphous mass of material is likely to be lost upon the reader, unless Dreiser has counted upon the cumulative effect of incident to be the same in a book of this kind as it is in a novel.

The book, I think, will be unacceptable to the general reader of the bourgeois type, not because of its radicalism but simply because it attempts to tell him, like the Seabury report, with so much data to make his head swim, that there has been skullduggery afoot—which is a fact he has known all along. This general reader accepts (usually at second hand) revelations of corruption, extortion, mendacity and the malefaction of great wealth as in the nature of things and only vaguely hopes that something will be done about it, as, in the past, something ameliorative has been done about things when sufficient hue and cry is raised, and in promises there is bait for votes.

The book will be unacceptable to statistically minded (i.e., to actuaries, accountants, economists, bankers, research clerks, &c., to whom the digit is more important than the moon) because Dreiser has dumped into his hopper nearly all the statistics he could beg, borrow, mooch or find, without regard to age or obsolescence. From Gustavus Myers's "The History of the Great American Fortunes," reports of the Pujo committee's investigation, old Senate inquiries, old biographies and old exposés he has taken moth-eaten impeachment material without bringing it up to date, even when to use the old figures together with the new ones would give emphasis to his arguments. . . .

The book will be unacceptable to the liberals, because it commits Dreiser to the doctrine of the complete reorganization of society for the benefit of the workers, with an oligarchy functioning with autocratic severity and punishing by death or exile any liberal criticism of its personnel or its functioning. The liberals can only lament with a pained anxiety the deflection to the extreme left of valuable minds from their course of sweet reasonableness and eternal vigilance for the preservation of individual rights and the well-being of the whole.

And the book, I suspect, will be unacceptable to the communists even as propaganda, because their ideology is much more concrete, rationalistic, systematized and ruthless than the sort of vague socialistic theories of the nineties which infiltrate Dreiser's new, passionate idealism. In the communist program, which involves a remaking of society from top to bottom, there is no place for idealism, humanitarianism or liberal half measures or compromises of any sort. The communists, of course, will make a show of welcoming Dreiser because he is an outstanding personality in the world of letters, and they will capitalize on his conversion for all it is worth. But they will be bound to laugh up their sleeves at his naïveté in the chapter on "New Statecraft Suggestions." The catchword of adverse criticism of Soviet Russia has been "You can't change human nature," and the Soviet oligarchs have been acting precisely on that principle—that you can't change human nature, i. e., the human nature conditioned by bourgeois capitalistic ideology, so the only thing to do is to "liquidate" it. There is far too much bourgeois thinking in Dreiser's expression of discontent with the present state of things in America, too much kindheartedness in it, for him and his work to escape "liquidation" in any properly organized communistic system.

Who remains, you ask, to whom the book might be acceptable? To the disinherited, perhaps, with whom Dreiser is now deeply concerned and to whom life is not a syllogism, a Five-Year Plan, a set of accountant's statistics, but a painful bread-and-butter struggle. And I suggest that it is a good book for American capitalists to take a peek into, if only to be reminded that this book is a symptom of something more than the psychic effects of the depression in the "business cycle."

Dreiser is not a young man: he is over 60 years of age. He has been through as many panics and depressions as most of the oldtimers in the banking fraternity who try to reassure us that depressions have happened before and the country has always come out all right. It is very uncommon for a man to change his ideas radically at the age of 60. Even at the age of 35 or 40 many men who started out in youth with faintly socialistic ideas become entrenched in a laissez-faire conservatism as soon as they have established their niché in the economic structure. And as a rule those who are by nature conformative have unbudgable ideas when they get to Dreiser's age.

What caused the recent change in his fundamental philosophy it is difficult to say. He paid a visit to Russia, but when he first came back at least he was so far from being converted to Communism that he could write of Russia in a frame of mind acceptable to the Saturday Evening Post. For a time when I was reading "Tragic America" I had the persistent notion that this whole book might have had its inception in an incompleted long-distance call for which Dreiser had to pay an unasked for report charge and that this minor instance of corporate gouging had so aroused his indignation as to make him reexamine all the charges, muckraking and otherwise, against our economic system, and to reserve his special indignation for the American Telephone and Telegraph Company.

But whatever may have been the

cause, major, trivial, the fact is that Dreiser's sympathies are now definitely communistic, even though he is probably unacceptable to the Communist party. His conversion, no doubt, is an emotional one, brought about by a feeling, all too common nowadays, that we have been badly let down, through incompetence and cupidity, by those who control our economic destiny. It is, as a general thing, an emotion that could be changed if serious thought were taken by the controllers of finance and industry to clean house and repair the damage by scientific plumbing and not by stopping the leaks with wads of chewing gum and old rags. It is well for them to consider the emotional force that is strong enough to swing a Theodore Dreiser to the extreme left, and not to waste too much time finding fault with Dreiser's statistics or picking holes in his logic. The communists will do that for him quickly enough. It would be ghastly for us and the manipulators of our economy to wake up some morning and find that Dreiser's deflection to the left was, in the light of the then known events, opportunistic or else a fine example of that tropism an earlier Dreiser adumbrated.

Rev. James M. Gillis. "Not So Tragic America." *Catholic News*, February 6, 1932, p. 5.

Theodore Dreiser is grouchy again or still. The man must be miserable. He has no peace within and he certainly does not find it without. In his new book "Tragic America," he vociferates his hatred of our country, our civilization, our banking system, our churches (especially the Catholic Church, from which he is an apostate), our schools, our police, our judiciary, our everything. North or South, he finds no comfort. All, all is rotten.

If such a man had no literary gift, no one would pay attention to him. We have such sour-bellies in every neighborhood. They live and they die soreheads. When they pass on it would take a Dante to allocate them to their proper place, but if they are permitted to ramble around and pester people in purgatory or in the Inferno, it must be terrible over there. Dante didn't know the half of it.

The fault in Dreiser's method is familiar. It is the one used by foreign critics who harp on the horrors of American civilization. They clip from our newspapers all stories of gangsters, racketeers, debauches and divorcees, asses, idiots and crooks in public life, the farcical features of prohibition, and its hypocrisy. They play up the inanities and asinities of Hollywood—mostly a mythical Hollywood. Reno is their mutton: they return to it again and again (like some of our actresses and society women). They pounce upon Mencken's "Americana" as a thesaurus of our lunacies. They judge us by the "necking," the slobbering and the clinching they see in our movies. In a word they isolate and concentrate upon all our crimes, sins and follies, and they say "This—this is America."

The method is easy. The answer is easier still: "This—this is not America." This is not America any more than a city is its sewers, or a human body its colon. There is more to a city and more to a body than that. And there is more to America than stupidity and sin.

Now Mr. Dreiser, you have so long and so exclusively paid attention to the baser things of life that you can neither see nor guess that there is anything else. You call your book, "Tragic America," an earlier one, "An American Tragedy." You really ought to ease away from all that heavy stuff. Shakespeare gave us, indeed, "Hamlet" and "Othello." But being a real artist and a genuine genius he didn't imagine, or try to persuade us to imagine, that life is all that way. He gave us "The Merry Wives of Windsor," "Twelfth Night" and "All's Well That Ends Well."

They say you are a genius, Mr. Dreiser. I have always doubted it. To me you seem a fanatic, and the most unpleasant kind of fanatic, the man with a fixed idea. If you are a genius, let's see it. Let's have a little demonstration of the fact that you "see life whole." That is the indispensable mark of a man of genius. Are you an all-around man, or simply a "nut"? Show us.

As Catholics, Mr. Dreiser, we lament the fact that you are a renegade from the faith. If any one needs true religion, you do. With your sense of the tragedy of life, your hypersensitiveness about the injustice and the savagery of this earthly life, you really ought to have, as a balance and a comfort, the assurance of another and better life.

You rejected religion. And don't fool yourself about the reason. As a boy, when you went to mass didn't you sometimes hear from the Gospels, "Blessed are the pure of heart for they shall see God?" And with your active mind didn't you realize that contrariwise "cursed are the impure of heart because they shall see only the devil!" That's your plight, Mr. Dreiser. You see all men as devils and all the earth as a hell, because you carry around the devil and hell inside you. It is not unkind or un-Christian to tell you this. You have said it yourself in your printed books a hundred times. In fact you really say nothing else in this unending series of long sprawling, painful autobiographies.

Snap out of it, Theodore. Look up at the sky. Take a squint at the sun. Go out on the hillside and inhale deeply. Get out of the gutters. Come up from those sewers. Be decent, be clean, and America will not seem so tragic.

Eliot Jones. "Dreiser vs. the U.S." *Saturday Review of Literature*, 8 (February 27, 1932), 555.

Mr. Dreiser's thesis in this book is that capitalism is a failure in this country. In more than four hundred pages of fine type he criticizes unsparingly the railroads, trusts, banks, courts, churches, charitable organizations, and police, in fact, most of our economic, social, and political institutions. In a concluding chapter he advocates the adoption of a communistic régime, similar to the Russian system, which he characterizes as a fascinating social development.

As an economist the reviewer realizes keenly the urgent need of reform in many directions. But he is literally amazed that Mr. Dreiser should have the effrontery to offer to the reading public such a conglomeration of inaccurate statements and irresponsible utterances as this book contains. With respect to the inaccuracies, many illustrations could be given, but two will suffice. Mr. Dreiser says that one telephone company (the American Telephone and Telegraph Company) owns all the telephone stations in the country, whereas in fact in 1930 there were 7,785 other telephone companies, not including more than thirty thousand rural telephone associations. He states also that the Interstate Commerce Commission reduced the wages of the railway employees in 1921, being apparently blissfully unaware of the fact that the Interstate Commerce Commission, great as is its power, has never had authority to fix railway wages.

The glaring misstatements scattered throughout the book, inexcusable though they be, are less striking than the irresponsible utterances of the author. He asserts that our capitalists welcome industrial depressions as a means of reducing wages and increasing dividends; indeed, they deliberately and regularly instigate them. Though "the common people (more than ninety-nine per cent of the population) never have prosperity, the corporations and their banks have it constantly." What welcome news this will be to the corporations and banks! He alleges that the Fords, du Ponts, and Insulls give nothing in return for the profits they glory in. He maintains that the railroads (ogre roads, he calls them) have not improved their service one whit in the last fifteen years. He says that the Interstate Commerce Commission must have known in July, 1930, that business activity would decline in 1931, or at least they could have known it had they taken the trouble to examine the several business indices open to them. He includes the Girl Scouts in a list of the "world's craziest, most inane bunch of hypocrites, loafers, and fools"; and he berates the Supreme Court of the United States for not letting a witness appear before it in his shirt sleeves. The American Telephone and Telegraph Company seems to stir him to particular fury. In the author's language, "courts, legislatures, bureaus, commissions, and what not, wherever functioning, all do the bidding of this shameless and bandit corporation." He sneeringly refers to the president of this "vulture" company as dear, darling Gifford; and calls J. P. Morgan sainted, Rockefeller a vulture, Harding a common thief, and the leaders of the American Federation of Labor leeches. And so on, *ad nauseam!*

The reviewer wonders whether any author, no matter how widely known, can honestly hope to contribute to the improvement (or even upsetting) of the economic and social order by writing a book that is so full of misstatement, misrepresentation, and vituperation; and reluctantly comes to the conclusion that the author's sincerity is open to question. In any event, the whole treatment is sophomoric, and quite unworthy of an author of note.

H. Eric Liljeholm. Albany *Knickerbocker Press*, March 20, 1932.

Another hymn of hate, a dark picture, Mr. Dreiser. Another David and Goliath—Dreiser against Capitalism. But no stone in the sling. Modern weapons—barrages of statistics, cannonade of astonishing incidents, and bombing with invective and appeals to logic, to action co-mixed.

The tone is a bit heavy-worded, as usual with Dreiser. The mass of statistics is forbidding, but indicative of the thoroughness but not necessarily the accuracy of the man. The multiplicity of incidents attests to combing of histories of our industrial rise—or fall, whichever way you look at it.

Some of the statistics and his knowledge of economies have been challenged by economists.

But whatever challenge, the sincerity of Dreiser is apparent, his desire to lend himself to the gigantic task of bettering the lives of a lethargic mass that will not act for itself is touching.

The book should be provocative of thought. And action. It is a sad commentary on the intelligence and common purpose of the American workingman that undoubtedly only a few of these probably will read the book. As Dreiser himself expresses it, they would rather "go to the ball game."

Dreiser strikes at Capitalism as fundamentally wrong and charges that changes in the system must be fundamental and drastic or the recurrent cycles of so-called prosperity and depression will continue. Not new, but well-put and backed by proofs.

Dreiser traces the history of railroads, shows them to be bloodleeches on the very porous skin of the public treasury. It is interesting to note in this connection the great grab being made for huge sums by the railroads throughout the country now from the "reconstruction fund." He hits the whole American scene—crooked politicians, "the corporation-minded" Supreme Court, "futile" voting, "chain-gang" corporations, "intermingling" of business and missions and religion, the Red Cross, everything.

He attacks those "grand old buccaneers" of our early history and portrays them as plain robbers of the government, and hence of the common people. He cites, "40,000 millionaires bestride the land and 130 corporations control $55,000,000,000." He charges and essays proof that "An oligarchical group of financial overlords is seeking to enslave the people, first seeking to debase it mentally."

He condemns sham battles with "surplus" eggs in California while children go undernourished in the land, and crys out in despair, "Is life really mad? Because there is too much food, must people starve?"

In substitution for Capitalism he offers state ownership of basic industries and a board of conscientious men untainted by greed to direct the energies of the nation toward happier and fuller lives. Another Utopian solution—a far-off practical one.

It's an "un-American" book. There is no molasses in it. The drab picture it paints makes one wonder—where is that "rugged, fearless, independent Americanism" once vaunted?—

S. C. C.
"Mr. Dreiser Astray." *Christian Science Monitor,* March 26, 1932, p. 14.

Probably few people in America today are so complacent or so ill-informed as to believe that all's right with the American world; but probably still fewer, after reading this book, will venture to assert that it will accomplish anything toward the amelioration of the conditions which it sets out to expose. "Tragic America" may do credit to Mr. Drieser's heart, but it certainly does no credit to his intelligence. The very qualities which, on the whole, have been assets to him in his works of fiction are terrible liabilities in this queer excursion into the realms of economics and sociology. He feels earnestly and profoundly; he thinks confusedly; he writes badly—often incredibly badly. Yet somehow in his novels he has generally managed to accomplish the effects after which he has striven so laboriously. This much must be admitted even by those who believe that his merits as a novelist have been much exaggerated.

But when he turns from the field of the emotions to the field of economies the result is almost as ludicrous as it is pathetic. Except that the writing is as bad as ever (or perhaps worse) and that the writer is evidently burdened with his indignation against capitalistic society, there is little in this volume to remind one of the novelist. He labors through masses of weighty and ill-digested statistics, often incorrect, not seldom misunderstood, occasionally obsolete. He has read Miss Ida Tarbell and he has had his own experiences of a textile strike. There is a great display of facts about oil and freight rates and telephone companies and profits and censuses; and about such matters as the alliance between capitalism and the churches. Some of his statistics may be correct; we don't pretend to have checked them all; but so many have been shown to be incorrect that it is safe to say that no reliance can be placed upon any of them.

The general impression left by the book is of confused, half-articulate indignation. The cure for the social and economic ills of the country is, Mr. Dreiser suggests, a reorganization (requiring, among other things, a new national constitution) along the lines of Soviet Russia. He believes that the masses of the American people are ready for this change. The book will disappoint and disconcert Mr. Dreiser's admirers and will be a weapon in the hands of his detractors.

Edmund Wilson. "Equity for Americans." *New Republic,* 70 (March 30, 1932), 185–186.

When the writers' committee recently went to Pineville, Kentucky, and attempted to give out some food to the striking miners, they found the leading citizens of the community still snarling over the visit of the Dreiser committee. At their first interview with the mayor of Pineville, Mr. Cleon Calvert, the able and avid attorney for the Straight Creek Coal Company, who sat as it were at the mayor's right hand, suddenly delivered himself apropos of nothing of the following statement: "Mr. Dreiser is very fond of tragedy"—in a tone which contemptuously implied that talking about tragedy was affectation—"he wrote 'An American Tragedy' and now he's written another book called 'Tragic America'—and he makes the assertion there that Morgan, Insull, Mellon and Ford have interests in Harlan County." And Mr. Calvert went on to point out that this statement was extremely inaccurate. Some of these interests were not in Harlan but in Knox County; some had ceased to exist, etc.

Now what Dreiser wrote in his book was this: "In Harlan County, Kentucky, the big Morgan, Insull, Ford, Mellon, etc., interests are grinding the coal miners to uncivilized living conditions. Corporation police have perpetrated lawless terror upon strikers, and denied them privileges guaranteed by Constitution and state laws." Mr. Calvert did not attempt to take up the question of the uncivilized living conditions of the miners or the denial of their constitutional rights. But Dreiser's slip about Harlan County had put him in a position to do something to discredit him. And Dreiser, in allowing it to occur, had exposed himself to the enemy. Stuart Chase, in reviewing "Tragic America," complained that there were other errors. If there are, it is a pity, and Dreiser should have them corrected. Anyone who takes up such a radical position as he does in his new book should be proof against attacks on grounds of accuracy on the part of the people he is sure to antagonize.

For such people will always try to make inaccuracies look like errors of fact. The fact is that the coal miners in Kentucky—and pretty much everywhere else in the United States—do live under uncivilized conditions and are denied their constitutional rights. And Dreiser does, in spite of his inaccuracies, succeed in getting over the basic truth about America—just as in spite of his inept and woolly writing he succeeds in being eloquent about it.

By all the rules of rhetoric and composition, "Tragic America" ought to be entirely ineffective. Never has Dreiser's prose seemed more slipshod, never have his sentences trailed and been blurred by more "to say the leasts," "as a matter of facts" and "as I see its." When there is a necessity for hitting the nail on the head, Dreiser usually manages to drive it in cockeyed: "The average individual today is really tortured; he is so numerous, so meaningless, so wholly confused and defeated. . . . More, this wildly individualistic, and hence wildly capitalistic, tension renders life at once so dull and insecure." And when he wants to bring something home to us with especial force, he is likely to produce an anticlimax: "In fact, as early as the middle of the last century, Lawrence Stone and Company, of Boston and New York, in order to have the duties on woolen and dye products lowered, disbursed bribes amounting to $87,000. Yet so widely was this type of thing practised by the affluent members of our dominant commercial class, that our history as a nation is most disagreeably colored thereby. . . . How's that for an honest, kind and true country of presumably democratic and yet wholly—as it would appear—individualistic and better still, corporate, and better still, imperial or in other words, financially tyrannical leanings? How?"

Yet in spite of Dreiser's curious wavering between a slightly pompous literary tone and a tone of extremely informal conversation—"Why, by God," he exclaims at one point, "they don't even give them a decent city government!" —his way of expressing himself never gets between us and what he wants to say. The style is always collapsing; but the man behind it remains sound. His prose has a long and steady rhythm which continues to convey his feelings and ideas even when the words don't quite make sense; and his very absurdities have the unmistakably idiosyncratic character of a genuine literary personality. And so "Tragic America," for all its crudenesses, gives a better picture of the present crisis than neater and more closely reasoned books.

Such books have a way of reducing life to statistical tables or abstract generalizations. But "Tragic America" has the imaginative scope and insight which have made Dreiser so remarkable a novelist. Dreiser talks always in terms of farmers and bankers, textile workers and white-collar workers, miners and millionaires; and—where he is particularly good—presents trusts and companies and banking operations as blind and uncouth organisms with a kind of life of their own which expand and contract, galvanize and kill, and fight each other on international arenas.

Taking up in successive chapters industry, the banks, the railways, the government, the Supreme Court, labor, the police, the church, organized charity and crime, he shows that the American people and their government are now at the mercy of the great trusts and banking houses, which are controlled by a very few rich persons. Not only have the farmers and the working class been broken for the capitalist's profit but they have been prevented by gag law and injunction, by club and gun and jail and gallows from protesting, and the time has come for the dispossessed people to turn and break the capitalists.

Here is Dreiser's conclusion: "Yet what can alleviate this corporate grip upon America? In this book, I have shown the uselessness of reform under the present methods of production and private property. Therefore, as I see it, nothing but a fundamental change in the whole system can do it. The present foundation is crumbling; the weakness is basic—absolutely at bottom and cannot be patched up or repaired. Hence, I now ask, how is it possible to change the foundation of the American economic structure? I would answer *for the masses to build themselves new institutions.* For under our present methods the working class is being destroyed —it is dying from insufferable conditions. This class must be joined by farmers and the entire middle class whom the financial barons have bled and defrauded. The cultural influences of the middle class with frequently slightly more leisure, must join up with the working class to whom they are far closer than they realize, and bolster it up.

"For indeed, the sacredness of private property is an illusion, as shown by change and death. Hence and instead, the proposed new government must have the power to confiscate and turn into state property all of the basic industries: coal, lumber, food, steel, etc., as well as the means of transportation. Some might think that those owning stock in these corporations might be paid for their holdings, but I do not agree. In my judgment, they must take pot luck with the rest of us, fall in with the necessary changes in the spirit of our early pioneers and make a new and better scene here and now. Too long have they been the beneficiaries of inequity, and must learn, however grimly, that that is true. Let them forget the past. It has been a fine dream for the few, but an evil one for the many, and must give way. Besides, what have they to fear? The fate and the life and the living and working conditions of every other man—improved as equity would improve them. And is that so bad? Only a coward or a parasite would say so. Personally, I welcome the change."

He proposes "an executive power for the American working masses not unlike the Communist Central Committee in Moscow, but composed of American men and women . . . who have made a thorough study of the social and economic ills that today engulf America."

"Tragic America" is thus a significant book which marks a definite new departure in the American intellectual world. Dreiser is the first American writer outside the Communist camp itself to come out flatly for Communism for America; and his book is a pioneering effort in what has now become the supremely important task of selling the Americans the idea of Communism. This means for one thing translating the Communist ideology, colored at present so largely by Russia, into terms of American life and substituting for the jargon of the official Communist propaganda in America a language which Americans can understand. Dreiser, in "Tragic America," has made a first brave stab at this. He has, for example, tried to take off the curse attached for the American mind to the word "Communism" by talking about Communism as "equity." Well, we shall probably in the long run have to call it Communism just the same. But it will be a Communism which is less preoccupied with echoing and aping Moscow than American Communism seems to be. It will have back of it the immediate conviction of such unrussianizable Americans as Dreiser and consequently a technique more appropriate for persuading the American mind.

Norman Thomas. "Dreiser as Economist." *Nation*, 134 (April 6, 1932), 402–403.

"Tragic America" is chiefly important because it was written by the author of "An American Tragedy." This book is Dreiser all the way through. In style most of it is Dreiser at his worst. And that is pretty bad. A meticulous English department in high school or college could have almost as much fun with the book as the economics department. Certainly there are very few pages which the statisticians and conservative economists cannot indict for some degree of misuse or misinterpretation of facts and figures. Even friendly critics have called attention to a few of the author's glaring errors and to his extraordinary inability to figure out percentages. I have no desire to add to this catalogue. Yet two or three characteristic bits of the statistical information, or misinformation, with which Dreiser loads up his book struck my eye and seem to deserve some comment. For instance, he says that in western Pennsylvania he found "unbelievable misery. Miners received wages of but from $14 to $24 for two weeks' work. Yet paying $25 a month for a shabby four-room house." I have seen in western Pennsylvania and elsewhere hundreds of pay slips, but I never saw any pay slip charging a miner $25 a month for a four-room shack. Often miners are charged more than $25 for rent plus other charges which are deducted from their wages, and that is probably what Mr. Dreiser means. He could have told the exact truth and made an even more impressive picture of misery.

Elsewhere he calmly says, without any qualifying explanation: "The Methodists, however, have 893,881 in the mission fields (conceive that!) functioning most extensively in China and India." The context makes it perfectly plain that the author thinks that this vast army is a paid army of propagandists. Actually there are only about 1,400 paid missionaries of the Methodist Church in foreign countries.

The author's Communist sympathies and enthusiasm for Russia do not make him accurate when discussing the Soviet Republic. Thus he says, or clearly implies, that the Russian clergy were not disfranchised for a period of ten years. As a matter of fact, they were disfranchised from the date of the promulgation of the first Soviet constitution.

The abundance of mistakes like this, and worse, does not deprive the book of a certain massive and deserved impressiveness. Mr. Dreiser is obviously in earnest. The situation he describes is so bad that many mistakes in detail do not make the total picture essentially untrue. They do make it unnecessarily vulnerable to critics. Moreover, it is not academic to insist that the leaders and builders of a new social order should justify confidence by a capacity for using facts and figures not only with subjective honesty but with objective competence.

In so far as Mr. Dreiser goes in for suggestions concerning a possible way out of America's tragedy, he shows strong Communist leanings. They are, however, literary rather than precise, and one feels that the Communist Party is well advised in refusing him membership but keeping him as an outside sympathizer. He is very scornful concerning the use the people can or will make of the ballot, and most of the time is rather skeptical about the workers to whom he must appeal. He wants an American approximation to the Russian system of government, but he sincerely says: "I would be the last to want the brutality which might accompany such a [revolutionary] change."

In short, neither the student nor the ordinary reader will turn to this book for an accurate statistical picture of America or for a well-thought-out guide to revolutionary change by violent or peaceful processes. Yet I repeat that the book is impressive, and I confess that for the life of me I could not decide as I read it how much of its weight was due to the fact that I knew Dreiser wrote it and how much to its own inherent quality. A shocking confession for a reviewer to make! I suspect, however, that some of its weight is due to the qualities that have made Theodore Dreiser in the field of fiction an extraordinarily significant figure.

Elmer Davis. "The Red Peril." *Saturday Review of Literature*, 8 (April 16, 1932), 661–662.

Even in these distressful times, it needs a lively imagination to see any serious danger (or hope, if you prefer) that America will go communist. What you read, and still more what you hear, among the intellectuals might lead you to think that the glorious day was at hand when, the awful summons hearing, the capitalist heaven and earth will pass away. But most of these ladies and gentlemen appear to have a somewhat vague notion of what communism is, in theory or practice, or why the ills we know not of are preferable to those we have. In fact, they would probably be among the first to be shot; when they saw communism in operation, in its early stages of gaining and consolidating power, they would be shocked; and being still under the influence of bourgeois ideology, they might give unguarded expression to their feelings before they realized that they were living in a new order which did not tolerate criticism.

However, they are not likely to be exposed to such a painful contrast between expectation and reality. The profit system as our ancestors knew it is apparently on the way out; the American economic order of the future, perhaps even the near future, will probably be something that would be unrecognizable to Alexander Hamilton or Commodore Vanderbilt. But unless a wholly improbable change occurs in the mentality of the American people, that order will be quite as alien to orthodox communism. Our communist intellectuals virtually admit that when they write cheerfully of the rivers of blood (other people's blood) that must flow before the apostles of the enlightenment succeed in giving the American proletariat what is good for them.

There begin to be signs, however, that American literature is going to have its Red peril, even though it is no more than a Red nuisance as yet. Germs that a healthy organism can throw off find a foothold in an enfeebled system, and while no part of American society looks any too vigorous at present, the intellectual group is about the sickest of the lot. In the nineteen twenties the intellectuals set up a great hullabaloo, most of which boiled down to the question, What is it all about? No satisfactory answer was found; and few intellectuals had sufficient sense of proportion or knowledge of history to realize that this misfortune was neither unprecedented nor necessarily fatal; to perceive that nobody has ever yet found a finally satisfactory answer but that somehow the human race has managed to worry along.

To admit that there are questions which even our so impressive intelligence is unable to answer, and at the same time not to despair of the ability of the human race to find, eventually, better answers than we can reach as yet —to recognize that there is nothing to do but keep on trying as well as we can, and to be as content as we can with the small gains that in the course of ages amount to something—that requires some courage and some balance; qualities which were not notably prevalent among the intellectuals of the 'twenties. Accordingly a good many of them have taken the easiest way out and yielded to the attraction of a system in which final and all-embracing truth is laid down in the sacred writings, to be authoritatively interpreted for the faithful by the communist church.

The merit of communism as an economic system is a technical question, requiring considerably more evidence than we now have before anybody can be sure of the answer. But so far as can be judged from their writings it is not communism as economics that has taken hold of the imaginations of its American intellectual converts; it is communism as a medicine for sick souls. Why not Catholicism, whose value as an anodyne has been proved by long experience? Well, for one thing (as I have argued in these pages before) because Catholicism is actually in operation in this country; a man who professed his conversion to Catholicism would be expected to behave as a Catholic and refrain from practising the seven deadly sins and from writing novels about some of them. (Not all Catholic novelists so restrict themselves, but those who do not are apt to find themselves involved in arguments with their stricter coreligionists.) But a man who professes communism may continue, pending the dawn of the red millennium over these states, to enjoy all the advantages of capitalist democracy; not the least of which, for the intellectual, is the rare felicity of being permitted to think what you like and say what you think, in print.

That is not all of it, of course. The man or woman whose intellectual background is immediately rationalist and more remotely Protestant has a subcutaneous emotional antipathy to Catholicism as faith, whereas communism is ostensibly a triumph of rationalism. That reason and faith are blended in about the same proportion in each does not disturb him; he takes them both at their face value. And finally a creed which sets the attainment of perfect felicity in the hereafter is less congenial to the contemporary spirit than one which (however recklessly) envisions the perfectibility of life on earth. People in whom the judgment outweighs the emotions are likely to be skeptical of the attainment of perfect felicity by the human race, at any rate within the next million years; but those are not the people who are looking around for a Rock of Ages.

Most of us are driven to strange shifts in these hard times, and the bourgeois ideologist may doubt his right to condemn people who save their emotional comfort at the expense of their capacity for disinterested thinking. They would deny, of course, that they pay any such price. The art of reconciling faith with reason is an old one, and the communists follow respectable precedent if they accomplish it by subordinating reason to faith and holding, in the end, that what appear as facts to the eye of the unsaved cannot be facts if they contradict revelation. It may be that they are the heirs of the future, but their inheritance cannot include very much of the stored intellectual treasure of the past. They do not want it; it is "bourgeois," that is, it is hard to reconcile with the lately revealed truth; and except in pure technology they are unfitted to grasp it exactly in so far as they are good communists. It is as true now as it ever was that submission to religious dogma is poisonous to any attempt at dispassionate thinking, or to intellectual appraisal of the ideas of other men.

For proof of that you need go no farther than the analyses of international politics currently appearing in the editorials of *Izvestiya* and *Pravda*. The French General Staff and the American Farm Board are allies in a foul conspiracy for an unprovoked assault on proletarian Russia; if no such assault takes place, it is presumably because vigilant Moscow editors have exposed the plot in time. The Japanese adventure at Shanghai is only the first step in a joint attack on China by the imperialistic capitalist powers, to be followed by the apocalyptically predicted crusade against the Soviet Union. Yet at the same time, almost in the same issue, the Japanese adventure in Shanghai is proof that the greed of the predatory capitalist powers is about to lead them into wars (also prophetically predicted) against one another. The bourgeois reader is likely to wonder if the men who concoct these theories are conscious liars or merely lunatics. They are neither, of course—only devotees of a dogmatic religion, frantically trying to twist the evidence to fit the sacred doctrines.

Or, if you want an example nearer home, look at Mr. Dreiser's "Tragic America." How sound Dreiser's communism may be, in the eye of the orthodox, I do not know; but it has evidently bitten deeply enough into him to rid him of the taint of bourgeois virtues. He used to be a good newspaperman, yet "Tragic America" is full of misstatements; in his novels he has analyzed character and motivated behavior as well as any man now writing, but his treatment of the character and motives of real people in "Tragic America" is often simply childish. Dreiser the artist knew a great deal about human beings; Dreiser the convert and missionary casts away the filthy rags of profane knowledge, and glories in the all-sufficient garment of faith.

This sort of thing is no doubt effective polemic, on the tabloid level; but people on the tabloid level are not going to take the considerable trouble involved in reading anything by Dreiser. There is plenty of valid evidence available for the indictment of a political and economic order which is not being very vociferously defended, at present, by anybody but Ralph Easley and Dolly Gann; and if Dreiser had confined himself to that evidence his argument would have more effect on the sort of people who would read a Dreiser book. But the appeal from reason to the passions seems, to the bourgeois critic, a pretty constant characteristic of Communist propaganda. The Communist denies that, of course. There is no truth, no beauty, but "proletarian" truth and beauty; *doemonum cibus est soecularis sapientia.* If Communism gets the upper hand all that has been thought and written in the past will be judged by new standards, and most of it condemned, as the church fathers judged the profane letters of Greece and Rome.

Bennett Stevens. "The Gnats and Dreiser." *New Masses,* 7 (May 1932), 24.

Dreiser throughout his literary career has grasped for values other than those maintained by dominant class interests. He has documented, through the characters of his novels, the shallowness and surface nature of personal behavior in a society in which life is inept because capitalism has failed to give it sufficient purpose. But in his novels, and in his autobiographic studies as well, the mood conveyed is that men are victims of an inexorable fate; in them he never made his readers feel that the masses have the power to transform the society that dwarfs them.

Dreiser's visit to the Soviet Union marked a significant change in his intellectual outlook. For although he failed to orientate himself completely to a society in which individualistic *laissez-faire* attitude had been replaced by Socialistic principles and objectives, he was impressed by the fact that these Socialistic values were enriching the lives of the masses in an incomparable manner by removing exploitation and its degrading consequences. He has since participated as an advocate of the workers against capitalist oppression; he has not only given the weight of his name to committees fighting for the defense of political prisoners but he has demonstrated through his investigating trips into the Pennsylvania and Kentucky coalfields where coal operators' terror prevailed against striking miners and their sympathizers, that his interest is not merely verbal. His experiences on these trips have stimulated him to supplement his personal observations through research and to publish this book as an expose of the functioning of capitalism in America. In it he describes the conditions under which the masses live and work, the control of the government and the courts by a few banks and corporations in whose hands the wealth of America is concentrated, the scandalous history of how this wealth was acquired by corporation greed, the terror and coercion that is employed that this concentration of wealth may continue, the perfidious role of the churches and charity agencies and the use of the schools and the press by capitalists to debase the workers mentally. As could be expected the capitalist press has sought to discredit the book by disparagement and ridicule; the two leading Sunday book review sections carried caricatures of Dreiser as illustrations accompanying the caviling reviews by Stuart Chase and Simeon Strunsky, who became as squeamish as Oxford dons in their search for inaccuracies, the number and importance of which they exaggerated. Norman Thomas also used the same tactic in an attempt to destroy confidence in Dreiser's research qualifications thus undermining faith in the value of the book's conclusions. The book actually teems with pertinent, verifiable data gleaned from reliable sources with which most of Dreiser's readers are unacquainted, and comprises a damning indictment of capitalist dominated, and thus tragic, America.

Yet Dreiser has not written an effective book. Facetious banter which he interjects in an effort to popularize his subject, and his awkward style, obscure the significant material which the book contains. But from a Communist point of view there are far more grievious errors in the book than Dreiser's failure to marshall and present his facts with proper clarity. In spite of his declaration of sympathy with Communist principles, he fails at times clearly to grasp them. He manifests repeatedly the liberal fallacy that the use of the American government by the capitalist class is merely an abuse of the "ideals of the Republic" which the "framers of the Constitution never contemplated." Disregarding all the evidence which he presents indicating the control of the federal government by corporations, he naively advocates that "all police used to supervise strike conditions anywhere . . . should be directed by our national government only and receive all orders from it." (Holy shades of the Pullman strike and other strikes broken by federal troops!) In his discussion of religion he is similarly inconsistent; he recognizes that religion by its emphasis on resignation, as well as by the churches' overt acts, is counter-revolutionary, but he at times seems to subscribe to the Christian Socialist blather about the need to return to the teachings of Jesus. In his discussion of labor unions, although he is vigorously critical of the officials of the American Federation of Labor, he regards them as "cabbage-heads" rather than as deliberate misleaders, and concludes in a defeatist strain that "American workers have as yet no real leaders anywhere"—thus ignoring the inspiring fights being waged by left-wing unions although he has on other occasions endorsed the leadership of these organizations.

In spite of its inadequacies this intrepid book marks an important development in the history of American letters. Dreiser by its publication offers a challenge to American artists and intellectuals awakened politically by the crisis, to declare themselves on the side of the revolutionary workers in the fierce struggles that are taking place and in the yet more bitter ones that loom ahead.

Checklist of Additional Reviews

Indianapolis *Star,* January 18, 1932.
William Soskin. "Reading and Writing." New York *Post,* March 26, 1932.
"Bookmarks." New York *World Telegram,* April 26, 1932.

Further Reviews: Bibliographic Information Incomplete

"Dreiser Places Himself." Kansas City *Times,* January, 1932 (?).
Gustav Davidson. *Sunday Mirror,* January 31, 1932.

Notes

THEODORE
DREISER

America Is Worth Saving

MODERN AGE BOOKS
NEW YORK

America Is Worth Saving

Quincy Howe. "Cooperative Monopolies." New York *Herald Tribune Books,* February 2, 1941, p. 12.

Theodore Dreiser's message to the American people might be summarized this way. Modern technology has created a world-wide revolution which is at last giving the common man a chance to enjoy the better things of life. To date, however, the "International of Privilege," which maintains headquarters in London but which has a thriving branch office in this country, has retained its privileges by artificially restricting production except when various cliques inside the International engage in modern war. Then, production zooms, war profits pile up, and the innocent millions go to the slaughter. The present war in Europe is primarily a repitition of the last one except that this time the British bungled things badly at the start when the hoped-for Russo-German conflict failed to materialize.

According to Mr. Dreiser compared with what the British have done to India, Hitler's offenses are nothing to get excited about; as for the Soviet Union, with all its faults and difficulties, it has measurably promoted human welfare within its frontiers. America's "Sixty Families" come off in some ways even worse than the British aristocrats for whom they have conceived such a slavish admiration as to blind themselves even to their own interests. But in spite of the fact that a good deal of the democracy we now enjoy is sham, we have a democratic tradition and our Constitution and Delcaration of Independence plus our immense natural resources put us in a position to liberate the common man.

Mr. Dreiser suggests that we either give real competition a chance or else establish "a co-operative system of monopolies" with the "social control" coming "from the botton." And by all means stay out of the imperialist war now raging in Europe.

This brief summary may not do full justice to Mr. Dreiser's thesis, but it should at least spare some of our more excited interventionists the attacks of apoplexy that will surely fell them if they try to read it. Mr. Dreiser has written this book in the same way he has written his novels. He has written from the passion of his own heart and with no regard for those who do not share that passion. Like his novels, the book is loosely organized, crudely written, ill-proportioned. Mr. Dreiser labors some weak points and does not make the most of all his strong ones. These faults as a matter of fact loom larger in the field of political literature than they do in the imaginative sphere. Mr. Dreiser's novels have the qualities of their defects; his political and social ideas, on the other hand, gain little from the style in which he has presented them. However, one feels that this book has been written with courage and sincerity.

"Counsel from Hollywood." *Time*, 37 (February 3, 1941), 74-76.

Many books end up in Hollywood. Last week, for a change, two books came out of Hollywood. Both carry identical counsel for the U. S. citizen on identical subjects: Defense, Democracy and World War II. *America Is Worth Saving* is a spiteful, wretchedly written tract by great, aging Theodore Dreiser *(The Titan, An American Tragedy)*, who lives in Hollywood, lectures to California's women's clubs. *The Remarkable Andrew* might well be Dreiser's tract scripted into a novel by its author, Screenwriter Dalton Trumbo. . . .

Dreiser's tract is largely an attack on this felonious isle, this seat of tyrants, this England. He is also so fearfully wrought up over the present state of the U. S. that *America is Worth Saving* reads like the definitive burlesque of Upton Sinclair. Like Trumbo, Dreiser is just a good guy trying to revive the Constitution and the Declaration of Independence. Last fall, during the Presidential campaign, he announced his support of Earl Browder and the Communist Party platform.

Robert L. Duffus. "Theodore Dreiser Mounts the Soapbox." New York *Times Book Review*, February 9, 1941, p. 22.

Readers who remember "Sister Carrie" and who know of its author's stubborn insistence on writing his own kind of novel, in his own way, with his own personal pity and imagination, will want to be patient with Theodore Dreiser. If they are not Communists, or fellow-travelers, or secretly inclined to like Mr. Hitler, or so constituted that the word England or Britain puts them in a rage, they will have to be patient with the present volume. This is not so much a book to be read as a long soap-box speech to be listened to. It is equipped with the devices of the Union Square orator who sees his crowd drifting away to another cornplaster vender: "Do we love England? Are you asking me? And does England love us? Are you asking me?" Or: "I am going to set down some facts and figures favorable to Russia. But please don't run out on me."

The facts and figures favorable to Russia do not turn out to be convincing for those not already convinced. The Russian plan, says Mr. Dreiser, "is a plan to produce goods for the people, just as much of everything as they need." To prove that the plan works he cites statistics which must have come from somewhere, and which one may believe if he believes all that Moscow tells him. He also seems to contend that since Stalin promises "democracy day after day, week after week, year after year to 170,000,000 people" and the people "submit so enthusiastically to dictatorship," Russia must have democracy. And since Mr. Dreiser, like the rest of us, has difficulty in defining democracy, this may be true. On the whole, however, Mr. Dreiser is more successful, has more fun and uses more truths and half-truths in damning the British Empire, the French Empire and some aspects of life in the United States than boosting Mr. Stalin's experiment in freedom.

There is much to be said against certain phases of life in the so-called democracies, and Mr. Dreiser says it. We do have "poverty in the midst of plenty." The British Empire was not reared entirely on altruism. Mr. Dreiser once visited an English "gentleman of title," who was outraged when a tradesman dared to wish him a Merry Christmas. Doubtless such gentlemen exist, though Mr. Dreiser need not visit them. There are certainly international tie-ups of armament firms and oil producers. Stupid and brutal Englishmen have had power in India and also in Ireland. British workers have not always been able to find work. British snobs are as bad as our own snobs. Quite a number of conspicuous Englishmen believed that it would be possible and desirable to conciliate Hitler, direct his energies eastward, and let him wipe out communism. The "non-intervention" policy followed by Britain and France during the Spanish civil war must be described as one of the high milk-and-water marks in modern hypocrisy, if not in the hyprocrisy of all time. And one could go on following Mr. Dreiser's indictment and agreeing with some of it.

But like the other soap-box operators —and indeed like many Republican and Democratic orators during Presidential campaigns and in the halls of Congress—Mr. Dreiser adulterates his truths with half-truths and his half-truths with things that are not so at all. It is not true that American Quakers have to enter the Army. It is not true that England has crushed democracy in South Africa, Canada and New Zealand. It is not true that England "spared no effort to support the slaveholding secessionists" during our Civil War: some members of the aristocracy and some others, including Thomas Carlyle, did support them and were beaten down by English public opinion. It is not true that there is now "vast unemployment" in England. It is a half-truth to tell the story of post-war England without once mentioning the enormous extension of publicly financed social services during that period. It is not true—and this Mr. Dreiser well knows—that "Russia and Germany * * * merely agreed not to attack each other." They agreed, among other things, to divide up Poland, and did so. And it is ludicrous to condemn England in bitter terms for surrendering at Munich and also for going to war a year later.

Whether Mr. Dreiser is a Communist or a fellow-traveler or something else is immaterial to the argument in his book and to the comments that have to be made upon it. There are many of us who are not frightened or impressed by labels and who do not consider them important. What is important at the moment is the effect of people's words and actions. The intended effect of Mr. Dreiser's words in this volume is obvious. It is to create a sentiment adverse to aid to England or sympathy for England in her struggle against Hitler. It is Mr. Dreiser's privilege to make this effort, yet its implications should be clearly understood.

"At this date, and to my positive personal knowledge," says Mr. Dreiser, "there is nowhere on earth a greater foe to the development, mental and physical, of the masses of the earth than the present ruling class of England." He says, again: "Hitler? If Hitler had never been, the job would have had to be done by some one else." He says, again: "There was no Jewish question in 1914, and there is none now in so far as these warriors are concerned. Neither is democracy, human liberty, nor any other truly and socially respectable thing being fought for. Power, wealth, dominance for one or the other is all that is sought."

Mr. Dreiser is no Bundist, full of racial venom and infantile insolence. He is certainly not that perhaps mythical capitalist who believes that Nazism would be a good thing in this country because it "shows those labor fellows where they get off." There is not the least doubt in this reviewer's mind that he loves his country, wishes its people well, stands up for what he takes to be the underdog, resents injustice, believes in the principles underlying the Declaration of Independence and the Constitution, longs for peace, hates the power, the sacrifice of liberty, the mass agony that go with war. Mr. Dreiser's heart is in the right place.

But his head? If it is in the right place, on top of his sturdy Middle Western shoulders, it is certainly performing in a curious way. For it is the happiness, freedom and well-being of the greatest number that he wants. And he seeks to attain these blessings for the American people by a course of action, or inaction, that would as surely as tomorrow's sunrise place the Western world under the domination of men who do not care about human happiness or well-being and who hate freedom with an undying hate. He gives comfort, whether he will or not, to the fomenters of Nazi pogroms, to the degenerate brutes who police Nazi prison camps, to the liars and butchers who dynamited Rotterdam after the city had surrendered, to the killers of women and children, to fanatics devoid of conscience.

It is his privilege to be wrong-headed. Let us hope that the time will never come when the spirit of Hitlerism will gain sufficient ground in America to deny him or any one else that privilege. But one feels like tolling the bell for the author of "Sister Carrie."

New Yorker, 16 (February 8, 1941), 66.

The author of "An American Tragedy" writes that we are being rushed into war because the monopoly system cannot solve the problems of peace; that we are having a "transatlantic love affair" with Britain, which he says is not a democracy but a ruthless imperial power; and that we have a chance for democracy here under the Constitution and must achieve it by breaking up the monopolies or placing them under social control. A bitterly sincere but loose-minded Leftist analysis, written in the author's now-familiar substitute for the English language.

Granville Hicks. "Dreiser to the Rescue." *Saturday Review of Literature*, 23 (February 22, 1941), 13.

Mr. Dreiser is not the kind of writer for whose least word one waits eagerly, for his minor works are very minor indeed. "America Is Worth Saving" does, however, break a ten years' silence, and if it adds nothing to Dreiser's stature, if there is nothing in it to suggest that it is the work of a man who has written novels of importance, it gives us some insight into the curiously involved workings of Dreiser's mind.

With much of the book many persons will agree. Dreiser maintains that capitalism has demonstrated its inefficiency, that poverty in an age of abundance is ridiculous and criminal, that democracy must solve the problem of full production and equitable distribution. This has all been said before, but it can do no harm to have it said again.

Dreiser dislikes capitalism, but there is something he hates even more—England. England is "this black widow of the nations," "an imperialist monster," and "our worst enemy." Of the British upper class he says: "At this date and to my positive personal knowledge—I have traveled in England a number of times and followed its structure and history with the greatest of care—there is nowhere on earth a greater foe to the development, mental and physical, of the masses of the earth, than the present ruling class of England." And for the lower class he has contempt: "There is no sense of democracy among the people by and large." He devotes one whole chapter to criticisms of England by the English themselves, from Jonathan Swift to Harold Laski. From the exploitation of India to the obsequiousness of servants he canvasses the sins of the British, and there is no charge too trivial or too far-fetched for him to raise: "They have an outright contempt for our architecture which the rest of the world recognizes as the most progressive and characteristic of our epoch, and scorn to erect any high buildings in England and so give us credit for any original achievement."

As even these brief sentences suggest, Mr. Dreiser has not lost his old fondness for using ten words where one would do as well. Nor is the book free from the confusions we expect of him. If the Civil War is on page 37 an example of our "save-the-world" complex, it is on page 155 part of our struggle for democracy. There is an entire chapter devoted to "that strange arrangement which according to our modern psychologists holds in nature . . . and that is that three per cent of the people born in the world, and *only* three percent, have the amazing ability to do what we call 'Think.'" The possessors of this amazing ability turn out to be the industrial and financial leaders. Almost as extraordinary is Mr. Dreiser's veneration for the Constitution.

In spite, however, of the wordiness and the occasional Menckenisms, the book drives ahead, and in spite of contradictions and all too characteristic nonsense, it has a position. That position is simply that British imperialism is even worse than Hitler fascism and therefore we must not take sides in the war.

Underlying this there is a more complicated argument, which is in part only implied but can be made explicit. Mr. Dreiser holds, first, that if we keep out of war, we may be able to make democracy work. But, second, if that hope fails, there is always the Soviet Union, of which he thinks well. And, third, even if Stalin can't save us, maybe fascism wouldn't be too bad.

Those who disagree with Mr. Dreiser's conclusions would be foolish to under-estimate the strength of some of his arguments. Though certain of the charges he brings against the British are ridiculous, and though his statistics are often open to question, much of what he says is undeniably true. Moreover, his account of the role of British—and American—capitalism in contributing to the rise of fascism is substantially accurate. No one serves democracy by ignoring these facts.

Yet the counter argument is perfectly clear. If England is defeated, there is not much to hope from either the Soviet Union or the United States. The former, even if it is not overrun by German armies, will yield to its own fascist tendencies. The latter will be faced by the task of building a gigantic military machine at a time when democratic morale is at its lowest and fascist prestige at its highest. Democracy is imperfect in both England and the United States, but recent history scarcely teaches us that the way to get more democracy is to abandon what we have.

Lester Leake Riley. "Along the Bookshelves." *Churchman,* 155 (April 1, 1941), 18.

The trenchant pen of Theodore Dreiser writes with all the power and passion of a tract for the times. And it is manifest that the most important fact in modern politics, and that the most obscured and least understood, is the social creation of those few to whom power and personality belong in the control of the world's surplus savings, which subject the destiny of the common welfare to profits and property. These things Dreiser would teach and exhort. No gentle reader, however, will like his voice. It is a voice, surely, that the world is increasingly hearing, beit ever so crass, as it becomes more articulate. So here is set forth the plan of salvation for America, but only the tough-minded can bear it now.

Max Gissen. "What Must America Do?" *New Republic,* 104 (May 26, 1941), 736-737.

It can be said of all these books [Stuart Cloete's *Yesterday is Dead,* Sir Norman Angell's *America's Dilemma: Alone or Allied?,* Clarence K. Streit's *Union Now With Britain,* and Theodore Dreiser's *America Is Worth Saving*] that between publication and review dates the course of events in a world at war has not importantly affected the essential position of each. When you are able to say this about such assorted discussions of a question as broad as What Must America Do, it becomes fairly evident that the basic problem, at least, is clearly defined. That problem is whether the United States can exist as a working democracy in a Hitler-dominated world. The general verdict here is a sincere and well documented No. Only Theodore Dreiser says Why Not, and I, for one, don't question *his* sincerity, even though it has become the fashion to tap the forehead and say poor Dreiser.

It is Stuart Cloete's book that suggests the logical beginning. He says that "Yesterday Is Dead," and on that point there is full, if variously stated, agreement. Yesterday is dead if for no other reason than that most of mankind is being forced to take sides in a conflict that grew out of even sharper recognition of that very fact. Mr. Cloete alone among these authors seems to regret it. His title is almost a lament; and his book, a rushing personal essay, is a partly confused, sometimes brilliant, but always melancholy search for an answer to the question: What ever got this potentially fine world into this awful mess? Cloete blames it on such diverse influences as modern man's excessive demand for material things, the greed of the reactionary rich, faulty education, insipid advertising and an unwholesome attitude toward sex; all of which gives him plenty of windmills to ride at and as often as not all that's left of his lance are the slivers in his hand. But he always has another lance. Cloete is a South African who knows and loves the frontier life which he described in "The Turning Wheels." And what he really dislikes is modern industrial society which comes between man and nature. But for all this nostalgia he can still read the signs. Yesterday is dead.

When it comes to fixing the more immediate causes behind the present war, and apportioning the blame, the authors present an impressive show of unanimity in spite of differences in approach. The one towering recognition is that Hitler's rise was backed and to some extent even engineered by the governments of the democracies. First by supplying the credits and raw materials that made it possible for Germany to arm; then by concurring in the mean and deliberate political surrenders that led to the final show-down. None of these writers is blind to the fact that Munich began in Manchuria and was hurried on by what happened in Ethiopia, Austria and Spain. It gives Dreiser his best opportunity to flay Britain and to question her democratic intent. Before you finish "America Is Worth Saving" you're apt to feel that you've been beaten about the ears with a sheaf of Daily Workers; but when Dreiser explores the fascist bent in English government and industry, it won't do merely to ignore him. Cloete knows the guilt of the democracies, too; and Sir Norman Angell, in "America's Dilemma: Alone or Allied," is less than convincing when he credits Chamberlain and Daladier with sincerity and patriotism, plays down the ideological character of the war and blames popular fear of decisive action in the democracies for the pro-Hitler game played by their reactionary governments.

It is not that Angell is disingenuous in his approach. It is simply that he emphasizes one point, the need for collective security, to the exclusion of the deep-seated factors that largely explain the nature of the present conflict. Mr. Streit, in "Union Now with Britain," to a certain extent runs the same narrow course. Angell argues, as he has many times before, that the United States missed a great chance in 1919 to help achieve a lasting international organization and permanent world peace. Cloete and Streit are of a similar mind. But Angell is careful to point out that the choice is not between bristling armaments and some kind of league; that collective security should mean the joint *use* of arms, if necessary, to defend any threatened member. But it is not so sure that Angell is wholly right in attributing Europe's collapse to the failure to agree on collective action at decisive points. It is at least as correct to say that, as far as England and France were concerned, there *was* collective action, but toward infamous ends.

Again, except for Mr. Dreiser, there is little difference of opinion as to what a victorious Hitler would mean to America. The forecast is by now familiar and probably is concurred in by most Americans. That through international-trade devices, economic penetration of Latin America, appeals to business men (whom Cloete labels the Achilles heel of America), encouragement of civil discord and possibly even direct attack, Hitler could ultimately destroy democracy in America. Dreiser disposes of the threat chiefly by ignoring it. Using the simplest of Marxist approaches, he sees this war as merely another imperialist squabble. To him the British Empire is a more vicious instrument of oppression than anything the Nazis could devise. As for Latin America, let Nazism establish itself there as firmly as it pleases, since we must realize that Latin Americans really have more in common with Germans and Italians than they ever could have with us. Let's stay in our own back yard and fix up the home place and we'll get along fine.

Dreiser's seeming complacence at the prospect of a Hitler-dominated world is due to more than shortsightedness. It is more probably the product of two deep hatreds. The first is a consuming Anglophobia which at times nearly unbalances him and leads to interim diatribes filled with half-truths and faulty interpretations of history. The second arises from the distress and want of millions of Americans resulting from the greed of those groups whose wealth and power depend on a national economy based on scarcity rather than plenty. And although a lot of this book dissolves at the approach of ordinary common sense (the assertion that economic democracy can be strengthened in America after a Hitler victory; the Anglophobia; the uncritical praise for life under Stalin, etc.), don't run out on Dreiser when he smashes away at the effort to smother democracy here and now under the guise of unity, defense etc. Have you seen the papers? . . .

R. G. Woolbert. "Recent Books." *Foreign Affairs*, (July 1941), 877.

The major part of this book, the first published in ten years by the well-known American novelist, is a garrulous and intemperate attack on England.

Christian Century, October 26, 1941.

The title itself is news—coming from Mr. Dreiser, some of whose earlier books might seem to cast considerable doubt on the proposition. But this book has far more to say about Great Britain than about America. It is a piece of trenchant pamphleteering designed to dissociate America from the British cause. Great Britain is not democratic, is therefore no trustworthy champion of democracy, has always hated and scorned America for at least trying to be democratic, and is bound to collapse as an imperial power. "If an empire built on such hypocrisy and blood can endure, then you and I might just as well abandon all our efforts to establish a decent world." Great Britain is not really fighting nazism, says Mr. Dreiser. "No, it is a scrap between Hitlerdum and Hitlerdee." Therefore, obviously, we should stay out of it and devote our attention to correcting the defects of our own democracy. There are plenty of them, but we have the power to correct them. "If Americans don't get what they feel they have a right to get, they will go out and take it—and every intelligent citizen of this world of potential plenty will say, more power to them. A man in the public eye who stands honestly and firmly for this idea is Harry Bridges, of the C.I.O. in the west." We need a "society based on abundance," not one based on monopoly and profits for the few. We must do something to make the Bill of Rights and the Declaration of Independence come true. Russia, he says, has been trying to do something like that. A favorable paragraph about the Russian experiment follows. But—"we in America have no time to waste arguing about Russia's plan. We need an American plan." One gathers that, while our Constitution would furnish the text of the plan, the saving substance of it, as conceived by Mr. Dreiser, would have much in common with Russian principles.

Social Studies, 32 (November 1941), 335.

A great novelist examines the issue of war and peace. Isolationist with a vengeance.

Theodore Dreiser

THE BULWARK

A Novel

Doubleday & Company Inc.

Garden City 1946 New York

The Bulwark

Edwin Seaver. "'The Bulwark'." *Book Find News*, 2 (March 1946), 3-5

The publication of a novel by Theodore Dreiser, his first novel in the generation that has elapsed since the appearance of *An American Tragedy*, is of course a literary event of prime importance. The fact that this novel is also Dreiser's last, that it was contemplated and actually begun many years ago, worked on and put aside at various intervals, and finally concluded in the ultimate year of his life, the fact that death intervened before the author could see his book in print—all this makes the occasion particularly solemn and perhaps prevents our reviewing *The Bulwark* at the moment with a measurable objectivity. Dreiser was the last of the old giants, and his passing marked the end of an entire epoch in American letters. *The Bulwark* should be considered not only as a novel but also as the aged author's spiritual legacy. It is difficult to deal with so much in the brief space and time allotted the reviewer.

Theodore Dreiser was always, in the deepest sense, a moralist. The fact that many people once considered his early works as quite scandalous, and indeed so immoral that his great *Sister Carrie*, for instance, had to be buried in the publisher's cellar lest its circulation contaminate its readers, means little to us today. Such and worse, is often the fate of the true moralist. We know now that Dreiser was always perplexed by the meaning of life, was determined to come to grips with it, scorned the easy escape, and dared to smash the current idols of morality in his stubborn quest for the truth of life and human motives. No American writer ever loved his fellow mortals more passionately, or probed more profoundly for the roots of human behavior, or searched more desperately for an answer to the riddle of existence. By nature he was deeply religious—which does not mean churchy—and his religious bent informed him with an enormous pity for our mortal lot. If at times he seemed blundering and clumsy and naive, his philosophy crude, his science worse, it was perhaps because he was exploring a region in which the familiar charts and compasses were useless, and this at a time when men no longer thought it necessary to explore such a region or had given up in despair. Dreiser the moralist, Dreiser the religious, Dreiser the novelist wanted to know why we are born and live and die, why we know what right is and do what we know is wrong, why we yearn for the light and lust after darkness, why we admire good and enjoy evil.

But if all this is basic to an understanding of Theodore Dreiser, it is also necessary to remember that he lived in the years when the United States was being transformed from the old order to the new, when the old industrial capitalism was giving way to finance capitalism and monopoly, when the old walls of isolationism were being smashed and our country was entering the world arena as one of the major contenders for global power. The very foundations of the established American way of life were being changed, and while we were still paying lip service to the old morality, it no longer sustained us. America was going to church one day a week and worshipping the golden calf seven days a week. In other words, at the same time that Dreiser was concerned with the timeless concept of what men live by, he was also concerned with the immediate conditioning of that concept by the changing social structure.

What we have in *The Bulwark* is a kind of summation of Dreiser's quest stated in its simplest terms, a religious acceptance of life and its trials and tribulations, a feeling of profound resignation and peace, an affirmation of faith in the divine order of things. There will be some, I know, there may indeed be many who will feel that *The Bulwark* was written by an old man who was tired of the fight for a better world, and that in this book he was not merely resigned, but had handed in his resignation; people may say with a sigh, ah well, he gave up before going to his long home. And it may be so. But I am not convinced that it is so.

In *The Bulwark*, Dreiser tells the story of a Quaker family, the story of the
upright and examplary Solon and Be
necia Barnes, and their children. In es
sence the story is this: If a man leads a
good life and walks in the paths of right
eousness, shall not his offspring follow
in his footsteps and enjoy also the fruit
of goodness and righteousness? The fa
ther has not eaten sour grapes; why
then should his children's teeth be set
on edge. And yet several of the children
do go astray, and one in particular, his
beloved son Stewart, learns to lie and to
steal, is involved in a murder and com
mits suicide. Dreiser was too wise a nov
elist to have all this happen in a
vacuum. All around Solon and Benecia
the world is changing; the children are
subject to temptations it was much
easier for the older generation to avoid
And yet the why remains, the anguish
and the agony remain. Unlike Job, So
lon does not curse God and wish to die
He strives to understand the meaning
of it all. "I know now," he tells his
daughter, "that we know so little of all
that infinite something of which we are
a part—and that there are more lan
guages spoken of than we have any
knowledge of." And again, Dreiser says
"For see how tragedy had descended
upon him, and still he had faith, and
would have." And this faith is in divine
love, "constant as nature itself, every
where the same, in sunshine and dark
ness . . . It was an intimate relation to
the very heart of being."

This reviewer, for one, is not pre
sumptuous enough to brush aside Drei
ser's final affirmation as something not
worth listening to. If I cannot accept his
farewell vision, if, as I think, it was a
reversion to the past rather than a leap
into the future, I can accept the integ
rity that gave it voice. Nor am I inclined
to argue with Dreiser's way of telling
this final story, although I think the firs

part of the book bears every evidence of being an unfinished job. But over the rest of the book, and particularly the third part, there is a kind of sunset glow, a kind of after sunset music that is beautifully evocative. I think *The Bulwark* shows that Theodore Dreiser was ready for his death, which is more, alas, than can be said for so many of his contemporaries.

Charles Poore. "Books of the Times." New York *Times*, March 21, 1946, p. 23.

The woods got to be so full of Dreiserites toward the end of his life that it was hard to see Dreiser. By the time he died last December in his seventy-fifth year there had already appeared two new generations of American novelists who followed in his footsteps and profited from the battles he had fought and won. Some of them had written novels in the naturalistic tradition that were attacked just as Dreiser's "Sister Carrie" and "The Genius" had been attacked, but never so vengefully, never so successfully; their paths were made easier because of his pioneering. Yet there was only one Dreiser, towering over his followers with all his own exasperating faults and strange abberations and rocky virtues, as we are reminded by the publication of "The Bulwark" this morning.

"The Bulwark" is the first new novel by Dreiser that has appeared in twenty years, and it gives the impression that he had been working on this surprising companion piece to "The Financier," "The Titan" and "The Genius" for at least that long. It has a curiously old-fashioned air about it, as though its prose had been written by gaslight, though the truth of the matter is that he was simply writing very much as he had always written.

The theme of "The Bulwark" is a religious one, and people who look to find in it an exposition of Dreiser's radical politics will be rather completely disappointed. Instead, they will find an exhausting study of the Quaker religion, presented from a sympathetic point of view. How accurately Dreiser knew the tenets of Quakerism I cannot say, but he certainly brings out its admirable qualities. In "The Bulwark" it is some of the characters who practice—or, rather, fail to practice—Quakerism who get into disasters; the faith itself endures.

Now it has long been a leading cliché of American criticism to say that Dreiser's style is lumpy with clichés, so it had better be said at once that this is true of "The Bulwark." Reading it is really a fairly rugged task. Dreiser was never one to make it too easy to plow through his novels; you get more insight than pleasure from them. Yet you do get insight, and you get it because, though the words he uses may be shopworn, the characters they create are true individuals. . . .

Lewis Gannett. "Books and Things." New York *Herald Tribune*, March 21, 1946, p. 23.

In 1900, in the Age of Innocence, Theodore Dreiser published "Sister Carrie," a kind of watershed in American literary history. Six big novels within the next quarter-century established Dreiser as a major American novelist. But after "An American Tragedy," which appeared in 1925 when he was fifty-four (and the autobiographical "Dawn" in 1931), Dreiser lapsed into all but silence. He had burned himself out. When he died last summer, his already seemed a voice of the past. And it is no service to his memory to publish today as "Dreiser's first novel in twenty years," a manuscript on which he is said to have worked off and on for twenty-five years, "The Bulwark."

For "The Bulwark" is a tired man's Sunday-school story, with all the faults that always marked Dreiser's writing and none of the force: it is muddled in time-setting as well as in philosophy. The simple fact is that, without Dreiser's magic name attached to it, it would hardly have passed a first reader for any publishing house. . . .

Sterling North. "Dreiser's Last Testament." New York *Post*, March 21, 1946.

From pulpits which branded with the scarlet letter "Sister Carrie" (1900) and "An American Tragedy" (1925) we may now expect impassioned sermons praising Theodore Dreiser's final lucid, poetic and deeply religious novel, "The Bulwark."

This is a celestial bit of irony which Dreiser himself would have enjoyed. Having been misunderstood throughout his life by sanctimonious illiterates, he now runs the danger of being canonized by the same motley crew.

Actually, of course, Dreiser was the great moralist of the twentieth century. He was the last American novelist to come to serious grips with the problems of "good" and "evil." He alone among contemporary writers considered man of sufficient importance to be worthy of classic tragedy.

Even when his prose was at its most ponderous and his logic at its murkiest, Dreiser was digging deeply into human motivations, was seeking with powerful blind instincts his way through the treacherous jungle of human society.

None of his plots were "set-ups." None of his solutions are easy or pretty or cheaply optimistic. Not even in his final novel, the moving, beautifully understated life story of a devout Quaker, does he allow himself the complete comfort of revealed "truth." Dreiser probably died still questing the Grail.

But if this book is not a last testament, no writer has ever left one.

Written and rewritten over a period of thirty-five years, this life of Solon Barnes, good, gray Philadelphian, seems to have brought Dreiser as near to an expression of belief as he would ever come.

"Good intent is of itself a universal language." Not the road to hell, but the road to heaven is paved with good intentions, or so thinks the chief protagonist of this quiet, thoughtful novel.

Despite the fact that at least two of his five children have disappointed him grievously (one so forgetting his Quaker teaching as to follow murder with suicide) Solon Barnes in his mental agony finds in God "His good intent toward all things—all of His created world."

Dreiser was an old man as he dictated that final sentence. But he was a man who had watched and studied humanity for three-quarters of a century. He had explored capitalism, socialism and communism in his search for the greater good for the greater number. Readers of his novel will wonder whether at heart he did not end life a member of the Society of Friends.

Harry Hansen. "Dreiser on Faith." New York *World Telegram*, March 31, 1946.

In March, 1910, Theodore Dreiser scribbled an outline for a novel The Bulwark, "on the back of a discarded letter to the critic Mencken." (His secretary, Marguerite Tjader, is speaking.) He was 33 years old; he had written Sister Carrie; he was in Who's Who. In the course of the next 35 years he wrote four or five versions of the novel but put them aside; in the meantime he finished that long line of books on which his reputation rests, from Jennie Gerhardt through The Titan, The Financier, The "Genius" to An American Tragedy and a dozen more. Today, nearly three months after he died in Glendale, Calif., a grave, pudgy-faced, white-haired man, The Bulwark appears.

Why this long delay, this culling of the best passages, this final dictation of the last third in 1945? Miss Tjader, writing for the Book Find News, says he had gone so deeply into the financial and family experiences that he had enough material for three books of the present size. But The Bulwark is strangely unlike the big novels—it has short chapters and ends on a note of spiritual faith, in which an American Quaker, who has been shocked by his son's suicide and his daughter's sexual laxness, reiterates his reliance on that Inner Light that draws men together in faith and makes each one his brother's keeper, finding contentment and peace in serving others, the religion of unselfish love experienced by John Woolman.

As a story The Bulwark is uninspired and routine; its characters are described but not brought to life; if published without Dreiser's name it would justify only passing mention. It must have been finished not because of an overwhelming urge to express it, but because Dreiser was constantly being asked about it. . . . Here, again, is Dreiser, the moralist, pondering the inscrutable behavior of human beings and relating his idea of the social responsibility of the individual to the old, Biblical truths, reiterating "our intimate relation to the very heart of being."

This will be welcome news to those who have looked upon Dreiser as lost among the radicals, and, as H. L. Mencken might say, they will now enroll Dreiser among the pious. On the other hand, radical admirers will be slightly disturbed, although holding fast to Dreiser as their giant among American authors. Edwin Seaver, reviewing the novel for the Book Find Club, remarks: "If I cannot accept his farewell vision; if, as I think, it is a reversion to the past rather than a leap into the future, I can accept the integrity that gave it voice." There is, he says, "a kind of sunset glow" in the third part, which shows that "Dreiser was ready for his death" . . . whatever that means.

The Bulwark gets its title from the mother's remark: "Thy father was a bulwark of our faith." Doubleday is publishing it in an edition of 60,000 at $2.-75, and the printing of the Book Find Club will be at least that many. It is extremely likely, however, that its future popularity will not be among the old Dreiser admirers and radicals but among the readers of Lloyd Douglas' books, which would be the final irony.

Robert E. Spiller. "Dreiser as Master Craftsman." *Saturday Review of Literature,* 29 (March 23, 1946), 23.

This is the first of two novels which Dreiser completed and put to press just before he died. Both were conceived and probably partly written thirty or more years ago. The third volume of the Cowperwood trilogy is yet to appear. "The Bulwark," a study of a Philadelphia Quaker family at the close of the last century, was first announced in 1916. It is possible, however, that the reception of "The Genius" one year earlier discouraged the completion of another major work at that time, for, until "An American Tragedy" in 1925, Dreiser gave to the world only short stories, essays, plays, and autobiography.

"The Bulwark" is a major novel, a substantial piece of work, well conceived and carefully executed, representing its author in his full creative power. If it may also be taken as a last will and testament, it presents an interesting biographical problem, for here is an answer in faith to the spiritual doubt of his best work. Another possible reason for its delay is that Dreiser at the age of forty-six was not ready for the affirmation which seemed logical to him at seventy-four. Perhaps it took him thus long to face his own challenge.

"The Bulwark" is the life story of Solon Barnes and of his family from the time when, at the age of ten, he left with his parents the small town of his birth, to his death in the now old family home in New Jersey not far from Trenton, his grown children about him. It is a quiet and solemn story, told with an almost heavy sincerity and an economy of incident. The moral issue which confronts Solon throughout is always before the reader. The characters move, as Dreiser characters must, through the shaping actions of their lives helpless in the hands of a fate beyond their control, but "The Bulwark" is unique among Dreiser novels in that the moral issue and the forces of which it is composed are clearly defined and never for a moment forgotten. Never is the reader lost in mere action; always he is weighing and evaluating the central problem: Does the simple way of the Friends provide a philosophy capable of dealing with the forces which so mangled the lives of Carrie and Jennie and Frank Cowperwood, and later Clyde Griffith? Had Solon the answer?

Emphasis on ideology involves a sacrifice in fictional vividness. When a novelist, in the manner of a Hawthorne, is interested rather in what his characters stand for than in what they are, there is an inevitable loss of the sense of reality. They become typed to the point of losing much of their actuality. The line between realism and allegory is crossed, and the characters are themselves controlled instead of controlling the action. This happens to Solon, and it happens even more so to Benecia his wife, and to his five children, their friends, business associates, and relatives. Each character moves only within the part in the ideological pattern assigned to him. Even Stewart and Etta, the youngest and most wayward of the children, lack the authenticity of Jennie Gerhardt and Clyde Griffith, although the course of their lives is closely drawn to the Dreiser formula of Sex and Wealth. The old stories are here repeated, but compressed so that their bearing upon Solon's problem alone is emphasized. Yet even minor characters, within these limitations, have a firmness of outline and a solidity which is Dreiser's greatest achievement always. There is nothing shadowy about his allegory; it is made of the stuff of life—and his people live.

The sacrifice of full character development is more than repaid in firmness of texture, a quality not so certain in Dreiser's work. This is the most solidly built of all his novels, in plot and ideology. The long pages of minutiae which stretch out the slim plots of his other works are here severely cut to essentials, and he is able to tell a much longer and more involved story than is usual with him, in half the space. And the uncertainty of direction which spoiled "The Genius" is no longer present. This is the work of a master craftsman who knows what he wishes to say and exactly how much writing is necessary to its saying.

For Quakers, the central issue of this story will have a profound and searching meaning; and for those others who have found in the way of the Quakers in wartime a hope and a promise, it will serve as a fair and non-partisan examination of their faith. For Solon's guidance by the Inner Light is constant if not always perfect. He falls into the error of substituting the dicta of "The Book of Discipline" for an ever fresh searching on his own part. He is too much Solon, the lawgiver; too little the lover of men. He fails with his children because his conviction is too rigid for a world in change; and he fails in his profession as banker because he listens to the false logic of his elder friend, Justus Wallin, that property may be acquired if administered in justice. The sense of guilt which pursues him through life is not laid aside until sorrow has taught its lesson. That in the end he is still able to distil the doctrine of love from his religious heritage makes it possible for him to die in peace.

In thus reconciling God with nature, Dreiser has not rejected the brutality of his own naturalism, but he endows Solon finally with a way of life which, for him at least, gives meaning if not always clear direction to the conflict in the natural world. Was this Dreiser's deathbed confession? Had the mysticism which always colored his dogged acceptance of the ugly with the beautiful finally taken a form and a control in religious awakening? His biographers must decide.

Edmund Wilson. "Theodore Dreiser's Quaker and Graham Greene's Priest." *New Yorker*, 22 (March 23, 1946), 88, 91, 92.

. . . As you read "The Bulwark," Theodore Dreiser's posthumous novel, you go through all the familiar experience of first groaning over the commonplace characters and the shoddy clichés of the style, then gradually finding yourself won by the candor and humanity of the author, then finally being moved by a powerful dramatic pathos which Dreiser has somehow built up. The people of "The Bulwark," when we start it, seem to be among the least promising that Dreiser has ever tackled: a family of Pennsylvania Quakers, hard-working and poor in the first generation, hard-working and well-to-do in the second, never adventurous, eccentric, or brilliant. Yet, even in its earlier and duller stretches, this is not one of Dreiser's most tedious books. He seems, by the time he wrote it, to have learned to cover ground more quickly. The language, too, is somewhat less oafish than it is in the worst of his work, and, here as elsewhere, the personal voice, the rhythm, carries off the vague and fumbling vocabulary. Yes, we say, when we come to the first love scene, Dreiser is still deeper and purer than most of the people who write so much more cleverly. . . .

Natalie H. Calderwood. "The Old and New Dreiser." Kansas City [Mo.] *Star*, March 23, 1946.

When Theodore Dreiser died in December, 1945, many critics made their final pronouncements on him. Indeed they had been making final pronouncements for twenty years. In the books on American literature written during the 1930s, Dreiser was given a chapter in the section on early American realism and was finished off exactly as if he had said his last word, almost as if he had written centuries ago.

This treatment of Dreiser is understandable. During the first quarter of the century he made a contribution to American literature and thought which was important enough to receive consideration all by itself, no matter what else he might do. The fact remains, however, that Dreiser had not said his last word, had not made his final contribution, and was certainly not ready to be finished off.

For at his death he left behind two unpublished novels. One of these, "The Bulwark," has just now been published. While it does not invalidate most of what has heretofore been said about Dreiser, it does invalidate some. More important than this, it adds a new note to the Dreiser legend and must certainly therefore be taken into account in the final estimate which cannot be made until the second of the unpublished novels appears. . . .

In "The Bulwark" there is some of the old Dreiser attack on the materialism of Americans. There is evidence too of the old conviction that life is a confusion of opposing motives and ideals, and that man is pretty much the pawn of fickle and perverse gods. There is also the fine old Dreiser pity and compassion for the suffering victims of the gods. But there is one important thing more.

Dreiser has often been berated for his negation—if anything so powerful as Dreiser's criticism of life could be called negation. At any rate he did swing out heavily without offering very many constructive suggestions, in his novels at least, for making life better. It was not his business to do so, especially if he had nothing constructive to offer. Objection is sometimes in itself constructive.

In "The Bulwark," however, there is a new note. There is a strong positive statement of belief that man can achieve not only peace but happiness in this troublous world. And he can achieve it in one way: by a love which transcends the material and the personal. . . .

John T. Flanagan. "Dreiser's Powerful Posthumous Novel." Chicago *Sun Book Week*, March 24, 1946.

. . . In this posthumous novel Theodore Dreiser reveals a modified form of the naturalistic philosophy which so impregnated his earlier work. He still sets himself against the status quo, he is still a vigorous enemy of materialistic capitalism and social repression, he still presents life as too strong for the human ants who throng this globe. But Solon Barnes is not a failure, nor is he false to his creed, and at his death he retains the faith which had been his solace during many a crisis. Religion cannot nullify economic determinism nor can it despoil capitalism of its prey, but more than anything else it can cushion the shocks of life. If in Marxist terminology it is the opiate of the masses, to Solon Barnes it is the one dependable thing in life.

"The Bulwark" can hardly increase the stature of the artist who conceived Sister Carrie and Frank Cowperwood, but Solon Barnes is a character finely imagined and admirably presented. And in his posthumous novel Theodore Dreiser proved that he could write simple and direct as well as vigorous English.

Mary Carter-Roberts. "Reviewing the New Books: Theodore Dreiser's Posthumous Novel Not His Best." Washington *Star*, March 24, 1946.

The posthumously published work of a famous author usually sells. Sometimes it is significant work, sometimes it is not, but the public which has read the author in his lifetime can be depended on to manifest its interest, even with a whetting of curiosity, in anything which appears bearing his name after his death. Seemingly an awareness of this dependability has led a publisher to bring out a new novel by the late Theodore Dreiser.

"The Bulwark" is not significant work. It is a mass of the famous Dreiser faults—bad writing, maudlin seriousness, dullness, crudity—without the compensating Dreiser virtues of contemporary reality and impressive characterization. It reads, indeed, like something which Harold Bell Wright might have perpetrated in about the year 1906. It will add nothing to Mr. Dreiser's quite sufficient glory. It will, at most, remind people that he did do better.

It is a pompous and dreary report on the history of a wealthy American Quaker family from the late years of the 19th century to the 1920s. The parents marry in idyllic love made purposeful by genuine religious faith. The five children grow up in a changing world and run into disaster of various kinds. The mother dies of grief. The father, though he is unable to understand where he failed, humbly accepts the will of God. It is an old and honorable theme. It requires character for its development, however, and Mr. Dreiser has neglected to furnish it therewith.

No person in the book has the faintest vestige of life. The people are wraithlike generalizations. Weighted with the groaning load of Mr. Dreiser's style they soon cease to be even approximations of human beings and become figures of demonstration in a completely obvious lecture.

I have said elsewhere that Dreiser wrote good books badly. Here he has written badly without producing anything of sufficient integration to deserve the name of book on any terms. I can find only one trace of significance in "The Bulwark," and that is this—it deals with its people, such as they are, on terms of conventional morality. Good and bad in it and defined in the manner of a generation ago, but without the hypocrisy which appertained to the definition in the time when it was sanctified by general acceptance, without smugness, that is to say. There is a good deal of evidence that moral values are being reinstated in the general consciousness and, in that connection, the theme of "The Bulwark" can claim to be significant. But a theme without characters or art, a theme that is merely stated and that badly, is no noticeable contribution to literature.

T.J.M.
" 'The Bulwark' Accentuates Dreiser's Loss to Letters." Atlanta [Ga.] *Constitution*, March 24, 1946.

Theodore Dreiser, in "The Bulwark," one of two novels before his death and his first in 20 years, has undertaken a social theme once more.

This time, however, he selected a topic far removed from that of his controversial "An American Tragedy," which emerged from the storm center of moralists' indignation to win the status of an American classic. "The Bulwark," a story of a Quaker household beset by the materialism of the 20th century, deals with the failure of the older generation to understand the younger and the subsequent maladjustment. . . .

Dreiser in the novel shows a keen awareness of the ever-widening gap between man's abandonment of religion and increasing dependence upon technological and materialistic standards. "The Bulwark," written in a rich, complex style marked by an author at full maturity, emphasizes Dreiser's death as a loss to American literature and the passing of a socially-conscious author of undoubted literary merit.

Horace Gregory. "In the Large Stream of American Thought." New York *Herald Tribune Weekly Book Review*, March 24, 1946, p. 1.

Theodore Dreiser died at seventy-four, in December, 1945. The publication of his long-awaited novel, "The Bulwark," has arrived at an unfashionable moment in his literary reputation. At the present hour younger critics have turned their attention to the glamorous and youthful memory of another Middle-Western novelist, F. Scott Fitzgerald, and the re-emergence of Dreiser's elderly, bulky figure, throwing its shadow across the scene, seems to interrupt an otherwise fortunate, though admittedly sentimental journey among the pitfalls and tarnished glories of the nineteen-twenties. Yet the publication of "The Bulwark" has its own elements of timely interest and the book re-establishes the obvious truth that Dreiser consciously wrote within the larger stream of an American tradition. "The Bulwark" may be described as a "Quaker novel," which is by no means inappropriate to the years that follow a second world war, for the unspectacular presence of the Quaker as well as his humane services here and in Europe have revived the saintly image of John Woolman whose teachings are closely associated with the central theme of Dreiser's book.

Those who have read "The Financier" and "The Titan" will find in the scenes of "The Bulwark" another aspect of the same locality that had witnessed the early rise and fall of Frank Cowperwood. "The Bulwark" is the life-story of Solon Barnes, a self-educated Philadelphia Quaker banker. It follows the career of its protagonist from farm boy to treasurer of a bank. Barnes's marriage was an outwardly successful one, and it is not until his younger daughter leaves home and follows a bohemian way of living and his youngest son commits suicide that Barnes realizes his own unhappy destiny. The entire book, which has the air of an historical novel, falls within the proximity of the late nineteenth century atmosphere that had been generated in the carriage-riding afternoons and gas-lit evenings of "The Financier." Barnes is looked upon as a solid man by his associates in a Philadelphia bank; he is of outwardly conventional appearance, yet his unarticulated, internal life follows the precepts of John Woolman's "Journals," and these are laws which contradict his material success and the amoral conduct of his own children. Barnes's "tragic flaw" is one of slow-mindedness, of being unable to adjust his inner life to "progress" and the ruthless character of American materalism —and that is the sermon, if we wish to state it baldly, of "The Bulwark."

In Solon Barnes's misunderstanding

of his children we have Dreiser's characteristic touch of pathos which in his other novels also showed the dividing line between fathers and daughters, mothers and sons. And it is in that revelation that Dreiser has so often made us aware of human bewilderment and waste, and recreated for his readers what is commonly called "the illusion of life."

It is in his understanding of human fatality that Dresier holds his place in the tradition of the great nineteenth century novelists. In all his writings he remained unaffected by twentieth century techniques in telling a story, and one is almost led to insist that his true master was Balzac, the Balzac whose power is felt through the screen of bad translations into English, and Balzac alone. The same power is felt in a memorable scene in "Sister Carrie," where Hurstwood robs his employers, in the hotel and courtroom scenes of "An American Tragedy," and in a room in "The Financier" where Cowperwood's enemies decided to wreck his financial career in Philadelphia. In these great scenes one is in the presence of a man who has something to say, and though he seems often to move far outside the province of art, when the moment arrives for him to say it, he writes supremely well. Whenever the warmth of action rises, whenever the scene is furthest removed from all thought of "literature," it is there that one finds the presence of Dreiser's "genius."

It is well known that the more important aspects of Dreiser's slow self-education were predominantly "unliterary" and that through the many pages of his novels one finds traces of the impressions left by his extra-mural readings of Darwin and Spencer, the elder Huxley and Thorstein Veblen. Each growing city in American (and particularly the Chicago of "Sister Carrie" and "The Titan") as Dreiser saw it was a battlefield, and the men within it, moved by economic and social forces greater than themselves, waged war side by side and against each other. Each town and city enclosed (in Robert Browning's phrase) "a world of men," men in streets and factories, courthouses and prisons, stock exchanges and hotels, in banks and brothels, lodges, "private" offices and bars. The world of Dreiser's novels is literally a man's world, and it is not at all surprising that Dreiser received his warmest admiration from the two critics, Henry Louis Mencken and Carl Van Doren. The same understanding of masculine psychology enters Van Doren's study of Benjamin Franklin's energetic political career. And the same insight illuminates the lively chapters of Mencken's autobiography. It was fortunate indeed that Mencken wrote the preface to the new memorial edition of "An American Tragedy," for the personal tribute to the memory of Dreiser says all that may be required of a completely candid and graceful epitaph.

I think we may accept it as a notorious fact that Dreiser never wrote a novel with the mere purpose of entertaining the reader or his wife. And none of his books seem to have been written for the delight of women who wish to identify themselves with the heroine of a latest novel. It is here that the legend of how "Sister Carrie" was virtually supressed by the wife of its original publisher has critical relevance. Was the lady shocked at Carrie's lack of sexual morals? Perhaps. Yet there have been many heroines from the earliest novel to the present date whose frailties and misadventures have been enjoyed by generations of respectable women. The deeper shock in "Sister Carrie" was the way Dreiser turned a blind eye to the sensibilities of his women characters. Dreiser's women are either the sorrowing mothers or pretty, vivacious mistresses of men—and should they happen to become men's wives, their attractiveness begins to fall away, and presently to disappear.

Of the ladies who rotate through the pages of Dreiser's "A Gallery of Women," and the girls who participate in the love affairs of "The Genius" the less said the better. In "Sister Carrie" it is Hurstwood, Carrie's lover, and not Carrie herself, who commands the center of the stage, and Jenny Gerhardt is seen only from a man's point of view. The only exceptions to this general rule (and the exceptions would not be flattering to a publisher's wife) are the figures of Aileen Butler, Cowperwood's mistress who became his wife, and Clyde Griffith's mother in "An American Tragedy." In these two figures Dreiser's women share in a man's world the three-dimensional qualities of life. His blindness to feminine motives and behavior also affects the women of "The Bulwark," and their lack of reality contributed to the reasons why Dreiser's discussions of sexual "freedom" and morality in his present book seem as curiously outmoded and as overweighted as in his earlier novels.

Even in its limitations, the very atmosphere of a Dreiser novel has its analogy to the writings of Dreiser's contemporary, Edgar Lee Masters—and nowhere is the relationship between the two men more clearly shown than in the pages of Master's autobiography, "Across Spoon River." In their lack of formal education, in their frequent awkwardness in writing prose, in their sincerely realized conviction of having something to say, in their late maturity, in their devotion to "scientific" cults and theories, and in their honest, unblinking, if somewhat limited and belligerent view of an America that expended its energy upon immediate and material gains, the resemblance between the two writers is so deeply marked that one cannot dismiss it as one of accidental origins. The likeness has its roots in a Middle Western environment, in the doubts and speculations of a people who were but one generation removed from a race of pioneers. Despite the rapid growth of cities and the hope of sharing large fortunes made, the era of Dreiser's youth was one of slowly awakening disillusionment among the many. Since Dreiser and Masters had become the spokesmen of the many, the emotional temper of their prose and verse reflected the darker aspects of an otherwise prosperous, outwardly placid American landscape, and it was as though the two writers, unknown to one another until both had reached middle age, shared in the secrets of a conspiracy.

Dreiser's "The Bulwark" lacks the energy and force that we associate with the writing of his Cowperwood novels and "Sister Carrie"; but the book carries with it a lyrical overtone and unexpected charm that is inspired by the quotations from John Woolman's "Journals." And even the most critical (as well as the most thoughtless) reader of "The Bulwark" cannot fail to be moved by the pathos of the scenes in which Solon Barnes faces his failure to live by the ethics of his faith. Here, as in his earlier novels, Dreiser is the great and critical biographer of that figure that was once called "the American business man," who was not the man of largest fortune but one who represented the aspiration of his civilization—Hurstwood in "Sister Carrie," or the glittering figure of Frank Cowperwood. Even in the pathetic character of Clyde Griffith the aspirations toward American wealth and power, the desires to conform to the standards of American "success" are clearly shown.

We are perhaps still too close to the date of Dreiser's death to measure his stature or to fix his claims upon the imagination of posterity. We know that critics at the time of Whitman's death in 1892 felt his loss and yet they were scarcely in a position to measure the orbit of his posthumous fame. In American fiction Dreiser's contribution is not unlike the impression left upon readers of Whitman's poetry; we know that Dreiser belongs to that division in American literature which places him, somewhat self-consciously, at Whitman's side, and at an opposite extreme from the prose and poetry of Edgar Allan Poe. In or out of fashion, Dreiser's notorious "artlessness" will remain what it was when Sherwood Anderson wrote "Heavy, heavy, the feet of Theodore. How easy to pick some of his books to pieces, to laugh at him for so much of his heavy prose." Yet if his flaws remain, so do his virtues. The seriousness of Dreiser's intentions, his understanding of a larger "world of men" than any of his contemporaries knew, have not failed their purpose. And no American novelist within living memory has equaled Dreiser's power to remind his readers of Wordsworth's emotion when he wrote of "thoughts" that "lie too deep for tears."

"Dreiser's Final Novel Is Recantation of Old Doubts." St. Louis *Globe-Democrat*, March 24, 1946.

Theodore Dreiser's posthumous novel, the life story of Solon Barnes and his wife, Benecia, a Quaker family guided by "the Inner Light" is a tragedy of the revolt of their children from the formal pietism of their faith. Solon is a sincere but thrifty financier who reconciles possessiveness with the doctrine of stewardship. A Philadelphia banker, preoccupied, reserved, honest, seeking to live simply according to Friends' discipline. He seeks to be just, and when banking associates skate on thin ice of speculation he calls in the bank examiners. Yet the strictness of his discipline is a bar to justice to his children. They rebel at being set apart from common custom.

The portrait of Solon partakes of Dreiser's recorded concept of his own Roman Catholic father and thus moulds the novel into autobiographic apologia. For when he writes of the rebellions which lead Dorothea into the social whirl, Etta into scandal, and Stewart into tragic suicide, he writes as one who has looked into his own heart.

This last testament in fiction is a personal recantation of that mumbo-jumbo of materialism Dreiser so ardently argued in the autobiographic books of his maturity. Life is no longer the jungle-strife of "claw and fang" he saw through his strabismic view of Darwin and set down in another Philadelphia story, "The Financier," as "Things live on each other—that was it." Nor merely the insensate "Rub-A-Dub-Dub" once echoing through his personal confession. Now he avows a conviction that "there must be a Creative Divinity, and so a purpose, in all this variety and beauty and tragedy of life."

Dreiser had seen the vision of John Woolman, and he knows now, with St. Paul, that "the greatest of these is Charity." He is not preoccupied with theories of social, economic or political relations—he probably never was except in a novelist's view as they mould character—but with loving kindness. His prose returns to the clarity of the earlier novels, but freed from its materialistic detail. Freed too of the turbulence which made his autobiographic writing seem to stumble and fumble in its search for truth. It, too, shines with the inner light, and he closes his tale on a note of pity as Etta sobs, crying not for herself or her father, but "weeping over life."

F. O. Matthiessen. "God, Mammon and Mr. Dreiser." New York *Times Book Review*, March 24, 1946, pp. 1, 42, 44.

When Dreiser died, he had not published a novel for twenty years, and only one, "An American Tragedy," in the past thirty. His pioneering work had been done at the very beginning of the century, and his one period of great productivity extended through the four years (1911–15) in which he brought to completion "Jennie Gerhardt," "The Financier," "The Titan," and "The 'Genius,' "

His first novel is still the one most frequently cited to demonstrate his historical function as the courageous opener of doors for later writers like Sherwood Anderson and Farrell. But "Sister Carrie" is not merely historically important. Dreiser did far more than break through the genteel tradition by insisting on frankness in dealing with sex. He was against all official versions of our life. He came himself from the other side of the tracks. The son of an unsuccessful German immigrant, and the twelfth of thirteen children, he knew, like so many of the characters he created, what it meant to be on the outside looking into the brilliantly lighted windows of American wealth and power.

The emotional force of his novels rises from his own involvement in his material. "Sister Carrie" exudes the glamour of a chromo, the glamour of the big cities as Carrie herself was drawn to them. The liability in what Santayana called the genteel tradition was due to its being the product of the mind apart from experience. Dreiser gave us the stuff of our common existence, not as it was hoped to be by any idealizing theorist, but as it actually was in its crudity.

This posthumous novel, "The Bulwark," was first announced thirty years ago—and he seems to have intended to fit it into the pattern inaugurated by "The Financier," into his study of American society as it was being transformed by finance capitalism near the end of the nineteenth century. His scene is again Philadelphia, against which he projected the beginning of Frank Cowperwood's career. But his material is very different; not the rise of a typical robber-baron, but the history of a Quaker family as it responded to the pressures of an increasingly complex world. What caused Dreiser to lay this novel aside I am in no position to say, but he is reported to have worked on it intermittently during his latest years and to have added his last touches not long before his death.

As it stands, "The Bulwark" is a whole cycle of taste away from "Sister Carrie." That book was virtually suppressed by its publisher because of its shock to conventional morality. This new novel, if it had been by an unknown writer instead of by Dreiser, might conceivably not have found a publisher at all. That is not a reflection on its value, but on its lack of accord with current formulas. It also breaks with Dreiser's previous work in being a religious novel. We have had currently a recrudescence of best-selling novels of religiosity, embellished by slick and sentimental handling. But "The Bulwark" is as bare as a parable.

Its style avoids some of the problems that have always confronted Dreiser's readers. As though in response to his Quaker material, he writes with greater simplicity and spareness, with fewer clumsy and broken-backed sentences than he used to grope his way through. But his word-sense can still be as cumbersome as ever. He can write of "talking enthusiastically of things Western" and of "a veritable figurine of a girl"; and for one of his most important moments, the suicide of a boy, he can summon no fresher resources of language than: "Thinking of his beloved mother, he opened the larger blade of the knife, and turning to the wall and whispering, 'Mother, forgive me,' plunged it into his heart."

Out of its context that is not easily distinguishable from the language of our earlier and simpler dime novels; and the question it raises is how can a novel with such a climax manage to be impressive? The quality which, despite all his imperfect control over his medium, has made Dreiser the most massive figure in our twentiety-century literature, was described in one of his own phrases: "My pride in a sturdy, passive acceptance of things." For that acceptance meant absorption, it meant the kind of patient knowledge that could alone yield naturalistic fiction. Dreiser's books have scored through their accumulation rather than their selection: their most memorable passages, Hurstwood in the breadline or Clyde Griffiths dazzled by the luxury of a hotel lobby, have depended upon our thorough if heavy immersion in all the material details.

The theme of this new book precludes any such immersion in the external world, since it is more strictly devoted to a crisis of the inner life. It is a study, to be sure, of Solon Barnes and his family in a shifting society, in which the Quaker values come to seem more and more obsolete. But the world of Philadelphia banking, in which Solon engages, is posited rather than developed. It is the same world that challenged the will to power in Cowperwood, but here Dreiser is concerned with the gradual transformation of his Quakers by growing prosperity and social conservatism.

Solon Barnes starts his career as a devout if unintellectual young man. He makes a marriage of love, but it also brings him greather wealth. He tries to hold to the belief that a business man should be a steward under the Lord, and he and his devoted wife keep up the Quaker patterns with their five children. But he becomes stolid and dull as he grows older. He is occasionally disturbed by a glimpse of "irreligious greed" in his associates, but he has no real discernment of the main drive of the age toward ruthless accumulation. When his younger children respond to the attraction of dancing and modern books, as the world moves down into the twentieth century, he treats them only with uncomprehending sternness. At this point it would seem that the title of the novel is ironic.

Its last half pivots on the tensions between father and children. The oldest daughter, who is rather plain, becomes studious and lonely; but the next boy and girl make their adjustments to the age. Their Quakerism is all on the surface, the boy in particular knows how to combine decorous behavior with a solid bank account. The two youngest, Etta and Stewart, are of the kind whom Dreiser has always treated most sympathetically. They are struck by the "romance" of life, by its "color, motion, beauty." When Etta has just finished boarding school, she is discovered by her father reading Daudet's "Sapho." Her response to his denunciation of her is to leave home and join a school friend at the University of Wisconsin, and to refuse to come back. As she says, "We simply want to know about life."

The passage that takes Etta subsequently to Greenowich Village and a love affair with an artist brings up certain anachronisms, which may throw light on when the book was planned. Dreiser tells us that his characters are now in the early Nineteen Twenties, but the automobile was no longer a possession merely of the rich at that time, nor was the two-step in vogue. The fact that Dreiser does not even mention the war of 1917–18 would seem to indicate that his plot was at least blocked out before the event.

Far more affecting than Etta's Bohemianism is the account of Stewart's disaster. His father's ways have become too fixed and dull "for frail, restless, hungry, human need." Stewart, like Clyde Griffiths, begins to feel the compelling fascination of clothes and money. (Dress has always been an important symbol for Dreiser.) Solon, berating him severely for attending a burlesque show, refuses to add to his small allowance, and Stewart begins stealing from his father's purse in order to go on week-end rides with the boys at school. When one of the girls they have picked up dies of a heart ailment and they are arrested, Stewart, overcome with adolescent fear and shame, kills himself.

Here, at the end, comes Solon's reversal. Shocked out of his complacency, he walks beside the peaceful stream near which he had courted his wife long ago, and broods upon the state into which he has drifted. His renewed distrust of luxury brings to the surface his latent doubts about his associates at the bank. He wants no further part in their acquisitive society, he denounces their mushroom development of holding companies, and resigns. He stands now as a bulwark, but his indictment draws no further comment from the other directors than that his principles are "too high for these days."

But Solon goes farther than that. After his wife's death from a stroke, he arrives at a reaffirmation of his faith. Since that is not the conduct we have grown to expect from Dreiser's characters, and since it will doubtless be attacked by those who believe that any renewal of Christianity marks a "new failure of nerve," it is important to relate the conclusion of this novel to the background of Dreiser's own thought.

He dwelt in his autobiography on the narrow and frustrating moralism of the Middle Western town in which he was reared. The Puritan taboos were made even harsher by the bigotry and intolerance of his Catholic father. Dreiser found his release through the rich, if formless, emotional life of his mother. He was to describe the end of his youth by saying: "Chronically nebulous, doubting, uncertain, I stared and stared at everything, only wondering, not solving." That attitude of mind, encountering then the school of Darwin, resulted in the mature Dreiser who could discern only "a vast compulsion which has nothing to do with the individual desires or tastes or impulses." This was the Dreiser whom Mencken hailed for his power to express with tragic dignity the immense "meaninglessness" of life.

At the beginning of "The Financier" he introduced a battle to the death between a lobster and a squid—which young Cowperwood watched with fascination—as a symbol of the brutal survival of the fittest. Dreiser has continued to meditate on natural science since that time, and his different emphasis now is symbolized by Solon's reaction, as he walks beside the stream, to a brilliant, emerald insect feeding upon and destroying the bud of a plant. Which was intended to live or die? Solon cannot answer, but he passes beyond the immediate struggle of existence, to an acceptance of natural order, of cosmic, if unfathomable, purpose.

Solon no longer sets himself up in judgment; he has been brought back to humility, and is far more open to life. He rejoices in the beauty of creation, and insists on "the need of love toward all created things." That is the core of his reaffirmation, and we are reminded that Dreiser's deepest attitudes toward suffering humanity have always been suffused with compassion and mercy. As if to answer those who might suspect that his sympathetic presentation of the faith that has given sanction to such attitudes involves some sort of abnegation, Dreiser has woven into his text at this point Solon's reading of one of the firmest of American radicals, John Woolman. An eighteenth-century Quaker, he insisted not at all on others belonging to that sect. He insisted on human brotherhood in its simplest and most revolutionary form, on the freeing of all slaves, on economic equality. Woolman was one of Rivera's American heroes when he did his frescoes for the workers' school on Fourteenth Street. He is the natural apostle for Solon's belated rediscovery of Christian love, for the Solon who dies mumbling: "The banks, the banks * * * the poor and the banks."

But Solon's is not the last word to this parable. Etta, reunited with her father at the end, is found crying by her cold brother, Orville, who is surprised that she should care, since he blames her for starting all the family's troubles. She does not bother to get angry at him, but answers simply: "Oh, I am not crying for myself, or for father—I am crying for *life.*" That suggest the emotional depth that Dreiser always strove to bring to expression. He wanted to cut through the dry formalism of the American mind, and to make, like Melville, a reassertion of the heart.

Burton Rascoe. "Does Dreiser's Final Novel Reveal Spiritual Creed?" Chicago *Sunday Tribune*, Pt. 4, March 24, 1946, pp. 3, 8.

The literary world, or at least that portion of it which considers Dreiser one of the great figures in American fiction, has been waiting 30 years for "The Bulwark." First announced for publication in the spring of 1916, it was listed in various publishers' catalogs as a forthcoming book over a period of 20-odd years.

Skeptics among Dreiser students and bibliographers had long doubted that the novel had progressed, or ever would progress, beyond the nine pages of the text printed and bound up in the salesmen's dummies by the now defunct John Lane company.

Posthumous publication of the novel [Dreiser died four days before the beginning of the present year, at the age of 71] starts many hares of speculation which this huntsman of the clews to Dreiser's mind and personality is not reluctant to pursue. For the novel is a freak production in Dreiser's literary output and it is perhaps to be considered more in the light of Dreiserian self-revelation than on its merits as a work of fiction.

Is "The Bulwark," as we have it now, practically a new work, begun prior to 1916 but laid aside and never returned to until a few months before the author died? Or is it, substantially, the text Dreiser wrote nearly 30 years ago but never released to the public? If the novel was finished in 1916, why was it not published at that time?

I may be going out on a limb but it is my theory, based upon a careful study of "The Bulwark" and a long familiarity with Dreiser's work and personal history, that the novel just published was finished long before 1916 and that the text, except for some minor alterations—none for the better and mainly anachronistic—is the same now as it was then. I believe the novel was the by-product of a profound religious [or emotional] experience, the validity of which Dreiser came to doubt after he had written it; that he withheld the novel upon the return of his physical health, following a nervous breakdown, and the consequent return of his anti-religious and mechanistic concept of life; and that, during his final illness, he not only reëxperienced some of the spiritual intimations disclosed in the book but became convinced, finally, of the novel's value and so released it.

"The Bulwark" is utterly unlike the main body of Dreiser's work and is closest akin to "The Doer of the Word," written in 1902 and included in "Twelve Men" [1919]. It is as simple, factual, unadorned as the Book of Ruth in the Old Testament. Its rhythm is largely Biblical, indicating, I think, the unconscious influence of Bible-reading at the time the novel was written.

Dreiser tells you about the characters in "The Bulwark" and relates what they did; he does not reveal them to you, except occasionally, by what they do, or say, or feel. This would indicate that he was still a reporter, when he wrote it, and not a creator and that he was more interested in conveying a message than in telling a story.

The message is simple: It is only in suffering that one finds God and learns of one's identity with the all-pervading spirit of God; and that once you understand the nature of love and humility you lose all fear and walk with God in righteousness. It is a message that Dreiser himself rejected, with anger and some blatancy, thruout the major portions of the articulate life; but his more violently expressed antipathies to religion and what he called "moralistic taboos" were, I think, only the shoutings of a religious apostate and a highly puritanical man who was trying to convince himself and never quite succeeding.

As originally announced, "The Bulwark" was to deal "with the struggle of the head of a Quaker family to bring up his children in the orthodox fashion and with the influence of modern society upon these children's beliefs and actions." The novel is just that. Solon Barnes, in the novel, is a pious and prosperous Quaker whose model of conduct was "The Journal of John Woolman." Two of his children, a boy and a girl, irked by ascetic restrictions of their home life, broke away from them with tragic consequences. The girl was abandoned by a painter to whom she had given the whole of her love; the boy, faced with a charge of rape and murder, committed suicide.

The novel is bare and matter-of-fact but with all the overtones of such narration. The story is Solon's rather than that of the children; and it is the effect of the shock of events upon Solon's concepts of God and of righteousness that Dreiser was most concerned with. John Woolman taught Solon in his hour of trial, as he must have taught Dreiser, that "God talks directly to man when His help is needed and man asks Him for it."

Ironically enough, it is probable that many, to whom Dreiser's name for many years was anathema, will find deep consolation and refreshment of spirit in this novel. Many Dreiserians, on the other hand, will say it is both the invocation and the *nunc dimittis* of the whole testimony about his life as embodied in his troubled and tortured search for meaning in what he had seen and thought and felt.

R. T. R.
"Books—New & Old: Dreiser's Posthumous Novel: Work Written in Desperation." Dallas *News*, March 24, 1946.

With the publication of "Sister Carrie" in 1900, Theodore Dreiser became the leading novelist of our time, and no other American writer has since successfully challenged his right to this position. More than his contempories, Dreiser had the qualities necessary to the novelist—perception, understanding, warmth and compassion. He added to these a remarkable insight into the dichotomies which have plagued modern society: theoretical political democracy and actual economic oligarchy, theoretical Christianity and actual materialism, cleavages upon which many individual personalities have been wrecked and by which the pattern of American culture has already been, perhaps irreparably, damaged. With these assets, in spite of his sometimes heavy and awkward style, Dreiser achieved a considerable measure of greatness.

But Dreiser never had sufficient breadth of vision (and intellectual courage?) to resolve, or to stimulate the reader to resolve, the problem. Dreiser must have perceived this weakness and, suffering from his knowledge, must have tried to rise above it. Doubtless one such effort was his association with the Communists, and now it seems obvious that this did not satisfy him. The present novel, his first in twenty years, must be viewed as another such effort.

"The Bulwark," of itself, does not merit attention. But it demands careful scrutiny because of its implications. . . .

It would be easy, and kind, to dismiss "The Bulwark" as the product of senility. But this is impossible. Though the characters are spiritless, the action meagerly motivated, the conflicts without passion, the novel shows competent structure. The style is adequate and clear, advancing the story along a steady and undeviating course. Often the telling is rich with an old-fashioned dignity and quaint felicity. No, "The Bulwark" is a last, vigorous reaching of a desperate man.

As they are of great importance, the sins of Solon's offspring must be examined. Two children marry from the Big to the Bigger Money. One, a boy under 20, commits suicide after being discovered an alleged accessory to rape and manslaughter. Another, a very plain girl, becomes a teacher and is left at the novel's end, struggling toward what one hopes will be a successful capture in marriage of another teacher. These four, it seems are to be pitied, and their sins half-forgiven.

But the sins of the beautiful Etta are so monstrous that Dreiser must finally let her partake of Solon's religious experience and become reconverted to Quakerism. For Etta descended to the Inferno's last and lowest circle: she became a Free Thinker and embraced Heresy. Specifically, she did, willfully and of her own malice aforethought, read the works of Daudet, Flaubert and Balzac.

Surely this is an artist destroying himself with a vengeance.

Yet Dreiser's act is not unique. Nor is it the first time we have seen this spectacle. In our time, when the struggle, already so far advanced, to preserve our waning hope for human dignity, freedom and intelligence cannot suffer further breaching of the defenses, so many of whom, as in the case of Dreiser, we respected and regarded as leaders, and not alone in the field of the arts, have made an equally destructive and equally cowardly exit. This is the implication of "The Bulwark" which is terrifying.

W. G. Rogers. "Does Dreiser's Last Novel Do His Best Work Credit?" New Haven *Register*, March 24, 1946.

Solon Barnes and his wife, Benecia, their four parents and their five children, all Quakers of varying degrees of fidelity, are the characters in this novel,

Dreiser's first in 20 years and completed just before his death in December.

The story spans the life of Solon, "bulwark" of his faith, born in modest circumstances but by his diligence amassing more earthly goods than, he fears, Fox and Woolman would have approved. Troubled by only occasional qualms, inspired by the noble examples of his father and mother, he works his way upward to a success which is as assured in his case as it was for an Alger hero.

But what goes up must come down. His children have these alternatives: To abide by the stern and simple precepts of their parents' faith, or to enjoy themselves by the use of their parents' money. When they so far forget the habitual "thee" and "thou" that they also forget the difference between thine and mine, as one of them does, they are lost to Quakerdom.

The original sinner among the Barneses may have been Solon, in Dreiser's opinion, for it was he who, while following the straight and narrow path for himself, piled up the wealth which helped to open the eyes of his sons and daughters to the vast gap between the social position and their social opportunities.

Yet it's hard to decide just what the author meant. He disapproves of one boy who is overly ambitious and worldly, and of another who sows his Quaker oats and reaps suicide. Does he also disapprove of a daughter who believes in the emancipation of her sex?

Both abstractly and historically one of the greatest American novelists, Dreiser is not at his best in this posthumous work. Thought his prose style is as clumsy as ever, it is not this time redeemed by forceful characterizations, crusading zeal and inevitable development.

It's not so much a novel as a tract, and for many pages a very dull one. Choice of the Book Find club for April, it deserves reading if only because Dreiser wrote it, but it is not one of the stories for which he will be remembered. Maybe you'd rather do him homage by rereading "Sister Carrie," "The Titan," or "An American Tragedy."

"Valedictory." *Time,* 47 (March 25, 1946), 102, 106.

Shortly before he died, the late, great Theodore Dreiser finished two novels, the first he had written in 20 years. *The Stoic,* which will not be published until fall, completes the towering trilogy on U.S. business which was begun with *The Financier* (1912) and continued in *The Titan* (1914). The *Bulwark,* which he had meditated for some 30 years, is an unpretentious, fitting valedictory.

For years, Puritans attacked most of Dreiser's novels tooth & nail for their frankness and coarseness. *The Bulwark* is Dreiser's tender tribute to all that was good in the forces which most bitterly attacked him.

Solon Barnes is a Quaker, brought up in unworldliness. He marries (for love) into a richer family of Friends and becomes a Philadelphia banker. For many years he floats along on uneasy rationalizations about the sacred stewardship of wealth (which he honestly tries to live up to). When his associates mire themselves and their bank deeper & deeper in crooked, within-the-law self-interest, he can stay silent no longer. In part the novel is a study of the losing struggle between the moribund U.S. religious sense and proliferating U.S. materialism.

But Dreiser was far less a theorist than a humanist; essentially his novel is not a social thesis but the timeless story of family life. Of Solon's five children, one is set apart by her homeliness; one is a born Pharisee; one is a self-conscious beauty; one is an artist; one is a natural cavalier. Dreiser is interested mainly in the two latter, the arch-rebels. Against them Solon Barnes finds sterness and tolerance equally ineffective. His son and daughter, in the struggle to come to life as autonomous human beings, become thieves, and worse. The soberly beautiful family group grows rigid with reluctant tyranny, ugly with fear and deceit. The beloved and charming home becomes, for some members of the family, a place of captivity, distaste and boredom. Finally the crime and suicide of the youngest child brings the repentance and ultimate religious conversion of another.

The story has been told many times, and more dramatically, but seldom with more balanced compassion or gentler insight. *The Bulwark's* closing chapters, in which Solon Barnes realizes what his good intentions have wrought, and is battered into a simpler, humbler kind of religious understanding, are of a searching, level, melancholy beauty which cannot be expected of any living American writer.

From first to last, self-schooled, slow-minded Theodore Dreiser was ridiculed as a turgid stylist and a ponderous craftsman. His critics will still find much to ridicule in this novel. Other readers may find that the slow, munching, rhythm, the tone-deaf iteration, the lifelessness of epithet, are of a rocklike unity with the earnest intelligence, the upright and enduring heart, which even Dreiser's detractors give him credit for. They may also find that Dreiser was capable of a remarkable purity of communication whenever he was deeply moved. For in the words of the American Quaker, John Woolman, which he quotes, Dreiser at his best lived and wrote in faithfulness to *"a principle placed in the human mind, which in different places and ages hath had different names; it is, however, pure and proceeds from God. It is deep and inward, confined to no forms of religion nor excluded from any, when the heart stands in perfect sincerity. In whomsoever this takes root and grows, they become brethren."*

Emerson Price. "Book Reviews." Cleveland *Press*, March 26, 1946.

The final work of the late Theodore Dreiser is touched only here and there with that majestic and noble quality of the genius who gave us AN AMERICAN TRAGEDY and SISTER CARRIE. Nevertheless, THE BULWARK is not only far superior to most novels but must inevitably take its place among the greatest books of our age.

This work seems to me to stand as a giant framework—a framework of great strength—about which the author, at an earlier time, might have built the novel which he unquestionably had conceived, but had not brought to its fullest conclusion.

The book is marked by many flashes

of the author's brilliance, as it bears evidence of his relentless searching for the obscure and deeply important causes for social tragedy. If this searching has not been as fully sustained as it once was, it has been accurately directed, and it has borne shocking and tragic fruit.

The story is that of a Quaker, Solon Barnes, reared in a heavily moralistic atmosphere. It is the story of Solon's unsuccessful attempt to inflict his severe moral code upon his children, and of the deep tragedy that ensues. In substance, this novel presents a vivid example of a moral code too narrow and too rigid in design to defeat the enormous problems engendered by the rising materialism of the Twentieth Century.

The book does not stand among Mr. Dreiser's best, but it has great importance and should be read by all who understand that the author, throughout his long career, gave rich substance, color and form to American literature. We cannot hope that his genius will be equaled for many years to come.

"Dreiser the Great." *Newsweek*, 27 (March 25, 1946), 102–103.

When Theodore Dreiser died last December, the 74-year-old author left behind the completed manuscripts of two novels. One, "The Bulwark," is published this week. As Dreiser's first novel in the generation that has passed since he wrote "An American Tragedy," its appearance is a literary event of major importance.

Whatever Dreiser's faults, and they were many, his virtues were overwhelming. At his best he stood head and shoulders above his contemporaries. A powerful, complex individual, he groped his uncertian way through the life of his time, one of the most understanding of human beings. What he wrote about the things he saw and the people he knew, stands with the best writing ever done in this country.

Dreiser's life was a quest. He was always trying the find out the why and wherefore of life. Sometimes, as in his first novel, "Sister Carrie," and in "An American Tragedy," he came close to succeeding at his almost-impossible task. His latest novel, over which he worked for many years, is a continuation of his search, and it, too, is a success. It stands with the best that came from his labored pen.

Dreiser was a courageous man, filled with a compassionate love for his fellow men, and nowhere in his writing are these qualities better expressed than in "The Bulwark." Edwin Seaver, reviewing this novel for the Book Find Club, says that "by nature he was deeply religious—which does not mean churchly—and his religious bent informed him with an enormous pity for our mortal lot."

It is necessary to recognize the religious in Dreiser in order to appreciate "The Bulwark" and it is also necessary to recall the times in which Dreiser came upon the American scene. Again to quote Seaver, Dreiser "lived in the years when the United States was being transformed from the old order to the new, when the old industrial capitalism was giving way to finance, capitalism, and monopoly, when the old walls of isolationism were being smashed and our country was entering the world arena . . ."

It is with this changing order that Dreiser deals in "The Bulwark." The moral and spiritual changes that came over America during this period are very much Dreiser's concern. At the same time he is attempting to sum up his own long search for some kind of sustaining religious faith. How convincing he is may, in the long run, depend upon how much the reader takes to this moving story. For "The Bulwark" is not an easy book either to read or to understand.

In "The Bulwark," Dreiser tells the story of a Quaker family through three generations. He is mainly concerned with the middle generation, with Solon and Benecia Barnes, and their struggle to hold to the faith through the changing years. It is the upright and solemn Solon's conviction that if he follows the path of righteousness all the days of his life, his children will follow in his footsteps and enjoy the good fruit of his goodness.

Solon Barnes is a good man. He has his faith and his religion, and he makes every effort to live up to the law of God as he understands it. But he is unable to impart his faith to all his children.

But Solon does not, in his tragic disappointment, turn bitter and curse his God who seemingly has forsaken him. Even at the end of his long life Solon (even as Dreiser himself did) keeps on seeking the meaning of things in this world. The old man turns in the moment of tragedy to his daughter and says: "I know now that we know so little of all of that infinite something of which we are a part."

"The Bulwark" is a profoundly moving book. It is, also, in many ways, a strange book to come from one who, like Dreiser, had fought the moralists all his life and turned for succor to the Communist cause. But even those who will be disappointed at his presumed desertion cannot fail to be stirred by the sheer beauty of this novel. For it is a beautiful and even profound book and it is written with a grace of style that is too often absent from Dreiser's powerful and awkward prose.

Edward Carberry. Cincinnati *Post*, March 30, 1946.

Perhaps the most astonishing manifestation of the "rediscovery" of religion is Theodore Dreiser's posthumous THE BULWARK.

If the fundamental quality of the novels of this blundering mammoth of American letters could be caught in a single phrase, it might be set down as a brooding pity over the meaninglessness of life. Dreiser was a 19th Century naturalist and Darwinism was in his very bones.

Yet in this novel—planned 30 years ago and worked on at intervals since—he chose to deal with a Quaker and his family. He has done so sympathetically, sensitively, tenderly even. His Solon Barnes learns the precedence of the Inner Light over the Book of Discipline the hard way—through suffering.

And, in following the spiritual growth of his character, Dreiser seems to be reversing the philosophy of a lifetime and his last public statements. For he died a professing Communist. He is admitting the possibility of meaning and accepting the reality of Christian love.

R. F. H.
"Theodore Dreiser on the Spiritual Values." Springfield [Mass.] *Republican*, March 31, 1946.

. . . ["The Bulwark"], the story of a Quaker family, will neither add to nor detract from Dreiser's fame, although it will add a puzzling dimension to an already confused attempt at evaluation of a great author who frequently wrote very poorly yet whose words carried a stunning impact. He had written no novel for a generation, yet his name is still among America's great; he had been torn to pieces by latter-day critics, yet possibly to no one man does American literature owe more.

"The Bulwark" at first does not seem like a Dreiser novel. It is too simply wrought, too tender toward the world, too sympathetic with spiritual faith to seem the work of the man who wrote "Jennie Gerhardt" and "Sister Carrie." Some of the paragraphs and even the chapters read as though they must be merely the outlines of a thought Dreiser intended to fill out later. In other books he would take pages in pursuit of a single point; in "The Bulwark" a single sentence suffices, and in one startling instance he even uses a rather banal quotation as a chapter heading.

But as the ending approaches it is realized that there is nothing wrong with the novel, it is complete and well rounded and from another author would be received with polite applause and probably forgotten. It is with Dreiser that something is wrong—it is not the same thundering Dreiser that we knew of old. Some of the rolling clumsy sentences are there, the old intense interest in human beings hasn't been lost, and occasionally there is a far-off rumbling of a rising storm. But somewhere there has been a metamorphosis; Dreiser is no longer man shaking his fist at the preacher, he is the preacher waving his finger at man. . . .

This is the first time in Dreiser's novels that spiritual values have been so warmly treated, even coddled, and probably by some this novel will be regarded as his last will and testament to the world. This is possibly true; perhaps Dreiser became alarmed at the widening gap between man and his religion, his increasing dependance on technology and material standards, and sought to point the way to salvation, not necessarily religious regeneration but the rescue of human dignity.

There is admittedly nothing wrong with such a stand; if a man has found faith he should proclaim it. But from a literary standpoint Dreiser's greatness must rest with what he found wrong with man and his world and not what he found right with them. The old towering indignations and thrilling concepts of man and Nature, roaring out in endless torrents of battering prose, are far more stimulating and valuable to mankind when Dreiser is wandering about in philosophical wilderness than when he has reached the calmness of an ecclesiastical garden.

Charles Brown. "Despite the Critics, Dreiser Is Secure on His Literary Hill." Daily *Oklahoman*, March 31, 1946.

The target of many critical attacks, both by men who hated him and by men who admired him, Theodore Dreiser nevertheless remains a monolithic character in American literature.

His early novels were viciously attacked by the moralists and he was accused of being sex-obsessed and a corrupter of American ideals; one critic called his books "explosions in a sewer." But he also suffered from his admirers, they ridiculed his efforts at "fine writing," declared no great writer ever wrote so badly.

"The Bulwark" is his first novel in 20 years, written just before he died at the age of 74 in California. It, too, will be attacked. The critics will say it is dull, that the style is slipshod and awkward, that Dreiser has gone soft in his old age.

But when the noise about the book subsides, Dreiser will still dominate the American literary landscape and "The Bulwark" will take its place beside "An American Tragedy," "Jennie Gerhardt," and "Sister Carrie" as among the finest contributions to American fiction.

The story of "The Bulwark" is not a new one for Dreiser. Even the philosophic approach is not new, although the impression left by the book is different from that of his earlier novels. The novel marks a growth in Dreiser's broad human understanding, and most of his critics have granted him that. Whereas in his earlier novels, the reader was oppressed by the hopelessness of Dreiser's naturalistic view of life, "The Bulwark" will leave him strengthened in hope and faith. . . .

The story and the characters are not new to readers of Dreiser; it is the religious implication and the acceptance of faith in God that set "The Bulwark" off from his earlier novels. Dreiser's attitude is summed up in the remark of one of the mourners at Solon's funeral: "I am not crying for myself, or for father —I am crying for Life."

Helen K. Farrall. "Strength and Compassion Set Dreiser's Posthumous Novel Apart." Des Moines [Iowa] *Register*, March 31, 1946.

When Theodore Dreiser died last winter at the age of 74 he left the completed manuscripts of two novels, one of which "The Bulwark" was published last week. Dreiser's first novel since "The American Tragedy," it is worthy to stand with his best, and its simple rugged strength and its compassion and humanity set it apart and above most contemporary fiction even as its main character Solon Barnes stood, a bulwark among men.

To read "The Bulwark" is a moving experience.

In his plodding often dull style, Dreiser has managed to achieve a reality which too often escapes the more facile writer. The awkward sentences, the naïveté, the fumbling reiterations which have always been the trademark of this great American novelist are still present but a new economy of words, and a swiftness of plot movement in the second half of the story make its telling powerful emotionally.

We are told that Dreiser meditated on this novel for 30 years and it is believable. His theme is the conflict of the old moralities and spiritual values of the nineteenth century with the crass materialism and the greed of the twentieth. His plot in content and manner of telling is almost Victorian and the reader will more than once be reminded of the nineteenth century English novelists. . . .

George Mayberry. "Dreiser: The Last Chapter." *New Republic*, 114 (April 1, 1946), 449–450.

The appearance of *The Bulwark*, three months after Dreiser's death and almost thirty years after it was first announced, coincides with the publication of a "memorial edition" of *An American Tragedy*, which appeared originally in 1925. The coincidence serves to illustrate the familiar observation that what is perhaps Dreiser's best book was also his last work of any great importance. (The announced posthumous publication of *The Soic*, the third volume of "A Triology of Desire"—*The Financier* and *The Titan* are the first two volumes—makes this necessarily a suspended judgment.) Certainly his infrequent political and literary journalism since 1925 adds little to the value of his work, although it contributes significantly to his biography. And it is to his biographers that we will have to turn eventually for an explanation of the delays surrounding the writing and publication of *The Bulwark* and *The Stoic*. As matters now stand we can examine *The Bulwark* with assurance only in itself and in relation to the earlier published novels. In this latter aspect it is at least interesting as a new portal to the recurring themes, preoccupations and techniques of Dreiser the novelist.

Solon Barnes is a "bulwark" of the Quaker faith and of the American way, devout in his religion and successful in his business undertakings. The son of a humble Maine farmer and tradesman, he has become a wealthy and powerful Philadelphia banker and patriarch. But his younger children, coming of age in the early 1920's, inevitably chafe at the restraints imposed upon them by their father's beliefs and values. (With heavy Dreiserian irony, the older son who shares the externals of Solon's faith is an inhuman prig and a cad.) The self-destructive career of his youngest son and revelation of dishonesty in his business associates bring Solon to spiritual and physical purgatory, but before his death he makes a reaffirmation of faith in the Inner Light.

Although shorter than Dreiser's other novels, *The Bulwark* sprawls with characters and overflows with incident. Apart from the opening chapters where the details of Solon's early life are filled in, and the closing pages which record his anguish, the book suggests a synopsis rather than a completed novel. The stories of his several children are taken up sporadically and inadequately explored. Where they should have had their proper existences in relation to the larger story of the father, they have only fitful and isolated lives. Indeed the structural failures of *The Bulwark* highlight successful parallels in Dreiser's earlier work and suggest again that it is from the cumulative effect of infinitely wrought details that much of his art as well as his power derives. . . .

Arnold Sroog. " 'The Bulwark' True Dreiser." *Daily Worker*, April 1, 1946.

The Dreiser method has always been to seize a segment of American life, tear it open pitilessly and lay it bare for all to see.

In his last published work—although there is much evidence that the work was begun as early as 30 years ago—Dreiser sets before us the Quakers of the Philadelphia area.

The Bulwark is Dreiser—with all the greatness and some of the crudities. . . .

Dreiser in this book grapples with the religious way of life according to Quaker doctrine. He counterposes the precepts of this way of life against the forces at work in modern capitalist America. In the long prologue-like opening section Dreiser gives you Solon, steeped as he is in Quaker doctrine of simplicity and opposition to the accumulation of wealth.

The story unfolds at the turn of the century, when all America was in the grip of a money fever, when money was the king and the rights and dignity of man all but forgotten. Solon enters the banking business as a result of his marriage and he adjusts his doctrine in this one respect—but this one only.

The impact of the capitalist mode of life—with its false and inhuman system of values—attacks first the unity of Solon's family. One by one Solon's children reject their father's doctrines, each in his own way—one in search of love, one for social success, one for financial success, one for art and one for sex and good times.

The suicide of his youngest son brings Solon to face with reality. He resigns from the bank and castigates his fellow directors. The comment of one of the directors is a Dreiser gem:

"The only trouble with his (Solon's) principles is that they're too high for these days . . ." (p. 305).

The Quaker values and virtues emerge defeated from their conflict with modern capitalist society. Solon dies at peace with himself but without having achieved any solution to his dilemma. Those children who returned to share his defeat in his late days—those disappointed in their grasp for life—achieve no permanent solution.

The book closes with the words of Emma [sic], youngest daughter and fourth child, who more than any other character in the novel sought a constructive and sound way out of the swamp. Here are her words:

"Oh, I am not crying for myself, or for father—I am crying for LIFE." (Dreiser's emphasis)'

Life was the loser in this struggle—for neither side could nurture it.

Dreiser hints at his own solution to the dilemma in citing the work of an early American radical and Quaker, John Woolman. He recalls Woolman's belief in the brotherhood of man regardless of creed and indicates his acceptance of this morality.

Some critics who have already judged *The Bulwark* believe that it is a poor work; others find in it unexpected charm and greater ease in style than is customary with Dreiser.

The fact is that this novel, because of its different subject matter, may not have the broad appeal of his earlier work. But it is true Dreiser, an unerring portrait of a section of the American scene.

One more thing must be said. Dreiser's wonderful and deep insight into people marks this novel as it does all his others. His great sympathy and real understanding of people stand alone in the works of American writers. *The Bulwark* is no exception.

Joseph Henry Jackson. "Bookman's Notebook." San Francisco *Chronicle,* April 3, 1946.

For almost half a century Theodore Dreiser was a force in American fiction.

That he possessed this influence was a triumph of some sort, for few men have had less technical equipment for the art of the novel. Dreiser's style was so awkward and bumbling that it could hardly be called a style at all. To the day of his death he never learned to write a single good sentence. He seized hungrily upon the most hackneyed turns of phrase; he pounced upon the obvious as though it were new and fresh—as perhaps it seemed to his faulty ear. Yet in spite of all this he was an important writer. Why?

Dreiser's importance derived from the fact that he had something to say. He was clumsy about getting it out, but eventually, in all of his books, he did get on to paper his profound understanding of human beings and his pity for their struggles. The reader must dig for it, but it is always there.

Now, after Dreiser's death, comes the first of two novels he left in manuscript form, **"The Bulwark."** It has all the faults of his other novels; you can peg them one by one as you go. But it has also the virtues of his other work, and you can find those, too. . . .

In spite of the fact that "The Bulwark" reads like an outline of a novel expanded beyond outline limits, in spite of Dreiser's plodding prose, "The Bulwark," like every other novel the man wrote, has something to say and says it. And there will be many to agree that the point Dreiser makes is a sound one. It becomes more evident all the time that the technologies, the material gains, the surface seeming of success, has not been enough and that the American Way of Life needs something more inside it to support the glossy outer framework of prosperity and mechanical progress. Solon Barnes found his own Inner Light, or at least recognized its necessity. Mr. Dreiser's demonstration that without some such Light there is nowhere to turn should bring assent from many a reader.

Keith Wilson. "Dreiser's Last Novel." Omaha [Neb.] *Sunday World Herald,* April 7, 1946.

After the first 30 pages of the last novel by Theodore Dreiser, many a bored and bewildered reader will begin to wonder whether this is a story or an exercise in verbal sporifics.

My advice is to stick with it. After all his fumbling, Dreiser had a story to tell —a thoughtful story of a man whose religious, idealistic way of life collided headon with the materialism of our day. . . .

It is disconcerting to find Theodore Dreiser so sincerely pious. For chapter after chapter one waits in vain for some hell-raising turn of events, some allusion to the common man and his oppressors, perhaps a condemnation of the old order accomplished in the ruthless, objective manner in which he could do these things.

The high spiritual plane on which Dreiser tells his story is lowered only in the sequences in which he tells of the escapades and crimes of Stewart, the wayward son. This is lurid melodrama, poorly done and out of keeping with the tone of the book.

I understand that the dull forepart of "The Bulwark" was written during Dreiser's last years but that much of the rest of it had been written 35 or 40 years ago. If this is true, Dreiser was a far better craftsman in his middle years.

It is scarcely necessary to add that the Dreiser style is heavy and ponderous, that the man had no ear for words or for prose rhythm. This book does have the intensity of purpose which carried him successfully through many another literary effort, and it tells a story. As for style and the rest, what do you expect, Hemingway?

Fred C. Whitney. "Books in Review." El Cajon [Calif.] *Valley News,* April 17, 1946.

Theodore Dreiser is an old man. It is more than twenty years since he wrote his last and greatest book, "An American Tragedy" in 1925. But last year saw him produce another. "The Bulwark." It is a matter of some speculation whether the "Bulwark" is a new manuscript written in his declining years, or whether it is an old one dug up out of some mouldy trunk of his prime. Be that as it may, "The Bulwark" is an old man's view of life, full of tolerance and understanding, it is a far cry from the socially militant Dreiser of a score of years ago.

The Bulwark is not a novel which might make any author, on the other hand it is not unworthy of Theodore Dreiser. It reaches a highly realistic level, and the tolerance which Solon attains before his death, may be Dreiser's tolerance too, for substantially there is little difference between the militant bespectacled reformer and the dreamy-eyed idealist.

Dreiser is the great enigma of American literature. Careful critics have been in unanimous accord that his work is clumsy and careless. Yet there is, all in all, an element of intangible beauty as yet undefinable. He has been called the most suppressed and the most unsuppressible American author ever since his first work "Sister Carrie" was supressed right after its publication in 1900. This was followed by "Jennie Gerhardt" in 1911.

His style is reportorial, a hangover probably from his newspaper days on the old St. Louis Republic and the Chicago Daily Globe where he was variously special feature writer, drama critic and editor. Perhaps it is because he tells the exact truth he is so well loved, perhaps it's because he has achieved an almost perfect detachment, but more probably it is because he was the first and so far the greatest of American humanists.

Lionel Trilling. "Dreiser and the Liberal Mind." *Nation,* 157 (April 20, 1946), 466, 468, 470, 472.

We are all a little tired of Henry James—or, rather, we are tired of the Henry James we have been creating by all our talk about him, by those intense and bitter conversations in which he existed as a symbol so glowingly but so passively, the martyr-hero of a certain kind of culture. It is now time, surely, to let him go back into privacy, releasing him from the deadly public life of polemic, to read him again in quiet. And yet I cannot help detaining him for a moment longer in the life-in-death of argument by mentioning him in connection with Theodore Dreiser, whose name has again been so much with us since his death and the appearance of his posthumous novel, "The Bulwark."

James and Dreiser: with that juxtaposition we are immediately at the dark and bloody crossroads where culture and politics meet. One does not go there gladly, but I found that I was there perforce, for as I read the new Dreiser novel my thoughts kept recurring to a pronouncement on James which I had come on some months ago. The passage had then struck me as so representative of a certain aspect of American intellect that I had saved it. Robert Gorham Davis is commenting on the belief, held by some, that there is a kind of political value in James's awareness, in his moral perceptiveness. Mr. Davis says, "Unfortunately, it is a little too late for this . . ." and then goes on:

> There has been a tremendous increase in our cultural awareness and achievement in recent decades, and American intellectuals need feel no inferiority before European culture or the ghost of Henry James. But these same decades have taught us that delicacy of perception, knowledge, a refinement of relationships within limited groups can coexist with the grossest evils and dangers and do almost nothing to counter them. The disasters that we have just barely escaped and the disasters that are certain to threaten demand a kind of self-committal, a going forth to battle with Apollyon and Giant Despair that James's experience, emotional and metaphysical, simply cannot help us with. . . .

Mr. Davis, as we know, is not the kind of critic who brushes aside delicacy of perception and knowledge—on the contrary, he is notable in his own work for these very qualities. And as the rest of Mr. Davis's review shows, he has great respect for James and takes no delight in throwing him to the wolves of political fate. He only wants to warn us that the moral and intellectual qualities which he and James have in common are not to be counted on in moments of crisis.

American intellectuals, especially when they are being American or political, are remarkably quick to warn us that perception and knowledge, although somehow valuable—"American intellectuals need feel no inferiority before European culture"—will never get us through gross dangers and difficulties. We are still haunted by a kind of social fear of intellect, the same uneasiness that Tocqueville observed in us more than a century ago.

This uneasiness is the more intense when intellect works as intellect ideally should, when its processes are vivacious or complex and its results are interesting and brilliant. It is then that we like to confront it with gross difficulties and dangers and challenge it to save us from disaster. What I suppose was meant by the idea Mr. Davis is commenting on, the political value of James's qualities, was not that they will set up an umbrella against the atomic bomb or solve political contradictions but that, within the natural limit of the art that contains them, they can suggest the moral and intellectual qualities that might save us and that certainly make salvation worth while. When intellect is awkward and dull, we do not put it to the question of ultimate or immediate practicality—no liberal critic would go out of his way to remark that "unfortunately it is a little too late" for what Dreiser gives us. James's style, characters, subjects, and especially his manner of personal life are looked upon with a hostile eye, no quarter given. But Dreiser's faults, we have always been given to understand, are essentially virtues. Parrington established the formula for the criticism of Dreiser by calling him a "peasant." When Dreiser thinks stupidly, it is because he has the slow stubbornness of a peasant; when he writes badly, it is because he is impatient of the literary gentility of the bourgeoisie. It is as if wit and flexibility of mind, as if perception and knowledge, were to be equated with aristocracy, while dulness and stupidity must naturally suggest a virtuous democracy, as in the old plays.

The liberal judgment of Dreiser and James goes back of politics, goes back to the moral assumptions that make politics. It is the fear of mind, much more than any explicit political meaning that can be drawn from the works of the two men, that accounts for the unequal justice they have received from our progressive critics. If it could be conclusively demonstrated—say, by documents in James's holograph—that James intended his books as pleas for cooperatives, labor unions, better housing, more equitable taxation, and closer relations with Russia, the American critic in his liberal and progressive character would, one feels, still be worried by James because his work shows so many of the electric qualities of mind. And if the opposite were proved of Dreiser, it would be brushed aside—as his anti-Semitism has in fact been brushed aside—because his books have the awkwardness, the chaos, the heaviness which we associate with "reality." In the American metaphysic, reality is always material reality, hard, resistant, unformed, impenetrable. And that work of mind is felt to be trustworthy which most resembles this reality by reproducing the sensations it affords.

Professor Beard in "The Rise of American Civilization" gives an ironic account of James's career and implies that we have the clue to its irrelevance when we know that James was "a whole generation removed from the odors of the shop." Or Granville Hicks in "The Great Tradition" comments on James's stories about artists and makes the point that such artists as James portrays, so concerned about art and their integrity in art, do not really exist. "Who has ever known such artists? Where are the Hugh Verekers, the Mark Ambients, the Neal Paradsys, the Overts, Linberts, Dencomes, Delaways?" The question, Mr. Hicks admits, had occurred to James himself, but how had James answered it? "If the life about us for the last thirty years refused warrant for these examples," James said, "then so much the worse for that life. . . . There are decencies that in the name of the general self-respect we must take for granted, there's a rudimentary intellectual honor to which we must, in the interest of civilization, at least pretend." And to this Mr. Hicks, shocked beyond argument, replies, "But this is the purest romanticism, this writing about what ought to be rather than what is!" James was a traitor to the reality of the odors of the shop. He betrayed the reality of *what is* for the projection of *what ought to be.* Dare we ever trust him again?

To Mr. Hicks, Dreiser is "clumsy" and "stupid" and "bewildered" and "crude in his statement of materialistic monism"; and in his personal life—which perhaps is in point because James' personal life is always supposed to be so much in point—not quite emancipated from "his boyhood longing for crass material success," showing "again and again a desire for the ostentatious luxury of the successful business man." The judgment is true, and so far as it is personal it is based on Dreiser's own statements. But Dreiser's faults are the sad, lovable, honorable faults of "reality" itself, or America itself—huge, inchoate, struggling toward expression, caught between the dream of power and the dream of morality.

Or again: "The liability in what Santayana called the genteel tradition was due to its being the product of mind apart from experience. Dreiser gave us the stuff of our common existence, not as it was hoped to be by any idealizing theorist, but as it actually was in its crudity." The author of this statement is a writer who certainly cannot be accused of any lack of feeling for what James represents; yet how easily Mr. Matthiessen, in his *Times* review of Dreiser's novel, falls into the liberal cliché which establishes as the criterion of Dreiser's value his difference from some "idealizing theorist," his opposition to the genteel tradition. This is the line on which has proceeded the long, wearisome defense of Dreiser's prose style. Everyone is aware that Dreiser's prose is full of roughness and ungainliness, and the critics who admire Dreiser tell us it does not matter. Of course it does not matter. No reader with a right sense of style would suppose it does matter, and he might even find it a virtue. But it has been taken for granted that the ungainliness of Dreiser's style is the only possible objection to be made to it, and that whoever finds any fault at all in it wants, instead, a prettified genteel style. For instance, Edwin Berry Burgum, in a leaflet on Dreiser put out by the Book Find Club, tells us that Dreiser was one of those who used—or, as he says, utilized—"the diction of the Middle West, pretty much as it was spoken, rich in colloquialism and frank in the simplicity and directness of the pioneer tradition"—a diction substituted for "the literary English, formal and bookish, of New England provincialism that was closer to the aristocratic spirit of the mother country than to the tang of everyday life in the new West." This is mere fantasy. Quite apart from the fact that Hawthorne, Thoreau, and Emerson were all remarkably colloquial—wrote, that is, in their own speaking tones—and specifically American in quality and quite simple and direct in manner, Dreiser is far from writing in the diction of the Middle West. If we are to talk of bookishness, it is Dreiser who is bookish; he is precisely literary in the bad sense; at hundreds of points his diction is not only genteel but fancy; he is full of flowers of rhetoric and he shines with paste gems.

Charles Jackson, the novelist, telling us, in the same leaflet, that Dreiser's style does not matter, reminds us how much still comes to us when we have lost by translation the stylistic brilliance of Thomas Mann or the Russians or Balzac. He is in part right. And he is right too when he says that a certain kind of conscious, supervised artistry is not appropriate to the novel of large dimensions. Yet it is the fact that the great novelists have usually written great prose, and what comes through even a bad translation is exactly the power of mind that made the well-hung sentence of the original text. In literature style is so little the mere clothing of thought—need it be said at this late date?—that we may say that from the novelist's prose spring his characters, his ideas, and even his story itself.

To the extent that Dreiser's style is defensible, his thought is also defensible. That is, when he thinks like a novelist, he is worth following—when by means of his rough and ungainly but effective style he creates rough, ungainly, but effective characters and events. But when he thinks like, as we say, a philosopher, he is likely to be not only foolish but vulgar. He thinks as the modern crowd thinks when it decides to think: religion is nonsense, "religionists" are fakes, tradition is a fraud, what is man but matter and impulses, mysterious "chemisms"?—"What, cooking, eating, coition, job holding, growing, aging, losing, winning, in so changeful and passing a scene as this, important? Bunk! It is some form of titillating illusion with about as much import to the superior forces that bring it all about as the functions and gyrations of a fly. No more. And maybe less." Thus Dreiser at sixty. And yet there is for him always the vulgarly saving suspicion that maybe there is Something Behind It All. It is much to the point of his vulgarity that Dreiser's anti-Semitism was not merely a social prejudice but an idea, a way of dealing with things.

No one, I suppose, has ever represented Dreiser as a masterly intellect. It is even a commonplace to say that his ideas are inconsistent or inadequate. But once that admission has been made, his ideas are hustled out of sight while his reality and great brooding pity are spoken of. (His pity is to be questioned—pity is to be judged not by amount but by kind.) Why has no one ever said that it was "unfortunately a little too late" for Dreiser's awkward, dim speculation, a little too late for so much self-pity, for so much lust for "beauty" and "sex" and "living" and "life itself"? With us it is always a little too late for mind, but never too late for honest stupidity; always a little too late for understanding, never too late for righteous, bewildered wrath; always too late for thought, never too late for naive moralizing. We seem to like to condemn our finest, but not our worst, qualities by pitting them against the exigency of time. It is perhaps not wholly accidental that the article on Literature in that compendium of liberal thought, the Encyclopedia of the Social Sciences, should be by Max Lerner, who gave us the phrase "It is later than you think," and that it should tell us that "literature faces . . . continually the need for rebarbarization."

What we will be patient of and find time for when we confront disasters is of course a matter of taste. But like every matter of taste, it is eventually a practical matter as well. It has its consequences and its issue. Their nature is suggested by Dreiser's posthumous novel—a work of some years back but revised and concluded recently—and by the reception given to it.

"The Bulwark" is a work not merely of piety but of pietism. It is a simple, didactic story recommending a simple Christian belief, the virtues of self-abnegation and self-control, of belief in and submission to the purposes of higher powers, those "superior forces that bring it all about," once, in Dreiser's opinion, so indifferent, now somehow benign. This is not the first occasion on which Dreiser has shown a tenderness toward religion. "Jennie Gerhardt" and the figure of the Reverend Duncan McMillan in "An American Tragedy" are in a way forecasts of the avowals of "The Bulwark." Yet they cannot prepare us for the blank pietism of the new novel, not after we have remembered how salient in Dreiser has been his long surly rage against the "religionists" and "moralists," the men who presume to think that life can be given any law and who dare to believe that faith or tradition can shape the savage and beautiful entity that Dreiser liked to call "life itself." For to Dreiser now nothing can be simpler than the control of life. For the safe conduct of the personal life we have only to follow the Inner Light according to the regimen of the Society of Friends, or, presumably, according to some other godly rule.

To find an analogue to "The Bulwark," we must go back to the moralizing novels of the eighteenth or early nineteenth century. Everything in the story is subordinated to the moment when the Quaker Solon Barnes sees that life has an obscure purpose and justification. Barnes's childhood and youth, his marriage of deep love, his business success in Philadelphia, the alienation of his children and the inadequacy and tragedy of their lives after they have rejected the Quaker faith, are all given in merest summary, with none of that often excessive circumstantiality that makes Dreiser's earlier novels so ineradicably memorable. All details of drama and development are rigorously suppressed to hasten the book toward the moment when Solon Barnes experiences faith and affirmation and his daughter turns from her life of free sexual experience to a chaste sadness for life itself.

I must not be taken to mean that the novel is wholly without power. After all, we cannot follow the life of a man up to the moment of his reconciliation and death without a sense of the majestic significance of the happening. But to take the book and its message in any other serious way than as a fact in Dreiser's biography is, I am sure, impossible.

Dreiser's mood of "acceptance" in the last year of his life is not a thing to be submitted to the tests of intellectual validity. It consists of a feeling of cosmic understanding, an overarching sense of reconciliation to the world with its evil as well as its good. Any reader of nineteenth-century literature will be perfectly familiar with it and, very likely, perfectly sympathetic. It is no more to be quarreled with or reasoned with than love itself—indeed, it is a form of love, not so much love of the world as love of oneself in the world. It is often what is meant by peace. Perhaps it is either the cessation of desire or the perfect balance of desires. If it was Dreiser's own emotion in the end of his life, who would not be happy that he achieved it? I am not even sure that our civilization and our political action would not be the better if more of us knew and cultivated such emotions of grave felicity.

Yet, granting the personal validity of the emotion, the book of which it is the issue and the point is a failure. In the light of Dreiser's past ideas, it is even an offensive failure. On the whole, our liberal critics have been willing to accept it. Mr. Matthiessen accepts it and warns us of the attack that will be made upon it by "those who believe that any renewal of Christianity marks a new 'failure of nerve.' " Life does not look to me the way it looks to the contributors to the "Failure of Nerve" symposium in the *Partisan Review,* and I am not inclined to make such a simple diagnosis as Mr. Matthiessen predicts. The failure of the book does not derive from a failure of nerve but from a failure of heart and mind.

I measure the resolution of "The Bulwark" by "Candide" and know that in the light of the Lisbon earthquake or any more recent catastrophe or holocaust no mood of reconciliation or acceptance can be rationalized into a social doctrine. Or I measure it by works more sympathetic to the religious mood —Ivan Karamazov's "giving back his ticket," his admission to the "harmony" of the universe, suggests that "The Bulwark" is not morally adequate; we dare not, as Solon Barnes does, "accept" the suffering of others; and from "The Book of Job" I know that it does not include enough in its exploration of evil and is not stern enough.

When I say that the book is a failure of thought and feeling I naturally do not mean that Dreiser got old and weak in his mind and heart. The weakness was always there. And in a sense it is not Dreiser who failed but a whole movement of ideas in which we have all been involved. Our liberal, progressive culture found the time to tolerate the vulgar materialist denial, the cry of "Bunk"; and now, almost as a a natural consequence, it has been given, and is willing to receive and find time for, this pietistic mood of reconciliation in all its thinness.

Dreiser, of course, was stronger than the culture that accepted him. He *meant* his ideas. But we, when it came to his ideas, talked about his great brooding pity and shrugged the ideas off. We are still doing it. Robert Elias, who is writing the biography of Dreiser, tells us (in the Book Find leaflet) that "it is part of the logic of [Dreiser's] life that he should have completed 'The Bulwark' at the same time that he joined the Communists." Just what kind of logic this is we learn from Mr. Elias's further statement: "When he supported left-wing movements and finally, last year, joined the Communist Party, he did so, not because he had examined the details of the party line and found them satisfactory, but because he agreed with a general program that represented a means for establishing his cherished goal, greater equality among men." Dreiser was perhaps following the logic of his own life, but certainly he was also following the logic of the progressive criticism that accepted him so heedlessly and so happily—the progressive criticism that first establishes the ultimate social responsibility of the writer and then goes on to say that he is not really responsible for anything, even his ideas. Ideas are but "details," and for details we have no time. With a "cherished goal" before our eyes dare we stop for piddling distinctions and discriminations? And is this not the moment, spiritually and politically, when it is so very late and men are gasping in their inequalities, to learn to accept without quibble the ultimate wisdom of the "superior forces"?

Annette T. Rubinstein. "A Pillar of Society." *New Masses*, 59 (April 30, 1946), 23–24

The material of *The Bulwark* provides an unusual and effective means of exploring an idea seldom presented in the novel. This is not, of course, the problem posed on the book's jacket of "the ever-widening gap which is left by modern man's abandonment of religion." Nor does the book's meaning center in the stereotyped conflict between Solon and his irreligious children. Their desertion merely restates the failure of his faith. And since in Solon, Dreiser has deliberately chosen an honest, intelligent, loving and practically successful bulwark of that faith, this failure indicates the essential unsoundness of a philosophy which may be described in historical and not sectarian terms (since all religions in our bourgeois world do, as a matter of fact, accept it) as the philosophy of protestantism; that is, a philosophy which sees in earthly success an earnest of heavenly approval and concerns itself rather with the parable of the ten talents than with that of the needle's eye.

Of course novelists from Fielding on have given us innumerable instances of the "Is the milk watered? The sugar sanded? The scales weighted? All right, then come in to prayers!" school, and almost as many studies of the still more significant self-deceived and self-righteous Gradgrinds and Dodsons. Here, however, Dreiser has chosen a more unusual example of the successful businessman, less realistic in being atypical, but all the more irrefutable as a logical demonstration of the necessary bankruptcy of individualistic ethics in a country of potential plenty. For this reason, if for no other, *The Bulwark*, while not a great book, is a most significant one.

The actual story is a simple one which follows Solon's life from early childhood through old age. An industrious, altruistic, self-denying and sincere Quaker father, who continues to work hard and begins to prosper more rapidly when fortune gives him the management of his sister-in-law's estate, a loving, deeply religious mother, a profoundly happy marriage, and a generous, devout, though somewhat worldly father-in-law, set the tone for Solon's unquestioning acceptance of an earnest, energetic, God-fearing, prosperous adult life.

Yet the intrinsic incompatibility of devotion to practical affairs for the sake of individual accumulation and real devotion to "The Inner Light" is tentatively indicated from the very beginning of the book. In early boyhood Solon has a troubled consciousness of the intangible difference between the poor Friends' School he first attends and that of the more prosperous community to which he then moves; he puzzles over the subtle change in his father's still helpful attitude to poorer neighbors, now mortgagees or tenants rather than customers; he unknowingly shares his father's uneasiness at the increasing distance between the family's former literal obedience to Quaker precepts and the unpretentious but real comfort, or modest luxury, of its later life.

Nor is the development of this theme confined to Solon. Both his father and his wealthy father-in-law are also repeatedly disturbed by recurrent contradictions between their growing prosperity and their seemingly unchanged ethics, and the latter even evolves a self-conscious theory of the rich man as God's steward which he is occasionally moved to utter at First Day Meetings. Yet the point at which prudence and industry and their natural results become absorption with material things instead of obedience to the divine will is as difficult to determine in advance as are most changes from difference of degree to difference of kind, and we are not surprised that there is no moment at which either Rufus or Justus or, later, Solon himself, finds any reason to interrupt the successful search for further profitable investments.

Solon's youthful marriage with his rather shadowy childhood sweetheart is a fortunate one in every way, and he and Benecia remain devoted to each other and to their much-loved five children. His public life is no less serene. Regular promotions, steady increase of income, growing respect from all church and business associates, and an undiminished conviction of the worth of good banking and bankers, which is barely ruffled by his distaste for certain over-adventurous new associates and the speculative practices they attempt to introduce, compose so idyllic a picture we may well be tempted to question it.

Surely there must have been some instances of internal conflict in the career of any good man who had to foreclose as many mortgages as Solon did! But Dreiser seems more concerned with logical than with artistic completeness, and the very assumption that Solon was uniformly kind, honest, and practically successful gives his failure a more universal significance. For despite the fact that he is almost invariably punctilious in obedience to all the tenets of his faith as interpreted by "The Inner Light," long before the book ends we perceive his essential surrender. He himself often suffers a half-formulated feeling that he has somehow lost the spiritual reality which moved in his mother's life and informed his own youth, and the full truth of this stifled suspicion is apparent when we see that his religion, carefully and sincerely observed throughout their childhood, has not vitality enough left to affect one of his five children!

An interesting sidelight here is Dreiser's insight into the unerring perception with which all the children sense the unrealistic nature of their elders' conscious values and resent standards of thrift and industry which no longer have a genuine social function. They have, however, nothing with which to replace these values and at least four of the five "come to no good." Their catastrophes are plausible and varied, including lonely spinsterhood, a cold and empty business marriage, an unhappy love affair and, for the youngest, a jail suicide at seventeen.

Throughout the book Dreiser's peculiarly matter-of-fact style, here applied to uncharacteristically conventional material, gives the effect of a summarized biography rather than a novel. His use of seemingly unselected incidents, carefully annotated lists of dinner guests who are never again referred to, and quick objective descriptions of plot characters on their first entrance all increase the resemblance to a sort of case history whose interpretation rests with the reader rather than with the reporter.

Except for a few reminiscent flashes of his early naive wonder at the lack of any moral structure in the physical universe—amazement that a child can cause pain with no evil intention, or that a beatufiul insect must destroy a beautiful plant in order to live—Dreiser maintains an utterly impersonal detachment throughout the book. I think it is this which leaves the reader with a curious feeling of incompleteness when he has first finished it. Rereading, or perhaps merely a reconsideration, will, I believe, show that it is only one's habitual expectation of the judge's summary which was disappointed—the verdict itself is directed by more than sufficient evidence.

For despite its seeming lack of deliberate intention or judgment, there are few American novels which so clearly illustrate the basic nature of economic phenomena in social life, the fundamental importance of the historical method in interpreting seemingly stable values, and the ethical irrelevance of subjective attitudes which find no commensurate objective expression. It is as a stimulus to such thinking in the field of Marxist ethics that this book makes its real contribution.

Howard Mumford Jones. "Dreiser Reconsidered." *Atlantic Monthly,* 177 (May 1, 1946), 162, 164, 166, 168, 170.

The publishers of *The Bulwark* announce with truth that this posthumous work is the first novel by Theodore Dreiser to appear in twenty years. As one toils through its cumbrous pages, they do, indeed, take one back to the twenties, when the wine of the puritans was being spilled on the ground. Any estimate of Dreiser must be based upon the revolt of which he was the embodiment and which conditions even his latest fiction. But first, *The Bulwark* itself.

The fable is standard. Solon Barnes, scion of a Quaker family, sober, industrious, inflexible, a child of the nineteenth century, marries a sober Quaker wife and rises by industry and frugality to being a minor personage in the banking world of Philadelphia. He rears a family. Convinced that God prospers the righteous, he is troubled by the contemporaneous prosperity of the wicked in the Gilded Age, a doubt that makes him stick more closely to Victorian values as the materialism of capital and the worldliness of Philadelphia society increase.

His children cannot accept the restrictions of the old ways, but their rebellion is disastrous. One daughter goes to live with an artist in Greenwich Village, a son turns out to be a prig, and another son kills himself because, on a wild party, he is involved in the death of a girl. Solon resigns from the bank in protest against shady practice. His death closes the book. One is reminded of the despairing cry of the father in Hebbel's *Maria Magdalena,* "I understand the world no more." Readers of Dreiser will recognize echoes of his earlier books in this plot.

The manuscript might have been written at almost any time in this writer's career. It retains all his peculiarities. A fecund author, he never mastered a style, so that the strength and weakness of *Sister Carrie,* which dates from 1900, are in this regard the strength and weakness of *An American Tragedy,* published in 1925. I open this vast novel at random, find myself in the middle of the Roberta-Clyde love affair, and read:—

> And this, in spite of the present indifference of the Griffiths, caused him to walk with even more of an air than had hitherto characterized him. Even though neither they nor any of those connected with them recognized him, still he looked at himself in his mirror from time to time with an assurance and admiration which before this he had never possessed. For now Roberta, feeling that her future was really dependent on his will and whim, had set herself to flatter him almost constantly, to be as obliging and convenient to him as possible. Indeed, according to her notion of the proper order of life, she was now his and his only as much as any wife is ever to a husband, to do with as he wished.

This is the average level of Dreiser's prose. Can writing be more gray, featureless, lacking in cogency? *An American Tragedy* is impressive for other reasons, but *The Bulwark,* lacking weight and onset, is not. The style is unaltered. The characters all talk alike. If it is possible to lug in a cliché, Dreiser is led as by enchantment to prefer it to something simpler and more direct. Indeed, *The Bulwark* in theme and style has the air of being a reprint for classes in the history of fiction; one almost expects some scholar to provide an introduction, glossary, and notes.

But the book is not insignificant, and Dreiser cannot be ignored. His clumsy, yet sympathetic, spirit embodies a phase of American thought. He is a characteristic product of our revolt against the nineteenth century. The publishers' instinct is therefore right in calling the attention of buyers to the fact that twenty years have elapsed since *An American Tragedy* was published.

The twenties were the triumph of the revolution against [sic]. During the previous ten years young and ardent writers, assembling for a crusade against tradition, began the attack; by the mid-twenties Jerusalem had been conquered. Jerusalem had been somewhat unhistorically defended by an army of "puritans," albeit "puritanism" had no connection with the seventeenth century, a moment of history the attackers never studied. "Puritanism" was a misnomer. The attack was upon the nineteenth century, and its timing simply marked a cultural lag between the United States and Europe, particularly Great Britain.

In England the last third of the last century had seen revolt, the record of which is the writings of Spencer, Huxley, and Tyndall, the biographical and historical studies of Leslie Stephen, Andrew Lang, and their kind, and the literary productions of writers as various as Stevenson, Wilde, G.B.S., and Samuel Butler. The Protestant God had been an oppressor (see Gosse's *Father and Son*); everybody therefore argued that if you could get rid of him, you would be happy (as in Butler's *The Way of All Flesh*). The assumption that literature should elucidate poetic justice (as in Tennyson and George Eliot) was so palpably absurd, it was comforting to discover there was no cosmic court of equity (for example, the end of *Tess of the d'Urbervilles*). Experimental science was obviously progressive; therefore theology was obviously wrong (as in *Robert Elsmere*). The practice of art and the freedom of the human instinct were better guides than philosophy or social custom *(Studies in the Rennaissance, The Critic as Artist, An Unsocial Socialist).*

In the United States the next century saw a parallel revolt, but the name was different—the "revolt from the village." In 1913 John Macy complained that American literature was "idealistic, sweet, delicate, nicely finished"—that is, devoted to a village concept of poetic justice. It was therefore immature. "Any child," he wrote, "can read American literature, and if it does not make a man of him, it at least will not lead him into forbidden realms." American books "too seldom come to grips with the problems of life."

Dreiser was the heir, not merely of determinism and the revolt from the village, but of the whole anti-Victorian movement. To him Spencer was a dazzling mind. Oppressed by a Catholic God as Gosse had been oppressed by a Protestant Deity, he adopted the agnostic axioms of Tyndall, Stephen, and the Victorian monists. The passage in *The Financier* in which Frank Cowperwood watches the lobster devour the squid shows how delightedly Dreiser substituted the crudest form of Darwinism for theology. If literary idealism had sophisticated the facts of life, Dreiser proposed to substitute brute fact for literary idealism. Whether his novels can survive the passing of these simple and primitive epistemological assumptions is a nice problem of literary history.

Sister Carrie and *An American Tragedy* seem destined to endure, whereas *The Financier, The Titan, The "Genius,"* and, as I think, *Jennie Gerhardt* have already faded. The difficulty with these lesser novels is that they illustrate the formula of the revolt they spring from. They exist only as documents. Life in them is merely aimless, merely the product of mechanical and chemical forces. Sexuality, which Dreiser valued highly, is tedious in these books, because it is simple and repetitive. Who now remembers the procession of women in and out of Frank Cowperwood's beds? Or the endless inamorata of Eugene Witla? The paradox of Dreiser's theory that sexual passion is a driving force is that his books lack sexual passion. They only catalogue, they do not participate. These females are mere objects in space like the paintings Cowperwood buys, the furnitue he acquires, the clothing of his mistresses, and all that vague, vulgar, gilt accumulation that, despite his affectation of scorn, really titillated Dreiser's imagination.

One can, I suppose, write a novel without believing in God, in art, or in idealism, but one cannot very well write a novel without believing in personality. Cowperwood, Witla, and Jennie Gerhardt are not personalities, but the products of force, themselves metamorphosed into force. The squid and the lobster would do as well. The result is not fiction but algebra. *The Bulwark* suffers from this fallacy. Solon Barnes is as he is because he is. His children are drawn after the same formula, and the climax is not conflict, but collision.

Usually what survives of a literary artist has little to do with his philosophy of the universe. We do not now care for Chaucer's astrological lore, Bunyan's theology, or George Eliot's positivism; but for the Wife of Bath, Apollyon, and Maggie Tulliver. Imaginative vision, the sympathetic presentation of character, it is commonplace, outlast general ideas. There were, I am convinced, two persons in Dresier: the rebel against nineteenth-century moralism, dogged, brooding, an evangelist of agnosticism; and the reporter, sensitive, sympathetic, curious, all things to all men, who, at certain levels of society (for example, the lower middle class), forgetting that in theory all men are blobs of random cells, took to humanity with Chaucerian delight.

Where in American prose is there better portraiture than that of Paul Dresser in *Twelve Men!* In the same volume consider the flexibility of temperament that gives you both "The Mighty Rourke" and "A Doer of the Word." There are equally vivid passages in the other autobiographical books. If this reporting sometimes failed (as it miserably did in *A Gallery of Women*), delight in experience informs the opening third of *An American Tragedy*, wherein, not yet hag-ridden by a social thesis, we experience the life of a street evangelist and the life of hotels. The same delight makes Drouet and Hurstwood credible in *Sister Carrie*. Cowperwood is lath and plaster by comparison.

Take from Dreiser his naturalistic philosophy, and what you have left curiously resembles Dickens—for it is thus the despised nineteenth century brings in its revenge. Like Dickens, Dreiser never comprehended and could not portray cultivated life. But like Dickens he moved sympathetically among the lower middle class, the poor, and the shabby-genteel denizens of that half world between the slums and success where Hurstwood runs saloons that Dick Swiveller would have liked, and Caroline Meeber's career as an actress so oddly suggests The Infant Phenomenon in *Nickleby*. For both writers, happiness was endless vitality, hearty vulgarity; and this sense of well-being could be increased by a Christmas philosophy of gifts. Thus Paul Dresser scatters vagabond kindness as if he were employed by the Cheeryble brothers.

Moreover, Dreiser's delight in melodrama is Dickens's delight; for example, the immense court scene in *An American Tragedy*—one can almost overhear Boz applauding in the wings. Finally, Dreiserian delicacy is like that of Dickens, who never says openly that Edith Dombey is Carker's mistress. So, despite the foolish censors, Dreiser dropped a Victorian curtain over Cowperwood's harem and extracts all the sensuality from *The "Genius."* But *The Bulwark* is without delight; the thesis (as my outline hints) has swallowed up the book.

It is these scattered scenes of imaginative vigor and real warmth that constitute Dreiser's chief claim to immortality. In them the style is still bad, but its badness is venial (like that of Dickens), it does not ruin achievement. Not here but elsewhere does Dreiser fail. The more he reflects, the worse he writes, except that when he tries to penetrate psychology and paint for us motive and impulse, he becomes still more dreadful. But where his problem is one of description and movement; where, as in the case of the biographical sketches and the autobiographical scenes, his purpose is principally to record, not to interpret, then his faulty grasp of medium is less disastrous. For he had the reporter's memory for spoken phrase, though he seems mainly to have interviewed powerful uneducated persons; just as he has the quick, reportorial eye for random detail.

The stolid, coarse-grained thesis novels, the naïve cosmology, the bad writing, the uneasy political radicalism—these are not essential and fine; what is fine is those parts of his books which are, as it were, reportorial, it being understood that the reporter was a genius whose sympathy contradicted the deterministic philosophy he seemed to accept.

Dreiser saw, felt, tasted, smelled, handled, and loved the visible world, a world with many goodly creatures in it, many weak men, some fools, no devil, much chemistry, and no God. In both senses of the word the invisible world was beyond him. He can therefore move us to pity (as in *An American Tragedy*) but he cannot move us to terror. His laughter was both gentle and Gargantuan, but as a satirist he is feeble and opaque. What he might have become in any other epoch is an open question: for us, he is the incarnation of our anti-Victorian mood.

Mason Wade. "Books of the Week." *Commonweal*, 44 (June 14, 1946), 220.

This posthumously published novel, the author's first in twenty years, adds nothing to Dreiser's reputation and will puzzle his ardent disciples. For "The Bulwark" is one of those half-born books which writers have a way of treasuring and at intervals reworking, but which seldom see the light of day in their own lifetimes. It is an unkind fate which permits the publication of unsuccessful work after the close of a distinguished career. "The Bulwark" was first announced thirty years ago, at the close of Dreiser's most productive period, and was to be part of his fictional study of the transformation of America by capitalism at the turn of the century. It is the story of Solon Barnes, an earnest young Quaker with an eye to the main chance, who sees his economic success made empty by the disintegration of the values he cherishes in the twentieth century world in which his children grow up. Their personal tragedies revive a faith that had become complacent with success, in a conclusion very different from that of most of Dreiser's books, which reflect his own naturalistic revolt against tradition and authority. But the book is largely lifeless; its drama undeveloped. It carries no conviction, for Dreiser was better at depicting revolt than affirmation. This is a book about Quakerism, but a far better picture of that faith emerge[s] from Jessamyn West's far less pretentious and more eloquent book, "The Friendly Persuasion." Either the subject or the unfinished character of the book is responsible for an unanticipated variation from Dreiser's wonted elephantine prose. "The Bulwark's" simplicity is the greatest strength of a weak book.

Granville Hicks. "The Library: Theodore Dreiser." *American Mercury,* 62 (June 1946), 751–756.

To appreciate Theodore Dreiser's posthumous novel, *The Bulwark,* we must see it in relation to his life and the body of his work. Certainly it is not the best of his novels, but it is a remarkably appropriate climax to his career. Taken by itself, it would add little to his reputation as a novelist, but it compels us to revise upward our estimate of the man.

The Bulwark is the story of a Quaker boy who grows up in the outskirts of Philadelphia, works hard, prospers in the banking business, marries the girl of his choice, raises a family, and wins an enviable position in the community. Only as his children approach maturity is this Solon Barnes confronted with problems to which the moral code of the Friends seems inadequate. One son and one daughter achieve conventional success, but Solon is too astute to believe that they have found the inner peace known to himself and his wife. The other three children are overt rebels, and all of them have their difficulties, with the youngest blundering into tragedy. Solon's faith is assailed by these disasters, but in the end doubts are dispelled and faith triumphs.

Although the emphases and conclusions seem almost startlingly new, the theme is that to which the whole of Dreiser's career was devoted. His great problem was always the problem of values, and, in particular, the problem of the inadequacy of the middle-class morality of the nineteenth century. He had been taught by his sternly Catholic father to work hard, live austerely, and expect his reward in the hereafter. In the world of his young manhood, he quickly discovered, most people did not live by these standards. What standards, he asked himself, did they live by, and what happened to them in the end? The questions never ceased to fascinate him.

Dreiser's contemporary, Lincoln Steffens, always talked about "my life of unlearning." Every generation has its share of unlearning to do, but perhaps Americans born in the 1860's and 1870's had more than ordinary difficulty in reconciling the world they grew up in with the account their parents and preceptors had given them of the world as it should be.

At least for public purposes Lincoln Steffens regarded the process of disillusionment as comedy. To Dreiser it was almost unmitigated tragedy. There was a difference in the economic stiuations of the Steffenses and the Dreisers, and a striking difference in the relations between parents and children. Perhaps, too, Steffens' study of ethics and philosophy helped to soften the shock. Dreiser had to make his own philosophy out of experience and accidental reading, without the straw of formal education. It is not surprising that the confused materialism at which he arrived seemed to him less satisfying than the emphatic certainties of his father's generation.

In *The Bulwark* Dreiser did something that he had never tried to do before and that psychologically he could not have done until time had completed his emancipation. The book, that is, portrays the values of the older generation from its own point of view. Because of this, the first part of the story is quite new. Here is a Dreiserian hero who believes what his parents teach him and sets his feet firmly on the path to respectability and wealth. Solon loves but once, marries the object of his love, and cherishes her until her death. A quiet, earnest, untroubled boyhood leads to a purposeful and, for some years, happy maturity.

In the second part of the novel, however, all the familiar motifs appear. The girls re-enact, in milder versions, the rebellions of Carrie Meeber and Jennie Gerhardt. Stewart, the youngest child, has all of Clyde Griffiths' longing for excitement and luxury, and, like Clyde, is the victim not only of his passions but also of an ironic and Hardyesque accident. Certain of Solon's business associates are cut from the same piece of goods as Frank Cowperwood, and Etta's lover is bloodbrother to Eugene Witla. Here, in short, is the unvarying Dreiserian drama: arrayed on one side are the ideals of pious, moralistic parents, who do not understand their children; on the other are the temptations of luxury and the consequent urge to get money by ruthlessness or dishonesty, together with the temptations of sex.

Dreiser's sympathetic portrayal of the older generation endows the conflict with a poignancy that one cannot feel in his earlier novels. His climax, moreover, goes beyond mere neutrality. Throughout most of the latter part of the book, Dreiser emphasizes Solon's narrowness, and the reader takes the side of Etta and even Stewart against their father, but the conclusion redresses the balance. When Solon sees a beautiful fly eating a beautiful bud—an episode that must have been intended to remind the reader of Cowperwood's famous meditation on the lobster and the squid—he is overcome with awe and wonder. "Surely," he thinks, "there must be a Creative Divinity, and so a purpose, behind all this variety and beauty and tragedy of life." In his business life Solon has remained true to his ideals at no small cost. In his relations with his family he has failed, but he faces his failures and tries to learn from them. Dreiser knew that the central problem remained unsolved, but he was nevertheless determined to make us appreciate Solon's personal triumph. Solon's faith is stronger than ever at the end, and the dignity of his death humbles the more sensitive of his children.

II

Did Dreiser get religion before he died? Those who were close to him in the last year of his life say that, in some sense or other, he did. There is something warmly personal in his description of Solon's reaffirmation of faith, and one gathers from Mrs. Tjader, his secretary, that Dreiser originally intended to have Solon die a disillusioned man and decided to restore his hero's faith only as his own was awakened. What he believed in is difficult to say, but the novel suggests that he had arrived at a kind of pantheism that he found emotionally satisfying.

Dreiser, as he once observed, was always confused. Although for many years he thought of himself as a materialist, there is not a clear statement of materialism in any of his books, and there are dozens of passages that are quite irreconcilable with any form of naturalism. His political career was a succession of inconsistencies, crowned by the farce of his joining the Communist Party a few months before he died. Every book in which he attempted to give a formal account of his views, from *Hey Rub-a-dub-dub* to *America Is Worth Saving,* is a congeries of contradictions.

In spite of all this, however, Dreiser came close to the root of several important matters. In the first place, he sensed more deeply than any other novelist the psychological consequences of the growth of large cities in America. Few writers have felt more keenly the excitement of the great city, or yearned more passionately for the urban fleshpots, and yet it is preeminently Dreiser who shows us the city as the destroyer of values. He knew as well as anyone the faults of the small communities, but he also knew that in such communities men had developed a way of life that brought some degree of security and satisfaction. The theme is developed early in *Sister Carrie,* and it recurs in every novel thereafter. Again and again Dreiser said in effect, "I cannot live by them, and it remains to be proven whether there are other standards that make a fruitful life possible." Because the industrialization and urbanization of America are such vast phenomena and so pervasive in their influence, we tend to ignore them as we ignore the climate, but they constitute the great revolution of modern times, more important than any political change, and Dreiser felt the impact of this revolution in every corner of his being.

In the second place, despite his failure to formulate a clear statement of naturalism, he never got very far away from the crux of the naturalistic problem. If one disregards all the verbose nonsense about "chemic forces" and the rest, one finds a resolute attempt to see human life as an integral part of a vast and only partly comprehensible natural process. The early materialists sought to reduce psychology to biology and biology to chemistry, and in his vocabulary and sometimes in his thinking Dreiser borrowed their concepts, but he was never satisfied, and though his dissatisfaction often led him into extravagant mysticism, it also kept his attention focused on the human being as such. There is a passage in *Sister Carrie,* muddy but interesting, in which he struggles with the problem of freedom of the will, and in the upshot agrees with the best of the naturalistic philosophers that freedom lies in the understanding of necessity. Dreiser felt strongly and portrayed fully the power of the inner and outer forces by which men are pulled this way and hauled that. His own life was not a life of reason, and few of his characters are reasonable beings. Yet they are always more than the total of the forces that drive them.

Finally we must say a word about Dreiser's humanitarianism. During his lifetime he supported a variety of causes, and, whatever mistakes he may have made, his indignation against injustice did rest firmly on his sense of the dignity of the individual human being. There are no contemptible persons in Dreiser's novels. Although at times he professed a Nietzschean scorn of the masses, and stated as a biological fact that less than 3 per cent of the population was capable of thinking, his sympathies were quickly roused, and he instinctively made the best case possible for any person he wrote about. Perhaps one reason why he made Solon Barnes a Quaker is that the Friends have always been the most generously humanitarian of the Christian sects. At any rate the quotations from John Woolman's *Journal* do not seem incongruous on Dreiser's pages. One could no more ask Dreiser for a program of reform than one could ask him for a system of philosophy, but he did have charity.

"I catch no meaning from all I have seen," Dreiser wrote some twenty years ago, "and pass quite as I came, confused and dismayed." Perhaps he changed in the last year or two, and felt both less confusion and less dismay. I am not sure, however, that too much importance should be attached to his conversion. What is important is that, in spite of all his vagaries, he remained true in essentials to the insights that were vouchsafed him.

III

Dreiser was a bewildered man, but he had the strength to bear his bewilderment. There is nothing new to be said about his style, for everyone recognizes its faults and almost everyone knows that they grew out of the man's basic qualities. Most novelists, if they have any skill with words, are tempted to say more than they know, but Dreiser, whose least encounter with the American language took on the appearance of a wrestling match, stubbornly refused to go beyond himself. I am not trying to suggest that good writing is a vice, but merely that Dreiser's awkwardness was integrally related to his tremendous honesty. Even his banalities do not seem the product of laziness but, rather, the desperate gestures of a man for whom mere words will never suffice.

The Bulwark has all of the old clumsiness, but what is the essentially Dreiserian style is somehow exhibited in a purer vein than ever before. The writing is so commonplace that it becomes austere and even dignified. There are plenty of the old trite phrases, and there are a few pretentious passages, but for the most part the novel is written with a simplicity that begins by being annoying and ends by being impressive. Dreiser never told a story better than in *The Bulwark*.

Yet I have said that *The Bulwark* is not the best of his novels, and in some ways it seems to me the poorest. Certain of his qualities are heightened in the book, but one of the most important of his attributes scarcely makes itself felt, and the novel suffers sharply as a result. What one misses is the sense of a time and a place. Can anyone forget the description of Fitzgerald and Moy's bar in *Sister Carrie* or the account of the Green-Davidson Hotel in *An American Tragedy?* Dreiser's documentation was laborious, and he relied on the piling up of detail, but he got his effect. In *The Bulwark*, on the other hand, the background is invariably a little vague, whether the scene is Solon's bank or Isobel's college or Etta's Greenwich Village. It has always been easy to make fun of Dreiser's concern with trivialities, but the truth is that the commonplace was not commonplace to him and that he could make it fresh and vivid to us. One came to know his people through the minutiae of their lives, and it is strange to read a book of his in which the figures are almost as removed from the vulgar circumstances of place and time as the characters of Henry James.

The explanation lies, at least in part, in the way in which the book was written. Mrs. Tjader tells us that it was begun as early as 1910 and that there were four or five early versions. When Dreiser took up the story again in the winter of 1945, he and Mrs. Tjader pieced the first part of the novel together out of the various fragments, and he then wrote and dictated the last third of the book. As a result, there is a very real uncertainty as to the period in which the action is taking place. The incidents of the latter part of the story are said to occur in the twenties, but there are a hundred details that belong to the years before the first World War. Even, however, if Dreiser had completely revised the novel or had written it afresh, I doubt if he could have documented it as he documented the earlier novels, for by the twenties he was the great American novelist and no longer immersed in the life of the people.

The Bulwark, at least in its final version, was the work of an old man, and its most moving pages portray the old age and death of Solon Barnes. Dreiser has portrayed pathetic old men before now. Solon, however, is not merely pathetic; he is meant to be and is a triumphant figure. As he rises above the vicissitudes of fate by virture of his inner resources, one believes in his triumph whether or not one believes in the Inner Light.

Whatever its philosophical implications, *The Bulwark* is certainly a rejection of naturalism as a literary theory. Dreiser, it is true, occasionally uses such characteristic phrases as "the import of sex as a force" and "the chemically radiated charm of her," and he even talks about Solon's "psychic religiosity," but these are mere matters of habit or, more probably, vestigial remains of an earlier version, for there is no serious attempt to explain anybody's behavior in terms of physics, chemistry, or biology.

The Bulwark might, indeed, be regarded as the death knell of literary naturalism. It was always a misbegotten theory. However enthusiastically Zola endorsed the formulas of Claude Bernard, he never in practice limited himself to them, and he would have been a mere parody of a novelist if he had. Dreiser owed more to Balzac than he did to Darwin, Spencer, and Haeckel, and even if he had had a more extensive and accurate knowledge of nineteenth century science, he still would not have been able to make great practical use of it. The theorists of naturalism held that the novel could become scientific, but the novelists, fortunately, knew better. Some of the wiser ones took from science what proved to be useful, but they found in science something to add to their art, not a substitute for it. In this country at least naturalism was chiefly a justification of a frankness that was not palatable to middle-class morality. Now that that battle is won, there is not much need for further talk about naturalism.

Dreiser in any case could never be brought comfortably within the naturalistic fold, no matter how hard academicians tried, and it is perhaps as well that *The Bulwark* has come along to make the attempt obviously futile. Even *The Financier* and *The Titan*, which he probably thought of as naturalistic, are Nietzschean rather than Darwinian.

Dreiser was Dreiser and not the exemplar of some theory. He was the lost, bewildered man of the turn of the century, caught between science and faith, between city and town, between the economics of monopoly capitalism and the economics of small-scale competition. With the most painful honesty he set forth the dilemmas of his generation and, by stating what he knew about men, said something about man.

James T. Farrell. "Dreiser's Posthumous Novel: A Major American Work." *Call*, 13 (July 1, 1946), 5.

Theodore Dreiser's posthumous work, The Bulwark, recounts the life story of a Quaker business man, Solon Barnes. This novel deals in terms of a problem of conscience. Solon Barnes discovers a growing lack of consistency between his own religious and social ideals, guided by his "inner light," and the practices of the business world as well as the customs of luxurious living of the successful people whom he knows.

The sum total of his life-experiences requires that he make a choice, and the essence of this story is found in the decision which he does reach.

It deals with conflicting social, economic and religious ideals, and with the consequences which this conflict creates in the lives of a family. On the one hand, it is a novel which dramatizes a problem of conscience: on the other hand, it is a social novel in the sense that it represents the role of social ideals and of social changes in the lives of its main characters.

The book is not as long as most of Dreiser's other novels, and in some parts, the story moves along in the pattern of an outline. Stylistically, there are not noticeable changes in this book: it is written in the manner which we have come to recognize as Dreiserian. The writing possesses greater simplicity than is the case in, say, The Financier. It is sometimes marred by a carelessness of phraseology and by long and involved sentences; but this book also contains sustained passages which are among the most moving and the most eloquent that Dreiser ever wrote.

The chief protagonist here, Solon Barnes was raised in the simple religious tradition of the Quakers.

There is a certain unstressed irony in the career of Solon, the business man, if this is seen in contrast with his experiences as a father. He is a successful business man: he is an unsuccessful parent. This irony cuts to the core of the business ideals of modern American civilization.

It is easier to make money, to rise in the world of business, than it is to fulfill one's duties as a parent. American civilization which has made such tremendous advances in solving the problems of the production of goods lags, and lags most pronouncedly in the "production" of human beings.

The children drift away from the religion of the parents. One girl goes to Wisconsin University, and then to Greenwich Village where she has an extra-marital love affair: a boy becomes involved in escapades which cause a public scandal, and commits suicide: the other children become in one sense or another, conventional.

And at the same time, the gambling and financially adventuristic practices which are becoming more pronounced in the business world, the way men make money—this causes in Solon an additional qualm of conscience.

He ends up a sick, dying old man. But all of this suffering, all of his disappointments deepens the sweetness and the genuineness of his nature. He has not been a bulwark in the world of practical realities, nor in the realm of the practical realities of personal family life. His love for his wife has been genuine and monagamous.

Yet he hasn't been able to mould the character and the lives of his children in consistency with his own faith. But he remains a "bulwark" of faith. His faith is mystical, and it conceives the entire universe and all that is in it as an arena of love. Some of the brotherly love which he felt, which he wished to express in real life this is, then, impedded in the entire universe.

His conviction of mystical love, illustrated when he is old and out walking and is endangered by a snake which does not attack him, endows him with resignation, a resignation which is not lacking in dignity. He dies with dignity.

The end of this book reveals a second irony, one which is patent in the work, although not, obviously, one of conscious intention on the part of the author. The "inner light," mystical love, the simplicity of a genuine man—this prepares him to meet death, but not to ride the storms of this life.

In evaluating this novel, in assessing its meaning and significance, we need to remember what happens in its pages, and not—as some reviews have done—merely to concentrate on the question of what was the faith of the author. There was always a mystical strain in Dreiser's thinking. There can be no doubt but that the mystical, religious ending of The Bulwark was dictated not only by the needs of the story and characterization, but also, by the personal attitude of the author.

However, once a book is published, it begins to live its own life, independent of its author. Besides the meanings which it possesses in relationship to the conviction, the perspective, the general intentions and orientations of the author, it also must be seen and grasped in terms of what story it tells, and what the events and characters of this novel reveal and mean.

Regarded from the standpoint of this second perspective, we can clearly see how this story reveals that a mysticism such as that of Solon Barnes equips one to die, but not to live and grapple with the practical realities of life in the form of society which prevails at the present time.

In this respect, the objectivity of Dreiser, his balanced and sympathetic manner of setting down characters and events, his consistent refusal to water down the facts concerning the pitilessness of circumstances, and the nature of the social and biological tragedies which man must face—all this shows the true and the serious artist. The ending is integrated in the story, and is not therefore, unwarranted.

What is most important about this novel is that it is a full and serious story which tells us of the complete life experience of a man. At the same time, it deals with the quality of ideals in modern America.

Dreiser was the great realistic writer of the ideals of American life in its period of most tremendous capitalist expansion and of greatest hope for the future. The Bulwark adds another massive panel to Dreiser's fictional recreation of the story of American ideals. And there is a further significance to The Bulwark. To paraphrase Goethe, we can repeat that gray is theory, but green is the tree of life.

Continuing the metaphor, The Bulwark can be said to possess the greenness of the tree of life. All theories, all values, all ideas, all social proposals must, in the last analysis, be referred to the way that men and women live. This story describes how men and women live.

In its revelation, it illustrates and depicts a simple human goodness which is of importance in any form of society, and in terms of any established set of social values. Without sentimentality, with no mawkishness whatsoever, Dreiser has here depicted the genuine goodness, the humanity of Solon Barnes and his wife, Benecia.

The description of their love and their loyalty is, in itself, touching and poignant. The character of Solon is marked by his dignity, his goodness, his nobility. One may disagree with his moral values and his choices, but one can not but recognize the depth of his humanity.

And there is a positive value in this. The characterization of Solon Barnes is a remarkable literary characterization; it can well stand alongside of the other creations in Dreiser's gallery of American figures. Theodore Dreiser's The Bulwark is a major American novel.

Orville Prescott. "Outstanding Books." *Yale Review*, 35 (Summer 1946), 767.

. . . This posthumous novel was written in fits and starts over a period of some thirty years. It is a study of Quakers and the problem of faith in a materialistic world. Mr. Dreiser approached it with the plodding, solemn thoroughness that marked all his work. The notorious clumsiness of his style is not quite so obtrusive as usual, but neither is there apparent here any of the crude strength and fierce power of his earlier works. Sincere, inept, mediocre, and superficial, *The Bulwark* has been sadly overpraised by those who are bemused by Dreiser's place in literary history as a pioneer of blunt realism. But judged solely on its own merits this book is much inferior to scores of current novels which are not seriously reviewed.

"Fiction." *Virginia Quarterly Review*, 22 (Summer 1946), lxxv.

This novel, Dreiser's first since "An American Tragedy," is in many ways his fullest, richest work, a sprawling Quaker saga centering around the life of Solon Barnes. . . . "The Bulwark" presents a wealth of characters and a depth of idea which more than compensate for Dreiser's frequently diffuse prose and labored structure.

Checklist of Additional Reviews

Kirkus Book Service, 14 (January 15, 1946), 21.

William McFee. "The Reviews." New York *Sun*, March 21, 1946.

"Theodore Dreiser's Last Novel." Newark *News*, March 21, 1946.

"New Dreiser." Worcester [Mass.] *Telegram*, March 23, 1946.

Publisher's Weekly, March 23, 1946.

John Hyde Preston. "Hero of Dreiser's Last Novel Resembles His Creator." New York *PM,* March 24, 1946.

Daphne Alloway McKicker. "Dreiser's Last Book Is Disappointing." Columbus [Ohio] *Citizen,* March 24, 1946.

Alex Stedman. "Books and Bookman." Fort Worth [Tex.] *Star-Telegram,* March 24, 1946.

P.J.S. "Decline in National Ideal of Honesty Told by Dreiser." Los Angeles [Cal.] *Times,* March 24, 1946.

Maude Robinson. "A Quaker Tragedy: Dreiser's Last Novel Will Stir No Storm." Salt Lake City [Utah] *Tribune,* March 24, 1946.

W.T.S. "Dreiser's Posthumous Novel." Providence [R.I.] *Journal,* March 24, 1946.

Eugene Phillips. "A Vigorous Human Novel, Theodore Dreiser's Last." Milwaukee *Journal,* March 24, 1946.

Frederic B. Hyde. "Pity Story of Quaker Life Rounds Out Dreiser's Life." Philadelphia *Inquirer,* March 24, 1946.

Dorothy T. Peckham. "Fails in His Family." Worcester [Mass.] *Telegram,* March 24, 1946.

E.A.L. "A Bulwark Overwhelmed." Boston *Globe,* March 27, 1946.

"Books on Parade." San Francisco *Call Bulletin,* March 29, 1946.

Ottumwa [Ia.] *Daily Courier,* March 30, 1946.

"Dreiser's Last Novel." Columbus [Ohio] *Dispatch,* March 31, 1946.

Akron [Ohio] *Beacon-Journal,* March 31, 1946.

"Dreiser's Last Book Unfolds Quaker's Life." Miami [Fla.] *Herald,* March 31, 1946.

New York *Wings,* April, 1946.

Roanoke [Va.] *Times,* April 1, 1946.

"Library Notes." Greenfield [Mo.] *Advocate,* April 4, 1946.

El Paso [Tex.] *Herald Post,* April 5, 1946.

Robert S. Nevin. "Novel By Theodore Dreiser Magnificently Written." Dayton [Ohio] *Journal Herald,* April 6, 1946.

Elizabeth North Hoyt. "A Quaker Background." Cedar Rapids [Ia.] *Gazette,* April 7, 1946.

R.O.F. "Posthumous Dreiser." Pasadena [Cal.] *Star-News,* April 7, 1946.

Clyde Beck. "Theodore Dreiser's Posthumous Novel." Detroit *News,* April 7, 1946.

Tulsa [Okla.] *World,* April 7, 1946.

Portland [Ore.] *Journal,* April 7, 1946.

John G. Fuller. Boston [Mass.] *Post,* April 7, 1946.

Richmond Beatty. "Family Disintegration." Nashville [Tenn.] *Banner,* April 10, 1946.

Theodore Smith. "Reviews and News of Books." San Francisco *News,* April 13, 1946.

Joseph J. Firebaugh. St. Louis *Post-Dispatch,* April 14, 1946.

Youngstown [Ohio] *Vindicator,* April 14, 1946.

S.A.Q. "Dreiser's Last Book." Richmond [Va.] *Times-Dispatch,* April 14, 1946.

Scranton [Pa.] *Best Sellers,* April 15, 1946.

Norman MacDonald. "Godly Quaker Dreiser's Theme." Boston [Mass.] *Herald,* April 17, 1946.

Hartford [Conn.] *Times,* April 18, 1946.

New Orleans *Times Picayune,* April 21, 1946.

Green Bay [Wis.] *Press Gazette,* April 26, 1946.

Beverly Hills [Cal.] *Script,* April 27, 1946.

El Paso [Tex.] *Times,* April 28, 1946.

Margaret Miller. "Novel of Quaker Life Issued Posthumously." San Diego [Cal.] *Union*, April 28, 1946.

Harvey Curtis Webster. "Dreiser Puts Down His Last Great Words." Louisville *Courier-Journal*, April 28, 1946.

New Haven [Conn.] *Journal-Courier*, May 1, 1946.

T.T.L. "In Faith We Stand." Columbia [Mo.] *Missourian*, May 2, 1946.

Marianna Willis. "Book Review." Glendora *Press-Gleaner*, May 3, 1946.

Lee Walsh. "Of Books and Writings." Washington *Daily News*, May 4, 1946.

Richard F. Sullivan. "Spencerism to Asceticism." Hartford [Conn.] *Courant*, May 5, 1946.

Marjorie Ragan. "Theodore Dreiser's Last Novel." Raleigh [N.C.] *Observer*, May 5, 1946.

Augusta [Ga.] *Chronicle*, May 12, 1946.

Burbank [Cal.] *Daily Review*, May 14, 1946.

Portland [Me.] *Press-Herald*, May 16, 1946.

Gladys Hoover. "Dreiser's Latest." San Jose [Cal.] *Mercury Herald and News*, May 19, 1946, p. 16.

Margaret P. Larsen. "Library Notes." Coleraine [Minn.] *Iron News*, May 23, 1946.

Corona [Cal.] *Independent*, May 31, 1946.

Los Altos [Cal.] *News*, May 30, 1946.

Charles Child Walcutt. "Naturalism in 1946: Dreiser and Farrell." *Accent*, 6 (Summer 1946), 263–268.

Wisconsin Library Bulletin, 42 (June 1946), 87.

Robert Match, *Tomorrow*, June, 1946.

United States Quarterly Booklist, 2 (June 1946), 89.

Helen Pride Craig. Columbia [S.C.] *Current Books in Review*, June 6, 1946.

St. Petersburg [Fla.] *Times*, June 16, 1946.

Gertrude Hall. "Book Review." Sausalito [Cal.] *News*, June 28, 1946.

Lee Bissinger. "Good Reading." New York *Pic*, July, 1946.

"Bound to be Read." Asbury [N.J.] *Sun*, July 1, 1946.

August Derleth. "Three Novels." Madison [Wis.] *Capitol Times*, July 14, 1946.

Marinette [Wis.] *Eagle Star*, September 19, 1946.

Alabama *Baptist*, October 10, 1946.

Harvey M. Campbell. "A New Dreiser." *Western Review*, 11 (Winter 1947), 106–108.

Notes

The Stoic

THEODORE DREISER

Garden City, New York
DOUBLEDAY & COMPANY, INC.
1947

The Stoic

Harry Hansen. "Dreiser Buries Cowperwood." New York *World Telegram*, November 7, 1947.

Few authors know when to stop writing, and even their best friends don't know when to stop printing them. Take the case of Theodore Dreiser. His great influence for naturalism and antipuritanism developed in the first 25 years of this century. In his middle years he wrote a heavy, documented style, leaning on newspaper reports and personal observation. Younger writers brought selection into their stories of American life; Dreiser, save in a few short stories, lumbered heavily on. When he died in 1945 he had outlived his period.

Yet his books continue to come, and today *The Stoic* is presented as the third of a trilogy telling the story of the predatory street railway magnate, Frank Algernon Cowperwood, of which the first two were *The Financier* and *The Titan*. Dreiser had almost completed the story the day before he died, and his widow has added what was indicated by his notes. . . .

There is nothing in the writing to tell a newcomer that the author had great influence on younger American writers. The author of *The Stoic* must have found completing it a chore, for it belongs to the early decades of the 20th century. Some of it is unconsciously amusing, as when a 20-year-old dancer visits Cowperwood in his hotel and introduces herself as a distant relative. After brief inquiries about her, "eyes said all that eyes could say. A few seconds more and he merely signalled with his finger. She rose . . . and threw herself into his arms." Well, maybe she did, at that.

Dorothee Carousso. "Theodore Dreiser's Final Novel." Brooklyn *Eagle*, November 9, 1947.

Together with "The Financier" and "The Titan," Theodore Dreiser's last novel, "The Stoic," published posthumously, completes the trilogy of nineteenth-century American materialism. . . .

Mr. Dreiser has, in his trilogy, portrayed an era and a way of life which has gone down into dust in the sudden passing of 50 years. The mores which human beings then held as inviolate are, in the light of present-day values, as superficial and ornate as the old homes which these people left behind as monuments. Today, driving past these old mansions in high-powered cars, we afford them only a passing glimpse, and give a shudder for the ornate monstrosities of design and exhibitionism.

So it is with the values and the social concepts of their builders. A passing glimpse, a shudder for the ugliness of their greed. It is no wonder that the twentieth century finds it necessary to travel in such high gear. Much speed is required if we are to stem the tides of social evil which an entire century permitted to accumulate while the few were preening themselves within their ornate palaces of marble and gold, and investing millions in art collections which they willed to the public much as they might throw a bone to a dog.

Personal wealth and social acceptance were the aims of that day, and any means for their attainment were understandable and pardonable in the nineteenth century. Frank Algernon Cowperwood depicts the last of a brutal, ruthless breed of men, who, with their mansions and mistresses and fortunes and follies, found little satisfaction out of 60 or 70 years of living.

One has the feeling as "The Stoic" draws to a close that a curtain is lowering . . . upon a great trilogy, upon the era that it depicts, upon Theodore Dreiser, who has left us a rich document of the life he saw and knew and was gifted to portray. Dreiser was undoubtedly crude in many respects, and his writing is often stilted in the light of new forms. And yet the thought which he leaves us is the nearest we have come to the truth of happiness . . . that no one man on earth shall ever know secure and lasting happiness so long as there is one hungry, unclothed, illiterate human being among us.

There was a time, many years ago, when Theodore Dreiser, himself poor, ill-clothed, blasted by all the literary world, felt that he had no place in the world. The faith that sustained him then shines out from his work, and makes "The Stoic" a memorable last work.

H.R.B.
"Dreiser Answers His Own Question In Final Novel."
St. Louis *Globe-Democrat*, November 9, 1947.

Theodore Dreiser, then a youthful reporter for the Globe-Democrat, went about St. Louis asking a question of his own: "What do you make of life?" He asked it of World's Champion John L. Sullivan, of Labor Leader Terence V. Powderly, of Editor Henry Watterson, and of Annie Besant, high priestess of theosophy. He still was voicing that query 50 years later when he died, the most distinguished American novelist of his time, but with the final pages of this posthumous novel incomplete.

This ends the trilogy, begun with "The Financier" and continued in "The Titan," which Dreiser founded upon the career of the traction tycoon, Charles T. Yerkes. In this volume the hero, Frank Cowperwood, driven out of Chicago by popular revolt, moves on to London to unify its underground system of transportation, and journeys through more of his vagrom loves and to his death. Exertions and errancy end his life. His millions vanish in litigation. As grass, his end.

Perhaps the novel's title, "The Stoic," carries the answer to that riddle of the Sphinx which Dreiser posed in his St. Louis interviews. The pantheistic philosophy of Zeno may serve as a clue. Dreiser in the final chapters relates it to the atom bomb and to the Brahmanistic teaching with which Annie Besant answered his question here.

This Cowperwood trilogy is, one suspects, a realistically factual record of Dreiser's dream life. He has described his father as a puritanical Catholic, his mother as an inherently sensual pagan.

A child of his time—born in 1871, he died in 1945—he worshipped success, and turned down the faith of his fathers to a belief in the materialistic jungle law of the then fashionable "Darwinism." In his symbolic Cowperwood he tried to justify the materialistic buccaneering of the time as a sort of inverted aestheticism.

Dreiser's middle years brought confusion confounded and his materialism developed a four-syllable interpretation of life's significance as "rub-a-dub-dub." Though his earlier Cowperwood is what Dreiser then would have liked to be, the years thus would change his view, and at the last he would discover that charity rather than envy, generosity rather than acquisitiveness, and spirituality rather than materialism, gave life meaning.

Contemplative and ruminative rather than dynamic and dramatic is its telling. Style and manner are those of "The Financier," but we are told of Cowperwood's acts and but faintly see him in action. Yet the story fascinates; and if incomplete in itself, the novel completes the epic of Theodore Dreiser's spiritual journeying.

Julian T. Sullivan. Indianapolis *Star*, November 9, 1947.

Although Theodore Dreiser wrote the final pages of "The Stoic" the day before his death on Dec. 28, 1945, at the age of 74, his powers as a novelist were undimmed. The penetrating observation, crude force and detachment which characterized the great Hoosier's earlier works are still evident and make this volume a fitting conclusion to the trilogy that began with "The Financier" and continued in "The Titan."

The thinking habits of a lifetime were strong chains that held both Mr. Dreiser and his creation, Frank Cowperwood, but the shifting of the author's basic philosophy that was apparent in "The Bulwark" develops to a climax in "The Stoic." The literary giant's naturalistic ideas were too deeply ingrained to be utterly cast aside. Frank Cowperwood in these final chapters of his life remains a victim of the animal desires for power and sexual satisfaction; but into his aggressive passage through life is injected a new element above and beyond the quests that had marked him a creature of fate. The change is brought to the financier by Berenice Fleming, who opens for him new visions of unselfish service . . .

"The Stoic" is a fine and absorbing story told in some of the simplest prose the Hoosier ever composed. It is less encumbered by debate and argumentation than many of his works. It is truly a monumental close to the career of one of the literary giants of the age.

"The Last of Dreiser." *Time*, 50 (November 10, 1947), 116.

Among the thousands of words the late Theodore Dreiser left behind are the 134,000 that went into this novel, which his publishers say is to be the last. He never quite finished it, though he certainly worked long at it. *The Stoic* completes a trilogy he began in 1912 with *The Financier*, and continued in *The Titan* (1914). Like all Dreiser novels, it is much chewed but badly digested: the product of his slow brooding on the injustices of life, clotted with unassimilated gobbets of ideas and massive lumps of earnest social purpose. *The Stoic* is as dated as a three day-old cake.

"Unfinished Trilogy." *Newsweek*, 30 (November 10, 1947), 85–86.

The greatness of Theodore Dreiser as a novelist is unchallenged. For all his faults, and they were many, he stood head and shoulders above most of his contemporaries. Behind the crudeness of his prose there was power. A deep understanding of the world he lived in and the people in it marked nearly everything he wrote.

The winnowing process of time may shorten the list of his major novels. It will leave "Sister Carrie" and among the others probably "The Financier" (1912) and "The Titan" (1914), Dreiser's two solid, realistic studies of a nineteenth-century "robber baron" in his ruthless struggle for wealth and power. Frank Cowperwood has never been bettered by any American novelist attracted to the exposition and exposure of a man of power.

For many years before his death Dreiser worked on what was to be the final volume of a trilogy devoted to Cowperwood. It was not finished at the time of his death in 1945. Had he lived a few months longer he would have brought the trilogy to a triumphant close. In its unfinished form this last novel, called "The Stoic," is one of Theodore Dreiser's better but not best books.

"The Stoic" has an old-fashioned quality about it and it exhibits most of Dreiser's worst faults as well as his better qualities. The sentimentality that always was an annoying part of Dreiser has a much more "corny" quality today than it had when he was presenting his prose to an often unwilling public 30 years ago. What John Chamberlain once called "the Ouida strain" still persists.

In spite of its clumsiness, however, "The Stoic" has a great deal of body to it as Dreiser follows the career of Cowperwood from his financial debacle in Chicago (see "The Titan") to his struggles in the City of London and to his death in America. Dominating the story is Berenice, Cowperwood's mistress. Like most of Dreiser's women she is sometimes a little difficult to believe in.

Dreiser left his book unfinished. He had intended to write an additional chapter and a summary of the trilogy in the form of a soliloquy. Mrs. Dreiser has furnished a résumé of how he had planned to end it according to his notes.

This adds little to the real interest of the book, the essential excitement of which lies in the dogged laying-bare of Cowperwood's character as an old-fashioned financial promoter as he battles with other titans. It is the tragic story of Cowperwood which holds the reader's attention, rather than the regeneration of Berenice, although Dreiser apparently intended to close the book with a "happy ending" in which Berenice, becoming socially conscious, atoned for Cowperwood's sins. According to Mrs. Dreiser's résumé of his notes, Berenice experienced a spiritual awakening which would enable her to acquire "a real and deep understanding of the meaning of life and its spiritual import."

"Unchanging Dreiser." Boston *Globe*, November 12, 1947.

. . . If this is the first Dreiser you have ever read you will be struck by one quality, its reporting. The two books that preceded it in the trilogy have been called the "best study we have of the predatory quest for power in American business." Substitute the word "report" for "study" and perhaps the statement is true.

The same pedestrian pace, the same styleless chronicle, the same banalities, but Dreiser is still a compelling writer. Why? Perhaps it is his seriousness, his sincerity, his objectivity. He impresses with these qualities, but he does not grip. The reader sits detached, watching these people and listening to the lecturer, Dreiser. For the student of literature, the book will be important for the record; for the average reader it will be old-fashioned.

Lisle Bell. "Books and Things." New York *Herald Tribune*, November 15, 1947, p. 9.

The appearance of Theodore Dreiser's posthumously published novel, "The Stoic," takes one back to the period between 1910 and 1920 when Dreiser's name carried high literary fame, if not distinction. . . . Reading it one is confronted with the lumbering, tortured and uninspired writing which is typically Dreiser, without the vitality and power which were also typically Dreiser.

Pat Colbert. Charleston [S.C.] *News*, November 16, 1947.

. . . Written in ponderous, Dreiserian prose, "The Stoic" is little more than an outdated report, poor in form, repetitious and disorganized in thought. Dreiser's contribution to American literature and to the generation of socially-conscious writers he inaugurated is unmistakable. Time may prove that his capacities as a thinker were limited in scope and overestimated in promise.

John K. Sherman. "Dreiser Power Holds in His Final Novel." Minneapolis *Tribune*, November 16, 1947.

It's like old times to read THE STOIC by Theodore Dreiser for this posthumous, unfinished novel is the last of the trilogy dealing with Frank Cowperwood, the financial genius, whom we last met years ago in the closing pages of "The Titan."

For readers who grew up on Dreiser, the spell of his writing exerts its pull every time they return to him. It is a spell cast by the dark, lumbering power of his art, that peered so deeply into human frailty, by the feeling of an inexorable fate which motivates and governs his characters, and by his patient, plodding style, so much criticized.

The style is the man, and with Dreisers' painstaking realism one must accept his awkward, unmusical prose as an integral part—even that graceless and oft-repeated phrase, "in connection with." One looks to Dreiser not for amenities of style but for the depth, understanding and pity of his vision. . . .

Malcolm Cowley. "Ending Dreiser's 'Trilogy of Desire'." New York *Times Book Review*, November 23, 1947, pp. 7, 57.

"The Financier" was published in 1912 and "The Titan" in 1914. These first two volumes in Theodore Dreiser's "trilogy of desire" had a lasting influence on American fiction, and they left many thousands of readers waiting for the volume to follow. Now that "The Stoic" has appeared, after more than thirty years, we can guess why Dreiser failed to publish it during his lifetime. He had worked on it patiently and had written two or three different endings, among which his literary executors were left to make their choice; but he had never succeeded in raising it to the level attained in the other two volumes.

The first of these remains the most impressive. "The Financier" is an interweaving of finance and politics with a love story that, besides being effective in itself, is also essential to the climax of the novel. There are two reasons, one public and one private, why Frank Algernon Cowperwood goes to prison. He has made and lost a fortune by gambling with the city's funds—that is the public reason—but he has also seduced the daughter of Edward Malia Butler, one of three political bosses who control Philadelphia. Butler, with his family affection and stubborn anger, is one of the most convincing figures in the whole trilogy—more convincing than Cowperwood himself, who is documented and philosophized, whereas Butler is presented almost without comments.

"The Titan," which came next, is inferior to its predecessor as a novel. Instead of being interwoven in the story, sex and finance are presented in alternate chapters—"to make a club sandwich," as Stuart P. Sherman said. The chapters about Cowperwood's successive mistresses have the monotony of variety, like the love life of a tomcat. One has to be more than ordinarily innocent and yearning to enjoy them today; but the business chapters are as good as ever, and they reach an overwhelming climax.

Look in "The Dictionary of American Biography" for the article on Charles Tyson Yerkes (1837–1905) and you will see how closely Dreiser has followed the life of that sturdy old pirate. Yerkes' story, like Cowperwood's, falls naturally into three volumes. First there were his adventures in Philadelphia, including his imprisonment, his second fortune—won by selling the market short during the Northern Pacific panic in 1873—and the scandal of his divorce and remarriage. Then came the series of patient maneuvers by which he gained control of the Chicago street railways and the battle of bribes—described vividly in "The Titan"—by which he tried to win a long-term franchise for all his lines.

There was, however, a third episode in Yerkes' career. After he lost the battle for Chicago—but retained $15,000,000 in booty from the sale of his street railways—he went to London and tried to give the city a unified rapid-transit system. He engaged in another battle of giants—this time against the House of Morgan for control of the London tubes—and meanwhile, with his beautiful ward, this ex-convict moved in social circles that were even higher than Dreiser in his latest novel has dared to suggest.

When he was almost at the point of victory in his financial struggle, he was stricken by illness; and his fortune melted away in litigation after his death. The free hospital he dreamed of was never built; the gallery of Old Masters that he had planned to present to the people of New York was sold at auction; the Chicago traction lines were hopelessly bankrupt; and the London tubes, which should have been his principal monument, were built and owned by others.

Here is the ready-made plot of Dreiser's last novel, a book that should have been as impressive as the two others in his trilogy; but somehow the subject failed to touch his imagination. He was unfamiliar with the London scene. Most of the story was less completely documented than Yerkes' American adventures, for the English libel laws had frightened away the muckraking journalists. These laws must have been an obstacle to Dreiser himself, when he first worked with the same material, for many of Yerkes' associates were then living and influential. Later it would seem that Dreiser brooded so long over the clearly available facts that he ended by losing most of his interest in them.

Like Thomas Wolfe, he left piles of manuscript for his literary executors, who seem to be handling them conscientiously. It is true that they let two or three of Dreiser's historical errors slip past them in preparing "The Stoic" for publication. When they read that Cowperwood mourned at the tomb of Sarah Bernhardt, they should have opened the nearest encyclopedia, where they would have learned that Bernhardt outlived him by eighteen years. But this error—with others like it—is of little importance compared with mistakes in planning the novel that could have been corrected only by the author himself. Let me list what seem to be the worst of them:

1. The title leads us to believe that Cowperwood at the end of his life will find some inner dignity to match his outward success. But he never becomes a stoic; at most he develops from simple hedonism or cynicism into a sort of resigned epicureanism.

2. The story arouses other expectations in the reader that it fails to satisfy. Characters like Lord Ettinge and Abington Scarr, the promoter, are introduced with trumpets, as if they were destined to play an important role; but then they silently vanish. A scene in Chapter 15 suggests that Berenice Fleming, his ward and mistress, will destroy Cowperwood just as she destroyed the snow image of him, but instead she is unfailingly loyal.

3. The story lacks the careful documentation one has learned to expect in Dreiser's novels. Episodes that should have been central, like the struggle between Cowperwood and Drake (Yerkes and Morgan) or the melting away of the hero's vast estate are dismissed each in a single chapter.

4. The author misses almost all the opportunities for drama that he would have seized upon in his earlier novels. There is no confrontation of Drake and Cowperwood; or of Cowperwood and Lord Stane, who is courting Berenice; or of Berenice and Cowperwood's wife (although the last two exchange a single look that carries them both to the edge of hysteria). Cowperwood's death is another lost opportunity; it results from an illness that is unconnected—except in its results—with either his business projects or his love affairs.

A final question concerns the last few chapters of the novel. We know that Dreiser wrote more than one ending to "The Stoic," and we assume that his editors chose the latest and best; but still it is unsatisfactory. It is simply the account of Berenice Fleming's visit to India, where she studies yoga under a holy man. This last episode might have cast light on the "trilogy of desire" if Berenice had ever reflected on Cowperwood's career from the standpoint of her new faith, which regards the world as an illusion. But, until her return to New York, he simply disappears from the story, with the result that we are given an elementary treatise on Indian mysticism instead of a proper conclusion to the novel. We feel after reading the treatise that Cowperwood's trilogy has simply broken off; it is ended but still unfinished.

Alan Branigan. "Profound Novel." Newark [N.J.] *News*, November 23, 1947.

Theodore Dreiser completed his great Cowperwood trilogy shortly before his death in December, 1945. "The Stoic" being the last of the series. The book shows that to the very end he retained the powerful, brooding imagination that made him one of the really profound American novelists of the realistic school. Like the previous, "The Financier" and "The Titan," the new work is a composition not without minor flaws but still magnificently successful in its large scheme.

Dreiser can be called the last of the pre-Joycean geniuses. Despite all the new discoveries in writing technique and psychological analysis, such as the stream-of-consciousness method, Dreiser adhered to the Henry James narrative style.

It was enough for him to set down an unvarnished, prosaic account of his hero's adventures, depending upon the vastness of enterprise and variety of love experience to carry the burden of story telling. The result may seem somewhat old-fashioned to the modern intellectual, but there are compensations in becoming interested in the details of a human being's life rather than in an author's dexterity with materials.

Frank Cowperwood, looked upon as a beaten old man when this volume begins, at once displays characteristics that prove his boundless energy. He takes a new mistress, a smart and beautiful creature named Berenice, as well as assuming the financial burden (and promise of profits) in the reorganization of London's subway system.

Into Dreiser's complex web of events are woven other grandiose schemes. Cowperwood selects a down-and-out society beau to squire Mrs. Cowperwood around Europe. He builds a pyramid of holding companies. He meets and impresses dozens of the British aristocracy with his clear business sense. Running parallel are plans to establish an art museum, a hospital and various charities after his death.

Dreiser's liberal views are not hurled at the reader. But in a deftly artistic way, he gets them across; especially the thought that at the end the hero's aggrandized plans go for naught. For the vultures of society—the trusts and the lawyers—descend on his estate and tear it to shreds. A man has lived and built and bettered society, and at the end there is only a heap of rubble.

Stewart Allen. "Dreiser's Last Novel: A Selected Anderson." Dallas *Times Herald*, November [23] 1947.

"The Stoic" is the last novel in the Dreiser trilogy that includes "The Financier" and "The Titan." Just as a fighter is said never to lose his punch, even after his legs desert him, so it may be said of Theodore Dreiser that he retained his power of expression to the end. The fire is here in this book no less than in the others. This unhurried strength, as always, provides a foundation for the structure, even when some of the actual framework of the plot seems out of plumb. . . .

Readers who have been distressed with the baldness of Dreiser's prose in the past will find no relief in this book. There is no more effort to turn a pretty phrase than there has ever been. If, occasionally, the reader becomes restive at the Olympian detachment of the teller, he must nevertheless marvel at the ability of his eye which saw so much from such a height.

Dreiser recorded what he saw without favor, without pity. The gift that has earned him his high place in American fiction will be missed. Few authors have the ability to give their characters the apparent freedom of will that Dreiser's appear to have. "Whatever they choose to do, I shall report," he seems to say.

"They must be people and not puppets."

The book was left unfinished at the time of the novelist's death. Mrs. Dreiser has prepared an appendix in which she sketches the remainder of the novel as based on Mr. Dreiser's notes. It is not the sort of story that requires a sharply definitive ending; the book suffers very little by stopping where it does.

Nelson Algren. "Dreiser's Despair Reaffirmed in 'The Stoic'." Philadelphia *Inquirer,* November 23, 1947.

"Let no one underestimate the need of pity," Theodore Dreiser wrote in "The Financier." "We live in a stony universe whose hard, brilliant forces rage fiercely. From the prowling hunger of the Hyrcan tiger to the concentric grip of Arcturus and Canopus there is the same ruthless, sightless disregard of the individual and the minor thing . . . And in the midst of the grip of desperate things—in odd crannies and chance flaws between forces—there spring and blossom these small flowers of sentiment. Tenderness! Mercy!"

Dreiser did not damn Cowperwood, his Hyrcan tiger hero of "The Stoic," for he felt that such a man's merciless quality sprang "out of conditions which life itself had created."

Cowperwood's conditions were those of America's economic frontiers at the turn of the century, when the great American dream was to acquire, each man for himself, as much of the world's goods as could possibly be labeled, in one man's lifetime, with one's own name.

Cowperwood was peculiarly fitted to realize such a dream: there were almost no restrictions, legal or ethical, to hinder his titanic vitality; and his cunning was matched only by his drive for power.

Yet, like Peer Gynt, he emerged a victim of his own powers and of his own times. The "chance flaw between forces" ruined his international coup, and the total of his maneuverings is summed up at last in an auction conducted over the wreckage of those lives he had laid waste.

As in the preceding volumes of this trilogy, Cowperwood's strategy is reported with a statistician's ardor, relieved only by accounts of conquests over women.

For though Dreiser remains the most representative of American naturalists, with his massive documentation and sense of the essential tragedy of our lives, he was less of a novelist than a reporter and more the disputant than the dramatist.

Writing on a one-dimensional plane, his pages follow upon each other as monotonously as those of a dated desk-calendar.

Dreiser, was, indeed, so absorbed by the vast, bleak chemistry of the universe that his men and women appear as germs under a microscope: characterless and remote, formless and almost indistinguishable in their grayness.

The similarity between Dreiser and Joseph Conrad has been noted by H. L. Mencken: "Both novelists see human existence as a seeking without a finding; both take refuge in 'I don't know.' The struggle of man is more than impotent; it is gratuitous and purposeless."

Yet in the pages following Cowperwood's death Dreiser records a search for a purpose to Cowperwood's life almost as if searching for a purpose to his own: a search that arrives at the Yogi concept: "Be grateful that by helping a poor man you are able to help yourself. If a man come to your door, go and meet yourself."

This belief is embraced by Cowperwood's bereaved mistress in planning a hospital in Cowperwood's name, with money left her by him.

This leaves us with the feeling that Dreiser, having carved a highway through the American literary wilderness almost single-handed, for other writers to follow, came at last to the dead-end he had predicted for himself as far back as 1930:

"I catch no meaning from all I have seen, and pass quite as I came, confused and dismayed."

Fanny Butcher. "Dreiser True Realist in His Final Novel." Chicago *Tribune*, November 23, 1947.

. . . How long Dreiser actually worked on "The Stoic" one does not know. Certainly it is not the result of thirty-odd years literary labor, altho that length of time has passed since its predecessors. Whether he would have considered the book finished, except for the last few chapters we also do not know. But as it is it bears all of the characteristic Dreiserian touches: the sternness of reality utterly unrelieved by even the most fleeting humor; reality at once powerful and impregnable; and the incredibly awkward style which, like the lack of even normal humor is overshadowed by the sheer structure of the story.

To present day readers "The Stoic" will probably seem more on the dull than on the impressive side, for they will either not know or will have forgotten that Dreiser's uncompromising realism, which today is a la mode, was pioneered 30 years ago by this author. The modern realists all either consciously or subconsciously are beholden to Dreiser for his titanic battle for the right of the writer to set down what his eyes saw and his ears heard instead of what his eyes had formerly read in romance and his ears had been trained to expect from the romantic figures of a novel.

Dreiser's "Sister Carrie," published in 1900 [at the editorial insistence, incidentally, of Frank Norris who was himself struggling to make the world read about what was actually in it] was a sensation, not to say a scandal in its day. It was withdrawn from circulation when the wife of the publisher read its, to her, shocking pages. But a quarter century later "Sister Carrie" seemed almost a gentle idyl of realism to readers by that time conditioned against shock by such writers as Hemingway, Faulkner and Steinbeck.

Today "The Stoic," which would have disturbed the romantic readers of thirty years ago for the ascendancy of the physical in the emotional life of the hero, and would certainly have surprised them for its analysis of superfinance and international business, seems almost a mild replica of some of the immoralistic tales of passion and big money which follows the pattern of "The Financier" and "The Titan." . . .

One critic once said of [Dreiser]: "He has little talent but much genius." And therein lies Dreiser's importance in the literature of America. He was a monumental influence, he yearned for the truth as some men yearn for God, and if he groped, his gropings were toward light.

I happen to be one of those who feel that posthumous books, unfinished, should remain in MSS, but I must confess that, with Cowperwood's life left unfinished for the reader at the end of "The Titan," it is interesting to know thirty years later, how Dreiser intended to resolve his hero's life. "The Stoic" somehow seems very old-fashioned, both economically and emotionally, and lacking in the zest of titanic power with which Dreiser's earlier work almost steam-rollered readers.

Brian Spinks. "Completing the Record of a Notable Career." Houston *Post*, November 23, 1947.

It would not have mattered greatly if Theodore Dreiser had not written this, the last work of his career. His niche in American literature already is secure, and whatever it may be, it was attained a long time ago. Nothing that might issue from the door of the tomb is likely to add to or detract from his position very much.

"The Stoic" is of interest primarily because it completes the record of a notable career. It also completes the trilogy which, in its final summary, was to state Dreiser's philosophy and conception of life. . . .

Whatever one's interest in Dreiser, as an admirer or as a member of the generation which he represents, this is a book that will be bought not so much for its merit as because it rounds out and completes the work of a man who unquestionably was one of the most remarkable American novelists of this century.

William H. Hickerson. "Dreiser's Last Novel Won't Add to His Fame." Cleveland *Plain Dealer*, November 30, 1947.

"The Stoic" . . . adds nothing to the repute achieved by the author with the publication in 1925 of "An American Tragedy," which established him as the leader of the fight for unrestricted freedom of expression in fiction and as the chief exemplar in America of the technique of Dostoevski, Zola and other Europeans of the naturalistic school.

Completing the ostensibly interpretive and thinly disguised story of the financier and traction magnate, Charles Tyson Yerkes (1837–1905), "The Stoic" covers the closing years of Frank Algernon Cowperwood, fin de siecle captain of industry, an authentic social product of that period, but as dated as a Gatling gun. . . .

Probably the most convincing figure in the novel is Mrs. Aileen Cowperwood, the deceived, humiliated, neglected second wife. Fat, dowdy, flashy, gauche and devoted, she is turned over to one Bruce Tollifer, a broken dandy, and paid squire of dames. The other characters, both English and American, are broad types, thinly sketched when they do not border upon caricature, as does the confidential agent, Sippens, an American financier in his own right, who deferentially addresses Cowperwood as "Chief."

In brief, the raw material for this novel remains essentially raw, undigested, unassimilated. The conversations rarely advance the story or illuminate the personalities of the participants. People appear and disappear without a trace. Possibilities for action develop, only to vanish into thin air.

By what courtesy Cowperwood may be called "The Stoic" it is difficult to comprehend. A stoic, whatever else he may have been, is a person who has formed a rather definite opinion of life and has developed a fortitude and a pattern of behavior in relation to it. The chief figure of this novel, however, is a mere opportunist, a gambler in money and love.

Had "The Stoic" been written in reasonable chronological proximity to the other novels in the trilogy it would have possessed an import impossible for it to possess at this late date. Mr. Dreiser's fame still rests squarely on "Sister Carrie," "Jennie Gerhardt," "The Titan" and "An American Tragedy."

W. T. S.
Providence [R.I.] *Journal*, November 30, 1947.

Readers now going into middle age, or older, have lately by a sort of common consent fallen to sighing for the brave days of American literature in the post-war era of a quarter-century ago. That was indeed an exciting era—filled with experiment in poetry, drama, biography, the novel; filled with exciting disillusion; filled with (for U. S. literature) a new frankness and daring. American writing has been over-earnest and generally a little dull by comparison, ever since.

But if the writing of that glittering era is re-examined, our longing will be seen to be, I think, about two parts critical wisdom to two parts uncritical nostalgia. A lot of that writing is already dead and dust. Some of it is only historically interesting. The best of it is often (not always) flawed with the immaturities which, after all, usually attend a self-consciously "new"—or young—literary era.

Both Dreiser, whose fumbling realisms antedated and instructed that post-war era, and [Sherwood] Anderson, one of his best descendants, show the ungainliness, the marked limitations, which circumscribe the fiction of their period. Both were honest, honorable men; they belong among the admirable seekers-for-truth in American literature. How far either can ultimately transcend a merely historical role is a serious question.

It is fashionable to say of Dreiser that though he wrote very badly his probing examination and his massive structures transcend his faults. In the long run I doubt if that can be true. So insensitive a style is not likely to guarantee survival as literature to documentation, however thorough. Perhaps I am being over-discouraged by "The Stoic," his last—unfinished—novel which brings to a raveling conclusion the trilogy of

Frank Cowperwood begun so many years ago in "The Financier" and "The Titan." The clumsy sentences, the lack of subtlety, the plodding mechanics of plot, the woodenness of characterization, the failure of it all to take fire with any great significance are insuperable faults. . . .

E. D. W. New Bedford [Mass.] *Standard*, November 30, 1947.

. . . It has been said with much truth that Frank Cowperwood is one of the great characters created by an extraordinary novelist. In "The Stoic," he undertakes what is perhaps his most daring venture, building of the London subway system. At the height of his career, he leaves America for London to seize control of that city's transportation system. His success therein is but temporary.

Basically, a symbolic figure, Cowperwood is made real by the skill of Dreiser. Yet, while the reader often feels with him, he less often feels for him.

Dreiser completed some 79 chapters of the book, in fact was practically finished with it, when he died in California at 74. The last sentence of the 79th chapter: "What a wonderful thought this was!" is the last line Dreiser ever wrote. It was written the day before his death, Dec. 28, 1945.

His widow states that he left notes for one additional chapter and for a summary of the books in the trilogy. The summary was to have been written as a soliloquy emphasizing to the reader the author's conceptions of life, strength and weakness, wealth and poverty and good and evil.

In an appendix, Mrs. Dreiser prepared from her husband's notes three or four pages to bring the novel to an ending approximately as her husband had planned it. It is somewhat abrupt, as might be expected, but the salient facts are there to bring the novel to a satisfactory conclusion.

The book itself amply demonstrates Dreiser's ability as a story-teller and while it cannot be called his greatest book, it certainly is one of them. The theme is a broad and a bold one and Dreiser handles it masterfully. It is not always clear just at what he is driving but the author was not one to write aimlessly and the purpose of his book is evident through most of its pages.

It is recommended to all thoughtful readers, as well as to those who would enjoy a well-written, interesting novel by a truly great novelist.

Jack Conroy. "Dreiser's Final Novel of Cowperwood Series." Chicago *Sun*, December 3, 1947.

Nearing 40 and with four unpublished novels written, Sherwood Anderson in 1916 wrote to Theodore Dreiser: "To any of us here in America the one really hopeful note of our times is your stout figure pounding at the wall. Our hats are off to you, captain."

The impress of the ungainly, brooding man who first came to Chicago as a gawky youth of 16, fleeing from a poverty-bitten home in Indiana, has been made upon the work of many other writers who usually are regarded as members of the "Chicago school" of realists.

Dreiser's principal contribution, however, has been a conceptual and thematic, not a stylistic, one. His stubborn, unyielding honesty, his refusal to retreat under fire, blazed the way for writers with more subtle literary gifts.

We have recent examples in Nelson Algren, with his savagely uncompromising portrayals of the socially submerged and harried and hunted in "Never Come Morning" and "The Neon Wilderness," and in Willard Motley, whose Nick Romano is the spiritual heir of Dreiser's unheroic protagonists, tormented and baffled by forces beyond their control.

Dreiser worked as a minor clerk in a wholesale hardware establishment, and in his employer's ornate mansion he occasionally was privileged to glimpse briefly the gaudy splendor toward which he yearned for a while. A little later he had a job as an installment collector, badgering people who could not afford to pay for gewgaws they had not needed when they had been cozened into making a down payment.

These experiences did much to sweep the cobwebs out of the future author's head, and there were compensations. "Chicago was like a great orchestra in a tumult of noble harmonies," he wrote. "I was like a guest at a feast, eating and drinking in a delirium of ecstacy."

Chicago did much to shape in Dreiser's mind his trilogy about Frank Cowperwood, financial giant of the late 19th century. Cowperwood, who gained his first conception of business ethics by watching a lobster leisurely devouring a helpless squid in a glass tank, came to Chicago after a Philadelphia imprisonment for his financial manipulations, as related in "The Financier," published in 1912.

He captured the traction system of Chicago in "The Titan," which appeared in 1914, but at the end of the volume had been refused a renewal of his 50-year franchise. His activities as an insatiable libertine had estranged Aileen, his second wife, who as his mistress had stood by him in his Philadelphia trouble.

Now, after all these years, "The Stoic" again takes up the career of Cowperwood. He has acquired a mistress half his age; his wife sulks and drinks immoderately in the New York mansion which houses his art collection. Berenice, his new inamorata, inspires Cowperwood, pushing 60, to make a try for control of the London subway system. Characteristically, he gets it as well as entree to the homes of a lot of British swells with titles and ancient estates in the country. But Death eventually deals him the cards in the deck for all those of over-weening ambition, and with his passing the fortune he has collected throughout his rapacious years dissolves like a mist.

It would be pleasant to say that "The Stoic" is a worthy ending to the trilogy, but as a matter of fact it is not. Dreiser's gaucheries have been forgiven in the past because they were powered by a massive and compelling passion. All his stereotypes and gracelessness are here: "Berenice's pretty mouth curled scornfully," the London City Council is "enthused" at Cowperwood's victory. Cowperwood is represented as gazing respectfully on the grave of Sarah Bernhardt 23 years before her death.

These are minor faults, to be sure, but they are embodied in a novel marked by haste and what appears to be a profound weariness. The final chapter has been supplied in synopsis by Dreiser's wife from his notes, since he died before he could complete "The Stoic." Part of the book reads as though it has been transcribed from a rough draft. The final conclusion is that Yogi mysticism holds whatever answer there may be to the world's problems.

For Dreiser's vast services to American literature, however, one can still read "The Stoic," even with its pallid reflection of Dreiser's rugged strength, and cry out with Sherwood Anderson: "Our hats are off to you, captain!"

James T. Farrell. "Dreiser's 'The Stoic' Powerful." Chicago *News*, December 3, 1947.

Theodore Dreiser completed "The Stoic," the final novel of the Cowperwood series in the last year of his life. He had worked on the revision on the day of his death, Dec. 28, 1947.

"The Stoic" begins where the preceeding volume, "The Titan"—published in 1947—leaves off. At the conclusion of the latter novel, Cowperwood, nearing 60 and still rich realizes that his career as a Chicago financier is over.

This novel deals with his business operations in London. It is also concerned with his love for a young girl, Berenice, and with the relationship between him and his wife, Aileen.

"THE STOIC" is, if anything, more moving and more powerful than its two predecessors. Dreiser has presented Cowperwood as both an individual and as a force, in fact, as a representative of a life-force.

The social and the biological tragedy of man, so pitilessly and yet so compassionately described in his books, in reality is an expression of this life force. There is universal creativity, whether it be for good or for evil. Even Cowperwood, in the end, is seen as a puppet controlled by this force.

"THE STOIC," his last book, is one final and powerful representation of that Dreiserian image of man.

Dr. Marcuson. "Books in the News." Macon [Ga.] *News*, December 4, 1947.

A whole generation has passed since the publication of the other two volumes of the Trilogy, The Financier and The Titan. The Stoic which was to be the third and concluding volume was never finished. Whether Dreiser's mood changed and he lost interest in the story or whether he realized that the public interest had changed, your reviewer cannot say. The Trilogy deals with those financial giants who exploited the public with stock in public utilities—a subject which is no longer of interest to the general public. The large traction companies have passed away and the foolish investors perhaps have grown wiser. . . .

The book of course is written in Dreiser's usual powerful style but the structure of the volume is weak. The author probably realized the lack of popular interest in the financial manipulations of his hero and so devoted most of the book to his questionable love entanglements. Even here he seemed unable to construct a satisfactory solution. The age had changed and the interest of America had turned in another direction. It would perhaps have been better for the reputation of Dreiser, who was undoubtedly one of the greatest American writers, had the volume never been published.

John Lydenberg. "The Anatomy of Exhaustion." *Saturday Review of Literature*, 30 (December 6, 1947), 36.

The final volume of Theodore Dreiser's "trilogy of desire" makes a sadly inappropriate epitaph for the father of American naturalism. "The Stoic" is a tired book. Theodore Dreiser and Frank Cowperwood are tired, and their contagious lassitude infects the reader on the first page. The fictional counterpart of Charles T. Yerkes, Philadelphia and Chicago traction magnate, makes the rounds of finance, fornication, and marital troubles marked out in "The Financier" and "The Titan," but the driving passion has been long since spent and both protagonist and author seem to be performing merely mechanical rituals as they await imminent death.

Although two world wars, a boom, a great depression, fascism, and the breakdown of capitalism in Europe changed the world between the publication of "The Titan" and that of "The Stoic," the weakness of the novel does not lie in the fact that it describes what now seems like ancient history. It would have been a failure had it appeared in 1914, and the two earlier Cowperwood stories would be significant if they appeared today. The trouble arises from Dreiser's own limitations: his inability to resolve his intellectual and emotional quandaries, and the deficiencies of his technique.

If there was any serious question as to the source of Dreiser's strength as a novelist, "The Bulwark" and "The Stoic" have answered it finally. Running to only half the length of his shortest preceding novels, they seem like skeletons, outlines, notes for a novel Dreiser planned to write when he could find time and inspiration. In the earlier novels Dreiser never managed to get quite inside his characters; he contented himself with telling about them, instead of making the reader live with them and participate imaginatively in their struggles. But the weight of the details heaped on details, indeed the very ponderousness of his lumbering presentation, made them real. Now his graceless style and his inability to invent stand out starkly and prove fatal, where they were but minor flaws before. In the first two books, Cowperwood came to life as a great character, the fullest, richest, and most convincing embodiment of the American industrialist of the Gilded Age. Here we recognize his old lineaments, but we see them only as belonging to a dummy manufactured by Dreiser.

His skeleton novels have failed in yet another way: they do not transmit the positive message that here for the first time Dreiser sought to present. He could successfully identify himself with the ruthless builders of American industry and transmute into fiction the drama of their reckless and undiscriminating drive for power. He could convey, as no one else in American literature could, the feeling of a moral jungle in which the great financiers and the little Carries and Clydes struggled blindly and for rewards that would give them no satisfaction. But he could not portray convincingly the good life which he yearned to see his society adopt.

"The Bulwark" is the more significant of his two posthumous novels because he there faced the problem squarely and tried to show the strength and serenity that could be attained by unwavering faith and by firm adherence to the ethical precepts of one's religion. But he was still under compulsion to report faithfully the actualities of American life, to stress the conflict between materialist business norms and ethical or democratic precepts. As a result the bulwark of a deeply-felt Quaker religion is, despite Dreiser's intentions, transformed into a frail, finally broken reed.

In "The Stoic" the moral is merely appended, instead of being woven into the story. Cowperwood dies with his unification of the London underground only partially completed. He has failed to attain that last earthly glory, and his huge fortune is dissipated (as was Yerkes's) by lawsuits, legal fees, and malefactions of his former associates. *Sic transit*. . . . Berenice—the mistress to whom he had, surprisingly, been faithful for all but a few chapters—awakens to the spiritual emptiness of their drive for mundane power, and rushes to India for a four-year course in yoga. Then she returns to the West, to dedicate herself to the management of a charity hospital which Cowperwood had wished to have established. And the book closes with her determination to "acquire, if possible, a real and deep understanding of the meaning of life and its spiritual import." To the reader her conversion seems like an irrelevant afterthought.

It hurts to have to write thus about Dreiser. His contribution to American literature is as great, for all his limitations, as that of any other novelist; he fought stubbornly and often alone a battle that had to be fought. And with but one exception his earlier novels can still be read, not merely as historical landmarks, but as living fiction. "The Stoic," unhappily, is of value only for the unneeded light it casts on the difficulties Dreiser overcame when he wrote his great novels.

Lloyd Morris. "Dreiser's Last." New York *Herald Tribune, Weekly Book Review*, December 7, 1947, p. 54.

Though its publication had been promised for many years, Theodore Dreiser was still working on "The Stoic" when he died in 1945. This novel was to complete the trilogy begun in 1912 with "The Financier" and carried forward in 1914 by "The Titan." It is now published as he left it, unfinished. An appendix by his widow, based upon Dreiser's notes, describes its projected conclusion. Whether Dreiser regarded this version of the novel as final, or whether he would have revised or perhaps largely rewritten it had he lived, we are not told. But it invites rather more melancholy than is usually called for by similar posthumous gleanings. As a novel it is a deeply disappointing book, a twilight work that betrays the failing of a major talent. "The Stoic" lacks the immense vitality, the power and sweep of its predecessors in the trilogy. Its impact is feeble.

But, notwithstanding its ineffectiveness, "The Stoic" has both a special interest and a bearing upon the whole body of Dreiser's fiction. Forty years ago, when he began his trilogy, Dreiser undertook to trace the working out in life of the unofficial American gospel of material success. The millionaire, he felt, represented what most Americans secretly wanted to become, and thus constituted the national ideal of greatness. Dreiser determined to give them a full-length portrait of a typical example. He went into the arena of finance capitalism for his model,—Charles T. Yerkes, the traction magnate—and produced, in two long novels, a documented biography of one of its ten outstanding exponents. Yerkes or, as Dreiser called him, Frank Cowperwood, in the course of his rise to power disrupted the economy and debauched the politics of two great American cities; repeatedly fleeced the public; wrecked nearly every enterprise that he participated in; brought tragedy into the lives of almost all with whom he was intimately associated. In "The Stoic," Dreiser reports the final phases of his hero's career: his fidelity to a wife whom he no longer loved; his elderly passion for a youthful mistress; his daring attempt to seize control of the London traction system; his futile dream of immortality through philanthropy and the public bequest of a great art collection; the collapse of his empire and melting away of his wealth after his death. Like its predecessors, "The Stoic" is more social history than fiction. Unlike them, however, it is not social indictment.

For, during the long silent years that followed the publication of "An American Tragedy," Dreiser's feeling and thought seem to have undergone a drastic change. Early in life he had patched together a mechanistic philosophy that comforted his conscience; it made life a tragic experience, but it largely absolved the individual of moral responsibility. In the end his bleak theory failed to satisfy either Dreiser's heart or his mind. He could not help feeling that life is a problem in social justice, and that behind it there must exist a creative divinity and cosmic purpose. In the concluding portions of "The Stoic"—as in his other posthumous novel "The Bulwark"—Dreiser attempted to record his quest for a spiritual meaning in life. His final conclusion was that, without an "inner light," without love toward all created things, achievement is mere illusion and failure. He had traveled the long road from mechanism to mysticism. He was persuaded that society must be reorganized upon some more equitable basis. But he was also convinced that what determines the structure of society is the spiritual life of men. Two seemingly contradictory acts attest Dreiser's muddled thinking and moral integrity. Just before his death he joined the Communist party as a protest against the injustices suffered by the masses under capitalism. But in his posthumous novels he left a confession of spiritual need and religious affirmation as candid and poignant as any in our literature. "The Stoic" is a testament.

Alex Stedman. "Theodore Dreiser's Last Book Ends the Cowperwood Saga." Fort Worth *Press*, December 14, 1947.

"The Stoic," the last novel of the late Theodore Dreiser, completes his trilogy about Frank Cowperwood, the great American financier. The first two were "The Financier" and "The Titan." Death comes to Cowperwood in the fruition of international operations, and his vast fortune meets speedy dissolution at the hands of vultures and jackals operating behind the shield of law.

The story begins with the typical Dresier tedium, but gradually matures until the reader realizes here is a great novel about American life. It is a curious quality of many rare works of fiction that they have that slow but certain growth as the narrative progresses. Tolstoy's "War and Peace" is another striking illustration of the point. . . . Here in "The Stoic" is a deep insight into the human element of tragedy. . . .

"The Stoic" is life as a great American saw it, a chronicle of the times, of a generation alien and lost in its materialism and struggle for the only progress it knows. It is an item for every Dreiser follower, and, for the beginner, may invite profitable explorations into earlier works of a writer who had a profound influence on the American novel.

Pittsburgh *Press*, December 14, 1947.

Make way, those of you who worship at the literary altars of Hemingway, Joyce, Faulkner and Steinbeck, for the High Priest of your "uncompromising realism." He is Theodore Dreiser, of course, and he strides with a pioneer's paces across the pages upon which men have written what they actually saw and heard, not what some long-dead romanticist decreed should be written.

Posthumous publication of "The Stoic," the last of Dreiser's novels, brings back to us his real place in American letters. But it does not bring back the strength, the vigor, and yes, the surprise, that were locked in his earlier books.

As a sequel to "The Financier" (published in 1912), and "The Titan" (published in 1914), this new book leaves a lot to be desired. Perhaps our appetites have been jaded by the super-realism that Hemingway, Steinbeck et. al have ground into us. Perhaps life, in the 47 years since the publication of the shocking "Sister Carrie," has become a lot more grim and a lot more realistic than any of Dreiser's "realism."

Whatever the cause, Frank Algernon Cowperwood, the hero of the "trilogy of desire," is neither as wicked, as amoral, as grasping, or as indecent as our fathers thought he was. In "The Stoic," the swashbuckling financial pirate has become something of an amatory dilettante and an esthete of the dinner table. . . .

["The Stoic"] is neither as important nor as imposing as the two preceding volumes in the trilogy. To modern readers, it may even seem dull and humorless. But Dreiser is a pioneer who cannot, who must not, be ignored.

John Hay. "Books of the Week." *Commonweal*, 47 (December 19, 1947), 260–261.

In "The Financier" and "The Titan," Theodore Dreiser put his hero on a high dramatic plane. With his own moral energy and his powerful urge to construct and to complete his conceptions in every detail, he turned Frank Algernon Cowperwood into an epic character.

"The Stoic" which finishes the trilogy, is a step down from power. Dreiser's treatment of Cowperwood's last adventure, an attempt to seize control of London's subway system, is diffident compared to the business chapters in "The Titan." Even though the novel is only completed through notes put together by Dreiser's executors, the chapters leading to the end seem unfinished and undecided. Still, one is grateful to be reminded again of Theodore Dreiser, and "The Stoic" is not without its moving passages. With no immediate artistic tradition to fall back on, he was in the line of the great American authors who, like Whitman or Melville, built new art with their own creative energy. You can reject Dreiser in part, for whatever clumsiness you choose, but you cannot reject him as a whole. He never turned aside from the honesty and the force with which he pursued his great conceptions.

Checklist of Additional Reviews

Bridgeport [Conn.] *Post*, November 2, 1947.

Martha MacGregor. "Theodore Dreiser's Last Novel." New York *Post*, November 6, 1947, p. 30.

Margaret Parsons. Worcester [Mass.] *Gazette*, November 8, 1947.

"Briefly Noted." *New Yorker*, 23 (November 15, 1947), 134.

William Hallain Bonner. Buffalo *Evening News*, November 15, 1947.

Washington [D.C.] *Star*, November 16, 1947.

"Last Novel By Dreiser." Worcester [Mass.] *Telegram*, November 16, 1947.

S.J.F. "The Bookshelf." *Harvard Crimson*, November 19, 1947.

Tulsa [Okla.] *World*, Nobember 23, 1947.

"Dreiser's Trilogy Complete." Columbus [Ohio] *Dispatch*, November 23, 1947.

Jackson [Miss.] *News*, November 30, 1947.

Washington [D.C.] *News*, December 3, 1947.

Booklist, December 15, 1947, p. 151.

John Fannelly. "Finis." *New Republic*, 117 (December 22, 1947), 28.

Los Angeles *Times*, December 28, 1947.

William Habich. "Dreiser's Last—Symbol of an Age." Louisville *Courier-Journal*, December 28, 1947.

John Cournos. New York *Sun*, December 28, 1947.

Further Reviews: Bibliographic Information Incomplete

Frances Stover. “The Last Days of a Titan.” Milwaukee. November 9, 1947.

Angus McStay. “Dreiser’s Undeviating Furrow Ends with Cowperwood’s Death.”

Index of Critics

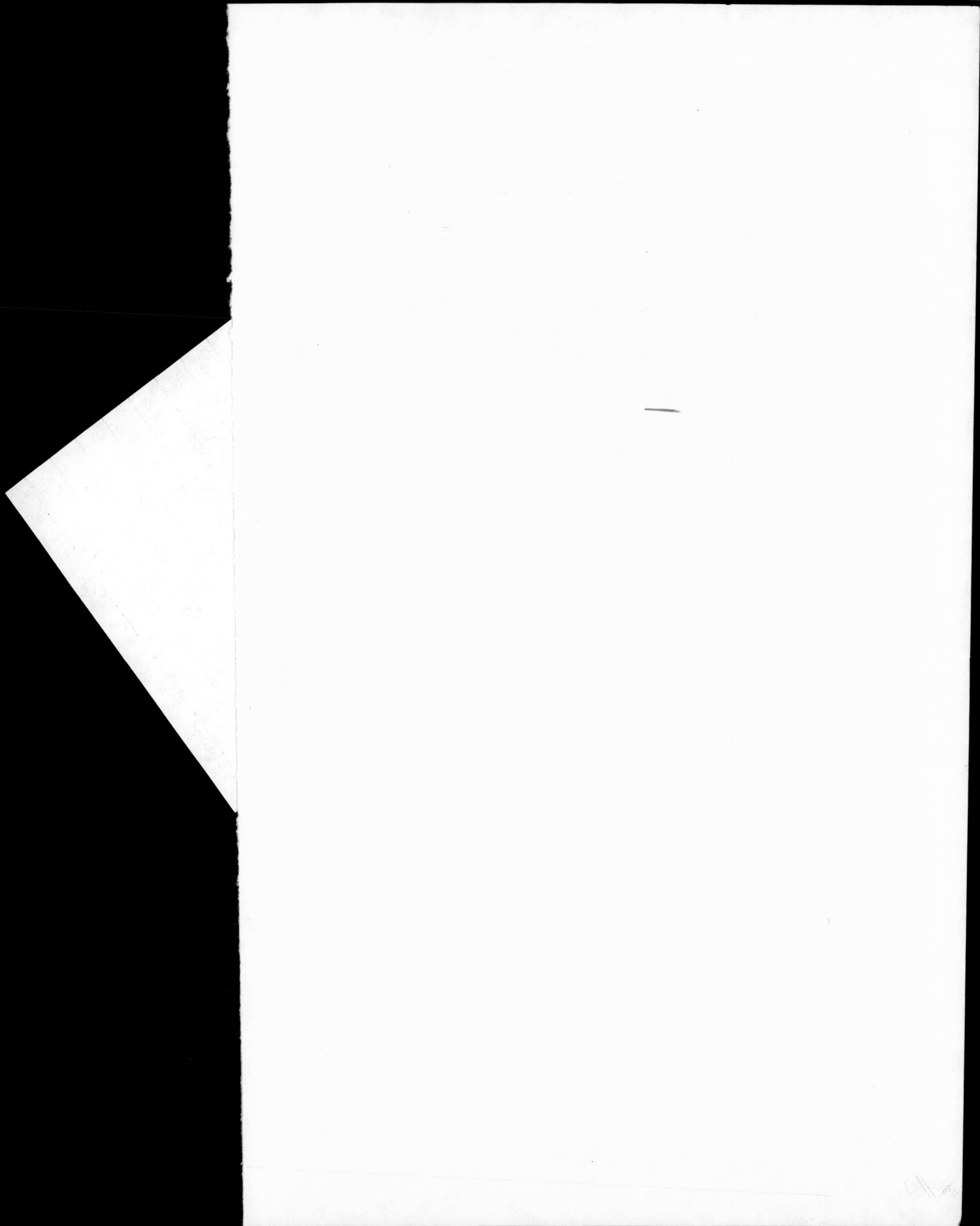

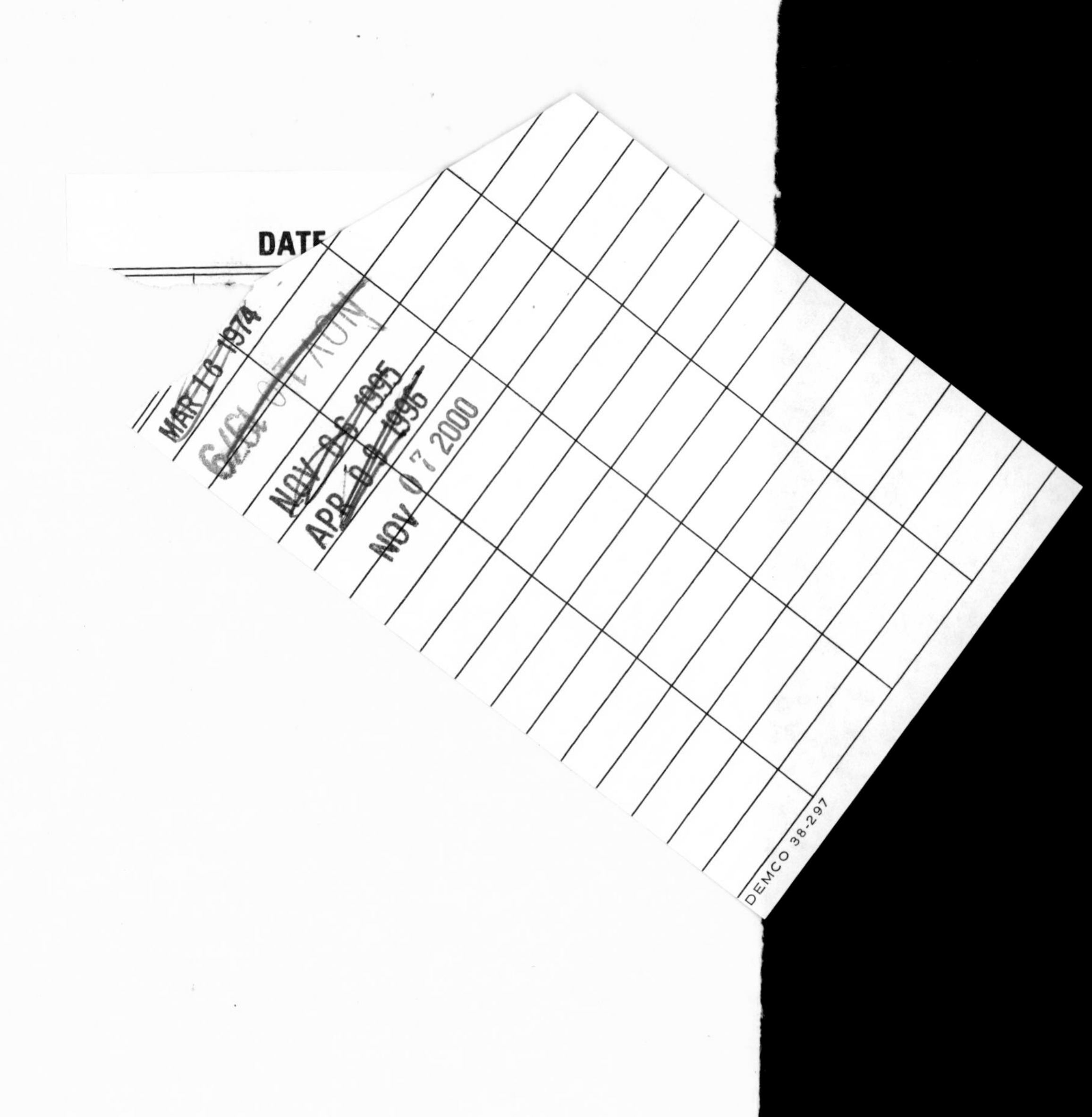
DATE
MAR 18 1974
NOV 06 1995
APR 04 1996
NOV 07 2000
DEMCO 38-297